"The Laudon & Laudon Web site includes technology updates, interactive Web exercises and study guide, a virtual tour of Electronic Commerce sites, and new case studies."

www.prenhall.com/laudon

"Available as a stand-alone item or in a PH Value Pack, this interactive student CD-ROM includes bullet text to assist students in their understanding of the material in the text, audio and video tours, and links to the student's Web site exercises and study guide so users can continually check their progress in mastering the material."

THIRD EDITION

Essentials of Management Information Systems

Transforming Business and Management

Kenneth C. Laudon

New York University

Jane Price Laudon

Azimuth Corporation

PRENTICE HALL Upper Saddle River, New Jersey 07458

Acquisitions Editor: David Alexander
Editor-in-Chief: PJ Boardman
Assistant Editor: Lori Cardillo
Editorial Assistant: Keith Kryszczun
Executive Marketing Manager: Nancy Evans
Senior Production Editor: Anne Graydon
Managing Editor: Dee Josephson
Production Coordinator: Carol Samet
Senior Manufacturing Supervisor: Paul Smolenski
Senior Manager, Manufacturing and Prepress: Vincent Scelta
Design Manager: Pat Smythe
Design Assistant: Michael Fruhbeis
Interior Design: Mary McDonnell
Cover Design: Cheryl Asherman
Cover Art: Ralph Mercer
Composition: Carlisle Communications, Inc.
Photo Research: Shirley Webster
Photo Permissions Supervisor: Kay Dellosa
Photo Permissions Editor: Elaine Estrada
Photo credits appear following the indexes.

A Simon & Schuster Company
Upper Saddle River, New Jersey 07458

ISBN 0-13-081973-5

Prentice-Hall International (UK) Limited, London
Prentice-Hall of Australia Pty. Limited, Sydney
Prentice-Hall Canada, Inc., Toronto
Prentice-Hall Hispanoamericana, S.A., Mexico
Prentice-Hall of India Private Limited, New Delhi
Prentice-Hall of Japan, Inc., Tokyo
Simon & Schuster Asia Pte. Ltd., Singapore
Editora Prentice-Hall do Brasil, Ltda., Rio de Janeiro

Printed in the United States of America

10 9 8 7 6 5 4 3 2 1

Kenneth C. Laudon is a Professor of Information Systems at New York University's Stern School of Business. He holds a B.A. in Economics from Stanford and a Ph.D. from Columbia University. He has authored 14 books dealing with information systems, organizations, and society. Professor Laudon has also written over forty articles concerned with the social, organizational, and management impacts of information systems, privacy, ethics, and multimedia technology.

Professor Laudon's current research is on the planning and management of large-scale information systems for the 1990s and multimedia information technology. He has received grants from the National Science Foundation to study the evolution of national information systems at the Social Security Administration, the IRS, and the FBI. A part of this research is concerned with computer-related organizational and occupational changes in large organizations, changes in management strategy, and understanding productivity change in the knowledge sector.

Ken Laudon has testified as an expert before the United States Congress. He has been a researcher and consultant to the Office of Technology Assessment (United States Congress) and to the Office of the President, several executive branch agencies, and Congressional Committees. Professor Laudon also acts as an in-house educator for several consulting firms and as a consultant to Fortune 500 firms on system infrastructure planning and longer term strategies. Ken works with the The Concours Group to provide advice to firms developing enterprise systems. His hobbies include celestial navigation and ocean sailboat racing.

Jane Price Laudon is a management consultant in the information systems area and the author of seven books. Her special interests include systems analysis, data management, MIS auditing, software evaluation, and teaching business professionals how to design and use information systems.

Jane received her Ph.D. from Columbia University, her M.A. from Harvard University, and her B.A. from Barnard College. She has taught at Columbia University and the New York University Stern School of Business. She maintains a lifelong interest in Oriental languages and civilizations.

The Laudons have two daughters, Erica and Elisabeth.

Essentials of Management Information Systems: Transforming Business and Management reflects a deep understanding of MIS research and teaching as well as practical experience designing and building real-world systems.

for Erica
and Elisabeth

Brief Contents

Contents

PART TWO Technical Foundations of Information Systems

Preface

Essentials of Management Information Systems: Transforming Business and Management (Third Edition) is based on the premise that it is difficult, if not impossible, to manage a modern organization without at least some knowledge of information systems—what they are, how they affect the organization and its employees, and how they can make businesses more competitive and efficient. Information systems have become essential for creating competitive firms, managing global corporations, and providing useful products and services to customers. This book provides an introduction to management information systems that undergraduate and MBA students will find vital to their professional success.

The Information Revolution in Business and Management: The New Role of Information Systems

Globalization of trade, the emergence of information economies, and the growth of the Internet and other global communications networks have recast the role of information systems in business and management. The Internet is becoming the foundation for new business models, new business processes, and new ways of distributing knowledge. Companies can use the Internet and networking technology to conduct more of their work electronically, seamlessly linking factories, offices, and sales forces around the globe. When corporate managers at firms such as the Marriott Corporation use information systems to examine their daily operations, they can find out exactly which rooms are occupied and what the revenue is from hundreds of hotels all over the world. This digital integration of the firm, from the warehouse to the executive suite, is becoming a reality. Accordingly we have changed the subtitle of this text to *Transforming Business and Management.*

New to the Third Edition

The Internet has created a universal platform for buying and selling goods. Its technology now also provides powerful capabilities for driving important business processes inside the company. This edition more fully explores the electronic business uses of the Internet for the internal management of the firm as well as the Internet's growing role in electronic commerce. It also provides a complete set of tools for integrating the Internet and multimedia technology into the MIS course. The following features and content reflect this new direction:

New Tools for Interactive Learning

A **Tools for Interactive Learning** section concluding each chapter shows students how they can extend their knowledge of each chapter with projects and exercises on the Laudon Web site and the optional CD-ROM multimedia edition.

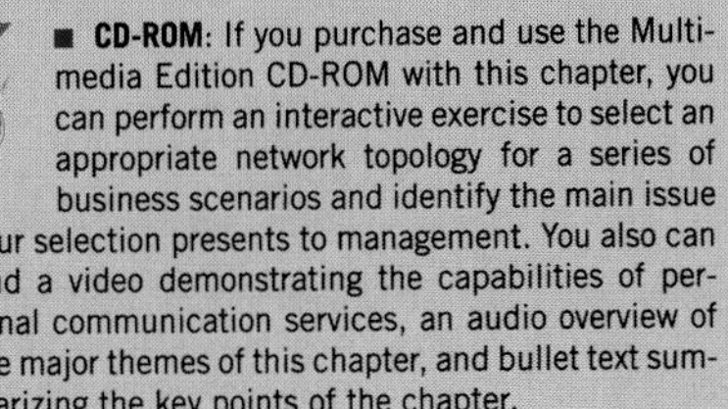

TOOLS FOR INTERACTIVE LEARNING

■ **INTERNET**: The Internet Connection for this chapter will take you to the Rosenbluth Travel Web site, where you can complete an exercise to analyze how Rosenbluth uses the Web and communications technology in its daily operations. You can use the interactive software at the Goodyear Web site in an Electronic Commerce project to assist customers in making tire purchases. You can also use the Interactive Study Guide to test your knowledge of the topics in the chapter and get instant feedback where you need more practice.

■ **CD-ROM**: If you purchase and use the Multimedia Edition CD-ROM with this chapter, you can perform an interactive exercise to select an appropriate network topology for a series of business scenarios and identify the main issue your selection presents to management. You also can find a video demonstrating the capabilities of personal communication services, an audio overview of the major themes of this chapter, and bullet text summarizing the key points of the chapter.

Students and instructors can see at a glance exactly how the Web can be used to enhance student learning for each chapter.

Students can also see immediately how the chapter can be used in conjunction with the optional CD ROM.

New Management Wrap-Up Overviews of Key Issues

Management Wrap-Up sections at the end of each chapter summarize key issues using the authors' management, organization, and technology framework for analyzing information systems.

Management Wrap-Up

To obtain meaningful benefits from the Internet, managers need to determine how its technologies can support their business goals. Planning should carefully consider network costs, the costs and benefits of Internet computing, and new personnel requirements. Managers also should anticipate making organizational changes to take advantage of these technologies and plan to maintain some measure of management control over the process.

The Internet can dramatically reduce transaction and agency costs and is fueling new business models. By using the Internet and other networks for electronic commerce, organizations can exchange purchase and sale transactions directly with customers and suppliers, eliminating inefficient middlemen. Organizational processes can be streamlined by using the Internet and intranets to make communication and coordination more efficient. To take advantage of these opportunities, organizational processes must be redesigned.

The Internet is creating a universal computing platform by using the TCP/IP network reference model and other standards for storing, retrieving, formatting, and displaying information. Web-based applications integrating voice, data, video, and audio are providing new products, services, and tools for communicating with employees and customers. Organizations can create intranets, internal networks based on Internet and Web technology, to reduce network costs and overcome connectivity problems. Key technology decisions should consider network reliability, security, bandwidth, and relationships to legacy systems, as well as the capabilities of Internet and other networking technologies.

MANAGEMENT

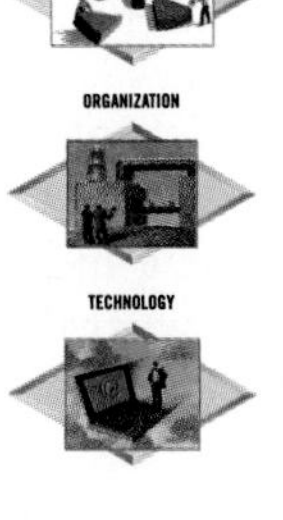

For Discussion:

1. The Internet is creating a business revolution and transforming the role of information systems in organizations. Do you agree? Why or why not?
2. What management, organization, and technology factors would you consider when deciding whether to build an intranet for your company?

Management Wrap-Up provides a quick overview of the key issues in each chapter, reinforcing the authors' management, organization, and technology framework.

Focus on Electronic Commerce and Electronic Business

The Internet, electronic commerce, and electronic business are introduced in Chapter 1 and integrated throughout the text and the entire learning package. A full chapter, entitled The Internet: Electronic Commerce and Electronic Business (Chapter 9), describes the underlying technology, capabilities, and benefits of the Internet, with expanded treatment of electronic commerce, Internet business models, and the use of intranets for the internal management of the firm.

Internet, Electronic Commerce, and Electronic Business Integrated into Every Chapter

Every chapter contains a Window On box, case study, or in-text discussion of electronic commerce, electronic business, or the use of the Internet in changing a particular aspect of information systems.

Enhanced Laudon & Laudon Web Site for Management Problem Solving and Interactive Learning

The Laudon & Laudon Web site has been enhanced to provide a wide array of capabilities for interactive learning and management problem solving that have been carefully prepared for use with the text. They include:

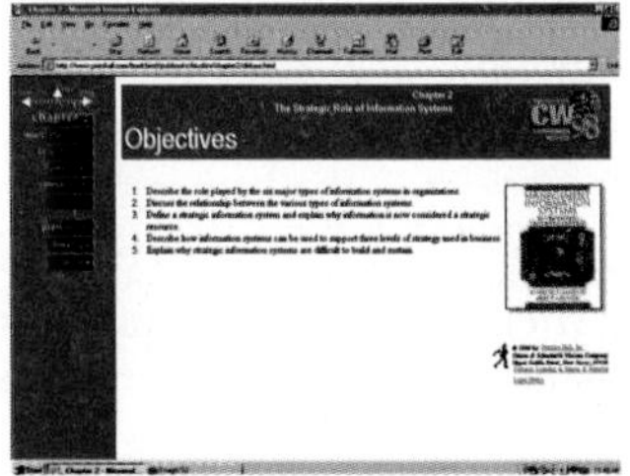

Student responses to questions are automatically graded and can be e-mailed to the instructor.

Interactive Study Guide and Internet Connections for Each Chapter For each chapter of the text, the Web site features an Interactive Study Guide and Internet Connection exercise.

- The on-line Interactive Study Guide helps students review and test their mastery of chapter concepts with a series of multiple-choice, true-false, and essay questions.
- Internet Connections noted by marginal icons in the chapter direct students to exercises and projects on the Laudon Web site related to organizations and

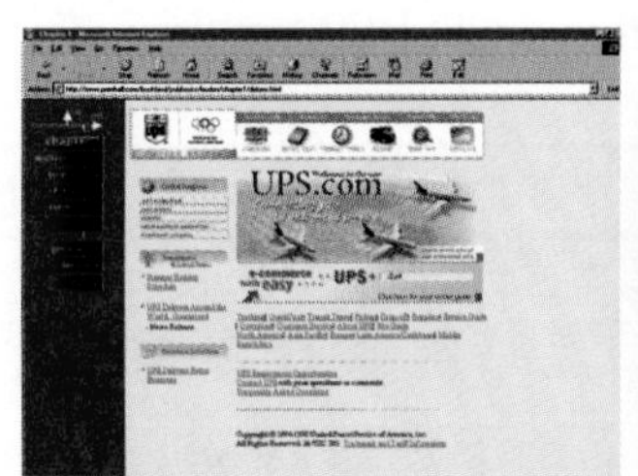

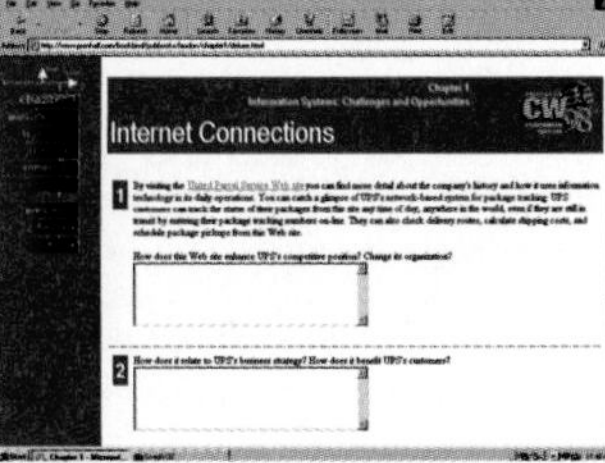

Students are presented with a problem to develop a budget for annual shipping costs. To obtain the information required by the solution, they can input data on-line and use the interactive software at this Web site to perform the required calculations or analysis.

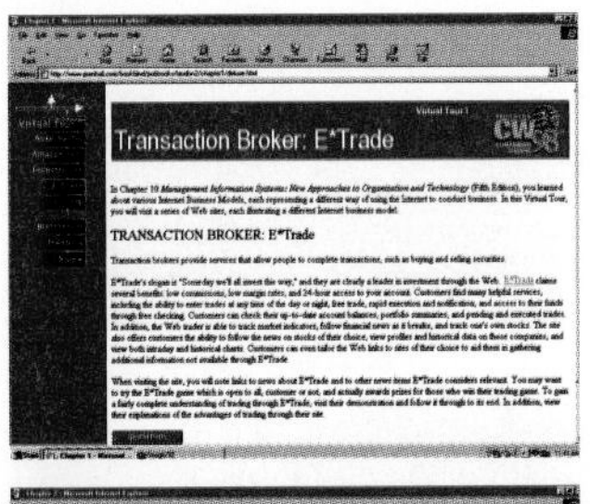

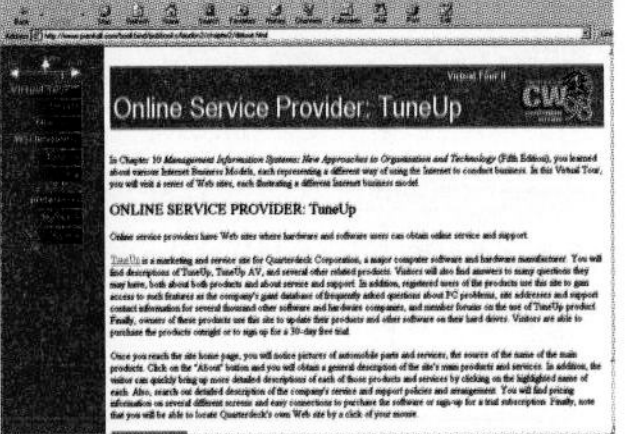

Students visit a series of Web sites illustrating different business uses of the Internet and then apply what they have learned to designing an Internet business strategy for a new company.

concepts in that chapter. Included are Web-based exercises and interactive Electronic Commerce exercises that apply chapter concepts to using the Web for management problem solving.

A Virtual Tour of Electronic Commerce Sites Students can take a tour of electronic commerce sites on the Web, where they can explore the various Internet business models and electronic commerce capabilities discussed in the text. Students can use what they have learned on the tour to complete a comprehensive electronic commerce project.

Additional Case Studies The Web site contains additional case studies with hyperlinks to the Web sites of the organizations they discuss.

Technology Updates The Web site provides technology updates to keep instructors and students abreast of leading-edge technology changes.

International Web Sites Links to Web sites of non-U.S. countries are provided for users interested in more international material.

Unique Features of This Text

Essentials of Management Information Systems: Transforming Business and Management (Third Edition) has many unique features designed to create an active, dynamic learning environment.

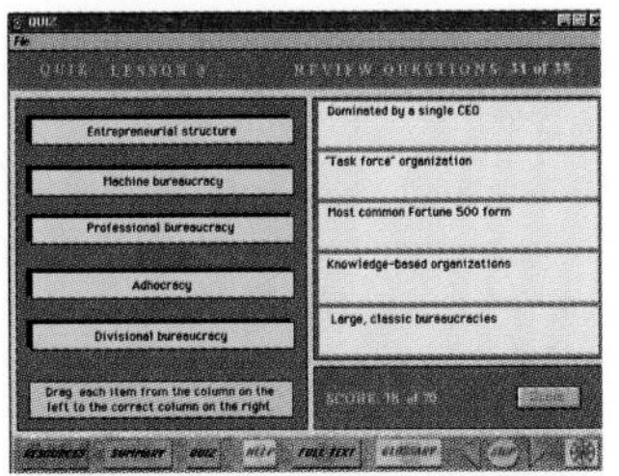

Students can reinforce and extend their knowledge of chapter concepts with interactive exercises on the CD-ROM.

Technology Integrated with Content

An interactive CD-ROM multimedia version of the text can be purchased as an optional item. In addition to the full text and bullet text summaries by chapter, the CD-ROM features interactive exercises, simulations, audio/video overviews explaining key concepts, on-line quizzes, hyperlinks to the exercises on the Laudon Web site, technology updates, and more. Students can use the CD-ROM as an interactive supplement or as an alternative to the traditional text.

Integrated Framework for Describing and Analyzing Information Systems

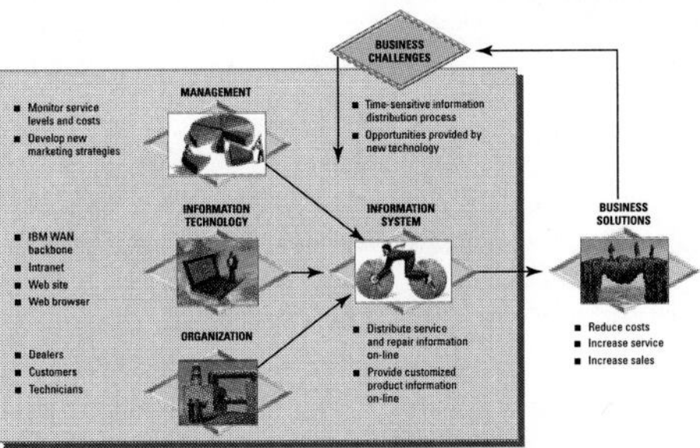

A special diagram accompanying each chapter-opening vignette graphically illustrates how management, organization, and technology elements work together to create an information system solution to the business challenges discussed in the vignette.

An integrated framework portrays information systems as being composed of management, organization, and technology elements. This framework is used throughout the text to describe and analyze information systems and information system problems.

Real-World Examples

Real-world examples drawn from business and public organizations are used throughout to illustrate text concepts. More than 100 companies in the United States and nearly 100 organizations in Canada, Europe, Australia, Asia, and Africa are discussed.

Each chapter contains three Window On boxes (Window on Management, Window on Organizations, Window on Technology) that present real-world examples illustrating the management, organization, and technology issues in the chapter. Each Window On box concludes with a section called *To Think About* containing questions for students to apply chapter concepts to management problem solving. The themes for each box are:

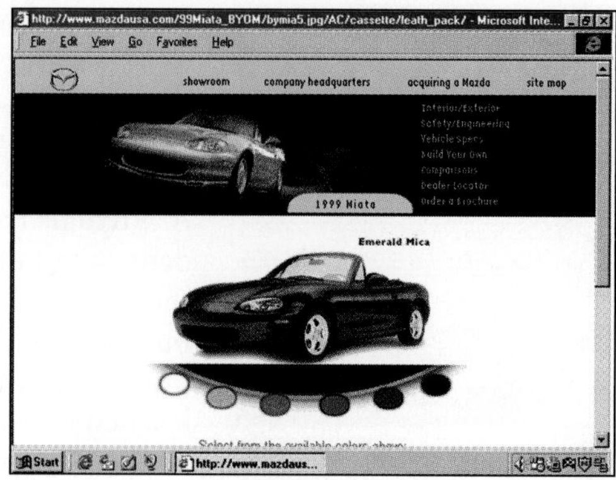

Each chapter opens with a vignette illustrating the themes of the chapter by showing how a real-world organization meets a business challenge using information systems.

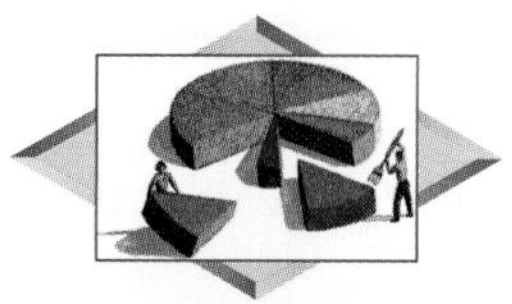

Window on Management: Management problems raised by systems and their solution; management strategies and plans; careers and experiences of managers using systems.

Window on Technology: Hardware, software, telecommunications, data storage, standards, and systems-building methodologies.

Window on Organizations: Activities of private and public organizations using information systems; experiences of people working with systems.

A Truly International Perspective

In addition to a full chapter on managing international information systems (Chapter 15), all chapters of the text are illustrated with real-world examples from nearly one hundred corporations in Canada, Europe, Asia, Latin America, Africa, Australia, and

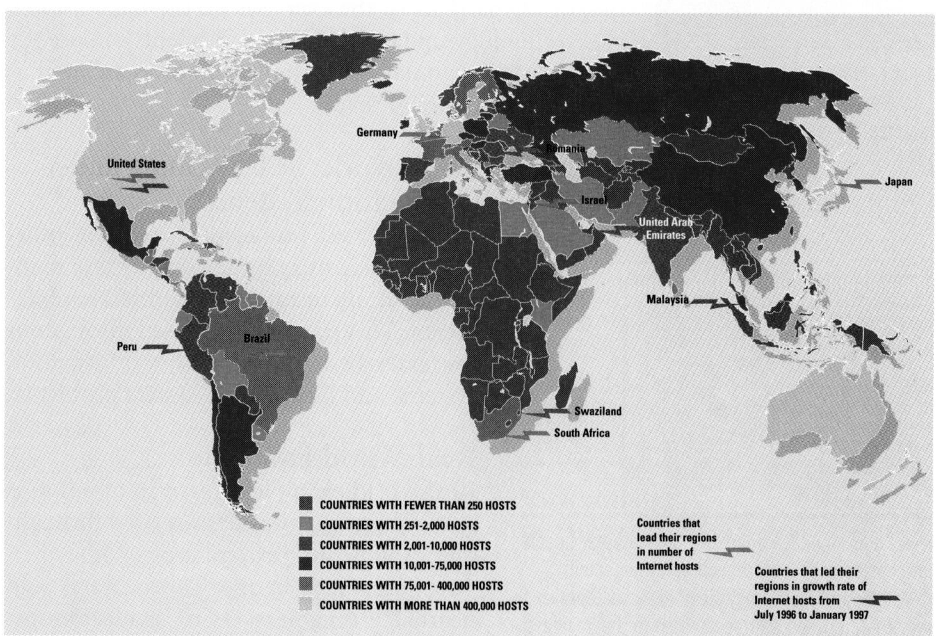

Each chapter contains at least one Window On box, case study, or opening vignette drawn from a non-U.S. firm, and often more.

the Middle East. The text concludes with five major international case studies contributed by leading MIS experts in Canada, Europe, Singapore, and Australia—Len Fertuck, University of Toronto (Canada); Helmut Krcmar, Stephan Wilczek, and Gerhard Schwabe, University of Hohenheim (Germany); Donald Marchand, Thomas Vollmann, and Kimberly Bechler, International Institute for Management Development (Switzerland); Boon Siong Neo and Christina Soh, Nanyang Technological University (Singapore); and Peter Weill and J. B. Barolsky, University of Melbourne, (Australia).

Attention to Small Businesses and Entrepreneurs

A diamond-shaped symbol identifies in-text discussions and specially designated chapter-opening vignettes, Window On boxes, and ending case studies that highlight the experiences and challenges of small businesses and entrepreneurs using information systems.

Pedagogy to Promote Active Learning and Management Problem Solving

Essentials of Management Information Systems: Transforming Business and Management (Third Edition) contains many features that encourage students to learn actively and to engage in management problem solving.

Group Projects: At the end of each chapter is a group project that encourages students to develop teamwork and oral and written presentation skills. The group projects have been enhanced in this edition to make even better use of the Internet. For instance, students might be asked to work in small groups to evaluate the Web sites of two competing businesses or to develop a corporate ethics code on privacy that considers e-mail privacy and the monitoring of employees using networks.

Management Challenges Section: Each chapter begins with several challenges relating to the chapter topic that managers are likely to encounter. These challenges are multifaceted and sometimes pose dilemmas. They make excellent springboards for class discussion. Some of these Management Challenges are: finding the right Internet business model; overcoming the organizational obstacles to building a database environment; and agreeing on quality standards for information systems.

Case Studies: Each chapter concludes with a case study based on a real-world organization. These cases help students synthesize chapter concepts and apply this new knowledge to concrete problems and scenarios. Major international case studies and electronic case studies at the Laudon & Laudon Web site provide additional opportunities for management problem solving.

Book Overview

Part One is concerned with the organizational foundations of systems and their emerging strategic role. It provides an extensive introduction to real-world systems, focusing on their relationship to organizations, management, and important ethical and social issues.

Parts Two and Three provide the technical foundation for understanding information systems, describing hardware, software, storage, and telecommunications technologies. Part Three concludes by describing how all of the information technologies work together through the Internet to support electronic commerce and electronic business.

Part Four focuses on the process of redesigning organizations using information systems, including reengineering of critical business processes. We see systems analysis and design as an exercise in organizational design, one that requires great sensitivity to the right tools and techniques, quality assurance, and change management.

Part Five describes the role of information systems in capturing and distributing organizational knowledge and in enhancing management decision making. It shows how knowledge management, work group collaboration, and individual and group decision making can be supported by the use of knowledge work, artificial intelligence, decision support, and executive support systems.

Part Six concludes the text by examining the special management challenges and opportunities created by the pervasiveness and power of contemporary information systems and the global connectivity of the Internet: ensuring security and control and developing global systems. Throughout the text emphasis is placed on using information technology to redesign the organization's products, services, procedures, jobs, and management structures; numerous examples are drawn from multinational systems and global business environments.

Chapter Outline

Each chapter contains the following:

- A detailed outline at the beginning to provide an overview
- An opening vignette describing a real-world organization to establish the theme and importance of the chapter
- A diagram analyzing the opening vignette in terms of the management, organization, and technology model used throughout the text
- A list of learning objectives
- Management Challenges related to the chapter theme
- Marginal glosses of key terms in the text
- An Internet Connection icon directing students to related material on the Internet
- A Management Wrap-Up tying together the key management, organization, and technology issues for the chapter, with questions for discussion
- A chapter summary keyed to the learning objectives
- A list of key terms that the student can use to review concepts
- Review questions for students to test their comprehension of chapter material
- A group project to develop teamwork and presentation skills
- A Tools for Interactive Learning section showing specifically how the chapter can be integrated with the Laudon Web site and optional CD-ROM edition of the text
- A chapter-ending case study that illustrates important themes

Instructional Support Materials

Instructor's Resource CD-ROM

Many of the support materials described below are now conveniently provided for adopters on the Instructor's Resource CD-ROM. The CD includes the Instructor's Resource Manual, Test Item File, Windows PH Custom Test, Transparencies, and the innovative lecture tool, *Presentation Manager, PowerPoint Edition.*

Instructor's Manual

The Instructor's Manual, written by Professor Glenn Bottoms of Gardner-Webb University, features not only answers to review, discussion, case study, and group project questions, but also an in-depth lecture outline, teaching objectives, key terms, teaching suggestions, and Internet resources. This supplement can be downloaded from the secure faculty section of the Laudon Web site, and is also available on the Instructor's Resource CD-ROM.

Test Item File

The Test Item File is a comprehensive collection of true-false, multiple choice, fill-in-the-blank, and essay questions, written by Dr. Lisa Miller of the University of Central Oklahoma. The questions are rated by difficulty level and answers are referenced by section. An electronic version of the Test Item File is available as the Windows PH Custom Test on the Instructor's Resource CD-ROM.

PowerPoint Slides

Over one hundred electronic color slides created by Dr. Edward Fisher of Central Michigan University are available in Microsoft PowerPoint, Versions 4.0 and 97. The slides illuminate and build upon key concepts in the text. In addition, the version 97 set contains hyperlinks to the Laudon Web site within each chapter. The PowerPoints can be downloaded from the Web site and are available on the Instructor's Resource CD-ROM within Presentation Manager.

Color Transparencies

One hundred full-color transparency acetates are available to adopters. These transparencies, taken from figures in the text, provide additional visual support to class lectures. The transparency masters are available as Acrobat files on the Web site and on the Instructor's Resource CD-ROM.

Presentation Manager, PowerPoint Edition

Presentation Manager, PowerPoint Edition is a truly user-friendly, PC-compatible presentation program that provides instructors with over one hundred images from the text, plus a prearranged set of PowerPoint slides, all to create dynamic classroom presentations. Figure and photo images are organized by chapter, as are the pre-made PowerPoint slides. Instructors can integrate their own images and modify or add notes for each image as well. This presentation program is available on the Instructor's Resource CD-ROM.

Video

Video clips are provided to adopters to enhance class discussion and projects. These clips highlight real-world corporations and organizations and illustrate key concepts found in the text.

Web Site

The Laudon/Laudon text is once again supported by an excellent Web site at **http://www.prenhall.com/laudon** that truly reinforces and enhances text material with Electronic Commerce Projects, Internet Exercises, an Interactive Study Guide, and International Resources. Please see its complete description found earlier in this preface.

Tutorial Software

For instructors looking for Application Software support to use with this text, Prentice Hall is pleased to offer CBT CD-ROMs for Microsoft Office 97 and, soon, for Office 2000. These exciting tutorial CDs are fully certified up to the expert level of the Microsoft Office User Specialist (MOUS) Certification Program. They are not available as stand-alone items but can be packaged with the Laudon/Laudon text at an additional charge. Please contact your local Prentice Hall representative for more details.

Software Cases

A series of optional management software cases called *Solve it! Management Problem Solving with PC Software* has been developed to support the text. *Solve it!* consists of 10 spreadsheet cases, 10 database cases, and 6 Internet projects drawn from real-world businesses, plus a data disk with the files required by the cases. The cases are graduated in difficulty. The case book contains complete tutorial documentation showing how to use spreadsheet, database, and Web browser software to solve the problems. A new version of *Solve it!* with all new cases is published every year. *Solve it!* must be adopted for an entire class. It can be purchased directly from the supplier, Azimuth Corporation, 124 Penfield Ave., Croton-on-Hudson, New York 10520 (telephone: 914-271-6321).

Acknowledgments

The production of any book involves many value contributions from a number of persons. We would like to thank all of our editors for encouragement, insight, and strong support for many years. Our editor David Alexander did an outstanding job in guiding the development of this edition, and we feel very fortunate to work with him. We remain grateful to PJ Boardman, Jim Boyd, and Sandy Steiner for their support of this project. We thank Executive Marketing Manager Nancy Evans for her superb marketing work and her continuing contributions to our texts. Thanks go as well to Sales Director Kris King for her suggestions for improving this edition. We commend Lori Cardillo for directing the preparation of ancillary materials and Anne Graydon for overseeing production of this text.

We remain deeply indebted to Marshall R. Kaplan for his invaluable assistance in the preparation of this edition. Special thanks to Dr. Glenn Bottoms of Gardner-Webb University, Dr. Edward Fisher of Central Michigan University, and Lisa Miller of the University of Central Oklahoma for their work on supporting materials.

The Stern School of Business at New York University and the Information Systems Department provided a very special learning environment, one in which we and others could rethink the MIS field. Special thanks to Professors Edward Stohr, Jon Turner, Vasant Dhar, Ajit Kambil, and Stephen Slade for providing critical feedback and support where deserved. Professor William H. Starbuck of the Management Department at NYU provided valuable comments and insights.

Professors Gordon Everest of the University of Minnesota, Al Croker and Michael Palley of Baruch College and NYU, Professor Kenneth Marr of Hofstra University, Professor Sassan Rahmatian of California State University, Fresno, Professor Lisa Friedrichsen of the Keller Graduate School of Management, and Dr. Edward Roche of the Concours Group provided additional suggestions for improvement. We continue to remember the late Professor James Clifford of the Stern School as a wonderful friend and colleague who also made valuable recommendations for improving our discussion of files and databases.

One of our goals was to write a book that was authoritative, synthesized diverse views in the MIS literature, and helped define a common academic field. A large number of leading scholars in the field were contacted and assisted us in this effort. Reviewers and consultants for *Essentials of Management Information Systems: Transforming Business and Managment* are listed in the back endpapers of the book. We thank them for their contributions. Consultants for this new edition include: Marianne Hill of Furman University; Jack Hogue of the University of North Carolina, Charlotte; Evans Adams of Fort Lewis College; Jack Powell of the University of South Dakota; Erma Wood of the University of Arkansas, Little Rock; Solomon Antony of Oakland University; Stephanie Robbins of the University of North Carolina, Charlotte; Marcel Robelis of the University of North Dakota; Patricia McQuaid of California Polytechnic Institute, and Jeff Zhang of Langston University. It is our hope that this group endeavor contributes to a shared vision and understanding of the MIS field.

—K.C.L.
J.P.L.

Essentials of Management Information Systems

CHAPTER 1

The Information Systems Revolution: Transforming Business and Management

chapter outline

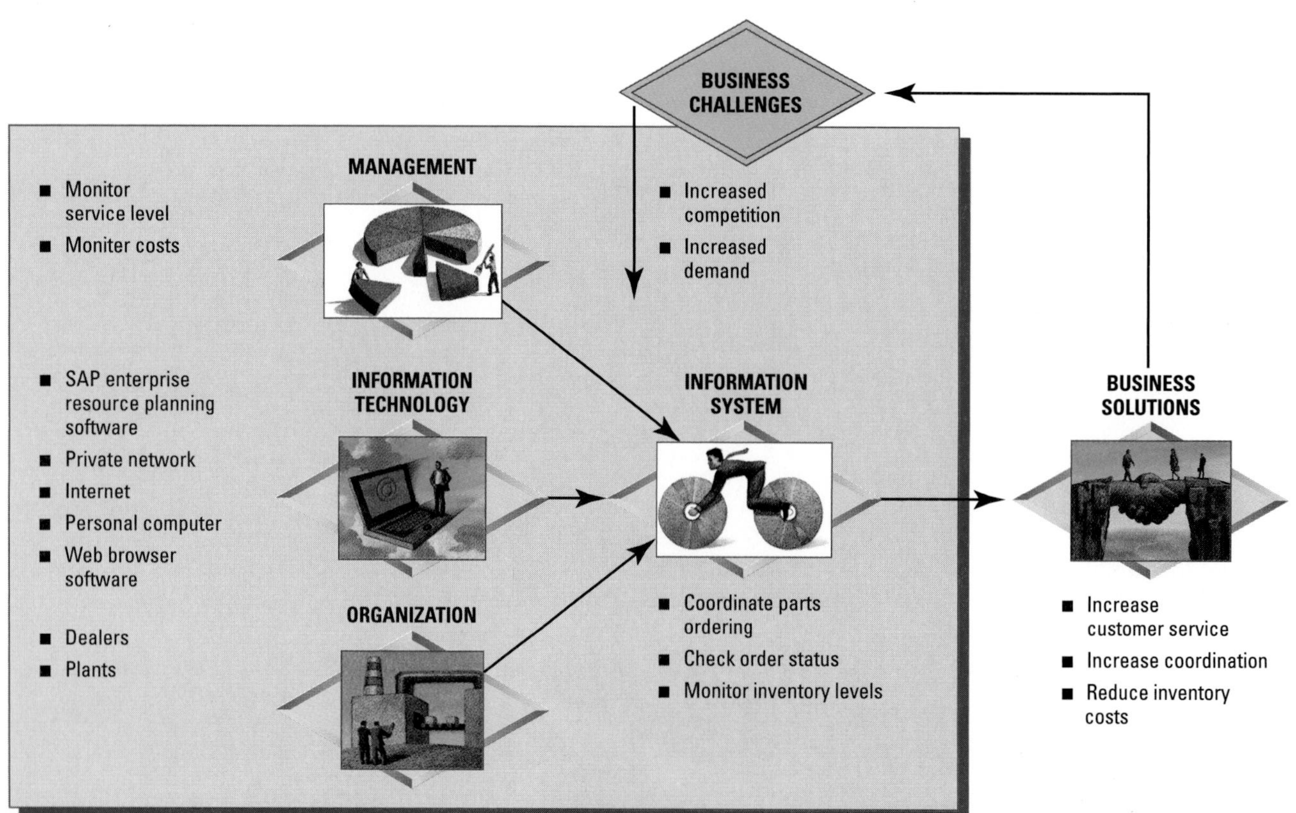

VW Mexico Shifts into High Gear with the Internet

Volkswagen of Mexico found it had to shift into high gear with its information systems: Competition was increasing, along with the demand for its autos. The Puebla plant, which produces Golfs, Jettas, and other Volkswagen models for North America and some overseas markets, had to add capacity to take on the production of new models such as VW's new Beetle. In March 1996, VW of Mexico implemented SAP's enterprise resource planning system in the Puebla plant to orchestrate all of the different areas of the parts-ordering and manufacturing processes—supplier orders, reception, warehousing, client orders, packing and billing. Its improvements in efficiency and coordination are as important to VW dealers as to the plant management itself. Dealers sometimes make more money on service than they do on selling cars, so increased efficiencies in ordering parts can translate into better customer service and more customers.

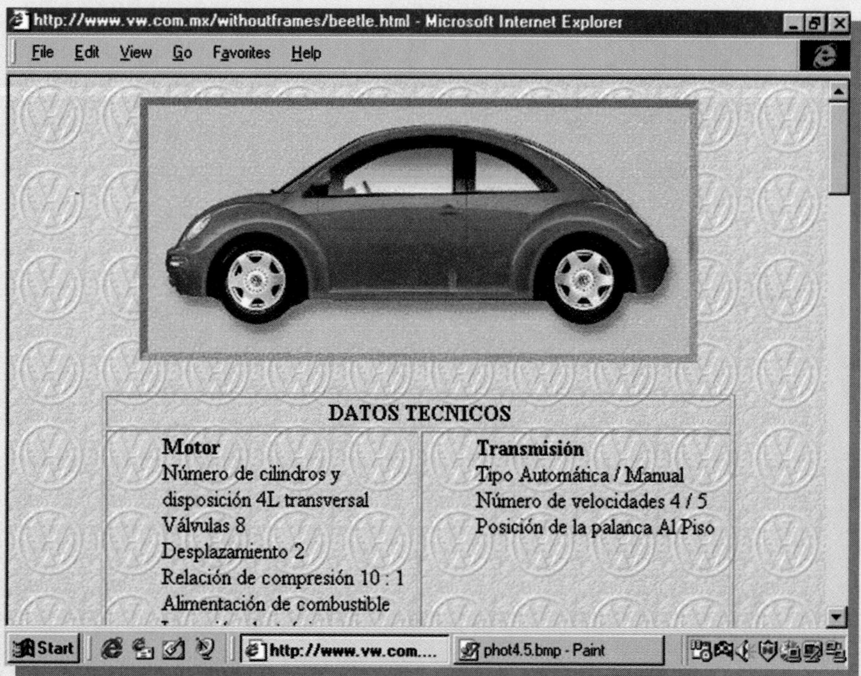

In the past, it would take about 10 days to have a spare part delivered from the plant. Dealers would have to call or fax the plant office between 8 A.M. and 4 P.M. Monday through Friday, or mail the plant a computer disk listing the needed inventory. Most dealers had no easy way of knowing if a part was available or if their orders were received. They would have to call the plant's distribution center and ask an office worker to track the order for them. Since there was no way to anticipate and coordinate parts orders, both dealers and the plant overstocked their inventories to make sure parts were always available, increasing their operating costs.

The new system eliminates the need for excess inventory by coordinating the parts-ordering process. Once an order for a part has been entered, people at every level of the company, from the plant floor to the dealer showroom can access the system to check its status. The plant can monitor inventory levels and replenish them before parts go out of stock. To make the system more easily available to dealers who had not yet computerized, the company created a private network based on Internet technology that allows its dealers to access information in the system using a personal computer and off-the-shelf browser software for accessing the World Wide Web.

VW Mexico dealers can now use their desktop computers to log onto the system via the Internet and supply an ID and password to access the company's private network. Then they can enter orders and check the progress of those orders. The system locates an order and reports its estimated time of delivery. Turnaround time for ordering parts has been reduced by more than half, giving dealers a decisive competitive advantage in customer service.

Dealers no longer have to maintain large local inventories of parts.

Some dealers have been reluctant to buy, install, and use computers to gain access to the system. VW Mexico management is counting on the ease and low cost of using Internet technology to win them over.

Source: Adapted from Aileen Crowley, "VW Mexico Shifting to High Gear," *PC Week*, January 9, 1998.

learning objectives

After completing this chapter, you will be able to:

1. Define an information system.
2. Distinguish between computer literacy and information systems literacy.
3. Explain why information systems are so important today and how they are transforming organizations and management.
4. Compare electronic commerce and electronic business and analyze their relationship to the Internet and digital technology.
5. Identify the major management challenges to building and using information systems in organizations.

VW Mexico's use of Internet technology in its parts ordering system illustrates how companies can use information systems and networks to conduct more of their business electronically to make them more efficient and competitive. In today's global business environment, information systems, the Internet, and other global networks are creating new opportunities for organizational coordination and innovation. Information systems can help companies extend their reach to faraway locations, offer new products and services, reshape jobs and work flows, and perhaps profoundly change the way they conduct business. As VW Mexico's experience also illustrates, systems pose challenges to management as well. This chapter starts our investigation of information systems and organizations by describing information systems from both technical and behavioral perspectives and by surveying the changes they are bringing to organizations and management.

1.1 WHY INFORMATION SYSTEMS?

Until recently, information itself was not considered an important asset for a firm. The management process was considered a face-to-face, personal art and not a far-flung, global coordination process. Today it is widely recognized that understanding information systems is essential for managers because most organizations need information systems to survive and prosper.

The Competitive Business Environment

Three powerful worldwide changes have altered the environment of business. The first change is the emergence and strengthening of the global economy. The second change is the transformation of industrial economies and societies into knowledge- and information-based service economies. The third is the transformation of the business

TABLE 1.1 The Changing Contemporary Business Environment
Globalization
Management and control in a global marketplace
Competition in world markets
Global work groups
Global delivery systems
Transformation of Industrial Economies
Knowledge- and information-based economies
Productivity
New products and services
Knowledge: a central productive and strategic asset
Time-based competition
Shorter product life
Turbulent environment
Limited employee knowledge base
Transformation of the Enterprise
Flattening
Decentralization
Flexibility
Location independence
Low transaction and coordination costs
Empowerment
Collaborative work and teamwork

enterprise. These changes in the business environment and climate, summarized in Table 1.1, pose a number of new challenges to business firms and their management.

Emergence of the Global Economy

A growing percentage of the American economy—and other advanced industrial economies in Europe and Asia—depends on imports and exports. Foreign trade, both exports and imports, accounts for a little over 25 percent of the goods and services produced in the United States, and even more in countries like Japan and Germany. The success of firms today and in the future depends on their ability to operate globally.

Globalization of the world's industrial economies greatly enhances the value of information to the firm and offers new opportunities to businesses. Today, information systems provide the communication and analytic power that firms need for conducting trade and managing businesses on a global scale. Controlling the far-flung global corporation—communicating with distributors and suppliers, operating 24 hours a day in different national environments, servicing local and international reporting needs—is a major business challenge that requires powerful information system responses.

Globalization and information technology also bring new threats to domestic business firms: Because of global communication and management systems, customers now can shop in a worldwide marketplace, obtaining price and quality information reliably, 24 hours a day. This phenomenon heightens competition and forces firms to play in open, unprotected worldwide markets. To become effective and profitable participants in international markets, firms need powerful information and communication systems.

Transformation of Industrial Economies

The United States, Japan, Germany, and other major industrial powers are being transformed from industrial economies to knowledge- and information-based service economies, while manufacturing has moved to low-wage countries. In a knowledge- and information-based economy, knowledge and information are key ingredients in creating wealth.

The knowledge and information revolution began at the turn of the twentieth century and has gradually accelerated. By 1976 the number of white-collar workers employed in offices surpassed the number of farm workers, service workers, and blue-collar workers employed in manufacturing (see Figure 1.1). Today, most people no longer work on farms or in factories but instead are found in sales, education, health care, banks, insurance firms, and law firms; they also provide business services like copying, computer programming, or making deliveries. These jobs primarily involve working with, distributing, or creating new knowledge and information. In fact, knowledge and information work now account for a significant 60 percent of the American gross national product and nearly 55 percent of the labor force.

knowledge- and information-intense products Products that require a great deal of learning and knowledge to produce.

Knowledge and information are becoming the foundation for many new services and products. **Knowledge- and information-intense products** such as computer games require a great deal of learning and knowledge to produce. Entire new information-based services have sprung up, such as Lexis, Dow Jones News Service and America Online. These fields are employing millions of people.

Intensification of knowledge utilization in the production of traditional products has increased as well. This trend is readily seen throughout the automobile industry where both design and production now rely heavily upon knowledge-intensive infor-

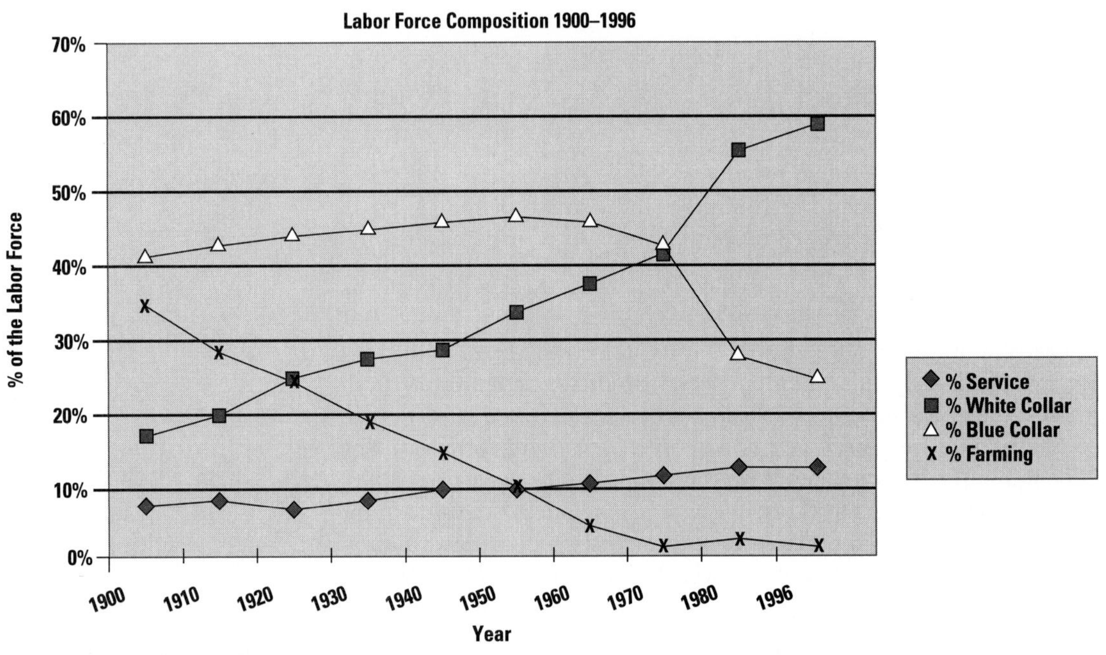

FIGURE 1.1

The growth of the information economy. Since the turn of the century, the United States has experienced a steady decline in the number of farm workers and blue-collar workers who are employed in factories. At the same time, the country is experiencing a rise in the number of white-collar workers who produce economic value using knowledge and information.

Sources: Adapted from U.S. Department of Commerce, Bureau of the Census, Statistical Abstract of the United States, 1997, *Table 645: 1900–1970 and* Historical Statistics of the United States, Colonial Times to 1970, *Vol. 1, Series D 182–232.*

mation technology. During the past decade, the automobile producers have sharply increased their hiring of computer specialists, engineers, and designers while reducing the number of blue-collar production workers.

New kinds of knowledge- and information-intense organizations have emerged that are devoted entirely to the production, processing, and distribution of information. For instance, environmental engineering firms, which specialize in preparing environmental impact statements for municipalities and private contractors, simply did not exist thirty years ago.

In a knowledge- and information-based economy, information technology and systems take on great importance. Knowledge-based products and services of great economic value, such as credit cards, overnight package delivery, and worldwide reservation systems, are based on new information technologies. Information technology constitutes more than 70 percent of the invested capital in service industries like finance, insurance, and real estate.

Across all industries, information and the technology that delivers it have become critical, strategic assets for business firms and their managers (Leonard-Barton, 1995). Information systems are needed to optimize the flow of information and knowledge within the organization and to help management maximize the firm's knowledge resources. Because the productivity of employees will depend on the quality of the systems serving them, management decisions about information technology are critically important to the prosperity and survival of a firm.

Transformation of the Business Enterprise

The third major change in the business environment is the very nature of organization and management. There has been a transformation in the possibilities for organizing and managing. Some firms have begun to take advantage of these new possibilities.

The traditional business firm was—and still is—a hierarchical, centralized, structured arrangement of specialists that typically relies on a fixed set of standard operating procedures to deliver a mass-produced product (or service). The new style of business firm is a flattened (less hierarchical), decentralized, flexible arrangement of generalists who rely on nearly instant information to deliver mass-customized products and services uniquely suited to specific markets or customers. This new style of organization is not yet firmly entrenched; it is still evolving. Nevertheless, the direction is clear, and this new direction would be unthinkable without information technology.

The traditional management group relied—and still does—on formal plans, a rigid division of labor, formal rules, and appeals to loyalty to ensure the proper operation of a firm. The new manager relies on informal commitments and networks to establish goals (rather than formal planning), a flexible arrangement of teams and individuals working in task forces, a customer orientation to achieve coordination among employees, and appeals to professionalism and knowledge to ensure proper operation of the firm. Once again, information technology makes this style of management possible.

Information technology is bringing about changes in organization that make the firm even more dependent than in the past on the knowledge, learning, and decision making of individual employees. Throughout this book, we describe the role that information technology is now playing in the transformation of the business enterprise form.

What Is an Information System?

An **information system** can be defined technically as a set of interrelated components that collect (or retrieve), process, store, and distribute information to support decision making and control in an organization. In addition to supporting decision making, coordination, and control, information systems may also help managers and workers analyze problems, visualize complex subjects, and create new products.

Information systems contain information about significant people, places, and things within the organization or in the environment surrounding it (see Figure 1.2). By

information system Interrelated components working together to collect, process, store, and disseminate information to support decision making, coordination, control, analysis, and visualization in an organization.

FIGURE 1.2

Functions of an information system. An information system contains information about an organization and its surrounding environment. Three basic activities—input, processing, and output—produce the information organizations need. Feedback is output returned to appropriate people or activities in the organization to evaluate and refine the input.

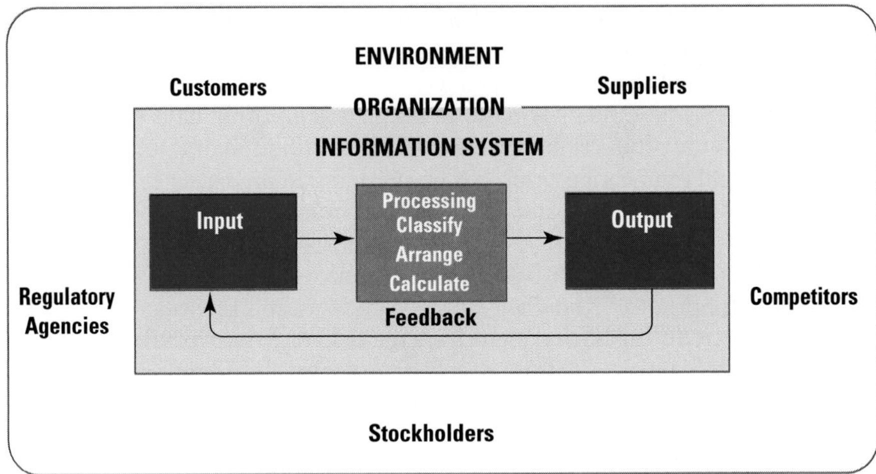

information Data that have been shaped into a form that is meaningful and useful to human beings.

data Streams of raw facts representing events occurring in organizations or the physical environment before they have been organized and arranged into a form that people can understand and use.

input The capture or collection of raw data from within the organization or from its external environment for processing in an information system.

processing The conversion, manipulation, and analysis of raw input into a form that is more meaningful to humans.

output The distribution of processed information to the people or activities where it will be used.

feedback Output that is returned to the appropriate members of the organization to help them evaluate or correct input.

computer-based information systems (CBIS) Information systems that rely on computer hardware and software for processing and disseminating information.

information we mean data that have been shaped into a form that is meaningful and useful to human beings. **Data,** in contrast, are streams of raw facts representing events occurring in organizations or the physical environment before they have been organized and arranged into a form that people can understand and use.

Three activities in an information system produce the information that organizations need for making decisions, controlling operations, analyzing problems, and creating new products or services. These activities are input, processing, and output. **Input** captures or collects raw data from within the organization or from its external environment. **Processing** converts this raw input into a more meaningful form. **Output** transfers the processed information to the people or activities where it will be used. Information systems also require **feedback,** which is output that is returned to appropriate members of the organization to help them evaluate or correct the input stage.

In the information system used by VW Mexico for ordering parts, the raw input from the dealer consists of the part number, part description, and number of each part ordered, along with the dealer's name and identification number. The computer processes these data by comparing each part number and amount of each part ordered to the quantity of each part available in inventory and scheduling the shipment of the part to the dealer. If the part is out of stock, the computer notifies the plant to manufacture more of that item. Shipping documents and on-line reports to the dealer confirming that the order has been received and its expected shipment date become output. The system thus provides meaningful information such as lists of which dealer ordered each part, the total number of parts ordered daily from the Puebla plant, the number and type of parts ordered by each dealer, or the number of parts in inventory.

Our interest in this book is in formal, organizational **computer-based information systems (CBIS)** like those designed and used by VW Mexico. **Formal systems** rest on accepted and fixed definitions of data and procedures for collecting, storing, processing, disseminating, and using these data. The formal systems we describe in this text are structured; that is, they operate in conformity with predefined rules that are relatively fixed and not easily changed. For instance, VW Mexico's system requires that all orders for parts include the dealer's name and identification number and a unique number for identifying each part.

Informal information systems (such as office gossip networks) rely, by contrast, on unstated rules of behavior. There is no agreement on what is information, or on how it will be stored and processed. Such systems are essential for the life of an organization, but an analysis of their qualities is beyond the scope of this text.

Formal information systems can be either computer-based or manual. Manual systems use paper-and-pencil technology. These manual systems serve important needs, but they too are not the subject of this text. Computer-based information systems, in contrast, rely on computer hardware and software technology to process and disseminate information. From this point on, when we use the term *information systems,* we will be referring to computer-based information systems—formal organizational systems that rely on computer technology. The Window on Technology describes some of the typical technologies used in computer-based information systems today.

formal system System resting on accepted and fixed definitions of data and procedures, operating with predefined rules.

Although computer-based information systems use computer technology to process raw data into meaningful information, there is a sharp distinction between a computer and a computer program on the one hand, and an information system on the other. Electronic computers and related software programs are the technical foundation, the tools and materials, of modern information systems. Computers provide the equipment for storing and processing information. Computer programs, or software, are sets of operating instructions that direct and control computer processing. Knowing how computers and computer programs work is important in designing solutions to organizational problems, but computers are only part of an information system. Housing provides an appropriate analogy. Houses are built with hammers, nails, and wood, but these do not make a house. The architecture, design, setting, landscaping, and all of the decisions that lead to the creation of these features are part of the house and are crucial for finding a solution to the problem of putting a roof over one's head. Computers and programs are the hammer, nails, and lumber of CBIS, but alone they cannot produce the information a particular organization needs. To understand information systems, one must understand the problems they are designed to solve, their architectural and design elements, and the organizational processes that lead to these solutions.

A Business Perspective on Information Systems

From a business perspective, an information system is an organizational and management solution, based on information technology, to a challenge posed by the environment. Examine this definition closely because it emphasizes the organizational and management nature of information systems: To understand information systems—to be information systems literate as opposed to computer literate—a manager must understand the broader organization, management, and information technology dimensions of systems (see Figure 1.3) and their power to provide solutions to challenges and problems in the business environment.

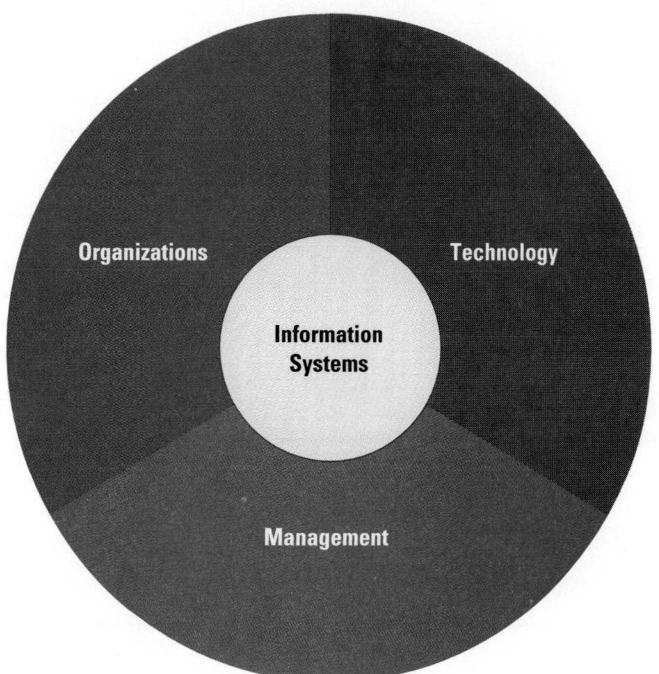

FIGURE 1.3

Information systems are more than computers. Using information systems effectively requires an understanding of the organization, management, and information technology shaping the systems. All information systems can be described as organizational and management solutions to challenges posed by the environment.

WINDOW ON TECHNOLOGY

UPS Competes Globally with Information Technology

United Parcel Service, the world's largest air and ground package-distribution company, started out in 1907 in a closet-sized basement office. Jim Casey and Claude Ryan—two teenagers from Seattle with two bicycles and one phone—promised the "best service and lowest rates." UPS has used this formula successfully for 90 years.

UPS still lives up to that promise today, delivering more than 3 billion parcels and documents each year to the United States and to more than 185 other countries and territories. Critical to the firm's success has been its investment in advanced information technology. Technology has helped UPS boost customer service while keeping costs low and streamlining its overall operations.

Using a handheld computer called a Delivery Information Acquisition Device (DIAD), UPS drivers automatically capture customers' signatures along with pickup, delivery, and time-card information. The drivers then place the DIAD into their truck's vehicle adapter, an information-transmitting device that is connected to the cellular telephone network. Package tracking information is then transmitted to UPS's computer network for storage and processing in UPS's main computer in Mahwah, New Jersey. From there, the information can be accessed worldwide to provide proof of delivery to the customer. The system can also generate a printed response to queries by the customer.

Through its automated package tracking system, UPS can monitor packages throughout the delivery process. At various points along the route from sender to receiver, a bar code device scans shipping information on the package label; the information is then fed into the central computer. Customer service representatives can check the status of any package from desktop computers linked to the central computer and are able to respond immediately to inquiries from customers. UPS customers can also access this information directly from their own computers, using either the World Wide Web of the Internet or special package tracking software supplied by UPS.

Anyone with a package to ship can access the UPS Web site to check delivery routes, calculate shipping rates, and schedule a pickup. Eventually they will be able use the Web to pay for their shipments using a credit card or a tab tracking on-line purchase orders for large regular customers. The data collected at the UPS Web site are transmitted to the UPS central computer and then back to the customer after processing. UPS recently started a new service called UPS Document Exchange to deliver business documents electronically using the Internet. The service provides a high level of security for these important documents and document tracking.

UPS's Inventory Express, launched in 1991, warehouses customers' products and ships them overnight to any destination the customer requests. Customers using this service can transmit electronic shipping orders to UPS by 1:00 A.M. and expect delivery by 10:30 that same morning. UPS is enhancing its information system capabilities so that it can guarantee that a particular package or group of packages will arrive at its destination at a specified time. If requested by the customer, UPS will be able to intercept a package prior to delivery and have it returned or rerouted.

To Think About: ***What are the inputs, processing, and outputs of UPS's package tracking system? What technologies are used? How are these technologies related to UPS's business strategy? What would happen if these technologies were not available?***

Sources: Barb Cole-Gomolski, "Need to Send Secure Documents via the Internet? See UPS," *Computerworld,* March 8, 1998; "UPS Launches New Delivery and Information Options," *UPS Public Relations,* January 2, 1997; and Kim Nash, "Overnight Services Duke It Out On-Line," *Computerworld,* April 22, 1996.

Review the diagram at the beginning of the chapter, which reflects this expanded definition of an information system. The diagram shows how VW Mexico's information system provides a solution to the business challenges of trying to increase customer service in the face of increased competition and demand. The diagram also illustrates how management, technology, and organization elements work together to create the system. We begin each chapter of the text with a diagram like this one to help you analyze the opening case. You can use this diagram as a starting point for analyzing any information system or information system problem you encounter.

Organizations

Information systems are a part of organizations. Indeed, for some companies, such as credit reporting firms, without the system there would be no business. The key elements of an organization are its people, structure and operating procedures, politics, and culture. We introduce these components of organizations here and describe them in greater detail in Chapter 3. Formal organizations are composed of different levels and specialties. Their structures reveal a clear-cut division of labor. Experts are employed and trained for different functions, including sales and marketing, manufacturing, finance, accounting, and human resources. Table 1.2 describes these functions.

An organization coordinates work through a structured hierarchy and formal, standard operating procedures. The hierarchy arranges people in a pyramidal structure of rising authority and responsibility. The upper levels of the hierarchy consist of managerial, professional, and technical employees, whereas the lower levels consist of operational personnel.

Standard operating procedures (SOPs) are formal rules for accomplishing tasks that have been developed over a long time; these rules guide employees in a variety of procedures, from writing an invoice to responding to complaining customers. Most procedures are formalized and written down, but many others are informal work practices. Many of a firm's SOPs are incorporated into information systems, such as how to pay a supplier or how to correct an erroneous bill.

Organizations require many different kinds of skills and people. In addition to managers, **knowledge workers** (such as engineers, architects, or scientists) design products or services and create new knowledge, and **data workers** (such as secretaries, bookkeepers, or clerks) process the organization's paperwork. **Production or service workers** (such as machinists, assemblers, or packers) actually produce the products or services of the organization.

Each organization has a unique *culture,* or fundamental set of assumptions, values, and ways of doing things, that has been accepted by most of its members. Parts of an organization's culture can always be found embedded in its information systems. For instance, the concern with putting service to the customer first is an aspect of the organizational culture of United Parcel Service that can be found in the company's package tracking systems.

standard operating procedures (SOPs) Formal rules for accomplishing tasks that have been developed to cope with expected situations.

knowledge workers People such as engineers or architects who design products or services and create knowledge for the organization.

data workers People such as secretaries or bookkeepers who process the organization's paperwork.

production or service workers People who actually produce the products or services of the organization.

TABLE 1.2 Major Organizational Functions

Function	Purpose
Sales and marketing	Selling the organization's products and services
Manufacturing	Producing products and services
Finance	Managing the organization's financial assets (cash, stocks, bonds, etc.)
Accounting	Maintaining the organization's financial records (receipts, disbursements, paychecks, etc.); accounting for the flow of funds
Human resources	Attracting, developing, and maintaining the organization's labor force; maintaining employee records

Different levels and specialties in an organization create different interests and points of view. These views often conflict. Conflict is the basis for organizational politics. Information systems come out of this cauldron of differing perspectives, conflicts, compromises, and agreements that are a natural part of all organizations. In Chapter 3 we will examine these features of organizations in greater detail.

Management

Managers perceive business challenges in the environment; they set the organizational strategy for responding; and they allocate the human and financial resources to achieve the strategy and coordinate the work. Throughout, they must exercise responsible leadership. Management's job is to "make sense" out of the many situations faced by organizations and formulate action plans to solve organizational problems. The business information systems described in this book reflect the hopes, dreams, and realities of real-world managers.

But less understood is the fact that managers must do more than manage what already exists. They must also create new products and services and even re-create the organization from time to time. A substantial part of management is creative work driven by new knowledge and information. Information technology can play a powerful role in redirecting and redesigning the organization. Chapter 3 describes the activities of managers and management decision making in detail.

senior managers People occupying the topmost hierarchy in an organization who are responsible for making long-range decisions.

middle managers People in the middle of the organizational hierarchy who are responsible for carrying out the plans and goals of senior management.

operational managers People who monitor the day-to-day activities of the organization.

It is important to note that managerial roles and decisions vary at different levels of the organization. **Senior managers** make long-range strategic decisions about products and services to produce. **Middle managers** carry out the programs and plans of senior management. **Operational managers** are responsible for monitoring the firm's daily activities. All levels of management are expected to be creative, to develop novel solutions to a broad range of problems. Each level of management has different information needs and information system requirements.

Technology

computer hardware Physical equipment used for input, processing, and output activities in an information system.

computer software Detailed, preprogrammed instructions that control and coordinate the work of computer hardware components in an information system.

storage technology Physical media and software governing the storage and organization of data for use in an information system.

communications technology Physical devices and software that link various computer hardware components and transfer data from one physical location to another.

network Two or more computers linked to share data or resources such as a printer.

Information technology is one of many tools available to managers for coping with change. **Computer hardware** is the physical equipment used for input, processing, and output activities in an information system. It consists of the following: the computer processing unit; various input, output, and storage devices; and physical media to link these devices together. Chapter 5 describes computer hardware in greater detail.

Computer software consists of the detailed preprogrammed instructions that control and coordinate the computer hardware components in an information system. Chapter 6 explains the importance of computer software in information systems.

Storage technology includes both the physical media for storing data, such as magnetic or optical disk or tape, and the software governing the organization of data on these physical media. More detail on physical storage media can be found in Chapter 5, whereas Chapter 7 treats data organization and access methods.

Communications technology, consisting of both physical devices and software, links the various pieces of hardware and transfers data from one physical location to another. Computers and communications equipment can be connected in networks for sharing voice, data, images, sound, or even video. A **network** links two or more computers to share data or resources such as a printer. Chapters 8 and 9 provide more details on communications and networking technology and issues.

Let us return to UPS's package tracking system in the Window on Technology and identify the organization, management, and technology elements. The organization element anchors the package tracking system in UPS's sales and production functions (the main product of UPS is a service—package delivery). It identifies the required procedures for identifying packages with both sender and recipient information, taking inventory, tracking the packages en route, and providing package status reports for UPS customers and customer service representatives. The system must also provide information to satisfy the needs of managers and workers. UPS drivers need to be trained in both package pickup and delivery procedures and in how to use the package tracking system so that they can work more efficiently and effectively. UPS customers may need some training to use UPS in-house package tracking software or the UPS World Wide Web site. UPS's management is responsible for monitoring service levels and costs and for promoting the company's strategy of combining low cost and superior service. Management decided to use automation to increase the ease of sending a package via UPS and of checking its delivery status, thereby reducing delivery costs and increasing sales revenues. The technology supporting this system consists of handheld computers, bar code scanners, wired and wireless communications networks, desktop computers, UPS's central computer, storage technology for the package delivery data, UPS in-house package tracking software, and software to access the World Wide Web. The result is an information system solution to a business challenge.

1.2 CONTEMPORARY APPROACHES TO INFORMATION SYSTEMS

Multiple perspectives on information systems show that the study of information systems is a multidisciplinary field; no single theory or perspective dominates. Figure 1.4 illustrates the major disciplines that contribute problems, issues, and solutions in the study of information systems. In general, the field can be divided into technical and behavioral approaches. Information systems are sociotechnical systems. Though they are composed of machines, devices, and "hard" physical technology, they require substantial social, organizational, and intellectual investments to make them work properly.

Technical Approach

The technical approach to information systems emphasizes mathematically based, normative models to study information systems, as well as the physical technology and formal capabilities of these systems. The disciplines that contribute to the technical approach are computer science, management science, and operations research. Computer science is concerned with establishing theories of computability, methods of computation, and methods of efficient data storage and access. Management science emphasizes the development of models for decision making and management practices. Operations research focuses on mathematical techniques for optimizing selected parameters of organizations such as transportation, inventory control, and transaction costs.

Behavioral Approach

An important part of the information systems field is concerned with behavioral issues that arise in the development and long-term maintenance of information systems. Issues such as strategic business integration, design, implementation, utilization, and

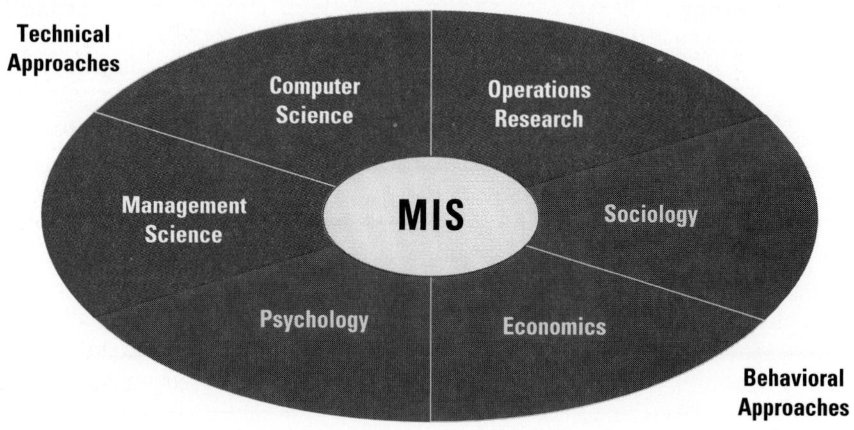

FIGURE 1.4
Contemporary approaches to information systems. The study of information systems deals with issues and insights contributed from technical and behavioral disciplines.

management cannot be explored usefully with the models used in the technical approach. Other behavioral disciplines contribute important concepts and methods. For instance, sociologists study information systems with an eye toward how groups and organizations shape the development of systems and also how systems affect individuals, groups, and organizations. Psychologists study information systems with an interest in how formal information is perceived and used by human decision makers. Economists study information systems with an interest in what impact systems have on control and cost structures within the firm and within markets.

The behavioral approach does not ignore technology. Indeed, information systems technology is often the stimulus for a behavioral problem or issue. But the focus of this approach is generally not on technical solutions; it concentrates rather on changes in attitudes, management and organizational policy, and behavior (Kling and Dutton, 1982).

Approach of This Text: Sociotechnical Systems

The study of management information systems (MIS) arose in the 1970s to focus on computer-based information systems aimed at managers (Davis and Olson, 1985). MIS combines the theoretical work of computer science, management science, and operations research with a practical orientation toward building systems and applications. It also pays attention to behavioral issues raised by sociology, economics, and psychology.

Our experience as academics and practitioners leads us to believe that no single perspective effectively captures the reality of information systems. Problems with systems—and their solutions—are rarely all technical or all behavioral. Our best advice to students is to understand the perspectives of all disciplines. Indeed, the challenge and excitement of the information systems field is that it requires an appreciation and tolerance of many different approaches.

A sociotechnical systems perspective helps to avoid a purely technological approach to information systems. For instance, the fact that information technology is rapidly declining in cost and growing in power does not necessarily or easily translate into productivity enhancement or bottom-line profits.

In this book, we stress the need to optimize the performance of the system as a whole. Both the technical and behavioral components need attention. This means that technology must be changed and designed in such a way as to fit organizational and individual needs. At times, the technology may have to be "de-optimized" to accomplish this fit. Organizations and individuals must also be changed through training, learning, and planned organizational change in order to allow the technology to operate and prosper (see, for example, Liker et al., 1987). People and organizations change to take advantage of new information technology. Figure 1.5 illustrates this process of mutual adjustment in a sociotechnical system.

FIGURE 1.5

A sociotechnical perspective on information systems. In a sociotechnical perspective, the performance of a system is optimized when both the technology and the organization mutually adjust to one another until a satisfactory fit is obtained.

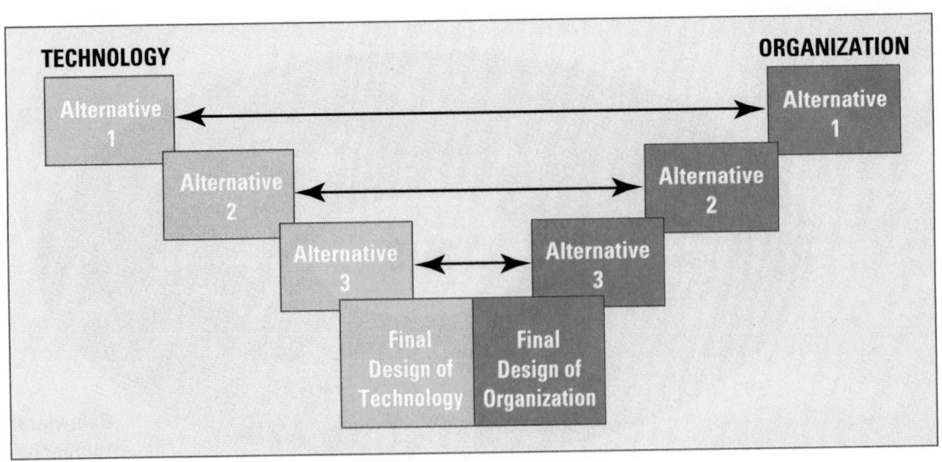

1.3 THE NEW ROLE OF INFORMATION SYSTEMS IN ORGANIZATIONS

Information systems cannot be ignored by managers because they play such a critical role in contemporary organizations. Digital technology is transforming business organizations. The entire cash flow of most Fortune 500 companies is linked to information systems. Today's systems directly affect how managers decide, how senior managers plan, and in many cases what products and services are produced (and how). They play a strategic role in the life of the firm. Responsibility for information systems cannot be delegated to technical decision makers.

The Widening Scope of Information Systems

Figure 1.6 illustrates the new relationship between organizations and information systems. There is a growing interdependence between business strategy, rules, and procedures on the one hand, and information systems software, hardware, databases, and telecommunications on the other. A change in any of these components often requires changes in other components. This relationship becomes critical when management plans for the future. What a business would like to do in five years is often dependent on what its systems will be able to do. Increasing market share, becoming the high-quality or low-cost producer, developing new products, and increasing employee productivity depend more and more on the kinds and quality of information systems in the organization.

A second change in the relationship of information systems and organizations results from the growing complexity and scope of system projects and applications. Building systems today involves a much larger part of the organization than it did in the past (see Figure 1.7). Whereas early systems produced largely technical changes that affected few people, contemporary systems bring about managerial changes (who has what information about whom, when, and how often) and institutional "core" changes (what products and services are produced, under what conditions, and by whom).

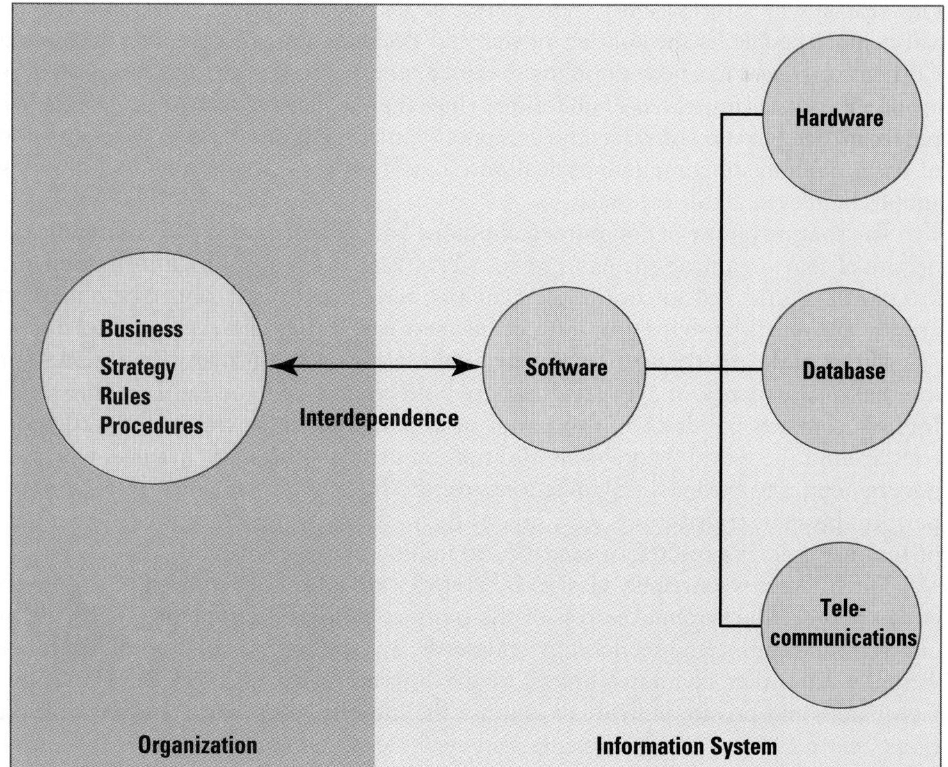

FIGURE 1.6

The interdependence between organizations and information systems. In contemporary systems there is a growing interdependence between organizational business strategy, rules, and procedures and the organization's information systems. Changes in strategy, rules, and procedures increasingly require changes in hardware, software, databases, and telecommunications. Existing systems can act as a constraint on organizations. Often, what the organization would like to do depends on what its systems will permit it to do.

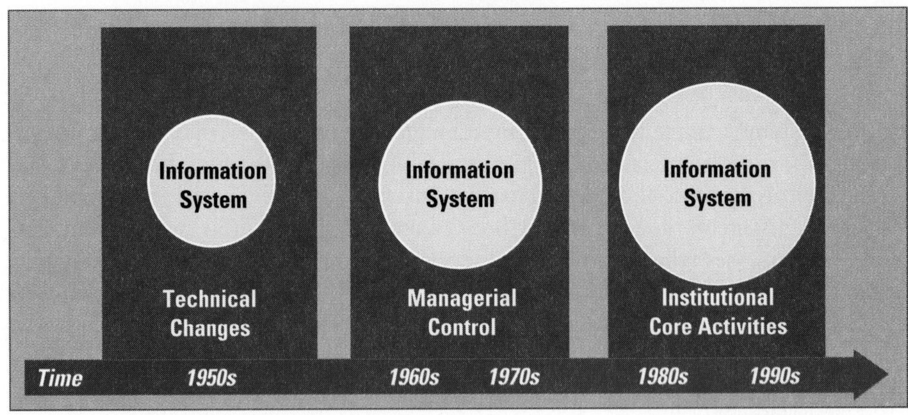

FIGURE 1.7
The widening scope of information systems. Over time, information systems have come to play a larger role in the life of organizations. Early systems brought about largely technical changes that were relatively easy to accomplish. Later systems affected managerial control and behavior; ultimately systems influenced "core" institutional activities concerning products, markets, suppliers, and customers.

In the 1950s, employees in the treasurer's office, a few part-time programmers, a single program, a single machine, and a few clerks might have used a computerized payroll system. The change from a manual to a computer system was largely technical: The computer system simply automated a clerical procedure such as check processing. In contrast, today's integrated human resources system (which includes payroll processing) may involve all major corporate divisions, the human resources department, dozens of full-time programmers, a flock of external consultants, multiple machines (or remote computers linked by telecommunications networks), and perhaps hundreds of end users in the organization who use payroll data to make calculations about benefits and pensions and to answer a host of other questions. The data, instead of being located in and controlled by the treasurer's office, are now available to hundreds of employees via desktop computers, each of which is as powerful as the large computers of the mid-1980s. This contemporary system embodies both managerial and institutional changes.

The Network Revolution and the Internet

One reason why information systems play a larger role in organizations, and why they affect more people, is the soaring power and declining cost of computer technology. Computing power has been doubling every 18 months, so that the performance of microprocessors has improved 25,000 times since their invention over 25 years ago. With powerful, easy-to-use software, the computer can crunch numbers, analyze vast pools of data, or simulate complex physical and logical processes with animated drawings, sounds, and even tactile feedback.

The soaring power of computer technology has spawned powerful communication networks that organizations can use to access vast storehouses of information from around the world and to coordinate activities across space and time. These networks are transforming the shape and form of business enterprises and even our society.

Internet International network of networks that is a collection of hundreds of thousands of private and public networks.

The world's largest and most widely used network is the **Internet**. The Internet is an international network of networks that are both commercial and publicly owned. The Internet connects hundreds of thousands of different networks from nearly 200 countries around the world. More than 100 million people working in science, education, government, and business organizations use the Internet to exchange information or perform business transactions with other organizations around the globe. The number of Internet users is expected to surpass 250 million by the year 2000.

The Internet is extremely elastic. If networks are added or removed or failures occur in parts of the system, the rest of the Internet continues to operate. Through special communication and technology standards, any computer can communicate with virtually any other computer linked to the Internet using ordinary telephone lines. Companies and private individuals can use the Internet to exchange business transactions, text messages, graphic images, and even video and sound, whether they are located next door or on the other side of the globe. Table 1.3 describes some of the Internet's capabilities.

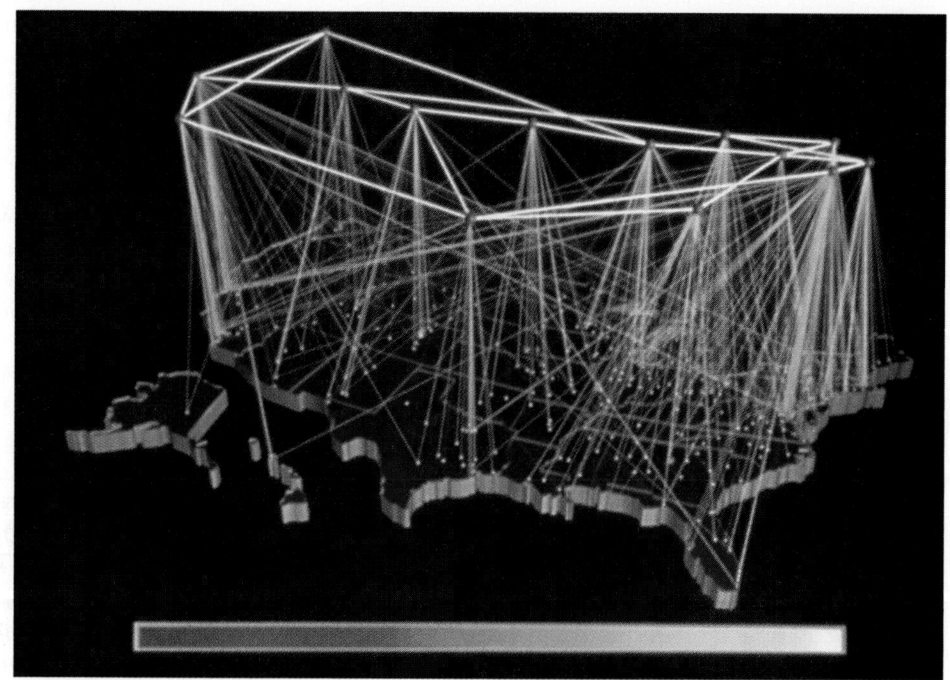

The Internet. This global network of networks provides a highly flexible platform for information-sharing. Digital information can be distributed at almost no cost to millions of people throughout the world.

TABLE 1.3 What You Can Do on the Internet

Function	Description
Communicate and collaborate	Send electronic mail messages; transmit documents and data
Access information	Search for documents, databases, and library card catalogues; read electronic brochures, manuals, books, and advertisements
Participate in discussions	Join interactive discussion groups; conduct primitive voice transmission
Obtain information	Transfer computer files of text, computer programs, graphics, animations, or videos
Find entertainment	Play interactive video games; view short video clips; read illustrated and even animated magazines and books
Exchange business transactions	Advertise, sell, and purchase goods and services

The Internet is creating a new "universal" technology platform upon which to build all sorts of new products, services, strategies, and organizations. It is reshaping the way information systems are being used in business and daily life. By eliminating many technical, geographic, and cost barriers obstructing the global flow of information, the Internet is accelerating the information revolution, inspiring new uses of information systems and new business models.

Of special interest to organizations and managers is the Internet capability known as the World Wide Web because it offers so many new possibilities for doing business. The **World Wide Web** is a system with universally accepted standards for storing, retrieving, formatting, and displaying information in a networked environment. Information is stored and displayed as electronic "pages" that can contain text, graphics, animations, sound, and video. These Web pages can be linked electronically to other Web pages, regardless of where they are located, and viewed by any type of computer. By clicking on highlighted words or buttons on a Web page, one can link to related pages to find additional information, software programs, or still more links to other points on the Web. The Web can serve as the foundation for new kinds of information systems.

World Wide Web A system with universally accepted standards for storing, retrieving, formatting, and displaying information in a networked environment.

All of the Web pages maintained by an organization or individual are called a **Web site.** (The chapter-opening vignette illustrates a page from VW Mexico's Web site.) Businesses are creating Web sites with stylish typography, colorful graphics, push-button interactivity, and often sound and video to disseminate product information widely, to "broadcast" advertising and messages to customers, to collect electronic orders and customer data, and increasingly to coordinate far-flung sales forces and organizations on a global scale.

Web site All of the World Wide Web pages maintained by an organization or an individual.

In Chapter 9 we describe the Web and other Internet capabilities in greater detail. We will also be discussing relevant features of the Internet throughout the text because the Internet affects so many aspects of information systems in organizations.

New Options for Organizational Design: The Networked Enterprise

The explosive growth in computing power and networks, including the Internet, is turning organizations into networked enterprises, allowing information to be instantly distributed within and beyond the organization. This capability can be used to redesign and reshape organizations, transforming their structure, scope of operations, reporting and control mechanisms, work practices, work flows, products, and services. New ways of conducting business electronically have emerged.

Flattening Organizations

Large, bureaucratic organizations, which primarily developed before the computer age are often inefficient, slow to change, and less competitive. Some of these organizations have downsized, reducing the number of employees and the number of levels in their organizational hierarchies. For example, by 1994 heavy equipment manufacturer Caterpillar, Inc., was producing the same level of output as it did 15 years earlier, but with 40,000 fewer employees.

Flatter organizations have fewer levels of management, with lower-level employees being given greater decision-making authority (see Figure 1.8). Those employees are empowered to make more decisions than in the past, they no longer work standard 9-to-5 hours, and they no longer necessarily work in an office. Moreover, such employees may be scattered geographically, sometimes working half a world away from the manager.

Contemporary information technology has made such changes possible. It can make more information available to line workers so they can make decisions that previously had been made by managers. Networked computers have made it possible for employees to work together as a team, another feature of flatter organizations. With the emergence of global networks such as the Internet, team members can collaborate

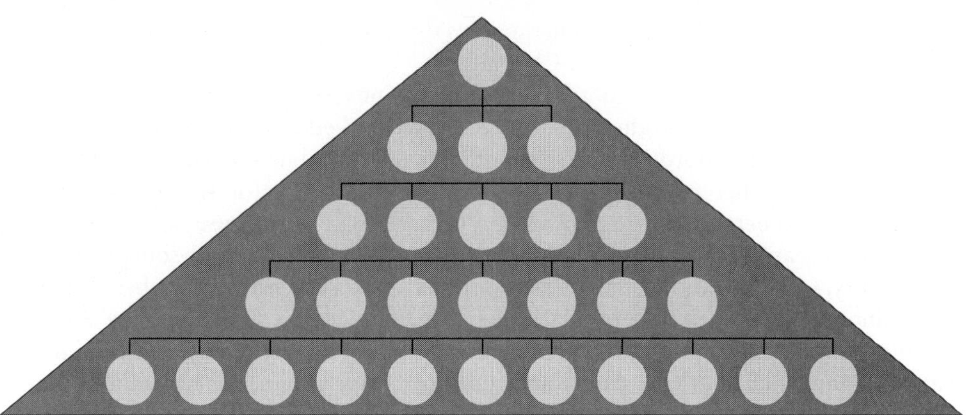

A traditional hierarchical organization with many levels of management

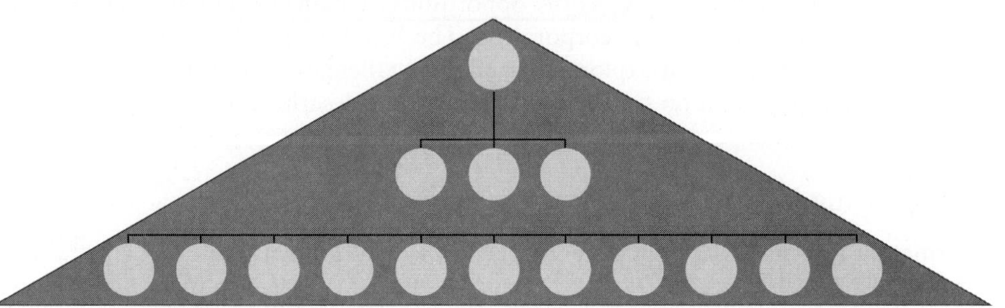

An organization that has been "flattened" by removing layers of management

FIGURE 1.8

Flattening organizations. Information systems can reduce the number of levels in an organization by providing managers with information to supervise larger numbers of workers and by giving lower-level employees more decision-making authority.

closely even from distant locations. These changes mean that the management span of control has also been broadened, allowing high-level managers to manage and control more workers spread over greater distances. Many companies have eliminated thousands of middle managers as a result of these changes. AT&T, IBM, and General Motors are just a few of the organizations that have eliminated more than thirty thousand middle managers in one fell swoop.

Separating Work from Location

It is now possible to organize globally while working locally: Information technologies such as e-mail, the Internet, and video conferencing to the desktop permit tight coordination of geographically dispersed workers across time zones and cultures. Entire parts of organizations can disappear: Inventory, and the warehouses to store it, can be eliminated as suppliers tie into the firm's computer systems and deliver just what is needed and just in time.

Communications technology has eliminated distance as a factor for many types of work in many situations. Salespersons can spend more time in the field with customers and yet have more up-to-date information with them while carrying much less paper. Many employees can work remotely from their homes or cars, and companies can reserve space at a much smaller central office for meeting clients or other employees.

Collaborative teamwork across thousands of miles has become a reality as designers work on the design of a new product together even if they are located on different continents. Ford Motor Co. has adopted a cross-continent collaborative model to design its automobiles. Supported by high-capacity communications networks and computer-aided design (CAD) software, Ford designers launched the Mustang design in Dunton, England. The design was worked on simultaneously by designers at Dearborn, Michigan, and Dunton, with some input from designers in Japan and Australia. Once the design was completed, Ford engineers in Turin, Italy, used it to produce a full-sized physical model. Ford now designs other models this way and is starting to use Web technology for global collaboration (see Chapter 12).

virtual organization Organization using networks linking people, assets, and ideas to create and distribute products and services without being limited by traditional organizational boundaries or physical location.

Companies are not limited to physical locations or their own organizational boundaries for providing products and services. Networked information systems are allowing companies to coordinate their geographically distributed capabilities and even coordinate with other organizations as virtual corporations (or **virtual organizations**), sometimes called *networked organizations*. Virtual organizations use networks to link people, assets, and ideas, allying with suppliers and customers, and sometimes even competitors, to create and distribute new products and services without being limited by traditional organizational boundaries or physical location. One company can take advantage of the capabilities of another company without actually physically linking to that company. Each company contributes its core competencies, the capabilities that it does the best. For example, one company might be responsible for product design, another for assembly and manufacturing, and another for administration and sales. These virtual organizations last as long as the opportunity remains profitable. Figure 1.9 illustrates the concept of a virtual corporation. The Window on Management describes a virtual organization for oil exploration and the challenges it poses for management. Another virtual organization for the utility industry is described in the chapter-ending case study.

Reorganizing Work Flows

Information systems have been progressively replacing manual work procedures with automated work procedures, work flows, and work processes. Electronic work flows have reduced the cost of operations in many companies by displacing paper and the manual routines that accompany it. Improved work-flow management has enabled many corporations not only to cut costs significantly but also to improve customer service at

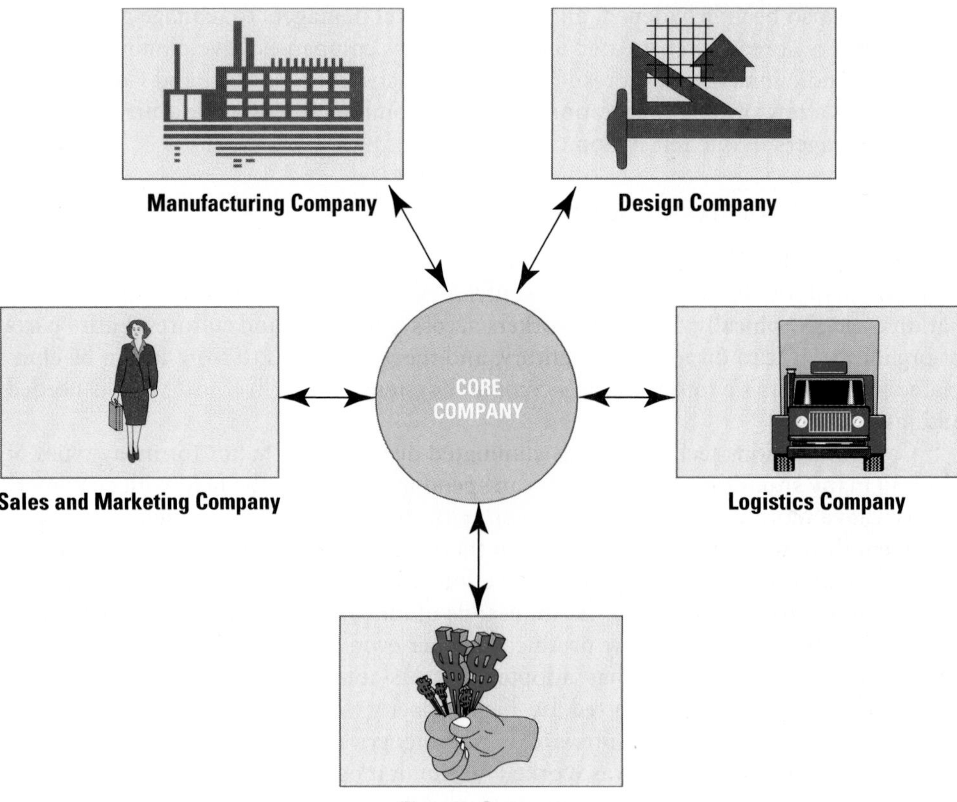

FIGURE 1.9

A virtual organization. Networked information systems enable different companies to join together to provide goods and services.

WINDOW ON MANAGEMENT

Managing a Virtual Oil Company

How does a wildcatting oil exploration company with only 65 employees grow to a billion-dollar valuation in only 12 years? The obvious answer is to find lots of oil. But how do you do that? Zilkha Energy Company of Houston, Texas, did it the hard way—they searched for oil in the Gulf of Mexico. As a source of oil, the Gulf has long been considered a "mature" area where the big fields have all been found. Production had been declining for years, and the big companies were no longer exploring for new drilling sites. However, Zilkha went its own way, relying heavily on information technology to find oil in areas thought to be uneconomical or topped out, to create a lean, focused virtual organization.

Zilkha is a virtual organization for oil exploration. Management knows what it is good at, and it does only that. Zilkha specializes in two areas only—analyzing data in order to find retrievable oil reserves and finding the financing to drill once those areas have been identified. The company does not generate the data it uses, and it does not drill for the oil itself. Zilkha owns no oil rigs, employs no drillers, maintains no structure of corporate executives. Management can outsource any of these services when it needs them. The company occupies a single floor in a building in downtown Houston. No one has a private office, and the huge monitors, the casual dress, and the obvious camaraderie make the visitor think he or she is visiting a startup software company in Silicon Valley. Employee pay is tied to performance, with 10 of the employees earning more than $500,000 each in 1997. Because the organization and methods have been so successful, in January 1998, Sonat Energy, one of the largest energy companies in the United States, paid $1 billion to purchase Zilkha.

The wildcatting industry has changed dramatically in recent years. Those who search for oil no longer rely on educated guesses made by trained geologists. Rather, after doing preliminary surveys, companies now mark out territory they believe has potential, and they buy up leases. Then they generate data on the territory before deciding whether to drill, and if so, where. Zilkha was dealing with an area that had all been leased before and had been explored. Therefore, it was able to re-order the standard process. Rather than surveying and buying leases first, the company began with the data. They purchased huge quantities of existing 3-D seismographic data from other companies for most of the continental shelf extending about 150 miles from the shore in the Gulf of Mexico. (Such data are generated by having ships bounce sound signals off underground formations, with computers translating the responses.) Zilkha would then perform its own analysis of the data to find the best drilling prospects.

Zilkha brought in the most advanced computer tools available, spending more than $1 million for its main computer alone. Management hired only top quality geologists to do the analysis for them. Their goal was to find the most likely spots for new drilling. Once those spots had been identified, they bought the leases giving them the right to drill. They were so confident of their results that they purchased the leases alone, bearing all the risk, instead of sharing the profits with other companies as a way to also share the risk. Their confidence has been justified. On 79 wells they have drilled, they have been successful 66 percent of the time, more than twice the success rate of the industry. What they are finding with improved computer analysis techniques and more modern drilling methods is oil and gas that either could not have been found years ago or could not have been retrieved economically with older drilling technology. Other companies are now doing the same thing in a number of areas around the world, and their discoveries have resulted in a Europe and a North America that are far less dependent upon Middle East oil than in the past.

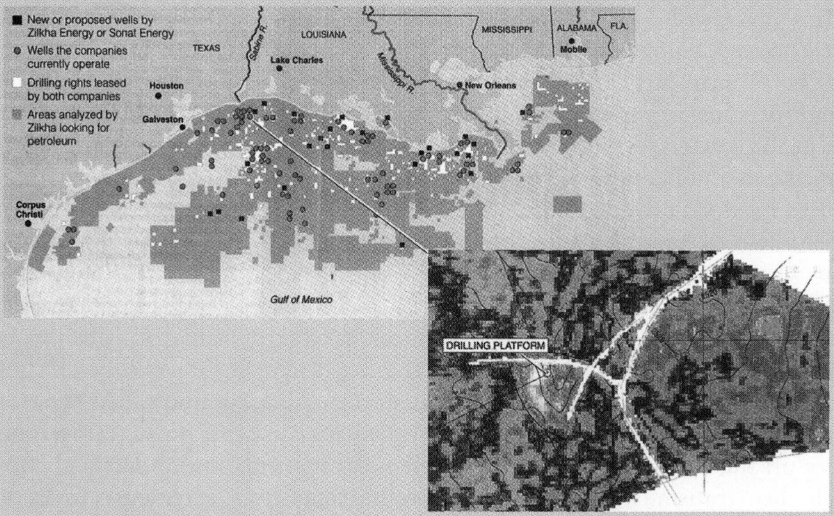

To Think About: ***How essential were information systems in the strategy and operation of this virtual business? What are the problems and the benefits of managing a virtual organization?***

Zilkha Energy is able to operate as a virtual energy company by purchasing and analyzing seismic data gathered by other companies.

Source: Adapted from Allen R. Myerson, "A Wildcatter on the Tame Side," *The New York Times*, March 20, 1998.

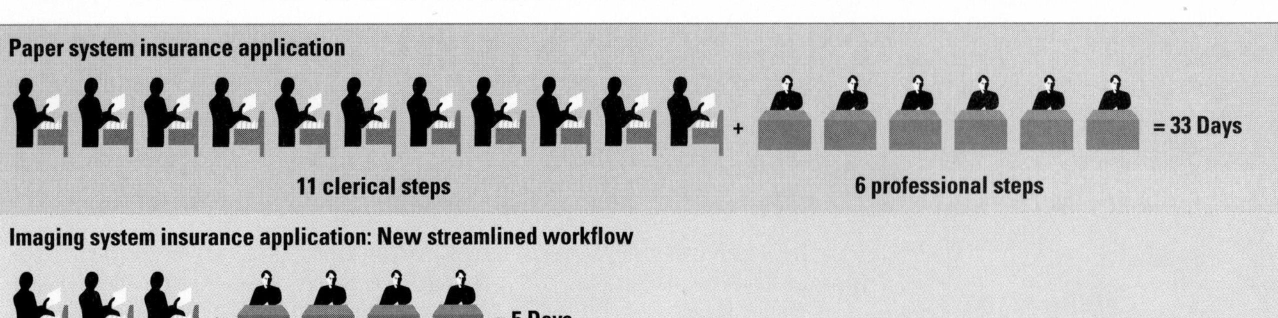

FIGURE 1.10

Redesigned work flow for insurance underwriting. An application requiring 33 days in a paper system would only take 5 days using computers, networks, and a streamlined work flow.

the same time. For instance, insurance companies can reduce processing of applications for new insurance from weeks to days (see Figure 1.10).

Redesigned work flows can have a profound impact on organizational efficiency and can even lead to new organizational structures, products, and services. We will be discussing the impact of restructured work flows on organizational design in greater detail in Chapters 3 and 10.

Increasing Flexibility of Organizations

Companies can use communications technology to organize in more flexible ways, increasing their ability to respond to changes in the marketplace and to take advantage of new opportunities. Information systems can give both large and small organizations additional flexibility to overcome some of the limitations posed by their size. Table 1.4 describes some of the ways in which information technology can help small companies act "big" and help big companies act "small." Small organizations can use information systems to acquire some of the muscle and reach of larger organizations. They can perform coordinating activities, such as processing bids or keeping track of inventory, and many manufacturing tasks with very few managers, clerks, or production workers. For example, Merig Design Equipment in Southcott Pines, Canada, is a one-man company that produces elaborate, intricate machine tool designs for the automotive industry using a Pentium personal computer and computer-aided design (CAD) software in the home of owner Roy Merkley. In the past, such work would have to be performed by teams of draftsmen and managers in conventional production offices (Warson, 1996).

mass customization Use of software and computer networks to finely control production so that products can be easily customized with no added cost for small production runs.

Large organizations can use information technology to achieve some of the agility and responsiveness of small organizations. One aspect of this phenomenon is **mass customization**, where software and computer networks are used to link the plant floor tightly with orders, design, and purchasing and to finely control production machines. The result is a dynamically responsive environment in which products can be turned out in greater variety and easily customized with no added cost for small production runs. For example, Levi Strauss has equipped its stores with an option called Personal Pair, which allows customers to design jeans to their own specifications, rather than picking them off the rack. Customers enter their measurements into a personal computer, which then transmits the customer's specifications over a network to Levi's plants. The company is able to produce the custom jeans on the same lines that manufacture its standard items. There are almost no extra production costs because the process does not require additional warehousing, production overruns, and inventories. A related trend is micromarketing, in which information systems can help compa-

TABLE 1.4 How Information Technology Increases Organizational Flexibility
Small Companies
Desktop machines, inexpensive computer-aided design (CAD) software, and computer-controlled machine tools provide the precision, speed, and quality of giant manufacturers.
Information immediately accessed by telephone and communications links eliminates the need for research staff and business libraries.
Managers can more easily obtain the information they need to manage larger numbers of employees in widely scattered locations.
Large Companies
Custom manufacturing systems allow large factories to offer customized products in small quantities.
Massive databases of customer purchasing records can be analyzed so that large companies can know their customers' needs and preferences as easily as local merchants.
Information can be easily distributed down the ranks of the organization to empower lower-level employees and work groups to solve problems.

nies pinpoint tiny target markets for these finely customized products and services—as small as individualized "markets of one." We discuss micromarketing in more detail in Chapter 2.

The Changing Management Process

Information technology is recasting the process of management, providing powerful new capabilities to help managers plan, organize, lead, and control. For instance, it is now possible for managers to obtain information on organizational performance down to the level of specific transactions from just about anywhere in the organization at any time. Product managers at Frito-Lay Corporation, the world's largest manufacturer of salty snack foods, can know within hours precisely how many bags of Fritos have sold on any street in America at its customers' stores, how much they sold for, and what the competition's sales volumes and prices are.

Many companies now use information technology for enterprise resource planning. **Enterprise resource planning (ERP)** is a business management system that integrates all facets of the business, including planning, manufacturing, sales, and finance so that they can become more closely coordinated by sharing information. ERP software models and automates many basic processes, such as filling an order or scheduling a shipment, with the goal of integrating information across the company and eliminating complex, expensive links between computer systems in different areas of the business. For instance, when a sale representative in Brussels enters a customer order, the data flows automatically to others in the company who need to see it. The factory in Hong Kong receives the order and begins production. The warehouse checks its progress on-line and schedules the shipment date. The warehouse can check its stock of parts and replenish whatever the factory has depleted. Updated sales and production data automatically flow to the accounting department. Corporate headquarters in London can view up-to-the-minute data on sales, inventory, and production at every step of the process. The chapter-opening vignette described an ERP system built by VW Mexico. This new intensity of information makes possible far more precise planning, forecasting, and monitoring than ever before.

enterprise resource planning (ERP) A business management system that integrates all facets of the business, including planning, manufacturing, sales, and finance, so that they can become more coordinated by sharing information with each other.

Redefining Organizational Boundaries

Networked information systems can enable transactions such as payments and purchase orders to be exchanged electronically among different companies, thereby reducing the cost of obtaining products and services from outside the firm. Organizations can also share business data, catalogues, or mail messages through such systems. These networked information systems can create new efficiencies and new relationships between an organization, its customers, and suppliers, redefining their organizational boundaries. For example, the Chrysler Corporation is networked to suppliers, such as the Budd Company of Rochester, Michigan. Through this electronic link, the Budd Company monitors Chrysler production and ships sheet metal parts exactly when needed, preceded by an electronic shipping notice. Chrysler and its suppliers have thus become linked business partners with mutually shared responsibilities.

The information system linking Chrysler and its suppliers is called an interorganizational information system. Systems linking a company to its customers, distributors, or suppliers are termed **interorganizational systems** because they automate the flow of information across organizational boundaries (Barrett, 1986-1987; Johnston and Vitale, 1988). Such systems allow information or processing capabilities of one organization to improve the performance of another or to improve relationships among organizations.

interorganizational systems Information systems that automate the flow of information across organizational boundaries and link a company to its customers, distributors, or suppliers.

Electronic Commerce and Electronic Business

The changes we have just described are creating new ways of conducting business electronically both inside and outside the firm. Increasingly, the Internet is providing the underlying technology for these changes. The Internet can link thousands of organizations into a single network, creating the foundation for a vast electronic marketplace. An **electronic market** is an information system that links together many buyers and sellers to exchange information, products, services, and payments. Through computers and networks, these systems function like electronic middlemen, with lowered costs for typical marketplace transactions such as selecting suppliers, establishing prices, ordering goods, and paying bills (Malone, Yates, and Benjamin, 1987). Buyers and sellers can complete purchase and sale transactions digitally, regardless of their location.

electronic market A marketplace that is created by computer and communication technologies that link many buyers and sellers.

A vast array of goods and services are being advertised, bought, and exchanged worldwide using the Internet as a global marketplace. Companies are furiously creating eye-catching electronic brochures, advertisements, product manuals, and order forms on the World Wide Web. All kinds of products and services are available on the Web, including fresh flowers, books, real estate, musical recordings, electronics, and steaks.

Many retailers maintain their own site on the Web, such as Virtual Vineyards (see Chapter 9). Others offer their products through electronic shopping malls, such as the Internet Shopping Network. Customers can locate products on this mall either by manufacturer, if they know what they want, or by product type, and then order them directly. Even electronic financial trading has arrived on the Web, offering electronic trading in stocks, bonds, mutual funds, and other financial instruments.

The Web is being increasingly used for business-to-business transactions as well. For example, airlines can use the Boeing Corporation's Web site to order parts electronically and check the status of their orders. The Window on Organizations illustrates how a small startup company created a Web site to link businesses trading in Asian goods.

The global availability of the Internet for the exchange of transactions between buyers and sellers is fueling the growth of electronic commerce. **Electronic commerce** is the process of buying and selling goods and services electronically with computerized business transactions using the Internet, networks, and other digital technologies. It also encompasses activities supporting those market transactions, such as advertising, marketing, customer support, delivery, and payment. By replacing manual and paper-based procedures with electronic alternatives, and by using information flows in new and dynamic ways, electronic commerce can accelerate ordering, delivery, and payment for goods and services while reducing companies' operating and inventory costs.

electronic commerce The process of buying and selling goods and services electronically involving transactions using the Internet, networks, and other digital technologies.

WINDOW ON ORGANIZATIONS

A Netrepreneur Promotes Asian Trade

Sarah Benecke, the CEO of Asia Sources Media (ASM) runs a Hong Kong company that offers services via the Internet that are badly needed by companies participating in global trade. She can cite many examples of the Net's benefits. For example, one Asian producer of sunglasses received an order for 6,000 pairs after exchanging only three e-mail messages with the buyer. A Lebanese importer has purchased over US $150,000 of communications and computer equipment from Asia using ASM services.

ASM began as an Asian trade magazine back in 1970, when U.S. and European trade with Asia was tiny and networking barely existed. Merle Hinrich, ASM's founder, realized the potential of the Net back in the 1980s, long before most of us had even heard of it. He began to search for software that could automate some of the buying and selling processes. His early efforts have evolved into a global electronic market for selling goods produced in Asia.

In 1991 ASM installed software that automated price quotes and trade documentation for both purchaser and vendor, including accounting reports. Next ASM offered an interactive catalog of products and factories on a CD-ROM. However, with the rapid development of the Web, it quickly converted its catalog to a Web site. Asian Sources Online is a Web site that now hosts more than 7,200 supplier sites with 37,000 products, receiving more than 10,000 inquiries each week. Users can view the products and then contact sellers when they are interested via e-mail. ASM is a matchmaker, helping buyers and sellers to find each other easily and bringing them together quickly without costly travel or telephone calls. ASM's next service, available by mid-1998, will enable transactions—money will actually change hands on-line.

Other services offered by the site include a trade show calendar and a product-alert capability that alerts users by e-mail when products of interest are available. A special section of the site is designed for factories to sell excess stock at discount prices. For example, here an importer was able to purchase 11,000 chocolate fondue sets for US $2.30 each. ASM is also about to offer large importers of Asian products the opportunity to place on-line a catalogue of the merchandise they are seeking so that sellers can contact them.

While it is clear that this electronic marketplace can benefit both exporters and importers, ASM needs to pay its costs and make a profit. To be able to support its growing electronic marketplace, in 1997 ASM spent more than $6 million to upgrade its hardware and software. Although some online marketplace sites charge a percentage of sales to pay their costs and make their profits, "We have never considered that," says Benecke. Instead, to earn revenue, ASM gets paid only for listings by sellers (and soon by buyers) and by accepting ads to be displayed on its Web site. The strategy has been successful. In 1997, the company took in $6 million, which happens to be the cost of the upgrade. In future years, with lower infrastructure expenditures and growing business, the company should prove to be quite profitable.

To Think About: ***How has the Internet changed international trade? In what ways can using the Internet as an electronic marketplace affect organizations?***

Source: Adapted from Art Jahnke, "Netrepreneurs, The Orient Express," *CIO WebBusiness Magazine,* March 1, 1998.

The Internet is emerging as the primary technology platform for electronic commerce. Equally important, Internet technology is being increasingly applied to facilitate the management of the rest of the business—publishing employee personnel policies, reviewing account balances and production plans, scheduling plant repairs and maintenance, and revising design documents. Companies are taking advantage of the connectivity and ease of use of Internet technology to create internal corporate networks called **intranets** that are based on Internet technology. Use of these private intranets for organizational communication, collaboration, and coordination is soaring. In this text, we use the term **electronic business** to distinguish these uses of Internet and digital technology for the management and coordination of other business processes from electronic commerce.

intranet An internal network based on Internet and World Wide Web technology and standards.

electronic business The use of the Internet and other digital technology for organizational communication and coordination and the management of the firm.

By distributing information through electronic networks, electronic business extends the reach of existing management. Managers can use e-mail, Web documents, and work-group software to effectively communicate frequently with thousands of employees, and even manage far-flung task forces and teams. These tasks would be impossible

At the Travelocity Web site, visitors can obtain information on airlines, hotels, vacation packages, and other travel and leisure topics, and they can make airline and hotel reservations online. The World Wide Web is fueling the growth of electronic commerce.

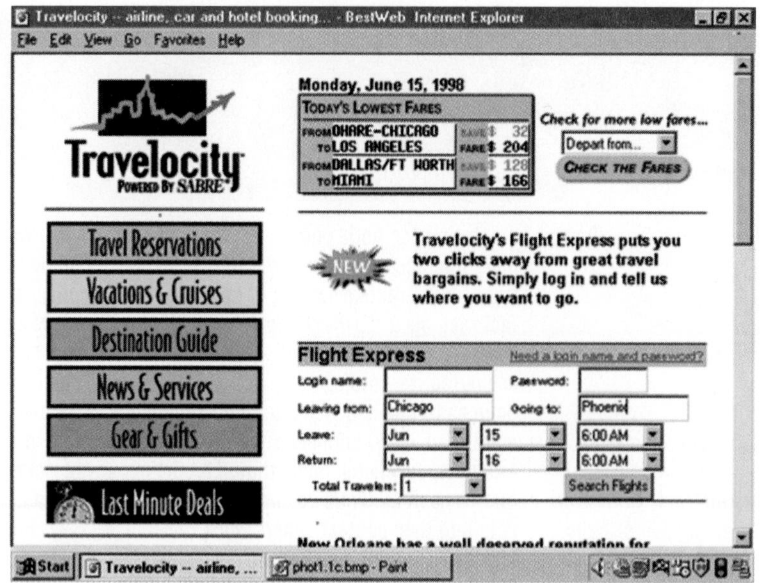

in face-to-face traditional organizations. Table 1.5 lists some examples of electronic commerce and electronic business.

Figure 1.11 illustrates an enterprise making intensive use of Internet and digital technology for electronic commerce and electronic business. Information can flow seamlessly among different parts of the company and between the company and external entities—its customers, suppliers, and business partners. Organizations will move toward this vision as they increasingly use the Internet and networks to manage their internal processes and their relationships with customers, suppliers, and other external entities.

Both electronic commerce and electronic business can fundamentally change the way business is conducted. To use the Internet and other digital technologies success-

TABLE 1.5 Examples of Electronic Commerce and Electronic Business

Examples
Electronic Commerce
Amazon.com operates a virtual storefront on the Internet offering over 2.5 million book titles for sale. Customers can input their orders via Amazon.com's Web site and have the books shipped to them.
Travelocity provides a Web site that can be used by consumers for travel and vacation planning. Visitors can find out information on airlines, hotels, vacation packages, and other travel and leisure topics, and they can make airline and hotel reservations on-line through the Web site.
Mobil Corporation created a private network based on Internet technology that allows its 300 lubricant distributors to submit purchase orders on-line.
Electronic Business
Roche Bioscience scientists worldwide use an intranet to share research results and discuss findings. The intranet also provides a company telephone directory and newsletter.
University of Texas Medical Branch at Galveston publishes nursing staff policies and procedures on an intranet. The intranet reduces paperwork and enhances the quality of nursing services by providing immediate notification of policy changes.
Dream Works SKG uses an intranet to check the daily status of projects, including animation objects, and to coordinate movie scenes.

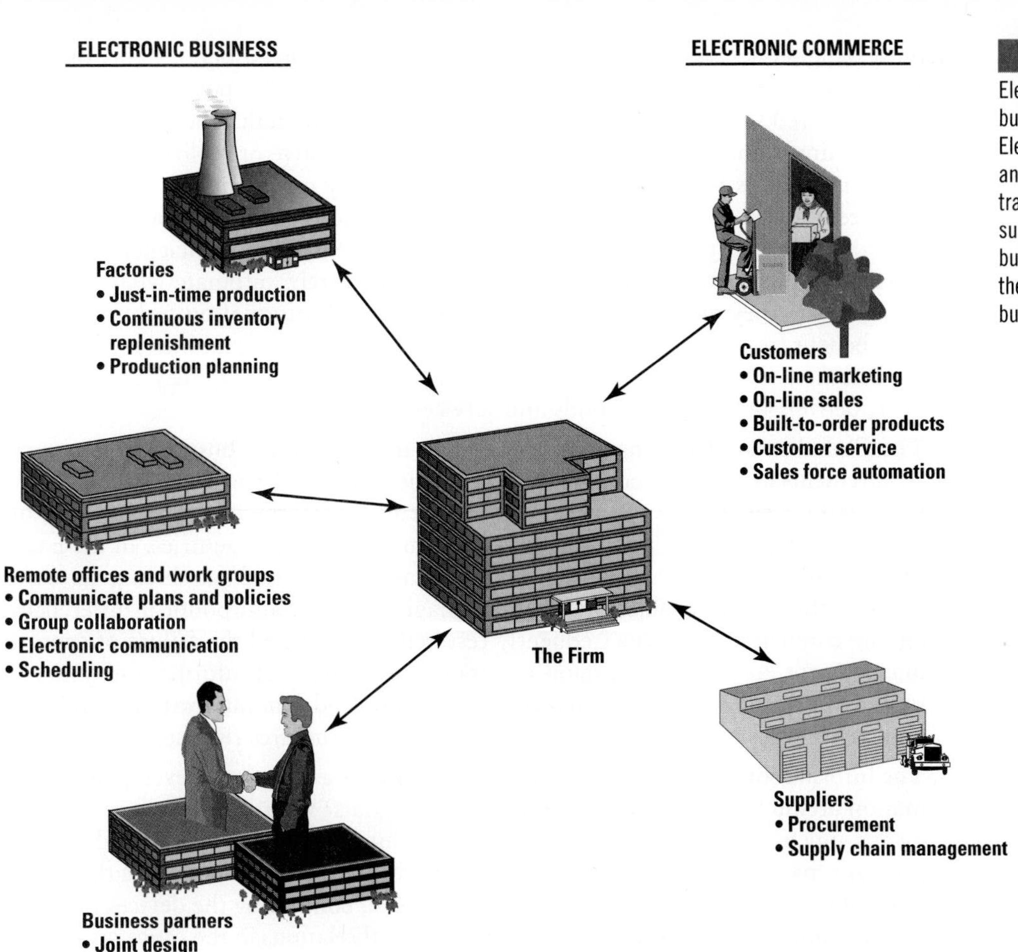

FIGURE 1.11
Electronic commerce and electronic business in the networked enterprise. Electronic commerce uses Internet and digital technology to conduct transactions with customers and suppliers, whereas electronic business uses these technologies for the managment of the rest of the business.

fully for electronic commerce and electronic business, organizations may have to redefine their business models, reinvent business processes, change corporate cultures, and create much closer relationships with customers and suppliers. We discuss these issues in greater detail in following chapters.

1.4 LEARNING TO USE INFORMATION SYSTEMS: NEW OPPORTUNITIES WITH TECHNOLOGY

Information systems today are creating many exciting opportunities for both businesses and individuals. They are also a source of new problems, issues and challenges for managers. In this course, you will learn about both the challenges and opportunities posed by information systems, and you will be able to use information technology to enrich your learning experience.

The Challenge of Information Systems: Key Management Issues

Although information technology is advancing at a blinding pace, there is nothing easy or mechanical about building and using information systems. There are five key challenges confronting managers:

1. **The Strategic Business Challenge: How can businesses use information technology to design organizations that are competitive and effective?** Investment in information technology amounts to more than half of the annual capital expenditures of

most large service-sector firms. Yet despite these heavy investments, many organizations are not obtaining significant business benefits. The power of computer hardware and software has grown much more rapidly than the ability of organizations to apply and use this technology. To stay competitive or realize genuine productivity benefits from information technology, many organizations actually need to be redesigned. They will have to make fundamental changes in organizational behavior, develop new business models, and eliminate the inefficiencies of outmoded organizational structures. If organizations merely automate what they are doing today, they are largely missing the potential of information technology. To fully benefit from information technology, including the opportunities provided by the Internet, organizations need to rethink and redesign the way they design, produce, deliver, and maintain goods and services.

2. **The Globalization Challenge: How can firms understand the business and system requirements of a global economic environment?** The rapid growth in international trade and the emergence of a global economy call for information systems that can support both producing and selling goods in many different countries. In the past, each regional office of a multinational corporation focused on solving its own unique information problems. Given language, cultural, and political differences among countries, this focus frequently resulted in chaos and the failure of central management controls. To develop integrated, multinational information systems, businesses must develop global hardware, software, and communications standards and create cross-cultural accounting and reporting structures (Roche, 1992).

3. **The Information Architecture Challenge: How can organizations develop an information architecture that supports their business goals?** Creating a new system now means much more than installing a new machine in the basement. Today, this process typically places thousands of terminals or personal computers on the desks of employees who have little experience with them, connecting the devices to powerful communications networks, rearranging social relations in the office and work locations, changing reporting patterns, and redefining business goals. Briefly, new systems today often require redesigning the organization and developing a new information architecture.

information architecture The particular form that information technology takes in a specific organization to achieve selected goals or functions.

Information architecture is the particular form that information technology takes in an organization to achieve selected goals or functions. Information architecture includes the extent to which data and processing power are centralized or distributed. Figure 1.12 illustrates the major elements of information architecture that managers will need to develop. Although the computer-systems base is typically operated by technical personnel, general management must decide how to allocate the resources it has assigned to hardware, software, and telecommunications. Resting upon the computer-systems base are the major business application systems, or the major islands of applications. Because managers and employees directly interact with these systems, it is critical for the success of the organization that these systems meet business functional requirements now and in the future.

Some MIS scholars prefer to use the term *IT infrastructure* rather than architecture, focusing on computer and communications technologies as the technical foundation of the organization's information systems capabilities (Weill and Broadbent, 1997 and 1998). Human knowledge and skills convert these components into information technology services, which then provide the foundation for the organization's information systems applications.

Here are typical questions regarding information architecture facing today's managers: Should the corporate sales data and function be distributed to each corporate remote site, or should they be centralized at headquarters? Should the organization purchase stand-alone personal computers or build a more powerful, centralized mainframe environment within an integrated telecommunications network? Should the organization build its own communications utility to link remote sites or rely on external providers like the telephone company? There is no one right

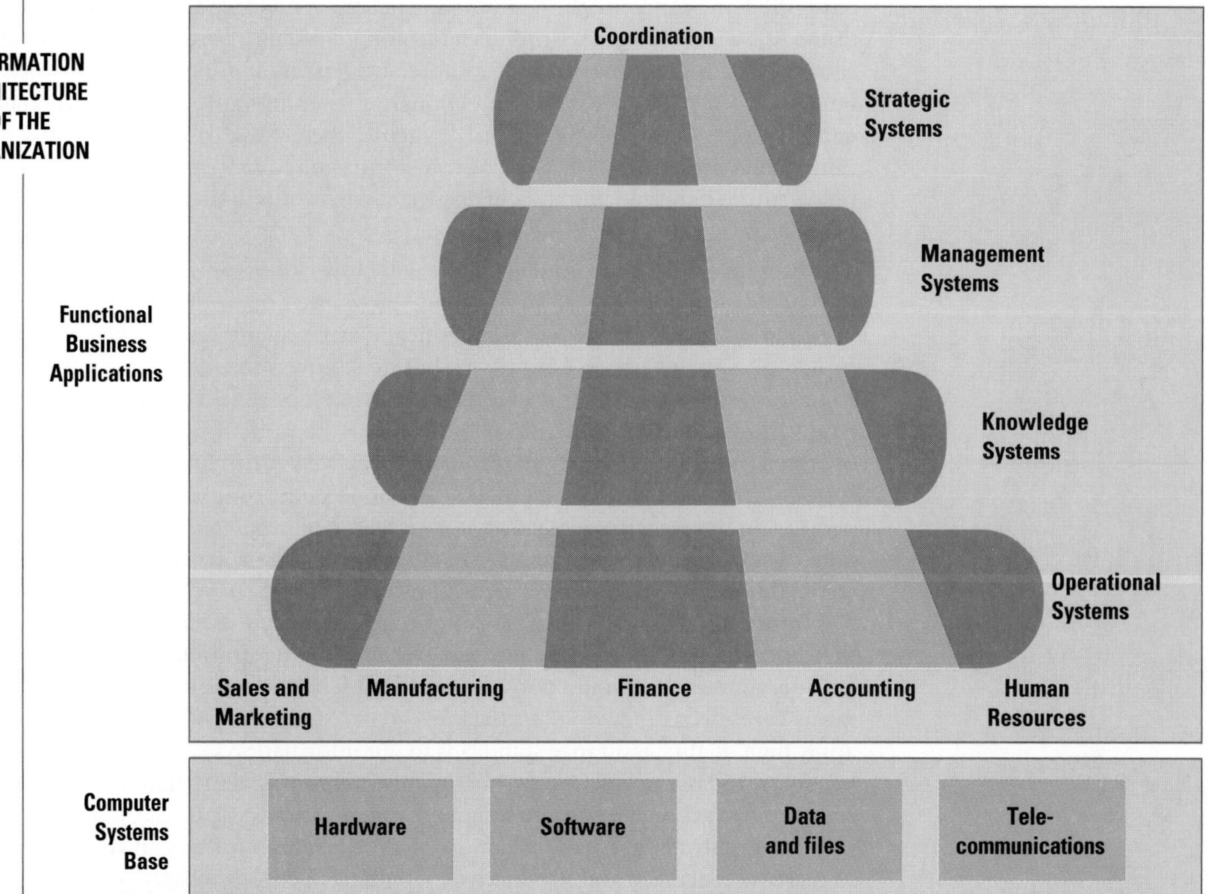

FIGURE 1.12

The information architecture of the firm. Today's managers must know how to arrange and coordinate the various computer technologies and business system applications to meet the information needs of each level of their organization, as well as the needs of the organization as a whole.

answer to these questions (see Allen and Boynton, 1991). Moreover, business needs are constantly changing, requiring the IT architecture to be reassessed (Feeny and Willcocks, 1998).

Even under the best of circumstances, combining knowledge of systems and the organization is itself a demanding task. For many organizations, the task is even more formidable because they are crippled by fragmented and incompatible computer hardware, software, telecommunications networks, and information systems. Although Internet standards have solved some of these connectivity problems, integration of diverse computing platforms is rarely as seamless as promised. Many organizations are still struggling to integrate islands of information and technology into a coherent architecture.

4. **The Information Systems Investment Challenge: How can organizations determine the business value of information systems?** A major problem raised by the development of powerful, inexpensive computers involves not technology but management and organizations. It's one thing to use information technology to design, produce, deliver, and maintain new products. It's another thing to make money doing it. How can organizations obtain a sizable payoff from their investment in information systems?

   Engineering massive organizational and system changes in the hope of positioning a firm strategically is complicated and expensive. Is this an investment that pays off? How can you tell? Senior management can be expected to ask these questions: Are we receiving the kind of return on investment from our systems that we should be? Do our competitors get more? Understanding the costs and benefits of building a single system is difficult enough; it is daunting to consider whether the entire systems effort is "worth it." Imagine, then, how a senior executive must think when presented with a major transformation in information architecture—a bold venture in organizational change costing tens of millions of dollars and taking many years.

5. **The Responsibility and Control Challenge: How can organizations design systems that people can control and understand?** How can organizations ensure that their information systems are used in an ethically and socially responsible manner? Information systems are so essential to business, government, and daily life that organizations must take special steps to ensure that they are accurate, reliable, and secure. Automated or semiautomated systems that malfunction or are poorly operated can have extremely harmful consequences. A firm invites disaster if it uses systems that don't work as intended, that don't deliver information in a form that people can interpret correctly and use, or that have control rooms where controls don't work or where instruments give false signals. The potential for massive fraud, error, abuse, and destruction is enormous.

   Information systems must be designed so that they function as intended and so that humans can control the process. When building and using information systems, organizations should consider health, safety, job security, and social well being as carefully as they do their business goals. Managers will need to ask: Can we apply high quality assurance standards to our information systems, as well as to our products and services? Can we build information systems that respect people's rights of privacy while still pursuing our organization's goals? Should information systems monitor employees? What do we do when an information system designed to increase efficiency and productivity eliminates people's jobs?

   This text is designed to provide future managers with the knowledge and understanding required to deal with these challenges. To further this objective, each succeeding chapter begins with a Management Challenges box that outlines the key issues of which managers should be aware.

Integrating Text with Technology: New Opportunities for Learning

In addition to the changes in business and management that we have just described, we believe that information technology creates new opportunities for learning that can make the MIS course more meaningful and exciting. We have provided a Web site and an interactive multimedia CD-ROM for integrating the text with leading-edge technology.

As you read each chapter of the text, you can visit the Prentice Hall Laudon Web site and use the Internet for interactive learning and management problem-solving. The Internet Connection icon in the chapter directs you to Web sites for which we have provided additional exercises and projects related to the concepts and organizations described in that chapter. For selected chapters, you will also find interactive Electronic Commerce projects, tours of Electronic Commerce sites, and a comprehensive Electronic Commerce project. A graded on-line interactive study guide contains questions to help you review what you have learned and test your mastery of chapter concepts. You can also use the Laudon Web site to find links to additional on-line case studies, international resources, technology updates, and on-line tutorials on how to use Web browsers and other Internet tools.

An interactive CD-ROM multimedia version of the text can be purchased as an optional item. The Multimedia Edition CD-ROM features interactive exercises, simulations, audio/video overviews explaining key concepts, on-line quizzes, hyperlinks to the exercises on the Laudon Web site, technology updates, and more. You can use the CD-ROM as an interactive study guide or as an alternative to the traditional text.

You will find a *Tools for Interactive Learning* section with this icon concluding every chapter to show how you can use the Web and interactive multimedia to enrich your learning experience.

Management Wrap-Up

MANAGEMENT

Managers are problem-solvers who are responsible for analyzing the many challenges confronting organizations and for developing strategies and action plans. Information systems are one of their tools, delivering the information required for solutions. Information systems both reflect management decisions and serve as instruments for changing the management process.

ORGANIZATION

Information systems are rooted in organizations, an outcome of organizational structure, culture, politics, work-flows, and standard operating procedures. They are instruments for organizational change, making it possible to recast these organizational elements into new business models and redraw organizational boundaries. Advances in information systems are accelerating the trend toward globalized, knowledge-driven economies and flattened, flexible, decentralized organizations.

TECHNOLOGY

A network revolution is under way. Information systems technology is no longer limited to computers but consists of an array of technologies that enable computers to be networked together to exchange information across great distances and organizational boundaries. The Internet provides global connectivity and a flexible platform for information-sharing, creating new uses for information systems and revolutionizing the role of information systems in organizations.

For Discussion:

1. Information systems are too important to be left to computer specialists. Do you agree? Why or why not?
2. As computers become faster and cheaper and the Internet becomes more widely used, most of the problems we have with information systems will disappear. Do you agree? Why or why not?

SUMMARY

1. **Define an information system.** The purpose of a CBIS is to collect, store, and disseminate information from an organization's environment and internal operations for the purpose of supporting organizational functions and decision making, communication, coordination, control, analysis, and visualization. Information systems transform raw data into useful information through three basic activities: input, processing, and output.

2. **Distinguish between computer literacy and information systems literacy.** Information systems literacy requires an understanding of the organizational and management dimensions of information systems as well as the technical dimensions addressed by computer literacy. Information systems literacy draws on both technical and behavioral approaches to studying information systems. Both perspectives can be combined into a sociotechnical approach to systems.

3. **Explain why information systems are so important today and how they are transforming organizations and management.** The kinds of systems built today are very important for the overall performance of the organization, especially in today's highly globalized and information-based economy. Information systems are driving both daily operations and organizational strategy. Powerful computers, software, and networks, including the Internet, have helped organizations become more flexible, eliminate layers of management, separate work from location, and restructure work flows, giving new powers to both line workers and management. Information technology allows managers to execute enterprise resource planning for more precise planning, forecasting, and monitoring of the major processes of the business. To maximize the advantages of information technology, there is a much greater need to plan for the overall information architecture of the organization.
4. **Compare electronic commerce and electronic business and analyze their relationship to the Internet and digital technology.** The Internet and other networks have made it possible for businesses to replace manual and paper-based processes with the electronic flow of information. In electronic commerce, businesses can exchange electronic purchase and sale transactions with each other and with individual customers. Electronic business uses the Internet and digital technology to expedite the exchange of information that can facilitate communication and coordination both inside the organization and between the organization and its business partners.
5. **Identify the major management challenges to building and using information systems in organizations.** There are five key management challenges in building and using information systems: (1) designing systems that are competitive and efficient; (2) understanding the system requirements of a global business environment; (3) creating an information architecture that supports the organization's goals; (4) determining the business value of information systems; and (5) designing systems that people can control, understand, and use in a socially and ethically responsible manner.

KEY TERMS

Communications technology, 12
Computer-based information systems (CBIS), 8
Computer hardware, 12
Computer software, 12
Data, 8
Data workers, 11
Electronic business, 25
Electronic commerce, 24
Electronic market, 24
Enterprise resource planning (ERP), 23
Feedback, 8
Formal system, 9
Information, 8
Information architecture, 28
Information system, 7
Input, 8
Internet, 16
Interorganizational systems, 24
Intranet, 25
Knowledge- and information-intense products, 6
Knowledge workers, 11
Mass customization, 22
Middle managers, 12
Network, 12
Operational managers, 12
Output, 8
Processing, 8
Production or service workers, 11
Senior managers, 12
Standard operating procedures (SOPs), 11
Storage technology, 12
Virtual organization, 20
Web site, 18
World Wide Web, 18

REVIEW QUESTIONS

1. Distinguish between a computer, a computer program, and an information system. What is the difference between data and information?
2. What activities convert raw data to usable information in information systems? What is their relationship to feedback?
3. What is information systems literacy?
4. What are the organization, management, and technology dimensions of information systems?
5. Distinguish between a behavioral and a technical approach to information systems in terms of the questions asked and the answers provided.
6. What major disciplines contribute to an understanding of information systems?
7. Why should managers study information systems?
8. What is the relationship between an organization and its information systems? How is this relationship changing over time?

9. What are the Internet and the World Wide Web? How have they changed the role played by information systems in organizations?
10. Describe some of the major changes that information systems are bringing to organizations.
11. How are information systems changing the management process?
12. What is the relationship between the network revolution, electronic commerce, and electronic business?
13. What do we mean by the information architecture of the organization?
14. What are the key management challenges involved in building, operating, and maintaining information systems today?

GROUP PROJECT

In a group with three or four classmates, find a description in a computer or business magazine of an information system used by an organization. Look for information about the company on the Web to gain further insight into the company and prepare a brief description of the business. Describe the system you have selected in terms of its inputs, processes, and outputs, and in terms of its organization, management, and technology features and the importance of the system to the company. Present your analysis to the class.

TOOLS FOR INTERACTIVE LEARNING

■ **INTERNET**: The Internet Connection for this chapter will take you to the United Parcel Service Web site, where you can complete an exercise to evaluate how UPS uses the Web and other information technology in its daily operations. You can use the interactive software at this Web site in an Electronic Commerce project to help a company calculate and budget for its shipping costs. You can also use the Interactive Study Guide to test your knowledge of the topics in this chapter, and get instant feedback where you need more practice.

■ **CD-ROM**: If you purchase and use the Multimedia Edition CD-ROM with this chapter, you will find a simulation showing you how the Internet works, a video clip illustrating UPS's package tracking system, interactive exercises, an audio overview of the major themes of this chapter, and bullet text summarizing the key points of the chapter.

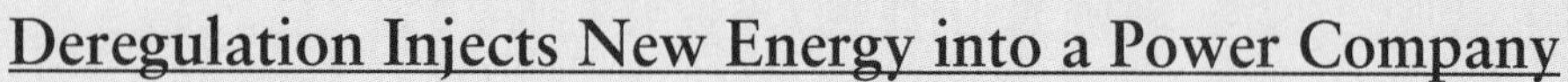

Deregulation Injects New Energy into a Power Company

The utilities industry is perhaps the least exciting of the major industries. Its job is to build, operate, and maintain power plants and power lines, using this infrastructure to supply power to thousands of nearly anonymous customers. These companies are state-regulated monopolies that have no need for a marketing or sales function because their customers have no choice as to who will supply their power. Prices change rarely, usually only after approval by a regulatory agency. The health of the company is usually measured by the value of its plants, generators, and power lines.

Deregulation is changing all that. Under deregulation, rates will no longer be set by the states; power suppliers will no longer have captive customers, and power consumers will be free to choose their power suppliers. As of March 1998, deregulation of the electric power industry went into effect in the state of California, and it will soon be spreading to other states. New companies competing in the deregulated market bear little resemblance to the lumbering dull companies we know as utilities.

Deregulation forces the separation of power generation from power retail sales. Some companies will continue to do both; others will generate power but sell it only to wholesale buyers; while other companies will generate no power, being retail suppliers only. Suddenly the need to compete will dominate the culture of these companies as they strive to acquire, satisfy, and keep customers. To hold on to current customers, these companies will have to emphasize service and price. Marketing and sales become critical—strategic—functions. Information about customers and potential customers will be central to success. These companies will set their own prices and will compete partially on the basis of price. Prices will change often based upon changing costs. The health of the company will be measured in sales and in numbers of customers, not in capital equipment. Because companies delivering power to retail customers will often purchase their power elsewhere, knowledge of the wholesale power supply market becomes critical. These companies will have no physical end-product to point to, making them service companies. Marketing and sales organizations must be flexible and able to react fast to changing competitive market conditions. Such organizations tend to be flatter (less hierarchical) than more traditional organizations. In such an environment, even the dress tends to be more relaxed.

How will these different power company cultures affect the look, role, and importance of information systems? In a traditional power company, information systems are used primarily to bill customers and collect from them, to restore power when outages occur, and to maintain its capital assets. Information systems comprise only a tiny percentage of its assets, with capital goods accounting for the overwhelming majority. Senior management seldom, if ever, concerns itself with the information systems of such companies.

On the other hand, information systems are strategic for companies operating in a highly competitive market. Employees in companies operating in a deregulated power supply market need to obtain, store, and access up-to-date, detailed information on customers and potential customers. Large databases to collect and store information from various sources become essential. Company computer systems are needed to enter customer information, while networks are necessary for gathering data about potential customers. Marketing and sales systems are needed to support those functions. Rapid repair of outages and downed lines become critical because quality service is essential in a competitive environment. Thus computer systems that locate and analyze power distribution problems become vital. To compete with low prices, these companies must control costs, which means automating many functions and establishing quality controls over these functions. In addition, locating and purchasing the cheapest power to sell is an essential function, and information systems using the Internet and electronic commerce networks are central to these functions.

Doug Hyde has seen both sides of the changing power company scene. As CEO of Green Mountain Power (GMP) in Vermont, he spent many years managing a traditional $150 million power company. His main responsibilities were to keep costs down and to satisfy regulators. The atmosphere in this hierarchical company was very traditional: To speak to him his subordinates had to call his secretary and make a formal appointment. Dress was "suits and ties." In this job, he seldom used computers and knew very little about them.

All of this changed in 1997. GMP established a new company meant to compete in the coming deregulated market, and Hyde moved over and became its CEO. The company, Green Mountain Energy Resources (GMER), located in South Burlington, Vermont, is a retail marketer of electric services. Technology is the heart and soul of the company. The company owns no generation or distribution facilities, but its startup costs included nearly $50 million for information technology. As Hyde explains, "In this new business, a lot of money had to be raised and then spent, creating an information system designed to produce not things but knowledge." The company maintains a relatively flat organization in which anybody can walk into anyone else's office at any time. The dress, not surprisingly, is very relaxed.

While located in Vermont, the company had to be ready to win its first customers in California when deregulation came into being. Hyde and his associates knew they would have to compete on price, but they decided to differentiate their product in another way so that many customers will prefer to buy from them. GMER is offering a customized product that is being marketed to environmentally conscious consumers in the hope that they will pay a small premium for "green goods" and will develop a loyalty to the GMER brand of electricity. The company buys its electricity from organizations that generate it from water, wind, solar, and geothermal sources. GMER individualizes its product so that, for example, a customer can request 60 percent solar energy and 40 percent wind energy.

To identify potential customers, the company has built a powerful data-gathering information system. Potential clients sign up with GMER by filling out an on-line form on the Web or by phoning a high-tech call center, providing name, address, meter number, type of home and energy-consuming appliances, and personal energy use. Using secured Internet connections, the meter number is transmitted electronically to the customer's former utility company, which returns a profile of the customer's 12-month energy use. GMER uses that information for customer analysis and also for a supply-forecasting program that guides purchases of electricity. GMER places orders with an electricity wholesaler. The process of supplying electricity requires about 40 electronic "conversations" per customer between GMER and its suppliers.

Additional information on customers comes from 23 outside contractors used for direct mailing and market research. GMER is also banking on high-tech methods of billing and customer support. For those who wish, for example, GMER will bill and accept payment via the Internet. According to Kevin Hartley, GMER's vice-president of marketing, "we create a product . . . that's not like anybody else's."

Source: Based on Emily Esterson, "A Shock to the System," *Inc. Technology*, No. 1, March 1998. Used by permission of *Inc.* magazine, Goldhirsh Group, Inc., 38 Commercial Wharf, Boston; permission acquired via Copyright Clearance Center, Inc.

Case Study Questions

1. To what extent is GMER a virtual organization? What is the role played by information systems in the way this company conducts its business?
2. How does GMER use the Internet for electronic commerce and electronic business?
3. What management, organization, and technology issues do you think a traditional power company would have to address to convert to a competitive company in the deregulated environment? How do you think some of these companies will succeed in making the transition? Explain your answer.
4. How might GMER have succeeded without its large investment in information systems? Are there benefits to not relying so totally upon computer systems, and if so, what are they?
5. What are some of the problems that GMER will face that technology cannot address?

CHAPTER 2

The Strategic Role of Information Systems

chapter outline

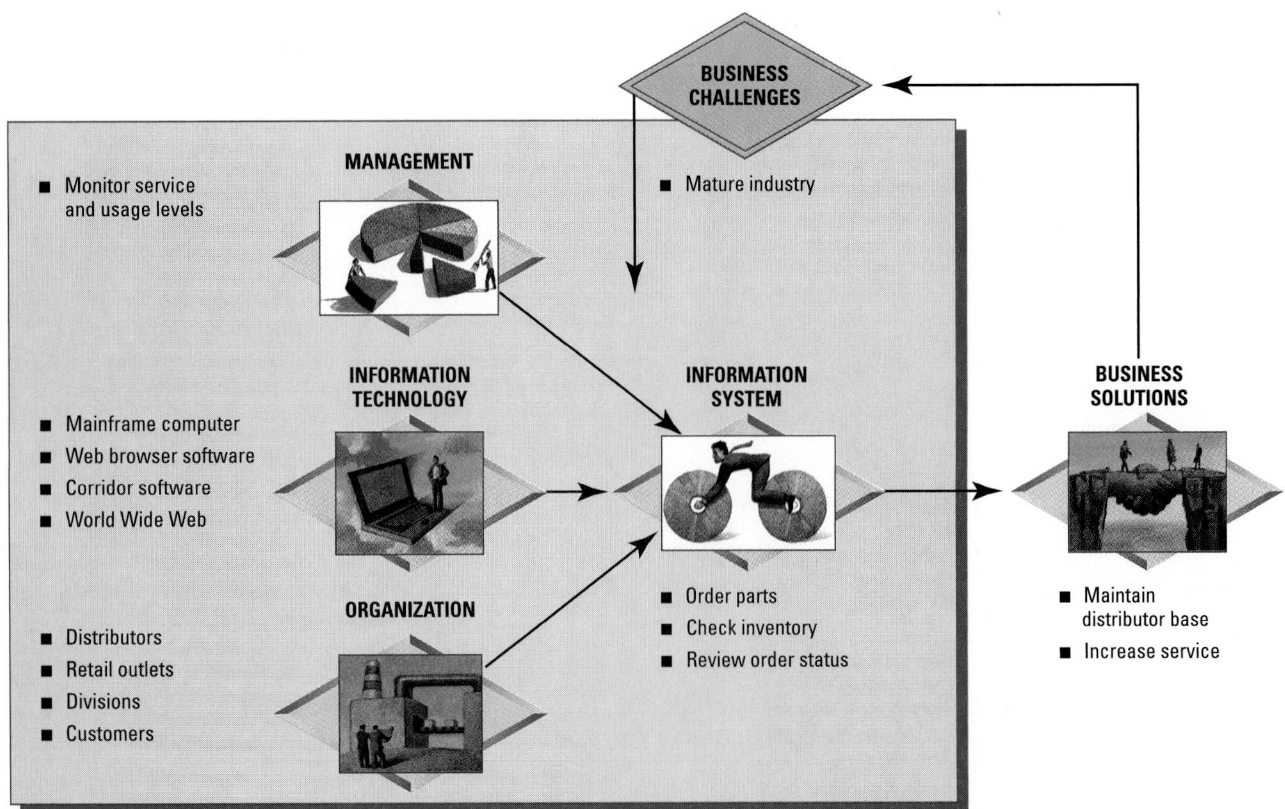

Hubbell Leapfrogs Competitors with the Web

In a mature, well-established industry, where there is little room for innovation, the differences between one vendor's products and those of the next are minimal. To compete successfully, companies must either provide their goods at the lowest cost or provide superior service. That's precisely what Hubbell, an Orange, Connecticut-based manufacturer of electrical devices is doing.

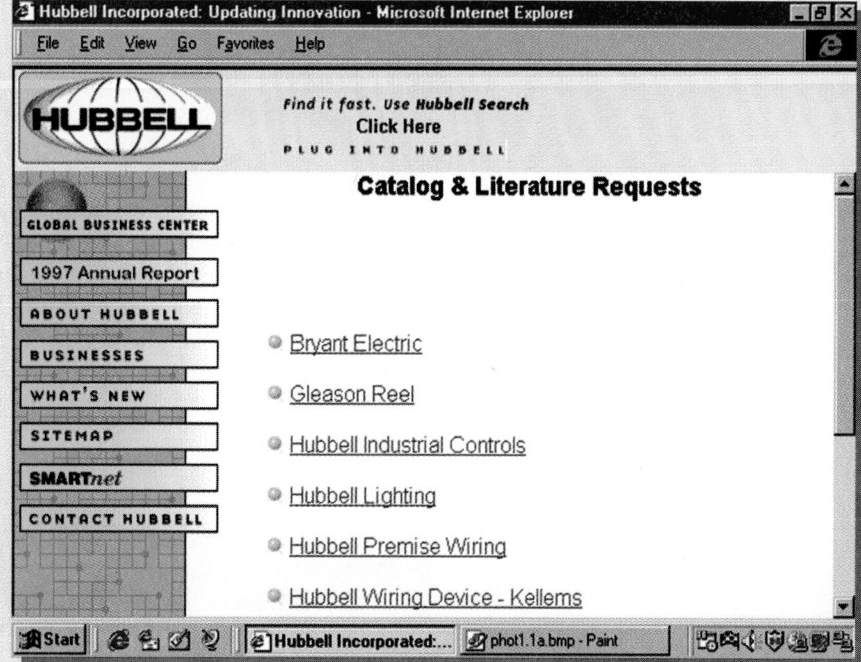

Hubbell markets electrical devices, lighting supplies and related equipment to distributors and some retail outlets. The company markets through multiple division brands, which include companies such as Bryant Electric, E.M. Wiegmann & Company, Killark Electrical Manufacturing Company, and The Ohio Brass Company. Hubbell has offices in Saudi Arabia, Asia, and Turkey and 8000 employees worldwide. All of these companies sell through distributors, and satisfying these distributors is key to maintaining market share.

To provide superior service, Hubbell launched SMARTnet, an Internet-based system that lets its distributors order parts, check inventory, and review order status for most of its divisions. At the opening menu, users select the company division they want to access and then fill out a query form to obtain the information they need. The Web-based application lets the distributor log on and stay connected the entire time they are working with a customer.

A software application called Corridor from Teubner & Associates of Stillwater, Oklahoma, allows data from Hubbell's mainframe computer to be put into Web page format. Users can access the data using the same standard Web browser software that they use to access Web pages. The system replaced an older networked application that was costly and difficult to use.

The system's ease of use and accessibility have kept Hubbell's distributors happy. Hubbell is experiencing a system usage growth of 50 percent to 75 percent per month.

Source: Adapted from Scott Wildemuth, "Hubbell Gets Smart Response from the Net," *Datamation*, March 1998.

Management Challenges

Hubbell's use of Internet technology illustrates how critical information systems have become for supporting organizational goals and for enabling firms to stay ahead of the competition. Hubbell has temporarily gained a market advantage over its competitors by offering a service others cannot. But something more than a single technological leap is required to sustain this competitive edge over many years. Specifically, managers need to address the following challenges:

1. **Integration:** Although it is necessary to design different systems serving different levels and functions in the firm, more and more firms are finding advantages in integrating systems; many are pursuing enterprise resource management. However, integrating systems for different organizational levels and functions to freely exchange information can be technologically difficult and costly. Managers need to determine what level of system integration is required and how much it is worth in dollars.

2. **Sustainability of competitive advantage:**The competitive advantages conferred by strategic systems do not necessarily last long enough to ensure long-term profits. Competitors can retaliate and copy strategic systems. Competitive advantage isn't always sustainable. Market conditions change. The business and economic environment changes. Technology and customers' expectations change. The classic strategic information systems—American Airlines' SABRE computerized reservation system, Citibank's ATM system, and Federal Express' package-tracking system—benefited by being the first in their respective industries. But then rival systems emerged. Information systems alone cannot provide an enduring business advantage (Mata et al., 1995; Kettinger et al., 1994; Hopper, 1990). Systems originally intended to be strategic frequently become tools for survival, something every firm has in order to stay in business, or they may even inhibit organizations from making the strategic changes required for future success (Eardley, Avison, and Powell, 1997).

learning objectives

After completing this chapter, you will be able to:

1. Analyze the role played by the six major types of information systems in organizations.
2. Describe the relationship between the various types of information systems.
3. Examine how the competitive forces and value chain models can be used to identify opportunities for strategic information systems.
4. Explain why strategic information systems are difficult to build and to sustain.
5. Describe how organizations can use information systems to enhance quality in their operations, products, and services.

In this chapter we show the role played by the various types of information systems in organizations. We then look at the problems firms face from competition and the ways in which information systems can provide competitive advantage. Hubbell used information systems to increase the quality of its service to distributors while keeping down costs. Information systems can be used to pursue other competitive strategies as well. And because quality has become so important in today's competitive environment, we describe the various ways that information systems can contribute to the quality goals of the firm.

2.1 KEY SYSTEM APPLICATIONS IN THE ORGANIZATION

Because there are different interests, specialties, and levels in an organization, there are different kinds of systems. No single system can provide all the information an organization needs. Figure 2.1 illustrates one way to depict the kinds of systems found in an organization. In the illustration, the organization is divided into strategic, management,

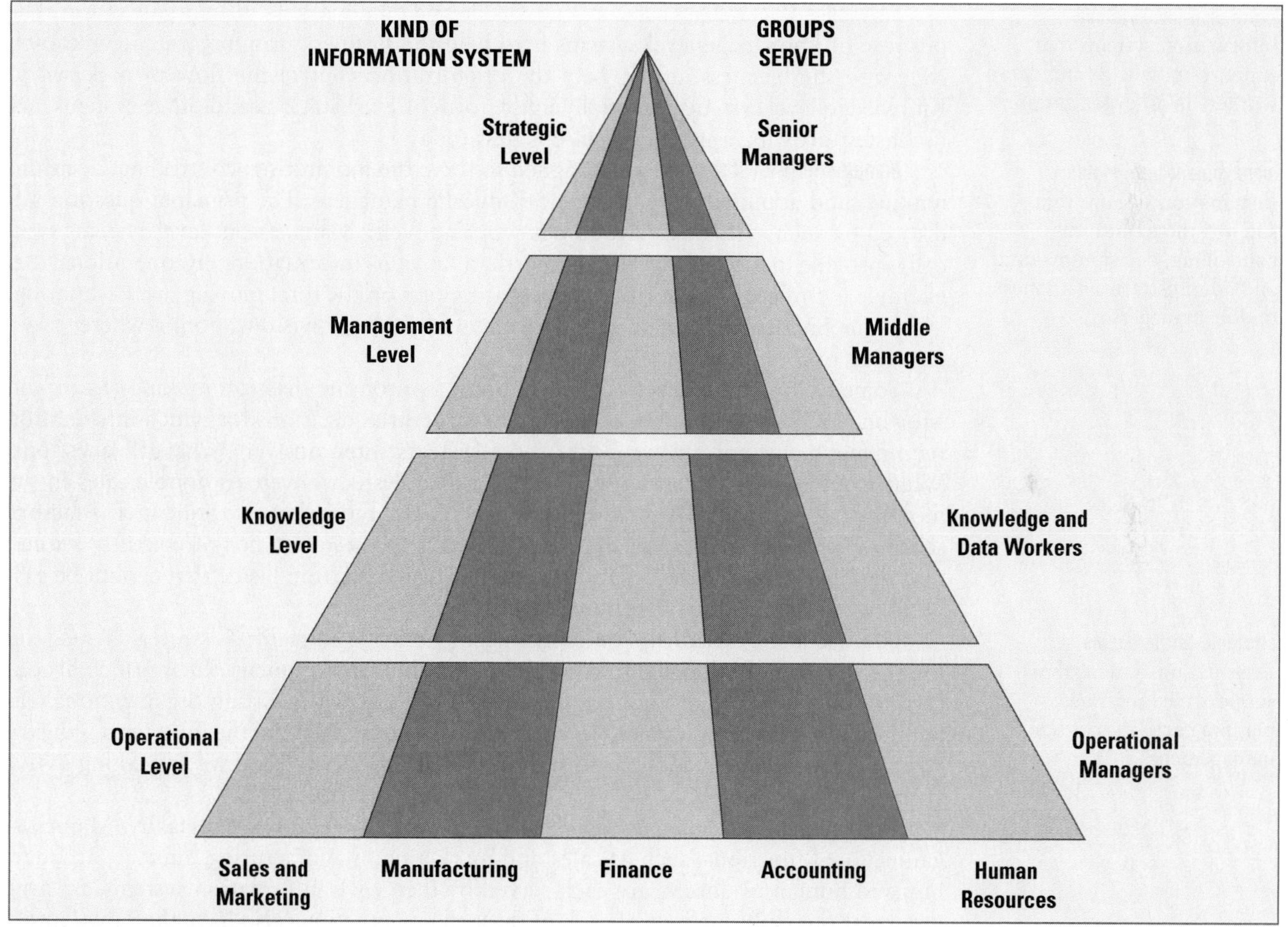

FIGURE 2.1

Types of information systems. Organizations and information systems can be divided into strategic, management, knowledge, and operational levels. They can be divided further into five functional areas: sales and marketing, manufacturing, finance, accounting, and human resources. Information systems serve each of these levels and functions. Strategic-level systems help senior managers with long-term planning. Management-level systems help middle managers monitor and control. Knowledge-level systems help knowledge and data workers design products, distribute information, and cope with paperwork. Operational-level systems help operational managers keep track of the firm's day-to-day activities.

knowledge, and operational levels and then is further divided into functional areas such as sales and marketing, manufacturing, finance, accounting, and human resources. Systems are built to serve these different organizational interests (Anthony, 1965).

Different Kinds of Systems

operational-level systems Information systems that monitor the elementary activities and transactions of the organization.

knowledge-level systems Information systems that support knowledge and data workers in an organization.

management-level systems Information systems that support the monitoring, controlling, decision-making, and administrative activities of middle managers.

strategic-level systems Information systems that support the long-range planning activities of senior management.

Four main types of information systems serve different organizational levels: operational-level systems, knowledge-level systems, management-level systems, and strategic-level systems. **Operational-level systems** support operational managers by keeping track of the elementary activities and transactions of the organization, such as sales, receipts, cash deposits, payroll, credit decisions, and the flow of materials in a factory. The principal purpose of systems at this level is to answer routine questions and to track the flow of transactions through the organization. How many parts are in inventory? What happened to Mr. Williams's payment? To answer these kinds of questions, information generally must be easily available, current, and accurate. Examples of operational-level systems include a system to record bank deposits from automatic teller machines or one that tracks the number of hours worked each day by employees on a factory floor.

Knowledge-level systems support knowledge and data workers in an organization. The purpose of knowledge-level systems is to help the business firm integrate new knowledge into the business and to help the organization control the flow of paperwork. Knowledge-level systems, especially in the form of workstations and office systems, are the fastest-growing applications in business today.

Management-level systems are designed to serve the monitoring, controlling, decision-making, and administrative activities of middle managers. The principal question addressed by such systems is: Are things working well? Management-level systems typically provide periodic reports rather than instant information on operations. An example is a relocation control system that reports on the total moving, house-hunting, and home financing costs for employees in all company divisions, noting wherever actual costs exceed budgets.

Some management-level systems support nonroutine decision making (Keen and Morton, 1978). They tend to focus on less-structured decisions for which information requirements are not always clear. These systems often answer "what if" questions: What would be the impact on production schedules if we were to double sales in the month of December? What would happen to our return on investment if a factory schedule were delayed for six months? Answers to these questions frequently require new data from outside the organization, as well as data from inside that cannot be easily drawn from existing operational-level systems.

Strategic-level systems help senior management tackle and address strategic issues and long-term trends, both in the firm and in the external environment. Their principal concern is matching changes in the external environment with existing organizational capability. What will employment levels be in five years? What are the long-term industry cost trends, and where does our firm fit in? What products should we be making in five years?

Information systems may also be differentiated by functional specialty. Major organizational functions, such as sales and marketing, manufacturing, finance, accounting, and human resources, are each served by their own information systems. In large organizations, subfunctions of each of these major functions also have their own information systems. For example, the manufacturing function might have systems for inventory management, process control, plant maintenance, computer-aided engineering, and material requirements planning.

A typical organization has operational-, management-, knowledge-, and strategic-level systems for each functional area. For example, the sales function generally has a sales system on the operational level to record daily sales figures and to process orders. A knowledge-level system designs promotional displays for the firm's products. A management-level system tracks monthly sales figures by sales territory and reports on territories where sales exceed or fall below anticipated levels. A system to forecast sales trends over a five-year period serves the strategic level.

Finally, different organizations have different information systems for the same functional areas. Because no two organizations have exactly the same objectives, structures, or interests, information systems must be custom-made to fit the unique characteristics of each. There is no such thing as a universal information system that can fit all organizations. Every organization does the job somewhat differently.

Information systems can thus be classified by functional specialty or by the organizational level they serve. Throughout this text are examples of systems supporting the various functional areas—sales systems, manufacturing systems, human resources systems, finance and accounting systems. For professors and students requiring deeper analysis of information systems from a functional perspective, we have included additional material on the Laudon and Laudon Web site. This chapter analyzes the key applications of the organization primarily in terms of the organizational level and types of decisions they support.

Six Major Types of Systems

In this section we describe the specific categories of systems serving each organizational level and their value to the organization. Figure 2.2 shows the specific types of information systems that correspond to each organizational level. The organization

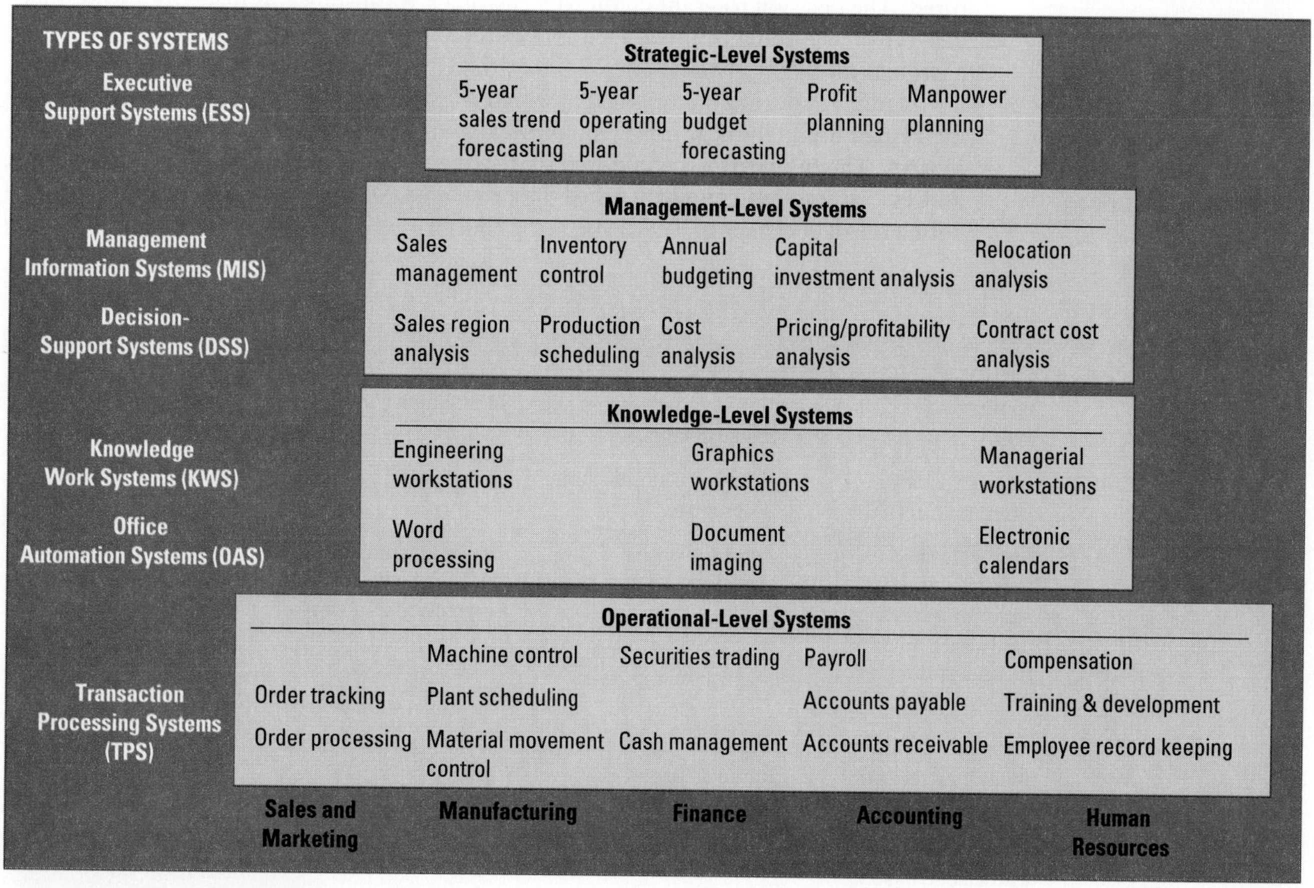

TYPES OF SYSTEMS

Executive Support Systems (ESS)

Strategic-Level Systems

5-year sales trend forecasting | 5-year operating plan | 5-year budget forecasting | Profit planning | Manpower planning

Management Information Systems (MIS)

Decision-Support Systems (DSS)

Management-Level Systems

Sales management | Inventory control | Annual budgeting | Capital investment analysis | Relocation analysis

Sales region analysis | Production scheduling | Cost analysis | Pricing/profitability analysis | Contract cost analysis

Knowledge Work Systems (KWS)

Office Automation Systems (OAS)

Knowledge-Level Systems

Engineering workstations | Graphics workstations | Managerial workstations

Word processing | Document imaging | Electronic calendars

Transaction Processing Systems (TPS)

Operational-Level Systems

Sales and Marketing	Manufacturing	Finance	Accounting	Human Resources
	Machine control	Securities trading	Payroll	Compensation
Order tracking	Plant scheduling		Accounts payable	Training & development
Order processing	Material movement control	Cash management	Accounts receivable	Employee record keeping

FIGURE 2.2

The six major types of information systems. Information systems are built to serve each of the four levels of an organization. Transaction processing systems (TPS) serve the operational level of an organization. Knowledge work systems (KWS) and office automation systems (OAS) serve the knowledge level of an organization. Decision-support systems (DSS) and management information systems (MIS) serve the management level of the organization. Executive support systems (ESS) serve the strategic level of an organization.

has executive support systems (ESS) at the strategic level; management information systems (MIS) and decision-support systems (DSS) at the management level; knowledge work systems (KWS) and office automation systems (OAS) at the knowledge level; and transaction processing systems (TPS) at the operational level. Systems at each level in turn are specialized to serve each of the major functional areas. Thus, the typical systems found in organizations are designed to assist workers or managers at each level and in the functions of sales and marketing, manufacturing, finance, accounting, and human resources.

Table 2.1 summarizes the features of the six types of information systems. It should be noted that each of the different kinds of systems may have components that are used by organizational levels and groups other than their main constituencies. A secretary may find information on an MIS, or a middle manager may need to extract data from a TPS.

Transaction Processing Systems

transaction processing systems (TPS) Computerized systems that perform and record the daily routine transactions necessary to conduct the business; they serve the operational level of the organization.

Transaction processing systems (TPS) are the basic business systems that serve the operational level of the organization. A transaction processing system is a computerized system that performs and records the daily routine transactions necessary to the conduct of the business. Examples are sales order entry, hotel reservation systems, payroll, employee record keeping, and shipping.

At the operational level, tasks, resources, and goals are predefined and highly structured. The decision to grant credit to a customer, for instance, is made by a lower-level supervisor according to predefined criteria. All that must be determined is whether the customer meets the criteria.

Figure 2.3 depicts a payroll TPS, which is a typical accounting transaction processing system found in most firms. A payroll system keeps track of the money paid to employees. The master file is composed of discrete pieces of information (such as a name, address, or employee number) called data elements. Data are keyed into the system, updating the data elements. The elements on the master file are combined in different ways

TABLE 2.1 Characteristics of Information Processing Systems

Type of System	Information Inputs	Processing	Information Outputs	Users
ESS	Aggregate data; external, internal	Graphics; simulations; interactive	Projections; responses to queries	Senior managers
DSS	Low-volume data or massive databases optimized for data analysis; analytic models and data analysis tools	Interactive; simulations; analysis	Special reports; decision analyses; responses to queries	Professionals; staff managers
MIS	Summary transaction data; high-volume data; simple models	Routine reports; simple models; low-level analysis	Summary and exception reports	Middle managers
KWS	Design specifications; knowledge base	Modeling; simulations	Models; graphics	Professionals; technical staff
OAS	Documents; schedules	Document management; scheduling; communication	Documents; schedules; mail	Clerical workers
TPS	Transactions; events	Sorting; listing; merging; updating	Detailed reports; lists; summaries	Operations personnel; supervisors

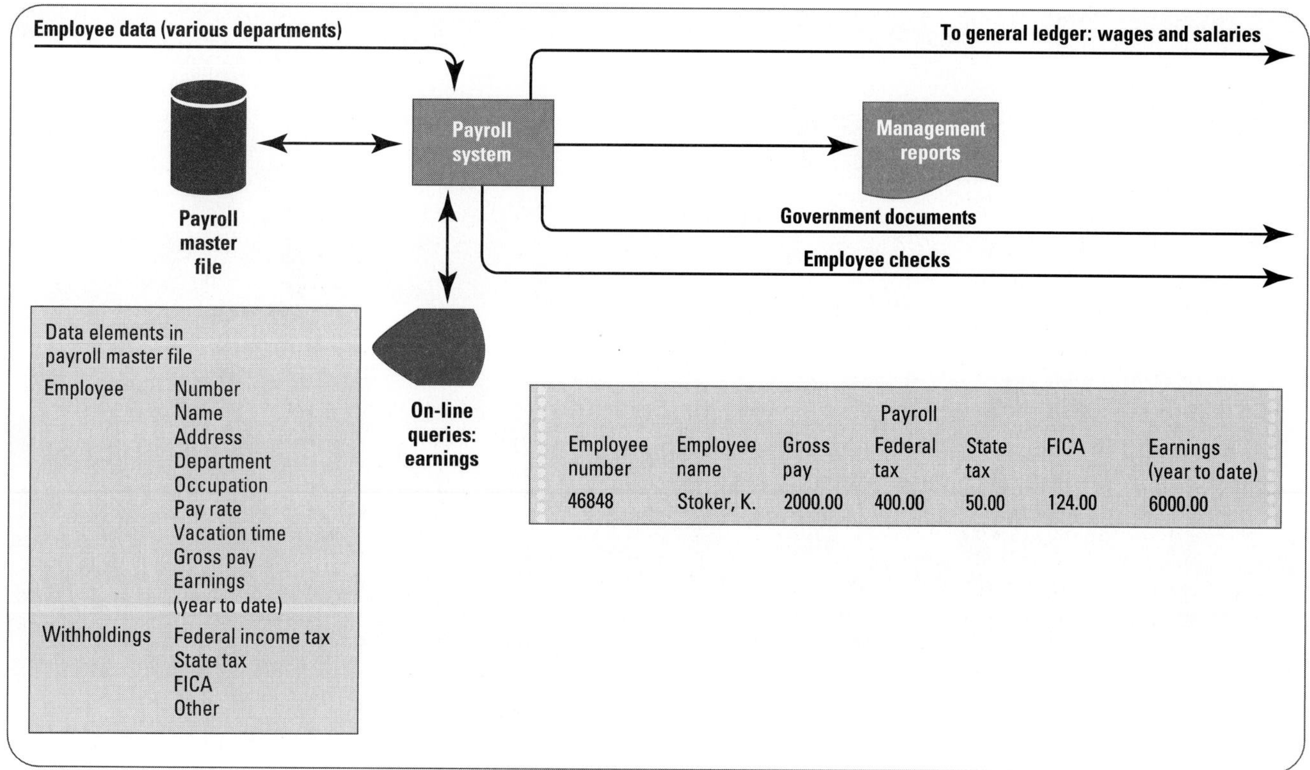

FIGURE 2.3

A symbolic representation for a payroll TPS.

to make up reports of interest to management and government agencies and paychecks sent to employees. These TPS can generate other report combinations of existing data elements.

Other typical TPS applications are identified in Figure 2.4. The figure shows that there are five functional categories of TPS: sales/marketing, manufacturing/production, finance/accounting, human resources, and other types of TPS that are unique to a particular industry. The UPS package tracking system described in Chapter 1 is an example of a manufacturing TPS. UPS sells package delivery services; the system keeps track of all of its package shipment transactions.

All organizations have these five kinds of TPS (even if the systems are manual). Transaction processing systems are often so central to a business that TPS failure for a few hours can spell the demise of a firm and perhaps other firms linked to it. Imagine what would happen to UPS if its package tracking system were not working! What would the airlines do without their computerized reservation systems?

Managers need TPS to monitor the status of internal operations and the firm's relations with the external environment. TPS are also major producers of information for the other types of systems. (For example, the payroll system illustrated here, along with other accounting TPS, supplies data to the company's general ledger system, which is responsible for maintaining records of the firm's income and expenses and for producing reports such as income statements and balance sheets.)

knowledge work systems (KWS) Information systems that aid knowledge workers in the creation and integration of new knowledge in the organization.

office automation systems (OAS) Computer systems, such as word processing, electronic mail systems, and scheduling systems, that are designed to increase the productivity of data workers in the office.

Knowledge Work and Office Automation Systems

Knowledge work systems (KWS) and **office automation systems (OAS)** serve the information needs at the knowledge level of the organization. Knowledge work systems aid knowledge workers, whereas office automation systems primarily aid data workers (although they are also used extensively by knowledge workers).

	TYPE OF TPS				
	Sales/ marketing systems	Manufacturing/ production systems	Finance/ accounting systems	Human resources systems	Other types (e.g., university)
Major functions of system	Sales management	Scheduling	Budgeting	Personnel records	Admissions
	Market research	Purchasing	General ledger	Benefits	Grade records
	Promotion	Shipping/receiving	Billing	Compensation	Course records
	Pricing	Engineering	Cost accounting	Labor relations	Alumni
	New products	Operations		Training	
Major application systems	Sales order information system	Materials resource planning systems	General ledger	Payroll	Registration system
	Market research system	Purchase order control systems	Accounts receivable/payable	Employee records	Student transcript system
	Pricing system	Engineering systems	Budgeting	Benefit systems	Curriculum class control systems
		Quality control systems	Funds management systems	Career path systems	Alumni benefactor system

FIGURE 2.4

Typical applications of TPS. There are five functional categories of TPS: sales/marketing, manufacturing/production, finance/accounting, human resources, and other types of systems specific to a particular industry. Within each of these major functions are subfunctions. For each of these subfunctions (e.g., sales management) there is a major application system.

In general, *knowledge workers* are people who hold formal university degrees and who are often members of a recognized profession, like engineers, doctors, lawyers, and scientists. Their jobs consist primarily of creating new information and knowledge. Knowledge work systems (KWS), such as scientific or engineering design workstations, promote the creation of new knowledge and ensure that new knowledge and technical expertise are properly integrated into the business. Examples of KWS are the computer-aided design and robotics systems used by Japanese shipbuilders described in the Window on Technology.

Data workers typically have less formal, advanced educational degrees and tend to process rather than create information. They consist primarily of secretaries, accountants, filing clerks, or managers whose jobs are principally to use, manipulate, or disseminate information. Office automation systems (OAS) are information technology applications designed to increase the productivity of data workers by supporting the coordinating and communicating activities of the typical office. Office automation systems coordinate diverse information workers, geographic units, and functional areas: The systems communicate with customers, suppliers, and other organizations outside the firm and serve as a clearinghouse for information and knowledge flows.

word processing Office automation technology that facilitates the creation of documents through computerized text editing, formatting, storing, and printing.

desktop publishing Technology that produces professional-quality documents combining output from word processors with design, graphics, and special layout features.

Typical office automation systems handle and manage documents (through word processing, desktop publishing, document imaging, and digital filing), scheduling (through electronic calendars), and communication (through electronic mail, voice mail, or videoconferencing). **Word processing** refers to the software and hardware that creates, edits, formats, stores, and prints documents (see Chapter 6). Word processing systems represent the single most common application of information technology to office work, in part because producing documents is what offices are all about. **Desktop publishing** produces professional publishing-quality documents by combining output from word pro-

WINDOW ON TECHNOLOGY

Technology Helps Japanese Shipbuilders Beat Back Competition

In the 1980s, Japan's shipbuilders and other smokestack industries looked like they were heading for the smelter. Countries like Korea and Taiwan threatened to overtake Japan because the strong yen made Japanese ships more expensive in foreign currencies. Japanese labor costs were high as well. Today, Japan has regained its No. 1 position in shipbuilding and ranks among the world's most profitable shipbuilders. It was able to convert labor-intensive ship factories into mass-assembly powerhouses by using information system technology.

Japan's shipbuilding process used to be heavily manual. For example, at Hitachi Zosen Corporation, one of Japan's large shipbuilders, workers pieced together ships from blocks of bulkheads and plates assembled mainly by hand. The blocks were trucked to dry dock and fused together with manual riveting and welding. Most ships were custom-produced.

Hitachi decided to lower costs by intensifying mass production and moving to a single basic ship design. It intensified its use of robotics. The company teamed up with Nippon Steel to develop more flexible welding robots that can weld along a curved surface slanting up 15 degrees. Each robot requires only two people to operate and performs this job twice as fast as manual welding. By the mid-1990s Hitachi had cut costs so low that it could offer as standard features items such as automatic engine valves, which other companies sold as extras.

After a decade of restructuring, a Japanese shipyard can look like both an assembly line and a design studio. At the Mitsubishi Heavy Industries yard in Nagasaki, robots cut bulkheads from inch-thick metal plates like a tailor cutting cloth. A machine emitting high-frequency radio waves along the length of a steel plate bends the plate into a preprogrammed shape. The machine replaces human welders that used to piece together many smaller plates to cover a curved surface and cuts the company's metal-bending time in half.

Mitsubishi made its computer system the brain of its shipyard, linking design, engineering, marketing, and assembly crews at every stage of production. Computer-aided design models provide the data driving much of this automation. Computer-aided design (CAD) eliminates much of the manual drafting and building of physical designs that used to slow down the design and production process by allowing the design work to be performed on the computer. The designs can then be revised electronically without having to rebuild any physical models. Data fed by designers into the Mitsubishi computer system tell the robot welder exactly where to weld a bulkhead to the hull and which type of rod to use. Buyers can inspect a virtual-reality image of the ship they have ordered on the computer. With just the click of a button, they can make sure that a water pump in the engine room is positioned far enough away from a bulkhead to be easily cleaned and repaired. The network has cut design time by one-third.

With automated shipyards the Japanese can build more ships faster with fewer workers than in the past. In 1987, Japan built 5.7 million tons of ships. In 1996, it built 10.2 million tons with 30 percent fewer full-time workers and 20 percent less capacity.

To Think About: ***How did information system technology change the way Japanese shipbuilders conducted business?***

Source: Adapted from Steve Glain, "Defying the Odds, Japan Shipbuilders Beat Back Their Hungry Competitors," *The Wall Street Journal*, February 12, 1998.

cessing software with design elements, graphics, and special layout features. Companies are now starting to publish documents in the form of Web pages for easier access and distribution. We describe Web publishing in more detail in Chapter 12.

Document imaging systems are another widely used knowledge application. **Document imaging systems** convert documents and images into digital form so that they can be stored and accessed by the computer. Figure 2.5 illustrates the imaging system used by the United Services Automobile Association, the fifth largest provider of auto insurance and the fourth largest provider of homeowner insurance in the United States. USAA receives more than 100,000 letters and mails more than 250,000 items daily. USAA has developed the largest imaging system in the world, storing 1.5 billion pages. All incoming mail received each day by the policy department is scanned and stored on optical disk. The original documents are thrown away. USAA's major regional offices across the country are hooked up to its imaging network. The network consists of image scanners, optical storage units, a mainframe computer, and a local area network to link service representatives' workstations and the scanner workstations located in the firm's mailroom. Service representatives can retrieve a client's file on-line and view documents from desktop computers. About 10,000 people use the network. Users believe that the imaging

document imaging systems Systems that convert documents and images into digital form so that they can be stored and accessed by the computer.

Computer-aided design (CAD) systems eliminate many manual steps in design and production by performing much of the design work on the computer.

system reduces the amount of time their work would take with a paper-based system by one-third, saving paper and storage costs. Customer service has been improved because electronic documents can be accessed more rapidly (Korzeniowski, 1997; Lasher, Ives, and Jarvenpaa, 1991; "USAA Insuring Progress," 1992).

Management Information Systems

management information systems (MIS) Information systems at the management level of an organization that serve the functions of planning, controlling, and decision making by providing routine summary and exception reports.

Management information systems (MIS) serve the management level of the organization, providing managers with reports and, in some cases, with on-line access to the organization's current performance and historical records. Typically, they are oriented almost exclusively to internal, not environmental or external, events. MIS primarily serve the functions of planning, controlling, and decision making at the management level. Generally, they are dependent on underlying transaction processing systems for their data.

MIS summarize and report on the basic operations of the company. The basic transaction data from TPS are compressed and are usually presented in long reports that are

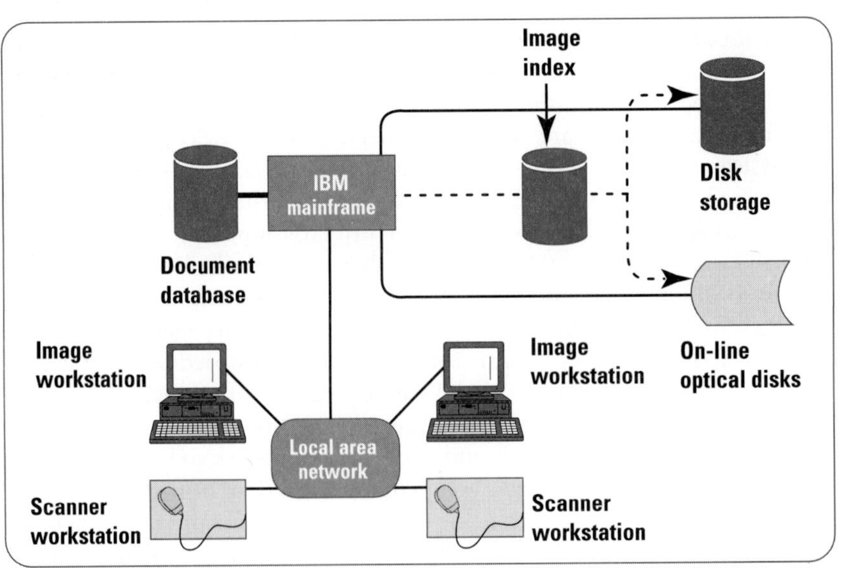

FIGURE 2.5
United Services Automobile Association's (USAA) imaging network. Scanners enter mail received by USAA's policy department into the imaging system, which stores and distributes the digitally processed image of the document electronically. Service representatives have immediate on-line access to clients' data.

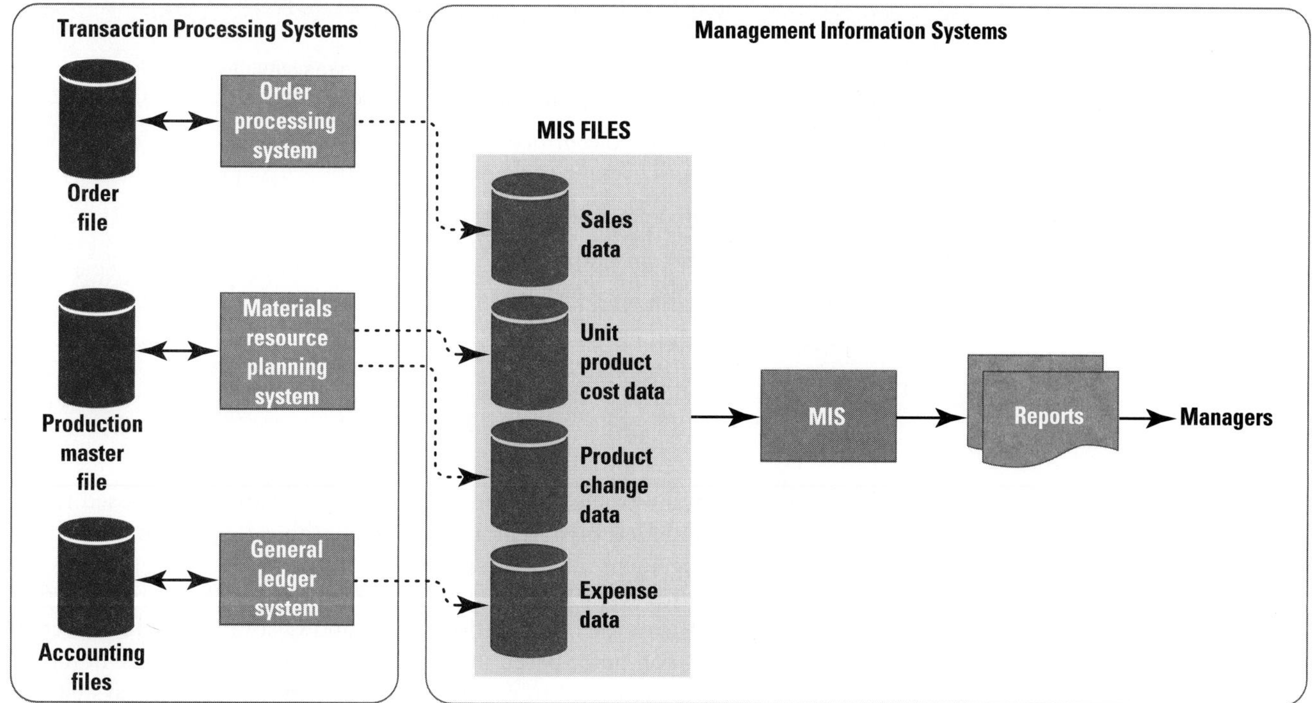

FIGURE 2.6

How management information systems obtain their data from the organization's TPS. In the system illustrated by this diagram, three TPS supply summarized transaction data at the end of the time period to the MIS reporting system. Managers gain access to the organizational data through the MIS, which provides them with the appropriate reports.

produced on a regular schedule. Figure 2.6 shows how a typical MIS transforms transaction level data from inventory, production, and accounting into MIS files that are used to provide managers with reports. Figure 2.7 shows a sample report from this system.

MIS usually serve managers interested in weekly, monthly, and yearly results—not day-to-day activities. MIS generally address structured questions that are known well in advance. These systems are generally not flexible and have little analytical capability.

Consolidated Consumer Products Corporation
Sales by Product and Sales Region: 1999

PRODUCT CODE	PRODUCT DESCRIPTION	SALES REGION	ACTUAL SALES	PLANNED	ACTUAL VS. PLANNED
4469	Carpet Cleaner	Northeast	4,066,700	4,800,000	0.85
		South	3,778,112	3,750,000	1.01
		Midwest	4,867,001	4,600,000	1.06
		West	4,003,440	4,400,000	0.91
	TOTAL		16,715,253	17,550,000	0.95
5674	Room Freshener	Northeast	3,676,700	3,900,000	0.94
		South	5,608,112	4,700,000	1.19
		Midwest	4,711,001	4,200,000	1.12
		West	4,563,440	4,900,000	0.93
	TOTAL		18,559,253	17,700,000	1.05

FIGURE 2.7

A sample report that might be produced by the MIS in Figure 2.6.

TABLE 2.2 Characteristics of Management Information Systems

1. MIS support structured decisions at the operational and management control levels. However, they are also useful for planning purposes of senior management staff.
2. MIS are generally reporting and control oriented. They are designed to report on existing operations and therefore to help provide day-to-day control of operations.
3. MIS rely on existing corporate data and data flows.
4. MIS have little analytical capability.
5. MIS generally aid in decision making using past and present data.
6. MIS are relatively inflexible.
7. MIS have an internal rather than an external orientation.

Most MIS use simple routines such as summaries and comparisons, as opposed to sophisticated mathematical models or statistical techniques. Table 2.2 describes the characteristics of typical management information systems.

Some researchers use the term MIS to include all of the information systems that support the functional areas of the organization (Davis and Olson, 1985). However, in this book we prefer to use computer-based information systems (CBIS) as the umbrella term for all information systems and to consider management information systems as those that are specifically dedicated to management-level functions.

Decision-Support Systems

decision-support systems (DSS) Information systems at the management level of an organization that combine data and sophisticated analytical models or data analysis tools to support semistructured and unstructured decision making.

Decision-support systems (DSS) also serve the management level of the organization. DSS help managers make decisions that are semistructured, unique, or rapidly changing, and not easily specified in advance. While DSS use internal information from TPS and MIS, they often bring in information from external sources, such as current stock prices or product prices of competitors. Table 2.3 shows how contemporary DSS differ from MIS and TPS systems.

Clearly, by design, DSS have more analytical power than other systems. They are built explicitly with a variety of models to analyze data, or they condense large amounts of data into a form where they can be analyzed by decision makers. DSS are designed so that users can work with them directly; these systems explicitly include user-friendly software. DSS are interactive; the user can change assumptions, ask new questions, and include new data.

An interesting, small, but powerful DSS is the voyage-estimating system of a subsidiary of a large American metals company that exists primarily to carry bulk cargoes of coal, oil, ores, and finished products for its parent company. The firm owns some vessels, charters others, and bids for shipping contracts in the open market to carry general cargo. A voyage-estimating system calculates financial and technical voyage details. Financial calculations include ship/time costs (fuel, labor, capital), freight rates for various types of cargo, and port expenses. Technical details include a myriad of factors such as ship cargo capacity, speed, port distances, fuel and water consumption, and

TABLE 2.3 Characteristics of Decision-Support Systems

1. DSS offer users flexibility, adaptability, and a quick response.
2. DSS operate with little or no assistance from professional programmers.
3. DSS provide support for decisions and problems whose solutions cannot be specified in advance.
4. DSS use sophisticated data analysis and modeling tools.

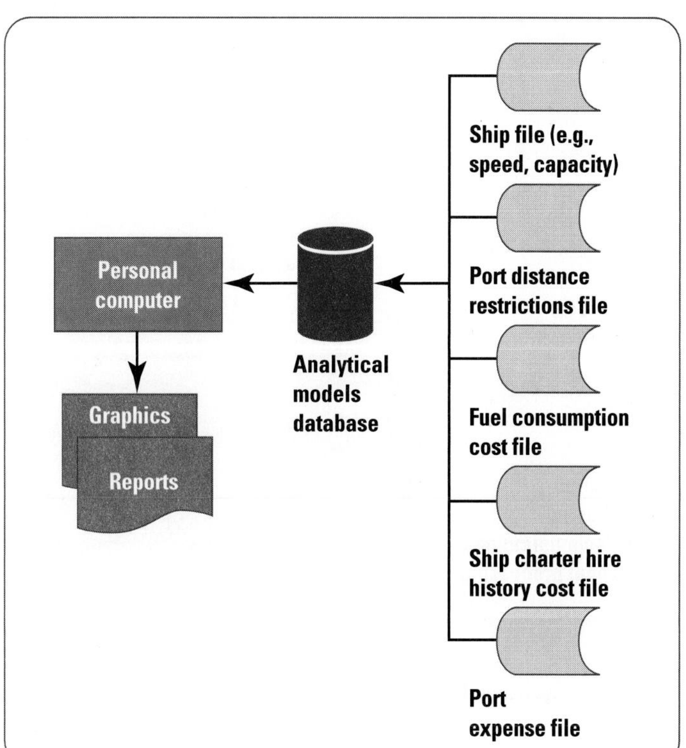

FIGURE 2.8

Voyage estimating decision-support system. This DSS operates on a powerful PC. It is used daily by managers who must develop bids on shipping contracts.

loading patterns (location of cargo for different ports). The system can answer questions such as the following: Given a customer delivery schedule and an offered freight rate, which vessel should be assigned at what rate to maximize profits? What is the optimum speed at which a particular vessel can optimize its profit and still meet its delivery schedule? What is the optimal loading pattern for a ship bound for the U.S. west coast from Malaysia? Figure 2.8 illustrates the DSS built for this company. The system operates on a powerful desktop personal computer, providing a system of menus that makes it easy for users to enter data or obtain information. We describe other types of DSS in Chapter 13.

Executive Support Systems

Senior managers use a category of information systems called **executive support systems (ESS)** to make decisions. ESS serve the strategic level of the organization. They address unstructured decisions and create a generalized computing and communications environment rather than providing any fixed application or specific capability. ESS are designed to incorporate data about external events such as new tax laws or competitors, but they also draw summarized information from internal MIS and DSS. They filter, compress, and track critical data, emphasizing the reduction of time and effort required to obtain information useful to executives. ESS employ the most advanced graphics software and can deliver graphs and data from many sources immediately to a senior executive's office or to a boardroom.

executive support systems (ESS) Information systems at the strategic level of an organization designed to address unstructured decision making through advanced graphics and communications.

Unlike the other types of information systems, ESS are not designed primarily to solve specific problems. Instead, ESS provide a generalized computing and telecommunications capacity that can be applied to a changing array of problems. While many DSS are designed to be highly analytical, ESS tend to make less use of analytical models.

Questions ESS assist in answering include the following: What business should we be in? What are the competitors doing? What new acquisitions would protect us from cyclical business swings? Which units should we sell to raise cash for acquisitions (Rockart and Treacy, 1982)? Figure 2.9 illustrates a model of an ESS. It consists of workstations with menus, interactive graphics, and communications capabilities that

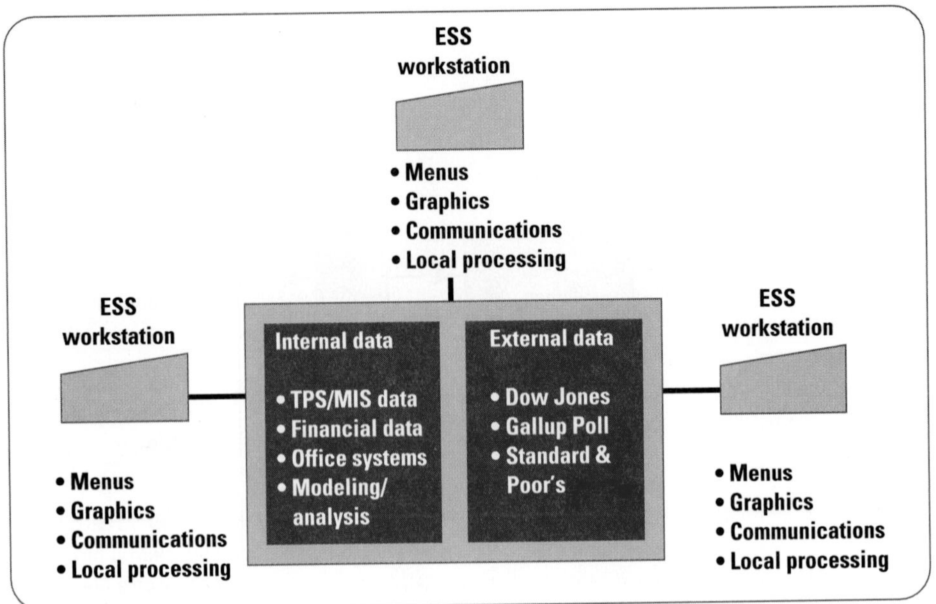

FIGURE 2.9

Model of a typical executive support system. This system pools data from diverse internal and external sources and makes them available to executives in an easy-to-use form.

can access historical and competitive data from internal corporate systems and external databases such as Dow Jones News/Retrieval or the Gallup Poll. Because ESS are designed to be used by senior managers who often have little, if any, direct contact or experience with computer-based information systems, they incorporate easy-to-use graphic interfaces. More details on leading-edge applications of DSS and ESS can be found in Chapter 13.

Relationship of Systems to One Another: Integration

Figure 2.10 illustrates how the various types of systems in the organization are related to one another. TPS are typically a major source of data for other systems, whereas ESS are primarily a recipient of data from lower-level systems. The other types of systems

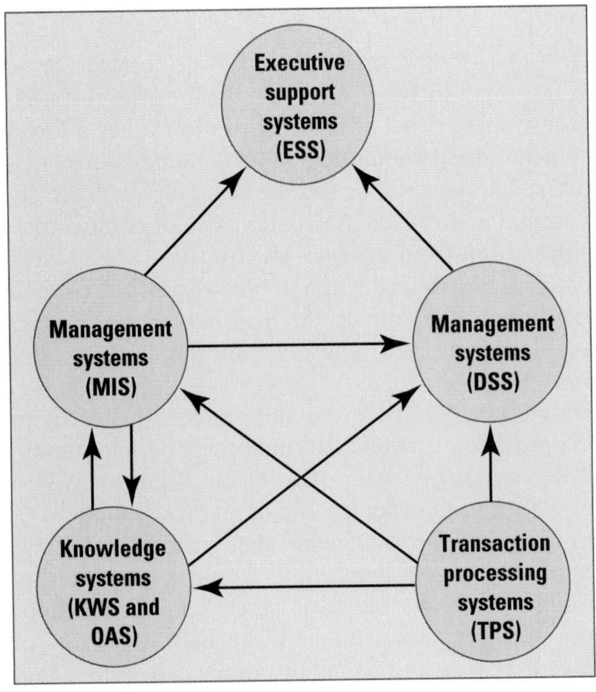

FIGURE 2.10

Interrelationships among systems. The various types of systems in the organization have interdependencies. TPS are a major producer of information that is required by the other systems which, in turn, produce information for other systems. These different types of systems are only loosely coupled in most organizations.

may exchange data with each other as well. Data may also be exchanged among systems serving different functional areas. For example, an order captured by a sales system may be transmitted to a manufacturing system as a transaction for producing or delivering the product specified in the order.

But how much can or should these systems be integrated? This is a very difficult question to answer. It is definitely advantageous to have some measure of integration so that information can flow easily among different parts of the organization. Chapter 1 has described how firms are using enterprise resource planning (ERP) systems to integrate information across the company. But integration costs money, and integrating many different systems is extremely time-consuming and complex. Each organization must weigh its needs for integrating systems against the difficulties of mounting a large-scale systems integration effort. There is no "one right level" of integration or centralization (Allen and Boynton, 1991; King, 1984).

2.2 THE STRATEGIC ROLE OF INFORMATION SYSTEMS

Each of the major types of information systems described previously is valuable for helping organizations solve an important problem. In the past few decades, some of these systems have become especially critical to firms' long-term prosperity and survival. Such systems, which are powerful tools for staying ahead of the competition, are called strategic information systems.

What Is a Strategic Information System?

Strategic information systems change the goals, operations, products, services, or environmental relationships of organizations to help them gain an edge over competitors. Systems that have these effects may even change the business of organizations. For instance, State Street Bank and Trust Co. of Boston transformed its core business from traditional banking services, such as customer checking and savings accounts and loans, to electronic record keeping, providing data processing services for securities and mutual funds, and services for pension funds to monitor their money managers (Rebello, 1995).

strategic information systems Computer systems at any level of the organization that change goals, operations, products, services, or environmental relationships to help the organization gain a competitive advantage.

Strategic information systems should be distinguished from strategic-level systems for senior managers that focus on long-term, decision-making problems. Strategic information systems can be used at all levels of the organization and are more far-reaching and deep-rooted than the other kinds of systems we have described. Strategic information systems fundamentally change a firm's goals, products, services, or internal and external relationships. Strategic information systems profoundly alter the way a firm conducts its business or the very business of the firm itself.

In order to use information systems as competitive weapons, one must first understand where strategic opportunities for businesses are likely to be found. Two models of a firm and its environment have been used to identify areas of the business where information systems can provide advantages over competitors. These are the competitive forces model and the value chain model.

Countering Competitive Forces

In the **competitive forces model,** which is illustrated in Figure 2.11 (Porter, 1980), a firm faces a number of external threats and opportunities: the threat of new entrants into its market, the pressure from substitute products or services, the bargaining power of customers, the bargaining power of suppliers, and the positioning of traditional industry competitors.

competitive forces model Model used to describe the interaction of external influences, specifically threats and opportunities, that affect an organization's strategy and ability to compete.

Competitive advantage can be achieved by enhancing the firm's ability to deal with customers, suppliers, substitute products and services, and new entrants to its market, which in turn may change the balance of power between a firm and other competitors in the industry in the firm's favor. Businesses can use four basic competitive strategies

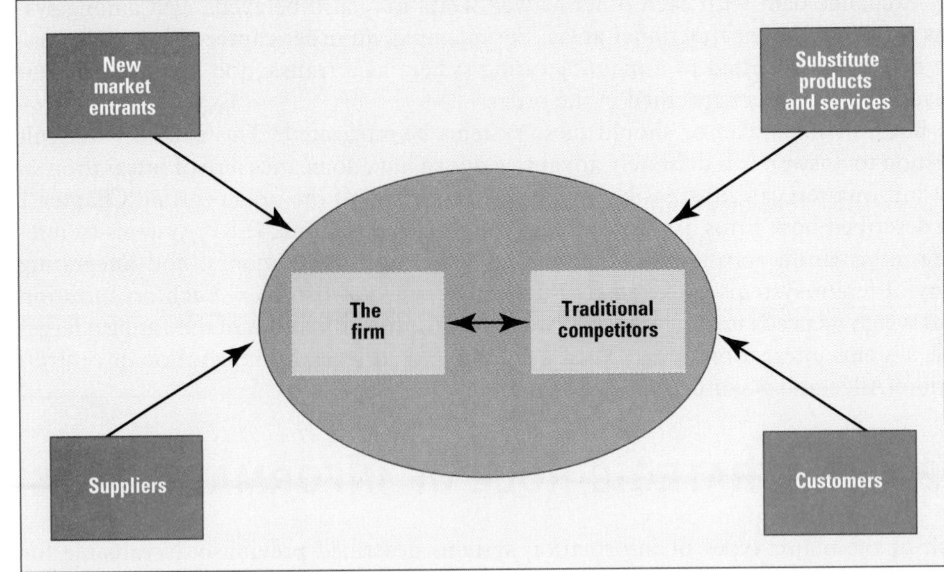

FIGURE 2.11

The competitive forces model. There are various forces that affect an organization's ability to compete and therefore greatly influence a firm's business strategy. There are threats from new market entrants and from substitute products and services. Customers and suppliers wield bargaining power. Traditional competitors constantly adapt their strategies to maintain their market positioning.

to deal with these competitive forces: product differentiation, focused differentiation, developing tight linkages to customers and suppliers, and becoming the low-cost producer. A firm may achieve competitive advantage by pursuing one of these strategies or by pursuing several strategies simultaneously. For instance, Hubbell, described earlier, is competing on quality and cost. We now describe how information systems can support these competitive strategies.

Product Differentiation

product differentiation Competitive strategy for creating brand loyalty by developing new and unique products and services that are not easily duplicated by competitors.

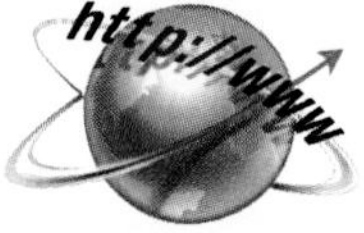

Firms can develop brand loyalty by **product differentiation**—creating unique new products and services that can easily be distinguished from those of competitors, and that existing competitors or potential new competitors can't duplicate.

Many of these information-technology-based products and services have been created by financial institutions. Citibank developed automatic teller machines (ATMs) and bank debit cards in 1977. As a leader in this area, Citibank became at one time the largest bank in the United States. Citibank ATMs were so successful that other banks were forced to counterstrike with their own ATM systems. Citibank, Wells Fargo bank and others have continued to innovate by providing on-line banking services so that customers can do most of their banking transactions with home computers linked to proprietary networks or the Internet. Some companies such as Security First Network Bank in Atlanta have used the Web to set up "virtual banks" offering a full array of banking services without any physical branches. Customers mail in their deposits.

Manufacturers are starting to use information systems to create products and services that are custom-tailored to fit the precise specifications of individual customers. Andersen Windows created a "Window of Knowledge" system that allows customers in hardware stores and retail outlets to design their own windows. Personal computers transmit customers' window specifications to Andersen's manufacturing plant in Bayport, Minnesota. Chapter 1 describes other examples of custom manufacturing where information technology is creating customized products while retaining the cost efficiencies of mass production techniques.

focused differentiation Competitive strategy for developing new market niches for specialized products or services where a business can compete in the target area better than its competitors.

Focused Differentiation

Businesses can create new market niches by **focused differentiation**—identifying a specific target for a product or service that it can serve in a superior manner. A firm can provide a specialized product or service that serves this narrow target market better than existing competitors and that discourages potential new competitors.

An information system can give companies a competitive advantage by producing data to improve their sales and marketing techniques. Such systems treat existing information as a resource that can be "mined" by the organization to increase profitability and market penetration. Information systems enable companies to finely analyze customer buying patterns, tastes, and preferences so that they can efficiently pitch advertising and marketing campaigns to smaller and smaller target markets.

Sophisticated **datamining** software tools find patterns in large pools of data and infer rules from them that can be used to guide decision making. For example, mining data about purchases at supermarkets might reveal that when potato chips are purchased, soda is also purchased 65 percent of the time. When there is a promotion, soda is purchased 85 percent of the time people purchase potato chips.

datamining Analysis of large pools of data to find patterns and rules that can be used to guide decision making and predict future behavior.

The data come from a range of sources—credit card transactions, purchase data from checkout counters, demographic data, and now information collected from visitors to Web sites. For example, the Web site for Stein Roe Investors, a mutual fund company, includes software that captures and analyzes data generated when people visit the site. The company can use these data to create and manage profiles of Web site visitors and to target potential customers with content, advertising, and incentives. For instance, if a visitor uses the retirement planning calculator on the Web site to plan investments, Stein Roe can send messages about its retirement accounts. Chapter 9 provides more detail on how the Web can be used for this purpose.

The Window on Organizations shows how datamining helps companies engage in one-to-one marketing, where personal or individualized messages can be created based on individualized preferences. The level of fine-grained customization provided by these datamining systems parallels that for mass customization described in Chapter 1.

The cost of acquiring a new customer has been estimated to be five times that of retaining an existing customer. By carefully examining transactions of customer purchases and activities, firms can identify profitable customers and win more of their business. Likewise, companies can use these data to identify nonprofitable customers (Clemons and Weber, 1994).

Datamining is both a powerful and profitable tool, but it poses challenges to the protection of individual privacy. Datamining technology can combine information from many diverse sources to create a detailed "data image" about each of us—our income, our driving habits, our hobbies, our families, and our political interests. The question of whether companies should be allowed to collect such detailed information about individuals is explored in Chapter 4.

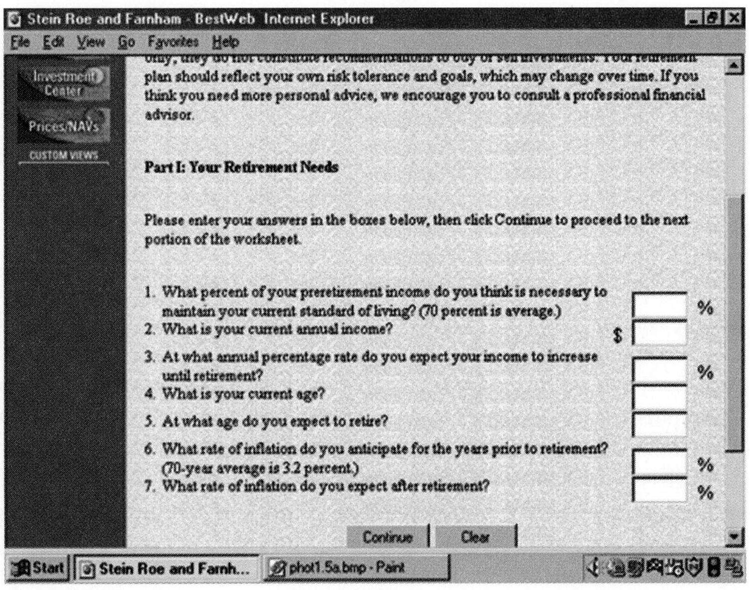
Stein Roe and Farnham - BestWeb Internet Explorer

File Edit View Go Favorites Help

plan should reflect your own risk tolerance and goals, which may change over time. If you think you need more personal advice, we encourage you to consult a professional financial advisor.

Part I: Your Retirement Needs

Please enter your answers in the boxes below, then click Continue to proceed to the next portion of the worksheet.

1. What percent of your preretirement income do you think is necessary to maintain your current standard of living? (70 percent is average.) %
2. What is your current annual income? $
3. At what annual percentage rate do you expect your income to increase until retirement? %
4. What is your current age?
5. At what age do you expect to retire?
6. What rate of inflation do you anticipate for the years prior to retirement? (70-year average is 3.2 percent.) %
7. What rate of inflation do you expect after retirement? %

Continue | Clear

Start | Stein Roe and Farnh... | phot1.5a.bmp - Paint

Stein Roe Investors uses data generated by visitors to its Web site to develop profiles that can target advertising more precisely to potential customers. People who express interest in retirement planning might be sent messages about Stein Roe retirement accounts.

WINDOW ON ORGANIZATIONS

Sears Canada Uses Datamining for One-to-One Marketing

Mass marketing is highly inefficient. A response rate of 3 percent to direct mail advertising is considered very good. Datamining and technologies for one-to-one marketing may be the answer.

About three years ago, Sears Canada noticed a disturbing trend. Although it had 110 retail stores and the largest catalog operation in Canada, its revenue and customer base had been shrinking since the late 1980s. Distribution of the famous Sears catalog was based primarily on whether a customer had purchased from a catalog in the previous 12 months, and customers who hadn't purchased anything in a year were dropped from Sears Canada's database. There was no systematic way of determining which prospective customer should receive a catalog, and no way to determine what a person might buy.

Sears decided to develop a customer planning and management system that would allow it to assemble more accurate knowledge about its customers for customer-centric one-to-one marketing. The company installed the Archer Retail Database Marketing System from Retail Target Marketing Systems and reorganized its customer database. Sears business analysts knew from past experience that the two most important predictors of whether someone would order from the catalog were how recently the customer had placed the last order and how much the person had ordered. The new system is able to sift through Sears Canada's customer database to find out what the most recent and biggest-spending customers had purchased. This information helps the company match catalog mailing lists to catalog content. For example, a catalog emphasizing women's clothing would be sent to a customer who purchased that category of merchandise in the past. Such information about customer buying patterns has helped Sears Canada maximize response rates and catalog sales while minimizing distribution expenses. Sales have been increasing with each new catalog mailing.

The new system also showed Sears Canada that its best catalog customers were also likely to be its best retail customers and that customers who shopped both retail and catalog spent significantly more than retail and catalog shoppers individually. This finding prompted the company to find ways to improve its service to retail customers.

San Francisco-based Bank of America wanted to improve its relationships with existing checking-account customers and to acquire new ones. It used datamining on its customer data to figure out which of its customers were using what products and services and to see whether a different mix of these products and services might better meet customer needs. Bank of America merged various behavior patterns into a more precise profile of its customers, clustering them into smaller, more understandable groups with similar interests and needs. When it found customers who were using the wrong products, it contacted them by telephone or mail. Datamining also helped the bank develop a new set of product ad promotions for its Hispanic customer base.

To Think About: ***How could datamining change the way organizations conduct business? What benefits does datamining provide? What problems might it create?***

Sources: Nick Wredon, "Building Brand Loyalty," *Beyond Computing,* January/February 1998; and "Strike It Rich!" *Datamation,* February 1997.

Developing Tight Linkages to Customers and Suppliers

switching costs The expense a customer or company incurs in lost time and expenditure of resources when changing from one supplier or system to a competing supplier or system.

Firms can create ties to customers and suppliers that "lock" customers into the firm's products and that tie suppliers into a delivery timetable and price structure shaped by the purchasing firm. This raises **switching costs** (the cost for customers to switch to competitors' products and services) and reduces customers' bargaining power and the bargaining power of suppliers.

Baxter Healthcare International, Inc. has developed a "stockless inventory" and ordering system to prevent customers from switching to competitors. Participating hospitals become unwilling to switch to another supplier because of the system's convenience and low cost. Baxter supplies nearly two-thirds of all products used by U.S. hospitals. Terminals tied to Baxter's own computers are installed in hospitals. When hospitals want to place an order, they do not need to call a salesperson or send a purchase order—they simply use a Baxter computer terminal on-site to order from the full Baxter supply catalogue. The system generates shipping, billing, invoicing, and inventory information, and the hospital terminals provide customers with an estimated delivery

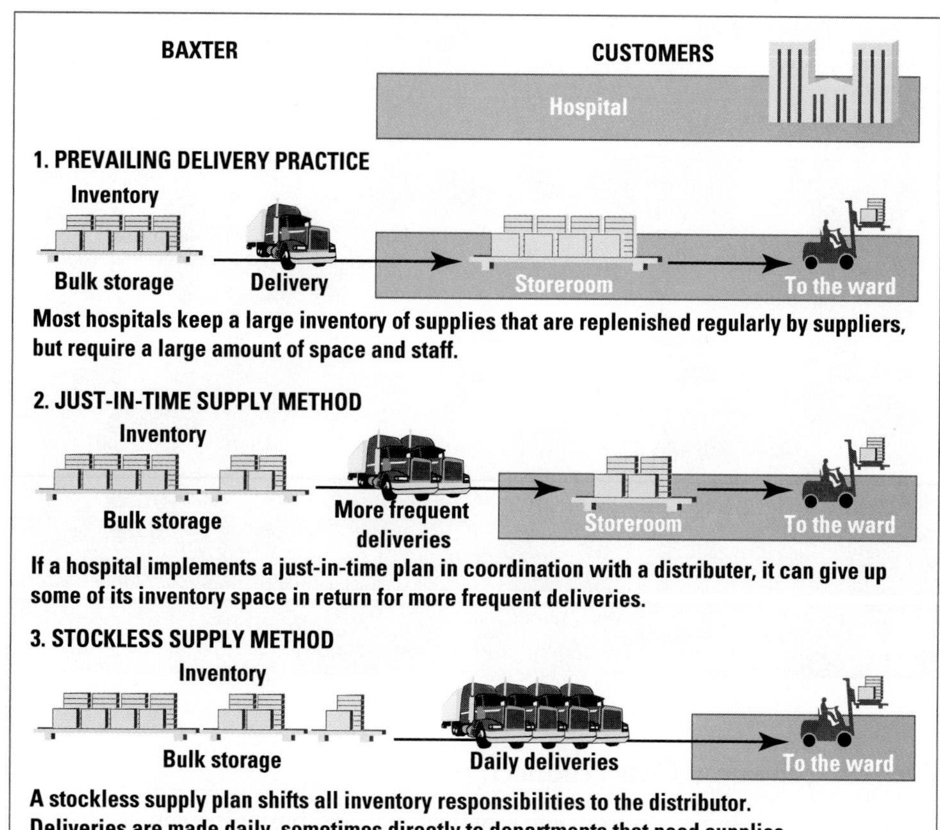
BAXTER
CUSTOMERS
Hospital
1. PREVAILING DELIVERY PRACTICE
Inventory
Bulk storage
Delivery
Storeroom
To the ward
Most hospitals keep a large inventory of supplies that are replenished regularly by suppliers, but require a large amount of space and staff.
2. JUST-IN-TIME SUPPLY METHOD
Inventory
Bulk storage
More frequent deliveries
Storeroom
To the ward
If a hospital implements a just-in-time plan in coordination with a distributer, it can give up some of its inventory space in return for more frequent deliveries.
3. STOCKLESS SUPPLY METHOD
Inventory
Bulk storage
Daily deliveries
To the ward
A stockless supply plan shifts all inventory responsibilities to the distributor. Deliveries are made daily, sometimes directly to departments that need supplies.

FIGURE 2.12
A comparison of traditional inventory and delivery practices to the *just-in-time supply method* and the *stockless inventory method.* Strategic systems for linking customers and suppliers have changed the way in which some companies handle the supply and inventory requirements of their businesses. The just-in-time supply method reduces inventory requirements of the customer while stockless inventory allows the customer to eliminate inventories entirely, resulting in a decided competitive advantage.
Adapted from "Removing the Warehouse from Cost-Conscious Hospitals," The New York Times, *March 3, 1991. Copyright © 1991 by The New York Times Co. Reprinted by permission.*

date. With more than 80 distribution centers in the United States, Baxter can make daily deliveries of its products, often within hours of receiving an order.

This system is similar to the just-in-time delivery systems developed in Japan and now being used in the American automobile industry. In these systems, automobile manufacturers such as General Motors or Chrysler enter the quantity and delivery schedules of specific automobile components into their own information systems. Then these requirements are automatically transmitted to a supplier's order entry information system. The supplier must respond with an agreement to deliver the materials at the time specified. Thus, automobile companies can reduce the cost of inventory, the space required for warehousing components or raw materials, and construction time.

Baxter has even gone one step further. Delivery personnel no longer drop off their cartons at a loading dock to be placed in a hospital storeroom. Instead, they deliver orders directly to the hospital corridors, dropping them at nursing stations, operating rooms, and stock supply closets. This has created in effect a "stockless inventory," with Baxter serving as the hospitals' warehouse (Caldwell, 1991). Figure 2.12 compares stockless inventory with the just-in-time supply method and traditional inventory practices.

While just-in-time inventory allows customers to reduce their inventories, stockless inventory allows them to eliminate their inventories entirely. All inventory responsibilities shift to the distributor, who manages the supply flow. The stockless inventory is a powerful instrument for binding customers, giving the supplier a decided competitive advantage.

Strategic systems aimed at suppliers are designed to maximize a firm's purchasing power (and minimize costs) by having suppliers interact with its information system to satisfy the firm's precise business needs. Suppliers who are unwilling to go along with this system may lose business to other suppliers who can meet these demands.

Wal-Mart's continuous inventory replenishment system uses sales data captured at the checkout counter to transmit orders to restock merchandise directly to its suppliers. The system enables Wal-Mart to keep costs low while fine-tuning its merchandise to meet customer demands.

Becoming the Low-Cost Producer

To prevent new competitors from entering their markets, businesses can produce goods and services at a lower price than competitors. Certain strategically oriented information systems help firms significantly lower their internal costs, allowing them to deliver products and services at a lower price (and sometimes with higher quality) than their competitors can provide.

By keeping prices low and shelves well-stocked, Wal-Mart has become the leading retail business in the United States. Wal-Mart uses a legendary inventory replenishment system triggered by point-of-sale purchases that is considered the best in the industry. The "continuous replenishment system" sends orders for new merchandise directly to suppliers as soon as consumers pay for their purchases at the cash register. Point-of-sale terminals record the bar code of each item passing the checkout counter and send a purchase transaction directly to a central computer at Wal-Mart headquarters. The computer collects the orders from all of the Wal-Mart stores and transmits them to suppliers. Because the system can replenish inventory with lightning speed, Wal-Mart does not need to spend much money on maintaining large inventories of goods in its own warehouses. The system also allows Wal-Mart to adjust purchases of store items to meet customer demands. Competitors such as Sears spend nearly 30 percent of each dollar in sales to pay for overhead (that is, expenses for salaries, advertising, warehousing, and building upkeep). Kmart spends 21 percent of sales on overhead. But by using systems to keep operating costs low, Wal-Mart pays only 15 percent of sales revenue for overhead.

supply chain management Integration of supplier, distributor, and customer logistics requirements into one cohesive process.

Both Baxter and Wal-Mart systems are examples of automated supply chain management. **Supply chain management** integrates supplier, distributor, and customer logistics requirements into one cohesive process. The supply chain is a collection of physical entities, such as manufacturing plants, distribution centers, conveyances, retail outlets, people, and information, that are linked through processes such as procurement or logistics to supply goods and services from source through consumption. To manage the supply chain, a company tries to eliminate delays and cut the amount of resources tied up along the way. Information systems make supply chain management more efficient by integrating demand planning, forecasting, materials requisition, order processing, inventory allocation, order fulfillment, transportation services, receiving, invoicing, and

TABLE 2.4 Strategic Uses of the Internet

Strategy	Internet Application
Product differentiation	Virtual banking: Security First Network Bank allows customers to view account statements, pay bills, check account balances, and obtain 24-hour customer service through the World Wide Web.
Focused differentiation	Hyatt Hotels can track the activities of visitors to the TravelWeb site, which provides electronic information on participating hotels. It can analyze these usage patterns to tailor hospitality-related products more closely to customer preferences.
Links to customers and suppliers	J.B. Hunt Transport Services manages the transportation logistics for J.C. Penney. Penney employees can access Hunt's Web site to check the status of any shipment.
Low-cost producer	Avex Electronics, Inc. is reducing costs by exchanging quotes, bills, and design drawings for electronics components and parts with customers and suppliers electronically using Internet technology and private networks.

payment. The enterprise resource planning systems described in Chapter 1, which have primarily focused on internal business processes, can be extended outside the firm to increase coordination with supply chain partners. Supply chain management can not only lower inventory costs but also can create efficient customer response systems that deliver the product or service more rapidly to the customer.

Table 2.4 shows how the Internet can be used to support each of the competitive strategies.

Leveraging Technology in the Value Chain

The **value chain model** highlights specific activities in the business where competitive strategies can be best applied (Porter, 1985) and where information systems are most likely to have a strategic impact. The value chain model can supplement the competitive forces model by identifying specific, critical leverage points where a firm can use information technology most effectively to enhance its competitive position. Exactly where can it obtain the greatest benefit from strategic information systems—what specific activities can be used to create new products and services, enhance market penetration, lock in customers and suppliers, and lower operational costs? This model views the firm as a series or "chain" of basic activities that add a margin of value to a firm's products or services. These activities can be categorized as either primary activities or support activities.

value chain model Model that highlights the primary or support activities that add a margin of value to a firm's products or services where information systems can best be applied to achieve a competitive advantage.

Primary activities are most directly related to the production and distribution of the firm's products and services that create value for the customer. Primary activities include inbound logistics, operations, outbound logistics, sales and marketing, and service. Inbound logistics include receiving and storing materials for distribution to production. Operations transforms inputs into finished products. Outbound logistics entail storing and distributing products. Marketing and sales includes promoting and selling the firm's products. The service activity includes maintenance and repair of the firm's goods and services. **Support activities** make the delivery of the primary activities possible and consist of organization infrastructure (administration and management), human resources (employee recruiting, hiring, and training), technology (improving products and the production process), and procurement (purchasing input).

primary activities Activities most directly related to the production and distribution of a firm's products or services.

support activities Activities that make the delivery of the primary activities of a firm possible. Consist of the organization's infrastructure, human resources, technology, and procurement.

FIGURE 2.13

Activities of the value chain. Various examples of strategic information systems for the primary and support activities of a firm that would add a margin of value to a firm's products or services.

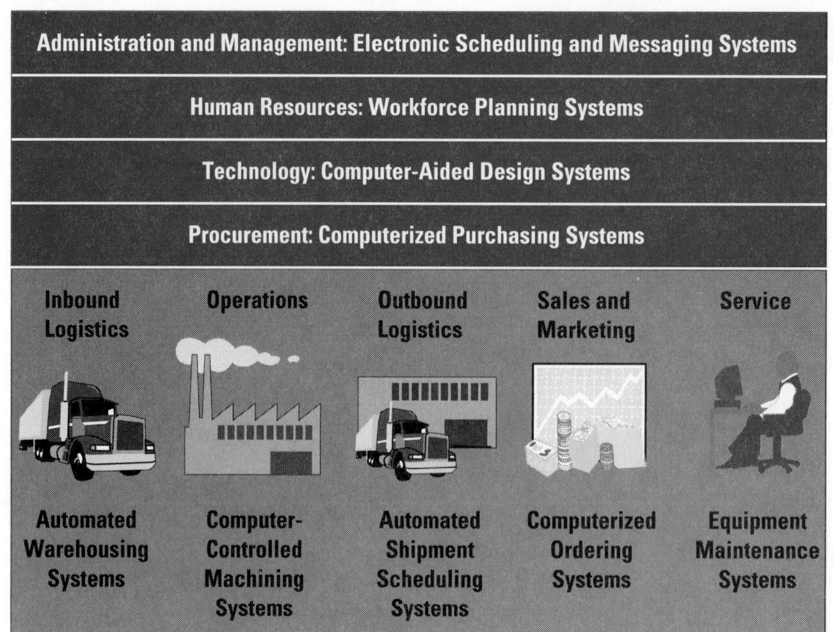

Organizations have a competitive advantage when they provide more value to their customers or when they provide the same value to customers at a lower price. An information system could have strategic impact if it helped the firm provide products or services at a lower cost than competitors or if it provided products and services at the same cost as competitors but with greater value. Hubbell's system, described earlier, creates value by both lowering operational costs and raising the level of quality of service. The value activities that add the most value to products and services depend on the features of each particular firm. Businesses should try to develop strategic information systems for the value activities that add the most value to their particular firm. Figure 2.13 illustrates the activities of the value chain, showing examples of strategic information systems that could be developed to make each of the value activities more cost effective.

For instance, a firm such as Wal-Mart could save money in the inbound logistics activity by having suppliers make daily deliveries of goods to its stores, thereby lowering the costs of warehousing and inventory. A computer-aided design system might support the technology activity, helping a firm to reduce costs and perhaps to design higher-quality products than the competition produces.

Implications for Managers and Organizations

Strategic information systems often change the organization as well as its products, services, and internal procedures, driving the organization into new behavior patterns. Such changes often require new managers, a new work force, and a much closer relationship with customers and suppliers.

Strategic Alliances and Information Partnerships

information partnership Cooperative alliance formed between two or more corporations for the purpose of sharing information to gain strategic advantage.

Companies are increasingly using information systems for strategic advantage by entering into strategic alliances with other companies in which both firms cooperate by sharing resources or services. Such alliances are often **information partnerships** in which two or more firms share data for mutual advantage (Konsynski and McFarlan, 1990). They can join forces without actually merging. American Airlines has an arrangement with Citibank to award one mile in its frequent flier program for every dollar spent using Citibank credit cards. American benefits from increased customer loyalty, while Citibank gains new credit card subscribers and a highly creditworthy customer base for cross-marketing. Northwest Airlines has a similar arrangement with U.S. Bank. American and Northwest have also allied with MCI, awarding frequent flier miles for each dollar of long-distance billing.

Managing Strategic Transitions

Adopting the kinds of systems described in this chapter generally requires changes in business goals, relationships with customers and suppliers, internal operations, and information architecture. These sociotechnical changes, affecting both social and technical elements of the organization, can be considered **strategic transitions**—a movement between levels of sociotechnical systems. Managers struggling to boost competitiveness will need to redesign various organizational processes to make effective use of leading-edge information systems technology. They will require new mechanisms for coordinating their firms' activities with those of customers and suppliers (Kambil and Short, 1994). Such changes often entail blurring of organizational boundaries, both external and internal. Suppliers and customers may become intimately linked and may share each other's responsibilities. For instance, in Baxter International's stockless inventory system, Baxter has assumed responsibility for managing its customers' inventories (Johnston and Vitale, 1988). Over time, Baxter has redesigned its work processes numerous times to continually improve its overall service level and business relationship with customers (Short and Venkatraman, 1992).

strategic transitions A movement from one level of sociotechnical system to another. Often required when adopting strategic systems that demand changes in the social and technical elements of an organization.

What Managers Can Do

Managers must take the initiative to identify the types of systems that would provide a strategic advantage to the firm. Some of the important questions managers should ask are

- How is the industry currently using information systems? Which organizations are the industry leaders in the application of information systems technology? How is the industry changing? Should the firm be looking at new ways of doing business?
- Are significant strategic opportunities to be gained by introducing new information systems technology? Where would new information systems provide the greatest value to the firm?
- What is the current business strategic plan, and how does that plan mesh with the current strategy for information services?
- Does the firm have the technology and capital required to develop a strategic information systems initiative? (Kettinger et al., 1994)

2.3 HOW INFORMATION SYSTEMS PROMOTE QUALITY

Global competition is forcing companies to focus more than ever on using quality in their competitive strategies. There are many ways in which information systems can help organizations achieve higher levels of quality in their products, services, and operations.

What Is Quality?

Quality can be defined from both producer and customer perspectives. From the perspective of the producer, **quality** signifies conformance to specifications (or the absence of variation from those specifications). A wristwatch manufacturer, for example, might include a specification for reliability which requires that 99.995 percent of the watches will neither gain nor lose more than one second per month. Simple tests will enable the manufacturer to measure precisely against these specifications.

quality Conformance to producer specifications and satisfaction of customer criteria such as quality of physical product, quality of service, and psychological aspects.

A customer definition of quality is much broader. First, customers are concerned with the quality of the physical product—its durability, safety, ease of use, and installation. Second, customers are concerned with the quality of service, by which they mean the accuracy and truthfulness of advertising, responsiveness to warranties, and ongoing product support. Finally, customer concepts of quality include psychological aspects:

the company's knowledge of its products, the courtesy and sensitivity of sales and support staff, and the reputation of the product.

total quality management (TQM) A concept that makes quality control a responsibility to be shared by all people in an organization.

Today more and more businesses are turning to an idea known as total quality management. **Total quality management (TQM)** is a concept that makes quality the responsibility of all people within an organization. TQM holds that the achievement of quality control is an end in itself. Everyone is expected to contribute to the overall improvement of quality—the engineer who avoids design errors, the production worker who spots defects, the sales representative who presents the product properly to potential customers, and even the secretary who avoids typing mistakes. Total quality management encompasses all of the functions within an organization.

TQM derives from quality management concepts developed by American quality experts such as W. Edwards Deming and Joseph Juran, but it was popularized by the Japanese. Japanese management adopted the goal of zero defects, focusing on improving their product or service prior to shipment rather than correcting them after they have been delivered. Japanese companies often give the responsibility for quality consistency to the workers who actually make the product or service, as opposed to a quality control department. Studies have repeatedly shown that the earlier in the business cycle a problem is eliminated, the less it costs the company. Thus the Japanese quality approach not only brought a shift in focus to the workers and an increased respect for product and service quality, but it also lowered costs.

How Information Systems Contribute to Total Quality Management

Information systems can help firms achieve their quality goals by helping them simplify products or processes, meet benchmarking standards, make improvements based on customer demands, reduce cycle time, and increase the quality and precision of design and production.

Simplifying the Product, the Production Process, or Both

Quality programs usually have a "fewer is better" philosophy—the fewer steps in a process, the less time and opportunity for an error to occur. The Carrier Corporation, the Syracuse, New York manufacturing giant, was faced with an eroding market share. One reason: a 70 percent error rate in using its manual order entry system, which was used to match customers and products when ordering Carrier's commercial air conditioning units. The system required so many steps to process an order that mistakes were all but inevitable. Errors sometimes went undetected until the end of the manufacturing line, where workers might discover a wrong coil or some other similar problem. Big mistakes occasionally affected customers. The company finally instituted a TQM program in which information technology played a large role. Carrier now coordinates everything from sales to manufacturing by using an artificial intelligence system (LaPlante, 1992). When information systems helped reduce the number of steps, the number of errors dropped dramatically, manufacturing costs dropped, and Carrier found itself with happier customers.

Benchmark

Many companies have been effective in achieving quality by setting strict standards for products, services, and other activities, and then measuring performance against those standards. This procedure is called benchmarking. Companies may use external industry standards, standards set by other companies, internally developed high standards, or some combination of the three. L.L. Bean, Inc., the Freeport, Maine mail order clothing company, uses benchmarking to achieve an order shipping accuracy of 99.9 percent.

To provide better information for benchmarking, information systems specialists can work with business specialists either to design new systems or to analyze quality-related data in existing systems. For instance, L.L. Bean carefully designed its informa-

WINDOW ON MANAGEMENT

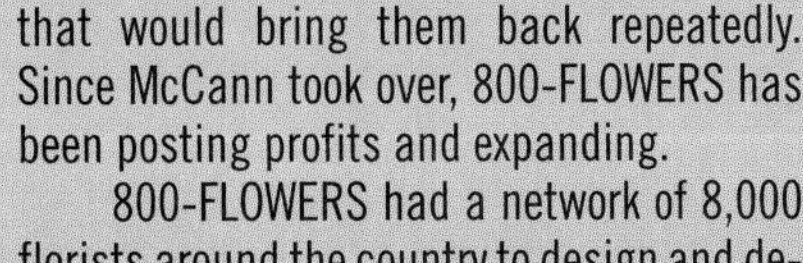

Building an Organization to Sell Flowers

Jim McCann bought 800-FLOWERS because it was the best marketing idea he had seen. But the company was $7 million in debt and spending way too much money on costly telemarketing national advertising to attract new customers. McCann recognized that selling flowers is a "nickel-and-dime business" that cannot afford expensive advertising. To be successful, he would have to rely on repeat customers. The underlying problem was that few customers came back because of poor service and inconsistent quality. So McCann rebuilt his organization to give customers quality service, service that would bring them back repeatedly. Since McCann took over, 800-FLOWERS has been posting profits and expanding.

800-FLOWERS had a network of 8,000 florists around the country to design and deliver all orders. McCann decided that he needed fewer florists, but these florists must be held to high standards for design, flower freshness, and delivery. He replaced the existing network with 2,500 florists who agreed to his standards, including a guarantee of same-day delivery for all orders received by 1 PM. McCann then hired a staff of 15 quality-control experts who spot-checked the florists to make certain they sold only fresh flowers. Next, he moved the 800-FLOWERS telemarketing center from its 55,000-square-foot facility in Dallas, Texas, to much smaller facilities in Bayside, New York. He added 30 more telereps to his staff and trained them in customer service, instructing them to personalize each conversation. 800-FLOWERS offered customer guarantees that wilted floral arrangements could be returned within seven days; arrangements the customer didn't like could be returned when they arrived.

Making a sale required a number of steps: writing the order; obtaining credit card approval; determining which 800-FLOWERS florist is closest to the delivery location; describing and deciding on a floral arrangement; and forwarding the order to the florist. Each step in the manual process increased the chance of human error and thus the possibility of a wrong delivery. McCann purchased a $4-million NCR midrange computer to centrally process orders more efficiently. The system reduces processing time from ten minutes to less than five. The computer system includes computer images of floral arrangements that the telereps can use to aid them as they talk with customers. The organization of 2,500 florists was brought into the whole process by being connected to the network. A computer, a modem (to connect them to the network), and a printer was installed in each florist's shop.

Florists can now obtain their orders by using 800-FLOWERS' Web site. The Web site allows them to ask questions about orders, such as whether delivery times can be altered or certain flowers substituted, and to confirm order deliveries on-line. This information is stored in the system for 800-FLOWERS to use in answering customer questions. Enhancements to the Web site include e-mail and on-line chat capabilities to allow florists to communicate with each other or receive training, as well as chat-based customer service. When customers access the 800-FLOWERS Web site, they are able to ask about orders and receive an immediate answer on-line from a customer service representative.

To Think About: ***How did technology promote quality at 800-FLOWERS? Could technology alone have solved 800-FLOWERS' quality problems? What was the relationship between quality, technology, and 800-FLOWERS' business strategy?***

Sources: Sharon Machlis, "Florists Use Web to Speed Deliveries," *Computerworld,* February, 9, 1998; and Richard D. Smith, "From One Little Shop, an 800-Flowers Garden Grows," *The New York Times,* January 8, 1995.

tion systems so it could analyze the data embedded in customer return transactions. Bean's return forms require customers to supply "reason codes" explaining why each item was returned. A report from these systems showing return transaction frequency and dollar value summarized by week or month and broken down by the reason for the returns helps management target areas where mistakes are being made.

Use Customer Demands as a Guide to Improving Products and Services

Improving customer service, making customer service the number one priority, will improve the quality of the product itself, as is clear from the Carrier example described earlier. The Window on Management shows how one small business, 1-800-FLOWERS, addressed the question of customer satisfaction in a quality program. It also shows the contribution of information systems in building a system and making needed information available when required.

Reduce Cycle Time

Experience indicates that the single best way to address quality problems is to reduce the amount of time from the beginning of a process to its end (cycle time). Reducing cycle time usually results in fewer steps. Shorter cycles mean that errors are often caught earlier in production (or logistics or design or whatever the function), often before the process is complete, eliminating many hidden costs. Iomega Corporation in Roy, Utah, a manufacturer of disk drives, was spending $20 million a year to fix defective drives at the end of its 28-day production cycle. Reengineering the production process allowed the firm to reduce cycle time to a day and a half, eliminating this problem and winning the prestigious Shingo Prize for Excellence in American Manufacturing in the process.

Improve the Quality and Precision of the Design

Quality and precision in design will eliminate many production problems. Computer-aided design (CAD) software has made dramatic quality improvements possible in a wide range of businesses from aircraft manufacturing to production of razor blades. Alan R. Burns, head of the Airboss Company in Perth, Australia, was able to use CAD to invent and design a new tire product. His concept was a modular tire made up of a series of replaceable modules or segments so that if one segment were damaged, only that segment, not the whole tire, would need replacing. Burns established quality performance measurements for such key tire characteristics as load, temperature, speed, wear life, and traction. He then entered these data into a CAD software package, which he used to design the modules. Using the software he was able iteratively to design and test until he was satisfied with the results. He did not need to develop an actual working model until the iterative design process was almost complete. Because of the speed and accuracy of the CAD software, the product he produced was of much higher quality than would have been possible through manual design and testing.

Increase the Precision of Production

For many products, one key way to achieve quality is to tighten production tolerances. Computer-aided design (CAD) software often includes a facility to translate design specifications into specifications both for production tooling and for the production process itself. In this way, products with more precise designs can also be produced more efficiently. Once his tire segment design was completed, Burns used the CAD software to design his manufacturing process. He was able to design a shorter production cycle, improving quality while increasing his ability to meet customer demand more quickly.

Komag of Milpitas, California, the world's largest supplier of 5¼-inch and smaller sputtered thin-film disks for disk drives in all types of computers, must control hundreds of variables in its manufacturing process, which transforms uncoated aluminum disks into highly technical precision products. Komag needed more precision in its production process. It implemented MESA, from Camstar Systems, Inc., a manufacturing execution system (MES), that allows Komag to monitor hundreds of process manufacturing execution steps. The system can analyze yield, productivity, and machine utilization, and respond to out-of-control process variances. Managers can obtain data on key production variables by product, process, machine, and shift. Within six months after implementing the new system, Komag doubled output (Komag, 1994).

Cerveceria y Malteria Quilmes, S.A., which makes Argentina's most popular beer, used Internet technology to increase the precision of its supply chain management. Some of its distributors are located more than 400 miles away from Quilmes' breweries. To make it easier for distributors to check production output before sending out their loading trucks, Quilmes added a Web interface to its production planning systems. Distributors can now instantly check the status of their orders in relation to how much Quilmes inventory is actually available and load their trucks more efficiently (Fabris, 1997).

Management Wrap-Up

MANAGEMENT

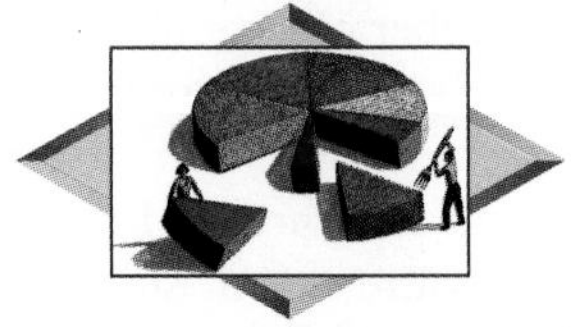

Management is responsible for developing the strategy and quality standards for the organization. Key management decisions include identifying the competitive strategies and the points in the value chain where information systems can provide the greatest benefit, as well as the principal areas for quality improvement.

ORGANIZATION

There are many types of information systems in an organization which serve different purposes, from transaction processing to knowledge management and management decision making. Each type of system can contribute a strategic edge. Systems that significantly promote competitive advantage and TQM often require extensive organizational change.

TECHNOLOGY

Information technology can be used to differentiate existing products, create new products and services, raise customer and supplier switching costs, and reduce operating costs. Selecting an appropriate technology for the firm's competitive strategy is a key decision.

For Discussion:

1. Several information systems experts have claimed that there is no such thing as a sustainable strategic advantage. Do you agree? Why or why not?
2. How can using information systems to promote quality provide a strategic advantage?

SUMMARY

1. **Analyze the role played by the six major types of information systems in organizations.** There are six major types of information systems in contemporary organizations that are designed for different purposes and different audiences. Operational-level systems are transaction processing systems (TPS), such as payroll or order processing, that track the flow of the daily routine transactions that are necessary to conduct business. Knowledge-level systems support clerical, managerial, and professional workers. They consist of office automation systems for increasing the productivity of data workers and knowledge work systems for enhancing the productivity of knowledge workers. Management-level systems (MIS and DSS) provide the management control level with reports and access to the organization's current performance and historical records. Most MIS reports condense information from TPS and are not highly analytical. Decision-support systems (DSS) support management decisions when these decisions are unique, rapidly changing, and not specified easily in advance. They have more advanced analytical models and data analysis capabilities than MIS and often draw on information from external as well as internal sources.

   Executive support systems (ESS) support the strategic level by providing a generalized computing and communications environment to assist senior management's decision making. They have limited analytical capabilities but can draw on sophisticated graphics software and many sources of internal and external information.

2. **Describe the relationship between the various types of information systems.** The various types of systems in the organization exchange data with one another. TPS are a major source of data for other systems, especially MIS and DSS. ESS is primarily a recipient of data from lower-level systems. However, the different systems in an organization are only loosely integrated. The information needs of the various functional areas and organizational levels are too specialized to be served by a single system.

3. **Examine how the competitive forces and value chain models can be used to identify opportunities for strategic information systems.** The competitive forces and value chain models can help identify areas of a business where information systems can supply a strategic advantage. The competitive forces model describes a number of external threats and opportunities faced by firms that they must counter with competitive strategies. Information systems can be developed to cope with the threat of new entrants into the market, the pressure from substitute products, the bargaining power of buyers, the bargaining power of suppliers, and the positioning of traditional industry competitors. The value chain model highlights specific activities in the business where competitive strategies can best be applied and where information systems are most likely to have a strategic impact. This model views the firm as a series or "chain" of basic activities that add a margin of value to a firm's products or services. Information systems can have a strategic impact on the activities that add the most value to the firm.

4. **Explain why strategic information systems are difficult to build and to sustain.** Not all strategic systems make a profit; they can be expensive and risky to build. Many strategic information systems are easily copied by other firms, so that strategic advantage is not always sustainable. Implementing strategic systems often requires extensive organizational change and a transition from one sociotechnical level to another. Such changes are called strategic transitions and are often difficult and painful to achieve.

5. **Describe how organizations can use information systems to enhance quality in their operations, products, and services.** Information systems can help organizations simplify their products and the production process, meet benchmarking standards, improve customer service, reduce production cycle time, and improve the quality and precision of design and production.

KEY TERMS

Competitive forces model, 51
Datamining, 53
Decision-support systems (DSS), 48
Desktop publishing, 44
Document imaging systems, 45
Executive support systems (ESS), 49
Focused differentiation, 52
Information partnership, 58
Knowledge-level systems, 40
Knowledge work systems (KWS), 43
Management information systems (MIS), 46
Management-level systems, 40
Office automation systems (OAS), 43
Operational-level systems, 40
Primary activities, 57
Product differentiation, 52
Quality, 59
Strategic information systems, 51
Strategic-level systems, 40
Strategic transitions, 59
Supply chain management, 56
Support activities, 57
Switching costs, 54
Total quality management (TQM), 60
Transaction processing systems (TPS), 42
Value chain model, 57
Word processing, 44

REVIEW QUESTIONS

1. Identify and describe the four levels of the organizational hierarchy. What types of information systems serve each level?
2. List and briefly describe the major types of systems in organizations. How are they related to one another?
3. What are the five types of TPS in business organizations? What functions do they perform? Give examples of each.
4. Describe the functions performed by knowledge work and office automation systems and some typical applications of each.
5. What are the characteristics of MIS? How do MIS differ from TPS? From DSS?
6. What are the characteristics of DSS? How do they differ from those of ESS?

7. What is a strategic information system? What is the difference between a strategic information system and a strategic-level system?
8. Define and compare the competitive forces and value chain models for identifying opportunities for strategic systems.
9. What are the four basic competitive strategies? How can information systems help firms pursue each of these strategies?
10. Why are strategic information systems difficult to build?
11. Explain the advantages of an information partnership.
12. How can managers find strategic applications in their firm?
13. What is total quality management?
14. How can companies use information systems to promote total quality management?

GROUP PROJECT

Form a group with two or three classmates. Research a business using annual reports or business publications such as *Fortune, Business Week,* and *The Wall Street Journal.* Visit the company Web site to gain further insights into the company. Analyze the business using the competitive forces and value chain models, including a description of the firm and its business strategies. Suggest strategic information systems for that particular business including those using the Internet, if appropriate. Present your findings to the class.

TOOLS FOR INTERACTIVE LEARNING

■ **INTERNET**: The Internet Connection for this chapter will take you to the Security First Network Bank (SFNB) Web site, where you can see how one company used the Internet to create an entirely new type of business. You can complete an exercise for analyzing the capabilities of this Web site and its strategic benefits. You can also use the Interactive Study Guide to test your knowledge of the topics in this chapter and get instant feedback where you need more practice.

■ **CD-ROM**: If you purchase and use the Multimedia Edition CD-ROM with this chapter, you can complete two interactive exercises. The first asks you to match various types of information systems described in the chapter to user information needs. The second asks you to perform a value chain analysis for a business. You can also find a video clip illustrating the strategic use of Alamo Rent-a-Car's reservation and rental system, interactive exercises, an audio overview of the major themes of this chapter, and bullet text summarizing the key points of the chapter.

CASE STUDY

Procter & Gamble: Finding the Right Business Model

Like many consumer products companies, Procter & Gamble, Co. embraced micromarketing. The world's preeminent consumer products company began using information technology in the late 1980s to support a traditional make-sell business strategy. P&G developed capabilities to electronically exchange orders with its largest customers and began to redevelop its order, billing, and shipping systems. But a major consolidation of grocery stores brought about by competition from large national chains such as Wal-Mart resulted in 40,000 retail outlets disappearing by the mid-1990s. P&G sales slowed.

P&G's answer was to (1) proliferate new products to give customers more choices, (2) develop marketing programs to push the product through the retail marketing channel to the customer, and (3) develop information systems that could track manufacturing, warehousing, shipping, and the hundreds of different price promotions used to push product down the channel to retailers. P&G used a series of information systems to collect and analyze retail sales data, using the information for finely tuned promotional campaigns. For example, by analyzing scanner-based sales data in relationship to regional weather patterns, P&G measured the effects of the cough and flu season on sales of its Vicks Formula 44 and Nyquil cold products. It then developed consumer response programs, such as special sales or coupon giveaways in cold regions. P&G developed 35 different varieties of Bounce fabric softener in North America, his and her baby diapers, 31 different varieties of hair shampoo, and 50 versions of Crest toothpaste.

To move all this new product down the retail channel, P&G developed 27 different types of promotions from bonus packs (two products put together in a single pack) to cents-off campaigns, to goldfish giveaways (unfortunately, most of the goldfish froze to death before customers could retrieve them). P&G made 55 price changes per day, affecting 110 products, and offered 440 price promotions per year. It was the micromarketing product model gone completely wild.

In this period of the early 1990s, information systems were developed to make the existing business processes and the business model more efficient. Marketing developed elaborate quota systems for salespeople and carefully tracked sales force performance. To make new products successful, any sales force has to be given sales targets, and P&G salespeople were told to move product no matter what. The sales force was credited with a sale when the product was shipped out of the P&G warehouse, not when a consumer actually bought the product. And the recently modernized order, shipping, and billing systems dutifully tracked how much product was shipped from the P&G warehouses. In fact, the sales force developed so many promotions and pricing formulas (17 different price lists for the same products) that it became difficult even with elaborate computer systems to keep the orders straight. Retailers would order cases at a promised $100 per case, but P&G would ship them at $125 a case; a special order-correction facility of 150 specialists was set up in Cincinnati to correct 27,000 orders per month, at a cost of $35 to $75 per order.

Retailers of course responded to aggressive price promotions. Economists call this a moral hazard: People are given incentives to do the wrong thing. Retailers built larger warehouses, and when P&G prices became very attractive, they would order trainloads of merchandise in what is called "forward buying." These huge orders presented P&G manufacturing with severe problems. Manufacturing began to build new plants, only to find that the new plants would sit idle as prices returned to normal. Meanwhile, retailers' warehouses were filled with aging coffee, shampoo, and diapers. Some items would be trapped for years in the warehouse system of retailers.

The combined result of the P&G business model, systems, and marketing strategy was to raise costs to everyone in the retail channel and to the consumer. Earnings of P&G fell and sales growth stopped. Consumers were confused. The average consumer, often a woman, takes only 21 minutes to do her supermarket shopping. In that time, she buys an average of 18 items from 30,000 to 40,000 choices, down 25 percent from five years ago. She doesn't bother to check prices, looking for the same product, in the same row, at the same price week after week.

Obviously a new business model with new business processes was needed, and in 1993 P&G began a major business strategy and process shift. The new business strategy had several components, according to Durk Jager, president and chief operating officer.

P&G began by eliminating one-third of its products, some of which were sold to others. It reduced its labor force by 13,000 and eliminated dozens of factories. P&G then greatly reduced price promotions and met with retail channel executives to explain the new policies. A new policy was adopted for new products: If they failed to rise to the top two-thirds of product sales in a division, they would be eliminated in one year. P&G moved from brand and product management toward customer management by assigning one P&G representative to a store to coordinate sales to individual supermarkets. Prior to this, up to seven P&G product managers would call on stores. To ensure the customer would always find the product they wanted on the shelf, P&G built systems that would trigger shipments only when customers actually bought products. Taking a cue from Wal-Mart, one of P&G's largest customers and well known for its continuous replenishment systems, P&G now uses point-of-sale data provided by retailers to generate orders. P&G trucks now deliver only what is needed based on customer sales. This has saved retailers over $250 million in inventory costs alone. Now, when dealing with highly automated retailers such as Wal-Mart, 40 percent of all orders are computer generated and based directly on actual sales recorded daily and weekly. The sales force was equipped with laptop computers, and they send daily reports to headquarters recording changes in customer buying habits—and the reasons for changes in those buying habits. At headquarters, sales and marketing specialists analyze the data and quickly adjust product schedules to both actual purchases and anticipated demand.

P&G recently began a program of sharing data with its retail customers to improve supply chain efficiency and the profits of its "channel partners." With the help of IBM, P&G runs a continuous replenishment system for 40 percent of its total goods shipped in North America. P&G business partners send electronic purchase orders to IBM, which processes them and routes them to P&G to replenish inventory.

P&G is also trying to obtain information directly from retail outlets. Along with three retailers, the company started piloting a Collaborative Planning, Forecasting, and Replenishment (CPFR) system aimed at reducing middlemen. Retailers will use their own planning and forecasting systems and directly share the data with their suppliers.

In some instances, P&G products were withdrawn from retail shelves because they did not sell well. Overall, P&G believes that sharing information with channel partners is the way to increase profits and stay in touch with what is actually selling in the marketplace.

Sources: Bruce Caldwell with John Foley, "IBM Means E-Business," *Information Week,* February 9, 1998; Raju Nariesetti, "P&G, Seeing Shoppers Were Being Confused, Overhauls Marketing," *The Wall Street Journal,* January 15, 1997; Zachary Schiller, Greg Burns, and Karen Lowry, "Make It Simple: That's P&G's New Mantra—and It Is Spreading," *Business Week,* September 9, 1996; and Ronald Henkoff, "P&G New and Improved," *Fortune,* October 14, 1996.

Case Study Questions

1. What was Procter & Gamble's business strategy during the 1980s and early 1990s?
2. How much strategic advantage was provided by P&G's information systems? Why?
3. What management, organization, and technology factors contributed to Procter & Gamble's problems?
4. How successful are the solutions Procter & Gamble developed? What kind of changes in strategy and systems did the solutions involve?

CHAPTER 3

Information Systems, Organizations, and Management

chapter outline

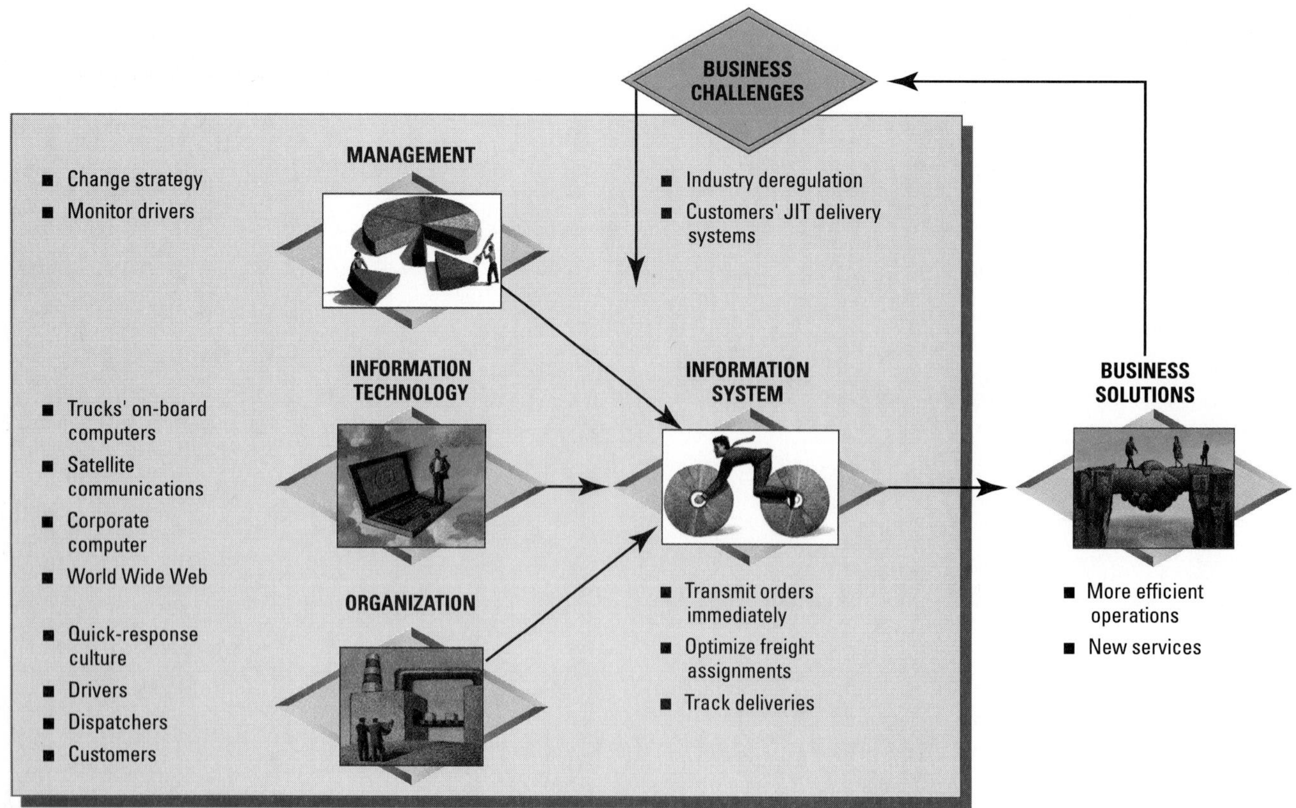

Schneider Responds to the New Rules of the Trucking Game

Deregulation revolutionized the business environment for the trucking industry overnight. Competition for customers heated up. Interstate trucking firms no longer had to follow the rules of a regulatory bureaucracy about what kinds of freight to carry and where to take them. These same rules had also made it difficult for customers to change carriers because only certain trucking firms could meet these regulations. Large retailers and manufacturers were installing just-in-time delivery systems. They wanted to use trucking firms that could transport their shipments right away.

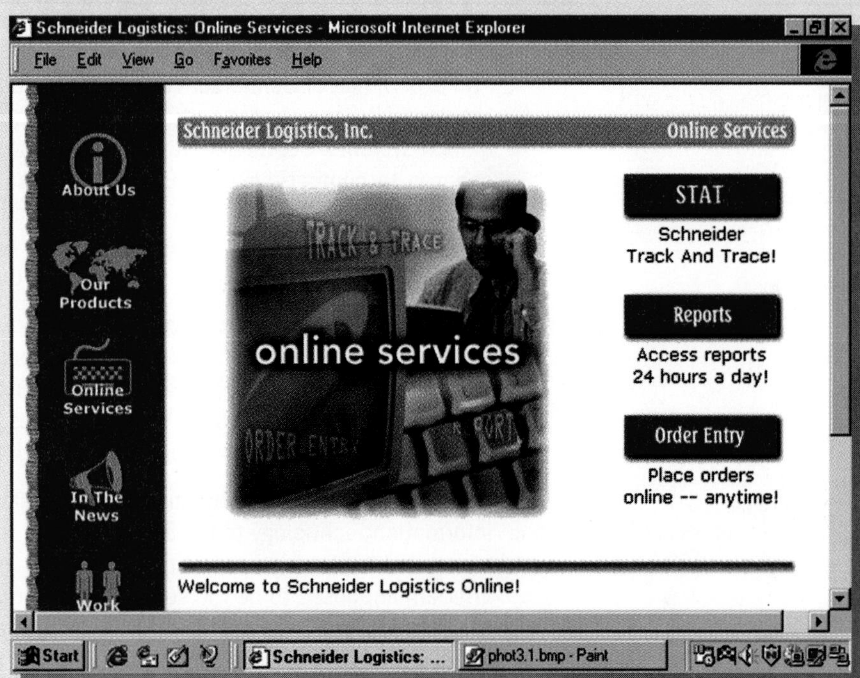

Schneider National, based in Green Bay, Wisconsin, one of North America's largest trucking, transportation, and logistics companies, responded to these demands with a multipronged strategy. First, it tried to make sweeping changes in its corporate culture. Schneider sought to replace its regulated-utility mentality with quick reflexes and an urgency to get things done. CEO Don Schneider democratized the organization by calling all employees "associates" and by removing status symbols like reserved parking places. He encouraged everyone, from drivers on up, to speak out on ways to improve operations. He also instituted an extra bonus paycheck based solely on performance.

Second, the firm deployed new information systems to support these changes. It equipped each truck with a computer and a rotating antenna. A satellite tracks every rig, making sure it adheres to schedule. When an order comes into headquarters, dispatchers know exactly which truck to assign to the job. The dispatchers send an order directly by satellite to the driver's onboard terminal, complete with directions to the destination and instructions on what gate to use and papers to collect with the merchandise. Within 15 to 30 minutes of sending an order to Schneider's computer, customers know which trucks to expect and when.

Schneider has started using its information systems to provide the logistics management function for other companies, setting up a separate division, Schneider Logistics, Inc., for this purpose. Among its clients is General Motors Corporation. Schneider manages all shipments of GM service parts, amounting to 435,000 outbound "order lines" daily to more than 9000 GM dealers, warehouse distributors, and mass merchandisers. While other providers use only their own trucks, planes, and trains, Schneider uses its information systems to provide solutions that use the best medium for moving freight, even if that isn't its own trucks.

To make shipment information more accessible to clients, Schneider Logistics created a Web site with electronic-commerce capabilities. Designated customers can use the Web site to "paperlessly" send new load requests directly to Schneider Logistics. Preassigned passwords are provided to customers, ensuring the security of confidential shipment information. The Web site is being enhanced so that clients can use it to track the status of their shipments and approved carriers can find available loads on-line.

Information systems now play such a powerful role in Schneider's operations that the firm has been described as "an information system masquerading as a trucking line." Don Schneider himself has observed that "people get the mistaken impression that our business is running trucks." Several other competitors responded to deregulation by merely lowering rates. They went bankrupt.

Sources: "Secure Website Goes Live for Schneider Brokerage," Schneider National, Inc., June 17, 1998; "Website Features Interactive Electronic Commerce Capabilities," Schneider National Logistics, February 18, 1997; Mark Levinson, "Riding the Data Highway," *Newsweek*, March 21, 1994; and Stephen Barr, "Delivering the Goods," *CFO*, August 1994.

Management Challenges

The experience of Schneider National illustrates the interdependence of business environments, organizational culture, management strategy, and the development of information systems. Schneider National developed new information systems in response to changes in competitive pressures from its surrounding environment, but it needed to change its organizational culture before it could use new systems successfully. The information systems, in turn, changed the way Schneider ran its business and made management decisions. Schneider's story raises the following management challenges:

1. **The difficulties of managing change.** Bringing about change through the development of information technology and information systems is slowed considerably by the natural inertia of organizations. Of course, organizations do change, and powerful leaders are often required to bring about these changes. Nevertheless, the process, as leaders eventually discover, is more complicated and much slower than is typically anticipated.
2. **Fitting technology to the organization (or vice-versa).** On the one hand, it is important to align information technology to the business plan, to senior management's strategic business plans, and to standard operating procedures in the business. Information technology is, after all, supposed to be the servant of the organization. On the other hand, these business plans, senior managers, and SOPs all may be very outdated or incompatible with the envisioned technology. In such instances, managers will need to change the organization to fit the technology or to adjust both the organization and the technology to achieve an optimal "fit."

learning objectives

After completing this chapter, you will be able to:

1. Identify the salient characteristics of organizations.
2. Analyze the relationship between information systems and organizations.
3. Contrast the classical and contemporary models of managerial activities and roles.
4. Describe how managers make decisions in organizations.
5. Assess the implications of the relationship between information systems, organizations, and management decision making for the design and implementation of information systems.

This chapter explores the complex relationships between organizations, management, and information systems. We introduce the features of organizations that you will need to understand when you design, build, and operate information systems. We also scrutinize the role of a manager and try to identify areas where information systems can enhance managerial effectiveness. The chapter concludes by examining the process of management decision making.

3.1 ORGANIZATIONS AND INFORMATION SYSTEMS

Information systems and organizations have a mutual influence on each other. On the one hand, information systems must be aligned with the organization to provide information needed by important groups within the organization. At the same time, the organization must be aware of and open itself to the influences of information systems in order to benefit from new technologies.

The interaction between information technology and organizations is very complex and is influenced by a great many mediating factors, including the organization's structure, standard operating procedures, politics, culture, surrounding environment, and management decisions (see Figure 3.1). Managers must be aware that information systems can markedly alter life in the organization. They cannot successfully design new systems or understand existing systems without understanding organizations. Managers do decide what systems will be built, what they will do, how they will be implemented, and so forth (see the Window on Management on page 73). Sometimes, however, the outcomes are the result of pure chance and of both good and bad luck.

What Is an Organization?

An **organization** is a stable, formal social structure that takes resources from the environment and processes them to produce outputs. This technical definition focuses on three elements of an organization. *Capital* and *labor* are primary production factors provided by the environment. The organization (the firm) transforms these inputs into products and services in a *production function*. The products and services are *consumed by environments* in return for supply inputs (see Figure 3.2). An organization is *more stable* than an informal group in terms of longevity and routineness. Organizations are *formal* legal entities, with internal rules and procedures, that must abide by laws. Organizations are also *social structures* because they are a collection of social elements, much as a machine has a structure—a particular arrangement of valves, cams, shafts, and other parts.

This definition of organizations is powerful and simple, but it is not very descriptive or even predictive of real-world organizations. A more realistic behavioral definition of an organization is that it is a collection of rights, privileges, obligations, and responsibilities that are delicately balanced over a period of time through conflict and

organization (technical definition) A stable, formal, social structure that takes resources from the environment and processes them to produce outputs.

organization (behavioral definition) A collection of rights, privileges, obligations, and responsibilities that are delicately balanced over a period of time through conflict and conflict resolution

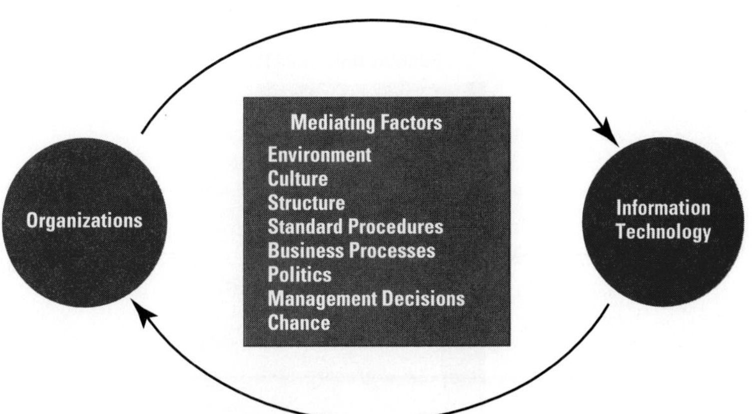

FIGURE 3.1

The two-way relationship between organizations and information technology. This complex two-way relationship is mediated by many factors, not the least of which are the decisions made—or not made—by managers. Other factors mediating the relationship are the organizational culture, bureaucracy, politics, business fashion, and pure chance.

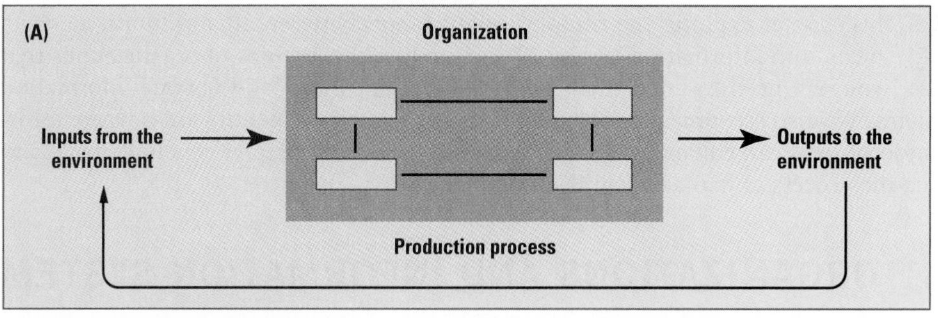

FIGURE 3.2 The technical microeconomic definition of the organization. In the microeconomic definition of organizations, capital and labor (the primary production factors provided by the environment) are transformed by the firm through the production process into products and services (outputs to the environment). The products and services are consumed by the environment, which supplies additional capital and labor as inputs in the feedback loop.

conflict resolution (see Figure 3.3). In this behavioral view of the firm, people who work in organizations develop customary ways of working; they gain attachments to existing relationships; and they make arrangements with subordinates and superiors about how work will be done, how much work will be done, and under what conditions. Most of these arrangements and feelings are not discussed in any formal rule book.

How do these definitions of organizations relate to information system technology? A technical view of organizations encourages us to focus upon the way inputs are combined into outputs when technology changes are introduced into the company. The firm is seen as infinitely malleable, with capital and labor substituting for each other quite easily. But the more realistic behavioral definition of an organization suggests that building new information systems or rebuilding old ones involves much more than a technical rearrangement of machines or workers—that some information systems change the organizational balance of rights, privileges, obligations, responsibilities, and feelings that has been established over a long period of time.

Technological change requires changes in who owns and controls information, who has the right to access and update that information, and who makes decisions about whom, when, and how. For instance, Schneider's information systems provide central managers with more information to monitor truck drivers. This more complex view forces us to look at the way work is designed and the procedures used to achieve outputs.

The technical and behavioral definitions of organizations are not contradictory. Indeed, they complement each other: The technical definition tells us how thousands of firms in competitive markets combine capital, labor, and information technology, whereas the behavioral model takes us inside the individual firm to see how that technology affects the inner workings of the organization. Section 3.2 describes how theo-

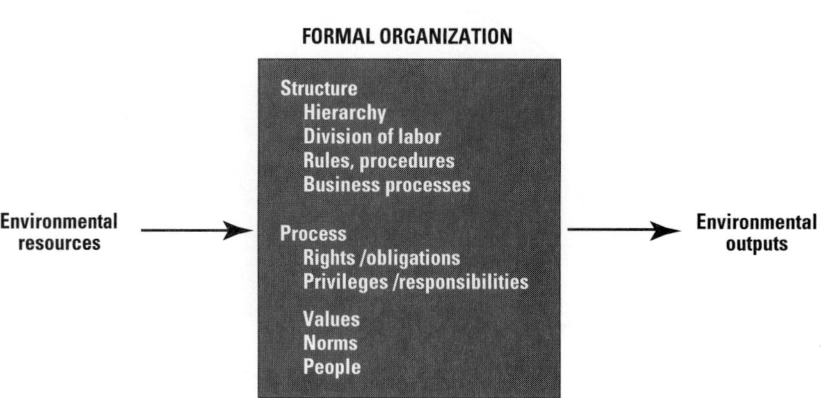

FIGURE 3.3 The behavioral view of organizations. The behavioral view of organizations emphasizes group relationships, values, and structures.

WINDOW ON MANAGEMENT

A Tale of Two Cities' Information Systems

For the past few years, media headlines have trumpeted the financial problems of Washington, D.C., some of which stem from the city government's information systems. School administrators have maintained two information systems, one for public and Congressional consumption and one that enables the administration to pay tens of millions of dollars to school officials whom the City Council had ordered laid off. System errors caused the city to overpay hospitals by $35 million. The city has mistakenly paid an extra $34 million to 20,000 people because the city's Medicaid and welfare computers are not linked. The city's Information Systems department returns new computer systems to manufacturers to have free, installed software removed, and then they accept bids to purchase the same software. Its information systems are antiquated, with some mission-critical systems running on ancient 286-based PCs that are housed in condemned buildings. The city's 80 data networks are not connected with each other. Forty percent of all telephones are rotary phones, and there is no government-wide phone directory. Procurement red tape is so bad that software for one critical system arrived two years before the hardware. Redundant computer centers are running at 40 percent of capacity. The city's mayor, Marion Barry, Jr., has admitted that senior officials overspend their budgets by millions of dollars by routinely overriding information system controls.

As bad as Washington sounds, however, it appears to be no worse than Philadelphia in 1992. At that time Philadelphia was running a budget deficit of $200 million per year and was rapidly heading into bankruptcy. *City and State* magazine designated Philadelphia as the city that "set the standard for municipal distress in the 1990s." Many city departments had their own computer systems or no automation at all. What systems existed were old, poorly supported, and stifled by layers of bureaucracy.

A turnaround began with the newly elected mayor, Edward Rendell. He balanced the city budget starting in 1993, and focused on improving information systems. By 1996 *Fortune* magazine ranked Philadelphia third in its annual list of "Best Cities for Family and Work." Antiquated systems were replaced, and a high-capacity, wide-area fiber-optic network was installed. The city outsourced much of its information systems work to private contractors, saving $450 million in just two years. Philadelphia's Chief Information Officer, John Carrow, focused zealously on cost-effective customer service. Staff was cut while services were maintained or improved. Carrow enforced his new management by meeting with his staff every Friday morning to review information system performance that week.

Washington, too, is beginning to address its problems, and its people are looking to Philadelphia for inspiration. City management consultants recently recommended 342 management-reform projects for the city, thirty to forty of which are for information systems. The city hired a new Chief Technology Officer (CTO), Michael T. Hernon. He is concerned about the "skill-impaired" workforce but says he may not even try to improve their skills. Instead, like Philadelphia, he is looking to outsource much of the work to save the city money and to improve services. He has obtained financing to centralize and standardize Information Systems, modernize computer and communication systems, and eliminate redundant facilities.

Washington reformers face special problems Philadelphia did not. For example, Washington does not have full power to govern itself. Instead, the city is governed by the United States Congress, which does interfere with city activities. Congress scrutinizes reform projects, not always acting in a nonpartisan manner. In addition, Washington does not have county and state governments with which to share its burdens, as do Philadelphia and other cities.

To Think About: ***How much of a role did management play in the condition of Washington's and Philadelphia's information systems? What other factors were involved?***

Source: Adapted from Gary H. Anthes, "A Tale of Two Cities," *Computerworld,* January 12, 1998.

ries based on each of these definitions of organizations can help explain the relationships between information systems and organizations.

Some features of organizations are common to all organizations; others distinguish one organization from another. Let us look first at the features common to all organizations.

Why Organizations Are So Much Alike: Common Features

You might not think that Apple Computer, United Airlines, and the Aspen, Colorado, Police Department have much in common, but they do. In some respects, all modern organizations are alike because they share the characteristics that are listed in Table 3.1. A German sociologist, Max Weber, was the first to describe these "ideal-typical"

TABLE 3.1 Structural Characteristics of All Organizations
Clear division of labor
Hierarchy
Explicit rules and procedures
Impartial judgments
Technical qualifications for positions
Maximum organizational efficiency

bureaucracy Formal organization with a clear-cut division of labor, abstract rules and procedures, and impartial decision making that uses technical qualifications and professionalism as a basis for promoting employees.

characteristics of organizations in 1911. He called organizations **bureaucracies** that have certain "structural" features. According to Weber, all modern bureaucracies:

- have a clear-cut *division of labor and specialization;*
- arrange specialists in a *hierarchy* of authority;
- limit authority and action by abstract *rules or procedures* (standard operating procedures, or SOPs);
- create a system of *impartial and universalistic decision making;*
- hire and promote employees on the basis of *technical qualifications and professionalism* (not personal connections);
- are devoted to the *principle of efficiency:* maximizing output using limited inputs.

According to Weber, bureaucracies are prevalent because they are the most efficient form of organization. Other scholars have supplemented Weber, identifying additional features of organizations. All organizations develop standard operating procedures, politics, and cultures.

Standard Operating Procedures

standard operating procedures (SOPs) Precise rules, procedures, and practices developed by organizations to cope with virtually all expected situations.

Organizations that survive over time become very efficient, producing a limited number of products and services by following standard routines. These standard routines become codified into reasonably precise rules, procedures, and practices called **standard operating procedures (SOPs)** that are developed to cope with virtually all expected situations. Some of these rules and procedures are written, formal procedures. Most are "rules of thumb" to be followed in selected situations.

These standard operating procedures have a great deal to do with the efficiency that modern organizations attain. For instance, in the assembly of a car, managers and workers develop complex standard procedures to handle the thousands of motions in a precise fashion, permitting the finished product to roll off the assembly line. Any change in SOPs requires an enormous organizational effort. Indeed, the organization may need to halt the entire production process before the old SOPs can be retired.

For example, difficulty in changing standard operating procedures is one reason Detroit auto makers have been slow to adopt Japanese mass-production methods. Until recently, U.S. auto makers followed Henry Ford's mass-production principles. Ford believed that the cheapest way to build a car was to churn out the largest number of autos by having workers repeatedly perform a simple task. By contrast, Japanese auto makers have emphasized "lean production" methods whereby a smaller number of workers, each performing several tasks, can produce cars with less inventory, less investment, and fewer mistakes. Workers have multiple job responsibilities and are encouraged to stop production in order to correct a problem.

Organizational Politics

People in organizations occupy different positions with different specialties, concerns, and perspectives. As a result, they naturally have divergent viewpoints about how resources, rewards, and punishments should be distributed. These differences matter to members of organizations, both managers and employees, and they result in political struggle, competition, and conflict within every organization. Political resistance is one of the great difficulties of bringing about change in organizations—especially the development of new information systems. Virtually all information systems that bring about significant changes in goals, procedures, productivity, and personnel are politically charged and will elicit serious political opposition.

Organizational Culture

All organizations have bedrock, unassailable, unquestioned (by the members) assumptions that define the goals and products of the organization. **Organizational culture** is this set of fundamental assumptions about what products the organization should produce, how it should produce them, where, and for whom. Generally, these cultural assumptions are taken totally for granted and are rarely publicly announced or spoken about. (Schein, 1985).

organizational culture The set of fundamental assumptions about what products the organization should produce, how and where it should produce them, and for whom they should be produced.

You can see organizational culture at work by looking around your university or college. Some bedrock assumptions of university life are that professors know more than students, the reason students attend college is to learn, and classes follow a regular schedule. Organizational culture is a powerful unifying force that restrains political conflict and promotes common understanding, agreement on procedures, and common practices. If we all share the same basic cultural assumptions, then agreement on other matters is more likely.

At the same time, organizational culture is a powerful restraint on change, especially technological change. Most organizations will do almost anything to avoid making changes in basic assumptions. Any technological change that threatens commonly held cultural assumptions usually meets a great deal of resistance. For instance, one key longstanding assumption—that management should be very authoritarian and does not need to listen to the opinions of workers—is another reason U.S. auto makers have been slow to switch to "lean production."

On the other hand, there are times when the only sensible way is to employ a new technology that directly opposes an existing organizational culture. When this occurs, the technology is often stalled while the culture slowly adjusts.

Why Organizations Are So Different: Unique Features and Business Processes

Although all organizations do have common characteristics, no two organizations are identical. Organizations have different structures, goals, constituencies, leadership styles, tasks, and surrounding environments.

Different Organizational Types

One important way in which organizations differ is in their structure or shape. The differences among organizational structures are characterized in many ways. Mintzberg's classification, described in Table 3.2, identifies five basic kinds of organizations (Mintzberg, 1979).

Organizations and Environments

Organizations reside in environments from which they draw resources and to which they supply goods and services. Organizations and environments have a reciprocal relationship. On the one hand, organizations are open to, and dependent on, the social and physical environment that surrounds them. Without financial and human resources—people willing to work reliably and consistently for a set wage or revenue from customers—organizations could not exist. But organizations can influence their environments as well, at least in the short term. Organizations form alliances with others to influence the political process; they advertise to influence customer acceptance of their products.

TABLE 3.2 Organizational Structures

Organizational Type	Description	Example
Entrepreneurial structure	Young, small firm in a fast-changing environment. It has a simple structure and is managed by an entrepreneur serving as its single chief executive officer.	Small startup business
Machine bureaucracy	Large bureaucracy existing in a slowly changing environment, producing standard products. It is dominated by a centralized management team and centralized decision making.	Midsized manufacturing firm
Divisionalized bureaucracy	Combination of multiple machine bureaucracies, each producing a different product or service, all topped by one central headquarters.	Fortune 500 firms such as General Motors
Professional bureaucracy	Knowledge-based organization where goods and services depend on the expertise and knowledge of professionals. Dominated by department heads with weak centralized authority.	Law firms, school systems, hospitals
Adhocracy	"Task force" organization that must respond to rapidly changing environments. Consists of large groups of specialists organized into short-lived multidisciplinary teams and has weak central management.	Consulting firms such as the Rand Corporation

Figure 3.4 shows that information systems play an important role in helping organizations perceive changes in their environments, and also in helping organizations act on their environments. Information systems are key instruments for *environmental scanning,* helping managers identify external changes that might require an organizational response.

Environments generally change much faster than organizations. The main reasons for organizational failure are an inability to adapt to a rapidly changing environment and a lack of resources—particularly among young firms—to sustain even short periods of troubled times (Freeman et al., 1983). New technologies, new products, and changing public tastes and values (many of which result in new government regulations) put strains on any organization's culture, politics, and people. Most organizations do not cope well with large environmental shifts. The inertia built into an organization's standard operating procedures, the political conflict raised by changes to the existing order, and the threat to closely held cultural values typically inhibit organizations from making significant changes. It is not surprising that only 10 percent of the Fortune 500 companies in 1919 still exist today.

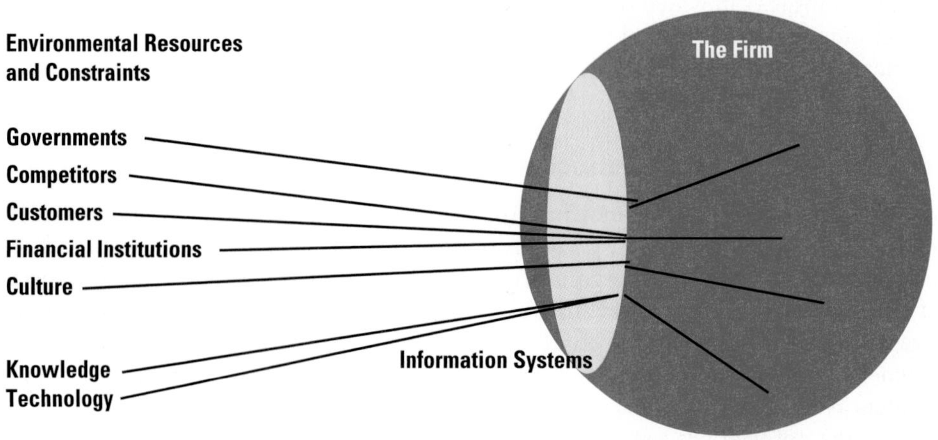

FIGURE 3.4
Environments and organizations have a reciprocal relationship. Environments shape what organizations can do, but organizations can influence their environments and decide to change environments altogether. Information technology plays a critical role in helping organizations perceive environmental change, and in helping organizations act on their environment. Information systems act as a filter between organizations and their environments. They do not necessarily reflect reality, but instead refract environmental change through a number of built-in biases.

Fast-changing technologies, such as information technology, are especially threatening to organizations. At times, technological changes occur so radically that they either enhance or destroy the competence of firms in an industry (Tushman and Anderson, 1986). When technological discontinuities happen, most organizations fail to adapt, go out of existence, and free up resources for new organizations. For instance, Wang Laboratories, a leading manufacturer of minicomputers and word processors, was a dominant force in the computer industry during the 1970s and early 1980s. But when powerful personal computers (PCs) reduced the need for minicomputers, Wang nearly went out of business because it failed to adapt its products to the new technology.

Other Differences Among Organizations

Organizations have different shapes or structures for many other reasons also. They differ in their ultimate goals and the types of power used to achieve them. Some organizations have coercive goals (e.g., prisons); others have utilitarian goals (e.g., businesses). Still others have normative goals (universities, religious groups). Organizations also serve different groups or have different constituencies, some primarily benefiting their members, others benefiting clients, stockholders, or the public. The nature of leadership differs greatly from one organization to another—some organizations may be more democratic or authoritarian than others.

Another way organizations differ is by the tasks they perform and the technology they use. In some cases, organizations use routine tasks that could be reduced to formal rules that require little judgment. (An example would be inventory reordering.) Organizations that primarily perform routine tasks are typically hierarchical and run according to standard procedures. In other cases, organizations work primarily with nonroutine tasks. (An example might be a consulting company that creates strategic plans for other companies.)

Business Processes

Business processes refer to the manner in which work is organized, coordinated, and focused to produce a valuable product or service. On the one hand, business processes are concrete workflows of material, information, and knowledge—sets of activities. But business processes also refer to the unique ways in which organizations coordinate work, information, and knowledge, and the ways in which management chooses to coordinate work.

business processes The unique ways in which organizations coordinate and organize work activities, information, and knowledge to produce a product or service.

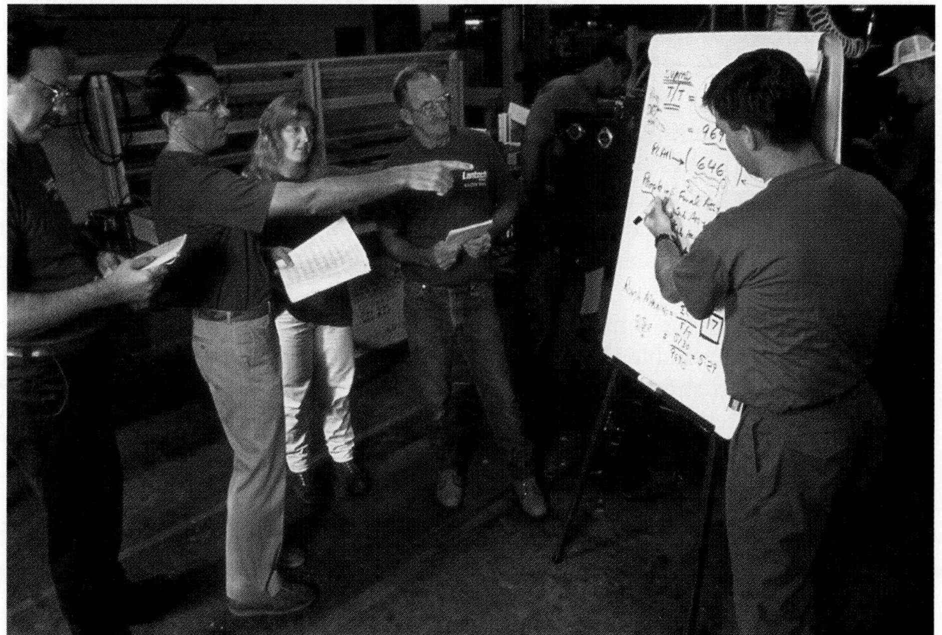

Lantech Inc. redesigned its manufacturing process, replacing the traditional assembly line with microlines where workers oversee all aspects of production. Well-designed business processes can contribute to organizational success.

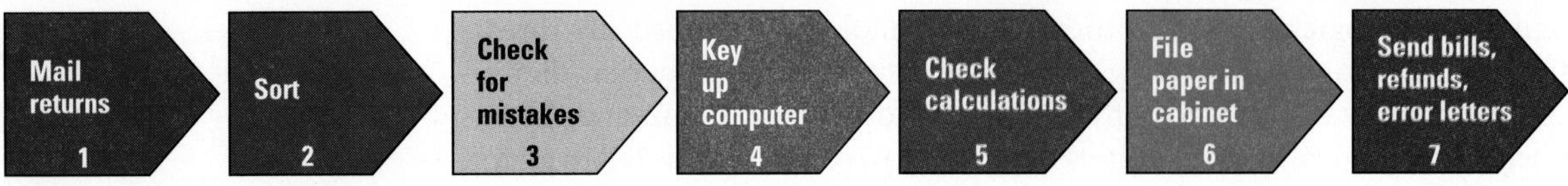

FIGURE 3.5 The Internal Revenue Service tax collection process. Collecting federal income taxes is a multistep process with many activities to coordinate.

The contemporary interest with business processes comes from the recognition that strategic success ultimately depends on how well firms execute their primary mission of delivering the lowest cost, highest quality goods and services to customers. Examples of processes are new-product development, which turns an idea into a manufacturable prototype, or order fulfillment, which begins with the receipt of an order and ends when the customer has received and paid for the product.

Business processes, by nature, are generally cross-functional, transcending the boundaries between sales, marketing, manufacturing, and research and development. Processes cut across the traditional organizational structure, grouping employees from different functional specialties to complete a piece of work. For example, the order fulfillment process at many companies requires cooperation among the sales function (receiving the order, entering the order), the accounting function (credit checking and billing for the order), and the manufacturing function (assembling and shipping the order).

The objectives for processes are more external and linked to meeting customer and market demands than are those for the traditional functional approach. Instead of evaluating how well each functional area is performing as a discrete business function, management would evaluate how well a group executes a process. For instance, instead of measuring the manufacturing department independently on how well it reduces the cost to produce each unit and the shipping department independently on how quickly it ships out each unit, management might look at the entire logistics process from receipt of raw material to receipt by the customer.

Figure 3.5 depicts the current income tax collection process at the United States Internal Revenue Service. Taxpayers mail their income tax returns (and payment checks) to the IRS (Step 1), where they are first sorted by type of return, by whether checks are enclosed, and other criteria (Step 2). IRS examiners look over the paper returns for mistakes, making sure all schedules are attached (Step 3). Thousands of people key only the most important pieces of information from each return into the IRS computer system (Step 4). The computers check the calculations and data on the returns, generating a report of returns with errors (Step 5). The paper returns are filed in cabinets (Step 6). The IRS sends out refunds, bills for additional payments, and letters to taxpayers informing them of errors on their returns (Step 7).

Information systems can help organizations achieve great efficiencies by automating parts of these processes or by helping organizations rethink and streamline these processes through the development of work-flow software. For example, experts have pointed out that the IRS tax collection process could be made more efficient—with taxpayer information more easily accessible—by eliminating some of the manual and paper-based activities. Instead of entering limited pieces of data from the returns into the computer system, the entire tax return could be scanned into the computer, with all of its information available for instant access. The computer could perform all of the returns examination and error checking instead of having people make preliminary examinations of the returns (Johnston, 1998). Chapter 10 will treat this subject in greater detail, since it is fundamental to systems analysis and design.

Automating business processes requires careful analysis and planning. When systems are used to strengthen the wrong business model or business processes, the business can become more efficient at doing what it should *not* do. And as a result, the strategic position of the firm suffers and it becomes vulnerable to competitors who may have discovered the right business model. Therefore, one of the most important

Organizational Level	Activity	Example Support System
Individual	Job, task	PC application; personal client database; decision-support systems
Team	Project	Product scheduling; access to mainframe data; access to external data sources; dynamic information requirements; group DSS; groupware
Department	Major function	Accounts payable; warehouse; payroll; human resources; marketing; stable information requirements; MIS; major transaction systems
Division	Major product or service	Systems to support production, marketing, administration, and human resources; access to organizational financial, and planning data; MIS; major transaction systems; on-line interactive systems
Organization	Multiple products, services, and goals	Integrated financial and planning systems; MIS; on-line interactive systems; ESS
Interorganization	Alliance Competition Exchange Contact	Communication systems; intelligence, observation, and monitoring systems
Organizational network	Sector of economy: related products, services; interdependencies	Informal communication systems; industry and sector-level formal reporting systems

FIGURE 3.6 Organizational levels and support systems. Systems are designed to support various levels of the organization.

strategic decisions that a firm can make is not deciding how to use computers to improve business processes, but instead to first understand what business processes need improvement (Keen, 1997). The choice of which business process to improve is critical.

Levels of Analysis

All organizations have different levels, occupations, divisions, and groups, each with different concerns. The impact of information systems will probably be different for different levels and groups within an organization. This can be seen in Figure 3.6, which describes typical organizational levels and the principal concerns at each level, providing examples of information systems that are appropriate for each level.

At the individual and small-group levels of organization, information systems apply to a particular job, task, or project. At the department and division levels, information systems deal with a particular business function, product, or service. At the organization, interorganization, and organizational network levels, information systems support multiple products, services, and goals and facilitate alliances and coordination between two or more different organizations or groups of organizations.

Much of the work of organizations is done by informal work groups such as task forces, interdepartmental committees, project teams, and committees. Recently developed system tools directed at support of work groups are discussed in Chapters 6, 9, and 12.

TABLE 3.3 A Summary of Salient Features of Organizations

Common Features	Unique Features
Formal structure	Organizational type
Standard operating procedures (SOPs)	Environments
Politics	Goals
Culture	Power
	Constituencies
	Function
	Leadership
	Tasks
	Technology
	Business processes
	Levels

As you can see in Table 3.3, the list of unique features of organizations is longer than the common features list. It stands to reason that information systems will have different impacts on different types of organizations. Different organizations in different circumstances will experience different effects from the same technology. Only by close analysis of a specific organization can a manager effectively design and manage information systems.

3.2 THE CHANGING ROLE OF INFORMATION SYSTEMS

You are now ready to look more closely at the relationship between information systems and organizations. We will begin by describing the developing role of information systems within organizations before we examine the effect that information system technology has upon organizations.

The Evolution of Information Systems

In Chapters 1 and 2 we described the expanding role information systems have been playing within organizations.

Supporting this widening role have been changes in the technical and organizational configuration of systems that have brought computing power and data much closer to the ultimate end users (see Figure 3.7). Isolated "electronic accounting machines" with limited functions in the 1950s gave way in the 1960s to large, centralized mainframe computers that served corporate headquarters and a few remote sites. In the 1970s, midsized minicomputers located in individual departments or divisions of the organization were networked to large, centralized computers. Desktop PCs first were used independently and then were linked to minicomputers and large computers in the 1980s.

In the 1990s, the architecture for a fully networked organization emerged. In this new enterprise-wide architecture, computers coordinate information flowing among desktops, between desktops, among minicomputers and mainframes, and perhaps among hundreds of smaller local networks. These networks can be connected into a network linking the entire enterprise or linking to external networks, including the Internet. Information systems have become integral, on-line, interactive tools deeply involved in the minute-to-minute operations and decision making of large organizations.

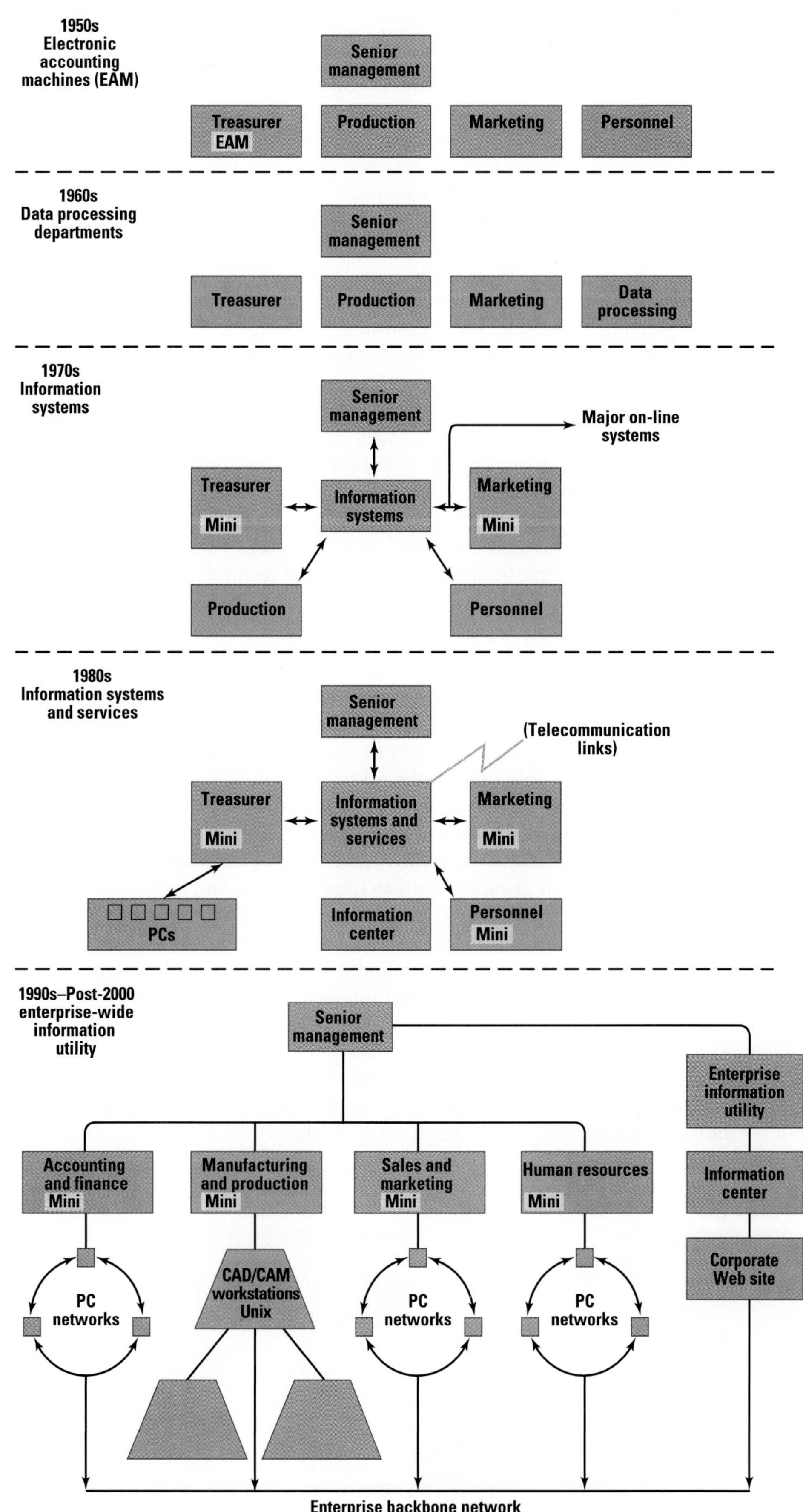

FIGURE 3.7

The development of information architecture of organizations. The last five decades have seen dramatic changes in the technical and organizational configurations of systems. During the 1950s organizations were dependent on computers for a few critical functions. The 1960s witnessed the development of large centralized machines. By the late 1970s and into the 1980s information architecture became complex, and information systems included telecommunications links to distribute information. During the 1990s information architecture is an enterprise-wide information utility, which in turn is connected to vendors and customers through the World Wide Web.

information systems department The formal organizational unit that is responsible for the information systems function in the organization.

programmers Highly trained technical specialists who write computer software instructions.

systems analysts Specialists who translate business problems and requirements into information requirements and systems, acting as liaison between the information systems department and the rest of the organization.

information systems managers Leaders of the various specialists in the information systems department.

end users Representatives of departments outside the information systems group for whom applications are developed.

chief information officer (CIO) Senior manager in charge of the information systems function in the firm.

The position and role of information system specialists also have evolved over time. The formal organizational unit or function that has emerged is called an **information systems department.** In the early years, the information systems group was composed mostly of **programmers,** highly trained technical specialists who wrote the software instructions for the computer. Today a growing proportion of staff members are **systems analysts,** who constitute the principal liaison between the information systems group and the rest of the organization. It is the systems analyst's job to translate business problems and requirements into information requirements and systems. **Information systems managers** are leaders of teams of programmers and analysts, project managers, physical facility managers, telecommunications managers, and heads of office automation groups. They are also managers of computer operations and data entry staff. **End users** are representatives of departments outside of the information systems group for whom applications are developed. These users are playing an increasingly large role in the design and development of information systems.

In many companies, the information systems department is headed by a **chief information officer (CIO).** The CIO is a senior management position to oversee the use of information technology in the firm. The size of the information systems department can vary greatly, depending on the role of information systems in the organization and on the organization's size. Today, information systems groups often act as powerful change agents within the organization, suggesting new business strategies and new information-based products and coordinating both the development of technology and the planned changes in the organization.

Why Organizations Build Information Systems

Obviously, organizations adopt information systems to become more efficient, to save money, and to reduce the work force. Information systems have become vitally important simply to stay in business and may even be a source of competitive advantage. However, this may not be the only or even the primary reason for adopting systems.

Some organizations build certain systems simply because they are more innovative than others. They have values that encourage any kind of innovation, regardless of its direct economic benefit to the company. In other cases, information systems are built to satisfy the ambitions of various groups within an organization. And in some cases such as that of Schneider National, described in the chapter-opening vignette, and organizations converting to the new euro currency, described in the Window on Organizations, changes in an organization's environment demand a system response. Information systems may need to be built to help the organization deal with government regulations, competitors' actions, and changing costs.

Figure 3.8 illustrates a model of the systems development process that includes many considerations other than economic. This model divides the explanations for why organizations adopt systems into two groups: *external environmental factors* and *internal institutional factors* (Laudon, 1985; King et al., 1994).

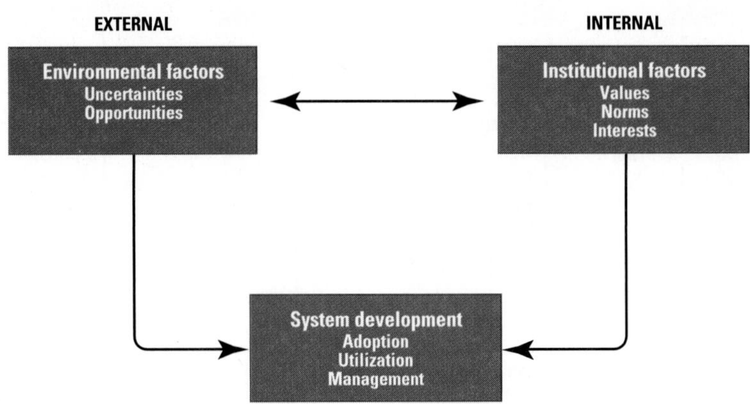

FIGURE 3.8

The systems development process. External environmental factors and internal institutional factors influence the types of information systems that organizations select, develop, and use.

WINDOW ON ORGANIZATIONS

European Currency Conversion Becomes a Systems Nightmare

Currency in Europe is about to undergo a revolutionary change, and organizations around the world must be ready. Europe is creating a single currency, with the soon-to-be-born euro replacing such venerable old currencies as the French franc and the German deutsche mark (DM). A three-and-one-half-year transition period will begin on January 1, 1999, during which people will be free to use either the euro or the currencies of the eleven (so far) eligible European countries. On July 1, 2002, those eleven national currencies will cease to be legal tender, and everyone will have no choice but to use the euro.

The decision by the European countries to replace their currencies with a single currency has hit organizations around the globe like a tidal wave. The number of organizations affected is staggering. Currency trading firms must adjust so their software will handle the euro, but they are just the proverbial tip of the iceberg. Tax software, software for banks, credit cards, and international trades of securities and goods must be modified. Automated teller machines must be upgraded. Ultimately, any business that relates to European currencies must make changes—even telephone booths and corner newspaper machines.

Because the euro will not replace the eleven currencies in one day, the problem is exceptionally complex. During the transition period, the national currencies and the euro will exist side-by-side. Anyone using the money of the eleven countries will be free to choose either the traditional national currency or the euro. Organizations must have systems that can handle transactions in both the local money and the euro.

Currently the value of each of the eleven national currencies is set by the marketplace, and those relationships are very complex. One deutsche mark may be worth 3.352 francs and 987.00 lira. Conversion values almost always have had to be cited in decimals, up to as many as six decimal places in some cases. Traditionally, to convert from one currency to another, you needed to multiply (or divide) the one currency by a given number. However, during the transition period, each national currency first will have to be converted to euros and then converted into the other currency. For example, to convert deutsche marks into francs, the deutsche marks first must be converted into euros and then the euros will be converted into francs. The European Monetary Union will set the value of the euro against each of the national currencies of the participating countries during the transition period.

One example of the difficulties organizations will face with the interim currency conversion is the rounding problem. Conversion ratios already stretch into seven, eight, ten or more decimal places, making rounding a necessity. In the new situation, rounding will have to occur on each of the conversion steps between two European currencies. Rounding twice makes the process unpredictable, causing one side to gain unexpectedly while the other one loses. If the amount being converted is very large, the windfall for one side can be quite substantial, as will the unplanned losses for the other.

Bond-trading systems face additional hurdles. A DM 10 million-denominated bond, for instance, would by January 1, 1999, become a 19.5xx,xxx.xxx euro-denominated bond. Most current systems can only deal with the issued value of a bond in whole numbers. They would have to be changed to handle numbers after the decimal point.

Decisions on how to deal with such issues have to be made very quickly, because programming must be completed months before January 1, 1999, to give organizations adequate time to test their newly programmed software. The costs are high. European corporations with worldwide operations may have to spend from $150 billion to $400 billion to upgrade their systems.

To Think About: ***How are organizations and information systems affected by the adoption of the euro?***

Sources: Andrew Ross Sorkin, "A Year Before the Millennium Bug, There's the Euro Problem," *The New York Times,* March 3, 1998, and Alan Lloyd Paris, "The Euro Dilemma," *Wall Street & Technology,* January 1998.

Environmental factors are factors external to the organization that influence the adoption and design of information systems. Examples of *external constraints* would be the rising costs of labor or other resources, the competitive actions of other organizations, and changes in government regulations. Examples of *external opportunities* include new technologies, new sources of capital, the demise of a competitor, or a new government program.

environmental factors Factors external to the organization that influence the adoption and design of information systems.

Institutional factors are factors internal to the organization that influence the adoption and design of information systems. They include values, norms, and vital interests that govern matters of strategic importance to the organization. For instance, the top management of a corporation can decide that it needs to exercise much stronger control over the inventory process and therefore decide to develop an inventory information system. (For a similar model, see Kraemer et al., 1989.)

institutional factors Factors internal to the organization that influence the adoption and design of information systems.

How Information Systems Affect Organizations

We shall now look at another question: How do information systems affect organizations? To find some answers, we need to summarize a large body of research and theory based on economic and behavioral approaches.

Economic Theories

From an economic standpoint, information system technology can be viewed as a factor of production that can be freely substituted for capital and labor. As the cost of information system technology falls, it is substituted for labor, which historically has been a rising cost. Hence, in microeconomic theory, information technology should result in a decline in the number of middle managers and clerical workers as information technology substitutes for their labor.

Information technology also helps firms contract in size because it can reduce transaction costs—the costs incurred when a firm buys on the marketplace what it cannot make itself. According to **transaction cost theory,** firms and individuals seek to economize on transaction costs, much as they do on production costs. Using markets is expensive (Williamson, 1985) because of coordination costs such as locating and communicating with distant suppliers, monitoring contract compliance, buying insurance, obtaining information on products, and so forth. Traditionally, firms have tried to reduce transaction costs by getting bigger, hiring more employees or buying their own suppliers and distributors, as General Motors used to do.

transaction cost theory Economic theory stating that firms grow larger because they can conduct marketplace transactions internally more cheaply than they can with external firms in the marketplace.

Information technology, especially the use of networks, can help firms lower the cost of market participation (transaction costs), making it worthwhile for firms to contract with external suppliers instead of using internal sources. For example, by using computer links to external suppliers, the Chrysler Corporation can achieve economies by obtaining more than 70 percent of its parts from the outside. Figure 3.9 shows that as transaction costs decrease, firm size (the number of employees) should shrink because it becomes easier and cheaper for the firm to contract the purchase of goods and services in the marketplace rather than to make the product or service itself. Firm size can stay constant or contract even if the company increases its revenues. (For example, General Electric reduced its work force from about 400,000 people in the early 1980s to about 230,000 while increasing revenues 150 percent.)

Information technology also can reduce internal management costs. According to **agency theory,** the firm is viewed as a "nexus of contracts" among self-interested individuals rather than as a unified, profit-maximizing entity (Jensen and Meckling, 1976). A principal (owner) employs "agents" (employees) to perform work on his or her behalf. However, agents need constant supervision and management because they other-

agency theory Economic theory that views the firm as a nexus of contracts among self-interested individuals who must be supervised and managed.

FIGURE 3.9

The transaction cost theory of the impact of information technology on the organization. Firms traditionally grew in size in order to reduce transaction costs. IT potentially reduces the costs for a given size, shifting the transaction cost curve inward, opening up the possibility of revenue growth without increasing size, or even revenue growth accompanied by shrinking size.

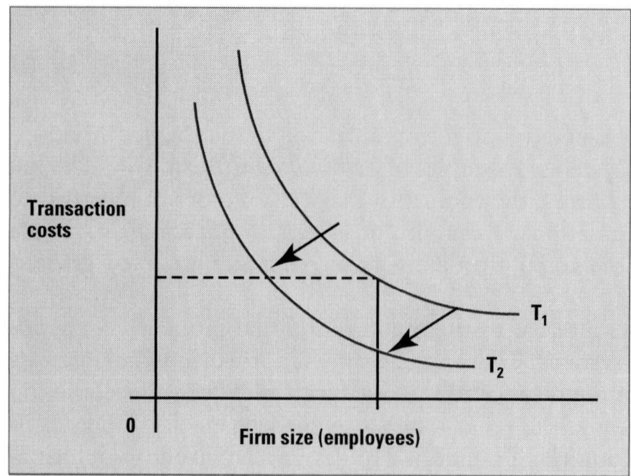

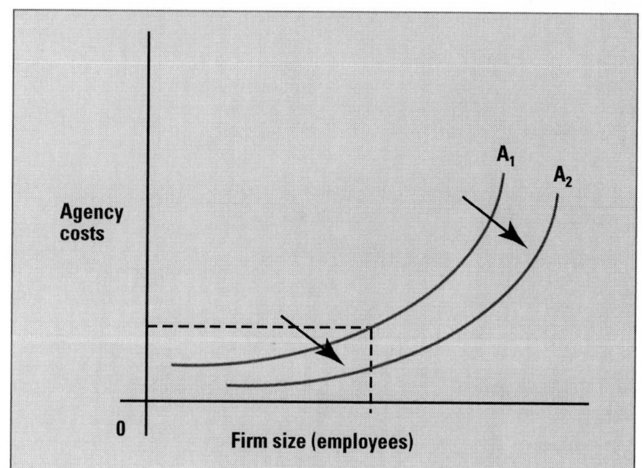

FIGURE 3.10

The agency cost theory of the impact of information technology on the organization. As firms grow in size and complexity, traditionally they experience rising agency costs. IT shifts the agency cost curve down and to the right, allowing firms to increase size while lowering agency costs.

wise will tend to pursue their own interests rather than those of the owners. As firms grow in size and scope, agency costs or coordination costs rise, because owners must expend more and more effort supervising and managing employees.

Information technology, by reducing the costs of acquiring and analyzing information, permits organizations to reduce agency costs because it becomes easier for managers to oversee a greater number of employees. Figure 3.10 shows that by reducing overall management costs, information technology allows firms to increase revenues while shrinking the numbers of middle management and clerical workers. We have seen examples in earlier chapters where information technology expanded the power and scope of small organizations by allowing them to perform coordinating activities such as processing orders or keeping track of inventory with very few clerks and managers.

Behavioral Theories

While economic theories try to explain how large numbers of firms act in the marketplace, behavioral theories from sociology, psychology, and political science are more useful for describing the behavior of individual firms. Behavioral research has found little evidence that information systems automatically transform organizations, although the systems may be instrumental in accomplishing this goal once senior management decides to pursue this end. Instead, researchers have observed an intricately choreographed relationship in which organizations and information technology mutually influence each other.

Behavioral researchers have theorized that information technology could change the hierarchy of decision making in organizations by lowering the costs of information acquisition and broadening the distribution of information (Malone, 1997). Information technology could bring information directly from operating units to senior managers, thereby eliminating middle managers and their clerical support workers. Information technology could permit senior managers to contact lower-level operating units directly through the use of networked telecommunications and computers, eliminating middle management intermediaries. Alternatively, information technology could distribute information directly to lower-level workers, who could then make their own decisions based on their own knowledge and information without any management intervention. Some research even suggests that computerization increases the information given to middle managers, empowering them to make more important decisions than in the past, thus reducing the need for large numbers of lower-level workers (Shore, 1983).

In postindustrial societies, authority increasingly relies on knowledge and competence, and not on mere formal position. Hence, the shape of organizations should "flatten," since professional workers tend to be self-managing; and decision making should

In virtual offices, employees do not work from a permanent location. Here, work spaces are temporary with employees moving from desk to desk as vacancies open.

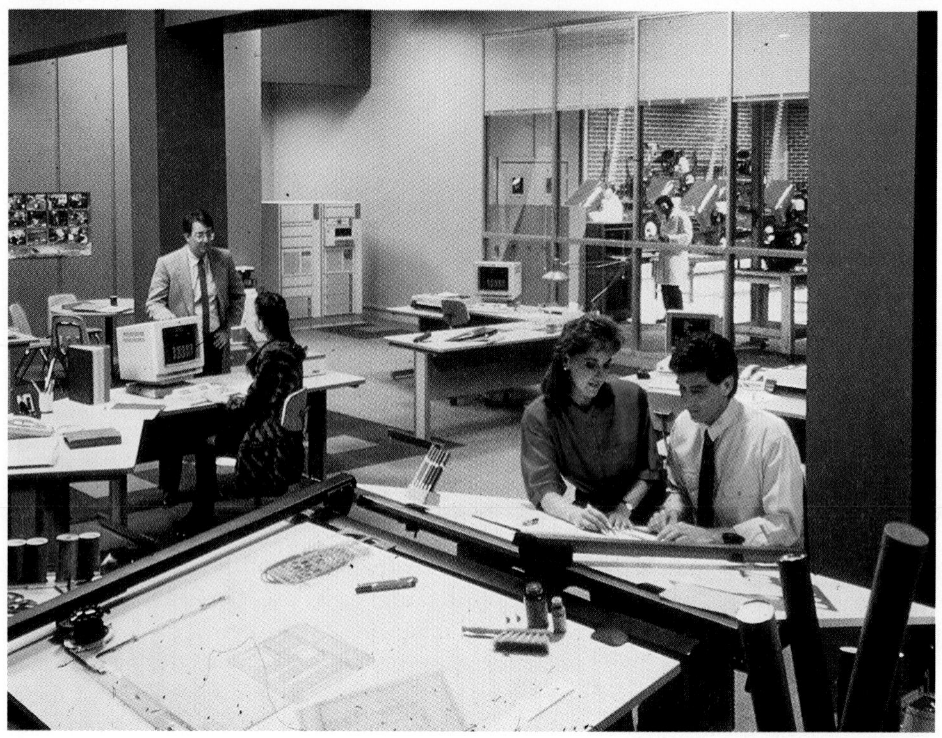

become more decentralized as knowledge and information become more widespread throughout (Drucker, 1988). Information technology may encourage "task force" networked organizations in which groups of professionals come together—face-to-face or electronically—for short periods of time to accomplish a specific task (e.g., designing a new automobile); once the task is accomplished, the individuals join other task forces. More firms may operate as virtual organizations, where work no longer is tied to geographic location.

Who makes sure that self-managed teams do not head off in the wrong direction? Who decides which person works on what team and for how long? How can managers judge the performance of someone who is constantly rotating from team to team? How do people know where their careers are headed? New approaches for evaluating, organizing, and informing workers are required; and not all companies can make virtual work effective (Davenport and Pearlson, 1998).

No one knows the answers to these questions, and it is not clear that all modern organizations will undergo this transformation—General Motors, for example, may have many self-managed knowledge workers in certain divisions, but it still will have a manufacturing division structured as a large, traditional bureaucracy. In general, the shape of organizations historically changes with the business cycle and with the latest management fashions. When times are good and profits are high, firms hire large numbers of supervisory personnel; when times are tough, they let go many of these same people (Mintzberg, 1979). It is not known if the shrinkage of some firms' middle management in the early 1990s resulted from hard times or from computerization.

Another behavioral approach views information systems as the outcome of political competition between organizational subgroups for influence over the policies, procedures, and resources of the organization (Laudon, 1974; Keen, 1981; Kling, 1980; Laudon, 1986). Information systems inevitably become bound up in the politics of organizations because they influence access to a key resource—namely, information. Information systems can affect who does what to whom, when, where, and how in an organization. For instance, a major study of the efforts of the FBI to develop a national computerized criminal history system (a single national listing of the criminal histories, arrests, and convictions of more than 36 million individuals in the United States) found

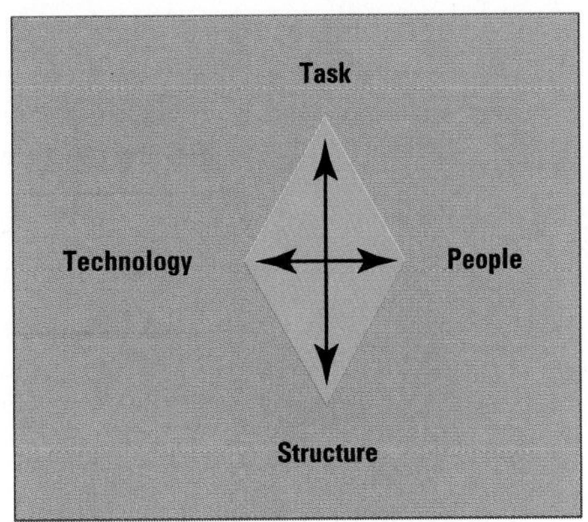

FIGURE 3.11
Organizational resistance and the mutually adjusting relationship between technology and the organization. Implementing information systems has consequences for task arrangements, structures, and people. According to this model, in order to implement change, all four components must be changed simultaneously. *Source: Leavitt, 1965.*

that the state governments strongly resisted the FBI's efforts. This information would give the federal government, and the FBI in particular, the ability to monitor how states use criminal histories. The states resisted the development of this national system quite successfully (Laudon, 1986).

Because information systems potentially change an organization's structure, culture, politics, and work, there is often considerable resistance to them when they are introduced. There are several ways to visualize organizational resistance. Leavitt (1965) used a diamond shape to illustrate the interrelated and mutually adjusting character of technology and organization (see Figure 3.11). Here, changes in technology are absorbed, deflected, and defeated by organizational task arrangements, structures, and people. In this model, the only way to bring about change is to change the technology, tasks, structure, and people simultaneously. Other authors have spoken about the need to "unfreeze" organizations before introducing an innovation, quickly implementing it, and "refreezing" or institutionalizing the change (Kolb, 1970; Alter and Ginzberg, 1978).

The Internet and Organizations

The Internet, especially the World Wide Web, is beginning to have an important impact on the relationships between firms and external entities, and even on the organization of business processes inside a firm. The Internet increases the accessibility, storage, and distribution of information and knowledge for organizations. In essence, the Internet is capable of dramatically lowering the transaction and agency costs facing most organizations. For instance, brokerage firms and banks in New York can now "deliver" their internal-operations procedures manuals to their employees at distant locations by posting them on their corporate Web site, saving millions of dollars in distribution costs. A global sales force can receive nearly instant price/product information updates via the Web or instructions from management via e-mail. Vendors of some large retailers can access retailers' internal Web sites directly for up-to-the-minute sales information and initiate replenishment orders instantly.

Businesses are slowly rebuilding some of their key business processes based on the new Internet technology. If prior networking is any guide, one result will be simpler business processes, fewer employees, and much flatter organizations than in the past.

Implications for the Design and Understanding of Information Systems

What is the importance of these theories of organizations? The primary significance of this section is to show that you cannot take a narrow view of organizations and their relationship to information systems. Experienced systems observers and managers approach systems change very cautiously. In order to reap the benefits of technology, organizational innovations—changes in the culture, values, norms, and interest-group alignments—must be managed with as much planning and effort as technology changes.

You should develop a checklist of factors to consider in your systems plans. In our experience, the central organizational factors are these:

The *environment* in which the organization must function.

The *structure* of the organization: hierarchy, specialization, standard operating procedures.

The *culture and politics* of the organization.

The *type* of organization.

The *nature and style* of leadership.

The extent of support and understanding of *top management.*

The *level* of organization at which the system resides.

The principal *interest groups* affected by the system.

The *kinds of tasks, decisions, and business processes* that the information system is designed to assist.

The *sentiments and attitudes* of workers in the organization who will be using the information system.

The *history of the organization:* past investments in information technology, existing skills, important programs, and human resources.

3.3 THE ROLE OF MANAGERS IN THE ORGANIZATION

Managers play a key role in organizations. Their responsibilities range from making decisions, to writing reports, to attending meetings, to arranging birthday parties. To determine how information systems can benefit managers, we must first examine what managers do and what information they need for decision making and their other functions. We must also understand how decisions are made and what kinds of decisions can be supported by formal information systems.

Classical Descriptions of Management

classical model of management Traditional description of management that focused on its formal functions of planning, organizing, coordinating, deciding, and controlling.

The **classical model of management,** which describes what managers do, was largely unquestioned for the more than 70 years since the 1920s. Henri Fayol and other early writers first described the five classical functions of managers as *planning, organizing, coordinating, deciding,* and *controlling.* This description of management activities dominated management thought for a long time, and it is still popular today.

But these terms actually describe managerial functions and are unsatisfactory as a description of what managers actually do. The terms do not address what managers do when they plan, decide things, and control the work of others. We need a more fine-grained understanding of how managers actually behave.

Behavioral Models

Contemporary behavioral scientists have discovered from observation that managers do not behave as the classical model of management led us to believe. Kotter (1982), for example, describes the morning activities of the president of an investment management firm.

7:35 A.M. Richardson arrives at work, unpacks her briefcase, gets some coffee, and begins making a list of activities for the day.

7:45 A.M. Bradshaw (a subordinate) and Richardson converse about a number of topics and exchange pictures recently taken on summer vacations.

8:00 A.M. They talk about a schedule of priorities for the day.

8:20 A.M. Wilson (a subordinate) and Richardson talk about some personnel problems, cracking jokes in the process.

8:45 A.M. Richardson's secretary arrives, and they discuss her new apartment and arrangements for a meeting later in the morning.

8:55 A.M. Richardson goes to a morning meeting run by one of her subordinates. Thirty people are there, and Richardson reads during the meeting.

11:05 A.M. Richardson and her subordinates return to the office and discuss a difficult problem. They try to define the problem and outline possible alternatives. She lets the discussion roam away from and back to the topic again and again. Finally, they agree on a next step.

In this example, it is difficult to determine which activities constitute Richardson's planning, coordinating, and decision making. **Behavioral models** state that the actual behavior of managers appears to be less systematic, more informal, less reflective, more reactive, less well-organized, and much more frivolous than students of information systems and decision making generally expect it to be.

behavioral models Descriptions of management based on behavioral scientists' observations of what managers actually do in their jobs.

Observers find that managerial behavior actually has five attributes that differ greatly from the classical description: First, managers perform a great deal of work at an unrelenting pace—studies have found that managers engage in more than 600 different activities each day, with no break in their pace. Second, managerial activities are fragmented; most activities last for less than 9 minutes; only 10 percent of the activities exceed one hour in duration. Third, managers prefer speculation, hearsay, gossip—they want current, specific, and ad hoc information (printed information often will be too old). Fourth, they prefer oral forms of communication to written forms because oral media provide greater flexibility, require less effort, and bring a faster response. Fifth, managers give high priority to maintaining a diverse and complex web of contacts that acts as an informal information system.

From his real-world observations, Kotter argues that effective managers are actually involved in only three critical activities:

- First, general managers spend significant time establishing personal agendas and goals, both short- and long-term.
- Second—and perhaps most important—effective managers spend a great deal of time building an interpersonal network composed of people at virtually all levels of the organization, from warehouse staff to clerical support personnel to other managers and senior management.
- Third, Kotter found that managers use their networks to execute personal agendas, to accomplish their own goals.

Analyzing managers' day-to-day behavior, Mintzberg found that it could be classified into ten managerial roles. **Managerial roles** are expectations of the activities that managers should perform in an organization. Mintzberg found that these managerial roles fell into three categories: interpersonal, informational, and decisional.

managerial roles Expectations of the activities that managers should perform in an organization.

INTERPERSONAL ROLES. Managers act as figureheads for the organization when they represent their companies to the outside world and perform symbolic duties such as giving out employee awards. Managers act as leaders, attempting to motivate, counsel, and support subordinates. Managers also act as a liaison between various levels of the organization; within each of these levels, they serve as a liaison among the members of the management team. Managers provide time and favors, which they expect to be returned.

interpersonal roles Mintzberg's classification for managerial roles where managers act as figureheads and leaders for the organization.

INFORMATIONAL ROLES. Managers act as the nerve centers of their organization, receiving the most concrete, up-to-date information and redistributing it to those who need to be aware of it. Managers are therefore information disseminators and spokespersons for their organization.

informational roles Mintzberg's classification for managerial roles where managers act as the nerve centers of their organizations, receiving and disseminating critical information.

WINDOW ON TECHNOLOGY

Schwab's Managers Turn to the Internet

Although giant discount broker Charles Schwab and Co. had many capabilities for providing electronic services and instant financial information to customers, it was much slower in providing essential information to its managers. Schwab once had a general ledger system that ran only at corporate headquarters in San Francisco and was very difficult to learn and use. Managers at regional centers could only obtain financial reports on paper through interoffice mail. Schwab found a way to provide this information more rapidly by using Internet technology to create a general ledger reporting system called FinWeb. Managers at any Schwab office now can access and print reports at any time in easy-to-digest form. In addition to providing managers with better information, FinWeb cut down Schwab's training and printing expenses.

Schwab then created a Web-based reporting and analysis application called SMART, which provides managers with a comprehensive view of Schwab activities. SMART, which stands for Schwab Metric and Analysis Reporting Tool, includes a risk-evaluation template that helps managers assess nine categories of risk. These risk categories include customer satisfaction and the value of proprietary assets at risk, such as market, credit, and operating risks. Access to all of this information will help managers in Schwab's Integrated Consulting and Audit Department become more productive and expert in their ability to perform risk analysis for the company. Another area of the SMART application called Virtual Training provides departmental news and information and introduces new employees to company policies and procedures.

Schwab now lets managers and other employees use The Sabre Group's Internet-based Travel Planner to book their travel reservations themselves. Travel Planner incorporates Schwab's travel rules and special business rates it has negotiated with airlines and hotels. Schwab employees make reservations and order tickets on-line. They charge expenses using Diners Club cards, and they can download expense information automatically into an electronic expense form. They then fill out the form, typing in items for which they have paid cash. Managers can review and approve these expense reports on-line, and the company electronically reimburses the credit card company and the employees. The system provides summary reports to help managers analyze companywide travel activity. Employees save time by doing all their travel booking themselves.

The application's summary reports help Schwab monitor its travel expenses and negotiate better deals with vendors. Schwab also achieves better discounts on travel by using the electronic ticketing capabilities of this system.

Unlike consumer-oriented Internet travel sites such as Microsoft's Expedia or Sabre's Travelocity, Internet systems for corporate travel allow companies to enforce their travel policies, such as preferred airlines or hotels with which they have negotiated discounted rates.

By using the Internet for travel planning, Schwab has reduced travel-related telephone inquiries from 350 five-minute calls per day to 224 calls and has reduced its internal Travel Division staff from 17 to 11 employees. Savings from Travel Planner amounted to $1.6 million in 1997. Before implementing electronic travel management, Schwab paid almost 40 cents per travel mile. Now Schwab pays 20 to 21 cents per mile. Other companies in the San Francisco area, where Schwab is headquartered, pay an average of 32 to 34 cents per mile.

To Think About: ***How has the Internet helped Schwab's managers manage? What managerial roles do the systems described here support?***

Sources: Carol Sliwa, "Schwab Saves with 'Net Travel Planning,' " *Computerworld,* April 13, 1998, and Laura DiDio, "Schwab Gets SMART with Reporting App," *Computerworld,* January 26, 1998.

decisional roles Mintzberg's classification for managerial roles where managers initiate activities, handle disturbances, allocate resources, and negotiate conflicts.

DECISIONAL ROLES. Managers make decisions. They act as entrepreneurs by initiating new kinds of activities; they handle disturbances arising in the organization; they allocate resources to staff members who need them; and they negotiate conflicts and mediate between conflicting groups in the organization.

The Window on Technology describes some of the ways that the Internet can support these managerial roles.

Table 3.4, based on Mintzberg's role classifications, is one look at where systems can and cannot help managers. The table shows that information systems do not yet contribute a great deal to important areas of management life. These areas will provide great opportunities for future systems efforts.

A corporate chief executive learns how to use a computer. Many senior managers lack computer knowledge or experience and require systems that are extremely easy to use.

TABLE 3.4 Managerial Roles and Supporting Information Systems

Role	Behavior	Support Systems
Interpersonal Roles		
Figurehead		→ None exist
Leader	Interpersonal	→ None exist
Liaison		→ Electronic communication systems
Informational Roles		
Nerve center		→ Management information systems, executive support systems
Disseminator	Information	→ Mail, office systems
Spokesperson	processing	→ Office and professional systems Workstations
Decisional Roles		
Entrepreneur		→ None exist
Disturbance handler	Decision	→ None exist
Resource allocator	making	→ DSS
Negotiator		→ None exist

Source: Authors and Henry Mintzberg, "Managerial Work: Analysis from Observation," *Management Science* 18 (October 1971).

3.4 MANAGERS AND DECISION MAKING

Decision making remains one of the more challenging roles of a manager. Information systems have helped managers communicate and distribute information; however, they have provided only limited assistance for management decision making. Because decision making is an area that system designers have sought most of all to affect (with mixed success), we now turn our attention to this issue.

strategic decision making Determining the long-term objectives, resources, and policies of an organization.

management control Monitoring how efficiently or effectively resources are utilized and how well operational units are performing.

The Process of Decision Making

Decision making can be classified by organizational level, corresponding to the strategic, management, knowledge, and operational levels of the organization introduced in Chapter 2. **Strategic decision making** determines the objectives, resources, and policies of the organization. Decision making for **management control** is principally concerned with how efficiently and effectively resources are used and how well operational units are performing.

operational control Deciding how to carry out specific tasks specified by upper and middle management and establishing criteria for completion and resource allocation.

knowledge-level decision making Evaluating new ideas for products, services, ways to communicate new knowledge, and ways to distribute information throughout the organization.

unstructured decisions Nonroutine decisions in which the decision maker must provide judgment, evaluation, and insights into the problem definition; there is no agreed-upon procedure for making such decisions.

Operational control decision making determines how to carry out the specific tasks set forth by strategic and middle-management decision makers. **Knowledge-level decision making** deals with evaluating new ideas for products and services, ways to communicate new knowledge, and ways to distribute information throughout the organization.

Within each of these levels of decision making, researchers classify decisions as *structured* and *unstructured,* as we do in this book. **Unstructured decisions** are those in which the decision maker must provide judgment, evaluation, and insights into the problem definition. Each of these decisions are novel, important, and nonroutine, and there is no well-understood or agreed-upon procedure for making them (Gorry and Scott-Morton, 1971). **Structured decisions,** by contrast, are repetitive and routine and involve a definite procedure for handling them so that they do not have to be treated each time as if they were new. Some decisions are semistructured; in such cases, only part of the problem has a clear-cut answer provided by an accepted procedure.

Combining these two views of decision making produces the grid shown in Figure 3.12. In general, operational control personnel face fairly well-structured problems. In contrast, strategic planners tackle highly unstructured problems. Many of the problems encountered by knowledge workers are fairly unstructured as well. Nevertheless, each level of the organization contains both structured and unstructured problems.

Stages of Decision Making

Making decisions consists of several different activities. Simon (1960) described four different stages in decision making: intelligence, design, choice, and implementation.

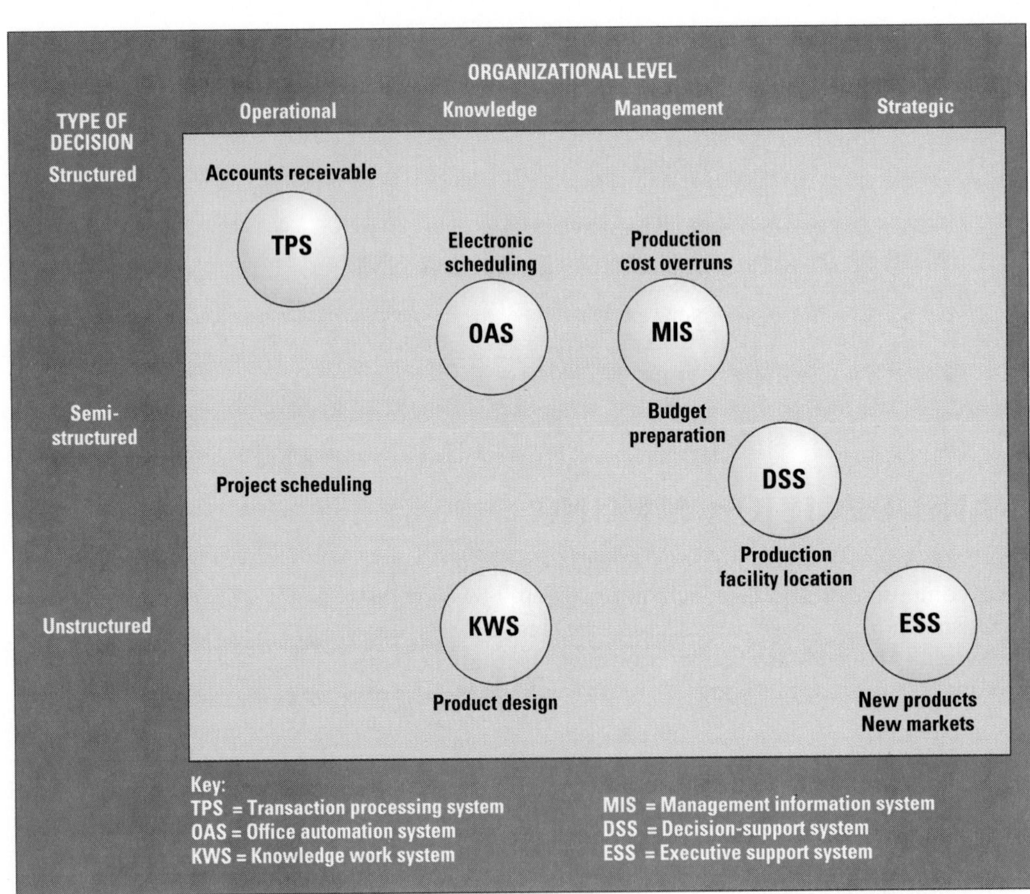

FIGURE 3.12 Different kinds of information systems at the various organization levels support different types of decisions.

Intelligence consists of *identifying and understanding* the problems occurring in the organization—why the problem, where, and with what effects. Traditional MIS systems that deliver a wide variety of detailed information can help identify problems, especially if the systems report exceptions.

During solution **design**, the individual *designs* possible solutions to the problems. Smaller DSS systems are ideal in this stage of decision making because they operate on simple models, can be developed quickly, and can be operated with limited data.

Choice consists of *choosing* among solution alternatives. Here the decision maker might need a larger DSS system to develop more extensive data on a variety of alternatives and complex models or data analysis tools to account for all of the costs, consequences, and opportunities.

During solution **implementation,** when the decision is put into effect, managers can use a reporting system that delivers routine reports on the progress of a specific solution. Support systems can range from full-blown MIS systems to much smaller systems, as well as project-planning software operating on personal computers.

In general, the stages of decision making do not necessarily follow a linear path. Think again about the decision you made to attend a *specific* college. At any point in the decision-making process, you may have to loop back to a previous stage (see Figure 3.13). For instance, one can often come up with several designs but may not be certain about whether a specific design meets the requirements for the particular problem. This situation requires additional intelligence work. Alternatively, one can be in the process of implementing a decision, only to discover that it is not working. In such a case, one is forced to repeat the design or choice stage.

structured decisions Decisions that are repetitive, routine, and have a definite procedure for handling them.

intelligence The first of Simon's four stages of decision making, when the individual collects information to identify problems occurring in the organization.

design Simon's second stage of decision making, when the individual conceives of possible alternative solutions to a problem.

choice Simon's third stage of decision making, when the individual selects among the various solution alternatives.

implementation Simon's final stage of decision making, when the individual puts the decision into effect and reports on the progress of the solution.

Individual Models of Decision Making

A number of models attempt to describe how people make decisions. Some of these models focus on individual decision making, whereas others focus on decision making in groups.

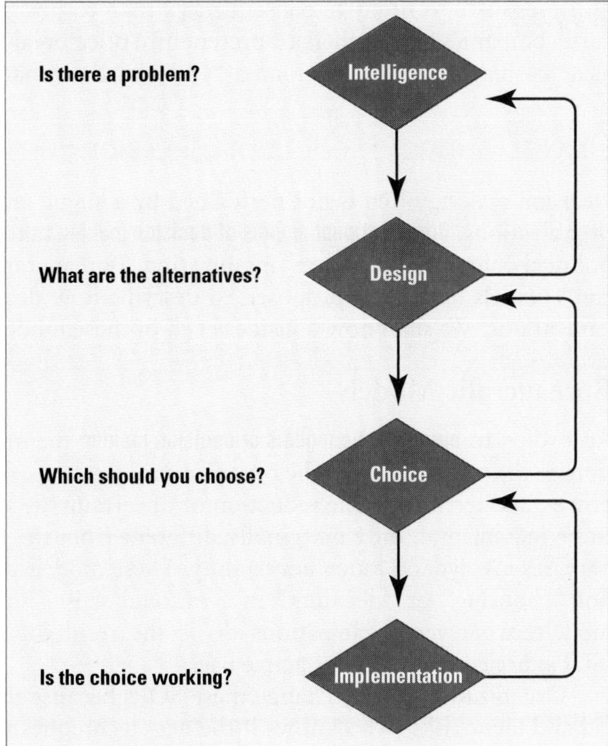

FIGURE 3.13

The decision-making process. Decisions are often arrived at after a series of iterations and evaluations at each stage in the process. The decision maker often must loop back through one or more of the stages before completing the process.

rational model Model of human behavior based on the belief that people, organizations, and nations engage in basically consistent, value-maximizing calculations or adaptations within certain constraints.

The basic assumption behind individual models of decision making is that human beings are in some sense rational. The **rational model** of human behavior is built on the idea that people engage in basically consistent, rational, value-maximizing calculations. Under this model, an individual identifies goals, ranks all possible alternative actions by their contributions to those goals, and chooses the alternative that contributes most to those goals.

Criticisms of this model show that in fact people cannot specify all of the alternatives, and that most individuals do not have singular goals and so are unable to rank all alternatives and consequences. Many decisions are so complex that calculating the choice (even if done by computer) is virtually impossible. One modification to the rational model states that instead of searching through all alternatives, people actually choose the first available alternative that moves them toward their ultimate goal. Another modification alters the rational model by suggesting that in making policy decisions, people choose policies most like the previous policy (Lindblom, 1959). Finally, some scholars point out that people do not make choices, but that decision making is a continuous process in which final decisions are always being modified.

cognitive style Underlying personality dispositions toward the treatment of information, selection of alternatives, and evaluation of consequences.

systematic decision makers Cognitive style that describes people who approach a problem by structuring it in terms of some formal method.

intuitive decision makers Cognitive style that describes people who approach a problem with multiple methods in an unstructured manner, using trial and error to find a solution.

Modern psychology has further qualified the rational model by research that finds that humans differ *in how they maximize their values* and in the *frames of reference* they use to interpret information and make choices. **Cognitive style** describes underlying personality dispositions toward the treatment of information, the selection of alternatives, and the evaluation of consequences. McKenney and Keen (1974) described two decision-making cognitive styles: systematic versus intuitive types. **Systematic decision makers** approach a problem by structuring it in terms of some formal method. They evaluate and gather information in terms of their structured method. **Intuitive decision makers** approach a problem with multiple methods, using trial and error to find a solution. They tend not to structure information gathering or evaluation. Neither style is considered superior to the other. There are different ways of being rational.

More recent psychological research shows that humans have built-in biases that can distort decision making. People can be manipulated into choosing alternatives that they might otherwise reject simply by changing the *frame of reference.* One example can be found in the research of Tversky and Kahneman (1981), who found that people are more sensitive to negative consequences than to positive ones. For this reason, credit card companies ask retailers to present any price break given to customers paying cash as a "cash discount" rather than a "credit card surcharge."

Organizational Models of Decision Making

organizational models of decision making Models of decision making that take into account the structural and political characteristics of an organization.

Decision making often is not performed by a single individual but by entire groups or organizations. **Organizational models of decision making** take into account the structural and political characteristics of an organization. Bureaucratic, political, and even "garbage can" models have been proposed to describe how decision making takes place in organizations. We shall now consider each of these models.

Bureaucratic Models

bureaucratic models of decision making Models of decision making where decisions are shaped by the organization's standard operating procedures (SOPs).

According to **bureaucratic models of decision making** the most important goal of organizations is the preservation of the organization itself (i.e., the maintenance of budget, manpower, and territory). The reduction of uncertainty is another major goal. Policy tends to be incremental, only marginally different from the past, because radical policy departures involve too much uncertainty. These models depict organizations generally as not "choosing" or "deciding" in a rational sense. Rather, according to bureaucratic models, whatever organizations do is the result of standard operating procedures (SOPs) honed over years of active use.

Organizations rarely change these SOPs because they may have to change personnel and incur risks (who knows if the new techniques work better than the old ones?). Although senior management and leaders are hired to coordinate and lead the organization, they are effectively trapped by the organization's standard solutions. As President John F. Kennedy discovered during the 1962 Cuban missile crisis, his actions were largely constrained not by his imagination but by what his naval commanders were trained to do (Allison, 1971).

Some organizations do, of course, change; they learn new ways of behaving; and they can be led. But all of these changes require a long time. Look around and you will find many organizations doing pretty much what they did 10, 20, or even 30 years ago.

Political Models of Organizational Choice

Power in organizations is shared; even the lowest-level workers have some power. At the top, power is concentrated in the hands of a few. For many reasons, leaders differ in their opinions about what the organization should do, and, as we made clear earlier in this chapter, these differences do matter.

Each individual in an organization, especially at the top, is a key player in the game of politics. In **political models of decision making**, what an organization does is a result of political bargains struck among key leaders and interest groups. Organizations do not come up with "solutions" that are "chosen" to solve some "problem." They come up with compromises that reflect the conflicts, the major stakeholders, the diverse interests, the unequal power, and the confusion that constitute politics.

political models of decision making Models of decision making where decisions result from competition and bargaining among the organization's interest groups and key leaders.

"Garbage Can" Model

A relatively new theory of decision making, called the **"garbage can" model**, states that organizations are not rational. Decision making is largely accidental and is the product of a stream of solutions, problems, and situations that are randomly associated.

"garbage can" model Model of decision making that states that organizations are not rational and that decisions are solutions that become attached to problems for accidental reasons.

If this model is correct, it should not be surprising that the wrong solutions are applied to the wrong problems in an organization or that, over time, a large number of organizations make critical mistakes that lead to their demise. The Exxon Corporation's delayed response to the 1989 Alaska oil spill is an example. Within an hour after the Exxon tanker *Valdez* ran aground in Alaska's Prince William Sound on March 29, 1989, workers were preparing emergency equipment; however, the aid was not dispatched. Instead of sending out emergency crews, the Alyeska Pipeline Service Company (which was responsible for initially responding to oil spill emergencies) sent the crews home. The first full emergency crew did not arrive at the spill site until at least 14 hours after the shipwreck, by which time the oil had spread beyond effective control. Yet enough equipment and personnel had been available to respond effectively. Much of the 10 million gallons of oil fouling the Alaska shoreline in the worst tanker spill in American history could have been confined had Alyeska acted more decisively (Malcolm, 1989).

Implications for System Design

The research on decision making shows that it is not a simple process even in the rational individual model. Decision situations differ from one another in terms of the clarity of goals, the types of decision makers present, the amount of agreement among them, and the frames of reference brought to a decision-making situation. Information systems do not make the decision for humans but rather support the decision-making process. How this is done will depend on the types of decisions, decision makers, and frames of reference.

Research on organizational decision making should alert students of information systems to the fact that decision making in a business is a group and organizational process. Systems must be built to support group and organizational decision making. Moreover, systems must do more than merely promote decision making. They must also make individual managers better managers of existing routines, better players in the bureaucratic struggle for control of an organization's agenda, and better political players.

As a general rule, research on decision making indicates that information systems designers should design systems that have the following characteristics:

- They are flexible and provide many options for handling data and evaluating information.
- They are capable of supporting a variety of styles, skills, and knowledge.
- They are powerful in the sense of having multiple analytical and intuitive models for the evaluation of data and the ability to keep track of many alternatives and consequences.
- They reflect understanding of group and organizational processes of decision making.
- They are sensitive to the bureaucratic and political requirements of systems.

Management Wrap-Up

MANAGEMENT

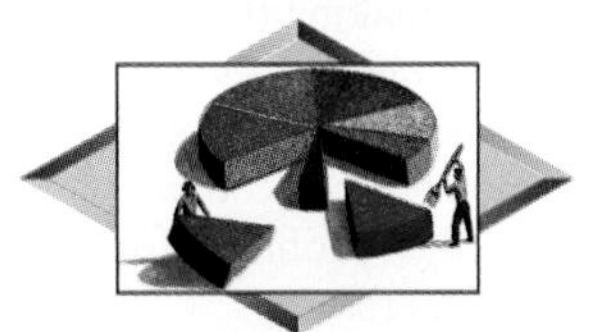

Information technology provides tools for managers to carry out both their traditional and newer roles, allowing them to monitor, plan, and forecast with more precision and speed than ever before and to respond more rapidly to the changing business environment. Managers will be required to overcome psychosocial biases and resistance to change to find meaningful ways to use the Internet and other information technologies to transform the management process.

ORGANIZATION

Each organization has a unique constellation of information systems that result from its interaction with information technology. Contemporary information technology can lead to major organizational changes—and efficiencies—by reducing transaction and agency costs, but its application in each organization will be a result of that organization's unique set of environmental and institutional factors.

TECHNOLOGY

Information technology changes far more rapidly than organizations, and for this reason, it is often a destroyer of organization competence. However, information technology offers managers new ways of organizing work that can promote organizational survival and prosperity. Managers have to keep a keen eye on changes in information technology in order to avoid losing organizational competencies, and in order to exploit the opportunities provided by new technology.

For Discussion:

1. It has been said that implementation of a new information system is always more difficult than anticipated. As an example, discuss some of the difficulties that might arise in developing a corporate Internet application that allowed customers to order products directly instead of working through the direct sales force or the retailers who traditionally carried your products.
2. How has the Internet changed the management process?

SUMMARY

1. **Identify the salient characteristics of organizations.** All modern organizations are hierarchical, specialized, and impartial. They use explicit standard operating procedures to maximize efficiency. All organizations have their own culture and politics arising from differences in interest groups. Organizations differ in goals, groups served, social roles, leadership styles, incentives, surrounding environments, and types of tasks performed. These differences create varying types of organizational structures.

2. **Analyze the relationship between information systems and organizations.** The impact of information systems on organizations is not unidirectional. Information systems and the organizations in which they are used interact with and influence each other. The introduction of a new information system will affect organizational structure, goals, work design, values, competition between interest groups, decision making, and day-to-day behavior. At the same time, information systems must be designed to serve the needs of important organizational groups and will be shaped by the structure, tasks, goals, culture, politics, and management of the organization. The power of information systems to transform organizations radically by flattening organizational hierarchies has not yet been demonstrated for all types of organizations. The Internet has a potentially large impact on organizational structure and business processes because it can dramatically reduce transaction and agency costs.

3. **Contrast the classical and contemporary models of managerial activities and roles.** Early classical models of management stressed the functions of planning, organizing, coordinating, deciding, and controlling. Contemporary research has examined the actual behavior of managers to show how managers get things done.

   Mintzberg found that managers' real activities are highly fragmented, variegated, and brief in duration, with managers moving rapidly and intensely from one issue to another. Other behavioral research has found that managers spend considerable time pursuing personal agendas and goals and that contemporary managers shy away from making grand, sweeping policy decisions.

4. **Describe how managers make decisions in organizations.** Decisions can be structured, semistructured, or unstructured, with structured decisions clustering at the operational level of the organization and unstructured decisions at the strategic planning level. The nature and level of decision making are important factors in building information systems for managers.

   Decision making itself is a complex activity at both the individual and the organizational level. Individual models of decision making assume that human beings can accurately choose alternatives and consequences based on the priority of their objectives and goals. The rigorous rational model of individual decision making has been modified by behavioral research that suggests that rationality is limited. People select alternatives biased by their cognitive style and frame of reference. Organizational models of decision making illustrate that real decision making in organizations takes place in arenas where many psychological, political, and bureaucratic forces are at work. Thus, organizational decision making may not necessarily be rational.

5. **Assess the implications of the relationship between information systems, organizations, and management decision making for the design and implementation of information systems.** Salient features of organizations that must be addressed by information systems include organizational levels, organizational structures, types of tasks and decisions, the nature of management support, and the sentiments and attitudes of workers who will be using the system. The organization's history and external environment must be considered as well.

   Implementation of a new information system is often more difficult than anticipated because of organizational change requirements. Because information systems potentially change important organizational dimensions, including the structure, culture, power relationships, and work activities, there is often considerable resistance to new systems.

   If information systems are built properly, they can support individual and organizational decision making. Up to now, information systems have been most helpful to managers for performing informational and decisional roles; the same systems have been of very limited value for managers' interpersonal roles. Information systems that are less formal and highly flexible will be more useful than large, formal systems at higher levels of the organization.

   Information systems can best support managers and decision making if such systems are flexible, with multiple analytical and intuitive models for evaluating data and the capability of supporting a variety of styles, skills, and knowledge.

KEY TERMS

Agency theory, 84
Behavioral models, 89
Bureaucracy, 74
Bureaucratic models of decision making, 94
Business processes, 77
Chief information officer (CIO), 82
Choice, 93
Classical model of management, 88
Cognitive style, 94
Decisional roles, 90
Design, 93
End users, 82
Environmental factors, 83
"Garbage can" model, 95
Implementation, 93
Information systems department, 82
Information systems managers, 82
Informational roles, 89
Institutional factors, 83
Intelligence, 93
Interpersonal roles, 89
Intuitive decision makers, 94
Knowledge-level decision making, 92
Management control, 91
Managerial roles, 89
Operational control, 92
Organization, 71
Organizational culture, 75
Organizational models of decision making, 94
Political models of decision making, 95
Programmers, 82
Rational model, 94
Standard operating procedures (SOPs), 74
Strategic decision making, 91
Structured decisions, 93
Systematic decision makers, 94
Systems analysts, 82
Transaction cost theory, 84
Unstructured decisions, 92

REVIEW QUESTIONS

1. What is an organization? How do organizations use information?
2. Compare the technical definition of organizations with the behavioral definition.
3. What features do all organizations have in common?
4. In what ways can organizations differ?
5. How have the roles of information systems and information systems specialists changed in organizations?
6. Describe the two factors that explain why organizations adopt information systems.
7. Describe the major economic theories that help explain how information systems affect organizations.
8. Describe the major behavioral theories that help explain how information systems affect organizations.
9. Why is there considerable organizational resistance to the introduction of information systems?
10. What are the five functions of managers described in the classical model?
11. Behavioral research has identified five characteristics of the modern manager. How do these characteristics relate to the classical model?
12. What specific managerial roles can information systems support? Where are information systems particularly strong in supporting managers, and where are they weak?
13. Define structured and unstructured decisions. Give three examples of each.
14. What are the four stages of decision making described by Simon?
15. Describe each of the organizational choice models. How would the design of systems be affected by the choice of model employed?
16. What is the impact of the Internet on organizations and the process of management?

GROUP PROJECT

With a group of three or four students, select a company described in *The Wall Street Journal, Forbes,* or another business publication. Visit the Web site of that company to find out additional information about that company and to see how the firm is using the Web. On the basis of this information, describe some of the features of this organization, such as important business processes, culture, structure, and environment. Assess the impact of this Web site on the organization. Is the Web site helping the company reduce transaction costs? What impact is it having, if any, on the firm's business processes? Present your findings to the class.

TOOLS FOR INTERACTIVE LEARNING

■ **INTERNET**: The Internet Connection for this chapter will take you to Application Demos on the Netscape Web site, where you can view interactive demonstrations of an intranet. You can complete an exercise to evaluate how companies can use intranets to reduce agency costs and make the management process more efficient. You can also use the Interactive Study Guide to test your knowledge of the topics in this chapter and get instant feedback when you need more practice.

■ **CD-ROM**: If you purchase and use the Multimedia Edition CD-ROM with this chapter, you will find two interactive exercises. The first asks you to analyze the work groups for dealing with several organizational problems, and the second asks you to apply the correct model of organizational decision making to solve another set of problems. You can also find a video clip illustrating the role of information systems in Schneider National's organization, an audio overview of the major themes of this chapter, and bullet text summarizing the key points of the chapter.

CASE STUDY

Greyhound Seeks Salvation in a Strategic Reservation System

Greyhound Lines, Inc., headquartered in Dallas, Texas, has long been the leading transcontinental bus company in the United States. However, the company share of interstate travel dropped from 30 percent in 1960 to 6 percent in the late 1980s, due to the rise in ownership of automobiles and discount airline service. The following chronology lists events that appear to be relevant to Greyhound's problems.

July 1991

- Frank Schmieder becomes Greyhound chief executive. Schmieder gains a reputation as an intelligent though volatile boss. Union negotiators find him to be affable and are pleased that he occasionally rides the bus.
- Michael Doyle, a former financial officer at Phillips Petroleum Co., becomes chief financial officer and works closely with Schmieder to run Greyhound.

August 1991

- Schmieder begins to cut costs, upgrade buses and facilities, and settle labor disputes. Policies of Schmieder and Doyle include cutting the bus fleet from 3700 to 2400 and replacing current regional executives. They also replace most terminal workers with part-time workers who are paid about $6 an hour, whether they sweep floors or serve customers. These part-time workers are offered little opportunity to get a raise. During the next three years, annual staff turnover of 30 percent becomes common, with some terminals reaching 100 percent.

October 1991

- The Greyhound business plan includes a commitment to a computerized reservation system that financial market analysts focus on as the key to a revitalized Greyhound. The plan includes system support for more efficient use of buses and drivers.

Bus customers traditionally do not reserve seats in advance but rather arrive at the terminal, buy a ticket, and take the next bus. Few buses ever reserve seats. The primary use of bus customer telephone lines has been to disseminate schedule information, not for reserving seats as in the airline industry. Traditionally, clerks plotted journeys manually from thick schedule log books; Greyhound buses stop in several thousand towns in the United States. The process was very slow. Computerizing all of the routes and stops would theoretically greatly reduce the time needed to plot journeys and issue tickets. The goals of an automated system were not only to speed the issuing of tickets, thereby reducing company service-counter costs, but also to improve customer service and customer relations.

The company had to manage several thousand buses and their drivers nationwide, making certain they were in the right locations at the right times. Greyhound assigned buses and bus drivers by hand, using data that were usually months old. The company kept buses and drivers in reserve in order to meet peak-period demand, thereby enabling the company to remain the premier continent-wide bus company.

The new system, called Trips, was to handle both reservations and bus and driver allocations because they were seen as tightly linked. The traditional bus strategy of no reservations, just walk-in riders meant that many times buses departed nearly empty. Management hoped that adopting a reservation approach would allow them to reduce the number of near-empty buses. They also expected that the reservation portion of the system would provide Greyhound with reliable readership data so schedules could be more efficiently organized and so planners could determine where and when to reduce prices in order to fill seats. The plan for Trips was received very positively in financial markets, giving Greyhound the ability to borrow funds and offer new stock shares to raise capital.

Early Spring 1992

- The Trips project begins with staff of about 40 and a $6 million budget. Thomas Thompson, Greyhound senior vice president for network planning and operations, is placed in charge of Trips development.

A bus reservation system, by the nature of the operation of buses, is far more complex than airline reservation systems. A passenger may make one or two stops on an airline flight across the United States, whereas bus passengers may make scores of stops on a cross-country trip. Greyhound technicians estimated that a bus management system would need to manage 10 times the number of daily vehicle stops as an airline vehicle-management system.

The average bus passenger also differs from the average airline passenger. Several Greyhound executives later claimed to have raised the questions of how many bus passengers would have credit cards to enable them to purchase tickets in advance by telephone, and even how many have telephones available. American Airlines' SABRE reservation system required three years to develop, at a cost of several hundred million dollars, and the project included a staff many times the size of the Trips staff.

November–December 1992

- Greyhound stock price reaches $13.50.
- Greyhound management actively promotes Trips to investors, lenders, and security analysts as a key to the future success of Greyhound. Management publicly promises to launch the system in time for the 1993 summer busy season.

The first version of Trips had been developed by a consulting firm. Planned users of the system, such as ticket clerks, required 40 hours of training to learn it. Clerks had to deal with many screens in order to plot a trip between any two points. The system data bank was incomplete so clerks often had to pull out the log books and revert to plotting a ticket purchaser's planned trip manually. Clerk time to issue tickets doubled when they used the system. The system also crashed repeatedly.

Thompson decided to redesign the system and introduce it in the Northeast corridor in the spring of 1993. After that initial introduction, no new sites would be added until the autumn of 1993, when the busiest travel season would be behind Greyhound. This approach would also give the team time to work out the bugs before the system was introduced nationally.

- Greyhound reports a profit of $11 million, its first profit since 1989.

May 1993

- Rollout of Trips begins, using the failed version because Thompson did not have enough time to develop the new version. When Trips reaches 50 locations, the computer terminals begin to freeze unpredictably.
- Greyhound stock hits a post Chapter 11 high of $22.75. Securities analysts have been praising Greyhound management for reengineering the company and for cutting costs.

June 1993

- The rollout of Trips continues.
- Doyle exercises an option to purchase 15,000 shares of Greyhound stock at $9.81.
- Greyhound stock holds above $20 as formal introduction of Trips nears.
- Doyle exercises options on 22,642 shares at $9.81 and immediately sells them at a profit of $179,000.
- A new 800 customer-service telephone number begins operating, replacing previous customer-information telephone systems; in Omaha, Nebraska, 400 operators answer the calls. The average number of calls per day prior to the new system is 60,000.

July 1993

- The toll-free telephone system begins serving the 220 terminals already hooked up to Trips for making reservations; over the past month calls have risen to an estimated 800,000 per day.

The system could not handle all the calls, with many customers receiving busy signals. Customers often had to call up to a dozen times to get through. The busy signals were caused by the switching mechanism and the slow response time of Trips. The computer in Dallas sometimes took as long as 45 seconds to respond to a single keystroke and could take up to five minutes to print a ticket. The system also crashed numerous times, causing tickets to be written manually.

At some bus terminals, the passengers who arrived with manual tickets were told to wait in line so they could be reissued a ticket by the computer. Long lines, delays, and confusion resulted. Many passengers missed their connections; others lost their luggage.

- On the same day as the initiation of the telephone system, Greyhound announces an increase in earnings per share and ridership and the introduction of a new discount-fare program; Greyhound stock rises 4.5 percent.

August 1993

- Doyle sells 15,000 shares of stock at $21.75 on August 4. Two other Greyhound vice presidents sell a total of 21,300 shares of stock.

September 1993

- Trips is closed down west of the Mississippi River because of its continuing problems and delays. No reports have appeared yet in the press of the Greyhound problems.
- On September 23, Greyhound announces ridership down by 12 percent in August and earnings also down; the press release does not mention Trips and blames the fall in ridership on the national economic environment.
- Greyhound stock, which was down 12 percent in August, falls to $11.75, or 24 percent, in one day.
- Thompson is relieved of his duties on Trips; another vice president takes over responsibility.

May 1994

- The company offers a $68 ticket for a trip anywhere in the United States with a three-day advance purchase. The crush of potential customers trying to take advantage of the offer brings Trips to a halt. Buses and drivers are not available in some cities, resulting in large numbers of frustrated passengers stranded in terminals.

July 1994

- On-time bus performance falls to 59 percent versus 81 percent at its peak.
- First-half operating revenues fall 12.6 percent, accompanied by a large drop-off in ridership; the nine largest regional carriers in the United States show an average rise in operating revenue of 2.6 percent.

August 1994

- Schmieder and Doyle resign.
- Thomas G. Plaskett, a 50-year-old Greyhound director, is appointed interim CEO; Plaskett was the chairman and CEO of Pan Am Corporation.

November 1994

- Greyhound creditors file suit to attempt to force Greyhound back into protection under Chapter 11 of the Federal Bankruptcy Act.
- Greyhound stock falls to $1.875 per share.
- Greyhound announces its fourth consecutive quarterly loss.
- A financial restructuring agreement is reached that gives creditors 45 percent ownership of Greyhound. The agreement allows the company to avoid Chapter 11 bankruptcy.
- Craig Lentzsch is appointed Greyhound's new permanent CEO.

January 1995

- Greyhound announces the Securities and Exchange Commission is investigating the company and former directors, officers, and employees for possible securities law violations. The investigation is examining possible insider trading, the adequacy of the firm's internal accounting procedures, and the adequacy of public disclosures related to the Trips system and the company's disappointing earnings in 1993. Greyhound says that it does not believe it has violated any securities laws and is cooperating fully. In addition to the SEC investigation, Greyhound is facing a raft of investors' lawsuits involving similar allegations and a Justice Department antitrust investigation into its terminal agreements with smaller carriers.

Lentzsch instituted a "back to basics" policy that unravelled many of his predecessors' strategies. He dismantled the "airline" model that relied on reservations. Greyhound today does not take reservations. If a bus fills up with passengers, Greyhound will roll out another until everyone has a seat. Lentzsch then changed the company's pricing structure. Schmieder had raised the walk-up prices as high as possible while lowering prices of advance-purchase tickets to compete with the airlines. Lentzsch realized Greyhound's core customers wanted low-cost, no-frills travel above all. Today Greyhound's maximum one-way walk-up fare averages half of airline discount-ticket prices.

Other steps toward profitability included adding more people to answer telephones and staff terminals, adding more buses to popular routes, such as New York to Boston, and restoring routes to long-haul areas that Schmieder had nearly abandoned. Greyhound's earnings have continued to improve. Passenger-ticket sales have increased for 34 months in a row, with ridership so strong that the company has been able to raise its average ticket price by 6.5 percent.

But challenges remain. Greyhound still shoulders $208 million in long-term debt. Greyhound will need to maintain good labor relations and continue improving its ridership and finances if it is to survive.

Sources: Robert Tomsho, "Greyhound Drives Down New Road in Quest of Success," *The Wall Street Journal,* February 25, 1998, and "How Greyhound Lines Re-Engineered Itself Right into a Deep Hole," *The Wall Street Journal,* October 20, 1994; and Wendy Zellner, "Leave the Driving to Lentzsch," *Business Week,* March 18, 1996.

Case Study Questions

1. What was Greyhound's business strategy? How were its business processes related to that strategy?
2. How compatible was Trips with Greyhound's business processes and other organizational features?
3. What management, organization, and technology factors contributed to Greyhound's problems?
4. If you were a Greyhound manager, what solutions would you recommend? Would you suggest new business processes or information systems applications? If so, what would they do?
5. Does this case raise any ethical issues? If so, describe them.

CHAPTER 4

Ethical and Social Impact of Information Systems

chapter outline

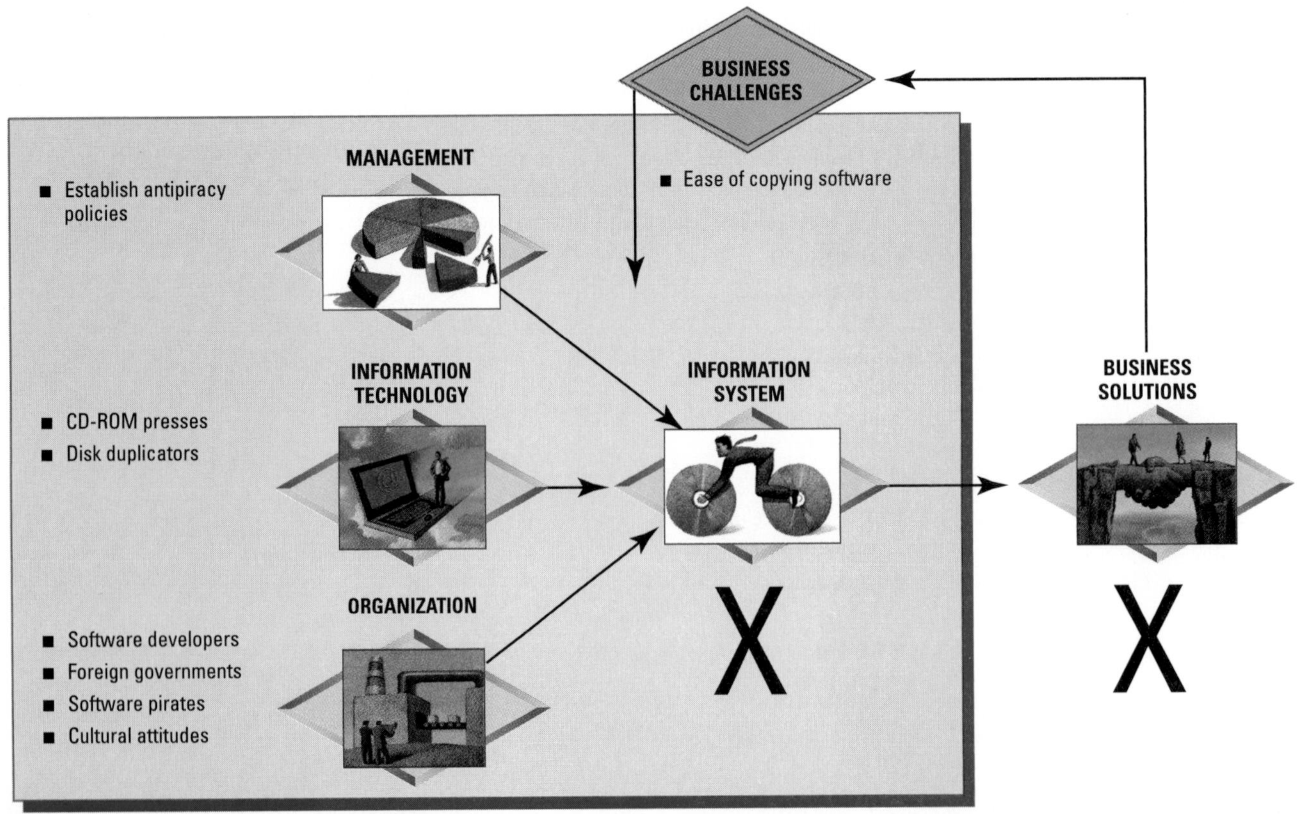

Software Piracy Is Big Business

Almost everyone has been tempted to copy software. You might be low on funds. You might be too pressed for time to go out and buy a copy for yourself. Your manager might tell you to buy one copy of a product for your department and make copies to keep costs down. Many people copy the software and keep on working without a second thought, even though it's illegal.

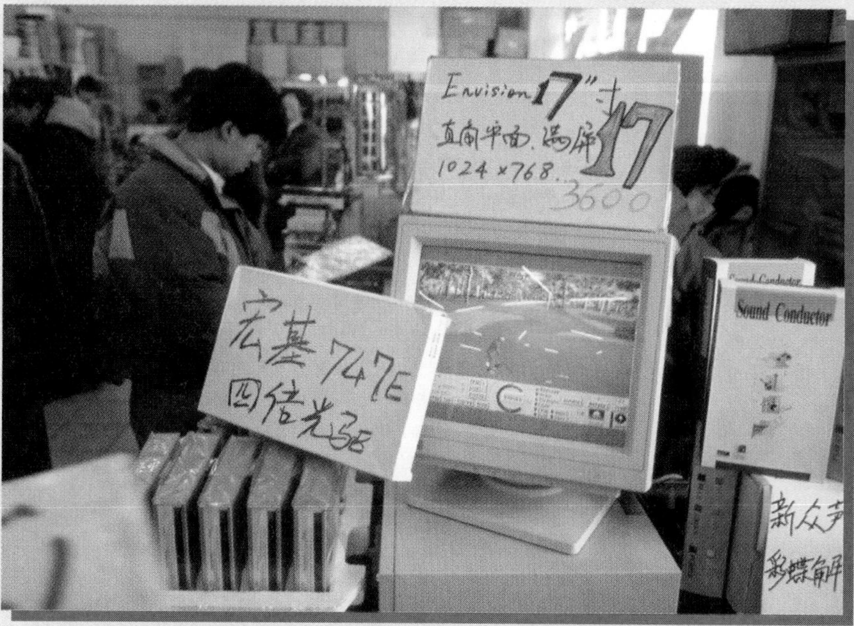

What would happen if everyone around the world copied the software they used? For one thing, they would be cheating software developers out of billions of dollars. In 1997, software piracy around the world created losses of over $11.4 billion, an amount exceeding the combined revenues of the ten largest PC software companies. And in some countries, software piracy is big business. In China, Russia, the Philippines, and El Salvador, more than 90 percent of the software in use was copied illegally. These are some key findings of a study released by the Software Publishers Association (SPA) and the Business Software Alliance. The SPA is the principal trade association of the desktop software industry and is active in protecting intellectual property rights around the world.

On another occasion, the SPA noted in its annual "Special 301" review of unfair international trade practices for the U.S. Trade Representative (USTR) that Indonesia and Vietnam have piracy rates of 98 percent. The SPA called them "one-copy" countries, where the entire country's demand could be satisfied by copying a single, legitimate piece of software.

SPA credited the Chinese government with raiding pirate CD-ROM factories and with trying to establish a software title verification program to deter them. Nevertheless, the software piracy rate in China remains 95 percent, virtually unchanged. The SPA applauded the raids reported by the Chinese government but noted that there were no reports indicating fines or prison sentences for the offenders, nor were there any indications that the pirated software was taken off the market.

Enforcement of antipiracy laws in Russia is impeded by the weakness of the country's police and court system. Despite a new criminal code, criminal penalties remain low. A huge "installed base" of pirated software cannot be eradicated because software created by U.S. authors before 1993 is unprotected by copyright.

Unlike most other Latin American countries, Argentina doesn't offer legal protection for software. Software makers believe that royalties are not paid on approximately 71 percent of the software sold in Argentina, resulting in $165 million in revenue lost annually. Most of the pirated software consists of easy-to-copy programs such as Microsoft Word. A Price Waterhouse & Co. study concluded that the biggest abusers are small private companies and Argentine federal and local government agencies. According to Claudia Segovia, president of the local unit of Unisys, "there's no culture in Argentina of assigning value to software." A February 1998 Argentine Supreme Court decision upheld a lower-court ruling that the country's antiquated copyright laws don't cover software.

The software piracy rate is lower in the United States. The culture respects intellectual property and there are effective enforcement mechanisms. According to Ken Wasch, president of

SPA, the only companies using illegally copied software who are unlikely to be detected "are those who have no disgruntled employees." About 95 percent of the calls SPA receives each day reporting software piracy come from current or former employees of the companies being reported.

Users are hurt by software piracy as well as the software developers because they pay higher prices to offset the losses. If piracy could be curbed, many software firms would have the resources to invest more in research and development to improve their products. Large software companies can survive piracy, but many small firms cannot afford to lose 30 percent to 50 percent of their revenue.

Sources: "Software Piracy Up," *Computerworld,* July 20, 1998; Jonathan Friedland, "Software Makers Assail Argentine Piracy Ruling," *The Wall Street Journal,* February 6, 1998; and Software Publishers Association, "Argentina, China and Russia Among Top Priorities in SPA 'Special 301' Report," February 18, 1997.

Management Challenges

Technology can be a double-edged sword. It can be the source of many benefits. One great achievement of contemporary computer systems is the ease with which digital information can be so easily transmitted and shared among many people. But at the same time, this powerful capability creates new opportunities for breaking the law or taking benefits away from others. Copying software and other digital media is one of the compelling ethical issues raised by contemporary information systems. As you read this chapter, you should be aware of the following management challenges:

1. **Understanding the moral risks of new technology.** Rapid technological change means that the choices facing individuals also rapidly change, and the balance of risk and reward and the probabilities of apprehension for wrongful acts change as well. Software copying has emerged as a new ethical issue precisely for this reason, in addition to other issues described in this chapter. In this environment it will be important for management to conduct an ethical and social impact analysis of new technologies. One might take each of the moral dimensions described in this chapter and briefly speculate on how a new technology will impact each dimension. There will not always be right answers for how to behave but management judgment should be considered on the moral risks of new technology.
2. **Establishing corporate ethics policies that include information systems issues.** As managers you will be responsible for developing corporate ethics policies and for enforcing them and explaining them to employees. Historically the information systems area is the last to be consulted and much more attention has been paid to financial integrity and personnel policies. But from what you will know after reading this chapter, it is clear your corporation should have an ethics policy in the information systems area covering such issues as privacy, property, accountability, system quality, and quality of life. The challenge will be in educating non-IS managers to the need for these policies, as well as educating your work force.

learning objectives

After completing this chapter, you will be able to:

1. Analyze the relationship among ethical, social, and political issues raised by information systems.
2. Identify the main moral dimensions of an information society and apply them to specific situations.
3. Apply an ethical analysis to difficult situations.
4. Examine specific ethical principles for conduct.
5. Design corporate policies for ethical conduct.

Software piracy challenges traditional protections of intellectual property rights and is one of the new ethical issues raised by the widespread use of information systems. Others include establishing information rights, including the right to privacy; establishing accountability for the consequences of information systems; setting standards to safeguard system quality that protect the safety of the individual and society; and preserving values and institutions considered essential to the quality of life in an information society. This chapter describes these issues and suggests guidelines for dealing with these questions.

4.1 UNDERSTANDING ETHICAL AND SOCIAL ISSUES RELATED TO SYSTEMS

Ethics refers to the principles of right and wrong that can be used by individuals acting as free moral agents to make choices to guide their behavior. Information technology and information systems raise new ethical questions for both individuals and societies because they create opportunities for intense social change, and thus threaten existing distributions of power, money, rights, and obligations. Like other technologies, such as steam engines, electricity, telephone, and radio, information technology can be used to achieve social progress, but it can also be used to commit crimes and threaten cherished social values. The development of information technology will produce benefits for many, and costs for others. In this situation, what is the ethical and socially responsible course of action?

ethics Principles of right and wrong that can be used by individuals acting as free moral agents to make choices to guide their behavior.

A Model for Thinking about Ethical, Social, and Political Issues

Ethical, social, and political issues are of course tightly coupled together. The ethical dilemma you may face as a manager of information systems typically is reflected in social and political debate. One way to think about these relationships is given in Figure 4.1. Imagine society as a more or less calm pond on a summer day, a delicate ecosystem in partial equilibrium with individuals and with social and political institutions. Individuals know how to act in this pond because social institutions (family, education, organizations) have developed well-honed rules of behavior, and these are backed by laws developed in the political sector that prescribe behavior and promise sanctions for violations. Now toss a rock into the center of the pond. But imagine instead of a rock that the disturbing force is a powerful shock of new information technology and systems hitting a society more or less at rest. What happens? Ripples, of course.

Suddenly individual actors are confronted with new situations often not covered by the old rules. Social institutions cannot respond overnight to these ripples—it may take years to develop etiquette, expectations, social responsibility, "politically correct" attitudes, or approved rules. Political institutions also require time before developing new laws and often require the demonstration of real harm before they act. In the meantime, you may have to act. You may be forced to act in a legal "gray area."

We can use this model as a first approximation to the dynamics that connect ethical, social, and political issues. This model is also useful for identifying the main moral dimensions of the "information society," which cut across various levels of action—individual, social, and political.

Five Moral Dimensions of the Information Age

A review of the literature on ethical, social, and political issues surrounding systems identifies five moral dimensions of the information age that we introduce here and explore in greater detail in Section 4.3. The five moral dimensions are as follows:

- *Information rights and obligations:* What **information rights** do individuals and organizations possess with respect to information about themselves? What can

information rights The rights that individuals and organizations have with respect to information that pertains to themselves.

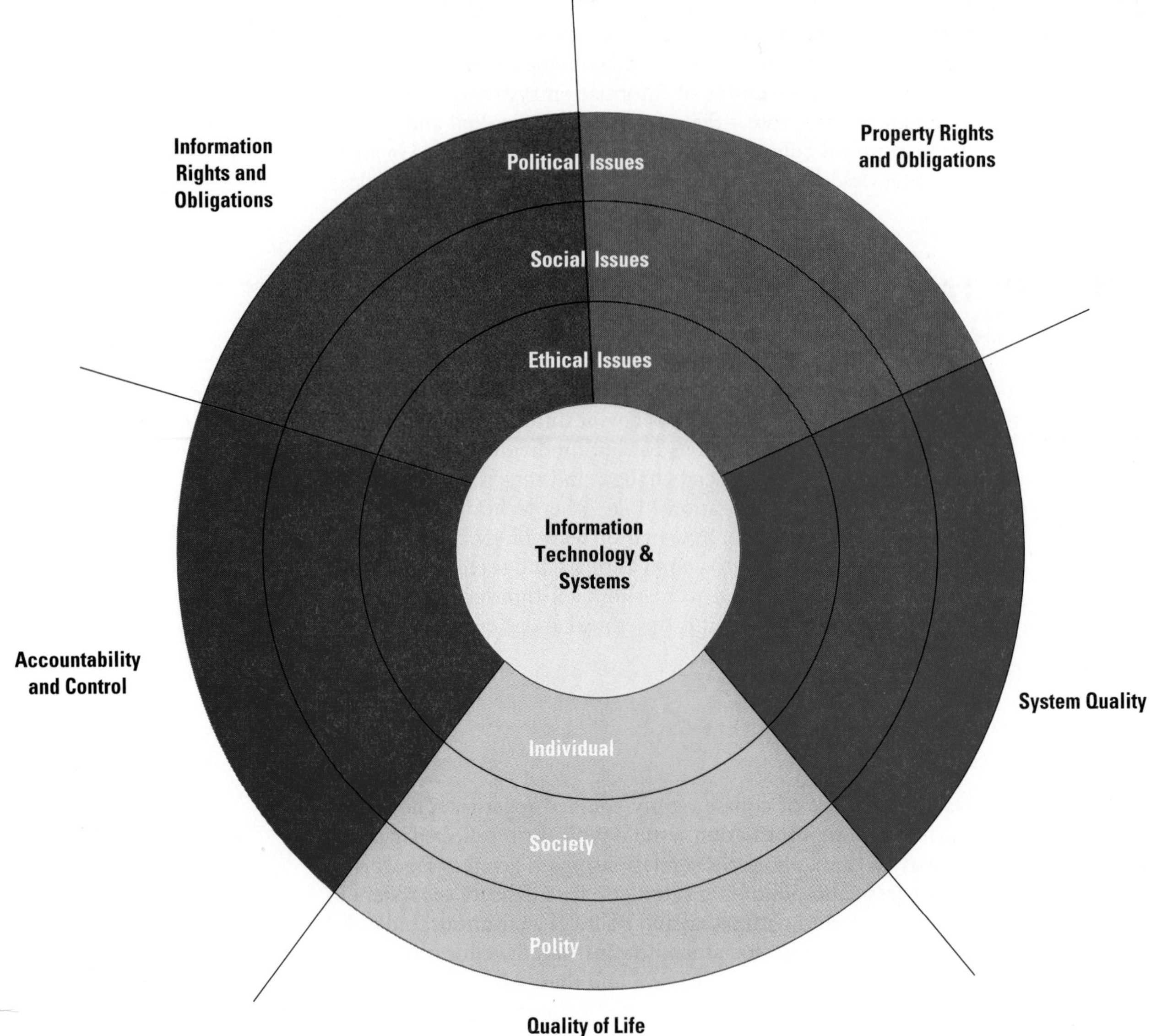

FIGURE 4.1 The relationship between ethical, social, and political issues in an information society. The introduction of new information technology has a ripple effect, raising new ethical, social, and political issues that must be dealt with on the individual, social, and political levels. These issues have five moral dimensions: information rights and obligations, property rights and obligations, system quality, quality of life, and accountability and control

they protect? What obligations do individuals and organizations have concerning this information?

- *Property rights:* How will traditional intellectual property rights be protected in a digital society in which tracing and accounting for ownership is difficult, and ignoring such property rights is so easy?
- *Accountability and control:* Who can and will be held accountable and liable for the harm done to individual and collective information and property rights?
- *System quality:* What standards of data and system quality should we demand to protect individual rights and the safety of society?
- *Quality of life:* What values should be preserved in an information- and knowledge-based society? What institutions should we protect from violation? What cultural values and practices are supported by the new information technology?

Before we analyze these dimensions let us briefly review the major technology and system trends that have heightened concern about these issues.

Key Technology Trends That Raise Ethical Issues

These ethical issues long preceded information technology—they are the abiding concerns of free societies everywhere. Nevertheless, information technology has heightened ethical concerns, put stress on existing social arrangements, and made existing laws obsolete or severely crippled. There are four key technological trends responsible for these ethical stresses.

The doubling of computing power every 18 months has made it possible for most organizations to utilize information systems for their core production processes. As a result, our dependence on systems and our vulnerability to system errors and poor data quality have increased. Occasional system failures heighten public concern over our growing dependence on some critical systems. Social rules and laws have not yet adjusted to this dependence. Standards for ensuring the accuracy and reliability of information systems (see Chapter 14) are not universally accepted or enforced.

Advances in data storage techniques and rapidly declining storage costs have been responsible for the multiplying databases on individuals—employees, customers, and potential customers—maintained by private and public organizations. These advances in data storage have made the routine violation of individual privacy both cheap and effective. For example, IBM has developed a wafer-sized disk that can hold the equivalent of more than 500 large novels (Mankoff, 1998). Already massive data storage systems are cheap enough for regional and even local retailing firms to use in identifying customers.

Advances in datamining techniques for large databases are a third technological trend that heightens ethical concerns, because they enable companies to find out much detailed personal information about individuals. With contemporary information systems technology, companies can assemble and combine the myriad pieces of information stored on you by computers much more easily than in the past. Think of all the ways you generate computer information about yourself—credit-card purchases, telephone calls, magazine subscriptions, video rentals, mail-order purchases, banking records, and local, state, and federal government records (including court and police

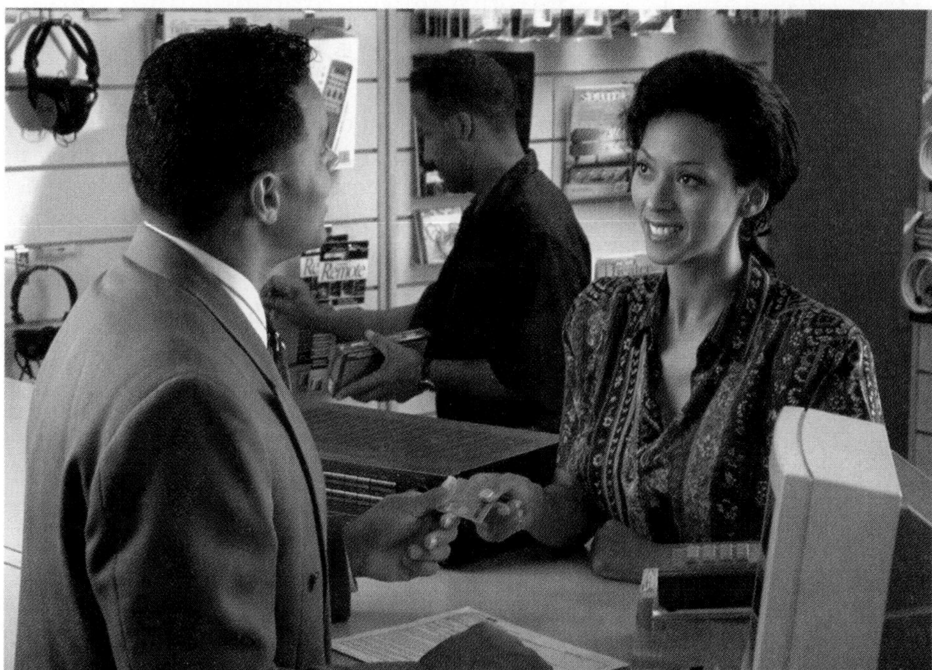

Making a purchase with a credit card can make personal information available to market researchers, telephone marketers, and direct mail companies. Advances in information technology facilitate the invasion of privacy.

records). Put together and mined properly, this information could reveal not only your credit information but also your driving habits, your tastes, your associations, and your political interests.

Companies with products to sell purchase relevant information from these sources to help them more finely target their marketing campaigns. For example, if you buy "upscale" merchandise from one catalogue, the catalogue company might sell your name to another catalogue mail-order company. The Window on Organizations in Chapter 2 describes how companies can use datamining on very large pools of data from multiple sources to rapidly identify buying patterns of customers and suggest individual responses.

Last, *advances in networking*, including the Internet, promise to reduce greatly the costs of moving and accessing large quantities of data, and open the possibility of mining large pools of data remotely using small desktop machines, permitting an invasion of privacy on a scale and precision heretofore unimaginable. The first Window on Organizations describes the privacy implications of allowing outsiders to access internal corporate data via the Web and combine that internal data with data from other sources.

The development of global digital-superhighway communication networks widely available to individuals and businesses poses many ethical and social concerns. Who will account for the flow of information over these networks? Will you be able to trace information collected about you? What will these networks do to the traditional relationships between family, work, and leisure? How will traditional job designs be altered when millions of "employees" become subcontractors using mobile offices that they themselves must pay for?

In the next section we will consider some ethical principles and analytical techniques for dealing with these kinds of ethical and social concerns.

4.2 ETHICS IN AN INFORMATION SOCIETY

Ethics is a concern of humans who have freedom of choice. Ethics is about individual choice: When faced with alternative courses of action, what is the correct moral choice? What are the main features of "ethical choice"?

Basic Concepts: Responsibility, Accountability, and Liability

responsibility Accepting the potential costs, duties, and obligations for the decisions one makes.

accountability The mechanisms for assessing responsibility for decisions made and actions taken.

liability The existence of laws that permit individuals to recover the damages done to them by other actors, systems, or organizations.

due process A process in which laws are well-known and understood and there is an ability to appeal to higher authorities to ensure that laws are applied correctly.

Ethical choices are decisions made by individuals who are responsible for the consequences of their actions. Responsibility is a feature of individuals and is a key element of ethical action. **Responsibility** means that you accept the potential costs, duties, and obligations for the decisions you make. **Accountability** is a feature of systems and social institutions: It means that mechanisms are in place to determine who took responsible action, who is responsible. Systems and institutions in which it is impossible to find out who took what action are inherently incapable of ethical analysis or ethical action. Liability extends the concept of responsibility further to the area of laws. **Liability** is a feature of political systems in which a body of law is in place that permits individuals to recover the damages done to them by other actors, systems, or organizations. **Due process** is a related feature of law-governed societies and is a process in which laws are known and understood and there is an ability to appeal to higher authorities to ensure that the laws were applied correctly.

These basic concepts form the underpinning of an ethical analysis of information systems and those who manage them. First, as discussed in Chapter 3, information technologies are filtered through social institutions, organizations, and individuals. Systems do not have "impacts" by themselves. Whatever information system impacts exist are products of institutional, organizational, and individual actions and behaviors. Second, responsibility for the consequences of technology falls clearly on the institutions, organizations, and individual managers who choose to use the technology. Using information technology in a "socially responsible" manner means that you can and will be

WINDOW ON ORGANIZATIONS

Linking Databases to the Web: A New Threat to Privacy?

The World Wide Web has opened new avenues for sharing and selling personal data. Organizations can link their internal databases to the World Wide Web, where they can be accessed by their business partners. Outsiders can query and analyze the data stored in the databases. A considerable amount of personal information can be obtained this way, especially when data about individuals from one company are combined with data from another.

MicroStrategy, Inc., in Vienna, Virginia, which sells on-line analytical processing (OLAP) software to work with databases, is promoting the idea of "consumerizing" large databases by making them accessible via the Web. Outsiders would be allowed to query and analyze stored data. Michael Saylor, MicroStrategy's CEO, believes that corporations will want to enrich their Web-accessible databases with demographic data on U.S. households including names, addresses, phone numbers, approximate incomes, and "psychographic" data such as hobbies and interests. MicroStrategy is working on an agreement with Acxiom Corporation in Conway, Arkansas, which accumulates data on 95 percent of U.S. households, to "content-enable" its decision-support software so that clients can combine their internal data with Acxiom's demographic data. According to Saylor, thousands of organizations would be interested in such information. Corporations could charge up to $100 per person per month to let others analyze warehouse data.

Source Informatics in Phoenix plans to use MicroStrategy's DSS Web to broaden its customer base by distributing data via the Web to thousands of pharmaceutical sales representatives. It has a database of pharmaceutical information gathered from pharmacies around the United States.

Some companies have found that marketing personal data has backfired. Word that the information service provider Lexis-Nexis was making critical information such as Social Security numbers and maiden names available for sale spread quickly by e-mail. The company's Dayton, Ohio, headquarters received a deluge of communications from individuals who requested that their names be deleted from Lexis-Nexis' P-Trak service. When the furor died down, it was revealed that the service only provided Social Security numbers for a very short time. The remainder of the data provided through P-Trak (name, address, two prior addresses, maiden name, birth date, and telephone numbers) are header information from credit reports, and are not protected by the Fair Credit Reporting Act. (The Fair Credit Reporting Act restricts the use of consumer credit data.) Furthermore, Lexis-Nexis screens its clients before allowing them to use P-Trak.

In response to the Lexis-Nexis incident, the Federal Trade Commission is proposing tighter rules on how personal data are used. The FTC has recommended extending the confidentiality guidelines of the Fair Credit Reporting Act to cover items such as Social Security numbers, birth dates, former addresses, and mothers' maiden names. The Senate even designated a subcommittee to explore the dangers of circulating personal data publicly. The subcommittee recognizes that a great deal of data has already reached the public arena, but it wants to investigate whether the data's presence on the Internet makes the problem much more severe because its information is easy to find and easy to access.

Privacy expert H. Jefferson Smith notes that most consumers are not informed about industry practices regarding the collection, use, and sharing of personal data. They do not understand that their purchase transactions can be collected and analyzed to create psychological purchasing profiles that can be shared with other merchants. He recommends that companies considering making internal customer data more widely available think about what constitutes fair play from the customer's standpoint. They should inform consumers about the intended uses of such data. Data collected from customers for one purpose should not be used for another purpose without the customer's permission.

To Think About: ***Should the Web be used to allow outsiders to view internal corporate data on people? Why or why not? What management, organization, and technology factors need to be addressed in using the Web for accessing internal corporate databases?***

Sources: H. Jefferson Smith, "How Much Privacy Do We Owe Customers?" *Beyond Computing,* January/February 1998; and John Foley and Bruce Caldwell, "Dangerous Data," *Information Week,* September 30, 1996.

held accountable for the consequences of your actions. Third, in an ethical political society, individuals and others can recover damages done them through a set of laws characterized by due process.

Ethical Analysis

When confronted with a situation that seems to present ethical issues, how should you analyze and reason about the situation? Following is a five-step process that should help:

- **Identify and describe clearly the facts.** Find out who did what to whom, and where, when, and how. You will be surprised in many instances at the errors in the initially reported facts, and often you will find that simply getting the facts straight helps define the solution. It also helps to get the opposing parties involved in an ethical dilemma to agree on the facts.

- **Define the conflict or dilemma and identify the higher-order values involved.** Ethical, social, and political issues always reference higher values. The parties to a dispute all claim to be pursuing higher values (e.g., freedom, privacy, protection of property, and the free enterprise system).

  Typically, an ethical issue involves a dilemma: two diametrically opposed courses of action that support worthwhile values. For example, the Window on Technology in this chapter illustrates two competing values: the need of companies to use marketing to become more efficient and the need to protect individual privacy.
- **Identify the stakeholders.** Every ethical, social, and political issue has stakeholders: players in the game who have an interest in the outcome, who have invested in the situation, and usually who have vocal opinions. Find out the identity of these groups and what they want. This will be useful later when designing a solution.
- **Identify the options that you can reasonably take.** You may find that none of the options satisfy all the interests involved, but that some options do a better job than others. Sometimes arriving at a "good" or ethical solution may not always be a "balancing" of consequences to stakeholders.
- **Identify the potential consequences of your options.** Some options may be ethically correct, but disastrous from other points of view. Other options may work in this one instance, but not be generalizable to other similar instances. Always ask yourself, "What if I choose this option consistently over time?"

Once your analysis is complete, what ethical principles or rules should you use to make a decision? What higher-order values should inform your judgment?

Candidate Ethical Principles

Although you are the only one who can decide which among many ethical principles you will follow, and how you will prioritize them, it is helpful to consider some ethical principles with deep roots in many cultures that have survived throughout recorded history.

1. Do unto others as you would have them do unto you (the Golden Rule). Putting yourself into the situation of others, and thinking of yourself as the object of the decision, can help you think about "fairness" in decision making.
2. If an action is not right for everyone to take, then it is not right for anyone (**Immanuel Kant's Categorical Imperative**). Ask yourself, "If everyone did this, could the organization, or society, survive?"
3. If an action cannot be taken repeatedly, then it is not right to be taken at any time (**Descartes' rule of change**). This is the slippery-slope rule: An action may bring about a small change now that is acceptable, but if repeated would bring unacceptable changes in the long run. In the vernacular, it might be stated as "once started down a slippery path you may not be able to stop."
4. Take the action that achieves the higher or greater value (the **Utilitarian Principle**). This rule assumes you can prioritize values in a rank order, and understand the consequences of various courses of action.
5. Take the action that produces the least harm, or the least potential cost (**Risk Aversion Principle**). Some actions have extremely high failure costs of very low probability (e.g., building a nuclear generating facility in an urban area) or extremely high failure costs of moderate probability (speeding and automobile accidents). Avoid these high failure cost actions, with greater attention obviously to high failure cost potential of moderate to high probability.

Immanuel Kant's Categorical Imperative A principle that states that if an action is not right for everyone to take, it is not right for anyone.

Descartes' rule of change A principle that states that if an action cannot be taken repeatedly, then it is not right to be taken at any time.

Utilitarian Principle Principle that assumes one can put values in rank order and understand the consequences of various courses of action.

Risk Aversion Principle Principle that one should take the action that produces the least harm or incurs the least cost.

6. Assume that virtually all tangible and intangible objects are owned by someone else unless there is a specific declaration otherwise. (This is the **ethical "no free lunch" rule.**) If something created by someone else is useful to you, it has value and you should assume the creator wants compensation for this work.

ethical "no free lunch" rule Assumption that all tangible and intangible objects are owned by someone else unless there is a specific declaration otherwise and that the creator wants compensation for this work.

Unfortunately, these ethical rules have too many logical and substantive exceptions to be absolute guides to action. Nevertheless, actions that do not easily pass these rules deserve some very close attention and a great deal of caution if only because the appearance of unethical behavior may do as much harm to you and your company as actual unethical behavior.

Professional Codes of Conduct

When groups of people claim to be professionals, they take on special rights and obligations because of their special claims to knowledge, wisdom, and respect. Professional codes of conduct are promulgated by associations of professionals such as the American Medical Association (AMA), the American Bar Association (ABA), the Data Processing Management Association (DPMA) and the Association of Computing Machinery (ACM). These professional groups take responsibility for the partial regulation of their professions by determining entrance qualifications and competence. Codes of ethics are promises by the profession to regulate themselves in the general interest of society. For example, avoiding harm to others, honoring property rights (including intellectual property), and respecting privacy are among the General Moral Imperatives of the ACM's Code of Professional Conduct (ACM, 1993).

Extensions to these moral imperatives state that ACM professions should consider the health, privacy, and general welfare of the public in the performance of their work and that professionals should express their professional opinion to their employer regarding any adverse consequences to the public (see Oz, 1994).

Some Real-World Ethical Dilemmas

The recent ethical problems described in this section illustrate a wide range of issues. Some of these issues are obvious ethical dilemmas, in which one set of interests is pitted against another. Others represent some type of breach of ethics. In either instance, there are rarely any easy solutions.

Continental Can: Based in Norwalk, Connecticut, Continental Can Company developed a human resources database with files on all of its employees. Besides the typical employee data, the system included the capability to "red flag" employees nearing retirement or approaching the age at which a pension would be vested in the individual. Throughout the 1980s, when the red flag went up, management would fire the person even after decades of loyal service. In 1991 a federal district court in Newark, New Jersey, awarded ex-employees $445 million for wrongful dismissal (McPartlin, 1992).

Downsizing with Technology at the Telephone Company: Many of the large telephone companies in the United States are using information technology to reduce the size of their work force. For example, AT&T is using voice recognition software to reduce the need for human operators by allowing computers to recognize a customer's responses to a series of computerized questions. New algorithms called "word spotting" allow the computer to recognize speech that is halting, stuttering, paused, or ungrammatical. AT&T expects that the new technology will eliminate 3000 to 6000 operator jobs nationwide, 200 to 400 management positions, and 31 offices in 21 states.

GTE Corporation reengineered its customer-service function to reduce the number of repair technicians. Customer-service workers who in the past had passed customer complaints on to repair technicians have been authorized to resolve the problems themselves by performing remote tests on customers' lines. The company also merged 12 operations centers into a single center to monitor the company's entire nationwide network. These and other changes have relied on technology to eliminate 17,000 jobs (Andrews, 1994; Levinson, 1994).

E-mail Privacy at EPSON: In March 1990, e-mail administrator Alana Shoars filed a suit in Los Angeles Superior Court alleging wrongful termination, defamation, and invasion of privacy by her former employer, Epson America Inc. of Torrance, California. She sought $1 million in damages. In July 1990, Shoars filed a class suit seeking $75 million for 700 Epson employees and approximately 1800 outsiders whose e-mail may have been monitored. Shoars contends that she was fired because she questioned the company's policy of monitoring and printing employee's e-mail messages. Epson claims that Shoars was fired because she opened an MCI:Mail account without permission. Many firms claim that they have every right to monitor the electronic mail of their employees because they own the facilities, intend their use to be for business purposes only, and create the facility for a business purpose (Bjerklie, 1994; Rifkin, 1991).

In each instance, you can find competing values at work, with groups lined on either side of a debate. A company may argue, for example, that it has a right to use information systems to increase productivity and reduce the size of its work force to keep down costs and stay in business. Employees displaced by information systems may argue that employers have some responsibility for their welfare. A close analysis of the facts can sometimes produce compromised solutions that give each side "half a loaf." Try to apply some of the described principles of ethical analysis to each of these cases. What is the right thing to do?

4.3 THE MORAL DIMENSIONS OF INFORMATION SYSTEMS

In this section, we take a closer look at the five moral dimensions of information systems first described in Figure 4.1. In each dimension we identify the ethical, social, and political levels of analysis and illustrate with real-world examples the values involved, the stakeholders, and the options chosen.

Information Rights: Privacy and Freedom in an Information Society

privacy The claim of individuals to be left alone, free from surveillance or interference from other individuals, organizations, or the state.

Privacy is the claim of individuals to be left alone, free from surveillance or interference from other individuals or organizations including the state. Claims to privacy are also involved at the workplace: Millions of employees are subject to electronic and other forms of high-tech surveillance. Information technology and systems threaten individual claims to privacy by making the invasion of privacy cheap, profitable, and effective.

The claim to privacy is protected in the U.S., Canadian, and German constitutions in a variety of different ways, and in other countries through various statutes. In the United States, the claim to privacy is protected primarily by the First Amendment guarantees of freedom of speech and association and the Fourth Amendment protections against unreasonable search and seizure of one's personal documents or home, and the guarantee of due process.

Due process has become a key concept in defining privacy. Due process requires that a set of rules or laws exist that clearly define how information about individuals will be treated, and what appeal mechanisms are available. Perhaps the best statement of due process in record keeping is given by the Fair Information Practices Doctrine developed in the early 1970s.

Fair Information Practices (FIP) A set of principles originally set forth in 1973 that governs the collection and use of information about individuals and forms the basis of most U.S. and European privacy laws.

Most American and European privacy law is based on a regime called Fair Information Practices (FIP) first set forth in a report written in 1973 by a federal government advisory committee (U.S. Department of Health, Education, and Welfare, 1973). **Fair Information Practices (FIP)** is a set of principles governing the collection and use of information about individuals. The five Fair Information Practices principles are shown in Table 4.1.

FIP principles are based on the notion of a "mutuality of interest" among the record holder and the individual. The individual has an interest in engaging in a transaction, and the record keeper—usually a business or government agency—requires information

TABLE 4.1 Fair Information Practices Principles

1. There should be no personal record system whose existence is secret.
2. Individuals have rights of access, inspection, review, and amendment to systems that contain information about them.
3. There must be no use of personal information for purposes other than those for which it was gathered without prior consent.
4. Managers of systems are responsible and can be held accountable and liable for the damage done by systems for their reliability and security.
5. Governments have the right to intervene in the information relationships among private parties.

about the individual to support the transaction. Once gathered, the individual maintains an interest in the record, and the record may not be used to support other activities without the individual's consent.

Fair Information Practices form the basis of 13 federal statutes listed in Table 4.2 that set forth the conditions for handling information about individuals in such areas as credit reporting, education, financial records, newspaper records, cable communications, electronic communications, and even video rentals. The Privacy Act of 1974 is the most important of these laws, regulating the federal government's collection, use, and disclosure of information. Most federal privacy laws apply only to the federal government. Only credit, banking, cable, and video rental industries have been regulated by federal privacy law.

In the United States, privacy law is enforced by individuals who must sue agencies or companies in court to recover damages. European countries and Canada define *privacy* in a similar manner to that in the United States, but they have chosen to enforce their privacy laws by creating privacy commissions or data protection agencies to pursue complaints brought by citizens.

TABLE 4.2 Federal Privacy Laws in the United States

1. General Federal Privacy Laws
Freedom of Information Act, 1968 as Amended (5 USC 552)
Privacy Act of 1974 as Amended (5 USC 552a)
Electronic Communications Privacy Act of 1986
Computer Matching and Privacy Protection Act of 1988
Computer Security Act of 1987
Federal Managers Financial Integrity Act of 1982
2. Privacy Laws Affecting Private Institutions
Fair Credit Reporting Act of 1970
Family Educational Rights and Privacy Act of 1978
Right to Financial Privacy Act of 1978
Privacy Protection Act of 1980
Cable Communications Policy Act of 1984
Electronic Communications Privacy Act of 1986
Video Privacy Protection Act of 1988

WINDOW ON TECHNOLOGY

Are the Cookies Eating Your Privacy?

When you surf the Net, you are being observed. The only questions are by whom and for what purposes? Tools to monitor your visits to the World Wide Web have been developed for commercial reasons—to help organizations determine how to better target their offerings, and to determine who is visiting their Web sites. For example, many commercial sites log the number of visitors and which site pages they visit to collect marketing information about user interests and behaviors. One key issue arises from this data collection—do they know who you are? If so, then what do they do with such data, and are these uses appropriate, legal, and ethical? In other words, is your privacy being improperly invaded?

Do they know who you are? The answer is—maybe! Of course you are known if you register at a site to purchase a product or service. This situation is the same as using a credit card to purchase any product or service. In addition some sites offer you a free service, such as information, in exchange for your agreeing to register, and when you register they have you identified. This is probably no different from your signing up for a supermarket's frequent shopper or discount card—you voluntarily give up some of your privacy in exchange for something you want. In both cases, the company collects the information to use in its own marketing research and to target specific offers to you. They also might sell it to other companies or organizations, raising the privacy issues discussed elsewhere in this chapter.

But what if you do not volunteer personal information at a site? Can they gather it anyway, without your consent and without your knowledge? The answer seems to be yes, with the help of Internet technology. Using click-stream tracking, a Web site owner can audit the files tracking usage of the Web site to see the path that users take through the site. For example, a merchant could use click-stream tracking to see which icons on the site attract people to click and which are bypassed. Marketers are especially interested in finding out which site the visitor came from before visiting that particular Web site. If a Web site is getting a lot of traffic from another Web site, it might pay to concentrate more advertising efforts there.

Cookies are tiny data files that are deposited on your computer by interested Web sites when you visit those sites. They identify your Web browser software and track your visits to the Web site. When you return to a site that has stored a cookie, it will search your computer, find the cookie, and "know" what you have done in the past. It may also update the cookie, depending on your activity this visit. In this way, the site can customize its contents for your interests (assuming your past activities indicate your current interest). If you are a regular Web user, search your hard drive for files named "cookie.txt" and you are

Internet Challenges to Privacy

The Internet introduces technology that poses new challenges to the protection of individual privacy. Information sent over this vast network of networks may pass through many different computer systems before it reaches its final destination. Each of these systems is capable of monitoring, capturing, and storing communications that pass through it.

It is possible to record many on-line activities, including which on-line newsgroups or files a person has accessed and which Web sites he or she has visited. This information can be collected by both a subscriber's own Internet service provider and the system operators of remote sites that a subscriber visits. E-mail addresses can be collected for the purpose of sending out unsolicited e-mail and electronic messages. This practice is called **spamming,** and it is growing because it only costs a few cents to send thousands of messages advertising one's wares to Internet users. Organizations and individuals can waste many hours filtering these unwanted messages (Cranor and La Macchia, 1998). The Window on Technology describes some of the challenges to individual privacy posed by this technology.

spamming The practice of sending unsolicited e-mail and other electronic communication.

Ethical Issues

The ethical privacy issue in this information age is as follows: Under what conditions should I (you) invade the privacy of others? What legitimates intruding into others' lives through unobtrusive surveillance, through market research, or by whatever means? Do we have to inform people that we are eavesdropping? Do we have to in-

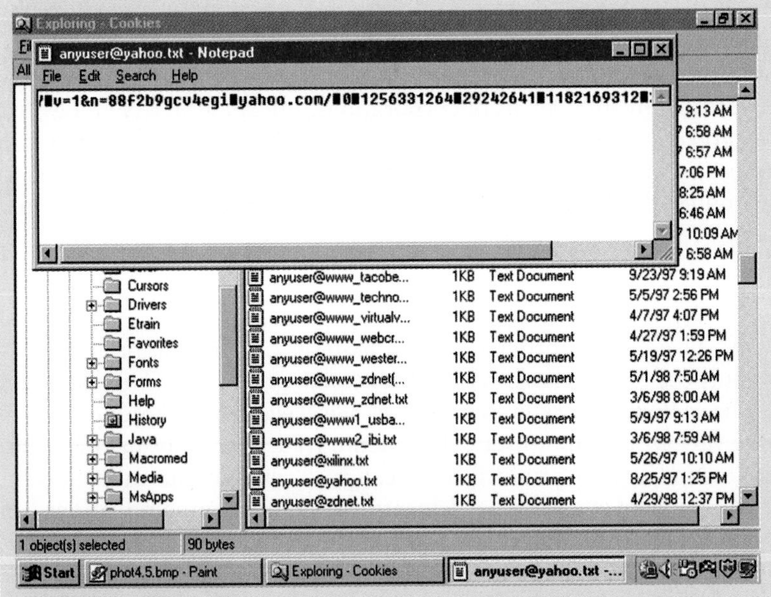

"Cookies" are tiny text files deposited on a computer hard drive when a user visits certain Web sites. Cookies provide information that helps companies track the activities and interests of their Web site visitors. Although it can provide valuable marketing information, the practice of collecting Web-site visitor data raises worries about protecting individual privacy.

likely to find some. The site may use the data from its cookies for itself, or it too may sell that data to others.

Web search engines are another source of privacy invasion. They monitor and store data on who searches and for what, and these data are becoming public. For example, you can visit McKinley's Magellan site to see a sample of what topics people have searched using Magellan (http://voyeur.mckinley.com/voyeur.cgi). While Magellan does not display the identity of the searchers, they have that technical capacity. And they could sell it to interested parties. You are also monitored as you use Usenet newsgroups. Deja News publicly catalogues 15,000 Usenet groups and monitors their visitors. Visit its site (http://dejanews.com) and you can view a profile of your own (or other person's) use of Usenet groups—how many times you posted messages and in which newsgroups. You may not want this information released. For example, you may be part of a political newsgroup that you want kept confidential. That information is available for others to see and may even be sold to interested parties.

To Think About: ***How would you balance the rights of individuals to privacy against the desire of companies to use this technology to improve their marketing and to better target their products to the interests of individuals?***

Sources: Rivka Tadjer, "Much Ado About Privacy," *Internet Computing,* March 1998; Matthew Hahn, "Easy Now to Keep Tabs on Users' Internet Postings," *The New York Times,* January 6, 1997; and Thomas E. Weber, "Browsers Beware: The Web is Watching," *The Wall Street Journal,* June 27, 1996.

form people that we are using credit history information for employment screening purposes?

Social Issues

The social issue of privacy concerns the development of "expectations of privacy" or privacy norms, as well as public attitudes. In what areas of life should we as a society encourage people to think they are in "private territory" as opposed to public view? For instance, should we as a society encourage people to develop expectations of privacy when using electronic mail, cellular telephones, bulletin boards, the postal system, the workplace, the street? Should expectations of privacy be extended to criminal conspirators?

Political Issues

The political issue of privacy concerns the development of statutes that govern the relations between record keepers and individuals. Should we permit the FBI to prevent the commercial development of encrypted telephone transmissions so they can eavesdrop at will (Denning et al., 1993)? Should a law be passed to require direct-marketing firms to obtain the consent of individuals before using their names in mass marketing (a consensus database)? Should e-mail privacy—regardless of who owns the equipment—be protected by law? In general, large organizations of all kinds—public and private—are reluctant to remit the advantages that come from the unfettered flow of information on individuals. Civil libertarians and other private groups have been the strongest voices supporting restraints on large organizations' information-gathering activities.

Property Rights: Intellectual Property

intellectual property Intangible property created by individuals or corporations that is subject to protections under trade secret, copyright, and patent law.

Contemporary information systems have severely challenged existing law and social practices that protect private intellectual property. **Intellectual property** is considered to be intangible property created by individuals or corporations. Information technology has made it difficult to protect intellectual property because computerized information can be so easily copied or distributed on networks. Intellectual property is subject to a variety of protections under three different legal traditions: trade secret, copyright, and patent law (Graham, 1984).

Trade Secrets

trade secret Any intellectual work or product used for a business purpose that can be classified as belonging to that business, provided it is not based on information in the public domain.

Any intellectual work product—a formula, device, pattern, or compilation of data—used for a business purpose can be classified as a **trade secret**, provided it is not based on information in the public domain. Trade secrets have their basis in state law, not federal law, and protections vary from state to state. In general, trade secret laws grant a monopoly on the ideas behind a work product, but it can be a very tenuous monopoly.

Software that contains novel or unique elements, procedures, or compilations can be included as a trade secret. Trade secret law protects the actual ideas in a work product, not only their manifestation. To make this claim, the creator or owner must take care to bind employees and customers with nondisclosure agreements and to prevent the secret from falling into the public domain.

The limitation of trade secret protection is that although virtually all software programs of any complexity contain unique elements of some sort, it is difficult to prevent the ideas in the work from falling into the public domain when the software is widely distributed.

Copyright

copyright A statutory grant that protects creators of intellectual property against copying by others for any purpose for a period of 28 years.

Copyright is a statutory grant that protects creators of intellectual property against copying by others for any purpose for a period of 28 years. Since the first Federal Copyright Act of 1790, and the creation of the Copyright Office to register copyrights and enforce copyright law, Congress has extended copyright protection to books, periodicals, lectures, dramas, musical compositions, maps, drawings, artwork of any kind, and motion pictures. The congressional intent behind copyright laws has been to encourage creativity and authorship by ensuring that creative people receive the financial and other benefits of their work. Most industrial nations have their own copyright laws, and there are several international conventions and bilateral agreements through which nations coordinate and enforce their laws.

In the mid-1960s the Copyright Office began registering software programs, and in 1980 Congress passed the Computer Software Copyright Act, which clearly provides protection for source and object code and for copies of the original sold in commerce, and sets forth the rights of the purchaser to use the software while the creator retains legal title.

Copyright protection is explicit and clear-cut: It protects against copying of entire programs or their parts. Damages and relief are readily obtained for infringement. The drawback to copyright protection is that the underlying ideas behind a work are not protected, only their manifestation in a work. A competitor can use your software, understand how it works, and build new software that follows the same concepts without infringing on a copyright.

"Look and feel" copyright infringement lawsuits are precisely about the distinction between an idea and its expression. For instance, in the early 1990s Apple Computer sued Microsoft Corporation and Hewlett-Packard Inc. for infringement of the expression of Apple's Macintosh interface. Among other claims, Apple claimed that the defendants copied the expression of overlapping windows. The defendants counterclaimed that the idea of overlapping windows can only be expressed in a single way, and therefore was not protectable under the "merger" doctrine of copyright law. When ideas and their expression merge, the expression cannot be copyrighted. In general, courts appear to be following the reasoning of a 1989 case—*Brown Bag Software* vs. *Symantec Corp.*—in which the court dissected the elements of software alleged to be infringing. The court found that neither similar concept, function, general functional features (e.g., drop-down menus), nor colors are protectable by copyright law (*Brown Bag* vs. *Symantec Corp.*, 1992).

Patents

A **patent** grants the owner an exclusive monopoly on the ideas behind an invention for 17 years. The congressional intent behind patent law was to ensure that inventors of new machines, devices, or methods receive the full financial and other rewards of their labor and yet still make widespread use of the invention possible by providing detailed diagrams for those wishing to use the idea under license from the owner of the patent. The granting of a patent is determined by the Patent Office and relies on court rulings.

patent A legal document that grants the owner an exclusive monopoly on the ideas behind an invention for 17 years; designed to ensure that inventors of new machines or methods are rewarded for their labor while making widespread use of their inventions.

The key concepts in patent law are originality, novelty, and invention. The Patent Office did not accept applications for software patents routinely until a 1981 Supreme Court decision that held that computer programs could be a part of a patentable process. Since that time hundreds of patents have been granted and thousands await consideration.

The strength of patent protection is that it grants a monopoly on the underlying concepts and ideas of software. The difficulty is passing stringent criteria of nonobviousness (e.g., the work must reflect some special understanding and contribution), originality, and novelty, as well as years of waiting to receive protection.

Challenges to Intellectual Property Rights

Contemporary information technologies, especially software, pose a severe challenge to existing intellectual property regimes, and therefore create significant ethical, social, and political issues. Digital media differ from books, periodicals, and other media in terms of ease of replication; ease of transmission; ease of alteration; difficulty classifying a software work as a program, book, or even music; compactness—making theft easy; and difficulties in establishing uniqueness.

The proliferation of electronic networks, including the Internet, has made it even more difficult to protect intellectual property. Before widespread use of networks, copies of software, books, magazine articles, or films had to be stored on physical media, such as paper, computer disks, or videotape, creating some hurdles to distribution. Using networks, information can be more widely reproduced and distributed (Johnson, 1997). With the World Wide Web in particular, one can easily copy and distribute virtually anything to thousands and even millions of people around the world, even if they are using different types of computer systems. Information can be illicitly copied from one place and distributed through other systems and networks even though these parties do not willingly participate in the infringement (Carazos, 1996). The Internet was designed to transmit information freely around the world, including copyrighted information. Intellectual property that can be easily copied is likely to be copied (Chabrow, 1996).

The manner in which information is obtained and presented on the Web further challenges intellectual property protections (Okerson, 1996). Web pages can be constructed from bits of text, graphics, sound, or video that may come from many different sources. Each item may belong to a different entity, creating complicated issues of ownership and compensation (see Figure 4.2). Web sites can also use a capability called "framing" to let one site construct an on-screen border around content obtained by linking to another Web site. The first site's border and logo stay on screen, making the content of the new Web site appear to be "offered" by the previous Web site. For example, TotalNews, Inc., based in Phoenix, maintains a Web site linked to the Web sites of more than 1100 news organizations and frames virtually all of them.

Mechanisms are being developed to sell and distribute books, articles, and other intellectual property on the Internet, but publishers continue to worry about copyright violations because intellectual property can now be copied so easily.

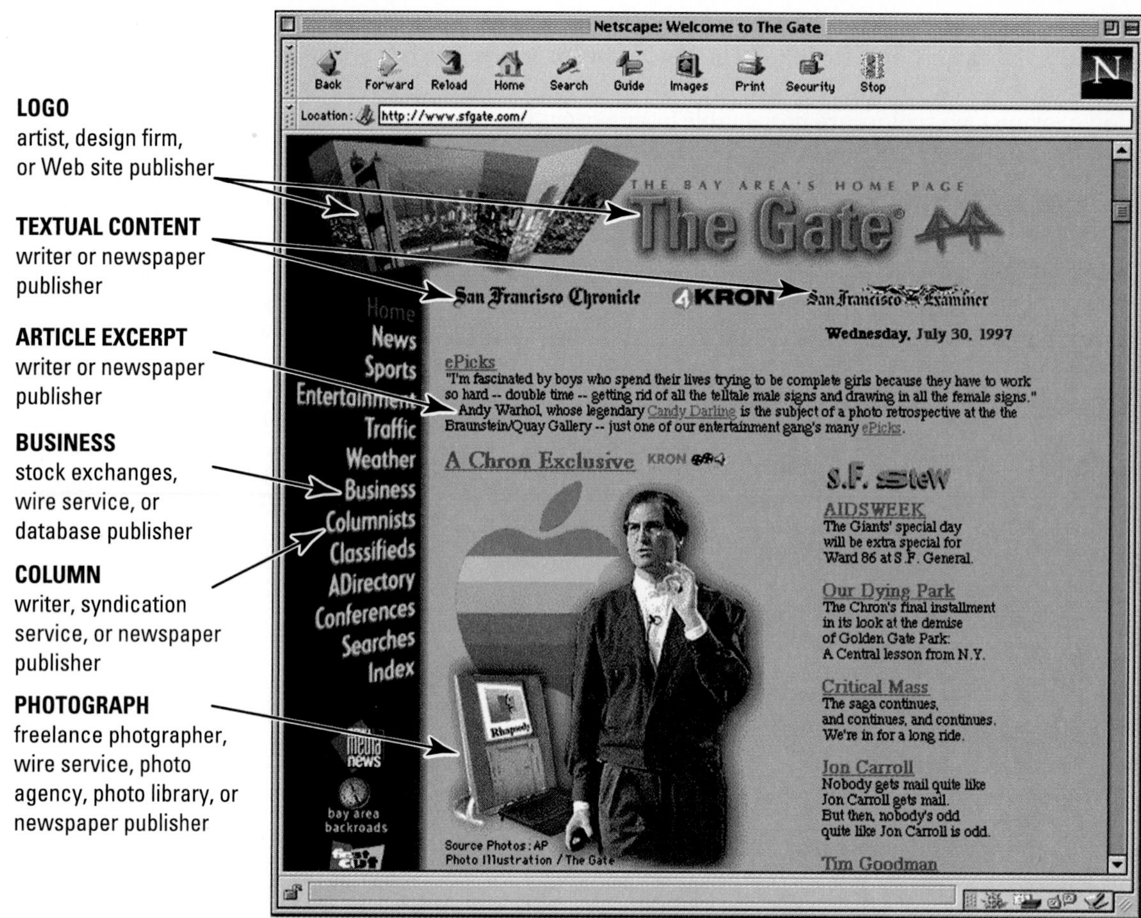

FIGURE 4.2 Who Owns the Pieces? Anatomy of a Web page. Web pages are often constructed with elements from many different sources, clouding issues of ownership and intellectual property protection. *Source: Web page from* The San Francisco Chronicle. *© San Francisco Chronicle. Reprinted with permission.*

Ethical Issues

The central ethical issue posed to individuals concerns copying software: Should I (you) copy for my own use a piece of software protected by trade secret, copyright, and/or patent law? In the information age, it is so easy to obtain perfect, functional copies of software, that the software companies themselves have abandoned software protection schemes to increase market penetration, and enforcement of the law is so rare. However, if everyone copied software, very little new software would be produced because creators could not benefit from the results of their work.

Social Issues

There are several property-related social issues raised by new information technology. Most experts agree that the current intellectual property laws are breaking down in the information age. The vast majority of Americans report in surveys that they routinely violate some minor laws—everything from speeding to taking paper clips from work to copying software. The ease with which software can be copied contributes to making us a society of lawbreakers. These routine thefts threaten significantly to reduce the speed with which new information technologies can and will be introduced, and thereby threaten further advances in productivity and social well-being (see the chapter-opening vignette).

Political Issues

The main property-related political issue concerns the creation of new property protection measures to protect investments made by creators of new software. Apple, Microsoft, and 900 other hardware and software firms formed the Software Publishers Association (SPA) to lobby for new protection laws and enforce existing laws. SPA has established a toll-free antipiracy hotline for employees to report on their corporations, staged numerous surprise audits or raids, sent hundreds of cease and desist letters, and filed more than 100 lawsuits (80 percent against corporations, 20 percent against bulletin board operators, training facilities, schools, and universities) since its inception. The SPA has developed model Employee Guidelines for Using Software, described in the Window on Organizations on page 120.

Allied against SPA are a host of groups and millions of individuals who resist efforts to strengthen antipiracy laws, and instead encourage situations in which software can be copied. These groups believe that software should be free, that antipiracy laws cannot in any event be enforced in the digital age, or that software should be paid for on a voluntary basis (shareware software). According to these groups, the greater social benefit results from the free distribution of software.

Accountability, Liability, and Control

Along with privacy and property laws, new information technologies are challenging existing liability law and social practices for holding individuals and institutions accountable. If a person is injured by a machine controlled, in part, by software, who should be held accountable and therefore held liable? Should a public bulletin board or an electronic service such as Prodigy or America Online permit the transmission of pornographic or offensive material (as broadcasters), or should they be held harmless against any liability for what users transmit (as is true of common carriers such as the telephone system)? What about the Internet? If you outsource your information processing, can you hold the external vendor liable for injuries done to your customers? Try some real-world examples.

Some Recent Liability Problems

On March 13, 1993, a blizzard hit the East Coast of the United States, knocking out an Electronic Data Systems Inc. (EDS) computer center in Clifton, New Jersey. The center operated 5200 ATM machines in 12 different networks across the country involving more than 1 million card holders. In the two weeks required to recover operations, EDS informed its customers to use alternative ATM networks operated by other banks or computer centers, and offered to cover more than $50 million in cash withdrawals. Because the alternative networks did not have access to the actual customer account balances, EDS was at substantial risk of fraud. Cash withdrawals were limited to $100 per day per customer to reduce the exposure. Most service was restored by March 26. Although EDS had a disaster-recovery plan, it did not have a dedicated backup facility. Who is liable for any economic harm caused individuals or businesses who could not access their full account balances in this period (Joes, 1993)?

In April 1990, a computer system at Shell Pipeline Corporation failed to detect a human operator error. As a result, 93,000 barrels of crude oil were shipped to the wrong trader. The error cost $2 million because the trader sold oil that should not have been delivered to him. A court ruled later that Shell Pipeline was liable for the loss of the oil because the error was due to a human operator who entered erroneous information into the system. Shell was held liable for not developing a system that would prevent the possibility of misdeliveries (King, 1992). Whom would you have held liable—Shell Pipeline? The trader for not being more careful about deliveries? The human operator who made the error?

These cases point out the difficulties faced by information systems executives who ultimately are responsible for the harm done by systems developed by their staffs. In

WINDOW ON ORGANIZATIONS

Employee Guidelines for Using Software

PURPOSE

All users will use software only in accordance with its license agreement. Unless otherwise provided in the license, any duplication of copyrighted software, except for backup and archival purposes, is a violation of copyright law. In addition to violating copyright law, unauthorized duplication of software is contrary to [organization's] standards of conduct. The following points are to be followed to comply with software license agreements:

1. We will use all software in accordance with its license agreements.
2. Legitimate software will promptly be provided to all users who need it. No [organization] user will make any unauthorized copies of any software under any circumstances. Anyone found copying software other than for backup purposes is subject to termination.
3. We will not tolerate the use of any unauthorized copies of software in our organization. Any person illegally reproducing software can be subject to civil and criminal penalties including fines and imprisonment. We do not condone illegal copying of software under any circumstances, and anyone who makes, uses, or otherwise acquires unauthorized software will be appropriately disciplined.
4. No user will give software to any outsiders including clients, customers, and others.
5. Any user who determines that there may be a misuse of software within the organization will notify the software manager, department manager, or legal counsel.
6. All software used by the organization on organization-owned computers will be purchased through appropriate procedures.

I have read [organization's] software code of ethics. I am fully aware of our software compliance policies and agree to abide by those policies. I understand that violation of any above policies may result in my termination.

____
User signature

____
Date

To Think About: ***Try to find out your university's policy regarding software. Is there a software code of ethics on campus? If an employee finds routine copying of software in a firm, should the person (a) call the firm's legal counsel or (b) call SPA on the antipiracy hotline? Are there any circumstances in which software copying should be allowed?***

Source: "Software Management Guide: A Guide for Software Asset Management, version 1.0." Reprinted by permission of the Software Publishers Association.

general, insofar as computer software is part of a machine, and the machine injures someone physically or economically, the producer of the software and the operator can be held liable for damages. Insofar as the software acts more like a book, storing and displaying information, courts have been reluctant to hold authors, publishers, and booksellers liable for content (the exception being instances of fraud or defamation), and hence courts have been wary of holding software authors liable for "booklike" software.

In general, it is very difficult (if not impossible) to hold software producers liable for their software products when those products are considered like books, regardless of the physical or economic harm that results. Historically, print publishers, books, and periodicals have not been held liable because of fears that liability claims would interfere with First Amendment rights guaranteeing freedom of expression.

What about "software as service"? ATM machines are a service provided to bank customers. Should this service fail, customers will be inconvenienced and perhaps harmed economically if they cannot access their funds in a timely manner. Should liability protections be extended to software publishers and operators of defective financial, accounting, simulation, or marketing systems?

Software is very different from books. Software users may develop expectations of infallibility about software; software is less easily inspected than a book, and more difficult to compare with other software products for quality; and software claims actually to perform a task rather than describe a task like a book; people come to depend on services essentially based on software. Given the centrality of software to everyday life, the chances are excellent that liability law will extend its reach to include software even when it merely provides an information service.

Telephone systems have not been held liable for the messages transmitted because they are regulated "common carriers." In return for their monopoly on telephone service, they must provide access to all, at reasonable rates, and achieve acceptable reliability. But broadcasters and cable television systems are subject to a wide variety of federal and local constraints on content and facilities. Organizations can be held liable for offensive content on their Web sites; and on-line services such as Prodigy or America Online might be held liable for postings by their users.

Ethical Issues

The central liability-related ethical issue raised by new information technologies is whether individuals and organizations who create, produce, and sell systems (both hardware and software) are morally responsible for the consequences of their use (see Johnson and Mulvey, 1995). If so, under what conditions? What liabilities (and responsibilities) should the user assume, and what should the provider assume?

Social Issues

The central liability-related social issue concerns the expectations that society should allow to develop around service-providing information systems. Should individuals (and organizations) be encouraged to develop their own backup devices to cover likely or easily anticipated system failures, or should organizations be held strictly liable for system services they provide? If organizations are held strictly liable, what impact will this have on the development of new system services? Can society permit networks and bulletin boards to post libelous, inaccurate, and misleading information that will harm many persons? Or should information service companies become self-regulating, self-censoring?

Political Issues

The leading liability-related political issue is the debate between information providers of all kinds (from software developers to network service providers), who want to be relieved of liability insofar as possible (thereby maximizing their profits), and service users—individuals, organizations, communities—who want organizations to be held responsible for providing high-quality system services (thereby maximizing the quality of service). Service providers argue they will withdraw from the marketplace if they are held liable, whereas service users argue that only by holding providers liable can we guarantee a high level of service and compensate injured parties. Should legislation impose liability or restrict liability on service providers? This fundamental cleavage is at the heart of numerous political and judicial conflicts.

System Quality: Data Quality and System Errors

The debate over liability and accountability for unintentional consequences of system use raises a related but independent moral dimension: What is an acceptable, technologically feasible level of system quality (see Chapter 14)? At what point should system managers say, "Stop testing, we've done all we can to perfect this software. Ship it!" Individuals and organizations may be held responsible for avoidable and foreseeable consequences, which they have a duty to perceive and correct. And the gray area is that some system errors are foreseeable and correctable only at very great expense, an expense so great that pursuing this level of perfection is not feasible economically—no one could afford the product. For example, although software companies try to debug their products before releasing them to the marketplace, they knowingly ship buggy products because the time and cost of fixing all minor errors would prevent these products from ever being released (Rigdon, 1995). What if the product was not offered on the marketplace, would social welfare as a whole not advance and perhaps even decline?

TABLE 4.3 Illustrative Reported Data Quality Problems

- An airline inadvertently corrupted its database of passenger reservations while installing new software and for months planes took off with half-loads.
- A manufacturer attempted to reorganize its customer files by customer number only to discover the sales staff had been entering a new customer number for each sale because of special incentives for opening new accounts. One customer was entered 7000 times. The company scrapped the software project after spending $1 million.
- A manufacturing company nearly scrapped a $12 million data warehouse project because of inconsistently defined product data.
- J. P. Morgan, a New York bank, discovered that 40 percent of the data in its credit-risk management database was incomplete, necessitating double-checking by users.
- Several studies have established that 5 to 12 percent of bar-code sales at retail grocery and merchandise chains are erroneous and that the ratio of overcharges to undercharges runs as high as 5:1, with 4:1 as a norm. The problem tends to be human error in keeping shelf prices accurate and corporate policy that fails to allocate sufficient resources to price checking, auditing, and development of error-free policies.

Source: Catherine Yang and Willy Stern, "Maybe They Should Call Them Scammers," *Business Week,* January 16, 1995; William Bulkeley, "Databases Plagued by a Reign of Error," *Wall Street Journal,* May 26, 1992; and Doug Bartholomew, "The Price Is Wrong," *Information Week,* September 14, 1992.

Carrying this further, just what is the responsibility of a producer of computer services—should they withdraw the product that can never be perfect, warn the user, or forget about the risk (let the buyer beware)?

Three principal sources of poor system performance are software bugs and errors, hardware or facility failures due to natural or other causes, and poor input data quality. Chapter 14 shows why zero defects in software code of any complexity cannot be achieved and the seriousness of remaining bugs cannot be estimated. Hence, there is a technological barrier to perfect software and users must be aware of the potential for catastrophic failure. The software industry has not yet arrived at testing standards for producing software of acceptable but not perfect performance (Collins et al., 1994).

Although software bugs and facility catastrophe are likely to be widely reported in the press, by far the most common source of business system failure is data quality. Few companies routinely measure the quality of their data but studies of individual organizations report data error rates ranging from 0.5 to 30 percent (Redman, 1998). Table 4.3 describes some of these data quality problems.

Ethical Issues

The central quality-related ethical issue raised by information systems is at what point should I (or you) release software or services for consumption by others? At what point can you conclude that your software or service achieves an economically and technologically adequate level of quality? What should you be obliged to know about the quality of your software, its procedures for testing, and its operational characteristics?

Social Issues

The leading quality-related social issue once again deals with expectations: Do we want as a society to encourage people to believe that systems are infallible, that data errors are impossible? Do we instead want a society where people are openly skeptical and questioning of the output of machines, where people are at least informed of the risk? By heightening awareness of system failure, do we inhibit the development of all systems, which in the end contributes to social well-being?

Political Issues

The leading quality-related political issue concerns the laws of responsibility and accountability. Should Congress establish or direct the National Institute of Science and Technology (NIST) to develop quality standards (software, hardware, data quality) and impose those standards on industry? Or should industry associations be encouraged to develop industry-wide standards of quality? Or should Congress wait for the marketplace to punish poor system quality, recognizing that in some instances this will not work (e.g., if all retail grocers maintain poor quality systems, then customers have no alternatives)?

Quality of Life: Equity, Access, Boundaries

The negative social costs of introducing information technologies and systems are beginning to mount along with the power of the technology. Many of these negative social consequences are not violations of individual rights, nor are they property crimes. Nevertheless, these negative consequences can be extremely harmful to individuals, societies, and political institutions. Computers and information technologies potentially can destroy valuable elements of our culture and society even while they bring us benefits. If there is a balance of good and bad consequences to the use of information systems, who do we hold responsible for the bad consequences? Next, we briefly examine *some* of the negative social consequences of systems, considering individual, social, and political responses.

Balancing Power Center versus Periphery

An early fear of the computer age was that huge, centralized mainframe computers would centralize power at corporate headquarters and in the nation's capital, resulting in a Big Brother society suggested in George Orwell's novel, *1984*. The shift toward highly decentralized computing, coupled with an ideology of "empowerment" of thousands of workers, and the decentralization of decision making to lower organizational levels, have reduced fears of power centralization in institutions. Yet much of the "empowerment" described in popular business magazines is trivial. Lower-level employees may be empowered to make minor decisions, but the key policy decisions may be as centralized as in the past.

Rapidity of Change: Reduced Response Time to Competition

Information systems have helped to create much more efficient national and international markets. The now more efficient global marketplace has reduced the normal social buffers that permitted businesses many years to adjust to competition. "Time-based competition" has an ugly side: The business you work for may not have enough time to respond to global competitors and may be wiped out in a year, along with your job. We stand the risk of developing a "just-in-time society" with "just-in-time jobs" and "just-in-time" workplaces, families, and vacations.

Maintaining Boundaries: Family, Work, Leisure

Parts of this book were produced on trains, planes, as well as on family "vacations" and what otherwise might have been "family" time. The danger to ubiquitous computing, telecommuting, nomad computing, and the "do anything anywhere" computing environment is that it might actually come true. If so, the traditional boundaries that separate work from family and just plain leisure will be weakened. Although authors have traditionally worked just about anywhere (typewriters have been portable for nearly a century), the advent of information systems, coupled with the growth of knowledge-work occupations, means that more and more people will be working when traditionally they would have been playing or communicating with family and friends. The "work umbrella" now extends far beyond the eight-hour day.

While some people may enjoy the convenience of working at home, the "do anything anywhere" computing environment can blur the traditional boundaries between work and family time.

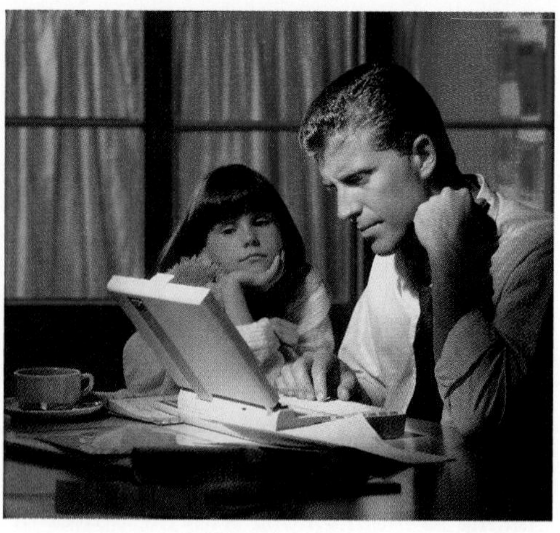

Weakening these institutions poses clear-cut risks. Family and friends historically have provided powerful support mechanisms for individuals, and they act as balance points in a society by preserving "private life," providing a place for one to collect one's thoughts, think in ways contrary to one's employer, and dream.

Dependence and Vulnerability

Our businesses, governments, schools, and private associations such as churches are incredibly dependent now on information systems and are therefore highly vulnerable if these systems should fail. With systems now as ubiquitous as the telephone system, it is startling to remember that there are no regulatory or standard-setting forces in place similar to telephone, electrical, radio, television, or other public-utility technologies. The absence of standards and the criticality of some system applications will probably call forth demands for national standards and perhaps regulatory oversight.

Computer Crime and Abuse

computer crime The commission of illegal acts through the use of a computer or against a computer system.

computer abuse The commission of acts involving a computer that may not be illegal but are considered unethical.

Many new technologies in the industrial era have created new opportunities for committing crime. Technologies including computers create new valuable items to steal, new ways to steal them, and new ways to harm others. **Computer crime** can be defined as the commission of illegal acts through the use of a computer or against a computer system. Computers or computer systems can be the object of the crime (destroying a company's computer center or a company's computer files), as well as the instrument of a crime (stealing computer lists by illegally gaining access to a computer system using a home computer). Simply accessing a computer system without authorization, or intent to do harm, even by accident, is now a federal crime. **Computer abuse** is the commission of acts involving a computer that may not be illegal but are considered unethical.

No one knows the magnitude of the computer crime problem—how many systems are invaded, how many people engage in the practice, or what the total economic damage is. Many companies are reluctant to report computer crimes because they may involve employees. The most economically damaging kinds of computer crime are introducing viruses, theft of services, disruption of computer systems, and theft of telecommunications services. Computer crime has been estimated to cost more than $1 billion in the United States, and an additional $1 billion if corporate and cellular phone theft is included. "Hackers" is the pejorative term for persons who use computers in illegal ways. Hacker attacks are on the rise, posing new threats to organizations linked to the Internet (see Chapter 14).

Computer viruses (see Chapter 14) have grown exponentially during the past decade. Thousands of viruses have been documented. The average corporate loss for a bad virus outbreak is $250,000, and the probability of a large corporation experiencing a significant computer virus infection in a single year is 50 percent according to some experts. Although many firms now use antivirus software, the proliferation of computer networks will surely increase the probability of infections.

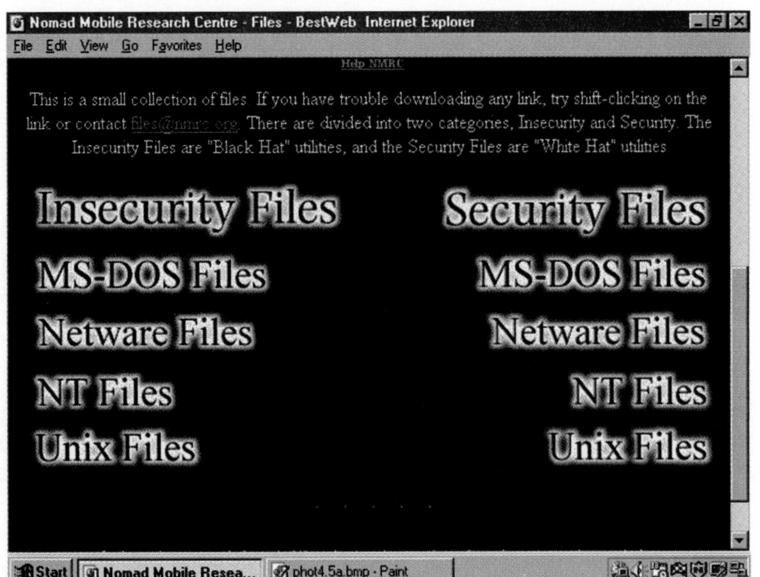

This Web site details security weaknesses in the major network operating systems that can be exploited by hackers. Hackers illegally accessing systems can create widespread disruption and harm.

Following are some illustrative computer crimes:

- On May 29, 1996, the Federal Trade Commission announced it had obtained a temporary restraining order to freeze the assets of Fortuna Alliance of Bellingham, Washington. Fortuna had allegedly taken in more than $6 million from thousands of people in an illegal investors' pyramid scheme advertised on the Internet. Fortuna placed ads at several Web sites inviting thousands of customers on the Web to invest $250 to $1750 with the promise of earning at least $5000 per month if they could persuade others to invest. The FTC called Fortuna its largest fraud case to date on the Internet (Wilder, 1996).
- Timothy Lloyd, a former chief computer network administrator at Omega Engineering Inc. in Bridgeport, New Jersey, was charged with planting a "logic bomb" that deleted all of the firm's software programs on July 30, 1996. A "logic bomb" is a malicious program that is set to trigger at a specified time. The company suffered $10 million in damages. Lloyd had been recently dismissed from his job. Federal prosecutors also charged Lloyd with stealing about $50,000 of computer equipment, which included a backup tape that could have allowed Omega to recover its lost files (Chen, 1998).
- In July 1992, a federal grand jury indicted a national network of 1000 hackers calling themselves MOD—Masters of Deception. Their's was one of the largest thefts of computer information and services in history. The hackers were charged with computer tampering, computer fraud, wire fraud, illegal wiretapping, and conspiracy. The group broke into over 25 of the largest corporate computer systems in the United States, including Equifax, Inc. (a credit reporting firm with 170 million records), Southwestern Bell Corporation, New York Telephone, and Pacific Bell. The group stole and resold credit reports, credit card numbers, and other personal information. The hackers—all of whom were under 22 years of age—pleaded guilty. Their convicted leader, Mark Abene, spent 10 months in prison (Gabriel, 1995; Tabor, 1992).

In general, it is employees—insiders—who have inflicted the most injurious computer crimes because they have the knowledge, access, and frequently a job-related motive to commit such crimes.

Congress responded to the threat of computer crime in 1986 with the Computer Fraud and Abuse Act. This act makes it illegal to access a computer system without authorization. Most states have similar laws, and nations in Europe have similar legislation. Other existing legislation covering wiretapping, fraud, and conspiracy by any

TABLE 4.4 Internet Crime and Abuse

Problem	Description
Hacking	Hackers exploit weaknesses in Web site security to obtain access to proprietary data such as customer information and passwords. They may use "Trojan horses" posing as legitimate software to obtain information from the host computer.
Jamming	Jammers use software routines to tie up the computer hosting a Web site so that legitimate visitors can't access the site.
Malicious software	Cyber vandals use data flowing through the Internet to transmit computer viruses, which can disable computers that they "infect" (see Chapter 14).
Sniffing	Sniffing is a form of electronic eavesdropping by placing a piece of software to intercept information passing from a user to the computer hosting a Web site. This information can include credit card numbers and other confidential data.
Spoofing	Spoofers fraudulently misrepresent themselves as other organizations, setting up false Web sites where they can collect confidential information from unsuspecting visitors to the site.

means, regardless of technology employed, is adequate to cover computer crimes committed thus far.

The Internet's ease of use and accessibility have created new opportunities for computer crime and abuse. Table 4.4 describes some of the most common areas where the Internet has been used for illegal or malicious purposes.

Employment: Trickle-Down Technology and Reengineering Job Loss

Reengineering work (see Chapter 10) is typically hailed in the information systems community as a major benefit of new information technology. It is much less frequently noted that redesigning business processes could potentially cause millions of middle-level managers and clerical workers to lose their jobs. Worse, if reengineering actually worked as claimed, these workers could not find similar employment in the society because of an actual decline in demand for their skills. One economist has raised the possibility that we will create a society run by a small "high tech elite of corporate professionals . . . in a nation of the permanently unemployed" (Rifkin, 1993). Some have estimated that if reengineering were seriously undertaken by the Fortune 1000 companies, about 25 percent of the U.S. labor force could be displaced. Reengineering has been seriously used at only 15 percent of American service and manufacturing companies.

Economists are much more sanguine about the potential job losses. They believe relieving bright, educated workers from reengineered jobs will result in these workers moving to better jobs in fast-growth industries. Left out of this equation are blue-collar workers, and older, less well-educated middle managers. It is not clear that these groups can be retrained easily for high-quality (high-paying) jobs. Careful planning and sensitivity to employee needs can help companies redesign work to minimize job losses, as illustrated in the Window on Management.

Equity and Access: Increasing Racial and Social Class Cleavages

Does everyone have an equal opportunity to participate in the digital age? Will the social, economic, and cultural gaps that exist in American and other societies be reduced by information systems technology? Or will the cleavages be increased, permitting the "better off" to become even better off relative to others? When and if computing becomes ubiquitous, does this include the poor as well as the rich?

The answers to these questions are clearly not known; the impact of systems technology on various groups in society is not well-studied. What is known is that infor-

WINDOW ON MANAGEMENT

The Internet for All?

The Internet is making dramatic changes within corporations. But what happens if some employees cannot reap Internet benefits simply because they have no access to a computer? Or because they lack the computer skills? Management in many companies is facing this problem today. If some employees cannot use the company's information systems based on Internet technology, the company could fail to gain from all their talents and creativity. The employees too might lose by not being able to develop their own skills and advance their own careers. Some management is sensitive to this issue and is responding by searching for ways to include all their employees, to the benefit of all.

The Tribune Company, a Chicago-based publishing and broadcasting firm, began in 1996 to focus on potential benefits of information systems based on Internet technology. Like many companies, the Tribune first reacted with an external search for people with the required information systems skills. Yet quality information systems development requires both creativity and technical knowledge. Given the nature of their business, the company already employed many creative people, such as graphic designers and artists. Management realized this and concluded creative, artistic people could be taught the technical skills needed to use information systems based on the Internet. They quit looking outside and instead gave their employees the opportunity to advance into a new field. The company quickly gained a very creative Internet development staff, which developed over 100 pages on the Tribune Company's Web site within the first two months. In addition, because the development staff was integrated into other company units, many Tribune employees quickly began using the Web-based system. According to Jeff Scherb, the company's senior vice president and chief technology officer, the Tribune's goal is to "get to the point where people don't think twice about Web publishing."

One problem many companies face is how to make Internet-based applications available to the whole staff. After all, not all employees have access to computers. *The Los Angeles Times* wanted to use Internet technology to establish an information system to expand human resources and workflow applications. Although most of its over 4000 employees have computer access, many do not. Some whole departments, such as printing, have no computers. The company is considering installing strategically placed kiosks as a solution to this problem.

Initiatives to use information technology to create and preserve jobs are taking place outside the United States as well. The European Commission is funding eight pilot projects designed to help local authorities use communications technologies to create jobs. Each project will help local authorities, such as the Welsh Development Agency and the Athens City Council analyze communications technologies in their area. The Commission hopes that their findings will help local authorities make wise policy decisions about future investments in communications technologies.

To carry out the project, local authorities are expected to link up with software providers and telecommunications service providers in their area. The European Commission is encouraging them to explore labor market applications such as linking job offers to job applications and creation of interenterprise communications networks.

To Think About: ***What are the arguments for and against companies and governments spending funds to create jobs with Internet and related information technology and to expand Internet access? Think about social and ethical issues as well as those relating to profit.***

Sources: Elizabeth de Bony, "European Commission Launches Effort to Create Jobs Through Technology Projects," *Computerworld,* April 14, 1997; and Julie Kings, "Tribune Co. Trains Net Pros In-house," *Computerworld,* January 20, 1997.

mation and knowledge, and access to these resources through educational institutions and public libraries, are inequitably distributed. Access to computers is distributed inequitably along racial and social class lines, as are many other information resources. Left uncorrected, we could end up creating a society of information haves, computer literate and skilled, versus a large group of information have-nots, computer illiterate and unskilled.

The Clinton administration and public interest groups want to narrow this "digital divide" by making digital information services—including the Internet—available to "virtually everyone" just as basic telephone service is now. An amendment to the Telecommunications Act of 1996, which widened telecommunications deregulation, stipulates subsidies for schools and libraries so that people of all backgrounds have access to the tools of information technology (Lohr, 1996). This is only a partial solution to the problem.

Health Risks: RSI, CVS, and Technostress

repetitive stress injury (RSI) Occupational disease that occurs when muscle groups are forced through repetitive actions with high-impact loads or thousands of repetitions with low-impact loads.

carpal tunnel syndrome (CTS) Type of RSI in which pressure on the median nerve through the wrist's bony carpal tunnel structure produces pain.

computer vision syndrome (CVS) Eye strain condition related to computer display screen use, with symptoms including headaches, blurred vision, and dry, irritated eyes.

technostress Stress induced by computer use whose symptoms include aggravation, hostility toward humans, impatience, and enervation.

The most important occupational disease today is **repetitive stress injury (RSI).** RSI occurs when muscle groups are forced through repetitive actions often with high-impact loads (such as tennis) or tens of thousands of repetitions under low-impact loads (such as working at a computer keyboard).

The single largest source of RSI is computer keyboards. Forty-six million Americans use computers at work, and 185,000 cases of RSI are reported each year, according to the National Center for Health Statistics. The most common kind of computer-related RSI is **carpal tunnel syndrome (CTS),** in which pressure on the median nerve through the wrist's bony structure called a "carpal tunnel" produces pain. The pressure is caused by constant repetition of keystrokes: In a single shift, a word processor may perform 23,000 keystrokes. Symptoms of carpal tunnel syndrome include numbness, shooting pain, inability to grasp objects, and tingling. So far, nearly two million workers have been diagnosed with carpal tunnel syndrome.

RSI is avoidable. Designing workstations for a neutral wrist position (using a wrist rest to support the wrist), proper monitor stands, and footrests all contribute to proper posture and reduced RSI. New, ergonomically correct keyboards are also an option, although their efficacy has yet to be clearly established. These measures should be backed by frequent rest breaks, rotation of employees to different jobs, and moving toward voice or scanner data entry.

RSI is not the only occupational illness caused by computers; back and neck pain, leg stress, and foot pain also result from poor ergonomic designs of workstations (see Tables 4.5 and 4.6).

Computer vision syndrome (CVS) refers to any eye strain condition related to computer display screen use. Its symptoms are headaches, blurred vision, and dry and irritated eyes. The symptoms are usually temporary (Furger, 1993).

The newest computer-related malady is **technostress,** defined as stress induced by computer use and whose symptoms are aggravation, hostility toward humans, impatience, and enervation. The problem according to experts is that humans working continuously with computers come to expect other humans and human institutions to behave like computers, providing instant response, attentiveness, and with an absence of emotion. Computer-intense workers are aggravated when put on hold during a phone call, become incensed or alarmed when their PCs take a few seconds longer to perform a task, lack empathy for humans, and seek out friends who mirror the characteristics of their machines. Technostress is thought to be related to high levels of job turnover in the computer industry, high levels of early retirement from computer-intense occupations, and elevated levels of drug and alcohol abuse.

Repetitive stress injury (RSI) is the leading occupational disease today. The single largest cause of RSI is computer keyboard work.

TABLE 4.5 OSHA Ergonomic Risk Factors
Intermittent keying
Intensive keying
Neck twisting/bending
Wrist bending
Prolonged mouse use
Prolonged sitting
Sitting without solid foot support
Lighting (poor illumination or glare)

Source: Mary E. Thyfault, "OSHA Clamps Down," *Information Week*, November 21, 1995.

The incidence of technostress is not known but is thought to be in the millions in the United States and growing rapidly. Although frequently denied as a problem by management, computer-related jobs now top the list of stressful occupations based on health statistics in several industrialized countries. The costs worldwide of stress are put at $200 billion.

To date the role of radiation from computer display screens in occupational disease has not been proved. Video display terminals (VDTs) emit nonionizing electric and magnetic fields at low frequencies. These rays enter the body and have unknown effects on enzymes, molecules, chromosomes, and cell membranes. Long term studies are investigating low-level electromagnetic fields and birth defects, stress, low birth weight, and other diseases. All manufacturers have reduced display screen emissions since the early 1980s, and European countries such as Sweden have adopted stiff radiation emission standards.

The computer has become a part of our lives—personally as well as socially, culturally, and politically. It is unlikely the issues and our choices will become easier as information technology continues to transform our world. The growth of the Internet and the information economy suggests that all the ethical and social issues we have described will be heightened further as we move into the first digital century.

Management Actions: A Corporate Code of Ethics

Some corporations have developed far-reaching corporate IS codes of ethics—Federal Express, IBM, American Express, and Merck and Co. Most firms, however, have not developed these codes of ethics, which leaves them at the mercy of fate, and leaves their employees in the dark about expected correct behavior. There is some dispute concerning a general code of ethics versus a specific information systems code of ethics. As managers, you should strive to develop an IS-specific set of ethical standards for each of the five moral dimensions:

TABLE 4.6 Computer-Related Diseases

Disease/Risk	Incidence
RSI	185,000 new cases a year
Other joint diseases	Unknown
Computer Vision Syndrome	10 million cases a year
Technostress	5 to 10 million cases
VDT radiation	Unknown impacts

- *Information rights and obligations.* A code should cover topics such as employee e-mail privacy, workplace monitoring, treatment of corporate information, and policies on customer information.
- *Property rights and obligations.* A code should cover topics such as software licenses, ownership of firm data and facilities, ownership of software created by employees on company hardware, and software copyrights. Specific guidelines for contractual relationships with third parties should be covered as well.
- *Accountability and control.* The code should specify a single individual responsible for all information systems, and underneath this individual others who are responsible for individual rights, the protection of property rights, system quality, and quality of life (e.g., job design, ergonomics, employee satisfaction). Responsibilities for control of systems, audits, and management should be clearly defined. The potential liabilities of systems officers and the corporation should be detailed in a separate document.
- *System quality.* The code should describe the general levels of data quality and system error that can be tolerated with detailed specifications left to specific projects. The code should require that all systems attempt to estimate data quality and system error probabilities.
- *Quality of life.* The code should state that the purpose of systems is to improve the quality of life for customers and for employees by achieving high levels of product quality, customer service, and employee satisfaction and human dignity through proper ergonomics, job and workflow design, and human resource development.

Management Wrap-Up

MANAGEMENT

ORGANIZATION

TECHNOLOGY

Managers are ethical rule makers for their organizations (Green, 1994). They are charged with creating the policies and procedures to establish ethical conduct, including the ethical use of information systems. Managers are also responsible for identifying, analyzing, and resolving the ethical dilemmas that invariably crop up as they balance conflicting needs and interests.

Rapid changes fueled by information technology are creating new situations where existing laws or rules of conduct may not be relevant. New "gray areas" are emerging in which ethical standards have not yet been codified into law. A new system of ethics for the information age is required to guide individual and organizational choices and actions.

Information technology is introducing changes that create new ethical issues for societies to debate and resolve. Increasing computing power, storage, and networking capabilities—including the Internet—can expand the reach of individual and organizational actions and magnify their impact. The ease and anonymity with which information can be communicated, copied, and manipulated in on-line environments are challenging traditional rules of right and wrong behavior.

For Discussion:

1. Should producers of software-based services such as ATMs be held liable for economic injuries suffered when their systems fail?
2. Should companies be responsible for unemployment caused by their information systems? Why or why not?

SUMMARY

1. **Analyze the relationship among ethical, social, and political issues raised by information systems.** Ethical, social, and political issues are closely related in an information society. Ethical issues confront individuals who must choose a course of action, often in a situation in which two or more ethical principles are in conflict (a dilemma). Social issues spring from ethical issues. Societies must develop expectations in individuals about the correct course of action, and social issues then are debates about the kinds of situations and expectations that societies should develop so that individuals behave correctly. Political issues spring from social conflict and have to do largely with laws that prescribe behavior and seek to use the law to create situations in which individuals behave correctly.
2. **Identify the main moral dimensions of an information society and apply them to specific situations.** There are five main moral dimensions that tie together ethical, social, and political issues in an information society. These moral dimensions are information rights and obligations, property rights, accountability and control, system quality, and quality of life.
3. **Apply an ethical analysis to difficult situations.** An ethical analysis is a five-step methodology for analyzing a situation. The method involves identifying the facts, values, stakeholders, options, and consequences of actions. Once completed, you can begin to consider what ethical principle you should apply to a situation to arrive at a judgment.
4. **Examine specific ethical principles for conduct.** Six ethical principles are available to judge your own conduct (and that of others). These principles are derived independently from several cultural, religious, and intellectual traditions. They are not hard-and-fast rules and may not apply in all situations. The principles are the Golden Rule, Immanuel Kant's Categorical Imperative, Descartes' rule of change, the Utilitarian Principle, the Risk Aversion Principle, and the ethical "no free lunch" rule.
5. **Design corporate policies for ethical conduct.** For each of the five moral dimensions, corporations should develop an ethics policy statement to assist individuals and to encourage the correct decisions. The policy areas are as follows. Individual information rights: spell out corporate privacy and due process policies. Property rights: clarify how the corporation will treat property rights of software owners. Accountability and control: clarify who is responsible and accountable for information. System quality: identify methodologies and quality standards to achieve. Quality of life: identify corporate policies on family, computer crime, decision making, vulnerability, job loss, and health risks.

KEY TERMS

Accountability, 108
Carpal tunnel syndrome (CTS), 128
Computer abuse, 124
Computer crime, 124
Computer vision syndrome (CVS), 128
Copyright, 116
Descartes' rule of change, 110
Due process, 108
Ethical "no free lunch" rule, 111
Ethics, 105
Fair Information Practices (FIP), 112
Immanuel Kant's Categorical Imperative, 110
Information rights, 105
Intellectual property, 116
Liability, 108
Patent, 117
Privacy, 112
Repetitive stress injury (RSI), 128
Responsibility, 108
Risk Aversion Principle, 110
Spamming, 114
Technostress, 128
Trade secret, 116
Utilitarian principle, 110

REVIEW QUESTIONS

1. In what ways are ethical, social, and political issues connected? Give some examples.
2. What are the key technological trends that heighten ethical concerns?
3. What are the differences between responsibility, accountability, and liability?
4. What are the five steps in an ethical analysis?
5. Identify six ethical principles.
6. What is a professional code of conduct?
7. What are meant by "privacy" and "fair information practices"? How is the Internet challenging the protection of individual privacy?
8. What are the three different regimes that protect intellectual property rights? What challenges to intellectual property rights are posed by the Internet?
9. Why is it so difficult to hold software services liable for failure or injury?
10. What is the most common cause of system quality problems?
11. Name and describe four "quality of life" impacts of computers and information systems.
12. What is technostress, and how would you measure it?
13. Name three management actions that could reduce RSI injuries.

GROUP PROJECT

With three or four of your classmates, develop a corporate ethics code on privacy that addresses both employee privacy and the privacy of customers and users of the corporate Web site. Be sure to consider e-mail privacy and employer monitoring of worksites, as well as corporate use of information about employees concerning their off-job behavior (e.g., lifestyle, marital arrangements, and so forth). Present your ethics code to the class.

TOOLS FOR INTERACTIVE LEARNING

■ **INTERNET**: The Internet Connection for this chapter will direct you to a series of Web sites where you can learn more about the privacy issues raised by the use of the Internet and the Web. You can complete an exercise to analyze the privacy implications of existing technologies for tracking Web site visitors. You can also use the Interactive Study Guide to test your knowledge of the topics in this chapter, and get instant feedback where you need more practice.

■ **CD-ROM**: If you purchase and use the Multimedia Edition CD-ROM with this chapter, you can complete an interactive exercise asking you to perform an ethical analysis of problems encountered by a business. You can also find a video clip on software piracy and the activities of the Software Publishers Association (SPA), an audio overview of the major themes of this chapter, and bullet text summarizing the key points of the chapter.

CASE STUDY

Profiling YOU!

Digital data about each of us are multiplying fast. Every time you do many things, including charge something on your credit card, buy something on time, fill out and send in a warranty card, buy a plane ticket, make a telephone call from your home or work, receive a traffic ticket, buy or sell stocks, or visit your doctor, someone is recording that action electronically. This list could go on and on. Recording these actions is absolutely not an invasion of privacy. After all, companies need records to bill you, to reserve your plane seat, or to report your purchases and sales for tax purposes. Your doctor must keep records on your health and the government must know when a ticket is issued, to whom it was issued, and when it was paid. Invasion of privacy does arise when these data are used for purposes other than the reasons for which they were collected. Even worse, someone may put several pieces of this data together and draw conclusions from it to your detriment.

How might others use these data about you? Assume, for example, that your credit card company analyzes your credit card transaction and finds that your expenditures on prescription drugs has risen, you have made several charges to a resume service, you are charging visits to a psychological counselor, and you are also buying gasoline more frequently but in smaller quantities than in the past. Your credit card issuer could easily conclude that you are having trouble (the counselor and prescription charges) and are possibly without a job (resume service and smaller gasoline purchases). The credit card issuer might logically conclude that you have lost your job and so are a bad credit risk. The result could easily be that you would find your credit limited or your credit account closed altogether.

The newest wrinkle in this privacy invasion is software for electronic profiling. Such software collects data about people, often from various sources, and uses aggressive data mining and artificial intelligence techniques to help an organization evaluate the risk you might present. One such system, Computer-Assisted Passenger Screening (CAPS), was adopted by the Federal Aviation Administration (FAA) and required to be used by all airlines in the United States by the end of 1998. The system was developed upon the recommendation of the White House Commission on Terrorism after the July 1996 explosion of TWA Flight 800. CAPS creates a profile on all purchasers of airline tickets. Its goal is to identify potential terrorists.

The specific data and the criteria CAPS uses are secret, although early uses have given observers some insights. Hassan Abbass, a Syrian-born United States citizen residing in Cleveland, recently sued US Airways, alleging discrimination because he and his family had been subjected to such actions as "humiliating" luggage searches. Abbass and his wife obviously were targeted because of their frequent visits to Syria, a country that the United States State Department has designated a source of terrorism. However the Abbasses claim their frequent trips are only to visit family, that they are not terrorists, and that they are being unfairly harassed. Greg Nojeim, an American Civil Liberties Union (ACLU) lawyer, claims that this type of targeting singles out people of Middle Eastern descent for special scrutiny and so is discriminatory. "A profile that targets as potential terrorists people who travel frequently to a country on the State Department's terrorist list would have a disparate impact on people who trace their national origin to that country," Nojeim insists. Abbass has settled his lawsuit against US Air but the ACLU predicts many more such suits. Nojeim claims that the ACLU has received "scores of complaints" from passengers, most of them claiming racial discrimination, whereas the U.S. Department of Transportation has investigated 46 complaints. All of these complaints were lodged in only the first few months the system was operating, and while it was being used by only a handful of airlines.

The fact that both the data used and the profile criteria are a secret is a major source of CAPS problems. An FAA spokesperson refused to state what criteria are used in the profile that selects potential terrorists, because, she claims, if the criteria were made public, actual terrorists would learn how to avoid being pinpointed. She does deny that race, religion, or ethnicity are included, because to use them would violate federal law.

Many acknowledge that electronic-profiling systems do produce benefits, helping corporations save money and reduce various types of risks. Sears, Roebuck and Co. began using electronic-profiling software after the company amassed losses of $688 million in credit-card fraud and uncollectable debt in one quarter in 1997. Early reports on the use of the system indicate that it can prevent 20 percent of the purchases by deadbeats and by fraudulent credit-card users, for a savings of nearly $550 million per year.

With savings like that, no wonder banks and other retailers are beginning to use similar systems to manage their credit risks. Several vendors of fraud-detection software offer products designed to check credit cards as they are being used for on-line purchases over the Internet. Companies engaged in electronic commerce have complained of swindles where shoppers place their orders, receive the merchandise and then dispute the sale, claiming that their credit card numbers were used fraudulently. The seller must give these "shoppers" refunds. IVS Fraud Screen, a detection service from CyberSource Corporation in San Jose, California, uses artificial intelligence to assess the likelihood that a proposed on-line transaction is fraudulent. The software examines the amount of the sale, the time of the day, and the source of the transaction, along with traditional data, and compares such data with a data pool of known fraudulent transactions to produce a fraud score. It flags suspect sales for further study.

The value of these systems is not being questioned. The ethics of these systems is. Profiling systems can invade peoples' privacy, resulting in discriminatory treatment; therefore, they raise fears among the general public. The Chicago Police Department developed a profiling system that was meant to locate police officers who might be likely to engage in police brutality. Selection criteria included, for example, officers who had been recently divorced. The system never came into use because of strong opposition from the police union.

Some computer ethics specialists believe that these systems can be used responsibly. One problem, they explain, is that people have too much faith in anything that comes from the computer. Ethicists usually advocate not allowing profiling systems to automatically trigger any action against anyone. Instead, action must be taken only after intervention by a responsible human being. In addition, they urge proper training of system users so the users will understand the sensitive legal and personal issues involved with profiling.

Sources: Kim S. Nash, "Electronic Profiling," *Computerworld*, February 9, 1998 and John M. Broder, "Making America Safe for Electronic Commerce," *The New York Times*, June 22, 1997.

Case Study Questions

1. Name the technologies that have enabled the emergence of electronic-profiling systems, and explain how each has contributed to their development.
2. Which ethical principles apply here? Explain your answer.
3. We have described five moral dimensions of the information age. Pick one of these dimensions and describe the ethical, social, and political aspects of electronic profiling.
4. Airline terrorism presents a special problem because of the number of deaths that could result from one overlooked terrorist. If you were a member of the White House Commission on Terrorism, charged with combating terrorism on airlines, what would your arguments be for the adoption of the CAPS system? Then, change yourself into a lawyer arguing for the Abbass family and explain your arguments against the CAPS system. Finally, having considered both sides, explain your personal position on this issue.

CHAPTER 5

Computers and Information Processing

chapter outline

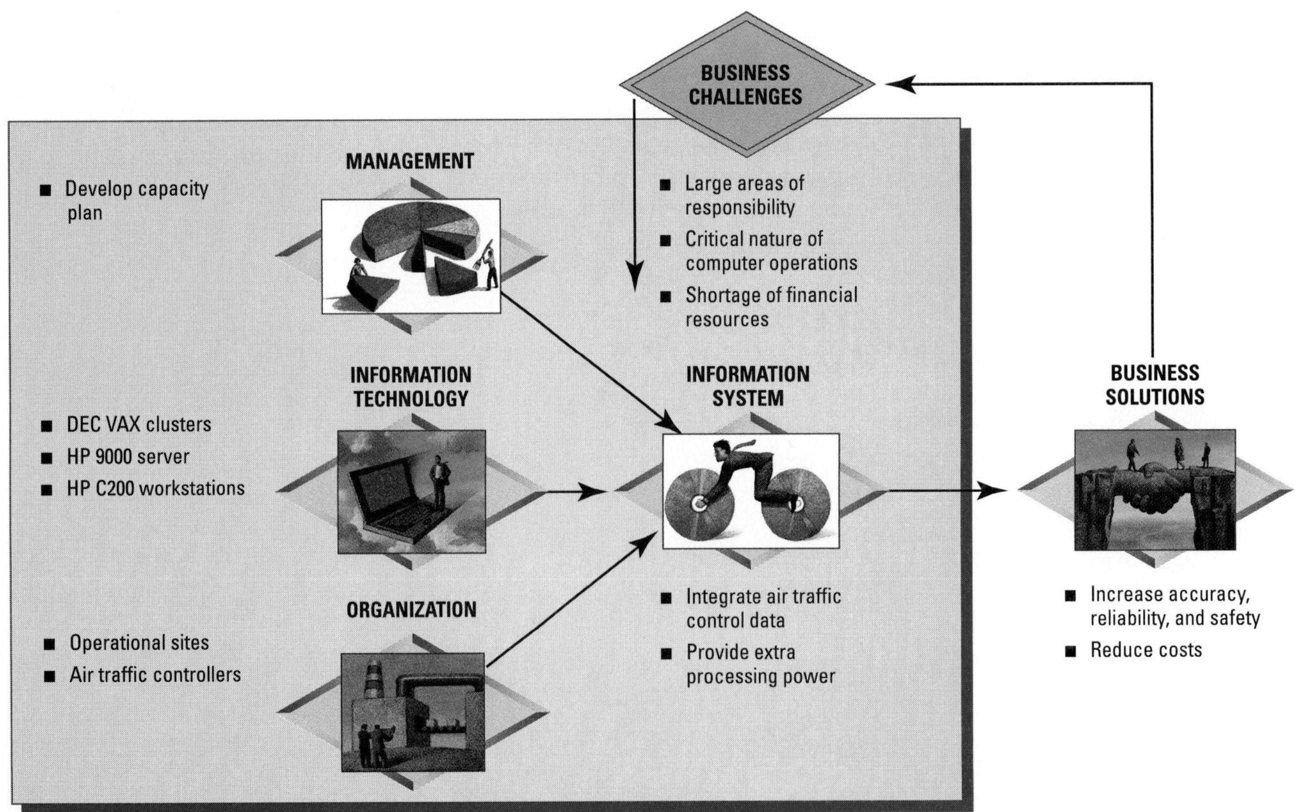

Navigation Canada Takes Flight with New Computers

The area that Canada's air traffic control system monitors is vast—more than 15 million square miles of airspace. Before privatization in November 1996, this responsibility was handled with outdated Digital Equipment Corporation VAX cluster computers that required air traffic controllers to hunt for information on six different systems. The air navigation system was funded by an Air Transportation Tax levied by the government, which did not provide sufficient funds for computer upgrades.

Then a new private, nonprofit company called Navigation Canada took over. Navigation Canada, because it could charge the airline industry fees for its services, was able to raise $600 million to upgrade the computers required to make the air traffic control system safer and more secure. The upgrade, called the Canadian Air Traffic Control System (CATTS), started in the summer of 1998 and will take three years to complete. Navigation Canada replaced the VAX clusters with HP 9000 server computers and HP C200 Unix-based workstations. Each of Navigation Canada's 23 operational sites is being outfitted with three servers—a primary server, a backup server and a third server for training purposes. The built-in redundancy is deliberate. If one of the servers fails, another can take over. Air navigation systems can't afford to be down even for five minutes. Software has been added to ensure that flight data are transmitted and received without modification or corruption.

CATTS gives air traffic controllers radar data, flight path information, computer-based conflict prediction, weather updates, and navigational aid data on a single system. CATTS also automatically routes flight plans to the appropriate people, reducing the chance of human error or loss of critical information. With these new capabilities, Navigation Canada can reduce flight delays and inefficiencies created by airplanes contending for the same runway. Air traffic controllers can support routes that are more direct and fuel-efficient. In addition to making the Canadian skies safer for flyers, Navigation Canada expects the efficiencies created by CATTS to cut annual operating costs by $135 million.

Source: Adapted from Laura DiDio, "$600M Net Upgrade Takes Flight," *Computerworld*, February 16, 1998.

Management Challenges

By shifting from old VAX cluster computers to HP servers and workstations, Navigation Canada was able to provide more computing power for its air traffic control operations and to integrate all of the information used by air traffic controllers. To make this decision, Navigation Canada's management needed to understand how much computer processing capacity was required by its business processes and how to evaluate the price and performance of various types of computers. It had to know why HP 9000 server computers and HP C200 workstations were appropriate for its processing needs, and it had to plan for future processing requirements. Management also had to understand how the computer worked with related storage, input/output, and communications technology. Selecting appropriate computer hardware raises the following management challenges:

1. **The centralization vs. decentralization debate.** A longstanding issue among information system managers and CEOs has been the question of how much to centralize or distribute computing resources. Should processing power and data be distributed to departments and divisions, or should they be concentrated at a single location using a large central computer? Client/server computing facilitates decentralization, but network computers and mainframes support a centralized model. Which is the best for the organization? Each organization will have a different answer. Managers need to make sure that the computing model they select is compatible with organizational goals.

2. **Making wise technology purchasing decisions.** Soon after having made an investment in information technology, managers find the completed system is obsolete and too expensive, given the power and lower cost of new technology. In this environment it is very difficult to keep one's own systems up-to-date. A considerable amount of time must be spent anticipating and planning for technological change.

learning objectives

After completing this chapter, you will be able to:

1. Identify the hardware components in a typical computer system.
2. Describe how information is represented and processed in a computer system.
3. Contrast the capabilities of mainframes, minicomputers, PCs, workstations, and supercomputers.
4. Compare different arrangements of computer processing, including the use of client/server computing and network computers.
5. Describe the principal media for storing data and programs in a computer system.
6. Compare the major input and output devices and approaches to input and processing.
7. Describe multimedia and future information technology trends.

In this chapter we describe the typical hardware configuration of a computer system, explaining how a computer works and how computer processing power and storage capacity are measured. We then compare the capabilities of various types of computers and related input, output, and storage devices.

5.1 WHAT IS A COMPUTER SYSTEM?

A contemporary computer system consists of a central processing unit, primary storage, secondary storage, input devices, output devices, and communications devices (see Figure 5.1). The central processing unit manipulates raw data into a more useful form and controls the other parts of the computer system. Primary storage temporarily stores data and program instructions during processing, whereas secondary storage devices (magnetic and optical disks, magnetic tape) store data and programs when they are not being used in processing. Input devices, such as a keyboard or mouse, convert data and instructions into electronic form for input into the computer. Output devices, such as printers and video display terminals, convert electronic data produced by the computer system and display them in a form that people can understand. Communications devices provide connections between the computer and communications networks. Buses are paths for transmitting data and signals among the parts of the computer system.

How Computers Represent Data

In order for information to flow through a computer system and be in a form suitable for processing, all symbols, pictures, or words must be reduced to a string of binary digits. A binary digit is called a **bit** and represents either a 0 or a 1. In the computer, the presence of an electronic or magnetic signal means one, and its absence signifies zero. Digital computers operate directly with binary digits, either singly or strung together to form bytes. A string of eight bits that the computer stores as a unit is called a **byte.** Each byte can be used to store a decimal number, a symbol, a character, or part of a picture (see Figure 5.2).

bit A binary digit representing the smallest unit of data in a computer system. It can only have one of two states, representing 0 or 1.

byte A string of bits, usually eight, used to store one number or character in a computer system.

Figure 5.3 shows how decimal numbers are represented using true binary digits. Each position in a decimal number has a certain value. Any number in the decimal system (base 10) can be reduced to a binary number. The binary number system (base 2) can express any number as a power of the number 2. The table at the bottom of the figure shows how the translation from binary to decimal works. By using a binary number system a computer can express all numbers as groups of zeroes and ones. True binary cannot be used by a computer because, in addition to representing numbers, a

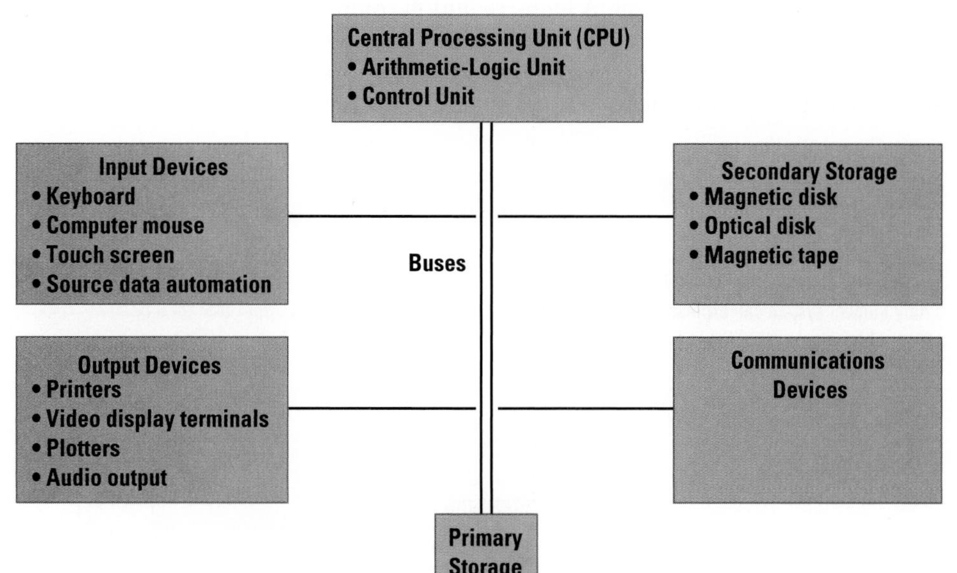

FIGURE 5.1

Hardware components of a computer system. A contemporary computer system can be categorized into six major components. The central processing unit manipulates data and controls the other parts of the computer system; primary storage temporarily stores data and program instructions during processing; secondary storage feeds data and instructions into the central processor and stores data for future use; input devices convert data and instructions for processing in the computer; output devices present data in a form that people can understand; and communications devices control the passing of information to and from communications networks.

FIGURE 5.2

Bits and bytes. Bits are represented by either a 0 or 1. A string of 8 bits constitutes a byte, which represents a character. The computer's representation for the word "ALICE" is a series of five bytes, where each byte represents one character (or letter) in the name.

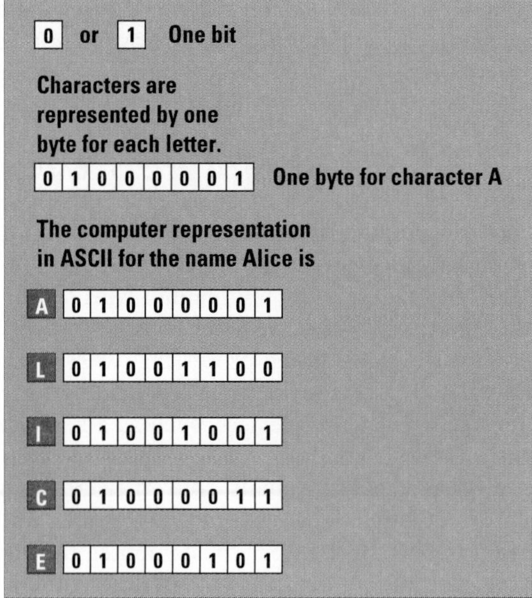

computer must represent alphabetic characters and many other symbols used in natural language, such as $ and &. This requirement led manufacturers of computer hardware to develop standard binary codes.

EBCDIC (Extended Binary Coded Decimal Interchange Code) Binary code representing every number, alphabetic character, or special character with 8 bits, used primarily in IBM and other mainframe computers.

ASCII (American Standard Code for Information Interchange) A 7- or 8-bit binary code used in data transmission, PCs, and some large computers.

pixel The smallest unit of data for defining an image in the computer. The computer reduces a picture to a grid of pixels. The term pixel comes from picture element.

Two common codes are EBCDIC and ASCII. The **Extended Binary Coded Decimal Interchange Code (EBCDIC**—pronounced ib-si-dick) was developed by IBM in the 1950s, and it represents every number, alphabetic character, or special character with eight bits. **ASCII,** which stands for the **American Standard Code for Information Interchange,** was developed by the American National Standards Institute (ANSI) to provide a standard code that could be used by many different manufacturers in order to make machinery compatible. ASCII was originally designed as a seven-bit code, but most computers use eight-bit versions. EBCDIC is used in IBM and other mainframe computers, whereas ASCII is used in data transmission, PCs, and some larger computers. Table 5.1 shows how some letters and numbers would be represented using EBCDIC and ASCII. Other coding systems are being developed to represent a wider array of foreign languages.

How can a computer represent a picture? The computer stores a picture by creating a grid overlay of the picture. In this grid or matrix, the computer measures the light or color in each box or cell, called a **pixel** (picture element). The computer then stores this information on each pixel. A high-resolution computer terminal has a 1024 × 768 VGA standard grid, creating more than 700,000 pixels. Whether pictures or text are stored, it is through this process of reduction that a modern computer is able to operate in a complex environment.

FIGURE 5.3

True binary digits. Each decimal number has a certain value that can be expressed as a binary number. The binary number system can express any number as a power of the number 2.

10100, which is equal to:

$0 \times 2^0 = 0$
$0 \times 2^1 = 0$
$1 \times 2^2 = 4$
$0 \times 2^3 = 0$
$1 \times 2^4 = 16$
20

Place	5	4	3	2	1
Power of 2	2^4	2^3	2^2	2^1	2^0
Decimal value	16	8	4	2	1

TABLE 5.1 Examples of ASCII and EBCDIC Codes

Character or Number	ASCII-8 Binary	EBCDIC Binary
A	01000001	11000001
E	01000101	11000101
Z	01011010	11101001
0	00110000	11110000
1	00110001	11110001
5	00110101	11110101

Time and Size in the Computer World

Table 5.2 presents some key levels of time and size that are useful in describing the speed and capacity of modern computer systems.

Very slow, old computers or hardware devices measure machine cycle times in milliseconds (thousandths of a second). More powerful machines use measures of **microseconds** (millionths of a second) or **nanoseconds** (billionths of a second). Very powerful computers measure machine cycles in picoseconds (trillionths of a second). A very large computer with multiple processors has a machine cycle time of less than one nanosecond. Such computers can execute one billion instructions per second, with each processor executing 100 MIPS. MIPS, or millions of instructions per second, is a common benchmark for measuring the speed of larger computers.

Computer storage capacity is measured in bytes. One thousand bytes (actually 1024 storage positions) is called a **kilobyte.** Small PCs used to have internal primary memories of 640 kilobytes. A large PC today can store 128 megabytes of information in primary memory. Each **megabyte** is approximately one million bytes. Large computers have gigabyte storage capacities. A **gigabyte** is approximately one billion bytes. External computer storage devices can store trillions of bytes of data. A **terabyte** is approximately one trillion bytes.

microsecond One-millionth of a second.

nanosecond One-billionth of a second.

kilobyte One thousand bytes (actually 1024 storage positions). Used as a measure of PC storage capacity.

megabyte Approximately one million bytes. Unit of computer storage capacity.

gigabyte Approximately one billion bytes. Unit of computer storage capacity.

terabyte Approximately one trillion bytes. Unit of computer storage capacity.

Computer Generations

There have been four major stages, or computer generations, in the evolution of computer hardware, each distinguished by a different technology for the components that do the computer's processing work. Each generation has dramatically expanded computer

TABLE 5.2 Time and Size in the Computer World

Time	
Millisecond	1/1000 second
Microsecond	1/1,000,000 second
Nanosecond	1/1,000,000,000 second
Picosecond	1/1,000,000,000,000 second
Storage Capacity	
Byte	String of 8 bits
Kilobyte	1000 bytes[a]
Megabyte	1,000,000 bytes
Gigabyte	1,000,000,000 bytes
Terabyte	1,000,000,000,000 bytes

[a] *Actually 1024 storage positions*

processing power and storage capabilities while simultaneously lowering costs. For instance, the cost of performing 100,000 calculations plunged from several dollars in the 1950s to less than $0.025 in the 1980s and approximately $.00004 in 1995. These generational changes in computer hardware have been accompanied by generational changes in computer software (see Chapter 6) that have made computers increasingly more powerful, inexpensive, and easy to use.

First Generation: Vacuum Tube Technology, 1946–1956

The first generation of computers relied on vacuum tubes to store and process information. These tubes were colossal in size, consumed a great deal of power, were short-lived, and generated a great deal of heat. First-generation computers had extremely limited memory and processing capability and were used for very limited scientific and engineering work. The maximum main memory size was approximately 2000 bytes (2 kilobytes), with a speed of 10 kiloinstructions per second. Rotating magnetic drums were used for internal storage and punched cards for external storage. Jobs such as running programs or printing output had to be coordinated manually.

Second Generation: Transistors, 1957–1963

In the second computer generation, transistors replaced vacuum tubes as the devices for storing and processing information. Transistors were smaller and more reliable than vacuum tubes, they generated less heat, and they consumed less power. Magnetic core memory was the primary storage technology. It was composed of small magnetic doughnuts (about 1 millimeter in diameter), which could be polarized in one of two directions to represent a bit of data. Wires were strung along and through these cores to both write and read data. Second-generation computers had up to 32 kilobytes of RAM memory and speeds reaching 200,000 to 300,000 instructions per second. Second-generation computers had enough memory and processing power to be used more widely for scientific work and for business tasks such as automating payroll and billing.

Third Generation: Integrated Circuits, 1964–1979

Third-generation computers relied on integrated circuits, which were made by printing hundreds and later thousands of tiny transistors on small silicon chips. These devices were called semiconductors. Computer memories expanded to 2 megabytes of RAM memory, and speeds accelerated to 5 million instructions per second. Third-generation computer technology introduced software that could be used by people without extensive technical training, making it possible for computers to enlarge their role in business.

Fourth Generation: Very Large-Scale Integrated Circuits, 1980–Present

The fourth generation extends from 1980 to the present. Computers in this period use very large-scale integrated circuits (VLSIC), which are packed with hundreds of thousands and often millions of circuits per chip. With VLSIC technology, the computer's memory, logic, and control can be integrated on a single chip; hence the name **microprocessor,** or computer on a chip. Microprocessor technology has put the power of a computer that once took up a large room on a small desktop or laptop computer, making computers inexpensive and widely available for use in business and everyday life. Computer memory sizes have mushroomed to the gigabyte range in large commercial machines; processing speeds have exceeded one billion instructions per second. In Section 5.6, we discuss the next generation of hardware trends.

microprocessor Very large-scale integrated circuit technology that integrates the computer's memory, logic, and control on a single chip.

5.2 THE CPU AND PRIMARY STORAGE

The **central processing unit (CPU)** is the part of the computer system where the manipulation of symbols, numbers, and letter occurs, and it controls the other parts of the computer system. The CPU consists of a control unit and an arithmetic-logic unit (see Figure 5.4). Located near the CPU is **primary storage** (sometimes called primary memory or main memory), where data and program instructions are stored temporarily during pro-

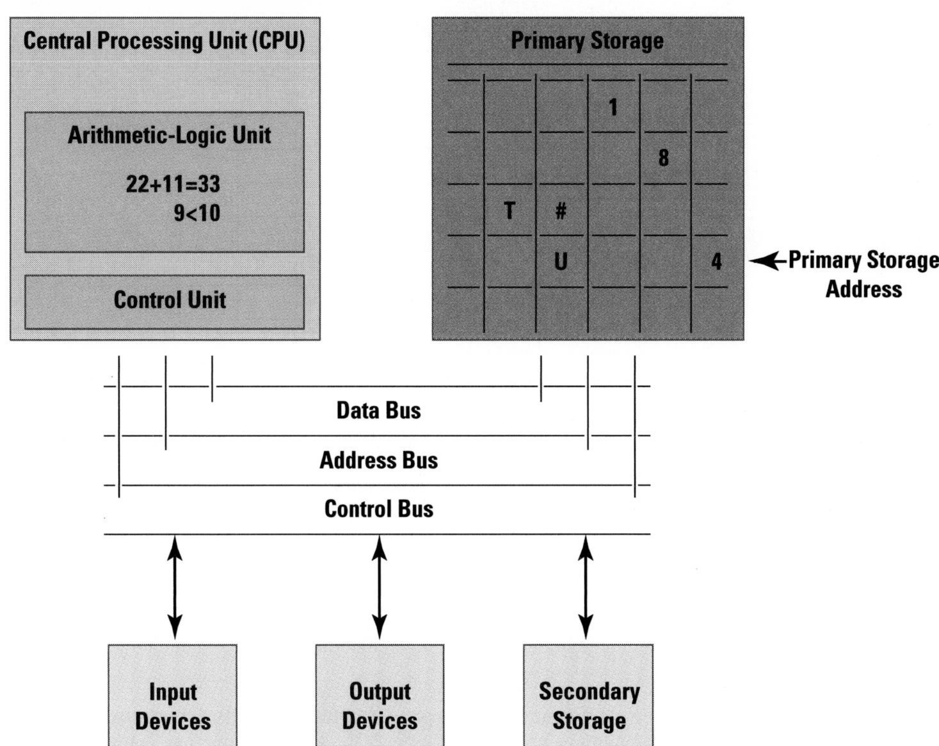

FIGURE 5.4

The CPU and primary storage. The CPU contains an arithmetic-logic unit and a control unit. Data and instructions are stored in unique addresses in primary storage that the CPU can access during processing. The data bus, address bus, and control bus transmit signals between the central processing unit, primary storage, and other devices in the computer system.

cessing. Three kinds of buses link the CPU, primary storage, and the other devices in the computer system. The data bus moves data to and from primary storage. The address bus transmits signals for locating a given address in primary storage. The control bus transmits signals specifying whether to read or write data to or from a given primary storage address, input device, or output device. The characteristics of the CPU and primary storage are very important in determining the speed and capabilities of a computer.

central processing unit (CPU) Area of the computer system that manipulates symbols, numbers, and letters, and controls the other parts of the computer system.

Primary Storage

primary storage Part of the computer that temporarily stores program instructions and data being used by the instructions.

Primary storage has three functions. It stores all or part of the program that is being executed. Primary storage also stores the operating system programs that manage the operation of the computer. (These programs are discussed in Chapter 6.) Finally, the primary storage area holds data that are being used by the program. Data and programs are placed in primary storage before processing, between processing steps, and after processing has ended, prior to being returned to secondary storage or released as output.

How is it possible for an electronic device such as primary storage to actually store information? How is it possible to retrieve this information from a known location in memory? Figure 5.5 illustrates primary storage in an electronic digital computer. Internal primary storage is often called **RAM, or random access memory.** It is called RAM because it can directly access any randomly chosen location in the same amount of time.

RAM (random access memory) Primary storage of data or program instructions that can directly access any randomly chosen location in the same amount of time.

Figure 5.5 shows that primary memory is divided into storage locations called bytes. Each location contains a set of eight binary switches or devices, each of which can store one bit of information. The set of eight bits found in each storage location is sufficient to store one letter, one digit, or one special symbol (such as $) using either EBCDIC or ASCII. Each byte has a unique address, similar to a mailbox, indicating where it is located in RAM. The computer can remember where the data in all of the bytes are located simply by keeping track of these addresses. Most of the information used by a computer application is stored on secondary storage devices such as disks and tapes, located outside of the primary storage area. In order for the computer to work on information, information must be transferred into primary memory for processing. Therefore, data are continually being read into and written out of the primary storage area during the execution of a program.

FIGURE 5.5

Primary storage in the computer. Primary storage can be visualized as a matrix. Each byte represents a mailbox with a unique address. In this example, mailbox [n,1] contains eight bits representing the number 0 (as coded in EBCDIC).

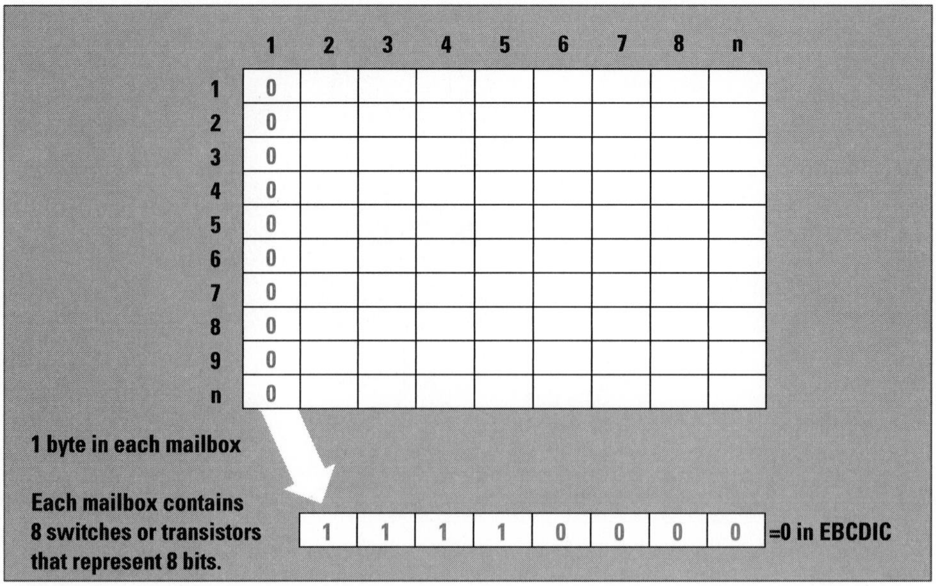

	1	2	3	4	5	6	7	8	n
1	0								
2	0								
3	0								
4	0								
5	0								
6	0								
7	0								
8	0								
9	0								
n	0								

1 byte in each mailbox

Each mailbox contains 8 switches or transistors that represent 8 bits.

1	1	1	1	0	0	0	0	=0 in EBCDIC

Types of Semiconductor Memory

semiconductor An integrated circuit made by printing thousands and even millions of tiny transistors on a small silicon chip.

ROM (read-only memory) Semiconductor memory chips that contain program instructions. These chips can only be read from; they cannot be written to.

PROM (programmable read-only memory) Subclass of ROM chip used in control devices because it can be programmed once.

EPROM (erasable programmable read-only memory) Subclass of ROM chip that can be erased and reprogrammed many times.

Primary storage is composed of semiconductors. A **semiconductor** is an integrated circuit made by printing thousands and even millions of tiny transistors on a small silicon chip. There are several different kinds of semiconductor memory used in primary storage. RAM is used for short-term storage of data or program instructions. RAM is volatile: Its contents will be lost when the computer's electric supply is disrupted by a power outage or when the computer is turned off. **ROM,** or **read-only memory,** can only be read from; it cannot be written to. ROM chips come from the manufacturer with programs already burned in, or stored. ROM is used in general-purpose computers to store important or frequently used programs, such as computing routines for calculating the square roots of numbers.

There are two other subclasses of ROM chips: **PROM,** or **programmable read-only memory,** and **EPROM,** or **erasable programmable read-only memory.** PROM chips are used by manufacturers as control devices in their products. They can be programmed once. In this way, manufacturers avoid the expense of having a specialized chip manufactured for the control of small motors, for instance; instead, they can program into a PROM chip the specific program for their product. PROM chips, therefore, can be made universally for many manufacturers in large production runs. EPROM chips are used for device control, such as in robots, where the program may have to be changed on a routine basis. With EPROM chips, the program can be erased and reprogrammed.

The Arithmetic-Logic Unit and Control Unit

arithmetic-logical unit (ALU) Component of the CPU that performs the principal logic and arithmetic operations of the computer.

control unit Component of the CPU that controls and coordinates the other parts of the computer system.

machine cycle Series of operations required to process a single machine instruction.

The **arithmetic-logic unit (ALU)** performs the principal logical and arithmetic operations of the computer. It adds, subtracts, multiplies, and divides, determining whether a number is positive, negative, or zero. In addition to performing arithmetic functions, an ALU must be able to determine when one quantity is greater than or less than another and when two quantities are equal. The ALU can perform logic operations on the binary codes for letters as well as numbers.

The **control unit** coordinates and controls the other parts of the computer system. It reads a stored program, one instruction at a time, and directs other components of the computer system to perform the tasks required by the program. The series of operations required to process a single machine instruction is called the **machine cycle.** As illustrated in Figure 5.6, the machine cycle has two parts: an instruction cycle and an execution cycle.

During the instruction cycle, the control unit retrieves one program instruction from primary storage and decodes it. It places the part of the instruction telling the ALU

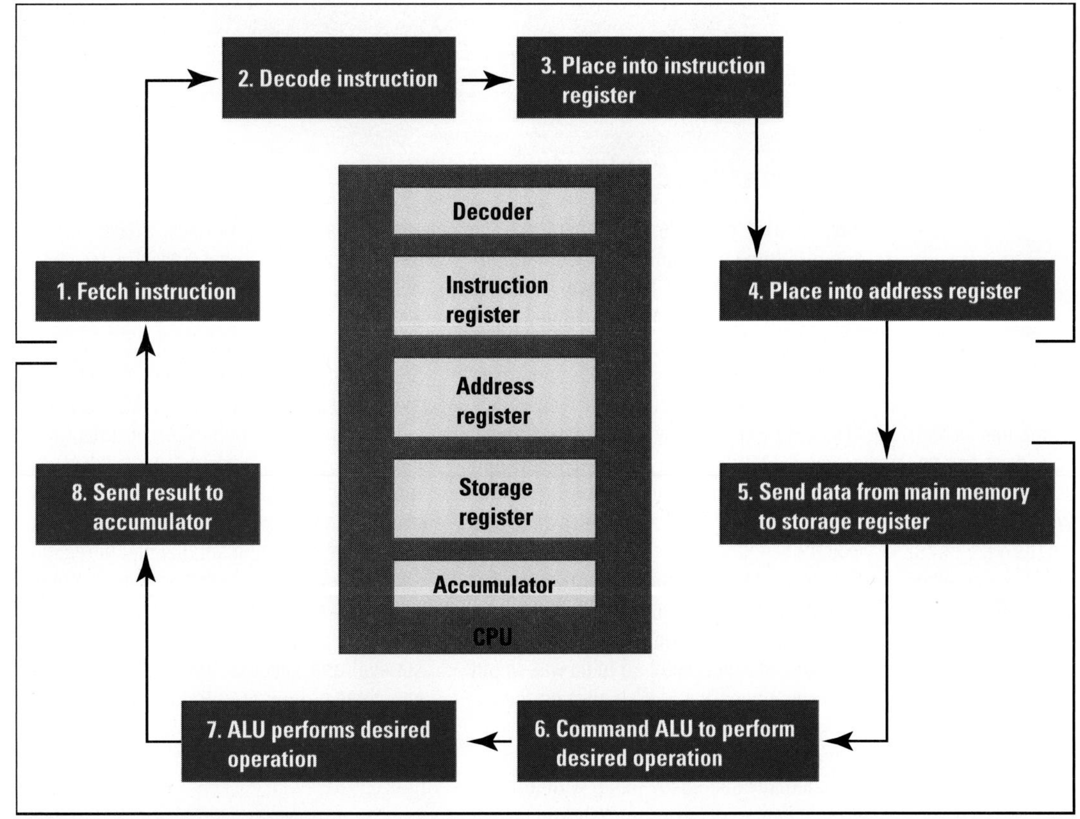

FIGURE 5.6 The various steps in the machine cycle. The machine cycle has two main stages of operation: the instruction cycle (I-cycle) and the execution cycle (E-cycle). There are several steps within each cycle required to process a single machine instruction in the CPU.

what to do next in a special instruction register and places the part specifying the address of the data to be used in the operation into an address register. (A **register** is a special temporary storage location in the ALU or control unit that acts like a high-speed staging area for program instructions or data being transferred from primary storage to the CPU for processing.)

register Temporary storage location in the ALU or control unit where small amounts of data and instructions reside for thousandths of a second just before use.

During the execution cycle, the control unit locates the required data in primary storage, places it in a storage register, instructs the ALU to perform the desired operation, temporarily stores the result of the operation in an accumulator, and finally places the result in primary memory. As each instruction is completed, the control unit advances to and reads the next instruction of the program.

5.3 COMPUTERS AND COMPUTER PROCESSING

Computers represent and process data the same way, but there are different classifications. We can use size and processing speed to categorize contemporary computers as mainframes, minicomputers, PCs, workstations, and supercomputers.

Categories of Computers

A **mainframe** is the largest computer, a powerhouse with massive memory and extremely rapid processing power. It is used for very large business, scientific, or military applications where a computer must handle massive amounts of data or many complicated processes. A **minicomputer** is a mid-range computer, about the size of an office desk, often used in universities, factories, or research laboratories. A **personal computer (PC)**, which is sometimes referred to as a microcomputer, is one that can be placed on a desktop or carried from room to room. Smaller laptop PCs are often used as portable desk-

mainframe Largest category of computer, used for major business processing.

minicomputer Middle-range computer.

personal computer (PC) Small desktop or portable computer.

WINDOW ON TECHNOLOGY

Mainframes Learn to Serve the Web

Isn't using a mainframe computer as your Web server overkill? After all, most companies are using servers for their Web sites that cost in the tens of thousands of dollars, or even less. Mainframes, on the other hand, will cost $500,000 or more. However, electronic commerce is driving certain companies to use a mainframe as a Web server.

Companies that communicate with their customers via the World Wide Web face the same issues as any other company: costs, responsiveness, up time, data storage, and security. Mainframes offer greater responsiveness, data storage, up time, and security than their smaller counterparts. The real issue is a huge cost differential. Some companies that have ended up using mainframes as Web servers asked themselves if a mainframe would really cost more. Others asked if they needed the extra performance enough to pay the difference in the cost of a mainframe.

Merrill Lynch & Co., the giant Wall Street firm, uses a mainframe to support its stock market Web site. Customers use the site to obtain stock quotes, track other market measures, follow their own portfolios and obtain information about traded companies. For Merrill Lynch, the decision was relatively easy—it was cheaper and easier to use the mainframe as their Web server. "The data were already on the mainframe," explains Merrill Lynch Vice President Jeff Savit. "The Web was the obvious way to liberate it." Placing the Web site anywhere else would have meant new hardware, installation costs, staff to support that hardware, and ongoing costs of moving the data from the mainframe to a smaller Web server. Instead, all Merrill Lynch had to do was to put the new application (a Web site) on the existing computer. By linking continuously updated market information to the Web server, the company can easily pump it to internal users, clients, and external Web users. Merrill Lynch's Web site drew 18 million hits in 1997.

For SpeedServe of La Vergne, Tennessee, the decision was much more difficult. SpeedServe sells books, videos, and games over the Web. They ran their site on a Windows NT server until recently. In 1997, when the company site started averaging 100,000 hits per day, their NT server no longer could handle the volume of traffic. The company hopes to reach a level of one million transactions per day in 1998, and adding a second or even a third NT server would not have solved their problem. So they looked to the future and brought in an IBM S/390 mainframe instead. For SpeedServe the short-run costs are greater, but they calculated that by going to a mainframe, their labor and support costs will be lower long-range, and they have no worries about room to grow, speed, or the other issues they would face by adding smaller computers. In addition, security is better on a mainframe, and with so many transactions per day, computer security will be critical to their survival and success. SpeedServe is using only three of their mainframe's 10 CPUs, so it has plenty of room for growth in its transaction volume.

To Think About: ***Suggest other situations where a company might prefer a mainframe to a network of smaller computers, and explain why the mainframe would be the better choice for management. What management, organization, and technology issues should be considered?***

Source: Adapted from Jaikumar Vijayan and Tim Ouellette, "Big Iron Gets a Case of Web Fever," *Computerworld,* January 26, 1998.

workstation Desktop computer with powerful graphics and mathematical capabilities and the ability to perform several complicated tasks at once.

supercomputer Highly sophisticated and powerful computer that can perform very complex computations extremely rapidly.

tops on the road. PCs are used as personal machines as well as in business. A **workstation** also fits on a desktop but has more powerful mathematical and graphics-processing capability than a PC and can perform more complicated tasks than a PC in the same amount of time. Workstations are used for scientific, engineering, and design work that requires powerful graphics or computational capabilities. A **supercomputer** is a highly sophisticated and powerful machine that is used for tasks requiring extremely rapid and complex calculations with hundreds of thousands of variable factors. Supercomputers traditionally have been used in scientific and military work, but they are starting to be used in business as well.

The problem with this classification scheme is that the capacity of the machines changes so rapidly. Powerful PCs have sophisticated graphics and processing capabilities similar to workstations. PCs still cannot perform as many tasks at once as mainframes, minicomputers, or workstations (see the discussion of operating systems in Chapter 6); nor can they be used by as many people simultaneously as these larger machines. Even these distinctions will become less pronounced in the future. The most powerful workstations have some of the capabilities of earlier mainframes and supercomputers (Thomborson, 1993).

Any of these categories of computers can be designed to support a computer network, enabling users to share files, software, peripheral devices, such as printers, or other network resources. **Server computers** are specifically optimized for network use, with large memory and disk-storage capacity, high-speed communications capabilities, and powerful CPUs. Powerful workstations are being further customized as Web servers for maintaining and managing Web sites. The Window on Technology explores how larger computers and mainframes can be used for this purpose.

server computer Computer specifically optimized to provide software and other resources to other computers over a network.

Supercomputers and Parallel Processing

A supercomputer is an especially sophisticated and powerful type of computer that is used primarily for extremely rapid and complex computations with hundreds or thousands of variable factors. Supercomputers traditionally have been used for classified weapons research, weather forecasting, and petroleum and engineering applications, all of which use complex mathematical models and simulations. Although extremely expensive, supercomputers are beginning to be employed in business. For instance, Trimark Investment Management, a Toronto, Canada, mutual funds company, switched to a Pyramid Technology Niles 150 with six processors when its account base shot up from 250,000 to 800,000 customers. The extra processing power could manage this massive amount of data more rapidly.

Supercomputers can perform complex and massive computations almost instantaneously because they can perform hundreds of billions of calculations per second—many times faster than the largest mainframes. Supercomputers do not process one instruction at a time but instead rely on **parallel processing.** As illustrated in Figure 5.7, multiple processing units (CPUs) break down a problem into smaller parts and work on it simultaneously. Some supercomputers use many thousands of processors. Getting a group of processors to attack the same problem at once requires both rethinking the problems and special software that can divide problems among different processors in the most efficient way possible, providing the needed data, and reassembling the many subtasks to reach an appropriate solution.

parallel processing Type of processing in which more than one instruction can be processed at a time by breaking down a problem into smaller parts and processing them simultaneously with multiple processors.

Some supercomputers can now perform more than a trillion mathematical calculations each second—a teraflop. The term *teraflop* comes from the Greek *teras*, which for mathematicians means one trillion, and flop, an acronym for floating point operations per second. (A floating point operation is a basic computer arithmetic operation, such as addition, on numbers that include a decimal point.) Work is under way to build supercomputers capable of 10 teraflops.

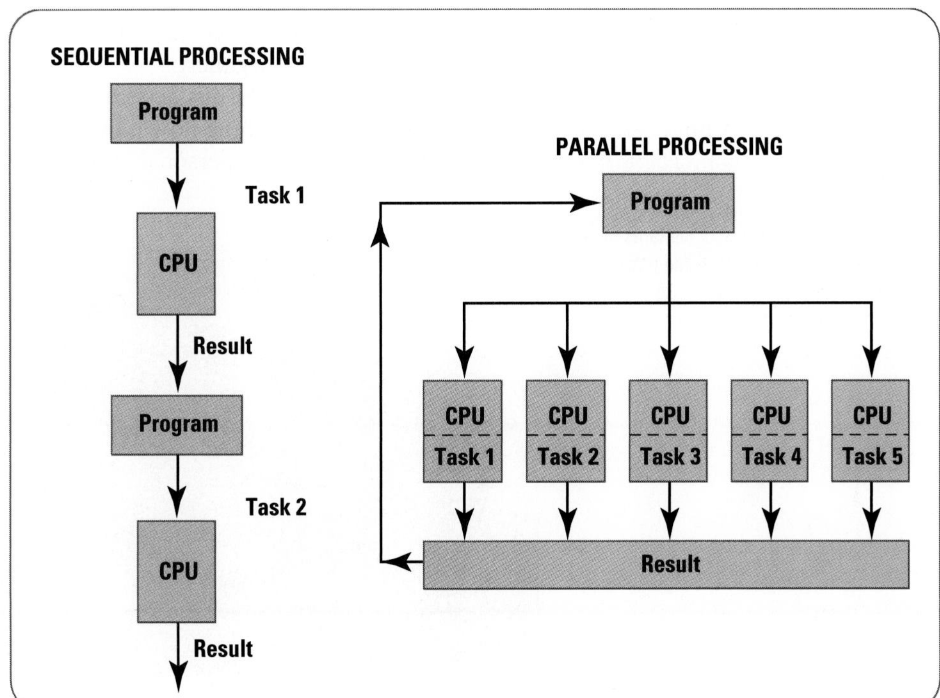

FIGURE 5.7

Sequential and parallel processing. During sequential processing, each task is assigned to one CPU that processes one instruction at a time. In parallel processing, multiple tasks are assigned to multiple processing units to expedite the result.

TABLE 5.3 Examples of Microprocessors

Name	Microprocessor Manufacturer	Word Length	Data Bus Width	Clock Speed (MHz)	Used In
80486	Intel	32	32	20–100	IBM and other PCs
68040	Motorola	32	32	25–40	Mac Quadras
Pentium	Intel	32	64	75–200	IBM and other PCs
Pentium Pro	Intel	32	64	150–200	IBM and other PCs
Pentium (MMX)	Intel	32	64	166–233	Multimedia PCs and workstations
Pentium II	Intel	32	64	233–450	High-end PCs and workstations
PowerPC	Motorola, IBM, Apple	32	64	100–400	High-end PCs and workstations
Alpha	DEC	64	64	600+	DEC workstations

Microprocessors and Processing Power

Computers' processing power depends in part on the speed and performance of their microprocessors. Some popular microprocessors are shown in Table 5.3. You will often see chips labeled as 8-bit, 16-bit, or 32-bit devices. These labels refer to the **word length,** or the number of bits that can be processed at one time by the machine. An 8-bit chip can process 8 bits, or 1 byte, of information in a single machine cycle. A 32-bit chip can process 32 bits or 4 bytes in a single cycle. The larger the word length, the greater the speed of the computer.

A second factor affecting chip speed is cycle speed. Every event in a computer must be sequenced so that one step logically follows another. The control unit sets a beat to the chip. This beat is established by an internal clock and is measured in **megahertz** (abbreviated MHz, which stands for millions of cycles per second). The Intel 8088 chip, for instance, originally had a clock speed of 4.47 megahertz, whereas the Intel Pentium II chip has a clock speed that ranges from 233 to 450 megahertz.

A third factor affecting speed is the **data bus width.** The data bus acts as a highway between the CPU, primary storage, and other devices, determining how much data can be moved at one time. The 8088 chip used in the original IBM personal computer, for

word length The number of bits that can be processed at one time by a computer. The larger the word length, the greater the speed of the computer.

megahertz A measure of cycle speed, or the pacing of events in a computer; one megahertz equals one million cycles per second.

data bus width The number of bits that can be moved at one time between the CPU, primary storage, and the other devices of a computer.

The Pentium II microprocessor contains more than seven million transistors and provides mainframe and supercomputer-like processing capabilities.

example, had a 16-bit word length but only an 8-bit data bus width. This meant that data were processed within the CPU chip itself in 16-bit chunks but could only be moved 8 bits at a time between the CPU, primary storage, and external devices. On the other hand, the Alpha chip has both a 64-bit word length and a 64-bit data bus width. To have a computer execute more instructions per second and work through programs or handle users expeditiously, it is necessary to increase the word length of the processor, the data bus width, or the cycle speed—or all three.

Microprocessors can be made faster by using **reduced instruction set computing (RISC)** in their design. Some instructions that a computer uses to process data are actually embedded in the chip circuitry. Conventional chips, based on complex instruction set computing, have several hundred or more instructions hard-wired into their circuitry, and they may take several clock cycles to execute a single instruction. In many instances, only 20 percent of these instructions are needed for 80 percent of the computer's tasks. If the little-used instructions are eliminated, the remaining instructions can execute much faster.

reduced instruction set computing (RISC) Technology used to enhance the speed of microprocessors by embedding only the most frequently used instructions on a chip.

Reduced instruction set (RISC) computers have only the most frequently used instructions embedded in them. A RISC CPU can execute most instructions in a single machine cycle and sometimes multiple instructions at the same time. RISC is most appropriate for scientific and workstation computing, where there are repetitive arithmetic and logical operations on data or applications calling for three-dimensional image rendering.

On the other hand, software written for conventional processors cannot be automatically transferred to RISC machines; new software is required. Many RISC suppliers are adding more instructions to appeal to a greater number of customers, and designers of conventional microprocessors are streamlining their chips to execute instructions more rapidly.

Microprocessors optimized for multimedia and graphics have been developed to improve processing of visually intensive applications. Intel's **MMX (MultiMedia eXtension)** microprocessor is a Pentium chip that has been modified to increase performance in many applications featuring graphics and sound. Multimedia applications such as games and video will be able to run more smoothly, with more colors, and be able to perform more tasks simultaneously. For example, multiple channels of audio, high-quality video or animation, and Internet communication could all be running in the same application.

MMX Pentium microprocessor modified to improve processing of multimedia applications. Stands for MultiMedia eXtension.

distributed processing The distribution of computer processing work among multiple computers linked by a communication network.

centralized processing Processing that is accomplished by one large central computer.

Computer Networks and Client/Server Computing

Today, stand-alone computers have been replaced by computers in networks for most processing tasks. The use of multiple computers linked by a communications network for processing is called **distributed processing.** In contrast with **centralized processing,** in which all processing is accomplished by one large central computer, distributed processing distributes the processing work among PCs, minicomputers, and mainframes linked together.

One form of distributed processing is the **client/server** model of computing. Client/server computing splits processing between "clients" and "servers." Both are on the network, but each machine is assigned functions it is best suited to perform. The **client** is the user point-of-entry for the required function and is normally a desktop computer, workstation, or laptop computer. The user generally interacts directly only with the client portion of the application, often to input data or retrieve data for further analysis. The **server** provides the client with services and might be anything from a supercomputer or mainframe to another desktop computer. Servers store and process shared data and also perform back-end functions not visible to users, such as managing network activities. Figure 5.8 illustrates the client/server computing concept. Computing on the Internet uses the client/server model (see Chapter 9).

Figure 5.9 illustrates five different ways that the components of an application could be partitioned between the client and the server. The *interface* component is

client/server computing A model for computing that splits processing between "clients" and "servers" on a network, assigning functions to the machine most able to perform the function.

client The user point-of-entry for the required function in client/server computing. Normally a desktop computer, workstation, or laptop computer.

server In client/server computing, the component that satisfies some or all of the user's request for data and/or functionality and that performs back-end functions not visible to users, such as managing network activities.

FIGURE 5.8

Client/server computing. In client/server computing, computer processing is split between client machines and server machines linked by a network. Users interface with the client machines.

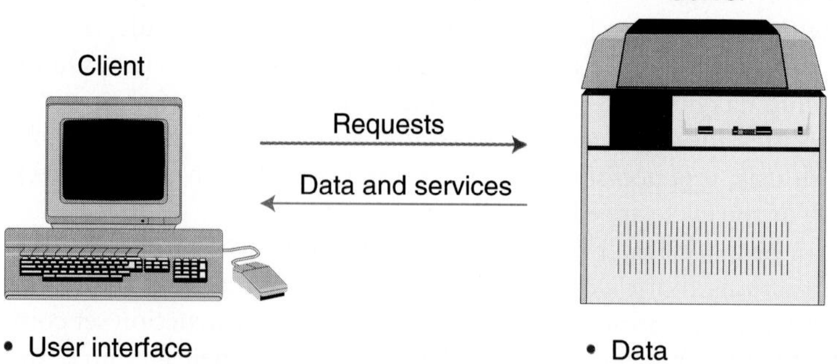

essentially the application interface—how the application appears visually to the user. The *application logic* component consists of the processing logic, which is shaped by the organization's business rules. (An example might be that a salaried employee is only to be paid monthly.) The *data management* component consists of the storage and management of the data used by the application.

The exact division of tasks depends on the requirements of each application, including its processing needs, the number of users, and the available resources. For example, client tasks for a large corporate payroll might include inputting data (such as enrolling new employees and recording hours worked), submitting data queries to the server, analyzing the retrieved data, and displaying results on the screen or on a printer. The server portion will fetch the entered data, and process the payroll. It also will control access so that only authorized users can view or update the data.

In some firms client/server networks with PCs have actually replaced mainframes and minicomputers. The process of transferring applications from large computers to smaller ones is called **downsizing.** Downsizing has many advantages. Memory and processing power on a PC cost a fraction of their equivalent on a mainframe. The decision to downsize involves many factors in addition to the cost of computer hardware, including the need for new software, training, and perhaps new organizational procedures.

downsizing The process of transferring applications from large computers to smaller ones.

FIGURE 5.9

Types of client/server computing. There are various ways in which an application's interface, logic, and data management components can be divided among the clients and servers in a network.

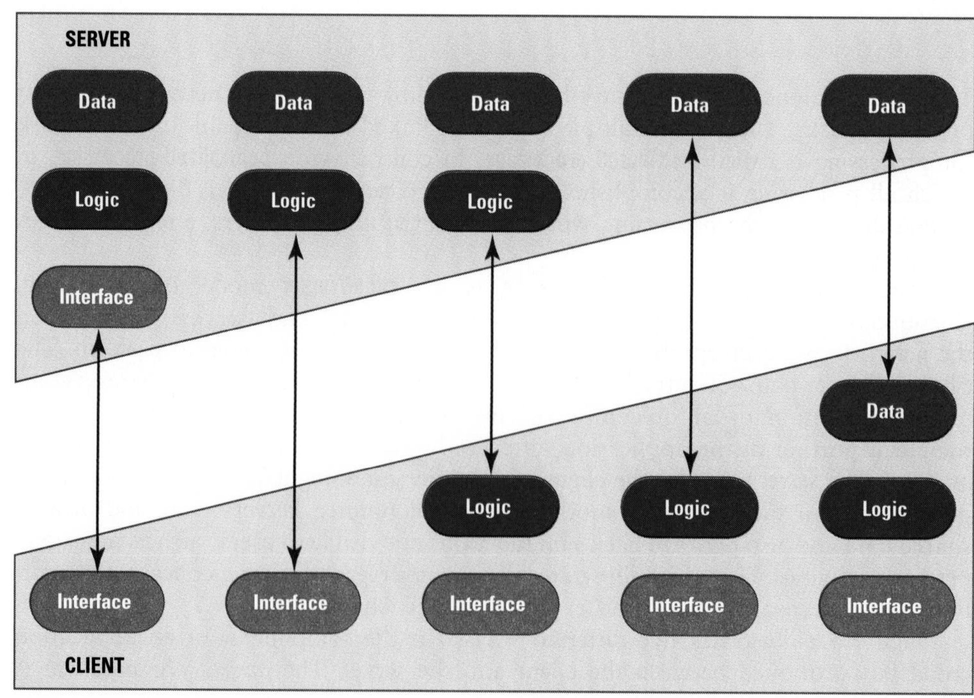

Network Computers and Total Cost of Ownership

In one form of client/server computing, the client is so small that the bulk of computer processing occurs on the server. The term *thin client* is sometimes used to refer to the client in this arrangement or to refer to network computers. **Network computers (NCs)** are smaller, simpler, and cheaper versions of the traditional personal computer with minimal storage and processing capabilities. The most simplified network computers do not store software programs or data permanently. Instead, users download whatever software or data they need from a central computer over the Internet or an organization's internal network. The central computer also saves information for the user and makes it available for later retrieval, effectively eliminating the need for secondary storage devices such as hard disks, floppy disks, CD-ROMs, and their drives. A network computer may consist of little more than a stripped-down PC, a monitor, a keyboard, and a network connection.

network computer (NC) Simplified desktop computer that does not store software programs or data permanently. Users download whatever software or data they need from a central computer over the Internet or an organization's own internal network.

If managed properly, both network computers and client/server computing can reduce the total cost of ownership (TCO) of information technology resources. **Total cost of ownership (TCO)** is a popular term to designate how much it costs to own technology resources, including the original cost of the computer and software, hardware and software upgrades, maintenance, technical support, and training.

total cost of ownership (TCO) Designates the total cost of owning technology resources, including initial purchase costs, the cost of hardware and software upgrades, maintenance, technical support, and training.

Proponents of network computers believe NCs can reduce TCO because they are less expensive to purchase than PCs with local processing and storage, and because they can be administered and updated from a central network server. (Network computers can cost between $500 and $1000 per unit.) Software programs and applications would not have to be purchased, installed, and upgraded for each user because software would be delivered and maintained from one central point. So much data and information are being delivered through the Web that computers do not necessarily need to store their own content. Network computers thus could increase management control over the organization's computing function.

Not everyone agrees that network computers will bring benefits. Some researchers believe that centralizing control over computing would stifle worker initiative and creativity. Several studies of the cost of owning PCs question whether the savings promised by network computers will actually be realized. Very little software has yet been designed for the network computing model. If a network failure occurs, hundreds or thousands of employees would not be able to use their computers, whereas people could keep on working if they had full-function PCs. A poorly supervised network computer system could prove to be just as inefficient as PCs sometimes are. Full-function PCs are more appropriate for situations where end users have varied application needs that require local processing. Companies should closely examine how network computers would fit into their information technology infrastructure. These issues are explored in the Window on Managment.

The Window on Organizations explores other TCO issues related to the purchase and use of laptop computers in the business.

Network computers have minimal local processing and storage capabilities because they download the software and data users need from a network.

WINDOW ON MANAGEMENT

Network Computers: A New Management Option

Are network computers the next phase in corporate computing? Some companies think so. Companies that have made the switch point to low purchase and maintenance costs as their rationale for switching to NCs.

General Accident Fire & Life Corporation decided on a wide-scale rollout of network computers in early 1998, installing 2200 IBM Network Station NCs in various locations. The British insurer had upgraded its text-based mainframe core processing system for tracking claims, underwriting, and other daily activities with one that displayed output on computer screens in color. With NCs, users can easily access this legacy system, as well as Web-like applications on the company's private intranet. PCs were rejected because they were considered too costly to be used primarily to access a centralized mainframe system. General Accident hasn't computed the cost savings from network computers because it would have to compare the cost of both purchasing and supporting NCs versus local PCs over a full year. The company selected NCs because management wanted more control over what applications run over users' machines and because the NCs worked with its back-end mainframe system.

Retired Persons Services Inc. in Alexandria, Virginia, the pharmaceutical arm of the American Association of Retired Persons (AARP), installed 1000 units of @ Workstation, a $700 network computing device from HDS Network Systems, at three locations, with 200 more to be installed later. According to Don Resh, the company's senior vice president and chief information officer (CIO), "There's nothing a user can do to screw them up." The NC system requires much less technical support than 1000 PCs. Resh calculates that five years of support and maintenance for 1000 PCs would cost $35 million, compared with $2.5 million for the network computer system.

The Evangelical Lutheran Good Samaritan Society, a nonprofit organization operating 235 nursing homes, long-term care facilities and low-income housing for senior citizens, turned to network computers for similar reasons. Facility directors and nurses at each of its sites had been supporting PC applications themselves, taking their time and concentration away from their primary responsibility of serving patients. The Society will be running its core financial, human resources, and other applications on a central server at company headquarters in Sioux Falls, South Dakota. Nursing homes and other sites will access the applications using Web browser software running on 1000 to 1500 IBM network computers.

Some managers have decided against NCs because of the unreliability of both internal networks and the Internet. Dayna Aronson, information systems manager at Norpac Food Sales, the Lake Oswego, Oregon, division of Norpac Foods, Inc., is not planning to adopt the NC model for many years to come. He worries about hundreds of users twiddling their thumbs if the network goes down. Having local processing power and data "provides a level of autonomy and redundancy worth far more than saving $1000."

John Holmwood, a technical analyst at Nova Gas Transmission in Calgary, British Columbia, believes that network computers save management and support costs. The majority of a company's total costs for networked desktop computers are at the desktop, particularly managing the various pieces of hardware and software maintained on each user's desktop throughout the company. Nevertheless, Nova is not committed to network computers. It is debating whether to use NCs or "dataless" workstations. These "dataless" workstations are standard PCs linked to a network, but most of the data and applications they use are stored on centralized computers. Nova will move to network computers only if it can prove that support and management costs will be significantly lower than such costs with standard PCs.

To Think About: ***If you were a manager, what people, organization, and technology factors would you consider in deciding whether to use network computers in your organization?***

Sources: Kristi Essick, "Insurer Picks NCs for Central Management," *Computerworld,* February 2, 1998; Randy Weston, "Health Care Organization Heals IS Wound with NCs," *Computerworld,* January 19, 1998; and Edward Cone, "NCs Impress," *Information Week,* March 31, 1997.

5.4 SECONDARY STORAGE

secondary storage Relatively long-term, nonvolatile storage of data outside the CPU and primary storage.

In addition to primary storage, where information and programs are stored for immediate processing, modern computer systems use other types of storage in order to accomplish their tasks. Information systems need to store information outside of the computer in a nonvolatile state (not requiring electrical power) and to store volumes of data too large to fit into a computer of any size today (such as a large payroll or the U.S. census). The relatively long-term storage of data outside the CPU and primary storage is called **secondary storage.**

Primary storage is where the fastest, most expensive technology is used. Access to information stored in primary memory is electronic and occurs almost at the speed of light. Secondary storage is nonvolatile and retains data even when the computer is

WINDOW ON ORGANIZATIONS

Selecting Laptop Computers: The Bottom Line for Organizations

Laptop technology is developing at a dizzying pace. All of the brands include the hottest technology, the fastest processors, the sharpest screens, the newest ports, the largest hard drives. Almost regardless of brand, the quality is so high that Fred Angelopolus, vice president of sales and support at Hitachi PC Corp. of San Jose, California, says that "Notebooks are becoming commodities, and there really isn't a huge variance between Vendor A and Vendor B anymore." So how can management of a corporation, large or small, choose which brand to purchase?

The answer for many is that choice is no longer based upon hardware. Purchasers are no longer much concerned whether the machine is fast enough, has enough memory or storage, or has an easy-to-read screen. They take these for granted, and instead they ask three key questions: How stable is the vendor, are the components interchangeable, and how good is the service and support wherever we need it? The question that underlies all three is: What is the total cost of ownership of this computer over several years? Or, put another way, how will this purchase affect our bottom line?

The purchase cost of a laptop is small compared to the cost of staff and the income that staff generates. Consultants of the Vancouver, British Columbia office of consulting and accounting firm, Price Waterhouse, bill customers as much as $250 an hour. If their computer is down a number of hours, it translates into a lot of lost income. Price Waterhouse Procurement Manager Michael Calyniuk, wants to make sure that all employees can work every day, that their productivity is not negatively impacted by a down computer. Calyniuk explains that, although in the past employees could get by for a couple of days without their computers, "Today we are looking at virtually same-day replacement, and that's a huge motivating factor in terms of notebook PC acquisitions. The bottom line is that we want as little downtime as possible." A down computer negatively results in lost revenue, a reduced bottom line.

Shortening laptop-computer downtime can be accomplished several ways. One approach that Calyniuk uses is interchangeable parts. When a computer fails, a compatible part can be installed so that problem computers can be up and running very quickly. If the problem cannot be fixed that way at once, users must be able to remove the hard disk and slip it into another computer of the same model. Computers "can't share components between manufacturers," Calyniuk points out, so Price Waterhouse has decreased the number of vendors from which it purchases.

A second approach is rapid service by the vendor. Calyniuk and others demand 24-hour-a-day, 7-day-a-week support from their vendors. For companies that operate around the world, as does Price Waterhouse, that support must be available worldwide. The company has about 30,000 employees, including 1800 in Canada. So many employees are mobile that Price Waterhouse buys very few desktop computers; its notebooks must be able to function as desktop replacements.

To Think About: ***Does the view that notebooks (and other computers) are becoming commodities mean that management no longer needs to pay attention to the technology and the company that produces that technology? Explain your response.***

Source: Adapted from Jon Pepper, "Beyond Speed," *Information Week*, February 2, 1998.

turned off. There are many kinds of secondary storage; the most common are magnetic disk, optical disk, and magnetic tape. These media can transfer large bodies of data rapidly to the CPU. However, secondary storage requires mechanical movement to gain access to the data, so in contrast to primary storage, it is relatively slow.

Magnetic Disk

The most widely used secondary-storage medium today is **magnetic disk.** There are two kinds of magnetic disks: floppy disks (used in PCs) and **hard disks** (used on commercial disk drives and PCs). Hard disks are thin steel platters with an iron oxide coating. In larger systems, multiple hard disks are mounted together on a vertical shaft. Figure 5.10 illustrates a commercial hard disk pack for a large system. It has 11 disks, each with two surfaces, top and bottom. However, although there are 11 disks, no information is recorded on the top or bottom surfaces; thus, there are only 20 recording surfaces on the disk pack. On each surface, data are stored on tracks.

magnetic disk A secondary storage medium in which data are stored by means of magnetized spots on a hard or floppy disk.

hard disk Magnetic disk resembling a thin steel platter with an iron oxide coating; used in large computer systems and in many PCs.

Read/write heads move horizontally over the spinning disks to any of 200 positions, called cylinders. At any one of these cylinders, the read/write heads can read or write information to any of 20 different concentric circles on the disk surface areas called

FIGURE 5.10

Disk pack storage. Large systems often rely on disk packs, which provide reliable storage for large amounts of data with quick access and retrieval. A typical removable disk-pack system contains 11 two-sided disks.

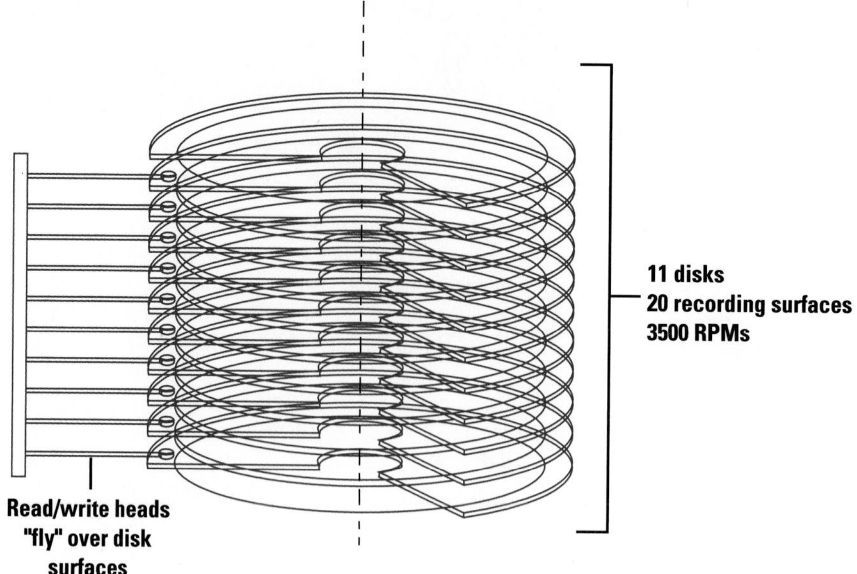

track Concentric circle on the surface area of a disk on which data are stored as magnetized spots; each track can store thousands of bytes.

cylinder Represents circular tracks on the same vertical line within a disk pack.

RAID (Redundant Array of Inexpensive Disks) Disk storage technology to boost disk performance by packaging more than 100 smaller disk drives with a controller chip and specialized software in a single large unit to deliver data over multiple paths simultaneously.

floppy disk Removable magnetic disk storage primarily used with PCs.

sector Method of storing data on a floppy disk in which the disk is divided into pie-shaped pieces or sectors. Each sector is assigned a unique number so that data can be located using the sector number.

direct access storage device (DASD) Refers to magnetic disk technology that permits the CPU to locate a record directly.

tracks. (Each track contains several records.) The **cylinder** represents the circular tracks on the same vertical line within the disk pack. Read/write heads are directed to a specific record using an address consisting of the cylinder number, the recording surface number, and the data record number.

The entire disk pack is housed in a disk drive or disk unit. Large mainframe or minicomputer systems have multiple disk drives because they require immense disk storage capacity.

Disk drive performance can be further enhanced by using a disk technology called **RAID (Redundant Array of Inexpensive Disks).** RAID devices package more than a hundred 6.25-inch disk drives, a controller chip, and specialized software into a single large unit. Traditional disk drives deliver data from the disk drive along a single path, but RAID delivers data over multiple paths simultaneously, accelerating disk access time. Small RAID systems provide 10 to 20 gigabytes of storage capacity, whereas larger systems provide more than 10 terabytes. RAID is potentially more reliable than standard disk drives because other drives are available to deliver data if one drive fails.

PCs usually contain hard disks, which can store more than 10 gigabytes. (Two gigabytes is currently the most common size.) PCs also use **floppy disks,** which are flat, 3.5-inch disks of polyester film with a magnetic coating (5.25-inch floppy disks are becoming obsolete). These disks have a storage capacity ranging from 360K to 2.8 megabytes and a much slower access rate than hard disks. Floppy disks and cartridges and packs of multiple disks use a **sector** method of storing data. As illustrated in Figure 5.11, the disk surface is divided into pie-shaped pieces. Each sector is assigned a unique number. Data can be located using an address consisting of the sector number and an individual data record number.

Magnetic disks on both large and small computers permit direct access to individual records. Each record can be given a precise physical address in terms of cylinders and tracks or sectors, and the read/write head can be directed to go directly to that address and access the information. This means that the computer system does not have to search the entire file, as in a sequential tape file, in order to find the record. Disk storage is often referred to as a **direct access storage device (DASD).**

For on-line systems requiring direct access, disk technology provides the only practical means of storage today. DASD is, however, more expensive than magnetic tape. Updating information stored on a disk destroys the old information because the old data on the disk are written over if changes are made. The disk drives themselves are susceptible to environmental disturbances. Even smoke particles can disrupt the movement of read/write heads over the disk surface, which is why disk drives are sealed from the environment.

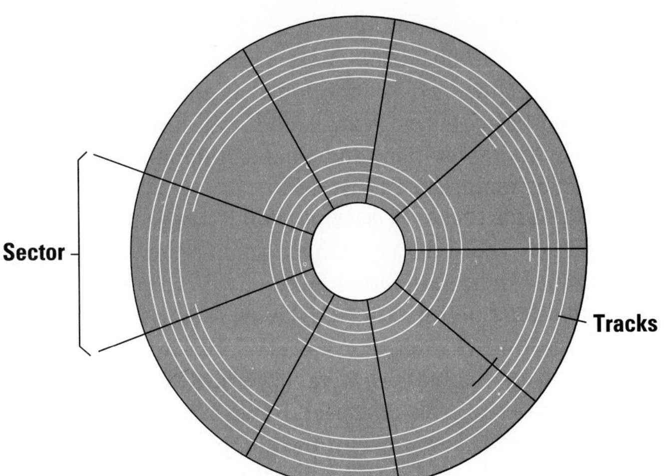

FIGURE 5.11

The sector method of storing data. Each track of a disk can be divided into sectors. Disk storage location can be identified by sector and data record number.

Optical Disks

Optical disks, also called compact disks or laser optical disks, store data at densities many times greater than those of magnetic disks and are available for both PCs and large computers. Data are recorded on optical disks when a laser device burns microscopic pits in the reflective layer of a spiral track. Binary information is encoded by the length of these pits and the space between them. Optical disks can store massive quantities of data, including not only text but also pictures, sound, and full motion video, in a highly compact form. The optical disk is read by having a low-power laser beam from an optical head scan the disk.

The most common optical disk system used with PCs is called **CD-ROM (compact disk read-only memory)**. A 4.75-inch compact disk for PCs can store up to 660 megabytes, nearly 300 times more than a high-density floppy disk. Optical disks are most appropriate for applications where enormous quantities of unchanging data must be stored compactly for easy retrieval, or for storing graphic images and sound. CD-ROM is also less vulnerable than floppy disks to magnetism, dirt, or rough handling.

CD-ROM (compact disk read-only memory) Read-only optical disk storage used for imaging, reference, and database applications with massive amounts of unchanging data and for multimedia.

Because a single CD-ROM can store vast quantities of data, the technology is often used for storing images, sound, and video, as well as text.

CD-ROM is read-only storage. No new data can be written to it; it can only be read. CD-ROM has been most widely used for reference materials with massive amounts of data, such as encyclopedias and directories, and for storing multimedia applications that combine text, sound, and images (see Section 5.6). For example, U.S. census demographic data and financial databases from Dow Jones or Dun and Bradstreet are available on CD-ROM.

WORM (write once/read many) Optical disk system that allows users to record data only once; data cannot be erased but can be read indefinitely.

CD-R (compact disk-recordable) Optical disk system that allows individuals and organizations to record their own CD-ROMs.

digital video disk (DVD) High-capacity optical storage medium that can store full-length videos and large amounts of data.

WORM (write once/read many) and **CD-R (compact disk-recordable)** optical disk systems allow users to record data only once on an optical disk. Once written, the data cannot be erased, but can be read indefinitely. CD-R (compact disk-recordable) technology allows individuals and organizations to create their own CR-ROMs at low cost using a special CD-R recording device. New *CD-RW (CD-ReWritable)* technology has been developed to allow users to create rewritable optical disks (Magneto-optical technology was developed earlier for this purpose). Rewritable optical disk drives are not yet competitive with magnetic disk storage for most applications. Their access speed is slower than that of magnetic disks and they are more expensive than magnetic media. Rewritable optical disks are useful primarily for applications requiring large volumes of storage where the information is only occasionally updated.

CD-ROM storage is likely to become more popular and more powerful in years to come, and access speeds will improve. **Digital video disks (DVDs),** also called Digital Versatile Disks, are optical disks the same size as CD-ROMs but of even higher capacity. They can hold a minimum of 4.7 gigabytes of data, enough to store a full-length, high-quality motion picture. DVDs are initially being used to store movies and multimedia applications using large amounts of video and graphics, but they may replace CD-ROMs because they can store large amounts of digitized text, graphics, audio, and video data.

Magnetic Tape

magnetic tape Inexpensive, older secondary-storage medium in which large volumes of information are stored sequentially by means of magnetized and nonmagnetized spots on tape.

Magnetic tape is an older storage technology that still is employed for secondary storage of large volumes of information. It is used primarily in old legacy mainframe batch applications and for archiving data. Reel-to-reel magnetic tape systems come in 14-inch reels that are up to 2400 feet long and 0.5 inches wide. Data can be stored on magnetic tape at different densities. Mass storage systems using libraries of tape cartridges with much higher density and storage capacity (up to 35 gigabytes) are replacing reel-to-reel tapes in mainframe and minicomputer systems. PCs and some minicomputers use small tape cartridges resembling home audiocassettes to store information.

The principal advantages of magnetic tape are that it is very inexpensive, it is relatively stable, and it can store very large volumes of information. Magnetic tape also can be reused many times.

The principal disadvantages of magnetic tape are that it stores data sequentially and is relatively slow compared with the speed of other secondary storage media. In order to find an individual record such as an employment record on a magnetic tape reel, the tape must be read from the beginning up to the location of the desired record. Hence, magnetic tape is not a good medium when it is necessary to find information rapidly, such as for an airline reservation system. Tape also can age over time and tape reels are labor intensive to mount and dismount. Tape represents a fading technology, but it continues to exist in changing forms.

5.5 INPUT AND OUTPUT DEVICES

Human beings interact with computer systems largely through input and output devices. Advances in information systems rely not only on the speed and capacity of the CPU but also on the speed, capacity, and design of the input and output devices. Input/output devices are often called *peripheral devices*.

Input Devices

Keyboards remain the principal method of data entry for entering text and numerical data into a computer. However, pointing devices, such as the computer mouse and touch screens, are becoming popular for issuing commands and making selections in today's highly graphic computing environment.

Pointing Devices

The point-and-click actions of the **computer mouse** have made it an increasingly popular alternative to keyboard and text-based commands. A mouse is a handheld device that is usually connected to the computer by a cable. The computer user moves the mouse around on a desktop to control the position of the cursor on a video display screen. Once the cursor is in the desired position, the user can push a button on the mouse to select a command. The mouse also can be used to "draw" images on the screen. *Trackballs* and *touch pads* often are used in place of the mouse as pointing devices on laptop PCs.

Touch screens are easy to use and appeal to people who can't use traditional keyboards. Users can enter limited amounts of data by touching the surface of a sensitized video display monitor with a finger or a pointer. With colorful graphics, sound, and simple menus, touch screens often are found in information kiosks in retail stores, restaurants, and shopping malls.

computer mouse Handheld input device whose movement on the desktop controls the position of the cursor on the computer display screen.

touch screen Input device technology that permits the entering or selecting of commands and data by touching the surface of a sensitized video display monitor with a finger or a pointer.

Source Data Automation

Source data automation captures data in computer-readable form at the time and place they are created. Point-of-sale systems, optical bar-code scanners used in supermarkets, and other optical character recognition devices are examples of source data automation. One of the advantages of source data automation is that the many errors that occur when people use keyboards to enter data are almost eliminated. Bar-code scanners make fewer than 1 error in 10,000 transactions, whereas skilled keypunchers make about 1 error for every 1000 keystrokes. The principal source data automation technologies are optical character recognition, magnetic ink character recognition, pen-based input, digital scanners, voice input, and sensors.

Optical character recognition (OCR) devices translate specially designed marks, characters, and codes into digital form. The most widely used optical code is the **bar code,** which is used in point-of-sale systems in supermarkets and retail stores. Bar codes also are used in hospitals, libraries, military operations, and transportation facilities. The codes can include time, date, and location data in addition to identification data. The information makes them useful for analyzing the movement of items and determining what has

source data automation Input technology that captures data in computer-readable form at the time and place the data are created.

optical character recognition (OCR) Form of source data automation in which optical scanning devices read specially designed data off source documents and translate the data into digital form for the computer.

bar code Form of OCR technology widely used in supermarkets and retail stores in which identification data are coded into a series of bars.

Touch screens allow users to enter small amounts of data by touching words, numbers, or specific points on the screen.

happened to them during production or other processes. (The discussion of the United Parcel Service in Chapter 1 shows how valuable bar codes can be for this purpose.)

magnetic ink character recognition (MICR) Input technology that translates characters written in magnetic ink into digital codes for processing.

Magnetic ink character recognition (MICR) technology is used primarily in check processing for the banking industry. The bottom portion of a typical check contains characters identifying the bank, checking account, and check number that are preprinted using a special ink. An MICR reader translates these characters into digital form for the computer.

Handwriting-recognition devices such as pen-based tablets, notebooks, and notepads are promising new input technologies, especially for people working in the sales or service areas or for those who have traditionally shunned computer keyboards. These **pen-based input** devices usually consist of a flat-screen display tablet and a pen-like stylus.

pen-based input Input devices such as tablets, notebooks, and notepads consisting of a flat-screen display tablet and a pen-like stylus that digitizes handwriting.

With pen-based input, users print directly onto the tablet-sized screen. The screen is fitted with a transparent grid of fine wires that detect the presence of the special stylus, which emits a faint signal from its tip. As users write letters and numbers on the tablet, they are translated into digital form, where they can be stored or processed and analyzed. For instance, the United Parcel Service replaced its drivers' familiar clipboard with a battery-powered Delivery Information Acquisition Device (DIAD) to capture signatures (see the Chapter 1 Window on Technology), along with other information required for pickup and delivery. This technology requires special pattern-recognition software to accept pen-based input instead of keyboard input. Most pen-based systems still cannot recognize freehand writing very well.

digital scanners Input devices that translate images such as pictures or documents into digital form for processing.

voice input devices Technology that converts the spoken word into digital form for processing.

Digital scanners translate images such as pictures or documents into digital form and are an essential component of image-processing systems. **Voice input devices** convert spoken words into digital form for processing by the computer. Voice recognition devices allow people to enter data into the computer without using their hands, making them useful for inspecting and sorting items in manufacturing and shipping and for dictation. (Documents can be created by speaking words into a computer rather than keying them in.) We describe advances in voice technology in the following section.

sensors Devices that collect data directly from the environment for input into a computer system.

Sensors are devices that collect data directly from the environment for input into a computer system. For instance, today's farmers can use sensors on their tractors to monitor speed and adjust the amount of fertilizer or pesticide sprayed on soil. Sensor-equipped combines can monitor, calculate, and record each field's yield as the combines harvest crops (Feder, 1998).

Batch and On-Line Input and Processing

batch processing A method of collecting and processing data in which transactions are accumulated and stored until a specified time when it is convenient or necessary to process them as a group.

on-line processing A method of collecting and processing data in which transactions are entered directly into the computer system and processed immediately.

The manner in which data are input into the computer affects how the data can be processed. Information systems collect and process information in one of two ways: through batch or through on-line processing. In **batch processing,** transactions such as orders or payroll time cards are accumulated and stored in a group or batch until the time when, because of some reporting cycle, it is efficient or necessary to process them. This was the only method of processing until the early 1960s, and it is still used today in older systems or some systems with massive volumes of transactions. In **on-line processing,** which is now very common, the user enters transactions into a device that is directly connected to the computer system. The transactions usually are processed immediately.

The demands of the business determine the type of processing. If the user needs periodic or occasional reports or output, as in payroll or end-of-the-year reports, batch processing is most efficient. If the user needs immediate information and processing, as in an airline or hotel reservation system, then the system should use on-line processing.

transaction file In batch systems, a file in which all transactions are accumulated to await processing.

master file A file that contains all permanent information and is updated during processing by transaction data.

Figure 5.12 compares batch and on-line processing. Batch systems often use tape as a storage medium, whereas on-line processing systems use disk storage, which permits immediate access to specific items. In batch systems, transactions are accumulated in a **transaction file,** which contains all the transactions for a particular time period. Periodically this file is used to update a **master file,** which contains permanent information on entities. (An example is a payroll master file with employee earnings and deductions data. It is updated with weekly time-card transactions.) Adding the transaction data to the existing master file creates a new master file. In on-line processing, transactions are entered into the system immediately using a keyboard, pointing device, or source data

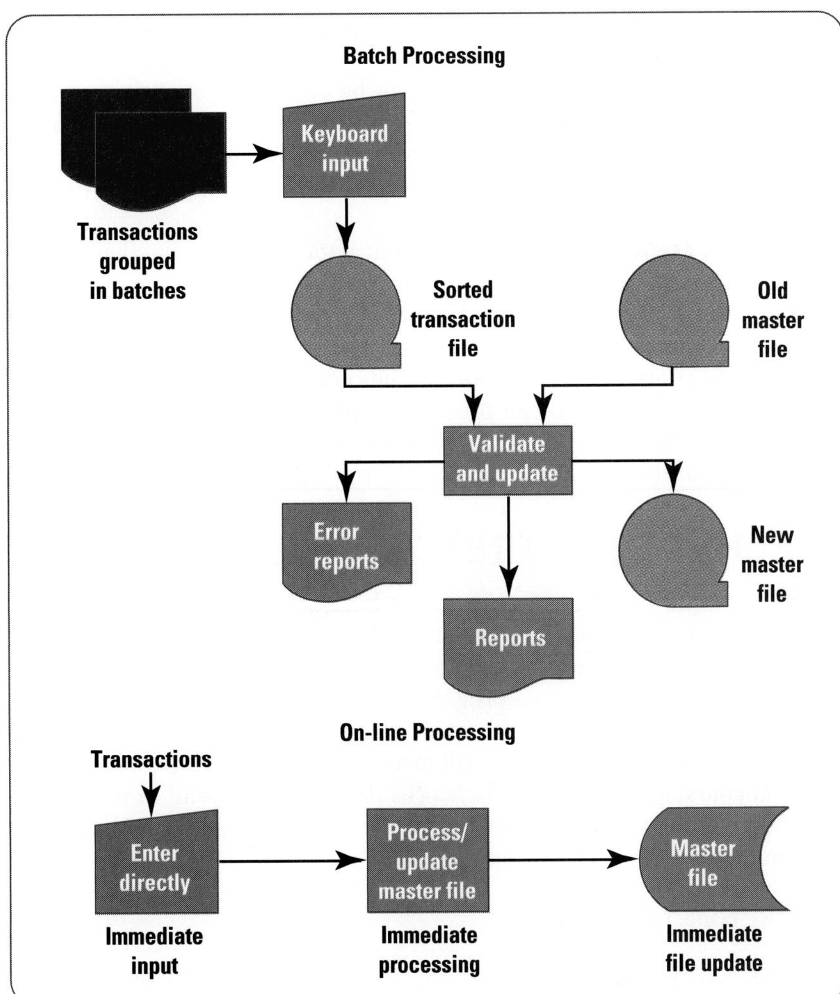

FIGURE 5.12

A comparison of batch and on-line processing. In batch processing, transactions are accumulated and stored in a group. Because batches are processed on a regular interval basis, such as daily, weekly, or monthly, information in the system will not always be up to date. A typical batch-processing job is payroll preparation. In on-line processing, transactions are input immediately and usually processed immediately. Information in the system is generally up to date. A typical on-line application is an airline reservation system.

automation, and the system usually responds immediately. The master file is updated continually. In on-line processing, there is a direct connection to the computer for input and output.

Output Devices

The major data output devices are cathode ray tube terminals (CRTs), sometimes called video display terminals or VDTs, and printers.

The **cathode ray tube (CRT)** is probably the most popular form of information output in modern computer systems. It works much like a television picture tube, with an electronic gun shooting a beam of electrons to illuminate the pixels on the screen. The more pixels per screen, the higher the resolution. CRT monitors can be classified as monochrome or color and by their display capabilities. Some display only text, whereas others display both text and graphics. Display devices for graphics often utilize bit mapping. **Bit mapping** allows each pixel on the screen to be addressed and manipulated by the computer (as opposed to blocks of pixels in character addressable displays). This requires more computer memory but permits finer detail and the ability to produce any kind of image on the display screen. Special-purpose graphics terminals used in CAD/CAM and commercial art have very high-resolution capabilities (1280 × 1024 pixels).

cathode ray tube (CRT) A screen, also referred to as a video display terminal (VDT). Provides a visual image of both user input and computer output. Displays text or graphics as either color or monochrome images.

bit mapping The technology that allows each pixel on the screen to be addressed and manipulated by the computer.

Printers and Plotters

Printers produce a printed hard copy of information output. They include impact printers (a standard typewriter or a dot matrix) and nonimpact printers (laser, inkjet, and thermal transfer printers). Most printers print one character at a time, but some

printer A computer output device that provides paper hard-copy output in the form of text or graphics.

commercial printers print an entire line or page at a time. In general, impact printers are slower than nonimpact printers.

plotter Output device using multicolored pens to draw high-quality graphic documents.

High-quality graphics documents can be created using **plotters** with multicolored pens to draw (rather than print) computer output. Plotters are much slower than printers, but are useful for outputting large-size charts, maps, or drawings.

Other Output Devices

voice output device A converter of digital output data into spoken words.

A **voice output device** converts digital output data back into intelligible speech. For instance, when you call for information on the telephone, you may hear a computerized voice respond with the telephone number you requested.

Audio output such as music and other sounds can be delivered by speakers connected to the computer. In addition to audio output, multimedia applications, including those on the Web, also can produce graphics or video as visual output. Microfilm and microfiche have been used to store large quantities of output as microscopic filmed documents, but they are being replaced by optical disk technology.

5.6 INFORMATION TECHNOLOGY TRENDS

During the last 30 years, computing costs have dropped by a factor of 10 each decade, and capacity has increased by a factor of at least 100 each decade. Today's microprocessors can put a mainframe on a desktop, and eventually into a briefcase or shirt pocket. As computers become progressively smaller, powerful, and easier to use, computer intelligence will be incorporated into more aspects of daily life. Computers and related information technologies will increasingly blend data, images, and sound, sending them coursing through vast networks that can process all of them with equal ease. We can see how this is possible through the use of interactive multimedia, superchips, microminiaturization, and social interfaces.

Interactive Multimedia

multimedia Technologies that facilitate the integration of two or more types of media such as text, graphics, sound, voice, full-motion video, or animation into a computer-based application.

Multimedia is defined as the technologies that facilitate the integration of two or more types of media, such as text, graphics, sound, voice, full-motion video, still video, or animation, into a computer-based application. Multimedia is becoming the foundation of new consumer products and services, such as electronic books and newspapers, electronic classroom-presentation technologies, full-motion video conferencing, imaging, graphics design tools, and video and voice mail. Many Web sites use mulitmedia.

A simple multimedia system consists of a personal computer with a 32-bit microprocessor, a high-resolution color monitor, a high-capacity hard disk drive, and a CD-

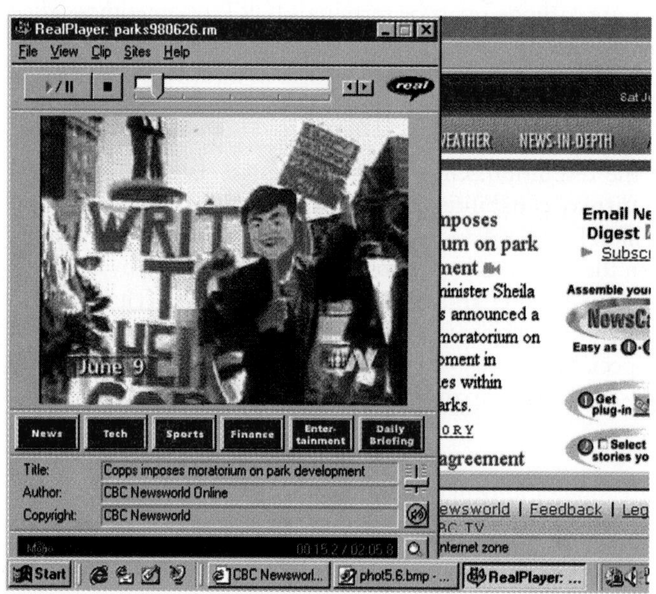

Newsworld Online is a multimedia Web site providing news from Canada, including live video, 24 hours a day. Web sites can incorporate multimedia elements such as graphics, sound, animation, and full-motion video.

TABLE 5.4 Examples of Multimedia Web Sites

Web Site	Description
Internet TV	Playlist includes live concerts, music videos, and hourly newscasts.
FedNet	Tracks Congressional activities with live and archived floor debates and proceedings.
Newsworld Online	Provides news from Canada, including live video, 24 hours a day.
Movielink	Provides sneak previews of movies in several formats and the ability to order tickets on-line.

ROM disk drive. (A five-inch optical disk holding more than 600 megabytes of information can store an hour of music, several thousand full-color pictures, several minutes of video or animation, and millions of words.) Stereo speakers are useful for amplifying audio output.

The most difficult element to incorporate into multimedia information systems has been full-motion video, because so much data must be brought under the digital control of the computer. The massive amounts of data in each video image must be digitally encoded, stored, and manipulated electronically, using techniques that compress the digital data. Special adapter cards are used to digitize sound and video.

The possibilities of this technology are endless, but multimedia seems especially well-suited for training and presentations. For training, multimedia is appealing because it is interactive and permits two-way communication. People can use multimedia training sessions any time of the day, at their own pace (Hardaway and Will, 1997). Instructors can easily integrate words, sounds, pictures, and both live and animated video to produce lessons that capture students' imaginations. For example, Duracell, the $2.6 billion battery manufacturer, used an interactive multimedia program to teach new employees at its Chinese manufacturing facility how to use battery-making machinery. Workers can use computer simulations to "stop," "start," and control equipment (Kay, 1997).

Interactive Web pages replete with graphics, sound, animations, and full-motion video have made multimedia popular on the Internet. For example, the TerraQuest Web site features "virtual explorations" on the Web to exotic destinations such as Antarctica or the Galapagos Islands. At Virtual Galapagos, an interactive tour of the Galapagos Islands, one can read letters from voyagers and comments by experts in natural history and expedition travel; view film clips, photos, or maps; or participate in on-line chat sessions with other visitors to the site. Table 5.4 lists examples of other multimedia Web sites.

Superchips and Fifth-Generation Computers

In addition to improving their design, microprocessors have been made to perform faster by shrinking the distance between transistors. This process gives the electrical current less distance to travel. The narrower the lines forming transistors, the larger the number of transistors that can be squeezed onto a single chip, and the faster these circuits will operate. The Pentium II microprocessor, for example, squeezes more than 7 million transistors on a postage-stamp-size silicon pad. Intel is now working on a 64-bit microprocessor known as the IA64 or the Merced, which contains more than 10 million transistors. It will have a clock speed exceeding 800 megahertz, twice as fast as today's fastest Pentium.

Researchers already have created semiconductors with circuits as small as .08 microns. Figure 5.13 shows the number of transistors on some prominent microprocessors and memory chips. The number of transistors that can fit economically onto a single silicon chip is doubling every 18 months. Between 50 million and 100 million transistors could soon conceivably be squeezed onto a single microprocessor. There are physical limits to this approach that soon may be reached, but researchers are experimenting with new materials to increase microprocessor speed.

FIGURE 5.13
The shrinking size and growth in number of transistors.

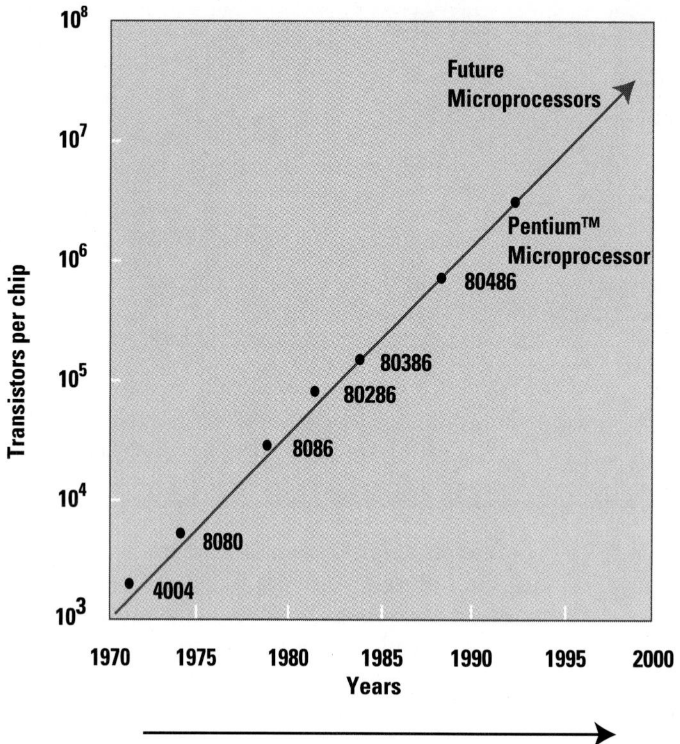

These advances in microprocessor and hardware technology are leading to ever-more-powerful and sophisticated computers. Conventional computers are based on the Von Neumann architecture, which processes information serially, one instruction at a time. In the future, more computers will use parallel processing and massively parallel processing to blend voice, images, and huge pools of data from diverse sources, using artificial intelligence and intricate mathematical models.

massively parallel computers Computers that use hundreds or thousands of processing chips to attack large computing problems simultaneously.

Massively parallel computers have huge networks of hundreds or even thousands of processor chips interwoven in complex and flexible ways to attack large computing problems. As opposed to parallel processing, where small numbers of powerful but expensive specialized chips are linked together, massively parallel machines chain hundreds or even thousands of inexpensive, commonly used chips to break problems into many small pieces and solve them. For instance, Wal-Mart Stores uses a massively parallel machine to sift through an inventory and sales trend database with 24 trillion bytes of data.

Intel's Merced microprocessor introduces a new style of processing, known as explicitly parallel instruction computing (EPIC), to high-performance computing. An EPIC processor can execute many different instructions at once inside a single processor, using software to sort instructions and decide which ones could be run simultaneously. The Merced is designed to push parallel computing into the mainstream.

Smart Cards and Microminiaturization

Microprocessor technology has fueled a growing movement toward microminiaturization—the proliferation of computers that are so small, fast, and cheap that they have become ubiquitous. For instance, many of the intelligent features that have made automobiles, stereos, toys, watches, cameras, and other equipment easier to use are based on microprocessors. The future will see even more intelligence built into everyday devices, with mainframe and perhaps even supercomputer-like computing power packed in a pocket- or notebook-sized computer. Pen, notebook, and palmtop computers will be as pervasive as handheld calculators.

smart card A credit-card–size plastic card containing embedded storage and a microprocessor.

Microminiaturization is making possible the use of smart cards for many everyday transactions. A **smart card** is a plastic card the size of a credit card that contains a small amount of storage and tiny microprocessor instead of a magnetic strip. The embedded chip can carry information, such as one's health records, identification data, or telephone numbers, and the cards can serve as "electronic purses" in place of cash. For example, New York City Transit Authority smart cards can be used as alternatives to subway and bus tokens and for paying tolls on highways and bridges. Although smart cards are not as popular in the United States as in Europe, they are very versatile and their uses are growing.

Social Interfaces

Potentially, computer technology could become so powerful and integrated into daily experiences that it would appear essentially invisible to the user (Weiser, 1993). More information and knowledge will be represented visually, through graphics (Lieberman, 1996). Social interfaces are being developed that model the interaction between people and computers using familiar human behavior. People increasingly will interact with the computer in more intuitive and effortless ways—through writing, speech, touch, eye movement, and other gestures (Selker, 1996).

Voice-recognition technology is moving closer to natural speech. Until recently, voice recognition only could be used for accepting simple commands. Voice-recognition devices had small vocabularies and could identify individual words. Now continuous-speech voice recognition is possible, using a type of artificial intelligence called natural language processing to identify phrases and sentences. Commercial continuous-speech voice-recognition products have vocabularies large enough for general business use. Computers increasingly are able to understand what is said to them and to talk back.

Management Wrap-Up

MANAGEMENT

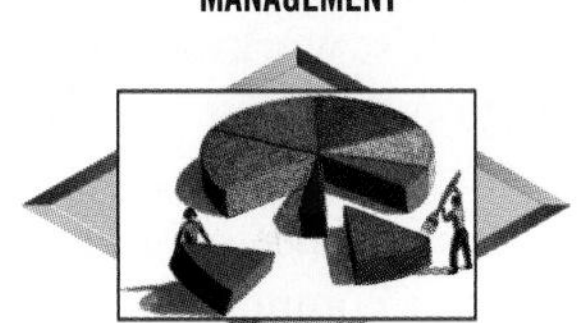

Selection of computer hardware technology for the organization is a key business decision, and it should not be left to technical specialists alone. General managers should understand the capabilities of various computer processing, input, output, and storage options, as well as price/performance relationships. They should be involved in hardware-capacity planning and decisions to distribute computing, downsize, or use network computers.

ORGANIZATION

Computer hardware technology can either enhance or impede organization performance. Selection of appropriate computer hardware technology should consider how well the technology meshes with the culture and structure of the organization, as well as its information-processing requirements.

TECHNOLOGY

Information technology today is not limited to computers but must be viewed as an array of digital devices networked together. Organizations have many computer processing options to choose from, including mainframes, workstations, PCs, and network computers and many different ways of configuring hardware components to create systems.

For Discussion:

1. What factors would you consider in deciding whether to switch from centralized processing on a mainframe to client/server processing?

2. A firm would like to introduce computers into its order entry process but feels that it should wait for a new generation of machines to be developed. After all, any machine bought now will be quickly out of date and less expensive a few years from now. Do you agree? Why or why not?

SUMMARY

1. **Identify the hardware components in a typical computer system.** The modern computer system has six major components: a central processing unit (CPU), primary storage, input devices, output devices, secondary storage, and communications devices.

2. **Describe how information is represented and processed in a computer system.** Digital computers store and process information in the form of binary digits called bits. A string of 8 bits is called a byte. There are several coding schemes for arranging binary digits into characters. The most common are EBCDIC and ASCII. The CPU is the center of the computer, where the manipulation of symbols, numbers, and letters occurs. The CPU has two components: an arithmetic-logic unit and a control unit. The arithmetic-logic unit performs arithmetic and logical operations on data, while the control unit controls and coordinates the other components of the computer.

   The CPU is closely tied to primary memory, or primary storage, which stores data and program instructions temporarily before and after processing. Several different kinds of semiconductor memory chips are used with primary storage: RAM (random access memory) is used for short-term storage of data and program instructions; whereas ROM (read-only memory) permanently stores important program instructions. Other memory devices include PROM (programmable read-only memory) and EPROM (erasable programmable read-only memory).

3. **Contrast the capabilities of mainframes, minicomputers, PCs, workstations, and supercomputers.** Depending on their size and processing power, computers are categorized as mainframes, minicomputers, PCs, workstations, or supercomputers. Mainframes are the largest computers; minicomputers are mid-range machines; PCs are desktop or laptop machines; workstations are desktop machines with powerful mathematical and graphic capabilities; and supercomputers are sophisticated, powerful computers that can perform massive and complex computations because they use parallel processing. The capabilities of microprocessors used in these computers can be gauged by their word length, data bus width, and cycle speed. Because of continuing advances in microprocessor technology, the distinctions between these types of computers are constantly changing. PCs are now powerful enough to perform much of the work that was formerly limited to mainframes and minicomputers.

4. **Compare different arrangements of computer processing, including the use of client/server computing and network computers.** Computers can be networked together to distribute processing among different machines. In the client/server model of computing, computer processing is split between "clients" and "servers" connected via a network. Each function of an application is assigned to the machine best suited to perform that function. The exact division of tasks between client and server depends on the application.

   Network computers are pared-down desktop machines with minimal or no local storage and processing capacity. They obtain most or all of their software and data from a central network server. Network computers help organizations maintain central control over computing. If managed properly, both network computers and client/server computing can reduce the total cost of ownership (TCO) of information technology resources.

5. **Describe the principal media for storing data and programs in a computer system.** The principal forms of secondary storage are magnetic tape, magnetic disk, and optical disk. Tape stores records in sequence and only can be used in batch processing. Disk permits direct access to specific records and is much faster than tape. Disk technology is used in on-line processing. Optical disks can store vast amounts of data compactly. CD-ROM disk systems can only be read from, but rewritable optical disk systems are becoming available.

6. **Compare the major input and output devices and approaches to input and processing.** The principal input devices are keyboards, computer mice, touch screens, magnetic ink and optical character recognition, pen-based instruments, digital scanners, sensors, and voice input. The principal output devices are video display terminals, printers, plotters, voice output devices, and microfilm and microfiche. In batch processing, transactions are accumulated and stored in a group until the time when it is efficient or necessary to process them. In on-line processing, the user enters transactions into a device that is directly connected to the computer system. The transactions are usually processed immediately.

7. **Describe multimedia and future information technology trends.** Multimedia integrates two or more types of media, such as text, graphics, sound, voice, full-motion video, still video, and/or animation into a computer-based application. The future will see faster chips that can package large amounts of computing power in very small spaces. Microminiaturization will embed intelligence in more everyday devices, including smart cards. Computers using massively parallel processing will be utilized more widely, and computers and related information technologies will be able to blend data, images, and sound. Social interfaces will make using computers more intuitive and natural.

KEY TERMS

Arithmetic-logic unit (ALU), 142
ASCII (American Standard Code for Information Interchange), 138
Bar code, 155
Batch processing, 156
Bit, 137
Bit mapping, 157
Byte, 137
Cathode ray tube (CRT), 157
CD-R (compact disk-recordable), 154
CD-ROM (compact disk read-only memory), 153
Central processing unit (CPU), 141
Centralized processing, 147
Client, 147
Client/server computing, 147
Computer mouse, 155
Control unit, 142
Cylinder, 152
Data bus width, 146
Digital scanner, 156
Digital video disk (DVD), 154
Direct access storage device (DASD), 153
Distributed processing, 147
Downsizing, 148
EBCDIC (Extended Binary Coded Decimal Interchange Code), 138
EPROM (erasable programmable read-only memory), 142
Floppy disk, 152
Gigabyte, 139
Hard disk, 151
Kilobyte, 139
Machine cycle, 142
Magnetic disk, 151
Magnetic ink character recognition (MICR), 156
Magnetic tape, 154
Mainframe, 143
Massively parallel computers, 160
Master file, 156
Megabyte, 139
Megahertz, 146
Microprocessor, 140
Microsecond, 139
Minicomputer, 143
MMX, 147
Multimedia, 158
Nanosecond, 139
Network computer, 149
On-line processing, 156
Optical character recognition (OCR), 155
Parallel processing, 145
Pen-based input, 156
Personal computer (PC), 143
Pixel, 138
Primary storage, 141
Printer, 157
Plotter, 158
PROM (programmable read-only memory), 142
RAM (random access memory), 141
RAID (Redundant Array of Inexpensive Disks), 152
Reduced instruction set computing (RISC), 147
Register, 143
ROM (read-only memory), 142
Secondary storage, 150
Sector, 152
Semiconductor, 142
Sensors, 156
Server, 147
Server computer, 145
Source data automation, 155
Smart card, 160
Terabyte, 139
Total cost of ownership (TCO), 149
Touch screen, 155
Track, 152
Transaction file, 156
Voice input device, 156
Voice output device, 158
Word length, 146
WORM (write once/read many), 154

REVIEW QUESTIONS

1. What are the components of a contemporary computer system?
2. Distinguish between a bit and a byte.
3. What are ASCII and EBCDIC, and why are they used?
4. Name and define the principal measures of computer time and storage capacity.
5. Describe the major generations of computers and the characteristics of each.
6. Name the major components of the CPU and the function of each.
7. Describe how information is stored in primary memory.
8. What are the four different types of semiconductor memory, and when are they used?
9. What is the difference between a mainframe, a minicomputer and a PC? Between a PC and a workstation?
10. Name and describe the factors affecting the speed and performance of a microprocessor.
11. What are downsizing and client/server processing?
12. What is a network computer? How does it differ from a conventional PC?
13. List the most important secondary storage media. What are the strengths and limitations of each?
14. List and describe the major input devices.
15. What is the difference between batch and on-line processing? Diagram the difference.
16. List and describe the major output devices.
17. What is multimedia? What technologies are involved?
18. Distinguish between serial, parallel, and massively parallel processing.

GROUP PROJECT

It has been predicted that notebook computers will become available that have 10 times the power of a current personal computer, with a touch-sensitive color screen that one can write on or draw on with a stylus or type on when a program displays a keyboard. Each will have a small compact, rewritable, removable CD-ROM disk that can store the equivalent of a set of encyclopedias. In addition, the computers will have voice-recognition capabilities, including the ability to record sound and give voice responses to questions. The computers will be able to carry on a dialogue by voice, graphics, typed words, and displayed video graphics. Thus, computers will be about the size of a thick pad of letter paper and just as portable and convenient, but with the intelligence of a computer and the multimedia capabilities of a television set. Such a computer is expected to cost about $2000. Form a group with three or four of your classmates and develop an analysis of the impacts such developments would have on one of these areas: university education, corporate sales and marketing, manufacturing, or management consulting. Explain why you think the impact will or will not occur.

TOOLS FOR INTERACTIVE LEARNING

■ **INTERNET**: The Internet Connection for this chapter will direct you to a series of Web sites where you can complete an exercise to survey the products and services of major computer hardware vendors and the use of Web sites in the computer hardware industry. You can also use the Interactive Study Guide to test your knowledge of the topics in this chapter and get instant feedback where you need more practice.

■ **CD-ROM**: If you purchase and use the Multimedia Edition CD-ROM with this chapter, you can complete an interactive exercise testing your knowledge of the machine cycle and view a simulation of a program executing on a computer. You can also find a video clip by Intel showing the evolution of computer hardware, an audio overview of the major themes of this chapter, and bullet text summarizing the key points of the chapter.

CASE STUDY

Storage and Strategy

No company wants to fix a system that isn't broken. But sometimes systems that have operated smoothly for many years come to a crossroads. Distributed computing, along with widespread use of the Internet and multimedia are putting new strains on firms' data storage capabilities. New technology arrangements are required because so much data is being generated.

A key part of the business of Schlumberger Geco Prakla, headquartered in Gatwick, England, is selling seismic data to oil and gas companies to guide their exploration. Sales of Schlumberger's reservoir of approximately 3 terabytes of on-line data are climbing rapidly since an automated data collection system and three-dimensional seismic mapping techniques and engineering applications, enabled by a more powerful internal communications network, became operational in 1997.

For the past 15 years, the company has stored its data using backup-tape technology. When a customer requested seismic data, an employee had to search among 1.5 million warehoused reels of tape and then copy the information to whatever storage format the customer needed. This inefficient, time-consuming process could take up to two weeks. Schlumberger experienced throughput problems because its storage capacity wasn't keeping up with the soaring power of its computers and networks.

The company installed Storage Computer's OmniRAID, a continuously available storage system. OmniRAID can move data at a rate of 12 megabytes per second. (Schlumberger's previous small-computer interface technology could only move data at 3 to 5 megabytes per second.) Also in use are Storage Technology's PowderHorn Automated Cartridge System silos, which house five thousand 50-gigabyte D3 tape cartridges. The silos and the OmniRAID system can deliver data very rapidly when requested by customers and transfer it to their choice of media for overnight delivery. Customers belonging to the ARIES network (a nationwide network linking NASA, supercomputing centers, and various private firms) can have their data delivered over the network almost instantaneously.

San Francisco-based Fritz Companies, an import/export broker that handles customs clearance and other logistics for Wal-Mart, Federal Express, Sears, and other companies, was forced to change its hardware technology. Fritz used a Unisys A16 mainframe for its major business transaction processing related to customs clearance and for its accounting system. Computer activity for its main business was very intense only a few hours each day. The accounting department was able to run its programs on the mainframe during other, less busy times.

The accounting department is responsible for tracking all of the firm's business activities in 110 countries. Enormous amounts of data are required to craft hundreds of customized reports for management and clients. These reports contain time-sensitive information, and how fast the system generates these reports is critical. The need for increasingly sophisticated reports, coupled with rapid business growth, strained the accounting department's resources. For instance, the monthly report summarizing the entire company's activities was nearly four hundred pages.

The accounting system used commercial software supplied by an external vendor. The vendor announced that it would stop supporting its software running on mainframes in favor of software running on midrange systems. Fritz's management wanted to keep using the vendor's accounting package, so it moved the accounting system to a Hewlett-Packard HP 9000 minicomputer. The rest of Fritz's business remained on the mainframe.

Performance on the HP 9000 system fell off drastically. Reports and batch operations that once took three or four hours on the mainframe were taking 20 or more hours on the midrange system. The time required to output reports necessary to manage field offices rose from one to three days. Both managers and rank-and-file employees were screaming.

The bottleneck proved not to be in the computer's processing speed but in its input/output activities, even though the system used high-performance disk controllers and HP Fast/Wide SCSI 2-gigabyte disk drives. Fritz then acquired a Zitel CASD-II/Enterprise storage system, which offers high capacity solid-state memory caching. Cache memory resides between the CPU and the array of disk drives. Data can be read into and out of the system at close to the speed of the CPU. Because the system no longer had to wait for an input/output event, processor utilization doubled. There was a 300 percent to 400 percent improvement in accounting operations. Performance returned to a level equal to when the system ran on the mainframe. The time required to run the company's month-end fixed-asset closing shrank from three hours to 45 minutes. A monthly closing report program that used to take 21 hours can now run in three to four hours.

Sources: Martin J. Garvey with James Governor and Mary Haynes, "Serious about Storage," *InformationWeek,* August 10, 1998; Nick Wreden, "Putting Data in Its Place," *Beyond Computing,* April 1997 and http://www.zitel.com/httdocs/estudst.htm.

Case Study Questions

1. What problems did Schlumberger Geco Prakla and Fritz Companies experience? What management, organization, and technology factors were responsible for these problems?
2. How are the capabilities of an information system affected by its input, output, and storage devices?
3. How were Fritz's and Schlumberger's business processes affected by their choice of data storage systems?
4. What management, organization, and technology issues should be considered when selecting a data storage system?

CHAPTER 6

Information Systems Software

chapter outline

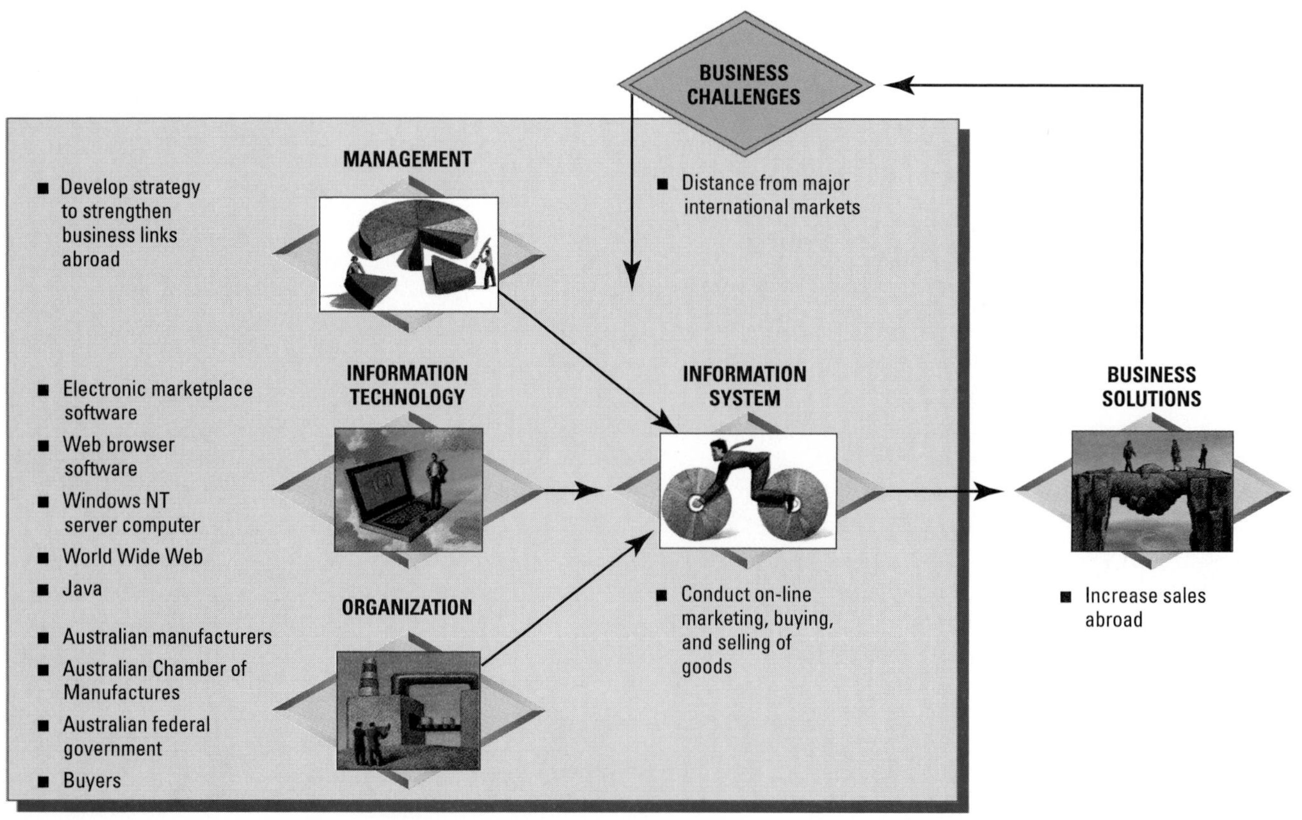

Software Overcomes Australia's Tyranny of Distance

Australian manufacturers are used to talking about the "tyranny of distance," their country's geographical isolation from the world's largest trade centers. Companies from "down under" typically require two years to break into international markets, a long time for small or medium-sized businesses without income. That time is usually spent conducting preliminary market research, establishing supply chains, and developing and growing their market.

Now, Australia's government and business leaders are hoping to use software and the Internet to shrink those distances from the rest of the world. The Australian federal government has launched an "Innovate Australia" initiative to strengthen Australian businesses' links to other countries. It funded a project to band together manufacturers to conduct trade over the Internet. The project created a "live" trading floor on which on-line marketing, bidding, buying, and selling of goods and services can take place on the Internet using Java-capable Web browser software. Trade'ex, a Tampa, Florida, vendor of electronic marketplace software, developed the system in cooperation with the Australian Chamber of Manufactures (ACM), the nation's largest multi-industry employer organization for manufacturers.

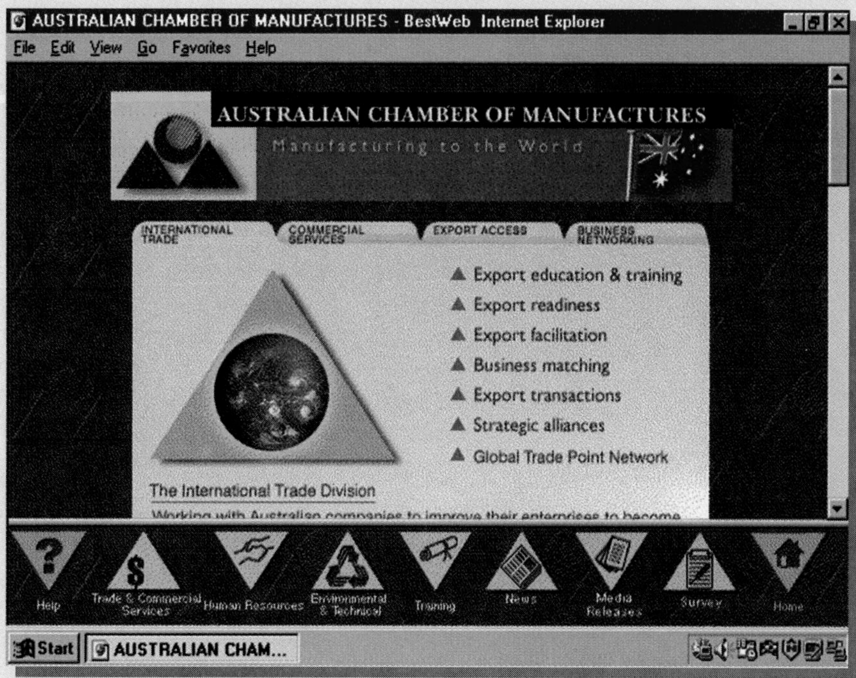

Here's how the system works: Trade'ex Marketplace Server software runs on a Windows NT server computer at ACM headquarters, storing information about the manufacturers' products such as product descriptions, pricing, and inventory figures. This computer also runs software that allows buyers to shop and place orders and sellers to fulfill those orders. Registered purchasers can purchase products directly on-line using a secure purchasing "swipe" debit card to which they have been assigned. Manufacturers can even use the Market Administrator system to customize their product information over the Internet. They can set up special promotions or multitiered pricing arrangements by company or region.

About 1500 Australian manufacturers from various industries, including information technology, telecommunications, printing, office equipment, and stationery, have participated. The government has invested about $462,000 in the project, whereas the time and resources invested by the ACM and its partners have been about double that amount. The ACM plans to collect a small percentage of each sales transaction. It predicts that by 2001, half of all purchasing transactions in the manufacturing sector will be made on-line, and it expects to capture a significant amount of this business.

The system was initially launched in a pilot version that was limited to domestic trading activities, but it is being widened for international trade. Pilot participants have been enthusiastic, noting that other systems could not provide information to distribution channels fast enough. The system also required much less effort and expense than having each manufacturer set up its own Web site. The ACM is now rebuilding the system with Sun Microsystems Java technology to enable larger manufacturers to link the system with their existing systems to facilitate invoicing, payment, and account collection.

Source: Adapted from Louisa Bryan, "Reaching Out from Down Under," *Computerworld Global Innovators,* March 10, 1997.

Management Challenges

To use the Internet and the World Wide Web for electronic commerce, Australian manufacturers had to develop special software. They had to know the capabilities of various types of software, including Web browsers and Java, and they had to select software that could provide a foundation for buying and selling on the Internet. Selecting and developing the right software can improve organizational performance, but it raises the following management challenges:

1. **Increasing complexity and software errors.** Although some software for desktop systems and for some Internet applications can be rapidly generated, a great deal of what software will be asked to do remains far-reaching and sophisticated, requiring programs that are large and complex. Citibank's automatic teller machine application required 780,000 lines of program code, written by hundreds of people, each working on small portions of the program. Large and complex systems tend to be error-prone, with software errors or "bugs" that may not be revealed for years until after exhaustive testing and actual use. Researchers do not know if the number of bugs grows exponentially or proportionately to the number of lines of code, nor can they tell for certain whether all segments of a complex piece of software will always work in total harmony. The process of designing and testing software that is reliable and "bug-free" is a serious quality control and management problem (see Chapter 14).

2. **The application backlog.** Advances in computer software have not kept pace with the breathtaking productivity gains in computer hardware. Developing software has become a major preoccupation for organizations. A great deal of software must be intricately crafted. Moreover, the software itself is only one component of a complete information system that must be carefully designed and coordinated with other people, as well as with organizational and hardware components. Managerial, procedural, and policy issues must be carefully researched and evaluated apart from the actual coding. The "software crisis" is actually part of a larger systems analysis, design, and implementation issue, which will be treated in detail later. Despite the gains from fourth-generation languages, personal desktop software tools, object-oriented programming, and software tools for the World Wide Web, many businesses continue to face a backlog of two to three years in developing the information systems they need, or they will not be able to develop them at all.

learning objectives

After completing this chapter, you will be able to:

1. Describe the major types of software.
2. Examine the functions of system software and compare leading PC operating systems.
3. Explain how software has evolved and how it will continue to develop.
4. Analyze the strengths and limitations of the major application programming languages and software tools.
5. Describe new approaches to software development.

The usefulness of computer hardware depends a great deal on available software and the ability of management to evaluate, monitor, and control the utilization of software in the organization. This chapter shows how software turns computer hardware into useful information systems, describes major software types, provides criteria for selecting software, and presents new approaches to software development.

6.1 WHAT IS SOFTWARE?

Software is the detailed instructions that control the operation of a computer system. Without software, computer hardware could not perform the tasks we associate with computers. The functions of software are to (1) manage the computer resources of the organization; (2) provide tools for human beings to take advantage of these resources; and (3) act as an intermediary between organizations and stored information. Selecting appropriate software for the organization is a key management decision.

software The detailed instructions that control the operation of a computer system.

Software Programs

A software **program** is a series of statements or instructions to the computer. The process of writing or coding programs is termed *programming,* and individuals who specialize in this task are called programmers.

The **stored program concept** means that a program must be stored in the computer's primary storage along with the required data in order to execute, or have its instructions performed by the computer. Once a program has finished executing, the computer hardware can be used for another task when a new program is loaded into memory.

program A series of statements or instructions to the computer.

stored program concept The idea that a program cannot be executed unless it is stored in a computer's primary storage along with required data.

Major Types of Software

There are two major types of software: system software and application software. Each kind performs a different function. **System software** is a set of generalized programs that manage the resources of the computer, such as the central processor, communications links, and peripheral devices. Programmers who write system software are called *system programmers.*

Application software describes the programs that are written for or by users to apply the computer to a specific task. Software for processing an order or generating a mailing list is application software. Programmers who write application software are called *application programmers.*

The types of software are interrelated and can be thought of as a set of nested boxes, each of which must interact closely with the other boxes surrounding it. Figure 6.1 illustrates this relationship. The system software surrounds and controls access to the hardware. Application software must work through the system software in order to operate. End users work primarily with application software. Each type of software must be specially designed to a specific machine to ensure its compatibility.

system software Generalized programs that manage the resources of the computer, such as the central processor, communications links, and peripheral devices.

application software Programs written for a specific application to perform functions specified by end users.

6.2 SYSTEM SOFTWARE

System software coordinates the various parts of the computer system and mediates between application software and computer hardware. The system software that manages and controls the activities of the computer is called the **operating system.** Other system software consists of computer language translation programs that convert programming languages into machine language and utility programs that perform common processing tasks.

operating system The system software that manages and controls the activities of the computer.

Functions of the Operating System

One way to look at the operating system is as the system's chief manager. Operating system software decides which computer resources will be used, which programs will be run, and the order in which activities will take place.

An operating system performs three functions. It allocates and assigns system resources; it schedules the use of computer resources and computer jobs; and it monitors computer system activities.

FIGURE 6.1

The major types of software. The relationship between the system software, application software, and users can be illustrated by a series of nested boxes. System software—consisting of operating systems, language translators, and utility programs—controls access to the hardware. Application software, such as the programming languages and "fourth-generation" languages, must work through the system software to operate. The user interacts primarily with the application software.

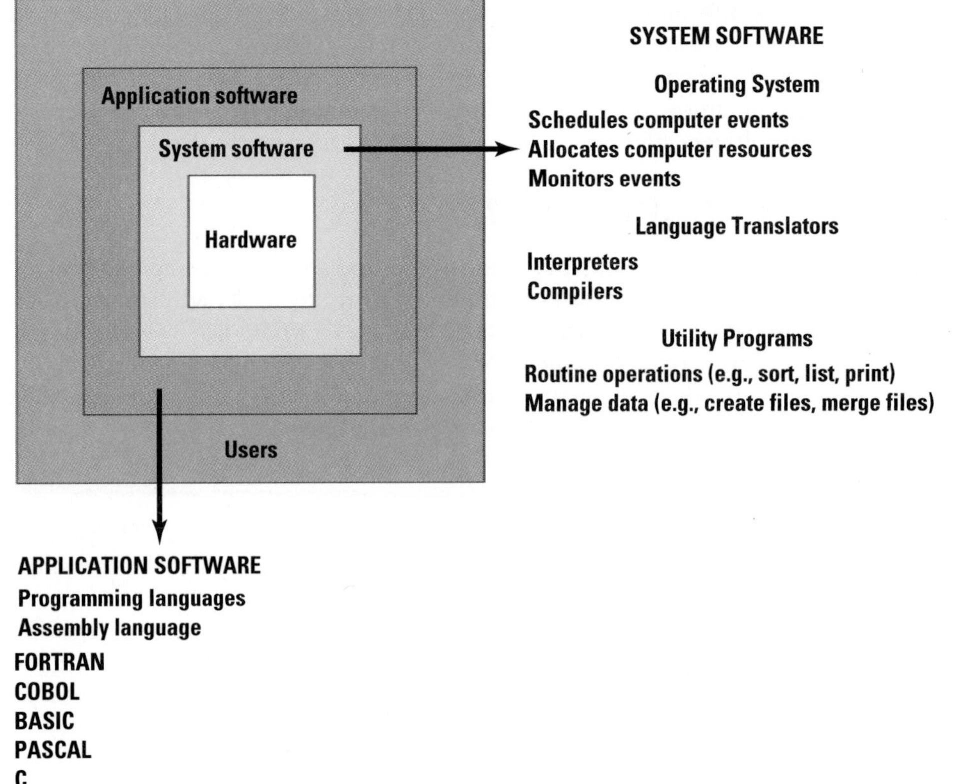

Allocation and Assignment

The operating system allocates resources to the application jobs in the execution queue. It provides locations in primary memory for data and programs and controls the input and output devices such as printers, terminals, and telecommunication links.

Scheduling

Thousands of pieces of work can be going on in a computer simultaneously. The operating system decides when to schedule the jobs that have been submitted and when to coordinate the scheduling in various areas of the computer so that different parts of different jobs can be worked on at the same time. For instance, while a program is executing, the operating system is scheduling the use of input and output devices. Not all jobs are performed in the order they are submitted; the operating system must schedule these jobs according to organizational priorities. On-line order processing may have priority over a job to generate mailing lists and labels.

Monitoring

The operating system monitors the activities of the computer system. It keeps track of each computer job and may also keep track of who is using the system, of what programs have been run, and of any unauthorized attempts to access the system. Information system security is discussed in detail in Chapter 14.

Multiprogramming, Virtual Storage, Time Sharing, and Multiprocessing

How is it possible for 1000 or more users sitting at remote terminals to use a computer information system simultaneously if, as we stated in the previous chapter, most computers can execute only one instruction from one program at a time? How can computers run thousands of programs? The answer is that the computer has a series of specialized operating system capabilities.

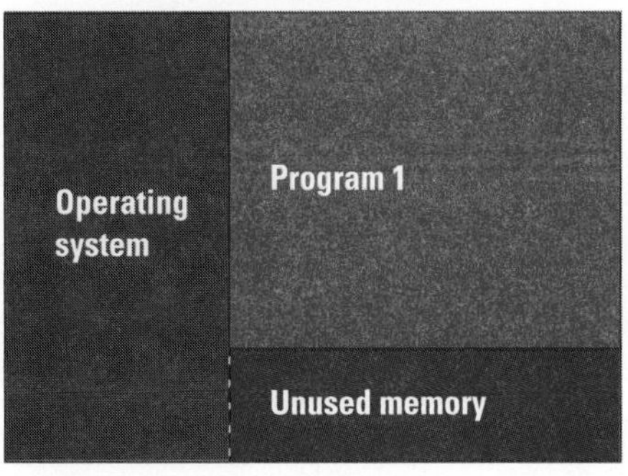

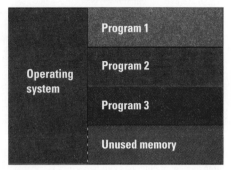

FIGURE 6.2

Single-program execution versus multiprogramming. In multiprogramming, the computer can be used much more efficiently because a number of programs can be executing concurrently. Several complete programs are loaded into memory. This memory management aspect of the operating system greatly increases throughput by better management of high-speed memory and input/output devices.

Multiprogramming

The most important operating system capability for sharing computer resources is **multiprogramming**. Multiprogramming permits multiple programs to share a computer system's resources at any one time through concurrent use of a CPU. By concurrent use, we mean that only one program is actually using the CPU at any given moment but that the input/output needs of other programs can be serviced at the same time. Two or more programs are active at the same time, but they do not use the same computer resources simultaneously. With multiprogramming, a group of programs takes turns using the processor.

multiprogramming A method of executing two or more programs concurrently using the same computer. The CPU executes only one program but can service the input/output needs of others at the same time.

Figure 6.2 shows how three programs in a multiprogramming environment can be stored in primary storage. The first program executes until an input/output event is read in the program. The operating system then directs a channel (a small processor limited to input and output functions) to read the input and move the output to an output device. The CPU moves to the second program until an input/output statement occurs. At this point, the CPU switches to the execution of the third program, and so forth, until eventually all three programs have been executed. In this manner, many different programs can be executing at the same time, although different resources within the CPU are actually being utilized.

The first operating systems executed only one program at a time. Before multiprogramming, when a program read data off a tape or disk or wrote data to a printer, the entire CPU came to a stop. This was a very inefficient way to use the computer. With multiprogramming, the CPU utilization rate is much higher.

Multitasking

Multitasking refers to multiprogramming on single-user operating systems such as those in older personal computers. One person can run two or more programs or program tasks concurrently on a single computer. For example, a sales representative could write a letter to prospective clients with a word processing program while simultaneously using a database program to search for all sales contacts in a particular city or geographic area. Instead of terminating the session with the word processing program, returning to the operating system, and then initiating a session with the database program, multitasking allows the sales representative to display both programs on the computer screen and work with them at the same time.

multitasking The multiprogramming capability of primarily single-user operating systems, such as those for older PCs.

Virtual Storage

Virtual storage handles programs more efficiently because the computer divides the programs into small fixed- or variable-length portions, storing only a small portion of the program in primary memory at one time. If only two or three large programs can be read into memory, a certain part of main memory generally remains underutilized because the programs add up to less than the total amount of primary storage space available. Given the limited size of primary memory, only a small number of programs can reside in primary storage at any given time.

virtual storage A way of handling programs more efficiently by the computer by dividing the programs into small fixed- or variable-length portions with only a small portion stored in primary memory at one time.

FIGURE 6.3

Virtual storage. Virtual storage is based on the fact that, in general, only a few statements in a program can actually be utilized at any given moment. In virtual storage, programs are broken down into small sections called pages. Individual program pages are read into memory only when needed. The rest of the program is stored on disk until it is required. In this way, very large programs can be executed by small machines, or a large number of programs can be executed concurrently by a single machine.

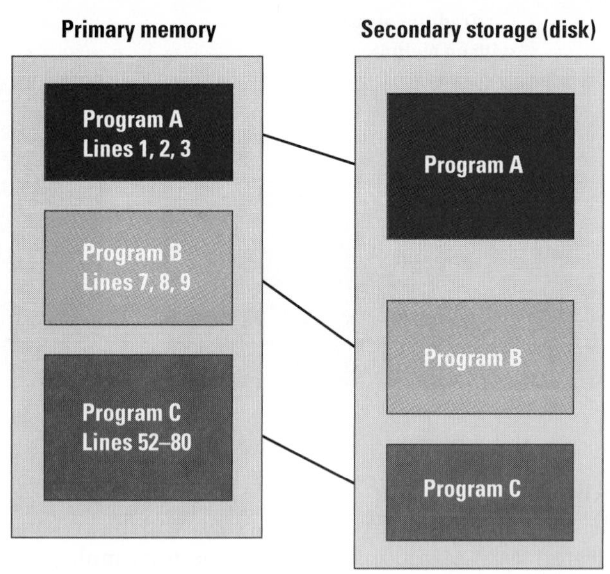

page A small fixed-length section of a program, which can be easily stored in primary storage and quickly accessed from secondary storage.

Only a few statements of a program actually execute at any given moment. Virtual storage breaks a program into a number of fixed-length portions called **pages** or into variable-length portions called *segments*. Each of these portions is relatively small (a page is approximately 2 to 4 kilobytes). This permits a very large number of programs to reside in primary memory, inasmuch as only one page of each program is actually located there (see Figure 6.3).

All other program pages are stored on a peripheral disk unit until they are ready for execution. Virtual storage provides a number of advantages. First, the central processor is utilized more fully. Many more programs can be in primary storage because only one page of each program actually resides there. Second, programmers no longer have to worry about the size of the primary storage area. With virtual storage, programs can be of infinite length and small machines can execute a program of any size (admittedly, small machines will take longer than big machines to execute a large program).

Time Sharing

time sharing The sharing of computer resources by many users simultaneously by having the CPU spend a fixed amount of time on each user's program before proceeding to the next.

Time sharing is an operating system capability that allows many users to share computer processing resources simultaneously. It differs from multiprogramming in that the CPU spends a fixed amount of time on one program before moving on to another. In a time-sharing environment, thousands of users are each allocated a tiny slice of computer time (2 milliseconds). In this time slot, each user is free to perform any required operations; at the end of this period, another user is given a 2-millisecond time slice of the CPU. This arrangement permits many users to be connected to a CPU simultaneously, with each receiving only a tiny amount of CPU time. But because the CPU is operating at the nanosecond level, a CPU can accomplish a great deal of work in 2 milliseconds.

Multiprocessing

multiprocessing An operating system feature for executing two or more instructions simultaneously in a single computer system by using multiple central processing units.

Multiprocessing is an operating system capability that links together two or more CPUs to work in parallel in a single computer system. The operating system can assign multiple CPUs to execute different instructions from the same program or from different programs simultaneously, dividing the work between the CPUs. While multiprogramming uses concurrent processing with one CPU, multiprocessing uses simultaneous processing with multiple CPUs.

Language Translation and Utility Software

When computers execute programs written in languages such as COBOL, FORTRAN, or C, the computer must convert these human-readable instructions into a form it can understand. System software includes special language translator programs that trans-

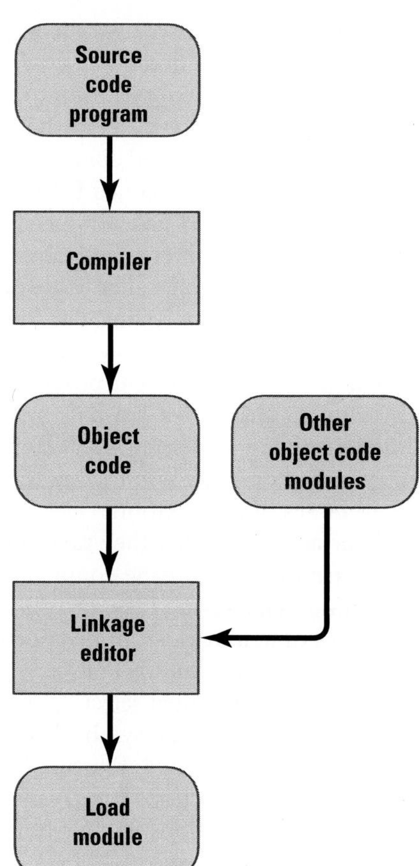

FIGURE 6.4

The language translation process. The source code, the program in a high-level language, is translated by the compiler into object code so that the instructions can be "understood" by the machine. These are grouped into modules. Prior to execution, the object code modules are joined together by the linkage editor to create the load module. It is the load module that is actually executed by the computer.

late higher-level language programs written in programming languages such as BASIC, COBOL, and FORTRAN into machine language that the computer can execute. This type of system software is called a *compiler* or *interpreter.* The program in the high-level language before translation into machine language is called **source code.** A **compiler** translates source code into machine code called **object code.** Just before execution by the computer, the object code modules are joined with other object code modules in a process called *linkage editing.* The resulting load module is what is actually executed by the computer. Figure 6.4 illustrates the language translation process.

Some programming languages such as BASIC do not use a compiler but an **interpreter,** which translates each source code statement one at a time into machine code and executes it. Interpreter languages such as BASIC provide immediate feedback to the programmer if a mistake is made, but they are very slow to execute because they are translated one statement at a time.

An assembler is similar to a compiler, but it is used to translate only assembly language (see Section 6.3) into machine code.

System software includes **utility programs** for routine, repetitive tasks, such as copying, clearing primary storage, computing a square root, or sorting. If you have worked on a computer and have performed such functions as setting up new files, deleting old files, or formatting diskettes, you have worked with utility programs. Utility programs are prewritten programs that are stored so that they can be shared by all users of a computer system and can be rapidly used in many different information system applications when requested.

Graphical User Interfaces

When users interact with a computer, even a PC, the interaction is controlled by an operating system. The user interface is the part of an information system that users interact with. Users communicate with an operating system through the user interface of that operating system. Early PC operating systems were command-driven, but the

source code Program instructions written in a high-level language that must be translated into machine language to be executed by the computer.

compiler Special system software that translates a higher-level language into machine language for execution by the computer.

object code Program instructions that have been translated into machine language so that they can be executed by the computer.

interpreter A special translator of source code into machine code that translates each source code statement into machine code and executes them, one at a time.

utility program System software consisting of programs for routine, repetitive tasks, which can be shared by many users.

graphical user interface (GUI) The part of an operating system that users interact with that uses graphic icons and the computer mouse to issue commands and make selections.

graphical user interface, often called a **GUI,** makes extensive use of icons, buttons, bars, and boxes to perform the same task. It has become the dominant model for the user interface of PC operating systems and for many types of application software.

Older PC operating systems such as DOS, described on the following page, are command-driven, requiring the user to type in text-based commands using a keyboard. For example, to perform a task such as deleting a file named DATAFILE, the user must type in a command such as *DELETE C:\DATAFILE.* Users need to remember these commands and their syntax to work with the computer effectively. An operating system with a graphical user interface uses graphic symbols called *icons* to depict programs, files, and activities. Commands can be activated by rolling a mouse to move a cursor about the screen and clicking a button on the mouse to make selections. Icons are symbolic pictures and they are also used in GUIs to represent programs and files. For example, a file could be deleted by moving the cursor to a Trash icon. Many graphical user interfaces use a system of pull-down menus to help users select commands and pop-up boxes to help users select among command options. Windowing features allow users to create, stack, size, and move around boxes of information.

Proponents of graphical user interfaces claim that they save learning time because computing novices do not have to learn different arcane commands for each application. Common functions such as getting help, saving files, or printing output are performed the same way. A complex series of commands can be issued simply by linking icons. On the other hand, GUIs may not always simplify complex tasks if the user has to spend too much time first pointing to icons and then selecting operations to perform on those icons (Morse and Reynolds, 1993). Graphic symbols themselves are not always easy to understand unless the GUI is well designed. Existing GUIs are modeled after an office desktop, with files, documents, and actions based on typical office behavior, making them less useful for nonoffice applications in control rooms or processing plants (Mandelkern, 1993).

PC Operating Systems

Like any other software, PC software is based on specific operating systems and computer hardware. A software package written for one PC operating system generally cannot run on another. Table 6.1 compares the leading PC operating systems: Windows 98 and Windows 95, Windows NT, Windows CE, OS/2, UNIX, the Macintosh operating system, and DOS.

TABLE 6.1 Leading PC Operating Systems

Operating System	Features
Windows 98 and Windows 95	32-bit operating system with a streamlined graphical user interface. Has multitasking and powerful networking capabilities and can be integrated with the information resources of the Web.
Windows NT	32-bit operating system for PCs, workstations, and network servers not limited to Intel microprocessors. Supports multitasking, multiprocessing, intensive networking.
Windows CE	Pared-down version of the Windows operating system for handheld computers and wireless communication devices.
OS/2 (Operating System/2)	Operating system for the IBM PCs. Can take advantage of the 32-bit microprocessor. Supports multitasking and networking.
UNIX	Used for powerful PCs, workstations, and minicomputers. Supports multitasking, multi-user processing, and networking. Is portable to different models of computer hardware.
Mac OS	Operating system for the Macintosh computer. Supports networking and multitasking and has powerful multimedia capabilities. Supports connecting to and publishing on the Internet.
DOS	Operating system for IBM (PC-DOS) and IBM-compatible (MS-DOS) PCs. Limits program use of memory to 640 K.

DOS was the most popular operating system for 16-bit PCs. It is used today with older PCs based on the IBM PC standard because so much available application software was written for systems using DOS. (PC-DOS is used exclusively with IBM PCs. MS-DOS, developed by Microsoft, is used with other 16-bit PCs that function like the IBM PC.) DOS itself does not support multitasking and limits the size of a program in memory to 640 K.

DOS Operating system for 16-bit PCs based on the IBM personal computer standard.

DOS is command-driven, but it can present a graphical user interface by using Microsoft **Windows,** a highly popular graphical user interface shell that runs in conjunction with the DOS operating system. Windows supports limited forms of multitasking and networking but shares the memory limitations of DOS. Early versions of Windows had some problems with application crashes when multiple programs competed for the same memory space.

Windows A graphical user interface shell that runs in conjunction with the DOS PC operating system. Supports multitasking and some forms of networking.

Microsoft's **Windows 98** and **Windows 95** are genuine 32-bit operating systems. A 32-bit operating system can run faster than DOS, which could only address data in 16-bit chunks, because it can address data in 32-bit chunks. Both Windows 98 and Windows 95 provide a streamlined graphical user interface that arranges icons to provide instant access to common tasks. They can support software written for DOS but can also run programs that take up more than 640 K of memory. Windows 98 and 95 feature multitasking, multithreading (the ability to manage multiple independent tasks simultaneously), and powerful networking capabilities, including the capability to integrate fax, e-mail, and scheduling programs.

Windows 98 Version of the Windows operating system that is more closely integrated with the Internet and that supports hardware technologies such as MMX, digital video disk, videoconferencing cameras, scanners, TV tuner-adapter cards, and joysticks.

Windows 95 A 32-bit operating system with a streamlined graphical user interface and multitasking, multithreading, and networking capabilities.

Windows 98 is faster and more integrated with the Internet than Windows 95, with support for new hardware technologies such as MMX, digital video disk (DVD—see Chapter 5), videoconferencing cameras, scanners, TV tuner-adapter cards, and joysticks. It provides capabilities for optimizing hardware performance and file management on the hard disk and enhanced three-dimensional graphics. The most visible feature of Windows 98 is the integration of the operating system with Web browser software. Users will be able to work with the traditional Windows interface or use the Web browser interface to display information. The user's hard disk can be viewed as an extension of the World Wide Web so that a document residing on the hard disk or on the Web can be accessed the same way. Small applet programs (see the discussion of Java in Section 6.4) on the Windows desktop can automatically retrieve information from specific Web sites whenever the user logs onto the Internet. These applets can automatically update the desktop with the latest news, stock quotes, or weather.

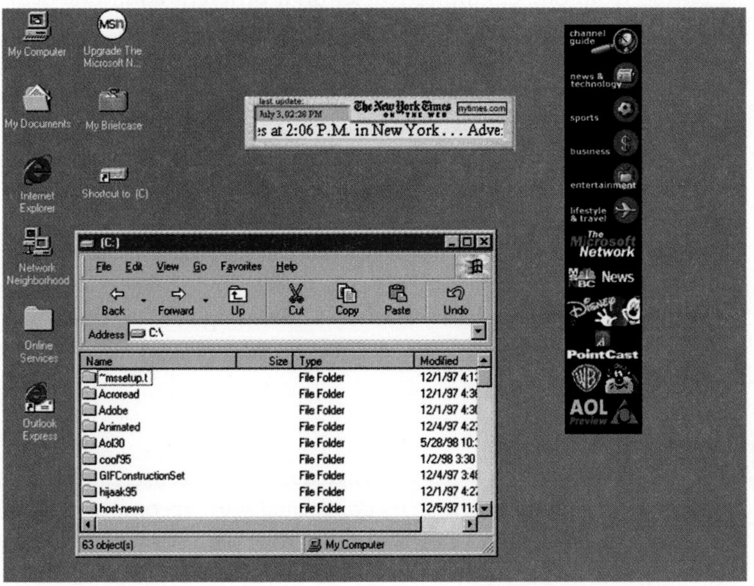

Microsoft's Windows 98 is a powerful operating system with a graphical user interface and capabilities to integrate the user's desktop with the information resources of the Internet.

Windows NT Powerful operating system developed by Microsoft for use with 32-bit PCs and workstations based on Intel and other microprocessors. Supports networking, multitasking, and multiprocessing.

Windows NT (for New Technology) is another 32-bit operating system developed by Microsoft with features that make it appropriate for applications in large networked organizations. It is used as an operating system for high-performance workstations and network servers. Windows NT shares the same graphical user interface as the other Windows operating systems, but it has more powerful networking, multitasking, and memory-management capabilities. Windows NT can support existing software written for DOS and Windows, and it can provide mainframe-like computing power for new applications with massive memory and file requirements. It can even support multiprocessing with multiple CPUs.

There are two versions of Windows NT—a Workstation version for users of standalone or client desktop computers and a Server version designed to run on network servers. Windows NT Server includes tools for creating and operating Web sites. Unlike OS/2, Windows NT is not tied to computer hardware based on Intel microprocessors.

Windows CE Portable and compact version of the Windows operating system designed to run on small handheld computers, personal digital assistants, or wireless communication devices.

Windows CE has some of the capabilities of Windows, including its graphical user interface, but it is designed to run on small handheld computers, personal digital assistants, or wireless communication devices such as pagers and cellular phones. It is a portable and compact operating system requiring very little memory. Non-PC and consumer devices can use this operating system to share information with Windows-based PCs and to connect to the Internet.

OS/2 Powerful operating system used with 32-bit IBM/PCs or workstations that supports multitasking, networking, and more memory-intensive applications than DOS.

OS/2 is a robust 32-bit operating system for powerful IBM or IBM-compatible PCs with Intel microprocessors. OS/2 is used for complex, memory-intensive applications or those that require networking, multitasking or large programs. OS/2 provides powerful desktop computers with mainframe-operating-system capabilities, such as multitasking and supporting multiple users in networks, and it supports networked multimedia and pen computing applications.

OS/2 supports applications that run under Windows and DOS and has its own graphical user interface. There are now two versions of OS/2. OS/2 Warp is for personal use. It can accept voice-input commands and run Java applications without a Web browser (see Sections 6.3 and 6.4). OS/2 Warp Server has capabilities similar to Windows NT for supporting networking, systems management, and Internet access.

UNIX Operating system for PCs, minicomputers, and mainframes, which is machine independent and supports multi-user processing, multitasking, and networking.

UNIX is an interactive, multi-user, multitasking operating system developed by Bell Laboratories in 1969 to help scientific researchers share data. Many people can use UNIX simultaneously to perform the same kind of task, or one user can run many tasks on UNIX concurrently. UNIX was developed to connect various machines together and is highly supportive of communications and networking. UNIX was designed for minicomputers but now has versions for PCs, workstations, and mainframes. It is often used on workstations and server computers. UNIX can run on many different kinds of computers and can be easily customized. Application programs that run under UNIX can be ported from one computer to run on a different computer with little modification. UNIX also can store and manage a large number of files.

UNIX is considered powerful but very complex, with a legion of commands. Graphical user interfaces have been developed for UNIX. UNIX cannot respond well to problems caused by the overuse of system resources such as jobs or disk space. UNIX also poses some security problems, because multiple jobs and users can access the same file simultaneously. Vendors have developed different versions of UNIX that are incompatible, thereby limiting software portability.

Mac OS Operating system for the Macintosh computer that supports multitasking, has access to the Internet, and has powerful graphics and multimedia capabilities.

Mac OS, the operating system for the Macintosh computer, features multitasking as well as powerful multimedia and networking capabilities, and a mouse-driven graphical user interface. New features of this operating system allow users to connect to, explore, and publish on the Internet and World Wide Web and to use Java software (see Section 6.4).

6.3 APPLICATION SOFTWARE

Application software is primarily concerned with accomplishing the tasks of end users. Many different languages can be used to develop application software. Each has different strengths and drawbacks.

Generations of Programming Languages

To communicate with the first generation of computers, specialized programmers wrote programs in **machine language**—the 0s and 1s of binary code. Programming in 0s and 1s (reducing all statements such as add, subtract, and divide into a series of 0s and 1s) made early programming a slow, labor-intensive process.

machine language A programming language consisting of the 1s and 0s of binary code.

As computer hardware improved and processing speed and memory size increased, computer languages changed from machine language to languages that were easier for humans to understand. Generations of programming languages developed to correspond with the generations of computer hardware. Figure 6.5 shows the development of programming languages during the last 50 years as the capabilities of hardware have increased. The major trend is to increase the ease with which users can interact with hardware and software.

Machine language was the first-generation programming language. The second generation of programming languages occurred in the early 1950s with the development of assembly language. Instead of using 0s and 1s, programmers could substitute language-like acronyms and words such as *add, sub* (subtract), and *load* in programming statements. A language translator called a *compiler* converted the English-like statements into machine language.

From the mid-1950s to the mid-1970s, the third generation of programming languages emerged. These languages, such as FORTRAN, COBOL, and BASIC, allowed programs to be written with regular words using sentence-like statements. These languages are called **high-level languages** because each statement generates multiple statements when it is translated into machine language. Programs became easier to create and started to be used more widely for scientific and business problems.

high-level language Programming languages in which each source code statement generates multiple statements at the machine-language level.

Beginning in the late 1970s, fourth-generation languages and tools were created. These languages dramatically reduce programming time and make software tasks so easy that many can be performed by nontechnical computer users without the help of professional programmers. Software such as word processing, spreadsheets, data management, and Web browsers became popular productivity tools for end users.

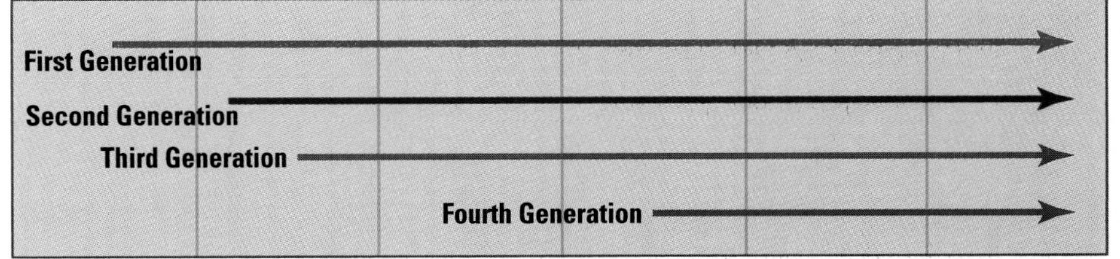

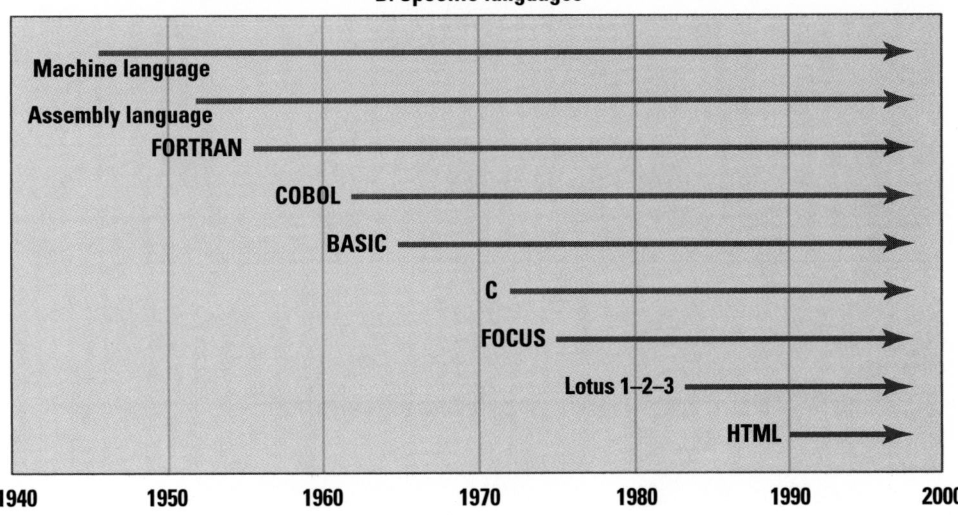

FIGURE 6.5

Generations of programming languages. As the capabilities of hardware increased, programming languages developed from the first generation of machine and second generation of assembly languages of the 1950s to 1960s, through the third-generation, high-level languages such as FORTRAN and COBOL developed in the 1960s and 1970s, to today's fourth-generation languages and tools.

Popular Programming Languages

Most managers need not be expert programmers, but they should understand how to evaluate software applications and to select programming languages that are appropriate for their organization's objectives. We will now briefly describe the more popular high-level languages.

Assembly Language

assembly language A programming language developed in the 1950s that resembles machine language but substitutes mnemonics for numeric codes.

Like machine language, **assembly language** (Figure 6.6) is designed for a specific machine and specific microprocessors. Each operation in assembly corresponds to a machine operation. On the other hand, assembly language makes use of certain mnemonics (e.g., *load, sum*) and assigns addresses and storage locations automatically. Although assembly language gives programmers great control, it is costly in terms of programmer time, difficult to read and debug, and difficult to learn. Assembly language is used primarily today in system software.

FORTRAN

FORTRAN (FORmula TRANslator) A programming language developed in 1956 for scientific and mathematical applications.

FORTRAN (FORmula TRANslator) (Figure 6.7) was developed in 1956 to provide an easier way of writing scientific and engineering applications. FORTRAN is especially useful in processing numeric data. Many kinds of business applications can be written in FORTRAN, and contemporary versions provide sophisticated structures for controlling program logic. FORTRAN is not very good at providing input/output efficiency or in printing and working with lists. The syntax is very strict and keying errors are common, making the programs difficult to debug.

COBOL

COBOL (COmmon Business Oriented Language) Major programming language for business applications because it can process large data files with alphanumeric characters.

COBOL (COmmon Business Oriented Language) (Figure 6.8) came into use in the early 1960s. It was developed by a committee representing both government and industry. Rear Admiral Grace M. Hopper was a key committee member who played a major role in COBOL development. COBOL was designed with business administration in mind, for processing large data files with alphanumeric characters (mixed alphabetic and numeric data), and for performing repetitive tasks such as payroll. It is poor at complex mathematical calculations. Also, there are many versions of COBOL, and not all are compatible with each other.

FIGURE 6.6
Assembly language. This sample assembly language command adds the contents of register 3 to register 5 and stores the result in register 5.

```
AR 5, 3
```

FIGURE 6.7
FORTRAN. This sample FORTRAN program code is part of a program to compute sales figures for a particular item.

```
READ (5,100) ID, QUANT, PRICE
TOTAL = QUANT * PRICE
```

FIGURE 6.8
COBOL. This sample COBOL program code is part of a routine to compute total sales figures for a particular item.

```
MULTIPLY QUANT-SOLD BY UNIT-PRICE GIVING SALES-TOTAL.
```

BASIC

BASIC (Beginners All-purpose Symbolic Instruction Code) was developed in 1964 by John Kemeny and Thomas Kurtz to teach students at Dartmouth College how to use computers. Today it is a popular programming language on college campuses and for PCs. BASIC can do almost all computer processing tasks from inventory to mathematical calculations. It is easy to use, demonstrates computer capabilities well, and requires only a small interpreter. The weakness of BASIC is that it does few tasks well even though it does them all. It has no sophisticated program logic control or data structures, which makes it difficult to use in teaching good programming practices. Different versions of BASIC exist.

BASIC (Beginners All-purpose Symbolic Instruction Code) A general-purpose programming language used with PCs and for teaching programming.

Pascal

Named after Blaise Pascal, the seventeenth-century mathematician and philosopher, **Pascal** was developed by the Swiss computer science professor Niklaus Wirth of Zurich in the late 1960s. Pascal programs can be compiled using minimal computer memory, so they can be used on PCs. With sophisticated structures to control program logic and a simple, powerful set of commands, Pascal is used primarily in computer science courses to teach sound programming practices. The language is weak at file handling and input/output and is not easy for beginners to use.

Pascal A programming language used on PCs and used to teach sound programming practices in computer science courses.

C and C++

C is a powerful and efficient language developed at AT&T's Bell Labs in the early 1970s. It combines machine portability with tight control and efficient use of computer resources, and it can work on a variety of different computers. It is used primarily by professional programmers to create operating system and application software, especially for PCs.

C++ is a newer version of C that is object-oriented (see Section 6.4). It has all the capabilities of C plus additional features for working with software objects. C++ is used for developing application software.

C A powerful programming language with tight control and efficiency of execution; is portable across different microprocessors and is used primarily with PCs.

C++ Object-oriented version of the C programming language.

Other Programming Languages

Other important programming languages include Ada, LISP, Prolog, and PL/1.

- **Ada** was developed in 1980 by the U.S. Defense Department to serve as a standard for all of its applications. Named after Ada, Countess of Lovelace, a nineteenth-century mathematician, it was designed to be executed in diverse hardware environments. Ada is used for both military and nonmilitary applications because it can operate on different brands of computer hardware.
- **LISP** (designating LISt Processor) and **Prolog** (designating PROgramming LOGic) are used for artificial-intelligence applications. LISP, created in the late 1950s, is oriented toward putting symbols such as operations, variables, and data values into meaningful lists. Prolog was introduced around 1970 and also is well-suited to manipulating symbols. It can run on a wider variety of computers than LISP.
- **PL/1 (Programming Language 1)** is a powerful general-purpose programming language developed by IBM in 1964. It can comfortably handle both mathematical and business problems, but it has not replaced COBOL or FORTRAN because organizations have already invested so heavily in COBOL and FORTRAN systems.

Ada A programming language that is portable across different brands of hardware; is used for both military and nonmilitary applications.

LISP Programming language used for artificial-intelligence applications. Stands for LISt Processor.

Prolog Programming language for artificial-intelligence applications.

PL/1 (Programming Language 1) A programming language developed by IBM for both business and scientific applications.

Fourth-Generation Languages and PC Software Tools

Fourth-generation languages consist of a variety of software tools that enable end users to develop software applications with minimal or no technical assistance or that enhance the productivity of professional programmers. Fourth-generation languages tend to be nonprocedural or less procedural than conventional programming languages. Procedural languages require specification of the sequence of steps, or procedures, that tell

fourth-generation language A programming language that can be employed directly by end users or less-skilled programmers to develop computer applications more rapidly than conventional programming languages.

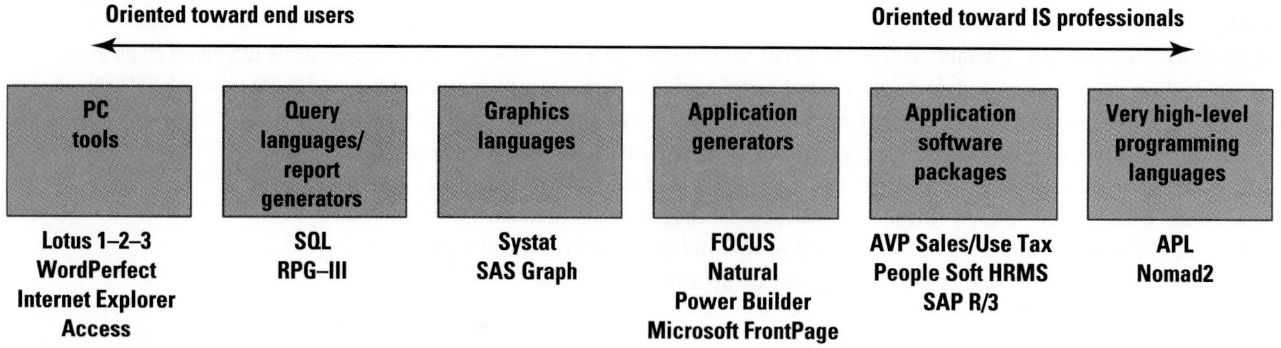

Oriented toward end users ⟷ Oriented toward IS professionals

PC tools	Query languages/ report generators	Graphics languages	Application generators	Application software packages	Very high-level programming languages
Lotus 1–2–3 WordPerfect Internet Explorer Access	SQL RPG–III	Systat SAS Graph	FOCUS Natural Power Builder Microsoft FrontPage	AVP Sales/Use Tax People Soft HRMS SAP R/3	APL Nomad2

FIGURE 6.9 Fourth-generation languages. The spectrum of major categories of fourth-generation languages and commercially available products in each category is illustrated. Tools range from those that are simple and designated primarily for end users to complex tools designed for information systems professionals.

the computer what to do and how to do it. Nonprocedural languages need only specify what has to be accomplished rather than provide details about how to carry out the task. Thus, a nonprocedural language can accomplish the same task with fewer steps and lines of program code than a procedural language.

There are seven categories of fourth-generation languages: query languages, report generators, graphics languages, application generators, very high-level programming languages, application software packages, and PC tools. Figure 6.9 illustrates the spectrum of these tools and some commercially available products in each category.

Query Languages

query language A high-level computer language used to retrieve specific information from databases or files.

Query languages are high-level languages for retrieving data stored in databases or files. They are usually interactive, on-line, and capable of supporting requests for information that are not predefined. They are often tied to database management systems (see Chapter 7) or some of the PC software tools described later in this section. For instance, the query

SELECT ALL WHERE age >40 AND name = "Wilson"

requests all records where the name is "Wilson" and the age is more than 40. Chapter 7 provides more detail on Structured Query Language (SQL), which has become a standard query language.

natural language Programming language that is very close to human language.

Available query tools have different kinds of syntax and structure, some being closer to natural language than others (Vassiliou, 1984–85). **Natural language** software allows users to communicate with the computer using conversational commands that resemble human speech. Natural language development is one of the concerns of artificial intelligence (see Chapter 12). Some consider the movement toward natural language as the next generation in software development.

Report Generators

report generator Software that creates customized reports in a wide range of formats that are not routinely produced by an information system.

Report generators are facilities for creating customized reports. They extract data from files or databases and create reports in many formats. Report generators generally provide more control over the way data are formatted, organized, and displayed than query languages. The more powerful report generators can manipulate data with complex calculations and logic before they are output. Some report generators are extensions of database or query languages.

Graphics Languages

graphics language A computer language that displays data from files or databases in graphic format.

Graphics languages retrieve data from files or databases and display them in graphic format. Users can ask for data and specify how they are to be charted. Some graphics software can perform arithmetic or logical operations on data as well. SAS and Systat are examples of powerful analytical graphics software.

Application Generators

Application generators contain preprogrammed modules that can generate entire applications, greatly speeding development. A user can specify what needs to be done, and the application generator will create the appropriate code for input, validation, update, processing, and reporting. Most full-function application generators consist of a comprehensive, integrated set of development tools: a database management system, data dictionary, query language, screen painter, graphics generator, report generator, decision support/modeling tools, security facilities, and a high-level programming language. Application generators now include tools for developing full-function Web sites.

application generator Software that can generate entire information system applications; the user needs only to specify what needs to be done, and the application generator creates the appropriate program code.

Very High-Level Programming Languages

Very high-level programming languages are designed to generate program code with fewer instructions than conventional languages such as COBOL or FORTRAN. Programs and applications based on these languages can be developed in much shorter periods of time. Simple features of these languages can be employed by end users. However, these languages are designed primarily as productivity tools for professional programmers. APL and Nomad2 are examples of these languages.

very high-level programming language A programming language that uses fewer instructions than conventional languages. Used primarily as a professional programmer productivity tool.

Application Software Packages

A **software package** is a prewritten, precoded, commercially available set of programs that eliminates the need for individuals or organizations to write their own software programs for certain functions. There are software packages for system software, but the vast majority of package software is application software.

software package A prewritten, precoded, commercially available set of programs that eliminates the need to write software programs for certain functions.

Application software packages consist of prewritten application software that is marketed commercially. These packages are available for major business applications on mainframes, minicomputers, and PCs. Although application packages for large complex systems must be installed by technical specialists, many application packages, especially those for PCs, are marketed directly to end users. Systems development based on application packages is discussed in Chapter 11.

The Window on Organizations provides examples of geographic information systems software, a type of leading-edge application software package that is proving very useful for businesses. **Geographic information systems (GIS)** can analyze and display data using digitized maps to enhance planning and decision making.

geographic information system (GIS) System with software that can display data using digitized maps to enhance planning and decision making.

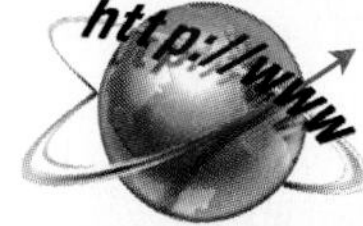

PC Software Tools

Some of the most popular and productivity-promoting software tools are the general-purpose application packages that have been developed for PCs, especially word processing, spreadsheet, data management, presentation graphics, integrated software packages, e-mail, Web browsers, and groupware.

WORD PROCESSING SOFTWARE. **Word processing software** stores text data electronically as a computer file rather than on paper. The word processing software allows the user to make changes in the document electronically in memory. This eliminates the need to retype an entire page to incorporate corrections. The software has formatting options to make changes in line spacing, margins, character size, and column width. Microsoft Word and WordPerfect are popular word processing packages. Figure 6.10 illustrates a Microsoft Word screen displaying text, graphics, and major menu options.

word processing software Software that handles electronic storage, editing, formatting, and printing of documents.

Most word processing software has advanced features that automate other writing tasks: spelling checkers, style checkers (to analyze grammar and punctuation), thesaurus programs, and mail merge programs, which link letters or other text documents with names and addresses in a mailing list. The newest versions of this software can create and access Web pages.

SPREADSHEETS. Electronic **spreadsheet** software provides computerized versions of traditional financial modeling tools such as the accountant's columnar pad, pencil, and calculator. An electronic spreadsheet is organized into a grid of columns and rows. The

spreadsheet Software displaying data in a grid of columns and rows, with the capability of easily recalculating numerical data.

WINDOW ON ORGANIZATIONS

Mapping Solutions with Geographic Information Systems

If you were a manager at a television station, would you want demographic information about your viewers presented as columns of numbers or in a graphic format? To Rod Brown of Big Horn Computer Services in Buffalo, Wyoming, the answer is clear. A graphic presentation of a complex set of numbers is unquestionably preferred. Brown is working on an application for a national television network. The network has collected a massive amount of demographic data on its viewers and wants management of its local affiliate stations to have access to that data. The application Brown is developing uses software technology known as *geographic information systems (GIS)*. The software maps any data that has a spatial quality. For the television station, the data will display maps that have areas shaded according to income, viewing habits, or whatever data the viewer wants to see. This particular application is prized by the network's management for another reason—the affiliated stations will be able to view the data through the Internet. As a result, the network need only install and keep up-to-date one copy of the software and data. The local stations will use their Web browser to view the data relevant to their own market.

Mapping tools are proving valuable as management tools in many ways. For example, to wireless telecommunications giant Bell South, the technology means lower customer support costs, whereas to its more than 50,000 wireless customers it means improved customer service. Bell South customers constantly want to know how far their service reaches. Traditionally, customer-service representatives took several minutes to rifle through paper files to find the answer—an expensive routine. Now, using a GIS system, the same representatives can see the answer displayed on a map in only seconds.

Managers in retail firms are finding many uses for mapping software. Johanna Dairies of Union, New Jersey, is using GIS software to display its customers on a map and then to design the most efficient delivery routes, creating savings of $100,000 per year for each route that can be eliminated. Quaker Oats uses GIS software to display and analyze sales and customer data by store locations. This information helps Quaker Oats customers to tailor the products they carry in their stores and to design advertising campaigns targeted specifically to each store's customers.

Retail stores also use GIS software to track their competition and, with the use of census data, to analyze their customer pool. Management at Sonny's Bar-B-Q, the Gainesville, Florida-based restaurant chain, uses mapping software to determine where to open new outlets. Sonny's well-thought-out growth plan specifies that the company will expand only into regions where barbecued food is very common but where the number of barbecue restaurants is small. The company also requires that location sites are no closer than seven miles from any other Sonny's. The company looks at a range of factors when determining the suitability of a given territory, including traffic count, median age, household income, total population, and population distribution. The data come from local and federal census bureaus and are purchasable in computer format. Reading and understanding mountains of statistics in numeric form is an almost impossible task. To Michael Turner, director of franchise services at Sonny's, the only answer was GIS software. That software has been central to Sonny's ability to open 15 to 20 restaurants a year (from a base of 83 in 1994).

To Think About: ***What are the organizational benefits of geographic information system software? What management, organization, and technology issues should be addressed when deciding whether to use GIS?***

Sources: April Jacobs, "Mapping Software Puts an End to Paper Chase," *Computerworld,* March 3, 1997; John Swenson, "Maps on the Web," *Information Week,* July 8, 1996; and Tony Seideman, "You Gotta Know the Territory," *Profit,* November–December 1994.

power of the electronic spreadsheet is evident when one changes a value or values, because all other related values on the spreadsheet will be automatically recomputed.

Spreadsheets are valuable for applications in which numerous calculations with pieces of data must be related to each other. Spreadsheets also are useful for applications that require modeling and what-if analysis. After the user has constructed a set of mathematical relationships, the spreadsheet can be recalculated instantaneously using a different set of assumptions. A number of alternatives can easily be evaluated by changing one or two pieces of data without having to rekey in the rest of the worksheet. Many spreadsheet packages include graphics functions that can present data in the form of line graphs, bar graphs, or pie charts. The most popular spreadsheet packages are Microsoft Excel and Lotus 1-2-3. The newest versions of this software can read and write Web files.

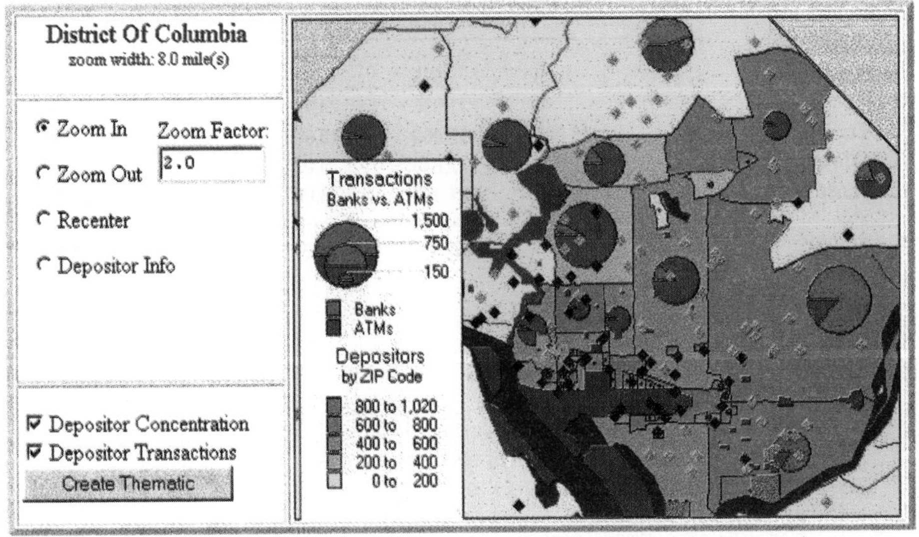

Geographic information system (GIS) software presents and analyzes data geographically, tying business data to points, lines, and areas on a map. GIS tools are available for use on the World Wide Web.

Figure 6.11 illustrates the output from a spreadsheet for a breakeven analysis and its accompanying graph.

DATA MANAGEMENT SOFTWARE. Although spreadsheet programs are powerful tools for manipulating quantitative data, **data management software** is more suitable for creating and manipulating lists and for combining information from different files. PC database management packages have programming features and easy-to-learn menus that enable nonspecialists to build small information systems.

data management software Software used for creating and manipulating lists, creating files and databases to store data, and combining information for reports.

Data management software typically has facilities for creating files and databases and for storing, modifying, and manipulating data for reports and queries. A detailed treatment of data management software and database management systems can be

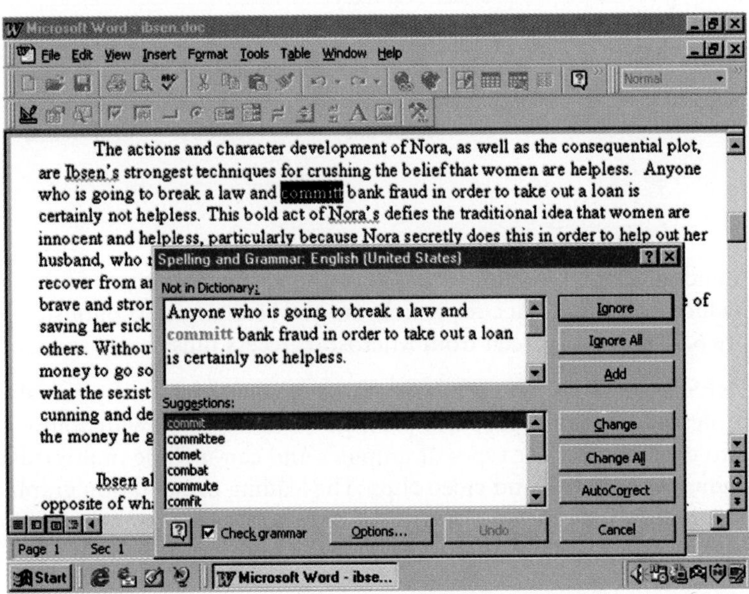

FIGURE 6.10

Text and the spell-checking option in Microsoft Word 97. Word processing software provides many easy-to-use options to create and output a text document to meet a user's specifications. *Courtesy of Microsoft.*

FIGURE 6.11

Spreadsheet software. Spreadsheet software organizes data into columns and rows for analysis and manipulation. Contemporary spreadsheet software provides graphing abilities for clear visual representation of the data in the spreadsheets. This sample breakeven analysis is represented as numbers in a spreadsheet as well as a line graph for easy interpretation.

Total fixed cost	**19,000.00**
Variable cost per unit	**3.00**
Average sales price	**17.00**
Contribution margin	**14.00**
Breakeven point	**1,357**

Custom Neckties Pro Forma Income Statement

Units sold	**0.00**	**679**	**1,357**	**2,036**	**2,714**
Revenue	**0**	**11,536**	**23,071**	**34,607**	**46,143**
Fixed cost	**19,000**	**19,000**	**19,000**	**19,000**	**19,000**
Variable cost	**0**	**2,036**	**4,071**	**6,107**	**8,143**
Total cost	**19,000**	**21,036**	**23,071**	**25,107**	**27,143**
Profit/Loss	**(19,000)**	**(9,500)**	**0**	**9,500**	**19,000**

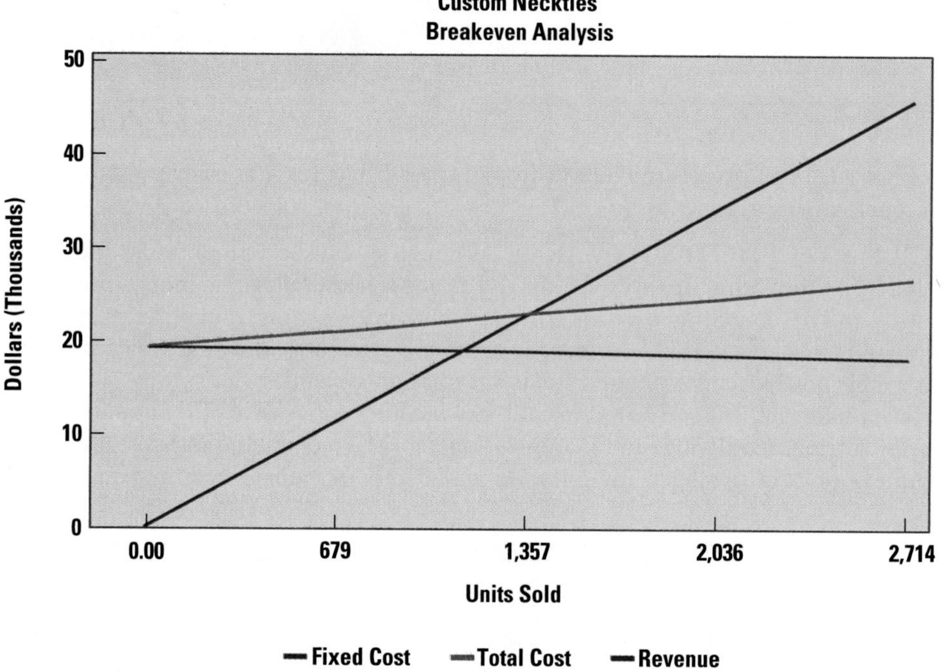

found in Chapter 7. Popular database management software for the personal computer includes Microsoft Access, which has been enhanced to publish data on the Web. Figure 6.12 shows a screen from Microsoft Access illustrating some of its capabilities.

presentation graphics Software to create professional-quality graphics presentations that can incorporate charts, sound, animation, photos, and video clips.

PRESENTATION GRAPHICS. **Presentation graphics** software allows users to create professional-quality graphics presentations. This software can convert numeric data into charts and other types of graphics and can include multimedia displays of sound, animation, photos, and video clips. The leading presentation graphics packages include capabilities for computer-generated slide shows and translating content for the Web. Microsoft PowerPoint, Lotus Freelance Graphics, and Aldus Persuasion are popular presentation graphics packages.

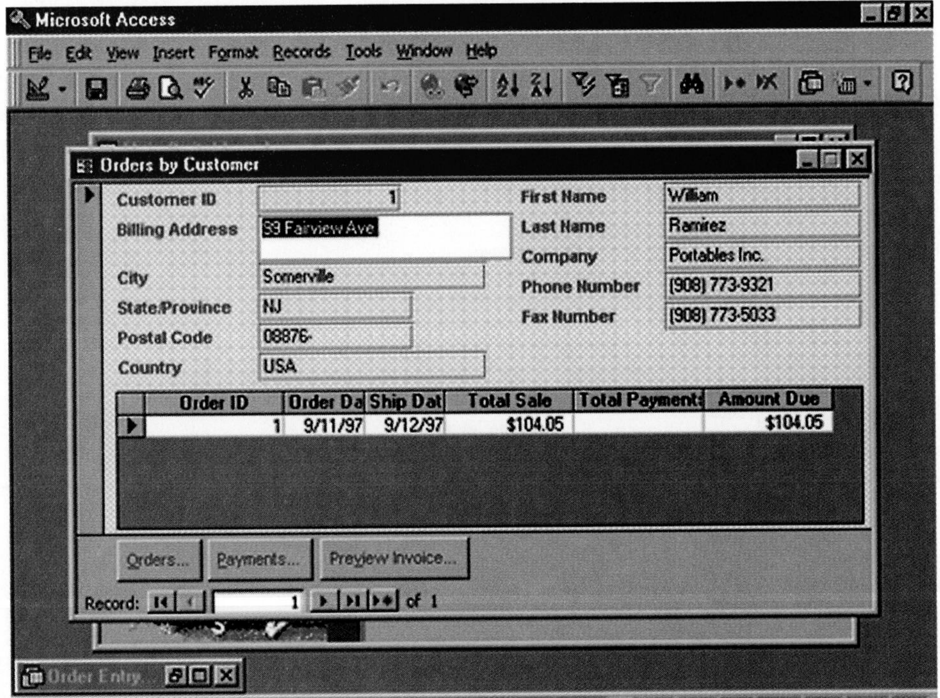

FIGURE 6.12

Data management software. This screen from Microsoft Access illustrates some of its powerful capabilities for managing and organizing information.

INTEGRATED SOFTWARE PACKAGES AND SOFTWARE SUITES. **Integrated software packages** combine the functions of the most important PC software packages, such as word processing, spreadsheets, presentation graphics, and data management. This integration provides a more general-purpose software tool and eliminates redundant data entry and data maintenance. For example, the breakeven analysis spreadsheet illustrated in Figure 6.11 could be reformatted into a polished report with word processing software without separately keying the data into both programs. Integrated packages are a compromise. Although they can do many things well, they generally do not have the same power and depth as single-purpose packages.

integrated software package A software package that provides two or more applications, such as word processing and spreadsheets, providing for easy transfer of data between them.

Integrated software packages should be distinguished from software suites, which are collections of applications software sold as a unit. Microsoft Office 97 is an example. This software suite contains Word word processing software, Excel spreadsheet software, Access database software, PowerPoint presentation graphics software, and Outlook, a set of tools for e-mail, scheduling, and contact management. Software suites have some features of integrated packages, such as the ability to share data among different applications, but they consist of full-featured versions of each type of software.

E-MAIL SOFTWARE. **Electronic mail (e-mail)** is used for the computer-to-computer exchange of messages and is an important tool for communication and collaborative work. A person can use a networked computer to send notes or lengthier documents to a recipient on the same network or a different network. Many organizations operate their own electronic-mail systems, but communications companies such as MCI and AT&T offer these services, along with commercial on-line information services such as America Online and Prodigy and public networks on the Internet.

electronic mail (e-mail) The computer-to-computer exchange of messages.

Web browsers and the PC software suites have e-mail capabilities, but specialized e-mail software packages such as Eudora are also available for use on the Internet. In addition to providing electronic messaging, many e-mail software packages have capabilities for routing messages to multiple recipients, message forwarding, and attaching text documents or multimedia to messages.

Web browser An easy-to-use software tool for accessing the World Wide Web and the Internet.

WEB BROWSERS. **Web browsers** are easy-to-use software tools for displaying Web pages and for accessing the Web and other Internet resources. Web browser software

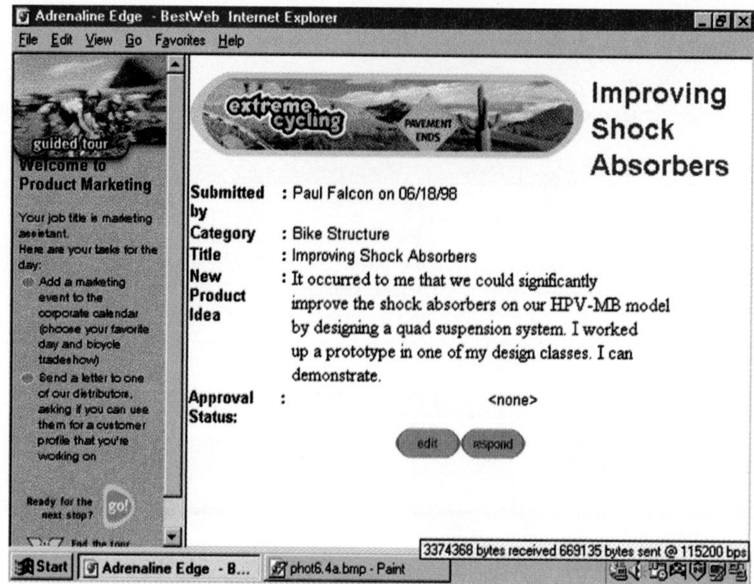

Lotus Notes groupware facilitates collaboration by enabling members of a group to share documents, schedule meetings, and discuss activities, events, and issues.

features a point-and-click graphical user interface that can be employed throughout the Internet to access and display information stored on computers at other Internet sites. Browsers can display or present graphics, audio, and video information as well as traditional text, and they allow you to click on-screen buttons or highlighted words to link to related Web sites. Web browsers have become the primary interface for accessing the Internet or for using networked systems based on Internet technology. You can see examples of Web browser software by looking at the illustrations of Web pages in each chapter of this text.

The two leading commercial Web browsers are Microsoft's Internet Explorer and Netscape Navigator, which is also available as part of the Netscape Communicator software suite. They include capabilities for using e-mail, file transfer, on-line discussion groups and bulletin boards, along with other Internet services. Newer versions of these browsers contain support for Web publishing and workgroup computing. (See the following discussion of groupware.)

groupware Software that provides functions and services that support the collaborative activities of work groups.

GROUPWARE. **Groupware** provides functions and services to support the collaborative activities of work groups. Groupware includes software for information sharing, electronic meetings, scheduling, and e-mail and a network to connect the members of the group as they work on their own desktop computers, often in widely scattered locations. Table 6.2 describes the capabilities of groupware.

Groupware enhances collaboration by allowing the exchange of ideas electronically. All the messages on a topic can be saved in a group, stamped with the date, time, and author. Any group member can review the ideas of others at any time and add to them, or individuals can post a document for others to comment upon or edit. Members can post requests for help, allowing others to respond. Finally, if a group so

TABLE 6.2 Groupware Capabilities
Group writing and commenting
Electronic mail distribution
Scheduling meetings and appointments
Shared files and databases
Shared timelines and plans
Electronic meetings

chooses, members can store their work notes on the groupware so that all others in the group can see what progress is being made, what problems occur, and what activities are planned.

The leading commercial groupware product has been Lotus Notes from the Lotus Development Corporation. The Internet is rich in capabilities to support collaborative work. Microsoft Internet Explorer 4.0 and Netscape Communicator include groupware functions, such as e-mail, electronic scheduling and calendaring, audio and data conferencing, and electronic discussion groups and databases (see Chapters 9 and 12). Microsoft's Office 2000 software suite includes groupware features using Web technology.

6.4 NEW SOFTWARE TOOLS AND APPROACHES

A growing backlog of software projects and the need for businesses to fashion systems that are flexible or that can run over the Internet have stimulated new approaches to software development with object-oriented programming tools and new programming languages such as Java and hypertext markup language (HTML).

Object-Oriented Programming

Traditional software development methods have treated data and procedures as independent components. A separate programming procedure must be written every time someone wants to take an action on a particular piece of data. The procedures act on data that the program passes to them.

What Makes Object-Oriented Programming Different?

Object-oriented programming combines data and the specific procedures that operate on those data into one *object*. The object combines data and program code. Instead of passing data to procedures, programs send a message for an object to perform a procedure that is already embedded into it. (Procedures are termed *methods* in object-oriented languages.) The same message may be sent to many different objects, but each will implement that message differently.

object-oriented programming An approach to software development that combines data and procedures into a single object.

For example, an object-oriented financial application might have Customer objects sending debit and credit messages to Account objects. The Account objects in turn might maintain Cash-on-Hand, Accounts-Payable, and Accounts-Receivable objects.

An object's data are hidden from other parts of the program and can only be manipulated from inside the object. The method for manipulating the object's data can be changed internally without affecting other parts of the program. Programmers can focus on what they want an object to do, and the object decides how to do it.

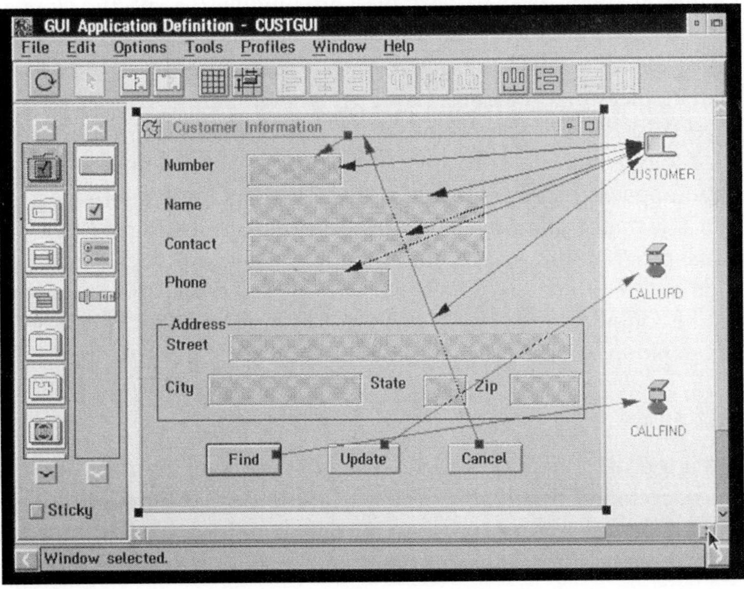

With visual programming tools such as IBM's Visual Age Generator, working software programs can be created by drawing, pointing, and clicking instead of writing program code.

An object's data are encapsulated from other parts of the system, so each object is an independent software building block that can be used in many different systems without changing the program code. Thus, object-oriented programming is expected to reduce the time and cost of writing software by producing reusable program code or software *chips* that can be reused in other related systems. Future software work can draw upon a library of reusable objects, and productivity gains from object-oriented technology could be magnified if objects were stored in reusable software libraries and explicitly designed for reuse (Fayad and Cline, 1996).

visual programming The construction of software programs by selecting and arranging programming objects rather than by writing program code.

Object-oriented programming has spawned a new programming technology known as **visual programming.** With visual programming, programmers do not write code. Rather, they use a mouse to select and move around programming objects, copying an object from a library into a specific location in a program, or drawing a line to connect two or more objects. Visual Basic is a widely used visual programming tool for creating applications that run under Microsoft Windows.

Object-Oriented Programming Concepts

Object-oriented programming is based on the concepts of class and inheritance. Program code is not written separately for every object but for classes, or general categories, of similar objects. Objects belonging to a certain class have the features of that class. Classes of objects in turn can inherit all the structure and behaviors of a more general class and then add variables and behaviors unique to each object. New classes of objects are created by choosing an existing class and specifying how the new class differs from the existing class, instead of starting from scratch each time.

class The feature of object-oriented programming meaning all objects belonging to a certain class have all of the features of that class.

Classes are organized hierarchically into superclasses and subclasses. For example, a *car* class might have a *vehicle* class for a superclass, so that it would inherit all the methods and data previously defined for *vehicle.* The design of the *car* class would only need to describe how cars differ from vehicles. A banking application could define a Savings-Account object that is very much like a Bank-Account object with a few minor differences. Savings-Account inherits all the Bank-Account's state and methods and then adds a few extras.

inheritance The feature of object-oriented programming in which a specific class of objects receives the features of a more general class.

We can see how class and **inheritance** work in Figure 6.13, which illustrates a tree of classes concerning employees and how they are paid. Employee is the common ancestor of the other four classes. Nonsalaried and salaried are subclasses of Employee, whereas Temporary and Permanent are subclasses of Nonsalaried. The variables for the class are in the top half of the box, and the methods are in the bottom half. Darker items in each box are inherited from some ancestor class. (For example, by following the tree upward, we can see that Name and ID in the Nonsalaried, Salaried, Temporary, and Permanent subclasses are inherited from the Employee superclass [ancestor class].) Lighter methods, or class variables, are unique to a specific class and they override, or redefine, existing methods. When a subclass overrides an inherited method, its object still responds to the same message, but it executes its definition of the method rather than its ancestor's. Whereas Pay is a method inherited from some superclass, the method Pay-OVERRIDE is specific to the Temporary, Permanent, and Salaried classes.

Object-oriented software can be custom-programmed or it can be developed with rapid-application development tools, which can potentially cost 30 percent to 50 percent less than traditional program development methods. Some of these tools provide visual programming environments in which developers can create ready-to-use program code by "snapping" together prebuilt objects. Other tools generate program code that can be compiled to run on a variety of computing platforms. The Window on Technology explores the use of such tools to speed up object-oriented software creation.

Java Programming language that can deliver only the software functionality needed for a particular task as a small applet downloaded from a network; can run on any computer and operating system.

Java

Java is a programming language named after the many cups of coffee its Sun Microsystems developers drank along the way. It is an object-oriented language, combining data with the functions for processing the data, and it is platform-independent. Java software is designed to run on any computer or computing device, regardless of the specific mi-

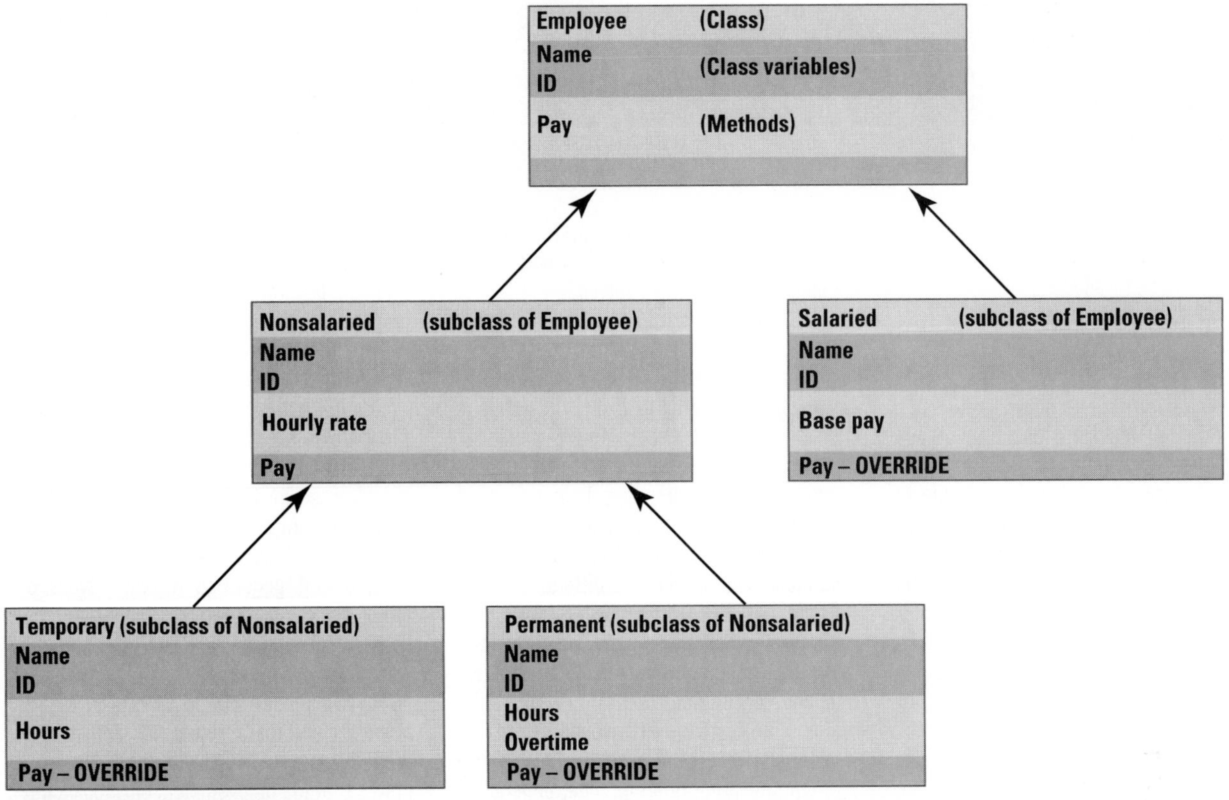

FIGURE 6.13 Class, subclasses, inheritance, and overriding. This figure illustrates how a message's method can come from the class itself or an ancestor class. Class variables and methods are shaded when they are inherited from above.

croprocessor or operating system it uses. A Macintosh Apple, an IBM personal computer running Windows, a DEC computer running UNIX, and even a smart cellular phone or personal digital assistant can share the same Java application.

Java can be used to create miniature programs called "applets" designed to reside on centralized network servers. The network delivers only the applets required for a specific function. With Java applets residing on a network, a user can download only the software functions and data that he or she needs to perform a particular task, such as analyzing the revenue from one sales territory. The user does not need to maintain large software programs or data files on his or her desktop machine. When the user is finished with processing, the data can be saved through the network. Java can be used with network computers because it enables all processing software and data to be stored on a network server, downloaded via a network as needed, and then placed back on the network server.

Java is also a very robust language that can handle text, data, graphics, sound, and video, all within one program if needed. Java applets often are used to provide interactive capabilities for Web pages. For example, Java applets can be used to create animated cartoons or real-time news tickers for a Web site, or to add a capability to a Web page to calculate a loan payment schedule on-line in response to financial data input by the user. (Microsoft's **ActiveX** sometimes is used as an alternative to Java for creating interactivity on a Web page. ActiveX is a set of controls that enables programs or other objects such as charts, tables, or animations to be embedded within a Web page. However, ActiveX lacks Java's machine independence and was designed for a Windows environment.)

ActiveX A set of controls for the Windows software environment that enables programs or other objects such as charts, tables, or animations to be embedded within a Web page.

Java also can be used to create more extensive applications that can run over the Internet or over a company's private network (see the Window on Management). Java

WINDOW ON TECHNOLOGY

Object Power Tools

Object-oriented tools are one type of advanced software technology that many companies are turning to when they decide to develop their own systems. These tools do not come without costs and problems, but they are proving to be an effective and efficient way for organizations to solve their business problems.

Stewart Enterprises in Metairie, Louisiana, decided to use Synon's Obsidian, an object-based development tool that automatically generates C++ program code. This company, which owns more than 500 funeral homes and cemeteries in seven countries, first used Obsidian to create an application called CAFÉ (Cemetery and Funeral Enabler). CAFÉ helps funeral homes make the necessary arrangements with families, fill out government forms, and print contracts. The company believes that Obsidian reduced program coding time by more than 50 percent.

When evaluating new system development tools, companies must consider a number of issues: What is the cost of the tools; what will the cost be to train the staff to use the tools; how quickly can systems be developed once the staff and software are ready; how will the tools fit in with the current or planned information systems infrastructure; and how well will the tools fit the business problem to be solved?

Highlights for Children, a children's magazine published in Columbus, Ohio, recently adopted IBM's Visual Age Generator as an object-oriented toolset for its application development. Programmers could develop applications by clicking on objects and dragging and dropping them onto other objects to build program logic.

Management knew that learning object technology would be a difficult process at first, but they felt the switch to the new technology would be helpful. One of the reasons is that their new object-oriented development tools enable the staff to write applications in English-like pseudo-code. The tools then convert the pseudo-code into the appropriate programming code, depending upon the software platform. In this way *Highlights* will not be restricted to a single platform in the future. The magazine also was pleased with the graphic-based technology used by the tools, making them easy to learn and use.

According to Steve Gilkerson, *Highlights'* director of information systems, the programmers were skilled in highly structured languages such as COBOL and would certainly have a problem switching to pseudo-code and object-oriented development. As Gilkerson put it, "Your first application will always be the toughest challenge." He decided on a transition approach that involved hiring a consulting firm that could train his staff, mentor them during the early development projects, and monitor them as they worked. At first he only had two programmers trained, but as they became skilled, they trained and mentored others. He summed up his approach by explaining, "You can't train 20 people at one time and expect results."

Gilkerson emphasized the need for experience, so he had his programmers develop small applications before tackling the big ones. For example, they developed a module that generated different types of billing notices before working on larger projects. In the end he believes his approach worked, and he is happy to report that between 80 percent and 95 percent of all the business application code developed runs properly on the target platform. He estimates that his programmers only took a day or two to do minor tweaking of the code to get it to operate properly. "Compare that with the weeks it could take to rewrite portions of a COBOL or C++ application."

To Think About: ***What problems should be anticipated when organizations start using object-oriented software technology? What management, organization, and technology issues should be addressed?***

Source: Adapted from Peter Ruker, "Today's Programming Tools," *Beyond Computing,* March 1998.

can let PC users manipulate data on networked systems using Web browsers, reducing the need to write specialized software. For example, Sprint PCS, the mobile-phone partnership, is using Java for an application that allows its employees to use Web browsers to analyze business data and send reports to colleagues via e-mail on an internal network. The system it replaces required specialized desktop software to accomplish these tasks and restricted these reports to a smaller number of employees (Clark, 1998).

To run Java software, a computer needs an operating system containing a Java Virtual Machine (JVM). (A JVM is incorporated into Web browser software such as Netscape Navigator or Microsoft Internet Explorer.) The Java Virtual Machine is a compact program that enables the computer to run Java applications. The JVM lets the computer simulate an ideal standardized Java computer, complete with its own repre-

WINDOW ON MANAGEMENT

Adding Java to the Programming Mix

For several years, Java has been the hot new language to enliven Web site programming, but there are other reasons to utilize the new language. Corporate managements are finding that using Java can cut programming time and costs compared with such languages as C++. In addition, Java is a genuine cross-platform language—the same code can be moved from computing platform to platform and still work—saving the organization programming time and expenses.

Atlanta-based Home Depot, with nearly 700 stores on its computer network, is using Java for many of its new applications. Its fundamental business requirement is to use network computers so a technician does not "have a hard drive to deal with every time I turn around," according to Curtis Chambers, the designer of the company's distributed applications. He explains that, with no hard drives, the hardware cost-per-unit is lower, and management has better control over which applications each store is using. Michael Anderson, Home Depot's director of information systems, adds that Java is an easier language to use and so speeds up development time. Perhaps most important in terms of reducing long-range cost, Anderson believes that by programming in Java, "We'll cut our support by 75 percent."

The company already has built a number of systems using Java. One application enables district managers to download sales and inventory information to their local PCs. No longer does each district have to create its own reports. Instead, the reports are automatically waiting for them when they log on to the company network. Java also is being used in the employment area. When a potential employee submits an application to one of the stores, one Java application automatically sends the application to all of Home Depot's 700 stores, making it more likely the company will find a good fit for the applicant while also saving job seekers considerable effort and time. In addition, the company is building an employment-tracking system. Management expects this system ultimately will become a paperless benefits system.

Daiwa Securities America, Inc. of New York is another convert to Java. The company wants to develop a system that will give it straight-through processing, which will move trade data from its entry when a trade is placed and completed through to all systems where that data is needed. Such a system would eliminate the cost of duplicate data entry. All financial trading companies have front-office (trading) systems and back-office (record keeping and accounting) systems. What is missing is a middle-office system that connects the two. Daiwa is using Java for several reasons. First, Java gives the applications platform independence—the Daiwa staff can develop each application only once and then run it on any platform, saving Daiwa a great deal in development and maintenance costs. In addition the company likes Java because it will be running many of its applications on internal and external networks, the kind of environment for which Java was created.

On the other hand, Bethesda Healthcare System, a health care provider in Boynton Beach, Florida, has no plans to switch from C++ to Java for its software development. Different versions of Java used by various software vendors include subtle differences in their Java Virtual Machines, which can cause errors in how applications behave. Glitches in how information is displayed by Web browsers could create life-or-death issues because physicians rely on such data to make treatment decisions. Bethesda transmits images such as X-rays to clinics and doctor's offices, which expect the images to be absolutely accurate. Bethesda Healthcare has no control over what hardware is used by the health care providers with whom it shares its data, so true cross-platform compatibility would be essential.

To Think About: ***What are the management benefits of using Java to develop software? What management organization and technology issues should be addressed when deciding whether to use Java?***

Sources: Sharon Gaudin, "Users Praise Business Benefits of Java," *Computerworld*, January 19, 1998; Ann Mallory, "Java Journeys," *Computerworld*, March 23, 1998; and Robert L. Scheier, "Jury's Still Out," *Computerworld*, May 12, 1997.

sentation of a CPU and its own instruction set. The Virtual Machine executes Java programs by interpreting their commands one by one and commanding the underlying computer to perform all the tasks specified by each command.

Management and Organizational Benefits of Java

Companies are starting to develop more applications in Java because such applications can potentially run in Windows, UNIX, IBM mainframe, Macintosh, and other environments without having to be rewritten for each computing platform. Sun Microsystems terms this phenomenon "write once, run anywhere." Java also could allow more software to be distributed and used through networks. Functionality could be stored with data on the network and downloaded only as needed. Companies might

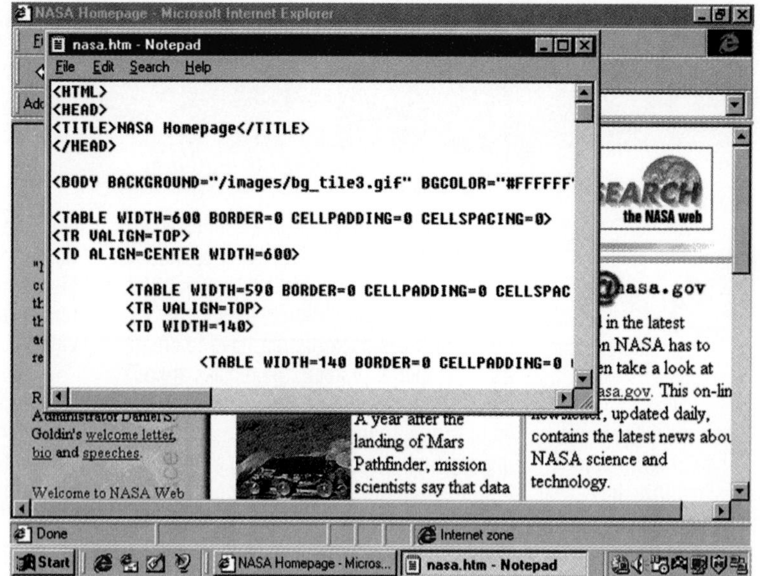

FIGURE 6.14

Sample of the HTML code used to create the NASA Web page displayed here.

not need to purchase thousands of copies of commercial software to run on individual computers; instead users could download applets over a network and use network computers.

Java is similar to C++ but considered easier to use. Java program code can be written more quickly than with other languages. Sun claims that no Java program can penetrate the user's computer, making it safe from viruses and other types of damage that might occur when downloading more conventional programs off a network.

Despite these benefits, Java has not yet fulfilled its early promise to revolutionize software development and use. Programs written in current versions of Java tend to run slower than "native" programs, which are written for a particular operating system, because they must be interpreted by the Java Virtual Machine. Vendors such as Microsoft are supporting alternative versions of Java that include subtle differences in their Virtual Machines that affect Java's performance in different pieces of hardware and operating systems. Without a standard version of Java, true platform independence cannot be achieved. The Window on Management explores the management issues posed by Java as companies consider whether to use this programming language.

Hypertext Markup Language (HTML)

hypertext markup language (HTML) Page description language for creating Web pages and other hypermedia documents.

Hypertext markup language (HTML) is a page description language for creating hypertext or hypermedia documents such as Web pages. (See the discussions of hypermedia in Chapter 7 and of Web pages in Chapter 9.) HTML uses instructions called *tags* (see Figure 6.14) to specify how text, graphics, video, and sound are placed on a document and to create dynamic links to other documents and objects stored in the same or remote computers. Using these links, a user need only point at a highlighted key word or graphic, click on it, and immediately be transported to another document.

HTML programs can be custom-written, but they also can be created by using the HTML authoring capabilities of Web browsers or of popular word-processing, spreadsheet, data management, and presentation graphics software packages. HTML editors such as Claris Home Page and Adobe PageMill are more powerful HTML authoring tool programs for creating Web pages.

Management Wrap-Up

MANAGEMENT

Management should be aware of the strengths and weaknesses of software tools, the tasks for which they are best suited, and whether these tools fit into the firm's long-term strategy and information architecture. Tradeoffs between efficiency, ease of use, and flexibility should be carefully analyzed. These organizational considerations have long-term cost implications.

ORGANIZATION

Software can either enhance or impede organizational performance, depending on the software tools selected and how they are used. Organizational needs should drive software selection. The software tool selected should be easy for the firm's IS staff to learn and maintain and flexible enough so that it can grow with the organization. Software for non-IS specialists should have easy-to-use interfaces and be compatible with the firm's other software tools.

TECHNOLOGY

A range of system and application software technologies is available to organizations. Key technology decisions include the appropriateness of the software tool for the problem to be addressed, compatibility with the firm's hardware, the efficiency of the software for performing specific tasks, vendor support of software packages, and other support capabilities for debugging, documentation, and reuse.

For Discussion:

1. Why is selecting both system and application software for the organization an important management decision?
2. Should organizations develop all of their systems with "fourth-generation" tools? Why or why not?

SUMMARY

1. **Describe the major types of software.** The major types of software are system software and application software. Each serves a different purpose. System software manages the computer resources and mediates between application software and computer hardware. Application software is used by application programmers and some end users to develop specific business applications. Application software works through system software, which controls access to computer hardware.

2. **Examine the functions of system software and compare leading PC operating systems.** System software coordinates the various parts of the computer system and mediates between application software and computer hardware. The system software that manages and controls the activities of the computer is called the operating system. Other system software includes computer-language translation programs that convert programming languages into machine language and utility programs that perform common processing tasks.

   The operating system acts as the chief manager of the information system, allocating, assigning, and scheduling system resources and monitoring the use of the computer. Multiprogramming, multitasking, virtual storage, time sharing, and multiprocessing enable system resources to be used more efficiently so that the computer can attack many problems at the same time.

   Multiprogramming (multitasking in PC environments) allows multiple programs to use the computer's resources concurrently. Virtual storage splits up programs into small portions so that main memory can be utilized more efficiently. Time sharing enables many users to share computer resources simultaneously by allocating each user a tiny slice of computing time. Multiprocessing is the use of two or more CPUs linked together working in tandem to perform a task.

   In order to be executed by the computer, a software program must be translated into machine language via special language-translation software—a compiler, an assembler, or an interpreter.

   PC operating systems have developed sophisticated capabilities such as multitasking and support for multiple users on networks. Leading PC operating systems include Windows 98 and 95, Windows CE, Windows NT, OS/2, UNIX, Mac OS, and DOS. PC operating systems with graphical user interfaces have gained popularity over command-driven operating systems. Windows is a popular graphical user interface shell for the DOS operating system.

3. **Explain how software has evolved and how it will continue to develop.** Software has evolved along with hardware. The general trend is toward user-friendly, high-level languages that both increase professional programmer productivity and make it possible for amateurs to use information systems. There have been four generations of software development: (1) machine language; (2) symbolic languages such as assembly language; (3) high-level languages such as FORTRAN and COBOL; and (4) fourth-generation languages, which are less procedural and closer to natural language than earlier generations of software. Software is starting to incorporate both sound and graphics and to support multimedia applications.

4. **Analyze the strengths and limitations of the major application programming languages and software tools.** The most popular conventional programming languages are assembly language, FORTRAN, COBOL, BASIC, Pascal, and C. Conventional programming languages make more efficient use of computer resources than fourth-generation languages and each is designed to solve specific types of problems.

   Fourth-generation languages include query languages, report generators, graphics languages, application generators, very high-level programming languages, application software packages, and PC software tools. They are less procedural than conventional programming languages and enable end users to perform many software tasks that previously required technical specialists. Popular PC software tools include word processing, spreadsheet, data management, presentation graphics, and e-mail software along with Web browsers and groupware.

5. **Describe new approaches to software development.** Object-oriented programming combines data and procedures into one *object,* which can act as an independent software building block. Each object can be used in many different systems without changing program code.

   Java is an object-oriented programming language designed to operate on the Internet. It can deliver precisely the software functionality needed for a particular task as a small applet that is downloaded from a network. Java can run on any computer and operating system. HTML is a page description language for creating Web pages.

KEY TERMS

ActiveX, 189
Ada, 179
Application generator, 181
Application software, 169
Assembly language, 178
BASIC (Beginners All-purpose Symbolic Instruction Code), 179
C, 179
C++, 179
Class, 188
COBOL (COmmon Business Oriented Language), 178
Compiler, 173
Data management software, 183
DOS, 175
Electronic mail (e-mail), 185
FORTRAN (FORmula TRANslator), 178
Fourth-generation language, 179
Geographic information system (GIS), 181
Graphical user interface (GUI), 174
Graphics language, 180
Groupware, 187
High-level language, 177
Hypertext markup language (HTML), 192
Inheritance, 189
Integrated software package, 185
Interpreter, 173
Java, 189
LISP, 179
Machine language, 177
Mac OS, 176
Multiprocessing, 172
Multiprogramming, 171
Multitasking, 171
Natural language, 180
Object code, 173
Object-oriented programming, 187
Operating system, 169
OS/2, 176
Page, 172
Pascal, 179
PL/1 (Programming Language 1), 179
Presentation graphics, 184
Program, 169
Prolog, 179
Query language, 180
Report generator, 180
Source code, 173
Software, 169
Software package, 181
Spreadsheet, 181
Stored program concept, 169
System software, 169
Time sharing, 172
UNIX, 176
Utility program, 173
Very high-level programming language, 181
Virtual storage, 171
Visual programming, 188
Web browser, 185
Windows, 175
Windows CE, 176
Windows 95, 175
Windows 98, 175
Windows NT, 176
Word processing software, 181

REVIEW QUESTIONS

1. What are the major types of software? How do they differ in terms of users and uses?
2. What is the operating system of a computer? What does it do?
3. Describe multiprogramming, virtual storage, time sharing, and multiprocessing. Why are they important for the operation of an information system?
4. What is the difference between an assembler, a compiler, and an interpreter?
5. Define and describe graphical user interfaces.
6. Compare the major PC operating systems.
7. What are the major generations of software and approximately when were they developed?

8. What is a high-level language? Name three high-level languages. Describe their strengths and weaknesses.
9. Define fourth-generation languages and list the seven categories of fourth-generation tools.
10. What is the difference between fourth-generation languages and conventional programming languages?
11. What is the difference between an application generator and an application software package? Between a report generator and a query language?
12. Name and describe the most important PC software tools.
13. What is object-oriented programming? How does it differ from conventional software development?
14. What is Java? How could it change the way software is created and used?
15. What is HTML? Why is it becoming important?

GROUP PROJECT

Which is the better Internet software tool, Internet Explorer 4.0 or Netscape Communicator? Your instructor will divide the class into two groups to research this question and present their findings to the class. To prepare your analysis, use articles from computer magazines and the Web and examine the software.

TOOLS FOR INTERACTIVE LEARNING

■ **INTERNET**: The Internet Connection for this chapter will direct you to a series of Web sites of various computer software vendors where you can complete an exercise to analyze the capabilities of various types of computer software. You can visit a Web site with interactive geographic information system (GIS) software to complete an Electronic Commerce project for logistics planning. You can also use the Interactive Study Guide to test your knowledge of the topics in this chapter and get instant feedback where you need more practice.

■ **CD-ROM**: If you purchase and use the Multimedia Edition CD-ROM with this chapter, you can complete an interactive exercise asking you to select the appropriate programming language or application software for a series of business problems. You can also find a video clip by illustrating the capabilities of geographic information system (GIS) software, an audio overview of the key themes of this chapter, and bullet text summarizing the key points of the chapter.

CASE STUDY

The Year 2000 Problem

The year 1999 is followed immediately by what year? That's easy for us—we all know that it is the year 2000, and we even know it is also a new century and a new millennium. But "ask" any computer and a great many of them will give a strange answer—1999 is followed by the year 1900. And this is an enormous problem. Let us see why.

Imagine that you were born in 1940 and are a citizen of the United States. You expect that when you turn 65 in the year 2005, you will collect Social Security benefits. But, if the computer calculates the year to be 1905, you will receive no payments, because you will not be eligible. In fact, you won't have even been born yet. Assume that you are in charge of maintenance for one of your company's large plants. Your computer runs a maintenance system that schedules plant equipment maintenance, and for that maintenance also schedules the purchase of supplies and allocates the staff time. You have scheduled maintenance in 1995, 1998, and 2001. If your computer jumps to 1900 and so never reaches the year 2000, your plant and your whole operation will be in chaos. Inability to recognize the right date could seriously affect airline operations, distribution of electrical power, billing records, and many other critical activities of everyday life.

Why do many computer programs fail to handle the turn of the century properly? Check your computer programs. You will probably find that for many date fields, the dates are stored as six digits, two digits each for the day, month, and year (MM-DD-YY). Programs have been written this way for decades because it saved data entry time and storage space if the century number "19" did not have to be entered. Imagine, for example, the data entry time needed just to enter 19 for every one of the millions of checks that each major bank processes each day. This presents no problem if the date is used only for display purposes. Human beings reading it will have no problem interpreting it. But if the date is used for calculations, it could mean confusion if not disaster.

To solve the problem before 2000 arrives, organizations need to comb through their programs to locate all coding in which dates are used. They then must determine whether each of those places is a problem. Many companies have computer programs amounting to many millions of lines of code, making this a daunting task. Where problems are found, they must be corrected. Two types of corrections are possible. One approach is to fix each date field by increasing the year field to four digits and inserting the century number. The other approach is to change the program code to compensate for the problem. The year 2000 affects all organizations—business, nonprofit, and government alike. We will look at two federal government agencies, the Department of Defense and the Federal Deposit Insurance Corporation (FDIC).

The Department of Defense (DOD) has more than 7000 computer systems with perhaps 360 million lines of code. These systems do everything from managing inventories to controlling weaponry. Failure to address the year 2000 problem could easily result in chaos. Transportation and other logistics systems, maintenance systems, accounting, and many other systems are very date dependent. Many weapons systems are also date dependent. The failure of these systems in a time of military crisis could easily be catastrophic. As explained by Bryce Ragland, the head of a year 2000 task force team at the Air Force Software Support Center, "There's a real risk that some wacko in another country might decide to launch an attack against the U.S. a few seconds after midnight just to see if our defenses can handle it."

One common approach to addressing the problem is first to review each system, placing each program into one of three groups. Group 1 applications are already year 2000 compliant (probably because they were developed within the past few years when people already were aware of the problem). Group 2 applications are those that are mission-critical, technically sound, and not going to be replaced, but not yet year 2000 compliant. These must be addressed. Group 3 applications are those not being kept (the DOD, like many organizations, sees the year 2000 problem also as an opportunity to eliminate a lot of dead wood). Next, the necessary changes for Group 2 systems must be made. Finally, all changes must be thoroughly tested, a massive job which will take up at least half the total year 2000 effort. All programs must be tested not only for how they handle the change from 1999 to 2000, but also for the years before and after 2000. In addition, all links to other programs must be tested so that programmers are certain that wrong data are neither sent to nor received from other programs and systems.

Changing programs or stored data presents a massive problem to the DOD because, like most of industry, it has had poor development practices over the years. The DOD used obscure, specialty programming languages, such as Jovial, for which few analytical and debugging tools are available to aid in solving the year 2000 problems. Quality documentation does not exist for most systems, documentation that would have enabled the staff to review the programs quickly or that would have enabled programmers to quickly make changes. Moreover, like most organizations, the DOD has had few programming standards, so that date calculations were written differently by different programmers, adding confusion to the problem.

The costs of scanning more than 7000 computer systems and identifying and fixing the trouble spots are enormous. The problem is so massive that, according to an April 1996 survey conducted by the House of Representatives, the DOD hadn't yet finished inventorying its roughly 358 million lines of program code. The DOD has an annual IT budget of $3 billion, but this is surely too little for such an enormous task. Congress, which is well aware of the year 2000 problem, has budgeted $2.3 billion to address the problem for the whole federal government. But a study of 24 federal agencies by Federal Sources Inc. estimates that it will cost about $5.6 billion for the federal government to rewrite all of its code to be year 2000 compliant. Without Congress allocating a major increase in funds, the DOD will have to focus on identifying the problems and making the changes, ignoring testing, or testing superficially at best. That means many systems will have to be put back in production with many hidden problems in them. Nor can the deadline for the changes be extended—the year 2000 will arrive on schedule, no matter what. By early 1997 the DOD had only 302 systems that were fully compliant with the year 2000. That actually puts them in better shape than not only most government agencies but also most businesses. Nonetheless, with nearly 7000 systems remaining, the task the department faces is gargantuan to say the least.

Even if organizations have made their systems fully year 2000 compliant, they still could face serious problems if the organizations with which they exchange data have not readied their systems. For example, the Federal Deposit Insurance Corporation (FDIC), which provides insurance to 6200 state-chartered banks, would not be able to fulfill its mission if the state-chartered banks it oversees do not fix their date problems on time. The FDIC would not be able to provide federal deposit insurance and these banks might face closure. They would have to return deposits to customers.

Ironically, the FDIC has fallen eight months behind in its year 2000 preparations. The agency was supposed to finish assessing its critical systems for year 2000 problems by July 1997, but it did not complete this task until April 1998. The FDIC has 500 systems with 15 million lines of program code, and it considers 40 of these systems critical. Five of these 40 systems are year 2000 compliant, and the others are being assessed, tested, or repaired. Testifying before a Senate subcommittee in February 1998, the FDIC said that 75 percent of its systems were already year 2000 compliant because it had been using four digits to express the year in date fields in all of its new software applications for the past five years. Senators at the hearing said they remained "deeply troubled" by the FDIC's delays. The FDIC is working on a contingency plan to address what will happen if its critical systems are not ready by January 1, 2000.

Sources: Matt Hamblen, "Y2K Shortcoming May Shutter Some Banks," *Computerworld*, February 16, 1998; Robert L. Scheier, Gary H. Anthes, and Allan E. Alter, "Year 2000 May Ambush U.S. Military," *Computerworld*, February 24, 1997; and Bruce Caldwell and Bob Violino, "Year 2000 Costs Climb," *Information Week*, April 7, 1997.

Case Study Questions

1. Why is the year 2000 problem a serious management issue?
2. What management, organization, and technology factors were responsible for causing the year 2000 problem at the Defense Department and FDIC?
3. How well are the Department of Defense and the FDIC handling the year 2000 problem?
4. What management, organizational, and technical issues must be considered when planning to address the year 2000 problem?
5. It has been said that if information systems were all thoroughly object oriented, the year 2000 problem would probably be a minor annoyance. Do you agree or disagree?

CHAPTER 7

Managing Data Resources

chapter outline

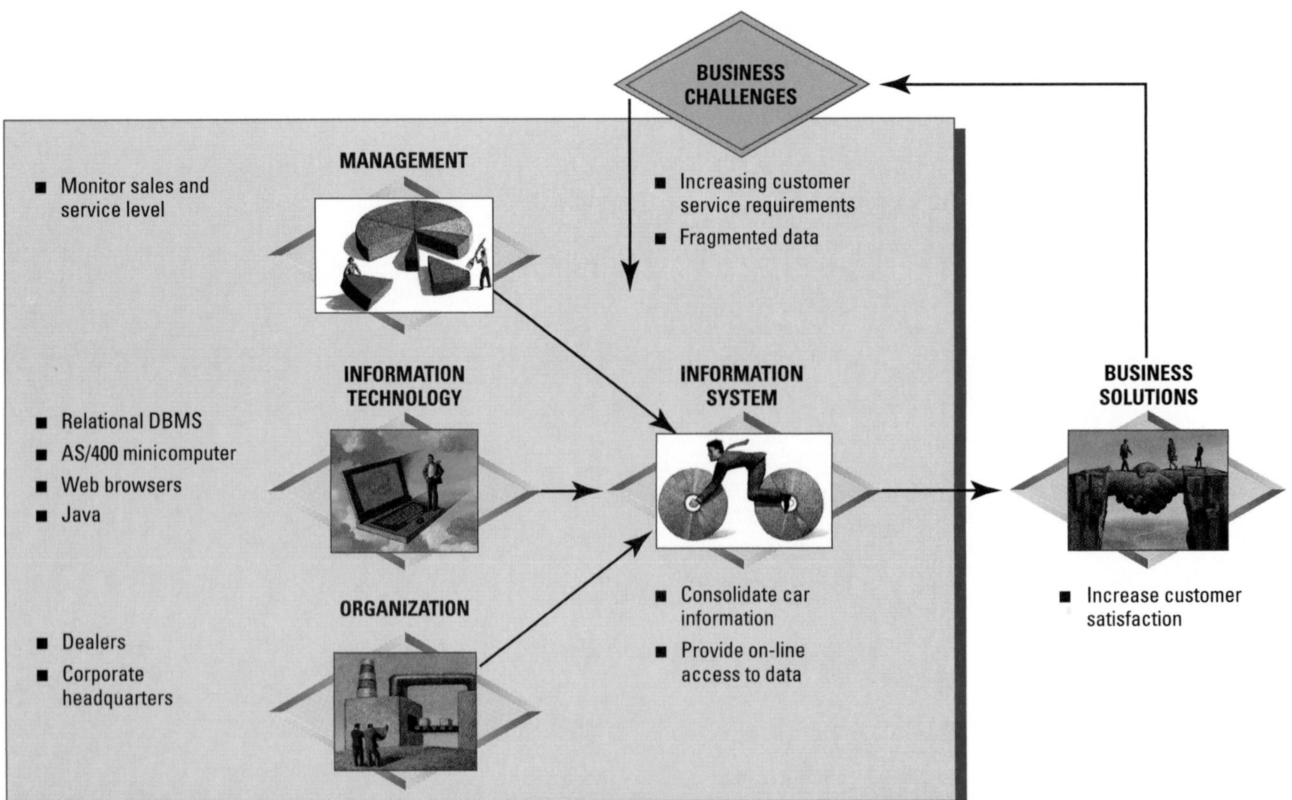

Saab Centralizes Customer Data

Saab Cars USA wants its dealers to be able have all the information they need to keep their customers happy—including the ability to track each car they sell, from assembly line to the junkyard. Until recently, this was an impossible task, because all of Saab's data concerning a specific car are not in one place. Records about service, ownership, warranties, and parts are scattered among three different systems. Some of the data are maintained on an AS/400 minicomputer at Saab's U.S. headquarters in Norcross, Georgia. Other pieces of data are on an IBM Systems 390 mainframe at Saab's parts distributor, and still other pieces are in dealer management systems at Saab's dealerships.

Several Saab dealers teamed up with Saab Cars USA representatives to solve this problem. They worked with IBM Global Services in White Plains, New York, to develop IRIS (Intranet Retail Information System). The system extracts data from Saab's corporate and dealer systems, as well as from the parts-distributor's mainframe, and stores these data in an IBM DB/400 relational database installed on Saab's AS/400 computer. The database acts as a central repository for customer information. Dealers can use their Web browser to access the data over an internal network based on Internet technology. A Java applet pulls the data from the DB/400 relational database and delivers them to the dealers' Web browsers.

Saab USA's managers and dealers believe the system will pay off by improving customer satisfaction. All of the information about a car, including ownership, service history, and warranty, is instantly available, so customer questions can be answered on the spot.

Source: Adapted from Justin Hibbard, "Saab's Driving Force," *Information Week,* January 26, 1998.

Management Challenges

Saab's IRIS system illustrates how much the effective use of information depends on how data are stored, organized, and accessed. Proper delivery of information not only depends on the capabilities of computer hardware and software but also on the organization's ability to manage data as an important resource. It has been very difficult for organizations to manage their data effectively. Two challenges stand out.

1. **Organizational obstacles to a database environment.** Implementing a database requires widespread organizational change in the role of information (and information managers), the allocation of power at senior levels, the ownership and sharing of information, and patterns of organizational agreement. A database management system (DBMS) challenges the existing power arrangements in an organization and for that reason often generates political resistance. In a traditional file environment, each department constructed files and programs to fulfill its specific needs. Now, with a database, files and programs must be built that take into account the full organization's interest in data. Although the organization has spent the money on hardware and software for a database environment, it may not reap the benefits it should because it is unwilling to make the requisite organizational changes.

2. **Cost/benefit considerations.**The costs of moving to a database environment are tangible, up front, and large in the short term (three years). Most firms buy a commercial DBMS package and related hardware. The software alone can cost $0.5 million for a full-function package with all options. New hardware may cost an additional $1 million to $2 million annually. It soon becomes apparent to senior management that a database system is a huge investment.

   Unfortunately, the benefits of the DBMS are often intangible, back loaded, and long term (five years). Several million dollars have been spent over the years designing and maintaining existing systems. People in the organization understand the existing system after long periods of training and socialization. For these reasons, and despite the clear advantages of the DBMS, the short-term costs of developing a DBMS often appear to be nearly as great as the benefits. When the short-term political costs are added to the equation, it is convenient for senior management to defer the database investment. The obvious long-term benefits of the DBMS tend to be severely discounted by managers, especially those unfamiliar with (and perhaps unfriendly to) systems. Moreover, it may not be cost effective to build organization-wide databases that integrate all the organization's data (Goodhue et al., September 1992).

learning objectives

After completing this chapter, you will be able to:

1. Compare traditional file organization and management techniques.
2. Explain the problems of the traditional file environment.
3. Describe how a database management system organizes information.
4. Identify the three principal database models and some principles of database design.
5. Discuss new database trends.
6. Analyze the managerial and organizational requirements for creating a database environment.

This chapter examines the managerial and organizational requirements as well as the technologies for managing data as a resource. First we describe the traditional file management technologies that have been used for arranging and accessing data on physical storage media and the problems they have created for organizations. Then we describe the technology of database management systems, which can overcome many of the drawbacks of traditional file management. We end the chapter with a discussion of the managerial and organizational requirements for successful implementation of database management systems.

7.1 ORGANIZING DATA IN A TRADITIONAL FILE ENVIRONMENT

An effective information system provides users with timely, accurate, and relevant information. This information is stored in computer files. When the files are properly arranged and maintained, users can easily access and retrieve the information they need.

You can appreciate the importance of file management if you have ever written a term paper using 3 × 5 index cards. No matter how efficient your storage device (a metal box or a rubber band), if you organize the cards randomly your term paper will have little or no organization. Given enough time, you could put the cards in order, but your system would be more efficient if you set up your organizational scheme early on. If your scheme is flexible enough and well documented, you can extend it to account for any changes in your viewpoint as you write your paper.

The same need for file organization applies to firms. Well-managed, carefully arranged files make it easy to obtain data for business decisions, whereas poorly managed files lead to chaos in information processing, high costs, poor performance, and little, if any, flexibility. Despite the use of excellent hardware and software, many organizations have inefficient information systems because of poor file management. In this section we describe the traditional methods that organizations have used to arrange data in computer files. We also discuss the problems with these methods.

File Organization Terms and Concepts

A computer system organizes data in a hierarchy that starts with bits and bytes and progresses to fields, records, files, and databases (see Figure 7.1). A *bit* represents the smallest unit of data a computer can handle. A group of bits, called a *byte,* represents a single character, which can be a letter, a number, or another symbol. A grouping of characters into a word, a group of words, or a complete number (such as a person's name or age) is called a **field**. A group of related fields, such as the student's name, the course taken, the date, and the grade comprise a **record**; a group of records of the same type is called a **file**. For instance, the student records in Figure 7.1 could constitute a course file. A group of related files make up a database. The student course file illustrated in Figure 7.1 could be grouped with files on students' personal histories and financial backgrounds to create a student database.

A record describes an entity. An **entity** is a person, place, thing, or event on which we maintain information. An order is a typical entity in a sales order file, which maintains information on a firm's sales orders. Each characteristic or quality describing a particular entity is called an **attribute**. For example, order number, order date, order amount, item number, and item quantity would each be an attribute of the entity order. The specific values that these attributes can have can be found in the fields of the record describing the entity *order* (see Figure 7.2).

Every record in a file should contain at least one field that uniquely identifies that record so that the record can be retrieved, updated, or sorted. This identifier field is called a **key field**. An example of a key field is the order number for the order record illustrated in Figure 7.2 or an employee number or social security number for a personnel record (containing employee data such as the employee's name, age, address, job title, and so forth).

field A grouping of characters into a word, a group of words, or a complete number, such as a person's name or age.

record A group of related fields.

file A group of records of the same type.

entity A person, place, thing, or event about which information must be kept.

attribute A piece of information describing a particular entity.

key field A field in a record that uniquely identifies instances of that record so that it can be retrieved, updated, or sorted.

FIGURE 7.1

The data hierarchy. A computer system organizes data in a hierarchy that starts with the bit, which represents either a 0 or a 1. Bits can be grouped to form a byte to represent one character, number, or symbol. Bytes can be grouped to form a field, and related fields can be grouped to form a record. Related records can be collected to form a file, and related files can be organized into a database.

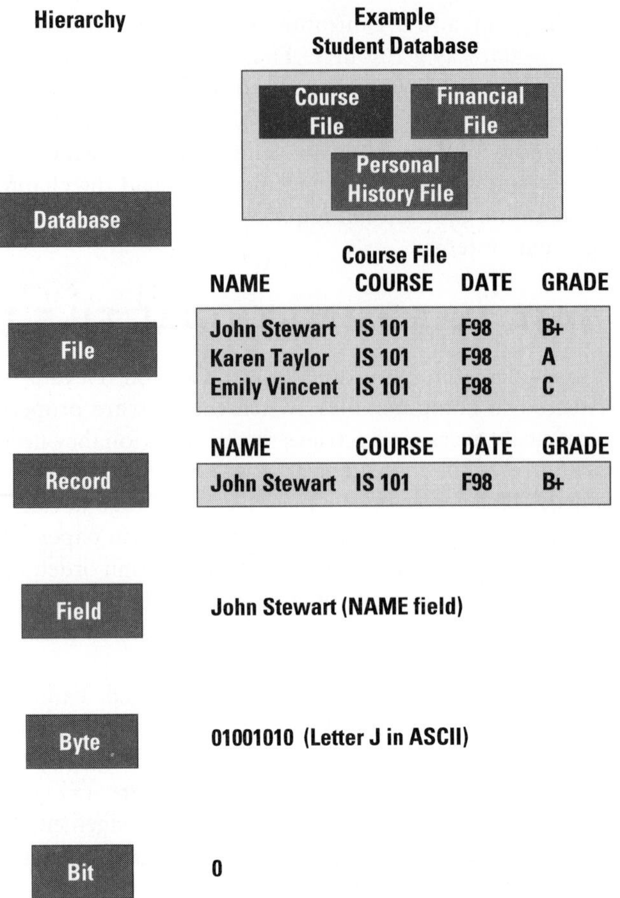

Accessing Records from Computer Files

sequential file organization A method of storing data records in which the records must be retrieved in the same physical sequence in which they are stored.

direct or **random file organization** A method of storing data records in a file so that they can be accessed in any sequence without regard to their actual physical order on the storage media.

Computer systems store files on secondary storage devices. Records can be arranged in several ways on storage media, and the arrangement determines the manner in which individual records can be accessed or retrieved. One way to organize records is sequentially. In **sequential file organization,** data records must be retrieved in the same physical sequence in which they are stored. In contrast, **direct** or **random file organization** allows users to access records in any sequence they desire, without regard to actual physical order on the storage media.

Sequential file organization is the only file organization method that can be used on magnetic tape. This file organization method is no longer popular, but some organizations still use it for batch processing applications in which they access and process each record sequentially. A typical application using sequential files is payroll, in which all employees in a firm must be paid one by one and issued a check. Direct or random file organization is utilized with magnetic disk technology (although records can be stored

FIGURE 7.2

Entities and attributes. This record describes the entity called ORDER and its attributes. The specific values for order number, order date, item number, quantity, and amount for this particular order are the fields for this record. Order number is the key field because each order is assigned a unique identification number.

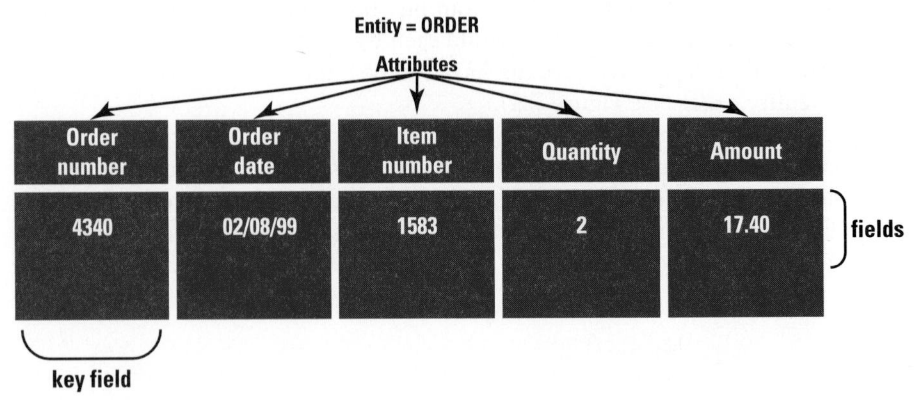

sequentially on disk if desired). Most computer applications today utilize some method of direct file organization.

The Indexed Sequential Access Method

Although records may be stored sequentially on direct access storage devices, individual records can be accessed directly using the **indexed sequential access method (ISAM).** This access method relies on an index of key fields to locate individual records. An **index** to a file is similar to the index of a book, as it lists the key field of each record and where that record is physically located in storage to expedite location of that record. Figure 7.3 shows how a series of indexes identifies the location of a specific record. Records are stored on disk in their key sequence. A cylinder index shows the highest value of the key field that can be found on a specific cylinder. A track index shows the highest value of the key field that can be found on a specific track. To locate a specific record, the cylinder index and then the track index are searched to locate the cylinder and track containing the record. The track itself is then sequentially read to find the record. If a file is very large, the cylinder index might be broken down into parts and a master index created to help locate each part of the cylinder index. ISAM is used in applications that require sequential processing of large numbers of records but that occasionally require direct access of individual records.

indexed sequential access method (ISAM) A file access method to directly access records organized sequentially using an index of key fields.

index A table or list that relates record keys to physical locations on direct access files.

Direct File Access Method

The **direct file access method** is used with direct file organization. This method uses a key field to locate the physical address of a record. However, the process is accomplished using a mathematical formula called a **transform algorithm** to translate the key field directly into the record's physical storage location on disk. The algorithm performs some mathematical computation on the record key, and the result of that calculation is the record's physical address. This process is illustrated in Figure 7.4.

This access method is most appropriate for applications in which individual records must be located directly and rapidly for immediate processing only. A few records in the

direct file access method A method of accessing records by mathematically transforming the key fields into the specific addresses for the records.

transform algorithm A mathematical formula used to translate a record's key field directly into the record's physical storage location.

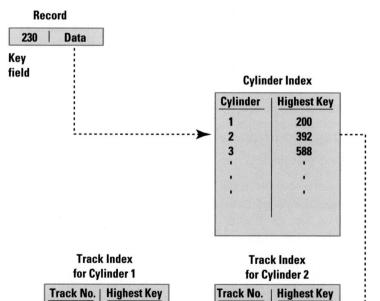

Record

230	Data

Key field

Cylinder Index

Cylinder	Highest Key
1	200
2	392
3	588
.	.
.	.
.	.

Track Index for Cylinder 1

Track No.	Highest Key
1	9
2	19
3	28
4	39
5	49
.	.
.	.
.	.

Track Index for Cylinder 2

Track No.	Highest Key
1	208
2	238
3	260
4	279
5	299
.	.
.	.
.	.

Track Index for Cylinder 3

Track No.	Highest Key
1	399
2	419
3	440
4	468
5	483
.	.
.	.
.	.

FIGURE 7.3

The indexed sequential access method (ISAM). To find a record with a key field of 230, the cylinder index would be searched to find the correct cylinder (in this case, cylinder 2). The track index for cylinder 2 would then be searched to find the correct track. Since the highest key on track 2 of cylinder 2 is 238 and the highest key on track 1 of cylinder 2 is 208, track 2 must contain the record. Track 2 of cylinder 2 would then be read to find the record with key 230.

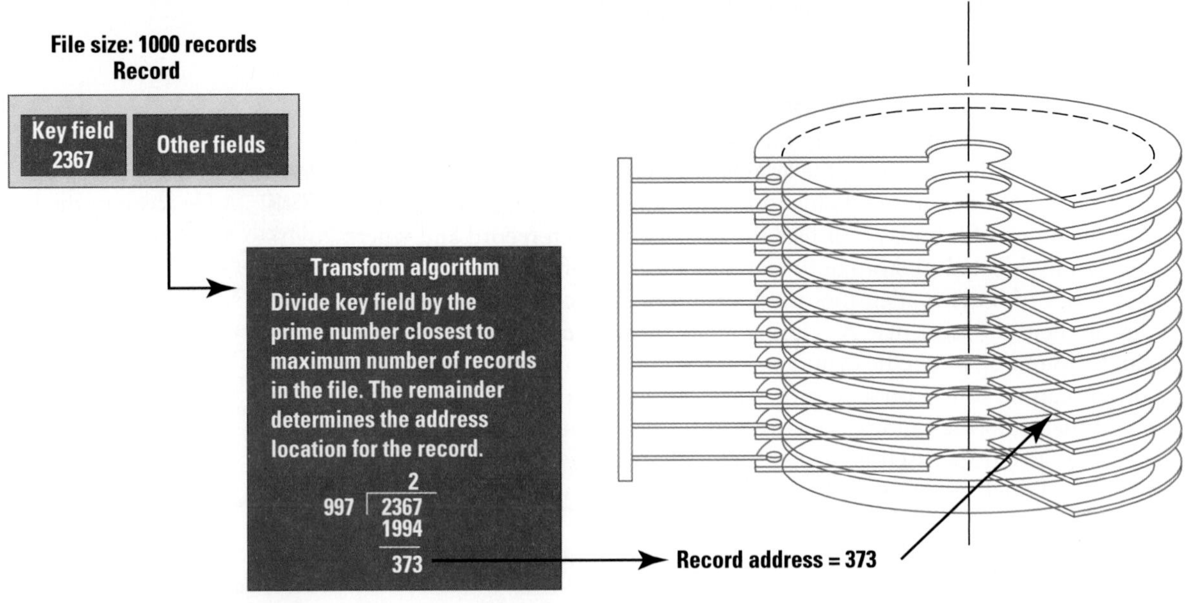

FIGURE 7.4 The direct file access method. Records are not stored sequentially on the disk but are arranged according to the results of some mathematical computation. Here, the transform algorithm divides the value in the key field by the prime number closest to the maximum number of records in the file (in this case, the prime number is 997). The remainder designates the storage location for that particular record.

file need to be retrieved at one time, and the required records are found in no particular sequence. An example might be an on-line hotel reservation system.

Problems with the Traditional File Environment

Most organizations began information processing on a small scale, automating one application at a time. Systems tended to grow independently, and not according to some grand plan. Each functional area tended to develop systems in isolation from other functional areas. Accounting, finance, manufacturing, human resources, and marketing all developed their own systems and data files. Figure 7.5 illustrates the traditional approach to information processing.

Each application, of course, required its own files and its own computer program to operate. For example, the human resources functional area might have a personnel master file, a payroll file, a medical insurance file, a pension file, a mailing list file, and so forth until tens, perhaps hundreds, of files and programs existed. In the company as a whole, this process led to multiple master files created, maintained, and operated by separate divisions or departments.

traditional file environment A way of collecting and maintaining data in an organization that leads to each functional area or division creating and maintaining its own data files and programs.

There are names for this situation: the **traditional file environment;** the *flat file organization* (because most of the data are organized in flat files); and the *data file approach* (because the data and business logic are tied to specific files and related programs). By any name, the situation results in growing inefficiency and complexity.

As this process goes on for five or ten years, the organization is saddled with hundreds of programs and applications, with no one who knows what they do, what data they use, and who is using the data. The organization is collecting the same information in far too many files. The resulting problems are data redundancy, program-data dependence, inflexibility, poor data security, and inability to share data among applications.

Data Redundancy and Confusion

data redundancy The presence of duplicate data in multiple data files.

Data redundancy is the presence of duplicate data in multiple data files. Data redundancy occurs when different divisions, functional areas, and groups in an organization independently collect the same piece of information. For instance, within the commercial

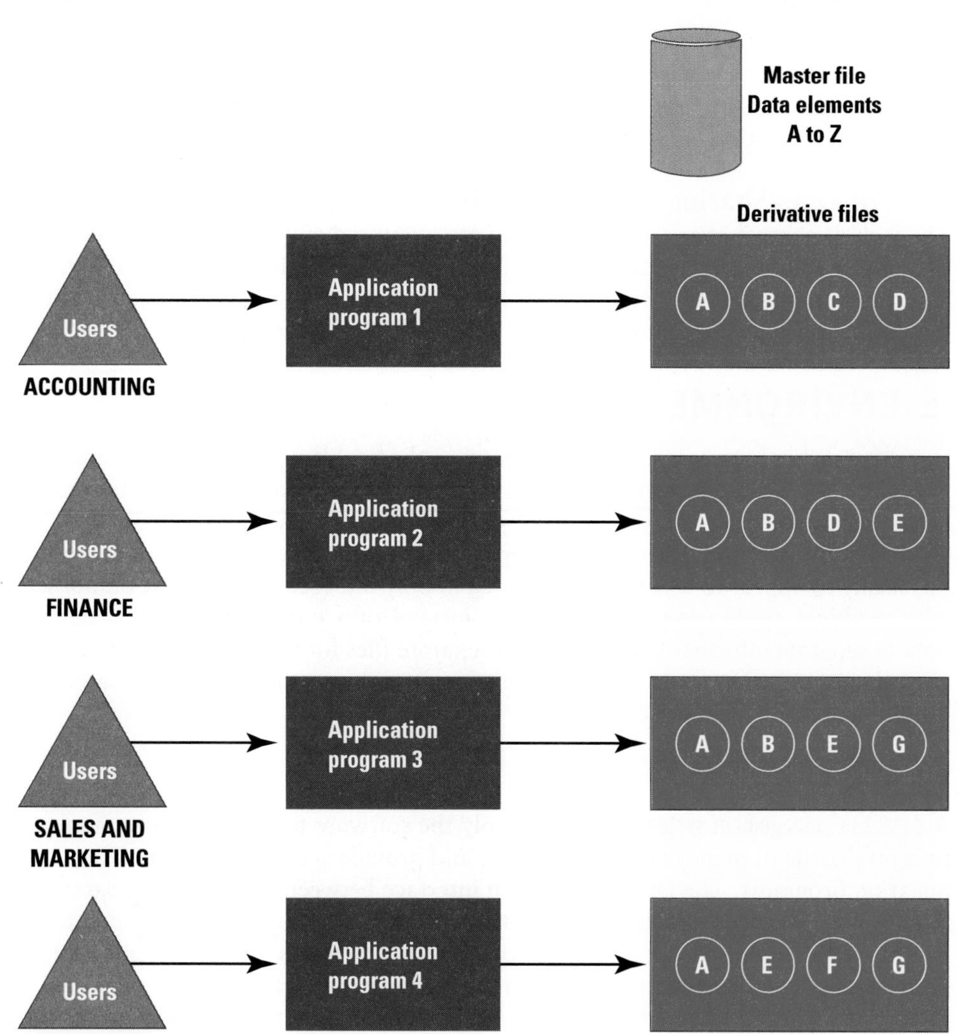

FIGURE 7.5

Traditional file processing. The use of a traditional approach to file processing encourages each functional area in a corporation to develop specialized applications. Each application requires a unique data file that is likely to be a subset of the master file. These subsets of the master file lead to data redundancy, processing inflexibility, and wasted storage resources.

loans division of a bank, the marketing and credit information functions might collect the same customer information. Because it is collected and maintained in so many different places, the same data item may have different meanings in different parts of the organization. Simple data items such as the fiscal year, employee identification, and product code can take on different meanings as programmers and analysts work in isolation on different applications.

Program-Data Dependence

Program-data dependence is the tight relationship between data stored in files and the specific programs required to update and maintain those files. Every computer program has to describe the location and nature of the data with which it works. In a traditional file environment, any change in data requires a change in all programs that access the data. Changes, for instance, in tax rates or ZIP-code length require changes in programs. Such programming changes may cost millions of dollars to implement in all the programs that require the revised data.

program-data dependence The close relationship between data stored in files and the software programs that update and maintain those files. Any change in data organization or format requires a change in all the programs associated with those files.

Lack of Flexibility

A traditional file system can deliver routine scheduled reports after extensive programming efforts, but it cannot deliver ad hoc reports or respond to unanticipated information requirements in a timely fashion. The information required by ad hoc requests is somewhere in the system but too expensive to retrieve. Several programmers would have to work for weeks to put together the required data items in a new file.

Poor Security

Because there is little control or management of data, access to and dissemination of information are virtually out of control. What limits on access exist tend to be the result of habit and tradition, as well as of the sheer difficulty of finding information.

Lack of Data Sharing and Availability

The lack of control over access to data in this confused environment does not make it easy for people to obtain information. Because pieces of information in different files and different parts of the organization cannot be related to one another, it is virtually impossible for information to be shared or accessed in a timely manner.

7.2 THE DATABASE ENVIRONMENT

database A collection of data organized to service many applications at the same time by storing and managing data so that they appear to be in one location.

Database technology can cut through many of the problems created by traditional file organization. A more rigorous definition of a **database** is a collection of data organized to serve many applications efficiently by centralizing the data and minimizing redundant data. Rather than storing data in separate files for each application, data are stored physically to appear to users as being stored in only one location. A single database services multiple applications. For example, instead of a corporation storing employee data in separate information systems and separate files for personnel, payroll, and benefits, the corporation could create a single common human resources database. Figure 7.6 illustrates the database concept.

Database Management Systems

database management system (DBMS) Special software to create and maintain a database and enable individual business applications to extract the data they need without having to create separate files or data definitions in their computer programs.

A **database management system (DBMS)** is simply the software that permits an organization to centralize data, manage them efficiently, and provide access to the stored data by application programs. The DBMS acts as an interface between application programs and the physical data files. When the application program calls for a data item such as gross pay, the DBMS finds this item in the database and presents it to the application program. Using traditional data files the programmer would have to define the data and then tell the computer where they were. A DBMS eliminates most of the data definition statements found in traditional programs.

A database management system has three components:

- A data definition language
- A data manipulation language
- A data dictionary

data definition language The component of a database management system that defines each data element as it appears in the database.

data manipulation language A language associated with a database management system that is employed by end users and programmers to manipulate data in the database.

Structured Query Language (SQL) The standard data manipulation language for relational database management systems.

data dictionary An automated or manual tool for storing and organizing information about the data maintained in a database.

The **data definition language** is the formal language used by programmers to specify the content and structure of the database. The data definition language defines each data element as it appears in the database before that data element is translated into the forms required by application programs.

Most DBMS have a specialized language called a **data manipulation language** that is used in conjunction with some conventional third- or fourth-generation programming languages to manipulate the data in the database. This language contains commands that permit end users and programming specialists to extract data from the database to satisfy information requests and develop applications. The most prominent data manipulation language today is **Structured Query Language,** or **SQL**. Complex programming tasks cannot be performed efficiently with typical data manipulation languages. However, most mainframe DBMS are compatible with COBOL, FORTRAN, and other third-generation programming languages, permitting greater processing efficiency and flexibility.

The third element of a DBMS is a **data dictionary.** This is an automated or manual file that stores definitions of data elements and data characteristics such as usage, physical representation, ownership (who in the organization is responsible for maintaining the data), authorization, and security. Many data dictionaries can produce lists and reports

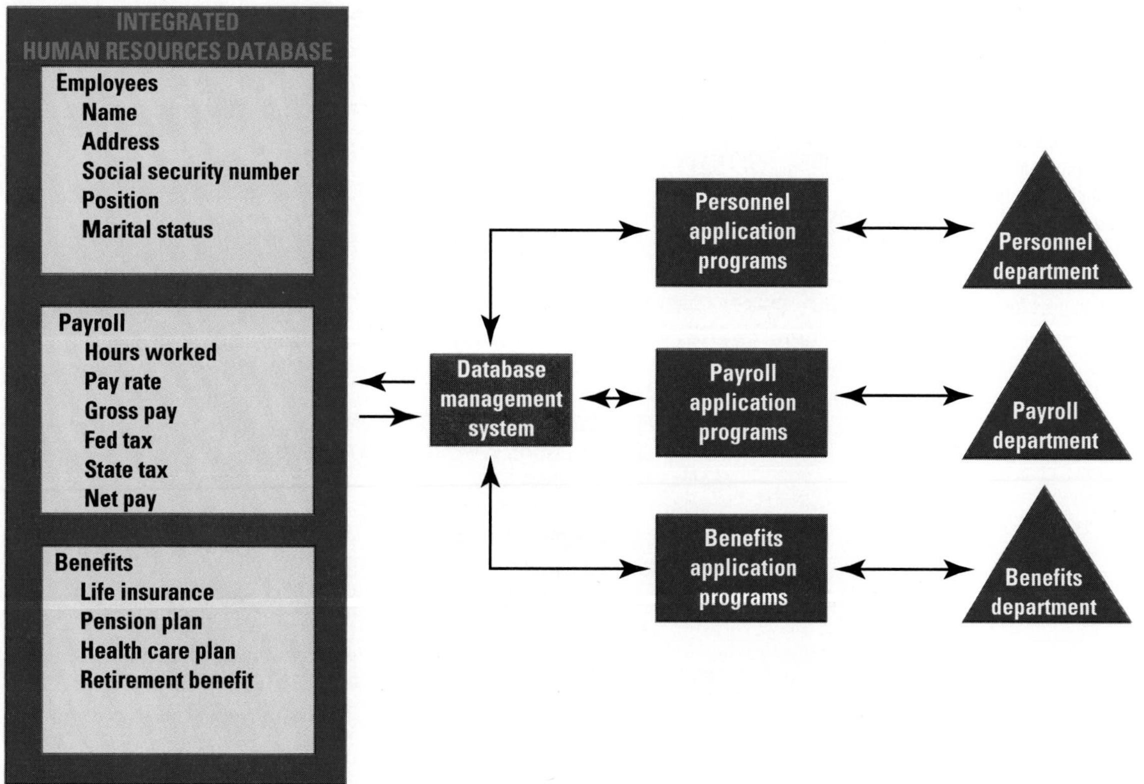

FIGURE 7.6 The contemporary database environment. A single human resources database serves multiple applications and also allows a corporation to easily draw together all the information on various applications. The database management system acts as the interface between the application programs and the data.

of data utilization, groupings, program locations, and so on. Figure 7.7 illustrates a sample data dictionary report that shows the size, format, meaning, and uses of a data element in a human resources database. A **data element** represents a field. In addition to listing the standard name (AMT-PAY-BASE), the dictionary lists the names that reference this element in specific systems and identifies the individuals, business functions, programs, and reports that use this data element.

data element A field.

By creating an inventory of data contained in the database, the data dictionary serves as an important data management tool. For instance, business users could consult the dictionary to find out exactly what pieces of data are maintained for the sales or marketing function or even to determine all the information maintained by the entire enterprise. The dictionary could supply business users with the name, format, and specifications required to access data for reports. Technical staff could use the dictionary to determine what data elements and files must be changed if a program is changed.

Most data dictionaries are entirely passive; they simply report. More advanced types are active; changes in the dictionary can be automatically utilized by related programs. For instance, to change ZIP codes from five to nine digits, one could simply enter the change in the dictionary without having to modify and recompile all application programs using ZIP codes.

In an ideal database environment, the data in the database are defined only once and used for all applications whose data reside in the database, thereby eliminating data redundancy and inconsistency. Application programs, which are written using a combination of the data manipulation language of the DBMS and a conventional programming language, request data elements from the database. Data elements called for by the application programs are found and delivered by the DBMS. The programmer does not have to specify in detail how or where the data are to be found.

FIGURE 7.7

Sample data dictionary report. The sample data dictionary report for a human resources database provides helpful information such as the size of the data element, which programs and reports use it, and which group in the organization is the owner responsible for maintaining it. The report also shows some of the other names that the organization uses for this piece of data.

```
NAME: AMT-PAY-BASE
FOCUS NAME: BASEPAY
PC NAME:      SALARY

DESCRIPTION: EMPLOYEE'S ANNUAL SALARY

SIZE: 9 BYTES
TYPE: N        (NUMERIC)
DATE CHANGED: 01/01/85
OWNERSHIP: COMPENSATION
UPDATE SECURITY: SITE PERSONNEL
ACCESS SECURITY: MANAGER, COMPENSATION PLANNING AND RESEARCH
                 MANAGER, JOB EVALUATION SYSTEMS
                 MANAGER, HUMAN RESOURCES PLANNING
                 MANAGER, SITE EQUAL OPPORTUNITY AFFAIRS
                 MANAGER, SITE BENEFITS
                 MANAGER, CLAIMS PAYING SYSTEMS
                 MANAGER, QUALIFIED PLANS
                 MANAGER, SITE EMPLOYMENT/EEO
BUSINESS FUNCTIONS USED BY: COMPENSATION
                            HR PLANNING
                            EMPLOYMENT
                            INSURANCE
                            PENSION
                            ISP

PROGRAMS USING: PI01000
                PI02000
                PI03000
                PI04000
                PI05000

REPORTS USING:  REPORT 124 (SALARY INCREASE TRACKING REPORT)
                REPORT 448 (GROUP INSURANCE AUDIT REPORT)
                REPORT 452 (SALARY REVIEW LISTING)
                PENSION REFERENCE LISTING
```

Use of a DBMS can reduce program-data dependence along with program development and maintenance costs. Access and availability of information can be increased because users and programmers can perform ad hoc queries of data in the database. The DBMS allows the organization to centrally manage data, utilization, and security.

Logical and Physical Views of Data

Perhaps the greatest difference between a DBMS and traditional file organization is that the DBMS separates the logical and physical views of the data, relieving the programmer or end user from the task of understanding where and how the data are actually stored.

logical view A representation of data as they would appear to an application programmer or end user.

physical view The representation of data as they would be actually organized on physical storage media.

The database concept distinguishes between logical and physical views of data. The **logical view** presents data as they would be perceived by end users or business specialists, whereas the **physical view** shows how data are actually organized and structured on physical storage media.

Suppose, for example, that a professor of information systems wanted to know at the beginning of the semester how students performed in the prerequisite computer literacy course (Computer Literacy 101) and the students' current majors. Using a database supported by the registrar, the professor would need something similar to the report shown in Figure 7.8.

Student Name	ID No.	Major	Grade in Computer Literacy 101
Lind	468	Finance	A-
Pinckus	332	Marketing	B+
Williams	097	Economics	C+
Laughlin	765	Finance	A
Orlando	324	Statistics	B

FIGURE 7.8

The report required by the professor. The report requires data elements that may come from different files but can easily be pulled together with a database management system if the data are organized into a database.

```
SELECT Stud_name, Stud.stud_id, Major, Grade
FROM Student, Course
WHERE Stud.stud_id = Course.stud_id
AND Course_id = "CL101"
```

FIGURE 7.9

The query used by the professor. This example shows how Structured Query Language (SQL) commands could be used to deliver the data required by the professor. These commands join two files, the student file (Student) and the course file (Course), and extract the specified pieces of information on each student from the combined file.

Ideally, for such a simple report, the professor could sit at an office terminal connected to the registrar's database and write a small application program using the data manipulation language to create this report. The professor first would develop the desired logical view of the data (Figure 7.8) for the application program. The DBMS would then assemble the requested data elements, which might reside in several different files and disk locations. For instance, the student major information might be located in a file called *Student,* whereas the grade data might be located in a file called *Course.* Wherever they were located, the DBMS would pull these pieces of information together and present them to the professor according to the logical view requested.

The query using the data manipulation language constructed by the professor might resemble that shown in Figure 7.9. Several DBMS working on both mainframes and PCs permit this kind of interactive report creation.

7.3 DESIGNING DATABASES

There are alternative ways of organizing data and representing relationships among data in a database. Conventional DBMS use one of three principal logical database models for keeping track of entities, attributes, and relationships. The three principal logical database models are hierarchical, network, and relational. Each logical model has certain processing advantages and certain business advantages.

Hierarchical Data Model

The earliest DBMS were hierarchical. The **hierarchical data model** presents data to users in a treelike structure. The most common hierarchical DBMS is IBM's IMS (Information Management System). Within each record, data elements are organized into pieces of records called *segments.* To the user, each record looks like an organization chart with one top-level segment called the *root.* An upper segment is connected logically to a lower segment in a parent-child relationship. A parent segment can have more than one child, but a child can have only one parent.

hierarchical data model One type of logical database model that organizes data in a treelike structure. A record is subdivided into segments that are connected to each other in one-to-many parent-child relationships.

Figure 7.10 shows a hierarchical structure that might be used for a human resources database. The root segment is Employee, which contains basic employee information such as name, address, and identification number. Immediately below it are three child segments: Compensation (containing salary and promotion data), Job Assignments (containing data about job positions and departments), and Benefits (containing data about beneficiaries and benefit options). The Compensation segment has two children below

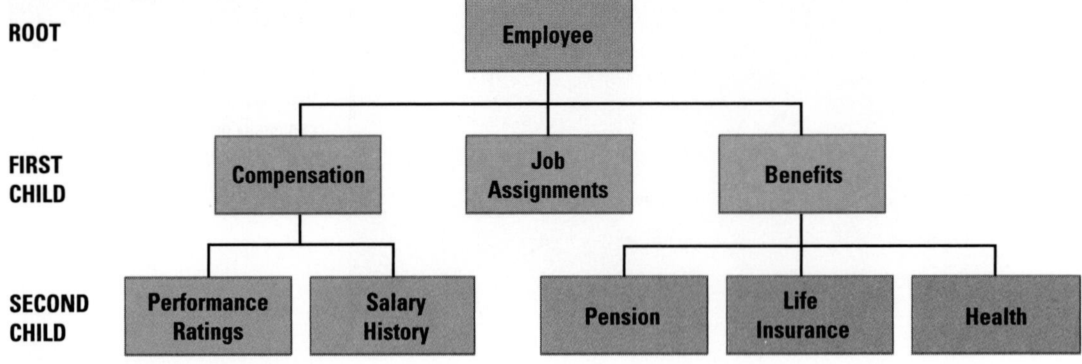

FIGURE 7.10 A hierarchical database for a human resources system. The hierarchical database model looks like an organizational chart or a family tree. It has a single root segment (Employee) connected to lower-level segments (Compensation, Job Assignments, and Benefits). Each subordinate segment, in turn, may connect to other subordinate segments. Here, Compensation connects to Performance Ratings and Salary History. Benefits connects to Pension, Life Insurance, and Health Care. Each subordinate segment is the child of the segment directly above it.

it: Performance Ratings (containing data about employees' job performance evaluations) and Salary History (containing historical data about employees' past salaries). Below the Benefits segment are child segments for Pension, Life Insurance, and Health, containing data about these benefit plans.

pointer A special type of data element attached to a record that shows the absolute or relative address of another record.

Behind the logical view of data are a number of physical links and devices to tie the information together into a logical whole. In a hierarchical DBMS the data are physically linked to one another by a series of **pointers** that form chains of related data segments. Pointers are data elements attached to the ends of record segments on the disk directing the system to related records. In our example, the end of the Employee segment would contain a series of pointers to all Compensation, Job Assignments, and Benefits segments. In turn, at the end of the Compensation and Benefits segments are pointers to their respective child segments.

Network Data Model

network data model A logical database model that is useful for depicting many-to-many relationships.

The **network data model** is a variation of the hierarchical data model. Indeed, databases can be translated from hierarchical to network and vice versa to optimize processing speed and convenience. Whereas hierarchical structures depict one-to-many relationships, network structures depict data logically as many-to-many relationships. In other words, parents can have multiple children, and a child can have more than one parent.

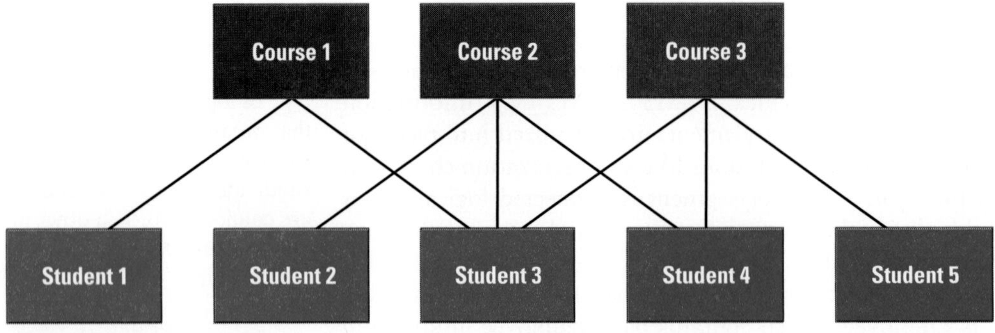

FIGURE 7.11 The network data model. This illustration of a network data model showing the relationship the students in a university have to the courses they take represents an example of logical many-to-many relationships. The network model reduces the redundancy of data representation through the increased use of pointers.

A typical many-to-many relationship in which a network DBMS excels in performance is the student-course relationship (see Figure 7.11). There are many courses in a university and many students. A student takes many courses and a course has many students. The data in Figure 7.11 could be structured hierarchically. But this could result in considerable redundancy and a slowed response to certain types of information queries; the same student would be listed on the disk for each class he or she was taking instead of only once. Network structures reduce redundancy and, in certain situations (when many-to-many relationships are involved), respond more quickly. However, there is a price for this reduction in redundancy and increased speed: The number of pointers in network structures rapidly increases, making maintenance and operation potentially more complicated.

Relational Data Model

The **relational data model,** the most recent of these three database models, overcomes some of the limitations of the other two models. The relational model represents all data in the database as simple two-dimensional tables called *relations*. The tables appear similar to flat files, but the information in more than one file can be easily extracted and combined. Sometimes the tables are referred to as files.

Figure 7.12 shows a supplier table, a part table, and an order table. In each table the rows are unique records and the columns are fields. Another term for a row or record in a relation is a **tuple.** Often a user needs information from a number of relations to produce a report. Here is the strength of the relational model: It can relate data in

relational data model A type of logical database model that treats data as if they were stored in two-dimensional tables. It can relate data stored in one table to data in another as long as the two tables share a common data element.

tuple A row or record in a relational database.

Table (Relation) — Columns (Fields) — Rows (Records, Tuples)

ORDER

ORDER-NUMBER	ORDER-DATE	DELIVERY-DATE	PART-NUMBER	PART-AMOUNT	ORDER-TOTAL
1634	02/02/99	02/22/99	152	2	144.50
1635	02/12/99	02/29/99	137	3	79.70
1636	02/13/99	03/01/99	145	1	24.30

PART

PART-NUMBER	PART-DESCRIPTION	UNIT-PRICE	SUPPLIER-NUMBER
137	Door latch	26.25	4058
145	Door handle	22.50	2038
152	Compressor	70.00	1125

SUPPLIER

SUPPLIER-NUMBER	SUPPLIER-NAME	SUPPLIER-ADDRESS
1125	CBM Inc.	44 Winslow, Gary IN 44950
2038	Ace Inc.	Rte. 101, Essex NJ 07763
4058	Bryant Corp.	51 Elm, Rochester NY 11349

FIGURE 7.12 The relational data model. Each table is a *relation* and each row or record is a *tuple.* Each column corresponds to a field. These relations can easily be combined and extracted to access data and produce reports, provided that any two share a common data element. In this example, the ORDER file shares the data element "PART-NUMBER" with the PART file. The PART and SUPPLIER files share the data element "SUPPLIER-NUMBER."

any one file or table to data in another file or table *as long as both tables share a common data element.*

To demonstrate, suppose we wanted to find in the relational database in Figure 7.12 the names and addresses of suppliers who could provide us with part number 137 or part number 152. We would need information from two tables: the supplier table and the part table. Note that these two files have a shared data element: SUPPLIER-NUMBER.

In a relational database, three basic operations are used to develop useful sets of data: select, project, and join. The *select* operation creates a subset consisting of all records in the file that meet stated criteria. *Select* creates, in other words, a subset of rows that meet certain criteria. In our example, we want to select records (rows) from the part table where the part number equals 137 or 152. The *join* operation combines relational tables to provide the user with more information than is available in individual tables. In our example we want to join the now shortened part table (only parts numbered 137 or 152 will be presented) and the supplier table into a single new result table.

The *project* operation creates a subset consisting of columns in a table, permitting the user to create new tables that contain only the information required. In our example, we want to extract from the new result table only the following columns: PART-NUMBER, SUPPLIER-NUMBER, SUPPLIER-NAME, and SUPPLIER-ADDRESS.

Leading mainframe relational database management systems include IBM's DB2 and Oracle from the Oracle Corporation. Microsoft Access is a PC relational database management system.

Advantages and Disadvantages of the Three Database Models

The principal advantage of the hierarchical and network database models is processing efficiency. For instance, a hierarchical model is appropriate for airline reservation transaction-processing systems, which must handle millions of structured routine requests each day for reservation information.

Hierarchical and network structures have several disadvantages. All the access paths, directories, and indices must be specified in advance. Once specified, they are not easily changed without a major programming effort. Therefore, these designs have low flexibility. For instance, if you queried the human resources database illustrated in Figure 7.10 to find out the names of the employees with the job title of administrative assistant, you would discover that there is no way that the system can find the answer in a reasonable amount of time. This path through the data was not specified in advance.

Both hierarchical and network systems are programming intensive, time consuming, difficult to install, and difficult to remedy if design errors occur. They do not support ad hoc, English language-like inquiries for information.

The strengths of relational DBMS are great flexibility in regard to ad hoc queries, power to combine information from different sources, simplicity of design and maintenance, and the ability to add new data and records without disturbing existing programs and applications. However, these systems are somewhat slower because they typically require many accesses to the data stored on disk to carry out the select, join, and project commands. Selecting one part number from among millions, one record at a time, can take a long time. Of course the database can be indexed and tuned to speed up prespecified queries. Relational systems do not have the large number of pointers carried by hierarchical systems.

Large relational databases may be designed to have some data redundancy to make retrieval of data more efficient. The same data element may be stored in multiple tables. Updating redundant data elements is not automatic in many relational DBMS. For example, changing the employee status field in one table will not automatically change it in all tables. Special arrangements are required to ensure that all copies of the same data element are updated together.

Hierarchical databases remain the workhorse for intensive high-volume transaction processing. Banks, insurance companies, and other high-volume users continue to use reliable hierarchical databases such as IBM's IMS, developed in 1969. Many or-

TABLE 7.1 Comparison of Database Alternatives

Type of Database	Processing Efficiency	Flexibility	End-User Friendliness	Programming Complexity
Hierarchical	High	Low	Low	High
Network	Medium–high	Low–medium	Low–moderate	High
Relational	Lower but improving	High	High	Low

ganizations have converted to DB2, IBM's relational DBMS for new applications, while retaining IMS for traditional transaction processing. For example, Dallas-based Texas Instruments depends on IMS for its heavy processing requirements, including inventory, accounting, and manufacturing. As relational products acquire more muscle, firms will shift away completely from hierarchical DBMS, but this will happen over a long period of time. Table 7.1 compares the characteristics of the different database models.

Creating a Database

To create a database, one must go through two design exercises: a conceptual design and a physical design. The conceptual or logical design of a database is an abstract model of the database from a business perspective, whereas the physical design shows how the database is actually arranged on direct access storage devices. Physical database design is performed by database specialists, whereas logical design requires a detailed description of the business information needs of actual end users of the database.

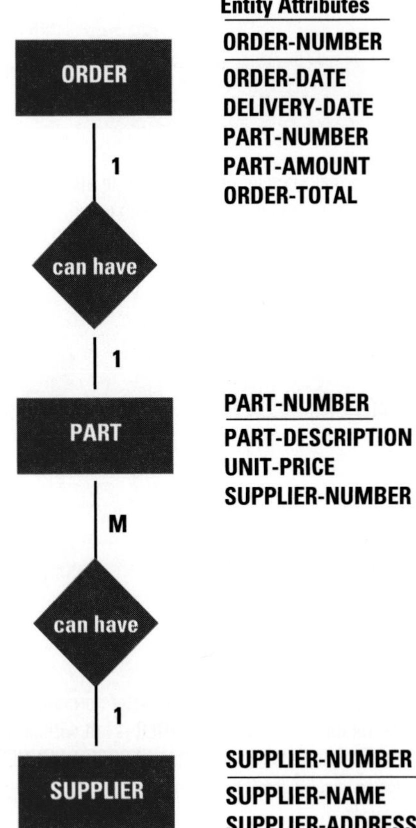

FIGURE 7.13

An entity-relationship diagram. This diagram shows the relationships between the entities ORDER, PART, and SUPPLIER that were used to develop the relational database illustrated in Figure 7.12.

Ideally, database design will be part of an overall organizational data planning effort (see Chapter 10).

The conceptual database design describes how the data elements in the database are to be grouped. The design process identifies relationships among data elements and the most efficient way of grouping data elements together to meet information requirements. The process also identifies redundant data elements and the groupings of data elements required for specific application programs. Groups of data are organized, refined, and streamlined until an overall logical view of the relationships among all the data elements in the database emerges.

entity-relationship diagram A methodology for documenting databases illustrating the relationship between various entities in the database.

Database designers document the conceptual data model with an **entity-relationship diagram,** illustrated in Figure 7.13. The boxes represent entities and the diamonds represent relationships. The *1* or *M* on either side of the diamond represents the relationship among entities as either one-to-one, one-to-many, or many-to-many. Figure 7.13 shows that the entity ORDER can have only one PART and a PART can only have one SUPPLIER. Many parts can be provided by the same supplier. The attributes for each entity are listed next to the entity and the key field is underlined.

normalization The process of creating small stable data structures from complex groups of data when designing a relational database.

To use a relational database model effectively, complex groupings of data must be streamlined to eliminate redundant data elements and awkward many-to-many relationships. The process of creating small, stable data structures from complex groups of data is called **normalization.** Figures 7.14 and 7.15 illustrate this process. In the particular business modeled here, an order can have more than one part but each part is provided by only one supplier. If we built a relation called ORDER with all the fields included here, we would have to repeat the name, description, and price of each part on the order and name and address of each part vendor. This relation contains what are called *repeating groups* because there can be many parts and suppliers for each order and it actually describes multiple entities—parts and suppliers as well as orders. A more efficient way to arrange the data is to break down ORDER into smaller relations, each of which describes a single entity. If we go step by step and normalize the relation ORDER, we emerge with the relations illustrated in Figure 7.15.

FIGURE 7.14 An unnormalized relation for ORDER. In an unnormalized relation there are repeating groups. For example, there can be many parts and suppliers for each order. There is only a one-to-one correspondence between ORDER-NUMBER and ORDER-DATE, ORDER-TOTAL, and DELIVERY-DATE.

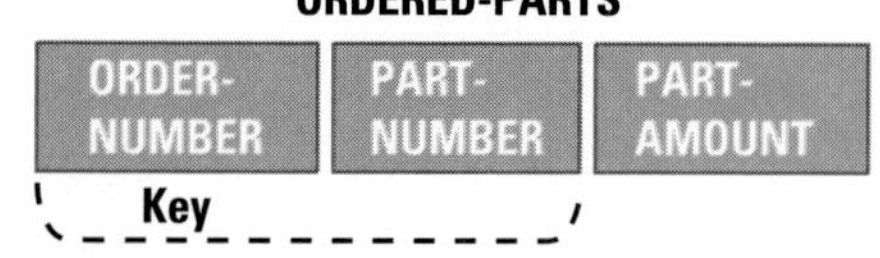

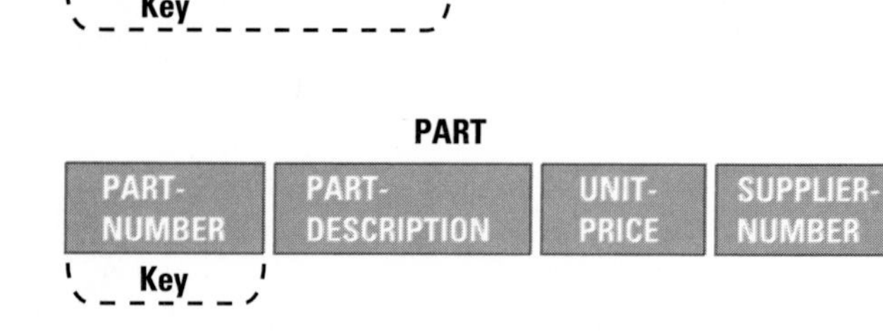

FIGURE 7.15 A normalized relation for ORDER. After normalization, the original relation ORDER has been broken down into four smaller relations. The relation ORDER is left with only three attributes and the relation ORDERED-PARTS has a combined, or concatenated, key consisting of ORDER-NUMBER and PART-NUMBER.

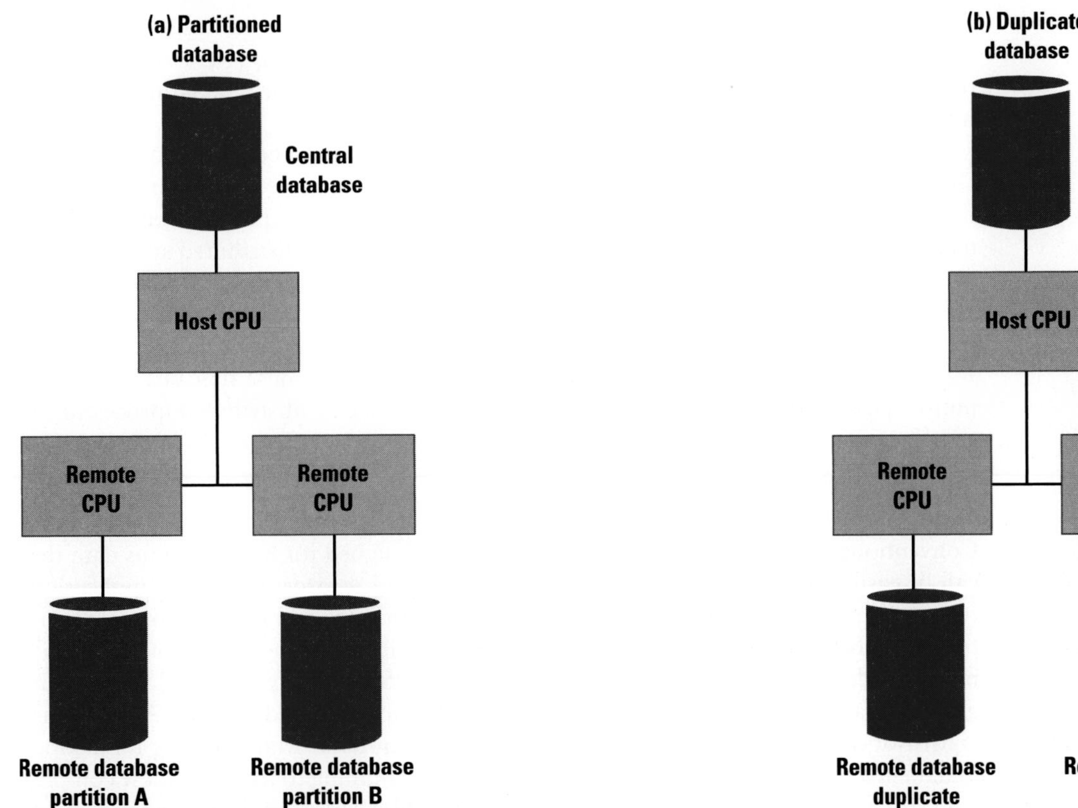

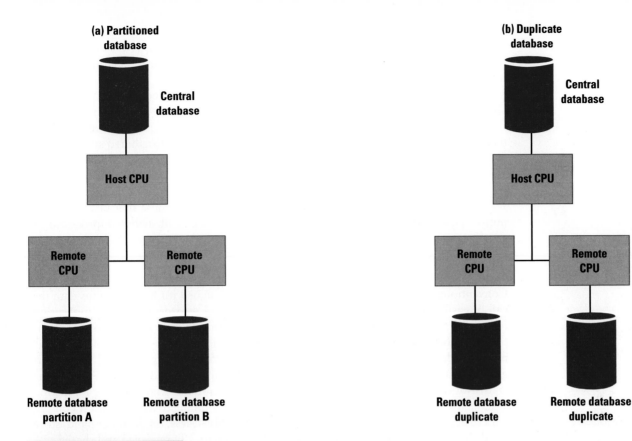

FIGURE 7.16 Distributed databases. There are alternative ways of distributing a database. The central database can be partitioned (a) so that each remote processor has the necessary data to serve its own local needs. The central database also can be duplicated (b) at all remote locations.

If a database has been carefully considered, with a clear understanding of business information needs and usage, the database model will most likely be in some normalized form. Many real-world databases are not fully normalized because this may not be the most sensible way to meet business information requirements. Note that the relational database illustrated in Figure 7.12 is not fully normalized because there could be more than one part for each order. The designers chose to not use the four relations described in Figure 7.15 because this particular business has a business rule specifying that a separate order must be placed for each part. The designers might have felt that there was no business need for maintaining four different tables.

7.4 DATABASE TRENDS

Recent database trends include the growth of distributed databases and the emergence of object-oriented and hypermedia databases.

Distributed Databases

The growth of distributed processing and networking has been accompanied by a movement toward distributed databases. A **distributed database** is one that is stored in more than one physical location. Parts of the database are stored physically in one location and other parts are stored and maintained in other locations. There are two main ways of distributing a database (see Figure 7.16). The central database (see Figure 7.16a) can be partitioned so that each remote processor has the necessary data to serve its local area. Changes in local files can be justified with the central database on a batch basis, often at night. Another strategy is to replicate the central database (Figure 7.16b) at all remote locations. For example, Lufthansa Airlines replaced its centralized mainframe

distributed database A database that is stored in more than one physical location. Parts or copies of the database are physically stored in one location, and other parts or copies are stored and maintained in other locations.

database with a replicated database to make information more immediately available to flight dispatchers. Any change made to Lufthansa's Frankfort DBMS is automatically replicated in New York and Hong Kong. This strategy also requires updating of the central database on off hours.

Both distributed processing and distributed databases have benefits and drawbacks. Distributed systems reduce the vulnerability of a single, massive central site. They permit increases in systems' power by purchasing smaller, less expensive computers. Finally, they increase service and responsiveness to local users. Distributed systems, however, are dependent on high-quality telecommunications lines, which themselves are vulnerable. Moreover, local databases can sometimes depart from central data standards and definitions, and pose security problems by widely distributing access to sensitive data. The economies of distribution can be lost when remote sites buy more computing power than they need. Despite these drawbacks, distributed processing is growing rapidly.

Object-Oriented and Hypermedia Databases

Conventional database management systems were designed for homogeneous data that can be easily structured into predefined data fields and records. But many applications today and in the future will require databases that can store and retrieve not only structured numbers and characters but also drawings, images, photographs, voice, and full-motion video (see Figure 7.17). Conventional DBMS are not well-suited to handling graphics-based or multimedia applications. For instance, design data in a CAD database consist of complex relationships among many types of data. Manipulating these kinds of data in a relational system requires extensive programming to translate these complex data structures into tables and rows. An **object-oriented database,** on the other hand, stores the data and procedures as objects that can be automatically retrieved and shared.

object-oriented database An approach to data management that stores both data and the procedures acting on the data as objects that can be automatically retrieved and shared; the objects can contain multimedia.

Object-oriented database management systems (OODBMS) are becoming popular because they can be used to manage the various multimedia components or Java applets used in Web applications, which typically integrate pieces of information from a variety of sources. OODBMS also are useful for storing data types such as recursive data. (An example would be parts within parts as found in manufacturing applications.) Finance and trading applications often use OODBMS because they require data models that must be easy to change to respond to new economic conditions. Motorola Corporation is using the Objectivity OODBMS to store complex celestial information required for its IRIDIUM satellite network because the object model allows navigation

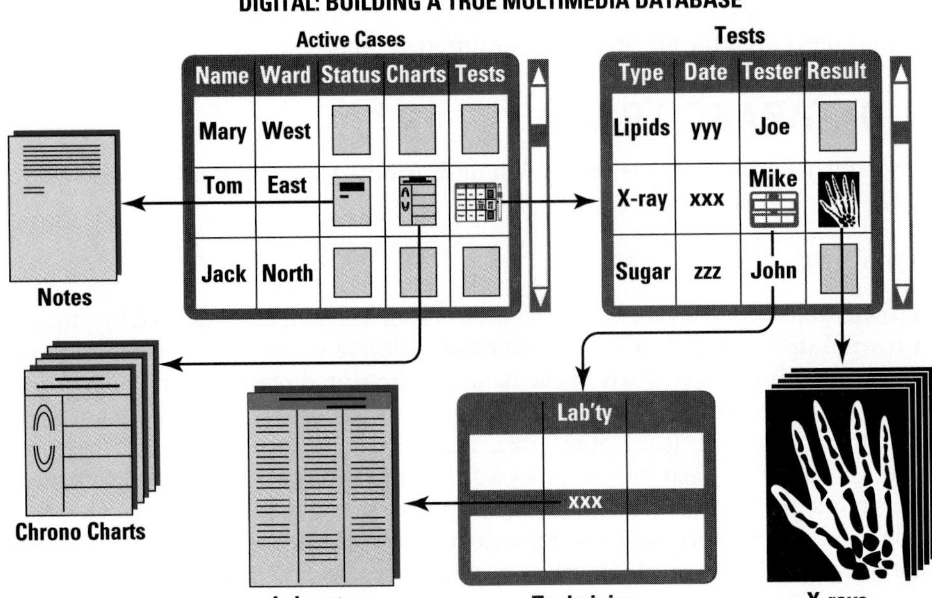

FIGURE 7.17

An object-oriented multimedia database. Medical data on patients in a hospital might likely be stored in a multimedia database such as this. Doctors could access patient files including vital medical images to generate the reports and derive the information they need to deliver quality health care quickly. *Reprinted by permission of Digital Equipment Corporation, Maynard, MA.*

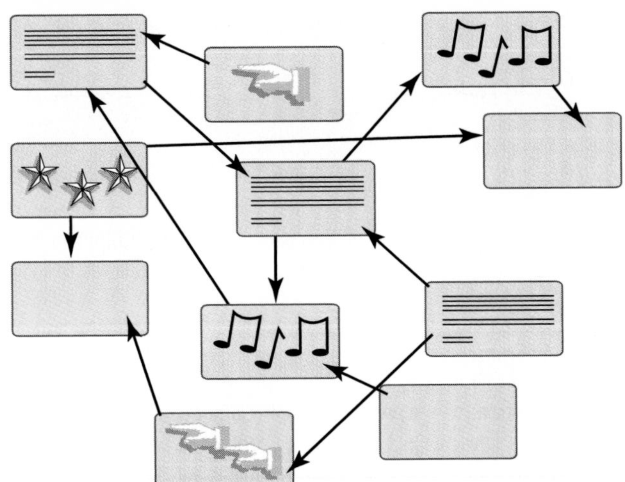

FIGURE 7.18

Hypermedia. In a hypermedia database, the user can choose his or her own path to move from node to node. Each node can contain text, graphics, sound, full-motion video, or executable programs. *Reprinted by permission of Digital Equipment Corporation, Maynard, MA.*

directly from data element to data element. A relational DBMS for this application would require extensive joining of separate tales to recombine their data (Watterson, 1998). The Window on Technology describes another application of OODBMS for a core transaction processing application.

The **hypermedia database** approach to information management transcends some of the limitations of traditional database methods by storing chunks of information in the form of nodes connected by links established by the user (see Figure 7.18). The nodes can contain text, graphics, sound, full-motion video, or executable computer programs. Searching for information does not have to follow a predetermined organization scheme. Instead, one can branch instantly to related information in any kind of relationship established by the author. The relationship between records is less structured than in a traditional DBMS. In most systems each node can be displayed on a screen. The screen also displays the links between the node depicted and other nodes in the database. Web sites use a hypermedia database approach to store information as interconnected pages containing text, sound, video, and graphics.

hypermedia database An approach to data management that organizes data as a network of nodes linked in any pattern established by the user; the nodes can contain text, graphics, sound, full-motion video, or executable programs.

Although object-oriented and hypermedia databases can store more complex types of information than relational DBMS, they are relatively slow compared with relational DBMS for processing large numbers of transactions. *Hybrid* object-relational systems are now available to provide capabilities of both object-oriented and relational DBMS. A hybrid approach can be accomplished in three different ways: by using tools that offer object-oriented access to relational DBMS, by using object-oriented extensions to existing relational DBMS, or by using a hybrid object-relational database management system.

Multidimensional Data Analysis

Sometimes managers need to analyze data in ways that cannot be represented by traditional database models. For example, a company selling four different products—nuts, bolts, washers, and screws—in three regions, East, West, and Central—might want to know actual sales by product for each region and might also want to compare them with projected sales. This analysis requires a multidimensional view of data.

To provide this type of information, organizations can use either a specialized multidimensional database or a tool that creates multidimensional views of data in relational databases. Multidimensional analysis enables users to view the same data in different ways using multiple dimensions. Each aspect of information—product, pricing, cost, region, or time period—represents a different dimension. So a product manager could use a multidimensional data analysis tool to learn how many washers were sold in the East in June, how that compares with the previous month and the previous June, and how it compares with the sales forecast. Another term for multidimensional data analysis is **on-line analytical processing (OLAP).**

on-line analytical processing (OLAP) Capability for manipulating and analyzing large volumes of data from multiple perspectives.

WINDOW ON TECHNOLOGY

Air France Flies with Object Technology

Can an object database help Air France increase its revenue by 1 percent? Management at the Paris-based airline thinks so, and so does AMR Corporation (parent of American Airlines). With a current revenue of about $7 billion, a 1 percent increase in Air France's revenue would mean an extra $70 million per year.

The problem the airline faces is that too many of its seats are filled by lower-paying customers, while higher-paying customers are often unable to find seats. The current mainframe-based reservation system enables the reservation personnel to track individual flight segments only, such as the nonstop Paris–to–New York segment. A customer whose trip originates elsewhere might be paying more money to fly and might need to connect to that same flight. The current system cannot check that segment in conjunction with flights originating elsewhere, and so that higher-paying customer will not be able to fill a seat on that flight. The seat instead may be filled by a lower-paying customer whose flight originates in Paris. If the airline can fill the same seat with a customer who is paying more for the ticket, it will increase Air France's revenue without any increase in the number of passengers. To address this problem, Air France is purchasing a new system using object database technology.

Like other airlines, Air France has depended on a mainframe to handle all reservations and to process all tickets. Air France will continue to keep its heavy transaction processing for reservations and tickets on its Unisys mainframe, but it will use a new system for revenue and yield management applications. According to Air France's Pierre Gandois, the manager of this project, the new system will be tracking "a combination of flights rather than looking at each flight as a single unit." In that way it will become easier for reservation clerks to sell seats to customers who purchase higher-priced tickets but are connecting from another flight.

This new system runs on a UNIX server and an object-oriented database. It will perform yield management to determine the best mix of full-fare and discount seat prices for a given flight to produce the highest revenue. The database sets parameters for ticket availability and discounts, automatically opening or closing discount offers as business conditions change. This will help the airline sell seats on a continuation flight for higher prices. The server will receive nightly updates on ticket sales from the mainframe. The system on the server will approve or deny bookings as flights are filling up. Once a request for a booking is approved by the new system, the mainframe will process the ticket as in the past. Thus the new system will increase revenue, not by increasing the passenger load but by filling some of the seats it is already filling with passengers who are paying higher prices for their tickets.

The reservation application was written and is being marketed by Sabre Decision Technologies, the software development company of AMR Corporation. Versant Object Technology Corporation supplied the object-oriented database. Air France's system represents one of the first companies outside the financial and telecommunications industries to use an object-oriented database for a core transaction processing application.

The new system will control about 20 percent of the airline's 500 daily flights. Sabre is also trying to market the system to other airlines, but they are having trouble. According to Vic Nilson, Sabre's Air France project director, managements at other airlines "are scared to go into an object database" because they believe the technology is too new. Many feel it is still unproved for heavy transaction processing applications such as flight reservations.

To Think About: ***Analyze Air France using the competitive forces and value chain models. Will the use of the object database reservation system enhance its competitive position? Why or why not? What management, organization, and technology issues did the new object-oriented system address?***

Source: Adapted from Craig Stedman, "Object Project Flies," *Computerworld*, February 10, 1997.

Figure 7.19 shows a multidimensional model that could be created to represent products, regions, actual sales, and projected sales. A matrix of actual sales can be stacked on top of a matrix of projected sales to form a cube with six faces. If you rotate the cube 90 degrees one way, the face showing will be product versus actual and projected sales. If you rotate the cube 90 degrees again, you can see region versus actual and projected sales. If you rotate 180 degrees from the original view, you can see projected sales and product versus region. Cubes can be nested within cubes to build complex views of data.

Data Warehouses

Decision makers need concise, reliable information about current operations, trends, and changes. What has been immediately available at most firms is current data only (historical data was available through special IS reports that took a long time to pro-

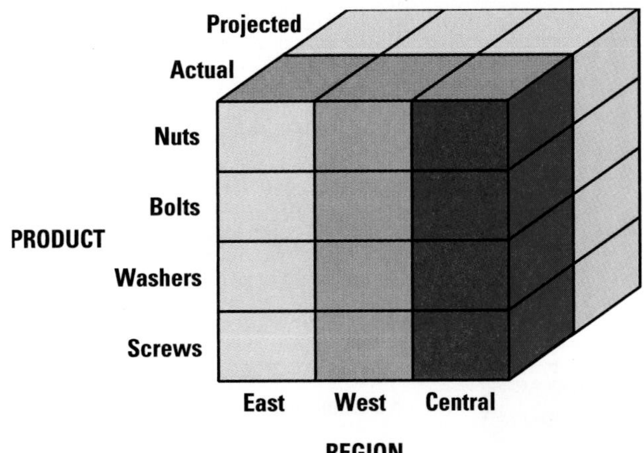

FIGURE 7.19

Multidimensional data model. The view that is showing is product versus region. If you rotate the cube 90 degrees, the face that will be showing is product versus actual and projected sales. If you rotate the cube 90 degrees again, you can see region versus actual and projected sales. Other views are possible. The ability to rotate the data cube is the main technique for multidimensional reporting. It is sometimes called "slice and dice."

duce). Data often are fragmented in separate operational systems such as sales or payroll so that different managers make decisions from incomplete knowledge bases. Users and information system specialists may have to spend inordinate amounts of time locating and gathering data (Watson and Haley, 1998). Data warehousing addresses this problem by integrating key operational data from around the company in a form that is consistent, reliable, and easily available for reporting.

What Is a Data Warehouse?

A **data warehouse** is a database, with tools, that stores current and historical data of potential interest to managers throughout the company. The data originate in many core operational systems and external sources and are copied into the data warehouse database as often as needed—hourly, daily, weekly, monthly. The data are standardized and consolidated so that they can be used across the enterprise for management analysis and decision making. The data are available for anyone to access as needed but cannot be altered. A data warehouse system includes a range of ad hoc and standardized query tools, analytical tools, and graphical reporting facilities. These systems can perform high-level analysis of patterns or trends, but they can also drill into more detail where needed. Figure 7.20 illustrates the data warehouse concept.

data warehouse A database, with reporting and query tools, that stores current and historical data extracted from various operational systems and consolidated for management reporting and analysis.

Companies can build enterprise-wide data warehouses where a central data warehouse serves the entire organization, or they can create smaller, decentralized warehouses called data marts. A **data mart** is a subset of a data warehouse in which a summarized or highly focused portion of the organization's data is placed in a separate database for a specific population of users. For example, a company might develop marketing and sales data marts to deal with customer information. A data mart typically focuses on a single subject area or line of business, so it usually can be constructed more rapidly and at lower cost than an enterprise-wide data warehouse. On the other hand, complexity, costs, and management problems will rise if an organization creates too many data marts (Francett, 1997).

data mart A small data warehouse containing only a portion of the organization's data for a specified function or population of users.

Benefits of a Data Warehouse

Data warehouses not only offer improved information, but they make it easy for decision makers to obtain it. They even include the ability to model and remodel the data. These systems also enable decision makers to access data as often as they need without affecting the performance of the underlying operational systems.

Through the use of on-line analytical processing (OLAP) and data marts, Office Depot was able to "refocus the business." Merchandisers, salespeople, and executives reviewed the retailer's PC business by generating detailed analyses of gross-margin return on investments by store and product type. They found that the company was carrying too much fringe stock in the wrong stores. Office Depot narrowed its inventory of PCs from 22 to 12 products. Profits rose from eliminating unnecessary inventory and avoiding markdowns on equipment that wasn't selling (Hoffman, 1998).

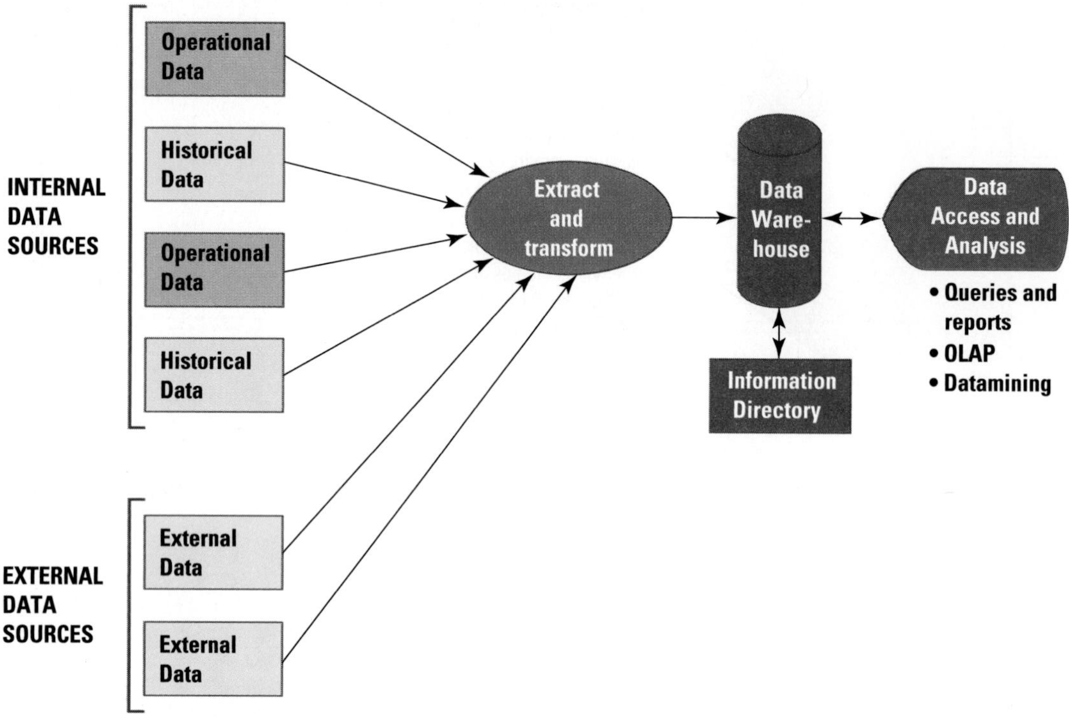

FIGURE 7.20 Components of a data warehouse. A data warehouse extracts current and historical data from operational systems inside the organization. These data are combined with data from external sources and reorganized into a central database designed for management reporting and analysis. The information directory provides users with information about the data available in the warehouse.

Victoria's Secret Stores was spending too much time trying to locate information and not enough time analyzing it. Through data warehousing, the lingerie chain learned that its system of allocating merchandise to its 678 shops, based on a mathematical store average, was wrong. For example, an average store sells equal pieces of black and ivory lingerie, but Miami-area consumers buy ivory designs by a margin of 10 to 1. Geographic demand patterns also showed that some stores did not need to discount merchandise. Data warehousing gave this firm a more precise understanding of customer behavior (Goldberg and Vijayan, 1996).

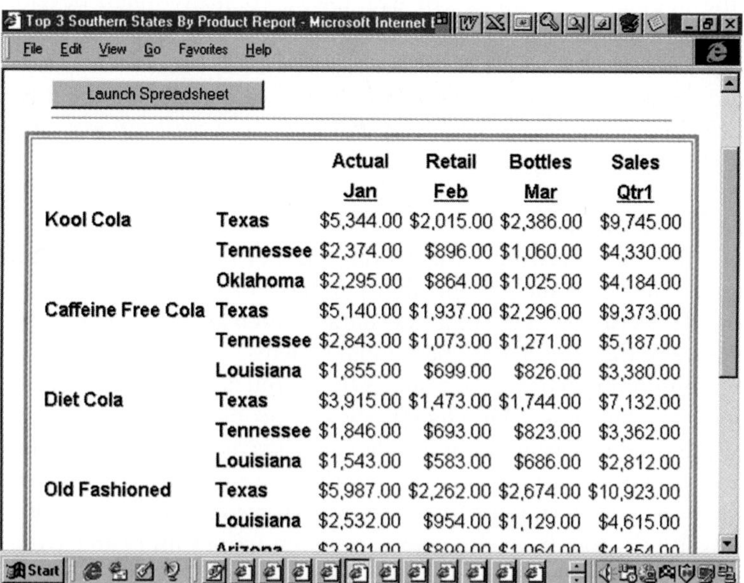

		Actual Jan	Retail Feb	Bottles Mar	Sales Qtr1
Kool Cola	Texas	$5,344.00	$2,015.00	$2,386.00	$9,745.00
	Tennessee	$2,374.00	$896.00	$1,060.00	$4,330.00
	Oklahoma	$2,295.00	$864.00	$1,025.00	$4,184.00
Caffeine Free Cola	Texas	$5,140.00	$1,937.00	$2,296.00	$9,373.00
	Tennessee	$2,843.00	$1,073.00	$1,271.00	$5,187.00
	Louisiana	$1,855.00	$699.00	$826.00	$3,380.00
Diet Cola	Texas	$3,915.00	$1,473.00	$1,744.00	$7,132.00
	Tennessee	$1,846.00	$693.00	$823.00	$3,362.00
	Louisiana	$1,543.00	$583.00	$686.00	$2,812.00
Old Fashioned	Texas	$5,987.00	$2,262.00	$2,674.00	$10,923.00
	Louisiana	$2,532.00	$954.00	$1,129.00	$4,615.00

Hyperion Essbase OLAP Server allows users to perform ad-hoc multidimensional data analysis on organizational databases through a Web interface. Users can work with OLAP applications such as planning, budgeting, and forecasting over corporate intranets or the Internet.

WINDOW ON MANAGEMENT

The EPA Cleans Up Its Own Mess Through the Internet

The Environmental Protection Agency (EPA) is charged with monitoring and cleaning up the environment. Nevertheless, it has had a longstanding mess of its own that needed cleaning up. The EPA's management recently decided to do just that. Part of its problem arose from the fact that over the years the EPA had built a series of databases in response to laws passed by Congress. Separate databases were established to support, among other things: the Clean Air Act; permits for waste water discharge; the Superfund Authorization Bill for cleaning up hazardous waste sites; the classification of more than 300 chemicals as toxic that have been or could be released into the environment; the issuing of more than 450,000 site permits for hazardous cleanup activities; record keeping on the more than 675,000 facilities regulated or monitored by the EPA; and an index of the chemical data in the various databases. These databases were so isolated from each other that they used five different database management systems, including Oracle and IBM's DB2.

The other EPA problem was the popularity of the data combined with their slow, expensive method of making the data available. Many thousands of people, such as EPA employees, chemical industry employees, environmental organizations, and residents of specific local areas, wanted some part of the information that was stored in those databases. However, because the data were not integrated, they were extremely difficult to access. Those who wanted access, including most EPA employees, had to call an EPA information systems specialist who then had to retrieve the data for them, a very slow, time-consuming, and expensive operation.

Management found a better way, relying on advanced information technology, including the Internet. The first issue, the need to integrate the data, was addressed through a data warehouse known as Envirofacts. While the independent databases remain, an integrated data warehouse database was completed in 1995. It combines data from five of the EPA databases, with more databases to be added soon. The data stored in Envirofacts are automatically updated monthly from the five isolated databases. EPA employees gain access through a proprietary EPA interface called Gateway. Using Gateway and Envirofacts, EPA employees are able to quickly access most of the data they need. The Gateway interface was installed on many of the EPA's 24,000 desktop PCs. They access Envirofacts through an EPA network. Nonemployees were also able to access the data directly through a dial-up line. The new system not only made it quicker for many people to procure the data they needed, but it also greatly reduced the workload for the EPA's information systems staff, freeing them for more productive work than simply retrieving data.

Nonetheless, problems remained. Support of Gateway, installed on thousands of machines, required a great deal of information systems staff time. Moreover, for those who were not EPA employees, access through a dial-up line was slow, difficult, and costly. So management has now turned to the Internet to allow access to anyone. The Internet offers several advantages. First, no special interface, such as Gateway, is needed. Instead, all anyone needs is the popular Netscape Navigator Web browser software that many people use for their Internet access. Moreover, the public no longer needs to gain access through an EPA dial-up line. Instead, they use their own Internet access providers. EPA employees have also been given access in this manner. Eventually, the EPA will phase out the use of Gateway. However, that will be done slowly so that employees who prefer to access that way can continue to do so. Ultimately Gateway will be retired and all access will be achieved through the Internet.

In addition to adding more databases to Envirofacts, the EPA has also launched another project to enhance access to the data people need. The agency will be adding to its Web site hot links to other government agencies and universities that also make environmental data available to the public. In that way, both the EPA and other organizations of all kinds will have quick and easy access to the data they need to help clean up and protect our environment.

To Think About: ***What are the management benefits of Envirofacts? Of making Envirofacts available through the Internet? What do you think might be management drawbacks?***

Source: Adapted from Richard Adhikari, "Saved by the Web," *InformationWeek*, March 17, 1997.

Linking Databases to the Web

It has been estimated that 70 percent of the world's business information resides on mainframe databases, many of which are for older legacy systems. Many of these legacy systems use hierarchical DBMS or even traditional flat files where information is difficult for users to access. A new series of software products has been developed to help users gain access to this mountain of legacy data through the Web.

There are a number of advantages to using the Web to access an organization's internal databases. Web browser software is extremely easy to use, requiring much less

The Environmental Protection Agency (EPA) created a Web site where employees and the general public can access its Envirofacts data warehouse. More and more organizations are using the World Wide Web to provide an interface to internal databases.

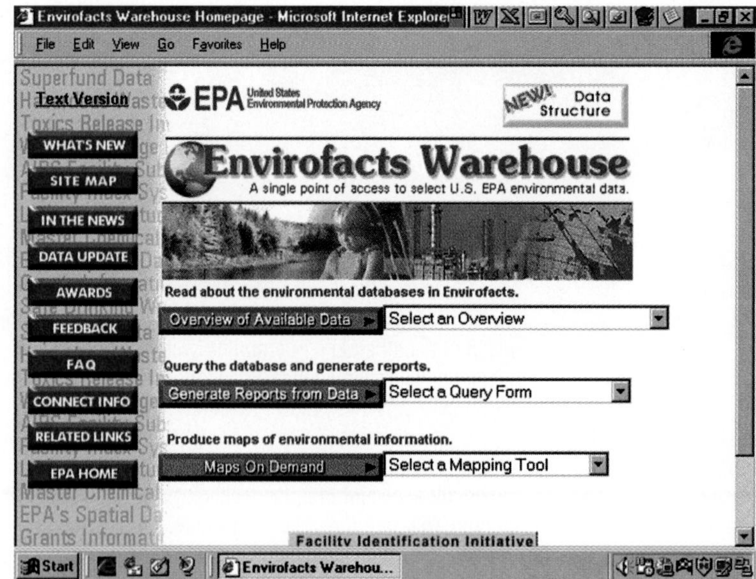

training than even user-friendly database query tools. The Web interface requires no changes to the legacy database. Companies leverage their investments in older systems because it costs much less to add a Web interface in front of a legacy system than to redesign and rebuild the system to improve user access.

Accessing corporate databases through the Web is creating new efficiencies and opportunities, in some cases even changing the way business is being done. For example, the Dreyfus Corporation, a New York mutual funds company, created a Web application that allows brokers to use Netscape Navigator Web browser software to access its mainframe database to obtain on-line prospectuses and fund histories (Garvey, 1997). The Window on Management describes some of the benefits of providing the general public with Web access to government databases.

7.5 MANAGEMENT REQUIREMENTS FOR DATABASE SYSTEMS

Much more is required for the development of database systems than simply selecting a logical database model. Indeed, this selection may be among the last decisions. The database is an organizational discipline, a method, rather than a tool or technology. It requires organizational and conceptual change.

Without management support and understanding, database efforts fail. The critical elements in a database environment are (1) data administration, (2) data planning and modeling methodology, (3) database technology and management, and (4) users. This environment is depicted in Figure 7.21 and now will be described.

Data Administration

Database systems require that the organization recognize the strategic role of information and begin actively to manage and plan for information as a corporate resource. This means that the organization must develop a **data administration** function with the power to define information requirements for the entire company and with direct access to senior management. The chief information officer (CIO) or vice president of information becomes the primary advocate in the organization for database systems.

data administration A special organizational function for managing the organization's data resources, concerned with information policy, data planning, maintenance of data dictionaries, and data quality standards.

Data administration is responsible for the specific policies and procedures through which data can be managed as an organizational resource. These responsibilities include developing information policy, planning for data, overseeing logical database design and data dictionary development, and monitoring the usage of data by information system specialists and end-user groups.

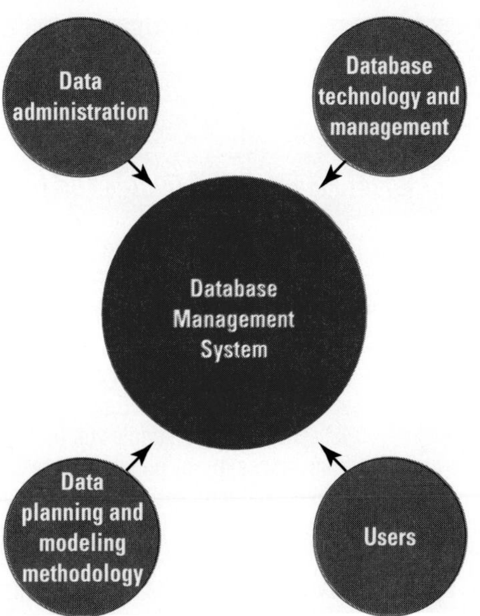

FIGURE 7.21

Key organizational elements in the database environment. For a database management system to flourish in any organization, data administration functions and data planning and modeling methodologies must be coordinated with database technology and management. Resources must be devoted to train end users to use databases properly.

The fundamental principle of data administration is that all data are the property of the organization as a whole. Data cannot belong exclusively to any one business area or organizational unit. All data are to be made available to any group that requires them to fulfill its mission. An organization needs to formulate an **information policy** that specifies its rules for sharing, disseminating, acquiring, standardizing, classifying, and inventorying information throughout the organization. Information policy lays out specific procedures and accountabilities, specifying which organizational units share information; where information can be distributed; and who has responsibility for updating and maintaining the information. Although data administration is a very important organizational function, it has proved very challenging to implement.

information policy Formal rules governing the maintenance, distribution, and use of information in an organization.

Data Planning and Modeling Methodology

The organizational interests served by the DBMS are much broader than those in the traditional file environment; therefore the organization requires enterprise-wide planning for data. Enterprise analysis, which addresses the information requirements of the entire organization (as opposed to the requirements of individual applications), is needed to develop databases. The purpose of enterprise analysis is to identify the key entities, attributes, and relationships that constitute the organization's data. These techniques are described in greater detail in Chapter 10.

Database Technology, Management, and Users

Databases require new software and a new staff specially trained in DBMS techniques, as well as new management structures. Most corporations develop a database design and management group within the corporate information system division that is responsible for the more technical and operational aspects of managing data. The functions it performs are called **database administration.** This group does the following:

database administration Refers to the more technical and operational aspects of managing data, including physical database design and maintenance.

- Defines and organizes database structure and content
- Develops security procedures to safeguard the database
- Develops database documentation
- Maintains the database management software

In close cooperation with users, the design group establishes the physical database, the logical relations among elements, and the access rules and procedures.

WINDOW ON ORGANIZATIONS

DNA Databases: Crime Fighters or Threats to Privacy?

DNA evidence has become a potent crime-fighting tool, allowing a criminal to be fingered by his or her own genes. Computer analysis can discover the identity of a killer or rapist by matching DNA from blood, saliva, or other body fluids left at a crime scene with a DNA profile in a database. DNA evidence is especially useful for solving violent crimes, where the people care deeply about identifying the perpetrators and getting them off the street.

Until recently DNA "hits" have been sporadic, because databases of DNA profiles were small and localized. The development of a national DNA database could change that. The Federal Bureau of Investigation and state laboratories have established new technical standards for testing DNA strands to support a national system of quicker, cheaper testing. In December 1997, eight states started to use FBI software to pool their data on-line, enabling them to identify criminals across their borders. Within minutes they scored their first hit, linking a convicted sex offender in Illinois to a 1989 offense and attempted murder in Wisconsin.

If DNA is such a powerful tool for identifying criminals, why hasn't a national DNA database been established already, such as one in Britain, which has scored thousands of hits? One obstacle is money—it is very costly to add the required equipment, gather hundreds of thousands of DNA samples, enter and analyze the data, and convert existing databases to the new technology.

Another obstacle is the fear that the creation of a national DNA database would pose threats to individual privacy. In February 1998 a Massachusetts judge halted the collection of blood samples for DNA profiling from thousands of prison inmates, probationers, and parolees. Several had sued the state, arguing that it was an illegal search and seizure conducted without proper safeguards. In other states, questions have arisen about exactly who must submit to DNA testing and who can have access to the data. The O. J. Simpson trial called attention to concerns about whether police and laboratory workers are properly trained to handle such powerful evidence.

Civil libertarians contend that the existence of a national DNA database represents more of a Big Brother invasion of privacy than a national computerized network of fingerprints. Taking blood is much more invasive than taking fingerprints, and DNA carries information that could be abused by insurance companies or even geneticists seeking a gene for something like pedophilia. Benjamin Keehn, a Boston public defender who represented some of the inmates who challenged DNA collection, believes it is dangerous to round up thousands of convicts, probationers and parolees, as Massachusetts did, on the assumption that they are more likely to commit a crime. If poor people are more likely to commit a crime, why not have their DNA on file, or even take samples at birth? he counters.

In South Dakota, DNA samples are taken routinely upon arrest, like fingerprints. Virginia now gathers samples from all convicted felons and some juveniles, and has created the most comprehensive DNA database in the nation with 160,000 samples. Dr. Paul Ferrera of Virginia's Division of Forensic Sciences notes that more than half of his "hits" from the crime scenes of rapes and murders came from felons who had previously been convicted only of breaking and entering or burglary.

Dr. George Rowe, a forensic sciences professor at Georgetown University, believes that a national DNA database could have enormous impact. Studies have shown that most violent crimes are committed by a very small number of individuals, many of whom are repeat offenders. "If we're able to identify these guys and send them away . . . think about the impact that will have on the safety of citizens."

DNA analysis also can benefit prisoners. The Innocence Project at Yeshiva University's School of Law already has exonerated 53 convicts after DNA testing was applied to the evidence in their cases. Project head Barry Scheck, who helped defend O. J. Simpson, believes that abuses can be avoided if states develop DNA database laws that carefully stipulate that the data can be used by law enforcement agencies for identification purposes only.

To Think About: ***Should we allow national DNA databases to be created? Why or why not? What management, organization, and technology issues should be addressed if such databases are created?***

Source: Adapted from Carey Goldberg, "DNA Databanks Giving Police a Powerful Weapon, and Critics," *The New York Times*, February 19, 1998.

A database serves a wider community of users than traditional systems. Relational systems with fourth-generation query languages permit employees who are not computer specialists to access large databases. In addition, users include trained computer specialists. To optimize access for nonspecialists, more resources must be devoted to training end users. Professional systems workers must be retrained in the DBMS language, DBMS application development procedures, and new software practices.

Database technology has provided many organizational benefits, but it allows firms to maintain large databases with detailed personal information that pose a threat to individual privacy. The Window on Organizations describes the privacy issues surrounding the creation of a national DNA database.

Management Wrap-Up

MANAGEMENT

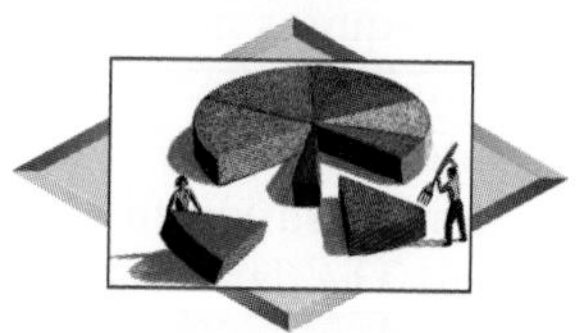

Selecting an appropriate data model and data management technology for the organization is a key management decision. Managers will need to evaluate the costs and benefits of implementing a database environment and the capabilities of various DBMS or file management technologies. Management should ascertain that organizational databases are designed to meet management information objectives and the organization's business needs.

ORGANIZATION

The organization's data model should reflect its key business processes and decision-making requirements. Data planning may need to be performed to make sure that the organization's data model delivers information efficiently for its business processes and enhances organizational performance. Designing a database is an organizational endeavor.

TECHNOLOGY

Many database and file management options are available for organizing and storing information. Key technology decisions should consider the efficiency of accessing information, flexibility in organizing information, the type of information to be stored and arranged, compatibility with the organization's data model, and compatibility with the organization's hardware and operating systems.

For Discussion:

1. It has been said that you do not need database management software to create a database environment. Discuss.
2. To what extent should end users be involved in the selection of a database management system and database design?

SUMMARY

1. **Compare traditional file organization and management techniques.** In a traditional file environment, data records are organized using either a sequential file organization or a direct or random file organization. Records in a sequential file can be accessed sequentially or they can be accessed directly if the sequential file is on disk and uses an indexed sequential access method. Records on a file with direct file organization can be accessed directly without an index.
2. **Explain the problems of the traditional file environment.** By allowing different functional areas and groups in the organization to maintain their own files independently, the traditional file environment creates problems such as data redundancy and inconsistency, program-data dependence, inflexibility, poor security, and lack of data sharing and availability.
3. **Describe how a database management system organizes information.** A database management system (DBMS) is the software that permits centralization of data and data management. A DBMS includes a data definition language, a data manipulation language, and a data dictionary capability. The most important feature of the DBMS is its ability to separate the logical and physical views of data. The user works with a logical view of data. The DBMS software translates user queries into queries that can be applied to the physical view of the data. The DBMS retrieves information so that the user does not have to be concerned with its physical location. This feature separates programs from data and from the management of data.
4. **Identify the three principal database models and some principles of database design.** There are three principal

logical database models: hierarchical, network, and relational. Each has unique advantages and disadvantages. Hierarchical systems, which support one-to-many relationships, are low in flexibility but high in processing speed and efficiency. Network systems support many-to-many relationships. Relational systems are relatively slow but are very flexible for supporting ad hoc requests for information and for combining information from different sources. The choice depends on the business requirements. Designing a database requires both a logical design and a physical design. The process of creating small, stable data structures from complex groups of data when designing a relational database is termed normalization.

5. **Discuss new database trends.** It is no longer necessary for data to be centralized in a single, massive database. A complete database or portions of the database can be distributed to more than one location to increase responsiveness and reduce vulnerability and costs. There are two major types of distributed databases: *replicated databases* and *partitioned databases.* Object-oriented, hypermedia, and multidimensional databases may be alternatives to traditional database structures for certain types of applications. Object-oriented and hypermedia databases can store graphics and other types of data in addition to conventional text data to support multimedia applications. Hypermedia databases allow data to be stored in nodes linked together in any pattern established by the user. A multidimensional view of data represents relationships among data as a multidimensional structure, which can be visualized as cubes of data and cubes within cubes of data, allowing for more sophisticated data analysis. Data can be more conveniently analyzed across the enterprise by using a data warehouse, in which current and historical data are extracted from many different operational systems and consolidated for management decision making. Databases can be linked to the Web or to Web browser software to facilitate user access to the data.

6. **Analyze the managerial and organizational requirements for creating a database environment.** Development of a database environment requires much more than selection of technology. It requires a change in the corporation's attitude toward information. The organization must develop a data administration function and a data planning methodology. The database environment has developed more slowly than was originally anticipated. There is political resistance in organizations to many key database concepts, especially to sharing of information that has been controlled exclusively by one organizational group. There are difficult cost/benefit questions in database management. Often, to avoid raising difficult questions, database use begins and ends as a small effort isolated in the information systems department.

KEY TERMS

Attribute, 201
Data administration, 222
Data definition language, 206
Data dictionary, 206
Data element, 207
Data manipulation language, 206
Data mart, 219
Data redundancy, 204
Data warehouse, 219
Database, 206
Database administration, 223
Database management system (DBMS), 206
Direct file access method, 203
Direct or random file organization, 202
Distributed database, 215
Entity, 201
Entity-relationship diagram, 213
Field, 201
File, 201
Hierarchical data model, 209
Hypermedia database, 217
Index, 203
Indexed sequential access method (ISAM), 203
Information policy, 223
Key field, 201
Logical view, 208
Network data model, 210
Normalization, 213
Object-oriented database, 216
On-line analytical processing (OLAP), 217
Physical view, 208
Pointer, 210
Program-data dependence, 205
Record, 201
Relational data model, 211
Sequential file organization, 202
Structured Query Language (SQL), 206
Traditional file environment, 204
Transform algorithm, 203
Tuple, 211

REVIEW QUESTIONS

1. Why is file management important for overall system performance?
2. Describe how indexes and key fields enable a program to access specific records in a file.
3. Define and describe the indexed sequential access method and the direct file access method.
4. List and describe some of the problems of the traditional file environment.
5. Define a database and a database management system.
6. Name and briefly describe the three components of a DBMS.

7. What is the difference between a logical and a physical view of data?
8. List some benefits of a DBMS.
9. Describe the three principal database models and the advantages and disadvantages of each.
10. What is normalization? How is it related to the features of a well-designed relational database?
11. What is a distributed database, and what are the two main ways of distributing data?
12. What are object-oriented and hypermedia databases? How do they differ from a traditional database?
13. Describe the capabilities of on-line analytical processing (OLAP) and multidimensional data analysis.
14. What is a data warehouse? How can it benefit organizations?
15. What are the four key elements of a database environment? Describe each briefly.
16. Describe and briefly comment on the major management challenges in building a database environment.

GROUP PROJECT

Review Figure 7.6, which provides an overview of a human resources database. Some additional information that might be maintained in such a database are an employee's date of hire, date of termination, number of children, date of birth, educational level, sex code, Social Security tax, Medicare tax, year-to-date gross pay and net pay, amount of life insurance coverage, health care plan payroll-deduction amount, life insurance plan payroll-deduction amount, and pension plan payroll-deduction amount.

Form a group with three or four of your classmates. Prepare two sample reports using the data in the database that might be of interest to either the employer or the employee. What pieces of information should be included on each report? In addition, prepare a data dictionary entry for one of the data elements in the database similar to the entry illustrated in Figure 7.7.

Your group's analysis should determine what business functions use this data element, which function has the primary responsibility for maintaining the data element, and which positions in the organization can access that data element. Present your findings to the class.

TOOLS FOR INTERACTIVE LEARNING

■ **INTERNET**: The Internet Connection for this chapter will direct you to a series of Web sites where you can complete an exercise to evaluate various commercial database management system products. You can also use the Interactive Study Guide to test your knowledge of the topics in this chapter and get instant feedback where you need more practice.

■ **CD-ROM**: If you purchase and use the Multimedia Edition CD-ROM with this chapter, you can complete an interactive exercise asking you to select the appropriate database management system for a series of business problems. You can also find a video clip illustrating the THOR satellite tracking application based on a relational database management system, an audio overview of the major themes of this chapter, and bullet text summarizing the key points of the chapter.

CASE STUDY

Glaxo's Data Warehouse Prescription

How can a pharmaceuticals manufacturer monitor its own sales in an era dominated by HMOs? GlaxoWellcome plc faced this question, and its response was the development and installation of a new data warehouse application. GlaxoWellcome is the world's largest pharmaceutical provider, the result of a merger between Britain's Glaxo and Wellcome companies. Headquartered in London and in Research Triangle, North Carolina, the firm has 54,000 employees in 70 countries with $12.6 billion in global sales in 1995. Its major drugs include: Zantac, used in the treatment of ulcers; Serevant and Flovent, used to treat asthma; and Epivir and Retrovir, used to treat AIDS.

Before the rise of HMOs (health maintenance organizations), the sale of pharmaceuticals was dominated by doctors who prescribed the drugs to be taken by their patients. Therefore, the marketing was directed entirely at them. Keeping track was fairly simple. Pharmaceutical firms only needed to keep track of what the doctors ordered.

Today, the market is dominated by HMOs, hospitals, insurance companies, and other third-party organizations that heavily influence what drugs are prescribed and in what quantity. The drug producers need to know which drugs (both their own and their competitors') are on the approved lists of these third-party groups, both for marketing purposes and for production planning. The drive toward managed care also has increased pressure to keep prices and inventories low.

To keep up with this information, GlaxoWellcome, like other pharmaceutical houses, relies on reports from two audited data services, IMS America in Philadelphia and Source Informatics in Phoenix. These two organizations report on such drug market statistics as the sales volume and wholesale and retail prices of each drug. They report on the shipment of drugs from wholesalers to retailers. They even publish the average dose and the number of tablets per prescription. Each month, GlaxoWellcome buys detailed reports summarizing this information.

In the past GlaxoWellcome analyzed these data manually, combining them with its own internal sales, shipment, and inventory information. The purchased market data came in a book-length, paper-based report. To access the data, company executives, marketers, and market analysts had to search through the report until they found the information they needed. The data then would be combined with GlaxoWellcome's internal data, frequently in a Microsoft Excel spreadsheet. "We couldn't get at the data easily, and it wasn't integrated," recalls Jay Short, the director of information marketing. Oftentimes this task was farmed out to an analyst. Preparation of such a report was a slow process, often taking analysts two or three days to complete. Such a process was also quite expensive. Each month the company created a 50-page product-performance report that would be distributed to about 110 people at an average cost of $100 per copy. Hundreds of other similar reports were also created monthly, making the overall company reporting cost extremely high. Worse, the reports would be outdated the moment they were printed, Short said. Management at GlaxoWellcome used this slow, expensive information system as best as they could to plan marketing; analyze sales, inventory, and prescription data; support its distribution process; and plan its production.

To attempt to give better information to management, the company built an information system called GWis (GlaxoWellcome Information System). The system is a data warehouse application based on MicroStrategy Inc.'s relational on-line analytical processing (ROLAP) technology. It works with a relational DBMS to integrate internal data with data from external sources. Users at their own desktop computers can easily access and combine internal sales, inventory, and prescription data with external market data. Users launch the process by entering various search criteria to create a report tailored to their own needs. They can, for example, quickly determine how a specific drug is selling. Using those criteria, the computer searches the data warehouse. It stores data collected from internal and external systems. Users get back tabular reports within a matter of seconds or a few minutes for the most complex queries. They do not need the involvement of an analyst.

The company paid special attention to the interface. It had to be easy for everyone to use—a difficult requirement given the varying skill levels of users. To meet the needs of their users, they designed a scalable interface that enables each user to select from three levels of complexity. As Julia Pastor, a project consultant from MicroStrategy, explained, "they needed something that was simple enough for novices, but wouldn't bore the power users."

The cost of the whole project was less than $500,000, but its benefits appear to be large. Because the reports are on-line and based on an up-to-date data warehouse, they are no longer out-of-date. GlaxoWellcome can use this information to closely monitor its distribution process and reduce operational costs. Moreover, reports can be produced without the need to rely on special analysts for preparing them. Gone are the $100-per-copy costs for many hundreds of reports. Even the information technology department has reaped major benefits because it was taken out of the daily reporting loop, according to Bill Almand, director of IT marketing. He claims that "all the reporting functions that fell on us as an organization are now pushed out to the business side." Although access to the new system was limited at first, the plan is to make it available to anyone who needs it, including 2500 salespeople in the field in the United States. The company is now constructing an internal network based on Internet technology, and the application will be made available through it when construction is complete.

How has the system worked? It faced its first major test during the summer of 1996 when GlaxoWellcome released studies showing that when Epivir and Retrovir are used in combination, they are effective in treating AIDS. Doctors began writing massive numbers of prescriptions for both drugs immediately. In the past the company would not have had a way to manage inventories when faced with such a deluge and would likely have ended up with shortages. But GWis made a difference. Using the new system, market analysts were able to monitor the sources of the demand and its size. Reports were often generated within minutes. Using these reports to manage production, inventories, and distribution, the company reports that its wholesalers around the world never ran out of either drug.

Sources: Steve Jefferson, "Cut and Paste Your Way to a Powerful Prototype," *Datamation,* October 1997; and Bronwyn Fryer, "Fast Data Relief," *InformationWeek,* December 2, 1996.

Case Study Questions

1. Analyze GlaxoWellcome from the viewpoint of the competitive forces and value chain models.
2. What management, organization, and technology problems did GlaxoWellcome have? What business processes were affected?
3. Did GWis enhance the company's competitive position, and if so, how?
4. Discuss the significance of the choices made in the interface.
5. What management, organization, and technology factors should have been considered when the company was deciding to develop and install the GWis system?
6. To what extent is the selection of a data warehouse application a decision to be made by technicians and to what extent is it an important business decision?

CHAPTER 8

Telecommunications and Networks

chapter outline

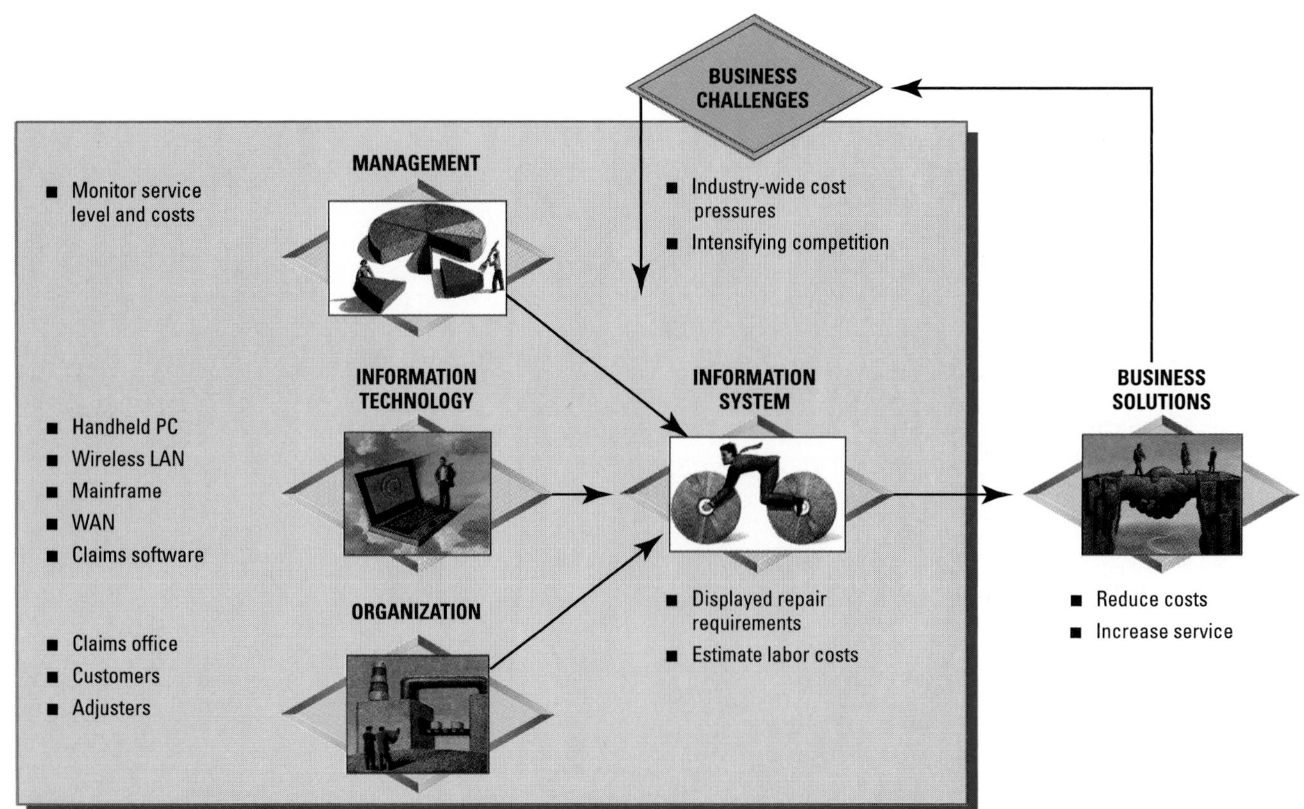

Manitoba Insurance Goes Wireless

Manitoba Public Insurance, which insures all cars in the Canadian province, turned to pen-based PCs with wireless links to improve customer service and efficiency. It created a drive-through claims center where claimants could instantly view their data and estimates for damage via a pen-based tablet PC linked to a wireless network.

Manitoba Public Insurance operates 19 claims offices throughout the province. Each claims office processes about 100 claims per day. In the past, claimants for auto accidents stood alone while the insurance adjuster input data into a PC. Now, as claimants drive into a bay at a claims center, an adjuster will enter the vehicle's license number onto the handheld PC. The data are transmitted via a wireless local-area network (LAN) to a server at the claims center, which communicates with the company's central mainframe. The system downloads information on the driver and the car that has been maintained in the system and transmits it to the adjuster's PC. After the adjuster appraises the damage from the accident, the PC screen displays a list of parts, prices, and the labor required for the repairs.

The software used by the system can spot ways to save money by using overlap logic to deduct labor time on common operations or performing calculations to estimate painting time. It was supplied by Mitchell International Inc., a San Diego reseller, and runs on a Fujitsu Stylistic 1000 tablet. This handheld PC measures 11 by 7.3 by 1.6 inches, has an 8-inch color screen and a 340-megabyte hard drive and weighs only 3.4 pounds.

The system has reduced customer waiting time while improving service. Pen-based computer systems with wireless links are proving so useful that other auto insurers are adopting them as well.

Source: Adapted from Tom Davey, "A Touch of Data," *InformationWeek,* January 26, 1998.

Management Challenges

Manitoba Public Insurance, like many companies all over the world, is finding ways to benefit from telecommunications technology to coordinate its internal activities and to communicate more efficiently with customers, suppliers, and other external organizations. Uses of networks and communications technology for electronic commerce and electronic business are multiplying, but they raise several management challenges:

1. **Managing LANs.** Although local area networks appear to be flexible and inexpensive ways of delivering computing power to new areas of the organization, they must be carefully administered and monitored. LANs are especially vulnerable to network disruption, loss of essential data, access by unauthorized users, and infection from computer viruses (see Chapter 14). Dealing with these problems requires special technical expertise that is not normally available in end-user departments and is in very short supply.
2. **Selecting a telecommunications platform for enterprise networking.** Internet technology can only provide limited connectivity. There are still major application areas where disparate hardware, software, and network components must be coordinated. Networks based on one standard may not be able to be linked to those based on another without additional equipment, expense, and management overhead. Networks that meet today's requirements may lack the connectivity for domestic or global expansion in the future. Managers may have trouble choosing the right telecommunications platform for the firm's information architecture.

learning objectives

After completing this chapter, you will be able to:

1. Describe the basic components of a telecommunications system.
2. Calculate the capacity of telecommunications channels and evaluate transmission media.
3. Compare the various types of telecommunications networks and network services.
4. Describe important connectivity standards for enterprise networking.
5. Identify principal telecommunications applications for supporting electronic commerce and electronic business.
6. Analyze the management problems raised by enterprise networking and suggest solutions.

Most of the information systems we use today require networks and communications technology. Companies, large and small from all over the world, are using networked systems and the Internet to locate suppliers and buyers, to negotiate contracts with them, and to service their trades. Uses of networks are multiplying for research, organizational coordination, and control. Networked systems are fundamental to electronic commerce and electronic business.

Today's computing tasks are so closely tied to networks that some believe "the network is the computer." This chapter describes the components of telecommunications systems, showing how they can be arranged to create various types of networks and network-based applications that can increase the efficiency and competitiveness of an organization. It also describes the management challenges introduced by the growth of vast enterprise-wide networks and suggests solutions so organizations can maximize the benefits of communications technology.

8.1 THE TELECOMMUNICATIONS REVOLUTION

Telecommunications can be defined as the communication of information by electronic means, usually over some distance. Previously, telecommunications meant voice transmission over telephone lines. Today, a great deal of telecommunications transmission is digital data transmission, using computers to transmit data from one location to another. We are currently in the middle of a telecommunications revolution that is spreading communications technology and telecommunications services throughout the globe.

telecommunications The communication of information by electronic means, usually over some distance.

The Marriage of Computers and Communications

Telecommunications used to be a monopoly of either the state or a regulated private firm. In the United States, American Telephone and Telegraph (AT&T) provided virtually all telecommunications services. Telecommunications in Europe and in the rest of the world, traditionally has been administered primarily by a state post, telephone, and telegraph authority (PTT). The United States monopoly ended in 1984, when the Justice Department forced AT&T to give up its monopoly and allow competing firms to sell telecommunications services and equipment. The 1996 Telecommunications Deregulation and Reform Act widened deregulation by freeing telephone companies, broadcasters, and cable companies to enter each other's markets. Other areas of the world are starting to open up their telecommunications services to competition as well.

Thousands of companies have sprung up to provide telecommunications products and services, including local and long-distance telephone services, cellular phones and wireless communication services, data networks, cable TV, communications satellites, and Internet services. Managers will be continually faced with decisions on how to incorporate these services and technologies into their information systems and business processes.

The Information Superhighway

Deregulation and the marriage of computers and communications also has made it possible for the telephone companies to expand from traditional voice communications into new information services, such as providing transmission of news reports, stock reports, television programs, and movies. These efforts are laying the foundation for the **information superhighway,** a vast web of high-speed digital telecommunications networks delivering information, education, and entertainment services to offices and homes. The networks comprising the highway are national or worldwide in scope and accessible by the general public rather than restricted to use by members of a specific organization or set of organizations such as corporations. Some analysts believe the information superhighway will have as profound an impact on economic and social life in the twenty-first century as railroads and interstate highways did in the past.

information superhighway High-speed digital telecommunications networks that are national or worldwide in scope and accessible by the general public rather than restricted to specific organizations.

The information superhighway concept is broad and rich, providing new ways for organizations and individuals to obtain and distribute information that virtually eliminate the barriers of time and place. Uses of this new superhighway for electronic commerce and electronic business are quickly emerging. The most well known and easily the largest implementation of the information superhighway is the Internet.

Another aspect of the information superhighway is the national computing network proposed by the U.S. federal government. The Clinton administration envisions this network linking universities, research centers, libraries, hospitals, and other institutions that need to exchange vast amounts of information while being accessible in homes and schools.

8.2 COMPONENTS AND FUNCTIONS OF A TELECOMMUNICATIONS SYSTEM

telecommunications system A collection of compatible hardware and software arranged to communicate information from one location to another.

A **telecommunications system** is a collection of compatible hardware and software arranged to communicate information from one location to another. Figure 8.1 illustrates the components of a typical telecommunications system. Telecommunications systems can transmit text, graphic images, voice, or video information. This section describes the major components of telecommunications systems. Subsequent sections describe how the components can be arranged into various types of networks.

Telecommunications System Components

The following are essential components of a telecommunications system:

1. Computers to process information
2. Terminals or any input/output devices that send or receive data
3. Communications channels, the links by which data or voice are transmitted between sending and receiving devices in a network. Communications channels use various communications media, such as telephone lines, fiber-optic cables, coaxial cables, and wireless transmission
4. Communications processors, such as modems, multiplexers, controllers, and front-end processors, which provide support functions for data transmission and reception
5. Communications software, which controls input and output activities and manages other functions of the communications network.

Functions of Telecommunications Systems

In order to send and receive information from one place to another, a telecommunications system must perform a number of separate functions. The system transmits infor-

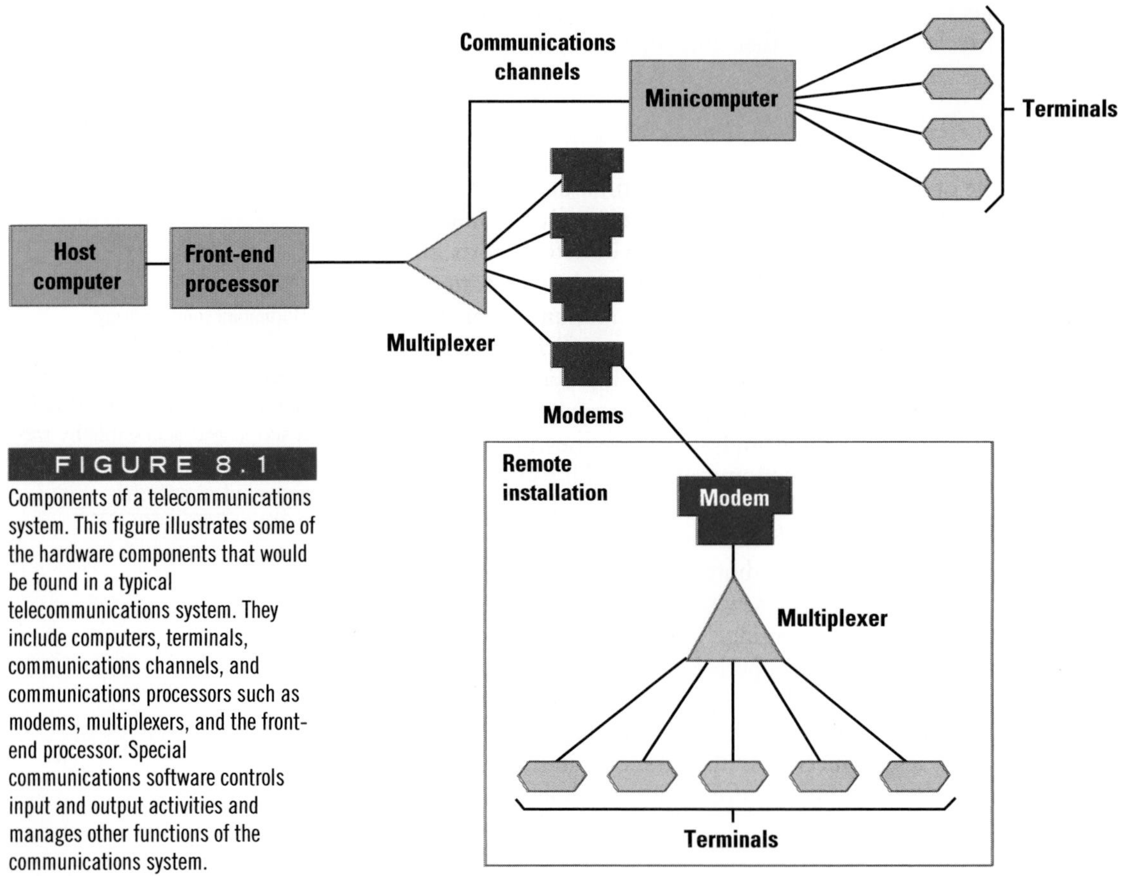

FIGURE 8.1

Components of a telecommunications system. This figure illustrates some of the hardware components that would be found in a typical telecommunications system. They include computers, terminals, communications channels, and communications processors such as modems, multiplexers, and the front-end processor. Special communications software controls input and output activities and manages other functions of the communications system.

mation, establishes the interface between the sender and the receiver, routes messages along the most efficient paths, performs elementary processing of the information to ensure that the right message gets to the right receiver, performs editorial tasks on the data (such as checking for transmission errors and rearranging the format), and converts messages from one speed (say, the speed of a computer) into the speed of a communications line or from one format to another. Finally, the telecommunications system controls the flow of information. Many of these tasks are accomplished by computer.

A telecommunications network typically contains diverse hardware and software components that need to work together to transmit information. Different components in a network can communicate by adhering to a common set of rules that enable them to talk to each other. This set of rules and procedures governing transmission between two points in a network is called a **protocol.** Each device in a network must be able to interpret the other device's protocol. The principal functions of protocols in a telecommunications network are to identify each device in the communication path, to secure the attention of the other device, to verify correct receipt of the transmitted message, to verify that a message requires retransmission because it cannot be correctly interpreted, and to perform recovery when errors occur.

protocol A set of rules and procedures that govern transmission between the components in a network.

Types of Signals: Analog and Digital

Information travels through a telecommunications system in the form of electromagnetic signals. Signals are represented in two ways: analog and digital signals. An **analog signal** is represented by a continuous waveform that passes through a communications medium. Analog signals are used to handle voice communications and to reflect variations in pitch.

A **digital signal** is a discrete, rather than a continuous, waveform. It transmits data coded into two discrete states: 1-bits and 0-bits, which are represented as on–off electrical pulses. Most computers communicate with digital signals, as do many local telephone companies and some larger networks. However, if a traditional telephone network is set up to process analog signals, a digital signal cannot be processed without some alterations. All digital signals must be translated into analog signals before they can be transmitted in an analog system. The device that performs this translation is called a **modem.** (Modem is an abbreviation for MOdulation/DEModulation.) A modem translates the digital signals of a computer into analog form for transmission over ordinary telephone lines, or it translates analog signals back into digital form for reception by a computer (see Figure 8.2).

analog signal A continuous waveform that passes through a communications medium; used for voice communications.

digital signal A discrete waveform that transmits data coded into two discrete states as 1-bits and 0-bits, which are represented as on–off electrical pulses; used for data communications.

modem A device for translating digital signals into analog signals and vice versa.

Communications Channels

Communications **channels** are the means by which data are transmitted from one device in a network to another. A channel can utilize different kinds of telecommunications transmission media: twisted wire, coaxial cable, fiber optics, terrestrial microwave, satellite, and other wireless transmission. Each has advantages and limitations. High-speed transmission media are more expensive in general, but they can handle higher volumes, which reduces the cost per bit. For instance, the cost per bit of data can be lower via satellite link than via leased telephone line if a firm uses the satellite link 100 percent of the time. There is also a wide range of speeds possible for any given medium depending on the software and hardware configuration.

channels The links by which data or voice are transmitted between sending and receiving devices in a network.

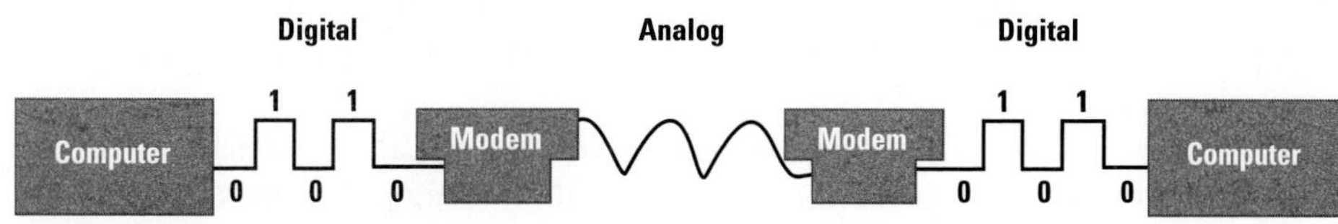

FIGURE 8.2 Functions of the modem. A modem is a device that translates digital signals from a computer into analog form so that they can be transmitted over analog telephone lines. The modem also is used to translate analog signals back into digital form for the receiving computer.

Twisted Wire

twisted wire A transmission medium consisting of pairs of twisted copper wires; used to transmit analog phone conversations but can be used for data transmission.

Twisted wire consists of strands of copper wire twisted in pairs and is the oldest transmission medium. Most of the telephone system in a building relies on twisted wires installed for analog communication, but they can be used for digital communication as well. Although it is low in cost and already is in place, twisted wire is relatively slow for transmitting data, and high-speed transmission causes interference called *crosstalk*. On the other hand, new software and hardware have raised the twisted-wire transmission capacity to make it useful for local- and wide-area computer networks as well as telephone systems.

Coaxial Cable

coaxial cable A transmission medium consisting of thickly insulated copper wire; can transmit large volumes of data quickly.

Coaxial cable, like that used for cable television, consists of thickly insulated copper wire, which can transmit a larger volume of data than twisted wire. It often is used in place of twisted wire for important links in a telecommunications network because it is a faster, more interference-free transmission medium, with speeds of up to 200 megabits per second. However, coaxial cable is thick, is hard to wire in many buildings, and cannot support analog phone conversations. It must be moved when computers and other devices are moved.

Fiber Optics

fiber-optic cable A fast, light, and durable transmission medium consisting of thin strands of clear glass fiber bound into cables. Data are transmitted as light pulses.

Fiber-optic cable consists of thousands of strands of clear glass fiber, each the thickness of a human hair, which are bound into cables. Data are transformed into pulses of light, which are sent through the fiber-optic cable by a laser device at a rate from 500 kilobits to several billion bits per second. Fiber-optic cable is considerably faster, lighter, and more durable than wire media and is well suited to systems requiring transfers of large volumes of data. However, fiber-optic cable is more difficult to work with, more expensive, and harder to install. In most networks fiber-optic cable is used as the high-speed backbone, while twisted wire and coaxial cable are used to connect the backbone to individual devices.

Wireless Transmission

Wireless transmission that sends signals through air or space without any physical tether has emerged as an important alternative to tethered transmission channels such as twisted wire, coaxial cable, and fiber optics. Today, common uses of wireless data transmission include pagers, cellular telephones, microwave transmissions, communication satellites, mobile data networks, personal communications services, personal digital assistants, and even television remote controls.

The wireless transmission medium is the electromagnetic spectrum, illustrated in Figure 8.3. Some types of wireless transmission, such as microwave or infrared, by nature occupy specific spectrum frequency ranges (measured in megahertz). Other types of wireless transmissions are actually functional uses, such as cellular telephones and paging devices, that have been assigned a specific range of frequencies by national regulatory agencies and international agreements. Each frequency range has its own strengths and limitations, and these have helped determine the specific function or data communications niche assigned to it.

microwave A high-volume, long-distance, point-to-point transmission in which high-frequency radio signals are transmitted through the atmosphere from one terrestrial transmission station to another.

satellite The transmission of data using orbiting satellites to serve as relay stations for transmitting microwave signals over very long distances.

Microwave systems, both terrestrial and celestial, transmit high-frequency radio signals through the atmosphere and are widely used for high-volume, long-distance, point-to-point communication. Microwave signals follow a straight line and do not bend with the curvature of the earth; therefore long-distance terrestrial transmission systems require that transmission stations be positioned 25 to 30 miles apart, adding to the expense of microwave.

This problem can be solved by bouncing microwave signals off **satellites,** enabling them to serve as relay stations for microwave signals transmitted from terrestrial stations. Communication satellites are cost effective for transmitting large quantities of data over long distances. Satellites are typically used for communications in large, geographically dispersed organizations that would be difficult to tie together through cabling media or terrestrial microwave. For instance, Amoco uses satellites for real-time

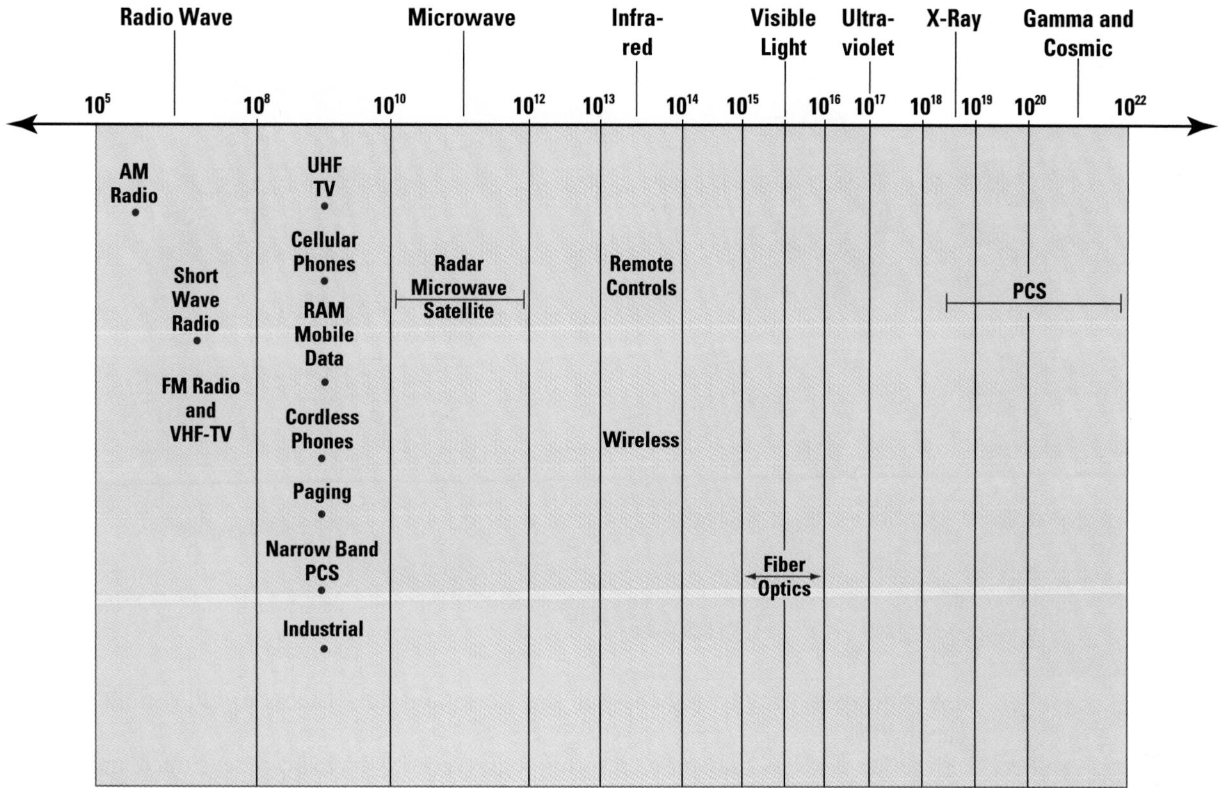

FIGURE 8.3 Frequency ranges for communications media and devices. Each telecommunications transmission medium or device occupies a different frequency range, measured in megahertz, on the electromagnetic spectrum.

data transfer of oil field exploration data gathered from searches of the ocean floor. Exploration ships transfer these data using geosynchronous satellites to central computing centers in the United States for use by researchers in Houston, Tulsa, and suburban Chicago. Figure 8.4 illustrates how this system works.

Conventional communication satellites move in stationary orbits approximately 22,000 miles above the earth. A newer satellite medium, the low-orbit satellite, is beginning to be deployed. These satellites travel much closer to the earth and are able to pick up signals from weak transmitters. They also consume less power and cost less to launch than conventional satellites. With such wireless networks, businesspeople will be

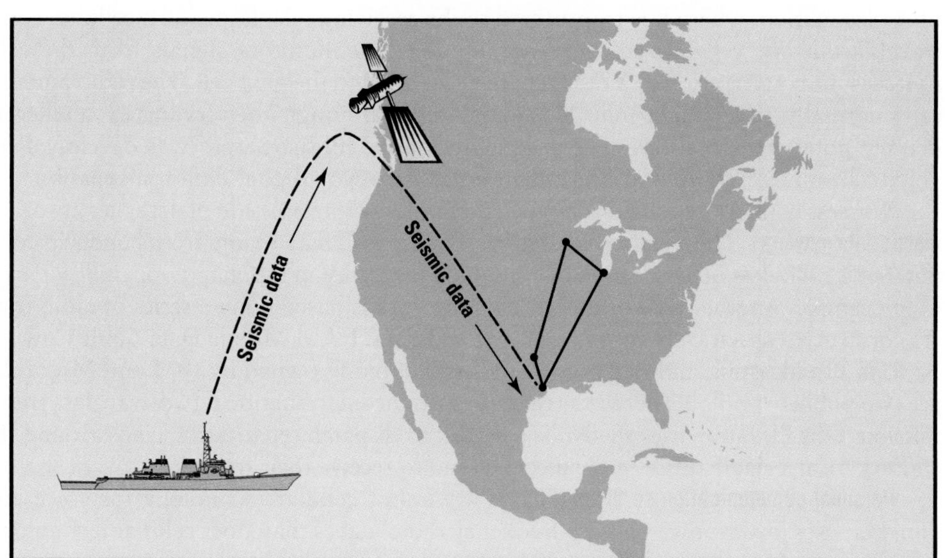

FIGURE 8.4 Amoco's satellite transmission system. Satellites help Amoco transfer seismic data between oil exploration ships and research centers in the United States.

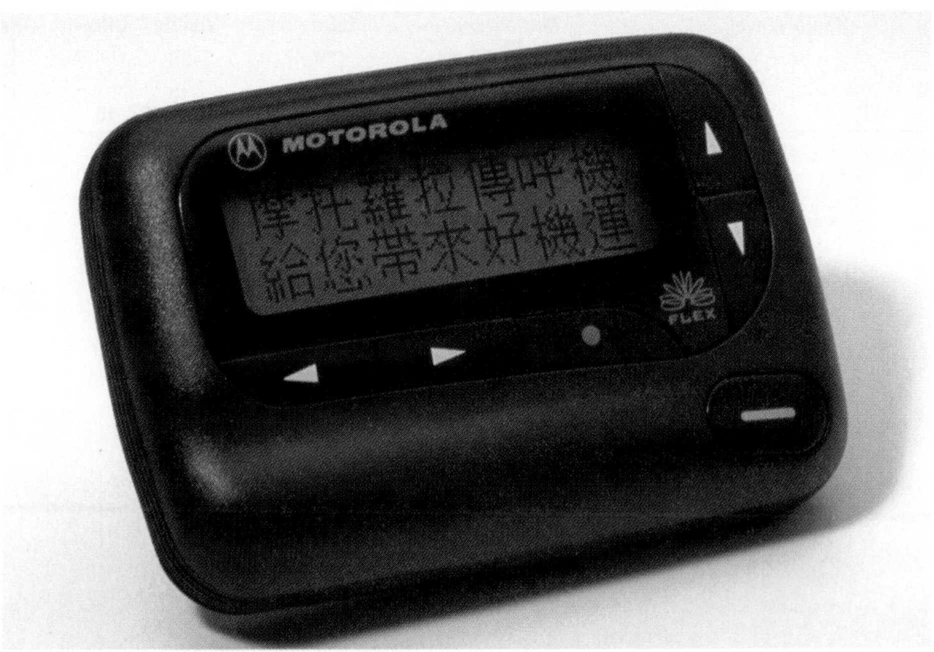

Pagers are increasingly used for wireless transmission of brief messages in China and throughout the globe.

able to travel virtually anywhere in the world and have access to full communication capabilities.

paging system A wireless transmission technology in which the pager beeps when the user receives a message; used to transmit short alphanumeric messages.

Other wireless transmission technologies recently have been developed and are being used in situations requiring mobile computing power. **Paging systems** have been in common use for several decades, originally just beeping when the user received a message and requiring the user to telephone an office to learn about the message. Today, paging devices can send and receive short alphanumeric messages that the user reads on the pager's screen. Paging is useful for communicating with mobile workers such as repair crews; one-way paging also can provide an inexpensive way of communicating with workers in offices. For example, Ethos Corporation in Boulder, Colorado, markets mortgage-processing software that uses a paging system that can deliver daily changes in mortgage rates to thousands of real estate brokers. The data transmitted through the paging network can be downloaded and manipulated, saving brokers approximately one and a half hours of work each week.

cellular telephone A device that transmits voice or data, using radio waves to communicate with radio antennas placed within adjacent geographic areas called cells.

Cellular telephones (sometimes called mobile telephones) work by using radio waves to communicate with radio antennas (towers) placed within adjacent geographic areas called cells. A telephone message is transmitted to the local cell by the cellular telephone and then is handed off from antenna to antenna—cell to cell—until it reaches the cell of its destination, where it is transmitted to the receiving telephone. As a cellular signal travels from one cell into another, a computer that monitors signals from the cells switches the conversation to a radio channel assigned to the next cell. The radio antenna cells normally cover eight-mile hexagonal cells, although their radius is smaller in densely populated localities. The cellular telephone infrastructure was developed for voice transmission, but it is being enhanced for two-way digital data transmission.

mobile data networks Wireless networks that enable two-way transmission of data files cheaply and efficiently.

Wireless networks explicitly designed for two-way transmission of data files are called **mobile data networks.** These radio-based networks transmit data to and from handheld computers. The wireless network used by Manitoba Insurance in the chapter-opening vignette is an example. Another type of mobile data network is based upon a series of radio towers constructed specifically to transmit text and data. RAM Mobile Data (jointly owned by Ram Broadcasting and Bell South) and Ardis (jointly owned by IBM and Motorola) are two publicly available networks that use such media for national two-way data transmission. Otis Elevators uses the Ardis network to dispatch repair technicians around the country from a single office in Connecticut and to receive their reports.

personal communication services (PCS) A wireless cellular technology that uses lower-power, higher-frequency radio waves than does cellular technology and so can be used with smaller-sized telephones.

Personal communication services (PCS) is a wireless cellular technology for voice and data that uses lower-power, higher-frequency radio waves than does cellular technology.

PCS cells are much smaller and more closely spaced. The higher-frequency signals enable PCS devices to be used in many places where cellular telephones are not effective, such as in tunnels and inside office buildings. Moreover, because PCS telephones need less power, they can be much smaller (shirt-pocket size) and less expensive than cellular telephones. They also operate at higher, less-crowded frequencies than cellular telephones (see Figure 8.3), so they will have the bandwidth to offer video and multimedia communication.

Personal digital assistants (PDA) are small, pen-based, handheld computers capable of entirely digital communications transmission. They have built-in wireless telecommunications capabilities as well as work-organization software. A well-known example is the 5.7 ounce PalmPilot by 3COM. It can display and compose e-mail messages (transmission requires additional software and an external modem) and can provide Internet access. The handheld device includes applications such as an electronic scheduler, address book, and expense tracker and can accept data entered with a special stylus through an on-screen writing pad.

personal digital assistants (PDA) Small, pen-based, handheld computers with built-in wireless telecommunications capable of entirely digital communications transmission.

Wireless networks can be more expensive, slower, and more error prone than wired networks. Bandwidth and energy supply in wireless devices require careful management from both hardware and software standpoints (Imielinski and Badrinath, 1994). Security and privacy will be more difficult to maintain because wireless transmission can be easily intercepted (see Chapter 14). Data cannot be transmitted seamlessly between different wireless networks if they use incompatible standards.

Transmission Speed

The total amount of information that can be transmitted through any telecommunications channel is measured in bits per second (BPS). Sometimes this is referred to as the *baud rate.* A **baud** is a binary event representing a signal change from positive to negative or vice versa. The baud rate is not always the same as the bit rate. At higher speeds a single signal change can transmit more than one bit at a time, so the bit rate generally will surpass the baud rate.

baud A change in signal from positive to negative or vice versa that is used as a measure of transmission speed.

One signal change, or cycle, is required to transmit one or several bits per second; therefore the transmission capacity of each type of telecommunications medium is a function of its frequency, the number of cycles per second that can be sent through that medium measured in *hertz* (see Chapter 5). The range of frequencies that can be accommodated on a particular telecommunications channel is called its **bandwidth.** The bandwidth is the difference between the highest and lowest frequencies that can be accommodated on a single channel. The greater the range of frequencies, the greater the bandwidth and the greater the channel's transmission capacity. Table 8.1 compares the transmission speed and relative costs of the major types of transmissions media.

bandwidth The capacity of a communications channel as measured by the difference between the highest and lowest frequencies that can be transmitted by that channel.

TABLE 8.1 Typical Speeds and Costs of Telecommunications Transmission Media

Medium	Speed	Cost
Twisted wire	300 BPS–10 MBPS	Low
Microwave	256 KBPS–100 MBPS	
Satellite	256 KBPS–100 MBPS	
Coaxial cable	56 KBPS–200 MBPS	
Fiber-optic cable	500 KBPS–10 GBPS	High

BPS = bits per second
KBPS = kilobits per second
MBPS = megabits per second
GBPS = gigabits per second

Communications Processors and Software

front-end processor A small computer managing communications for the host computer in a network.

concentrator Telecommunications computer that collects and temporarily stores messages from terminals for batch transmission to the host computer.

controller A specialized computer that supervises communications traffic between the CPU and the peripheral devices in a telecommunications system.

multiplexer A device that enables a single communications channel to carry data transmissions from multiple sources simultaneously.

Communications processors, such as front-end processors, concentrators, controllers, multiplexers, and modems, support data transmission and reception in a telecommunications network. In a large computer system, the **front-end processor** is a small computer dedicated to communications management and is attached to the main, or host, computer. The front-end processor performs communications processing such as error control, formatting, editing, controlling, routing, and speed and signal conversion.

A **concentrator** is a programmable telecommunications computer that collects and temporarily stores messages from terminals until enough messages are ready to be sent economically. The concentrator bursts signals to the host computer.

A **controller** is a specialized computer that supervises communications traffic between the CPU and peripheral devices such as terminals and printers. The controller manages messages from these devices and communicates them to the CPU. It also routes output from the CPU to the appropriate peripheral device.

A **multiplexer** is a device that enables a single communications channel to carry data transmissions from multiple sources simultaneously. The multiplexer divides the communications channel so that it can be shared by multiple transmission devices. The multiplexer may divide a high-speed channel into multiple channels of slower speed or may assign each transmission source a very small slice of time for using the high-speed channel.

Special telecommunications software residing in the host computer, front-end processor, and other processors in the network is required to control and support network activities. This software is responsible for functions such as network control, access control, transmission control, error detection/correction, and security. More detail on security software can be found in Chapter 14.

8.3 COMMUNICATIONS NETWORKS

topology The shape or configuration of a network.

A number of different ways exist to organize telecommunications components to form a network and hence provide multiple ways of classifying networks. Networks can be classified by their shape, or **topology.** Networks also can be classified by their geographic scope and the type of services provided. This section will describe the ways of looking at networks and the management and technical requirements of creating networks linking entire enterprises.

Network Topologies

One way of describing networks is by their shape, or topology. As illustrated in Figures 8.5 to 8.7, the three most common topologies are the star, bus, and ring.

The Star Network

star network A network topology in which all computers and other devices are connected to a central host computer. All communications between network devices must pass through the host computer.

The **star network** (see Figure 8.5) consists of a central host computer connected to a number of smaller computers or terminals. This topology is useful for applications where some processing must be centralized and some can be performed locally. One problem with the star network is its vulnerability. All communication between points in the network must pass through the central computer. Because the central computer is the traffic controller for the other computers and terminals in the network, communication in the network will come to a standstill if the host computer stops functioning.

The Bus Network

bus network Network topology linking a number of computers by a single circuit with all messages broadcast to the entire network.

The **bus network** (see Figure 8.6) links a number of computers by a single circuit made of twisted wire, coaxial cable, or fiber-optic cable. All of the signals are broadcast in both directions to the entire network, with special software to identify which components receive each message (there is no central host computer to control the network). If one of the computers in the network fails, none of the other components in the network are affected. However, the channel in a bus network can handle only one message at a time,

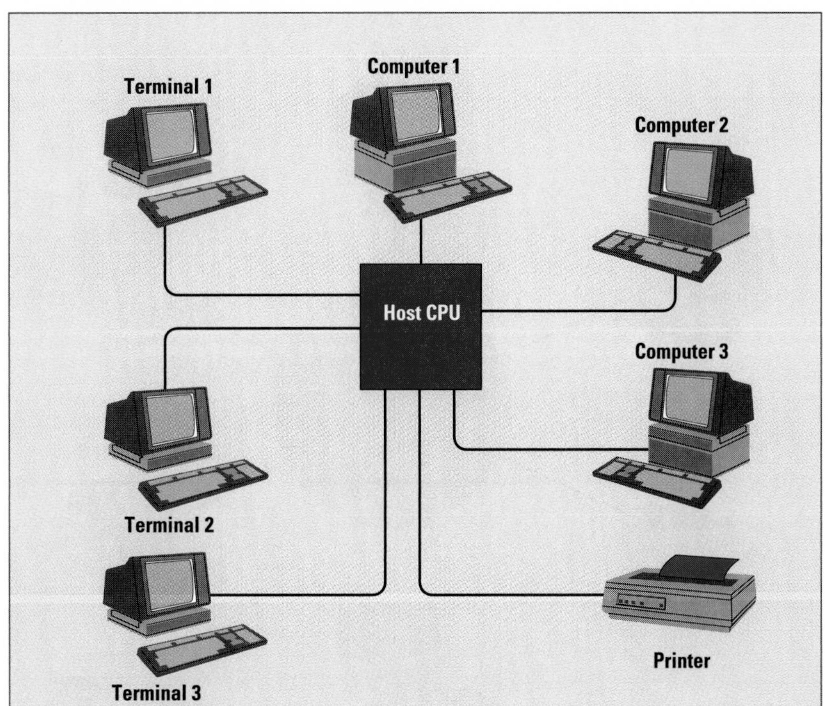

FIGURE 8.5

A star network topology. In a star network configuration a central host computer acts as a traffic controller for all other components of the network. All communication between the smaller computers, terminals, and printers must first pass through the central computer.

so performance can degrade if there is a high volume of network traffic. When two computers transmit messages simultaneously, a "collision" occurs, and the messages must be re-sent.

The Ring Network

Like the bus network, the **ring network** (see Figure 8.7) does not rely on a central host computer and will not necessarily break down if one of the component computers malfunctions. Each computer in the network can communicate directly with any other computer, and each processes its own applications independently. However, in ring topology, the connecting wire, cable, or optical fiber forms a closed loop. Data are passed along the ring from one computer to another and always flow in one direction. Both ring and bus topologies are used in local area networks (LANs), discussed in the next section.

ring network A network topology in which all computers are linked by a closed loop in a manner that passes data in one direction from one computer to another.

Private Branch Exchanges and Local Area Networks (LANs)

Networks may be classified by geographic scope into local networks and wide-area networks. Wide-area networks encompass a relatively wide geographic area, from several miles to thousands of miles, whereas local networks link local resources such as computers and terminals in the same department or building of a firm. Local networks consist of private branch exchanges and local area networks.

FIGURE 8.6

A bus network topology. This topology allows for all messages to be broadcast to the entire network through a single circuit. There is no central host, and messages can travel in both directions along the cable.

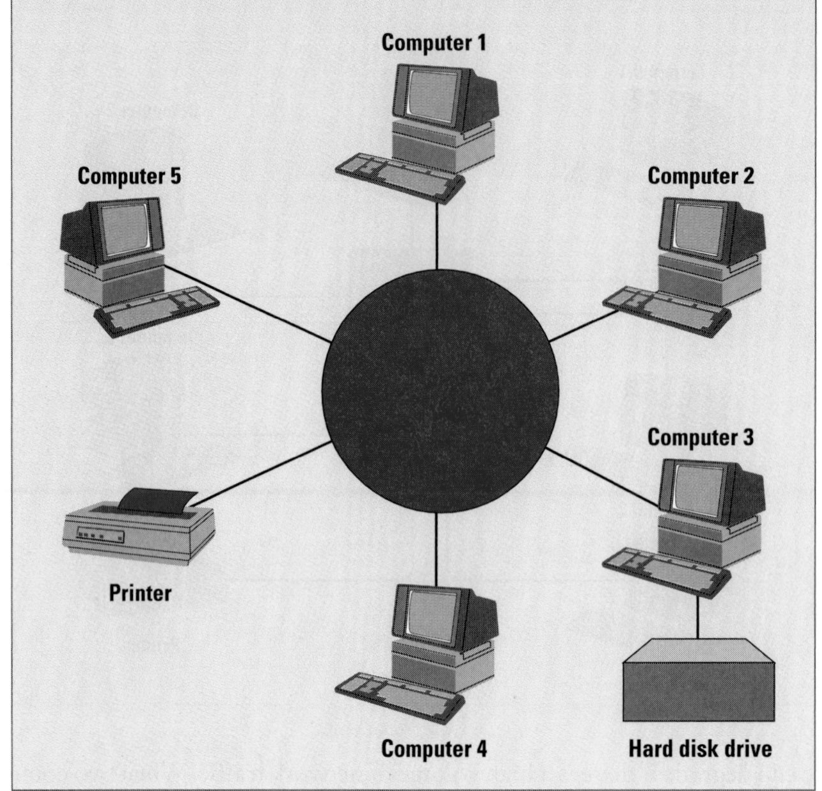

FIGURE 8.7

A ring network topology. In a ring network configuration, messages are transmitted from computer to computer, flowing in a single direction through a closed loop. Each computer operates independently so that if one fails, communication through the network is not interrupted.

Private Branch Exchanges

private branch exchange (PBX) A central switching system that handles a firm's voice and digital communications.

A **private branch exchange (PBX)** is a special-purpose computer designed for handling and switching office telephone calls at a company site. Today's PBXs can carry voice and data to create local networks. PBXs can store, transfer, hold, and redial telephone calls, and they also can be used to switch digital information among computers and office devices. Using a PBX, you can write a letter on a PC in your office, send it to the printer, then dial up the local copying machine and have multiple copies of your letter created.

The advantage of digital PBXs over other local networking options is that they do not require special wiring. A PC connected to a network by telephone can be plugged or unplugged anywhere in a building, utilizing the existing telephone lines. PBXs also are supported by commercial vendors, so the organization does not need special expertise to manage them.

The geographic scope of PBXs is limited, usually to several hundred feet, although the PBX can be connected to other PBX networks or to packet-switched networks (see the discussion of value-added networks in this section) to encompass a larger geographic area. The primary disadvantages of PBXs are that they are limited to telephone lines and they cannot easily handle very large volumes of data.

Local Area Networks

local area network (LAN) A telecommunications network that requires its own dedicated channels and that encompasses a limited distance, usually one building or several buildings in close proximity.

A **local area network (LAN)** encompasses a limited distance, usually one building or several buildings in close proximity. Most LANs connect devices located within a 2000-foot radius, and they have been widely used to link PCs. LANs require their own communications channels.

LANs generally have higher transmission capacities than PBXs, using bus or ring topologies and a high bandwidth. They are recommended for applications transmitting high volumes of data and high transmission speeds, including video transmissions and graphics. LANs often are used to connect PCs in an office to shared printers and other resources or to link computers and computer-controlled machines in factories.

LANs are more expensive to install than PBXs and are more inflexible, requiring new wiring each time a LAN is moved. One way to solve this problem is to create a

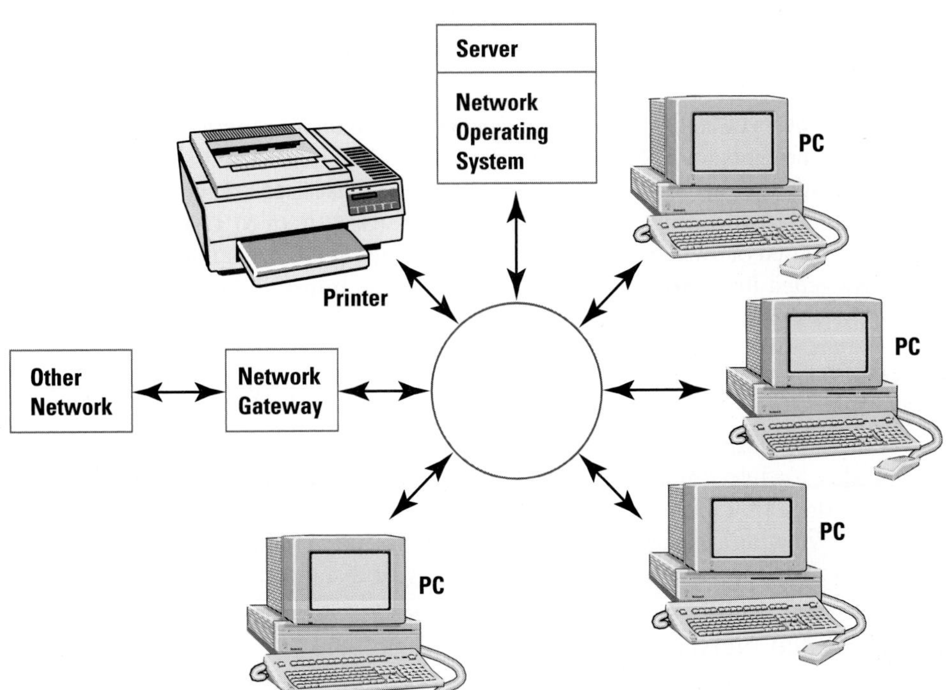

FIGURE 8.8
A local area network (LAN). A typical local area network connects computers and peripheral devices that are located close to each other, often in the same building.

wireless LAN, such as that used by Manitoba Public Insurance described in the chapter-opening vignette. LANs are totally controlled, maintained, and operated by end users. This means that the user must know a great deal about telecommunications applications and networking.

Figure 8.8 illustrates one model of a LAN. The *server* acts as a librarian, storing programs and data files for network users. The server determines who gets access to what and in what sequence. Servers may be powerful PCs with large hard-disk capacity, workstations, minicomputers, or mainframes, although specialized computers are available for this purpose.

The network gateway connects the LAN to public networks, such as the telephone network, or to other corporate networks so that the LAN can exchange information with networks external to it. A **gateway** is generally a communications processor that can connect dissimilar networks by translating from one set of protocols to another. (A bridge connects two networks of the same type. A router is used to route messages through several connected LANs or to a wide area network.)

gateway A communications processor that connects dissimilar networks by providing the translation from one set of protocols to another.

LAN technology consists of cabling (twisted wire, coaxial, or fiber-optic cable) or wireless technology that links individual computer devices, network interface cards (which are special adapters serving as interfaces to the cable), and software to control LAN activities. The LAN network interface card specifies the data transmission rate, the size of message units, the addressing information attached to each message, and network topology (Ethernet utilizes a bus topology, for example).

LAN capabilities also are defined by the **network operating system (NOS).** The network operating system can reside on every computer in the network, or it can reside on a single designated server for all the applications on the network. The NOS routes and manages communications on the network and the sharing of network resources. Novell NetWare, Microsoft Windows NT Server, and IBM's OS/2 Warp Server are popular network operating systems.

network operating system (NOS) Special software that routes and manages communications on the network and the sharing of network resources.

LANs may take the form of client/server networks, in which the server provides data and application programs to "client" computers on the network (see the Chapter 5 discussion of client/server computing) or they may use a peer-to-peer architecture. A **peer-to-peer** network treats all processors equally and is used primarily in small networks. Each computer on the network has direct access to each other's workstations and shared peripheral devices.

peer-to-peer Network architecture that gives equal power to all computers on the network; used primarily in small networks.

Wide Area Networks (WANs), Value-Added Networks (VANs), and Network Services

wide area network (WAN) Telecommunications network that spans a large geographical distance. May consist of a variety of cable, satellite, and microwave technologies.

switched lines Telephone lines that a person can access from a terminal to transmit data to another computer, the call being routed or switched through paths to the designated destination.

dedicated lines Telephone lines that are continuously available for transmission by a lessee. Typically conditioned to transmit data at high speeds for high-volume applications.

value-added network (VAN) Private, multipath, data-only, third-party-managed network that is used by multiple organizations on a subscription basis.

Wide area networks (WANs) span broad geographical distances, ranging from several miles to entire continents. WANs may consist of a combination of switched and dedicated lines, microwave, and satellite communications. **Switched lines** are telephone lines that a person can access from his or her terminal to transmit data to another computer, the call being routed or switched through paths to the designated destination. **Dedicated lines,** or nonswitched lines, are continuously available for transmission, and the lessee typically pays a flat rate for total access to the line. The lines can be leased or purchased from common carriers or private communications media vendors. Most existing WANs are switched. Amoco's network for transmitting seismic data illustrated in Figure 8.4 is a WAN.

Individual business firms may maintain their own wide area networks. The firm is responsible for telecommunications content and management. However, private wide area networks are expensive to maintain, or firms may not have the resources to manage their own wide area networks. In such instances, companies may choose to use commercial network services to communicate over vast distances.

Value-Added Networks (VANs)

Value-added networks are an alternative to firms designing and managing their own networks. **Value-added networks (VANs)** are private, multipath, data-only, third-party-managed networks that can provide economies in the cost of service and in network management because they are used by multiple organizations. The value-added network is set up by a firm that is in charge of managing the network. That firm sells subscriptions to other firms wishing to use the network. Subscribers pay only for the amount of data they transmit plus a subscription fee. The network may utilize twisted-pair lines, satellite links, and other communications channels leased by the value-added carrier.

The term *value added* refers to the extra value added to communications by the telecommunications and computing services these networks provide to clients. Customers do not have to invest in network equipment and software or perform their own error checking, editing, routing, and protocol conversion. Subscribers may achieve savings in line charges and transmission costs because the costs of using the network are shared among many users. The resulting costs may be lower than if the clients had leased their own lines or satellite services.

The leading international value-added networks provide casual or intermittent users international services on a dial-up basis and can provide a private network using dedicated circuits for customers requiring a full-time network. (Maintaining a private network may be most cost-effective for organizations with a high communications volume.)

International VANs have representatives with language skills and knowledge of various countries' telecommunications administrations. The VANs already have leased lines from foreign telecommunications authorities or can arrange access to local networks and equipment abroad. The Window on Organizations on page 244 illustrates some of the business benefits of using a VAN for global operations.

Network Services

packet switching Technology that breaks blocks of text into small, fixed bundles of data and routes them in the most economical way through any available communications channel.

Packet switching is a basic switching technique that can be used to achieve economies and higher speeds in WANs. **Packet switching** breaks up a lengthy block of text into small, fixed bundles of data called packets (see Figure 8.9). (The X.25 packet switching standard uses packets of 128 bytes each.) The packets include information for directing the packet to the right address and for checking transmission errors along with the data. Data are gathered from many users, divided into small packets, and transmitted via various communications channels. Each packet travels independently through the network. Packets of data originating at one source can be routed through different paths

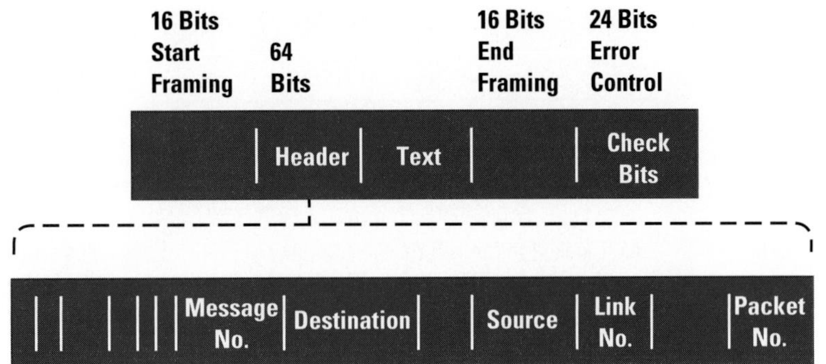

FIGURE 8.9
Packet switched networks and packet communications. Data are grouped into small packets, framed by identifying information, which are transmitted independently via various communication channels to maximize the potential of the paths in a network.

in the network before being reassembled into the original message when they reach their destination.

Frame relay is a shared network service that is faster and less expensive than packet switching and can achieve transmission speeds up to 1.544 megabits per second. Frame relay packages data into frames that are similar to packets, but it does not perform error correction. It works well on reliable lines that do not require frequent retransmissions because of error.

frame relay A shared network service technology that packages data into bundles for transmission but does not use error-correction routines. Cheaper and faster than packet switching.

Most corporations today use separate networks for voice, private-line services, and data, each of which is supported by a different technology. A service called **asynchronous transfer mode (ATM)** may overcome some of these problems because it can seamlessly and dynamically switch voice, data, images, and video between users. ATM also promises to tie LANs and wide-area networks together more easily. (LANs generally are based on lower-speed protocols, whereas WANs operate at higher speeds.) ATM technology parcels information into uniform cells, each with 53 groups of eight bytes, eliminating the need for protocol conversion. It can pass data between computers from different vendors and permits data to be transmitted at any speed the network handles (Vetter, 1995). ATM can transmit up to 2.5 GBPS.

asynchronous transfer mode (ATM) A networking technology that parcels information into 8-byte cells, allowing data to be transmitted between computers from different vendors at any speed.

Integrated Services Digital Network (ISDN) is an international standard for dial-up network access that integrates voice, data, image, and video services in a single link. There are two levels of ISDN service: Basic Rate ISDN and Primary Rate ISDN. Each uses a group of B (bearer) channels to carry voice or data along with a D (delta) channel for signaling and control information. Basic Rate ISDN can transmit data at a rate of 128 kilobits per second on an existing local telephone line. Organizations and individuals requiring high-bandwidth transmission or the ability to provide simultaneous voice or data transmission over one physical line might choose this service. Primary Rate ISDN offers transmission capacities in the megabit range and is designed for large users of telecommunications services.

Integrated Services Digital Network (ISDN) International standard for transmitting voice, video, image, and data to support a wide range of service over the public telephone lines.

digital subscriber line (DSL) A group of technologies providing high capacity transmission over existing copper telephone lines.

Other high-capacity services include digital subscriber line (DSL) technologies, cable modems, and T1 lines. Like ISDN, **digital subscriber line (DSL)** technologies also operate over existing copper telephone lines, to carry voice, data, and video, but they have higher transmission capacities than ISDN. There are several categories of DSL. Asymmetric digital subscriber line (ADSL) supports a transmission rate of 1.5–9 MBPS when receiving data and up to 640 KBPS when sending data. Symmetric digital subscriber line (SDSL) supports the same transmission rate for sending and receiving data of up to 3 MBPS. **Cable modems** are modems designed to operate over cable TV lines. They can provide high-speed access to the Web or corporate intranets of up to 10 MBPS. Most cable networks only let users receive data, so the usefulness of this technology will be limited until the cable companies upgrade their networks for two-way transmission. A **T1 line** is a dedicated telephone connection comprising 24 channels that can support a data transmission rate of 1.544 megabits per second. Each of these 64-kilobit-per-second channels can be configured to carry voice or data traffic. These services often are used for high-capacity Internet connections. Table 8.2 summarizes these network services.

cable modem Modem designed to operate over cable TV lines to provide high-speed access to the Web or corporate intranets.

T1 line A dedicated telephone connection comprising 24 channels that can support a data transmission rate of 1.544 megabits per second. Each channel can be configured to carry voice or data traffic.

WINDOW ON ORGANIZATIONS

Capespan's Global Network Delivers Fresh Produce

The emergence of the supermarket in Europe, combined with the growing economic unity of Europe, has forced Capespan International PLC to examine its organization and turn to a new telecommunications network in order to meet its customers' needs. Although Capespan is headquartered in Farnham Royal, England, it is jointly owned by Outspan International in Pretoria and Unifruco Ltd. in Capetown, two South African fruit-exporting firms. Their major exports include oranges, plums, apples, mangos, and avocados. In 1995, the company recorded $825 million in sales, and they expect that number to increase to $1.5 billion by the year 2000.

Traditionally the company loaded its tens of millions of cartons of produce on its ships in South African ports with the products being tracked only by the number of cartons of each product. When the shipment arrived in a European port, the sales staff sold the cartons to customers and then they were distributed. Most information was gathered manually. There was no time for last-minute decisions such as customer-specific labeling requests or changes in delivery times.

As it looked to the future, the company realized it had to change its whole method of sales and distribution. The supermarket environment places an emphasis upon quality, so products must arrive on time and in good condition. Name branding became important. "When you walk into a supermarket in the UK, every apple has a label on it," points out Gwynne Foster, Capespan's manager of information services. No longer can the supplier simply distribute and ship massive numbers of cartons of products. The products now need specific brands, and specific cartons must go to designated customers—Unifruco's Granny Smith apples and Outspan's navel oranges must get to specific stores labeled in a precise way.

Capespan developed a new information system to help it thrive in the new market. The new Capespan system maintains details on each carton, including such details as the grower, the packaging, the chemical treatment of the product, and inspection information. The data are fed into the system at the South African shipping dock where each carton is scanned using a hand-held scanner. The product is tracked as it travels to Europe and eventually to customers. Also, a manifest is created listing what is on each vessel. The manifest data are transmitted to Europe as soon as they become available, using Capespan's new network. The network operates through IBM Global Network and ties the organization together, linking more than half of its 200 trading partners.

Each sales office and receiving port receives the manifest, enabling the sales office to know what is available for sale and the port to arrange for the off-loading of the goods. The sales office sells the products to customers, and both the seller and the customers can plan for customer-specific labeling. Delivery to customers is timed, and the customers know what to expect.

The new system has given the company the flexibility to respond to changes in the market as Europe continues to unify. No one knows what market changes will occur, although a new system of buying based upon pan-European fruit buyers already has emerged. Before the installation of this system, Capespan had little flexibility and little capacity to respond rapidly to pan-European buyers or to any other coming changes. Now, the company believes, although its technology certainly will have to change as the market evolves, it has the foundation to enable Capespan to make those changes.

To Think About: ***How did market changes force Capespan to make changes in its business processes? What management, organization, and technology issues did Capespan have to face in order to make the required changes?***

Source: Adapted from Jeannette Borzo, "African-European Network Means Peachy Prospects for Capespan," *Computerworld Global Innovators,* March 10, 1997.

Enterprise Networking and Standards

enterprise networking An arrangement of the organization's hardware, software, telecommunications, and data resources to put more computing power on the desktop and create a companywide network linking many smaller networks.

Organizations can link their LANs and WANs to create networks that link entire enterprises. In **enterprise networking,** the organization's hardware, software, telecommunications, and data resources are arranged to put more computing power on the desktop and to create a companywide network linking many smaller networks. These enterprise networks also may be linked to the networks of other organizations outside the firm or to the Internet.

Figure 8.10 illustrates the implementation of enterprise networking at the National Basketball Association (NBA). As this diagram shows, NBA employees may work at its main offices in Manhattan and Secaucus, New Jersey, or in regional and international offices. The computers in the main offices are linked in local area networks (LANs). An enterprise-wide network links all of these sites, NBA teams, and sports arenas into one large network. Operating on these networks are a range of hardware, including IBM server computers, desktop Pentium Pro PCs running Windows NT, a Digital Equip-

TABLE 8.2 Network Services

Service	Description	Bandwidth
X.25	Packet switching standard that parcels data into packets of 128 bytes	Up to 1.544 MBPS
Frame Relay	Packages data into frames for high-speed transmission over reliable lines but does not use error-correction routines	Up to 1.544 MBPS
ATM (Asynchronous Transfer Mode)	Parcels data into uniform cells to allow high-capacity transmission of voice, data, images, and video between different types of computers	25MBPS–2.5 GBPS
ISDN	Digital dial-up network access standard that can integrate voice, data, and video services	Basic Rate ISDN: 128 KBPS Primary Rate ISDN: 1.5 MBPS
DSL (Digital Subscriber Line)	Series of technologies for high-capacity transmission over copper wires	ADSL—up to 9MBPS for receiving and up to 640 KBPS for sending data SDSL—up to 3 MBPS for both sending and receiving
T1	Dedicated telephone connection with 24 channels for high capacity transmission	1.544 MBPS
Cable Modem	Service for high-speed transmission of data over cable TV lines that is primarily one way	Up to 10 MBPS

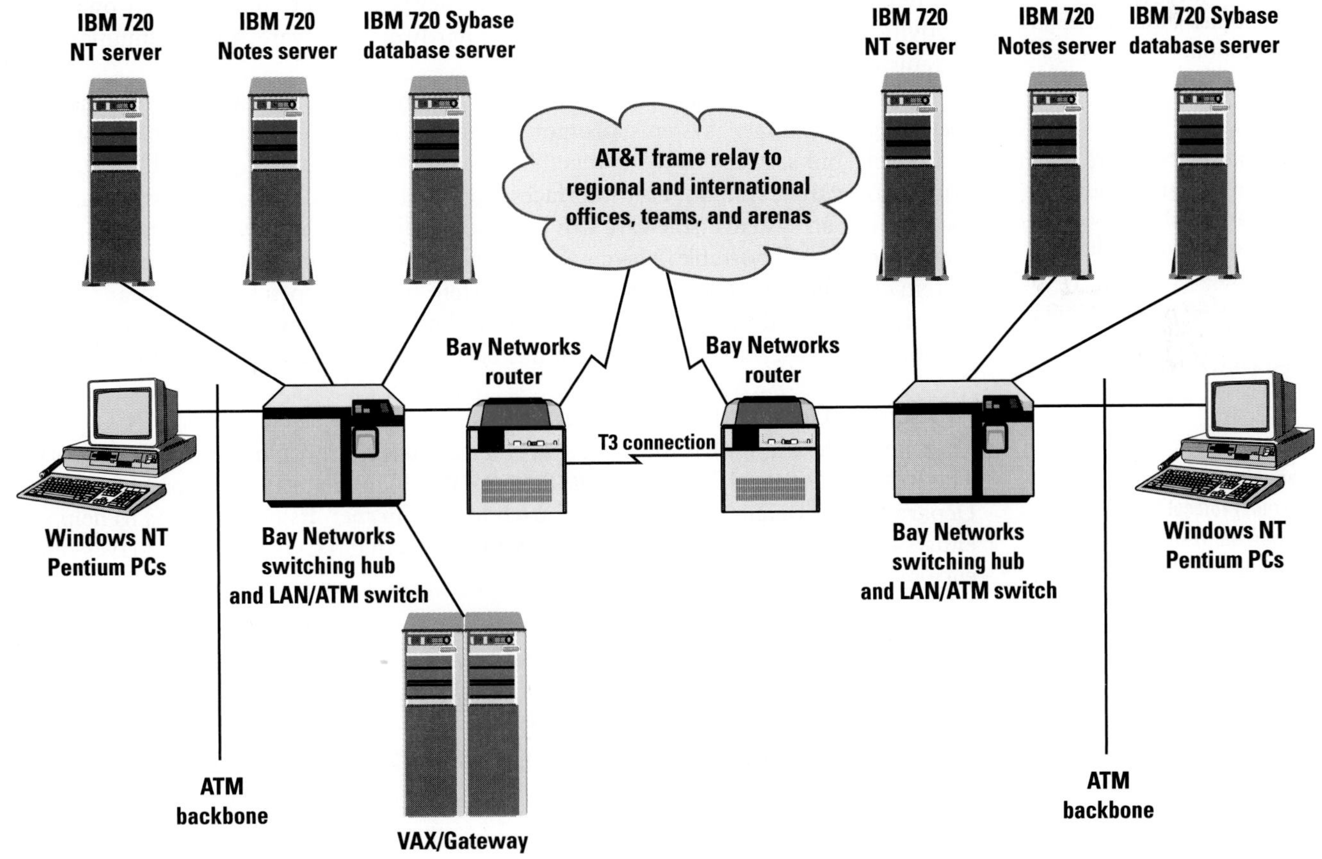

FIGURE 8.10 Enterprise networking at the National Basketball Association (NBA). The NBA's enterprise-wide network links desktop workstations and servers at its main, regional, and international offices, providing information to NBA employees, teams, and arenas. *Source: From "The NBA's Newest Star" by Bruce Caldwell from* InformationWeek, *June 24, 1996. Copyright © 1996 by CMP Media, Inc., 600 Community Drive, Manhasset, NY 11030. Reprinted from* InformationWeek *with permission.*

ment Corporation (DEC) VAX computer used as a gateway, and various routers and switching hubs. These networked systems run applications such as a player-contract management system and an information kiosk for fans with full-motion video based on Lotus Notes groupware.

In this enterprise architecture, the NBA uses a mixture of computer hardware supplied by different vendors. Large, complex databases that need central storage are found on mainframes, minis, or specialized servers, whereas smaller databases and parts of large databases are loaded on PCs and workstations. Client/server computing often is used to distribute more processing power to the desktop.

The system is a network. In fact, for all but the smallest organizations the system is composed of multiple networks. A high-capacity backbone network connects many local area networks and devices. The backbone may be connected to external networks like the Internet. The linking of separate networks, each of which retains its own identity, into an interconnected network, is called **internetworking.**

internetworking The linking of separate networks, each of which retains its own identity, into an interconnected network.

Connectivity and Standards

Enterprise networking is most likely to increase productivity and competitive advantage when digitized information can move seamlessly through the organization's web of electronic networks, connecting different kinds of machines, people, sensors, databases, functional divisions, departments, and work groups. This ability of computers and computer-based devices to communicate with one another and "share" information in a meaningful way without human intervention is called **connectivity.** Internet technology and Java software provide some of this connectivity, but the Internet cannot be used as a foundation for all of the organization's information systems. Most organizations still will require their own proprietary networks. They will need to develop their own connectivity solutions to make different kinds of hardware, software, and communications systems work together.

connectivity A measure of how well computers and computer-based devices communicate and share information with one another without human intervention.

Achieving connectivity requires standards for networking, operating systems, and user interfaces. Open systems promote connectivity because they enable disparate equipment and services to work together. **Open systems** are built upon public, nonproprietary operating systems, user interfaces, application standards, and networking protocols. In open systems, software can operate on different hardware platforms and in that sense can be "portable." Java software, described in Chapter 6, can create an open system environment. The UNIX operating system supports open systems because it can operate on many different kinds of computer hardware. However, there are different versions of UNIX, and no one version has been accepted as an open systems standard.

open systems Software systems that can operate on different hardware platforms because they are built on public nonproprietary operating systems, user interfaces, application standards, and networking protocols.

Models of Connectivity for Networks

There are different models for achieving connectivity in telecommunications networks. The **Transmission Control Protocol/Internet Protocol (TCP/IP)** model was developed by the U.S. Department of Defense in 1972 and is used in the Internet. Its purpose was to help scientists link disparate computers. Figure 8.11 shows that TCP/IP has a five-layer reference model.

Transmission Control Protocol/Internet Protocol (TCP/IP) U.S. Department of Defense reference model for linking different types of computers and networks; used in the Internet.

1. *Application:* Provides end-user functionality by translating the messages into the user/host software for screen presentation.
2. *Transmission Control Protocol (TCP):* Performs transport, breaking application data from the end user down into TCP packets called datagrams. Each packet consists of a header with the address of the sending host computer, information for putting the data back together, and information for making sure the packets do not become corrupted.
3. *Internet Protocol (IP):* The Internet Protocol receives datagrams from TCP and breaks the packets down further. An IP packet contains a header with address information and carries TCP information and data. IP routes the individual datagrams from the sender to the recipient. IP packets are not very reliable, but the TCP level can keep resending them until the correct IP packets get through.

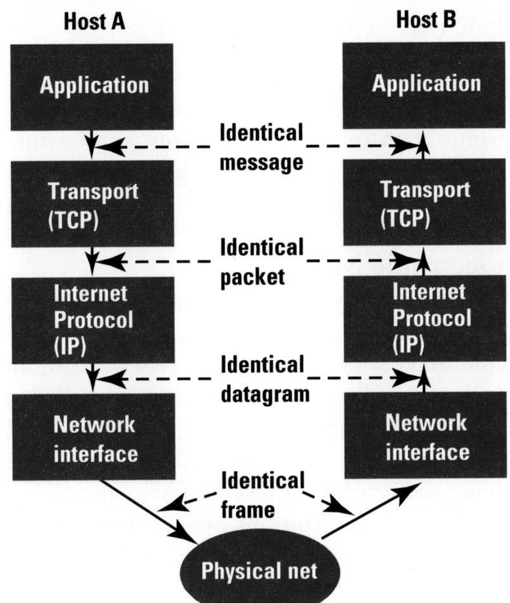

FIGURE 8.11

The Transmission Control Protocol/Internet Protocol (TCP/IP) reference model. This figure illustrates the five layers of the TCP/IP reference model for communications.

4. *Network interface:* Handles addressing issues, usually in the operating system, as well as the interface between the initiating computer and the network.
5. *Physical net:* Defines basic electrical-transmission characteristic for sending the actual signal along communications networks.

Two computers using TCP/IP would be able to communicate, even if they were based on different hardware and software platforms. Data sent from one computer to the other would pass downward through all five layers, starting with the application layer of the sending computer and passing through the physical net. After the data reached the recipient host computer, they would travel up the layers. The TCP level would assemble the data into a format the receiving host computer could use. If the receiving computer found a damaged packet, it would ask the sending computer to retransmit it. This process would be reversed when the receiving computer responded.

The **Open Systems Interconnect (OSI)** model is an alternative model developed by the International Standards Organization for linking different types of computers and networks. It was designed to support global networks with large volumes of transaction processing. Like TCP/IP, OSI enables a computer connected to a network to communicate with any other computer on the same network or a different network, regardless of the manufacturer, by establishing communication rules that permit the exchange of information between dissimilar systems. OSI divides the telecommunications process into seven layers.

Open Systems Interconnect (OSI) International reference model for linking different types of computers and networks.

Other connectivity-promoting standards have been developed for graphical user interfaces, electronic mail, packet-switching, and electronic data interchange (see the next section). Any manager wishing to achieve some measure of connectivity in his or her organization should try to use these standards when designing networks, purchasing hardware and software, or developing information system applications.

8.4 ELECTRONIC COMMERCE AND ELECTRONIC BUSINESS TECHNOLOGIES

Baxter International, described in Chapter 2, realized the strategic significance of telecommunications. The company placed its own computer terminals in hospital supply rooms. Customers could dial up a local VAN and send their orders directly to the company. Other companies also are achieving strategic benefits by developing electronic commerce and electronic business applications based on telecommunications technology.

Facilitating Applications

Electronic mail (e-mail), voice mail, facsimile machines (fax), digital information services, teleconferencing, dataconferencing, videoconferencing, groupware, and electronic data interchange are key applications for electronic commerce and electronic business because they provide network-based capabilities for communication, coordination, and speeding the flow of purchase and sale transactions.

Electronic Mail

We already have described the capabilities of electronic mail, or e-mail, in Chapter 6. E-mail eliminates telephone tag and costly long-distance telephone charges, expediting communication between different parts of an organization. Nestlé SA, the Swiss-based multinational food corporation, installed an electronic-mail system to connect its 60,000 employees in 80 countries. Nestlé's European units can use the electronic-mail system to share information about production schedules and inventory levels to ship excess products from one country to another.

Many organizations operate their own internal electronic-mail systems, but communications companies such as GTE, MCI, and AT&T offer these services, as do commercial on-line information services such as America Online and Prodigy and public networks on the Internet (see Chapter 9).

The Window on Management looks at the privacy of e-mail messages from a different perspective, examining whether monitoring employees using e-mail, the Internet, and other network facilities is ethical.

Voice Mail

voice mail A system for digitizing a spoken message and transmitting it over a network.

A **voice mail** system digitizes the spoken message of the sender, transmits it over a network, and stores the message on disk for later retrieval. When the recipient is ready to listen, the messages are reconverted to audio form. Various store-and-forward capabilities notify recipients that messages are waiting. Recipients have the option of saving these messages for future use, deleting them, or routing them to other parties.

Facsimile Machines (fax)

facsimile (fax) A machine that digitizes and transmits documents with both text and graphics over telephone lines.

Facsimile (fax) machines can transmit documents containing both text and graphics over ordinary telephone lines. A sending fax machine scans and digitizes the document image. The digitized document is transmitted over a network and reproduced in hard copy form by a receiving fax machine. The process results in a duplicate, or facsimile, of the original.

Digital Information Services

Powerful and far-reaching digital electronic services enable networked PC and workstation users to obtain information from outside the firm instantly without leaving their desks. Stock prices, periodicals, competitor data, industrial supplies catalogs, legal research, news articles, reference works, and weather forecasts, are some of the information that can be accessed on-line. Many of these services provide capabilities for electronic mail, electronic bulletin boards, on-line discussion groups, shopping, and travel reservations as well as Internet access. Table 8.3 describes the leading commercial digital information services. The following chapter describes how organizations can access even more information resources by using the Internet.

Teleconferencing, Dataconferencing, and Videoconferencing

teleconferencing The ability to confer with a group of people simultaneously using the telephone or electronic-mail group communication software.

dataconferencing Teleconferencing in which two or more users are able to edit and modify data files simultaneously.

People can meet electronically, even though they are hundreds or thousands of miles apart, by using teleconferencing, dataconferencing, or videoconferencing. **Teleconferencing** allows a group of people to confer simultaneously via telephone or via electronic-mail group communication software. Teleconferencing that includes the ability of two or more people at distant locations to work on the same document or data simultaneously is called **dataconferencing.** With dataconferencing, users at distant locations are able to edit and modify data (text, such as word processing documents; numeric, such as spreadsheets;

WINDOW ON MANAGEMENT

Monitoring Employees on Networks: Unethical or Good Business?

Should managers monitor employees using networks? Is it unethical? Or is it just good business? Although many view monitoring employee e-mail as unethical and even an illegal invasion of privacy, many companies consider it to be legitimate. They claim they need to know that the business facilities they own are being used to further their business goals. Some also argue that they need to be able to search electronic-mail messages for evidence of illegal activities, racial discrimination, or sexual harassment. Others argue that the company needs access to business information stored in e-mail files the same as if it were stored in paper file cabinets.

E-mail privacy within a company is not covered by U.S. federal law. The Electronic Communications Privacy Act of 1986 only prohibits interception or disclosure of e-mail messages by parties outside the company where the messages were sent without a proper warrant. Lawsuits so far have failed to limit the right of companies to monitor e-mail. For example, when Alana Shoars, a former e-mail administrator at Epson America Inc., discovered that her supervisor was copying and reading employees' e-mail, she sued in the Los Angeles, California, courts, alleging invasion of privacy. Later she filed a class action suit in the name of 700 Epson employees and 1800 outsiders also charging privacy invasion. Both cases were dismissed on the grounds that e-mail does not fall within the state's wiretapping laws.

Despite the lack of legal restrictions, many observers see electronic-mail privacy as serious. Michael Godwin, legal adviser for the Electronic Frontier Foundation, recommends that employers who intend to monitor e-mail establish a stated policy to that effect. Some companies have such policies, including Nordstrom, Eastman Kodak, and Federal Express, all of which claim the right to intercept and read employee e-mail. General Motors and Hallmark Cards have policies that grant employees greater privacy.

The Internet presents different issues—the use of company facilities not only for nonbusiness purposes but also for illegal uses such as retrieving pornography. Management can use new Web monitoring tools to monitor what employees are doing on the Internet. This software can track what Web sites users visit, the files they download, and even the categories of information they search. Some of these tools can block access to Web sites that employers consider inappropriate. Companies may use these tools to ensure that their employees are not wasting company time surfing the Web or that valuable network resources are not being wasted on nonbusiness activities.

Some employers take a tough stance. Sixty-four employees at Sandia Labs in Albuquerque, New Mexico, were disciplined for reading pornography at work on company time, or on their own time. Many were suspended without pay. Other firms, including Eli Lilly, publish a clear policy and then leave it to individual managers to enforce it if they choose. Many, however, take a middle-of-the-road position. At Chicago's WMS Industries, the IS department logs the amount of time each employee spends on the Net and sends the reports to managers to use as they wish.

To Think About: ***Do you believe management should have the right to monitor employee e-mail and Internet usage? Why or why not? Describe the problems such monitoring might present to management.***

Sources: Lawrence Magid, "Little Brother Is Watching," *Information Week,* February 16, 1998; Sharon Machlis, "Gotcha! Monitoring Tools Check Web Surfing at Work," *Computerworld,* April 7, 1997; Alice LaPlante, "Firms Spell Out Appropriate Use of Internet for Employees," *Computerworld,* February 5, 1996; "Does E-Mail Mean Everyone's Mail?" *Information Week,* January 3, 1994.

TABLE 8.3 Commerical Digital Information Services

Provider	Type of Service
America Online	General interest/business information
Prodigy	General interest/business information
Microsoft Network	General interest/business information
Dow Jones News Retrieval	Business/financial information
Dialog	Business/scientific/technical information
Lexis	Legal research
Nexis	News/business information

America Online gives subscribers access to extensive information, including news reports, travel, weather, education, financial services, and information from the World Wide Web. Companies and individuals can use such digital information services to obtain information instantly from their desktops.

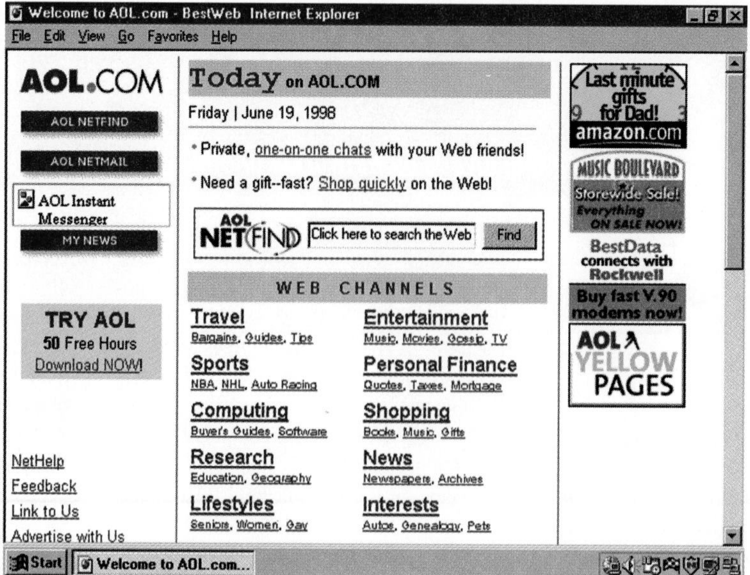

videoconferencing Teleconferencing with the capability of participants to see each other over video screens.

and graphic) files. Teleconferencing that has the capability to let participants see each other over video screens is termed *video teleconferencing,* or **videoconferencing.**

These forms of electronic conferencing are growing in popularity because they save travel time and cost. Legal firms might use videoconferencing to take depositions and to convene meetings between lawyers in different branch offices. The cosmetics manufacturer Estée Lauder is using desktop videoconferencing for remote collaboration. Staff in Manhattan and Melville, Long Island, view products under design as well as other meeting participants. Hospitals, universities, and corporate researchers are using videoconferencing to fill in personnel expertise gaps (Brandel, 1995; Frye, 1995). Electronic conferencing is useful for supporting telecommuting, enabling home workers to meet with or collaborate with their counterparts working in the office or elsewhere.

Videoconferencing usually has required special video conference rooms and videocameras, microphones, television monitors, and a computer equipped with a codec device that converts video images and analog sound waves into digital signals and compresses them for transfer over communications channels. Another codec on the receiving end reconverts the digital signals back into analog for display on the receiving monitor. PC-based, desktop videoconferencing systems in which users can see each other and simultaneously work on the same document are reducing videoconferencing costs so that more organizations can benefit from this technology.

Desktop videoconferencing systems typically provide a local window, in which you can see yourself, and a remote window to display the individual with whom you are communicating. Most desktop systems provide audio capabilities for two-way, real-

With PC desktop videoconferencing systems, users can see each other and simultaneously work on the same document. Organizations are using videoconferencing technology to improve coordination and to save travel time and costs.

Liz Claiborne uses e-mail and EDI to coordinate activities between U.S. corporate headquarters and factories in the Far East. By helping companies coordinate their supply chains, telecommunications applications can provide a competitive advantage.

time conversations and a whiteboard. The whiteboard is a shared drawing program that lets multiple users collaborate on projects by modifying images and text on-line. Software is available for desktop videoconferencing over the Internet, as described in the Window on Technology.

Groupware

Chapter 6 described the capabilities of groupware for supporting collaborative work. Individuals, teams, and work groups at different locations in the organization can use groupware to participate in discussion forums and work on shared documents and projects. More detail on the use of groupware for collaborative work can be found in Chapter 12.

Electronic Data Interchange and Electronic Commerce

Electronic data interchange (EDI) is a key technology for electronic commerce because it allows the computer-to-computer exchange between two organizations of standard transaction documents such as invoices, bills of lading, or purchase orders. EDI lowers transaction costs because transactions can be automatically transmitted from one information system to another through a telecommunications network, eliminating the printing and handling of paper at one end and the inputting of data at the other. EDI also may provide strategic benefits by helping a firm lock in customers, making it easier for customers or distributors to order from them rather than from competitors. Chapter 2 also shows how EDI can curb inventory costs by minimizing the amount of time components are in inventory.

electronic data interchange (EDI) The direct computer-to-computer exchange between two organizations of standard business transaction documents.

EDI differs from electronic mail in that it transmits an actual structured transaction (with distinct fields such as the transaction date, transaction amount, sender's name, and recipient's name) as opposed to an unstructured text message such as a letter. Figure 8.12 illustrates how EDI works.

FIGURE 8.12

Electronic data interchange (EDI). Companies can use EDI to automate electronic commerce transactions. Purchase orders and payments can be transmitted directly from the customer's computer to the seller's computer. The seller can transmit shipping notices, price changes, and invoices electronically back to the customer.

WINDOW ON TECHNOLOGY

Videoconferencing on the Internet

The Internet has opened many new ways for people to communicate, and videoconferencing is one of the most exciting. For the cost of a local telephone call, you can have a conference or work collaboratively on a whiteboard with anyone in the world. Among the leading Internet videoconferencing products are CU-SeeMe and Microsoft NetMeeting. (CU-SeeMe was developed by Cornell University. A pared-down version is available as free shareware, but many businesses prefer Enhanced CU-SeeMe, a full-function version marketed by White Pine Software.)

These products are inexpensive to purchase and require little extra equipment. Those with a Windows PC system who need to be an active part of a meeting would need a videocamera, a video capture board (if not bundled with their camera), a sound card, and a microphone (if one is not bundled with their computer system). These tools are well suited for "talking head" applications, in which people are sitting at their desks and not giving elaborate presentations.

The World Bank, the Washington D.C.-based development institution, has offices or partner organizations in 180 countries and thus an urgent need for global communications. It operates with tight budgets and limited travel resources. The World Bank uses the White Pines commercial version of CU-SeeMe to conduct small meetings and "virtual seminars" among employees in the United States, Egypt, Russia, and other countries. Although the video images that CU-SeeMe produces do not measure more than four inches square, and the feed does not always appear very smooth, the low cost allows the World Bank to let more employees work collaboratively from faraway locations. Users can brainstorm on a common electronic whiteboard. For large group meetings and training sessions, the World Bank uses Picture Tel's videoconferencing system, which is a high-end desktop product.

To Think About: ***What business processes can be streamlined through videoconferencing? What management, organization, and technology factors would you consider to decide whether to use Internet-based videoconferencing?***

Sources: Chris Devoney, "Go for the Bandwidth," *Computerworld,* April 13, 1998; Jose Alvear and Ronen Yaari, "You've Got a Video Call on Your Desktop," *NetGuide,* February 1997; and Lynda Radosevich, "Sizzle and Steak," *WebMaster,* November 1996.

Organizations can most fully benefit from EDI when they integrate the data supplied by EDI with applications such as accounts payable, inventory control, shipping, and production planning (Premkumar, Ramamurthy, and Nilakanta, 1994), and when they have carefully planned for the organizational changes surrounding new business processes. Management support and training in the new technology are essential (Raymond and Bergeron, 1996). Companies also must standardize the form of the transactions they use with other firms and comply with legal requirements for verifying that the transactions are authentic. Many organizations prefer to use private networks for EDI transactions, but use of the Internet is growing for this purpose (see Chapter 9).

8.5 MANAGEMENT ISSUES AND DECISIONS

Telecommunications technology and networking are so deeply embedded in the core processes of businesses today that they require careful management and planning.

The Challenge of Managing Enterprise Networking

Implementing enterprise networking has created problems as well as opportunities for organizations. Managers need to address these problems as they design and build networks for their organizations.

Problems Posed by Enterprise Networking

The rapid, often unplanned, development of networks and distributed computing has created some of the problems. We already have described the connectivity problems created by incompatible network components and standards. Four additional problems stand out: loss of management control over information systems, the need for organi-

TABLE 8.4 Problems Posed by Enterprise Networking
Connectivity problems
Loss of management control over systems
Organizational change requirements
Hidden costs of client/server computing
Network reliability and security

zational change, the hidden costs of client/server computing, and the difficulty of ensuring network reliability and security (see Table 8.4).

Loss of Management Control

Managing information systems technology and corporate data are proving much more difficult in a distributed environment because of the lack of a single central point where needed management can occur. Client/server computing and networks have empowered end users to become independent sources of computing power capable of collecting, storing, and disseminating data and software. Data and software no longer are confined to the mainframe and under the management of the traditional information systems department.

Under enterprise networking, it becomes increasingly difficult to determine where data are located and to ensure that the same piece of information, such as a product number, is used consistently throughout the organization (see Chapter 7). User-developed applications may combine incompatible pieces of hardware or software. However, observers worry that excess centralization and management of information resources will stifle the independence and creativity of end users and reduce their ability to define their own information needs. The dilemma posed by enterprise networking is one of central-management control versus end-user creativity and productivity.

Organizational Change Requirements

Decentralization also results in changes in corporate culture and organizational structure. Enterprise-wide computing is an opportunity to reengineer the organization into a more effective unit, but it will only create problems or chaos if the underlying organizational issues are not fully addressed (Duchessi and Chengalur-Smith, 1998).

Hidden Costs of Client/Server Computing

Many companies have found that the savings they expected from client/server computing did not materialize because of unexpected costs. Hardware-acquisition savings resulting from significantly lower costs of MIPS on PCs often are offset by high annual operating costs for additional labor and time required for network and system management.

The most difficult to evaluate and control are the hidden costs that accompany a decentralized client/server system. Considerable time must be spent on tasks such as network maintenance, data backup, technical problem solving, and hardware, software, and software-update installations. As illustrated in Figure 8.13, the largest cost component for both large and small client/server systems is operations staff.

Network Reliability and Security

Network technology is still immature and highly complex. The networks themselves have dense layers of interacting technology and the applications, too, are often intricately layered. Enterprise networking is highly sensitive to different versions of operating systems and network management software, with some applications requiring specific versions of each. It is difficult to make all of the components of large, heterogeneous networks work together as smoothly as management envisions. **Downtime**—periods of time in which the system is not operational—remains much more frequent in client/server

downtime Periods of time in which an information system is not operational.

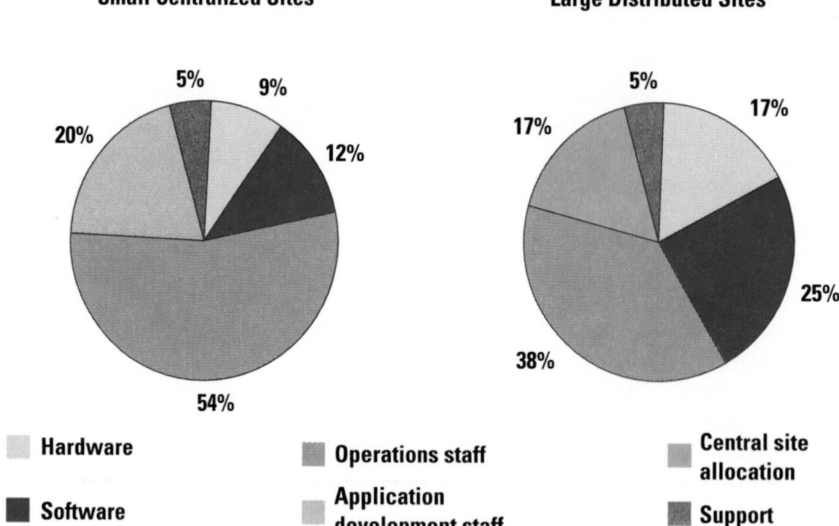

FIGURE 8.13

Cost breakdowns for client/server computing. The cost of operations staff, the largest cost component in client/server computing, is frequently underestimated when organizations downsize. *Source: Maximizing Return-on-Investment of Network Computing" by International Data Corporation in* Computerworld, *April 30, 1996. Copyright © 1998 Computerworld, Inc., Framingham, MA 01701. Rights reserved. Reprinted with permission of* Computerworld *Magazine.*

systems than in established mainframe systems and should be considered carefully before taking essential applications off a mainframe.

Security is of paramount importance in organizations where information systems make extensive use of networks. Networks present end users, hackers, and thieves with many points of access and opportunities to steal or modify data in networks. Systems linked to the Internet are even more vulnerable because the Internet was designed to be open to everyone. We discuss these issues in greater detail in Chapter 14.

Some Solutions

Organizations can counteract problems created by enterprise networking by planning for and managing the business and organizational changes, increasing end-user training, asserting data administration disciplines, and considering connectivity and cost controls when planning their information architecture.

MANAGING THE CHANGE To gain the full benefit of any new technology, organizations must carefully plan for and manage the change. Business processes may need to be reengineered to ensure that the organization fully benefits from the new technology (see Chapter 10). The company's information architecture must be redrawn to shape the new client/server environment. Management must address the organizational issues that arise from shifts in staffing, function, power, and organizational culture.

EDUCATION AND TRAINING A well-developed training program can help end users overcome problems resulting from the lack of management support and understanding of desktop computing (Westin et al., 1985; Bikson et al., 1985). Technical specialists will need training in client/server development and network support methods.

DATA ADMINISTRATION DISCIPLINES The role of data administration (see Chapter 7) becomes even more important when networks link many different applications and business areas. Organizations must systematically identify where their data are located, which group is responsible for maintaining each piece of data, and which individuals and groups are allowed to access and use that data. They need to develop specific policies and procedures to ensure that their data are accurate, available only to authorized users and properly backed up.

PLANNING FOR CONNECTIVITY Senior management must take a long-term view of the firm's information architecture and must make sure that its systems have the right degree of connectivity for its current and future information needs. It is usually too expensive to achieve complete connectivity in most organizations. It is far more sensible to identify classes of connectivity problems and specific application groups (such as critical electronic commerce and electronic business applications) that can be enhanced through increased connectivity.

A longer-term strategy recognizes that incompatible systems cannot be eliminated overnight and focuses on achieving connectivity for future applications. New systems should then be developed only if (1) they support the firm's connectivity standards and (2) they build upon existing networks and user applications in a seamless fashion. Management can establish policies to keep networks as homogeneous as possible, limiting the number of hardware, software, and network operating systems from different vendors.

The Telecommunications Plan

A telecommunications plan is more likely to succeed if it advances the key business goals of the company. During the planning process, managers can investigate ways of using telecommunications technology to enhance the firm's competitive position. Managers need to ask how telecommunications can reduce agency costs by increasing the scale and scope of operations without additional management. They need to determine if telecommunications technology can help them differentiate products and services, or if it can improve the firm's cost structure by eliminating intermediaries such as distributors or by accelerating business processes.

There are steps to implement a strategic telecommunications plan. First, start with an audit of the communications functions in your firm. What are your voice, data, video, equipment, staffing, and management capabilities? Identify priorities for improvement.

Second, you must know the long-range business plans of your firm. Your plan should include an analysis of how telecommunications will contribute to the specific five-year goals of the firm and to its longer-range strategies (e.g., cost reduction, distribution enhancement).

Third, identify critical areas where telecommunications currently does or can have the potential to make a large difference in performance. In insurance, these may be systems that give field representatives quick access to policy and rate information; in retailing, inventory control and market penetration; and in industrial products, rapid, efficient distribution and transportation.

Implementing the Plan

Once an organization has developed a telecommunications plan, it must determine the initial scope of the telecommunications project. Managers should take eight factors into account when choosing a telecommunications network.

The first and most important factor is distance. If communication will be largely local and entirely internal to the organization's buildings and social networks, there is little or no need for VANs, leased lines, or long-distance communications.

Along with distance, one must consider the range of services the network must support, such as electronic mail, EDI, internally generated transactions, voice mail, videoconferencing, or imaging, and whether these services must be integrated in the same network.

A third factor to consider is security. The most secure means of long-distance communications is through lines that are owned by the organization. The next secure form of telecommunications is through dedicated leased lines. VANs and ordinary telephone lines are less secure.

A fourth factor to consider is whether multiple access is required throughout the organization or whether it can be limited to one or two nodes within the organization. A multiple-access system requirement suggests that there will be perhaps several thousand users throughout the corporation; therefore, a commonly available technology such as installed telephone wire is recommended. However, if access is restricted to fewer than 100 high-intensity users, a more advanced technology such as a high-bandwidth LAN may be recommended.

TABLE 8.5 Implementation Factors in Telecommunications Systems
Distance
Range of services
Security
Multiple access
Utilization
Cost
Installation
Connectivity

A fifth and most difficult factor to judge is utilization. There are two aspects of utilization that must be considered when developing a telecommunications network: the frequency and the volume of communications. Together, these two factors determine the total load on the telecommunications system. On the one hand, high-frequency, high-volume communications suggest the need for high-speed LANs for local communication and leased lines for long-distance communication. On the other hand, low-frequency, low-volume communications suggest dial-up, voice-grade telephone circuits operating through a traditional modem.

A sixth factor is cost. How much does each option cost? Total costs should include development, operations, maintenance, expansion, and overhead. Which cost components are fixed? Which are variable? Are there any hidden costs to anticipate? It is wise to recall the thruway effect. The easier it is to use a communications path, the more people will want to use it. Most telecommunications planners estimate future needs on the high side yet still often underestimate the actual need. Underestimating the cost of telecommunications projects or uncontrollable telecommunications costs are principal causes of network failure.

Seventh, managers must consider the difficulties of installing the telecommunications system. Are the organization's buildings properly constructed to install fiber optics? In some instances, buildings have inadequate wiring channels underneath the floors, which makes installation of fiber-optic cable extremely difficult.

Eighth, management must consider how much connectivity would be required to make all of the components in a network communicate with each other or to tie together multiple networks. We already have described some of the major connectivity standards. Internet technology could be used for this purpose. Table 8.5 summarizes these implementation factors.

Management Wrap-Up

MANAGEMENT

ORGANIZATION

TECHNOLOGY

Managers need to be continuously involved in telecommunications decisions because many important business processes today are based on telecommunications and networks. Management should identify the business opportunities linked to telecommunications technology and establish the business criteria for selecting the firm's telecommunications platform. Planning should carefully consider network costs, the costs and benefits of client/server computing, and connectivity issues. Some measure of management control should be maintained as computing power is distributed throughout the organization.

Telecommunications technology enables organizations to reduce transaction and coordination costs, promoting electronic commerce and electronic business. The organization's telecommunications infrastructure should support its business processes and business strategy.

Telecommunications technology is intertwined with all the other information technologies and deeply embedded in contemporary information systems. Networks are becoming more pervasive and powerful, with capabilities to transmit voice, data, and video over long distances. Key technology decisions should consider network reliability, security, bandwith, and connectivity.

For Discussion:

1. Network design is a key business decision as well as a technology decision. Why?
2. If you were an international company with global operations, what criteria would you use to determine whether to use a value-added network (VAN) or a private wide area network (WAN)?

SUMMARY

1. **Describe the basic components of a telecommunications system.** A telecommunications system is a set of compatible devices that are used to develop a network for communication from one location to another by electronic means. The essential components of a telecommunications system are computers, terminals, other input/output devices, communications channels, communications processors (such as modems, multiplexers, controllers, and front-end processors), and telecommunications software. Different components of a telecommunications network can communicate with each other with a common set of rules termed protocols. Data are transmitted throughout a telecommunications network using either analog signals or digital signals. A modem is a device that translates analog to digital and vice versa.
2. **Calculate the capacity of telecommunications channels and evaluate transmission media.** The capacity of a telecommunications channel is determined by the range of frequencies it can accommodate. The higher the range of frequencies, called bandwidth, the higher the capacity (measured in bits per second). The principal transmission media are twisted copper telephone wire, coaxial copper cable, fiber-optic cable, and wireless transmission utilizing microwave, satellite, low frequency radio, or infrared waves.
3. **Compare the various types of telecommunications networks and network services.** Networks can be classified by their shape or configuration or by their geographic scope and type of services provided. The three common network topologies are the star network, the bus network, and the ring network. In a star network, all communications must pass through a central computer. The bus network links a number of devices to a single channel and broadcasts all of the signals to the entire network, with special software to identify which components receive each message. In a ring network, each computer in the network can communicate

directly with any other computer but the channel is a closed loop. Data are passed along the ring from one computer to another.

Local area networks (LANs) and private branch exchanges (PBXs) are used to link offices and buildings in close proximity. Wide area networks (WANs) span a broad geographical distance, ranging from several miles to continents and are private networks that are independently managed. Value-added networks (VANs) also encompass a wide geographic area but are managed by a third party, which sells the services of the network to other companies. Important network services include packet switching, frame relay, asynchronous transfer mode (ATM), ISDN, DSL, cable modem, and T1 lines.

4. **Describe important connectivity standards for enterprise networking.** Connectivity is a measure of how well computers and computer-based devices can communicate with one another and "share" information in a meaningful way without human intervention. It is essential in enterprise networking, in which different hardware, software, and network components must work together to transfer information seamlessly from one part of the organization to another. TCP/IP and OSI are important reference models for achieving connectivity in networks. Each divides the communications process into layers. UNIX is an operating system standard that can be used to create open systems. Connectivity also can be achieved by using Internet technology and Java.
5. **Identify the principal telecommunications applications for supporting electronic commerce and electronic business.** The principal telecommunications applications for electronic commerce and electronic business are electronic mail, voice mail, fax, digital information services, teleconferencing, dataconferencing, videoconferencing, electronic data interchange (EDI), and groupware. Electronic data interchange is the computer-to-computer exchange between two organizations of standard transaction documents such as invoices, bills of lading, and purchase orders.
6. **Analyze the management problems raised by enterprise networking and suggest solutions.** Problems posed by enterprise networking include: loss of management control over systems; the need to carefully manage organizational change; connectivity issues; difficulty of ensuring network reliability and security; and controlling the hidden costs of client/server computing.

Solutions include planning for and managing the business and organizational changes associated with enterprise-wide computing, increasing end-user training, asserting data administration disciplines, and considering connectivity and cost controls when planning their information architecture. A connectivity audit identifies existing capabilities and future needs. Although many corporations have assumed connectivity as a strategic goal, a more reasonable strategy would be to move incrementally toward greater connectivity while not giving up the vision of connectivity. Firms should develop strategic telecommunications plans to ensure that their telecommunications systems serve business objectives and operations. Important factors to consider are distance, range of services, security, access, utilization, cost, installation, and connectivity.

KEY TERMS

Analog signal, 235
Asynchronous transfer mode (ATM), 245
Bandwidth, 239
Baud, 239
Bus network, 240
Cable modem, 245
Cellular telephone, 238
Channels, 235
Coaxial cable, 236
Concentrator, 240
Connectivity, 248
Controller, 240
Dataconferencing, 250
Dedicated lines, 244
Digital signal, 235
Digital subscriber line (DSL), 245
Downtime, 255
Electronic data interchange (EDI), 253
Enterprise networking, 246
Facsimile (fax), 250
Fiber-optic cable, 236
Frame relay, 245
Front-end processor, 240
Gateway, 243
Information superhighway, 233
Integrated Services Digital Network (ISDN), 245
Internetworking, 248
Local area network (LAN), 242
Microwave, 236
Mobile data networks, 238
Modem, 235
Multiplexer, 240
Network operating system (NOS), 243
Open systems, 248
Open Systems Interconnect (OSI), 249
Packet switching, 244
Paging system, 238
Peer-to-peer, 243
Personal communication services (PCS), 238
Personal digital assistants (PDA), 239
Private branch exchange (PBX), 242
Protocol, 235
Ring network, 241
Satellite, 236
Star network, 240
Switched lines, 244
T1 line, 245
Telecommunications, 233
Telecommunications system, 234
Teleconferencing, 250
Topology, 240
Transmission Control Protocol/Internet Protocol (TCP/IP), 248
Twisted wire, 236
Value-added network (VAN), 244
Videoconferencing, 252
Voice mail, 250
Wide area network (WAN), 244

REVIEW QUESTIONS

1. What is the significance of telecommunications deregulation for managers and organizations?
2. What is a telecommunications system? What are the principal functions of all telecommunications systems?
3. Name and briefly describe each of the components of a telecommunications system.
4. Distinguish between an analog and a digital signal.
5. Name the different types of telecommunications transmission media and compare them in terms of speed and cost.
6. What is the relationship between bandwidth and the transmission capacity of a channel?
7. Name and briefly describe the different kinds of communications processors.
8. Name and briefly describe the three principal network topologies.
9. Distinguish between a PBX and a LAN.
10. List and describe the various network services.
11. Define the following: modem, baud, wide area network (WAN), value-added network (VAN), and open systems.
12. What is enterprise networking? Why does it require connectivity?
13. Name and describe the telecommunications applications that can support electronic commerce and electronic business.
14. Give four examples of problems posed by enterprise networking.
15. What are some solutions to enterprise networking problems?
16. What are the principal factors to consider when developing a telecommunications plan?

GROUP PROJECT

With a group of two or three of your fellow students, describe in detail the ways that telecommunications technology can provide a firm with competitive advantage. Use the companies described in Chapter 2 or other chapters you have read so far to illustrate the points you make, or select examples of other companies using telecommunications from business or computer magazines. Present your findings to the class.

TOOLS FOR INTERACTIVE LEARNING

■ **INTERNET**: The Internet Connection for this chapter will take you to the Rosenbluth Travel Web site, where you can complete an exercise to analyze how Rosenbluth uses the Web and communications technology in its daily operations. You can use the interactive software at the Goodyear Web site in an Electronic Commerce project to assist customers in making tire purchases. You can also use the Interactive Study Guide to test your knowledge of the topics in the chapter and get instant feedback where you need more practice.

■ **CD-ROM**: If you purchase and use the Multimedia Edition CD-ROM with this chapter, you can perform an interactive exercise to select an appropriate network topology for a series of business scenarios and identify the main issue your selection presents to management. You also can find a video demonstrating the capabilities of personal communication services, an audio overview of the major themes of this chapter, and bullet text summarizing the key points of the chapter.

CASE STUDY

Rosenbluth International Travels a Telecommunications Route to Success

The travel-service industry is in trouble. Airlines have capped the commissions they will pay to travel agents, and these commissions have been the main source of their income. Travel agents can no longer afford to pay major corporate clients for the right to handle their travel business. In addition, global competition has forced many corporations to cut back on all expenses, including travel. Finally, the World Wide Web now makes it easy for individuals, whether as private persons or employees, to investigate and book their own travel. Management at Rosenbluth International had to face this formidable reality and find a way to thrive.

Rosenbluth, a privately held, family-owned company, is the third (some say second) largest travel-services firm in the world, with American Express being number one. It has $2.5 billion in annual sales and nearly 3500 employees. Headquartered in Philadelphia, Pennsylvania, the company was founded in 1892, and it was a relatively small company when Hal Rosenbluth joined the firm in 1974. In 1984, he obtained a contract to provide all of DuPont Corporation's travel services, and the company's explosive growth began. Rosenbluth was a success with DuPont because he managed to save the company $150 million in travel and entertainment (T&E) expenses.

Hal Rosenbluth believes that by creating a humane working environment, and by genuinely putting employees (called "associates" at Rosenbluth) first, they will give more to the company, resulting in the company offering better service to its customers. "Our only sustainable competitive advantages," Rosenbluth maintains, "are the associates and the environment in which we work." Although his approach remains central to the company, by itself it would not continue to make the company successful in the radically new environment. The strategy that has worked begins with understanding the value that Rosenbluth International can give to its clients by helping them manage costs.

How can Rosenbluth help companies manage T&E costs? The company relies heavily upon cutting-edge information technology. First, at the level of the individual trip, it has lowered airline costs by developing a way to search for the lowest fares that will meet the requirements of the traveler. DACODA is Rosenbluth's yield-management system. The software focuses on the client company's optimal air program worldwide. One of its functions is to sort through all the complex airline databases, analyzing their pricing and discounting schemes. Travelers are given a list of choices to select from within the time, date and location parameters they have selected. Through its software, Rosenbluth also tracks and manages a series of qualitative preferences that can offer clients a better trip for the same cost. For example, the system combines personal preference information with flight data to enable many travelers to spend less time on the ground between connections. The software also maintains such data as seating preferences for each client, including traveler concerns about placement related to plane wings.

As client employees travel, much of their travel data, both booked and billed, is automatically stored in Rosenbluth's databases, making it very easy for travelers and their employers to record and monitor expenses. VISION is the proprietary Rosenbluth real-time software package that instantly collects client travel data. The traveler is presented with a simple, easy-to-use interface to enter, submit, and track expenses during the trip. This software package even enforces the client company's travel policies for each trip. It integrates the data regardless of where the reservation is made or which airline reservation system is used. This software is the source of management reports that are customized to meet client-specific needs. Thus, management can easily monitor and control all of its corporate travel and entertainment expenses.

Rosenbluth's Global Distribution Network (GDN) is a worldwide telecommunications network through which the airline reservation systems are accessible. All Rosenbluth agents are connected to GDN, as are most of the company's travel software applications. Clients planning trips can either use the network to research and book their travel arrangements, or they can work through a Rosenbluth agent. Moreover, clients can choose to use a local Rosenbluth agent, or they can turn to specific agents of their choice anywhere in the world.

Wal-Mart is a good example of a satisfied customer. Every traveler within the giant retailing company has access to a Rosenbluth reservation through a desktop or laptop computer connected to Wal-Mart's local area network. The company's 7000 frequent travelers book their own hotel, air, and auto-rental reservations by calling up Rosenbluth's reservation system. They enter their name, travel dates, times, and cities of origin, destination, and stopover. Rosenbluth's software creates a grid of flight options that adhere to Wal-Mart travel policies. The employee clicks a few buttons and the reservations are completed. Some other companies accomplish the same thing by having their employees access Rosenbluth software through Rosenbluth's new World Wide Web site. This approach is particularly cost effective for Rosenbluth clients because all the clients need to do is give their employees Web browser software and a connection to the Internet. Business travelers on the go can obtain information from the Web site, such as airline numbers or the location of restaurants and copy centers at their destinations, using a handheld PalmPilot personal digital assistant.

The BOC group is another satisfied customer, one of many companies that have turned to Rosenbluth because of what they offer in this new travel environment. BOC is a British-based company with specialties in gases, vacuum technology, and health care. It is a giant, with sales of more than $6 billion and 40,000 employees in more than 1200 sites within 60 countries. By 1998 Rosenbluth expected to handle all BOC travel throughout the world.

In addition to helping clients, Rosenbluth has been forced to cut its own costs to the bone in order to survive. To accomplish this, they also have relied heavily upon technology. For example, the agents use the same software as clients so that they, too, can easily and quickly locate the lowest fares, book flights, and serve clients quickly. The company also has examined the working methods of their agents in order to find ways for them to work more efficiently. Rosenbluth noticed that his agents typed the same words over and over, so he ordered their computer interface be modified where possible to present prompts that required only "yes" and "no" responses. The developers also changed the programs to display the client company's travel guidelines on the screen so that the agent would not waste time creating options for a client that were outside the company guidelines. As a result of these changes, agents experienced a 75 percent reduction in keystrokes, a significant increase in productivity.

The global network also makes an enormous contribution to reducing Rosenbluth costs. Because of the network, it does not matter where the travel agent is physically located. As a result Rosenbluth has been able to establish a series of centralized reservation centers, known as "intellicenters." These centers are located in North Dakota, Delaware, and Allentown, Pennsylvania, all locations where labor costs are low but the work ethic is high. Costs are low enough in these centers that Rosenbluth is able to offer clients a significant reduction in costs for booking through one of the intellicenters. The network also is managed so that if one reservation center becomes overloaded, excess calls are immediately and automatically routed to another center where current volume is lower. For example, during the great East Coast blizzard of January 1996, about 21,000 calls were rerouted without any problem. Customers did not even know they were being rerouted.

Sources: Kim Girard, "AvantGo Gives Handheld Users Intranet Access," *Computerworld,* February 23, 1998; Rob Walker, "Back to the Farm," *Smart Money,* February/March 1997; and http://www.rosenbluth.com.

Case Study Questions

1. What problems did Rosenbluth Travel face? Analyze the company using the competitive forces and value chain models.
2. What competitive strategy did the company follow to address its problems?
3. How did the DACODA, VISION, and related systems fit in with and contribute to its strategy? What was the significance of the systems being available on a worldwide network? On the Internet? How did these systems change the company's business processes?
4. What management, organization, and technology issues were addressed when Rosenbluth implemented the DACODA, VISION, and related systems?
5. What management, organization, and technology issues were addressed when Rosenbluth implemented its Global Distribution Network?

CHAPTER 9

The Internet: Electronic Commerce and Electronic Business

chapter outline

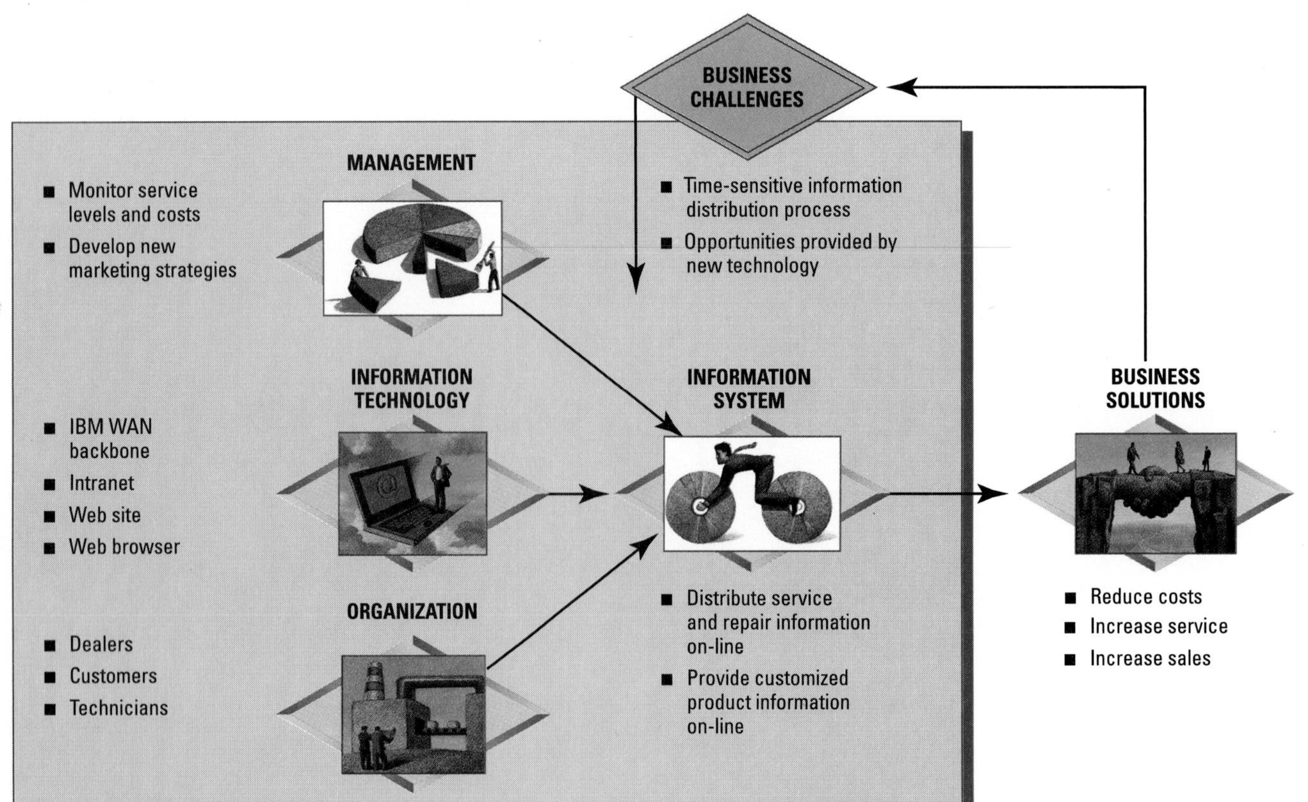

Mazda Drives Forward with the Internet

Every week, Mazda prepares bulletins with the latest vehicle service and repair information for its 840 North American dealers. By the time the dealers have received them, 12 days have elapsed because printing and distribution take so much time. Extensive workshop manuals to help with vehicle repairs take three to four weeks to reach technicians. To deliver this information more rapidly, Mazda created an intranet that publishes the material on-line. Dealers and technicians can access these documents through a conventional Web browser, easily locating documents and sending feedback via e-mail.

Mazda used its existing IBM Global Services wide area network as the backbone for the intranet. Every North American dealer already uses this network to order cars and parts, so it was not difficult to extend the existing infrastructure to intranet services.

Mazda still publishes the manuals on paper as well as on the intranet, but its goal is to eliminate printing and distribution of the bulky, expensive paper versions, which total 8.5 million pages per year. (Service bulletins are four inches thick; repair manuals are even thicker.)

Mazda also operates a public Web site with separate sections for the United States, Canada, the United Kingdom, Austria, Japan, and Australia. Visitors can view pictures of the latest models, review vehicle specifications and safety information, and order a brochure. The site has a series of interactive features, which visitors can use to calculate monthly car loan payments, locate their nearest Mazda dealer, or compare the Mazda model of their choice to models of competitors in a number of key categories. Using Mazda's Deal Direct on-line quote service, visitors can select a new car model that interests them and use an interactive "build-your-own" tool to determine the trim level and optional features that meet their needs. When finished, the session will display the vehicle they have chosen and the MSRP. They can obtain a price quote from a local Mazda dealer by clicking on a "Deal Direct" button to submit their request. The dealer will contact them via telephone or e-mail with a quote.

Sources: Adapted from Carol Sliwa, "Mazda Intranet Drives Good Service," *Computerworld,* February 23, 1998; and http://www.mazda.com

Management Challenges

Mazda's Web site and private intranet illustrate some of the features of Web and Internet technology that are allowing companies to benefit from electronic commerce and electronic business—interactivity, customization, standard technology that is easy to use, and the ability to transmit information electronically to streamline business processes. The Internet, the Web, and intranets can help companies achieve new levels of competitiveness and efficiency, but they raise the following management challenges:

1. **Internet computing requires a complete change of mindset.** To implement Internet technology for electronic commerce and electronic business successfully, companies may need to make organizational changes. They must examine and perhaps redesign an entire business process rather than throw new technology at existing business practices. Companies must consider a different organizational structure, changes in organizational culture, a different support structure for information systems, and different procedures of managing employees and networked processing functions.

2. **Finding a successful Internet business model.** Companies are racing to put up Web sites in the hope of increasing earnings through electronic commerce. However, many electronic commerce sites have yet to turn a profit or to make a tangible difference in firms' sales and marketing efforts (Halper, 1997). Cost savings or access to new markets promised by the Web may not materialize. Companies need to think carefully about whether they can create a genuinely workable business model on the Internet and how the Internet relates to their overall business strategy.

learning objectives

After reading this chapter you will be able to:

1. Describe how the Internet works and its major capabilities.
2. Identify the benefits the Internet offers organizations.
3. Demonstrate how the Internet can be used for electronic commerce.
4. Demonstrate how Internet technology can be used to create private intraorganizational and interorganizational networks and the use of these networks for electronic business.
5. Examine the challenges posed by the Internet to businesses and society.

The Internet has opened up many exciting possibilities for organizing and running a business that are transforming organizations and the use of information systems in everyday life. It is creating a universal platform for buying and selling goods and for driving important business processes inside the firm. Along with bringing many new benefits and opportunities, the Internet has created a new set of management challenges. We describe these challenges so that organizations can understand the management, organization, and technology issues that must be addressed to benefit from the Internet, electronic commerce, and electronic business.

9.1 THE INTERNET

The Internet is perhaps the most well-known, and the largest, implementation of internetworking, linking hundreds of thousands of individual networks all over the world. The Internet has a range of capabilities that organizations are using to exchange information internally or to communicate externally with other organizations. This giant network of networks has become a major catalyst for both electronic commerce and electronic business.

What Is the Internet?

The Internet began as a U.S. Department of Defense network to link scientists and university professors around the world. Even today individuals cannot connect directly to the Net, although anyone with a computer, a modem, and the willingness to pay a small monthly usage fee can access it through an Internet Service Provider (ISP). An **Internet Service Provider (ISP)** is a commercial organization with a permanent connection to the Internet that sells temporary connections to subscribers. Individuals also can access the Internet through such popular on-line services as Prodigy and America Online and through networks established by such giants as Microsoft and AT&T.

Internet Service Provider (ISP) A commercial organization with a permanent connection to the Internet that sells temporary connections to subscribers.

One of the most puzzling aspects of the Internet is that no one owns it and it has no formal management organization. As a creation of the Defense Department for sharing research data, this lack of centralization was purposeful, to make it less vulnerable to wartime or terrorist attacks. To join the Internet, an existing network needs only to pay a small registration fee and agree to certain standards based on the TCP/IP (Transmission Control Protocol/Internet Protocol) reference model, which we described in Chapter 8. Costs are low because the Internet owns nothing and so has no costs to offset. Each organization, of course, pays for its own networks and its own telephone bills, but those costs usually exist independent of the Internet. Regional Internet companies have been established to which member networks forward all transmissions. These Internet companies route and forward all traffic, and the cost is still only that of a local telephone call. The result is that the costs of e-mail and other Internet connections tend to be far lower than equivalent voice, postal, or overnight delivery, making the Net a very inexpensive communications medium. It is also a very fast method of communication, with messages arriving anywhere in the world in a matter of seconds or a minute or two at most. We will now briefly describe the most important Internet capabilities.

Internet Technology and Capabilities

The Internet is based upon client/server technology. Users of the Net control what they do through client applications, using graphical user interfaces or character-based products that control all functions. All the data, including e-mail messages, databases, and Web sites, are stored on servers. Servers dedicated to the Internet or even to specific Internet functions are the heart of the information on the Net (see Figure 9.1).

Major Internet capabilities include e-mail, Usenet newsgroups, LISTSERVs, chatting, Telnet, FTP, Archie, gophers, Veronica, WAIS, and the World Wide Web. They can be used to retrieve and offer information. Table 9.1 lists these capabilities and describes the functions they support.

Internet Tools for Communication

ELECTRONIC MAIL (E-MAIL) The Net has become the most important e-mail system in the world because it connects so many people worldwide, creating a productivity gain that observers have compared to Gutenberg's development of movable type in the fifteenth century. Organizations use it to facilitate communication between employees and offices, and to communicate with customers and suppliers.

Researchers use this facility to share ideas, information, even documents. E-mail over the Net also has made possible many collaborative research and writing projects, even though the participants are thousands of miles apart. With proper software, the user will find it easy to attach documents and multimedia files when sending a message

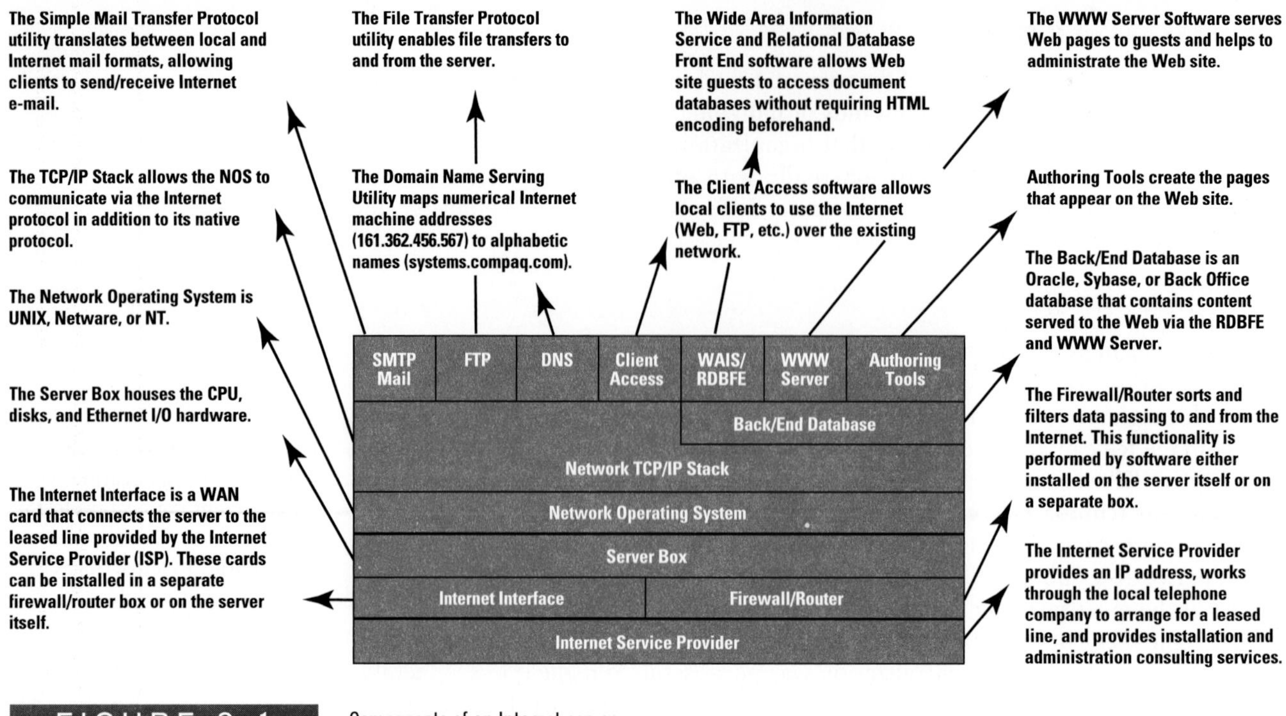
The Simple Mail Transfer Protocol utility translates between local and Internet mail formats, allowing clients to send/receive Internet e-mail.
The File Transfer Protocol utility enables file transfers to and from the server.
The Wide Area Information Service and Relational Database Front End software allows Web site guests to access document databases without requiring HTML encoding beforehand.
The WWW Server Software serves Web pages to guests and helps to administrate the Web site.
The TCP/IP Stack allows the NOS to communicate via the Internet protocol in addition to its native protocol.
The Domain Name Serving Utility maps numerical Internet machine addresses (161.362.456.567) to alphabetic names (systems.compaq.com).
The Client Access software allows local clients to use the Internet (Web, FTP, etc.) over the existing network.
Authoring Tools create the pages that appear on the Web site.
The Network Operating System is UNIX, Netware, or NT.
The Back/End Database is an Oracle, Sybase, or Back Office database that contains content served to the Web via the RDBFE and WWW Server.
The Server Box houses the CPU, disks, and Ethernet I/O hardware.
The Firewall/Router sorts and filters data passing to and from the Internet. This functionality is performed by software either installed on the server itself or on a separate box.
The Internet Interface is a WAN card that connects the server to the leased line provided by the Internet Service Provider (ISP). These cards can be installed in a separate firewall/router box or on the server itself.
The Internet Service Provider provides an IP address, works through the local telephone company to arrange for a leased line, and provides installation and administration consulting services.
SMTP Mail
FTP
DNS
Client Access
WAIS/ RDBFE
WWW Server
Authoring Tools
Back/End Database
Network TCP/IP Stack
Network Operating System
Server Box
Internet Interface
Firewall/Router
Internet Service Provider

FIGURE 9.1 Components of an Internet server.

Source: © Copyright 1994, 1995, 1996, 1997 Compaq Computer Corporation.

to someone or to broadcast a message to a predefined group. Figure 9.2 illustrates the components of an Internet e-mail address.

domain name The unique name of a collection of computers connected to the Internet.

The portion of the address to the left of the @ symbol in Net e-mail addresses is the name or identifier of the specific individual or organization. To the right of the @ symbol is the domain name. The **domain name** is the unique name of a collection of computers connected to the Internet. The domain contains subdomains separated by a period. The domain that is farthest to the right is the top level domain, and each domain to the left helps further define the domain by network, department, and even specific computer. The top level domain name may be either a country indicator or a function indicator, such as *com* for a commercial organization or *gov* for a government institution.

TABLE 9.1 Major Internet Capabilities

Capability	Functions Supported
E-mail	Person-to-person messaging; document sharing
Usenet Newsgroups	Discussion groups on electronic bulletin boards
LISTSERVs	Discussion groups using e-mail mailing list servers
Chatting	Interactive conversations
Telnet	Log on to one computer system and do work on another
FTP	Transfer files from computer to computer
Archie	Search database of documents, software, and data files available for downloading
Gophers	Locate information using a hierarchy of menus
Veronica	Speed searching of gopher sites by using keywords
WAIS	Locate files in databases using keywords
World Wide Web	Retrieve, format, and display information (including text, audio, graphics, and video) using hypertext links

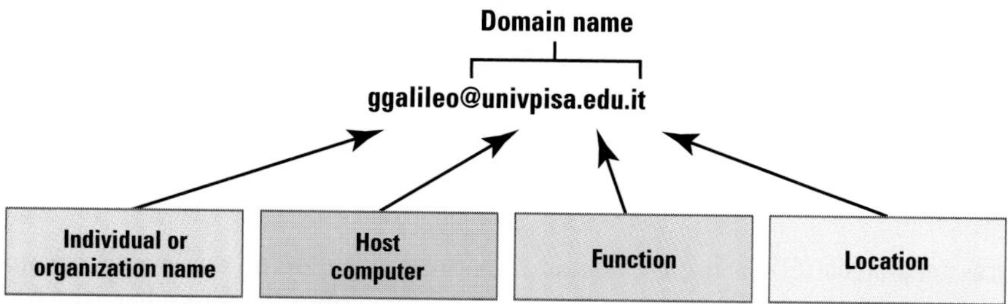

FIGURE 9.2 Analysis of an Internet address. In English, the e-mail address of physicist and astronomer Galileo Galilei would be translated as 'G. Galileo @ University of Pisa, educational institution, Italy'. The domain name to the right of the @ symbol contains a country indicator, a function indicator, and the location of the host computer.

All e-mail addresses end with a country indicator except those in the United States, which ordinarily does not use one. In Figure 9.2, *it,* the top level domain, is a country indicator, indicating that the address is in Italy. *Edu* indicates that the address is an educational institution; *univpisa* (in this case, University of Pisa) indicates the specific location of the host computer.

USENET NEWSGROUPS (FORUMS) **Usenet** newsgroups are worldwide discussion groups in which people share information and ideas on a defined topic such as radiology or rock bands. Discussion takes place in large electronic bulletin boards where anyone can post messages for others to read. Almost 20,000 groups exist discussing almost all conceivable topics. Each Usenet site is financed and administered independently.

Usenet Forums in which people share information and ideas on a defined topic through large electronic bulletin boards where anyone can post messages on the topic for others to see and respond to.

LISTSERV A second type of public forum, **LISTSERV,** allows discussions to be conducted through predefined groups but uses e-mail mailing list servers instead of bulletin boards for communications. If you find a LISTSERV topic you are interested in, you may subscribe. From then on, through your e-mail, you will receive all messages sent by others concerning that topic. You can, in turn, send a message to your LISTSERV and it will automatically be broadcast to the other subscribers. Tens of thousands of LISTSERV groups exist.

LISTSERV On-line discussion groups using e-mail broadcast from mailing list servers instead of bulletin boards for communications.

CHATTING **Chatting** allows two or more people who are simultaneously connected to the Internet to hold live, interactive, written conversations. Internet Relay Chat (IRC) is a general chat program for the Internet. Chat groups are divided into channels, each assigned its own topic of conversation. Chatting can be an effective business tool if people who can benefit from interactive conversations set an appointed time to "meet" and "talk" on a particular topic.

chatting Live, interactive conversations over a public network.

TELNET **Telnet** allows someone to be on one computer system while doing work on another. Telnet is the protocol that establishes an error-free, rapid link between the two computers, allowing you, for example, to log on to your business computer from a remote computer when you are on the road or working from your home. You can also log in and use third-party computers that have been made accessible to the public, such as using the catalogue of the U.S. Library of Congress. Telnet will use the computer address you supply to locate the computer you want to reach and connect you to it.

Telnet Network tool that allows someone to log on to one computer system while doing work on another.

Information Retrieval on the Internet

Information retrieval is a second basic Internet function. Many hundreds of library catalogues are on-line through the Internet, including those of such giants as the Library of Congress, the University of California, and Harvard University. In addition, users are able to search many thousands of databases that have been opened to the public by corporations, governments, and nonprofit organizations. Individuals can gather information on almost any conceivable topic stored in these databases and libraries. Many use the Internet to locate and download some of the free, quality computer software that has been made available by developers on computers all over the world.

The Internet is a voluntary, decentralized effort with no central listing of participants or sites, much less a listing of the data located at those sites, so a major problem is finding what you need from among the storehouses of data found in databases and libraries. Here we will introduce five major methods of accessing computers and locating files. We will discuss additional information-retrieval methods in our section on the World Wide Web.

file transfer protocol (FTP) Tool for retrieving and transferring files from a remote computer.

FTP **File transfer protocol (FTP)** is used to access a remote computer and retrieve files from it. FTP is a quick and easy method if you know the remote computer site where the file is stored. After you have logged on to the remote computer, you can move around directories that have been made accessible for FTP to search for the file(s) you want to retrieve. Once located, FTP makes transfer of the file to your own computer very easy.

Archie A tool for locating data on the Internet that performs keyword searches on a database of documents, software, and data files available for downloading from servers around the world.

ARCHIE **Archie** is a tool that can be used to search the files at FTP sites. It monitors hundreds of FTP sites regularly and updates a database on software, documents, and data files available for downloading called an Archie server. Clicking on a listing from one Archie server will bring you to another computer system where other relevant files are stored. There, the Archie server may allow you to continue your search for files until you locate what you need. Archie database searches use subject key words you enter, such as "Beijing," "telecommuting," "polymers," or "inflation," resulting in lists of sites that contain files on those topics.

gopher A tool for locating data on the Internet that enables the user to locate information stored on Internet servers through a series of easy-to-use, hierarchical menus.

GOPHERS Most files and digital information that are accessible through FTP also are available through gophers. A **gopher** is a computer client tool that enables the user to locate information stored on Internet gopher servers through a series of easy-to-use, hierarchical menus. The Internet has thousands of gopher server sites throughout the world. Each gopher site contains its own system of menus listing subject-matter topics, local files, and other relevant gopher sites. One gopher site might have as many as several thousand listings within its menus. When you use gopher software to search a specific topic and select a related item from a menu, the server will automatically transfer you to the appropriate file on that server or to the selected server wherever it is located. Once on that server, the process continues; you are presented with more menus of files and other gopher site servers that might interest you. You can move from site to site, narrowing your search as you go, locating information anywhere in the world. With descriptive menu listings linked to other gopher sites, you do not need to know in advance where relevant files are stored or the exact FTP address of a specific computer.

Veronica Capability for searching for text that appears in gopher menus by using keywords.

VERONICA **Veronica** (Very Easy Rodent-Oriented Netwide Index to Computer Archives) is an additional capability for searching for text that appears in gopher menus. When the user enters a key word, Veronica will search through thousands of gopher sites to find titles containing that keyword. It places these files on a temporary menu on your own local server so you can browse through them, making file retrieval by topic much easier.

WAIS A tool for locating data on the Internet that requires the name of the databases to be searched based upon key words.

WAIS **WAIS** (Wide Area Information Servers) is a fourth way to handle the problem of locating files around the world. WAIS is the most thorough way to locate a specific file, but it requires that you know the name of the databases you want searched. After you specify database names and key identifying words, WAIS searches for the key words in all the files in those databases. When the search has been completed, you will be given a menu listing all the files that contain your key words.

The World Wide Web

The World Wide Web (the Web) is at the heart of the explosion in the business use of the Net. The Web is a system with universally accepted standards for storing, retrieving, formatting, and displaying information using a client/server architecture. It was developed to allow collaborators in remote sites to share their ideas on all aspects of a common project. If the Web was used for two independent projects and later relationships were found between the projects, information could flow smoothly between the projects without making major changes (Berners-Lee et al., 1994).

The Web combines text, hypermedia, graphics, and sound. It can handle all types of digital communication while making it easy to link resources that are half-a-world apart. The Web uses graphical user interfaces for easy viewing. It is based upon a standard hypertext language called Hypertext Markup Language (HTML), which formats documents and incorporates dynamic links to other documents and pictures stored in the same or remote computers. (We have described HTML in Chapter 6.) Using these links, the user need only point at a highlighted key word or graphic, click on it, and immediately be transported to another document, probably on another computer somewhere else in the world. Users are free to jump from place to place following their own logic and interest.

Web browser software is programmed according to HTML standards (see Chapter 6). The standard is universally accepted, so anyone using a browser can access any of the millions of Web sites. Browsers use hypertext's point-and-click ability to navigate or *surf*—move from site to site on the Web—to another desired site. The browser also includes an arrow or back button to enable the user to retrace his steps, navigating back, site by site.

Those who offer information through the Web must establish a **home page**—a text and graphical screen display that usually welcomes the user and explains the organization that has established the page. For most organizations, the home page will lead the user to other pages, with all the pages of a company being known as a *Web site*. For a corporation to establish a presence on the Web, therefore, it must set up a Web site of one or more pages. Most Web pages offer a way to contact the organization or individual. The person in charge of an organization's Web site is called a **Webmaster.**

home page A World Wide Web text and graphical screen display that welcomes the user and explains the organization that has established the page.

Webmaster The person in charge of an organization's Web site.

To access a Web site, the user must specify a **uniform resource locator (URL),** which points to the address of a specific resource on the Web. For instance, the URL for Prentice Hall, the publisher of this text, is:

uniform resource locator (URL) The address of a specific resource on the Internet.

http://www.prenhall.com

Http stands for **hypertext transport protocol,** which is the communications standard used to transfer pages on the Web. HTTP defines how messages are formatted and transmitted and what actions Web servers and browsers should take in response to various commands. *Www.prenhall.com* is the domain name identifying the web server storing the Web pages.

hypertext transport protocol The communications standard used to transfer pages on the Web. Defines how messages are formatted and transmitted.

Searching for Information on the Web

Locating information on the Web is a critical function given the tens of millions of Web sites in existence and growth estimated at 300,000 pages per week. No comprehensive catalog of Web sites exists. The principal methods of locating information on the Web are Web site directories, search engines, and broadcast or "push" technology.

Several companies have created directories of Web sites and their addresses, providing search tools for finding information. Yahoo! is an example. People or organizations submit sites of interest, which then are classified. To search the directory, you enter one or more keywords and will see displayed a list of categories and sites with those key words in the title (see Figure 9.3).

Other search tools do not require Web sites to be preclassified and will search Web pages on their own automatically. Such tools, called **search engines,** can find Web sites that may be little known. They contain software that looks for Web pages containing one or more of the search terms; then it displays matches ranked by a method that usually involves the location and frequency of the search terms. These search engines do not display information about every site on the Web, but they create indexes of the Web pages they visit. The search engine software then locates Web pages of interest by searching through these indexes. AltaVista, Lycos, and Infoseek are examples of these search engines. Some are more comprehensive or current than others, depending on how their components are tuned. Some also classify Web sites by subject categories.

search engine A tool for locating specific sites or information on the Internet. Primarily used to search the World Wide Web.

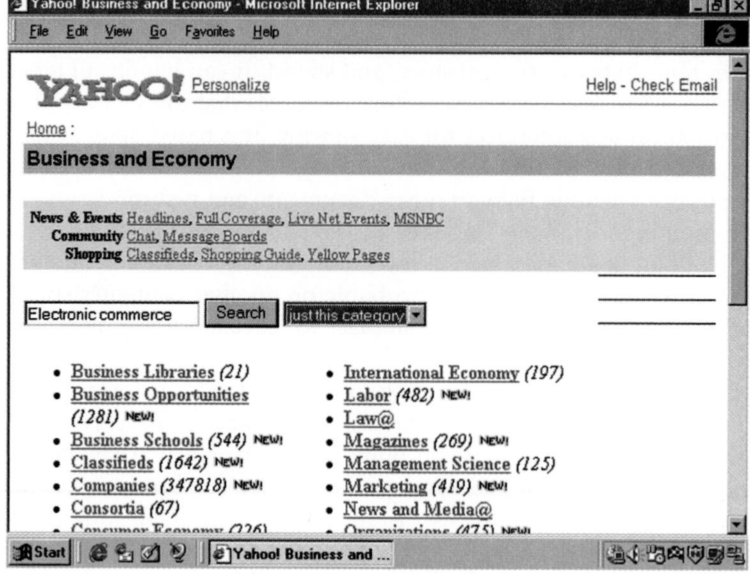

FIGURE 9.3

Yahoo! provides a directory of Web sites classified into categories. Users can search for sites of interest by entering keywords or exploring the categories.

Broadcast and "Push" Technology

"push" technology Method of obtaining relevant information on networks by having a computer broadcast information directly to the user based on prespecified interests.

Instead of spending hours surfing the Web, users can have the information they are interested in delivered automatically to their desktops through **"push" technology.** A computer broadcasts information of interest directly to the user, rather than having the user "pull" content from Web sites.

"Push" comes from *server push,* a term used to describe the streaming of Web page contents from a Web server to a Web browser. Special client software allows the user to specify the categories of information he or she wants to receive, such as news, sports, financial data, and so forth, and how often this information should be updated. The software runs in the background of the user's computer while the computer performs other tasks. Upon finding the kind of information requested, push programs serve it to the push client, notifying him or her by sending e-mail, playing a sound, displaying an icon on the desktop, sending full articles or Web pages, or displaying headlines on a screen saver. The streams of information distributed through push technology are also known as *channels* and can include private intranet channels and extranet channels, as well as channels from the public Internet (see Figure 9.4). Microsoft's Internet Explorer 4 and Netscape Communicator include push

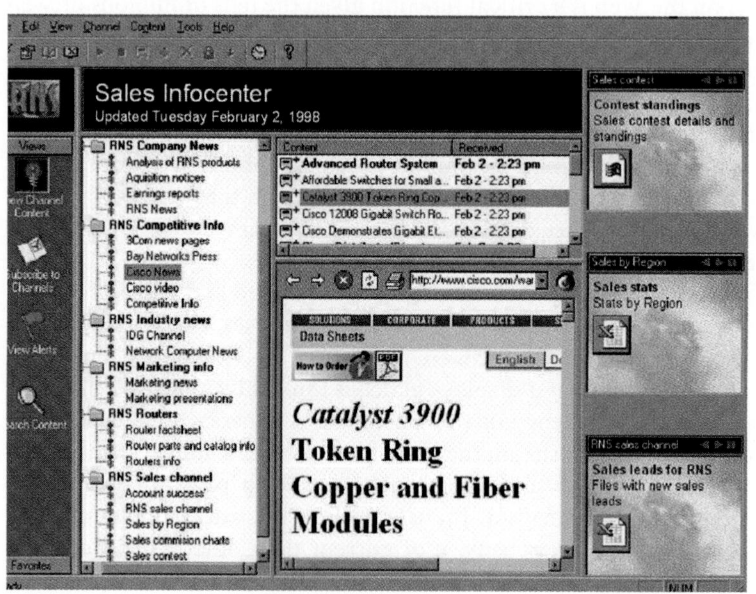

FIGURE 9.4

Delivering information through "push" technology. In this Sales Infocenter, the BackWeb push delivery service was used to create channels that automatically deliver information of interest to sales representatives, such as industry news, updates on competitors, market presentations, and files of new sales leads.

tools that automatically download Web pages, inform the user of updated content, and create channels of user-specified sites.

The audience for push technology is not limited to individual users. Companies are using push technology to set up their own channels to broadcast important internal information via corporate intranets or extranets. For example, Fruit of the Loom is using Pointcast push technology to alert managers to updated inventory information stored on its IBM AS/400 intranet Web server (Maddox, 1997). Lufthansa is using the BackWeb push delivery service to alert consumers to fare discounts.

Intranets and Extranets

Organizations can use Internet networking standards and Web technology to create private networks called intranets. We introduced intranets in Chapter 1, explaining that an intranet is an internal organizational network that can provide access to data across the enterprise. It uses the existing company network infrastructure along with Internet connectivity standards and software developed for the World Wide Web. Intranets can create networked applications that can run on many different kinds of computers throughout the organization.

Intranet Technology

The principal difference between the Web and an intranet is that whereas the Web is open to anyone, the intranet is private and is protected from public visits by **firewalls**—security systems with specialized software to prevent outsiders from invading private networks. The firewall consists of hardware and software placed between an organization's internal network and an external network, including the Internet. The firewall is programmed to intercept each message packet passing between the two networks, examine its characteristics, and reject unauthorized messages or access attempts. We provide more detail on firewalls in Chapter 14.

firewall Hardware and software placed between an organization's internal network and an external network to prevent outsiders from invading private networks.

Intranets require no special hardware and can run over any existing network infrastructure. Intranet software technology is the same as that of the World Wide Web. Intranets use HTML to program Web pages and to establish dynamic, point-and-click hypertext links to other sites. The Web browser and Web server software used for intranets are the same as those on the Web. A simple intranet can be created by linking a client computer with a Web browser to a computer with Web server software via a TCP/IP network. A firewall keeps unwanted visitors out.

Extranets

Some firms are allowing people and organizations outside the firm to have limited access to their internal intranets. Private intranets that are extended to users outside the company are called **extranets.** For example, authorized buyers could link to a portion of a company's intranet from the public Internet to obtain information about the cost and features of its products. The company can use firewalls to ensure that access to its internal data is limited, and remains secure; and to authenticate users, making sure that only those who are authorized to access the site can be identified.

extranet Private intranet that is accessible to select outsiders.

Extranets are especially useful for linking organizations with customers or business partners. They often are used for providing product-availability, pricing, and shipment data, and electronic data interchange (EDI), or for collaborating with other companies on joint development or training efforts. Figure 9.5 illustrates one way that an extranet might be set up.

Internet Benefits to Organizations

The Internet, intranets, and extranets are becoming the principal platforms for electronic commerce and electronic business because this technology provides so many benefits. The Internet's global connectivity, ease of use, low cost, and multimedia capabilities can be used to create interactive applications, services, and products. By using Internet technology, organizations can reduce communication and transaction costs,

FIGURE 9.5

Model of an extranet. In this model of an extranet, selected customers, suppliers, and business partners can access a company's private intranet from the public Internet. A firewall allows access only to authorized outsiders.

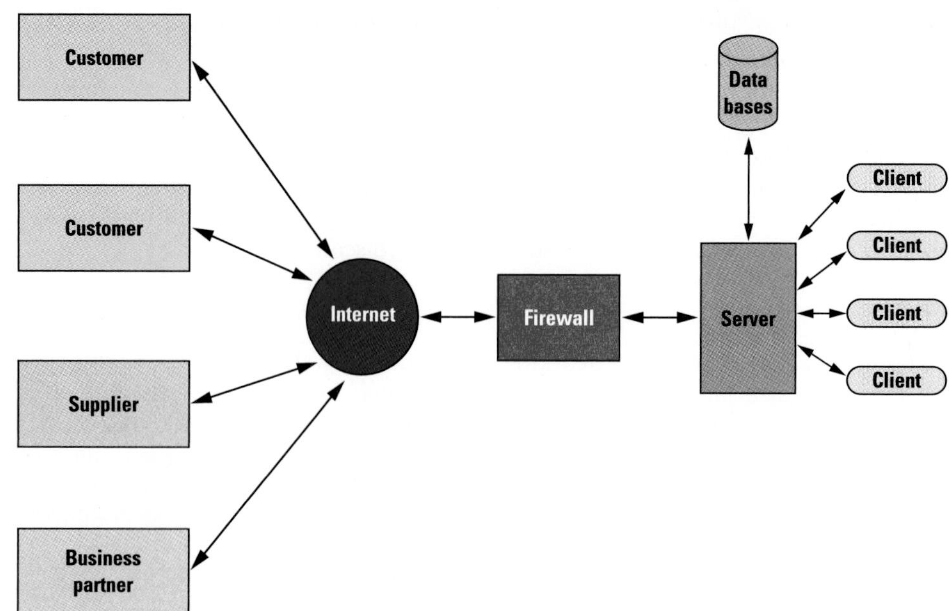

enhance coordination and collaboration, and accelerate the distribution of knowledge. Table 9.2 summarizes these benefits.

Connectivity and Global Reach

The value of the Internet lies in its ability to easily and inexpensively connect so many people from so many places all over the globe. Anyone who has an Internet address can log on to a computer and reach any other computer on the network, regardless of location, computer type, or operating system.

The Internet's global connectivity and ease of use can provide companies with access to businesses or individuals who normally would be outside their reach. Companies can link directly to suppliers, business partners, or individual customers at the same low cost, even if they are halfway around the globe. Businesses can find new outlets for their products and services abroad because the Internet facilitates cross-border transactions and information flows (Quelch and Klein, 1996). The Internet provides a low-cost medium for forming global alliances and virtual organizations. The Web provides a standard interface and inexpensive global access which can be used to create interorganizational systems among almost any organizations (Isakowitz, Bieber, and Vitali, 1998).

The Internet has made it easier and less expensive for companies to coordinate their staffs when opening new markets or working in isolated places because they do not have to build their own networks. Small companies who normally would find the cost of operating or selling abroad too expensive will find the Internet especially valuable.

Reduced Communication Costs

Before the Net, organizations had to build their own wide area networks or subscribe to a value-added network service. Employing the Internet, although far from cost-free,

TABLE 9.2 Internet Benefits to Organizations
Connectivity and global reach
Reduced communication costs
Lower transaction costs
Reduced agency costs
Interactivity, flexibility, and customization
Accelerated distribution of knowledge

is certainly more cost-effective for many organizations than building one's own network or paying VAN subscription fees. One estimate is that a direct mailing or faxing to 1200 customers within the United States will cost $1200 to $1600, whereas the same coverage through the Net will cost only about $9. Adding 600 more recipients who are spread through six other countries would increase the cost only another $9. Thus, the Internet can help organizations reduce operational costs or minimize operational expenses while extending their activities.

Schlumberger Ltd., the New York and Paris oil-drilling equipment and electronics producer, operates in 85 countries, and in most of them employees are in remote locations. To install its own network for so few people at each remote location would have been prohibitively expensive. Using the Net, Schlumberger engineers in Dubai (on the Persian Gulf) can check e-mail and stay in close contact with management at a very low cost. The field staff also are able to follow research projects as well as personnel within the United States.

Schlumberger has found that since it converted to the Net from its own network, overall communications costs are down in spite of a major increase in network and IT infrastructure spending. The main reason for these savings is the dramatic drop in voice traffic and in overnight-delivery service charges (they attach complete documents to their e-mail messages).

Hardware and software have been developed for **Internet telephony,** allowing companies to use the Internet for telephone voice transmission. (Internet telephony products sometimes are called IP telephony products.) For example, Universal Sewing Supply, which provides sewing services to firms such as Fruit of the Loom and Levi Strauss, added an IP telephony gateway supplied by VocalTec Communications Ltd. to its private network in the fall of 1997. The monthly telephone bill for communications between its St. Louis corporate office and its factories in the Dominican Republic, which ranged from $4000 to $7000 plummeted by 80 percent. Although Internet telephony can help firms reduce their high charges for international calls, the Internet is currently not well-suited to this purpose, having been designed for data communications, in which there are delays as data are downloaded. Most companies will not use Internet telephony services until the quality of telephone service improves (Korzeniowski, 1998).

Internet telephony The use of the Internet for telephone voice service.

Lower Transaction Costs

Businesses have found that conducting transactions electronically can be done at a fraction of the cost of paper-based processes. For instance, the paper and human cost of producing and processing an invoice might cost $100, compared with $10 if processed electronically (Price Waterhouse, 1996). The average retail banking transaction costs $1.50, compared with 15 to 25 cents for an electronic version. Using the Internet reduces these transaction costs even further. Here are some examples:

- BeamScope Canada Inc. of Richmond Hill, Ontario, finds it can process Web orders for about 80 cents versus $5 to $15 for live orders. Customers appreciate the convenience of on-line shopping as well.
- Each time Federal Express clients use FedEx's Web site to track the status of their packages instead of inquiring by telephone, FedEx saves $8.00, amounting to a $2 million savings in operating costs each year.
- Pharmaceuticals manufacturer Merck and Co. Inc. found that having a human resources representative handle a transaction personally cost $16.96, and tracking down and fixing a mistake amounted to $128. Employee self-service over an intranet only cost $2.32 per transaction, with almost no cost to correct mistakes (Row, 1996).

Reduced Agency Costs

As organizations expand and globalization continues, the need to coordinate activities in far-flung locations is becoming more critical. The Internet reduces agency costs—the cost of managing employees and coordinating their work— by providing low-cost networks and inexpensive communication and collaboration tools that can be used on a global scale.

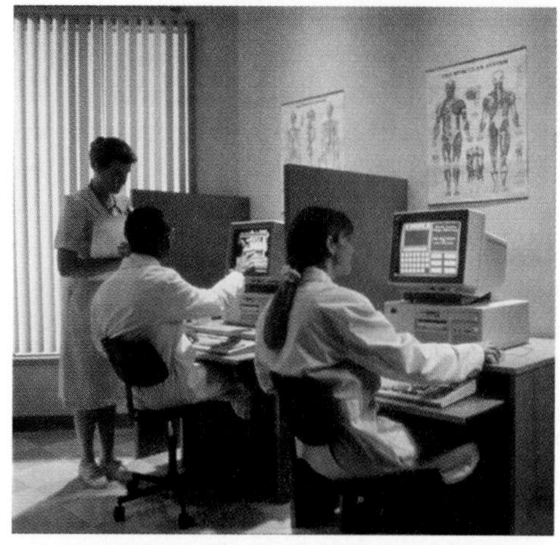

By enabling scientists, physicians, and other professionals to exchange information and ideas instantaneously, the Internet is accelerating the pace of scientific collaboration and the spread of knowledge.

Schlumberger uses the Net for this purpose, as does Cygnus Support, a software developer with only 125 employees with offices in Mountain View, California, and Somerville, Massachusetts. Cygnus originally turned to the Internet to link its offices inexpensively via e-mail. It later developed an intranet to keep employees informed about company developments and to help manage the large number of telecommuters who work for the company.

Interactivity, Flexibility, and Customization

Internet tools can create interactive applications that can be customized for multiple purposes and audiences. Web pages have capabilities for interacting with viewers that cannot be found in traditional print media. Visitors attracted by alluring displays of text, graphics, video, and sound also can click on hot buttons to make selections, take actions, or pursue additional information. Companies can use e-mail, chat rooms, and electronic discussion groups to create ongoing dialogues with their customers, using the information they have gathered to tailor communication precisely to fit the needs of each individual. Internet applications can be scaled up or down as the size of their audience changes because the technology works with the firm's existing network infrastructure.

Accelerated Distribution of Knowledge

In today's information economy, rapid access to knowledge is critical to the success of many companies. The Internet helps with this problem. Organizations are using e-mail and access to databases to gain immediate access to information resources in key areas such as business, science, law, and government. With blinding speed, the Internet can link a lone researcher sitting at a computer screen to mountains of data (including graphics) all over the world, otherwise too expensive and too difficult to tap. For example, scientists can obtain photographs taken by NASA space probes within an hour of the picture being taken. It has become easy and inexpensive for corporations to obtain the latest U.S. Department of Commerce statistics, current weather data, and laws of legal entities worldwide.

In addition to accessing public knowledge resources on the Internet and the Web, companies can create internal Web sites as repositories of their own organizational knowledge. Multimedia Web pages can organize this knowledge, giving employees easier access to information and expertise. Web browser software provides a universal interface for accessing information resources from internal corporate databases as well as external information sources.

9.2 THE INTERNET AND ELECTRONIC COMMERCE

In earlier chapters, we described an array of information technologies that are transforming the way products are produced, marketed, shipped, and sold. Companies have been using their own WANs, VANs, electronic data interchange (EDI), e-mail, shared databases, digital image processing, bar coding, and interactive software to replace telephone calls and paper-based procedures for product design, marketing, ordering, delivery, payment, and customer support. Trading partners can directly communicate with each other, bypassing middlemen and inefficient multilayered procedures. The Internet provides a public and universally available set of technologies for these purposes.

The Internet is rapidly becoming the technology of choice for electronic commerce because it offers businesses an even easier way to link with other business and individuals at very low cost. Web sites are available to consumers 24 hours a day. New marketing and sales channels can be created. Handling transactions electronically can reduce transaction costs and delivery time for some goods, especially those that are purely digital (such as software, text products, images, or videos). Retail sales via the Web reached $4 billion in 1997 and are expected to grow to $17 billion by 2001.

Internet Business Models

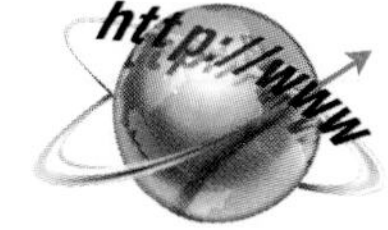

Companies large and small are using the Internet to make product information, ordering, and customer support immediately available and to help buyers and sellers make contact. Some of these Internet electronic commerce initiatives represent automation of traditional paper-based business processes, while others are new business models. For example, Gardener's Eden uses the Web to advertise its traditional print catalogue. Orders still must be placed by fax or telephone using the print catalogue. But Amazon.com represents a new type of business, as does Virtual Vineyards, which is discussed in the Case Study. Both are on-line storefronts that sell only over the Web. Another new business is Security First Network Bank, the virtual bank described in Chapter 2.

New business models have been created using the rich communication capabilities of the Internet. Onsale is an on-line auction forum, using e-mail and other interactive features of the Web. People can make on-line bids for items such as computer equipment, sports collectibles, wines, rock-concert tickets, and electronics. The system accepts bids for items entered on the Internet, evaluates the bids, and notifies the highest bidder. Bid.com in Toronto, which started out hosting consumer cyberauctions, now has Web-based auction services for business-to-business sales of items such as agricultural equipment.

The Internet has created on-line communities, where people can exchange ideas and opinions with people with similar interests in many different locations. Some of these virtual communities are providing the foundation for new businesses. Electric Minds, a cyberspace community for people interested in technology and culture generates revenue from advertisers who place banners on its Web site. In exchange, the sponsors have access to pockets of potential customers. Tripod attracts college students and young college graduates by providing "tools for life"—practical information about careers, health,

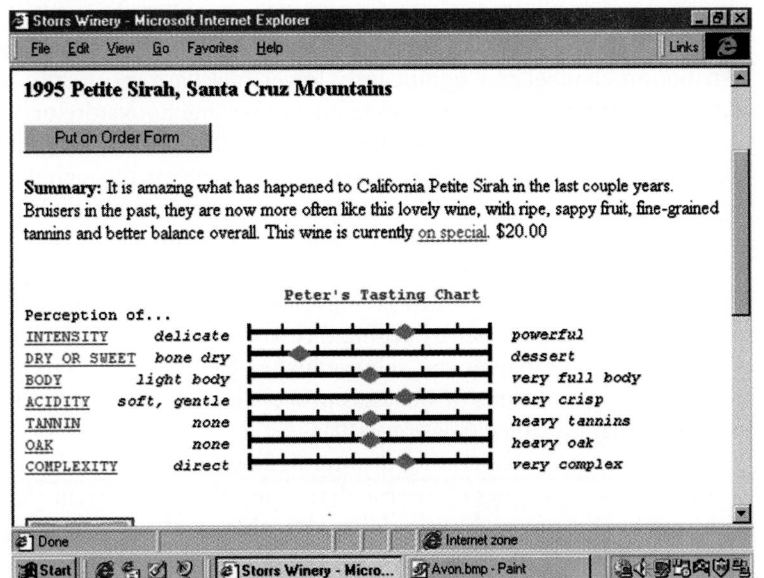

Peter's Tasting Chart on the Virtual Vineyards Web site provides evaluations of wines according to dimensions of taste to help visitors make informed wine selections. By providing this information along with the ability to purchase wine on-line, Virtual Vineyards has created a successful new business model for wine retailing.

Tripod is a new type of Internet business based on an on-line community for college students and young college graduates, with "pods" for specific interests such as health and fitness. The company generates revenue from advertising banners on its Web pages and from providing ways for corporate clients to target customers who are aged 18 to 30.

personal finance, and travel, a resume-distribution service, and a facility to maintain a personal Web page. Members can participate in on-line discussion groups on women's issues, work and money, or the arts. Tripod's revenue comes from providing ways for corporate clients to target customers in the 18- to 30-year-old age group. In addition to selling electronic advertising space, Tripod allows corporate customers to sell products on the Web site and receives a percentage of each transaction (Eckerson, 1996).

Table 9.3 compares some of these Internet-based business models, which also are described in the Laudon Web site. Some replace internal organizational processes, some replace existing businesses, and some represent completely new kinds of businesses. All in one way or another add *value:* They provide the customer with a new product or service; they provide additional information or service along with a traditional product or service; or they provide a product or service at much lower cost than traditional means.

Customer-Centered Retailing

The Internet provides companies with new channels of communication and interaction that can create closer yet more cost-effective relationships with customers in sales, marketing, and customer support.

Direct Sales over the Web

Manufacturers can sell their products and services directly to retail customers, bypassing intermediaries such as distributors or retail outlets. Eliminating middlemen in the distribution channel can significantly lower purchase transaction costs. Operators of virtual storefronts such as the Amazon.com on-line bookstore or Virtual Vineyards do not have expenditures for rent, sales staff, and the other operations of a traditional retail store. Airlines can sell tickets directly to passengers through their own Web sites or through travel sites such as Travelocity without paying commissions to travel agents.

To pay for all the steps in a traditional distribution channel, a product may have to be priced as high as 135 percent of its original cost to manufacture (Mougayar, 1998). Figure 9.6 illustrates how much savings can result from eliminating each of these layers in the distribution process. By selling directly to consumers or reducing the number of intermediaries, companies can achieve higher profits while charging lower prices. The removal of organizations or business process layers responsible for intermediary steps in a value chain is called **disintermediation.**

disintermediation The removal of organizations or business process layers responsible for certain intermediary steps in a value chain.

The Internet is accelerating disintermediation in some industries and creating opportunities for new types of intermediaries in others. In certain industries, distributors with warehouses of goods or middlemen such as real estate agents may be replaced by new intermediaries specializing in helping Internet users efficiently obtain product and

TABLE 9.3 Internet Business Models

Category	Description	Examples
Virtual Storefront	Sells physical goods or services on-line instead of through a physical storefront or retail outlet. Delivery of nondigital goods and services takes place through traditional means.	Amazon.com Virtual Vineyards Security First Network Bank
Marketplace Concentrator	Concentrates information about products and services from multiple providers at one central point. Purchasers can search, comparison-shop, and sometimes complete the sales transaction.	Internet Mall DealerNet Industrial Marketplace InsureMarket
Information Brokers	Provide product, pricing, and availability information. Some facilitate transactions, but their main value is the information they provide.	PartNet Travelocity Auto-by-Tel
Transaction Brokers	Buyers can view rates and terms, but the primary business activity is to complete the transaction.	E*Trade Ameritrade
Electronic Clearinghouses	Provide auction-like settings for products where price and availability are constantly changing, sometimes in response to customer actions.	Bid.com Onsale
Reverse Auction	Consumers submit a bid to multiple sellers to buy goods or services at a buyer-specified price.	Priceline.com
Digital Product Delivery	Sell and deliver software, multimedia, and other digital products over the Internet.	Build-a-Card PhotoDisc SonicNet
Content Provider	Creates revenue by providing content. The customer may pay to access the content or revenue may be generated by selling advertising space or by having advertisers pay for placement in an organized listing in a searchable database.	Wall Street Journal Interactive Quote.com Tripod
On-line Service Provider	Provide service and support for hardware and software users.	Cyber Media Tune Up.com

price information or locate on-line sources of goods and services. The information brokers listed in Table 9.3 are examples. In businesses impacted by the Internet, middlemen will have to adjust their services to fit the new business model or create new services based on the model.

Interactive Marketing

Marketers can use the interactive features of Web pages to hold consumers' attention or to capture information about their tastes and interests. Some of this information may be obtained by asking visitors to "register" on-line and provide information about

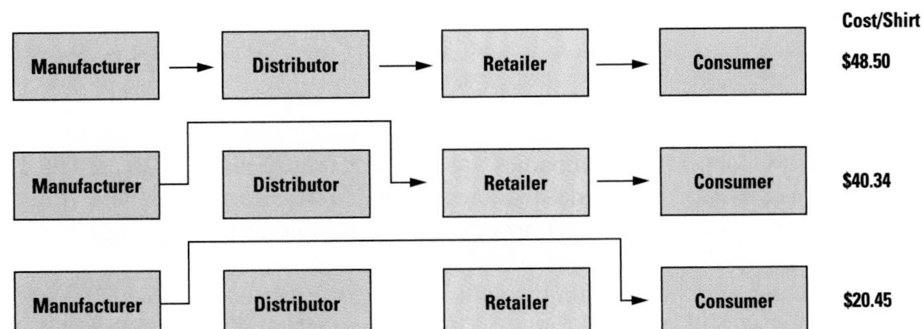

FIGURE 9.6

The benefits of disintermediation to the consumer. The typical distribution channel has several intermediary layers, each of which adds to the final cost of a product, such as a shirt. Removing each layer lowers the final cost to the consumer.

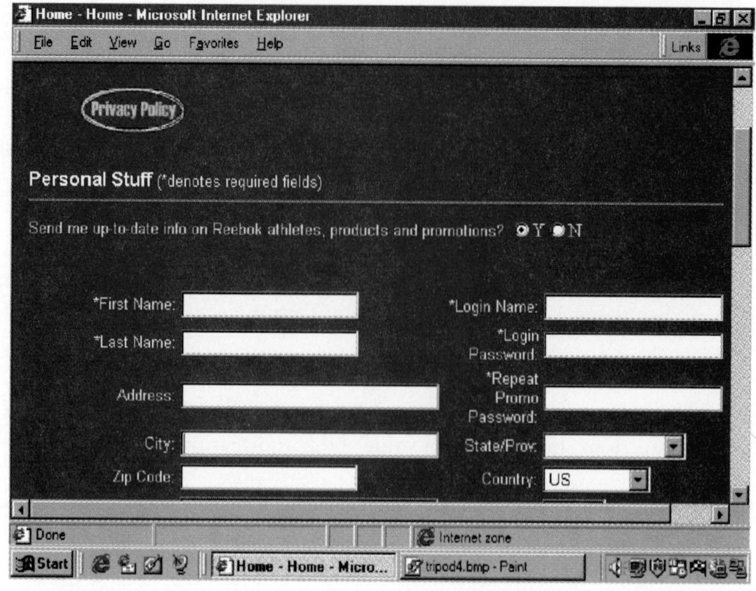

Reebok International uses its Web site to maintain an ongoing dialogue with customers and learn more about their tastes and interests. Visitors to the Web site can obtain profiles of athletes, customized workout tips, and other information by filling out an on-line profile form.

hit An entry into the log file of a Web server generated by each request to the server for a file.

themselves. Companies also can use special Web site auditing software capable of tracking the number of hits to their Web sites and the Web pages of greatest interest to visitors after they have entered the sites. (A **hit** is an entry into the log file of a Web server generated by each request to the server for a file.) They can analyze this information to develop more precise profiles of their customers. For instance, TravelWeb, a Web site offering electronic information on more than 16,000 hotels in 138 countries and an on-line reservation capability, tracks the origin of each user and the screens and hypertext links he or she uses to learn about customer preferences. The Hyatt hotel chain found that Japanese users are most interested in the golf facilities of a resort, valuable information in shaping market strategies and for developing hospitality-related products.

Companies can even use the Web and Internet capabilities such as electronic discussion groups, mailing lists, and e-mail to create ongoing dialogues with their customers. Communications and product offerings can be tailored precisely to individual customers (Bakos, 1998). For example, visitors to the Web site for Reebok International Ltd. can obtain profiles of athletes and training tips from coaches in fitness categories of their preference. If they fill out profile forms asking them to list their favorite sports, they also will receive customized workout tips, news updates about their sports, and other information on future visits. By becoming site "members," they can send e-mail "postcards" to their favorite athletes. Reebok further enhanced its Web site with e-mail, discussion-group, and bulletin-board capabilities to create a community of users (Cole-Gomolski, 1998).

The cost of customer survey and focus groups is very high. Learning what customers feel about one's products or services through electronic visits to Web sites is much cheaper. Web sites providing product information also lower costs by shortening the sales cycle, reducing the amount of time sales staff must spend in customer education (Sterne, 1995). The Web shifts more marketing and selling activities to the customer, as customers fill out their own on-line order forms (Hoffman, Novak, and Chatterjee, 1995).

Customer Self-Service

The Web and other network technologies are inspiring new approaches to customer service and support. Many companies are using their Web sites and e-mail to answer customer questions or to provide customers with helpful information. The Window on Technology describes the experiences of companies using chat rooms and Web-linked call centers for this purpose.

The Web provides a medium through which customers can interact with the company, at their convenience, and find information on their own that previously required

WINDOW ON TECHNOLOGY

Interacting with the Customer

Internet chat rooms have had a somewhat unsavory reputation as havens for teenagers, misfits, and virtual pick-up scenes, but companies have found that the interactive qualities of this technology can be harnessed in many valuable ways, especially in customer service and support.

Software maker Symantec, which deals with about 24,000 user queries per week, employs about 500 people to handle phone calls at its customer service center in Eugene, Oregon. The company has been encouraging people to solve their own problems by using a self-help database on its Web site because such support costs 40 percent to 60 percent less than telephone-based support. The database contains product information and discussion groups where customers can post questions. However, the average response time to questions submitted this way is 24 hours. To address this problem, Symantec recently added chat to its Web site to provide customers with more immediate feedback. Software from Business Evolution allows customers to click on a button on Symantec's Web site and enter a "room" to chat one-on-one with a customer service representative.

Other companies are experimenting with chat as a way to interact more closely with customers on the Internet. IBM used chat sessions with its top executives and customers to help promote the introduction of its line of specialized AS/400e midrange computers for Internet commerce. More than 2000 customers participated in the sessions, which were repeated three times to cover time differences in Europe and Asia. Merrill Lynch used a chat session with brokerage chief John Steffens to calm investors rattled by the October 1997 stock market plunge. The brokerage giant now regularly hosts chat seminars. Egghead Software's Web site lets customers chat with a "sales egg" as they shop in its on-line store or chat with other customers in a "virtual lounge."

If customers still need to speak with a human representative, Web sites can be enhanced to connect them to corporate call centers. New software products such as Web Agent from Aspect Telecommunications Inc. in San Jose, California, allow Web sites to be browsed simultaneously by customers and customer service agents. They can talk to each other over a separate telephone line or an Internet connection to compare products or discuss their features. WebAgent synchronizes Web screens viewed by both parties as they talk and even lets each draw circles around words or pictures for both to see. This feature is useful for explaining how a complex device, such as a router, works while a diagram is viewed on-screen.

Such benefits prompted Logistix Inc., a Fremont, California, logistics technology company, to use Web Agent in conjunction with its 120-person call center. Logistix and other companies like the fact that the technology can turn the call center into a central point for customer contact where agents can answer customer inquiries from a number of sources—telephone, fax, e-mail, or the Web site.

To Think About: ***How does the Internet change business relationships with customers and the customer support process?***

Sources: Matt Hamblen, "Call Centers and Web Sites Cozy Up," *Computerworld,* March 2, 1998; Gordon Arnaut, "No Frills, Just Service with a Screen," *The New York Times,* January 26, 1998; and Lisa Bransten, "Companies Are Talking Up Chat Rooms as Way to Improve Customer Service," *The Wall Street Journal,* December 15, 1997.

a human customer-support expert. Some companies are realizing substantial cost savings from Web-based customer self-service applications. American, Northwest, and other major airlines have created Web sites where customers can review flight departure and arrival times, seating charts, and airport logistics, check frequent-flyer miles, and purchase tickets on-line.

These Web sites allow companies to engage in ongoing dialogues with their customers that can provide information for other purposes. For example, Dell Computer has established a Dell news group on the Net and other on-line services to receive and handle customer complaints and questions. They answer about 90 percent of the questions within 24 hours. Dell also does market research for free through these news groups rather than paying a professional for the same information.

Business-to-Business Electronic Commerce: New Efficiencies and Relationships

Many believe that the most promising area of electronic commerce is not retailing to individuals but the automation of purchase and sale transactions from business to business. For a number of years, companies have used proprietary electronic data interchange (EDI) systems for this purpose; now they are turning to the Web and extranets.

Cisco Systems, a leading manufacturer of networking equipment, conducts 40 percent of its sales electronically, with more than $1 billion in sales per year through its Web site. Order-taking, credit checking, production scheduling, technical support, and routine customer-support activities are handled on-line.

Marshall Industries' Virtual Distribution System

Marshall Industries, the world's fourth-largest distributor of industrial electronic components and production supplies, created a "virtual" distribution environment in which almost all of the processes it performed physically have been converted to a digital service on the Net.

Marshall's customers and suppliers can access its intranet to obtain customized information. For example, high-tech suppliers can see information about their own accounts, such as sales reports, inventory levels, and design data. They also can accept or reject price quotes or order training materials. A personal knowledge-assistant process called Plugged-In allows customers to specify the product categories they are interested in. They only receive information specific to their interests.

Visitors can view more than 100,000 pages of data sheets, up-to-date pricing, and inventory information from 150 major suppliers, and information on 170,000 parts numbers. They can quickly locate products in Marshall's on-line catalogue using a sophisticated search engine. The site links to the United Parcel Service (UPS), where customers can track the status of their shipments. Sales representatives have secure intranet access so they can check sales and activity status only in their territory.

When a customer places an order, the system verifies price and quantity and initiates a real-time credit authorization and approval. As soon as the order is approved, the system sends an automated request to the warehouse for scheduling. The system then sends the customer an order acknowledgment accompanied by relevant shipping and logistics information from UPS. Messages about order status are automatically "pushed" to the customer. The system thus integrates the entire process of placing and receiving an order.

Other features of Marshall's Web site provide additional service and value. Visitors can access a free "Electronic Design Center" to test and run their designs over the Internet. For example, an engineer might use Marshall's Web site to test Texas Instruments' (TI) digital signal processors (DSPs) for the design of a new piece of multimedia hardware. (DSP chips improve the performance of high-tech products such as computer hard disks, headphones, and power steering in cars.) At the site, the engineer can find technical specifications and even simulate designs using TI chips. The engineer would

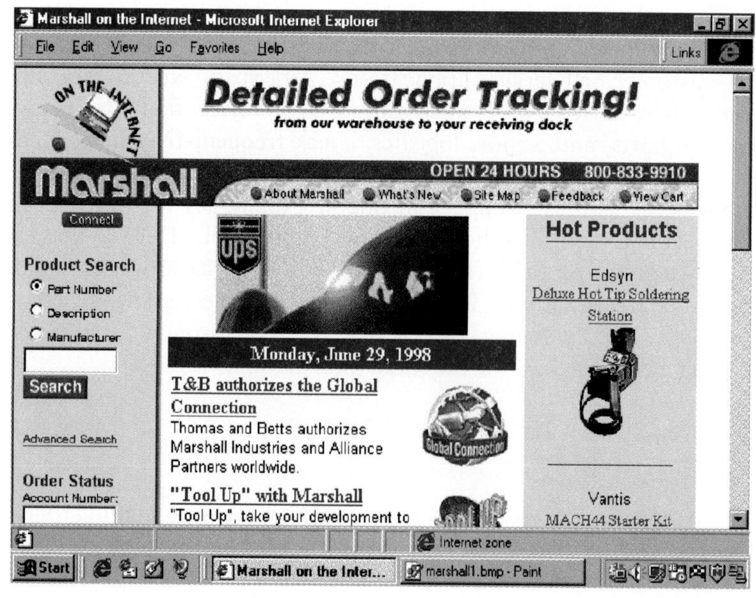

The Marshall Industries Web site supports a "virtual" distribution environment that automates the entire process of placing and receiving an order. Customers can use the Web site to review pricing information and product descriptions, input orders, and obtain customized information about their accounts and the status of their shipments with United Parcel Service. Marshall's Web site provides additional service and value by allowing visitors to test and run their designs over the Internet, obtain training, and access industry news.

download sample code, modify the code to suit the product being built, test it on a "virtual chip" attached to the Web, and analyze its performance. If the engineer liked the results, Marshall could download his or her code, burn it into physical chips and send back samples for designing prototypes. The entire process would take minutes.

Marshall's Web site provides after-sale training so that engineers do not have to attend special training classes or meetings in faraway locations. Marshall links to NetSeminar, a Web site where Marshall's customers can register for and receive educational programs developed for them by their suppliers using video, audio, and real-time chat capabilities.

For business-to-business electronic commerce, companies can use their own Web sites, like Cisco Systems and Marshall Industries, or they can conduct sales through Web sites set up as on-line marketplaces. (Marketplace concentrators are among the new Internet business models we introduced earlier in this chapter.) Industrial malls such as Industrial Marketplace bring together a large number of suppliers in one place, providing search tools so that buyers can quickly locate what they need. They make money by collecting fees from their "tenant" vendors. Companies also can sell to other companies through Web sites that run cyberauctions for electronic parts and industrial and scientific equipment. The auctions' operations are similar to those described earlier in this section (Deutsch, 1998). Figure 9.7 illustrates one way that a business-to-business purchase transaction might take place.

Corporate purchasing traditionally has been based on long-term relationships with one or two suppliers. The Internet makes information about alternative suppliers more accessible so that companies can find the best deal from a wider range of sources, including those overseas. For example, Mike Maiorano, the purchasing manager for XLNT Designs Inc., a manufacturer of networking technologies, consults the Web when he is asked to buy from an unfamiliar supplier or locate a new type of part. It is not surprising that identifying and researching potential trading partners is the most common procurement activity on the Internet (Buchanan, 1997). Suppliers themselves can use the Web to research competitors' prices on-line.

Organizations also can use the Web to solicit bids from suppliers by advertising requests for proposal (RFPs) on-line. Government organizations, especially military agencies and state governments, have been quick to adopt this model. Table 9.4 describes other examples of business-to-business electronic commerce.

Electronic Commerce Support Systems

A business interested in setting up a system to support electronic commerce has three options: (1) using a Web server with a toolkit to build its own system, (2) purchasing a packaged commerce Web server system, or (3) outsourcing the system to an e-commerce service provider. A number of commerce or merchant Web server systems are available. They typically provide a Web storefront, usually with some type of on-line catalogue support, and a means for taking orders. Some of these systems link to financial networks to complete payment processing. Table 9.5 describes some of these products.

For companies that are not ready to operate their own electronic commerce sites, companies such as AT&T, MCI, Best Internet Communications, and BBN Planet offer Web hosting services that process electronic commerce transactions for other organizations. A **Web hosting service** maintains a large Web server or series of servers and provides fee-paying subscribers with space to maintain their Web sites. The subscribing companies may create their own Web pages or have the hosting service or a Web design firm create them. Web hosting services offer solutions to small companies that do not have the resources to operate their own commerce servers or companies that still are experimenting with electronic commerce.

Integrating all of the processes associated with electronic commerce requires additional software and tools, such as software providing interfaces between Web servers and the company's core-transaction databases and electronic payment systems. **Electronic payment systems** use technologies such as electronic funds transfer, credit cards, smart

Web hosting service Company maintaining large Web servers to maintain the Web sites of fee-paying subscribers.

electronic payment system The use of digital technologies such as electronic funds transfer, credit cards, smart cards and debit cards, and Internet-based payment systems to pay for products and services electronically.

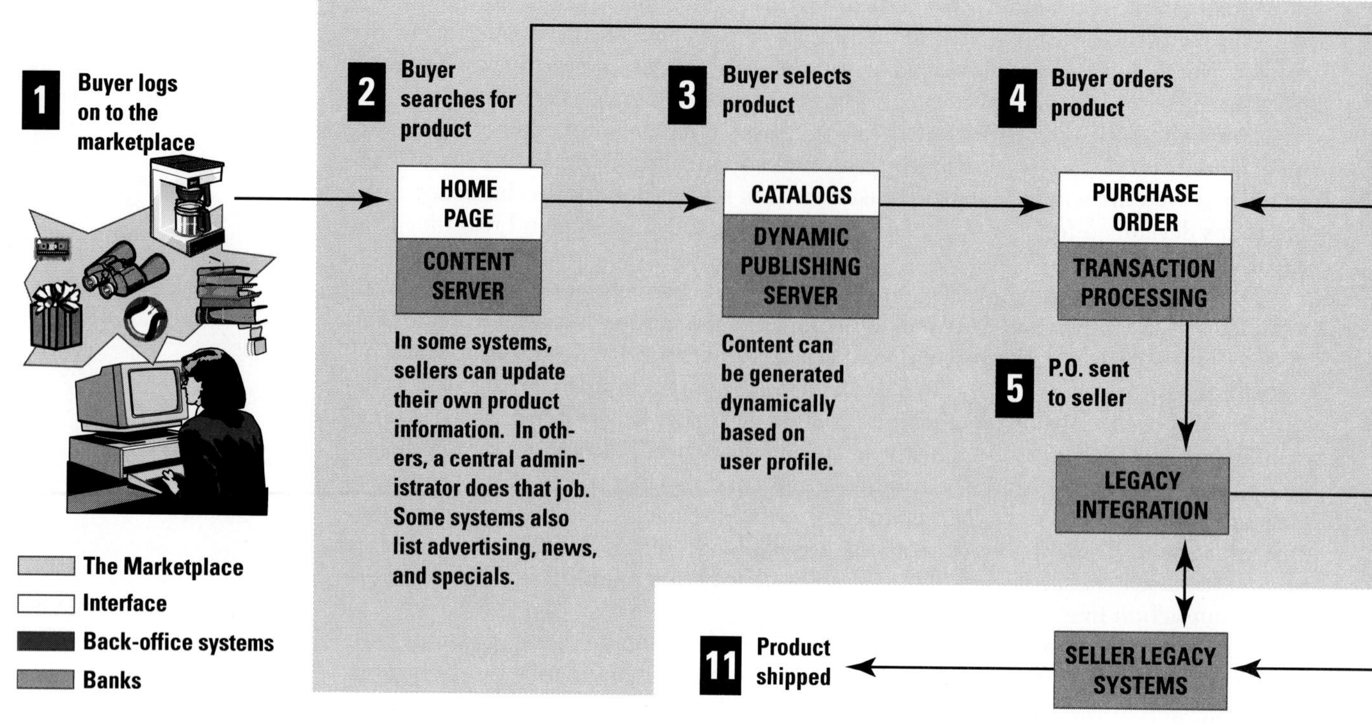

cards and debit cards, and new Internet-based payment systems to pay for products and services electronically. Software to track and monitor Web site usage for marketing analysis also is desirable.

The process of paying for products and services purchased on the Internet is complex and merits additional discussion. Many security issues are involved, and there are a large number of payment systems. We discuss secure electronic payment systems in detail in Chapter 14.

TABLE 9.4 Examples of Business-to-Business Electronic Commerce

Business	Electronic Commerce Application
U.S. General Services Administration	The procurement arm of the U.S. federal government created an ordering system called GSA Advantage, which allows federal agencies to buy everything through its Web site. The Web site lists 220,000 products and accounts for annual sales of $12 million. By using the Web, agencies can see all of their purchasing options and make choices based on price and delivery.
AMP Inc.	By placing its 400 catalogues on the Web, this electrical-components manufacturer hopes to reduce and eventually eliminate $8 million to $10 million per year in printing and shipping costs while offering catalogues that are always up-to-date. AMP created a new division called AMPeMerce Internet Solutions to help manufacturers and other companies develop Internet-based product catalogues and selling mechanisms.
General Electric Information Services	Operates a Trading Process Network (TPN) where GE and other subscribing companies can solicit and accept bids from selected suppliers over the Internet. TPN is a secure Web site developed for internal GE use that now is available to other companies for customized bidding and automated purchasing. GE earns revenue by charging subscribers for the service and by collecting a fee from the seller if a transaction is completed.

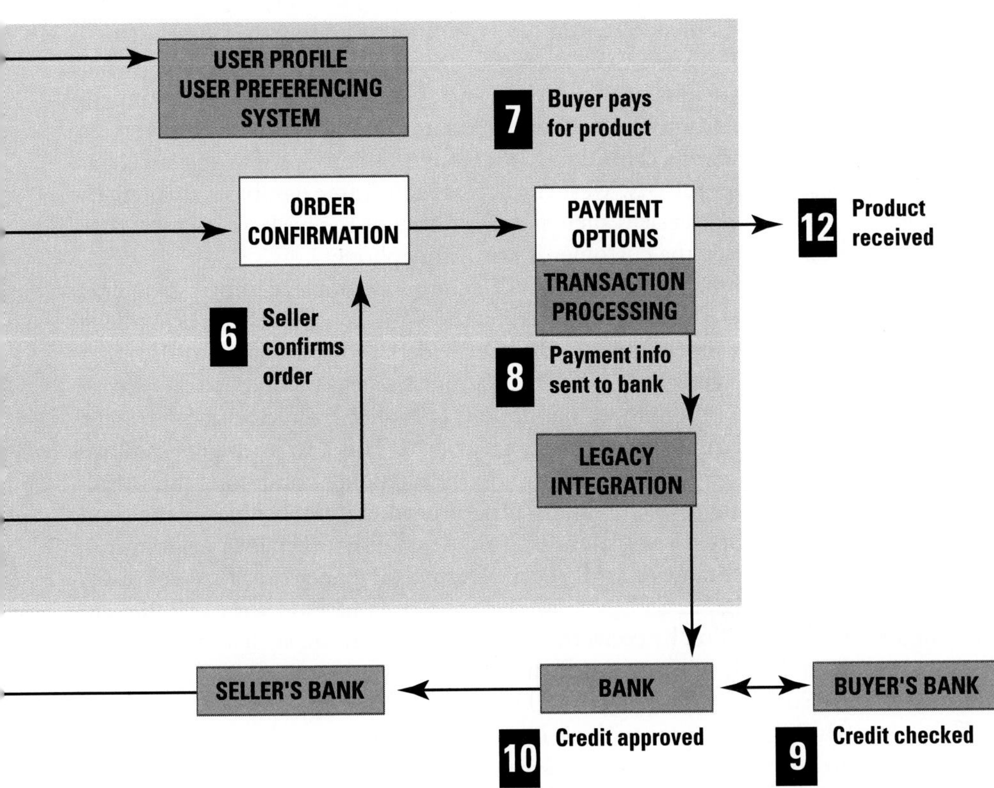

FIGURE 9.7

Portrait of an electronic commerce marketplace. Buyers can locate, order, and pay for products through an electronic mall, such as the one illustrated here, or through an individual vendor's Web site. *Source: "Portrait of an Electronic Marketplace,"* Computerworld, *April 28, 1997. Copyright © 1998 Computerworld, Inc., Framingham, MA 01701. Rights reserved. Reprinted with permission from* Computerworld Magazine.

9.3 INTRANETS AND ELECTRONIC BUSINESS

Businesses are finding some of the greatest benefits of Internet technology come from applications that lower agency and coordination costs. Although companies have used internal networks for many years to manage and coordinate internal business processes, intranets quickly are becoming the technology of choice for electronic business.

How Intranets Support Electronic Business

Intranets are inexpensive, scalable to expand or contract as needs change, and accessible from most computing platforms. Whereas most companies, particularly the larger ones, must support a multiplicity of computer platforms that cannot communicate with

TABLE 9.5 Examples of Electronic Commerce Servers and Toolkits

Product	Description	Vendor
Icat Electronic Commerce Server	Provides on-line catalogue shopping and order placement	Icat
Net.Commerce	Merchant server supporting the SET (Secure Electronic Transactions) protocol	IBM
MerchantXpert	Provides a full set of retailing services, including product displays, sales, promotions, electronic "shopping carts," tax calculations, and customer support and reporting	Netscape
Open MarketTransact	End-to-end commerce services, including on-line customer authentication, order and payment processing, tax calculations, and customer service	Open Market
PC-Charge	Works with PC-based Web servers for credit card processing	Go Software

each other, intranets provide instant connectivity, uniting all computers into a single, virtually seamless, network system. Web software presents a uniform interface, which can be used to integrate many different processes and systems throughout the company. Companies can connect their intranet to company databases just as with the Web, enabling employees to take actions central to a company's operations. For instance, customer service representatives for U.S. West can access mainframe databases through the corporate intranet to turn on services such as call waiting or to check installation dates for new phone lines, all while the customer is on the telephone.

Intranets can help organizations create a richer, more responsive information environment. Internal corporate applications based on the Web page model can be made interactive using a variety of media, text, audio, and video. A principal use of intranets has been to create on-line repositories of information that can be updated as often as required. Product catalogues, employee handbooks, telephone directories, or benefits information can be revised immediately as changes occur. This "event-driven" publishing allows organizations to respond more rapidly to changing conditions than traditional paper-based publishing, which requires a rigid production schedule. Made available via intranets, documents always can be up-to-date, eliminating paper, printing, and distribution costs. Some estimates put the cost of using the paper-based model of distributing information as high as $15 per employee. An organization with 100,000 employees might save $1.5 million by converting a single application, such as an employee policy and benefits manual, to electronic form on an intranet (Levitt, 1996).

Intranets have provided cost savings in other application areas as well. For instance, U.S. West saves $300,000 per year with an intranet application that automatically notifies service representatives of expiring service contracts. The intranet only cost $17,000 to build (Jahnke, 1998). KeyCorp's knowledge-bank intranet for distributing job postings, information on best practices, marketing material, and newsletters produces $1.8 million in annual cost savings for an initial development cost of $300,000 (*Computerworld,* 1997). Conservative studies of returns on investment (ROIs) from intranets show ROIs of 23 percent to 85 percent, and some companies have reported ROIs of more than 1000 percent. More detail on the business value of intranets can be found in Chapter 10.

For companies with an installed network infrastructure, intranets are very inexpensive to build and run. Programming Web pages is quick and easy with Web page authoring tools; employees can create Web pages on their own. The intranet provides a universal e-mail system, remote access, group collaboration tools, electronic library, application-sharing system, and company communications network. Some companies are using their intranets for virtual conferencing. Intranets are simple, cost-effective communication tools. Table 9.6 summarizes the organizational benefits of using intranets.

Intranets and Group Collaboration

Intranets and other network technologies provide a rich set of tools for creating collaborative environments in which members of an organization can exchange ideas, share information, and work together on common projects and assignments, regardless

TABLE 9.6 Organizational Benefits of Intranets
Connectivity: Accessible from most computing platforms
Can be tied to legacy systems and core transaction databases
Can create interactive applications with text, audio, and video
Scalable to larger or smaller computing platforms as requirements change
Easy to use, universal Web browser interface
Low start-up costs
Richer, more responsive information environment
Reduced information distribution costs

of their physical location. These tools include e-mail, fax, voice mail, teleconferencing, videoconferencing, dataconferencing, groupware, chat systems, newsgroups, and teamware. We already have described the capabilities of most of these tools.

Teamware consists of intranet-based applications for building a work team, sharing ideas and documents, brainstorming, scheduling, and archiving decisions made or rejected by a project for future use. It is similar to groupware, but more customized for team work. (Lotus's Instant TeamRoom is based on the Domino server version of Lotus Notes groupware.) Teamware and groupware frequently are used as support tools for the short-lived projects staffed by knowledge workers. Chapter 12 provides a detailed description of groupware and intranets for managing and distributing organizational knowledge resources.

teamware Group collaboration software that is customized for teamwork.

Some companies are using intranets to create enterprise collaboration environments linking diverse groups, projects, and activities throughout the organization. The U.S. West Global Village intranet is a prominent example. Here are just a few of its capabilities:

- A sales consultant in Chicago can check events throughout the company. He pulls up News of the Day, an internal newsletter.
- A project manager can click on the lab page to inspect software being developed for a new service. He can test the software from his own computer.
- Repair technicians can share a map showing damage to phone lines caused by ice storms and explore a strategy for repairing them.
- An executive can log onto the intranet from her home after dinner to catch up with e-mail and check out the next day's schedule for her project team.
- An engineer researching the design of a new network component can link to the public Internet via a gateway built into the Global Village home page. She surfs the Web to locate possible suppliers, then returns to the company intranet to inform her colleagues via e-mail about what she has found.

These intranet applications have enabled U.S. West to improve communications and streamline business processes, saving the company millions of dollars each year.

Intranet Applications for Electronic Business

Intranets are springing up in all the major functional areas of the business, allowing them to manage more of their business processes electronically. Figure 9.8 illustrates some of the intranet applications that have been developed for finance and accounting, human resources, sales and marketing, and manufacturing and production.

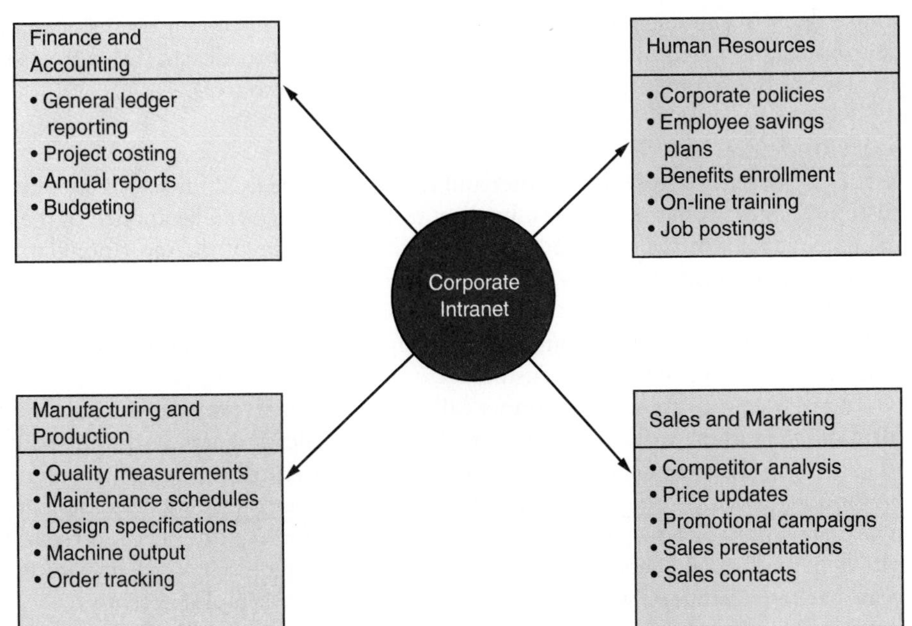

FIGURE 9.8

Functional applications of intranets. Intranet applications have been developed for each of the major functional areas of the business.

TABLE 9.7 Intranets in Finance and Accounting

Organization	Intranet Application
Charles Schwab	SMART reporting and analysis application provides managers with a comprehensive view of Schwab financial activities, including a risk-evaluation template that helps managers assess nine categories of risk. Schwab's intranet also delivers the FinWeb General Ledger reporting system on-line in easy-to-digest format.
Jeffries & Co.	Intranet-based data marts consolidate data from different legacy systems to provide a unified view of customer accounts. Sales staff and executives can access data marts that consolidate trading and financial data using Netscape Web browsers to view summary-level reports or drill down for further detail. The data marts help support the investment bank's expansion into new markets such as corporate finance and research.
Pacific Northwest National Laboratory	Intranet Web Reporting System provides financial statistics for laboratory activities, including current costs charged to each project, the number of hours spent on each project by individual employees, and how actual costs compare to projected costs. Lab employees can use Web browsers to perform ad-hoc queries on financial data.

Finance and Accounting

Many organizations have extensive TPS that collect operational data on financial activities, but their traditional management reporting systems, such as general ledger systems and spreadsheets, often cannot bring this detailed information together for decision making and performance measurement. Intranets can be very valuable for finance and accounting because they can provide an integrated view of financial and accounting information on-line in an easy-to-use format. Table 9.7 provides some examples.

Human Resources

One of the principal responsibilities of human resources departments is to keep employees informed of company issues as well as to provide information about their personnel records and employee benefits. Human resources can use intranets for on-line publishing of corporate policy manuals, job postings and internal job transfers, company telephone directories, and training classes. Employees can use an intranet to enroll in health care, employee savings and other benefit plans if it is linked to the firm's human resources or benefits database or to take on-line competency tests. Human resource departments can rapidly deliver information about upcoming events or company developments to employees using newsgroups or e-mail broadcasts. Table 9.8 lists examples of how intranets are used in the area of human resources.

Sales and Marketing

Earlier we described how the Internet and the Web can be used for selling to individual customers and to other businesses. Internet technology also can be applied to the internal management of the sales and marketing function. One of the most popular applications for corporate intranets is to oversee and coordinate the activities of the sales force. Sales staff can dial in for updates on pricing, promotions, rebates, or customers or obtain information about competitors. They can access presentations and sales documents and customize them for customers.

Wang Software created an intranet called Knowledge Exchange, which includes information about the work-flow products Wang sells, sales contacts, corporate strategies of existing and potential customers, case studies of current Wang customers, and troubleshooting tips for software implementations. The intranet includes discussion groups, which are scanned by help desk staff for information of interest to sales representatives. The help desk documents telephone transactions with representatives and feeds solutions back to a database where they can be used to help others. Representatives can use

TABLE 9.8	Intranets in Human Resources
Organization	**Intranet Application**
Genentech	An on-line employee handbook provides company announcements and an employee directory along with information on research seminars, commuting options, benefits, child care, how to obtain business cards, and safety equipment.
Public Service & Gas Co. of New Jersey	Employees can use an intranet to access information on company savings plans, track historical performance, and reallocate funds in their 401K savings plans, taking advantage of asset-allocation models to make decisions. They also can use the intranet to choose a health plan, reviewing reports on HMO providers to guide their selection, and even select their physicians.
TRW Inc.	Employees can view job postings on-line through an intranet.
Documentum Inc.	System engineers and consultants in the United States and Europe can receive on-line training on how to use the company's document management software products.

the site's search engine to pull up PowerPoint electronic presentations, documents, or spreadsheets based on specified keywords (Dahle, 1997).

Case Corp., a Racine, Wisconsin, manufacturer of earth-moving and farming equipment, supports its sales and marketing teams with intranet collaboration tools for contact management, discussion forums, document management, and calendars. Marketsmarter LLC develops customized intranet applications for marketing and sales personnel based on a proprietary process called PRAISE. (PRAISE stands for Purpose, Research, Analyze, Implement, Strategize, and Evaluate.) PRAISE applications facilitate sharing of information on competitors, potential product-development products, and research tasks and includes time-sensitive accountability to measure results (Sterne, 1998).

Manufacturing and Production

In manufacturing, information-management issues are highly complex, involving massive inventories, capturing and integrating real-time production data flows, changing relationships with suppliers, and volatile costs. The manufacturing function typically uses multiple types of data, including graphics as well as text, which are scattered in many disparate systems. Manufacturing information is often very time-sensitive and difficult to retrieve when files must be continuously updated. Developing intranets that integrate manufacturing data under a uniform user interface is more complicated than in other functional areas.

Despite these difficulties, companies are launching intranet applications for manufacturing. Intranets coordinating the flow of information between lathes, controllers, inventory systems, and other components of a production system can make manufacturing information more accessible to different parts of the organization, increasing precision, and lowering costs. Table 9.9 describes some of these uses.

Coordination and Supply Chain Management

Intranets and extranets also can be used to simplify and integrate business processes spanning more than one functional area. These cross-functional processes can be coordinated electronically, increasing organizational efficiency and responsiveness. One area of great interest to companies is the use of intranets and extranets to facilitate supply chain management.

Chapter 2 introduced the concept of supply chain management, which integrates procurement, production, and logistics processes to supply goods and services from their source to final delivery to the customer. The supply chain can be thought of as an "extended enterprise" linking material suppliers, distributors, retailers, and customers, as well as manufacturing facilities.

TABLE 9.9 Intranets in Manufacturing and Production

Organization	Intranet Application
Nortel Technologies	Intranet publishes three-dimensional models and animations for faster exploration of ideas, better feedback, and shorter development cycles. The application reduces miscommunication between process engineers and the shop floor because animations show how to fit different pieces together.
Sony Corporation	Intranet delivers financial information to manufacturing personnel so that workers can monitor the profit-and-loss performance of the production line and adapt performance accordingly. The intranet also provides data on quality measurements, such as defects and rejects, as well as maintenance and training schedules.
Duke Power	Intranet provides on-line access to a computer-aided engineering tool for retrieving equipment designs and operating specifications that allows employees to view every important system in the plant at various levels of detail. Different subsets of systems can be formatted together to create a view of all the equipment in a particular room. Maintenance technicians, plant engineers, and operations personnel can use this tool with minimal training.
Rockwell International	Intranet improves process and quality of manufactured circuit boards and controllers by establishing home pages for its Milwaukee plant's computer-controlled machine tools that are updated every 60 seconds. Quality control managers can check the status of a machine by calling up its home page to learn how many pieces the machine output that day, what percentage of an order that output represents, and to what tolerances the machine is adhering.

In the pre-Internet environment, supply chain coordination was hampered by the difficulties of making information flow smoothly between many different kinds of systems servicing different parts of the supply chain, such as purchasing, materials management, manufacturing, and distribution. Internet technology provides the connectivity to overcome these barriers. Firms can use intranets to improve coordination among their internal supply chain processes, and they can use extranets to coordinate supply chain processes shared with their business partners (see Figure 9.9). Marshall Industries' extranet, described earlier, has many powerful supply chain management capabilities, as does the extranet for supply chain management developed by Chrysler Corporation.

Chrysler's Supplier Partner Information Network (SPIN) allows 3500 of Chrysler's 12,000 suppliers selective access to portions of its intranet, where they can access the most current data on design changes, parts shortages, packaging information, and invoice tracking. Chrysler believes that by streamlining product delivery and shortening the time to communicate process or design changes, SPIN has reduced the time to complete various business processes by 25 percent to 50 percent. Chrysler can use the in-

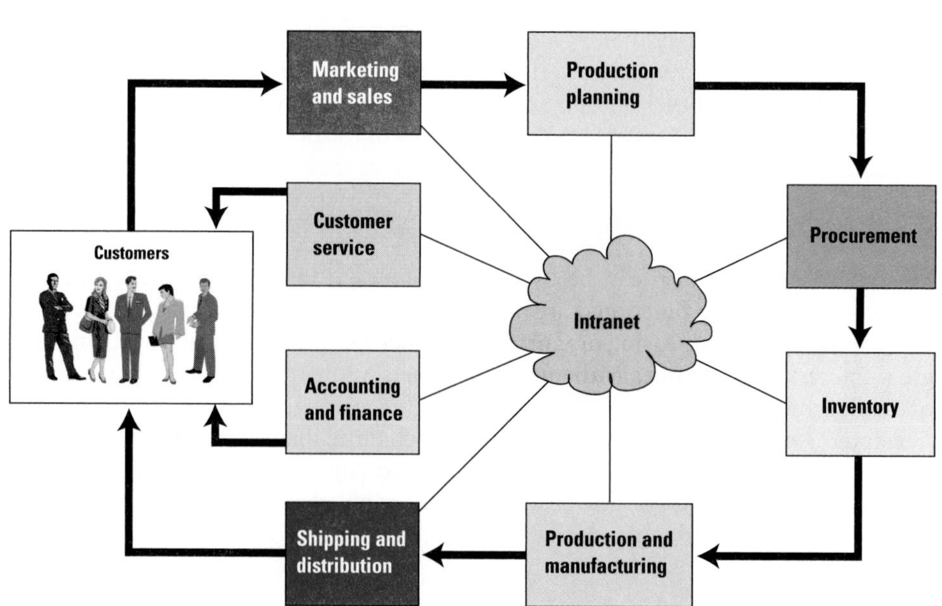

FIGURE 9.9

Intranet linking supply chain functions. Intranets can be used to integrate information from isolated business processes so that they can be coordinated for supply chain management. *Source: Kalakota and Whinston,* Electronic Commerce: A Manager's Guide. © 1997 by *Addison-Wesley Publishing Company. Reprinted by permission of Addison Wesley Longman. (p. 293).*

WINDOW ON ORGANIZATIONS

The Supply Chain Goes Global

Managing one's supply chain has been difficult enough in the past. But now, growing business globalization finds many companies obtaining supplies from all over the world. One might think that this would make the task of managing one's global supply chain impossible. Not so. The Internet is proving to be a tool that not only makes management of a global supply chain possible, but actually may even improve it.

What does the Internet offer the supply chain management function? Benefits begin with cost savings. Private networks are very expensive. For many companies, the cost of private networks makes obtaining supplies globally prohibitive. However, the Net is ubiquitous and only requires a Web browser to be able to use it. Neither seller nor buyer need build an expensive infrastructure. Suppliers and customers everywhere can easily afford to use it in their drive to participate in the global market. But cost savings is only one benefit of using the Net. The Net is fast, often dramatically cutting cycle times for sourcing, production and delivery. Faster cycle times mean companies can be more responsive to the market while also lowering inventory costs and errors. Let's look at a few examples of how it is working.

Adaptec Inc. is a Silicon Valley-based computer chip and board maker that obtains many of its products in East Asia. It is using the Internet to make available to its suppliers purchase orders and factory-status updates. The company says using the Net has cut the manufacturing cycle from 12 weeks to 8, making it a more responsive organization. At the same time, it claims savings of $10 million in inventory costs in only 4 months because of the Net. As Adaptec Electronic Commerce Manager Steve Robinson explains it, "It means data getting to the right people much faster, all in support of our No. 1 business driver—reducing cycle times."

Manufacturer Dell Computer is linking its entire supply chain via the Web. One benefit they already see, even before the links are completed, is they can get any new overseas partners on-line quickly and inexpensively. The Web is everywhere and easy to access, so fewer Dell IT staff are being used to help suppliers get on-line, and fewer Dell IT staff are being sent overseas.

The combined automobile industry presents an unusually ambitious example. The automotive supply chain already is global, and in response to this, the industry has created the Automotive Network Exchange (ANX), which began operating over the Internet in the summer of 1998. This partnership ultimately could enable as many as 40,000 automobile producers, parts suppliers, dealerships, and financial services companies to communicate worldwide. Auto industry experts estimate that by using this network, costs will be cut by $1 billion annually, or about $70 per vehicle produced. Jim Lloyd, vice president of network and information resources at UT Automotive in Dearborn, Michigan, explains that ANX will help save money on basic telecommunications costs because companies do not have to build the telecommunications infrastructure. "But," he adds, "that is just the tip of the iceberg." Other expected benefits include rapid response to changes in production and delivery schedules, a more rapid model development cycle, improved accuracy, and even higher product quality. To Abdallah Shanti, vice president of IT at LucasVarity plc, a $7 billion London-based company that supplies brake systems to auto makers in 20 countries, that has higher value than the immediate savings in communications costs.

To Think About: ***Suggest other ways the Internet can be used to improve supply chain management. What problems do you see in using the Internet in this way?***

Source: Adapted from Clinton Wilder, Gregory Dalton, and Beth Davis, "Global Links," *InformationWeek,* March 25, 1998.

formation from SPIN to manage employees more efficiently. A critical parts tracking application permits reassignment of workers so that shortages do not hold up assembly lines. Chrysler added invoice tracking to SPIN so that it spends less time fielding phone calls from suppliers inquiring about payments. SPIN has been revised to incorporate Chrysler's proprietary EDI system and push technology. SPIN can automatically notify suppliers of critical parts shortages.

Not all Internet-based supply chain applications are as ambitious as those of Chrysler or Marshall Industries, but they are changing the way businesses work internally and with each other (Kalakota and Whinston, 1996). Along with reducing costs, these supply chain management systems are providing more responsive customer service, allowing the workings of the business to be more driven by customer demand. Earlier supply chain management systems were driven by production master schedules based on forecasts or best guesses of demand for products. With new flows of information made possible by intranets and extranets, supply chain management can follow a demand-driven model.

Some companies are starting to use the Internet for supply chain management on a global scale, as described in the Window on Organizations.

9.4 MANAGEMENT CHALLENGES AND OPPORTUNITIES

Although the Internet offers a wealth of new opportunities for electronic commerce and electronic business, it also presents managers with a series of challenges. These challenges largely stem from the fact that Internet technology and its business functions are relatively new.

Unproven Business Models

Not all companies make money on the Web. We can point to a number of Web sites that have closed because they failed to return benefits that could justify the outlay of hundreds of thousands and even millions of dollars. Industry.net, the comprehensive industrial mall run by IBM and Nets.Inc no longer is in business. As of the writing of this chapter, such widely heralded sites as Amazon.com had yet to turn a profit. Business models built around the Internet are new and largely unproven. The greatest benefit of Internet technology for many firms may be the use of intranets to reduce internal operating costs.

Business Process Change Requirements

Electronic commerce and electronic business require careful orchestration of the firm's divisions, production sites, and sales offices, as well as close relationships with customers, suppliers, banks, and other trading partners. Essential business processes must be redesigned and more closely integrated, especially those for supply chain management.

Channel Conflicts

Using the Web for on-line sales and marketing may create channel conflict with the firm's traditional channels, especially for less information-intensive products that require physical intermediaries to reach buyers (Palmer and Griffith, 1998). Its sales force and distributors may fear that their revenues will drop as customers make purchases directly from the Web or that they will be displaced by this new channel. The use of alternative channels created by the Internet requires very careful planning and management. The Window on Management describes how several companies are dealing with this problem.

Technology Hurdles

To make extensive use of the Internet, some companies need more expensive telecommunications connections, workstations, or high-speed computers that can handle transmission of bandwidth-hungry graphics and perhaps special computers dedicated

Avon sells its beauty products through its Web site as well as through its sales force. The company found that the Web site primarily attracts new customers and does not compete with its traditional sales channel of using door-to-door representatives.

WINDOW ON MANAGEMENT

Avoiding Channel Conflict

Gibson Musical Instruments of Nashville, Tennessee, struck a sour chord with its distributors when it opened a Web site to sell its electric guitars. Why sell on the Web? Well, for starters, selling via the Web is less costly. Gibson decided to offer its guitars through the Web at a 10 percent discount. The problem was that it did this without consulting Gibson dealers. Not surprisingly, the dealers were irate. Gibson was so dependent upon them that it eliminated online sales within a month.

Selling on-line can be tricky for established companies. After all, they were selling their products before the Web site, and retailers, distributors, and sales representatives were making a living that way. Few if any existing companies can expect to replace their current sales chain with the Web any time soon. Gibson could not hope to replace its sales chain with only Web sales at any time in the foreseeable future. In fact, Gibson only hoped to reach new customers through the Web. They did not expect a Web site to threaten their current distributors, so they never asked, and, as it turned out, their distributors had a very different view.

It is not uncommon for companies like Gibson to act hastily by putting up a Web site without thinking through their Web strategy properly and without consulting their sales partners. However, other companies have turned to a Web site after proper planning and found the move to be a positive one. One company that successfully followed the Gibson approach was Avon, the New York City-based producer of beauty products. Avon did not have the problem of a sales staff or of retail stores because it works primarily through more than 2.3 million independent sales representatives selling door-to-door. Company management did not expect the Web site to compete with door-to-door sales. Nonetheless, to be sure, they undertook a lot of research that showed the Web site would not persuade existing customers to leave their personal sales representatives. Instead, research indicated that the site would attract new customers. Only then did they put up a Web site.

Apparel manufacturer VFCorp., producer of Jantzen swimwear and Lee and Wrangler jeans, took another approach, deciding not to attempt retail sales on the Web. Instead, their strategy has been to use their Web site to boost sales at their retail outlets. Potential customers can use their sites to help to find better fits through their Lee fitFinder, and to locate the nearest retail stores.

Computer-game producer Sega of America, Inc. followed a different strategy. They decided to sell from their Web site, but only after intensive consultations with their sales department. To allay fears from their sales staff and their retailers, products sold via the Web will not be discounted. Sega also will charge a sales-and-handling fee for on-line sales, making the products more expensive when purchased via the Web. Sega did reserve the right to offer special promotions over the Web as long as those promotions do not revolve around price discounts. For example, they e-mailed 15,000 customers, offering them a package of games that includes a T-shirt not for sale elsewhere. About 25 percent of those customers purchased the special offer.

Gibson eventually came up with a Web strategy that it believes will boost sales without alienating dealers. It put its parts catalog on the Web, using the Web only to sell strings, accessories, and items such as chrome- or nickel-plated screws that were previously available only to dealers and repairers. The company finds that the Web site is an excellent way to service customers who cannot find these items at their dealers. Dealers also benefit because they can use the Web to order parts at a discount.

To Think About: ***What management, organization, and technology issues should be addressed when considering whether to use the Web for direct sales to consumers?***

Source: Adapted from Sari Kalin, "Conflict Resolution," *CIO Magazine,* February 1, 1998.

as Web servers. Individuals and organizations in less-developed countries with poor telephone lines, limited hardware and software capacity, or government controls on communications will not be able to take full advantage of Internet resources (Goodman, Press, Ruth, and Rutkowski, 1994).

Bandwidth is another major technology issue. With the success of the Web, sound, graphics, and full-motion video are now important aspects of network computing. However, these all require immense quantities of data, greatly slowing down transmission and the downloading of screens. Some Web servers become overloaded with servicing requests and may be impossible to access during busy periods. The existing telecommunications infrastructure was not set up to handle large numbers of people using its services for hours at a time. (Current telephone systems were designed and priced under the assumption that 10 percent of all phones would be in use at any time and the average voice call lasted three to four minutes. The average Internet session lasts for 22 minutes, with many people connected for hours.) During peak periods of usage, Internet traffic slows to a crawl, and Internet service providers (ISPs) cannot keep up with the demand. Higher bandwidth alternatives are under development, but the public Internet in its current form is not reliable enough for many business-critical applications.

Web-based systems themselves are too slow for high-speed transaction processing. They can provide a useful interface, however, to core-transaction processing systems, such as order processing. Making this integration requires special software to link these systems and special technical expertise. Integrating data from multiple systems on an intranet can be a complex undertaking.

Legal Issues

Laws governing electronic commerce are mostly nonexistent or just being written. Legislatures, courts, and international agreements will have to settle such still-open questions as the legality and force of e-mail contracts, including the role of electronic signatures, and the application of copyright laws to electronically copied documents. Moreover, the Internet is global, and is used by individuals and organizations in hundreds of different countries. If a product were offered for sale in Thailand via a server in Singapore and the purchaser lived in Hungary, whose law would apply? Until greater clarity brings stability to these and other critical legal questions, doing business on the Internet will bring a level of unreliability that some will find unacceptable.

Security and Privacy

We already have described some of the potential security and privacy problems created by networked computing in previous chapters. Internet-based systems are even more vulnerable than those in private networks because the Internet was designed to be open to everyone. Many people have the skill and technology to intercept and spy upon streams of electronic information as they flow through the Internet and all other open networks. Any information, including e-mail, passes through many computer systems on the Net before it reaches its destination. It can be monitored, captured, and stored at any of these points along the route. Valuable data that might be intercepted include credit card numbers and names, private personnel data, marketing plans, sales contracts, product development and pricing data, negotiations between companies and other data that might be of value to competition. Concern over the security of electronic payments is one reason that electronic commerce has not grown more rapidly on the Net. We explore Internet security and the state of technology for secure electronic payments in greater detail in Chapter 14.

Chapter 4 described some of the ways that hackers, vandals, and computer criminals have exploited Internet weaknesses to break into computer systems. Stealing passwords, obtaining sensitive information, electronic eavesdropping or "jamming" corporate Web servers to make them inaccessible can cause serious disruptions and harm.

Chapter 4 also described some of the threats to individual privacy raised by the Internet. Through the use of "cookies" and Web-site monitoring software, companies can gather information about individuals without their knowledge. In other instances, Website visitors knowingly supply personal information such as their name, address, e-mail address, and special interests in exchange for access to the site without realizing how the organization owning the Web site may be using the information.

Effective use of the Internet, intranets, and extranets requires careful management planning (*IS/Analyzer,* May 1996). Table 9.10 lists what we believe are the top questions managers should ask when exploring the use of the Internet for electronic commerce and electronic business.

TABLE 9.10 Using the Internet in Business: Top Questions for Managers

1. What value will the Internet and intranets provide the business? Will the benefits outweigh the costs? How can we measure success?
2. How will business processes have to be changed to use this technology for electronic commerce or electronic business? How much process integration is required?
3. What technical skills and employee training will be required to use Internet technology?
4. Do we have the appropriate information technology infrastructure and bandwidth for using the Internet and intranets?
5. How can we integrate Internet applications with existing applications and data?
6. How can we make sure our intranet is secure from entry by outsiders? How secure is the electronic payment system we are using for electronic commerce?
7. Are we doing enough to protect the privacy of customers we reach electronically?

Management Wrap-Up

MANAGEMENT

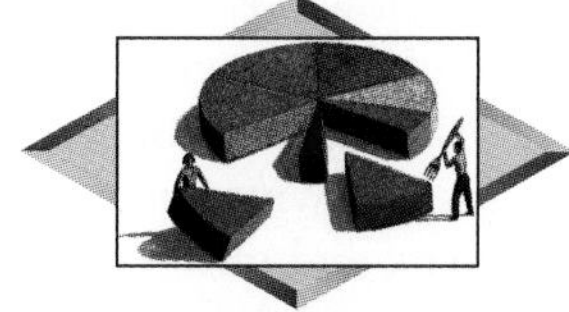

To obtain meaningful benefits from the Internet, managers need to determine how its technologies can support their business goals. Planning should carefully consider network costs, the costs and benefits of Internet computing, and new personnel requirements. Managers also should anticipate making organizational changes to take advantage of these technologies and plan to maintain some measure of management control over the process.

ORGANIZATION

The Internet can dramatically reduce transaction and agency costs and is fueling new business models. By using the Internet and other networks for electronic commerce, organizations can exchange purchase and sale transactions directly with customers and suppliers, eliminating inefficient middlemen. Organizational processes can be streamlined by using the Internet and intranets to make communication and coordination more efficient. To take advantage of these opportunities, organizational processes must be redesigned.

TECHNOLOGY

The Internet is creating a universal computing platform by using the TCP/IP network reference model and other standards for storing, retrieving, formatting, and displaying information. Web-based applications integrating voice, data, video, and audio are providing new products, services, and tools for communicating with employees and customers. Organizations can create intranets, internal networks based on Internet and Web technology, to reduce network costs and overcome connectivity problems. Key technology decisions should consider network reliability, security, bandwidth, and relationships to legacy systems, as well as the capabilities of Internet and other networking technologies.

For Discussion:

1. The Internet is creating a business revolution and transforming the role of information systems in organizations. Do you agree? Why or why not?
2. What management, organization, and technology factors would you consider when deciding whether to build an intranet for your company?

SUMMARY

1. **Describe how the Internet works and its major capabilities.** The Internet is a worldwide network of networks that uses the client/server model of computing and the TCP/IP network reference model. Using the Net, any computer can communicate with any other computer connected to the Net throughout the world. The Internet has no central management. The Internet is used for communications, including e-mail, public forums on thousands of topics, and live, interactive conversations. It also is used for information retrieval from hundreds of libraries and thousands of library, corporate, government, and nonprofit databases. It has developed into an effective way for individuals and organizations to offer information and products through a Web of graphical user interfaces and easy-to-use links worldwide. Major Internet capabilities include e-mail, Usenet, LISTSERV, chatting, Telnet, FTP, gophers, Archie, Veronica, WAIS, and the World Wide Web.

2. **Identify the benefits the Internet offers organizations.** Many organizations use the Net to reduce communications costs when they coordinate organizational activities and communicate with employees. Researchers and knowledge workers are finding the Internet a quick, low-cost way to gather and disperse knowledge. The global connectivity and low cost of the Internet helps organizations lower transaction and agency costs, allowing them to link directly to suppliers, customers, and business partners and to coordinate activities on a global scale with limited resources. The Web provides interactive multimedia capabilities that can be used to create new products and services and closer relationships with customers. Communication can be customized to specific audiences.

3. **Demonstrate how the Internet can be used for electronic commerce.** The Internet provides a universally available set of technologies for electronic commerce that can be used to create new channels for marketing, sales, and customer support and to eliminate intermediaries in buy and sell transactions. There are many different business models for electronic commerce on the Internet, including virtual storefronts, marketplace concentrators, information brokers, content providers, digital content delivery, and electronic clearinghouses. Interactive capabilities such as the Web, e-mail, and discussion groups can be used to build closer relationships with customers in marketing and customer support.

4. **Explain how Internet technology can be used to create private intraorganizational and interorganizational networks and the use of these networks for electronic business.** Private, internal corporate networks called intranets can be created using Internet connectivity standards, Web browsers, and Web servers. Extranets are private intranets that are extended to selected organizations or individuals outside the firm. Intranets and extranets are forming the underpinnings of electronic business by providing a low-cost technology that can run on almost any computing platform. Organizations can use intranets to create collaboration environments for coordinating work and information sharing, and they can use intranets to make information flow between different functional areas of the firm. Extranets are used in business-to-business electronic commerce, joint development projects between organizations, and supply chain management.

5. **Examine the challenges posed by the Internet to businesses and society.** Use of the Internet for electronic commerce and electronic business is in its infancy. Some of the new business models based on the Internet have not yet found proven ways to generate profits or reduce costs. Organizational change, including redesign of business processes and new roles for employees is often required; channel conflicts may erupt as the firm turns to the Internet as an alternative outlet for sales. Security, privacy, legal issues, network reliability, bandwidth, and integration of Internet-based applications with the firm's legacy systems pose additional challenges in Internet computing.

KEY TERMS

Archie, 270
Chatting, 269
Disintermediation, 278
Domain name, 268
Electronic payment system, 283
Extranet, 273
File transfer protocol (FTP), 270
Firewall, 273
Gopher, 270
Hit, 280
Home page, 271
Hypertext transport protocol, 271
Internet Service Provider (ISP), 267
Internet telephony, 275
LISTSERV, 269
"Push" technology, 272
Search engine, 271
Teamware, 287
Telnet, 269
Uniform resource locator (URL), 271
Usenet, 269
Veronica, 270
WAIS, 270
Web hosting service, 283
Webmaster, 271

REVIEW QUESTIONS

1. What is the Internet? List and describe its principal capabilities.
2. Why is the World Wide Web so useful for individuals and businesses?
3. Describe the ways of locating information on the Web.
4. What are intranets and extranets? How do they differ from the Web?
5. Describe the benefits of the Internet to organizations.
6. How can the Internet facilitate electronic commerce and electronic business?
7. Describe six Internet business models for electronic commerce.
8. How can the Internet support sales and marketing to individual customers?
9. How can the Internet help provide customer service?
10. How can Internet technology support business-to-business electronic commerce?
11. Why are intranets so useful for electronic business?
12. How can intranets support organizational collaboration?
13. Describe the uses of intranets for electronic business in sales and marketing, human resources, finance and accounting, and manufacturing.
14. How can companies use extranets and Internet technology for supply-chain management?
15. Describe the management challenges posed by electronic commerce and electronic business on the Internet.
16. What is channel conflict? Why is it becoming a growing problem in electronic commerce?

GROUP PROJECT

Form a group with three or four of your classmates. Select two businesses that are competitors in the same industry and using their Web sites for electronic commerce. Visit their Web sites. You might compare, for example, the Web sites of Amazon.com and Barnes and Noble, the Web sites for virtual banking created by Citibank and Wells Fargo Bank, or the Web sites of E*Trade and Ameritrade. Prepare an evaluation of each business's Web site in terms of its functions, user-friendliness, and how well it supports the company's business strategy. Which Web site does a better job? Why? Can you make some recommendations to improve these Web sites?

TOOLS FOR INTERACTIVE LEARNING

■ **INTERNET**: You can take a virtual tour of Electronic Commerce sites illustrating each of the Internet business models described in this chapter. Once you have finished the tour, you can start the comprehensive Electronic Commerce project in which you will select an Internet business model and develop an Internet strategy for a new business. The Internet Connection for this chapter will take you to Virtual Vineyards and other Web sites where you can complete an exercise to evaluate virtual storefronts and see interactive demonstrations of intranets. You can find an on-line case study entitled "Electronic Commerce Strategies: A Tale of Two Companies." You can also use the Interactive Study Guide to test your knowledge of the topics in this chapter and get instant feedback where you need more practice.

■ **CD-ROM**: If you purchase and use the Multimedia Edition CD-ROM with this chapter, you can complete an interactive exercise that requires you to select the appropriate Internet service for a series of problems. You can also find a video demonstrating the Internet services provided by Apple Computer, an audio overview of the major themes of this chapter, and bullet text summarizing the key points of the chapter.

Virtual Vineyards' Virtual Storefront

Peter Granoff spent the better part of two decades serving various functions in the wine industry, working as a teacher, taster, consultant, and sommelier in San Francisco's restaurants and clubs. He is the thirteenth American to be admitted to the British Court of Master Sommeliers. He watched sadly as the wine industry followed the lead of other retail-oriented businesses by creating superstores appealing to the consumers' calls for lower prices. Such stores kept an abundance of wines in stock, but they purchased fewer varieties, using their clout to squeeze lower prices from wine producers. Also, by simplifying their stock, they could substitute regular sales clerks for wine experts who received higher wages. These savings were passed on to the customers, most of whom were willing to sacrifice knowledgeable service for convenient shopping and savings. The retail outlets relied on the large producers with advertising budgets to educate consumers.

As a result, smaller wineries had no one to sell their product to because they could not provide the output or the discounts that superstores demanded. Small wine producers were responsible for many of the industry's best wines, but they couldn't survive under the new order. Hundreds of small wineries producing fewer than 5000 cases of wine per year were abandoned by their distributors.

Granoff knew that a market still existed for specialty labels and quality wines. The question was how to tap it, because it was geographically diffuse and too fragmented to be addressed by superstores. He found his answer by teaming up with his brother-in-law, Robert Olson, who had headed a Silicon Graphics marketing team selling software for interactive television. Olson wanted to apply what he knew to on-line retailing, and the World Wide Web seemed like the perfect medium.

Olson and Granoff believed that there were three advantages to using the Web for on-line retailing: (1) Computers are perfectly suited for the task of searching for key words and comparing numbers; (2) on-line retail reduces marketing costs because it is available to potential customers 24 hours a day, 365 days a year (at very low cost compared to the price of placing four half-page ads per year in *The New York Times;* (3) a Web site can sell directly to customers, eliminating middlemen and distribution costs.

Olson and Granoff pooled their expertise to found Virtual Vineyards, an on-line store that would serve as an agent for both the vineyard and the consumer. Its proprietor would taste and evaluate everything in stock. Earnings would be based on commissions on sales. In essence, Olson and Granoff would be selling wines traditionally using the most leading-edge technology.

Virtual Vineyards opened its virtual storefront in late January 1995. Since then, business has been increasing by approximately 20 percent per month, and sales have topped $1 million. It is not the only Web site selling wine. What it offers, in addition to convenience and low prices, is information, the expertise supplied by Peter Granoff, an authority in his field.

Other Web sites retailing goods typically feature links to reviews by other experts, mailing lists and on-line discussion groups, newsletters, journals, and so forth. Virtual Vineyards has none of these—only a clean line running to Granoff. Virtual Vineyards does not even have links to the wine producers' sites where customers can wander to read product presentations from different vendors. The information comes only from one source.

Granoff provides the winery descriptions, which demonstrate his knowledge of the industry and the operations of specific producers. For example, "The tiny Ahlgren Vineyard in the Santa Cruz Mountains . . . has earned a reputation for producing wines that balance concentrated varietal character with finesse and complexity. Total production is approximately 2000 cases, and vineyards in the Livermore Valley, the Santa Clara Valley, and the Santa Cruz Mountains are sources for the small lots of handmade wines . . . Dexter Ahlgren's philosophy is to interfere as little as possible during the entire winemaking process. The results speak volumes about the wisdom of a minimalist approach." In the Virtual Vineyards advice column, Granoff answers questions on topics ranging from investment to wineglass selection and wine storage methods. Virtual Vineyards wants to educate its visitors as well as sell them products. Visitors learn as they shop. For example, the Portfolio option describing wines on sale describes each label with a few sentences but also provides information about the class of wine. The Portfolio Option includes Peter's Tasting Chart for each label, with seven parallel horizontal lines, each representing a dimension of wine taste (intensity, sweetness or dryness, body, acidity, tannin, oak, and complexity). Each line represents a range. A red diamond, placed anywhere from far left to far right, indicates where the label under discussion falls within that range for that particular dimension. The chart conveys a great deal of information at a glance.

Virtual Vineyard's Web pages are clean and load quickly. The menus are uncluttered with links, the graphics compact. The look and feel of the site and the performance of its software reinforce its message of a strong voice tied to a specific person. Virtual Vineyards stocks about 250 labels from 50 wineries. The company is now using Java to make the Web site even more interactive and helpful.

Virtual Vineyards' information-based approach to sales and marketing presents some difficulties. Once past a certain level of detail, the expert's command of his product starts to weaken, and the software becomes too elaborate to use easily. The information-based model raises prices. The expert must be paid, adding to the retailer's mark-up. Customers theoretically could use the site to find out information and then purchase what they like somewhere else—at a lower price.

Virtual Vineyards hopes to surmount these difficulties by personalizing its service. For instance, Olson can learn about customer preferences from their order histories and then use that information to suggest new labels to try. Virtual Vineyards recently added food and gift items to its wares. It is considering opening a gourmet farmer's market to sell produce during peak seasons, but first must overcome transportation problems.

Sources: "Java User Survey: Case Studies," *Computerworld,* March 23, 1998; Fred Hapgood, "What Makes Virtual Vineyards Rule?" *Inc. Technology,* No. 2, 1996; and Mark Glaser, "Selling Online: Electronic Storefronts that Work," *New Media,* October 28, 1996.

Case Study Questions

1. Analyze Virtual Vineyards using the value chain and competitive forces models.
2. Why is Virtual Vineyards successful? What role does the Web play in its business model? How does Virtual Vineyards provide value?
3. What management, organization, and technology issues were addressed in building Virtual Vineyards' Web site?
4. Visit the Virtual Vineyards Web site [http://www.virtualvin.com] and evaluate it in terms of how successfully you believe it meets its business objectives. Could the site be improved? If so, how?
5. Can Virtual Vineyards serve as a model for other retailers on the Web? Why or why not?
6. One observer has noted that Virtual Vineyards "makes electronic commerce look all too easy." Explain.

CHAPTER 10

Redesigning the Organization with Information Systems

chapter outline

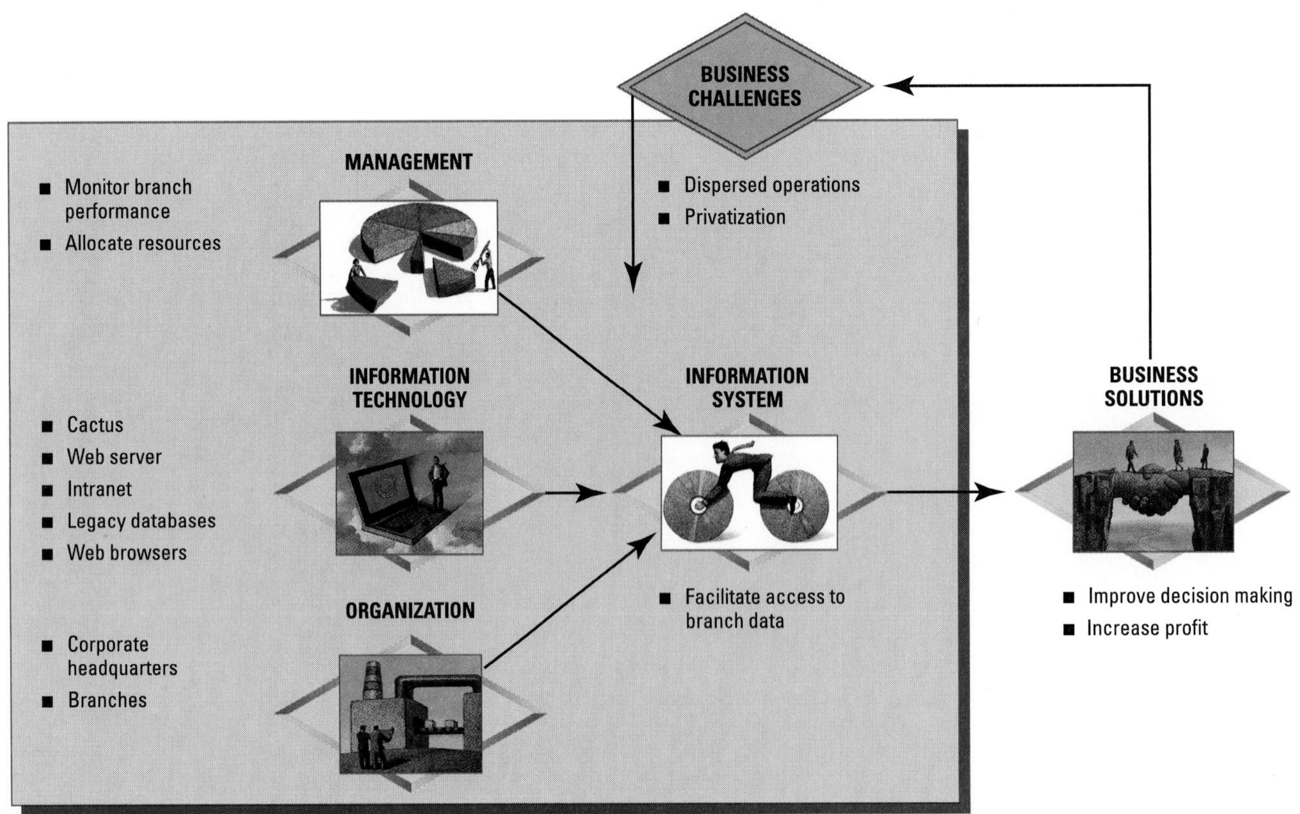

Grupo Financiero Bital Moves to Private Banking Systems

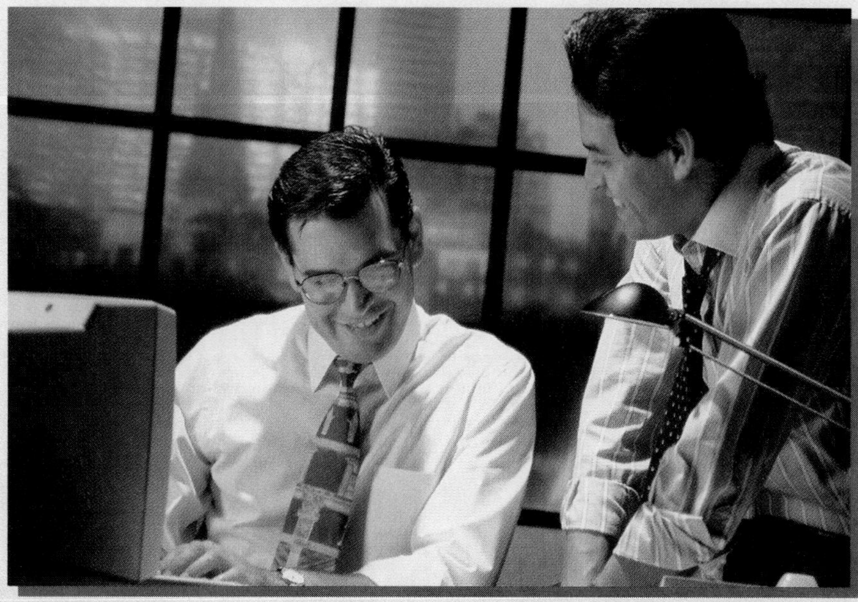

Grupo Financiero Bital controls assets of about $9 billion, making it one of the largest financial holding companies in Mexico. Bital is also a full-service retail bank with almost 1200 branches serving more than 3 million customers. Servicing this customer base requires intensive use of information systems, a task that grew larger when the bank was privatized in 1992. The business is so dispersed that Bital had trouble maintaining its technology infrastructure. New technology upgrades were installed manually by technicians who visited the widely scattered branch offices. This meant that some branches might have a new version of software running within a week, but others might not have the software installed and running for a month or more.

The situation grew more serious when the bank was privatized. Bital's information architecture was more appropriate for a government agency than for a profit-driven business. Branch managers could query Bital's massive databases for information, but the result might be a 500-page deluge of statistics rather than the exact information required. Bital's information systems group was charged with making its systems more stable and adding the functionality required to support profit-driven banking.

Bital's information systems staff decided that the easiest way to solve these problems was to implement an intranet. The intranet would provide a Web-based application for querying the database that could generate compact reports on an individual branch without altering Bital's underlying, centralized database for existing systems. The information was arranged so that a branch manager could examine information for his or her branch and make intelligent branch-level decisions concerning resources, time, and money. By being able to look at each branch as a separate business, the branch manager could take the necessary measures to make the branch more profitable, benefiting the entire bank.

A team of information systems specialists led by Jorge Sosa, director of Bital's branch systems development, used the Cactus application development workbench from Information Builders to implement a system that accesses data from Bital's legacy databases. The data are extracted from the database and stored on the company's Web server. Branch managers use their Web browsers to build queries against the extracted data.

Sosa's group created a special Web page called the "tablero" to help top management get a handle on the business. The tablero allows executives to examine aspects of Bital's business, as well as the performance of bank branches. Bital's management can use this information to balance resources and make decisions about which branches to shrink and which to expand.

Source: Adapted from Geoffrey James, "Intranets Give New Life to BPR," *Datamation,* March 1998.

Management Challenges

Grupo Financiero Bital's new intranet reporting system illustrates the many factors at work in the development of a new information system. Building the new system entailed analyzing the company's problems with existing information systems, assessing people's information needs, selecting appropriate technology, and redesigning procedures and jobs. Management had to monitor the system-building effort and to evaluate its benefits and costs. The new information system represented a process of planned organizational change.

However, building information systems, especially those on a large scale, presents many challenges. Here are some challenges to consider:

1. **Major risks and uncertainties in systems development.** Information systems development has major risks and uncertainties that make it difficult for the systems to achieve their goals. One problem is the difficulty of establishing information requirements, both for individual end users and for the organization as a whole. The requirements may be too complex or subject to change. Another problem is that the time and cost factors to develop an information system are very difficult to analyze, especially in large projects. A third problem is the difficulty of managing the organizational change associated with a new system. Although building a new information system is a process of planned organizational change, this does not mean that change can always be planned or controlled. Individuals and groups in organizations have varying interests, and they may resist changes in procedures, job relationships, and technologies. Although this chapter describes some ways of dealing with these risks and uncertainties, the issues remain major management challenges.
2. **Determining benefits of a system when they are largely intangible.** As the sophistication of systems grows, they produce fewer tangible and more intangible benefits. By definition, there is no solid method for pricing intangible benefits. Organizations could lose important opportunities if they only use strict financial criteria for determining information systems benefits. On the other hand, organizations could make very poor investment decisions if they overestimate intangible benefits.

learning objectives

After completing this chapter, you will be able to:

1. Demonstrate how building new systems can produce organizational change.
2. Explain how the organization can develop information systems that fit its business plan.
3. Identify the core activities in the systems development process.
4. Analyze the organizational change requirements for building successful systems.
5. Describe models for determining the business value of information systems.

This chapter describes how new information systems are conceived, built, and installed, with special attention to the issues of organizational design, business reengineering, and organizational change. It describes the core systems development activities and the organizational change process of implementing a new information system. The chapter explains how to establish the business value of information systems (including those based on the Internet) and how to ensure that new systems are linked to the organization's business plan and information requirements.

10.1 SYSTEMS AS PLANNED ORGANIZATIONAL CHANGE

This text has emphasized that an information system is a sociotechnical entity, an arrangement of both technical and social elements. The introduction of a new information system involves much more than new hardware and software. It also includes changes in jobs, skills, management, and organization. In the sociotechnical philosophy, one cannot install new technology without considering the people who must work with it (Bostrom and Heinen, 1977). When we design a new information system, we are redesigning the organization.

One of the most important things to know about building a new information system is that this process is one kind of planned organizational change. System builders must understand how a system will affect the organization as a whole, focusing particularly on organizational conflict and changes in the locus of decision making. Builders must also consider how the nature of work groups will change under the impact of the new system. Builders determine how much change is needed.

Systems can be technical successes but organizational failures because of a failure in the social and political process of building the system. Analysts and designers are responsible for ensuring that key members of the organization participate in the design process and are permitted to influence the ultimate shape of the system. This activity must be carefully orchestrated by information system builders (see Section 10.3).

Linking Information Systems to the Business Plan

Deciding which new systems to build should be an essential component of the organizational planning process. Organizations need to develop an information systems plan that supports their overall business plan and in which strategic systems are incorporated into top-level planning (Grover, Teng, and Fiedler, 1998). Once specific projects have been selected within the overall context of a strategic plan for the business and the systems area, an **information systems plan** can be developed. The plan serves as a road map indicating the direction of systems development, the rationale, the current situation, the management strategy, the implementation plan, and the budget (see Table 10.1).

information systems plan A road map indicating the direction of systems development: the rationale, the current situation, the management strategy, the implementation plan, and the budget.

The plan contains a statement of corporate goals and specifies how information technology supports the attainment of those goals. The report shows how general goals will be achieved by specific systems projects. It lays out specific target dates and milestones that can be used later to judge the progress of the plan in terms of how many objectives were actually attained in the time frame specified in the plan. The plan indicates the key management decisions concerning hardware acquisition; telecommunications; centralization/decentralization of authority, data, and hardware; and required organizational change. Organizational changes are also usually described, including management and employee training requirements; recruiting efforts; changes in business processes; and changes in authority, structure, or management practice.

Establishing Organizational Information Requirements

In order to develop an effective information systems plan, the organization must have a clear understanding of both its long- and short-term information requirements. Two principal methodologies for establishing the essential information requirements of the organization as a whole are enterprise analysis and critical success factors.

Enterprise Analysis (Business Systems Planning)

Enterprise analysis (also called *business systems planning*) argues that the information requirements of a firm can only be understood by looking at the entire organization in terms of organizational units, functions, processes, and data elements. Enterprise analysis can help identify the key entities and attributes of the organization's data. This method starts with the notion that the information requirements of a firm or a division can be specified only with a thorough understanding of the entire organization. This method was developed by IBM in the 1960s explicitly for establishing the relationship among large system-development projects (Zachman, 1982).

enterprise analysis An analysis of organization-wide information requirements by looking at the entire organization in terms of organizational units, functions, processes, and data elements; helps identify the key entities and attributes in the organization's data.

TABLE 10.1 Information Systems Plan

1. **Purpose of the Plan**
   Overview of plan contents
   Changes in firm's current situation
   Firm's strategic plan
   Current business organization
   Key business processes
   Management strategy
2. **Strategic Business Plan**
   Current situation
   Current business organization
   Changing environments
   Major goals of the business plan
3. **Current Systems**
   Major systems supporting business functions and processes
   Major current capabilities
      Hardware
      Software
      Database
      Telecommunications
   Difficulties meeting business requirements
   Anticipated future demands
4. **New Developments**
   New system projects
      Project descriptions
      Business rationale
   New capabilities required
      Hardware
      Software
      Database
      Telecommunications and Internet
5. **Management Strategy**
   Acquisition plans
   Milestones and timing
   Organizational realignment
   Internal reorganization
   Management controls
   Major training initiatives
   Personnel strategy
6. **Implementation Plan**
   Detailed implementation plan
   Anticipated difficulties in implementation
   Progress reports
7. **Budget Requirements**
   Requirements
   Potential savings
   Financing
   Acquisition cycle

The central method used in the enterprise analysis approach is to take a large sample of managers and ask them how they use information, where they get the information, what their environments are like, what their objectives are, how they make decisions, and what their data needs are.

The results of this large survey of managers are aggregated into subunits, functions, processes, and data matrices. Data elements are organized into *logical application groups*—groups of data elements that support related sets of organizational processes. Figure 10.1 is an output of enterprise analysis conducted by the Social Security Administration as part of a massive systems redevelopment effort. It shows what information is required to support a particular process, which processes create the data, and which use them. The shaded boxes in the figure indicate a logical application group. In this case, actuarial estimates, agency plans, and budget data are created in the planning process, suggesting that an information system should be built to support planning.

The weakness of enterprise analysis is that it produces an enormous amount of data that is expensive to collect and difficult to analyze. Most of the interviews are conducted with senior or middle managers, with little effort to collect information from clerical workers and supervisory managers. Moreover, the questions frequently focus not on the critical objectives of management and where information is needed, but rather on what *existing* information is used. The result is a tendency to automate whatever exists. But in many instances, entirely new approaches to how business is conducted are needed, and these needs are not addressed.

critical success factors (CSFs) A small number of easily identifiable operational goals shaped by the industry, the firm, the manager, and the broader environment that are believed to assure the success of an organization. Used to determine the information requirements of an organization.

Strategic Analysis or Critical Success Factors

The strategic analysis, or critical success factors, approach argues that the information requirements of an organization are determined by a small number of **critical success factors (CSFs)** of managers. If these goals can be attained, the success of the firm or organization is assured (Rockart, 1979; Rockart and Treacy, 1982).

Logical application groups	Processes \ Data classes	Actuarial estimates	Agency plans	Budget	Program regs./policy	Admin. regs./policy	Labor agreements	Data standards	Procedures	Automated systems documentation	Educational media	Public agreements	Intergovernmental agreements	Grants	External	Exchange control	Administrative accounts	Program expenditures	Audit reports	Organization/position	Employee identification	Recruitment/placement	Complaints/grievances	Training resources	Security	Equipment utilization	Space utilization	Supplies utilization	Workload schedules	Work measurement	Enumeration I.D.	Enumeration control	Earnings	Employer I.D.	Earnings control	Claims characteristics	Claims control	Decisions	Payment	Collection/waiver	Notice	Inquiries control	Quality appraisal
PLANNING	Develop agency plans	C	C	C	U	U									U																												
PLANNING	Administer agency budget	C	C	C	U	U						U	U	U		U	U	U		U	U					U	U	U		U		U			U		U			U		U	U
PLANNING	Formulate program policies	U	U		C				U						U				U				U															U					U
PLANNING	Formulate admin. policies		U		U	C	C		U						U				U	U			U																				
PLANNING	Formulate data policies		U	U		U		C	U	U															U	U	U	U															
PLANNING	Design work processes		U		U	U			C	C		U	U						U																			U					U
GENERAL MANAGEMENT	Manage public affairs		U		U	U			U		C	C	C																														
GENERAL MANAGEMENT	Manage intrgovt. affairs	U	U		U	U			U		U		C	C	C															U	U		U	U		U			U				
GENERAL MANAGEMENT	Exchange data				U				U			U	U	U	U	C	U	U												U													
GENERAL MANAGEMENT	Maintain admin. accounts			U		U			U			U	U				C				U					U	U	U								U			U				
GENERAL MANAGEMENT	Maintain prog. accounts			U	U				U			U	U					C														U			U		U	U	U	U		U	
GENERAL MANAGEMENT	Conduct audits				U	U			U	U							U	U	C		U								U														
GENERAL MANAGEMENT	Establish organizations			U		U			U											C	U								U	U													U
GENERAL MANAGEMENT	Manage human resources			U		U	U		U											C	C	C	C	C																			
GENERAL MANAGEMENT	Provide security				U	U		U	U	U															C	C	C	C		U													
GENERAL MANAGEMENT	Manage equipment			U		U		U	U	U															C	C	C	C															
GENERAL MANAGEMENT	Manage facilities			U		U			U																U	U	C																
GENERAL MANAGEMENT	Manage supplies			U		U			U																C	U	U	C															
GENERAL MANAGEMENT	Manage workloads	U		U	U	U			U							U										U	U	U	C	C		U			U		U					U	U
PROGRAM ADMIN.	Issue Social Security nos.								U				U		U																C	C											
PROGRAM ADMIN.	Maintain earnings								U				U	U	U																U		C	C	C	U							
PROGRAM ADMIN.	Collect claims information				U	U			U						U																U	U				C	C	U	U	U			
PROGRAM ADMIN.	Determine elig./entlmt.								U																						U	U	U			U		C	U	U			
PROGRAM ADMIN.	Compute payments				U				U									U													U		U			U		U	C	C			
PROGRAM ADMIN.	Administer debt mgmt.				U				U									U																					U	C			
SUPPORT	Generate notices								U						U																U		U			U		U	U	U	C		
SUPPORT	Respond to prog. inquiries				U				U		U																				U		U	U		U		U	U	U	U	C	
SUPPORT	Provide quality assessment				U	U			U	U																					U		U			U		U			U		C

KEY
C = creators of data U = users of data

FIGURE 10.1 Process/data class matrix. This chart depicts which data classes are required to support particular organizational processes and which processes are the creators and users of data.

CSFs are shaped by the industry, the firm, the manager, and the broader environment. This broader focus, in comparison with that of previous methods, accounts for the description of this technique as *strategic*. An important premise of the strategic analysis approach is that there is a small number of objectives that managers can easily identify and information systems can focus on.

The principal method used in CSF analysis is personal interviews—three or four—with a number of top managers to identify their goals and the resulting CSFs. These personal CSFs are aggregated to develop a picture of the firm's CSFs. Then systems are built to deliver information on these CSFs. (See Table 10.2 for an example of CSFs. For the method of developing CSFs in an organization, see Figure 10.2.)

The strength of the CSF method is that it produces a smaller data set to analyze than does enterprise analysis. Only top managers are interviewed, and the questions focus on a small number of CSFs rather than a broad inquiry into what information is used or needed. This method can be tailored to the structure of each industry, with different competitive strategies producing different information systems. Therefore, this method produces systems that are more custom-tailored to an organization.

TABLE 10.2 Critical Success Factors and Organizational Goals

Example	Goals	CSF
Profit concern	Earnings/share Return on investment Market share New product	Automotive industry Styling Quality dealer system Cost control Energy standards
Nonprofit	Excellent health care Meeting government regulations Future health needs	Regional integration with other hospitals Efficient use of resources Improved monitoring of regulations

Source: Rockart (1979).

A unique strength of the CSF method is that it takes into account the changing environment with which organizations and managers must deal. This method explicitly asks managers to look at the environment and consider how their analysis of it shapes their information needs. It is especially suitable for top management and for the development of DSS and ESS. Unlike enterprise analysis, the CSF method focuses organizational attention on how information should be handled.

The primary weakness of this method is that the aggregation process and the analysis of the data are art forms. There is no particularly rigorous way in which individual CSFs can be aggregated into a clear company pattern. Second, there is often confusion among interviewees (and interviewers) between *individual* and *organizational* CSFs. They are not necessarily the same. What can be critical to a manager may not be im-

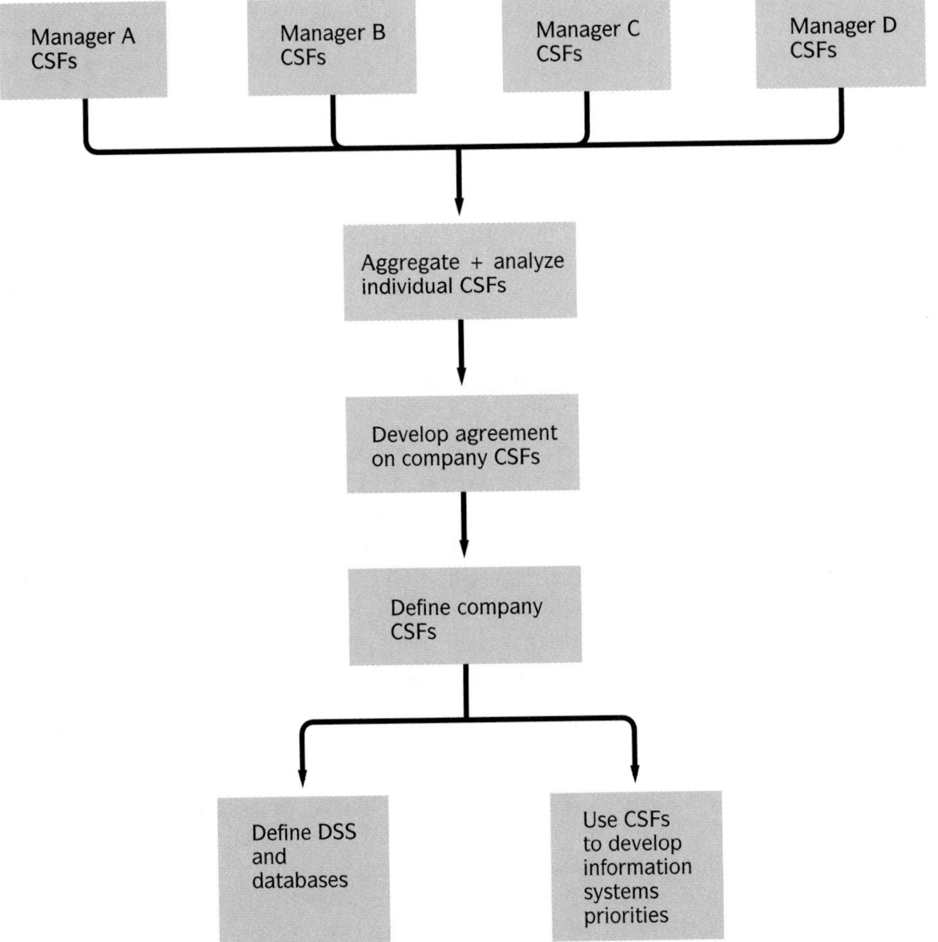

FIGURE 10.2 Using CSFs to develop systems. The CSF approach relies on interviews with key managers to identify their CSFs. Individual CSFs are aggregated to develop CSFs for the entire firm. Systems can then be built to deliver information on these CSFs.

portant for the organization. Moreover, this method is clearly biased toward top managers because they are the ones (generally the only ones) interviewed. Last, it should be noted that this method does not necessarily overcome the impact of a changing environment or changes in managers. Environments and managers change rapidly, and information systems must adjust accordingly. The use of CSFs to develop a system does not mitigate these factors.

Systems Development and Organizational Change

New information systems can be powerful instruments for organizational change, enabling organizations to redesign their structure, scope, power relationships, workflows, products, and services. Table 10.3 describes some of the ways that information technology is being used to transform organizations.

The Spectrum of Organizational Change

Information technology can promote various degrees of organizational change, ranging from incremental to far-reaching. Figure 10.3 shows four kinds of structural organizational change that are enabled by information technology: (1) automation, (2) rationalization, (3) reengineering, and (4) paradigm shifts. Each carries different rewards and risks.

The most common form of IT-enabled organizational change is **automation**. The first applications of information technology involved assisting employees to perform their tasks more efficiently and effectively. Calculating paychecks and payroll registers, giving bank tellers instant access to customer deposit records, and developing a nationwide network of airline reservation terminals for airline reservation agents are all examples of early automation.

A deeper form of organizational change—one that follows quickly from early automation—is **rationalization of procedures**. Automation frequently reveals new bottlenecks

automation Using the computer to speed up the performance of existing tasks.

rationalization of procedures The streamlining of standard operating procedures, eliminating obvious bottlenecks, so that automation makes operating procedures more efficient.

TABLE 10.3 How Information Technology Can Transform Organizations

Information Technology	Organizational Change
Global networks	International division of labor: The operations of a firm are no longer determined by location; the global reach of firms is extended; costs of global coordination decline. Transaction costs decline.
Enterprise networks	Collaborative work and teamwork: The organization of work can now be coordinated across divisional boundaries; a customer and product orientation emerges; widely dispersed task forces become the dominant work group. The costs of management (agency costs) decline. Business processes are changed.
Distributed computing	Empowerment: Individuals and work groups now have the information and knowledge to act. Business processes are redesigned, streamlined. Management costs decline. Hierarchy and centralization decline.
Portable computing	Virtual organizations: Work is no longer tied to geographic location. Knowledge and information can be delivered anywhere they are needed, anytime. Work becomes portable. Organizational costs decline as real estate is less essential for business.
Graphical user interfaces	Accessibility: Everyone in the organization—even senior executives—can access information and knowledge; work-flows can be automated, contributed to by all from remote locations. Organizational costs decline as work-flows move from paper to digital image, documents, and voice.

FIGURE 10.3

Organizational change carries risks and rewards. The most common forms of organizational change are automation and rationalization. These relatively slow-moving and slow-changing strategies present modest returns but little risk. Faster and more comprehensive change—like reengineering and paradigm shifts—carry high rewards but offer a substantial chance of failure.

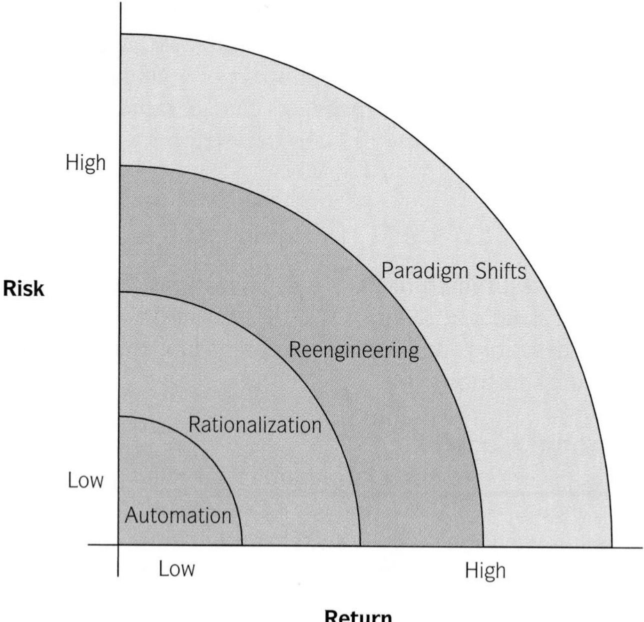

in production and makes the existing arrangement of procedures and structures painfully cumbersome. Rationalization of procedures is the streamlining of standard operating procedures, eliminating obvious bottlenecks, so that automation can make operating procedures more efficient. For example, Grupo Financiero Bital's banking system is effective not just because it utilizes state-of-the-art computer technology but also because its design allows its bank to operate more efficiently. The procedures of Bital, or of any organization, must be rationally structured to achieve this result. Before Bital could automate its banking system, it had to have identification numbers for all accounts and standard rules for calculating interest and account balances. Without a certain amount of rationalization in Grupo Bital's organization, its computer technology would have been useless.

business reengineering The radical redesign of business processes, combining steps to cut waste and eliminating repetitive, paper-intensive tasks in order to improve cost, quality, and service, and to maximize the benefits of information technology.

A more powerful type of organizational change is **business reengineering**, in which business processes are analyzed, simplified, and redesigned. Reengineering involves radically rethinking the flow of work and the business processes used to produce products and services, with a mind to radically reduce the costs of business (see Table 10.4). Using information technology, organizations can rethink and streamline their business processes to improve speed, service, and quality. Business reengineering reorganizes work-flows, combining steps to cut waste and eliminating repetitive, paper-intensive tasks (sometimes the new design eliminates jobs as well). It is much more ambitious than rationalization of procedures, requiring a new vision of how the process is to be organized.

An widely-cited example of business reengineering is Ford Motor Company's *invoiceless processing*. Ford employed more than 500 people in its North American Accounts Payable organization. The accounts payable clerks spent most of their time resolving discrepancies between purchase orders, receiving documents, and invoices. Ford reengineered its accounts payable process, instituting a system wherein the purchasing department enters a purchase order into an on-line database that can be checked by the receiving department when the ordered items arrive. If the received goods match the purchase order, the system automatically generates a check for accounts payable to send to the vendor. There is no need for vendors to send invoices. After reengineering, Ford was able to reduce headcount in accounts payable by 75 percent and produce more accurate financial information (Hammer and Champy, 1993).

Rationalizing procedures and redesigning business processes are limited to specific parts of a business. New information systems can ultimately affect the design of the entire organization, by transforming how the organization carries out its business or even the nature of the business itself. For instance, Schneider National (described in

TABLE 10.4 IT Capabilities and Their Organizational Impacts

Capability	Organizational Impact/Benefit
Transactional	IT can transform unstructured processes into routinized transactions.
Geographical	IT can transfer information with rapidity and ease across large distances, making processes independent of geography.
Automational	IT can replace or reduce human labor in a process.
Analytical	IT can bring complex analytical methods to bear on a process.
Informational	IT can bring vast amounts of detailed information into a process.
Sequential	IT can enable changes in the sequence of tasks in a process, often allowing multiple tasks to be worked on simultaneously.
Knowledge management	IT allows the capture and dissemination of knowledge and expertise to improve the process.
Tracking	IT allows the detailed tracking of task status, inputs, and outputs.
Disintermediation	IT can be used to connect two parties within a process who would otherwise communicate through an intermediary (internal or external).

Source: Thomas H. Davenport and James E. Short, "The New Industrial Engineering: Information Technology and Business Process Redesign," *Sloan Management Review 11,* Summer 1990.

Chapter 3) used new information systems to create a competitive on-demand shipping service and to develop a new business managing the logistics for other companies. Baxter International's stockless inventory system (described in Chapter 2) transformed Baxter into a working partner with hospitals and into a manager of its customers' supplies. This more radical form of business change is called a **paradigm shift.** A paradigm shift involves rethinking the nature of the business and the nature of the organization itself.

paradigm shift Radical reconceptualization of the nature of the business and the nature of the organization.

The Window on Technology illustrates how Internet technology can be used for making these organizational changes.

Paradigm shifts and reengineering often fail because extensive organizational change is so difficult to orchestrate (see Section 10.3). Why then do so many corporations entertain such radical change? Because the rewards are equally high (see Figure 10.3). In many instances firms seeking paradigm shifts and pursuing reengineering strategies

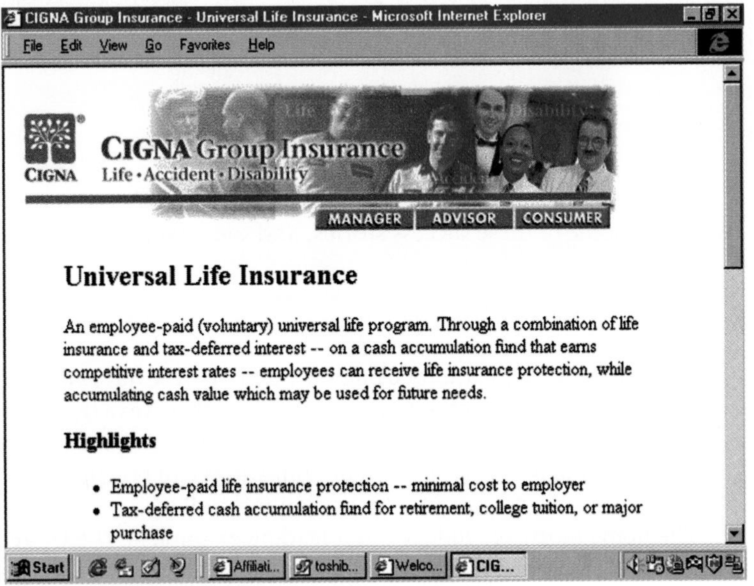

Cigna Corporate Insurance uses intranets and extranets to streamline its communication with brokers and case managers. Internet technology and the Web provide a flexible platform for redesigning work-flows, products, and services.

WINDOW ON TECHNOLOGY

Redesigning with the Internet

It has been said that Internet and Web technology provide so much flexibility that organizations can reengineer their business processes without modifying their legacy systems or switching to new technology platforms. Web browsers run on many types of computers and operating systems, so an organization can develop a Web application that runs on a mix of operating environments. Applications can be developed to facilitate business process reengineering using Web pages and interfaces to the organization's legacy systems on the Web server without changing the underlying systems themselves. Here are two examples.

Baylor Healthcare System is a north Texas-based, nonprofit network of hospitals, acute-care facilities, and family health care centers. The organization has grown through a series of mergers and associations, and some of its problems were based upon the legacy systems it inherited as it grew. Each organization brought to Baylor its own systems that supported its unique way of operating. Each constituent organization negotiated its own contract with pharmaceutical vendors, so Baylor was unable to obtain the large discounts it could receive if the orders were pooled. Looking at the potential cost savings, Baylor tried to pool the orders but found it required many meetings and numerous hours of costly manual time because of the incompatible systems.

To solve the problem inexpensively, management determined that the pharmaceutical-purchase process needed to be reengineered, placing much of the process on an intranet. The intranet portion of the new system was divided into three parts. The contract database made every contract available to all who needed to see it by storing a high-level executive summary of every contract, including the price and quantity of each drug. It also contained either the full text or a scanned image of the contract. The work-flow system was placed on the intranet to help keep the process moving. Every proposed purchase contract was put on-line where it was reviewed by medical analysts and others in the approval process. Thus review and approval could be achieved without delay. Finally, the intranet included a discussion forum where Baylor health providers could discuss appropriate drugs and resolve conflicts on what to order. The system has been a success. According to project manager Marylynn Henry, "The new system has had a substantial impact on Baylor's cost control." She adds that by making accurate information easily available, the system is "making it easier for employees to do their jobs."

CIGNA Corporate Insurance, an arm of Hartford, Connecticut-based CIGNA, sells life insurance, primarily to corporations, insuring their highly paid employees. These policies are sold by independent insurance brokers. Problems emerge each year when its life insurance policies come up for renewal. Records on each policy must be updated, and both the broker and CIGNA have part of the information needed. The updating process in the past was done through communications between the brokers and CIGNA staff, and it was labor-intensive, time-consuming, and costly. However, when the process was completed, much of the policy data remained out-of-date.

To enable the policies to be fully and accurately updated in a more efficient and less costly manner, CIGNA built an intranet and an extranet. Brokers use the extranet to retrieve information they need on CIGNA policy and investment offerings and to input required data for each policy sold. CIGNA case managers use the intranet to obtain the information they need on individual policies. This use, too, has been a success. According to Diana Rolny, a CIGNA business analyst, "Not only are we saving hundreds of thousands of dollars, but we're positioning ourselves to service the brokers and the customers more effectively."

To Think About: ***How are these companies using the Internet for organizational design? What types of organizational change are taking place?***

Sources: Adapted from Geoffrey James, "Baylor Pulls It Together" and "CIGNA Saves a Bundle," *Datamation,* March 1, 1998.

achieve stunning, order-of-magnitude increases in their returns on investment (or productivity). Some of these success stories, and some failure stories, are included throughout this book.

Business Process Reengineering

Many companies today are focusing on building new information systems where they can redesign business processes. Table 10.4 describes ways that information technology can streamline and consolidate business processes. If the business process is redesigned before computing power is applied, organizations can potentially obtain very large payoffs from their investments in information technology.

The home mortgage industry is a leading example in the United States of how major corporations have implemented business reengineering. The application process for a home mortgage currently takes about six to eight weeks and costs about $3000. The goal of many mortgage banks is to lower that cost to $1000 and the time to obtain a mortgage to about one week. Leading mortgage banks such as BancBoston, Countrywide Funding Corporation, and Banc One Corporation have redesigned the mortgage application process.

The mortgage application process is divided into three stages: origination, servicing, and secondary marketing. Figure 10.4 illustrates how business process redesign has been used in each of these stages.

In the past, a mortgage applicant filled out a paper loan application. The bank entered the application into its computer system. Specialists such as credit analysts and underwriters from perhaps eight different departments accessed and evaluated the application individually. If the loan application was approved, the closing was scheduled. After the closing, bank specialists dealing with insurance or funds in escrow serviced the loan. This "desk to desk" assembly-line approach might take up to 17 days.

Leading banks have replaced the sequential desk-to-desk approach with a speedier "work cell" or team approach. Now, loan originators in the field enter the mortgage application directly into laptop computers. Software checks the application transaction to make sure that all of the information is correct and complete. The loan originators transmit the loan applications using a dial-up network to regional production centers. Instead of working on the application individually, the credit analysts, loan underwriters, and other specialists convene electronically, working as a team to approve the mortgage. Some banks provide customers with a nearly instant credit lock-in of a guaranteed mortgage so they can find a house that meets their budget immediately. Such preapproval of a credit line is truly a radical reengineering of the traditional business process.

After closing, another team of specialists sets up the loan for servicing. The entire loan application process can take as little as two days. Loan information is easier to access than before, when the loan application could be in eight or nine different departments. Loan originators also can dial into the bank's network to obtain information on mortgage loan costs or to check the status of a loan for the customer.

By redesigning their approach to mortgage processing, mortgage banks have achieved remarkable efficiencies. They have not focused on redesigning a single business process but instead they have reexamined the entire set of logically connected processes required to obtain a mortgage. Instead of automating the previous method of mortgage processing, the banks have completely rethought the entire mortgage application process.

Work-Flow Management

To streamline the paperwork in the mortgage application process, banks have turned to work-flow and document management software. By using this software to store and process documents electronically, organizations can redesign their work-flow so that documents can be worked on simultaneously or moved more easily and efficiently from one location to another. The process of streamlining business procedures so that documents can be moved easily and efficiently is called **work-flow management.** Work-flow and document management software automates processes such as routing documents to different locations, securing approvals, scheduling, and generating reports. Two or more people can work simultaneously on the same document, allowing much quicker completion time. Work need not be delayed because a file is out or a document is in transit. And with a properly designed indexing system, users will be able to retrieve files in many different ways, based on the content of the document. Chapter 2 describes how the United Services Automobile Association (USAA) developed a document imaging system to obtain such benefits.

work-flow management The process of streamlining business procedures so that documents can be moved easily and efficiently from one location to another.

Steps in Effective Reengineering

To reengineer effectively, senior management needs to develop a broad strategic vision that calls for redesigned business processes. For example, Mitsubishi Heavy Industries management looked for breakthroughs to lower costs and accelerate product development that would enable the firm to regain market leadership in ship building.

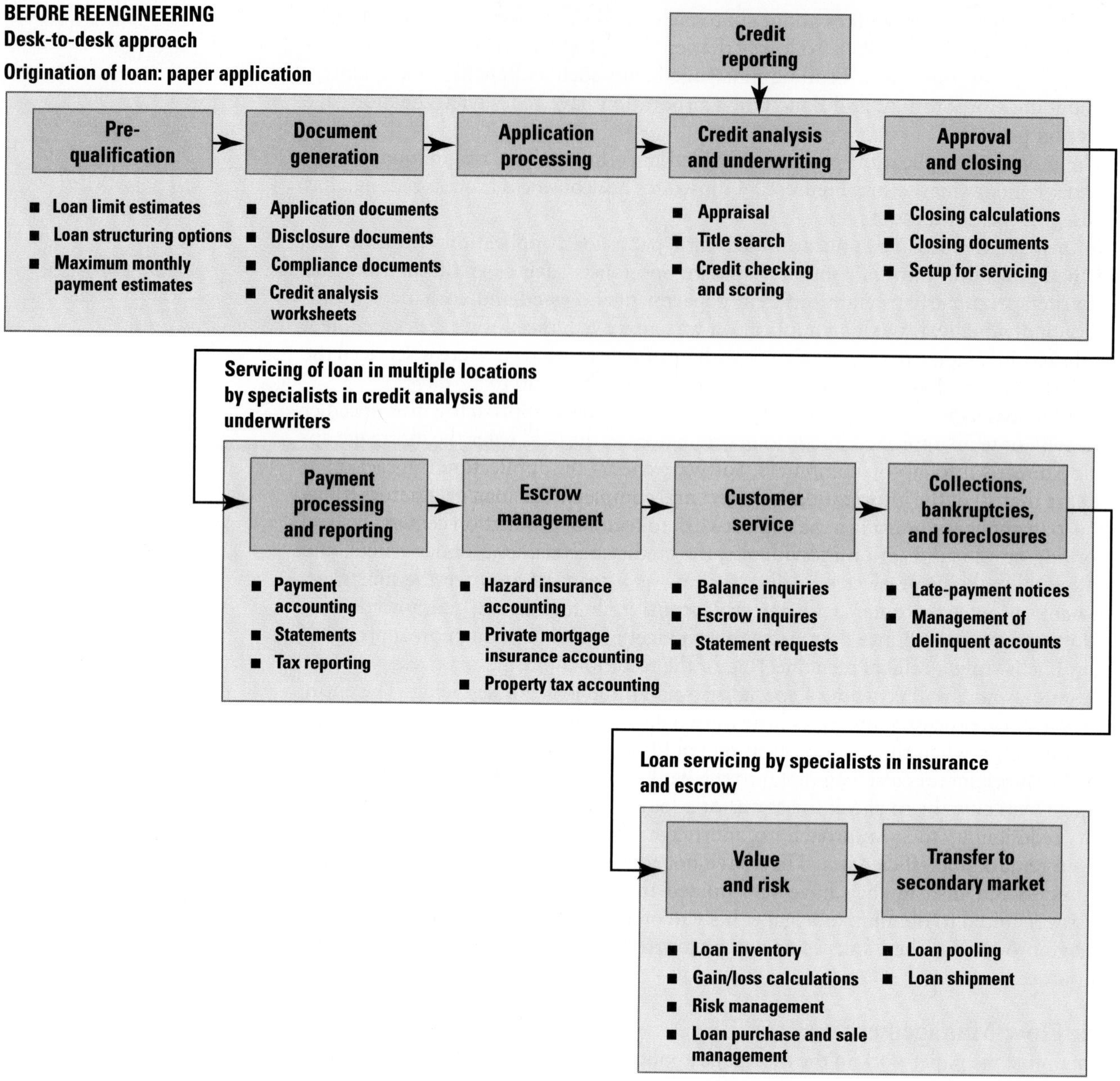

BEFORE REENGINEERING
Desk-to-desk approach

Origination of loan: paper application

Credit reporting → Credit analysis and underwriting

Pre-qualification → **Document generation** → **Application processing** → **Credit analysis and underwriting** → **Approval and closing**

Pre-qualification:
- Loan limit estimates
- Loan structuring options
- Maximum monthly payment estimates

Document generation:
- Application documents
- Disclosure documents
- Compliance documents
- Credit analysis worksheets

Credit analysis and underwriting:
- Appraisal
- Title search
- Credit checking and scoring

Approval and closing:
- Closing calculations
- Closing documents
- Setup for servicing

Servicing of loan in multiple locations by specialists in credit analysis and underwriters

Payment processing and reporting → **Escrow management** → **Customer service** → **Collections, bankruptcies, and foreclosures**

Payment processing and reporting:
- Payment accounting
- Statements
- Tax reporting

Escrow management:
- Hazard insurance accounting
- Private mortgage insurance accounting
- Property tax accounting

Customer service:
- Balance inquiries
- Escrow inquires
- Statement requests

Collections, bankruptcies, and foreclosures:
- Late-payment notices
- Management of delinquent accounts

Loan servicing by specialists in insurance and escrow

Value and risk → **Transfer to secondary market**

Value and risk:
- Loan inventory
- Gain/loss calculations
- Risk management
- Loan purchase and sale management

Transfer to secondary market:
- Loan pooling
- Loan shipment

AFTER REENGINEERING
Team approach

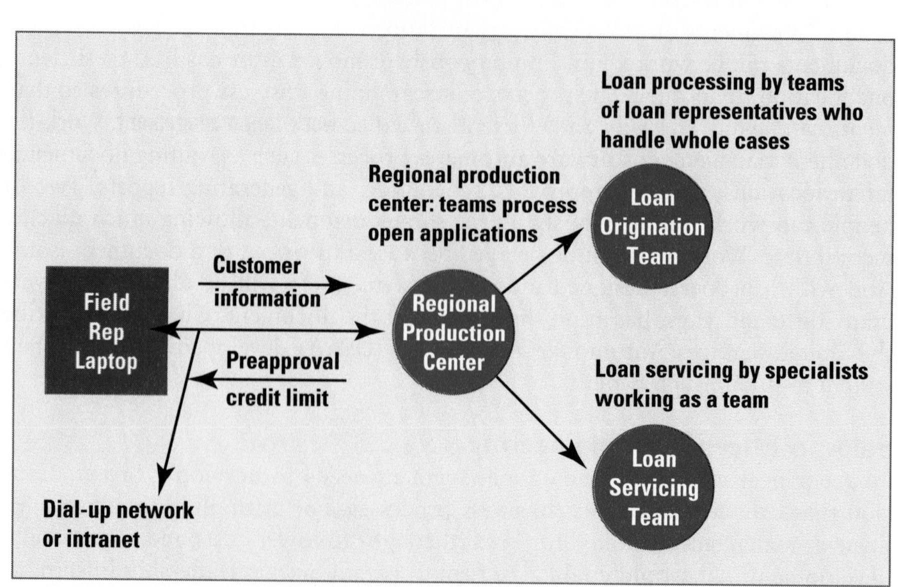

FIGURE 10.4

Redesigning mortgage processing in the United States. By redesigning their mortgage processing systems and the mortgage application process, mortgage banks will be able to reduce the costs of processing the average mortgage from $3000 to $1000, and reduce the time of approval from six weeks to one week or less. Some banks are even preapproving mortgages and locking interest rates on the same day as the customer applies.

TABLE 10.5 New Process Design Options with Information Technology

Assumption	Technology	Option	Examples
Field personnel need offices to receive, store, and transmit information.	Wireless communications	Personnel can send and receive information wherever they are.	Manitoba Insurance Price Waterhouse
Information can appear only in one place at one time.	Shared databases	People can collaborate on the same project from scattered locations; information can be used simultaneously wherever it is needed.	U.S. West Banc One
People are needed to ascertain where things are located.	Automatic identification and tracking technology	Things can tell people where they are.	United Parcel Service Schneider National
Businesses need reserve inventory to prevent stockouts.	Telecommunications networks and EDI	Just-in-time delivery and stockless supply.	Wal-Mart Baxter International

Companies should identify a few core business processes to be redesigned, focusing on those with the greatest potential payback (Davenport and Short, 1990).

Management must understand and measure the performance of existing processes as a baseline. If, for example, the objective of process redesign is to reduce time and cost in developing a new product or filling an order, the organization needs to measure the time and cost consumed by the unchanged process. For example, before reengineering, it cost C.R. England & Sons Inc. $5.10 to send an invoice; after processes were reengineered the cost per invoice dropped to 15 cents (Davidson, 1993).

The conventional method of designing systems establishes the information requirements of a business function or process and then determines how they can be supported by information technology. However information technology can create new design options for various processes because it can be used to challenge longstanding assumptions about work arrangements that used to inhibit organizations. Table 10.5 provides examples of innovations that have overcome these assumptions using companies discussed in the text. Information technology should be allowed to influence process design from the start.

Following these steps does not automatically guarantee that reengineering will always be successful. In point of fact, the majority of reengineering projects do not achieve breakthrough gains in business performance, with reengineering failure rates estimated as high as 70 percent (Hammer and Stanton, 1995; King, 1994; Moad, 1993). Problems with reengineering are part of the larger problem of orchestrating organizational change, a problem that attends the introduction of all new innovations, including information systems. Managing change is neither simple nor intuitive. A reengineered business process or a new information system inevitably affects jobs, skill requirements, work-flows, and reporting relationships (Teng, Jeong, and Grover, 1998). Fear of these changes breeds resistance, confusion, and even conscious efforts to undermine the change effort. We examine these organizational change issues more carefully in Section 10.3.

10.2 OVERVIEW OF SYSTEMS DEVELOPMENT

Whatever their scope and objectives, new information systems are an outgrowth of a process of organizational problem solving. A new information system is built as a solution to some type of problem or set of problems the organization perceives it is facing. The problem may be one where managers and employees realize that the organization is not performing as well as expected, or it may come from the realization that the organization should take advantage of new opportunities to perform more successfully.

FIGURE 10.5

The systems development process. Each of the core systems development activities entails interaction with the organization.

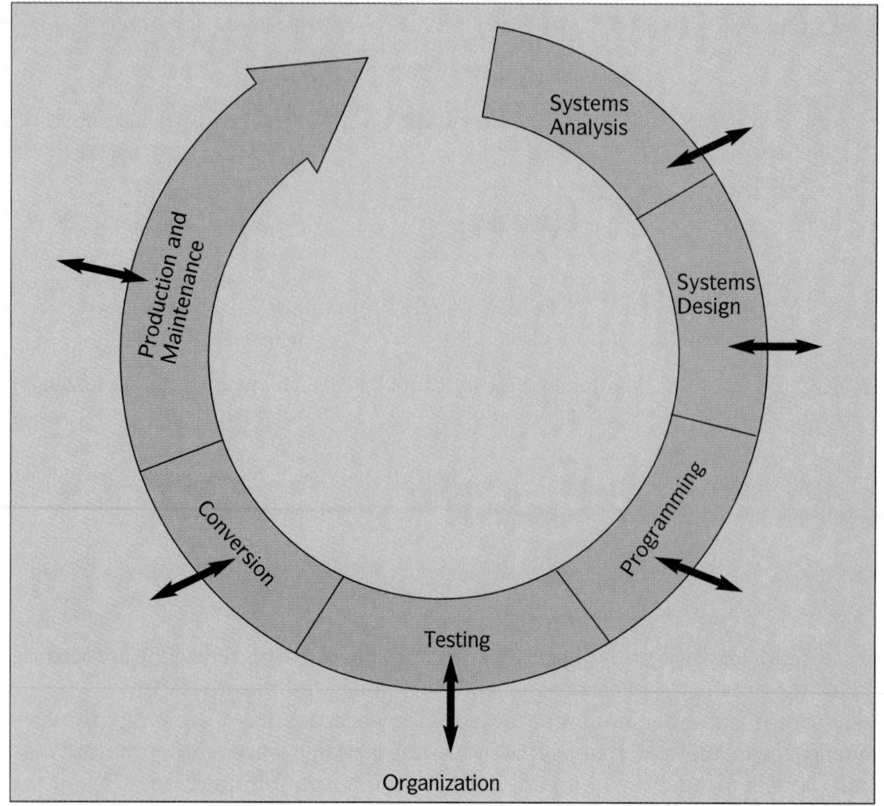

Review the diagrams at the beginning of each chapter of this text. They show an information system that is a solution to a particular set of business challenges or problems. The resulting information system is an outgrowth of a series of events called *systems development.* **Systems development** refers to all the activities that go into producing an information systems solution to an organizational problem or opportunity. Systems development is a structured kind of problem solving with distinct activities. These activities consist of systems analysis, systems design, programming, testing, conversion, and production and maintenance.

systems development The activities that go into producing an information systems solution to an organizational problem or opportunity.

Figure 10.5 illustrates the systems development process. The systems development activities depicted here usually take place in sequential order. But some of the activities may need to be repeated or some may be taking place simultaneously, depending on the approach to system building that is being employed (see Chapter 11). Note also that each activity involves interaction with the organization. Members of the organization participate in these activities and the systems development process creates organizational changes.

Systems Analysis

systems analysis The analysis of a problem that the organization will try to solve with an information system.

Systems analysis is the analysis of the problem that the organization will try to solve with an information system. It consists of defining the problem, identifying its causes, specifying the solution, and identifying the information requirements that must be met by a system solution.

The systems analyst creates a road map of the existing organization and systems, identifying the primary owners and users of data in the organization. These stakeholders have a direct interest in the information affected by the new system. In addition to these organizational aspects, the analyst also briefly describes the existing hardware and software that serve the organization.

From this organizational analysis, the systems analyst details the problems of existing systems. By examining documents, work papers, and procedures; observing system operations; and interviewing key users of the systems, the analyst can identify the

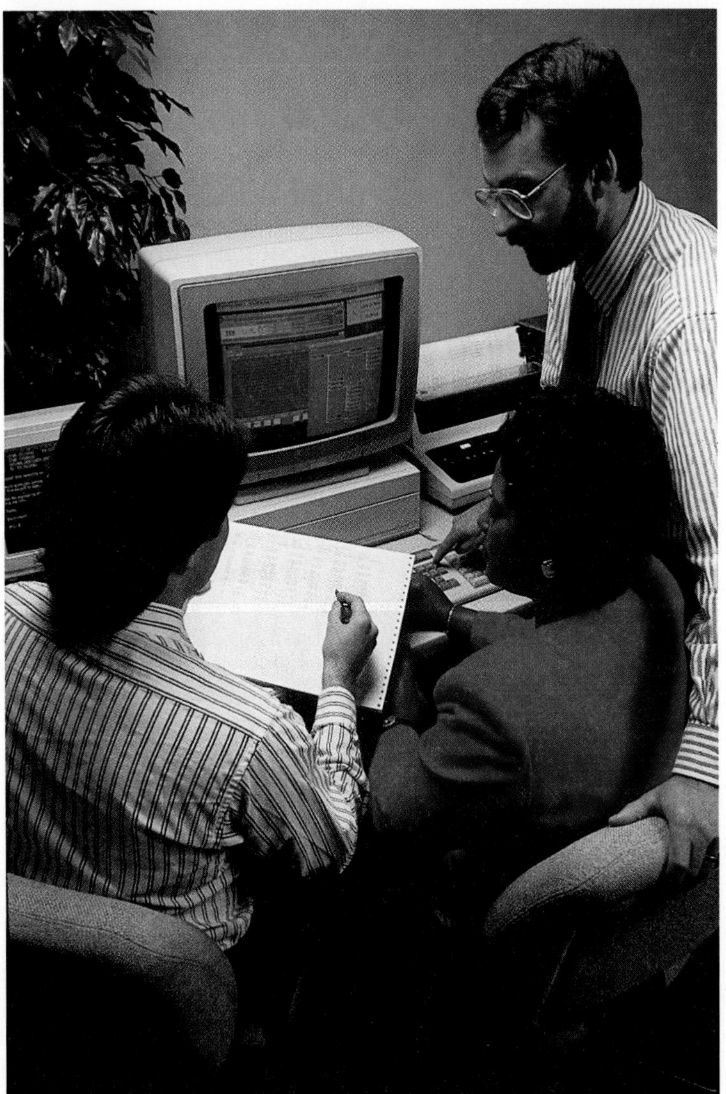

Building successful information systems requires close cooperation among end users and information systems specialists throughout the systems development process.

problem areas and objectives to be achieved by a solution. Often the solution requires building a new information system or improving an existing one.

Feasibility

In addition to suggesting a solution, systems analysis involves a **feasibility study** to determine whether that solution is feasible, or achievable, given the organization's resources and constraints. Three major areas of feasibility must be addressed:

1. **Technical feasibility:** whether the proposed solution can be implemented with the available hardware, software, and technical resources.
2. **Economic feasibility:** whether the benefits of the proposed solution outweigh the costs. We explore this topic in greater detail in Section 10.4, Understanding the Business Value of Information Systems.
3. **Operational feasibility:** whether the proposed solution is desirable within the existing managerial and organizational framework.

Normally the systems analysis process will identify several alternative solutions that can be pursued by the organization. The process then will assess the feasibility of each. A written systems proposal report will describe the costs and benefits, advantages and disadvantages of each alternative. It is up to management to determine which mix of costs, benefits, technical features, and organizational impacts represents the most desirable alternative.

feasibility study As part of the systems analysis process, the way to determine whether the solution is achievable, given the organization's resources and constraints.

technical feasibility Determines whether a proposed solution can be implemented with the available hardware, software, and technical resources.

economic feasibility Determines whether the benefits of a proposed solution outweigh the costs.

operational feasibility Determines whether a proposed solution is desirable within the existing managerial and organizational framework.

Establishing Information Requirements

information requirements A detailed statement of the information needs that a new system must satisfy; identifies who needs what information, and when, where, and how the information is needed.

Perhaps the most difficult task of the systems analyst is to define the specific information requirements that must be met by the system solution selected. At the most basic level, the **information requirements** of a new system involve identifying who needs what information, where, when, and how. Requirements analysis carefully defines the objectives of the new or modified system and develops a detailed description of the functions that the new system must perform. Requirements must consider economic, technical, and time constraints, as well as the goals, procedures, and decision processes of the organization. Faulty requirements analysis is a leading cause of systems failure and high systems development costs. A system designed around the wrong set of requirements will either have to be discarded because of poor performance or will need to be heavily revised. Therefore, the importance of requirements analysis cannot be overstated.

Developing requirements specifications may involve considerable research and revision. To derive information systems requirements, analysts may be forced to work and rework requirements statements in cooperation with users. There are also alternative approaches to eliciting requirements that help minimize these problems (see Chapter 11).

In many instances, building a new system creates an opportunity to redefine how the organization conducts its daily business. Some problems do not require an information system solution but instead need an adjustment in management, additional training, or refinement of existing organizational procedures. If the problem is information related, systems analysis still may be required to diagnose the problem and arrive at the proper solution.

Systems Design

systems design Details how a system will meet the information requirements as determined by the systems analysis.

Systems analysis describes what a system should do to meet information requirements, and **systems design** shows how the system will fulfill this objective. The design of an information system is the overall plan or model for that system. Like the blueprint of a building or house, it consists of all the specifications that give the system its form and structure.

The systems designer details the system specifications that will deliver the functions identified during systems analysis. These specifications should address all of the managerial, organizational, and technological components of the system solution. Table 10.6 lists the types of specifications that would be produced during systems design.

Logical and Physical Design

logical design Lays out the components of the information system and their relationship to each other as they would appear to users.

physical design The process of translating the abstract logical model into the specific technical design for the new system.

The design for an information system can be broken down into logical and physical design specifications. **Logical design** lays out the components of the system and their relationship to each other as they would appear to users. It shows what the system solution will do as opposed to how it is actually implemented physically. It describes inputs and outputs, processing functions to be performed, business procedures, data models, and controls. (Controls specify standards for acceptable performance and methods for measuring actual performance in relation to these standards. They are described in detail in Chapter 14.)

Physical design is the process of translating the abstract logical model into the specific technical design for the new system. It produces the specifications for hardware, software, physical databases, input/output media, manual procedures, and specific controls. Physical design provides the remaining specifications that transform the abstract logical design plan into a functioning system of people and machines.

Like houses or buildings, information systems may have many possible designs. They may be centralized or distributed, on-line or batch, partially manual, or heavily automated. Each design represents a unique blend of all of the technical and organizational factors that shape an information system. What makes one design superior to others is the ease and efficiency with which it fulfills user requirements within a specific set of technical, organizational, financial, and time constraints.

TABLE 10.6 Design Specifications

Output Medium Content Timing	Controls Input controls (characters, limit, reasonableness) Processing controls (consistency, record counts) Output controls (totals, samples of output) Procedural controls (passwords, special forms)
Input Origins Flow Data entry	Security Access controls Catastrophe plans Audit trails
User interface Simplicity Efficiency Logic Feedback Errors	Documentation Operations documentation Systems documents User documentation
Database design Logical data relations Volume and speed requirements File organization and design Record specifications	Conversion Transfer files Initiate new procedures Select testing method Cut over to new system
Processing Computations Program modules Required reports Timing of outputs	Training Select training techniques Develop training modules Identify training facilities
Manual procedures What activities Who performs them When How Where	Organizational changes Task redesign Job design Process design Office and organization structure design Reporting relationships

The Role of End Users

User information requirements drive the entire system-building effort. Users must have sufficient control over the design process to ensure that the system reflects their business priorities and information needs, not the biases of the technical staff (Hunton and Beeler, 1997.) Working on design increases users' understanding and acceptance of the system, reducing problems caused by power transfers, intergroup conflict, and unfamiliarity with new system functions and procedures. As we describe later in this chapter, insufficient user involvement in the design effort is a major cause of system failure.

The nature and level of user participation in design vary from system to system. There is less need for user involvement in systems with simple or straightforward requirements than in those with requirements that are elaborate, complex, or vaguely defined. Less structured systems need more user participation to define requirements and may necessitate many versions of design before specifications can be finalized. Different levels of user involvement in design are reflected in different systems development methods. Chapter 11 describes how user involvement varies with each development approach.

Completing the Systems Development Process

The remaining steps in the systems development process translate the solution specifications established during systems analysis and design into a fully operational information system. These concluding steps consist of programming, testing, conversion, production, and maintenance.

Programming

The process of translating design specifications into software for the computer constitutes a smaller portion of the systems development cycle than design and, perhaps, the testing activities. But it is here, in providing the actual instructions for the machine, that the heart of the system takes shape. During the **programming** stage, system specifications that were prepared during the design stage are translated into program code. On the basis of detailed design documents for files, transaction and report layouts, and other design details, specifications for each program in the system are prepared.

programming The process of translating the system specifications prepared during the design stage into program code.

Testing

Exhaustive and thorough **testing** must be conducted to ascertain whether the system produces the right results. Testing answers the question, "Will the system produce the desired results under known conditions?"

testing The exhaustive and thorough process that determines whether the system produces the desired results under known conditions.

The amount of time needed to answer this question has been traditionally underrated in systems project planning (see Chapter 14). As much as 50 percent of the entire software development budget can be expended in testing. Testing is also time consuming: Test data must be carefully prepared, results reviewed, and corrections made in the system. In some instances parts of the system may have to be redesigned. The risks of glossing over this step are enormous.

Testing an information system can be broken down into three types of activities:

Unit testing, or program testing, consists of testing each program separately in the system. It is widely believed that the purpose of such testing is to guarantee that programs are error-free, but this goal is realistically impossible. Testing should be viewed instead as a means of locating errors in programs, focusing on finding all the ways to make a program fail. Once pinpointed, problems can be corrected.

unit testing The process of testing each program separately in the system. Sometimes called *program testing*.

System testing tests the functioning of the information system as a whole. It tries to determine if discrete modules will function together as planned and whether discrepancies exist between the way the system actually works and the way it was conceived. Among the areas examined are performance time, capacity for file storage and handling peak loads, recovery and restart capabilities, and manual procedures.

system testing Tests the functioning of the information system as a whole in order to determine if discrete modules will function together as planned.

Acceptance testing provides the final certification that the system is ready to be used in a production setting. Systems tests are evaluated by users and reviewed by management. When all parties are satisfied that the new system meets their standards, the system is formally accepted for installation.

acceptance testing Provides the final certification that the system is ready to be used in a production setting.

It is essential that all aspects of testing be carefully thought out and that they be as comprehensive as possible. To ensure this, the development team works with users to devise a systematic test plan. The **test plan** includes all of the preparations for the series of tests previously described.

test plan Prepared by the development team in conjunction with the users; it includes all of the preparations for the series of tests to be performed on the system.

Figure 10.6 shows an example of a test plan. The general condition being tested is a record change. The documentation consists of a series of test-plan screens maintained on a database (perhaps a microcomputer database) that is ideally suited to this kind of application.

Conversion

Conversion is the process of changing from the old system to the new system. It answers the question, "Will the new system work under real conditions?" Four main conversion strategies can be employed: the parallel strategy, the direct cutover strategy, the pilot study strategy, and the phased approach strategy.

conversion The process of changing from the old system to the new system.

In a **parallel strategy** both the old system and its potential replacement are run together for a time until everyone is assured that the new one functions correctly. This is the safest conversion approach because, in the event of errors or processing disruptions, the old system can still be used as a backup. However, this approach is very expensive, and additional staff or resources may be required to run the extra system.

parallel strategy A safe and conservative conversion approach where both the old system and its potential replacement are run together for a time until everyone is assured that the new one functions correctly.

The **direct cutover** strategy replaces the old system entirely with the new system on an appointed day. At first glance, this strategy seems less costly than the parallel conversion strategy. However, it is a very risky approach that can potentially be more costly than parallel activities if serious problems with the new system are found. There is no

direct cutover A risky conversion approach where the new system completely replaces the old one on an appointed day.

Procedure	Address and Maintenance "Record Change Series"		Test Series 2		
	Prepared By:	Date:	Version:		
Test Ref.	**Condition Tested**	**Special Requirements**	**Expected Results**	**Output On**	**Next Screen**
2	Change records				
2.1	Change existing record	Key field	Not allowed		
2.2	Change nonexistent record	Other fields	"Invalid key" message		
2.3	Change deleted record	Deleted record must be available	"Deleted" message		
2.4	Make second record	Change 2.1 above	OK if valid	Transaction file	V45
2.5	Insert record		OK if valid	Transaction file	V45
2.6	Abort during change	Abort 2.5	No change	Transaction file	V45

FIGURE 10.6

A sample test plan to test a record change. When developing a test plan, it is imperative to include the various conditions to be tested, the requirements for each condition tested, and the expected results. Test plans require input from both end users and information system specialists.

other system to fall back on. Dislocations, disruptions, and the cost of corrections may be enormous.

The **pilot study** strategy introduces the new system to only a limited area of the organization, such as a single department or operating unit. When this pilot version is complete and working smoothly, it is installed throughout the rest of the organization, either simultaneously or in stages.

The **phased approach** strategy introduces the new system in stages, either by functions or by organizational units. If, for example, the system is introduced by functions, a new payroll system might begin with hourly workers who are paid weekly, followed six months later by adding salaried employees (who are paid monthly) to the system. If the system is introduced by organizational units, corporate headquarters might be converted first, followed by outlying operating units four months later.

A formal **conversion plan** provides a schedule of all the activities required to install the new system. The most time-consuming activity is usually the conversion of data. Data from the old system must be transferred to the new system, either manually or through special conversion software programs. The converted data then must be carefully verified for accuracy and completeness.

Moving from an old system to a new one requires that end users be trained to use the new system. Detailed **documentation** showing how the system works from both a technical and end-user standpoint is finalized during conversion time for use in training and everyday operations. Lack of proper training and documentation contributes to system failure, so this portion of the systems development process is very important.

Production and Maintenance

After the new system is installed and conversion is complete, the system is said to be in **production.** During this stage the system will be reviewed by both users and technical specialists to determine how well it has met its original objectives and to decide whether any revisions or modifications are in order. Changes in hardware, software, documentation, or procedures to a production system to correct errors, meet new requirements, or improve processing efficiency are termed **maintenance.**

Studies of maintenance have examined the amount of time required for various maintenance tasks (Lientz and Swanson, 1980). Approximately 20 percent of the time is devoted to debugging or correcting emergency production problems; another 20 percent is concerned with changes in data, files, reports, hardware, or system software. But 60 percent of all maintenance work consists of making user enhancements, improving documentation, and recoding system components for greater processing efficiency. The

pilot study A strategy to introduce the new system to a limited area of the organization until it is proven to be fully functional; only then can the conversion to the new system across the entire organization take place.

phased approach Introduces the new system in stages either by functions or by organizational units.

conversion plan Provides a schedule of all activities required to install a new system.

documentation Descriptions of how an information system works from either a technical or end-user standpoint.

production The stage after the new system is installed and the conversion is complete; during this time the system is reviewed by users and technical specialists to determine how well it has met its original goals.

maintenance Changes in hardware, software, documentation, or procedures to a production system to correct errors, meet new requirements, or improve processing efficiency.

TABLE 10.7 Systems Development

Core Activity	Description
Systems analysis	Identify problem(s) Specify solution Establish information requirements
Systems design	Create logical design specifications Create physical design specifications Manage technical realization of system
Programming	Translate design specifications into program code
Testing	Unit test Systems test Acceptance test
Conversion	Plan conversion Prepare documentation Train users and technical staff
Production and maintenance	Operate the system Evaluate the system Modify the system

amount of work in the third category of maintenance problems could be reduced significantly through better systems analysis and design practices. Table 10.7 summarizes the systems development activities.

Systems differ in terms of their size and technological complexity, and in terms of the organizational problems they are meant to solve. Because there are different kinds of systems, a number of methods have been developed to build systems. We describe these various methods in the next chapter.

10.3 SYSTEM IMPLEMENTATION: MANAGING CHANGE

The introduction or alteration of an information system has a powerful behavioral and organizational impact. It transforms the way various individuals and groups perform and interact. Changes in the way information is defined, accessed, and used to manage the resources of the organization often lead to new distributions of authority and power (Lucas, 1975). This internal organizational change breeds resistance and opposition and can lead to the demise of an otherwise good system.

A very large percentage of information systems fail to deliver benefits or to solve the problems for which they were intended because the process of organizational change associated with system-building was not properly addressed. Successful system-building requires careful planning and change management. We now turn to the problem of change management by examining patterns of implementation.

Implementation Success and Failure

implementation All of the organizational activities working toward the adoption, management, and routinization of an innovation.

change agent The individual acting as the catalyst during the change process to ensure successful organizational adaptation to a new system or innovation.

In the context of change management, **implementation** refers to all of the organizational activities working toward the adoption, management, and routinization of an innovation such as a new information system. In the implementation process, the systems analyst is a **change agent.** The analyst not only develops technical solutions but redefines the configurations, interactions, job activities, and power relationships of various organizational groups. The analyst is the catalyst for the entire change process and is responsible for ensuring that the changes created by a new system are accepted by all parties involved. The change agent communicates with users, mediates between competing interest groups, and ensures that the organizational adjustment to such changes is complete.

Whether system implementations are successful or not depends largely on managerial and organizational factors. The role of users, the degree of management support, the manner in which the systems project handles complexity and risk, and the management of the implementation process itself all have a profound impact on system outcome.

User Involvement and Influence

Heavy user involvement in the design and operation of information systems afford them more opportunities to mold the system according to their priorities and business requirements. In addition, they are more likely to react positively to the completed system because they have been active participants in the change process.

Communication problems between end users and designers are a major reason why user requirements are not properly incorporated into information systems and why users are driven out of the implementation process. Users and information system specialists tend to have different backgrounds, interests, and priorities and often pursue different goals. This is referred to as the **user-designer communications gap.** These differences are manifested in divergent organizational loyalties, approaches to problem solving, and vocabularies. Information system specialists, for example, often have a highly technical or machine orientation to problem solving. They look for elegant and sophisticated technical solutions in which hardware and software efficiency is optimized at the expense of ease of use or organizational effectiveness. Users, on the other hand, prefer systems that are oriented to solving business problems or facilitating organizational tasks. Often the orientations of both groups are so at odds that they appear to speak in different tongues. These differences are illustrated in Table 10.8, which depicts the typical concerns of end users and technical specialists (information system designers) regarding the development of a new information system.

user-designer communications gap The difference in backgrounds, interests, and priorities that impede communication and problem solving among end users and information systems specialists.

Management Support

If an information systems project has the backing and approval of management at various levels, it is more likely to be perceived positively by both users and the technical information services staff. Both groups will feel that their participation in the development process will receive higher-level attention, priority, and reward. Management backing also ensures that a systems project will receive sufficient funding and resources to be successful. Furthermore, all of the changes in work habits and procedures and any organizational realignments associated with a new system depend on management backing to be enforced effectively.

Level of Complexity and Risk

Systems differ dramatically in their size, scope, level of complexity, and organizational and technical components. Some systems development projects are more likely to fail because they carry a much higher level of risk than others. Researchers have identified three key dimensions that influence the level of project risk (McFarlan, 1981).

TABLE 10.8 The User-Designer Communications Gap

User Concerns	Designer Concerns
Will the system deliver the information I need for my work?	How much disk storage space will the master file consume?
How quickly can I access the data?	How many lines of program code will it take to perform this function?
How easily can I retrieve the data?	How can we cut down on CPU time when we run the system?
How much clerical support will I need to enter data into the system?	What is the most efficient way of storing this piece of data?
How will the operation of the system fit into my daily business schedule?	What database management system should we use?

TABLE 10.9 Dimensions of Project Risk

Project Structure	Project Technology Level	Project Size	Degree of Risk
High	Low	Large	Low
High	Low	Small	Very low
High	High	Large	Medium
High	High	Small	Medium-low
Low	Low	Large	Low
Low	Low	Small	Very low
Low	High	Large	Very high
Low	High	Small	High

PROJECT SIZE. The larger the project—as indicated by the dollars spent, the size of the implementation staff, the time allocated to implementation, and the number of organizational units affected—the greater the risk.

PROJECT STRUCTURE. Projects that are more highly structured run a much lower risk than those whose requirements are relatively undefined, fluid, and constantly changing; when requirements are clear and straightforward, outputs and processes can be easily defined. Users in highly structured projects tend to know exactly what they want and what the system should do; there is a much lower possibility of their changing their minds.

EXPERIENCE WITH TECHNOLOGY. The project risk will rise if the project team and the information system staff are unfamiliar with the hardware, system software, application software, or database management system proposed for the project.

These dimensions of project risk will be present in different combinations for each implementation effort. Table 10.9 shows that eight different combinations are possible, each with a different degree of risk. The higher the level of risk, the more likely it is that the implementation effort will fail.

Management of the Implementation Process

The conflicts and uncertainties inherent in any implementation effort will be magnified when an implementation project is poorly managed and organized. Under poor management basic elements of success may be omitted. Training to ensure that end users are comfortable with the new system and fully understand its potential uses is often sacrificed, in part because the budget is strained toward the end of a project. A systems development project without proper management will most likely suffer vast cost overruns, major time slippages, and technical performances that fall significantly below the estimated level.

How badly are projects managed? On average, private-sector projects are underestimated by one-half in terms of budget and time required to deliver the complete system promised in the system plan. A very large number of projects are delivered with missing functionality (promised for delivery in later versions). Government projects suffer about the same failure level, sometimes worse (Laudon, 1989; Helms and Weiss, 1986).

Managing Implementation

Not all aspects of the implementation process can be easily controlled or planned (Alter and Ginzberg, 1978). However, the chances for system success can be increased by anticipating potential implementation problems and applying appropriate corrective strategies. Strategies have also been devised for ensuring that users play an appropriate role throughout the implementation period and for managing the organizational change process. Various project management, requirements gathering, and planning methodologies have been developed for specific categories of problems.

Increasing User Involvement

The level of user involvement should vary depending upon both the development methodology being used and the risk level of the project. Tools to involve users—**external integration tools**—consist of ways to link the work of the implementation team to users at all organizational levels. For example, users can be made active members or leaders of systems development project teams or placed in charge of system training and installation.

external integration tools Project management technique that links the work of the implementation team to that of users at all organizational levels.

Overcoming User Resistance

Systems development is not an entirely rational process. Users leading design activities have used their position to further private interests and to gain power rather than to promote organizational objectives (Franz and Robey, 1984). Participation in implementation activities may not be enough to overcome the problem of user resistance. The implementation process demands organizational change. Such change may be resisted because different users may be affected by the system in different ways. Some users may welcome a new system because it brings changes they perceive as beneficial to them, while others may resist these changes because they believe the shifts are detrimental to their interests (Joshi, 1991).

If use of a system is voluntary, users may tend to avoid it. If use is mandatory, resistance will take the form of increased error rates, disruptions, turnover, and even sabotage. Implementation strategy must address the issue of counterimplementation (Keen, 1981). **Counterimplementation** is a deliberate strategy to thwart the implementation of an information system or an innovation in an organization.

counterimplementation A deliberate strategy to thwart the implementation of an information system or an innovation in an organization.

Strategies to overcome user resistance include user participation (to elicit commitment as well as to improve design), user education (training), management coercion (edicts, policies), and user incentives. User resistance can be addressed through changes to the new system, such as improved human factors (user/system interface). Finally, users will be more cooperative if organizational problems are solved prior to introducing the new system.

Managing Technical Complexity

Projects with high levels of technology benefit from **internal integration tools.** The success of such projects depends on how well their technical complexity can be managed. Project leaders need both heavy technical and administrative experience. They must be able to anticipate problems and develop smooth working relationships among a predominantly technical team. Team members should be highly experienced. Team meetings should take place frequently, with routine distribution of meeting minutes concerning key design decisions. Essential technical skills or expertise not available internally should be secured from outside the organization.

internal integration tools Project management technique that ensures that the implementation team operates as a cohesive unit.

Formal Planning and Control Tools

Large projects will benefit from appropriate use of **formal planning and control tools.** With project management techniques such as PERT (Program Evaluation and Review Technique) or Gantt charts, a detailed plan can be developed. (PERT lists the specific activities that make up a project, their duration, and the activities that must be completed before a specific activity can start. A Gantt chart such as that illustrated in Figure 10.7 visually represents the sequence and timing of different tasks in a development project, as well as their resource requirements.) Tasks can be defined and resources budgeted.

formal planning tools Project management technique that structures and sequences tasks; budgeting time, money, and technical resources required to complete the tasks.

formal control tools Project management technique that helps monitor the progress toward completion of a task and fulfillment of goals.

These project management techniques can help managers identify bottlenecks and determine the impact problems will have on project completion times. Standard control techniques can be used to chart project progress against budgets and target dates, so that deviations can be spotted and the implementation team can make adjustments to meet their original schedule. Periodic formal status reports against the plan will show the extent of progress.

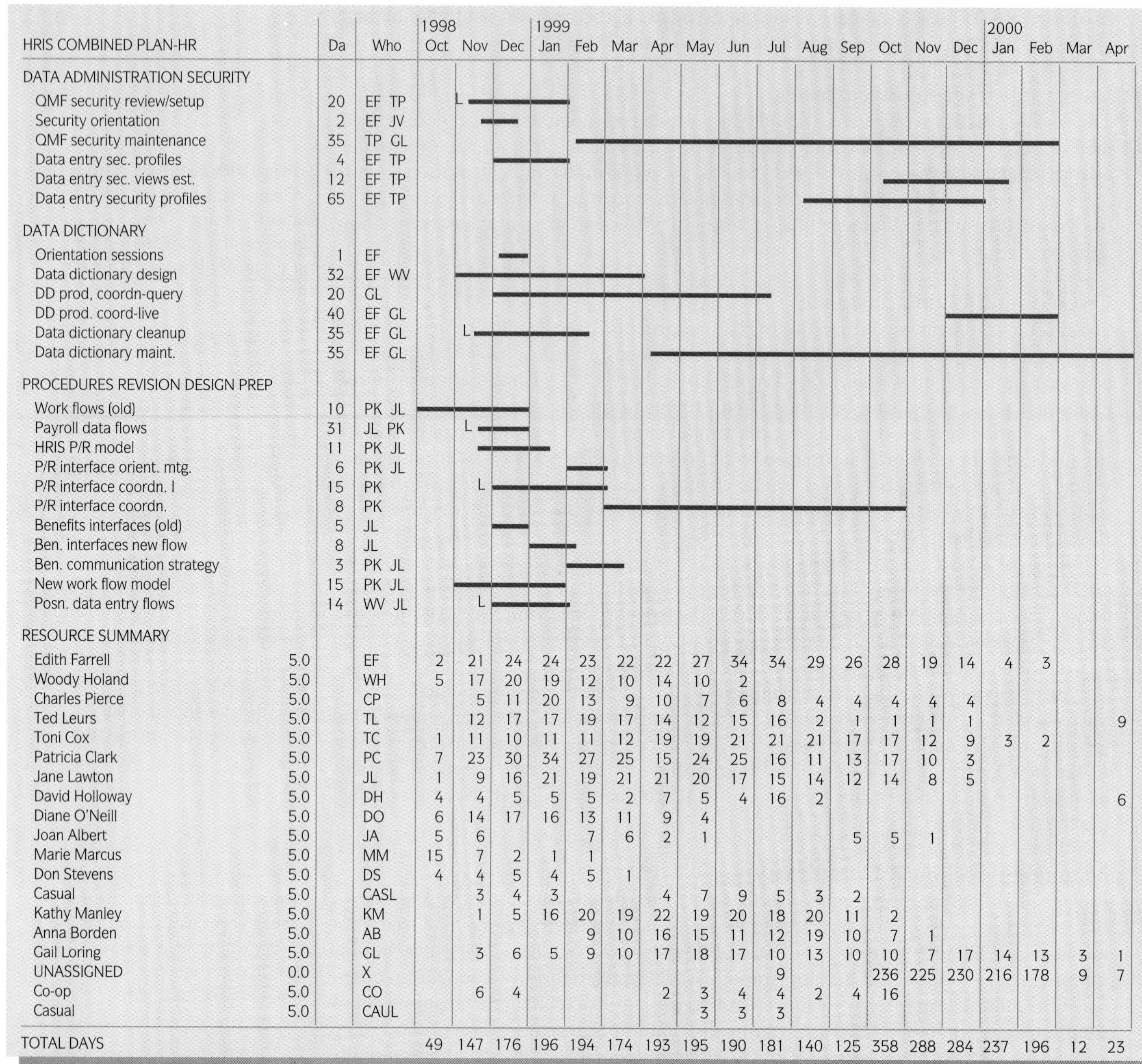

HRIS COMBINED PLAN-HR	Da	Who
DATA ADMINISTRATION SECURITY		
QMF security review/setup	20	EF TP
Security orientation	2	EF JV
QMF security maintenance	35	TP GL
Data entry sec. profiles	4	EF TP
Data entry sec. views est.	12	EF TP
Data entry security profiles	65	EF TP
DATA DICTIONARY		
Orientation sessions	1	EF
Data dictionary design	32	EF WV
DD prod, coordn-query	20	GL
DD prod. coord-live	40	EF GL
Data dictionary cleanup	35	EF GL
Data dictionary maint.	35	EF GL
PROCEDURES REVISION DESIGN PREP		
Work flows (old)	10	PK JL
Payroll data flows	31	JL PK
HRIS P/R model	11	PK JL
P/R interface orient. mtg.	6	PK JL
P/R interface coordn. I	15	PK
P/R interface coordn.	8	PK
Benefits interfaces (old)	5	JL
Ben. interfaces new flow	8	JL
Ben. communication strategy	3	PK JL
New work flow model	15	PK JL
Posn. data entry flows	14	WV JL

RESOURCE SUMMARY		Who	1998 Oct	Nov	Dec	1999 Jan	Feb	Mar	Apr	May	Jun	Jul	Aug	Sep	Oct	Nov	Dec	2000 Jan	Feb	Mar	Apr
Edith Farrell	5.0	EF	2	21	24	24	23	22	22	27	34	34	29	26	28	19	14	4	3		
Woody Holand	5.0	WH	5	17	20	19	12	10	14	10	2										
Charles Pierce	5.0	CP		5	11	20	13	9	10	7	6	8	4	4	4	4	4				
Ted Leurs	5.0	TL		12	17	17	19	17	14	12	15	16	2	1	1	1	1				9
Toni Cox	5.0	TC	1	11	10	11	11	12	19	19	21	21	21	17	17	12	9	3	2		
Patricia Clark	5.0	PC	7	23	30	34	27	25	15	24	25	16	11	13	17	10	3				
Jane Lawton	5.0	JL	1	9	16	21	19	21	21	20	17	15	14	12	14	8	5				
David Holloway	5.0	DH	4	4	5	5	5	2	7	5	4	16	2								6
Diane O'Neill	5.0	DO	6	14	17	16	13	11	9	4											
Joan Albert	5.0	JA	5	6			7	6	2	1				5	5	1					
Marie Marcus	5.0	MM	15	7	2	1	1														
Don Stevens	5.0	DS	4	4	5	4	5	1													
Casual	5.0	CASL		3	4	3			4	7	9	5	3	2							
Kathy Manley	5.0	KM		1	5	16	20	19	22	19	20	18	20	11	2						
Anna Borden	5.0	AB					9	10	16	15	11	12	19	10	7	1					
Gail Loring	5.0	GL		3	6	5	9	10	17	18	17	10	13	10	10	7	17	14	13	3	1
UNASSIGNED	0.0	X										9			236	225	230	216	178	9	7
Co-op	5.0	CO		6	4				2	3	4	4	2	4	16						
Casual	5.0	CAUL								3	3	3									
TOTAL DAYS			49	147	176	196	194	174	193	195	190	181	140	125	358	288	284	237	196	12	23

FIGURE 10.7 Formal planning and control tools help to manage information systems projects successfully. The Gantt chart in this figure was produced by a commercially available project management software package. It shows the task, person-days, and initials of each responsible person, as well as the start and finish dates for each task. The resource summary provides a good manager with the total person-days for each month and for each person working on the project to successfully manage the project. The project described here is a data administration project.

Controlling Risk Factors

One way implementation can be improved is by adjusting the project management strategy to the risk level inherent in each project. Thus, projects with little structure may involve users fully at all stages, whereas more formal projects may need to adjust user involvement according to the project phase. User participation may not be appropriate at all in some situations. For example, users may react negatively to a new design even though its overall benefits outweigh its drawbacks. Some individuals may stand to lose power as a result of design decisions (Robey and Markus, 1984), so that participation in design may actually exacerbate resentment and resistance.

Projects using complex, new technology are riskier and require more emphasis upon internal integration tools. Large projects can reduce risk by an increased use of formal planning and control tools.

Designing for the Organization

The systems development process must explicitly address the ways in which the organization will change when the new system is installed. In addition to procedural changes, transformations in job functions, organizational structure, power relationships, and behavior will all have to be carefully planned.

This is true of Internet-based systems as well as traditional systems. Although Web sites and intranets may not require major changes in an organization's technology infrastructure, they can create new business processes that require traditional functional areas such as marketing, sales, and customer service, to collaborate more closely in new ways. The Window on Organizations describes how Toshiba America handled these organizational-change issues when it implemented its Web site.

Although systems analysis and design activities are supposed to include an organizational impact analysis, this area has traditionally been neglected. An **organizational impact analysis** explains how a proposed system will affect organizational structure, attitudes, decision making, and operations. To integrate information systems successfully with the organization, thorough and fully documented organizational impact assessments must be given more attention in the development effort.

organizational impact analysis Study of the way a proposed system will affect organizational structure, attitudes, decision making, and operations.

Allowing for the Human Factor

The quality of information systems should be evaluated in terms of user criteria rather than just the technical criteria of the information systems staff. For example, a project objective might be that data entry clerks be able to learn the procedures and codes for four new on-line data entry screens in a half-day training session.

Areas where users interface with the system should be carefully designed, with sensitivity to ergonomic issues. **Ergonomics** refers to the interaction of people and machines in the work environment. It considers the design of jobs, health issues, and the end-user interface of information systems. The impact of the application system on the work environment and job dimensions must be carefully assessed. One noteworthy study of 620 Social Security Administration claims representatives showed that the representatives with on-line access to claims data experienced greater stress than those with serial access to the data via teletype. Even though the on-line interface was more rapid and direct

ergonomics The interaction of people and machines in the work environment, including the design of jobs, health issues, and the end-user interface of information systems.

Before

After

A well-designed user interface can make a system easy to use, whereas one that is cluttered or confusing will add to users' frustrations. Bellevue Industries, a distributor of O'Brien & Co. meat snacks, redesigned its Web pages to make its Web site more inviting.

WINDOW ON ORGANIZATIONS

Toshiba America Implements Its Web Site

Adding electronic commerce to a Web site, even when necessary, can be very disruptive to an organization. In 1997, when Nick Roberts became the Webmaster at the Computer Systems Division of Toshiba America Information Systems Inc., he found a Web site that was static and producing few if any sales. Visitors to the site could collect information on the company, and even request a sales call; however, they could not order on-line, and the requested sales call often took weeks to arrive. Meanwhile, Dell Computer Corp. and Gateway 2000 Inc., two top competitors, were closing millions of dollars in sales daily through the Web. Clearly, something had to change.

It was not that no one at Toshiba was interested in Web sales. The hiring of Roberts proved the company's interest. In addition, the division's Education Sales Group already had hired their own Web developer because they believed the company was procrastinating on the issue of Web-based sales. Neither Roberts nor Toshiba management believed that multiple Web sites was the proper strategy. Technically Roberts could easily build and install a unified site that would be at least as effective as those of Dell and Gateway. The problems were organizational. Toshiba sells many of its computers through resellers, and it was concerned about their reaction to a Toshiba Web site that enabled visitors to bypass resellers and order on-line. Also, what about Toshiba's own sales staff? How would the site affect their sales and commissions?

The solution required building a management partnership within Toshiba. Roberts approached Greg Cygan, vice president of Toshiba sales, and Rocco Valente, vice president of corporate reseller sales. The three formed a team and together they designed a site that satisfied all. They also pushed the Toshiba site capabilities beyond that of its competitors. The team agreed on two principles. First, Toshiba would monitor all leads coming through the Web and make sure they were resulting in sales. Second, customers would have as many ordering choices as possible, meaning the Web visitor would be able to order on-line, through a sales representative, or through a reseller.

The reseller issue was perhaps the most difficult. The team decided to establish a link to only one reseller at a time. They requested proposals from potential electronic commerce Web partners and selected one, but only for six months. They decided to open the bidding to other resellers every six months so that Toshiba could always be working with the best possible partner. Roberts used exciting new technology, AT&T's Interactive Answers Service, to address customers who wanted to talk with a sales representative. When a visitor elected to be contacted, they first entered some information, including how many units they wished to purchase, and the number of employees in their company. Then, if they clicked on the "call me right now" button, their telephone would ring almost instantly. At the other end would be either a Toshiba sales representative or someone from Toshiba's partner reseller. Criteria were developed to enable the computer automatically to determine which of the two would be given the opportunity to make the sale.

To Think About: ***What implementation issues had to be addressed by Toshiba to create a successful Web site?***

Source: Adapted from Lauren Gibbons Paul, "Over the Line," *CIO WebBusiness*, March 1, 1998.

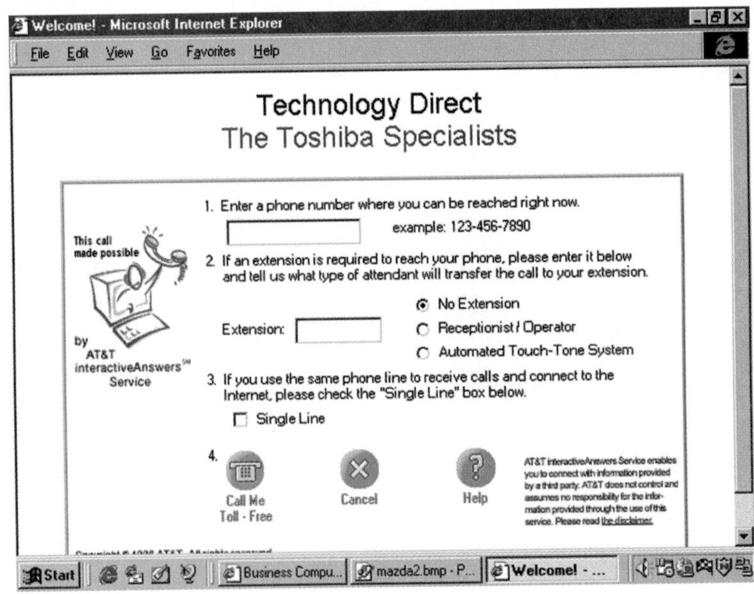

Toshiba America carefully designed a Web site for on-line sales that allows its sales, marketing, and customer service areas to work together closely. The Web site uses At&T's Interactive Answers Service technology to allow customers to talk on the telephone to Toshiba sales representatives or reseller partners.

than teletype, it created much more frustration. Claims representatives with on-line access could interface with a larger number of clients per day, which changed the dimensions of their jobs. The restructuring of work—involving tasks, quality of working life, and performance—had a more profound impact than the nature of the technology itself (Turner, 1984).

Management and organizational researchers have suggested a sociotechnical approach to information systems design and organizational change. **Sociotechnical design** aims to produce information systems that blend technical efficiency with sensitivity to organizational and human needs, leading to high job satisfaction (Mumford and Weir, 1979). The sociotechnical design process emphasizes participation by individuals most affected by a new system. The design plan establishes human objectives for the system that lead to increased job satisfaction. Designers set forth separate sets of technical and social design solutions. The social design plans explore different work group structures, allocation of tasks, and the design of individual jobs. The design solution that best fulfills both technical and social objectives is selected for the final design.

sociotechnical design Design to produce information systems that blend technical efficiency with sensitivity to organizational and human needs.

10.4 UNDERSTANDING THE BUSINESS VALUE OF INFORMATION SYSTEMS

Information systems can have several different values for business firms. A consistently strong information technology infrastructure can, over the longer term, play an important strategic role in the life of the firm. Looked at less grandly, information systems can permit firms simply to survive. The value of systems from a financial view comes down to one question: Does a particular information system investment produce sufficient returns to justify its costs? There are many issues to consider with this approach.

Capital Budgeting Models

Capital budgeting models are one of several techniques used to measure the value of investing in long-term capital investment projects. The process of analyzing and selecting various proposals for capital expenditures is called **capital budgeting.** Firms invest in capital projects in order to expand production to meet anticipated demand, or to modernize production equipment in order to reduce costs. Information systems are considered long-term capital investment projects.

capital budgeting The process of analyzing and selecting various proposals for capital expenditures.

Alternative methods are available to compare different projects with one another, and to make a decision about the investment. Three that are widely used are the cost-benefit ratio, the net present value, and the accounting rate of return on investment (ROI).

Cost-Benefit Ratio

A simple method for calculating the returns from a capital expenditure is to calculate the **cost-benefit ratio,** which is the ratio of benefits to costs. The formula is as follows:

$$\frac{\text{Total benefits}}{\text{Total costs}} = \text{Cost-benefit ratio}$$

cost-benefit ratio A method for calculating the returns from a capital expenditure by dividing the total benefits by total costs.

Table 10.10 lists some of the more common costs and benefits of systems. **Tangible benefits** can be quantified and assigned a monetary value. **Intangible benefits,** such as more efficient customer service or enhanced decision making, cannot be immediately quantified but may lead to quantifiable gains in the long run.

Some firms establish a minimum cost-benefit ratio that must be attained by capital projects, looking primarily at tangible benefits.

tangible benefits Benefits that can be quantified and assigned monetary value; they include lower operational costs and increased cashflows.

intangible benefits Benefits that are not easily quantified; they might include more efficient customer service or enhanced decision making.

Net Present Value

Evaluating a capital project requires that the cost of an investment be compared with the net cash inflows that occur many years later as the investment produces returns. But these two kinds of inflows are not directly comparable because of the time value of money. Money you have been promised to receive three, four, and five years from now is not worth as much as money received today. Money received in the future has to be discounted by some appropriate percentage rate—usually the prevailing interest rate, or

TABLE 10.10 Costs and Benefits of Information Systems

Costs	Tangible Benefits (cost savings)	Intangible Benefits
Hardware Telecommunications Software Services Personnel	Increased productivity Lower operational costs Reduced work force Lower computer expenses Lower outside vendor costs Lower clerical and professional costs Reduced rate of growth in expenses Reduced facility costs	Improved asset utilization Improved resource control Improved organizational planning Increased organizational flexibility More timely information More information Increased organizational learning Legal requirements attained Enhanced employee goodwill Increased job satisfaction Improved decision making Improved operations Higher client satisfaction Better corporate image

present value The value, in current dollars, of a payment or stream of payments to be received in the future.

sometimes the cost of capital. **Present value** is the value in current dollars of a payment or stream of payments to be received in the future. It can be calculated by using the following formula:

$$\text{Payment} \times \frac{1 - (1 + \text{interest})^{-n}}{\text{Interest}} = \text{Present value}$$

net present value The amount of money an investment is worth, taking into account its cost, earnings, and the time value of money.

Thus, in order to compare the investment (made in today's dollars) with future savings or earnings, you need to discount the earnings to their present value and then calculate the net present value of the investment. The **net present value** is the amount of money an investment is worth, taking into account its cost, earnings, and the time value of money. The formula for net present value is as follows:

$$\text{Present value of expected cash flows} - \text{Initial investment cost} = \text{Net present value}$$

Accounting Rate of Return on Investment (ROI)

Firms make capital investments to earn a satisfactory rate of return. In the long run, the desired rate of return must equal or exceed the cost of borrowing money in the marketplace. The accounting rate of return on investment (ROI) calculates the rate of return from an investment by adjusting the cash inflows produced by the investment for depreciation. It gives an approximation of the accounting income earned by the project.

To find the ROI, first calculate the average net benefit. The formula for the average net benefit is as follows:

$$\frac{(\text{Total benefits} - \text{Total cost} - \text{Depreciation})}{\text{Useful Life}} = \text{Net benefit}$$

This net benefit is divided by the total initial investment to arrive at ROI (rate of return on investment). The formula is:

$$\frac{\text{Net benefit}}{\text{Total initial investment}} = \text{ROI}$$

The Window on Management illustrates the use of ROI in assessing the value of intranets.

Limitations of Financial Models

Financial models assume that all relevant alternatives have been examined, that all costs and benefits are known, and that these costs and benefits can be expressed in a common metric, specifically, money. However, financial models do not express the risks and uncertainty of their own cost and benefit estimates. Costs and benefits do not occur in the same time frame—costs tend to be up front and tangible, while benefits tend to be

WINDOW ON MANAGEMENT

Intranets with 1000 Percent ROIs?

It may be difficult to make money on the Web, but making money on corporate intranets appears to be a hard proposition to lose. Recent research claims that corporations such as Amdahl Corporation, Booz, Allen and Hamilton, Southern California Gas, Silicon Graphics, and Lockheed—to name a few—are getting returns on investment of 1000 percent! Here's why: Corporations, for better or worse, print more paper than all the publishers in all markets in the United States put together. In other words, most corporations are publishing machines. Corporate intranets turn out to be an ideal electronic distributor of information. But buyer beware! The costs are often hidden, and what you improve may not be worth improving all that much in the long run. But you decide.

Costs. The major cost categories of intranet sites are the hardware, software, telecommunications, management, design, content, and staff required to keep the site up to date. Many firms fail to include one or more of these costs, and especially they fail to account for the costs of developing the content in the first place (or second place if it must be rekeyed and reformatted to fit Web software). Information is definitely not free.

Benefits. There are two business benefits: new revenue and cost reduction. And then there are the intangibles. New revenues will include direct sales, accepting advertising fees for banners, and fees for Web-based services. Generally, intranet sites are cost reducers: reduced printing costs, reduction in work force, scaled back use of proprietary networks, lower management costs, reduced transaction costs, cheaper electronic data sharing with vendors, and so forth. Intangibles may include better customer service, marketing value, and better employee access to corporation information.

An example of the tremendous returns possible from an intranet site is Amdahl Corporation, a California-based mainframe computer manufacturer. Prior to the corporate intranet, Amdahl relied on paper and e-mail over proprietary networks. In 1995 Amdahl began a corporate expansion out of the mainframe niche into data center management software, services, and consulting. In two years it doubled in size. Amdahl's strategy involved creating a Web Council of representatives from all the major business units and divisions. The Web Council decided to build a unified corporate electronic library, which would permit all the divisions to share needed information. In 1995 senior management supported building a Web infrastructure—servers, software, and networks. Each division and unit is responsible for maintaining its Web pages in over 100 separate intranet directories. Today over 6500 pages are maintained on the intranet.

Some benefits of the corporate library are to make information from research firms available throughout the corporation, to reduce calls to the help desk by putting reference material on hand, to increase accuracy and currency of information, and to widely distribute a competitive analysis book (which before the intranet was a monthly three-inch-thick publication!). Time savings for employees is one of the biggest benefits. To calculate this, International Data Corporation sent a questionnaire to a sample of users and asked them to compare how much time the intranet saved them. IDC realized that only about 70 percent of this estimated time saving resulted in additional work being done (because many employees could just waste time saved). Nevertheless, time saving was the largest benefit of the system.

The spreadsheet illustrated in Figure 10.8 shows how Amdahl calculated its ROI of 2063 percent.

To Think About: ***Do you think Amdahl has correctly estimated all the important costs of their site? The time savings of employees is a big element in the benefits column, but how much of the time saved by an employee is actually translated into useful work?***

Source: http://home.netscape.com/comprod/announce/roi.html. See the report by Ian Campbell entitled "The Intranet: Slashing the Cost of Doing Business," International Data Corporation.

back-loaded and intangible. Inflation may affect costs and benefits differently. Technology—especially information technology—can change during the course of the project, causing estimates to vary greatly. Intangible benefits are difficult to quantify.

The difficulties of measuring intangible benefits give financial models an *application bias:* Transaction and clerical systems that displace labor and save space always produce more measurable, tangible benefits than management information systems, decision-support systems, or computer-supported collaborative work systems (see Chapter 12).

Nonfinancial and Strategic Considerations

Other methods of selecting and evaluating information system investments involve nonfinancial and strategic considerations. When the firm has several alternative investments to select from, it can employ portfolio analysis and scoring models. Several of these methods can be used in combination.

Financial Worksheet For:
Amdahl

Annual Savings	Base	Year 1	Year 2	Year 3
Personnel Savings	$0	$6,000,000	$6,000,000	$6,000,000
ISO 9000	$0	$28,246	$28,246	$28,246
Document Distribution	$0	$334,000	$334,000	$334,000
Total Savings Per Period	$0	$6,362,246	$6,362,246	$6,362,246

Depreciation Schedule*	Initial	Year 1	Year 2	Year 3**
Software	$110,000	$22,000	$22,000	$22,000
Total Per Period	$110,000	$22,000	$22,000	$22,000

Expensed Costs	Initial	Year 1	Year 2	Year 3
Maintenance	$0	$23,750	$23,750	$23,750
Network Upgrades	$45,000	$15,000	$15,000	$15,000
Hardware	$30,000	$0	$0	$0
Personnel	$384,358	$1,110,000	$1,110,000	$1,080,000
Training	$0	$133,923	$76,923	$76,923
Total Per Period	$459,358	$1,282,673	$1,225,673	$1,195,673

Basic Financial Assumptions	
All Federal and State Taxes	50%
Discount Rate	15%
Depreciation * Straight Line (Years)	5

Net Cash Flows	Initial	Year 1	Year 2	Year 3
Total Benefits		$6,362,246	$6,362,246	$6,362,246
Less: Total Costs	$569,358	$1,282,673	$1,225,673	$1,195,673
Less: Depreciation		$22,000	$22,000	$22,000
Net Profit Before Tax	$569,358	$5,057,573	$5,114,573	$5,144,573
Net Profit After Tax	$284,679	$2,528,787	$2,557,287	$2,572,287
Add: Depreciation		$22,000	$22,000	$22,000
Net Cash Flow After Taxes	($284,679)	$2,550,787	$2,579,287	$2,594,287

Financial Analysis	Results	Year 1	Year 2	Year 3
Annual ROI		779%	146%	206%
3-Year ROI	2063%			
Payback (Years)	0.13			
3-Year IRR	896%			
3-Year NPV	$5,589,493			

*Hardware and software costs totalling more than $100,000 are depreciated over five years on a straight-line basis. All other costs are treated as expenses in the initial year.

**Any software upgrade is treated as a depreciable asset if greater than $100,000; otherwise it is included as an expensed cost for the year.

FIGURE 10.8 Amdahl achieved a three-year ROI of 2063 percent from its corporate intranet investment. This spreadsheet shows how the company arrived at this figure.

Portfolio Analysis

Rather than using capital budgeting, a second way of selecting among alternative projects is to consider the firm as having a portfolio of potential applications. Each application carries risks and benefits. The portfolio can be described as having a certain profile of risk and benefit to the firm (see Figure 10.9). Although there is no ideal profile for all firms, information-intensive industries (e.g., finance) should have a few high-risk–high-benefit projects to ensure that they stay current with technology. Firms in noninformation-intensive industries should focus on high-benefit–low-risk projects.

Some of the major risks in system-building are that benefits may not be obtained; system-building may exceed the organization's budget and time frame; or the system does not perform as expected. Risks are not necessarily bad. They are tolerable as long as the benefits are commensurate.

Once strategic analyses have determined the overall direction of system development, a **portfolio analysis** can be used to select alternatives. Obviously, one can begin by focusing on systems of high benefit and low risk. These promise early returns and low risks. Second, high-benefit–high-risk systems should be examined. Low-benefit–high-risk systems should be totally avoided, and low-benefit–low-risk systems should be reexamined for the possibility of rebuilding and replacing them with more desirable systems having higher benefits.

portfolio analysis An analysis of the portfolio of potential applications within a firm to determine the risks and benefits and select among alternatives for information systems.

Scoring Models

A quick, and sometimes compelling, method for arriving at a decision on alternative systems is a **scoring model.** Scoring models give alternative systems a single score based on the extent to which they meet selected objectives (the method is similar to the *objective attained* model) (Matlin, 1989; Buss, 1983).

scoring models A quick method for deciding among alternative systems based on a system of ratings for selected objectives.

In Table 10.11 the firm must decide among three alternative office automation systems: (1) an IBM, AS/400 client/server system with proprietary software; (2) a UNIX-based client server system using an Oracle database; and (3) a Windows NT client/server system using Lotus Notes. Column 1 lists the criteria that decision makers may apply to the systems. These criteria are usually the result of lengthy discussions among the decision-making group. Often the most important outcome of a scoring model is not the score but simply agreement on the criteria used to judge a system (Ginzberg, 1979; Nolan, 1982).

Column 2 lists the weights that decision makers attach to the decision criterion. The scoring model helps to bring about agreement among participants concerning the rank of the criteria.

Columns 3 to 5 use a 1-to-5 scale (lowest to highest) to express the judgments of participants on the *relative* merits of each system. For example, concerning the percentage of user needs that each system meets, a score of 1 for a system argues that this system when compared to others being considered will be low in meeting user needs.

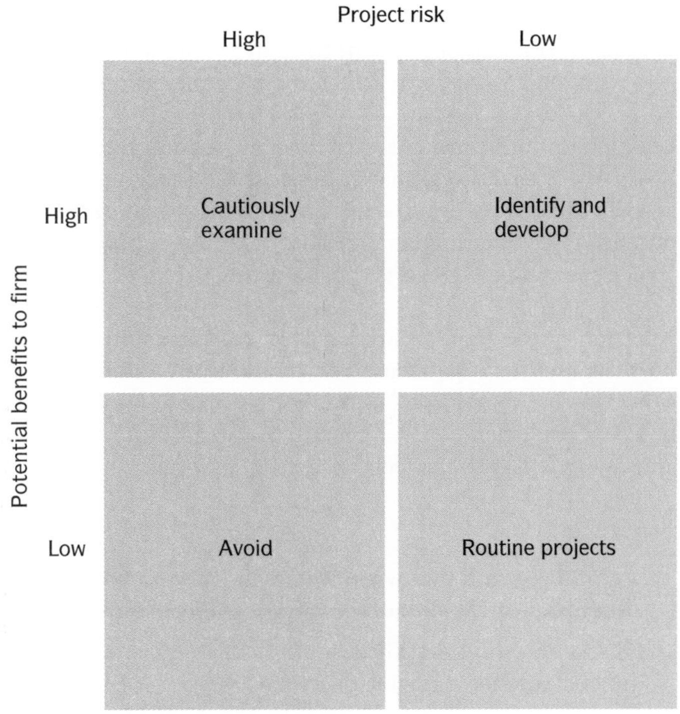

FIGURE 10.9

A system portfolio. Companies should examine their portfolio of projects in terms of potential benefits and likely risks. Certain kinds of projects should be avoided altogether and others developed rapidly. There is no ideal mix. Companies in different industries have different profiles.

TABLE 10.11 Scoring Model Used to Choose Among Alternative Office Automation Systems*

Criterion	Weight		AS/400		UNIX		Windows NT
Percentage of user needs met	0.40	2	0.8	3	1.2	4	1.6
Cost of the initial purchase	0.20	1	0.2	3	0.6	4	0.8
Financing	0.10	1	0.1	3	0.3	4	0.4
Ease of maintenance	0.10	2	0.2	3	0.3	4	0.4
Chances of success	0.20	3	0.6	4	0.8	4	0.8
Final score			1.9		3.2		4.0

Scale: 1 = low, 5 = high.
**One of the major uses of scoring models is in identifying the criteria of selection and their relative weights. In this instance an office automation system based on Windows NT appears preferable.*

As with all objective techniques, there are many qualitative judgments involved in using the scoring model. This model requires experts who understand the issues and the technology. It is appropriate to cycle through the scoring model several times, changing the criteria and weights, to see how sensitive the outcome is to reasonable changes in criteria. Scoring models are used most commonly to confirm, to rationalize, and to support decisions, rather than being the final arbiters of system selection.

Management Wrap-Up

MANAGEMENT

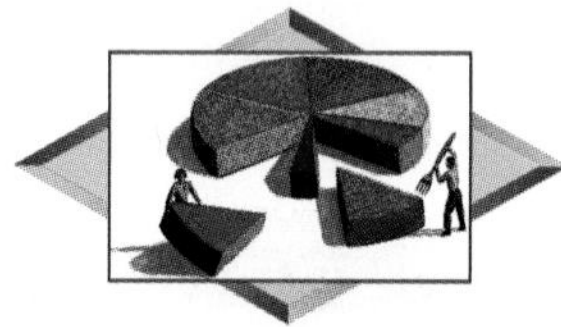

The key management issues in building systems are to stay in control of the process (to avoid runaway systems) and to lead the effort toward planned and sustained organizational change. Managers must link systems development to the strategy of the firm, and identify precisely which systems should be changed to achieve large-scale benefits for the organization as a whole. Understanding what process to improve from the firm perspective is more important than blindly reengineering whatever business process happens to need fixing or happens to yield a large return on investment (ROI). Many projects with huge ROIs have little impact on the business as a whole.

ORGANIZATION

Building an information system is a process of planned organizational change. Many levels of organizational change are possible. Redesigning business processes is especially risky because it requires far-reaching changes that often are resisted by members of the organization. Eliciting management and user support and maintaining an appropriate level of user involvement throughout the system-building process is essential.

TECHNOLOGY

Selection of the right technology for a system solution that fits the constraints of the problem and the organization's overall information architecture is a key business decision. Systems sometimes fail because the technology is too complex or sophisticated to be easily implemented. Managers and systems builders should be fully aware of the risks and rewards of various technologies as they make their technology selections.

For Discussion:

1. It has been said that when we design an information system, we are redesigning the organization. What are the ramifications of this statement?
2. It has been said that the reason most systems fail is because system builders ignore organizational behavior problems. Why?

SUMMARY

1. **Demonstrate how building new systems can produce organizational change.** Building a new information system is a form of planned organizational change that involves many different people in the organization. Because information systems are sociotechnical entities, a change in information systems involves changes in work, management, and the organization. Four kinds of technology-enabled change are (1) automation, (2) rationalization of procedures, (3) business reengineering, and (4) paradigm shift, with far-reaching changes carrying the greatests risks and rewards. Many organizations are attempting business reengineering to redesign work-flows and business processes in the hope of achieving dramatic productivity breakthroughs.

2. **Explain how the organization can develop information systems that fit its business plan.** Organizations should develop information systems plans that describe how information technology supports the attainment of their business goals. The plans indicate the direction of systems development, the rationale, implementation strategy, and budget. Enterprise analysis and critical success factors (CSFs) can be used to elicit organization-wide information requirements that must be addressed by the plans.

3. **Identify the core activities in the systems development process.** The core activities in systems development are systems analysis, systems design, programming, testing, conversion, production, and maintenance. Systems analysis is the study and analysis of problems of existing systems and the identification of requirements for their solution. Systems design provides the specifications for an information system solution, showing how its technical and organizational components fit together.

4. **Analyze the organizational change requirements for building successful systems.** From an organizational and behavioral standpoint, the major causes of information system failure are (1) insufficient or improper user participation in the systems development process, (2) lack of management support, (3) poor management of the implementation process, and (4) high levels of complexity and risk in systems development projects.

   Implementation is the entire process of organizational change surrounding the introduction of a new information system. One can better understand system success and failure by examining different patterns of implementation. Especially important is the relationship between participants in the implementation process, notably the interactions between system designers and users. The success of organizational change can be determined by how well information systems specialists, end users, and decision makers deal with key issues at various stages in implementation.

   Management support and control of the implementation process are essential, as are mechanisms for dealing with the level of risk in each new systems project. The level of risk in a systems development project is determined by three key dimensions: (1) project size, (2) project structure, and (3) experience with technology. The risk level of each project will determine the appropriate mix of external integration tools, internal integration tools, formal planning tools, and formal control tools to be applied.

   Appropriate strategies can be applied to ensure the correct level of user participation in the systems development process and to minimize user resistance. Information system design and the entire implementation process should be managed as planned organizational change. Sociotechnical design emphasizes the participation of the individuals most affected by a new system and aims for an optimal blend of social and technical design solutions.

5. **Describe models for determining the business value of information systems.** Capital budgeting models such as the cost/benefit ratio, net present value, and ROI are widely used financial models for determining the business value of information systems. Portfolio analysis and scoring models include nonfinancial considerations and can be used to evaluate alternative information systems projects.

KEY TERMS

Acceptance testing, 318
Automation, 307
Business reengineering, 308
Capital budgeting, 327
Change agent, 320
Conversion, 318
Conversion plan, 319
Cost-benefit ratio, 327
Counterimplementation, 323
Critical success factors (CSFs), 304
Direct cutover, 318
Documentation, 319
Economic feasibility, 315
Enterprise analysis, 303
Ergonomics, 325
External integration tools, 323
Feasibility study, 315
Formal planning and control tools, 323
Implementation, 320
Information requirements, 316
Information systems plan, 303
Intangible benefits, 327
Internal integration tools, 323
Logical design, 316

Maintenance, 319
Net present value, 328
Operational feasibility, 315
Organizational impact analysis, 325
Paradigm shift, 309
Parallel strategy, 318
Phased approach, 319
Physical design, 316
Pilot study, 319
Portfolio analysis, 331
Present value, 328
Production, 319
Programming, 318
Rationalization of procedures, 307
Scoring models, 331
Sociotechnical design, 327
System testing, 318
Systems analysis, 314
Systems design, 316
Systems development, 314
Tangible benefits, 327
Technical feasibility, 315
Test plan, 318
Testing, 318
Unit testing, 318
User-designer communications gap, 321
Work-flow management, 311

REVIEW QUESTIONS

1. Why can a new information system be considered planned organizational change?
2. What are the major categories of an information systems plan?
3. How can enterprise analysis and critical success factors be used to establish organization-wide information system requirements?
4. Describe each of the four kinds of organizational change that can be promoted with information technology.
5. What is *business reengineering?* What steps are required to make it effective?
6. What is the difference between *systems analysis* and *systems design?*
7. What is *feasibility?* Name and describe each of the three major areas of feasibility for information systems.
8. What are *information requirements?* Why are they difficult to determine correctly?
9. What is the difference between the *logical design* and the *physical design* of an information system?
10. Why is the testing stage of systems development so important? Name and describe the three stages of testing for an information system.
11. What is *conversion?* Why is it important to have a detailed conversion plan?
12. What role do programming, production, and maintenance play in systems development?
13. What is *implementation?* How is it related to information system success or failure?
14. Describe the ways that implementation can be managed to make the organizational change process more successful.
15. Name and describe the principal capital budgeting methods used to evaluate information systems projects. What are their limitations?
16. Describe how portfolio analysis and scoring models can be used to establish the worth of systems.

GROUP PROJECT

With three or four of your classmates, select a description of another system in this text. (Examples might be Glaxo's GWis system in Chapter 7; Rosenbunth Travel's DACODA or VISION system in Chapter 8; or the 800-FLOWERS order-taking system in Chapter 2.) Prepare a report describing (on the basis of the information provided) some of the design specifications that might be appropriate for the system you select. Present your findings to the class.

TOOLS FOR INTERACTIVE LEARNING

■ **INTERNET**: The Internet Connection for this chapter will direct you to a series of Web sites where you can complete an exercise to analyze the capabilities of various tools for work-flow management and business process reengineering. You can visit the TravelWeb site to explore its capabilities and complete an Electronic Commerce project for sales planning. You can also use the Interactive Study Guide to test your knowledge of the topics in this chapter and get instant feedback when you need more practice.

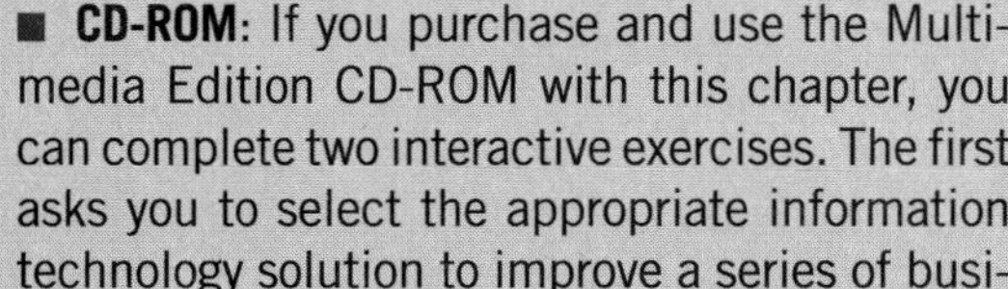

■ **CD-ROM**: If you purchase and use the Multimedia Edition CD-ROM with this chapter, you can complete two interactive exercises. The first asks you to select the appropriate information technology solution to improve a series of business processes. The second exercise requires you to perform a systems analysis for a multidivisional corporation experiencing revenue slowdown. You can also find a video clip on Andersen Consulting's Smart Store and Retail Place illustrating the innovative use of technology to rethink the delivery of goods and services, an audio overview of the major themes of this chapter, and bullet text summarizing the key points of the chapter.

CASE STUDY

Tackling the Nightmare of Data Gridlock

It sounds like a great deal of money—$10.8 billion—for only seven-and-a-half miles of highway, but the cost may seem small when one considers the size and complications of the highway-building project. Downtown Boston has been a traffic nightmare; the congestion and the gridlock are chronic. The new highway is meant to relieve the problem. When completed, it will travel through the heart of the city and will include elevated highways, tunnels and bridges. Before it is finished, workers will have excavated 13 million yards of earth and poured 3.8 million cubic yards of concrete. The project, known as Boston's Central Artery/Tunnel project (CA/T), is the largest and most technically challenging public infrastructure project the United States has ever experienced.

Knowledgeable observers compare the project to the construction of the English Channel tunnel (the Chunnel) and the new Hong Kong airport, except, they point out, CA/T is more complex in some key ways. Planning alone took ten years. The execution will involve more than 100 contractors, 36 simultaneous field offices and 45 contracts ranging in cost from $40 million to $400 million each. In early 1998 about 12,000 field engineers were submitting daily reports. CA/T is so complex that two giant, international construction engineering firms, Bechtel and Parsons Brinckerhoff (together called B/PB) were selected to jointly manage it.

Like any project of this size and complexity, CA/T has hit a number of snags, and it has been under close scrutiny by politicians and the press. Its friends refer to it as Big Dig, but its opponents call it Big Pig. "Big," if anything, understates not only the overall project size but also the size and complexity of the organization and of the data that must be stored and shared if the project is to succeed. The issue of data sharing in CA/T is the nightmare we want to examine in this case study.

CA/T goes back a long way. The Massachusetts Highway Department, the original project owner, began planning for the project years ago, and design began in 1986. Computer technology was much more primitive then. The hot new desktop computer was the 386, now many years outmoded and extremely slow compared to today's PCs. Networking, the basic technology underlying data sharing, almost did not exist. As a result, no information technology planning occurred for data integration or data storage; no one foresaw the need for them. Also, because computer systems were isolated from each other, no one understood the need to standardize software requirements. Each contractor used whatever software he or she wanted.

The first software tools used within CA/T were CAD (computer-aided design) systems used by the project managers and engineers who were doing or supervising the design work. These systems enabled project managers and the project owner to exchange design plans and drawings. Bechtel used GDS CAD, a very powerful tool for those days, one that had many facilities, including the ability to generate three-dimensional models, solve right-of-way problems, and even track the movement of rats that would be displaced as the excavation and construction proceeded. However, GDS was expensive, and so most contractors used less-expensive packages, the most popular being AutoCAD. The data formats of the two CAD packages were incompatible. When, with much effort, staff successfully made translations between the two, much of the detail of the drawings was lost. Tony Stucchi, the CAD manager for one of the project contractors, Perini Company, complained that he could not use converted GDS files due to their low quality, so he had to go around and use what files he could collect from individual designers. Feniosky Peña-Mora, a Massachusetts Institute of

Technology (MIT) professor of information technology and project management, who eventually became a consultant to CA/T, described the negative cost and time impact of the problem, saying, "There were a lot of people working overtime to translate things, and there was a lot of backlog because of the translation."

Unlike federal agencies and large companies, who have the power to dictate the software used by vendors to build their information systems, state governments are more reluctant to specify the software contractors must adopt. Project management was another key function with early data problems. CA/T project management required contractors to use Primavera Project Planner (P3), but only as part of CA/T's master schedule. Each unit of the project kept its own progress-tracking and expenditures records in its own way, some using project-management software tools, many using spreadsheets, others only using pencil and paper. "Everybody was developing their own tools and creating the balkanization of data," according to Peña-Mora. Walter Erb, who later joined the project as the B/PB manager of information services and technology, described why project management failed to require that the technology be updated over time. "When the job started," he explained, "Lotus and Word Perfect were the standards of the time and probably were very good products. But coming from the outside, I thought I had stepped back in time." Even data that was exchanged between the project management partners, Bechtel and Parsons Brinckerhoff, created problems because each used different spreadsheets to manage their project data.

Integrating these data manually was an extremely slow process, but even worse, project management reports contradicted reports from the contractors. As Peña-Mora described the process to merge the data, "Someone would say, 'We are in this stage' and another person would say, 'No, we are in this stage.' " The ultimate result of this lack of adequate electronic data-sharing was near gridlock. Finally, in 1992, Bechtel decided it needed to build a new system, which it called the Construction Information System (CIS). The main goal of this Oracle-based system was to produce standardized reports using SQL (Structured Query Language—see Chapter 7). Bechtel chose the Oracle database management system and software because the company already had a corporate Oracle license, and it had five years' experience building and operating financial systems with Oracle. CIS came into full operation in 1996.

Once the Oracle system was up and running, it offered two major advantages: Reports became standardized and all the organizations participating in the project were able to share their information. However, project management and contractors quickly realized the solution was inadequate. One problem was that Oracle programmers became an obstruction. The CIS project had failed to build interfaces for the various systems used in the field, and so field data were not automatically fed into the Oracle system. Instead, Oracle programmers were used to enter the data manually, thus reducing their availability for development work. At the same time, staff in many of the organizations participating in CA/T became aware of the capabilities of the Oracle system, and they began to submit requests for programming for other functions. Thus, as the availability of programmers declined, demand for Oracle programming rose, creating a serious bottleneck.

A second problem was the lack of adequate digital data sharing. The contractors and project managers kept their own records for work progress and cost estimates. Project management kept its records on Oracle whereas the contractors used their own systems. In essence, CA/T had an expensive, redundant duplicate-entry system. Accurate data are critical for many reasons, not the least of which is that contractor pay is tied directly to progress. To keep the data up-to-date and accurate, project management validated cost and progress data every two weeks with the contractors. This was a very labor-intensive, wasteful system. Dale Payate, president of J. Cashman Inc., a project contractor, estimated that on a typical large job the field office and the contractor exchange at least 10,000 documents. Given this circumstance, the current project was in danger of drowning in paperwork, and the Oracle system did not address this problem. The crying need was for contractors to input their daily project data directly into the Oracle system. "It would eliminate a lot of redundancy of work," Payate explained. "It would cut down on data verifications and everything would run a lot smoother."

By early 1998, many problems had been addressed. Legacy files still were being converted to Oracle, but the project required that all new development be done as part of CIS using Windows 95 or NT. An application was built that enabled contractors to query B/PB engineers through Oracle. One Oracle application tracked deficient materials. Daily engineering data was entered directly into the Oracle system, and all 12,000 daily engineers' reports were issued via Oracle. These reports not only included changes in materials and equipment, but weather information as well. According to the B/PB Oracle database administrator, Brian Straesser, the reports allowed "engineers to come in the morning, print a draft and carry it out to the field, then come in the afternoon and mark off the changes rather than writing a new report."

Under the supervision of the new project owner, the Massachusetts Turnpike Authority, a project master schedule was created. It uses P3 software and manages 8000 activities, including design, procurement, permit applications, and utility relocations. It interfaces with the Oracle database, the Boston subway system, and Amtrak. Peña-Mora, who was hired by the project in 1994, was brought in to create an IT integration plan for the project. The plan is called the IT Enable Office project. The project requires that all software be compatible not only with the Oracle database, but also with certain applications that some contractors already are using, such as P3. It has introduced document-management concepts that are new to construction companies. Now, rather than sending documents back and forth, the relevant data is entered directly into Oracle by the contractors.

Source: Adapted from Ann Harrison, "Unsnarling Information for the Real Superhighway," *Software Magazine*, March 1998.

Case Study Questions

1. As an outside consultant on information systems in 1991, prepare a report for submission to the CA/T

project ownership. Describe the problems you see, and define the management, organization, and technology factors responsible.

2. If you were asked to be a systems analyst in early 1992, working to design a system to solve the problems defined in question 1, list whom you would interview and the questions you would ask them.

3. Was the Bechtel Oracle project in 1992 an appropriate response to the problems existing at that time? Why or why not? What management, organization, and technology factors do you think were responsible for the shape of the response?

4. Suggest other current technology that B/PB might want to consider using to improve the data management, and describe the use of each, explaining why it would be superior to what is being done today.

5. Think about the differences between the state of computer and network technology in 1986 and today. If today you were asked to manage a large project that is expected to last for a number of years, explain how you would plan to be able to take advantage of new technology as it develops.

CHAPTER 11

Approaches to Systems-Building

chapter outline

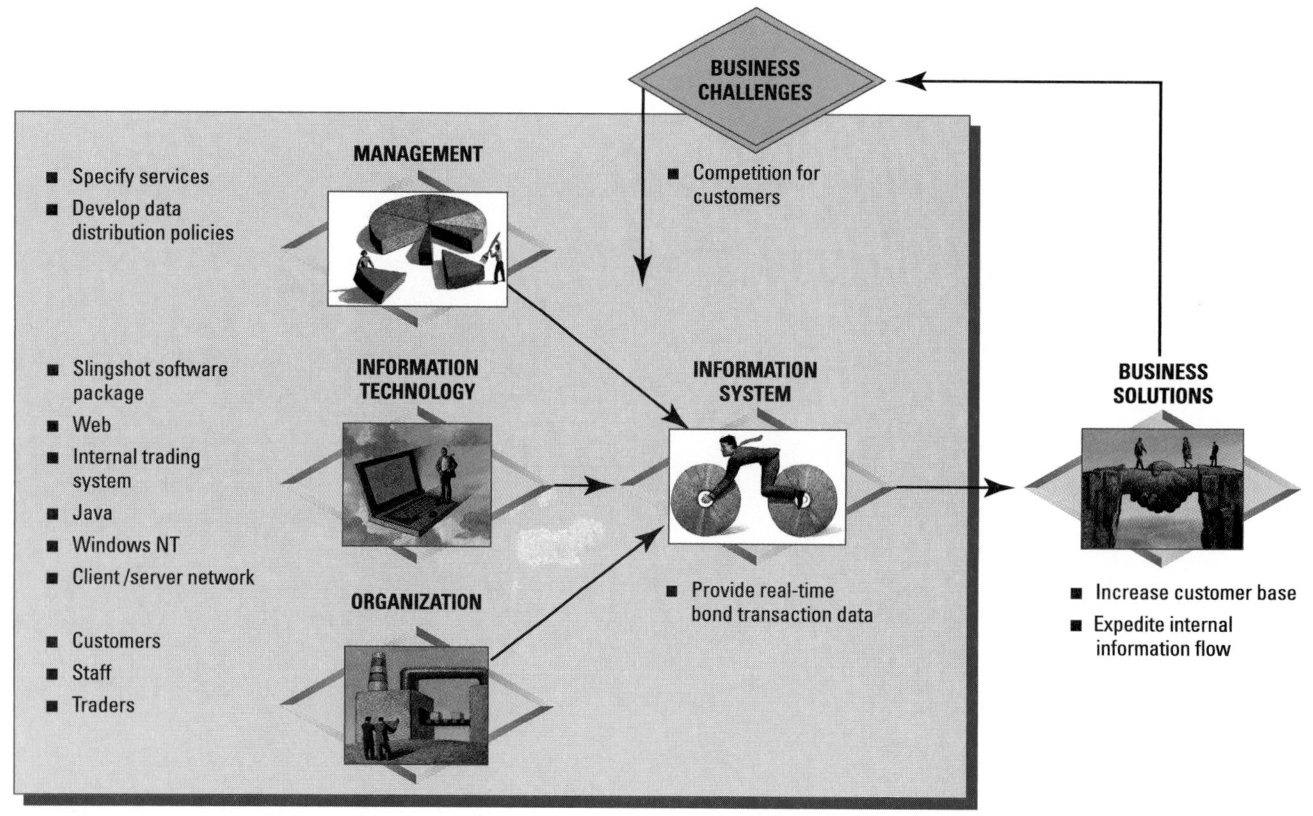

Euro Brokers Lures New Clients on the Net

Euro Brokers Investment Corporation, a fixed-income interdealer broker based in New York City, wanted to find a way to attract new customers using the Web. It decided to expand its real-time services and make them available to selected prospective customers. It implemented CSK Software's Slingshot real-time data-publishing software package to provide prospective customers with access to up-to-the-minute, emerging-markets transaction information, which previously only was available to company insiders.

Data generated by traders on Euro Brokers' internal trading system are processed by Slingshot and fed onto a public Web site, where prospective customers provided with passwords can take a look at the data. Euro Brokers considered building its own system to accomplish this function, but realized it lacked the in-house expertise and resources to do so. The Slingshot software package provided a solution.

Euro Brokers also is using Slingshot to distribute its real-time, emerging-markets bonds transaction data internally. Staff members access the data by clicking on icons on their computer desktop. This action opens up Java clients linked to Slingshot's mechanism for collecting and distributing the data from the firm's internal trading system. Slingshot runs only on NT servers.

Although only a handful of people at Euro Brokers currently use the system, the firm plans to use Slingshot to publish all of its real-time securities transaction information on the intranet and on the Internet.

Source: Adapted from Sarah Stirland, "Euro Brokers Shoots for Clients with Slingshot," *Wall Street and Technology Product Review,* Spring 1998.

Management Challenges

Like Euro Brokers, many organizations are examining alternative methods of building new information systems. Although they are designing and building some applications on their own, they also are turning to software packages, rapid application development tools, external consultants, and other strategies to reduce time, cost, and inefficiency. They also are experimenting with alternative tools to document, analyze, design, and implement systems. The availability of alternative systems-building approaches raises the following management challenges:

1. **Controlling information systems development outside the information systems department.** There may not be a way to establish standards and controls for systems development that is not managed by the information systems department, such as end-user development or outsourcing. Standards and controls that are too restrictive may not only generate user resistance but also may stifle end-user innovation. If controls are too weak, the firm may encounter serious problems with data integrity and connectivity. It is not always possible to find the right balance.

2. **Enforcing a standard methodology.** Although structured methodologies have been available for twenty-five years, very few organizations have been able to enforce them. It is impossible to use CASE or object-oriented methods effectively unless all participants in system-building adopt a common development methodology as well as common development tools. Methodologies are organizational disciplines.

learning objectives

After completing this chapter, you will be able to:

1. Appraise system-building alternatives: the traditional systems lifecycle, prototyping, application software packages, end-user development, and outsourcing.
2. Compare the strengths and limitations of each approach.
3. Assess the solutions to the management problems created by these approaches.
4. Describe the principal tools and methodologies used for systems development.

This chapter examines the use of prototyping, application software packages, end-user development, and outsourcing as systems-building alternatives to the traditional systems lifecycle method of building an entire information system from scratch. It also looks at various systems development methodologies and tools. There is no one approach that can be used for all situations and types of systems. Each of these approaches has advantages and disadvantages, and each provides managers with a range of choices. We describe and compare the system-building approaches and methodologies so that managers know how to choose among them.

11.1 THE TRADITIONAL SYSTEMS LIFECYCLE

The **systems lifecycle** is the oldest method for building information systems and is still used today for medium or large complex systems projects. This methodology assumes that an information system has a lifecycle similar to that of any living organism, with a beginning, middle, and end. The lifecycle for an information system has six stages: (1) project definition, (2) systems study, (3) design, (4) programming, (5) installation, and (6) post-implementation. Figure 11.1 illustrates these stages. Each stage consists of basic activities that must be performed before the next stage can begin.

systems lifecycle A traditional methodology for developing an information system that partitions the systems development process into six formal stages that must be completed sequentially with a very formal division of labor between end users and information systems specialists.

The lifecycle methodology has a very formal division of labor between end users and information systems specialists. Technical specialists such as systems analysts and programmers are responsible for much of the systems analysis, design, and implementation work; end users are limited to providing information requirements and reviewing the work of the technical staff. Formal sign-offs or agreements between end users and technical specialists are required as each stage is completed. Figure 11.1 also shows the product or output of each stage of the lifecycle that is the basis for such sign-offs. We now describe the stages of the lifecycle in detail.

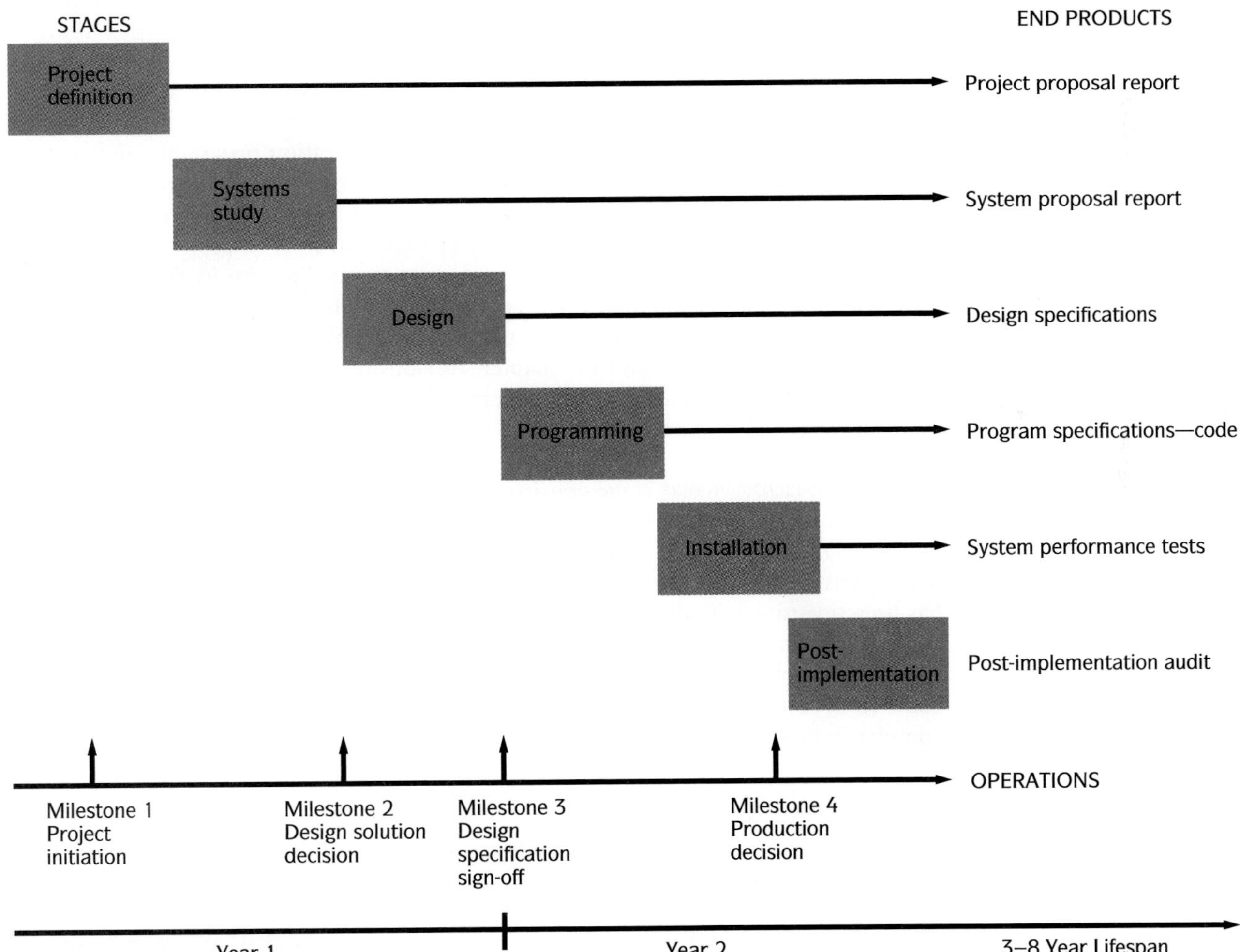

FIGURE 11.1 The lifecycle methodology for systems development. The lifecycle methodology divides systems development into six formal stages with specifics for milestones and end products at each stage. A typical medium-sized development project requires two years to deliver and has an expected life span of three to eight years.

Stages of the Systems Lifecycle

project definition A stage in the systems lifecycle that determines whether the organization has a problem and whether the problem can be solved by launching a system project.

systems study A stage in the systems lifecycle that analyzes the problems of existing systems, defines the objectives to be attained by a solution, and evaluates various solution alternatives.

design A stage in the systems lifecycle that produces the logical and physical design specifications for the systems solution.

programming A stage in the systems lifecycle that translates the design specifications produced during the design stage into software program code.

installation A stage in the systems lifecycle consisting of testing, training, and conversion; the final steps required to put a system into operation.

post-implementation The final stage of the systems lifecycle in which the system is used and evaluated while in production and is modified to make improvements or meet new requirements.

The **project definition** stage tries to answer the questions, "Why do we need a new system project?" and "What do we want to accomplish?" This stage determines whether the organization has a problem and whether that problem can be solved by building a new information system or by modifying an existing one. If a system project is called for, this stage identifies its general objectives, specifies the scope of the project, and develops a project plan that can be shown to management.

The **systems study** stage analyzes the problems of existing systems (manual or automated) in detail, identifies objectives to be attained by a solution to these problems, and describes alternative solutions. The systems study stage examines the feasibility of each solution alternative for review by management.

Systems study requires extensive information gathering and research; sifting through documents, reports, and work papers produced by existing systems; observing how these systems work; polling users with questionnaires; and conducting interviews. All of the information gathered during the systems study phase will be used to determine information system requirements. Finally, the systems study stage describes in detail the remaining lifecycle activities and the tasks for each phase.

The **design** stage produces the logical and physical design specifications for the solution. The lifecycle emphasizes formal specifications and paperwork, so many of the design and documentation tools described in Section 11.3, such as data flow diagrams, program structure charts, or system flowcharts, are likely to be utilized.

The **programming** stage translates the design specifications produced during the design stage into software program code. Systems analysts work with programmers to prepare specifications for each program in the system. Programmers write customized program code, typically using a conventional third-generation programming language such as COBOL or FORTRAN or a high-productivity fourth-generation language. Large systems have many programs with hundreds of thousands of lines of program code, and entire teams of programmers may be required.

The **installation** stage consists of the final steps to put the new or modified system into operation: testing, training, and conversion. The software is tested to make sure it performs properly from both a technical and a functional business standpoint. (More detail on testing can be found in Chapter 10.) Business and technical specialists are trained to use the new system. A formal conversion plan provides a detailed schedule of all of the activities required to install the new system, and the old system is converted to the new one.

The **post-implementation** stage consists of using and evaluating the system after it is installed and is in production. Users and technical specialists will go through a formal post-implementation audit that determines how well the new system has met its original objectives and whether any revisions or modifications are required. After the system has been fine-tuned, it will need to be maintained while it is in production to correct errors, meet requirements, or improve processing efficiency. Over time, the system may require so much maintenance to remain efficient and meet user objectives that it will come to the end of its useful lifespan. Once the system's lifecycle comes to an end, a completely new system is called for and the cycle may begin again.

Limitations of the Lifecycle Approach

The systems lifecycle is still used for building large transaction processing systems (TPS) and management information systems (MIS) where requirements are highly structured and well defined (Ahituv and Neumann, 1984). It will also remain appropriate for complex technical systems such as space launches, air traffic control, and refinery operations. Such applications need a rigorous and formal requirements analysis, predefined specifications, and tight controls over the systems-building process.

However, the systems lifecycle approach is costly, time-consuming, and inflexible. Volumes of new documents must be generated and steps repeated if requirements and specifications need to be revised. The lifecycle approach is inflexible and discourages change. Because of the time and cost to repeat the sequence of lifecycle activities, the methodology encourages freezing of specifications early in the development process. The lifecycle method is ill-suited to decision-oriented applications. Decision makers may need to experiment with concrete systems to clarify the kinds of decisions they wish to make. Formal specification of requirements may inhibit system-builders from exploring and discovering the problem structure (Fraser et al., 1994). Likewise, the lifecycle approach is not suitable for many small desktop systems, which tend to be less structured and more individualized.

11.2 ALTERNATIVE SYSTEM-BUILDING APPROACHES

Some of the problems of the traditional systems lifecycle can be solved by alternative system-building approaches. These approaches include prototyping, application software packages, end-user development, and outsourcing.

Prototyping

Prototyping consists of building an experimental system rapidly and inexpensively for end users to evaluate. By interacting with the prototype, users can get a better idea of their information requirements. The prototype endorsed by the users can be used as a template to create the final system.

prototyping The process of building an experimental system quickly and inexpensively for demonstration and evaluation so that users can better determine information requirements.

The **prototype** is a working version of an information system or part of the system, but it is meant to be only a preliminary model. Once operational, the prototype will be further refined until it conforms precisely to users' requirements. Once the design has been finalized, the prototype can be converted to a polished production system.

The process of building a preliminary design, trying it out, refining it, and trying again has been called an **iterative** process of systems development because the steps required to build a system can be repeated over and over again. Prototyping is more explicitly iterative than the conventional lifecycle, and it actively promotes system design changes. It has been said that prototyping replaces unplanned rework with planned iteration, with each version more accurately reflecting users' requirements.

prototype The preliminary working version of an information system for demonstration and evaluation purposes.

iterative A process of repeating over and over again the steps to build a system.

Steps in Prototyping

Figure 11.2 shows a four-step model of the prototyping process, which consists of the following:

Step 1: *Identify the user's basic requirements.* The system designer (usually an information systems specialist) works with the user only long enough to capture his or her basic information needs.

Step 2: *Develop an initial prototype.* The system designer creates a working prototype quickly, most likely using the fourth-generation software tools described in Chapter 6 that speed application development. Some features of computer-aided software engineering (CASE) tools described later in this chapter can be used for prototyping as can multimedia software tools that present users with interactive storyboards that sketch out the tasks of the proposed system for evaluation and modification (Madsen and Aiken, 1993).

Step 3: *Use the prototype.* The user is encouraged to work with the system in order to determine how well the prototype meets his or her needs and to make suggestions for improving the prototype.

Step 4: *Revise and enhance the prototype.* The system builder notes all changes requested by the user and refines the prototype accordingly. After the prototype has been revised, the cycle returns to step 3. Steps 3 and 4 are repeated until the user is satisfied.

When no more iterations are required, the approved prototype then becomes an operational prototype that furnishes the final specifications for the application. Sometimes the prototype itself is adopted as the production version of the system.

FIGURE 11.2

The prototyping process. The process of developing a prototype can be broken down into four steps. Because a prototype can be developed quickly and inexpensively, the developers can go through several iterations, repeating steps 3 and 4, in order to refine and enhance the prototype before arriving at the final operational one.

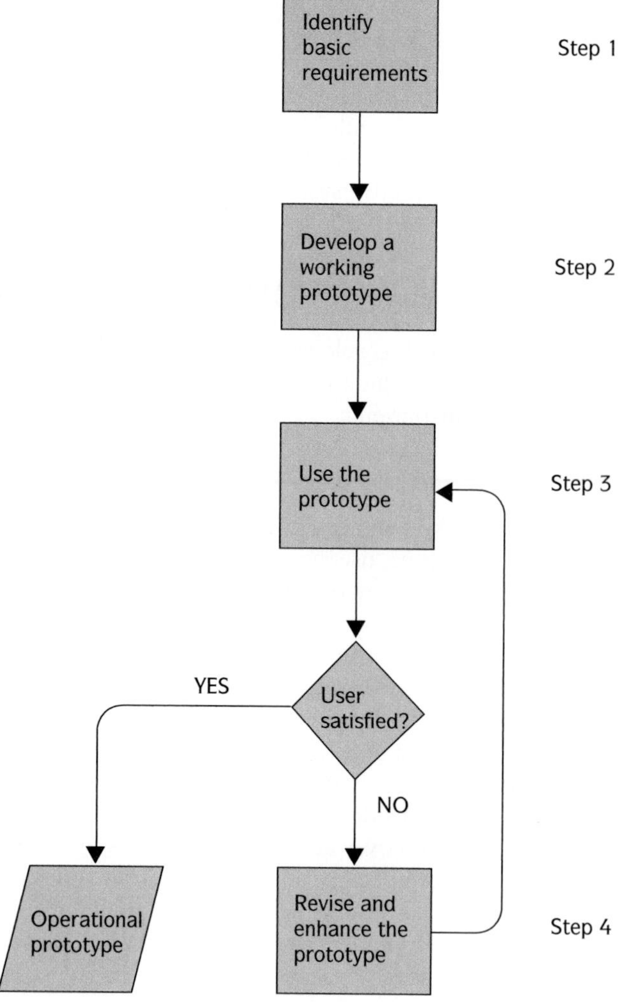

Advantages and Disadvantages of Prototyping

Prototyping is most useful when there is some uncertainty about requirements or design solutions. For example, a major securities firm requests consolidated information to analyze the performance of its account executives. But what should the measures of performance be? Can the information be extracted from the personnel system alone, or must data from client billings be incorporated as well? What items should be compared on reports? Users may not be initially able to see how the system will work.

end-user interface The part of an information system through which the end user interacts with the system, such as on-line screens and commands.

Prototyping is especially valuable for the design of the **end-user interface** of an information system (the part of the system that end users interact with, such as on-line display and data-entry screens, reports, or Web pages). The prototype enables users to react immediately to the parts of the system they will be dealing with. Figure 11.3 illustrates the prototyping process for an on-line calendar for retail securities brokers. The first version of the screen was built according to user-supplied specifications for a calendar to track appointments and activities. But when users actually worked with the calendar screen, they suggested adding labels for the month and year to the screen and a box to indicate whether the appointment had been met or an activity completed. The brokers also found that they wanted to access information that was maintained in the system about clients with whom they had appointments. The system designer added a link enabling brokers to move directly from the calendar screen to client records.

Prototyping encourages intense end-user involvement throughout the systems development lifecycle (Cerveny et al., 1986). Prototyping is more likely to produce systems that fulfill user requirements. For instance, when the DuPont Company used pro-

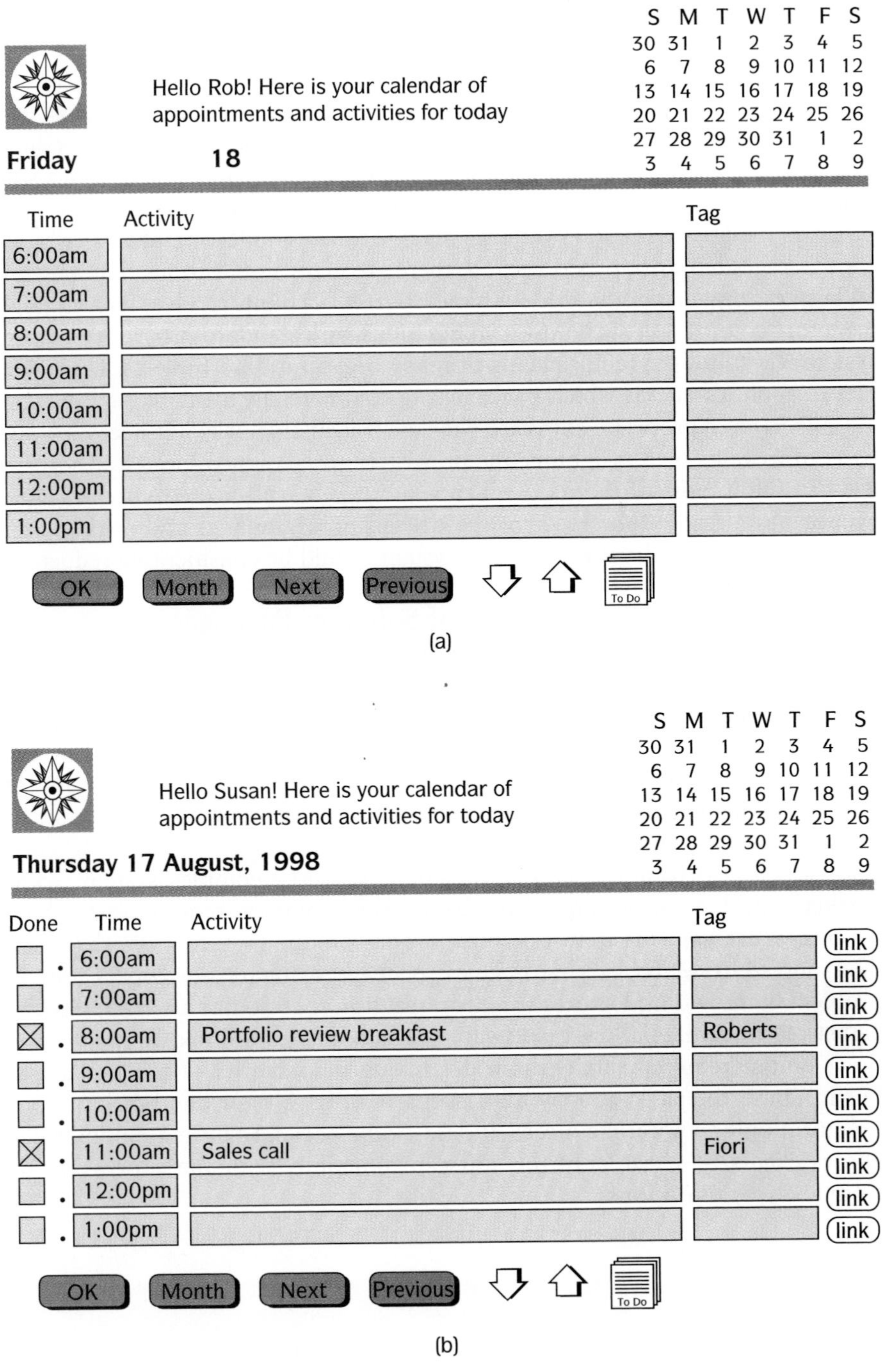

FIGURE 11.3

Prototyping a portfolio management application. This figure illustrates the process of prototyping one screen for the Financial Manager, a client and portfolio management application for securities brokers. Figure 11.3a shows an early version of the on-line appointment screen. Based on the special needs of a client, Figure 11.3b has two enhancements: a *done* indicator to show whether the task has been completed and a link to reference information maintained by the system on the client with whom the broker has an appointment.

totyping to build its systems, it produced more than 400 new programs with no failures (Arthur, 1992).

Prototyping is better suited for smaller applications. Large systems would have to be subdivided so that prototypes could be built one part at a time (Alavi, 1984), which may not be possible without a thorough requirements analysis using the conventional approach.

Rapid prototyping can gloss over essential steps in systems development. Once finished, if the prototype works reasonably well, management may not see the need for reprogramming, redesign, or full documentation and testing. Some of these hastily constructed systems may not easily accommodate large quantities of data or a large number of users in a production environment. Successful prototyping requires management and mechanisms for defining expectations, assigning resources, signaling problems, and measuring progress (Baskerville and Stage, 1996).

Application Software Packages

application software package A set of prewritten, precoded application software programs that are commercially available for sale or lease.

Another alternative strategy is to develop an information system by purchasing an application software package. As introduced in Chapter 6, an **application software package** is a set of prewritten, precoded application software programs that are commercially available for sale or lease. Application software packages may range from a simple task (e.g., printing address labels from a database on a microcomputer) to more than 400 program modules with 500,000 lines of code for a complex mainframe system.

Packages have flourished because there are many applications that are common to all business organizations—for example, payroll, accounts receivable, general ledger, or inventory control. For such universal functions with standard procedures, a generalized system will fulfill the requirements of many organizations. Table 11.1 provides examples of applications for which packages are commercially available.

When an appropriate software package is available, it is not necessary for a company to write its own programs; the prewritten, predesigned, pretested software package can fulfill most of the requirements and can be substituted instead. The package vendor has already done most of the design, programming, and testing, so the time frame and costs for developing a new system should be considerably reduced.

Advantages and Disadvantages of Software Packages

Using other development strategies, design activities may easily consume up to 50 percent or more of the development effort. However, with packages, most of the design work has been accomplished in advance. Software package programs are pretested before they are marketed so that purchaser testing can be accomplished in a relatively shorter period. Vendors supply much of the ongoing maintenance and support for the system, supplying enhancements to keep the system in line with ongoing technical and business developments.

Package disadvantages can be considerable with a complex system. To maximize market appeal, packages are geared to the most common requirements of all organizations. What happens if an organization has unique requirements that the package does not address? To varying degrees, package software developers anticipate this problem by providing features for customization that do not alter the basic software. **Customization** features allow a software package to be modified to meet an organization's unique requirements without destroying the integrity of the package software. For instance, the package may allocate parts of its files or databases to maintain an organization's own unique pieces of data. Some packages have a modular design that allows clients to select only the software functions with the processing they need from an array of options.

customization The modification of a software package to meet an organization's unique requirements without destroying the integrity of the package software.

TABLE 11.1 Examples of Application Software Packages

Accounts receivable	Job costing
Bond and stock management	Library systems
Computer-aided design (CAD)	Life insurance
Document imaging	Mailing labels
E-mail	Mathematical/statistical modeling
Enterprise resource planning (ERP)	Order processing
Groupware	Payroll
Health care	Process control
Hotel management	Tax accounting
Internet telephone	Web browser
Inventory control	Word processing

WINDOW ON TECHNOLOGY

Enterprise Resource Planning Systems: Benefits and Headaches

Enterprise resource planning (ERP) systems are increasingly the software of choice for organizations that are both large and complex (see Chapter 1). They help companies integrate all facets of the business, including planning, manufacturing, sales, and marketing. ERP software systems, such as SAP's R/3 (described in the chapter-ending Case Study), integrate modules for such differing functions as production, factory automation, finance, sales, purchasing, and personnel. However, many companies who swear by ERP systems find they are not robust or flexible enough to deliver the special budgeting, international consolidation, or other financial features that their managements expect. The predominant solution has been to install a separate, purchased financial system that meets the company's requirements to run alongside the ERP system. That solution, however, creates another problem.

Companies try to choose what they consider to be the best available ERP and financial software systems. They rarely select both systems because they fit well together. Unfortunately, making two such systems work together can be a difficult task because they usually present major difficulties arising from differing data structures. The way that data are represented in vendor files, for example, may not correspond to the way that data are represented in customer files. It may be difficult, if not impossible, to integrate financial, statistical, and operational information. The cost in money and time to integrate the two systems can be daunting. The effort can easily cost between $200,000 and $2 million and take up to six months. Even then, the job is not done. Each time the producer of either the ERP or the financial system releases a new version of their product, extensive work must be done to re-integrate the two systems, so addressing the lack in financial reporting only leads to other problems.

One approach to the data integration problem is a software interface—middleware—installed between the two systems. Commercial middleware software is available, but here, a similar problem exists—getting the middleware to work well with the ERP and financial systems that have been chosen. A better remedy, in the minds of some companies, is to build your own middleware. When completed, the middleware system will pass the data between the ERP and financial systems, enabling the organization to use the ERP system it needs to integrate its many functions, and allowing management to obtain the data it desires.

Motorola Corp. used this approach and did improve its reporting cycle, reducing the time to produce management reports from 48 hours down to 29 hours. The company's messaging product division created a UNIX-based middleware system that funnels data extracted monthly from 20 general-ledger systems worldwide into Walker financial-reporting and consolidation software, which then is used to generate management reports.

When Fujitsu Microelectronics, Inc., faced this integration problem with its SAP R/3 system installed in 1995, it used Microsoft Corp.'s Excel spreadsheets to analyze budget information, but users found the system inadequate. Analyzing data to compare, for example, a ratio of line-item expenses with revenue, could take weeks. Then Fujitsu found that Hyperion, a vendor of financial software that would meet its needs, also offered an accompanying set of tools to help create the interface between its system and R/3. The Hyperion utilities enabled Fujitsu to build a middleware system within four days. When completed, it transferred data between SAP's R/3 and Hyperion's Enterprise. Fujitsu now has switched from a monthly reporting system to a weekly system, enabling the company to react much faster to market changes.

To Think About: ***What management, organization, and technology issues are raised by installing ERP package software systems in large, complex organizations?***

Source: Adapted from Thomas Hoffman, "Extending ERP's Reach," *Computerworld,* February 9, 1998.

An alternative way of satisfying organizational information requirements unmet by a software package is to supplement the package with another piece of software. The Window on Technology describes how problems can result from trying to integrate the data from the two systems, requiring the organization to use special software called middleware to act as a bridge between the two systems. **Middleware** is a software product that connects two otherwise separate applications to pass data between them. One growing use for middleware products is to link a database system to a Web server. This allows users to request data from the database using forms displayed on a Web browser, and it enables the Web server to return dynamic Web pages based on the user's information request.

middleware Software that allows two different applications to exchange data.

Ultimately, required customization and additional programming may become so expensive and time-consuming that they eliminate many of the advantages of software packages. Figure 11.4 shows how package costs in relation to total implementation

FIGURE 11.4

The effects of customizing a software package on total implementation costs. As the modifications to a software package rise, so does the cost of implementing the package. Sometimes the savings promised by the package are whittled away by excessive changes. As the number of lines of program code changed approaches 5 percent of the total lines in the package, the costs of implementation rise fivefold.

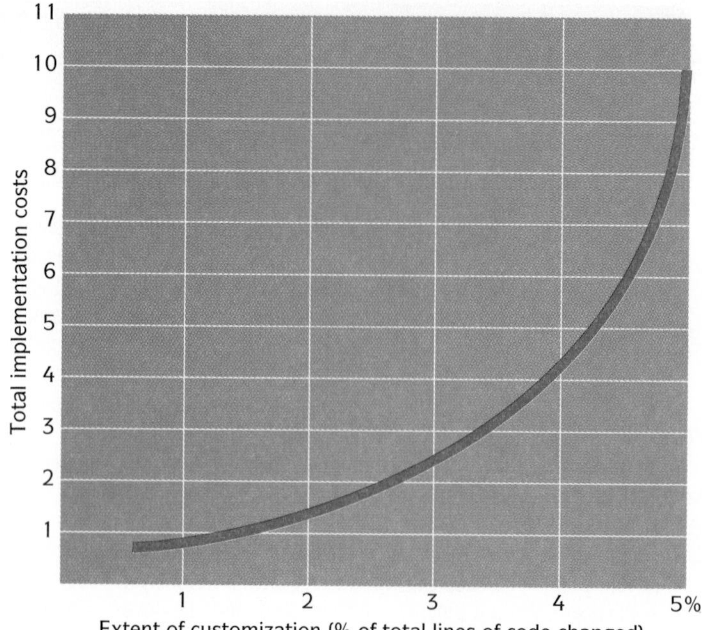

costs rise with the degree of customization. The initial purchase price of the package can be deceptive because of these hidden implementation costs.

Selecting Software Packages

Application software packages must be thoroughly evaluated before they can be used as the foundation of a new information system. The most important evaluation criteria are the functions provided by the package, flexibility, user-friendliness, hardware and software resources, database requirements, installation and maintenance effort, documentation, vendor quality, and cost. The package evaluation process often is based on a **Request for Proposal (RFP)**, which is a detailed list of questions submitted to vendors of packaged software.

Request for Proposal (RFP) A detailed list of questions submitted to vendors of packaged software or other services to determine if the vendor's product can meet the organization's specific requirements.

When a system is developed using an application software package, systems analysis will include a package evaluation effort. Design activities will focus on matching requirements to package features. Instead of tailoring the system design specifications directly to user requirements, the design effort will consist of trying to mold user requirements to conform to the features of the package.

When a software package solution is selected, the organization no longer has total control over the system design process. At best, packages can meet only 70 percent of most organizations' requirements. If the package cannot adapt to the organization, the organization will have to adapt to the package and change its procedures.

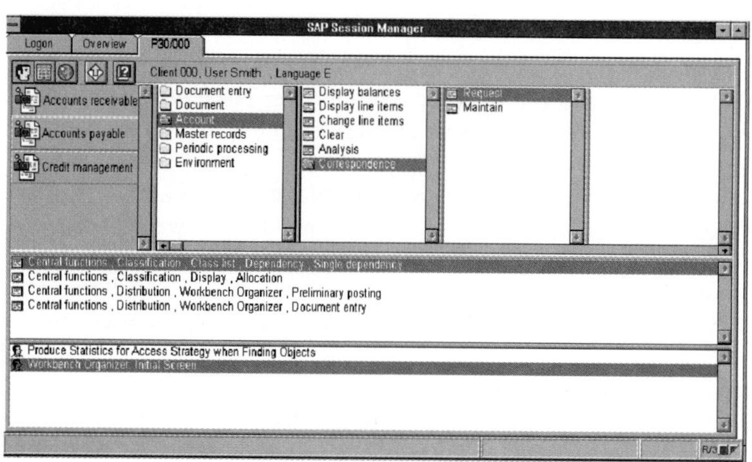

SAP's R/3 software package runs in a client/server environment and can be customized to accommodate different languages, currencies, tax laws, and accounting practices. *Copyright by SAP AG. All rights reserved.*

End-User Development

In many organizations end users are developing a growing percentage of information systems with little or no formal assistance from technical specialists. This phenomenon is called **end-user development.** End-user development has been made possible by the special fourth-generation software tools introduced in Chapter 6. With fourth-generation languages, graphics languages, and microcomputer tools, end users can access data, create reports, and develop entire information systems on their own, with little or no help from professional systems analysts or programmers. Many of these end-user developed systems can be created much more rapidly than with the traditional systems lifecycle. Figure 11.5 illustrates the concept of end-user development.

end-user development The development of information systems by end users with little or no formal assistance from technical specialists.

End-User Computing Tools: Strengths and Limitations

Many organizations have reported appreciable gains in application development productivity by using fourth-generation tools. Productivity enhancements based on conventional programming languages, such as structured programming (see Section 11.3), have resulted in a maximum productivity improvement of only 25 percent (Jones, 1979). In contrast, some studies of organizations developing applications with fourth-generation tools have reported productivity gains of 300 percent to 500 percent (Green, 1984–85; Harel, 1985). Fourth-generation tools have new capabilities, such as graphics, spreadsheets, modeling, and ad hoc information retrieval, that meet important business needs.

Unfortunately, fourth-generation tools still cannot replace conventional tools for some business applications because their capabilities remain limited. Fourth-generation processing is relatively inefficient, processing individual transactions too slowly and at too high a cost to make these systems suitable for very large transaction-processing systems. Slow response time and computer performance degradation often result when very large files are used.

Most fourth-generation tools are more nonprocedural than conventional programming languages. They cannot easily handle applications with extensive procedural logic and updating requirements, such as systems used for optimal production

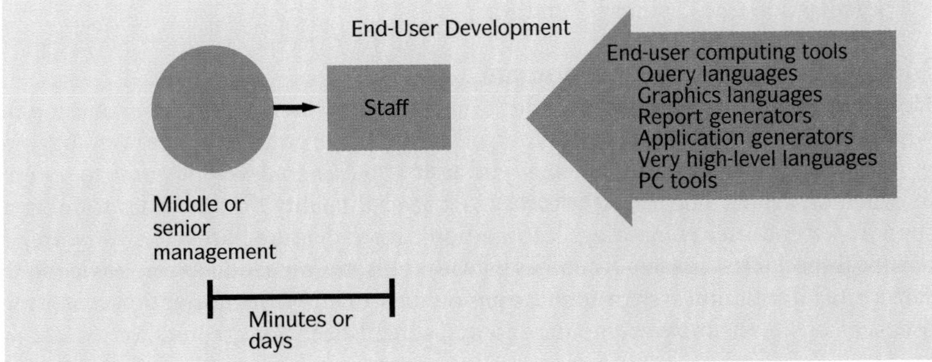

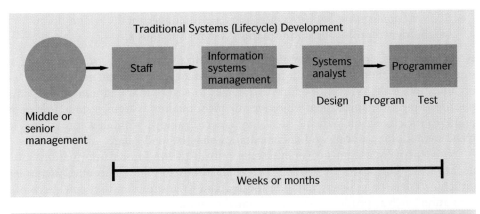

FIGURE 11.5

End-user versus systems lifecycle development. End users can access computerized information directly or develop information systems with little or no formal technical assistance. On the whole, end-user developed systems can be completed more rapidly than those developed through the conventional systems lifecycle. *From* Applications Development Without Programmers *by Martin, James, © 1982. Reprinted by permission of Prentice-Hall, Inc., Upper Saddle River, NJ.*

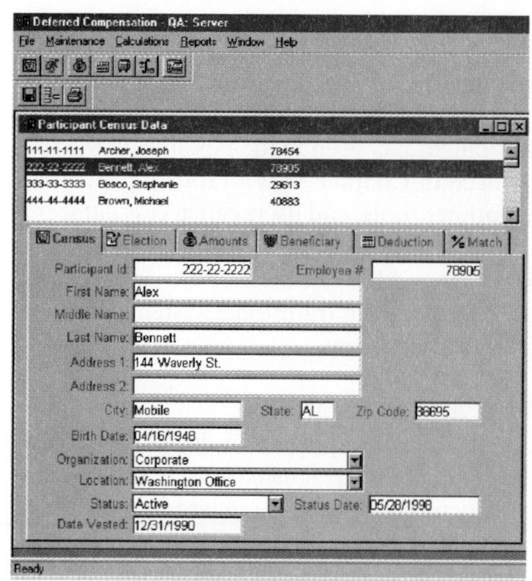

Emboss Technologies, which provides outsourcing services, leading edge software products, and consulting for employee benefits and executive compensation programs, developed an early version of an executive compensation system using PowerBuilder as a fourth-generation software tool. This screen lists individual participants in a deferred compensation plan.

scheduling, or tracking daily trades of stocks, bonds, and other securities that require complex processing and often the matching of multiple files. Fourth-generation tools make their greatest contribution to the programming and detail-design aspects of the systems development process but have little impact on other system-building activities.

Management Benefits and Problems

Without question, end-user development provides many benefits to organizations. These include the following:

- *Improved requirements determination* as users specify their own business needs.
- *Increased user involvement and satisfaction.* As users develop their systems themselves and control the system development process, they are more likely to use the system.
- *Reduced application backlog* when users are no longer totally reliant upon overburdened professional information systems specialists.

At the same time, end-user computing poses organizational risks because it occurs outside of traditional mechanisms for information systems management and control. Most organizations have not yet developed strategies to ensure that end-user-developed applications meet organizational objectives or meet quality assurance standards appropriate to their function. When systems are created rapidly, without a formal development methodology, testing and documentation may be inadequate.

Control over data can be lost in systems outside the traditional information systems department. When users create their own applications and files, it becomes increasingly difficult to determine where data are located and to ensure that the same piece of information (such as product number or annual earnings) is used consistently throughout the organization (see Chapters 7 and 8).

Managing End-User Development

How can organizations maximize the benefits of end-user applications development while keeping it under management control? A number of strategies have been suggested.

information center A special facility within an organization that provides training and support for end-user computing.

One way to facilitate and manage end-user application development is to set up an information center. The **information center** is a special facility that provides training and support for end-user computing. Information centers feature hardware, software, and technical specialists that supply end users with tools, training, and expert advice so they can create information system applications on their own. With information center tools, users can create their own computer reports, spreadsheets, or graphics, or extract data

Retail staff receive instructions in this New Jersey computer management class. An important function of information centers is to make end users feel proficient with computers.

for decision making and analysis with minimal technical assistance. Information-center consultants are available to instruct users and to assist in the development of more complex applications.

Information centers provide many management benefits. They can help end users find tools and applications that will make them more productive. They prevent the creation of redundant applications. They promote data sharing and minimize integrity problems (see Chapter 7). They ensure that the applications developed by end users meet audit, data quality, and security standards. They can help establish and enforce standards for hardware and software so that end users do not introduce many disparate and incompatible technologies into the firm (Fuller and Swanson, 1992; see Chapter 8). The information center will assist users with only hardware and software that have been approved by management.

In addition to using information centers, managers can pursue other strategies to ensure that end-user computing serves larger organizational goals (see Alavi, Nelson, and Weiss, 1987–88; Rockart and Flannery, 1983). Management should control the development of end-user applications by incorporating them into its strategic systems plans. Training and support should consider individual users' attitudes toward computers, educational levels, cognitive styles, and receptiveness to change (Harrison and Rainer, 1992). Management should also develop controls on critical end-user development, such as insisting on cost justification of end-user information system projects and establishing hardware, software, and quality standards for user-developed applications.

Outsourcing

If a firm does not want to use its internal resources to build or operate information systems, it can hire an external organization that specializes in providing these services to do the work. The process of turning over an organization's computer center operations, telecommunications networks, or applications development to external vendors is called **outsourcing**. In firms where the cost of the information systems function has risen rapidly, managers are turning to outsourcing to control these costs.

outsourcing The practice of contracting computer center operations, telecommunications networks, or applications development to external vendors.

Outsourcing is becoming popular because some organizations perceive it as being more cost-effective than maintaining their own computer center and information systems staff. The provider of outsourcing services can benefit from economies of scale (the same knowledge, skills, and capacity can be shared with many different customers) and is likely to charge competitive prices for information systems services. Outsourcing allows a company with fluctuating needs for computer processing to pay for only what it uses rather than to build its own computer center to stand underutilized when there is no peak load. Some firms outsource because their internal information systems staff

WINDOW ON MANAGEMENT

VISA's Outsourcing Triumph

When information systems management awards a multimillion-dollar outsourcing contract for a highly visible strategic project, and the winner has been underbid by several other companies, management must have good reasons. And the project must prove to be a success. That was precisely the situation when VISA International, Inc. offered a large and critical development project to DMR Consulting of Montreal, Canada.

VISA International's commercial card division, which is based in San Francisco, California, decided it needed to offer VISA's large corporate customers worldwide a way for them to produce reports related to their VISA expenditures. The goal was to enable the customers to easily summarize and analyze all VISA charges through a report that each corporation could customize. A project was established to develop the customizable software system so that it could be distributed to customers. This extra service could be a strategic advantage for VISA.

According to Ronald Prather, vice president of information services at VISA's commercial card division, the company originally planned to develop the system itself. Although VISA's 1000-person IS staff did not have the necessary skills, the intent was for them to learn the technology so they could support the new system after it was in use. However, after the project began, according to Prather, VISA found "We didn't have enough resources to do everything we wanted." Ultimately he decided to outsource the whole project, despite the fact that quality and on-time delivery were critical, because the final product was to be distributed to customers.

Outsourcing was a risky alternative. First, this was a large, mission-critical project, the kind that most companies want to develop themselves. In addition, studies have shown that almost 25 percent of outsourcing projects are canceled due to high costs and/or poor quality. Nonetheless, Prather proceeded and in the end received about ten bids on the project. DMR was selected despite the fact that several bids were lower. What were the keys to DMR's successful bid submission? First, DMR's proposal included a full-blown development project methodology. Prather was able to know how the project would proceed, how he and his staff would relate to the project, and what kinds of reports would be submitted. In addition, where many bids answered request-for-proposal questions with a simple "yes," DMR added a full explanation of how it would accomplish the task. Prather felt comfortable knowing exactly what he was buying and how it would be done. The DMR responses gave him confidence in the quality of its work and in the likelihood of a positive outcome. Also, all the programming was to be done in Quebec City, which saved VISA the expense of supplying DMR's 40 staffers office space. Prather also was pleased to find that the project would have two managers, one each from VISA and DMR. In that way Prather (who became the VISA project manager) always would know what was happening and be able to ensure a quality product.

The project was a success. VISA was able to maintain control over the project, being able, for example, to review designs before they were implemented. DMR met its plan dates, and the project ended on time and within budget. More than three hundred large corporations now are using the system. Ultimately, VISA awarded DMR a long-term contract to maintain the system.

To Think About: ***Do you consider Prather's choice to outsource and then to award the project to DMR to have been risky? Do you think you would have done the same in his position? Explain your responses.***

Source: Adapted from Julia King, "VISA Expands Outsourcing Deal," *Computerworld*, January 26, 1998.

cannot keep pace with technological change or because they want to free up scarce and costly talent for activities with higher payback (see the Window on Management.)

Not all organizations benefit from outsourcing, and the disadvantages of outsourcing can create serious problems for organizations if they are not well understood and managed (Earl, 1996). When a firm farms out the responsibility for developing and operating its information systems to another organization, it can lose control over its information systems function. Outsourcing can place the vendor in an advantageous position where the client has to accept whatever the vendor does and whatever fees the vendor charges. This dependency eventually could result in higher costs or loss of control over technological direction. Trade secrets or proprietary information may leak out to competitors because a firm's information systems are being run or developed by outsiders. This could be especially harmful if a firm allows an outsourcer to develop or to operate applications that give it some type of competitive advantage.

When to Use Outsourcing

If systems development and operations functions are well managed and productive, there may not be much immediate benefit in using an external vendor. However, there are a number of circumstances under which outsourcing makes a great deal of sense.

- *When there is limited opportunity for the firm to distinguish itself competitively through a particular information systems application or series of applications.* Applications such as payroll, for which the firm obtains little competitive advantage from excellence, are strong candidates for outsourcing. However, applications such as airline reservations or plant scheduling could impact profits, customers, or market share if such systems have problems. Such applications where the rewards for excellence are high and where the penalties for failure are high should probably be developed and operated internally.
- *When the predictability of uninterrupted information systems service is not very important.* For instance, airline reservations or catalogue shopping systems are too critical to be trusted outside. If these systems failed to operate for a few days or even a few hours, they could close down the business (see Chapter 2). On the other hand, a system to process employee insurance claims could be more easily outsourced because uninterrupted processing of claims is not critical to the survival of the firm.
- *When the firm's existing information system capabilities are limited, ineffective, or technically inferior.* Some organizations use outsourcers as an easy way to revamp their information systems technology. For instance, they might use an outsourcer to help them make the transition from traditional mainframe-based computing to a distributed client/server computing environment. On the other hand, outsourcing new technology projects can be risky because the organization may lack the expertise to negotiate a sound contract and may remain too dependent on the vendor after implementation (Lacity, Willcocks, and Feeny, 1996).

Organizations need to manage the outsourcer as they would manage their own internal information systems department by setting priorities and guaranteeing that information systems are running smoothly. They should establish criteria for evaluating the outsourcing vendor. Firms should design outsourcing contracts carefully so that the outsourcing services can be adjusted if the nature of the business changes. The firm's relationship with the vendor specified in the outsourcing contract, decision rights, performance measures, and assessment of risks and rewards should be aligned with the strategic intent for outsourcing (DiRomualdo and Gurbaxani, 1998).

Table 11.2 compares the advantages and disadvantages of each of the system-building alternatives described in this chapter.

11.3 SYSTEM-BUILDING METHODOLOGIES AND TOOLS

Various tools and development methodologies have been employed to help system builders document, analyze, design, and implement information systems. A **development methodology** is a collection of methods, one or more for every activity within every phase of a systems development project. Some development methodologies are suited to specific technologies, while others reflect different philosophies of systems development. The most widely-used methodologies and tools include the traditional structured methodologies, object-oriented software development, computer-aided software engineering (CASE), and software reengineering.

development methodology A collection of methods, one or more for every activity within every phase of a development project.

Structured Methodologies

Structured methodologies have been used to document, analyze, and design information systems since the 1970s and remain an important methodological approach. **Structured** refers to the fact that the techniques are step-by-step, with each step building upon the previous one. Structured methodologies are top-down, progressing from the highest, most abstract level to the lowest level of detail—from the general to the specific. For example, the highest level of a top-down description of a human resources system would show the main human resources functions: personnel, benefits, compensation, and Equal Employment Opportunity (EEO). Each of these would be

structured Refers to the fact that techniques are instructions that are carefully drawn up, often step-by-step, with each step building upon a previous one.

TABLE 11.2 Comparison of Systems-Development Approaches

Approach	Features	Advantages	Disadvantages
Systems lifecycle	Sequential step-by-step formal process Written specification and approvals Limited role of users	Necessary for large complex systems and projects	Slow and expensive Discourages changes Massive paperwork to manage
Prototyping	Requirements specified dynamically with experimental system Rapid, informal, and iterative process Users continually interact with the prototype	Rapid and inexpensive Useful when requirements are uncertain or when end-user interface is important Promotes user participation	Inappropriate for large, complex systems Can gloss over steps in analysis, documentation, and testing
Application software package	Commercial software eliminates need for internally developed software programs	Design, programming, installation, and maintenance work reduced Can save time and cost when developing common business applications Reduces need for internal information systems resources	May not meet organization's unique requirements May not perform many business functions well Extensive customization raises development costs
End-user development	Systems created by end users using fourth-generation software tools Rapid and informal Minimal role of information systems specialists	Users control systems-building Saves development time and cost Reduces application backlog	Can lead to proliferation of uncontrolled information systems Systems do not always meet quality assurance standards
Outsourcing	Systems built and sometimes operated by external vendors	Can reduce or control costs Can produce systems when internal resources not available or technically deficient	Loss of control over the information systems function Dependence on the technical direction and prosperity of external vendors

broken down into the next layer. Benefits, for instance, might include pension, employee savings, health care, and insurance. Each of these layers in turn would be broken down until the lowest level of detail could be depicted.

The traditional structured methodologies are process-oriented rather than data-oriented. Although data descriptions are part of the methods, the methodologies focus on how the data are transformed rather than on the data themselves. These methodologies are largely linear; each phase must be completed before the next one can begin. Structured methodologies include structured analysis, structured design, and the use of flowcharts.

structured analysis A method for defining system inputs, processes, and outputs and for partitioning systems into subsystems or modules that show a logical graphic model of information flow.

data flow diagram (DFD) A primary tool in structured analysis that graphically illustrates the system's component processes and the flow of data between them.

Structured Analysis

Structured analysis is widely used to define system inputs, processes, and outputs. It offers a logical graphic model of information flow, partitioning a system into modules that show manageable levels of detail. It rigorously specifies the processes or transformations that occur within each module and the interfaces that exist between them. Its primary tool is the **data flow diagram (DFD)**, a graphic representation of a system's component processes and the interfaces (flow of data) between them.

Figure 11.6 shows a simple data flow diagram for a mail-in university course registration system. The rounded boxes represent processes, which portray the transformation of data. The square box represents an external entity, which is an originator or receiver of information located outside the boundaries of the system being modeled. The open rectangles represent data stores, which are either manual or automated in-

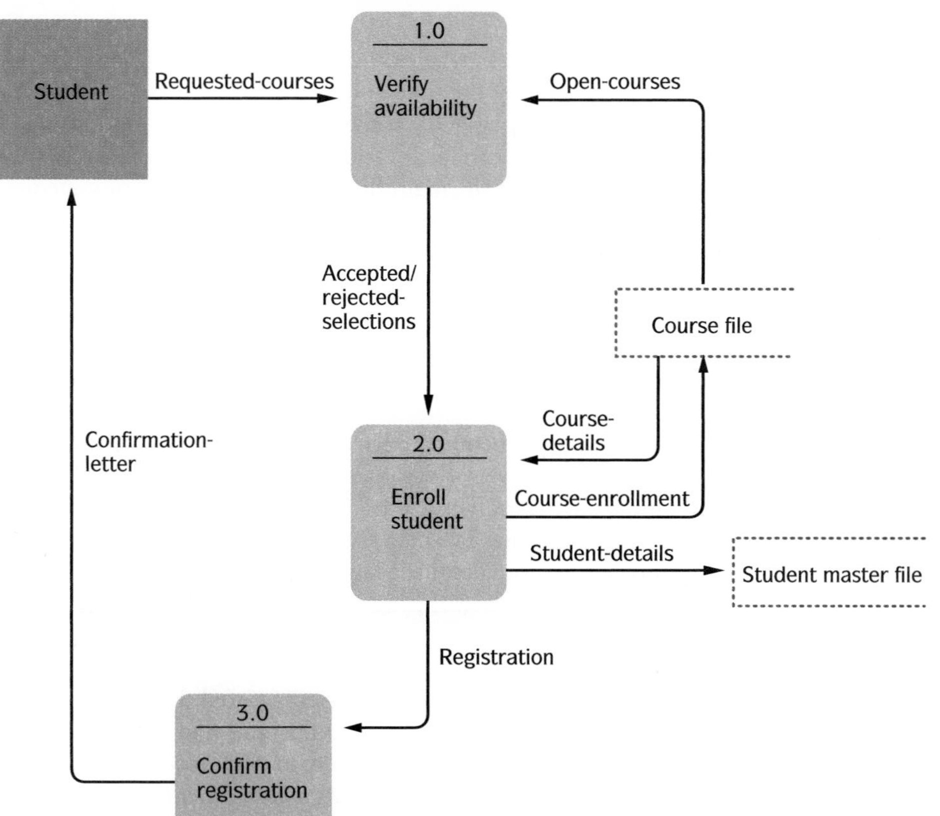

FIGURE 11.6
Data flow diagram for mail-in university registration system. The system has three processes: Verify availability (1.0), Enroll student (2.0), and Confirm registration (3.0). The name and content of each of the data flows appear adjacent to each arrow. There is one external entity in this system: the student. There are two data stores: the student master file and the course file.

ventories of data. The arrows represent data flows, which show the movement between processes, external entities, and data stores. They always contain packets of data, with the name or content of each data flow listed beside the arrow.

This data flow diagram shows that students submit registration forms with their name, identification number, and the numbers of the courses they wish to take. In process 1.0 the system verifies that each course selected is still open by referencing the university's course file. The file distinguishes courses that are open from those that have been canceled or filled. Process 1.0 then determines which of the student's selections can be accepted or rejected. Process 2.0 enrolls the student in the courses for which he or she has been accepted. It updates the university's course file with the student's name and identification number and recalculates the class size. If maximum enrollment has been reached, the course number is flagged as closed. Process 2.0 also updates the university's student master file with information about new students or changes in address. Process 3.0 then sends each student applicant a confirmation-of-registration letter listing the courses for which he or she is registered and noting the course selections that could not be fulfilled.

The diagrams can be used to depict higher-level processes as well as lower-level details. Through leveled data flow diagrams, a complex process can be broken down into successive levels of detail. An entire system can be divided into subsystems with a high-level data flow diagram. Each subsystem, in turn, can be divided into additional subsystems with second-level data flow diagrams, and the lower-level subsystems can be broken down again until the lowest level of detail has been reached.

Another tool for structured analysis is a data dictionary, which contains information about individual pieces of data and data groupings within a system (see Chapter 7). The data dictionary defines the contents of data flows and data stores so that system builders understand exactly what pieces of data they contain. **Process specifications** describe the transformation occurring within the lowest level of the data flow diagrams. They express the logic for each process.

process specifications Describes the logic of the processes occurring within the lowest levels of the data flow diagrams.

Structured Design

structured design Software design discipline, encompassing a set of design rules and techniques for designing a system from the top down in a hierarchical fashion.

structure chart System documentation showing each level of design, the relationship among the levels, and the overall place in the design structure; can document one program, one system, or part of one program.

structured programming A discipline for organizing and coding programs that simplifies the control paths so that the programs can be easily understood and modified. Uses the basic control structures and modules that have only one entry point and one exit point.

module A logical unit of a program that performs one or several functions.

sequence construct The sequential single steps or actions in the logic of a program that do not depend on the existence of any condition.

Structured design encompasses a set of design rules and techniques that promotes program clarity and simplicity, thereby reducing the time and effort required for coding, debugging, and maintenance. The main principle of structured design is that a system should be designed from the top down in hierarchical fashion and refined to greater levels of detail. The design should first consider the main function of a program or system, then break this function into subfunctions and decompose each subfunction until the lowest level of detail has been reached. The lowest-level modules describe the actual processing that will occur. In this manner all high-level logic and the design model are developed before detailed program code is written. If structured analysis has been performed, the structured specification document can serve as input to the design process. Our earlier human resources top-down description is also a good overview example of structured design.

As the design is formulated, it is documented in a structure chart. The **structure chart** is a top-down chart, showing each level of design, its relationship to other levels, and its place in the overall design structure. Figure 11.7 shows a structure chart that can be used for a payroll system. If a design has too many levels to fit onto one structure chart, it can be broken down further on more detailed structure charts. A structure chart may document one program, one system (a set of programs), or part of one program.

Structured Programming

Structured programming extends the principles governing structured design to the writing of programs to make software programs easier to understand and modify. It is based upon the principle of modularization, which follows from top-down analysis and design. Each of the boxes in the structure chart represents a component **module** that is usually directly related to a bottom-level design module. It constitutes a logical unit that performs one or several functions. Ideally, modules should be independent of each other and should have only one entry to and exit from their parent modules. They should share data with as few other modules as possible. Each module should be kept to a manageable size. An individual should be able to read and understand the program code for the module and easily keep track of its functions.

Proponents of structured programming have shown that any program can be written using three basic control constructs, or instruction patterns: (1) simple sequence, (2) selection, and (3) iteration. These control constructs are illustrated in Figure 11.8.

The **sequence construct** executes statements in the order in which they appear, with control passing unconditionally from one statement to the next. The program will execute statement A and then statement B.

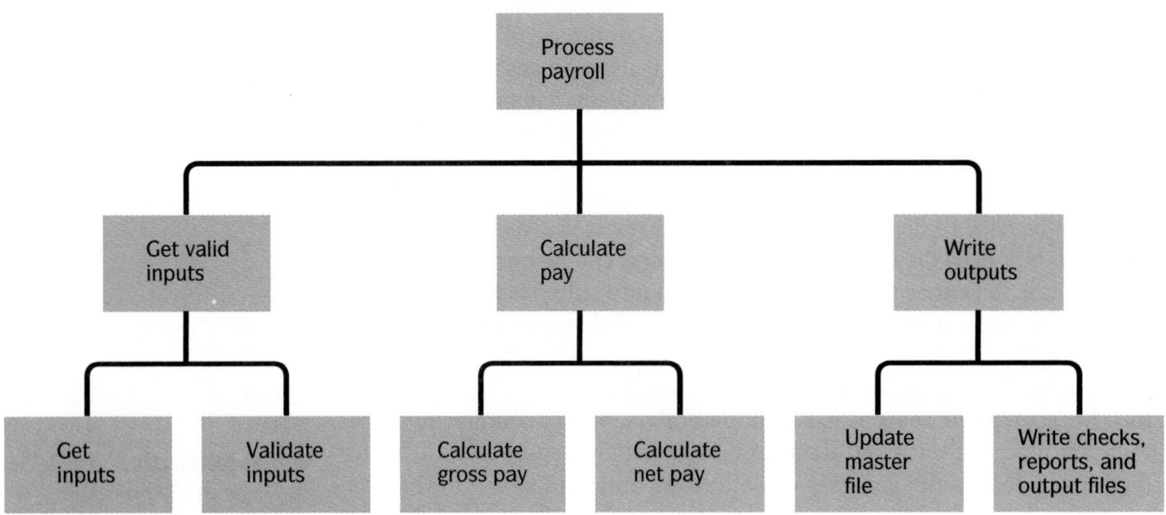

FIGURE 11.7 High-level structure chart for a payroll system. This structure chart shows the highest or most abstract level of design for a payroll system, providing an overview of the entire system.

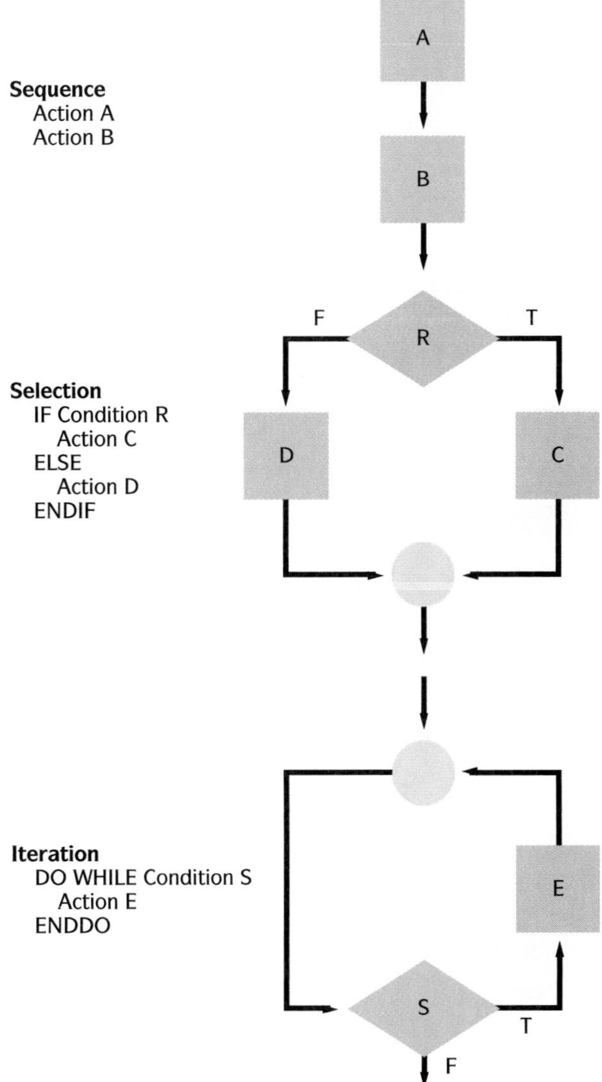

FIGURE 11.8

Basic control constructs. The three basic control constructs used in structured programming are sequence, selection, and iteration.

The **selection construct** tests a condition and executes one of the two alternative instructions based on the results of the test. Condition R is tested. If R is true, statement C is executed. If R is false, statement D is executed. Control then passes to the next statement.

The **iteration construct** repeats a segment of code as long as a conditional test remains true. Condition S is tested. If S is true, statement E is executed and control returns to the test of S. If S is false, E is skipped and control passes to the next statement.

selection construct The logic pattern in programming where a stated condition determines which of two or more actions can be taken, depending on which satisfies the stated condition.

iteration construct The logic pattern in programming where certain actions are repeated while a specified condition occurs or until a certain condition is met.

Flowcharts

Flowcharting is an old design tool that is still in use. **System flowcharts** detail the flow of data throughout an entire information system. Program flowcharts describe the processes taking place within an individual program in the system and the sequence in which they must be executed. Flowcharting is no longer recommended for program design because it does not provide top-down modular structure as effectively as other techniques. However, system flowcharts still may be used to document physical design specifications because they can show all inputs, major files, processing, and outputs for a system and they can document manual procedures.

system flowchart A graphic design tool that depicts the physical media and sequence of processing steps used in an entire information system.

Using specialized symbols and flow lines, the system flowchart traces the flow of information and work in a system, the sequence of processing steps, and the physical media on which data are input, output, and stored. Figure 11.9 shows some of the basic symbols for system flowcharting. The plain rectangle is a general symbol. Flow lines

FIGURE 11.9

Basic system flowchart symbols. Use these symbols and interconnecting lines to show the sequence of processing taking place within a system and the physical media used in each step.

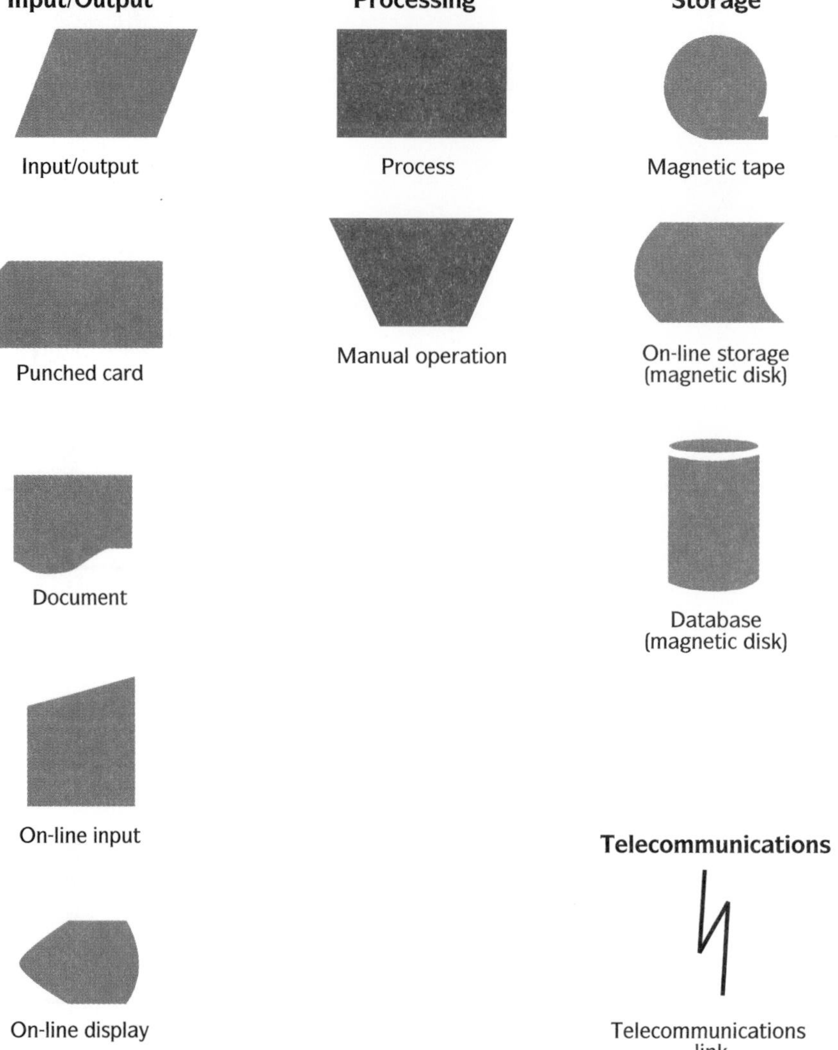

show the sequence of steps and the direction of information flow. Arrows are employed to show direction if it is not apparent in the diagram. Figure 11.10 illustrates a high-level system flowchart for a payroll system.

Limitations of Traditional Methods

Although traditional methods are valuable, they can be inflexible and time-consuming. Completion of structured analysis is required before design can begin, and programming must await the completed deliverables from design. A change in specifications requires that first the analysis documents and then the design documents must be modified before the programs can be changed to reflect the new requirement. Structured methodologies are function-oriented, focusing on the processes that transform the data. Yet business management has come to understand that most information systems must be data-oriented. Consequently, system builders are turning to object-oriented software development, computer-aided software engineering (CASE), and software reengineering to deal with these issues.

object-oriented software development An approach to software development that deemphasizes procedures and shifts the focus from modeling business processes and data to combining data and procedures to create objects.

Object-Oriented Software Development

In Chapter 6 we explained that object-oriented programming combines data and the specific procedures that operate on those data into one object. Object-oriented programming is part of a larger approach to systems development called *object-oriented software development*. **Object-oriented software development** differs from traditional method-

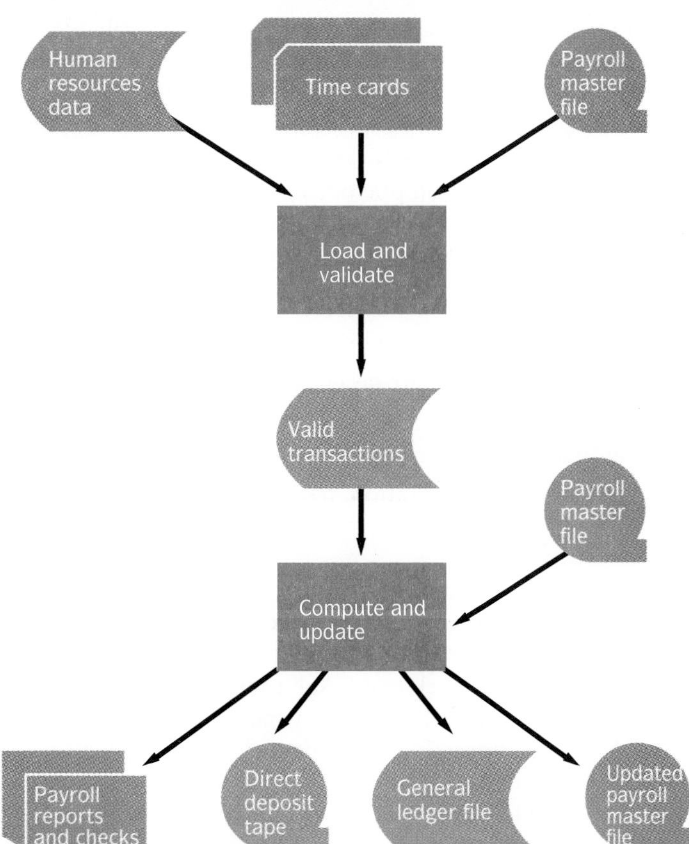

FIGURE 11.10

System flowchart for a payroll system. This is a high-level system flowchart for a batch payroll system. Only the most important processes and files are illustrated. Data are input from two sources: time cards and payroll-related data (such as salary increases) passed from the human resources system. The data are first edited and validated against the existing payroll master file before the payroll master is updated. The update process produces an updated payroll master file, various payroll reports (such as the payroll register and hours register), checks, a direct deposit tape, and a file of payment data that must be passed to the organization's general ledger system. The direct deposit tape is sent to the automated clearinghouse that serves the banks offering direct deposit services to employees.

ologies by shifting the focus from separately modeling business processes and data to combining data and procedures into unified objects. The system is viewed as a collection of classes and objects and relationships among them. The objects are defined, programmed, documented, and saved as building blocks for future applications.

Objects are easily reusable, so object-oriented software development directly addresses the issue of reusability and is expected to reduce the time and cost of writing software. Of course, no organization will see savings from reusability until it builds up a library of objects to draw upon and understands which objects have broader use (Pancake, 1995). In theory, design and programming can begin as soon as requirements are completed through the use of iterations of rapid prototyping. Object-oriented frameworks have been developed to provide reusable semicomplete applications that can be further customized by the organization into finished applications (Fayad and Schmidt, 1997).

Although the demand for training in object-oriented techniques and programming tools is exploding, object-oriented software development is still in its infancy (Fayad and Tsai, 1995). No agreed-upon object-oriented development methodology exists. Information systems specialists must learn a completely new way of modeling a system. Conversion to an object-oriented approach may require large-scale organizational investments, which management must balance against the anticipated payoffs.

Computer-Aided Software Engineering (CASE)

Computer-aided software engineering (CASE)—sometimes called *computer-aided systems engineering*—is the automation of step-by-step methodologies for software and systems development to reduce the amount of repetitive work the developer needs to do. Its adoption can free the developer for more creative problem-solving tasks. CASE tools also facilitate creation of clear documentation and the coordination of team development efforts. Team members can share their work more easily by accessing each other's files to review or modify what has been done. Systems developed with CASE and the

computer-aided software engineering (CASE) The automation of step-by-step methodologies for software and systems development to reduce the amount of repetitive work the developer needs to do.

newer methodologies have been found to be more reliable and require repairs less often (Dekleva, 1992). Many CASE tools are PC-based, with powerful graphical capabilities.

CASE tools provide automated graphics facilities for producing charts and diagrams, screen and report generators, data dictionaries, extensive reporting facilities, analysis and checking tools, code generators, and documentation generators. Most CASE tools are based on one or more of the popular structured methodologies. Some are starting to support object-oriented development. In general, CASE tools try to increase productivity and quality by doing the following:

- Enforce a standard development methodology and design discipline.
- Improve communication between users and technical specialists.
- Organize and correlate design components and provide rapid access to them via a design repository.
- Automate tedious and error-prone portions of analysis and design.
- Automate code generation, testing, and control rollout.

CASE Tools

Many CASE tools have been classified in terms of whether they support activities at the front end or the back end of the systems development process. Front-end CASE tools focus on capturing analysis and design information in the early stages of systems development, whereas back-end CASE tools address coding, testing, and maintenance activities. Back-end tools help convert specifications automatically into program code.

CASE tools automatically tie data elements to the processes where they are used. If a data flow diagram is changed from one process to another, the elements in the data dictionary would be altered automatically to reflect the change in the diagram. CASE tools also contain features for validating design diagrams and specifications. CASE tools thus support iterative design by automating revisions and changes and providing prototyping facilities.

A CASE information repository stores all the information defined by the analysts during the project. The repository includes data flow diagrams, structure charts, entity-relationship diagrams, data definitions, process specifications, screen and report formats, notes and comments, and test results.

CASE tools now have features to support client/server applications, object-oriented programming, and business process redesign. Figure 11.11 illustrates the use of Scitor's Process Charter for Windows, a flowcharting and process-analysis tool that lets developers diagram business processes with information such as resource requirements, costs, efficiencies, and delays. Developers can use this tool to visualize how processes are affected by internal and external factors.

The Challenge of Using CASE

To be used effectively, CASE tools require organizational discipline. Every member of a development project must adhere to a common set of naming conventions, standards, and development methodology. The best CASE tools enforce common methods and standards, which may discourage their use in situations where organizational discipline is lacking.

CASE is not a magic cure-all. It does not enable systems to be designed automatically or ensure that business requirements are met. Systems designers still have to understand what a firm's business needs are and how the business works. Systems analysis and design still are dependent upon the analytical skills of the analyst/designer.

Rapid Application Development (RAD)

rapid application development (RAD) Process for developing systems in a very short time period by using prototyping, fourth-generation tools, and close teamwork among users and systems specialists.

CASE tools, reusable software, object-oriented software tools, prototyping, and fourth-generation tools are helping system builders create working systems much more rapidly than using traditional structured approaches. The term **rapid application development (RAD)** is used to describe this process of creating workable systems in a very short period of time. RAD can include the use of visual programming and other tools for building graph-

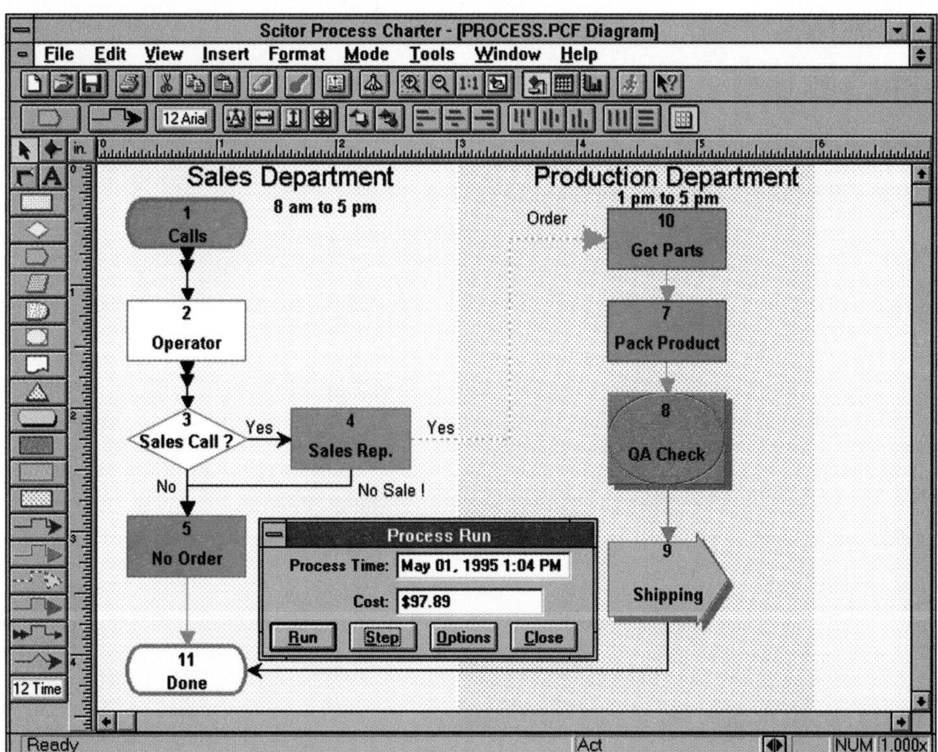

FIGURE 11.11

Process Charter provides tools to map out business processes and to simulate the processes in real-time with flashing colors. The process models include time and cost information.

ical user interfaces, iterative prototyping of key system elements, the automation of program code generation, and close teamwork among end users and information systems specialists. Simple systems often can be assembled from prebuilt components. The process does not have to be sequential, and key parts of development can occur simultaneously.

The Window on Organizations shows some of the benefits of using rapid application development. In this instance, Gulf Canada Resources was able to use an object-oriented application development tool to create a budgeting system in only a few months.

joint application design (JAD) Process to accelerate the generation of information requirements by having end users and information systems specialists work together in intensive interactive design sessions.

Sometimes a technique called **JAD (joint application design)** will be used to accelerate the generation of information requirements and develop the initial systems design. JAD brings end users and information systems specialists into a room together for an interactive design of the system. Properly prepared and facilitated, JAD sessions can significantly speed up the design phase while involving users at an intense level.

This Web-based Inventory Ordering System was developed using Information Builders' Cactus, a development toolset that can cut development time for complex applications by more than 50 percent. Rapid application development (RAD) tools allow developers to build systems much more rapidly than conventional methods.

WINDOW ON ORGANIZATIONS

Gulf Canada Refines Budgeting with Object-Oriented Software

How can a company control its cash flow when its estimates differ greatly from its actual expenditures? If that company is Gulf Canada Resources, Ltd., it solves the problem by building an object-oriented budgeting system known as Odin, to be run over its corporate intranet.

Gulf Canada is a $4.48 billion oil and natural gas drilling and refining company that is headquartered in Calgary, Alberta. It has a few thousand active drilling sites scattered throughout the vast regions of northwestern Alberta. Traditionally the field foremen managing these sites have compiled and submitted budget forecasts for each site annually. But the foremen were stationed in such remote locations that it was difficult for them to submit their estimates directly. Instead, they sent their estimates to their managers to be passed on to the corporate accountants. Their managers customarily "adjusted" the numbers to conform with their own views. Problems arose because history indicated that the estimates from the foremen, who were at the drilling sites, were much more accurate than the revisions made by managers. Corporate management decided that the site foremen needed a way to submit their estimates directly, a decision that resulted in Gulf Canada's new intranet-based budgeting system.

The timing of the decision to build a new budgeting system created a development problem because there were only three months remaining in the 1997 fiscal year. Management wanted the system ready for the 1998 fiscal year, so IT had to develop it on a crash basis. IT decided to bypass the traditional request-for-proposal process used to purchase a package and chose to develop its own system. The project staff used Cactus object-oriented development tools from Information Builders, Inc. The system uses a Sun Microsystems SPARC3000 server running an Oracle database.

Cactus is an application-development environment useful for business applications that can combine transaction processing, decision support, and batch processing. It provides visual object-based development tools that can create highly reusable components for distributed client/server or Web environments.

Gulf Canada met the deadline, and according to Kevin Rasmussen, applications coordinator, the company now has "an application that allows us to assemble all our corporate production and cost forecasts within our system." Outfitted with Web browsers, the company's field force can forecast costs on a well-by-well basis.

With the existence of the new system, the company no longer needs to rely on an annual cost estimate to compare to annual expenditures. Instead, the new plan is to use the system on a rolling 12-month basis, enabling appropriate staffers regularly to check field-level production figures against cost forecasts. Now, according to Rasmussen, the company can react to expense variances more effectively, adding or removing capital from projects where needed. In addition to the field foremen, employees from accounting, corporate services, IT, legal, and financial departments are also using the new system. Rasmussen claims that before the system, "The budget cycle was a hellish time, because we had to add everything up from scratch. Now, we're able to run scenarios in a matter of minutes."

To Think About: ***Why do you think the choice of an object-oriented development tool was critical to this project? What are the technology, organization, and management implications of the move to this new system?***

Sources: Hakhi Alakhun El, "Content by Committee," *Information Week,* January 12, 1998; and Thomas Hoffman, "Gulf Canada Refines Budgeting," *Computerworld,* January 12, 1998.

Software Reengineering

software reengineering A methodology that addresses the problem of aging software by salvaging and upgrading it so that the users can avoid a long and expensive replacement project.

reverse engineering The process of converting existing programs, files, and database descriptions into corresponding design-level components that can then be used to create new applications.

Software reengineering is a methodology that addresses the problem of aging software. A great deal of the software that organizations use was written without the benefit of a methodology such as structured analysis, design, and programming. Such software is difficult to maintain or update. However, the software serves the organization well enough to continue to be used, if only it could be more easily maintained. The purpose of software reengineering is to salvage such software by upgrading it so that users can avoid a long and expensive replacement project. In essence, developers use reengineering to extract design and programming intelligence from existing systems, thereby creating new systems without starting from scratch. Reengineering involves three steps: (1) reverse engineering, (2) revision of design and program specifications, and (3) forward engineering.

Reverse engineering entails extracting the underlying business specifications from existing systems. Older, nonstructured systems do not have structured documentation of the business functions the system is intended to support. Nor do they have adequate

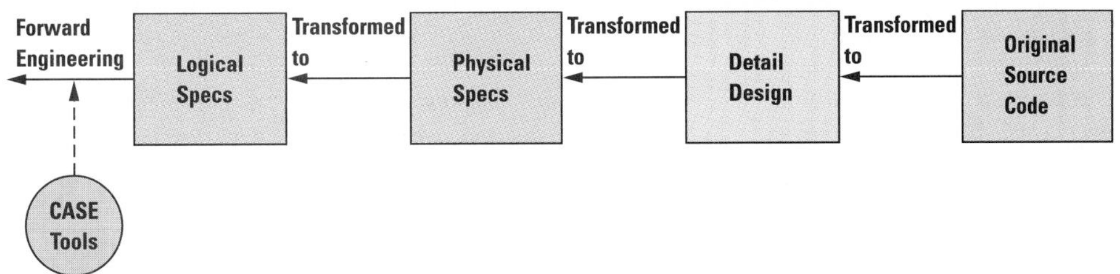

FIGURE 11.12 The reverse engineering process. Reverse engineering captures an existing system's functional capabilities and processing logic in a simplified form that can be revised and updated as the basis of a new replacement system. CASE tools can be used during forward engineering.

documentation of either the system design or the programs. Reverse engineering tools read and analyze the program's existing code, file, and database descriptions and produce structured documentation of the system. The output will show design-level components, such as entities, attributes, and processes. With structured documentation to work from, the project team can then revise the design and specifications to meet current business requirements. In the final step, **forward engineering,** the revised specifications are used to generate new, structured code for a structured and now maintainable system. In Figure 11.12, you can follow the reengineering process.

forward engineering The final step in reengineering when the revised specifications are used to generate new, structured program code for a structured and maintainable system.

Although software reengineering can reduce system development and maintenance costs, it is a very complex undertaking. Additional research and analysis are usually required to determine all of the business rules and data requirements for the new system (Aiken, Muntz, and Richards, 1994).

Management Wrap-Up

Selection of a systems-building approach can have a large impact on the time, cost, and end product of systems development. Managers should be aware of the strengths and weaknesses of each systems-building approach and the types of problems for which each is best suited.

MANAGEMENT

Organizational needs should drive the selection of a systems-building approach. The impact of application software packages and of outsourcing should be carefully evaluated before they are selected because these approaches give organizations less control over the systems-building process.

ORGANIZATION

Various tools and methodologies are available to support the systems-building process. Key technology decisions should be based on the organization's familiarity with the methodology or technology and its compatibility with the organization's information requirements and information architecture. Organizational discipline is required to use these technologies effectively.

TECHNOLOGY

For Discussion:

1. Why is selecting a systems development approach an important business decision? Who should participate in the selection process?
2. Some have said that the best way to reduce system development costs is to use application software packages or fourth-generation tools. Do you agree? Why or why not?

SUMMARY

1. **Appraise system-building alternatives: the traditional systems lifecycle, prototyping, application software packages, end-user development, and outsourcing.** The traditional systems lifecycle—the oldest method for building systems—breaks the development of an information system into six formal stages: (1) project definition, (2) systems study, (3) design, (4) programming, (5) installation, and (6) post-implementation. The stages must proceed sequentially, have defined outputs, and require formal approval before the next stage can commence.

   Prototyping consists of building an experimental system rapidly and inexpensively for end users to interact with and evaluate. The prototype is refined and enhanced until users are satisfied that it includes all of their requirements and can be used as a template to create the final system.

   Developing an information system using an application software package eliminates the need for writing software programs when developing an information system. Using a software package cuts down on the amount of design, testing, installation, and maintenance work required to build a system.

   End-user development is the development of information systems by end users, either alone or with minimal assistance from information systems specialists. End-user-developed systems can be created rapidly and informally using fourth-generation software tools.

   Outsourcing consists of using an external vendor to build (or operate) a firm's information systems. The system may be custom-built or may use a software package. In either case, the work is done by the vendor rather than by the organization's internal information systems staff.

2. **Compare the strengths and limitations of each approach.** The traditional system lifecycle is still useful for large projects that need formal specifications and tight management control over each stage of system-building. However, the traditional method is very rigid and costly for developing a system, and is not well suited for unstructured, decision-oriented applications where requirements cannot be immediately visualized.

   Prototyping encourages end-user involvement in systems development and iteration of design until specifications are captured accurately. The rapid creation of prototypes can result in systems that have not been completely tested or documented or that are technically inadequate for a production environment.

   Application software packages are helpful if a firm does not have the internal information systems staff or financial resources to custom-develop a system. To meet an organization's unique requirements, packages may require extensive modifications that can substantially raise development costs. A package may not be a feasible solution if implementation necessitates extensive customization and changes in the organization's procedures.

   The primary benefits of end-user development are improved requirements determination, reduced application backlog, and increased end-user participation in, and control of, the systems development process. However, end-user development, in conjunction with distributed computing, has introduced new organizational risks by propagating information systems and data resources that do not necessarily meet quality assurance standards and that are not easily controlled by traditional means.

   Outsourcing can save application development costs or allow firms to develop applications without an internal information systems staff, but it can also make firms lose control over their information systems and make them too dependent on external vendors.

3. **Assess the solutions to the management problems created by these approaches.** Organizations can overcome some of the limitations of using software packages by performing a thorough requirements analysis and using rigorous package selection procedures to determine the extent to which a package will satisfy its requirements. The organization can customize the package or modify its procedures to ensure a better fit with the package.

   Information centers help promote and control end-user development. They provide end users with appropriate hardware, software, and technical expertise to create their own applications and encourage adherence to application development standards. Organizations can also develop new policies and procedures concerning system development standards, training, data administration, and controls to manage end-user computing effectively.

   Organizations can benefit from outsourcing by only outsourcing part of their information systems, by thoroughly understanding which information systems functions are appropriate to outsource, by designing outsourcing contracts carefully, and by trying to build a working partnership with the outsourcing vendor.

4. **Describe the principal tools and methodologies used for systems development.** Structured analysis highlights the flow of data and the processes through which data are transformed. Its principal tool is the data flow diagram. Structured design and programming are software design disciplines that produce reliable, well-documented software with a simple, clear structure that is easy for others to understand and maintain. System flowcharts are useful for documenting the physical aspects of system design.

Computer-aided software engineering (CASE) automates methodologies for systems development. It promotes standards and improves coordination and consistency during systems development. CASE tools help system builders build a better model of a system and facilitate revision of design specifications to correct errors. Object-oriented software development is expected to reduce the time and cost of writing software and of making maintenance changes because it models a system as a series of reusable objects that combine both data and procedures. Software reengineering helps system builders reconfigure aging software to conform to structured design principles, making it easier to maintain.

KEY TERMS

Application software package, 346
Computer-aided software engineering (CASE), 359
Customization, 346
Data flow diagram (DFD), 354
Design, 342
Development methodology, 353
End-user development, 349
End-user interface, 344
Forward engineering, 363
Information center, 350
Installation, 342
Iteration construct, 357
Iterative, 343
Joint application design (JAD), 361
Middleware, 347
Module, 356
Object-oriented software development, 358
Outsourcing, 350
Post-implementation, 342
Process specifications, 355
Programming, 342
Project definition, 342
Prototype, 343
Prototyping, 343
Rapid application development (RAD), 360
Request for Proposal (RFP), 348
Reverse engineering, 362
Selection construct, 357
Sequence construct, 356
Software reengineering, 362
Structure chart, 356
Structured, 353
Structured analysis, 354
Structured design, 356
Structured programming, 356
System flowchart, 357
Systems lifecycle, 341
Systems study, 342

REVIEW QUESTIONS

1. What is the traditional systems lifecycle? Describe each of its steps.
2. What are the advantages and disadvantages of building an information system using the traditional systems lifecycle?
3. What do we mean by information system prototyping? What are its benefits and limitations?
4. List and describe the steps in the prototyping process.
5. What is an application software package? What are the advantages and disadvantages of developing information systems based on software packages?
6. What do we mean by end-user development? What are its advantages and disadvantages?
7. What is an information center? How can information centers solve some of the management problems created by end-user development?
8. Name some policies and procedures for managing end-user development.
9. What is outsourcing? Under what circumstances should it be used for building information systems?
10. What is structured analysis? What is the role of the data flow diagram in structured analysis?
11. What are the principles of structured design? How is it related to structured programming?
12. Describe the use of system flowcharts.
13. What is the difference between object-oriented software development and traditional structured methodologies?
14. What is CASE? How can it help system builders?
15. What is rapid application development (RAD)? What system-building tools and methods can be used in RAD?
16. What are software reengineering and reverse engineering? How can they help system builders?

GROUP PROJECT

With a group of your classmates, obtain product information for two similar PC application software packages. You might compare Dac/Easy Accounting/Payroll and QuickBooks for small business accounting or Quicken and Microsoft Money for personal finance. You can obtain some of this information from the Web and perhaps find demonstration versions of the packages on the vendor Web sites. Evaluate the strengths and limitations of the packages you select. Present your findings to the class.

TOOLS FOR INTERACTIVE LEARNING

■ **INTERNET:** The Internet Connection for this chapter will direct you to the SAP Web site where you can complete an exercise to evaluate the capabilities of this major multinational software package and learn more about enterprise resource planning. You can also use the Interactive Study Guide to test your knowledge of the topics in this chapter, and get instant feedback where you need more practice.

■ **CD-ROM:** If you purchase and use the Multimedia Edition CD-ROM with this chapter, you can complete two interactive exercises. The first asks you to construct a data flow diagram and the second asks you to select an appropriate systems development approach for various business scenarios. You can also find a video clip illustrating the use of Lotus Notes as an application development platform, an audio overview of the major themes of this chapter, and bullet text summarizing the key points of the chapter.

CASE STUDY

Can a German Software Giant Provide Enterprise Solutions?

SAP A.G., based in Walldorf, Germany, is Europe's largest vendor of software running on IBM mainframe computers and is an emerging leader in software packages for client/server environments. It has mushroomed into the world's fourth-largest software company. Among its clients are the Dow Chemical Company, E.I. du Pont de Nemours & Company, Chevron Corporation, Apple Computer, IBM, Intel, and the Exxon Corporation.

SAP's R/3 software package for client/server environments automates a wide range of business processes in human resources, plant management, and manufacturing. The software modules are integrated so they can automatically share data between them, and they have their own database-management system. The programs come in twelve different languages. Specific versions are tailored to accommodate different currencies, tax laws, and accounting practices. Managers can generate reports in their own local languages and currencies and have the same reports generated in the language and currency that are used as the corporate standard by top management. R/3 is considered one of the leading packages for enterprise resource planning (ERP) to integrate all facets of a business.

Businesses appreciate the multinational flavor of the software, especially its ability to overcome language and currency barriers fluently and to connect divisions and operating units spread around the world. Marion Merrel Dow Inc. is using SAP software for its financial and sales-and-service departments because it believes that no other available packages can handle its global business needs. Nearly 7000 companies use R/3.

Despite being a standard software package, SAP software can be customized approximately 10 percent to handle multinational currencies and accounting practices. SAP makes this flexibility one of its key selling points. As another selling point, SAP promotes the package as a platform for business reengineering.

R/3 is an integrated, client/server, distributed system with a graphical user interface. It can operate on a wide range of computers, including UNIX-based machines, Power PC-enabled IBM AS/400 minicomputers, and other servers. The back-end server and front-end client portions of R/3 can run on several different operating systems, including five variations of UNIX, Digital Equipment Corporation's VAX/VMS operating system, Hewlett-Packard's MPE operating system, OS/2, and Windows NT.

The R/3 package includes integrated financial accounting, production planning, sales and distribution, cost-center accounting, order-costing, materials management, human resources, quality assurance, fixed assets management, plant maintenance, and project planning applications. Users do not have to shut down one application to move to another; they can click on a menu choice. R/3 also provides word processing, filing systems, e-mail, and other office support functions.

R/3 can be configured to run on a single hardware platform, or it can be partitioned to run on separate machines (in whatever combination users choose) in order to minimize network traffic and place data where users need it the most. For instance, a firm could put the data used most frequently by its accounting department on a server located close to the accounting department to minimize network traffic. A central data dictionary keeps track of data and its location to maintain the integrity of distributed data. SAP will sell clients a blueprint of R/3's information, data, and function models and software tools to facilitate custom development and integration of existing applications into R/3.

The management of SAP America, Inc. (the Lester, Pennsylvania, subsidiary of SAP A.G.), thinks that the most important feature of R/3 may be the way it helps organizations automate and even redesign their business processes. By adopting the system design offered by the package, companies can evaluate and streamline their business processes. The promise of reengineering was what attracted the Eastman Kodak Company to SAP software. Kodak launched a pilot project in 1991 that installed SAP programs to redefine the job of order taking. The SAP package lets order takers make immediate decisions about granting customers credit and lets them access production data on-line so that they can tell customers exactly when their orders will be available for shipment. The project resulted in a 70 percent reduction in the amount of time it took to deliver products; response time to customers also was cut in half. These results prompted Kodak to use SAP software as the global architecture for all of its core systems.

The intricate and sophisticated features of SAP software deeply affect the infrastructure of a corporation. Installing SAP's fully integrated suite of software modules with all the business alterations required is a complex process with many interdependent options, which can overwhelm smaller firms lacking the resources of top-tier large corporations. Forrester Research, in Cambridge, Massachusetts, estimates that for every dollar spent on SAP R/3 software, five more must be spent on training and systems integration.

Owens-Corning Fiberglass Corporation adopted R/3 as an engine for broad company overhaul. Until recently, customers had to call an Owens-Corning shingle plant for a load of shingles and place additional calls to order insulation or siding. Each plant had its own product lines, pricing schedules, and trucking carriers. Factories limped along with antiquated PCs. The company operated like a collection of autonomous fiefdoms.

R/3 demanded that the corporation adopt a single product list and a single price list. Staff members initially resisted. The company grossly underestimated the cost of installing the system and of training employees to use the new system. (Actual training costs were expected to reach 13 percent, compared with initial estimates of 6 percent.) For example, when the system was installed, order-entry transactions took ten times longer to process than they had before. It took several weeks of research and the use of a special software tool to track transactions through a network to diagnose and fix the problem.

On the other hand, Owens-Corning expected R/3 to save the company $18 million in 1997 and $50 million in 1998 by streamlining business processes and eliminating jobs. Factory-floor employees would be able to use R/3 to confirm shipments of insulation or roofing shingles as the products left the plant. The shipping information would automatically update the general ledger. But if someone made a mistake and did not catch it right away, R/3's internal logic would force the company's finance staff to hunt for that transaction to balance the books.

SAP has a large internal staff to support its software packages, but it also uses legions of consultants from large consulting firms such as Price Waterhouse, Andersen Consulting, EDS Corporation, and Coopers & Lybrand, as well as smaller consulting firms. These external consultants work with SAP clients to install the SAP packages. SAP is growing so fast that there is a worldwide shortage of SAP experts with experience implementing R/3.

One reason for the shortage of consultants is that it can take years for even experienced technologists to understand all of the complexities and methodologies of SAP software. It takes about three years, or two or three installations of the package, before a consultant becomes an expert in the software. (R/3 was built with SAP's own internally-developed programming language called Abap. Users must work with Abap to modify or extend the SAP software package.) SAP pairs one or more of its seasoned eight- to ten-year German veterans with less-experienced U.S. consultants at each installation. However, the SAP experts tend to be troubleshooters or product experts, rather than business consultants, so clients do not necessarily get the best advice on how to integrate the software into their business operations efficiently and painlessly. The perception remains among some U.S. companies that even an on-site SAP expert who knows the financial accounting module cannot correct a problem in the sales and distribution module.

To augment the ranks of qualified consultants, SAP built a world training headquarters in Walldorf, costing an estimated $50 million to $60 million. It recruited more consultants by signing agreements with new consulting firms, such as Cap Gemini America.

SAP recently introduced Accelerated SAP (ASAP), a program that promises to cut implementation time by as much as half. ASAP provides tools, templates, and questionnaires for companies to create a step-by-step road map that lets users clearly define each task. The templates incorporate "best practices" that show how things are done and help users figure out where to begin.

To make installations easier, SAP has broken down the R/3 system into independent modules. Earlier versions of R/3 required users to implement the entire package and then turn on what they need. The new releases will let users upgrade selected pieces instead of the entire package.

Sources: Randy Weston, "Users Gravitate to 'Broken' Software," *Computerworld,* February 23, 1998; "This German Software is Complex, Expensive—and Wildly Popular," *The Wall Street Journal,* March 4, 1997; Caryn Gillolly, "Almost Up and Running," *InformationWeek,* October 13, 1997; Tom Stein, "Fast Deployment," *InformationWeek,* February 3, 1997; Doug Bartholomew, "SAP America: R/2 + R/3 = 5?" *InformationWeek,* January 10, 1994.

Case Study Questions

1. What advantages and disadvantages of application software packages are illustrated by SAP?
2. Analyze the specific strengths and weaknesses of the SAP software package.
3. If you were the manager of a corporation looking for new business application software, would you choose SAP? Would you choose another package? Why or why not? What management, organization, and technology factors would you consider?

CHAPTER 12

Managing Knowledge

chapter outline

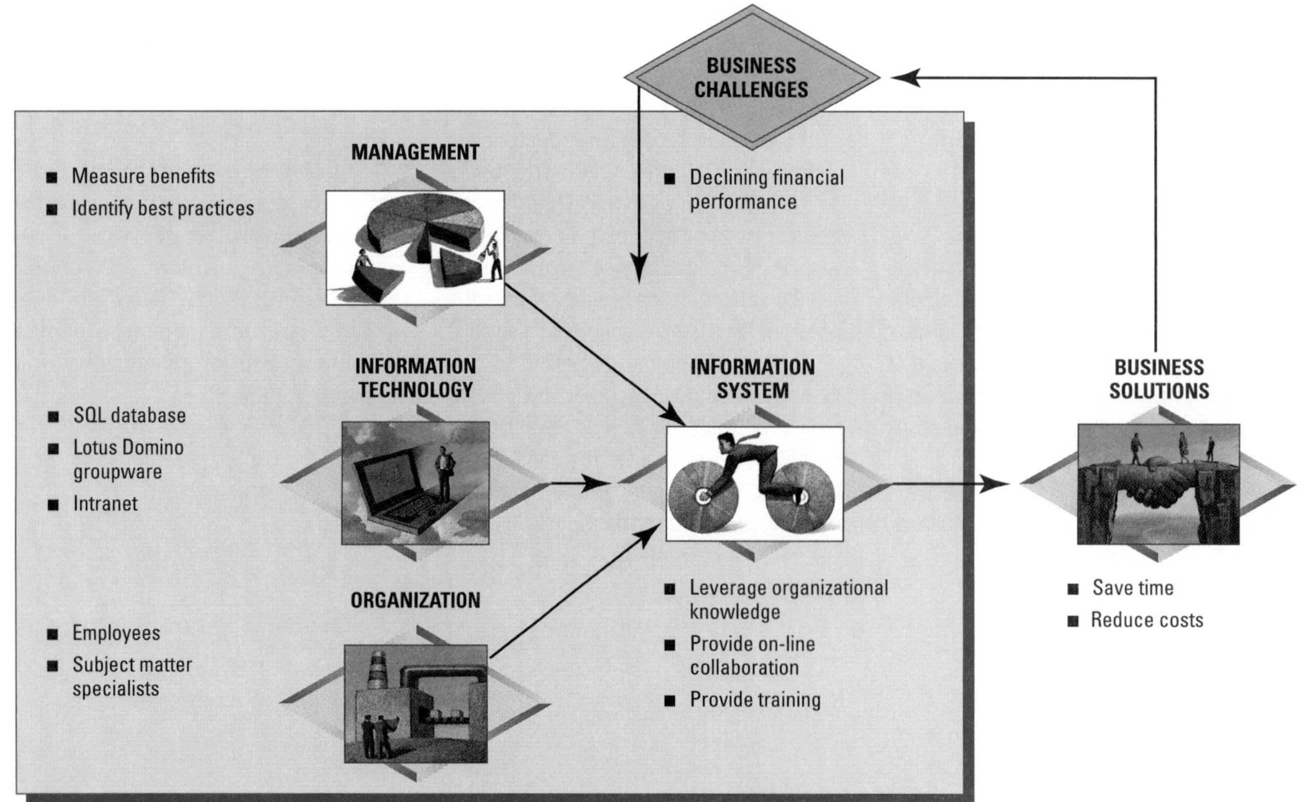

Shell Wakes Up with Knowledge Management

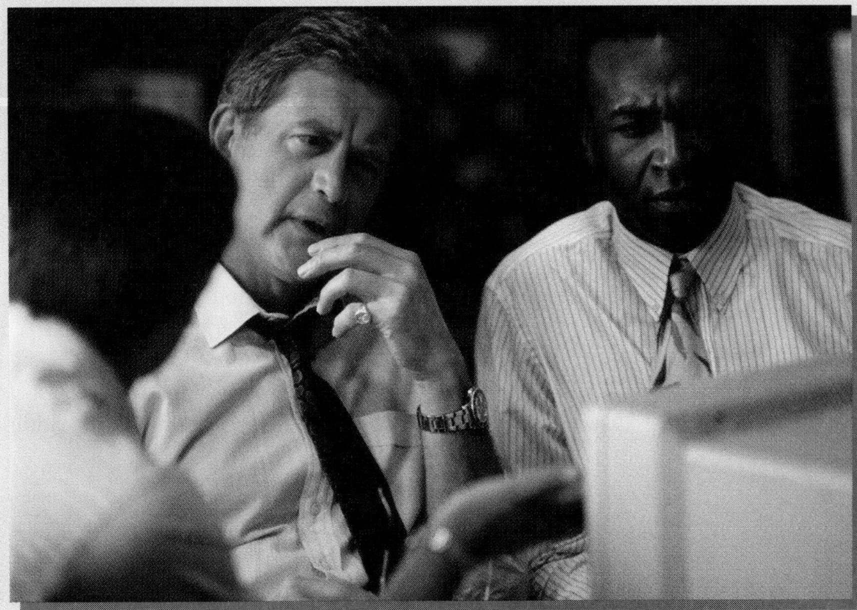

In 1991, Shell Oil Co. reported the worst financial results in its history. That news became a wake-up call to make some serious changes in the way it ran its business. One solution was to put more emphasis on making better use of the knowledge and experience of its employees. If Shell's entire work force of 21,000 could learn about the "best practice" of a single person, the company might reap enormous savings in time and effort and perhaps use these ideas to innovate further.

Shell used information systems to create a communications and collaboration environment that would act as a "knowledge multiplier." Ten subject-matter specialists scoured Shell sources and external sources such as universities, consultants, other companies, and research literature for leading-edge practices and ideas to populate a Knowledge Management System (KMS). The KMS contains knowledge in three areas: business models, leadership, and engagement, or human interactions. Its repository contains 1000 documents and 50 "best practices," such as a model developed by a university professor to help an organization meet its goals. The model was adopted by all of Shell's four major operating units. Other groups at Shell, such as geologists, use similar knowledge management systems.

The Knowledge Management System was developed by Shell and a systems integrator and became operational in September 1997. Its knowledge repository uses an SQL database. A Lotus Domino groupware application allows employees to carry on dialogues through the company intranet. The author of a best practice in the repository might use this tool to talk with colleagues about his or her experiences.

Sandi Fitch, a senior executive at Shell Services International, uses the KMS to mentor technical subordinates in business leadership. By using the KMS, she can walk through a business model, review concepts, do some exercises with her team, and then examine the best practices of others.

About 15,000 Shell employees currently use the system, and it soon will be available to all. Shell is only starting to analyze the benefits of its knowledge system. Initially, management will measure benefits in terms of usage and the number of best practices posted to the database. Later it will track the ideas from the system that actually are put into practice.

Source: Adapted from Gary H. Anthes, "Learning How to Share," *Computerworld,* February 23, 1998.

Management Challenges

Shell Oil Co.'s use of its Knowledge Management System is one example of how systems can be used to leverage organizational knowledge by making it more easily available. Collaborating and communicating with practitioners and experts and sharing ideas and information have become essential requirements in business, science, and government. In an information economy, capturing and distributing intelligence and knowledge and enhancing group collaboration have become vital to organizational innovation and survival. Special systems can be used for managing organizational knowledge, but they raise the following management challenges:

1. **Designing information systems that genuinely enhance the productivity of knowledge workers.** Information systems that truly enhance the productivity of knowledge workers may be difficult to build because the manner in which information technology can enhance higher-level tasks such as those performed by managers and professionals (i.e., scientists or engineers) is not always clearly understood (Sheng et al., 1989/90). Some aspects of organizational knowledge cannot be captured easily or codified, or the information that organizations finally manage to capture may become outdated as environments change (Malhotra, 1998). High-level knowledge workers may resist the introduction of any new technology, or they may resist knowledge work systems because such systems diminish personal control and creativity.

2. **Creating robust expert systems.** Expert systems must be changed every time there is a change in the organizational environment. Each time there is a change in the rules used by experts, they must be reprogrammed. It is difficult to provide expert systems with the flexibility of human experts. Many thousands of businesses have undertaken experimental projects in expert systems, but only a small percentage have created expert systems that actually can be used on a production basis.

learning objectives

After completing this chapter, you will be able to:

1. Explain the importance of knowledge management in contemporary organizations.
2. Describe the applications that are most useful for distributing, creating, and sharing knowledge in the firm.
3. Evaluate the role of artificial intelligence in knowledge management.
4. Demonstrate how organizations can use expert systems and case-based reasoning to capture knowledge.
5. Demonstrate how organizations can use neural networks and other intelligent techniques to improve their knowledge base.

This chapter examines information system applications specifically designed to help organizations create, capture, and distribute knowledge and information. First, we examine information systems for supporting information and knowledge work. Then we look at the ways that organizations can use artificial intelligence technologies for capturing and storing knowledge and expertise.

12.1 KNOWLEDGE MANAGEMENT IN THE ORGANIZATION

Chapter 1 described the emergence of the information economy, in which the major source of wealth and prosperity is the production and distribution of information and knowledge. For example, 55 percent of the U.S. labor force consists of knowledge and information workers, and 60 percent of the gross domestic product of the United States comes from the knowledge and information sectors, such as finance and publishing. Knowledge-intensive technology is vital to these information-intense sectors, but it also plays a major role in traditional industrial sectors such as the automobile and mining industries.

In an information economy, knowledge and core competencies—the two or three things that an organization does best—are key organizational assets. Producing unique products or services or producing them at a lower cost than competitors is based on superior knowledge of the production process and superior design. Knowing how to do things effectively and efficiently in ways that other organizations cannot duplicate is a primary source of profit. Some management theorists believe that these knowledge assets are as important, if not more important, than physical and financial assets in ensuring the competitiveness and survival of the firm. Management of organizational knowledge may be especially important in flattened or network organizations where layers of management have been eliminated to help members of teams and task forces maintain ties to other specialists in their field (Favela, 1997).

As knowledge becomes a central productive and strategic asset, the success of the organization increasingly depends on its ability to gather, produce, maintain, and disseminate knowledge. Developing procedures and routines to optimize the creation, flow, learning, and sharing of knowledge and information in the firm becomes a central management responsibility. The process of systematically and actively managing and leveraging the stores of knowledge in an organization is called **knowledge management.** Information systems can play a valuable role in knowledge management, helping the organization optimize its flow of information and capture its knowledge base.

knowledge management The process of systematically and actively managing and leveraging the stores of knowledge in an organization.

Information Systems and Knowledge Management

All the major types of information systems described so far facilitate the flow of information and have organizational knowledge embedded in them. However, office automation systems (OAS), knowledge work systems (KWS), group collaboration systems, and artificial intelligence applications are especially useful for knowledge management because they focus on supporting information and knowledge work and on defining and capturing the organization's knowledge base. This knowledge base may include (1) structured internal knowledge, such as product manuals or research reports; (2) external knowledge, such as competitive intelligence; and (3) informal internal knowledge, often called *tacit* knowledge, which resides in the minds of organizational members but has not been documented in structured form (Davenport, DeLong, and Beers, 1998).

Figure 12.1 illustrates the array of information systems specifically designed to support knowledge management. Office automation systems (OAS) help disseminate and coordinate the flow of information in the organization. Knowledge work systems (KWS) support the activities of highly skilled knowledge workers and professionals as they create new knowledge and try to integrate it into the firm. Group collaboration and support systems support the creation and sharing of knowledge among people working in groups. Artificial intelligence systems provide organizations and managers with codified knowledge that can be reused by others in the organization.

Knowledge Work and Productivity

In information economies, organizational productivity depends on increasing the productivity of information and knowledge workers. Consequently, companies have made massive investments in technology to support information work. Information technology now accounts for 41 percent of total business expenditures on capital equipment in

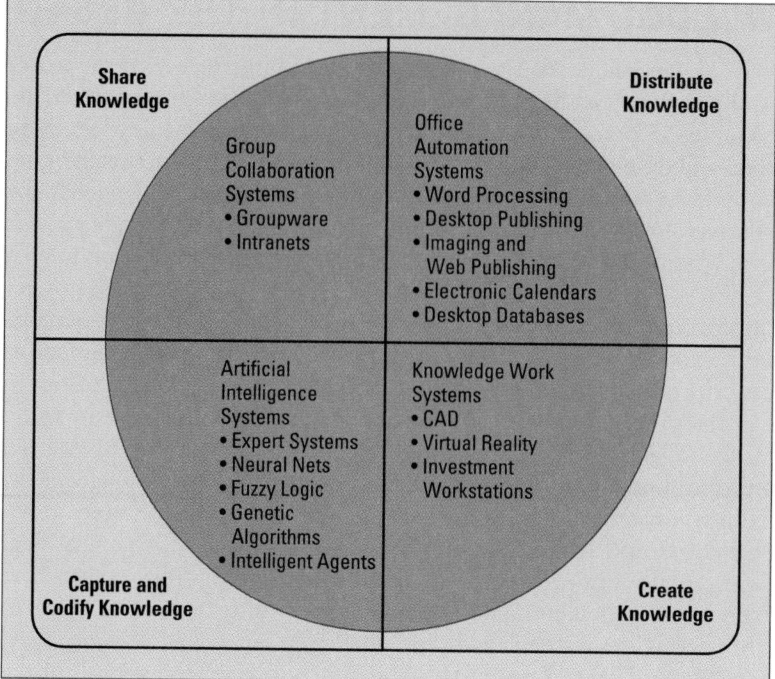

FIGURE 12.1

A number of contemporary information systems are designed to give close-in support to information workers at many levels in the organization.

the United States (Roach, 1996). Much of that information technology investment has poured into offices and the service sector. Office automation and professional work systems are among the fastest-growing information system applications.

Although information technology has increased productivity in manufacturing, the extent to which computers have enhanced the productivity of information workers is under debate. Some studies show that investment in information technology has not led to any appreciable growth in productivity among office workers. The average white-collar productivity gain from 1980 to 1990 was only 0.28 percent each year. Corporate downsizings and cost-reduction measures have increased worker efficiency but have not yet led to sustained enhancements signifying genuine productivity gains (Roach, 1988 and 1996). Other studies suggest that information technology investments are starting to generate a productivity payback. Brynjolffson and Hitt's examination of information systems spending at 380 large firms during a five-year period found that return on investment (ROI) averaged more than 50 percent per year for computers of all sizes (Brynjolfsson and Hitt, 1993). It is too early to tell whether these gains are short-term or represent a genuine turnaround in service-sector productivity.

Productivity changes among information workers are difficult to measure because of the problems of identifying suitable units of output for information work (Panko, 1991). How does one measure the output of a law office? Should one measure productivity by examining the number of forms completed per employee (a measure of physical unit productivity), or by examining the amount of revenue produced per employee (a measure of financial unit productivity) in an information- and knowledge-intense industry?

In addition to reducing costs, computers may increase the quality of products and services for consumers. These intangible benefits are difficult to measure and consequently are not addressed by conventional productivity measures. Moreover, because of competition, the value created by computers may primarily flow to customers rather than to the company making the investments (Brynjolffson, 1996).

Introduction of information technology does not automatically guarantee productivity. Desktop computers, e-mail, and fax applications actually can generate more drafts, memos, spreadsheets, and messages—increasing bureaucratic red tape and paperwork. Firms are more likely to produce high returns on information technology investments if they rethink their procedures, processes, and business goals.

12.2 INFORMATION AND KNOWLEDGE WORK SYSTEMS

Information work is work that consists primarily of creating or processing information. It is carried out by information workers who usually are divided into two subcategories: **data workers**, who primarily process and disseminate information; and **knowledge workers**, who primarily create knowledge and information.

Examples of data workers include secretaries, sales personnel, accountants, and draftsmen. Researchers, designers, architects, writers, and judges are examples of knowledge workers. Data workers usually can be distinguished from knowledge workers because knowledge workers usually have higher levels of education and membership in professional organizations. In addition, knowledge workers exercise independent judgment as a routine aspect of their work. Data and knowledge workers have different information requirements and different systems to support them.

information work Work that primarily consists of creating or processing information.

data workers People such as secretaries or bookkeepers who process and disseminate the organization's information and paperwork.

knowledge workers People such as engineers, scientists, or architects who design products or services or create knowledge for the organization.

Distributing Knowledge: Office and Document Management Systems

Most data work and a great deal of knowledge work takes place in offices, including most of the work done by managers. The office plays a major role in coordinating the flow of information throughout the entire organization. The office has three basic functions (see Figure 12.2):

- Managing and coordinating the work of data and knowledge workers
- Connecting the work of the local information workers with all levels and functions of the organization
- Connecting the organization to the external world, including customers, suppliers, government regulators, and external auditors.

Office workers span a very broad range of workers—professionals, managers, sales, and clerical workers working alone or in groups. Their major activities include the following:

- Managing documents, including document creation, storage, retrieval, and dissemination
- Scheduling for individuals and groups
- Communicating, including initiating, receiving, and managing voice, digital, and document-based communications for individuals and groups
- Managing data, such as on employees, customers, and vendors.

These activities can be supported by office automation systems (see Table 12.1). **Office automation systems (OAS)** can be defined as any application of information technology that intends to increase productivity of information workers in the office. Fifteen

office automation systems (OAS) Computer systems, such as word processing, voice-mail systems, and imaging, that are designed to increase the productivity of information workers in the office.

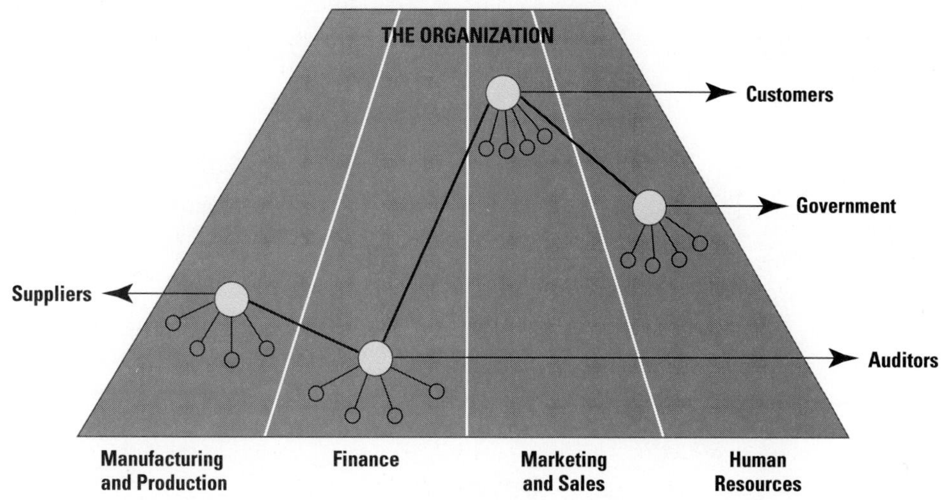

FIGURE 12.2

The three major roles of offices. Offices perform three major roles. [1] They coordinate the work of local professionals and information workers. [2] They coordinate work in the organization across levels and functions. [3] They couple the organization to the external environment.

TABLE 12.1 Typical Office Automation Systems

Office Activity	Technology
Managing documents	Word processing; desktop publishing; document imaging; Web publishing; work-flow managers
Scheduling	Electronic calendars; groupware; intranets
Communicating	E-mail; voice mail; digital answering systems; groupware; intranets
Managing data	Desktop databases; spreadsheets; user-friendly interfaces to mainframe databases

years ago, office automation meant only the creation, processing, and management of documents. Today professional knowledge and information work remains highly document-centered. However, digital image processing—words and documents—is also at the core of systems, as are high-speed digital communications services. Because office work involves many people jointly engaged in projects, contemporary office automation systems have powerful group assistance tools like networked digital calendars. An ideal office environment would be based on a seamless network of digital machines linking professional, clerical, and managerial work groups and running a variety of types of software.

Although word processing and desktop publishing address the creation and presentation of documents, they only exacerbate the existing paper avalanche problem. Work-flow problems arising from paper handling are enormous. It has been estimated that up to 85 percent of corporate information is stored on paper. Locating and updating information in that format is a great source of organizational inefficiency.

document imaging systems Systems that convert documents and images into digital form so that they can be stored and accessed by the computer.

jukebox A device for storing and retrieving many optical disks.

One way to reduce problems stemming from paper work-flow is to employ document imaging systems. **Document imaging systems** are systems that convert documents and images into digital form so they can be stored and accessed by a computer. Such systems store, retrieve, and manipulate a digitized image of a document, allowing the document itself to be discarded. The system must contain a scanner that converts the document image into a bit-mapped image, storing that image as a graphic. If the document is not in active use, it usually is stored on an optical disk system. Optical disks, kept on-line in a **jukebox** (a device for storing and retrieving many optical disks), require up to a minute to retrieve the document automatically.

Essex County Massachusetts implemented an automated document imaging and retrieval system for many of its records. Processing of mortgages, liens, deeds, and other land records has been streamlined and made more cost effective.

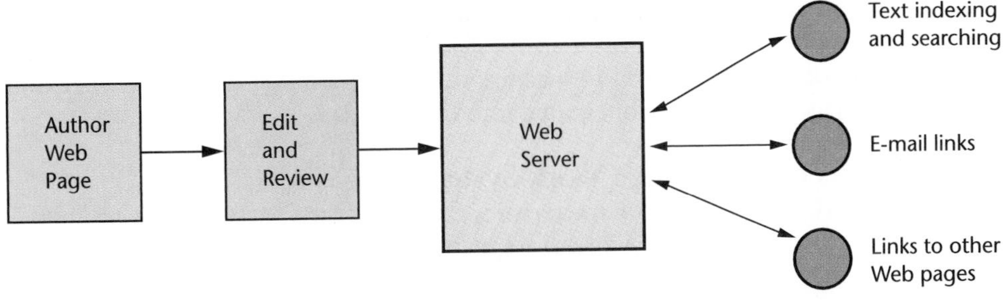

FIGURE 12.3
Web publishing and document management. An author can post information on an intranet Web server, where it can be accessed through a variety of mechanisms.

An imaging system also requires an **index server** to contain the indexes that will allow users to identify and retrieve a document when needed. Index data are entered so that a document can be retrieved in a variety of ways, depending upon the application. For example, the index may contain the document scan date, the customer name and number, the document type, and some subject information. Finally, the system must include retrieval equipment, primarily workstations capable of handling graphics, although printers usually are included. USAA's imaging system in Chapter 2 illustrates the kinds of benefits imaging technology can provide.

index server In imaging systems, a device that stores the indexes that allow a user to identify and retrieve a specific document.

Traditional document-management systems can be expensive, requiring proprietary client/server networks, special client software, and storage capabilities. Intranets provide a low-cost and universally available platform for basic document publishing, and many companies are using them for this purpose. Employees can publish information using Web-page authoring tools and post it to an intranet Web server where it can be shared and accessed throughout the company with standard Web browsers. These Web-like "documents" can be multimedia objects combining text, graphics, audio, and video along with hyperlinks. After a document has been posted to the server, it can be linked to other documents (see Figure 12.3).

For more sophisticated document-management functions, such as controlling changes to documents, maintaining histories of activity and changes in the managed documents, and the ability to search documents on either content or index terms, commercial Web-based systems such as those from IntraNet Solutions or Open Text are available. Vendors such as FileNet and Documentum have enhanced their traditional document-management systems with Web capabilities.

To achieve the large productivity gains promised by imaging technology, organizations must redesign their work-flow. In the past, the existence of only one copy of a document largely shaped work-flow. Work had to be performed serially; two people could not work on the same document at the same time. Significant staff time was devoted to filing and retrieving documents. After a document has been stored electronically, work-flow management can change the traditional methods of working with documents (see Chapter 10).

Creating Knowledge: Knowledge Work Systems

Knowledge work is that portion of information work that creates new knowledge and information. For example, knowledge workers create new products or find ways to improve existing ones. Knowledge work is segmented into many highly specialized fields, and each field has a different collection of **knowledge work systems (KWS)** that are specialized to support workers in that field. Knowledge workers perform three key roles that are critical to the organization and to the managers who work within the organization:

knowledge work systems (KWS) Information systems that aid knowledge workers in the creation and integration of new knowledge in the organization.

- Keeping the organization up-to-date in knowledge as it develops in the external world—in technology, science, social thought, and the arts
- Serving as internal consultants regarding the areas of their knowledge, the changes taking place, and the opportunities
- Acting as change agents evaluating, initiating, and promoting change projects.

Knowledge workers and data workers have somewhat different information systems support needs. Most knowledge workers rely upon office automation systems such as word processors, voice-mail systems, and calendaring systems, but they also require more specialized knowledge work systems. Knowledge work systems are specifically designed to promote the creation of knowledge and to ensure that new knowledge and technical expertise are properly integrated into the business.

Requirements of Knowledge Work Systems

Knowledge work systems have characteristics that reflect the special needs of knowledge workers. First, knowledge work systems must give knowledge workers the specialized tools they need, such as powerful graphics, analytical tools, and communications and document-management tools. These systems require great computing power in order to handle rapidly the sophisticated graphics or complex calculations necessary to such knowledge workers as scientific researchers, product designers, and financial analysts. Because knowledge workers are so focused on knowledge in the external world, these systems also must give the worker quick and easy access to external databases.

A user-friendly interface is very important to a knowledge worker's system. User-friendly interfaces save time by allowing the user to perform needed tasks and get to required information without having to spend a lot of time learning how to use the computer. Saving time is more important for knowledge workers than for most other employees because knowledge workers are highly paid—wasting a knowledge worker's time is simply too expensive. Figure 12.4 summarizes the requirements of knowledge work systems.

Knowledge workstations often are designed and optimized for the specific tasks to be performed, so a design engineer will require a different workstation than a lawyer. Design engineers need graphics with enough power to handle three-dimensional computer-aided design (CAD) systems. On the other hand, financial analysts are more interested in having access to a myriad of external databases and in optical disk technology so they can access massive amounts of financial data very quickly.

Examples of Knowledge Work Systems

Major knowledge work applications include computer-aided design (CAD) systems, virtual reality systems for simulation and modeling, and financial workstations. **Computer-aided design (CAD)** automates the creation and revision of designs, using computers and sophisticated graphics software. Using a more traditional physical design methodology, each design modification requires a mold to be made and a prototype to be physically tested. That process must be repeated many times, which is a very expensive and time-consuming process. Using a CAD workstation, the designer only needs to make a physical prototype toward the end of the design process because the design can be easily tested and changed on the computer. The ability of CAD software to provide design specifications for the tooling and the manufacturing process also saves a great

computer-aided design (CAD) Information system that automates the creation and revision of designs using sophisticated graphics software.

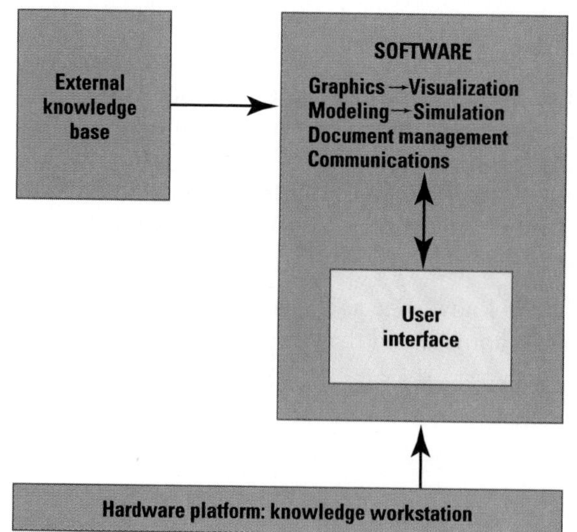

FIGURE 12.4

Requirements of knowledge work systems. Knowledge work systems require strong links to external knowledge bases in addition to specialized hardware and software.

deal of time and money while producing a manufacturing process with far fewer problems. For example, The Maddox Design Group of Atlanta, Georgia, uses MicroArchitect CAD software from IdeaGraphix for architectural design. Designers can quickly put the architectural background in, popping in doors and windows, and then do the engineering layout. The software can generate door and window schedules, time accounting reports, and projected costs. Additional descriptions of CAD systems can be found in Chapter 2.

Virtual reality systems have visualization, rendering, and simulation capabilities that go far beyond those of conventional CAD systems. They use interactive graphics software to create computer-generated simulations that are so close to reality that users believe they are participating in a real-world situation. In many virtual reality systems, the user dons special clothing, headgear, and equipment, depending upon the application. The clothing contains sensors that record the user's movements and immediately transmit that information back to the computer. For instance, to walk through a virtual reality simulation of a house, you would need garb that monitors the movement of your feet, hands, and head. You also would need goggles that contain video screens and sometimes audio attachments and feeling gloves so that you can be immersed in the computer feedback.

virtual reality systems Interactive graphics software and hardware that create computer-generated simulations that provide sensations that emulate real-world activities.

Virtual reality is just starting to provide benefits in educational, scientific, and business work. AB Volvo, the Swedish automobile and truck manufacturer, allows prospective buyers of its latest models of garbage trucks to "test drive" them in virtual reality. Burger King used a virtual reality version of a futuristic restaurant to show franchisees new store and equipment designs (Adhikari, 1996).

Surgeons at Boston's Brigham and Women's Hospital are using a virtual reality system in which a three-dimensional representation of the brain using CT and MRI scans is superimposed on live video. With this version of X-ray vision, surgeons can pinpoint the location of a tumor in the brain with 0.5 millimeter accuracy (Ditlea, 1998).

Virtual reality applications are being developed for the Web using a standard called **Virtual Reality Modeling Language (VRML).** VRML is a set of specifications for interactive, three-dimensional modeling on the World Wide Web that can organize multiple media types, including animation, images, and audio to put users in a simulated real-world environment. VRML is platform-independent, operates over a desktop computer, and requires little bandwidth. Users can download a three-dimensional virtual world designed using VRML from a sever over the Internet using their Web browser. (Recent versions of Netscape Navigator and Microsoft Internet Explorer are VRML-compliant.)

Virtual Reality Modeling Language (VRML) A set of specifications for interactive 3-D modeling on the World Wide Web.

Lockheed Martin Missile & Space is using VRML in a three-dimensional training environment to show employees how to operate large pieces of machinery. Dupont, the Wilmington, Delaware, chemical company, created a VRML application called HyperPlant, which allows users to access three-dimensional data over the Internet with

Planet 9 Studios, which specializes in providing 3-D content on the Internet, used Virtual Reality Modeling Language (VRML) to model Treasure Island for KMD San Francisco's bid at master planning for the island. Planet 9 produced fly-over animation, plan graphics, and dissolves between existing aerial photos and the animated project.

TABLE 12.2 Examples of Knowledge Work Systems

Knowledge Work System	Function in Organization
CAD/CAM (Computer-aided design/ computer-aided manufacturing)	Provides engineers, designers, and factory managers with precise control over industrial design and manufacturing
Virtual reality systems	Provide drug designers, architects, engineers, and medical workers with precise, photorealistic simulations of objects
Investment workstations	High-end PCs used in financial sector to analyze trading situations instantaneously and facilitate portfolio management

Netscape Web browsers. Engineers can go through three-dimensional models as if they were physically walking through a plant, viewing objects at eye level. This level of detail reduces the number of mistakes they make during construction of oil rigs, oil plants, and other structures.

Tower Records in West Sacramento, California, is using VRML to build a virtual store to serve buyers over the Internet. Sales clerks will be figure representations with the real clerk's face, and buyers will be able to hear the clerk's voice in real time over the Net (Adhikari, 1997).

investment workstation Powerful desktop computer for financial specialists, which is optimized to access and manipulate massive amounts of financial data.

The financial industry is using specialized **investment workstations** to leverage the knowledge and time of its brokers, traders, and portfolio managers. Firms such as Merrill Lynch and Paine Webber have installed investment workstations that integrate a wide range of data from both internal and external sources, including contact management data, real-time and historical market data, and research reports (Stirland, 1998). Previously, financial professionals had to spend considerable time accessing data from separate systems and piecing together the information they needed. By providing one-stop information faster and with fewer errors, the workstations streamline the entire investment process from stock selection to updating client records.

Table 12.2 summarizes the major types of knowledge work systems.

Sharing Knowledge: Group Collaboration Systems and Intranet Knowledge Environments

Although many knowledge and information work applications have been designed for individuals working alone, organizations have an increasing need to support people working in groups. Chapters 8 and 9 have introduced key technologies that can be used for group coordination and collaboration: e-mail, teleconferencing, dataconferencing, videoconferencing, groupware, and intranets. Groupware and intranets are especially valuable for this purpose.

Groupware

groupware Software that recognizes the significance of groups in offices by providing functions and services that support the collaborative activities of work groups.

Until recently, **groupware** (which we introduced in Chapter 6) was the primary tool for creating collaborative work environments. Groupware is built around three key principles: communication, collaboration, and coordination. It allows groups to work together on documents, schedule meetings, route electronic forms, access shared folders, develop shared databases, and send e-mail. Table 12.3 lists the capabilities of major commercial groupware products that make them such powerful platforms for capturing information and experiences, coordinating common tasks, and distributing work through time and place.

Information-intensive companies such as consulting firms and law firms have found groupware a valuable tool for leveraging their knowledge assets. For example, Ernst & Young, one of the Big Five accounting firms, used Lotus Notes to create a worldwide collaboration environment to help staff work together on projects that required teams

TABLE 12.3	Knowledge Management Capabilities of Groupware
Capability	**Description**
Publishing	Posting documents as well as simultaneous work on the same document by multiple users along with a mechanism to track changes to these documents
Replication	Maintaining and updating identical data on multiple PCs and servers
Discussion tracking	Organizing discussions by many users on different topics
Document management	Storing information from various types of software in a database
Work-flow management	Moving and tracking documents created by groups
Security	Preventing unauthorized access to data
Portability	Availability of the software for mobile use to access the corporate network from the road
Application development	Developing custom software applications with the software

assembled from different locations. Its offices in the United States, United Kingdom, Canada, the Netherlands, and Australia linked Lotus Notes to Oracle relational databases, eliminating the need for multiple copies of files. Employees can share a diary, access a common prospect-and-client database, and work on projects requiring regional and international teamwork (Black, 1995).

Intranet Knowledge Environments

Chapter 9 has described how some organizations are using intranets and Internet technologies for group collaboration, including e-mail, discussion groups, and multimedia Web documents. Some of these intranets are providing the foundation for knowledge environments in which information from a variety of sources and media, including text, sound, video, and even digital slides, can be shared, displayed, and accessed across an enterprise through a simple common interface. Shell Oil Company's Knowledge Management System (see the chapter-opening vignette) is one example. Another is the enterprise-wide knowledge environment developed by Ford Motor Company.

Ford's intranet connects 95,000 professional employees worldwide. It was built as one way to shorten the product-development cycle for automobiles. The intranet delivers a wealth of information that previously would have required several telephone calls or a library visit. On the enterprise home page, called the Ford Hub, is a directory of categories, including News, People, Processes, Products, and Competition. Also on-line are training registration forms, maps, the company telephone directory, building layouts, human resource information, a PointCast "push" channel with automatic news and stock updates, and text feeds from the Ford Communications Network, an internal closed-circuit telephone network. Employees can access on-line libraries and a Web Center of Excellence with information on best practices, standards, and recommendations. Ford believes it can shave weeks off design processes because engineers can access images on an intranet from wherever they are in the world instead of waiting for project documentation to arrive by mail. Ford says this comprehensive network transformed decades-old processes, allowing people to disseminate information, share best practices, communicate, conduct research, and collaborate in ways that were never before possible (Stuart, 1997).

These features of intranets, combined with their low cost, have made them attractive alternatives to proprietary groupware for collaborative work, especially among small and medium-sized businesses. For simple tasks such as sharing documents or document publishing, an intranet generally is less expensive to build and maintain than applications based on commercial products such as Lotus Notes, which requires proprietary software and client/server networks.

WINDOW ON ORGANIZATIONS

Multimedia Education for Learning Organizations

Should companies scrap human instructors for computers to train their employees? Many think so, and a few are using them to fulfill most of their employee training needs. One reason is the shortage of skilled workers in most fields, leading to the conclusion that workers need more education, even computer-based. For example, in the information-technology field alone, 346,000 positions were unfilled due to a lack of qualified candidates, according to a 1998 study done by the Information Technology Association of Arlington, Virginia. Also, corporate managements have come to realize that because we are in an information age, an educated work force is pivotal. Ernest Deavenport, CEO of $4 billion Eastman Chemical Co. in Kingsport, Tennessee, explains that his industry "must invest in our work force by enhancing the knowledge and skills of our employees." In addition, the emergence of new multimedia technology and new educational approaches, such as collaborative training, have improved the quality of computer-based education.

Eli Lilly & Co., the $8.5 billion pharmaceuticals company, has developed Spin (Scientific Performance Improvement Network), a network-based educational system that is built upon the concept of embedding collaborative education in work processes. Spin is designed for Lilly's research scientists who access the system either through a Lilly network or through the Web. Spin differs from most on-line education systems in that it not only aims to deliver current knowledge to the scientist/student but also to create new knowledge through interaction with other scientists. Each Spin course is linked to a discussion database so scientists can discuss what they are learning with each other, with teachers and with other scientists. In addition, every course requires that all students carry out a project that will apply the concepts learned in the course. In doing their studying or research, the students have access to an index of relevant Web sites, including proprietary databases stored in Eli Lilly's own databases. Students are able to customize their own Spin interface to include links to commonly used Web sites and databases. They also can make their own links available to other Spin students.

General Motors has established an electronic performance support system (EPSS) that takes the Eli Lilly concept a step further because its system captures knowledge that is created when employees are working while learning. The targets of this system are mechanics who need training as they work. The system relies heavily upon the latest voice-recognition technology. It runs on notebook-sized PCs, which are worn on the mechanics' belts. The system delivers learning materials directly to the user based upon the difficulty of the problem and the knowledge level of the learner. When users of this system complete their repair work, they verbally describe the procedure they followed into the computer, including any undocumented problems or solutions they discovered. The computer converts the words into text that eventually reaches technicians at GM headquarters. If students discover any new knowledge that the headquarter's technicians deem as widely useful, they can change service procedures and training materials. According to Jim Roach, the program manager of GM's service technology group, this system will not only change the way mechanics learn, but also will change the way they work. Mechanics will be able to work on a wider variety of vehicles than in the past because the knowledge they need will be built into the training equipment they use. "We get smarter workers with more transferable work skills," Roach claims.

To Think About: ***Discuss the role and value of organizational knowledge in the information age. How do these systems enhance organizational knowledge? How do they make the organization more effective? What drawbacks do you see for the Spin and EPSS systems?***

Source: Adapted from Justin Hibbard, "The Learning Revolution," *Information Week*, March 9, 1998.

However, for applications requiring extensive coordination and management, groupware software such as Notes has important capabilities that intranets cannot yet provide. Notes is more flexible when documents must be changed, updated, or edited on the fly. It can track revisions to a document as it moves through a collaborative editing process. Internal Notes-based networks are more secure than intranets. Web sites are more likely to crash or to have their servers overloaded when there are many requests for data. Notes is thus more appropriate for applications requiring production and publication of documents by many authors, frequent updating and document tracking, and high security and replication.

Intranet technology works best as a central repository with a small number of authors and relatively static information that does not require frequent updating, although intranet tools for group collaboration are improving. Netscape Communications' Communicator software bundles a Web browser with messaging and collaboration tools, including e-mail, newsgroup discussions, a group scheduling and calendaring tool, and point-to-point conferencing. Web technology is most useful for publishing information across multiple types of computer platforms and for displaying knowledge as multimedia objects linked to other knowledge objects in hyperlinks.

At the same time, Notes and other groupware products are being enhanced so they can be integrated with the Internet or private intranets. Recent versions of Domino, a server version of Notes, allow Notes to act as a Web server, providing an easy route for companies to take their document-based data to the Internet or an intranet. Notes clients can act as Web browsers to access information on the World Wide Web. Notes servers and data can be accessed by Web browsers as well as by Notes clients; Notes databases can contain HTML pages as well as Notes documents.

Collaborative work and organizational learning also can be enhanced by using intranets and other multimedia platforms for employee training and knowledge acquisition. The Window on Organizations describes some of these interactive multimedia training systems.

Group collaboration technologies alone cannot promote information-sharing if team members do not feel it is in their interest to share, especially in organizations that encourage competition among employees. This technology can best enhance the work of a group if the applications are properly designed to fit the organization's needs and work practices and if management encourages a collaborative atmosphere. The Window on Management describes how one company overcame these hurdles.

12.3 ARTIFICIAL INTELLIGENCE

Organizations are using artificial intelligence technology to capture individual and collective knowledge and to codify and extend their knowledge base.

What Is Artificial Intelligence?

Artificial intelligence can be defined as the effort to develop computer-based systems (both hardware and software) that behave as humans. Such systems would be able to learn natural languages, accomplish coordinated physical tasks (robotics), use a perceptual apparatus that informs their physical behavior and language (visual and oral perception systems), and emulate human expertise and decision making (expert systems). Such systems also would exhibit logic, reasoning, intuition, and the just-plain-common-sense qualities that we associate with human beings. Figure 12.5 on page 383 illustrates the elements of the artificial intelligence family. Another important element is intelligent machines, the physical hardware that performs these tasks.

artificial intelligence The effort to develop computer-based systems that can behave like humans, with the ability to learn languages, accomplish physical tasks, use a perceptual apparatus, and emulate human expertise and decision making.

Successful artificial intelligence systems are based on human expertise, knowledge, and selected reasoning patterns, but they do not exhibit the intelligence of human beings. Existing artificial intelligence systems do not come up with new and novel solutions to problems. Existing systems extend the powers of experts but in no way substitute for them or capture much of their intelligence. Briefly, existing systems lack the common sense and generality of naturally intelligent human beings.

Human intelligence is vastly complex and much broader than computer intelligence. A key factor that distinguishes human beings from other animals is their ability to develop associations and to use metaphors and analogies such as *like* and *as*. Using metaphor and analogy, humans create new rules, apply old rules to new situations, and at times act intuitively and/or instinctively without rules. Much of what we call common sense or generality in humans resides in the ability to create metaphor and analogy.

Human intelligence also includes a unique ability to impose a conceptual apparatus on the surrounding world. Meta-concepts such as cause-and-effect and time, and concepts of a lower order such as breakfast, dinner, and lunch, are all imposed by human beings on the world around them. Thinking in terms of these concepts and acting on them are central characteristics of intelligent human behavior.

WINDOW ON MANAGEMENT

Collective Knowledge Brings Power

Both business and information systems management at Monsanto Company believe that collaboration and shared (and so reusable) knowledge are necessary for creating better processes for key activities. It is these processes that drive the company; therefore, it is no surprise that the company has become involved with knowledge-management teams whose jobs are to create more sharing of information among Monsanto employees.

Monsanto, a giant agricultural chemical and pharmaceuticals company, faced a real challenge, however, when dealing with their Protiva division. St. Louis-based Protiva is a small (150-person) dairy company that produces one product, Posilac, a dairy enhancer. Protiva was selected to be the site for one of the four knowledge-management pilot projects set up to introduce the concept into Monsanto. The company probably chose Protiva because it had remained a one-product unit and needed to find ways to contribute more; however, the Protiva knowledge-management team knew that its workers were fiercely independent and not at all interested in collaboration. The team had to find ways to completely change Protiva's culture.

Michael Plummer, a consultant to Protiva, characterized the interaction between co-workers as "dysfunctional." He said observers at presentation meetings to review someone's work would notice that those present were more interested in showing off their own knowledge than in serious inquiry. Susan O'Neill, the Coopers & Lybrand partner in charge of the knowledge-strategies group, said the problem stemmed from a system that rewarded people for specialized knowledge. She described the thought process of employees who developed this problem as "I get my power and value through expertise; therefore, I want to hold on to it." The problem was made more difficult at Protiva because the multiple downsizings and reorganizations the current employees had experienced resulted in a pervasive mistrust of management.

To address the mistrust, the knowledge-management team established on-going lines of communication between management and employees. Management used these sessions to make clear how each individual contributed to the overall mission of the company. Management also listened, giving the employees a greater voice in decision making. The meetings also were used to improve everyone's communications skills.

Information technology staff also participated in this process, and they were required to work on their own communications skills. The team felt this was necessary if IT was to better understand the needs of the users. Ultimately, this changed the way IT developed software because the process became more interactive with users playing a larger role.

After many discussions, a number of employees made clear to the knowledge-management team that they were inundated with electronic information and needed an on-line place to store and organize it. In response, IT built a database system called Integrated Workspace. The system is meant to provide one-stop access to all the information that employees need to do their jobs. The knowledge-management team hopes that this system will encourage employees with common interests and expertise to share more freely. IT will be adding a free-form area where people can hold open discussions on relevant issues, such as how a chemical compound being used by one group might be useful to another group. Plummer also hopes that the "nutty ideas" people often come up with will be recorded rather than forgotten so they can be addressed.

The results have been surprising and encouraging. About 60 percent of Protiva's work force are using Integrated Workspace and the atmosphere seems to be changing. "What we managed to do," says Bullock, "is convince [the group] that it is their collective knowledge that brings power," not what any individual knows.

To Think About: ***Why do you think the team began with addressing the company's culture rather than simply introducing the Integrated Workspace? What management, organization, and technology issues did this project present?***

Source: Adapted from Julekha Dash, "Cultivating Collaboration," *Software Magazine,* March 1998.

Why Business Is Interested in Artificial Intelligence

Although artificial intelligence applications are much more limited than human intelligence, they are of great interest to business for the following reasons:

- To preserve expertise that might be lost through the retirement, resignation, or death of an acknowledged expert
- To store information in an active form—to create an organizational knowledge base—that many employees can examine, much like an electronic textbook or manual, so that others may learn rules of thumb not found in textbooks
- To create a mechanism that is not subject to human feelings such as fatigue and worry. This may be especially useful when jobs may be environmentally, physically, or mentally dangerous to humans. These systems also may be useful advisers in times of crisis.

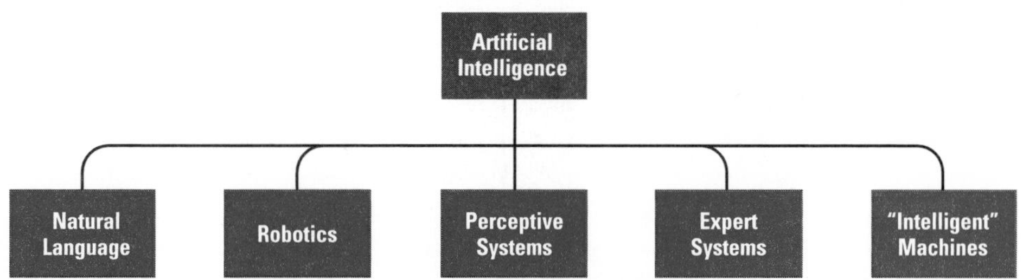

FIGURE 12.5

The artificial intelligence family. The field of AI currently includes many initiatives: natural language, robotics, perceptive systems, expert systems, and intelligent machines.

- To eliminate routine and unsatisfying jobs held by people
- To enhance the organization's knowledge base by suggesting solutions to specific problems that are too massive and complex to be analyzed by human beings in a short period of time.

Capturing Knowledge: Expert Systems

In limited areas of expertise, such as diagnosing a car's ignition system or classifying biological specimens, the rules of thumb used by real-world experts can be understood, codified, and placed in a machine. Information systems that solve problems by capturing knowledge for a very specific and limited domain of human expertise are called **expert systems.** An expert system can assist decision making by asking relevant questions and explaining the reasons for adopting certain actions.

expert system Knowledge-intensive computer program that captures the expertise of a human in limited domains of knowledge.

Expert systems lack the breadth of knowledge and the understanding of fundamental principles of a human expert. They are quite narrow, shallow, and brittle. They typically perform very limited tasks that can be performed by professionals in a few minutes or hours. Problems that cannot be solved by human experts in the same short period of time are far too difficult for an expert system. However, by capturing human expertise in limited areas, expert systems can provide benefits, helping organizations make higher-quality decisions with fewer people.

How Expert Systems Work

Human knowledge must be modeled or represented in a way that a computer can process. The model of human knowledge used by expert systems is called the **knowledge base.** Two ways of representing human knowledge and expertise are rules and knowlege frames.

knowledge base Model of human knowledge that is used by expert systems.

A standard structured programming construct (see Chapter 11) is the IF–THEN construct, in which a condition is evaluated. If the condition is true, an action is taken. For instance,

IF INCOME > $45,000 (condition)

THEN PRINT NAME AND ADDRESS (action)

A series of these rules can be a knowledge base. Any reader who has written computer programs knows that virtually all traditional computer programs contain IF–THEN statements. The difference between a traditional program and a **rule-based expert system** program is one of degree and magnitude. AI programs can easily have 200 to 10,000 rules, far more than traditional programs, which may have 50 to 100 IF–THEN statements. Moreover, in an AI program the rules tend to be interconnected and nested to a far larger degree than in traditional programs, as shown in Figure 12.6. Hence the complexity of the rules in a rule-based expert system is considerable.

rule-based expert system An AI program that has a large number of interconnected and nested IF–THEN statements, or rules, that are the basis for the knowledge in the system.

Could you represent the knowledge in the Encyclopedia Britannica this way? Probably not, because the **rule base** would be too large, and not all the knowledge in the encyclopedia can be represented in the form of IF–THEN rules. In general, expert systems can be efficiently used only in those situations in which the domain of knowledge is highly restricted (such as in granting credit) and involves no more than a few thousand rules.

rule base The collection of knowledge in an AI system that is represented in the form of IF–THEN rules.

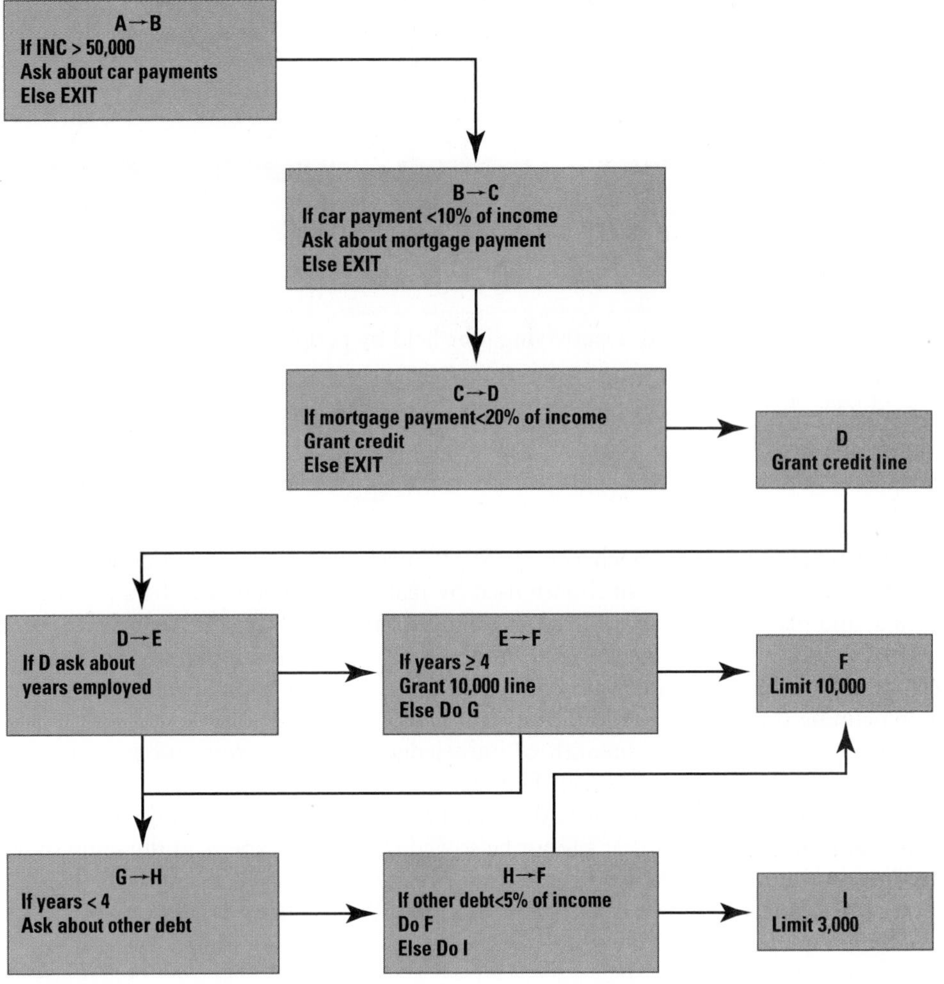

FIGURE 12.6

Rules in an AI program. An expert system contains a number of rules to be followed when utilized. The rules themselves are interconnected; the number of outcomes is known in advance and is limited; there are multiple paths to the same outcome; and the system can consider multiple rules at a single time. The rules illustrated are for simple credit-granting expert systems.

knowledge frames A method of organizing expert system knowledge into chunks; the relationships are based on shared characteristics determined by the user.

AI shell The programming environment of an expert system.

inference engine The strategy used to search through the rule base in an expert system; can be forward or backward chaining.

forward chaining A strategy for searching the rule base in an expert system that begins with the information entered by the user and searches the rule base to arrive at a conclusion.

Knowledge frames can be used to represent knowledge by organizing information into chunks of interrelated characteristics. The relationships are based on shared characteristics rather than a hierarchy. This approach is grounded in the belief that humans use frames, or concepts, to make rapid sense out of perceptions. For instance, when a person is told, "Look for a tank and shoot when you see one," experts believe that humans invoke a concept, or frame, of what a tank should look like. Anything that does not fit this concept of a tank is ignored. In a similar fashion, AI researchers can organize a vast array of information into frames. The computer then is instructed to search the database of frames and list connections to other frames of interest. The user can follow the pathways pointed to by the system.

Figure 12.7 shows a part of a knowledge base organized by frames. A "CAR" is defined by characteristics or slots in a frame as a vehicle, with four wheels, a gas or diesel motor, and an action such as rolling or moving. This frame could be related to almost any other object in the database that shares any of these characteristics, such as the tank frame.

The **AI shell** is the programming environment of an expert system. In the early years of expert systems, computer scientists used specialized programming languages such as LISP or Prolog that could process lists of rules efficiently. Today a growing number of expert systems use AI shells that are user-friendly development environments. AI shells can quickly generate user-interface screens, capture the knowledge base, and manage the strategies for searching the rule base.

The strategy used to search through the rule base is called the **inference engine.** Two strategies are commonly used: forward chaining and backward chaining (see Figure 12.8).

In **forward chaining** the inference engine begins with the information entered by the user and searches the rule base to arrive at a conclusion. The strategy is to fire, or carry

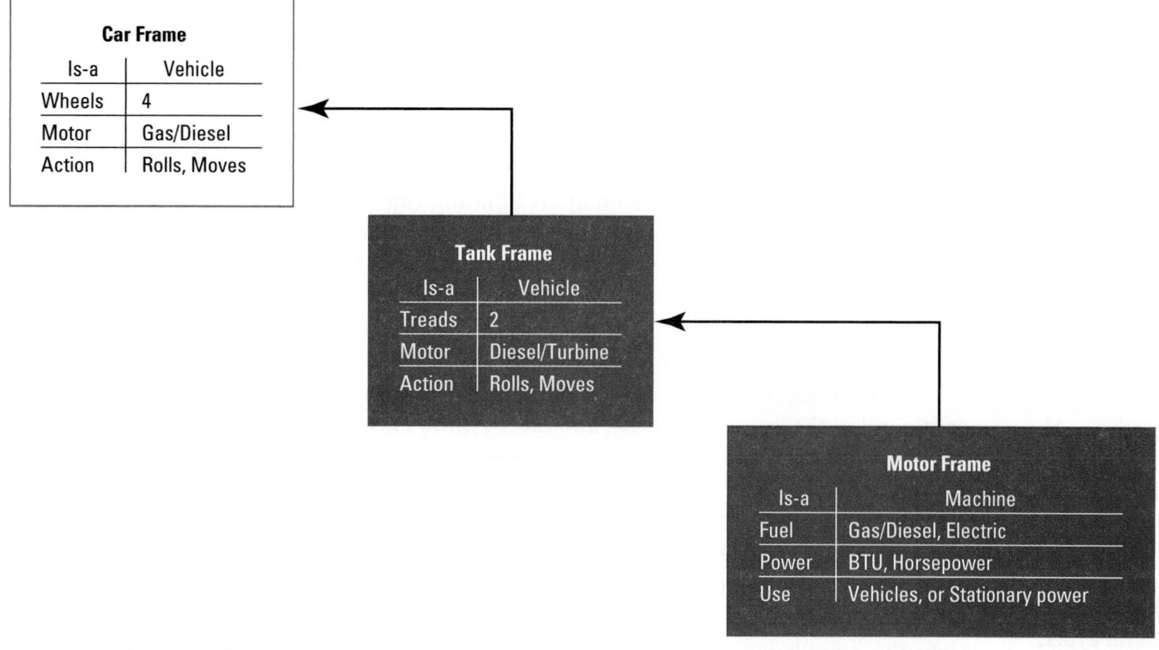

FIGURE 12.7 Frames to model knowledge. Knowledge and information can be organized into frames. Frames capture the relevant characteristics of the objects of interest. This approach is based on the belief that humans use "frames" or concepts to narrow the range of possibilities when scanning incoming information to make rapid sense out of perceptions.

out, the action of the rule when a condition is true. In Figure 12.8, beginning on the left, if the user enters a client with income greater than $100,000, the engine will fire all rules in sequence from left to right. If the user then enters information indicating that the same client owns real estate, another pass of the rule base will occur and more rules will fire. Processing continues until no more rules can be fired.

In **backward chaining** the strategy for searching the rule base starts with a hypothesis and proceeds by asking the user questions about selected facts until the hypothesis is either confirmed or disproved. In our example in Figure 12.8, ask the question, "Should

backward chaining A strategy for searching the rule base in an expert system that acts like a problem solver by beginning with a hypothesis and seeking out more information until the hypothesis is either proved or disproved.

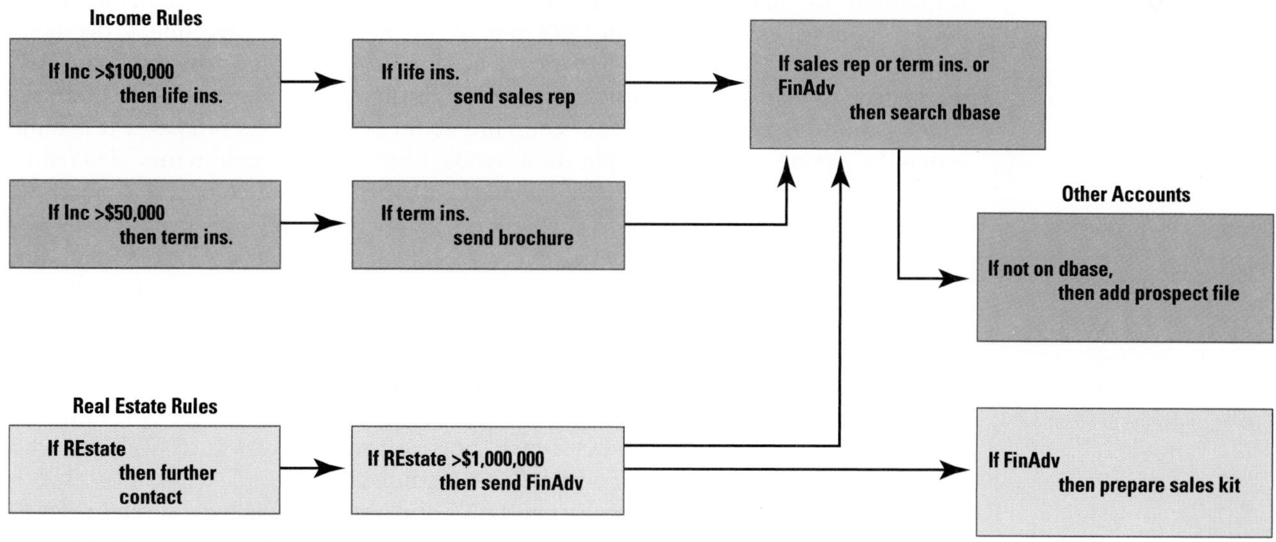

FIGURE 12.8 Inference engines in expert systems. An inference engine works by searching through the rules and "firing" those rules that are triggered by facts gathered and entered by the user. Basically, a collection of rules is similar to a series of nested "IF" statements in a traditional software program; however, the magnitude of the statements and degree of nesting are much greater in an expert system.

we add this person to the prospect database?" Begin on the right of the diagram and work toward the left. You can see that the person should be added to the database if a sales representative is sent, term insurance is granted, or a financial advisor visits the client.

Building an Expert System

Building an expert system is similar to building other information systems, although building expert systems is an iterative process with each phase possibly requiring several iterations before a full system is developed. Typically the environment in which an expert system operates is continually changing so that the expert system must also continually change. Some expert systems, especially large ones, are so complex that in a few years the maintenance costs will equal the development costs.

An AI development team is composed of one or more experts, who have a thorough command of the knowledge base, and one or more knowledge engineers, who can translate the knowledge (as described by the expert) into a set of rules or frames. A **knowledge engineer** is similar to a traditional systems analyst but has special expertise in eliciting information and expertise from other professionals.

knowledge engineer A specialist who elicits information and expertise from other professionals and translates it into a set of rules, frames, or semantic nets for an expert system.

The team members must select a problem appropriate for an expert system. The project will balance potential savings from the proposed system against the cost. The team members will develop a prototype system to test assumptions about how to encode the knowledge of experts. Next, they will develop a full-scale system, focusing mainly on the addition of a very large number of rules. The complexity of the entire system grows with the number of rules, so the comprehensibility of the system may be threatened. Generally the system will be pruned to achieve simplicity and power. The system is tested by a range of experts within the organization against the performance criteria established earlier. Once tested, the system will be integrated into the data flow and work patterns of the organization.

Examples of Successful Expert Systems

There is no accepted definition of a successful expert system. What is successful to an academic ("It works!") may not be successful to a corporation ("It costs a million dollars!"). The following are examples of expert systems that provide organizations with an array of benefits, including reduced errors, reduced cost, reduced training time, improved decisions, and improved quality and service.

Countrywide Funding Corp. in Pasadena, California, is a loan-underwriting firm with about 400 underwriters in 150 offices around the country. The company developed a PC-based expert system in 1992 to make preliminary creditworthiness decisions on loan requests. The company had experienced rapid, continuing growth and wanted the system to help ensure consistent, high-quality loan decisions. CLUES (Countrywide's Loan Underwriting Expert System) has about 400 rules. Countrywide tested the system by having every loan application handled by a human underwriter also fed to CLUES. The system was refined until it agreed with the underwriter in 95 percent of the cases.

Countrywide will not rely on CLUES to reject loans, because the expert system cannot be programmed to handle exceptional situations such as those involving a self-employed person or complex financial schemes. An underwriter will review all rejected loans and will make the final decision. CLUES has other benefits. Traditionally, an underwriter could handle six or seven applications a day. Using CLUES, the same underwriter can evaluate at least sixteen per day (Nash, 1993). Countrywide now is using the rules in its expert system to answer e-mail inquiries from visitors to its Web site who want to know if they qualify for a loan (Cole-Gomolski, 1998).

The Digital Equipment Corporation (DEC) and Carnegie-Mellon University developed XCON in the late 1970s to configure VAX computers on a daily basis. The system configures customer orders and guides the assembly of those orders at the customer site. XCON has been used for major functions such as sales and marketing, manufacturing and production, and field service, and played a strategic role at DEC (Sviokla, June 1990; Barker and O'Conner, 1989). It is estimated that XCON and related sys-

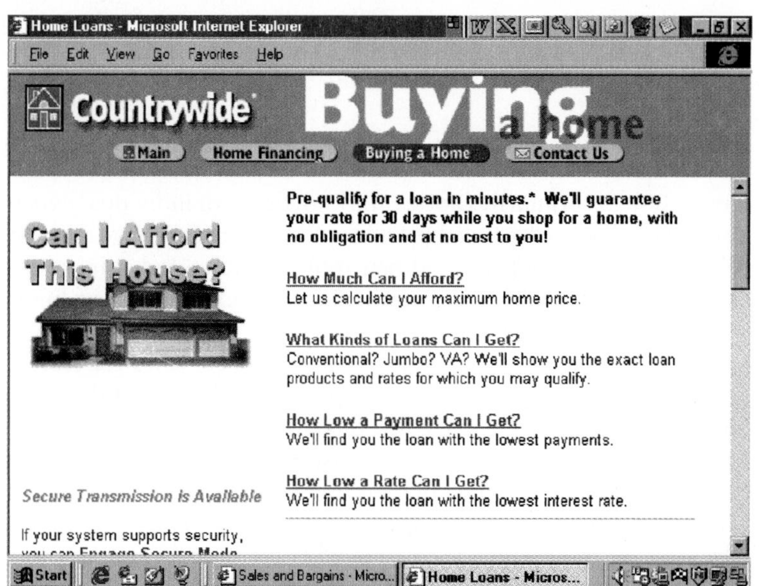

Countrywide Funding Corporation developed an expert system called CLUES to evaluate the creditworthiness of loan applicants. Countrywide is using the rules in this system to answer inquiries from visitors to its Web site who want to know if they can qualify for a loan.

tems saved DEC approximately $40 million per year. XCON started out with 250 rules but expanded to about 10,000.

Whirlpool uses the Consumer Appliance Diagnostic System (CADS) to help its customer service representatives handle its 3 million annual telephone inquiries. The system expedites customer service by directing customers to a single source of help without delay. Previously, customers who had a problem or question about Whirlpool products might have been put on hold or directed to two or three different customer representatives before their questions could be answered. Whirlpool developed CADS using Aion's Development System for OS/2 as its expert system shell. Two knowledge engineers worked with one programmer and three of the company's customer service experts to capture 1000 rules for 12 product lines. By 1999, Whirlpool expects to use CADS to respond to 9 million calls annually.

Problems with Expert Systems

Although expert systems lack the robust and general intelligence of human beings, they can provide benefits to organizations if their limitations are well understood. Only certain classes of problems can be solved using expert systems. Virtually all successful expert systems deal with problems of classification in which there are relatively few alternative outcomes and in which these possible outcomes are all known in advance. Many expert systems require large, lengthy, and expensive development efforts. Hiring or training more experts may be less expensive than building an expert system.

The knowledge base of expert systems is fragile and brittle; they cannot learn or change over time. In fast-moving fields such as medicine or the computer sciences, keeping the knowledge base up to date is a critical problem.

Expert systems can only represent limited forms of knowledge. IF–THEN knowledge exists primarily in textbooks. There are no adequate representations for deep causal models or temporal trends. No expert system, for instance, can write a textbook on information systems or engage in other creative activities not explicitly foreseen by system designers. Many experts cannot express their knowledge using an IF–THEN format. Expert systems cannot yet replicate knowledge that is intuitive, based on analogy and on a sense of things.

Contrary to early promises, expert systems are most effective in automating lower-level clerical functions. They can provide electronic checklists for lower-level employees in service bureaucracies such as banking, insurance, sales, and welfare agencies. The applicability of expert systems to managerial problems is very limited. Managerial problems generally involve drawing facts and interpretations from divergent sources, evaluating the facts, and comparing one interpretation of the facts with another, and do not involve analysis or simple classification. Expert systems based on the prior knowledge of a few known alternatives are unsuitable to the problems managers face on a daily basis.

Organizational Intelligence: Case-Based Reasoning

case-based reasoning (CBR) Artificial intelligence technology that represents knowledge as a database of cases.

Expert systems primarily capture the knowledge of individual experts, but organizations also have collective knowledge and expertise that they have built up over the years. This organizational knowledge can be captured and stored using case-based reasoning. In **case-based reasoning (CBR),** descriptions of past experiences of human specialists, represented as cases, are stored in a database for later retrieval when the user encounters a new case with similar parameters. The system searches for stored cases similar to the new one, finds the closest fit, and applies the solutions of the old case to the new case. Successful solutions are tagged to the new case and both are stored together with the other cases in the knowledge base. Unsuccessful solutions also are appended to the case database along with explanations as to why the solutions did not work (see Figure 12.9).

Expert systems work by applying a set of IF–THEN–ELSE rules against a knowledge base, both of which are extracted from human experts. Case-based reasoning, in contrast, represents knowledge as a series of cases, and this knowledge base is continuously expanded and refined by users.

For example, let us examine Compaq Computer of Houston, Texas, a company that operates in a highly competitive, customer service-oriented business environment and is

FIGURE 12.9

How case-based reasoning works. Case-based reasoning represents knowledge as a database of past cases and their solutions. The system uses a six-step process to generate solutions to new problems encountered by the user.

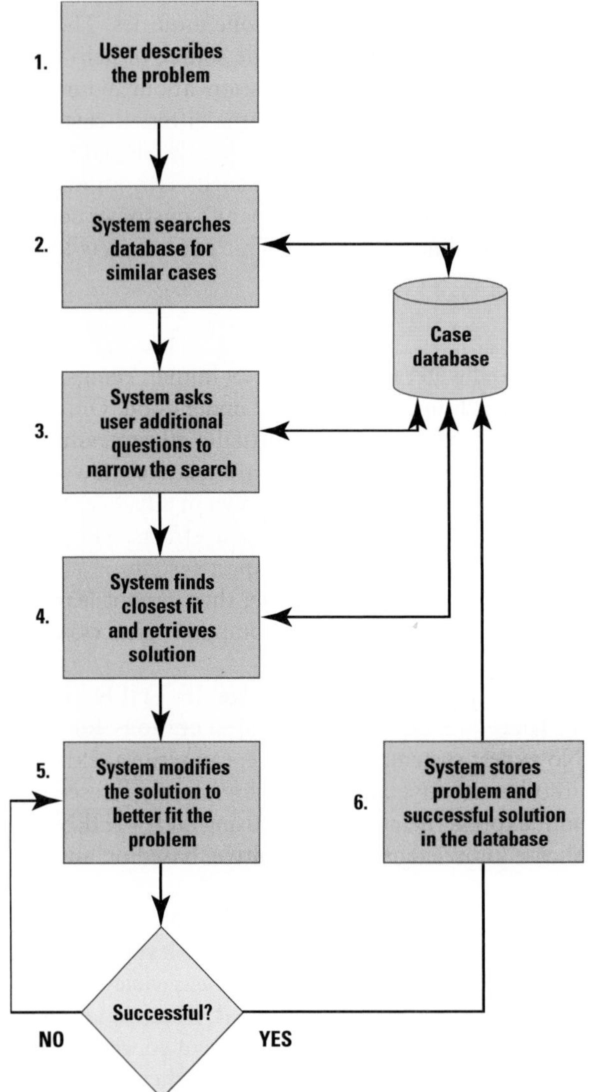

WINDOW ON TECHNOLOGY

Case-Based Reasoning Teams Up with Intranets

Information and knowledge may be pivotal, but what does an organization do when it has so much information that it cannot make use of it? One company faced with immense information-overload problems has been Kansas City, Missouri-based Cerner Corp. Cerner provides services and software to the health care industry throughout the world. The company fields a software development and support staff of approximately 2000 people worldwide. One technology that is proving particularly useful is a case-based reasoning system that is simply called CKR (pronounced "seeker"), which stands for Cerner Knowledge Reference. CKR uses case-based reasoning software from Inference Corp., Microsoft Office, and an intranet. The system was designed primarily to help those staffing Cerner's two help desks, one that supports Cerner's internal users and one that supports Cerner's clients.

Although the system is new, it already has a knowledge base of 13,000 cases. When a caller contacts a help desk, the person at the desk types a simple, English-text question into CKR. CKR responds with its own questions until it has enough information to offer solutions that come from similar problems stored in the database. The technology makes everyone smarter. As knowledge-management team leader Rhonda Dalzell explains, "You can get an answer without a deep knowledge about similar situations." One of the exciting features of this system is the ease with which new cases can be added to the database. All the user must do is click on a "feedback" button and then type in his or her experiences concerning the problem. The information will automatically be sent to the case author for consideration. The case author will examine the new input and, if it is deemed appropriate, add the new case with appropriate questions.

This system has benefits beyond the fact that knowledge is easily stored in an organized way so that it is quickly accessed. It also is useful to the organization because it solves the problem faced in earlier times when support staffs in different locations had to reinvent the same wheel. Now, when a solution to a specific problem is found in one location, the knowledge is quickly made available at all other locations through CKR. For instance, one group can study how best to implement Windows NT and immediately share what they have learned with others. The system helps staff in different locations to specialize, because management knows the knowledge gained at each location will be easy for staff everywhere to access. Groups of employees with common problems have formed "communities of interest" similar to Internet newsgroups on the intranet.

One unexpected benefit is that Cerner is finding that incoming staff can be trained in half the time. Dalzell claims that whereas it took six months to train new employees in the past, using CKR enables them to be trained in three months. In addition, that training now concentrates on understanding concepts rather than on memorizing details, making the employees more effective in their work.

To Think About: ***What were the business benefits of using a case-based reasoning system? How did using this system change the way Cerner ran its business? What other types of problems do you think cased-based reasoning can be used to solve?***

Source: Adapted from Gary H. Anthes, "Learning How to Share," *Computerworld,* February 23, 1998.

daily flooded with customer phone calls crying for help. Keeping those customers satisfied requires Compaq to spend millions of dollars annually to maintain large, technically skilled, customer-support staffs. When customers call with problems, they must describe the problems to the customer service staff, and then wait on hold while customer service transfers the calls to appropriate technicians. The customers then describe the problem all over again while the technicians try to come up with answers—all in all, a most frustrating experience. To improve customer service while reining in costs, Compaq began giving away expensive case-based reasoning software to customers purchasing their Pagemarq printer.

The software knowledge base is a series of several hundred actual cases of Pagemarq printer problems—actual war stories about smudged copies, printer memory problems, jammed printers—all the typical problems people face with laser printers. Trained CBR staff entered case descriptions in textual format into the CBR system. They entered key words necessary to categorize the problem, such as smudge, smear, lines, streaks, paper jam. They also entered a series of questions that might be needed to allow the software to further narrow the problem. Finally, solutions also were attached to each case.

With the Compaq-supplied CBR system running on their computer, owners no longer need to call Compaq's service department. Instead they run the software and describe the problem to the software. The system swiftly searches actual cases, discarding

FIGURE 12.10

Typical Web-based customer service system. *Source: Anne Bilodeau Zeiger, "Help Desks Make the Web Connection," Byte, April 1998. Used by permission of CMPnet.*

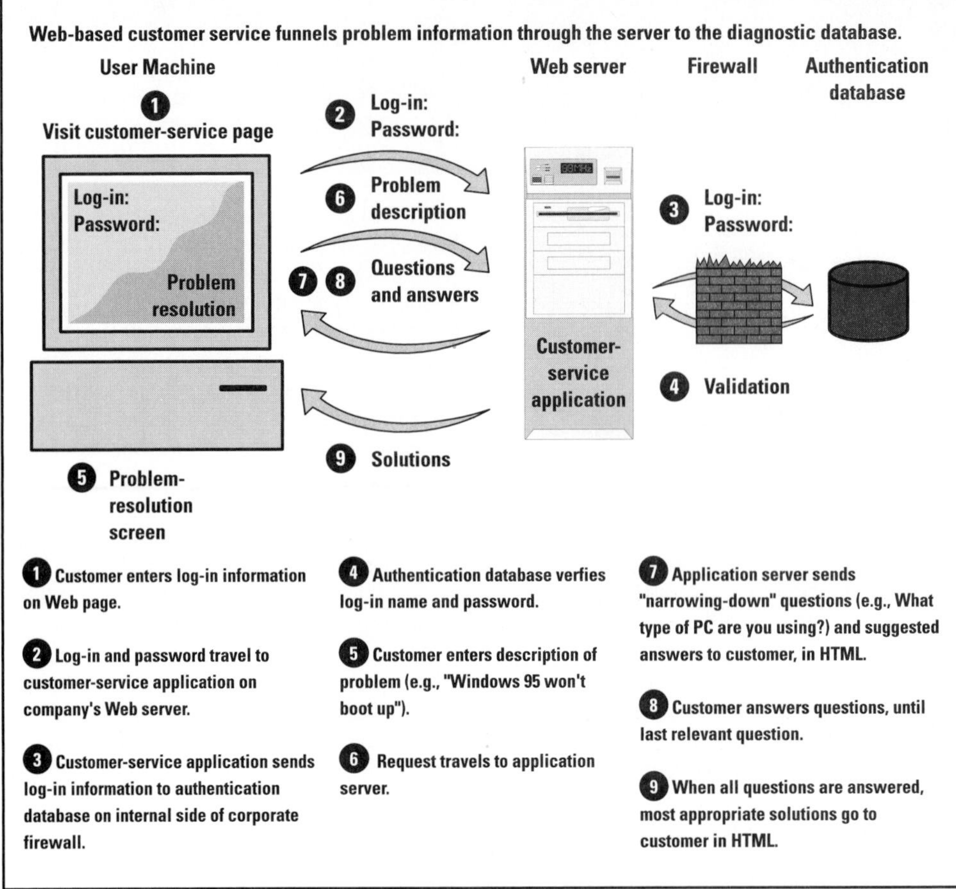

Web-based customer service funnels problem information through the server to the diagnostic database.
User Machine
Web server
Firewall
Authentication database
1 Visit customer-service page
2 Log-in: Password:
Log-in: Password:
Problem resolution
6 Problem description
7 8 Questions and answers
3 Log-in: Password:
Customer-service application
4 Validation
9 Solutions
5 Problem-resolution screen
1 Customer enters log-in information on Web page.
2 Log-in and password travel to customer-service application on company's Web server.
3 Customer-service application sends log-in information to authentication database on internal side of corporate firewall.
4 Authentication database verfies log-in name and password.
5 Customer enters description of problem (e.g., "Windows 95 won't boot up").
6 Request travels to application server.
7 Application server sends "narrowing-down" questions (e.g., What type of PC are you using?) and suggested answers to customer, in HTML.
8 Customer answers questions, until last relevant question.
9 When all questions are answered, most appropriate solutions go to customer in HTML.

unrelated ones, selecting related ones. If necessary to further narrow the search results, the software will ask the user for more information. In the end, one or more cases relevant to the specific problem are displayed, along with their solutions. Now, customers can solve most of their own problems quickly without a telephone call, while Compaq saves $10 million to $20 million annually in customer support costs.

New commercial software products, such as Inference's CasePoint WebServer, allow customers to access a case database through the Web. Using case-based reasoning, the server asks customers to answer a series of questions to narrow down the problems. CasePoint then extracts solutions from the database and passes them on to customers. Audio-product manufacturer Kenwood USA used this tool to put its manuals and technical-support solutions on the Web. Figure 12.10 illustrates how a Web-based customer service system with case-based reasoning might work.

The Window on Technology on page 389 describes another case-based reasoning application for an intranet.

12.4 OTHER INTELLIGENT TECHNIQUES

Organizations are using other intelligent computing techniques to extend their knowledge base by providing solutions to problems that are too massive or complex to be handled by people with limited resources. Neural networks, fuzzy logic, genetic algorithms, and intelligent agents are developing into promising business applications.

Neural Networks

There has been an exciting resurgence of interest in bottom-up approaches to artificial intelligence in which machines are designed to imitate the physical thought process of the biological brain. Figure 12.11 shows two neurons from a leech's brain. The soma, or nerve cell at the center, acts like a switch, stimulating other neurons and being stim-

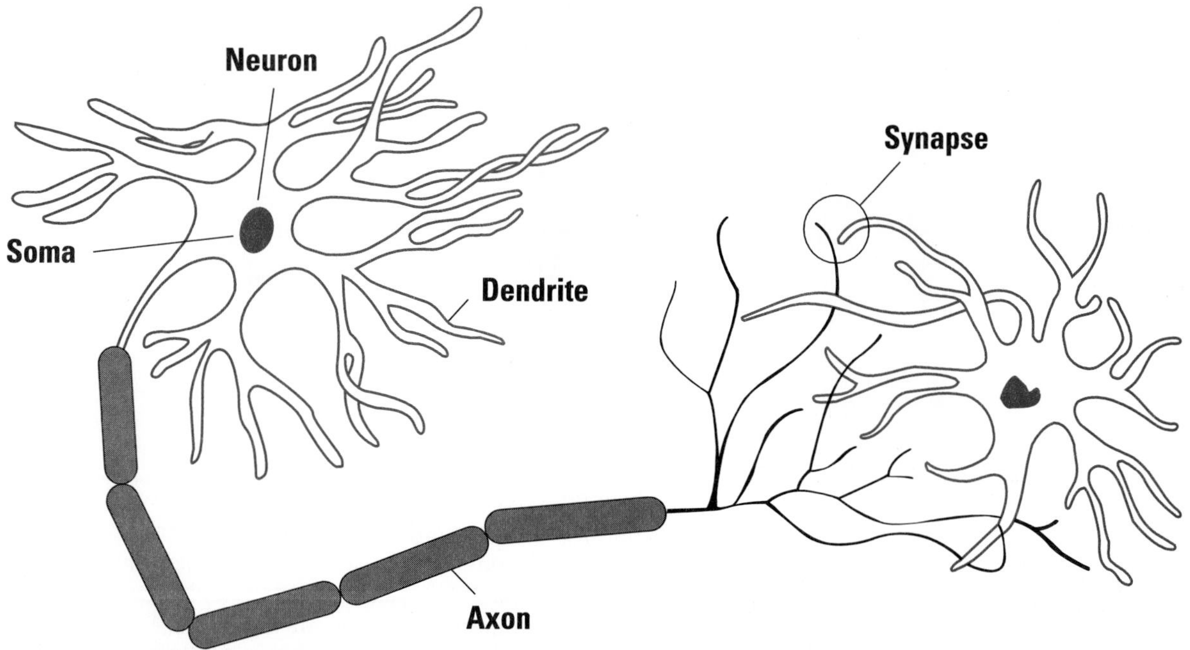

FIGURE 12.11 Biological neurons of a leech. Simple biological models, like the neurons of a leech, have influenced the development of artificial or computational neural networks in which the biological cells are replaced by transistors or entire processors. *Source: Defense Advance Research Projects Agency (DARPA), 1988. Unclassified. Hereinafter "DARPA, 1988."*

ulated in turn. Emanating from the neuron is an axon, which is an electrically active link to the dendrites of other neurons. Axons and dendrites are the "wires" that electrically connect neurons to one another. The junction of the two is called a synapse. This simple biological model is the metaphor for the development of neural networks. A **neural network** consists of hardware or software that attempts to emulate the processing patterns of the biological brain.

neural network Hardware or software that attempts to emulate the processing patterns of the biological brain.

The human brain has about 100 billion (10^{11}) neurons, each having about 1000 dendrites, which form 100,000 billion (10^{14}) synapses. The brain's neurons operate in parallel, and the human brain can accomplish about 10^{16}, or ten million billion, interconnections per second. This far exceeds the capacity of any known machine or any machine planned or ever likely to be built with current technology.

However, complex networks of neurons have been simulated on computers. Figure 12.12 shows an artificial neural network with two neurons. The resistors in the

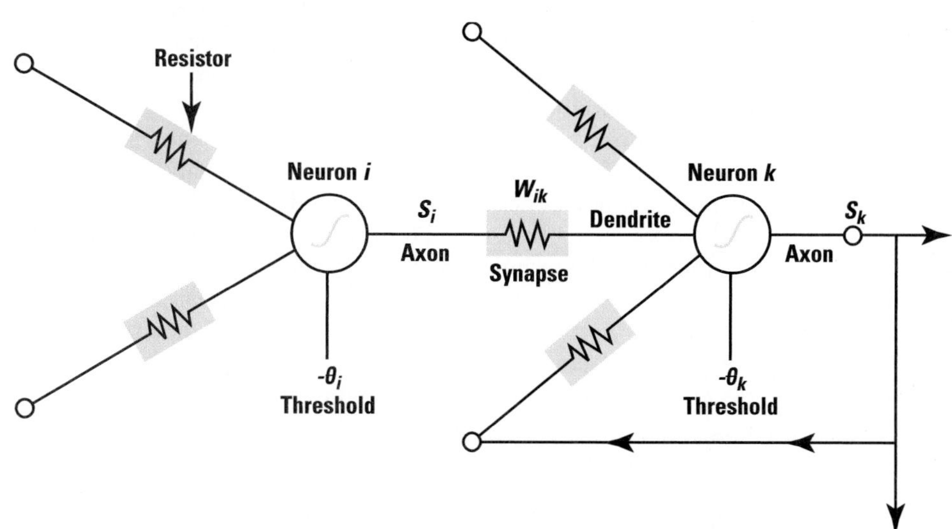

FIGURE 12.12 Artificial neural network with two neurons. In artificial neurons, the biological neurons become processing elements (switches), the axons and dendrites become wires, and the synapses become variable resistors that carry weighted inputs (currents) that represent data. *Source: DARPA, 1988. Unclassified.*

FIGURE 12.13

A neural network uses rules it "learns" from patterns in data to construct a hidden layer of logic. The hidden layer then processes inputs, classifying them based on the experience of the model. *Source: Herb Edelstein, "Technology How-To: Mining Data Warehouses,"* InformationWeek, *Jan. 8, 1998. Copyright © 1996 CMP Media, Inc., 600 Community Drive, Manhasset, NY 11030. Reprinted with permission.*

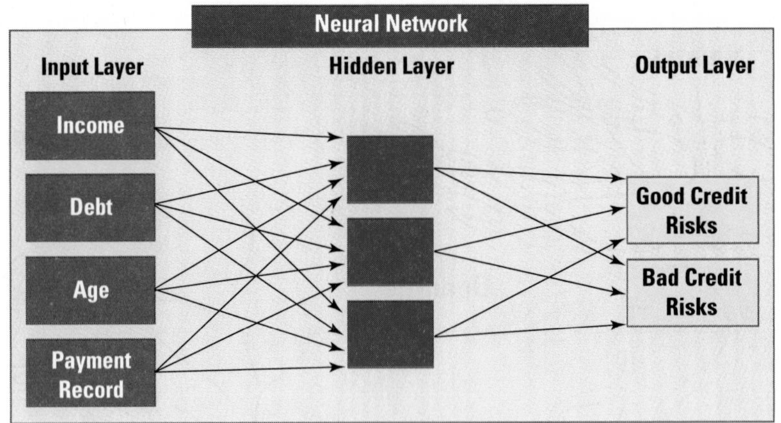

circuits are variable and can be used to teach the network. When the network makes a mistake (i.e., chooses the wrong pathway through the network and arrives at a false conclusion), resistance can be raised on some circuits, forcing other neurons to fire. If this learning process continues for thousands of cycles, the machine learns the correct response. The neurons are highly interconnected and operate in parallel.

A neural net has a large number of sensing and processing nodes that continuously interact with each other. Figure 12.13 represents a neural network comprising an input layer, an output layer, and a hidden processing layer. The network is fed a training set of data for which the inputs produce a known set of outputs or conclusions. This helps the computer learn the correct solution by example. As the computer is fed more data, each case is compared with the known outcome. If it differs, a correction is calculated and applied to the nodes in the hidden processing layer. These steps are repeated until a condition, such as corrections being less than a certain amount, is reached. The neural network in Figure 12.13 has "learned" how to identify a good credit risk.

The Difference Between Neural Networks and Expert Systems

What is different about neural networks? Expert systems seek to emulate or model a human expert's way of solving problems, but neural network builders claim that they do not model human intelligence, do not program solutions, and do not aim to solve specific problems per se. Instead, neural network designers seek to put intelligence into the hardware in the form of a generalized capability to learn. In contrast, the expert system is highly specific to a given problem and cannot be easily retrained.

Take a simple problem like identifying a cat. An expert system approach would interview hundreds of people to understand how humans recognize cats, resulting in a large set of rules, or frames, programmed into an expert system. In contrast, a trainable neural network would be brought to a test site, connected to a television, and started on the process of learning. Every time a cat was not correctly perceived, the system's interconnections would be adjusted. When cats were correctly perceived, the system would be left alone and another object scanned.

Neural network applications are emerging in medicine, science, and business to address problems in pattern classification, prediction and financial analysis, and control and optimization. Papnet is a neural net-based system to distinguish between normal and abnormal cells when examining Pap smears for cervical cancer, with far greater accuracy than visual examination by technicians. The computer is not able to make a final decision, so a technician will review any selected abnormal cells. Using Papnet a technician requires one-fifth the time to review a smear while attaining perhaps ten times the accuracy of the existing manual method.

Neural networks are being used by the financial industry to discern patterns in vast pools of data that might help investment firms predict the performance of equities, corporate bond ratings, or corporate bankruptcies (Lin, 1993). Japanese firms are using neural networks for prediction of securities ratings, timing of stock buying and selling, future yields of securities, inspection of flaws in steel plate, classification of welding defects, sound analysis, and identification of parts on a lens production line (Asakawa and Takagi, 1994). VISA International Inc. is using a neural network to help detect credit card fraud by monitoring all VISA transactions for sudden changes in the buying patterns of cardholders (Fryer, 1996).

Unlike expert systems, which typically provide explanations for their solutions, neural networks cannot always explain why they arrived at a particular solution. Moreover, they cannot always guarantee a completely certain solution, arrive at the same solution again with the same input data, or always guarantee the best solution (Trippi and Turban, 1989–1990). They are very sensitive and may not perform well if their training covers too little or too much data. In most current applications, neural networks are best used as aids to human decision makers instead of substitutes for them.

Fuzzy Logic

Traditional computer programs require precision—on–off, yes–no, right–wrong. However, we human beings do not experience the world this way. We might all agree that +120 degrees is hot and −40 degrees is cold; but is 75 degrees hot, warm, comfortable, or cool? The answer depends on many factors: the wind, the humidity, the individual experiencing the temperature, one's clothing, and one's expectations. Many of our activities also are inexact. Tractor-trailer drivers would find it nearly impossible to back their rig into a space precisely specified to less than an inch on all sides.

Fuzzy logic, a relatively new, rule-based development in AI, tolerates imprecision and even uses it to solve problems we could not have solved before. Fuzzy logic consists of a variety of concepts and techniques for representing and inferring knowledge that is imprecise, uncertain, or unreliable. Fuzzy logic can create rules that use approximate or subjective values and incomplete or ambiguous data. By expressing logic with some carefully defined imprecision, fuzzy logic is closer to the way people actually think than traditional IF–THEN rules.

fuzzy logic Rule-based AI that tolerates imprecision by using nonspecific terms called membership functions to solve problems.

Ford Motor Co. has developed a fuzzy logic application that backs a simulated tractor-trailer into a parking space. The application uses the following three rules:

IF the truck is *near* jackknifing, THEN *reduce* the steering angle.

IF the truck is *far away* from the dock, THEN steer *toward* the dock.

IF the truck is *near* the dock, THEN point the trailer *directly* at the dock.

This logic makes sense to us as human beings, for it represents how we think as we back that truck into its berth.

How does the computer make sense of this programming? The answer is relatively simple. The terms (known as *membership functions*) are imprecisely defined so that, for example, in Figure 12.14 cool is between 50 degrees and 70 degrees, although the temperature is most clearly cool between about 60 degrees and 67 degrees. Note that *cool* is overlapped by *cold* or *norm*. To control the room environment using this logic, the programmer would develop similarly imprecise definitions for humidity and other factors such as outdoor wind and temperature. The rules might include one that says: "*If the temperature is cool or cold and the humidity is low while the outdoor wind is high and the outdoor temperature is low, raise the heat and humidity in the room.*" The computer would combine the membership function readings in a weighted manner and, using all the rules, raise and lower the temperature and humidity.

Fuzzy logic is widely used in Japan and is gaining popularity in the United States. Its popularity has occurred partially because managers find they can use it to reduce costs and shorten development time. Fuzzy logic code requires fewer IF–THEN rules, making it simpler than traditional code. The rules required in the previous trucking example, plus its term definitions, might require hundreds of IF–THEN statements to implement in traditional logic. Compact code requires less computer capacity, allowing Sanyo Fisher USA to implement camcorder controls without adding expensive memory to their product.

Fuzzy logic also allows us to solve problems not previously solvable, thus improving product quality. In Japan, Sendai's subway system uses fuzzy logic controls to

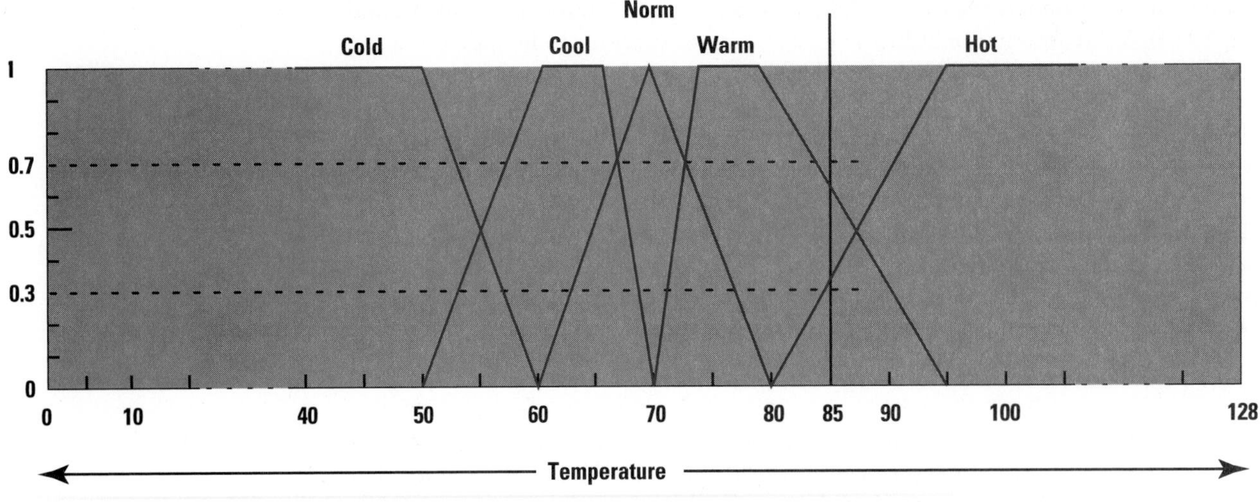

FIGURE 12.14

Implementing fuzzy logic rules in hardware. The membership functions for the input called temperature are in the logic of the thermostat to control the room temperature. Membership functions help translate linguistic expressions such as "warm" into numbers that can be manipulated by the computer. *Source: James M. Sibigtroth, "Implementing Fuzzy Expert Rules in Hardware,"* AI Expert, *April 1992. © 1992 Miller Freeman, Inc. Reprinted with permission.*

accelerate so smoothly that standing passengers need not hold on. Mitsubishi Heavy Industries in Tokyo has been able to reduce the power consumption of its air conditioners by 20 percent through implementing control programs in fuzzy logic. The auto-focus device in our cameras is only possible because of fuzzy logic. Williams-Sonoma sells an "intelligent" steamer made in Japan that uses fuzzy logic. A variable heat setting detects the amount of grain, cooks it at the preferred temperature, and keeps food warm up to 12 hours.

Management also has found fuzzy logic useful for decision making and organizational control. A Wall Street firm had a system developed that selects companies for potential acquisition, using the language stock traders understand. Recently a system has been developed to detect possible fraud in medical claims submitted by health care providers anywhere in the United States.

Genetic Algorithms

genetic algorithms Problem-solving methods that promote the evolution of solutions to specified problems using the model of living organisms adapting to their environment.

Genetic algorithms (also referred to as *adaptive computation*) refer to a variety of problem-solving techniques that are conceptually based on the method that living organisms use to adapt to their environment—the process of evolution. They are programmed to work the way populations solve problems—by changing and reorganizing their component parts using processes such as reproduction, mutation, and natural selection. Thus, genetic algorithms promote the evolution of solutions to particular problems, controlling the generation, variation, adaptation, and selection of possible solutions using genetically based processes. As solutions alter and combine, the worst ones are discarded and the better ones survive to go on to produce even better solutions. Genetic algorithms breed programs that solve problems even when no person can fully understand their structure (Holland, 1992).

Genetic algorithms originated in the work of John H. Holland, a professor of psychology and computer science at the University of Michigan, who devised a genetic code of binary digits that could be used to represent any type of computer program with a 1 representing true and a 0 representing false. With a long enough string of digits, any object can be represented by the right combination of digits. The genetic algorithm provides methods of searching all possible combinations of digits to identify the right string representing the best possible structure for the problem.

In one method, the programmer first randomly generates a population of strings consisting of combinations of binary digits. Each string corresponds to one of the variables in the problem. One applies a test for fitness, ranking the strings in the population according to their level of desirability as possible solutions. After the initial population is evaluated for fitness, the algorithm then produces the next generation of strings, consisting of strings that survived the fitness test plus offspring strings produced from mating pairs of strings, and tests their fitness. The process continues until a solution is reached (see Figure 12.15).

Like neural networks, genetic algorithms are ideal applications for massively parallel computers. Each processor can be assigned a single string. Thus, the entire population of a genetic algorithm can be processed in parallel, offering growing potential for solving problems of enormous complexity.

Solutions to certain types of problems in areas of optimization, product design, and the monitoring of industrial systems are especially appropriate for genetic algorithms. Many business problems require optimization because they deal with issues such as minimization of costs, maximization of profits, most efficient scheduling, and use of resources. If these situations are very dynamic and complex, involving hundreds of variables or hundreds of formulas, genetic algorithms are suitable for solving them because they can attack a solution from many directions at once.

Commercial applications of genetic algorithms are emerging. Engineers at General Electric used a genetic algorithm to help them design jet turbine aircraft engines, a complex problem involving about 100 variables and 50 constraint equations. The engineers evaluated design changes on a workstation that ran a simulation of the engine in operation. Because each design change required a new simulation to test its effectiveness, the designers could spend weeks on solutions that might not be optimal. Using an expert system reduced the time to produce a satisfactory design from several weeks to several days, but it would produce solutions only up to a point. Further improvements required simultaneous changes in large numbers of variables. At that point GE introduced a genetic algorithm that took the initial population of designs produced by the expert system and generated a design that contained three times the number of improvements over the best previous version in a period of only two days. Other organizations using genetic algorithms include the Coors Brewing Company, which uses genetic algorithms for scheduling the fulfillment and shipment of orders, and the U.S. Navy, which uses genetic algorithms for scheduling F-16 tryouts (Burtka, 1993).

Hybrid AI Systems

GE's system for jet engine design achieved impressive results by combining genetic algorithm and expert system technology. Genetic algorithms, fuzzy logic, neural networks, and expert systems can be integrated into a single application to take advantage of the best features of these technologies. Such systems are called **hybrid AI systems.** Hybrid applications in business are growing. In Japan, Hitachi, Mitsubishi, Ricoh, Sanyo, and others are starting to incorporate hybrid AI in products such as home appliances, factory machinery, and office equipment. Matsushita has developed a "neurofuzzy" washing machine that combines fuzzy logic with neural networks. Nikko Securities has been working on a neurofuzzy system to forecast convertible-bond ratings.

hybrid AI systems Integration of multiple AI technologies into a single application to take advantage of the best features of these technologies.

Intelligent Agents

Intelligent agents are software programs that work in the background to carry out specific, repetitive, and predictable tasks for an individual user, business process, or software application. The agent uses a built-in or learned knowledge base to accomplish tasks or make decisions on behalf of the user. Intelligent agents can be programmed to make decisions based on the user's personal preferences—for example, to delete junk e-mail, schedule appointments, or travel over interconnected networks to find the cheapest airfare to California. The agent can be likened to a personal digital assistant collaborating with the user in the same work environment. It can help the user by performing tasks on the user's behalf, training or teaching the user, hiding the complexity of difficult tasks, helping the user collaborate with other users, or monitoring events and procedures (Maes, 1994).

intelligent agent Software program that uses a built-in or learned knowledge base to carry out specific, repetitive, and predictable tasks for an individual user, business process, or software application.

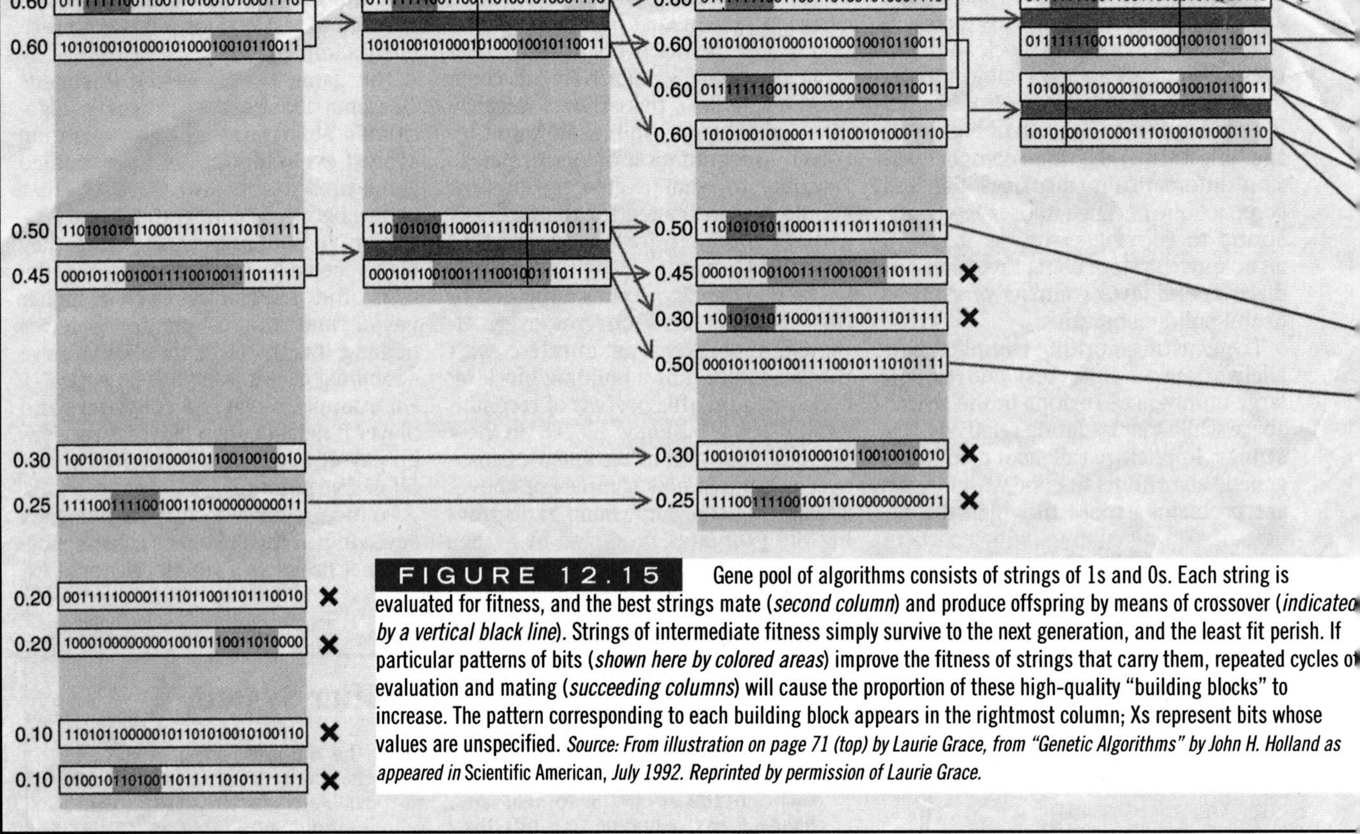

FIGURE 12.15 Gene pool of algorithms consists of strings of 1s and 0s. Each string is evaluated for fitness, and the best strings mate (*second column*) and produce offspring by means of crossover (*indicated by a vertical black line*). Strings of intermediate fitness simply survive to the next generation, and the least fit perish. If particular patterns of bits (*shown here by colored areas*) improve the fitness of strings that carry them, repeated cycles of evaluation and mating (*succeeding columns*) will cause the proportion of these high-quality "building blocks" to increase. The pattern corresponding to each building block appears in the rightmost column; Xs represent bits whose values are unspecified. *Source: From illustration on page 71 (top) by Laurie Grace, from "Genetic Algorithms" by John H. Holland as appeared in* Scientific American, *July 1992. Reprinted by permission of Laurie Grace.*

There are many intelligent agent applications today in operating systems, application software, e-mail systems, mobile computing software, and network tools. For example, the Wizards found in Microsoft Office software tools have built-in capabilities to show users how to accomplish various tasks, such as formatting documents or creating graphs, and to anticipate when users need assistance. (Search engines for locating information on the World Wide Web do not actually qualify as agents even though they sometimes are classified as such. These engines do not search the Internet for a query. They simply sort through a massive database of Web pages that the search engine has gathered.)

At IBM's Almaden Research Center, Dr. Ted Selker created an agent that actually facilitates the learning process for computer programmers who are learning the programming language LISP. COACH (Cognitive Adaptive Computer Help) contains three knowledge components that make it function. One compiles information about the user's LISP abilities including frequent mistakes and which coaching techniques proved effective. Another component maintains information about LISP itself. The final component stores strategies for coaching. COACH ensures that students of LISP receive a more thorough learning experience than they would otherwise.

Of special interest to business are intelligent agents used to cruise networks, including the Internet, in search of information. They are being used in electronic commerce applications to help consumers find products they want and assist them in comparing prices and other features. Yahoo! and Excite, two of the major Web search services, now offer "shopping agents" for a few merchandise categories, such as music, books, electronics, and toys. To use these agents, the consumer enters the desired product into an on-line shopping form. Using this information, the shopping agent searches

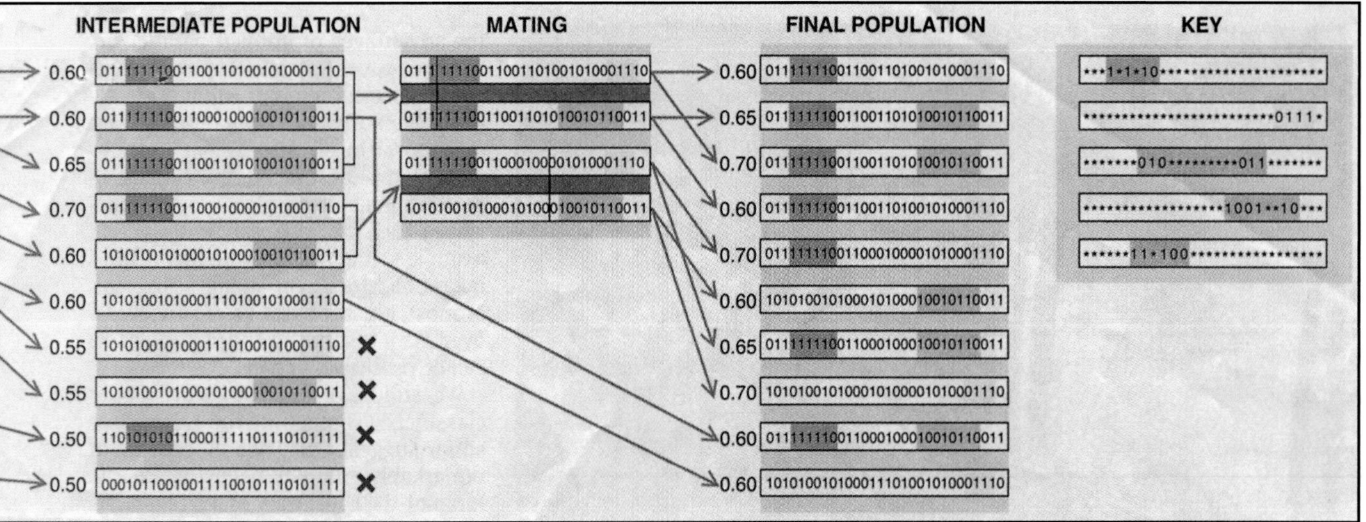

the Web for product pricing and availability. It returns a list of sites that sell the item along with pricing information and a purchase link.

"Eyes" is an automated personal-notification service from the Amazon.com on-line bookstore that performs agent functions by automatically sending e-mail notices to users concerning new books that might be of interest to them. After the user provides information on his or her specific interests, "Eyes" tracks every newly released book pertaining to those interests, automatically alerting the user to new arrivals.

Verity Inc. has developed server software that permits the release of an agent for the purpose of researching Web sites and databases. The product also provides means for the agent to brief a user on its findings by way of a pager, e-mail, or Web page. The Verity agent rates the importance of its findings according to the user's preferences, and uses those ratings in its reports. It already has turned out customized editions of the *San Jose Mercury*'s on-line newspaper in tests. Table 12.4 provides examples of other agents used in electronic commerce.

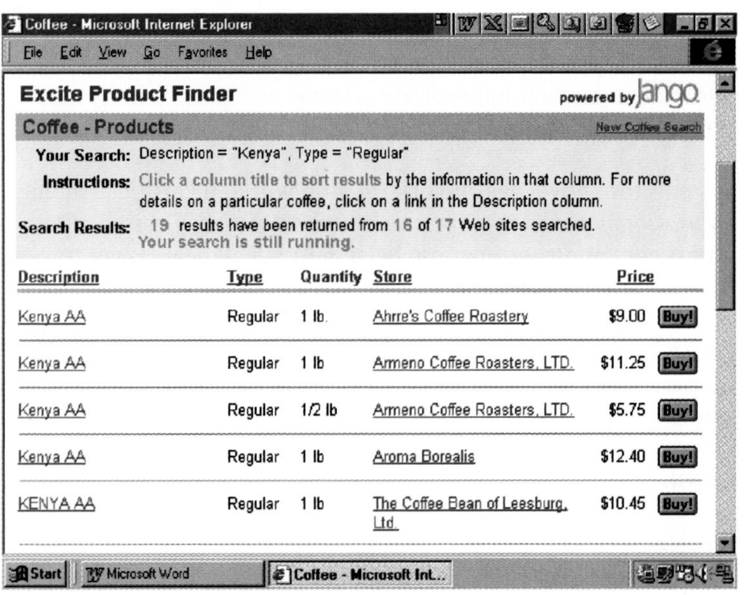

Excite's Product Finder uses Jango intelligent agent technology to search virtual retailers for price and availability of products specified by the user. Displayed here are the results of a search for sources of Kenya regular coffee.

TABLE 12.4 Examples of Intelligent Agents for Electronic Commerce

Product	Description	Vendor
Firefly	Helps users find music or films of interest. Users send critiques of movies and music to the Firefly Web site. When they want to select a new movie to see or a CD to buy, they supply data on their personal favorites, and Firefly will produce a list of similar items based on the critiques. The service is being extended to books, restaurants, and mutual funds.	Agents Inc.
IDML Tags	Can tag products and pages on a Web site to help users locate them.	Identify
Smart NewsReader	Windows application that provides access to Usenet newsgroups based on interests specified by the user. It can read through an article and score each thread of conversation based on the user's past interests.	Intel
BargainFinder and Lifestyle-Finder	BargainFinder does real-time comparison shopping among on-line participating CD music stores and returns the names of vendors that offer the lowest price. LifestyleFinder recommends Web sites to users based on information they provide about their lifestyles.	Andersen Consulting
Jango	Automatically consults Web sites and prepares reports for the shopper to find information and products such as books, clothing, wine, and PCs.	NetBot

Management Wrap-Up

MANAGEMENT

Leveraging and managing organizational knowledge have become core management responsibilities. Managers need to identify the knowledge assets of their organizations and make sure that appropriate systems and processes are in place to maximize their utilization.

ORGANIZATION

Systems for knowledge and information work and artificial intelligence can enhance organizational processes in a number of ways. They can facilitate communication, collaboration, and coordination, bring more analytical power to bear in the development of solutions, or reduce the amount of human intervention in organizational processes.

TECHNOLOGY

An array of technologies is available to support knowledge management, including artificial intelligence technologies and tools for knowledge and information work and group collaboration. Managers should understand the costs, benefits, and capabilities of each technology and the knowledge management problem for which each is best suited.

For Discussion:

1. Discuss some of the ways that knowledge management provides organizations with strategic advantage. How strategic are knowledge management systems?
2. How much can the use of artificial intelligence change the management process?

SUMMARY

1. **Explain the importance of knowledge management in contemporary organizations.** Knowledge management is the process of systematically and actively managing and leveraging the stores of knowledge in an organization. Knowledge is a central productive and strategic asset in an information economy. Information systems can play a valuable role in knowledge management, helping the organization optimize its flow of information and capture its knowledge base. Office automation systems (OAS), knowledge work systems (KWS), group collaboration systems, and artificial intelligence applications are especially useful for knowledge management because they focus on supporting information and knowledge work and on defining and codifying the organization's knowledge base.

2. **Describe the applications that are most useful for distributing, creating, and sharing knowledge in the firm.** Offices coordinate information work in the organization, link the work of diverse groups in the organization, and couple the organization to its external environment. Office automation systems (OAS) support these functions by automating document management, communications, scheduling, and data management. Word processing, desktop publishing, Web publishing, and digital imaging systems support document management activities. Electronic-mail systems and groupware support communications activities. Electronic calendar applications and groupware support scheduling activities. Desktop data-management systems support data management activities.

   Knowledge work systems (KWS) support the creation of knowledge and its integration into the organization. KWS require easy access to an external knowledge base; powerful computer hardware that can support software with intensive graphics, analysis, document management, and communications capabilities; and a friendly user interface. Knowledge work systems often run on workstations that are customized for the work they must perform. Computer-aided design (CAD) systems and virtual reality systems, which create interactive simulations that behave like the real world, require graphics and powerful modeling capabilities. Knowledge work systems for financial professionals provide access to external databases and the ability to analyze massive amounts of financial data very quickly.

   Groupware is special software to support information-intensive activities where people work collaboratively in groups. Intranets can perform many group collaboration and support functions and allow organizations to use Web publishing capabilities for document management.

3. **Evaluate the role of artificial intelligence in knowledge management.** Artificial intelligence is the development of computer-based systems that behave like humans. There are five members of the artificial intelligence family tree: natural language, robotics, perceptive systems, expert systems, and intelligent machines. Artificial intelligence lacks the flexibility, breadth, and generality of human intelligence but it can be used to capture and codify organizational knowledge.

4. **Demonstrate how organizations can use expert systems and case-based reasoning to capture knowledge.** Expert systems are knowledge-intensive computer programs that solve problems that heretofore required human expertise. The systems capture a limited domain of human knowledge using rules or frames. The strategy to search through the knowledge base, called the inference engine, can use either forward or backward chaining. Expert systems are most useful for problems of classification or diagnosis. Case-based reasoning represents organizational knowledge as a database of cases that can be continually expanded and refined. When the user encounters a new case, the system searches for similar cases, finds the closest fit, and applies the solutions of the old case to the new case. The new case is stored with successful solutions in the case database.

5. **Demonstrate how organizations can use neural networks and other intelligent techniques to improve their knowledge base.** Neural networks consist of hardware and software that attempt to mimic the thought processes of the human brain. Neural networks are notable for their ability to learn without programming and to recognize patterns that cannot be easily described by humans. They are being used in science, medicine, and business primarily to discriminate patterns in massive amounts of data.

   Fuzzy logic is a software technology that expresses logic with some carefully defined imprecision so that it is closer to the way people actually think than traditional IF–THEN rules. Fuzzy logic has been used for controlling physical devices and is starting to be used for limited decision-making applications.

   Genetic algorithms develop solutions to particular problems using genetically based processes such as fitness, crossover, and mutation to breed solutions. Genetic algorithms are beginning to be applied to problems involving optimization, product design, and monitoring industrial systems.

   Intelligent agents are software programs with built-in or learned knowledge bases that carry out specific, repetitive, and predictable tasks for an individual user, business process, or software application. Intelligent agents can be programmed to search for information or conduct transactions on networks, including the Internet.

KEY TERMS

AI shell, 384
Artificial intelligence, 381
Backward chaining, 385
Case-based reasoning (CBR), 388
Computer-aided design (CAD), 376
Data workers, 373
Document imaging systems, 374
Expert system, 383
Forward chaining, 384
Fuzzy logic, 393
Genetic algorithms, 394
Groupware, 378
Hybrid AI systems, 395
Index server, 375
Inference engine, 384
Information work, 373
Intelligent agent, 395
Investment workstation, 378
Jukebox, 374
Knowledge base, 383
Knowledge engineer, 386
Knowledge frames, 384
Knowledge management, 371
Knowledge workers, 373
Knowledge work systems (KWS), 375
Neural network, 391
Office automation systems (OAS), 373
Rule base, 383
Rule-based expert system, 383
Virtual Reality Modeling Language (VRML), 377
Virtual reality systems, 377

REVIEW QUESTIONS

1. What is knowledge management? List and briefly describe the information systems that support it.
2. What is the relationship between information work and productivity in contemporary organizations?
3. Describe the roles of the office in organizations. What are the major activities that take place in offices?
4. What are the principal types of information systems that support information worker activities of the office?
5. What are the generic requirements of knowledge work systems? Why?
6. Describe how the following systems support knowledge work: computer-aided design (CAD), virtual reality, investment workstations.
7. How does groupware support information work? Describe its capabilities and Internet and intranet capabilities for collaborative work.
8. What is artificial intelligence? Why is it of interest to business?
9. What is the difference between artificial intelligence and natural or human intelligence?
10. Define an expert system and describe how it can help organizations use their knowledge assets.
11. Define and describe the role of the following in expert systems: rule base, frames, inference engine.
12. What is case-based reasoning? How does it differ from an expert system?
13. Describe three problems of expert systems.
14. Describe a neural network. With what kinds of tasks would a neural network excel?
15. Define and describe fuzzy logic. What kinds of applications is it suited for?
16. What are genetic algorithms? How can they help organizations solve problems? What kinds of problems are they suited for?
17. What are intelligent agents? How can they be used to benefit businesses?

GROUP PROJECT

With a group of classmates, select two Web sites that provide intelligent agent technologies for electronic commerce and compare their capabilities; you can find lists of intelligent agent software by using Yahoo! to search for "intelligent software agents." Or compare two of the intelligent agent products described in this chapter. Present your findings to the class.

TOOLS FOR INTERACTIVE LEARNING

■ **INTERNET**: The Internet Connection for this chapter will take you to the National Aeronautics and Space Administration (NASA) Web site, where you can complete an exercise showing how this Web site can be used by knowledge workers. You can also use the Interactive Study Guide to test your knowledge of the topics in this chapter and get instant feedback where you need more practice.

■ **CD-ROM**: If you purchase and use the Multimedia Edition CD-ROM with this chapter, you will find two interactive exercises. The first asks you to choose the proper software tools for solving a series of knowledge management problems. The second asks you to select an appropriate AI technology to solve another series of problems. You can also find a video clip illustrating how the Papnet neural network is used for medical testing, an audio overview of the major themes of this chapter, and bullet text summarizing the key points of the chapter.

CASE STUDY

The United Nations Turns to Expert Systems

The United Nations has a payroll that would give most multinational corporations nightmares. Its 15,000 employees hold positions in more than 100 locations worldwide. They must pay in dozens of currencies. However, the worst complication is not the salary itself but the entitlements that accompany the salary.

Pay for U.N. employees is determined by a base salary plus entitlements. These entitlements include benefits based on location of work and the terms of a staff member's contract. All of these factors affect each employee's entitlements, and they constitute a significant portion of an employee's pay. The entitlements are so complex that they fill three volumes of several hundred pages each. Calculations of these entitlements were manual and often were described as "tedious." The United Nations decided to address these and other administrative computing matters in 1990 with its new Integrated Management Information System (IMIS).

Until IMIS, computing at the United Nations was based on aging mainframe systems. When the United Nations decided to modernize, it went all the way and moved to a client-server system. The new system's infrastructure includes Windows and UNIX operating systems and several thousand PC clients connected to HP9000 servers. IMIS is a series of client-server application modules that integrate accounting, payroll, personnel management, procurement and transportation functions. The project's staff throughout its development has included 30 to 60 developers. In addition, Price Waterhouse supplied consultants to the Entitlements project. All-in-all, it was a most ambitious project.

The first two years were spent gathering requirements, designing the system, and implementing the networks. In late 1993 they began to address the complex payroll. For the entitlements portion they designed the Entitlements System, using object-oriented technology to build an expert system that was capable of interpreting the complex salary regulations. The project selected PowerModel of IntelliCorp of Mountain View, California, for the development tool. Project members thought the tool fit well with the U.N.'s Windows–UNIX client-server environment. It integrates object-oriented programming, rule-based reasoning, a graphical user interface, and dynamic links to databases and other applications. It includes a fourth-generation tool for building a rule base and a knowledge base. PowerModel allowed developers to automate the parts of the system that were objectively quantifiable and to build a waiving process into the system for exceptions.

The entitlements project very early faced the enormous task of translating the three volumes of paper rules into a rules-based knowledge base. The developers organized the requirements into a class structure of objects. Establishing the requirements was one of the most difficult parts of the project because users in different locations saw and applied the requirements in different ways. After they designed the rules base, the team translated them into on-line rules.

The knowledge base for the system is online and is capable of applying entitlements automatically. The system also reassesses whenever a change to an employee's status is approved. Thus the system automates the tedious entitlement process and generates the appropriate salary for the next payroll after status changes are entered.

The new system had to be able to deal with promotions that do not reach the appropriate payroll office until long after they have been awarded. Whenever a promotion is entered, the system must recalculate the entitlements based upon the promotion date so that entitlements will be appropriate for the time between the promotion and the date it is entered into the system. Sometimes, however, events that merit a change in an individual's entitlements, such as a promotion, are not recorded until months later, but adding that entitlement at a later date might negate or modify other changes made to that individual's personnel status since the time of the promotion.

One of the reasons the project decided to use an object-oriented expert system is that the entitlement rules change so often. With traditional programming each rule change would result in changes to program code followed by recompiling the whole program. However, given the software technology being used, all the support staff must do to implement a rule change is go into the specific object and make the change and then return the new object into the rule base.

The system maintains the data on all U.N. employees and their dependents. It automatically manages such relevant events as promotions, relocations, and dependency-status changes. As a result, entitlement determination is more consistent than in the past, making the process more equitable. When IMIS processes a change to someone's entitlements, it offers an explanation of why the change was made, how it determined the change and what the value of the entitlements becomes. One result is that the U.N. now has much greater accuracy in the way entitlements are handled. In addition, whereas traditional systems usually compute entitlements when a payroll is run, in IMIS, personnel officers can make changes and see immediately what effect those changes will have on a staff member's pay. The system also allows its users to generate reports on the data, perform what-if scenarios, and project costs, making it an important planning tool.

The U.N. spent $85 million and eight years on IMIS, but it still isn't finished. The human resources module is operational only for some agencies, and the finance portion runs only at headquarters. IMIS's payroll system was scheduled to be operating in some divisions in late 1998. Some U.N. agencies are growing impatient, and they believe the system could have been built more rapidly at lower cost with commercial software packages such as SAP and PeopleSoft. But when the project began in 1990, commercial software packages were not robust enough to handle the United Nation's complex business rules.

Meanwhile, several thousand U.N. staff members around the world are straddling the old manual system and the incomplete IMIS. Even after IMIS is finished, much work remains. Maintenance probably will be difficult because the system was assembled in a patchwork fashion.

Sources: Gregory Dalton, "Slow Start for U.N. Project," *Information Week,* February 9, 1998; and David Baum, "U.N. Automates Payroll with AI System," *Datamation,* November 1996.

Case Study Questions

1. Was an expert system an appropriate technology for the United Nations to use with its payroll system? Why or why not?
2. How could IMIS change the way the United Nations conducted its business? How important is it for the United Nations? Why?
3. What management, organization, and technology factors were responsible for the problems encountered by the IMIS project?

CHAPTER 13

Enhancing Management Decision Making

chapter outline

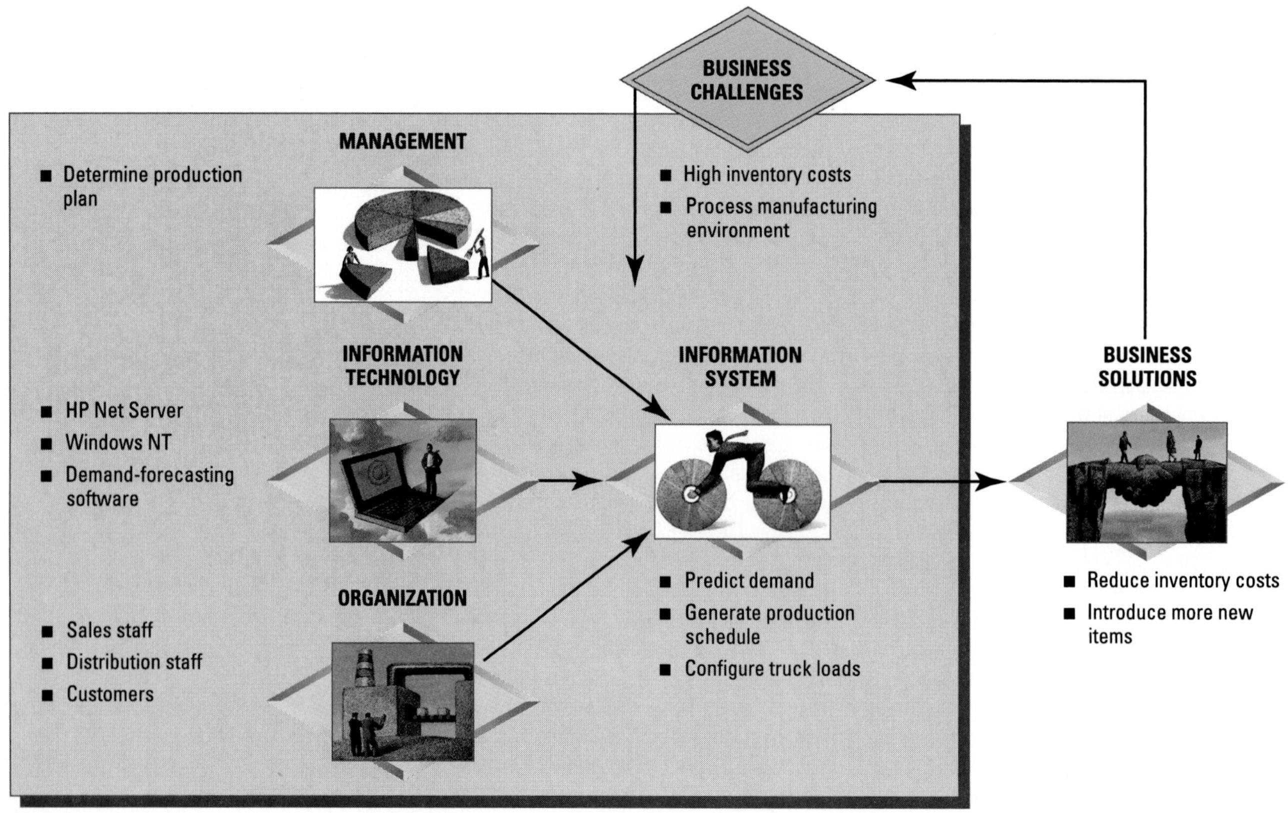

Foiling Bad Forecasts with a DSS

For the Reynolds Metal Company, aluminum sitting on the warehouse shelf is lost revenue. The company's foodservice division wanted to find a way to keep aluminum foil and plastic wrap moving more efficiently from the production line to restaurants and schools worldwide. Like most process manufacturers, who make goods from raw materials, Reynolds must base its production on the demand it forecasts rather than the orders it receives. Dave Seibert, the foodservice division's director of marketing, likened this process to "a roll of the dice." When Reynolds puts the product in a box, it is hoping the customers will buy it.

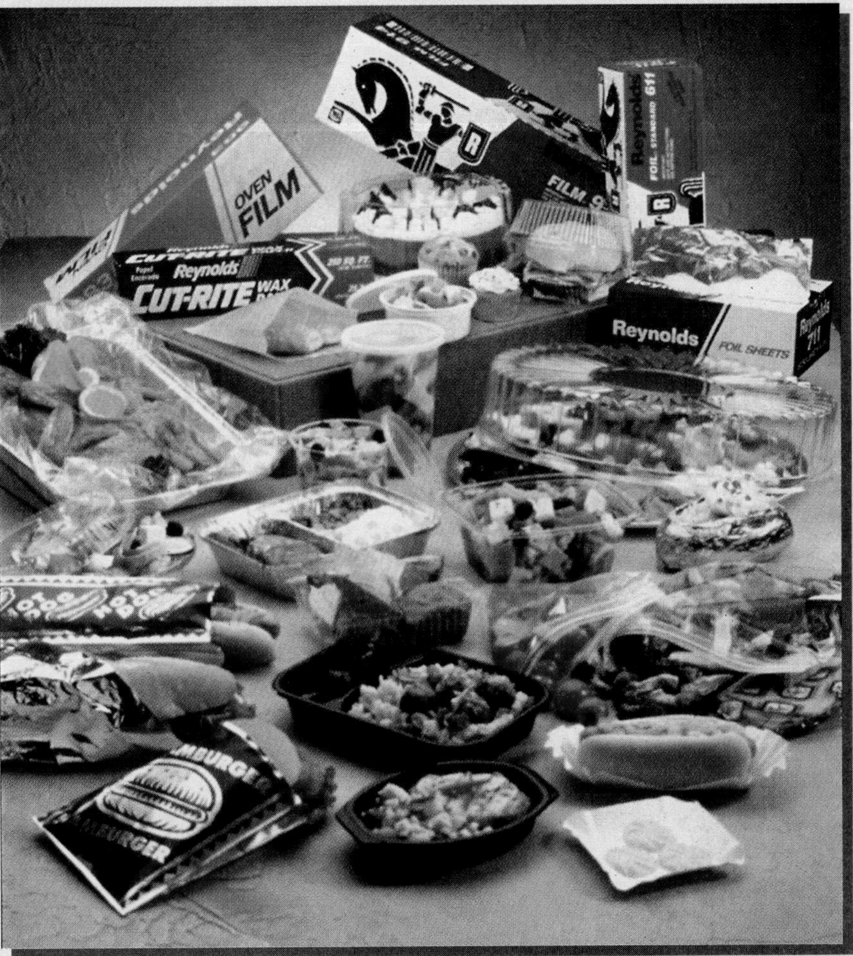

About 99 percent of the foodservice division's manufacturing plan is based on these forecasts, so accuracy is paramount. Reynolds had been using demand-forecasting software to help its production planning, but the software was more than twenty years old and ran on an IBM 9672 mainframe. It limited the company's ability to introduce items because the system only could be updated once a month. Error rates hovered in the mid-teens.

Reynolds decided to install a new demand-forecasting system that would provide a higher degree of precision when predicting customer needs. The new system runs on a Hewlett-Packard NetServer LS 100 running Microsoft's Windows NT operating system. The system can be updated daily if required.

Information such as sales history is entered into the system and used to make a preliminary prediction of the month's demand. The initial forecast is passed on to a distribution-planning module and combined with inventory and customer order projections. The system then generates requirements for when and where to ship a projected order. The distribution staff uses this information to help them configure the loads for the trucks. Managers in the manufacturing plants use the information to see what needs to be produced and where. The system has helped Reynolds reduce forecasting errors by 1 percent to 2 percent, and each percentage point translates into about 500,000 pounds of inventory that does not have to be maintained.

The foodservice division hopes to make the forecasting information more available to regional sales staff and even key customers by putting it on an extranet. A customer, for instance, could use a Web browser to review a forecast against its purchase plans and keep Reynolds' projections updated.

Source: Adapted from "Reynolds Foils Forecasting Errors," *Computerworld,* February 23, 1998.

Management Challenges

Reynolds' demand-forecasting system is an example of a decision-support system (DSS). Such systems have powerful analytic capabilities to support managers during the process of arriving at a decision. Other systems in this category are group decision-support systems (GDSS), which support decision making in groups, and executive support systems (ESS), which provide information for making strategic-level decisions. These systems can enhance organizational performance, but they raise the following management challenges:

1. **Building information systems that can actually fulfill executive information requirements.** Even with the use of Critical Success Factors and other information requirements determination methods, it may still be difficult to establish information requirements for ESS and DSS serving senior management. Chapter 3 has already described why certain aspects of senior management decision making cannot be supported by information systems because the decisions are too unstructured and fluid. Even if a problem can be addressed by an information system, senior management may not fully understand its actual information needs. For instance, senior managers may not agree on the firm's critical success factors, or the critical success factors they describe may be inappropriate or outdated if the firm is confronting a crisis requiring a major strategic change.

2. **Integrating DSS and ESS with existing systems in the business.** Even if system builders do know the information requirements for DSS or ESS, it may not be possible to fulfill them using data from the firm's existing information systems. Various MIS or TPS may define important pieces of data, such as the time period covered by the fiscal year, in different ways. It may not be possible to reconcile data from incompatible internal systems for analysis by managers even through data cleansing and data warehousing. A significant amount of organizational change may be required before the firm can build and install effective DSS and ESS.

learning objectives

After completing this chapter, you will be able to:

1. Differentiate a decision-support system (DSS) and a group decision-support system (GDSS).
2. Describe the components of decision-support systems and group decision-support systems.
3. Demonstrate how decision-support systems and group decision-support systems can enhance decision making.
4. Describe the capabilities of an executive support system (ESS).
5. Assess the benefits of executive support systems.

Most information systems described throughout this text help people make decisions in one way or another, but DSS, GDSS, and ESS are part of a special category of information systems that are explicitly designed to enhance managerial decision making. This chapter describes the characteristics of each of these types of information systems and shows how each enhances the managerial decision-making process.

DSS, GDSS, and ESS can support decision making in a number of ways. They can automate certain decision procedures (for example, determining the highest price that can be charged for a product to maintain market share). They can provide information about different aspects of the decision situation and the decision process, such as what opportunities or problems triggered the decision process, what solution alternatives were generated or explored, and how the decision was reached. Finally, they can stimulate innovation in decision making by helping managers question existing decision procedures or explore different solution designs (Dutta, Wierenga, and Dalebout, 1997).

13.1 DECISION-SUPPORT SYSTEMS (DSS)

As noted in Chapter 2, a **decision-support system (DSS)** assists management decision making by combining data, sophisticated analytical models and tools, and user-friendly software into a single powerful system that can support semistructured or unstructured decision making. A DSS provides users with a flexible set of tools and capabilities for analyzing important blocks of data.

decision-support system (DSS) Computer system at the management level of an organization that combines data, analytical tools, and models to support semistructured and unstructured decision making.

DSS and MIS

DSS are more targeted than MIS systems. An MIS provides managers with reports based on routine flows of data and assists in the general control of the organization. In contrast, a DSS is tightly focused on a specific decision or classes of decisions such as routing, queueing, evaluating, predicting, and so forth. In philosophy, a DSS promises end-user control of data, tools, and sessions. An MIS focuses on structured information flows, whereas a DSS emphasizes change, flexibility, and a quick response. With a DSS there is less of an effort to link users to structured information flows and a correspondingly greater emphasis on models, assumptions, ad hoc queries, and display graphics. Both the DSS and MIS rely on professional analysis and design. However, whereas an MIS usually follows a traditional systems development methodology, freezing information requirements before design and throughout the life cycle, a DSS is consciously iterative and never frozen.

Chapter 3 introduced the distinction between structured, semistructured, and unstructured decisions. Structured problems are repetitive and routine, for which known algorithms provide solutions. Unstructured problems are novel and nonroutine, for which there are no algorithms for solutions. One can discuss, decide, and ruminate about unstructured problems, but they are not solved in the sense that one finds an answer to an equation (Henderson and Schilling, 1985). Semistructured problems fall between structured and unstructured problems. A DSS is designed to support semistructured and unstructured problem analysis.

Chapter 3 also introduced Simon's description of decision making, which consists of four stages: intelligence, design, choice, and implementation. Decision-support systems are intended to help design and evaluate alternatives and monitor the adoption or implementation process.

Types of Decision-Support Systems

The earliest DSS tended to draw on small subsets of corporate data and were heavily model driven. Recent advances in computer processing and database technology have expanded the definition of a DSS to include systems that can support decision making by analyzing vast quantities of data.

Today there are two basic types of decision-support systems, model driven and data driven (Dhar and Stein, 1997). Early DSS developed in the late 1970s and 1980s were model driven. **Model-driven DSS** were primarily stand-alone systems isolated from major organizational information systems that used some type of model to perform "what-if" and other kinds of analyses. Such systems were often developed by end-user divisions or groups not under central IS control. Their analysis capabilities were based on a strong theory or model combined with a good user interface that made the model easy to use. The voyage-estimating DSS described in Chapter 2 is an example of a model-driven DSS.

model-driven DSS Primarily stand-alone system that uses some type of model to perform "what-if" and other kinds of analyses.

data-driven DSS A system that supports decision making by allowing users to extract and analyze useful information that was previously buried in large databases.

datamining Technology for finding hidden patterns and relationships in large databases and inferring rules from them to predict future behavior.

The second type of DSS is a **data-driven DSS.** These systems analyze large pools of data found in major organizational systems. They support decision making by allowing users to extract useful information that previously was buried in large quantities of data. Often data from transaction processing systems (TPS) are collected in data warehouses for this purpose. On-line analytical processing (OLAP) and datamining can then be used to analyze the data.

Traditional database queries answer such questions as, "How many units of product number 403 were shipped in November 1998?" On-line analytical processing (OLAP), or multidimensional analysis, supports much more complex requests for information, such as, "Compare sales of product 403 relative to plan by quarter and sales region for the past two years." We described on-line analytical processing (OLAP) and multidimensional data analysis in Chapter 7. With OLAP and query-oriented data analysis, users need to have a good idea about the information for which they are looking.

Datamining is more discovery driven. **Datamining** provides insights into corporate data that cannot be obtained with OLAP by finding hidden patterns and relationships in large databases and inferring rules from them to predict future behavior. The patterns and rules then can be used to guide decision making and forecast the effect of those decisions. The types of information that can be yielded from datamining include associations, sequences, classifications, clusters, and forecasts (Edelstein, 1996).

Associations are occurrences linked to a single event. For instance, a study of supermarket purchasing patterns might reveal that when corn chips are purchased, a cola drink is purchased 65 percent of the time, but when there is a promotion, cola is purchased 85 percent of the time. With this information, managers can make better decisions because they have learned the profitability of a promotion.

In *sequences,* events are linked over time. One might find, for example, that if a house is purchased, then a new refrigerator will be purchased within two weeks 65 percent of the time and an oven will be bought within one month of the home purchase 45 percent of the time.

Classification recognizes patterns that describe the group to which an item belongs by examining existing items that have been classified and by inferring a set of rules. For example, businesses such as credit card or telephone companies worry about the loss of steady customers. Classification can help discover the characteristics of customers who are likely to leave and can provide a model to help managers predict who they are so that they can devise special campaigns to retain such customers.

Clustering works in a manner similar to classification when no groups have yet been defined. A datamining tool will discover different groupings within data, such as finding affinity groups for bank cards or partitioning a database into groups of customers based on demographics and types of personal investments.

Although these applications involve predictions, *forecasting* uses predictions in a different way. It uses a series of existing values to forecast what other values will be. For example, forecasting might find patterns in data to help managers estimate the future value of continuous variables such as sales figures.

Datamining uses statistical analysis tools as well as neural networks, fuzzy logic, genetic algorithms, or rule-based and other intelligent techniques (described in Chapter 12).

As noted in Chapter 3, it is a mistake to think that decisions are only made by individuals in large organizations. In fact, most decisions are made collectively. Chapter 3 describes the rational, bureaucratic, political, and "garbage can" models of organizational decision making. Frequently, decisions must be coordinated with several groups before being finalized. In large organizations, decision making is inherently a group process, and a DSS can be designed to facilitate group decision making. Section 13.2 deals with this issue.

Components of DSS

Figure 13.1 illustrates the components of a DSS. They include a database of data used for query and analysis, a software system with models, datamining, and other analytical tools and a user interface.

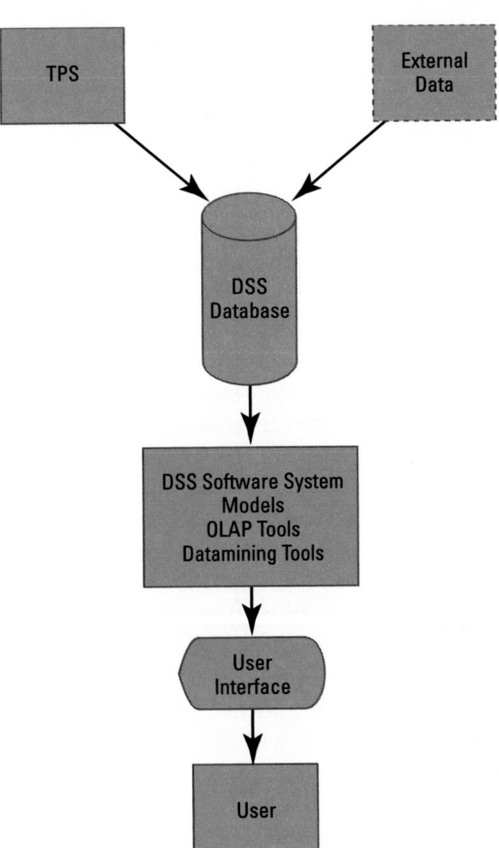

FIGURE 13.1

Overview of a decision-support system (DSS). The main components of the DSS are the DSS database, the DSS software system, and the user interface. The DSS database may be a small database residing on a PC or a massive data warehouse.

The **DSS database** is a collection of current or historical data from a number of applications or groups. It may be a small database residing on a PC that contains a subset of corporate data that has been downloaded and possibly combined with external data. Alternatively, the DSS database may be a massive data warehouse that is continuously updated by major organizational TPS. The data in DSS databases are generally extracts or copies of production databases so that using the DSS does not interfere with critical operational systems.

DSS database A collection of current or historical data from a number of applications or groups. Can be a small PC database or a massive data warehouse.

The **DSS software system** contains the software tools that are used for data analysis. It may contain various OLAP tools, datamining tools, or a collection of mathematical and analytical models that easily can be made accessible to the DSS user. A **model** is an abstract representation that illustrates the components or relationships of a phenomenon. A model can be a physical model (such as a model airplane), a mathematical model (such as an equation), or a verbal model (such as a description of a procedure to write up an order). Each decision support system is built for a specific set of purposes and will make different collections of models available depending on those purposes.

DSS software system Collection of software tools that are used for data analysis, such as OLAP tools, datamining tools, or a collection of mathematical and analytical models.

model An abstract representation that illustrates the components or relationships of a phenomenon.

Perhaps the most common models are libraries of statistical models. Such libraries usually contain the full range of expected statistical functions including means, medians, deviations, and scatter plots. The software has the ability to project future outcomes by analyzing a series of data. Statistical modeling software can be used to help establish relationships, such as relating product sales to differences in age, income, or other factors between communities. Optimization models, often using linear programming, determine optimal resource allocation to maximize or minimize specified variables such as cost or time. The Advanced Planning System (discussed in the next section) uses such software to determine the effect that filling a new order will have on meeting target dates for existing orders. A classic use of optimization models is to determine the proper mix of products within a given market to maximize profits.

Forecasting models often are used to forecast sales. The user of this type of model might supply a range of historical data to project future conditions and the sales that might result from those conditions. The decision maker could vary those future conditions (entering, for example, a rise in raw materials costs or the entry of a new, low-priced competitor in the market) to determine how these new conditions might affect sales. Companies often use this software to attempt to predict the actions of competitors. Model libraries exist for specific functions, such as financial and risk analysis models.

sensitivity analysis Models that ask "what-if" questions repeatedly to determine the impact of changes in one or more factors on outcomes.

Among the most widely used models are **sensitivity analysis** models that ask "what-if" questions repeatedly to determine the impact of changes in one or more factors on outcomes. "What-if" analysis—working forward from known or assumed conditions—allows the user to vary certain values to test results in order to better predict outcomes if changes occur in those values. "What happens if" we raise the price by 5 percent or increase the advertising budget by $100,000? What happens if we keep the price and advertising budget the same? Desktop spreadsheet software, such as Lotus 1-2-3 or Microsoft Excel, often is used for this purpose. Backward sensitivity analysis software is used for goal seeking: If I want to sell one million product units next year, how much must I reduce the price of the product?

The DSS user interface permits easy interaction between users of the system and the DSS software tools. A graphic, easy-to-use, flexible user interface supports the dialogue between the user and the DSS. The DSS users are usually corporate executives or managers, persons with well-developed working styles and individual preferences. Often they have little or no computer experience and no patience for learning to use a complex tool, so the interface must be relatively intuitive. In addition, what works for one may not work for another. Many executives, offered only one way of working (a way not to their liking), will simply not use the system. To mimic a typical way of working, a good user interface should allow the manager to move back and forth between activities at will. Building successful DSS requires a high level of user participation and, often, the use of prototyping to ensure these requirements are met.

Examples of DSS Applications

There are many ways in which DSS can be used to support decision making. Table 13.1 lists examples of DSS in well-known organizations. To illustrate the range of capabilities of a DSS, we will describe some successful DSS applications. The Advanced Planning System and Reynolds' demand-forecasting system described in the chapter-opening vignette are examples of a model-driven DSS. Southern California Gas Co., ShopKo Stores, and Barclay's Group Portfolio Management System are examples of a data-driven DSS.

TABLE 13.1 Examples of Decision-Support Systems

Organization	DSS Application
American Airlines	Price and route selection
Equico Capital Corporation	Investment evaluation
General Accident Insurance	Customer buying patterns and fraud detection
Bank of America	Customer profiles
Frito-Lay, Inc.	Price, advertising, and promotion selection
Burlington Coat Factory	Store location and inventory mix
National Gypsum	Corporate planning and forecasting
Southern Railway	Train dispatching and routing
Texas Oil and Gas Corporation	Evaluation of potential drilling sites
United Airlines	Flight scheduling
U.S. Department of Defense	Defense contract analysis

The Advanced Planning System—A Manufacturing DSS

To support most kinds of manufacturing, companies use a type of software known as manufacturing resources planning (MRPII). The typical MRPII system includes such applications as master production scheduling, purchasing, material requirements planning, and even general ledger. Many MRPII systems are too large and slow to be used for "what-if" simulations and too procedural to be modified into decision-support software. A Canadian company, Carp Systems International of Kanata, Ontario, sells the Advanced Planning System (APS) to give the user DSS functionality using the data from existing MRPII systems.

APS allows a range of "what-if" processing by pulling the relevant data from the manufacturing software and performing calculations based on user-defined variables. After Hurricane Andrew hit south Florida in 1992, Trane's Unitary Productions division in Fort Smith, Arkansas, was asked to quickly ship 114 five-ton air conditioning systems to small businesses in the affected area. Using APS, within minutes Trane could determine not only how long it would take to build the units but also how the added production would affect its existing customer commitments. The company found that it was able to fit the added production in without disrupting existing orders. It delivered the units weeks before the competition did.

Pitney Bowes, the $3.3 billion business equipment manufacturer, uses the software to simulate supply changes. Pitney Bowes carries enough manufacturing inventory to satisfy demand for 30 days. Using APS, the firm asked to see the impact if it would reduce the inventory to 15 days. APS responded with an answer within five minutes, including an estimate of what Pitney Bowes would save.

Southern California Gas Company

Southern California Gas Company needed to be more competitive in a recently deregulated industry. It created a marketing department and used data mining to focus the company's marketing efforts. Southern California Gas created a data mart—a departmental data warehouse consisting of billing records combined with credit data from Equifax and U.S. census records. Using data-mining techniques, the marketing department was able to identify a segment of customers most likely to sign up for a level payment plan.

Southern California Gas also used the system to decrease churn, or customers who were most likely to leave. Marketers learned that small, heating-only commercial customers were more sensitive to price increases than had been imagined. If the company were to raise its rates, this group of customers would switch to electric heating (mostly through space heaters). The company then performed a cost-benefit analysis to find out how much it cost to have such customers leave. Management decided that the company was not losing enough money from churn from this group of customers to warrant spending much money to keep them. It did, however, change its marketing approach to this group. It receives different literature that addresses the issue (Varney, 1996).

ShopKo Stores

ShopKo Stores, a $2 billion regional discounter, based in Green Bay, Wisconsin, competes head-to-head with Wal-Mart. The company started using datamining in about 1994 to discover cause-and-effect relationships between store items and customer buying habits. By using IBM's Intelligent Miner software across its advertising and merchandising departments, it discovered that customers who come in to purchase one product often buy another associated product, but that many associations are one-way streets. For example, a camera sale often triggers a film sale, but a film sale usually doesn't cause a camera sale.

ShopKo also learned that sales increased when merchandise was arranged in the store to match the way items were advertised in local circulars. Sometimes, however, the company ignores the results of data mining to maintain a high level of customer service. For example, ShopKo did increase sales by displaying baby formula next to baby clothes, but customers reported that they felt manipulated by that layout. ShopKo returned baby formula to its original location (Gerber, 1996).

The Window on Technology describes a data-driven decision-support system used in the financial industry.

WINDOW ON TECHNOLOGY

Utilizing Barclays' Bulging Data Warehouse

Data warehousing has become so successful that corporations often find they have more data than they can profitably use with their existing technology. The data warehouse of Barclays, the United Kingdom banking giant, was bulging, but they could not get the data they needed from all of it without new software. For example, they urgently needed to better manage their credit risk. They estimated that slicing just a few basis points from their average loan-default rate would result in millions of dollars more in profits each year, but to accomplish this they would need to examine huge quantities of data. Although it was possible to do, the time required to analyze the data was unacceptably slow. One model they wanted to use required 72 hours to run. Moreover, the model required that all the data be read from the warehouse database and loaded into the computer's memory before it could be processed. This would require that their hardware have immense amounts of very expensive computer memory.

Barclays was able to solve this problem by taking advantage of new features of on-line analytical processing (OLAP) software. This software was designed to enable the computer to dig deeply into the data warehouse, extracting large quantities of data at the very bottom of the data hierarchy. For example, in the past, for certain applications Barclays only could analyze its data at the regional level. With new software, they would be able to drill down to approximately 2000 branches and even beyond that to individual accounts.

To meet its needs, Barclay joined forces with WhiteLight Systems, an emerging software company based in Palo Alto, California. They knew about WhiteLight because Barclays had been looking for ways to solve its problems for several years and had briefly used a WhiteLight earlier product. This time, however, they allied with WhiteLight to complete development of the company's newest, most powerful version. Initial tests of the new software showed that processing time for the model described here was cut to about one hour, an amazing reduction of 96 percent. Barclay's new data-driven decision-support system, called the Group Portfolio Management System (GPMS) used a Teradata database, an NCR 4300 quad processor, a Pentium Pro 200 server with 1 gigabyte of memory, and client computers using Pentium 200s with 128 megabytes of memory. With this less-expensive hardware arrangement, using the model became feasible.

A bonus feature of the new software was that it supplied a highly detailed audit trail of the processing. With this audit trail, the bank staff was able to understand precisely how the calculations were being performed. In this way they could better understand the meaning of the information produced by WhiteLight. Barclays could begin the process of analyzing its giant quantity of data to find ways to reduce the risk of loan defaults.

To Think About: ***Suggest ways the success of this new technology at Barclays might affect the company's business strategy, technology commitment, and organization.***

Source: Adapted from Andy Webb, "Slice & Dice Massive Data Sets," *Wall Street & Technology,* Spring 1998 Edition.

Web-Based DSS

customer decision-support system (CDSS) System to support the decision-making process of an existing or potential customer.

DSS based on the Web and the Internet are being developed to support decision-making, providing on-line access to various databases and information pools along with software for data analysis. Some of these DSS are targeted toward management, but some have been developed to attract customers by providing information and tools to assist their decision-making as they select products and services. Companies are finding that deciding which products and services to purchase has become increasingly information-intensive. People use more information from multiple sources to make purchasing decisions (such as purchasing a car or computer) before they interact with the product or sales staff. **Customer decision-support systems (CDSS)** support the decision-making process of an existing or potential customer.

Figure 13.2 illustrates generic Internet facilities for a customer DSS. People interested in purchasing a product or service can use Internet search engines, intelligent agents, on-line catalogs, Web directories, newsgroup discussions, e-mail, and other tools to help them locate the information they need to help with their decision. Information brokers, such as Auto-by-Tel, described in Chapter 9, are also sources of summarized, structured information for specific products or industries and may provide models for evaluating the information.

Companies also have developed specific customer Web sites where all the information, models, or other analytical tools for evaluating alternatives are concentrated in one location. Some examples would be General Electric Plastics, Fidelity Investment's On-line Investor Center and Pedestal Capital's Bond Network.

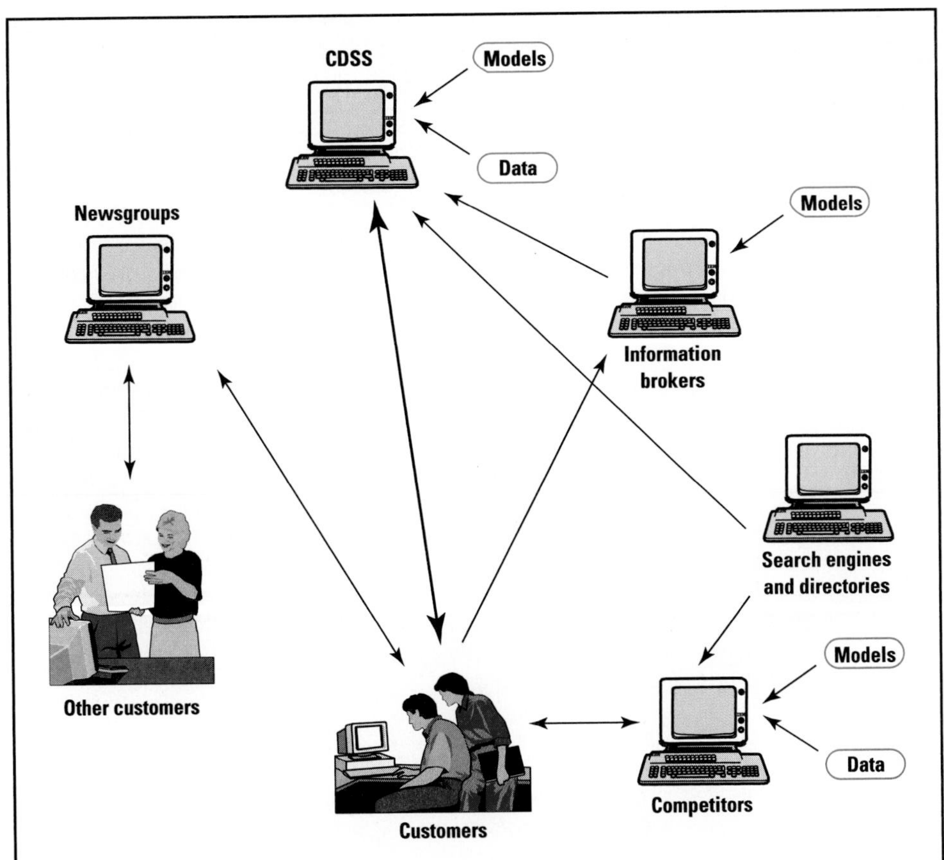

FIGURE 13.2

Customer decision support on the Internet. The Internet provides many sources of information and tools to assist customer purchasing decisions, including Web sites customized for this purpose. *Source: Robert M. O'Keefe and Tim McEachern, "Web-Based Customer Decision Support Systems,"* Communications of the ACM, *41, No. 3 (March 1998). Reprinted by permission.*

General Electric Plastics' DSS on the Web

General Electric Plastics (GEP) makes raw plastics that are packaged for specific uses such as bathroom sealants or that are used in the manufacture of other products. One of its ongoing problems is the need to constantly update product-specification information, which is vital to engineers using plastics in product design. GEP decided to use its Web site to provide a searchable repository of product-specification information that could be updated weekly. When launched, the site contained more than 15,000 pages of technical information. An e-mail capability allows visitors to forward technical questions to engineers, who then contact the customer.

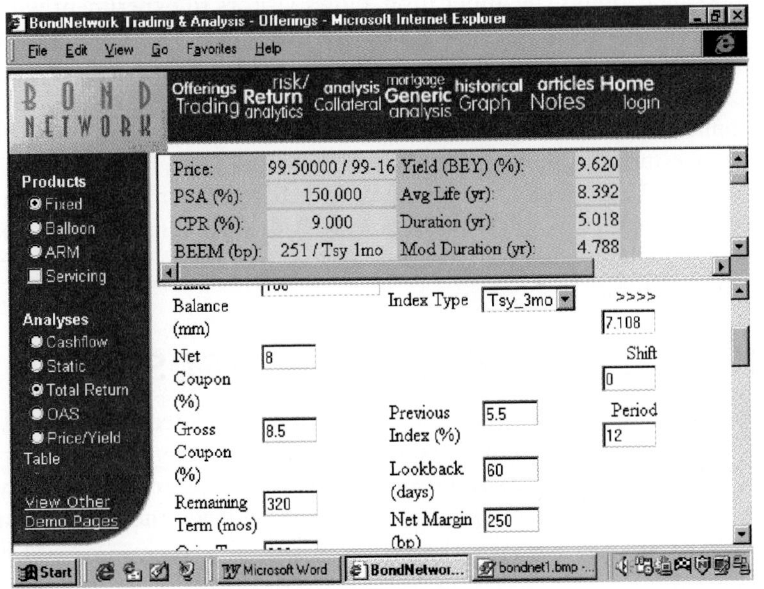

Bond Network is a Web-based financial DSS that visitors can use to evaluate alternative investments in mortgage portfolios. DSS based on the Web can provide information from multiple sources and analytical tools to help potential customers select products and services.

WINDOW ON ORGANIZATIONS

Bond Network: A Web-Based Financial DSS

Pedestal Capital Inc. is a New York-based brokerage firm that specializes in reselling loans, servicing, and other financial products related to mortgages. Its clients include banks, broker/dealers and other financial service institutions. It is the first brokerage firm to offer these types of portfolios on the Internet. Products ranging from one-year, adjustable-rate mortgages to 30-year, fixed-rate mortgage portfolios can be bought and sold this way.

Yung Lim, Pedestal's president and founder, believes his company's clients can benefit from the ability to analyze offerings on-line. He realizes that the power of the Internet can be harnessed to create a more efficient marketplace for the purchase and sale of mortgage-loan financial products. By providing clients with access to its staff and the use of its Web site, Pedestal hopes to improve information transfer and the valuation of mortgage products.

Pedestal's Web site, called Bond Network (www.bondnetwork.com), offers the ability to perform in a few minutes a number of tasks that often take hours with a spreadsheet. For instance, if a potential buyer wants to determine the level of prepayments that can be expected of a portfolio, they go to the Web, access Bond Network, and click on one of the displayed menu options. The numbers are analyzed and the answer appears in a few seconds. Pedestal's Web servers store all of the required product information and analytical software tools.

Pedestal's DSS is the first system to offer live on-line pricing of whole loan portfolios on the Internet. Whole loans are the raw mortgage products that financial service companies offer to home buyers or builders. They are pooled to become mortgage-backed bonds that trade very actively on Wall Street. Bond Network provides investors with information and the analysis to help them make better decisions regarding the buying and selling of whole loans and servicing.

To Think About: ***What kind of DSS is illustrated here? How can using a Web-based customer DSS help promote a company's business strategy? Suggest other applications for Web-based DSS.***

Source: Adapted from Alex Knight, "Whole Loans on the Net," *Wall Street and Technology*, January 1998.

Much of the data in the technical specifications are generated by continuous-simulation models. For example, a simulation model would be used to find out how a particular plastic might behave at very high temperatures. GEP's Web site was enhanced to make these simulation models available to customers so they could perform their own analysis. The Web site could dynamically generate graphs and diagrams in response to customer inputs (O'Keefe and McEachern, 1998).

Web-Based Financial DSS: Fidelity Investments and Pedestal Capital

Fidelity Investments' Web site features an on-line, interactive decision-support application to help clients make decisions about investment savings plans and investment portfolio allocations. The application allows visitors to experiment with numerous "what-if" scenarios to design investment savings plans for retirement or a child's college education. If the user enters information about his or her finances, time horizon, and tolerance for risk, the system will suggest appropriate portfolios of mutual funds. The application performs the required number-crunching and displays the changing return on investment as the user alters these assumptions.

The Window on Organizations describes another Web-based customer DSS for financial services. Bond Network is a Web site providing data on potential investments and financial models that visitors can use to evaluate alternative investments in mortgage portfolios.

13.2 GROUP DECISION-SUPPORT SYSTEMS (GDSS)

Early DSS focused largely on supporting individual decision making. However, because so much work is accomplished in groups within organizations, system developers and scholars began to focus on how computers can support group and organizational decision making. A new category of systems developed, known as group decision-support systems (GDSS).

What Is a GDSS?

A **group decision-support system (GDSS)** is an interactive computer-based system to facilitate the solution of unstructured problems by a set of decision makers working together as a group (DeSanctis and Gallupe, 1987). The GDSS was developed in response to a growing concern over the quality and effectiveness of meetings. The underlying problems in group decision making have been the explosion of decision-maker meetings, the growing length of those meetings, and the increased number of attendees. Estimates on the amount of a manager's time spent in meetings range from 35 percent to 70 percent.

group decision-support system (GDSS) An interactive computer-based system to facilitate the solution to unstructured problems by a set of decision makers working together as a group.

Meeting facilitators, organizational development professionals, and information systems scholars have been focusing on this issue and have identified a number of discrete meeting elements that need to be addressed (Grobowski et al., 1990; Kraemer and King, 1988; Nunamaker et al., 1991). Among these elements are the following:

1. *Improved preplanning,* to make meetings more effective and efficient.
2. *Increased participation,* so that all attendees will be able to contribute fully even if the number of attendees is large. Free riding (attending the meeting but not contributing) must also be addressed.
3. *Open, collaborative meeting atmosphere,* in which attendees from various organizational levels feel able to contribute freely. The lower-level attendees must be able to participate without fear of being judged by their management; higher-status participants must be able to participate without having their presence or ideas dominate the meeting and result in unwanted conformity.
4. *Criticism-free idea generation,* enabling attendees to contribute without undue fear of feeling personally criticized.
5. *Evaluation objectivity,* creating an atmosphere in which an idea will be evaluated on its merits rather than on the basis of the source of the idea.
6. *Idea organization and evaluation,* which require keeping the focus on the meeting objectives, finding efficient ways to organize the many ideas that can be generated in a brainstorming session, and evaluating those ideas not only on their merits but also within appropriate time constraints.
7. *Setting priorities and making decisions,* which require finding ways to encompass the thinking of all the attendees in making these judgments.
8. *Documentation of meetings* so that attendees will have as complete and organized a record of the meeting as may be needed to continue the work of the project.
9. *Access to external information,* which will allow significant, factual disagreements to be settled in a timely fashion, thus enabling the meeting to continue and be productive.
10. *Preservation of "organizational memory,"* so that those who do not attend the meeting can also work on the project. Often a project will include teams at different locations who will need to understand the content of a meeting at only one of the affected sites.

One response to the problems of group decision making has been the adoption of new methods of organizing and running meetings. Techniques such as facilitated meetings, brainstorming, and criticism-free idea generation have become popular and are now accepted as standard. Another response has been the application of technology to the problems resulting in the emergence of group decision-support systems.

Characteristics of GDSS

How can information technology help groups to arrive at decisions? Scholars have identified at least three basic elements of a GDSS: hardware, software tools, and people. *Hardware* refers to the conference facility itself, including the room, the tables, and the chairs. Such a facility must be physically laid out in a manner that supports group collaboration. It also must include some electronic hardware, such as electronic display boards, as well as audiovisual, computer, and networking equipment.

FIGURE 13.3
Illustration of the Gjensidige Insurance collaborative meeting room. There is one microphone for every two seats and a speaker system on the wall. This equipment is used for same-time meetings between Gjensidige's offices in Oslo and Trondheim. *© 1996–1997. All rights reserved. Ventana Corporation.*

A wide range of *software tools,* including tools for organizing ideas, gathering information, ranking and setting priorities, and other aspects of collaborative work are being used to support decision-making meetings. We describe these tools in the next section. *People* refers not only to the participants but also to a trained facilitator and often to a staff that supports the hardware and software. Together these elements have led to the creation of a range of different kinds of GDSS, from simple electronic boardrooms to elaborate collaboration laboratories. In a collaboration laboratory, individuals work on their own desktop PCs or workstations. Their input is integrated on a file server and is viewable on a common screen at the front of the room; in most systems the integrated input is also viewable on the individual participant's screen. See Figure 13.3 for an illustration of an actual GDSS collaborative meeting room.

GDSS Software Tools

Some features of groupware tools for collaborative work described in Chapters 6 and 12 can be used to support group decision making. There also are specific GDSS software tools for supporting group meetings. These tools were originally developed for meetings in which all participants are in the same room, but they also can be used for networked meetings in which participants are in different locations. Specific GDSS software tools include the following:

- *Electronic questionnaires* aid the organizers in premeeting planning by identifying issues of concern and by helping to ensure that key planning information is not overlooked.
- *Electronic brainstorming tools* allow individuals simultaneously and anonymously to contribute ideas on the topics of the meeting.
- *Idea organizers* facilitate the organized integration and synthesis of ideas generated during brainstorming.
- *Questionnaire tools* support the facilitators and group leaders as they gather information before and during the process of setting priorities.
- *Tools for voting or setting priorities* make available a range of methods from simple voting, to ranking in order, to a range of weighted techniques for setting priorities or voting (see Figure 13.4).
- *Stakeholder identification and analysis tools* use structured approaches to evaluate the impact of an emerging proposal on the organization, and to identify stakeholders and evaluate the potential impact of those stakeholders on the proposed project.

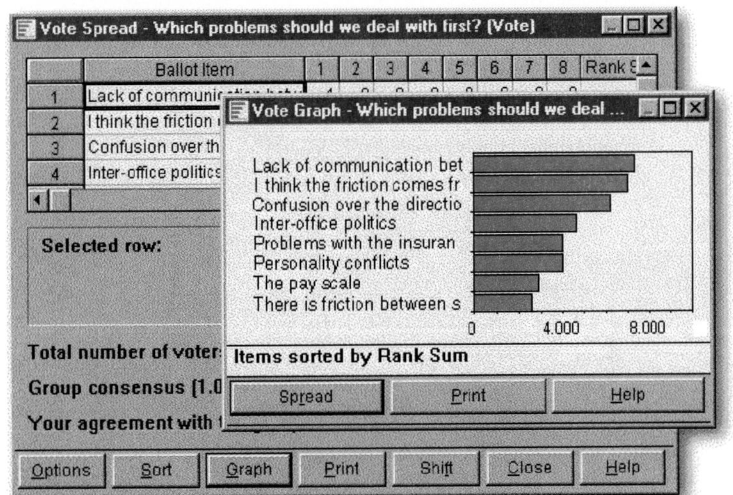

FIGURE 13.4

GDSS software tools. The Ventana Corporation's Group Systems electronic meeting software helps people create, share, record, organize, and evaluate ideas in meetings, between offices, or around the world.

- *Policy formation tools* provide structured support for developing agreement on the wording of policy statements.
- *Group dictionaries* document group agreement on definitions of words and terms central to the project.

Additional tools are available, such as group outlining and writing tools, software that stores and reads project files, and software that allows the attendees to view internal operational data stored by the organization's production computer systems.

Overview of a GDSS Meeting

An **electronic meeting system (EMS)** is a type of collaborative GDSS that uses information technology to make group meetings more productive by facilitating communication as well as decision making. It supports any activity in which people come together, whether at the same place at the same time or in different places at different times (Dennis et al., 1988; Nunamaker et al., 1991). IBM has a number of EMSs installed at various sites. Each attendee has a workstation. The workstations are networked and are connected to the facilitator's console, which serves as both the facilitator's workstation and control panel and the meeting's file server. All data that the attendees forward from their workstations to the group are collected and saved on the file server. The facilitator is able to project computer images onto the projection screen at the front center of the room. The facilitator also has an overhead projector available. Whiteboards are visible on either side of the projection screen. Many electronic meeting rooms are arranged in a semicircle and are tiered in legislative style to accommodate a larger number of attendees.

electronic meeting system (EMS) A collaborative GDSS that uses information technology to make group meetings more productive by facilitating communication as well as decision making. Supports meetings at the same place and time or at different places and times.

The facilitator controls the use of tools during the meeting, often selecting from a large tool box that is part of the organization's GDSS. Tool selection is part of the premeeting planning process. Which tools are selected depends on the subject matter, the goals of the meeting, and the facilitation methodology the facilitator will use.

Attendees have full control over their own desktop computers. An attendee is able to view the agenda (and other planning documents), look at the integrated screen (or screens as the session progresses), use ordinary desktop PC tools (such as a word processor or a spreadsheet), tap into production data that have been made available, or work on the screen associated with the current meeting step and tool (such as a brainstorming screen). However, no one can view anyone else's screens so participants' work is confidential until they release it to the file server for integration with the work of others. All input to the file server is anonymous—at each step everyone's input to the file server (brainstorming ideas, idea evaluation and criticism, comments, voting, etc.) can be seen by all attendees on the integrated screens, but no information is available to identify the source of specific inputs. Attendees enter their data simultaneously rather than in round-robin fashion as is done in meetings that have little or no electronic systems support.

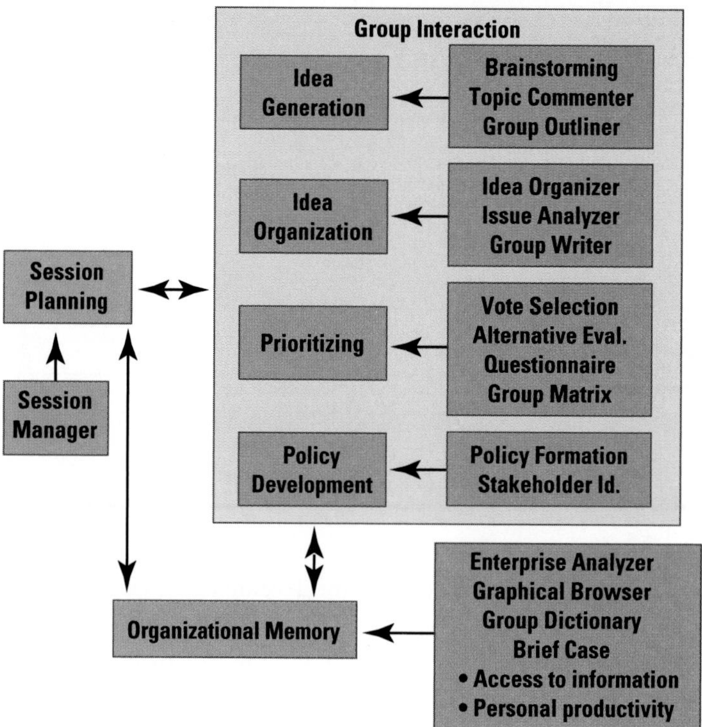

FIGURE 13.5

Group system tools. The sequence of activities and collaborative support tools used in an electronic meeting system (EMS) facilitates communication among attendees and generates a full record of the meeting. *Source: From Nunamaker, et al., "Electronic Meeting Systems to Support Group Work" in* Communications of the ACM, *July 1991. Reprinted by permission.*

Figure 13.5 shows the sequence of activities at a typical EMS meeting. For each activity it also indicates the type of tools used and the output of those tools. During the meeting all input to the integrated screens is saved on the file server. As a result, when the meeting is completed, a full record of the meeting (both raw material and resultant output) is available to the attendees and can be made available to anyone else with a need for access.

How GDSS Can Enhance Group Decision Making

GDSS are being used more widely, so we are able to understand some of their benefits and evaluate some of the tools. We look again at how a GDSS affects the 10 group meeting issues raised earlier.

1. *Improved preplanning.* Electronic questionnaires, supplemented by word processors, outlining software, and other desktop PC software, can structure planning, thereby improving it. The availability of the planning information at the actual meeting also can serve to enhance the quality of the meeting. Experts seem to feel that these tools add significance and emphasis to meeting preplanning.
2. *Increased participation.* Studies show that in traditional decision-making meetings without GDSS support the optimal meeting size is three to five attendees. Beyond that size, the meeting process begins to break down. Using GDSS software, studies show the meeting size can increase while productivity also increases. One reason for this is that attendees contribute simultaneously rather than one at a time, and can make more efficient use of the meeting time. Interviews of GDSS meeting attendees indicate that the quality of participation is higher than in traditional meetings.
3. *Open, collaborative meeting atmosphere.* A GDSS contributes to a more collaborative atmosphere in several ways. First, anonymity of input is essentially guaranteed. Individuals need not be afraid of being judged by their boss for contributing a possibly offbeat idea. Anonymity also reduces or eliminates the deadening effect that often occurs when high-status individuals contribute. Even the numbing pressures of social cues are reduced or eliminated.
4. *Criticism-free idea generation.* Anonymity ensures that attendees can contribute without fear of personally being criticized or of having their ideas rejected because

of the identity of the contributor. Several studies show that interactive GDSS meetings generate more ideas and more satisfaction with those ideas than verbally interactive meetings (Nunamaker et al., 1991). GDSS can help reduce unproductive interpersonal conflict (Miranda and Bostrum, 1993–1994).

5. *Evaluation objectivity.* Anonymity prevents criticism of the source of ideas, thus supporting an atmosphere in which attendees focus on evaluating the ideas themselves. The same anonymity allows participants to detach from their own ideas so they are able to view them from a critical perspective. Evidence suggests that evaluation in an anonymous atmosphere increases the free flow of critical feedback and even stimulates the generation of new ideas during the evaluation process.
6. *Idea organization and evaluation.* GDSS software tools used for this purpose are structured and are based on methodology. They usually allow individuals to organize and then submit their results to the group (still anonymously). The group then iteratively modifies and develops the organized ideas until a document is completed. Attendees generally have viewed this approach as productive.
7. *Setting priorities and making decisions.* Anonymity helps lower-level participants have their positions taken into consideration along with the higher-level attendees.
8. *Documentation of meetings.* Evidence at IBM indicates that postmeeting use of the data is crucial. Attendees use the data to continue their dialogues after the meetings, to discuss the ideas with those who did not attend, and even to make presentations (Grobowski et al., 1990). Some tools enable the user to zoom in to more details on specific information.
9. *Access to external information.* Often a great deal of meeting time is devoted to factual disagreements. More experience with GDSS will indicate whether GDSS technology reduces this problem.
10. *Preservation of "organizational memory."* Specific tools have been developed to facilitate access to the data generated during a GDSS meeting, allowing nonattendees to locate needed information after the meeting. The documentation of a meeting by one group at one site has also successfully been used as input to another meeting on the same project at another site.

Experience to date suggests that GDSS meetings can be more productive, make more efficient use of time, and produce the desired results in fewer meetings. One problem with understanding the value of GDSS is their complexity. A GDSS can be configured in an almost infinite variety of ways. In addition, the effectiveness of the tools will partially depend on the effectiveness of the facilitator, the quality of the planning, the cooperation of the attendees, and the appropriateness of tools selected for different types of meetings. GDSS can enable groups to exchange more information, but can't always help participants process the information effectively or reach better decisions (Dennis, 1996).

Researchers have noted that the design of an electronic meeting system and its technology is only one of a number of contingencies that affect the outcome of group meetings. Other factors, including the nature of the group, the task, the manner in which the problem is presented to the group, and the organizational context (including the organization's culture and environment) also affect the process of group meetings and meeting outcomes (Fjermestad, 1998; Caouette and O'Connor, 1998; Dennis et al., 1988 and 1996; Nunamaker et al., 1991; Watson, Ho, and Raman, 1994).

13.3 EXECUTIVE SUPPORT SYSTEMS (ESS)

We have described how DSS and GDSS help managers make unstructured and semistructured decisions. **Executive support systems (ESS)** also help managers with unstructured problems, focusing on the information needs of senior management. Combining data from internal and external sources, ESS creates a generalized computing and communications environment that can be focused and applied to a changing array of problems.

executive support system (ESS) Information system at the strategic level of an organization designed to address unstructured decision making through advanced graphics and communications.

ESS helps senior executives monitor organizational performance, track activities of competitors, spot problems, identify opportunities, and forecast trends.

The Role of ESS in the Organization

Before ESS, it was common for executives to receive numerous fixed-format reports, often hundreds of pages every month (or even every week). By the late 1980s, analysts found ways to bring together data from throughout the organization and allow the manager to select, access, and tailor them easily as needed. Today, an ESS is apt to include a range of easy-to-use desktop analytical tools and on-line data displays. Use of the systems has migrated down several organizational levels so that the executive and any subordinates are able to look at the same data in the same way.

drill down The ability to move from summary data down to lower and lower levels of detail.

Today's systems try to avoid the problem of data overload so common in paper reports because the data can be filtered or viewed in graphic format (if the user so chooses). Systems have the ability to **drill down,** moving from a piece of summary data to lower and lower levels of detail.

One limitation in an ESS is that it uses data from systems designed for very different purposes. Often data that are critical to the senior executive are simply not there. For example, sales data coming from an order-entry transaction processing system are not linked to marketing information, a linkage the executive would find useful. External data now are much more available in many ESS systems. Executives need a wide range of external data, from current stock market news to competitor information, industry trends, and even projected legislative action. Through their ESS, many managers have access to news services, financial market databases, economic information, and whatever other public data they may require. Managers can also use the Internet for this purpose, as described in the Window on Management.

ESS today includes tools for modeling and analysis. For example, many ESS use Excel or other spreadsheets as the heart of their analytical tool base. With only a minimum of experience, most managers find they can use these common software packages to create graphic comparisons of data by time, region, product, price range, and so on. Costlier systems include more sophisticated specialty analytical software. (Whereas DSS uses such tools primarily for modeling and analysis in a fairly narrow range of decision situations, ESS uses them primarily to provide status information about organizational performance.) Some ESS are being developed for use with the Web.

Developing ESS

ESS are executive systems, and executives create special systems development problems (we introduced this topic in Chapter 3). Because executives' needs change so rapidly, most executive support systems are developed through prototyping. A major difficulty for developers is that high-level executives expect success the first time. Developers must be certain that the system will work before they demonstrate it to the user. In addition, the initial system prototype must be one that the executive can learn very rapidly. Finally, if executives find that the ESS offers no added value, they will reject it.

One area that merits special attention is the determination of executive information requirements. ESS need to have some facility for environmental scanning. A key information requirement of managers at the strategic level is the capability to detect signals of problems in the organizational environment that indicate strategic threats and opportunities (Walls et al., 1992). The ESS needs to be designed so that both external and internal sources of information can be used for environmental scanning purposes. The Critical Success Factor methodology for determining information requirements (see Chapter 10) is recommended for this purpose.

ESS potentially could give top executives the capability of examining other managers' work without their knowledge, so there may be some resistance to ESS at lower levels of the organization. Implementation of ESS should be carefully managed to neutralize such opposition (see Chapter 10).

Cost justification presents a different type of problem with an ESS. Because much of an executive's work is unstructured, how does one quantify benefits for a system that

WINDOW ON MANAGEMENT

Netting Information on Your Competition

Keeping track of the competition is probably as old as business itself. Companies are always anxious to learn anything they can about a change in strategy, the release of new products, a change in management, or anything else that will help get the jump on them. In the past, gathering competitive intelligence involved lots of legwork and reams of paper. Today, managers can find an astonishing amount of competitive intelligence without leaving their desktops—much of it for free—by using the Internet.

The Internet is quick to use, easy to search, and offers a breathtaking array of information. Many companies have Web sites, enabling you to monitor them regularly. Companies often place more on their Web sites than they release publicly in any other way, making the sites a potentially rich source of information or at least providing clues to what is happening. Organization charts, customer lists, and news releases can be analyzed for clues to strategies, new products, and possible mergers. Net search engines allow the researcher to locate a great deal of information on corporate executives, often including some of their speeches and articles. Government sites on the Web provide public documents, such as patent applications, financial filings, and documents filed with regulatory agencies, that may be of value.

Usenet discussion groups often become a gold mine in the search for meaningful data. Usenet groups are specialized, allowing researchers to focus on specific issues of interest to the target companies. Participating in or just monitoring them might tell you much about your competition, and they are fully public. They even make available names and e-mail addresses to anyone interested. A new search tool, Deja News, allows individuals to search news groups by e-mail address, enabling researchers to determine which news groups the target person reads and all postings of that person to those groups. Thus, researchers can target an area of interest, locate individuals from companies about which they are interested, and trace all discussions of those people. Usenet groups also can lead researchers to individuals who have similar interests as themselves and so can be of help.

Staff at Fuld & Co., a Cambridge, Massachusetts, firm specializing in competitive intelligence issues, once noticed that a high-technology hardware producer was searching via Usenet for software engineers to hire. Fuld was able to conclude that the hardware company was making a strategic shift in its product line.

Many companies also keep up with customers and even business partners via the Net. Proper research can enable you to be knowledgeable about the issues your customers are facing. BellSouth Corporation's Leadership Institute started a market dynamics program that teaches executives how to study customers using the Internet before calling them.

One tactic being used by more companies is to have their information technology group build Web pages for their employees that include links that would be helpful in gathering information about competitors or customers. Thus, those with a need to know can gather much of the information themselves without delay and with no need to rely on others. For example, BBN Systems and Technologies built a Web page with links to statistics, published news accounts, press releases, Federal Communications Commission documents, a map of cable TV provider locations, and information about interactive cable TV trials. BBN employees could use this Web page to do their own research on the Internet and cable television from their desktops.

One warning about the process, however. Collecting data is only the beginning. The data usually will come in bits and pieces that require a major analytical effort. In addition, gathering data this way does have its problems. The information gathered on the Net is often stale, incomplete, tainted, or from questionable sources. Moreover, the huge quantities of data found on the Net, most of it irrelevant, can make the task of gathering useful information daunting and tedious. In addition, companies conducting this research under their corporate Internet account can be identified. The way around this last problem is to not use a corporate Net account but rather an account from a commercial service provider and use an e-mail address that cannot be linked to the firm.

To Think About: ***How important do you think competitive intelligence is to senior management and why? How does it support decision making? What are the management benefits of using the Web for this purpose?***

Sources: Sreenath Sreeinvasan, "Corporate Intelligence: A Cloakhold on the Web," *The New York Times,* March 2, 1998; and Anne Stuart, "Click & Dagger," *Webmaster,* July/August 1996.

primarily supports such unstructured work? An ESS often is justified in advance by the intuitive feeling that it will pay for itself (Watson et al., 1991). If ESS benefits can ever be quantified, it is only after the system is operational.

Benefits of ESS

How do executive support systems benefit managers? As we stated earlier, it is difficult at best to cost-justify an executive support system. Nonetheless, interest in these systems is growing, so it is essential to examine some of the potential benefits scholars have identified.

The Web site of this competitive intelligence firm provides guidance for developing a competitive intelligence strategy. The Web is a rich repository of information on competitors and the external environment.

Much of the value of ESS is found in their flexibility. These systems put data and tools in the hands of executives without addressing specific problems or imposing solutions. Executives are free to shape the problems as necessary, using the system as an extension of their own thinking processes. These are not decision-making systems; they are tools to aid executives in making decisions.

The most visible benefit of ESS is their ability to analyze, compare, and highlight trends. The easy use of graphics allows the user to look at more data in less time with greater clarity and insight than paper-based systems can provide. In the past, executives obtained the same information by taking up days and weeks of their staffs' valuable time. By using ESS, those staffs and the executives themselves are freed up for the more creative analysis and decision making in their jobs. ESS capabilities for drilling down and highlighting trends also may enhance the quality of such analysis and can speed up decision making (Leidner and Elam, 1993–1994).

Executives are using ESS to monitor performance more successfully in their own areas of responsibility. Some are using these systems to monitor key performance indicators. The timeliness and availability of the data result in needed actions being identified and taken earlier. Problems can be handled before they become too damaging; opportunities also can be identified earlier.

Platinum Technology's Forest & Trees enables organizations to create quickly executive information system (EIS) and decision-support system (DSS) applications that let users slice and dice business data any way they want and present the data in a format that is easy to view and understand. These intuitive applications can alert managers graphically to business problems and pinpoint details that require action.

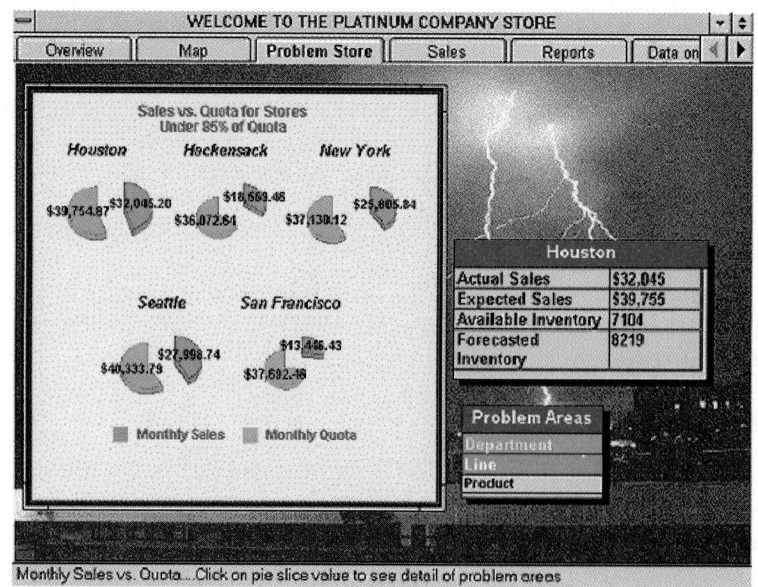

Executive support systems can and do change the workings of organizations. Immediate access to so much data allows executives to better monitor activities of lower units reporting to them. That very monitoring ability often allows decision making to be decentralized and to take place at lower operating levels. Executives are often willing to push decision making further down into the organization as long as they can be assured that all is going well. ESS can enable them to get that assurance. A well-designed ESS could dramatically improve management performance and increase upper management's span of control.

Examples of ESS

To illustrate the ways in which an ESS can enhance management decision making, we now describe two executive support systems, one for private industry and one for the public sector. These systems were developed for very different reasons and serve their organizations in different ways.

Sutter Home Winery: ESS for Business Intelligence

Unlike other businesses, Sutter Home Winery cannot analyze its sales data to determine consumer buying patterns. The Twenty-first Amendment to the U.S. Constitution ended Prohibition, but it also created laws forbidding producers of alcoholic beverages from selling directly to retailers. Because of this restriction, Sutter can only find out how much and what types of products its distributors sold, and such information is often a month old. Sutter needs more data about who buys its wines and who buys its competitors' wines. In order to comply with the law, this $200 million producer of wine and food products must collect information in other ways.

Sutter's management compensates by using information systems to combine business intelligence from external sources, including data from the Internet and point-of-sale data about consumer purchasing from market data-collection firms such as A.C. Nielsen or Information Resources, with the company's internal sales data. A variety of tools and technologies transform a motley collection of information into valuable insights that can be used to guide long-term planning and forecasting by senior management.

Sutter's salespeople who work with distributors and retailers provide information about what products are selling best and why, along with competitors' activities in pricing and promotional campaigns. They enter this information into a Lotus Notes database that can be accessed by sales managers and by management at corporate headquarters, including the company president. Occasionally the company adds data from focus groups and market research, especially when it is launching a new product. The data are organized and analyzed using AS/400 and PC databases, spreadsheets, groupware, and OLAP decision-support tools such as Cognos' PowerPlay. Sutter executives use this information for short- and long-term sales forecasts, marketing campaigns, and capital investment plans.

Sutter has assigned an employee to monitor Web sites that are industry-specific or related to the company's products and distribute reports two or three times a week to winery staff and senior managers. Business intelligence from the Internet has proven a useful and timely source of industry news (Wreden, 1997).

The U.S. General Services Administration

The General Services Administration (GSA) manages the vast real estate holdings of the U.S. government. In a period of tight federal budget restraints and as part of Vice President Al Gore's "reinventing government" initiatives, the organization needed to find ways to optimize the use of the government's multibillion-dollar inventory of 16,000 properties worldwide. Yet GSA managers facing this challenge had no system that would support them by making easily available to them the 4 gigabytes of data stored in their computers. The data were available only in old-fashioned printed reports and through slow, expensive custom programming. Analysis of the data was nearly impossible. GSA's response was GAMIS (Glenn Asset Management Information System), an executive support system based primarily on Lotus Notes that puts the needed data and analysis at the fingertips of the GSA's nontechnical managers.

The main purpose of the system was to give management quick and easy views of the organization's assets. Managers now can easily use ad hoc queries and perform "what-if" analysis, receiving the results on screen, in graphics format when desired. After indicating a specific office building, for example, the user will be offered 13 choices of data on that building, such as who occupies it, its financials, information on the congressional district it is in (if it is in the United States), and even a scanned photograph of the building. The data can be accessed via geographic information system (GIS) software from MapInfo Corp. (see Chapter 6). Through this software interface, the user begins with a national map and drills down into regional and city maps that show detail on location and type of property. Another click of the mouse and the user will pull up all the data on that piece of property. Users can limit the data at the outset, specifying, for example, that they want to look only at Justice Department properties with more than 50,000 square feet of floor space. All data are available to about 100 GSA employees in Washington, and about 50 employees in each of the 10 regions have access to all data for their own region. Washington employees also have available a database of commercial properties with rental space available.

With GAMIS, nontechnical managers can access and analyze gigabytes of information that were formerly available only via printouts and custom programming. The system has received high marks from many officials, including John Glenn, Democratic senator from Ohio and long a vocal critic of the GSA's antiquated computer system. When Glenn saw the system demonstrated, he was reported to have been so impressed that the GSA named the system after him. Observers have also praised the system because it was built from off-the-shelf software, making it quick and inexpensive to develop, providing high returns with minimum investments (Anthes, 1994).

Management Wrap-Up

MANAGEMENT

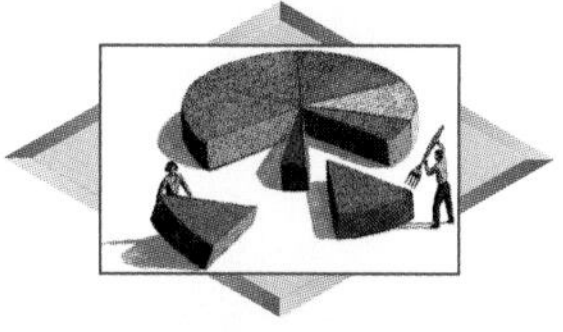

Management is responsible for determining where management support systems can make their greatest contribution to organizational performance and for allocating the resources to build them. At the same time, management needs to work closely with system builders to make sure that these systems effectively capture their information requirements and decision processes.

ORGANIZATION

Management support systems can improve organizational performance by speeding up decision making or improving the quality of management decisions themselves. However, some of these decision processes may not be clearly understood. A management support system will be most effective when system builders have a clear idea of its objectives, the nature of the decisions to be supported, and how the system will actually support decision making.

TECHNOLOGY

Systems to support management decision making can be developed with a range of technologies, including the use of large databases, modeling tools, graphics tools, datamining and analysis tools, and electronic meeting technology. Identifying the right technology for the decision or decision process to be supported is a key technology decision.

For Discussion:

1. As a manager or user of information systems, what would you need to know to participate in the design and use of a DSS or an ESS? Why?
2. If businesses used DSS, GDSS, and ESS more widely, would they make better decisions? Explain.

SUMMARY

1. **Differentiate a decision-support system (DSS) and a group decision-support system (GDSS).** A decision-support system (DSS) is an interactive system under user control that combines data, sophisticated analytical models and tools, and user-friendly software into a single powerful system that can support semistructured or unstructured decision making. There are two kinds of DSS: model-driven DSS and data-driven DSS. DSS targeted toward customers as well as managers are becoming available on the Web. A group decision-support system (GDSS) is an interactive computer-based system to facilitate the solution of unstructured problems by a set of decision makers working together as a group rather than individually.

2. **Describe the components of decision-support systems and group decision-support systems.** The components of a DSS are the DSS database, the DSS software system, and the user interface. The DSS database is a collection of current or historical data from a number of applications or groups that can be used for analysis. The DSS software system consists of OLAP and datamining tools or mathematical and analytical models that are used for analyzing the data in the database. The user interface allows users to interact with the DSS software tools directly.

   Group decision-support systems (GDSS) have hardware, software, and people components. Hardware components consist of the conference room facilities, including seating arrangements and computer and other electronic hardware. Software components include tools for organizing ideas, gathering information, ranking and setting priorities, and documenting meeting sessions. People components include participants, a trained facilitator, and staff to support the hardware and software.

3. **Demonstrate how decision-support systems and group decision-support systems can enhance decision making.** Both DSS and GDSS support steps in the process of arriving at decisions. A DSS provides results of model-based or data-driven analysis that help managers design and evaluate alternatives and monitor the progress of the solution that was adopted. A GDSS helps decision makers meeting together to arrive at a decision more efficiently and is especially useful for increasing the productivity of meetings larger than four or five people. However, the effectiveness of GDSS is contingent on the nature of the group, the task, and the context of the meeting.

4. **Describe the capabilities of executive support systems (ESS).** Executive support systems (ESS) help managers with unstructured problems that occur at the strategic level of management. ESS provides data from both internal and external sources and provides a generalized computing and communications environment that can be focused and applied to a changing array of problems. ESS helps senior executives spot problems, identify opportunities, and forecast trends. These systems can filter out extraneous details for high-level overviews, or they can drill down to provide senior managers with detailed transaction data if required.

5. **Assess the benefits of executive support systems.** ESS helps senior managers analyze, compare, and highlight trends so that they more easily may monitor organizational performance or identify strategic problems and opportunities. ESS may increase the span of control of senior management and allow decision making to be decentralized and to take place at lower operating levels.

KEY TERMS

Customer decision-support system (CDSS), 410
Data-driven DSS, 406
Datamining, 406
Decision-support system (DSS), 405
Drill down, 418
DSS database, 407
DSS software program, 407
Electronic meeting system (EMS), 415
Executive support system (ESS), 417
Group decision-support system (GDSS), 413
Model, 407
Model-driven DSS, 405
Sensitivity analysis, 408

REVIEW QUESTIONS

1. What is a decision-support system (DSS)? How does it differ from a management information system (MIS)?
2. How can a DSS support unstructured or semistructured decision making?
3. What is the difference between a data-driven DSS and a model-driven DSS? Give examples.
4. What are the three basic components of a DSS? Briefly describe each.
5. What is a customer decision-support system? How can the Internet be used for this purpose?
6. What is a group decision-support system (GDSS)? How does it differ from a DSS?

7. What are the three underlying problems in group decision making that have led to the development of GDSS?
8. Describe the three elements of a GDSS.
9. Name five GDSS software tools.
10. What is an electronic meeting system (EMS)? Describe its capabilities.
11. For each of the three underlying problems in group decision making referred to in question 7, describe one or two ways GDSS can contribute to a solution.
12. Define and describe the capabilities of an executive support system.
13. How can the Internet be used to enhance executive support systems?
14. In what ways is building executive support systems different from building traditional MIS systems?
15. What are the benefits of ESS? How do these systems enhance managerial decision making?

GROUP PROJECT

With three or four of your classmates, identify several groups in your university that could benefit from a GDSS. Design a GDSS for one of those groups, describing its hardware, software, and people elements. Present your findings to the class.

TOOLS FOR INTERACTIVE LEARNING

■ **INTERNET**: The Internet Connection for this chapter will take you to a series of Web sites where you can complete an exercise using Web-based DSS for buying or financing a home. You can use the interactive software at the Fidelity Investments Web site in an Electronic Commerce project using a Web-based DSS for investment portfolio analysis. You can also use the Interactive Study Guide to test your knowledge of the topics in this chapter and get instant feedback where you need more practice.

■ **CD-ROM**: If you purchase and use the Multimedia Edition CD-ROM with this chapter, you can complete an interactive exercise asking you to design a group decision-support system (GDSS). You can also find a video clip illustrating the use of Intel videoconferencing technology, an audio overview of the major themes of this chapter, and bullet text summarizing the key points of the chapter.

CASE STUDY

Zeneca Searches for Decisions

Staying competitive in the pharmaceuticals business requires a great deal of information. Zeneca PLC, the British pharmaceuticals manufacturer, must compete against much larger drug companies and dozens of successful products if it is to grow. In today's health care market, price is a key factor as governments, insurance companies, and patients all are exerting great pressure on pharmaceutical companies, HMOs, and all types of health care companies to lower their prices. To the deliverers of health care services, lower prices mean they must have lower costs. While remaining profitable, Zeneca must be able to compete with lower costs, and be more aggressive, creative, and innovative than its competitors in marketing its products. Since 1996, Zeneca has launched 10 new products, accelerating its prescription drug sales in the U.S. market, which accounts for more than 40 percent of drug-division sales. To market these drugs, Zeneca spent heavily to expand its sales force. Management needs this sales effort to pay off so it can generate funds for research and new product development.

Zeneca's U.S. facility in Wilmington, Delaware, has no shortage of data. In the early 1990s its IBM mainframe already held 6 million records, which were the source of the six-inch-thick reports that were distributed monthly to 200 marketing and sales managers. The paper reports contained current and historical details about customers, products, contracts, drug pricing, and sales. Given their size, the reports required great patience and perseverance to locate and identify specific information needed by a user. According to senior systems engineer Keith Magay, "It could take as long as two days for a manager to find the pertinent data" because of the size of the paper reports. Once the needed data were located (if they were), they still were paper-based static data and difficult to use and analyze.

However, use of marketing and sales data is vital to Zeneca if it is to compete successfully. For example, Zeneca's prostate cancer treatment drug, Zolodex, has been outsold by its more expensive competitor, Lupron. Given the pressures by their customers to lower costs, one would expect that Zolodex would be the leader rather than Lupron. But Zeneca managers only were able to find out which drug was selling the most through analysis of their stored data, and that was a daunting task when it was delivered in monthly paper reports.

To address the problem, Zeneca management decided to build a decision-support system that would enable managers to mine the data quickly. The system, known as ZICS (Zeneca Integrated Contracting System), draws its data from multiple mainframe databases as if those databases were a single data warehouse. Marketing and sales managers gain access to the data through their desktop computers or portable laptops. They can easily obtain information on account types, customers, product classes, contract terms, prescription drug pricing, and sales and contract histories.

The system itself is sophisticated, using on-line analytical processing (OLAP) technology that enables users to analyze multiple factors simultaneously. Zeneca business managers can obtain a multidimensional view of data to manipulate product and customer information. Because the system is interactive and supports complex many-to-many comparisons, users can find indirect correlations that would otherwise not be visible. The analysis takes place on-line and interactively. Users can view the data from several perspectives, including by product, by account type, or by broad market segment. A manager might tap into the system to see how much of a given prescription drug an HMO purchased during six months. The manager could click on a cell for the account name, then click on other cells to view the time period and sales information, then click on still other cells to view the products. The manager could use menu-based navigational tools to shop around for better data comparisons.

In 1995, using this system, managers at Zeneca discovered that Zolodex was being outsold by Lupron. Sales managers were able to pull together sales data by customer so they would be able to demonstrate to their customers how many tens of thousands of dollars they could save by purchasing Zolodex rather than Lupron. According to Bob Bogle, Zeneca's vice president of information systems, "With this kind of system, we can analyze large volumes of data in ways that let us reach intelligent competitive decisions." The company intends to use the data to help its staff demonstrate to customers how a contract with Zeneca can increase the customers' profits. ZICS cost Zeneca only about $30,000 to build, although they also had to pay $200,000 for the underlying DSS software. However, that software can be used as the basis for other decision-support systems, and ZICS has garnered such glowing reports from its users that the company planned to build others, including one to serve their 27 corporate account managers and another to support the company's 50 national managers.

Source: Stephen D. Moore, "Zeneca Pretax Profit Rose 13% in Half but Currency Fluctuation Hurt Results," *The Wall Street Journal,* March 6, 1998; and Bronwyn Fryer, "Zeneca Takes Its Medicine," *InformationWeek,* March 18, 1996.

Case Study Questions

1. What problems did Zeneca face in trying to make good decisions?
2. What was Zeneca's business strategy and how was decision making related to it?
3. What kind of decision-support system did Zeneca develop? What kinds of decisions did the DSS support?
4. What management, organization, and technology issues had to be addressed when building the new system?

CHAPTER 14

Information Systems Security and Control

chapter outline

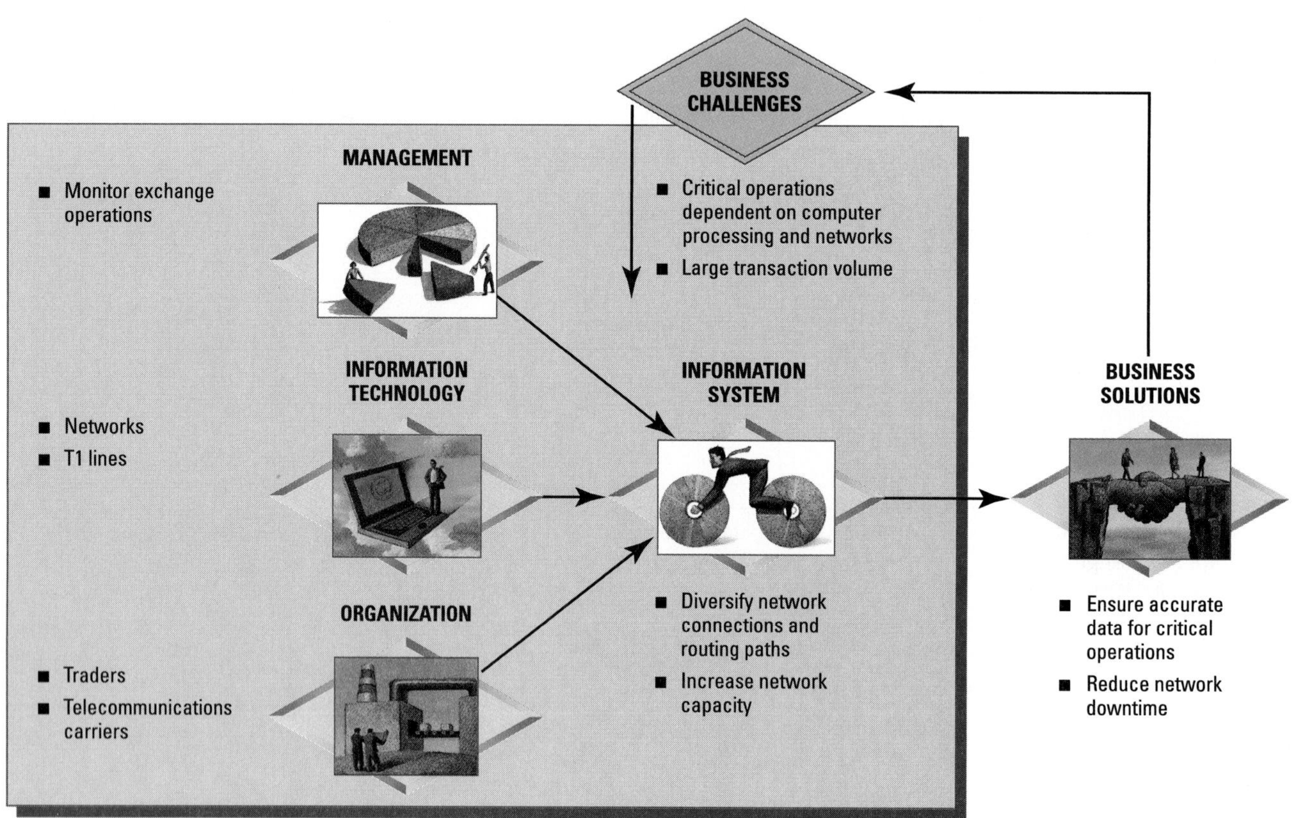

The Pacific Exchange Invests in Uptime

On July 16, 1997, construction workers at Barstow, California, inadvertently cut a major fiber-optic backbone, severing two of the Pacific Exchange's T1 links to New York and California. (T1 are dedicated, high-capacity phone lines supporting transmission rates of 1.544 megabits per second.) The backbone was quickly repaired. Then on July 17, construction near Baltimore cut the exchange's other T1 line. This too was repaired. Then on July 18, construction in Barstow again severed the fiber trunk that carried all of the exchange's trading information between California and New York.

One would think that there would be minimal impact on the stock exchange's network, because each of its T1 lines had been bought from different telecommunications carriers. Presumably their fiber cables had different locations; however, all of the exchange's New York–San Francisco traffic wound up on the same line. This meant that the third-largest stock exchange in the United States was handling all of its business on a single cable.

Dave Eisenlohr, the Exchange's vice president for data center operations, observed that "downtime is not an option." The Exchange's profitability is directly related to the reliability of its systems and networks. A network outage of only 30 to 60 minutes could cost millions in lost trades.

The Exchange had diversified its network connections so that no single point of failure was permitted; instead of using a single large link, it used multiple T1 lines from different carriers. Network administrators from the exchange personally inspected the links and routes for its communications traffic. What they failed to investigate was how their carriers handled spare bandwidth. It turned out that these carriers leased spare capacity on their backbones to other carriers. Several of these carriers rerouted their lines through the same concentration points. In Baltimore, lines from Cable & Wireless and Sprint converged, and fiber from WilTel and Cable & Wireless ran through Barstow. There were no alternative routing paths when the lines got cut.

The Exchange concluded that the carriers were not sufficiently coordinated to guarantee diverse routing paths. Management ordered the Exchange to install additional capacity—four times the amount needed. It also demanded that carriers guarantee they could ensure route diversity to keep the Exchange's business.

Source: Adapted from Laura DiDio, "An Investment in Uptime," *Computerworld,* February 23, 1998.

Management Challenges

The experience of the Pacific Exchange illustrates one of many problems that organizations relying on computer-based information systems may face. Hardware and software failures, communication disruptions, natural disasters, employee errors, and use by unauthorized people may prevent information systems from running properly or running at all. As you read this chapter, you should be aware of the following management challenges.

1. **Designing systems that are neither overcontrolled nor undercontrolled.** The biggest threat to information systems is posed by authorized users, not outside intruders. Most security breaches and damage to information systems come from organizational insiders. If a system requires too many passwords and authorizations to access information, the system will go unused. On the other hand, there is a growing need to create secure systems based on distributed multiuser networks and the Internet. Controls that are effective but that do not prevent authorized individuals from using a system are difficult to design.
2. **Applying quality assurance standards in large systems projects.** This chapter explains why the goal of zero defects in large, complex pieces of software is impossible to achieve. If the seriousness of remaining bugs cannot be ascertained, what constitutes acceptable—if not perfect—software performance? And even if meticulous design and exhaustive testing could eliminate all defects, software projects have time and budget constraints that often prevent management from devoting as much time to thoroughly testing as it should. Under such circumstances it will be difficult for managers to define a standard for software quality and to enforce it.

learning objectives

After completing this chapter you will be able to:

1. Demonstrate why information systems are so vulnerable to destruction, error, abuse, and system quality problems.
2. Compare general controls and application controls for information systems, including controls to safeguard use of the Internet.
3. Select the factors that must be considered when developing the controls for information systems.
4. Describe the most important software quality-assurance techniques.
5. Demonstrate the importance of auditing information systems and safeguarding data quality.

Computer systems play such a critical role in business, government, and daily life that organizations must take special steps to protect their information systems and to ensure that they are accurate and reliable. This chapter describes how information systems can be *controlled* and made secure so that they serve the purposes for which they are intended.

14.1 SYSTEM VULNERABILITY AND ABUSE

Before computer automation, data about individuals or organizations were maintained and secured as paper records dispersed in separate business or organizational units. Information systems concentrate data in computer files that potentially can be accessed more easily by large numbers of people and by groups outside the organization. Consequently, automated data are more susceptible to destruction, fraud, error, and misuse.

When computer systems fail to run or work as required, firms that depend heavily on computers experience a serious loss of business function. For example, it costs brokerage firms more than $6 million for every hour their computer systems are not working. The longer computer systems are down, the more serious the consequences for the firm. Some firms relying on computers to process their critical business transactions might experience a total loss of business function if they lose computer capability for more than a few days.

Why Systems Are Vulnerable

When large amounts of data are stored in electronic form they are vulnerable to many more kinds of threats than when they exist in manual form. Table 14.1 lists the most common threats against computerized information systems. They can stem from technical, organizational, and environmental factors compounded by poor management decisions.

Computerized systems are especially vulnerable to such threats for the following reasons:

- A complex information system cannot be replicated manually.
- Computerized procedures appear to be invisible and are not easily understood or audited.
- Although the chances of disaster in automated systems are no greater than in manual systems, the effect of a disaster can be much more extensive. In some cases all of a system's records can be destroyed and lost forever.
- On-line information systems are directly accessible by many individuals. Legitimate users may gain easy access to computer data that they are not authorized to view. Unauthorized individuals can also gain access to such systems.

Advances in telecommunications and computer software have magnified these vulnerabilities. Through telecommunications networks, information systems in different locations can be interconnected. The potential for unauthorized access, abuse, or fraud is not limited to a single location but can occur at any access point in the network.

Additionally, more complex and diverse hardware, software, organizational, and personnel arrangements are required for telecommunications networks, creating new areas and opportunities for penetration and manipulation. Wireless networks using radio-based technology are even more vulnerable to penetration because radio frequency bands are easy to scan. The Internet poses special problems because it was explicitly designed to be accessed easily by people on different computer systems. The vulnerabilities of telecommunications networks are illustrated in Figure 14.1.

TABLE 14.1 Threats to Computerized Information Systems

Hardware failure	Fire
Software failure	Electrical problems
Personnel actions	User errors
Terminal access penetration	Program changes
Theft of data, services, equipment	Telecommunications problems

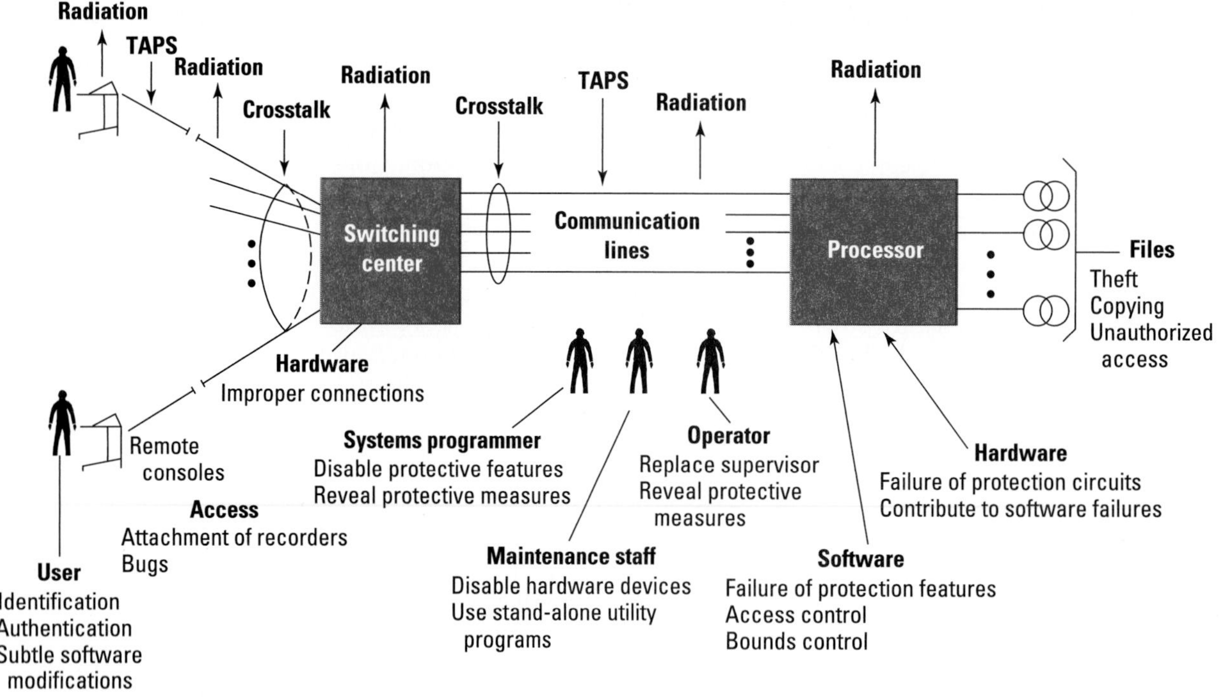

FIGURE 14.1 Telecommunications network vulnerabilities. Telecommunications networks are highly vulnerable to natural failure of hardware and software and to misuse by programmers, computer operators, maintenance staff, and end users. It is possible to tap communications lines and illegally intercept data. High-speed transmission over twisted wire communications channels causes interference called *crosstalk*. Radiation can disrupt a network at various points as well.

hacker A person who gains unauthorized access to a computer network for profit, criminal mischief, or personal pleasure.

computer virus Rogue software programs that are difficult to detect that spread rapidly through computer systems, destroying data or disrupting processing and memory systems.

Hackers and Computer Viruses

The efforts of hackers to penetrate computer networks have been widely publicized. A **hacker** is a person who gains unauthorized access to a computer network for profit, criminal mischief, or personal pleasure. The potential damage from intruders is frightening. The Window on Organizations describes problems created by hackers for organizations that use the Internet.

Most recently, alarm has risen over hackers propagating **computer viruses,** rogue software programs that spread rampantly from system to system, clogging computer memory or destroying programs or data. Nearly 12,000 viruses are known to exist, with 200 or more new viruses created each month. Table 14.2 describes the characteristics of the most common viruses. Many newer viruses are "macro" viruses, which exist inside ex-

TABLE 14.2 Common Computer Viruses

Virus Name	Description
Concept	Macro virus that attaches itself to Microsoft word documents and can be spread when Word documents are attached to e-mail. Can copy itself from one document to another and delete files.
Form	Makes a clicking sound with each keystroke but only on the 18th day of the month. May corrupt data on the floppy disks it infects.
One_Half	Encrypts the hard disk so that only the virus can read the data there, flashing "One_Half" on the computer screen when its activity is half-completed. Very destructive because it can mutate, making it difficult to identify and eliminate.
Monkey	Makes the hard disk look like it has failed because Windows will not run.
Junkie	A "multipartite" virus that can infect files as well as the boot sector of the hard drive (the section of a PC hard drive that the PC first reads when it boots up). May cause memory conflicts.
Ripper (or Jack the Ripper)	Corrupts data written to a PC's hard disk about one time in every thousand.

WINDOW ON ORGANIZATIONS

Uprooting the Internet Hackers

Business use of the Internet and electronic commerce have been growing rapidly during the past few years. However, the Internet has no central authority or management, and no one to install the technology or establish network-wide security policies. Reports of Internet security breaches are rising.

The main concern comes from unwanted intruders—hackers—who use the latest technology and their skill to break into supposedly secure computers or disable them. Hackers have been launching attacks on World Wide Web servers and browsers, exploiting backdoor holes in network operating systems, and planting logic bombs and Trojan horses, malicious pieces of software that can hide in a system or network until they execute at a specified time.

In denial-of-service attacks, hackers flood a network server or Web server with data in order to crash the network. Panix, a pioneering Internet service provider that hosts almost 1000 corporate Web sites, was virtually shut down for four days in September 1996 because a hacker bombarded its computer with requests for information. The intruder had alternately invaded Panix's computers that control pages on the Web, others that store e-mail, and still others that link Internet addresses to Panix subscribers, blocking them from receiving communications. The hacker used a special computer program to send up to 150 requests per second to Panix's computers, seeking to establish a connection or to obtain information. The requests contained fake Internet addresses, which Panix computers had to sort out before they could reject them. Panix computers were overwhelmed by the deluge and could not handle legitimate Web or e-mail requests. Panix is trying to find the source of the attack, but there is no easy way to trace it.

Panix suffered another serious attack in October 1993 that forced it to shut down for three days. Hackers collected passwords from legitimate Panix users. With those passwords, they were able to access other computers connected to the Internet to steal data and more passwords. The security of the whole system was compromised.

Government agencies have suffered Internet attacks as well. Intruders have broken into the networks of the National Institutes of Health to observe traffic and to copy password files. In 1994, hackers broke into Pentagon computers and attached "sniffers" (programs monitoring data flowing across a network) to switches connecting Air Force computers to the Internet. The hackers were searching for passwords they could use to access Air Force databases.

Hackers do not have to be as skillful as in the past to cause damage. The Web has many sites with step-by-step instructions on how to perpetrate various "hacks." A query to the Alta Vista search engine on how to launch a denial-of-service attack turned up 17,000 matches.

Organizations such as the Computer Emergency Response Team (CERT) have been set up explicitly to address security on the Internet. CERT helps determine who is breaking in to the Internet, and it devises solutions to the method used for the break-in. When an Internet user reports a new break-in, CERT does not publicize it until a solution has been found. With the increase in break-ins, the U.S. Defense Department's Advanced Research Projects Agency (ARPA) is planning to add funding to CERT in order to double their staff. The Federal Bureau of Investigation (FBI) also investigates computer crimes reported to them, 80 percent of which are on the Internet.

To Think About: ***How can break-ins from the Internet harm organizations? In light of these security problems, what management, organization, and technology issues would you consider in developing an Internet security plan?***

Sources: Laura DiDio, "Internet Security Holes Widen," *Computerworld,* March 2, 1998; Dean Tomasula, "Tighter Security Loosens the Constraints on Electronic Commerce," *Wall Street and Technology,* February 1997; Bart Ziegler, "Savvy Hacker Tangles Web for Net Host," *The Wall Street Journal,* September 12, 1996; and Bob Violino, "Your Worst Nightmare," *InformationWeek,* February 19, 1996.

ecutable programs, also called macros, that provide functions within programs such as Microsoft Word.

In addition to spreading via computer networks, viruses can invade computerized information systems from "infected" diskettes from an outside source, through infected machines, from files of software downloaded via the Internet or files attached to e-mail transmissions. The potential for massive damage and loss from future computer viruses remains.

Organizations can use antivirus software and screening procedures to reduce the chances of infection. **Antivirus software** is special software designed to check computer systems and disks for the presence of various computer viruses. Often the software can eliminate the virus from the infected area. However, most antivirus software is only effective against viruses already known when the software is written—to protect their systems, management must continually update their antivirus software.

antivirus software Software designed to detect, and often eliminate, computer viruses from an information system.

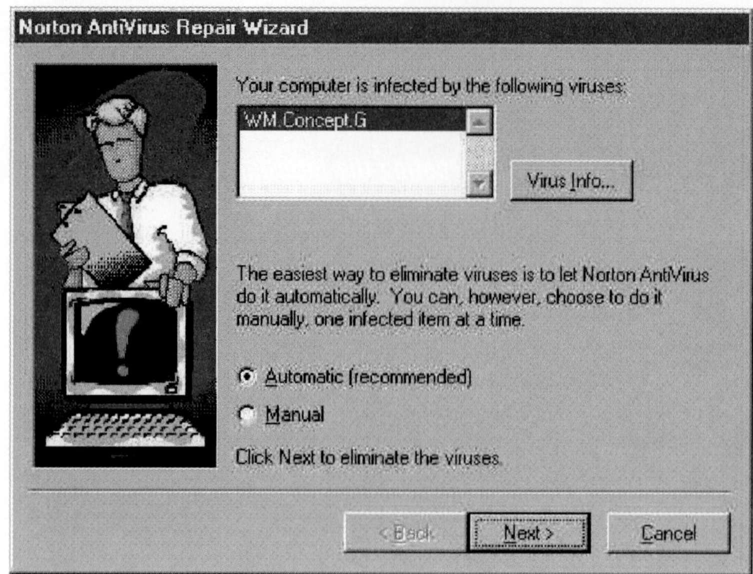

Companies can detect and eliminate computer viruses in their systems by using antivirus software regularly.

Concerns for System Builders and Users

The heightened vulnerability of automated data has created special concerns for the builders and users of information systems. These concerns include disaster, security, and administrative error.

Disaster

Computer hardware, programs, data files, and other equipment can be destroyed by fires, power failures, or other disasters. It may take many years and millions of dollars to reconstruct destroyed data files and computer programs. If an organization needs them to function on a day-to-day basis, it will no longer be able to operate. This is why companies such as VISA USA Inc. and National Trust employ elaborate emergency backup facilities. VISA USA Inc. has duplicate mainframes, duplicate network pathways, duplicate terminals, and duplicate power supplies. VISA even uses a duplicate data center in McLean, Virginia, to handle half of its transactions and to serve as an emergency backup to its primary data center in San Mateo, California. National Trust, a large bank in Ontario, Canada, uses uninterruptable power supply technology provided by International Power Machines (IPM) because electrical power at its Mississauga location fluctuates frequently.

fault-tolerant computer systems Systems that contain extra hardware, software, and power supply components that can back a system up and keep it running to prevent system failure.

Fault-tolerant computer systems contain extra hardware, software, and power supply components that can back the system up and keep it running to prevent system failure. Fault-tolerant computers contain extra memory chips, processors, and disk storage devices. They can use special software routines or self-checking logic built into their circuitry to detect hardware failures and automatically switch to a backup device. Parts from these computers can be removed and repaired without disruption to the computer system.

on-line transaction processing Transaction processing mode in which transactions entered on-line are immediately processed by the computer.

Fault-tolerant technology is used by firms for critical applications with heavy on-line transaction processing requirements. In **on-line transaction processing,** transactions entered on-line are immediately processed by the computer. Multitudinous changes to databases, reporting, or requests for information occur each instant.

Rather than build their own backup facilities, many firms contract with disaster recovery firms, such as Comdisco Disaster Recovery Services in Rosemont, Illinois, and Sungard Recovery Services headquartered in Wayne, Pennsylvania. These disaster recovery firms provide *hot sites* housing spare computers at locations around the country where subscribing firms can run their critical applications in an emergency. Disaster recovery services offer backup for client/server systems as well as traditional mainframe applications.

Security

Security refers to the policies, procedures, and technical measures used to prevent unauthorized access or alteration, theft, and physical damage to information systems. Security can be promoted with an array of techniques and tools to safeguard computer hardware, software, communications networks, and data. We already have discussed disaster protection measures. Other tools and techniques for promoting security will be discussed in subsequent sections.

security Policies, procedures, and technical measures used to prevent unauthorized access, alteration, theft, or physical damage to information systems.

Errors

Computers also can serve as instruments of error, severely disrupting or destroying an organization's record keeping and operations. For instance, on February 25, 1991, during Operation Desert Storm, a Patriot missile defense system operating at Dharan, Saudi Arabia, failed to track and intercept an incoming Scud missile because of a software error in the system's weapons control computer. The Scud hit an army barracks, killing 28 Americans. Errors in automated systems can occur at many points in the processing cycle: through data entry, program error, computer operations, and hardware. Figure 14.2 illustrates all of the points in a typical processing cycle where errors can occur.

System Quality Problems: Software and Data

In addition to disasters, viruses, and security breaches, defective software and data pose a constant threat to information systems, causing untold losses in productivity. An undiscovered error in a company's credit software or erroneous financial data can result in millions of dollars of losses. Several years ago, a hidden software problem in AT&T's long distance system brought down that system, bringing the New York-based financial exchanges to a halt and interfering with billions of dollars of business around the country for a number of hours. Modern passenger and commercial vehicles are increasingly dependent upon computer programs for critical functions. A hidden software defect in a braking system could result in the loss of lives.

Bugs and Defects

A major problem with software is the presence of hidden **bugs** or program code defects. Studies have shown that it is virtually impossible to eliminate all bugs from large programs. The main source of bugs is the complexity of decision-making code. Even a relatively small program of several hundred lines will contain tens of decisions leading to hundreds or even thousands of different paths. Important programs within most corporations are usually much larger, containing tens of thousands or even millions of lines of code, each with many times the choices and paths of the smaller programs. Such complexity is difficult to document and design—designers document some reactions wrongly or fail to consider some possibilities. Studies show that about 60 percent of errors discovered during testing are a result of specifications in the design documentation that were missing, ambiguous, in error, or in conflict.

bugs Program code defects or errors.

Zero defects, a goal of the total quality management movement, cannot be achieved in larger programs. Complete testing simply is not possible. Fully testing programs that contain thousands of choices and millions of paths would require thousands of years. Eliminating software bugs is an exercise in diminishing returns, because it would take proportionately longer testing to detect and eliminate obscure residual bugs (Littlewood and Strigini, 1993). Even without rigorous testing, one could not know for sure that a piece of software was dependable until the product proved itself after much operational use. The message? We cannot eliminate all bugs, and we cannot know with certainty the seriousness of the bugs that do remain.

The Maintenance Nightmare

Another reason that systems are unreliable is that computer software traditionally has been a nightmare to maintain. Maintenance, the process of modifying a system in production use, is the most expensive phase of the systems development process. In most

FIGURE 14.2

Points in the processing cycle where errors can occur. Each of the points illustrated in this figure represents a control point where special automated and/or manual procedures should be established to reduce the risk of errors during processing.

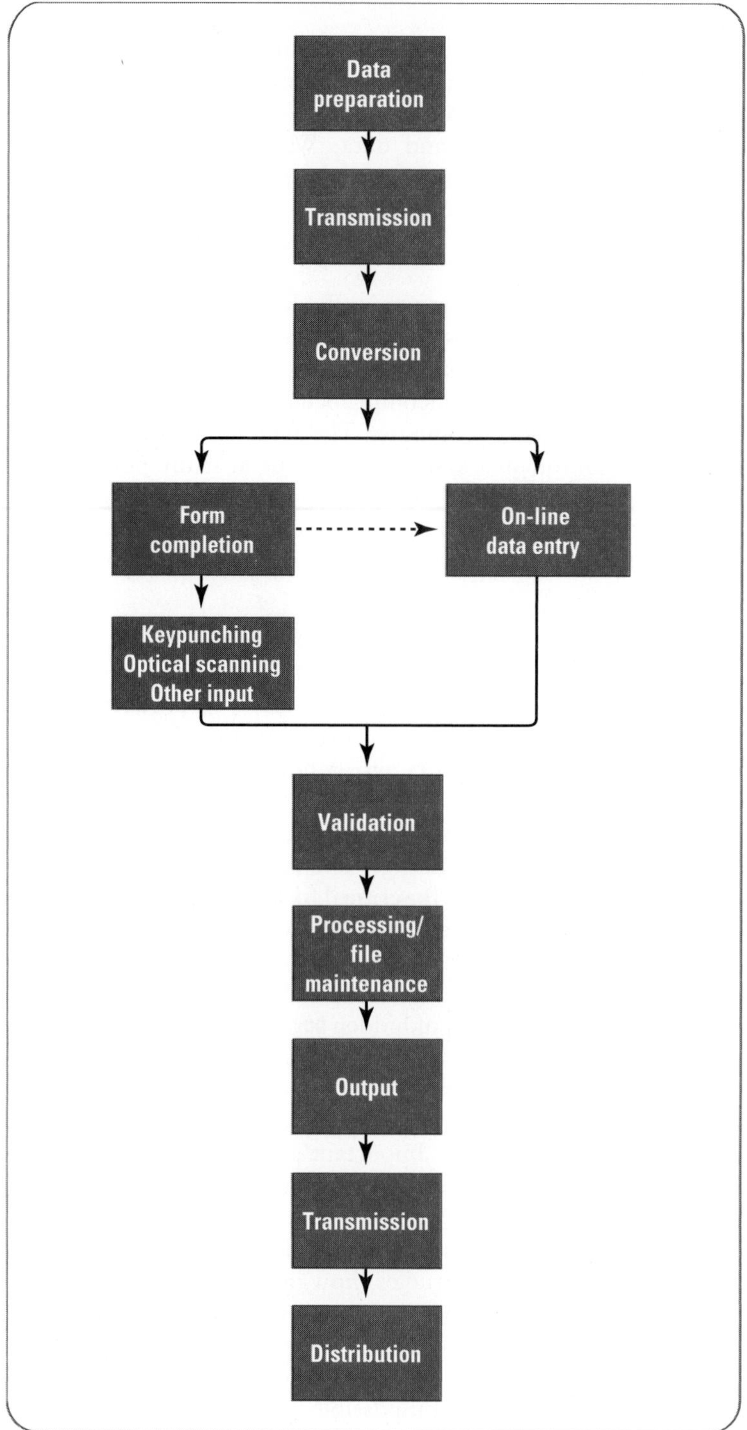

organizations nearly half of information systems staff time is spent in the maintenance of existing systems.

Why are maintenance costs so high? One major reason is organizational change. The firm may experience large internal changes in structure or leadership, or change may come from its surrounding environment. These organizational changes affect information requirements. Another reason appears to be software complexity, as measured by the number and size of interrelated software programs and subprograms and the complexity of the flow of program logic between them (Banker, Datar, Kemerer, and Zweig, 1993). A third common cause of long-term maintenance problems is faulty sys-

Estimate of the relative cost of repairing errors based on consultant reports and the popular trade literature

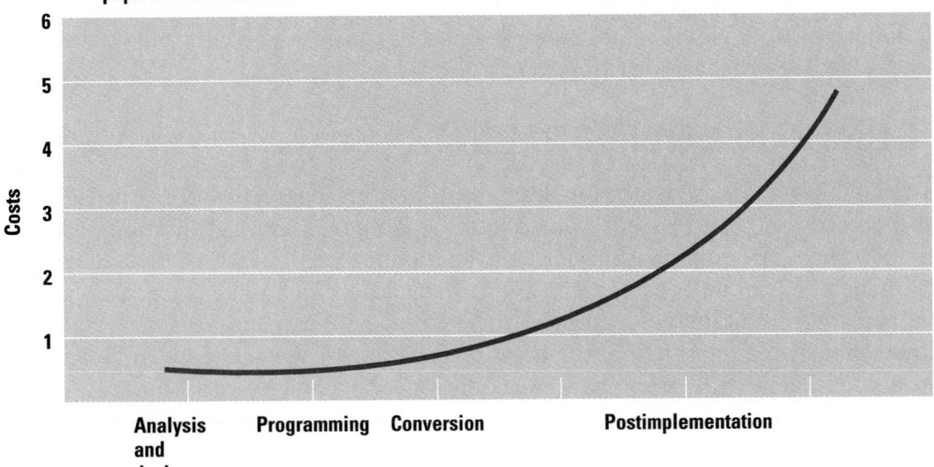

FIGURE 14.3

The cost of errors over the systems development cycle. The most common, most severe, and most expensive system errors develop in the early design stages. They involve faulty requirements analysis. Errors in program logic or syntax are much less common, less severe, and less costly to repair than design errors. *Source: Alberts, 1976.*

tems analysis and design, especially information requirements analysis. Some studies of large TPS systems by TRW, Inc., have found that a majority of system errors—64 percent—result from early analysis errors (Mazzucchelli, 1985).

Figure 14.3 illustrates the cost of correcting errors based on the experience of consultants reported in the literature.

If errors are detected early, during analysis and design, the cost to the systems development effort is small. But if they are not discovered until after programming, testing, or conversion has been completed, the costs can soar astronomically. A minor logic error, for example, that could take one hour to correct during the analysis and design stage could take 10, 40, and 90 times as long to correct during programming, conversion, and postimplementation, respectively.

Data Quality Problems

Chapter 4 has pointed out that the most common source of information system failure is poor data quality. Data that are inaccurate, untimely, or inconsistent with other sources of information can create serious operational and financial problems for businesses. When bad data go unnoticed, they can lead to bad decisions, product recalls, and even financial losses (Redman, 1998).

Data quality problems plague the public sector as well. A study of the FBI's computerized criminal record systems found a total of 54.1 percent of the records in the National Crime Information Center System to be inaccurate, ambiguous, or incomplete, and 74.3 percent of the records in the FBI's semi-automated Identification Division system exhibited significant quality problems. A summary analysis of the FBI's automated Wanted-Persons File also found that 11.2 percent of the warrants were invalid. A study by the FBI itself found that 6 percent of the warrants in state files were invalid and that 12,000 invalid warrants are sent out nationally each day.

The FBI has taken some steps to correct these problems, but low levels of data quality in these systems have disturbing implications. In addition to their use in law enforcement, computerized criminal history records are increasingly being used to screen employees in both the public and private sectors. Many of these records are incomplete and show arrests but no court disposition; that is, they show charges without proof of conviction or guilt. Many individuals may be denied employment unjustifiably because these records overstate their criminality. These criminal record systems are not limited to violent felons. They contain the records of 36 million people, about one-third of the labor force. Inaccurate and potentially damaging information is being maintained on many law-abiding citizens. The level of data quality in these systems threatens citizens' constitutional rights to due process and impairs the efficiency and effectiveness of any law enforcement programs in which these records are used (Laudon, 1986a).

Poor data quality may stem from errors during data input or faulty information system and database design (Wand and Wang, 1996; Strong, Lee, and Wang, 1997). In the following sections we examine how organizations can deal with data and software quality problems as well as other threats to information systems.

14.2 CREATING A CONTROL ENVIRONMENT

To minimize errors, disaster, computer crime, and breaches of security, special policies and procedures must be incorporated into the design and implementation of information systems. The combination of manual and automated measures that safeguard information systems and ensure that they perform according to management standards is termed *controls*. **Controls** consist of all the methods, policies, and organizational procedures that ensure the safety of the organization's assets, the accuracy and reliability of its accounting records, and operational adherence to management standards.

controls All of the methods, policies, and procedures that ensure protection of the organization's assets, accuracy and reliability of its records, and operational adherence to management standards.

In the past, the control of information systems was treated as an afterthought, addressed only toward the end of implementation, just before the system was installed. Today, however, organizations are so critically dependent on information systems that vulnerabilities and control issues must be identified as early as possible. The control of an information system must be an integral part of its design. Users and builders of systems must pay close attention to controls throughout the system's life span.

Computer systems are controlled by a combination of general controls and application controls.

General controls are those that control the design, security, and use of computer programs and the security of data files in general throughout the organization. On the whole, general controls apply to all computerized applications and consist of a combination of system software and manual procedures that create an overall control environment.

general controls Overall controls that establish a framework for controlling the design, security, and use of computer programs throughout an organization.

Application controls are specific controls unique to each computerized application, such as payroll, accounts receivable, and order processing. They consist of controls applied from the user functional area of a particular system and from programmed procedures.

application controls Specific controls unique to each computerized application.

General Controls

General controls are overall controls that ensure the effective operation of programmed procedures. They apply to all application areas. General controls include the following:

- Controls over the system implementation process
- Software controls
- Physical hardware controls
- Computer operations controls
- Data security controls
- Administrative disciplines, standards, and procedures

Implementation Controls

Implementation controls audit the systems development process at various points to ensure that the process is properly controlled and managed. The systems development audit should look for the presence of formal review points at various stages of development that enable users and management to approve or disapprove the implementation.

implementation controls The audit of the systems development process at various points to make sure that it is properly controlled and managed.

The systems development audit also should examine the level of user involvement at each stage of implementation and check for the use of a formal cost/benefit methodology in establishing system feasibility. The audit should look for the use of controls and quality assurance techniques for program development, conversion, and testing and for complete and thorough system, user, and operations documentation.

Software Controls

software controls Controls to ensure the security and reliability of software.

Controls are essential for the various categories of software used in computer systems. **Software controls** monitor the use of system software and prevent unauthorized access of software programs, system software, and computer programs. System software is an important control area because it performs overall control functions for the programs that directly process data and data files.

Hardware Controls

Hardware controls ensure that computer hardware is physically secure, and they check for equipment malfunction. Computer hardware should be physically secured so that it can be accessed only by authorized individuals. Computer equipment should be specially protected against fires and extremes of temperature and humidity. Organizations that are critically dependent on their computers also must make provisions for emergency backup in case of power failure.

hardware controls Controls to ensure the physical security and correct performance of computer hardware.

Many kinds of computer hardware contain mechanisms that check for equipment malfunction. Parity checks detect equipment malfunctions responsible for altering bits within bytes during processing. Validity checks monitor the structure of on–off bits within bytes to make sure that it is valid for the character set of a particular computer machine. Echo checks verify that a hardware device is performance ready. Chapter 5 discussed computer hardware in detail.

Computer Operations Controls

Computer operations controls apply to the work of the computer department and help ensure that programmed procedures are consistently and correctly applied to the storage and processing of data. They include controls over the setup of computer processing jobs, operations software, and computer operations, and backup and recovery procedures for processing that ends abnormally.

computer operations controls Procedures to ensure that programmed procedures are consistently and correctly applied to data storage and processing.

Instructions for running computer jobs should be fully documented, reviewed, and approved by a responsible official. Controls over operations software include manual procedures designed to both prevent and detect error. Specific instructions for backup and recovery can be developed so that in the event of a hardware or software failure, the recovery process for production programs, system software, and data files does not create erroneous changes in the system.

Data Security Controls

Data security controls ensure that valuable business data files on either disk or tape are not subject to unauthorized access, change, or destruction. Such controls are required for data files when they are in use and when they are being held for storage.

data security controls Controls to ensure that data files on either disk or tape are not subject to unauthorized access, change, or destruction.

When data can be input on-line through a terminal, entry of unauthorized input must be prevented. For example, a credit note could be altered to match a sales invoice on file. In such situations, security can be developed on several levels:

- Terminals can be physically restricted so that they are available only to authorized individuals.
- System software can include the use of passwords assigned only to authorized individuals. No one can log on to the system without a valid password.
- Additional sets of passwords and security restrictions can be developed for specific systems and applications. For example, data security software can limit access to specific files, such as the files for the accounts receivable system. It can restrict the type of access so that only individuals authorized to update these specific files will have the ability to do so. All others will only be able to read the files or will be denied access altogether.

Systems that allow on-line inquiry and reporting must have data files secured. Figure 14.4 illustrates the security allowed for two sets of users of an on-line personnel database with sensitive information such as employees' salaries, benefits, and medical histories. One set of users consists of all employees who perform clerical functions such as inputting employee data into the system. All individuals with this type of profile can update the system but can neither read nor update sensitive fields such as salary, medical history, or earnings data. Another profile applies to a divisional manager, who cannot update the system but who can read all employee data fields for his or her division,

FIGURE 14.4

Security profiles for a personnel system. These two examples represent two security profiles or data security patterns that might be found in a personnel system. Depending upon the security profile, a user would have certain restrictions on access to various systems, locations, or data in an organization.

SECURITY PROFILE 1

User: Personnel Dept. Clerk

Location: Division 1

Employee Identification Codes with This Profile:	00753, 27834, 37665, 44116
Data Field Restrictions	**Type of Access**
All employee data for Division 1 only	Read and Update
• Medical history data	None
• Salary	None
• Pensionable earnings	None

SECURITY PROFILE 2

User: Divisional Personnel Manager

Location: Division 1

Employee Identification Codes with This Profile:	27321
Data Field Restrictions	**Type of Access**
All employee data for Division 1 only	Read Only

including medical history and salary. These profiles would be established and maintained by a data security system. The data security system illustrated in Figure 14.4 provides very fine-grained security restrictions, such as allowing authorized personnel users to inquire about all employee information except in confidential fields such as salary or medical history.

Companies with global operations have additional security requirements, as described in the Window on Management on page 440.

Administrative Controls

administrative controls Formalized standards, rules, procedures, and disciplines to ensure that the organization's controls are properly executed and enforced.

segregation of functions The principle of internal control to divide responsibilities and assign tasks among people so that job functions do not overlap, to minimize the risk of errors and fraudulent manipulation of the organization's assets.

Administrative controls are formalized standards, rules, procedures, and control disciplines to ensure that the organization's general and application controls are properly executed and enforced. The most important administrative controls are (1) segregation of functions, (2) written policies and procedures, and (3) supervision.

Segregation of functions means that job functions should be designed to minimize the risk of errors or fraudulent manipulation of the organization's assets. The individuals responsible for operating systems should not be the same ones who can initiate transactions that change the assets held in these systems. A typical arrangement is to have the organization's information systems department responsible for data and program files and end users responsible for initiating transactions such as payments or checks.

Written policies and procedures establish formal standards for controlling information system operations. Procedures must be formalized in writing and authorized by the appropriate level of management. Accountabilities and responsibilities must be clearly specified.

Supervision of personnel involved in control procedures ensures that the controls for an information system are performing as intended. Without adequate supervision, the best-designed set of controls may be bypassed, short-circuited, or neglected.

Weakness in each of these general controls can have a widespread effect on programmed procedures and data throughout the organization. Table 14.3 summarizes the effect of weaknesses in major general control areas.

TABLE 14.3 Effect of Weakness in General Controls

Weakness	Impact
Implementation controls	New systems or systems that have been modified will have errors or fail to function as required.
Software controls (program security)	Unauthorized changes can be made in processing. The organization may not be sure of which programs or systems have been changed.
Software controls (system software)	These controls may not have a direct effect on individual applications. Other general controls depend heavily on system software, so a weakness in this area impairs the other general controls.
Physical hardware controls	Hardware may have serious malfunctions or may break down altogether, introducing numerous errors or destroying computerized records.
Computer operations controls	Random errors may occur in a system. (Most processing will be correct, but occasionally it may not be.)
Data file security controls	Unauthorized changes can be made in data stored in computer systems or unauthorized individuals can access sensitive information.
Administrative controls	All of the other controls may not be properly executed or enforced.

Application Controls

Application controls are specific controls within each separate computer application, such as payroll or order processing. They include automated and manual procedures that ensure that only authorized data are completely and accurately processed by that application. The controls for each application should encompass the whole sequence of processing.

Not all of the application controls discussed here are used in every information system. Some systems require more of these controls than others, depending on the importance of the data and the nature of the application.

Application controls can be classified as (1) input controls, (2) processing controls, and (3) output controls.

Input Controls

Input controls check data for accuracy and completeness when they enter the system. There are specific input controls for input authorization, data conversion, data editing, and error handling.

Input must be properly authorized, recorded, and monitored as source documents flow to the computer. For example, formal procedures can be set up to authorize only selected members of the sales department to prepare sales transactions for an order entry system.

Input must be properly converted into computer transactions, with no errors as it is transcribed from one form to another. Transcription errors can be eliminated or reduced by keying input transactions directly into computer terminals or by using some form of source data automation.

Control totals can be established beforehand for input transactions. These totals can range from a simple document count to totals for quantity fields such as total sales amount (for a batch of transactions). Computer programs count the totals from transactions input.

Edit checks include various programmed routines that can be performed to edit input data for errors before they are processed. Transactions that do not meet edit crite-

input controls The procedures to check data for accuracy and completeness when they enter the system.

control totals A type of input control that requires counting transactions or quantity fields prior to processing for comparison and reconciliation after processing.

edit checks Routines performed to verify input data and correct errors prior to processing.

WINDOW ON MANAGEMENT

Security Goes Global

When companies go international, so do concerns about security. Server crashes, natural disasters, and even industrial espionage can create global risks. One weak link in a global information system can result in staggering losses, because so many operating units are tied together with networked systems. Vulnerability may increase when companies consolidate hundreds of local computer centers in various countries into a handful of transnational data centers.

According to Professor Edward Roche, author of *Managing Information Technology in Multinational Corporations* (1992), companies need to devise a security plan that addresses their global systems, and they need to rehearse coordination between headquarters and their local operations throughout the world.

Supporting this coordinated security policy approach, IBM and Comdisco, Inc. have developed global business recovery services. Companies can put their entire organization under one umbrella policy rather than contract disaster recovery services on a regional basis.

Forward-looking global organizations are setting up a small, central security team at company headquarters and then appointing someone to take charge of security for each business unit around the world. The central team conducts a risk analysis for the entire organization and then selects a methodology to use worldwide. For example, European operations might emphasize physical computer security, because computer theft is higher there than elsewhere.

The challenge is creating a security policy that can work across international boundaries. Only a small percentage of companies actually have security departments—as low as 18 percent among Asian-Pacific countries and 21 percent in Europe. There are different regional attitudes about the importance of security, making it difficult for employees to pay attention to the problem.

Less stringent security requirements in Europe and Asia allow banks to be less diligent about disaster recovery plans than in other parts of the world. The availability of software can also add to difficulties in implementing worldwide security strategies. Through a series of virus attacks, Otis Elevator learned that its European subsidiaries used antivirus software with a lower level of protection than that used by corporate headquarters in Farmington, Connecticut.

Global security planning paid off for Young & Rubicam Advertising. When the main server in its Sao Paulo, Brazil, office crashed one morning in December 1996, it could have created a catastrophe. Instead, it set off some well-laid plans. A copy of Lotus Notes (which this international advertising firm uses for its creative work, media plans, and strategy) was downloaded from its New York office on its wide area network (WAN). The Sao Paulo office was operational by the end of the business day. No data had been lost.

When Young & Rubicam launched its WAN in Latin America, it developed a single security plan for its diverse network needs in Argentina, Brazil, Mexico, and the United States. However, procedures differ slightly in each country. For example, in Brazil and Argentina, daily backup tapes are delivered to a storage vault, whereas in Mexico, backup tapes are delivered to the home of a Mexican executive because no similar pickup services exist.

To Think About: ***What are the management benefits of having a global security plan? What are the management, organizational, and technology challenges to implementing such a plan?***

Source: Adapted from Tom Duffy, "Avoiding a Transnational Breakdown," *Computerworld Global Innovators,* March 10, 1997.

processing controls The routines for establishing that data are complete and accurate during updating.

run control totals The procedures for controlling completeness of computer updating by generating control totals that reconcile totals before and after processing.

computer matching The processing control that matches input data to information held on master files.

ria will be rejected. The edit routines can produce lists of errors to be corrected later. Important types of edit techniques are summarized in Table 14.4.

Processing Controls

Processing controls establish that data are complete and accurate during updating. The major processing controls are run control totals, computer matching, and programmed edit checks.

Run control totals reconcile the input control totals with the totals of items that have updated the file. Updating can be controlled by generating control totals during processing. The totals, such as total transactions processed or totals for critical quantities, can be compared manually or by computer. Discrepancies are noted for investigation.

Computer matching matches the input data with information held on master or suspense files, with unmatched items noted for investigation. Most matching occurs during input, but under some circumstances it may be required to ensure completeness of updating. For example, a matching program might match employee time cards with a payroll master file and report missing or duplicate time cards.

TABLE 14.4 Important Edit Techniques

Edit Technique	Description	Example
Reasonableness checks	To be accepted, data must fall within certain limits set in advance, or they will be rejected.	If an order transaction is for 20,000 units and the largest order on record was 50 units, the transaction will be rejected.
Format checks	Characteristics of the contents (letter/digit), length, and sign of individual data fields are checked by the system.	A nine-position Social Security number should not contain any alphabetic characters.
Existence checks	The computer compares input reference data to tables or master files to make sure that valid codes are being used.	An employee can have a Fair Labor Standards Act code of only 1, 2, 3, 4, or 5. All other values for this field will be rejected.
Dependency checks	The computer checks whether a *logical* relationship is maintained between data for the *same* transaction. When it is not, the transaction is rejected.	A car loan initiation transaction should show a logical relationship between the size of the loan, the number of loan repayments, and the size of each installment.

Most edit checking occurs at the time data are input. However, certain applications require some type of reasonableness or dependency check during updating. For example, consistency checks might be utilized by a utility company to compare a customer's electric bill with previous bills. If the bill was 500 percent higher this month compared to last month, the bill would not be processed until the meter was rechecked.

Output Controls

Output controls ensure that the results of computer processing are accurate, complete, and properly distributed. Typical output controls include the following:

output controls Measures that ensure that the results of computer processing are accurate, complete, and properly distributed.

- Balancing output totals with input and processing totals
- Reviews of the computer processing logs to determine that all of the correct computer jobs executed properly for processing
- Formal procedures and documentation specifying authorized recipients of output reports, checks, or other critical documents

Security and the Internet

Linking to the Internet or transmitting information via intranets and extranets require special security measures. Large public networks, including the Internet, are more vulnerable because they are virtually open to anyone and because they are so huge that when abuses do occur, they can have an enormously widespread impact. Chapter 9 described the use of *firewalls* to prevent unauthorized users from accessing private networks. As growing numbers of businesses expose their networks to Internet traffic, firewalls are becoming a necessity.

A firewall is generally placed between internal LANs and WANs and external networks such as the Internet. The firewall controls access to the organization's internal networks by acting like a "Checkpoint Charlie" that examines each user's credentials before they can access the network. The firewall identifies names, Internet Protocol (IP) addresses, applications, and other characteristics of incoming traffic. It checks this

NetGuard's Guardian firewall software provides a simple, user-friendly graphical interface for defining security rules. Guardian provides tools to monitor and control Internet access to private corporate networks.

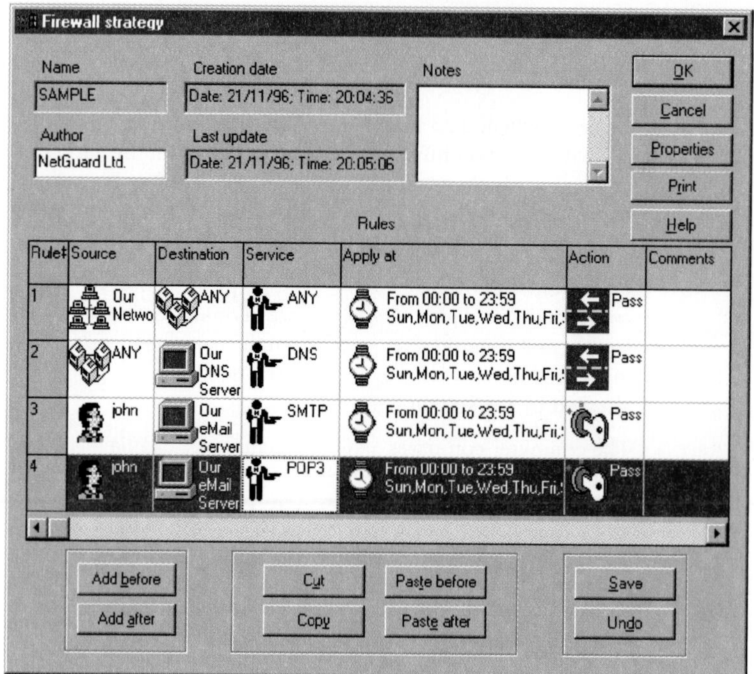

information against the access rules that have been programmed into the system by the network administrator. The firewall prevents unauthorized communication into and out of the network, allowing the organization to enforce a security policy on traffic flowing between its network and the Internet (Oppliger, 1997). Table 14.5 describes different types of firewall products and compares their capabilities. Hybrid products are being developed that combine these features.

To create a good firewall, someone must write and maintain the internal rules identifying the people, applications, or addresses that are allowed or rejected in very fine detail. Firewalls can deter, but not completely prevent network penetration from outsiders, and should be viewed as one element in an overall security plan.

TABLE 14.5 Categories of Firewall Products

Type of Firewall Product	Description
Packet-Filtering Firewall	A router examines each incoming Internet Protocol (IP) packet, checking its source or destination addresses or services. User-defined access rules must identify every type of packet that the organization does not want to admit.
Application Gateway and Proxy Service	A host computer called an application gateway sits between the Internet and an organization's internal network, providing middleman services to users on either side. If a user outside the company wants to communicate with a user inside the organization, the first user "talks" to the proxy application on the application gateway and the proxy application then communicates with the internal computer. Likewise, a computer user inside the organization goes through the proxy to "talk" to computers on the outside.
Hardened Firewall Host	A stripped-down computer is specially configured to protect against unauthenticated log-ins from outside the organization. Users inside or outside the organization must connect to trusted applications on the firewall machine before connecting further.

Security and Electronic Commerce

Security of electronic communications is a major control issue for companies engaged in electronic commerce. It is essential that commerce-related data of buyers and sellers be kept private when they are transmitted electronically. The data being transmitted also must be protected against being purposefully altered by someone other than the sender, so that, for example, stock market execution orders or product orders accurately represent the wishes of the buyer and seller.

Many organizations rely on encryption to protect sensitive information transmitted over networks. **Encryption** is the coding and scrambling of messages to prevent unauthorized access to or understanding of the data being transmitted. A message can be encrypted by applying a secret numerical code called an encryption key so that it is transmitted as a scrambled set of characters. (The key consists of a large group of letters, numbers, and symbols.) In order to be read, the message must be decrypted (unscrambled) with a matching key. A number of encryption standards exist, including Data Encryption Standard (DES), which is used by the U.S. government, RSA (by RSA Data Security), SSL (Secure Sockets Layer), and S-HTTP (Secure Hypertext Transport Protocol). SSL and S-HTTP are used for Web-based traffic.

encryption The coding and scrambling of messages to prevent their being read or accessed without authorization.

There are several alternative methods of encryption, but "public key" encryption is becoming popular. Public key encryption, illustrated in Figure 14.5, uses two different keys, one private and one public. The keys are mathematically related so that data encrypted with one key only can be decrypted using the other key. To send and receive messages, communicators first create separate pairs of private and public keys. The public key is kept in a directory and the private key must be kept secret. The sender encrypts a message with the recipients' public key. Upon receiving the message, the recipient uses his or her private key to decrypt it.

Encryption is especially useful to shield messages on the Internet and other public networks because they are less secure than private networks. Encryption helps protect transmission of payment data, such as credit card information, and addresses problems of authentication and message integrity. **Authentication** refers to the ability of each party to know that the other parties are who they claim to be. In the nonelectronic world, we use our signatures. Bank-by-mail systems avoid the need for signatures on checks they issue for their customers by using well-protected private networks where the source of the request for payment is recorded and can be proven. **Message integrity** is the ability to be certain that the message that is sent arrives without being copied or changed.

authentication The ability of each party in a transaction to ascertain the identity of the other party.

message integrity The ability to ascertain that a transmitted message has not been copied or altered.

Experts are working on methods that involve encryption for creating agreed-upon certified digital signatures. A **digital signature** is a digital code attached to an electronically transmitted message that is used to verify the origins and contents of a message. It provides a way to associate a message with the sender, performing a function similar to a written signature. A recipient of data can use the digital signature to verify who sent the data and that the data were not altered after being "signed."

digital signature A digital code that can be attached to an electronically transmitted message to uniquely identify the sender.

Authentication can be further reinforced by attaching a **digital certificate** to an electronic message. A digital certificate system uses a trusted third party known as a

digital certificate An attachment to an electronic message to verify the identity of the sender and to provide the receiver with the means to encode a reply.

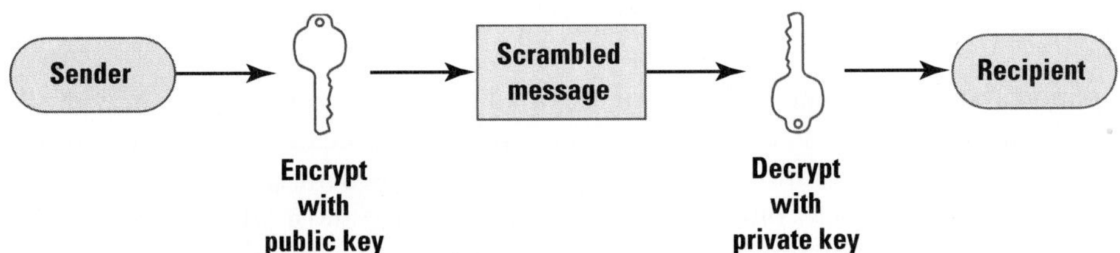

FIGURE 14.5 Public key encryption. A public key encryption system can be viewed as a series of public and private keys that lock data when they are transmitted and unlock the data when they are received. The sender locates the recipient's public key in a directory and uses it to encrypt a message. The message is sent in encrypted form over the Internet or a private network. When the encrypted message arrives, the recipient uses his or her private key to decrypt the data and read the message.

DigiCash's eCash™ is a software-based payments system that allows users to send electronic cash payments from any personal computer (PC) to any other PC or workstation, using any computer network including the Internet. This screen illustrates a transaction log with the user's account history.

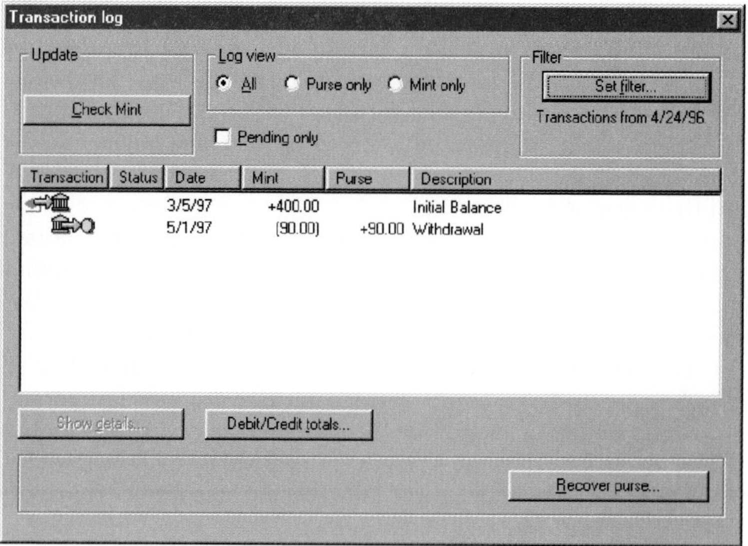

certificate authority (CA) to verify a user's identity. The CA system can be run as a function inside an organization or by an outside company such as VeriSign Inc. in Mountain View, California. The CA verifies a digital certificate user's identity off-line, by telephone, postal mail, or in person. This information is put into a CA server, which generates an encrypted digital certificate containing owner identification information and a copy of the owner's public key. The certificate authenticates that the public key belongs to the designated owner. The CA makes its own public key available publicly either in print or perhaps on the Internet. The recipient of an encrypted message uses the CA's public key to decode the digital certificate attached to the message, verifies it was issued by the CA, and then obtains the sender's public key and identification information contained in the certificate. Using this information, the recipient can send an encrypted reply. The digital certificate system would enable, for example, a credit card user and merchant to validate that their digital certificates were issued by an authorized and trusted third party before they exchange data.

Much on-line commerce continues to be handled through private EDI networks, usually run over VANs. VANs (value-added networks) are relatively secure and reliable. However, because they have to be privately maintained and run on high-speed private lines, VANs are expensive, easily costing a company $100,000 per month. They also are inflexible, being connected only to a limited number of sites and companies. As a result, the Internet is emerging as the network technology of choice. EDI transactions on the Internet run from one-half to one-tenth the cost of VAN-based transactions (Knowles, 1997). Special electronic-payment systems have been developed for the Internet. The capabilities and security features of leading payment systems are described in the Window on Technology.

Developing a Control Structure: Costs and Benefits

Information systems can make exhaustive use of all the control mechanisms previously discussed. But they may be so expensive to build and so complicated to use that the system is economically or operationally unfeasible. Some cost/benefit analysis must be performed to determine which control mechanisms provide the most effective safeguards without sacrificing operational efficiency or cost.

One of the criteria that determine how much control is built into a system is the *importance of its data.* Major financial and accounting systems, for example, such as a payroll system or one that tracks purchases and sales on the stock exchange, must have higher standards of controls than a *tickler* system to track dental patients and remind them that their six-month checkup is due. For instance, Swissair invested in additional

WINDOW ON TECHNOLOGY

Securing Electronic Payments on the Internet

Almost everyone agrees that the biggest piece of the Internet commerce puzzle is how to get paid. Many companies and individuals are reluctant to use the Internet for electronic payments because Internet communication is so difficult to secure. On the other hand, stock trading on the Internet is flourishing, and companies such as Virtual Vineyards or Amazon.com booksellers are busy selling their wares on-line with Internet electronic-payment systems. Here's how the most popular payment-processing systems work.

VISA International, MasterCard International, American Express, and other major credit card companies and banks have adopted the **Secure Electronic Transaction (SET)** protocol for encrypting credit card payment data over the Internet and other open networks. A user acquires a digital certificate and digital wallet from his or her bank, which acts like a middleman in an e-commerce transaction. The wallet and certificate specify the identity of the user and the credit card being used. When the user shops at a Web site and selects the SET payment method, the merchant's servers send a signal over the Internet that invokes the user's SET wallet. The digital wallet encrypts the payment information and sends it to the merchant. The merchant verifies that the information is a SET packet and adds its digital certificate to the message. The merchant then encrypts this information and passes it on to the bank, which verifies the transaction. The financial institution approves or denies the transaction based on credit standing and passes that information over the Internet to the merchant and back to the user's wallet.

CyberCash/Checkfree Wallet gives away client software that encrypts and forwards transaction and credit card information to a Web-based merchant. The merchant in turn forwards the information to a CyberCash server. The server takes the information behind a firewall, decrypts it, and sends it to the merchant's bank. The merchant's bank then forwards an authorization request to the bank that issued the credit card. After verifying the information, the bank issuing the card forwards either an approval or denial of payment to CyberCash. CyberCash transmits this information back to the merchant, who notifies the customer. The chance of a security breach is lessened because the merchant on the Web never sees or stores a credit card number.

DigiCash uses "e-cash," or electronic cash, for anonymous on-line purchasing. **Electronic cash** is currency represented in electronic form that is moving outside the normal network of money (paper currency, coins, checks, credit cards) and for now is not under the purview of the Federal Reserve within the United States. Users are supplied with client software and can exchange money with another e-cash user over the Internet. When they make an on-line purchase, the e-cash software creates a "coin" in an amount specified by the user and sends it to the bank wrapped in a virtual "envelope." The bank withdraws the amount requested from the user's account, puts a validating stamp on the "envelope" to validate the coin's value and returns it to the user. When the user receives the envelope back, he or she can spend the coin.

First Virtual Internet Payment System takes a different approach from the others. Instead of devising a secure way to transmit information over the Internet, they avoid it entirely. Prospective customers must apply for a unique alphanumeric personal identification number called a VirtualPIN that can be used at any participating site. The VirtualPIN is stored with the user's credit card number off-line, on a secure computer. That means that only First Virtual has access to sensitive data. Merchants using this system must obtain a Seller's VirtualPIN and set up an account. When a customer makes a purchase over the Internet, all that travels on the Internet is the customer's VirtualPIN number. To process a payment, the merchant submits its Seller's VirtualPIN along with the shopper's VirtualPIN to First Virtual. First Virtual then e-mails the customer to confirm the purchase. If the customer approves the transaction, First Virtual processes the transaction, sending confirmation to the seller. The seller then ships the purchased item to the buyer.

To Think About: ***What management, organization, and technology issues would you consider in selecting an Internet payment system?***

Sources: Bill Roberts, "On Your Mark, Get SET, Wait!" *Datamation,* April 1998; Mitch Wagner, "Get SET to Secure Transactions," *Computerworld,* July 28, 1997; and Robert Keenan, "Are We There Yet?: A Developer's Guide to Internet Commerce Solutions," *Interactivity,* February 1997.

hardware and software to increase its network reliability because it was running critical reservation and ticketing applications.

The cost effectiveness of controls also will be influenced by the efficiency, complexity, and expense of each control technique. For example, complete one-for-one checking may be time-consuming and operationally impossible for a system that processes hundreds of thousands of utilities payments daily. But it might be possible to use this technique to verify only critical data such as dollar amounts and account numbers, while ignoring names and addresses.

Secure Electronic Transaction (SET) A standard for securing credit card transactions over the Internet and other networks.

electronic cash Currency represented in electronic form that moves outside the normal network of money, preserving the anonymity of its users.

TABLE 14.6 On-Line Order Processing Risk Assessment

Exposure	Probability of Occurrence (%)	Loss Range/ Average ($)	Expected Annual Loss ($)
Power failure	30	5000–200,000 (102,500)	30,750
Embezzlement	5	1000–50,000 (25,500)	1,275
User error	98	200–40,000 (20,100)	19,698

This chart shows the results of a risk assessment of three selected areas of an on-line order processing system. The likelihood of each exposure occurring over a one-year period is expressed as a percentage. The next column shows the highest and lowest possible loss that could be expected each time the exposure occurred and an average loss calculated by adding the highest and lowest figures together and dividing by 2. The expected annual loss for each exposure can be determined by multiplying the average loss by its probability of occurrence.

risk assessment Determining the potential frequency of the occurrence of a problem and the potential damage if the problem were to occur. Used to determine the cost/benefit of a control.

A third consideration is the *level of risk* if a specific activity or process is not properly controlled. System builders can undertake a **risk assessment**, determining the likely frequency of a problem and the potential damage if it were to occur. For example, if an event is likely to occur no more than once a year, with a maximum of $1000 loss to the organization, it would not be feasible to spend $20,000 on the design and maintenance of a control to protect against that event. However, if that same event could occur at least once a day, with a potential loss of more than $300,000 a year, $100,000 spent on a control might be entirely appropriate.

Table 14.6 illustrates sample results of a risk assessment for an on-line order processing system that processes 30,000 orders per day. The probability of a power failure occurring in a one-year period is 30 percent. Loss of order transactions while power is down could range from $5000 to $200,000 for each occurrence, depending on how long processing was halted. The probability of embezzlement occurring over a yearly period is about 5 percent, with potential losses ranging from $1000 to $50,000 for each occurrence. User errors have a 98 percent chance of occurring over a yearly period, with losses ranging from $200 to $40,000 for each occurrence. The average loss for each event can be weighted by multiplying it by the probability of its occurrence annually to determine the expected annual loss. Once the risks have been assessed, system builders can concentrate on the control points with the greatest vulnerability and potential loss. In this case, controls should focus on ways to minimize the risk of power failures and user errors.

In some situations, organizations may not know the precise probability of threats occurring to their information systems, and they may not be able to quantify the impact of events that disrupt their information systems. In these instances, management may choose to describe risks and their likely impact in a qualitative manner (Rainer, Snyder, and Carr, 1991).

To decide which controls to use, information system builders must examine various control techniques in relation to each other and to their relative cost-effectiveness. A control weakness at one point may be offset by a strong control at another. It may not be cost-effective to build tight controls at every point in the processing cycle if the areas of greatest risk are secure or if compensating controls exist elsewhere. The combination of all of the controls developed for a particular application will determine its overall control structure.

The Role of Auditing in the Control Process

How does management know that information system controls are effective? To answer this question, organizations must conduct comprehensive and systematic *audits*. An

Function: Personal Loans	Prepared by: J. Ericson	Received by: T. Barrow
Location: Peoria, Ill.	Preparation date: June 16, 1998	Review date: June 28, 1998

Nature of Weakness and Impact	Chance for Substantial Error		Effect on Audit Procedures	Notification to Management	
	Yes/ No	Justification	Required Amendment	Date of Report	Management Response
Loan repayment records are not reconciled to borrower's records during processing.	Yes	Without a detection control, errors in individual client balances may remain undetected.	Confirm a sample of loans.	5/10/98	Interest Rate Compare Report provides this control.
There are no regular audits of computer-generated data (interest charges).	Yes	Without a regular audit or reasonableness check, widespread miscalculations could result before errors are detected.		5/10/98	Periodic audits of loans will be instituted.
Programs can be put into production libraries to meet target deadlines without final approval from the Standards and Controls group.	No	All programs require management authorization. The Standards and Controls group controls access to all production systems, and assigns such cases to a temporary production status.			

FIGURE 14.6 Sample auditor's list of control weaknesses. This chart is a sample page from a list of control weaknesses that an auditor might find in a loan system in a local commercial bank. This form helps auditors record and evaluate control weaknesses and shows the result of discussing those weaknesses with management, as well as any corrective actions taken by management.

MIS audit identifies all of the controls that govern individual information systems and assesses their effectiveness. To accomplish this, the auditor must acquire a thorough understanding of operations, physical facilities, telecommunications, control systems, data security objectives, organizational structure, personnel, manual procedures, and individual applications.

MIS audit Identifies all the controls that govern individual information systems and assesses their effectiveness.

The auditor usually interviews key individuals who use and operate a specific information system concerning their activities and procedures. Application controls, overall integrity controls, and control disciplines are examined. The auditor should trace the flow of sample transactions through the system and perform tests, using, if appropriate, automated audit software.

The audit lists and ranks all control weaknesses and estimates the probability of their occurrence. It then assesses the financial and organizational impact of each threat. Figure 14.6 is a sample auditor's listing of control weaknesses for a loan system. It includes a section for notifying management of such weaknesses and for management's response. Management is expected to devise a plan for countering significant weaknesses in controls.

14.3 ENSURING SYSTEM QUALITY

Organizations can improve system quality by using software quality assurance techniques and by improving the quality of their data.

Software Quality Assurance

Solutions to software quality problems include using an appropriate systems development methodology; proper resource allocation during systems development; the use of metrics; attention to testing; and the use of quality tools.

Methodologies

Chapter 11 has already described widely used systems development methodologies. The primary function of a development methodology is to provide discipline to the entire development process. A good development methodology establishes organization-wide standards for requirements gathering, design, programming, and testing. To produce quality software, organizations must select an appropriate methodology and then enforce its use. The methodology should call for systems requirement and specification documents that are complete, detailed, accurate, and documented in a format the user community can understand before they approve it. Specifications also must include agreed upon measures of system quality so that the system can be evaluated objectively while it is being developed and once it is completed.

Resource Allocation During Systems Development

resource allocation The determination of how costs, time, and personnel are assigned to different phases of a systems development project.

Views on **resource allocation** during systems development have changed significantly over the years. Resource allocation determines the way the costs, time, and personnel are assigned to different phases of the project. In earlier times, developers focused on programming, with only about 1 percent of the time and costs of a project being devoted to systems analysis (determining specifications). More time should be spent in specifications and systems analysis, decreasing the proportion of programming time and reducing the need for so much maintenance time. Current literature suggests that about one-quarter of a project's time and cost should be expended in specifications and analysis, with perhaps 50 percent of its resources being allocated to design and programming. Installation and postimplementation ideally should require only one-quarter of the project's resources. Investments in software quality initiatives early in a project are likely to provide the greatest payback (Slaughter, Harter, and Krishnan, 1998).

Software Metrics

software metrics The objective assessments of the software used in a system in the form of quantified measurements.

Software metrics can play a vital role in increasing system quality. **Software metrics** are objective assessments of the system in the form of quantified measurements. Ongoing use of metrics allows the IS department and the user jointly to measure the performance of the system and identify problems as they occur. Examples of software metrics include the number of transactions that can be processed in a specified unit of time, on-line response time, the number of payroll checks printed per hour, and the number of known bugs per hundred lines of code. Unfortunately, most manifestations of quality are not so easy to define in metric terms. In those cases developers must find indirect measurements. For example, an objective measurement of a system's ease of use might be the number of calls for help the IS staff receives per month from system users.

For metrics to be successful, they must be carefully designed, formal, and objective. They must measure significant aspects of the system. In addition, metrics are of no value unless they are used consistently and users agree to the measurements in advance.

Testing

walkthrough A review of a specification or design document by a small group of people carefully selected based on the skills needed for the particular objectives being tested.

debugging The process of discovering and eliminating the errors and defects—the bugs—in program code.

Early, regular, and thorough testing will contribute significantly to system quality. In general, software testing is often misunderstood. Many view testing as a way to prove the correctness of work they have done. In fact, we know that all sizable software is riddled with errors, and we must test to uncover these errors.

Testing begins at the design phase. Because no coding yet exists, the test normally used is a **walkthrough**—a review of a specification or design document by a small group of people carefully selected based on the skills needed for the particular objectives being tested. Once coding begins, coding walkthroughs also can be used to review program code. However, code must be tested by computer runs. When errors are discovered, the source is found and eliminated through a process called **debugging.**

Chapter 10 described the stages of testing required to put an information system in operation—program testing, system testing, and acceptance testing. Testing will be successful only if planned properly.

Quality Tools

Finally, system quality can be significantly enhanced by the use of quality tools. Many tools have been developed to address every aspect of the systems development process. Information systems professionals are using project management software to manage their projects. Products exist to document specifications and system design in text and graphic forms. Programming tools include data dictionaries, libraries to manage program modules, and tools that actually produce program code (see Chapters 6 and 11). Many types of tools exist to aid in the debugging process. The most recent set of tools automates much of the preparation for comprehensive testing.

Data Quality Audits

Information system quality also can be improved by identifying and correcting faulty data, making error detection a more explicit organizational goal (Klein, Goodhue, and Davis, 1997). The analysis of data quality often begins with a **data quality audit**, which is a structured survey of the accuracy and level of completeness of the data in an information system. Data quality audits are accomplished by the following methods:

data quality audit A survey of files and samples of files for accuracy and completeness of data in an information system.

- Surveying end users for their perceptions of data quality
- Surveying entire data files
- Surveying samples from data files

Unless regular data quality audits are undertaken, organizations have no way of knowing to what extent their information systems contain inaccurate, incomplete, or ambiguous information. Unfortunately, many organizations are not giving data quality the priority it deserves (Tayi and Ballou, 1998). Some organizations, such as the Social Security Administration, have established data quality audit procedures. These procedures control payment and process quality by auditing a 20,000-case sample of beneficiary records each month. The FBI, on the other hand, did not conduct a comprehensive audit of its record systems until 1984. With few data quality controls, the FBI criminal record systems were found to have serious problems.

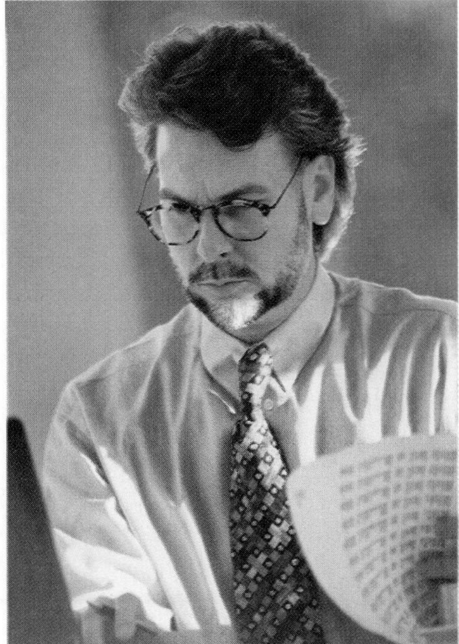

Auditors can analyze the quality of data in a system by conducting a survey of data files for accuracy.

Management Wrap-Up

MANAGEMENT

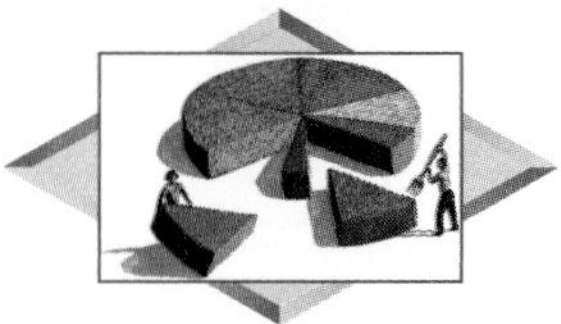

ORGANIZATION

TECHNOLOGY

Management is responsible for developing the control structure and quality standards for the organization. Key management decisions include establishing standards for systems accuracy and reliability, determining an appropriate level of control for organizational functions, and establishing a disaster recovery plan.

The characteristics of the organization play a large role in determining its approach to quality assurance and control issues. Some organizations are more quality and control conscious than others. Their cultures and business processes support high standards of quality and performance. Creating high levels of security and quality in information systems can be a process of lengthy organizational change.

A number of technologies and methodologies are available for promoting system quality and security. Technologies such as antivirus and data security software, firewalls, and programmed procedures can be used to create a control environment, whereas software metrics, systems development methodologies, and automated tools for systems development can be used to improve software quality. Organizational discipline is required to use these technologies effectively.

For Discussion:

1. It has been said that controls and security should be one of the first areas to be addressed in the design of an information system. Do you agree? Why or why not?
2. How much software testing is "enough"? What management, organization, and technology issues should you consider in answering this question?

SUMMARY

1. **Demonstrate why information systems are so vulnerable to destruction, error, abuse, and system quality problems.** With data easily concentrated into electronic form and many procedures invisible through automation, computerized information systems are vulnerable to destruction, misuse, error, fraud, and hardware or software failures. The effect of disaster in a computerized system can be greater than in manual systems because all of the records for a particular function or organization can be destroyed or lost. On-line systems and those utilizing the Internet are especially vulnerable because data and files can be immediately and directly accessed through computer terminals or at many points in the network. Computer viruses can spread rampantly from system to system, clogging computer memory or destroying programs and data. Software presents problems because of the high costs of correcting errors and because software bugs may be impossible to eliminate. Data quality can also severely impact system quality and performance.

2. **Compare general controls and application controls for information systems, including controls to safeguard use of the Internet.** Controls consist of all the methods, policies, and organizational procedures that ensure the safety of the organization's assets, the accuracy and reliability of its accounting records, and adherence to management standards. There are two main categories of controls: general controls and application controls.

   General controls handle the overall design, security, and use of computer programs and files for the organization as a whole. They include physical hardware controls, system software controls, data file security controls, computer operations controls, controls over the system implementation process, and administrative disciplines. Firewalls help safeguard private networks from unauthorized access when organizations use intranets or link to the Internet. Encryption is a widely used technology for securing electronic payment systems.

   Application controls are those unique to specific computerized applications. They focus on the completeness and accuracy of input, updating and maintenance, and the validity of the information in the system. Application controls consist of (1) input controls, (2) processing controls, and (3) output controls.

3. **Select the factors that must be considered when developing the controls for information systems.** To determine which controls are required, designers and users of systems must identify all of the control points and control weaknesses and perform risk assessment. They must also perform a cost/benefit analysis of controls and design controls that can effectively safeguard systems without making them unusable.
4. **Describe the most important software quality assurance techniques.** The quality and reliability of software can be improved by using a standard development methodology, software metrics, thorough testing procedures, quality tools, and by reallocating resources to put more emphasis on the analysis and design stages of systems development.
5. **Demonstrate the importance of auditing information systems and safeguarding data quality.** Comprehensive and systematic MIS auditing can help organizations to determine the effectiveness of the controls in their information systems. Regular data quality audits should be conducted to help organizations ensure a high level of completeness and accuracy of the data stored in their systems.

KEY TERMS

Administrative controls, 438
Antivirus software, 431
Application controls, 436
Authentication, 443
Bugs, 433
Computer matching, 440
Computer operations controls, 437
Computer virus, 430
Control totals, 439
Controls, 436
Data quality audit, 449
Data security controls, 437
Debugging, 448
Digital certificate, 443
Digital signature, 443
Edit checks, 439
Electronic cash (e-cash), 445
Encryption, 443
Fault-tolerant computer system, 432
General controls, 436
Hacker, 430
Hardware controls, 437
Implementation controls, 436
Input controls, 439
Message integrity, 443
MIS audit, 447
On-line transaction processing, 432
Output controls, 441
Processing controls, 440
Resource allocation, 448
Risk assessment, 446
Run control totals, 440
Secure Electronic Transaction (SET), 445
Security, 433
Segregation of functions, 438
Software controls, 436
Software metrics, 448
Walkthrough, 448

REVIEW QUESTIONS

1. Why are computer systems more vulnerable than manual systems to destruction, fraud, error, and misuse? Name some of the key areas where systems are most vulnerable.
2. Name some features of on-line information systems that make them difficult to control.
3. What are *fault-tolerant computer systems?* When should they be used?
4. How can bad software and data quality affect system performance and reliability? Describe two software quality problems.
5. What are *controls?* Distinguish between *general controls* and *application controls.*
6. Name and describe the principal general controls for computerized systems.
7. List and describe the principal application controls.
8. How does MIS auditing enhance the control process?
9. What is the function of risk assessment?
10. Name and describe four software quality assurance techniques.
11. Why are data quality audits essential?
12. What is security? List and describe controls that promote security for computer hardware, computer networks, computer software, and computerized data.
13. What special security measures must be taken by organizations linking to the Internet?
14. Describe the role of firewalls and encryption systems in promoting security.

GROUP PROJECT

Form a group with two or three other students. Select a system described in one of the chapter-ending cases. Write a description of the system, its functions, and its value to the organization. Then write a description of both the general and application controls that should be used to protect the organization. Present your findings to the class.

TOOLS FOR INTERACTIVE LEARNING

■ **INTERNET:** The Internet Connection for this chapter will take you to a series of Web sites where you can complete an exercise to evaluate various secure electronic payment systems for the Internet. You can also use the Interactive Study Guide to test your knowledge of the topics in this chapter and get instant feedback where you need more practice.

■ **CD-ROM:** If you purchase and use the Multimedia Edition CD-ROM with this chapter, you can complete an interactive exercise asking you to identify the security and control problems faced by a company and select appropriate solutions. You can also find a video clip illustrating the Comdisco disaster recovery service, an audio overview of the major themes of this chapter, and bullet text summarizing the key points of the chapter.

CASE STUDY

NASD Files Do a Disappearing Act

The National Association of Securities Dealers (NASD) is the self-regulatory organization of the brokerage industry and the operator of NASDAQ, the over-the-counter stock trading system that has evolved into the second-largest stock market in the United States and the third largest in the world. On March 26, 1998, the NASD launched a public-disclosure system that will allow investors to access the disciplinary history of all NASD brokers and firms through the Internet or NASD's toll-free hotline. Investors will be able to log onto the Internet, punch up the name of a broker or firm, and immediately see if there are any pending customer complaints, arbitration claims, arbitration awards, court awards paid to customers, or settlements of account disputes exceeding $10,000. The system also will provide information on brokers' work histories and where they are registered to do business.

The system is based on regulatory records on the nation's 535,000 stock brokers maintained in a central registration depository (CRD) system. An earlier system allowed investors to obtain some of this information from an 800-number hotline, but the information that could be obtained that way was much more limited. (For example, investors could not learn whether there was a backlog of complaints against their broker. To obtain more complete data, including pending complaints, investors had to check with their state securities department.) Moreover, some data that were supposed to be included in the NASD central registration depository system were missing. In early 1997, NASD disclosed that as many as 20,000 pieces of regulatory data on stockbrokers could have been inadvertently purged from this system. NASD at first said only 1100 files had been purged, but later revised the figure to around 3000. State regulators, on the other hand, insist the number was 20,000. The NASD said the 20,000 figure represented the potential number of purged filings as opposed to actual ones.

Despite the leading-edge technology available to Wall Street, the CRD works much like a library card catalog. Material about brokers and firms must be entered into computers manually by NASD clerks. The NASD reported that these clerks were following faulty guidelines that it had inadvertently issued when the deletions occurred. These guidelines, which NASD no longer uses, were spelled out in an internal memorandum obtained by *The Wall Street Journal.* The NASD memo informed staffers that "revised" guidelines allowed them to delete a broad range of disciplinary data from the CRD system, including instances in which a customer, court, or arbitration panel had withdrawn or dismissed a broker as a named party in a lawsuit or arbitration filing before a judgment was entered. Most of the purged data dealt with this information.

Under a contract with state regulators, NASD is not allowed to delete such information, but the states were not informed about the revised guidelines. Elisse Walter, chief operating officer at NASD's regulatory arm, admitted that "it was an error—a serious error at that," but she stated that NASD quickly established steps and controls to make sure the problem would not happen again.

While NASD restored the purged records, investors could call a NASD hotline to find out about pending and resolved disciplinary cases against brokers or firms. (State securities offices can give investors additional data about pending court cases and arbitration.)

Attorneys representing investors were not satisfied. The NASD, as a self-regulatory organization disseminating data, should at the minimum have been able to inform people that the information they provided might not be complete.

The problem was accidentally uncovered a year earlier by a state regulator. John Deden, a Colorado investigator, printed out a CRD report of a stockbroker he was investigating. When he tapped into the CRD files a few months later to update the investigation, he found that two complaints that were on the original printout had disappeared from the file. Checking on other investigatory files, Deden found that a felony conviction on another broker's record had vanished as well. As he dug further, he found more missing data.

In September 1996, a group of NASD executives and regulators developed a "restoration protocol" for correcting the purged files. The group examined 300 pieces of purged data and determined what needed to be restored. It found 20,000 pieces of regulatory data that had been deleted from a sample of records between January 1995 and August 1996 alone.

Determining what data are missing can be difficult. For example, NASD purged a customer complaint that Joseph Kathrein, Jr., a broker from Quick and Reilly Group Inc., in Newport Beach, California, had conducted unauthorized options trading. NASD had purged the complaint because it did not allege fraud. Kathrein denied the allegation and stated that the case had been resolved in arbitration, with no finding of guilt on either side. However, he noted that it was part of his record and that everything should be on file for investors and regulators to view.

The purged Kathrein data will be restored to the CRD system, but other purges will be more difficult to reinstate. NASD allowed disciplinary records of brokers to be expunged as part of private settlement pacts with investors. According to Denise Crawford, the Texas securities commissioner, this practice raises the issue of whether the states can rely on the CRD. "If we can't rely on this information, the public isn't being served," she said.

State regulators have been negotiating with the NASD on ways to overhaul the CRD system, including instituting procedures to erase stale complaints against brokers. The NASD and the states have agreed that certain complaints can be excised, such as those settled in favor of a broker or those that are not resolved within two years.

Sources: Deborah Lohse and Michael Siconolfi, "NASD System to Tell More About Brokers," *The Wall Street Journal,* March 9, 1998; and Michael Siconolfi, "NASD Error Results in a Purge of Broker Data," *The Wall Street Journal,* February 7, 1997.

Case Study Questions

1. Evaluate the importance of the CRD system for the NASD, for the financial community, and for investors.
2. Identify control weaknesses in the CRD system. What management, organization, and technology factors were responsible for those weaknesses?
3. Design controls for the CRD system to deal with these problems.

CHAPTER 15

Managing International Information Systems

chapter outline

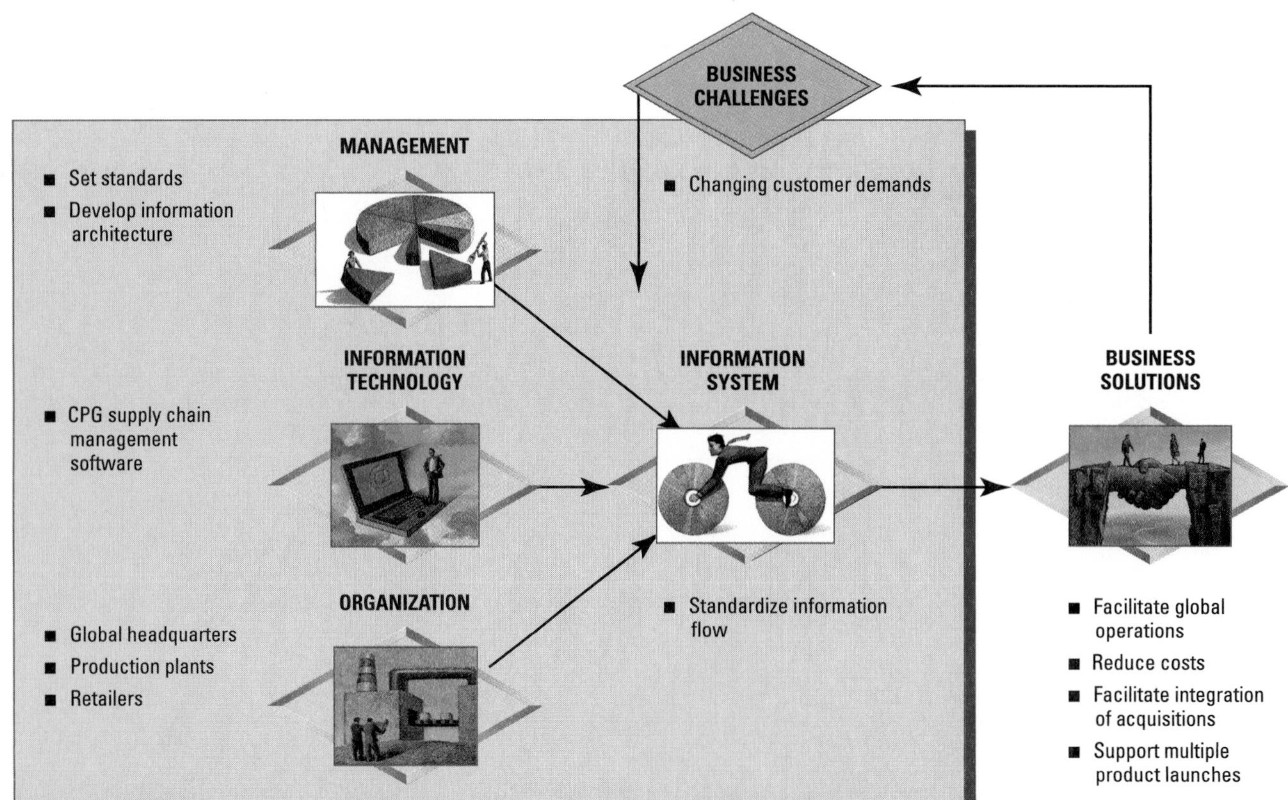

Kellogg Seeks Global Coordination

Kellogg Company, the maker of Kellogg's Corn Flakes® and Kellogg's Rice Krispies® cereals and Kellogg's Pop Tarts® toaster pastries, practically owns breakfast, holding more than 40 percent of the breakfast-food market. In a decade, it has grown from a $3.3 billion company to a $6.8 billion company and it doesn't want to stop. Kellogg wants to meet the demands of customers such as Wal-Mart as they expand outside the United States. To accomplish this goal, the company will need new business processes and new information systems.

Kellogg is investing millions in new global information system technology to support its global operations. Wal-Mart and other sophisticated retailers and grocery chains are setting up shop in every corner of the globe. These companies want their key suppliers, such as Kellogg, to provide them with the same level of service that they provide domestically. According to Doug Wenger, Kellogg's global program director, Kellogg will need globally integrated systems in which data can be entered at one place and flow seamlessly to another. The company would like to take an order anywhere, make the product anywhere, and ship it from any place in the world.

Kellogg selected Oracle Corporation's Consumer Packaged Goods (CPG) software, which allows it to distribute systems while standardizing on one product. CPG includes Oracle's financial and manufacturing management software bundled with software from niche vendors such as Manugistics, Inc., from Rockville, Maryland; Industri-Matematik International Corporation in Tarrytown, New York; Indus International Inc. in San Francisco; and Information Resources Inc. in Chicago. The components are separate software products, so CPG is not as tightly integrated as Kellogg would wish, but the company hopes that future versions will allow data to flow effortlessly through the system.

Kellogg plans to implement the system region by region in North America, Latin America, Europe, and Asia-Pacific. Each region will implement the same software but make its own decisions about the priority of each component. Kellogg is not insisting on central control. Jay Shreiner, Kellogg's chief information officer in Battle Creek, Michigan, distinguishes between central and global systems. Global systems give people in various areas "the tools to make the right decisions for Kellogg's. Headquarters needs access to certain information, but we do not believe in running the worldwide supply chain explicitly from Battle Creek."

Kellogg sees several benefits from implementing a global supply chain system, including improved inventory management, support for multiple product launches, and easier integration of acquisitions into the system.

Source: Adapted from Randy Weston, "Software to Tame Supply Chain Tiger," *Computerworld,* February 16, 1998.

Management Challenges

Kellogg Co. is one of many business firms moving toward global forms of organization that transcend national boundaries. Kellogg could not make this move unless it reorganized its information systems and standardized some of its information systems so that the same information could be used by disparate business units in different countries. Such changes are not always easy to make, and they raise the following management challenges:

1. **Lines of business and global strategy.** Firms must decide whether some or all of their lines of business should be managed on a global basis. There are some lines of business in which locale variations are slight, and the possibility exists to reap large rewards by organizing globally. PCs and power tools may fit this pattern, as well as industrial raw materials. Other consumer goods may be quite different by country or region. It is likely that firms with many lines of business will have to maintain a very mixed organizational structure.
2. **The difficulties of managing change in a multicultural firm.** Although engineering change in a single corporation in a single nation can be difficult, costly, and long term, bringing about significant change in very-large-scale global corporations can be daunting. Both the agreement on "core business processes" in a transnational context and the decision on common systems requires either extraordinary insight, a lengthy process of consensus building, or the exercise of sheer power.

learning objectives

After completing this chapter, you will be able to:

1. Identify the main factors behind the growing internationalization of business.
2. Compare global strategies for developing business.
3. Demonstrate how information systems support different global strategies.
4. Plan the development of international information systems.
5. Evaluate the main technical alternatives in developing global systems.

The changes Kellogg seeks are some of the changes in international information systems infrastructure—the basic systems needed to coordinate worldwide trade and other activities—that organizations need to consider if they want to operate across the globe. This chapter explores how to organize, manage, and control the development of international information systems.

15.1 THE GROWTH OF INTERNATIONAL INFORMATION SYSTEMS

We already have described two powerful worldwide changes driven by advances in information technology that have transformed the business environment and posed new challenges for management. One is the transformation of industrial economies and societies into knowledge- and information-based economies. The other is the emergence of a global economy and global world order.

The new world order will sweep away many national corporations, national industries, and national economies controlled by domestic politicians. Much of the Fortune 500—the 500 largest U.S. corporations—will disappear in the next 50 years, mirroring past behavior of large firms since 1900. Many firms will be replaced by fast-moving networked corporations that transcend national boundaries. The growth of international trade has radically altered domestic economies around the globe. About $1 trillion worth of goods, services, and financial instruments—one-fifth of the annual U.S. gross national product—changes hands each day in global trade.

Consider a laptop computer as an example: The CPU is likely to have been designed and built in the United States; the DRAM (or dynamic random access memory, which makes up the majority of primary storage in a computer) was designed in the United States but built in Malaysia; the screen was designed and assembled in Japan, using American patents; the keyboard was from Taiwan; and it was all assembled in Japan, where the case also was made. Management of the project was located in Silicon Valley along with marketing, sales, and finance that coordinated all the activities from financing and production to shipping and sales efforts. None of this would be possible without powerful international information and telecommunication systems, an international information systems infrastructure.

To be effective, managers need a global perspective on business and an understanding of the support systems needed to conduct business on an international scale.

Developing the International Information Systems Infrastructure

This chapter describes how to go about building an international information systems infrastructure suitable for your international strategy. An infrastructure is the constellation of facilities and services, such as highways or telecommunications networks, required for organizations to function and prosper. An **international information systems infrastructure** consists of the basic information systems required by organizations to coordinate worldwide trade and other activities. Figure 15.1 illustrates the reasoning we will follow throughout the chapter and depicts the major dimensions of an international information systems infrastructure.

international information systems infrastructure The basic information systems required by organizations to coordinate worldwide trade and other activities.

The basic strategy to follow when building an international system is to understand the global environment in which your firm is operating. This means understanding the overall market forces, or business drivers, that are pushing your industry toward global competition. A **business driver** is a force in the environment to which businesses must respond and that influences the direction of the business. Likewise, examine carefully the inhibitors or negative factors that create *management challenges*—factors that could scuttle the development of a global business. Once you have examined the global environment, you will need to consider a corporate strategy for competing in that environment. How will your firm respond? You could ignore the global market and focus on domestic competition only, sell to the globe from a domestic base, or organize production and distribution around the globe. There are many in-between choices.

business driver A force in the environment to which businesses must respond and that influences the direction of business.

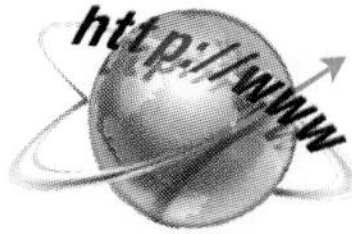

After you have developed a strategy, it is time to consider how to structure your organization so it can pursue the strategy. How will you accomplish a division of

Businesses need an international information systems infrastructure to coordinate the activities of their sales, manufacturing, and warehouse units worldwide.

FIGURE 15.1

International information systems infrastructure. The major dimensions for developing an international information systems infrastructure are the global environment, the corporate global strategies, the structure of the organization, the management and business procedures, and the technology platform.

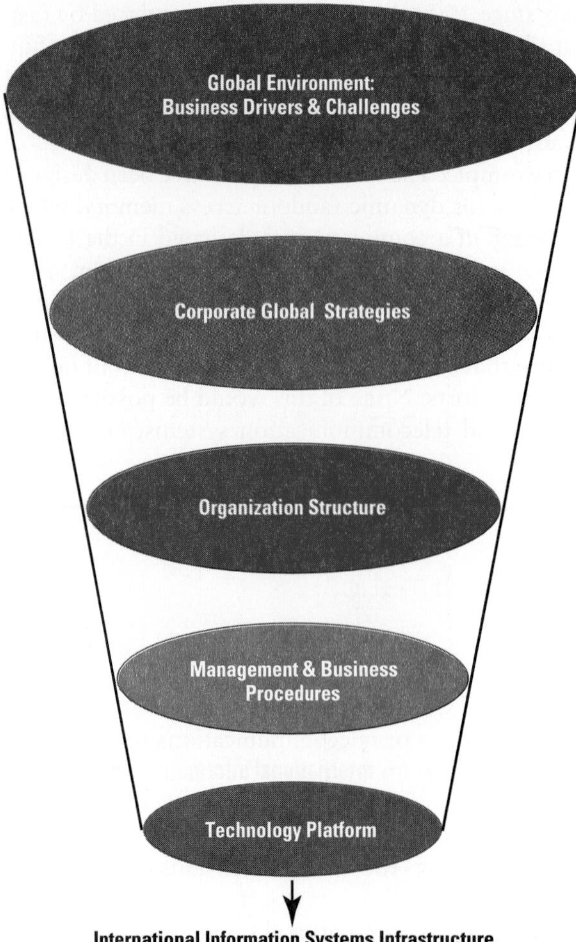

labor across a global environment? Where will production, administration, accounting, marketing, and human resource functions be located? Who will handle the systems function?

Next, you must consider the management issues in implementing your strategy and making the organization design come alive. Key here will be the design of business procedures. How can you discover and manage user requirements? How can you induce change in local units to conform to international requirements? How can you reengineer on a global scale, and how can you coordinate systems development?

The last issue to consider is the technology platform. Although changing technology is a key driving factor leading toward global markets, you need to have a corporate strategy and structure before you can rationally choose the right technology.

After you have completed this process of reasoning, you will be well on your way toward an appropriate international information infrastructure capable of achieving your corporate goals. Let us begin by looking at the overall global environment.

The Global Environment: Business Drivers and Challenges

Table 15.1 illustrates the business drivers in the global environment that are leading all industries toward global markets and competition.

The global business drivers can be divided into two groups: general cultural factors and specific business factors. There are easily recognized general cultural factors driving internationalization since World War II. Information, communication, and transportation technologies have created a *global village* in which communication (by telephone, television, radio, or computer network) around the globe is no more difficult and not much more expensive than communication down the block. Moving goods and services to and from geographically dispersed locations has fallen dramatically in cost.

TABLE 15.1 The Global Business Drivers

General Cultural Factors
Global communication and transportation technologies
Development of global culture
Emergence of global social norms
Political stability
Global knowledge base
Specific Business Factors
Global markets
Global production and operations
Global coordination
Global workforce
Global economies of scale

The development of global communications has created a global village in a second sense: There is now a **global culture** created by television and other globally shared media such as movies that permits different cultures and peoples to develop common expectations about right and wrong, desirable and undesirable, heroic and cowardly. The collapse of the Eastern bloc has speeded up the growth of a world culture enormously, increased support for capitalism and business, and reduced the level of cultural conflict considerably.

global culture The development of common expectations, shared artifacts, and social norms among different cultures and peoples.

A last factor to consider is the growth of a global knowledge base. At the end of World War II, knowledge, education, science, and industrial skills were highly concentrated in North America, Europe, and Japan, with the rest of the world euphemistically called the *Third World.* This is no longer true. Latin America, China, Southern Asia, and Eastern Europe have developed powerful educational, industrial, and scientific centers, resulting in a much more democratically and widely dispersed knowledge base.

These general cultural factors leading toward internationalization result in specific business globalization factors that affect most industries. The growth of powerful communications technologies and the emergence of world cultures create the condition for *global markets*—global consumers interested in consuming similar products that are culturally approved. Coca-Cola, American sneakers (made in Korea but designed in Los Angeles), and CNN News (a television show) can now be sold in Latin America, Africa, and Asia.

Responding to this demand, global production and operations have emerged with precise on-line coordination between far-flung production facilities and central headquarters thousands of miles away. At Sealand Transportation, a major global shipping company based in Newark, New Jersey, shipping managers in Newark can watch the loading of ships in Rotterdam on-line, check trim and ballast, and trace packages to specific ship locations as the activity proceeds. This is all possible through an international satellite link.

The new global markets and pressure toward global production and operation have called forth whole new capabilities for global coordination of all factors of production. Not only production but also accounting, marketing and sales, human resources, and systems development (all the major business functions) can be coordinated on a global scale. Frito Lay, for instance, can develop a marketing sales force automation system in the United States, and, once provided, may try the same techniques and technologies in Spain. Micromarketing—marketing to very small geographic and social units—no longer means marketing to neighborhoods in the United States, but to neighborhoods throughout the world! These new levels of global coordination permit for the first time in history the location of business activity according to comparative advantage. Design should be located where it is best accomplished, as should marketing, production, and finance.

Finally, global markets, production, and administration create the conditions for powerful, sustained global economies of scale. Production driven by worldwide global demand can be concentrated where it can be best accomplished, fixed resources can be allocated over larger production runs, and production runs in larger plants can be scheduled more efficiently and precisely estimated. Lower cost factors of production can be exploited wherever they emerge. The result is a powerful strategic advantage to firms that can organize globally. These general and specific business drivers have greatly enlarged world trade and commerce.

Not all industries are similarly affected by these trends. Clearly, manufacturing has been much more affected than services that still tend to be domestic, and highly inefficient. However, the localism of services is breaking down in telecommunications, entertainment, transportation, financial services, and general business services including law. Clearly those firms within an industry that can understand the internationalization of the industry and respond appropriately will reap enormous gains in productivity and stability.

Business Challenges

Although the possibilities of globalization for business success are significant, fundamental forces are operating to inhibit a global economy and to disrupt international business. Table 15.2 lists the most common and powerful challenges to the development of global systems.

particularism Making judgments and taking actions on the basis of narrow or personal characteristics.

At a cultural level, **particularism,** making judgments and taking action on the basis of narrow or personal characteristics, in all its forms (religious, nationalistic, ethnic, regionalism, geopolitical position) rejects the very concept of a shared global culture and rejects the penetration of domestic markets by foreign goods and services. Differences among cultures produce differences in social expectations, politics, and ultimately legal rules. In certain countries, such as the United States, consumers expect domestic name-brand products to be built domestically and are disappointed to learn that much of what they thought of as domestically produced is in fact foreign made.

Different cultures produce different political regimes. Among the many different countries of the world there are different laws governing the movement of information, information privacy of their citizens, origins of software and hardware in systems, and radio and satellite telecommunications. Even the hours of business and the terms of business trade vary greatly across political cultures. These different legal regimes complicate global business and must be considered when building global systems.

transborder data flow The movement of information across international boundaries in any form.

For instance, European countries have very strict laws concerning transborder data flow and privacy. **Transborder data flow** is defined as the movement of information across

TABLE 15.2 Challenges and Obstacles to Global Business Systems

General
Cultural particularism: regionalism, nationalism
Social expectations: brand-name expectations; work hours
Political laws: transborder data and privacy laws
Specific
Standards: different EDI, e-mail, telecommunications standards
Reliability: phone networks not reliable
Speed: data transfer speeds differ, slower than United States
Personnel: shortages of skilled consultants

WINDOW ON ORGANIZATIONS

Marine Power Europe's Extranet Challenge

Building an extranet overseas can be rewarding, but it poses challenges for companies at all phases of globalization. Boat-engine company Marine Power Europe learned this lesson when it decided to implement a multilingual extranet in about a dozen European countries. Marine Power Europe is a subsidiary of Brunswick Corp.

The extranet cost $500,000 to build. It allows the company's independent dealers to check prices and then submit and track orders. Mercury Marine, the company's U.S. counterpart, had much less difficulty implementing a similar extranet because it was based on one language and one set of business rules. The European extranet, in contrast, had to operate with eight different languages and account for local differences such as an oil tax in Italy and a horsepower tax in Norway. Marine Power Europe's Managing Director Randy Gray warns that a global extranet will take three times as long and cost three times as much as comparable projects in the United States because of such regulatory and cultural complexities. "It requires very intricate local knowledge," he asserts.

Marine Power's extranet runs on IBM AS/400 servers with Web server software provided by Click Interactive Inc., a Chicago-based company. The extranet is supported by a 14-person information systems development and logistics staff at the company's regional headquarters in Brussels.

Marine Power believes that its extranet effort was helped by users' experience with France's Minitel system. Minitel is a government information service dating back to the early 1980s. Consumers use dumb terminals to look up telephone numbers, send personal ads, and conduct other on-line transactions from their homes. About 85 percent of Marine Power's French customers use Minitel to place orders, making them comfortable conducting business on-line.

Although the Internet provided a common set of technical standards, Marine Power Europe still had to grapple with an array of differences in the 11 countries where it sells engines. For example, information systems problems were fixed quickly in Belgium, but in Italy it could take an entire month to repair a broken printer. European countries have different levels of technological acceptance. In Italy, where PCs are not widely used by small businesses, Marine Power had relatively greater difficulty getting dealers to invest in information technology. In contrast, 90 percent of Marine Power's dealers already owned PCs in Scandinavian countries. Unlike the United States, European Internet service providers (ISPs) charge for Internet usage by the minute.

As a result, Marine Power decided not to impose the extranet on its small dealers. Instead of putting its catalogs on the Web, it offered them on CD-ROMs that dealers could use without network connections. Only price lists are on Marine Power's Web site for now.

To Think About: ***What management, organization, and technology issues did Marine Power Europe have to address in implementing its extranet?***

Source: Adapted from Gregory Dalton, "Ready to Go Global?" *InformationWeek*, February 9, 1998.

international boundaries in any form. Some European countries prohibit the processing of financial information outside their boundaries or the movement of personal information to foreign countries. The European Union Data Protection Directive, which went into effect in October 1998, restricts the flow of any information to countries (such as the United States) that do not meet strict European information laws on personal information. That means, for instance, that a French marketing manager might not be able to use a credit card in New York because the credit information cannot be forwarded to the United States, given its privacy laws. In response, most multinational firms develop information systems within each European country to avoid the cost and uncertainty of moving information across national boundaries.

Cultural and political differences profoundly affect organizations' standard operating procedures. A host of specific barriers arise from the general cultural differences, everything from different reliability of phone networks to the shortage of skilled consultants (see Steinbart and Nath, 1992). The Window on Organizations illustrates how such differences can affect efforts to implement an extranet globally.

National laws and traditions have created disparate accounting practices in various countries, which impact the way profits and losses are analyzed. German companies generally do not recognize the profit from a venture until the project is completely finished and they have been paid. British firms, on the other hand, begin posting profits before a project is completed, when they are reasonably certain they will get the money.

These accounting practices are tightly intertwined with each country's legal system, business philosophy, and tax code. British, U.S., and Dutch firms share a predominantly Anglo-Saxon outlook that separates tax calculations from reports to shareholders to focus on showing shareholders how fast profits are growing. Continental European accounting practices are less oriented toward impressing investors, focusing on demonstrating compliance with strict rules and minimizing tax liabilities. These diverging accounting practices make it difficult for large international companies with units in different countries to evaluate their performance.

Cultural differences can also affect the way organizations use information technology. For example, Japanese firms fax extensively but have been reluctant to take advantage of the capabilities of e-mail. One explanation is that the Japanese view e-mail as poorly suited for much intragroup communication and depiction of the complex symbols used in the Japanese written language (Straub, 1994).

Language remains a significant barrier. Although English has become a kind of standard business language, this is truer at higher levels of companies and not throughout the middle and lower ranks. Software may have to be built with local language interfaces before a new information system can be successfully implemented.

Currency fluctuations can play havoc with planning models and projections. A product that appears profitable in Mexico or Japan may actually produce a loss due to changes in foreign exchange rates.

These inhibiting factors must be taken into account when you are designing and building an international infrastructure for your business. For example, companies trying to implement "lean production" systems spanning national boundaries typically underestimate the time, expense, and logistical difficulties of making goods and information flow freely across different countries (Levy, 1997).

State of the Art

One might think, given the opportunities for achieving competitive advantages as outlined previously and the interest in future applications, that most international companies have rationally developed marvelous international systems architectures. Nothing could be further from the truth. Most companies have inherited patchwork international systems from the distant past, often based on concepts of information processing developed in the 1960s—batch-oriented reporting from independent foreign divisions to corporate headquarters, with little on-line control and communication. Corporations in this situation increasingly will face powerful competitive challenges in the marketplace from firms that have rationally designed truly international systems. Still other companies have recently built technology platforms for an international infrastructure but have nowhere to go because they lack global strategy.

As it turns out, there are significant difficulties in building appropriate international infrastructures. The difficulties involve planning a system appropriate to the firm's global strategy, structuring the organization of systems and business units, solving implementation issues, and choosing the right technical platform. Let us examine these problems in greater detail.

15.2 ORGANIZING INTERNATIONAL INFORMATION SYSTEMS

There are three organizational issues facing corporations seeking a global position: choosing a strategy, organizing the business, and organizing the systems management area. The first two are closely connected, so we will discuss them together.

Global Strategies and Business Organization

Four main global strategies form the basis for global firms' organizational structure. These are domestic exporter, multinational, franchiser, and transnational. Each of these strategies is pursued with a specific business organizational structure (see Table 15.3). For simplicity's sake, we describe three kinds of organizational structure or governance: centralized (in the home country), decentralized (to local foreign units), and coordi-

TABLE 15.1 Global Business Strategy and Structure

Business Function	Strategy: Domestic Exporter	Multinational	Franchiser	Transnational
Production	Centralized	Dispersed	Coordinated	Coordinated
Finance/Accounting	Centralized	Centralized	Centralized	Coordinated
Sales/Marketing	Mixed	Dispersed	Coordinated	Coordinated
Human Resources	Centralized	Centralized	Coordinated	Coordinated
Strategic Management	Centralized	Centralized	Centralized	Coordinated

nated (all units participate as equals). There are other types of governance patterns observed in specific companies (e.g., authoritarian dominance by one unit, a confederacy of equals, a federal structure balancing power among strategic units, and so forth; see Keen, 1991).

The **domestic exporter** strategy is characterized by heavy centralization of corporate activities in the home country of origin. Nearly all international companies begin this way, and some move on to other forms. Production, finance/accounting, sales/marketing, human resources, and strategic management are set up to optimize resources in the home country. International sales are sometimes dispersed using agency agreements or subsidiaries, but even here foreign marketing is totally reliant on the domestic home base for marketing themes and strategies. Caterpillar Corporation and other heavy capital-equipment manufacturers fall into this category of firm.

domestic exporter A strategy characterized by heavy centralization of corporate activities in the home country of origin.

The **multinational** strategy concentrates financial management and control out of a central home base while decentralizing production, sales, and marketing operations to units in other countries. The products and services on sale in different countries are adapted to suit local market conditions. The organization becomes a far-flung confederation of production and marketing facilities in different countries. Many financial service firms, along with a host of manufacturers such as General Motors, Chrysler, and Intel, fit this pattern.

multinational A global strategy that concentrates financial management and control out of a central home base while decentralizing production, sales, and marketing operations to units in other countries.

Franchisers are an interesting mix of old and new. On the one hand, the product is created, designed, financed, and initially produced in the home country, but for product-specific reasons must rely heavily on foreign personnel for further production, marketing, and human resources. Food franchisers such as McDonald's, Mrs. Fields Cookies, and Kentucky Fried Chicken fit this pattern. McDonald's created a new form of fast-food chain in the United States and continues to rely largely on the United States for inspiration of new products, strategic management, and financing. Nevertheless, because the product must be produced locally—it is perishable—extensive coordination and dispersal of production, local marketing, and local recruitment of personnel are required. Generally, foreign franchisees are clones of the mother country units, but fully coordinated worldwide production that could optimize factors of production is not possible. For instance, potatoes and beef can generally not be bought where they are cheapest on world markets but must be produced reasonably close to the area of consumption.

franchiser A firm where product is created, designed, financed, and initially produced in the home country, but for product-specific reasons must rely heavily on foreign personnel for further production, marketing, and human resources.

Transnational firms are the stateless, truly globally managed firms that may represent a larger part of international business in the future. Transnational firms have no single national headquarters but instead have many regional headquarters and perhaps a world headquarters. In a **transnational** strategy, nearly all the value-adding activities are managed from a global perspective without reference to national borders, optimizing sources of supply and demand wherever they appear, and taking advantage of any local competitive advantages. Transnational firms take the globe, not the home country, as their management frame of reference. The governance of these firms has been likened to a federal structure in which there is a strong central management core of decision making, but considerable dispersal of power and financial muscle throughout the global divisions. Few companies have actually attained transnational status, but Citicorp, Sony, Ford, and others are attempting this transition.

transnational Truly globally managed firms that have no national headquarters; value-added activities are managed from a global perspective without reference to national borders, optimizing sources of supply and demand and taking advantage of any local competitive advantage.

Information technology and improvements in global telecommunications are giving international firms more flexibility to shape their global strategies. Protectionism and a need to serve local markets better encourage companies to disperse production facilities and at least become multinational. At the same time, the drive to achieve economies of scale and take advantage of short-term local advantages moves transnationals toward a global management perspective and a concentration of power and authority. Hence, there are forces of decentralization and dispersal, as well as forces of centralization and global coordination (Ives and Jarvenpaa, 1991).

Global Systems to Fit the Strategy

The configuration, management, and development of systems tend to follow the global strategy chosen (Roche, 1992; Ives and Jarvenpaa, 1991). Figure 15.2 depicts the typical arrangements. By *systems* we mean the full range of activities involved in building information systems: conception and alignment with the strategic business plan, systems development, and ongoing operation. For the sake of simplicity, we consider four types of systems configuration. *Centralized systems* are those in which systems development and operation occur totally at the domestic home base. *Duplicated systems* are those in which development occurs at the home base but operations are handed over to autonomous units in foreign locations. *Decentralized systems* are those in which each foreign unit designs its own unique solutions and systems. *Networked systems* are those in which systems development and operations occur in an integrated and coordinated fashion across all units. As can be seen in Figure 15.2, domestic exporters tend to have highly centralized systems in which a single domestic systems development staff develops worldwide applications. Multinationals offer a direct and striking contrast: Here foreign units devise their own systems solutions based on local needs with few if any applications in common with headquarters (the exceptions being financial reporting and some telecommunications applications). Franchisers have the simplest systems structure: Like the products they sell, franchisers develop a single system usually at the home base and then replicate it around the world. Each unit, no matter where it is located, has the identical applications. Last, the most ambitious form of systems development is found in the transnational: Networked systems are those in which there is a solid, singular global environment for developing and operating systems. This usually presupposes a powerful telecommunications backbone, a culture of shared applications development, and a shared management culture that crosses cultural barriers. The networked systems struc-

FIGURE 15.2

Global strategy and systems configurations. The large *X*'s show the dominant pattern, and the small *x*'s show the emerging patterns. For instance, domestic exporters rely predominantly on centralized systems, but there is continual pressure and some development of decentralized systems in local marketing regions.

SYSTEM CONFIGURATION	STRATEGY			
	Domestic Exporter	Multinational	Franchiser	Transnational
Centralized	X			
Duplicated			X	
Decentralized	x	X	x	
Networked		x		X

ture is most visible in financial services where the homogeneity of the product—money and money instruments—seems to overcome cultural barriers.

Reorganizing the Business

How should a firm organize itself for doing business on an international scale? To develop a global company and an information systems support structure, a firm needs to follow these principles:

1. Organize value-adding activities along lines of comparative advantage. For instance, marketing/sales functions should be located where they can best be performed, for least cost and maximum impact; likewise with production, finance, human resources, and information systems.
2. Develop and operate systems units at each level of corporate activity—national, regional, and international. To serve local needs, there should be *host country systems units* of some magnitude. *Regional systems units* should handle telecommunications and systems development across national boundaries that take place within major geographic regions (European, Asian, American). *Transnational systems units* should be established to create the linkages across major regional areas and coordinate the development and operation of international telecommunications and systems development (Roche, 1992).
3. Establish at world headquarters a single office responsible for development of international systems, a global chief information officer (CIO) position.

Many successful companies have devised organizational systems structures along these principles. The success of these companies relies not only on the proper organization of activities, but also on a key ingredient—a management team that can understand the risks and benefits of international systems and that can devise strategies for overcoming the risks. We turn to these management topics next.

15.3 MANAGING GLOBAL SYSTEMS

Table 15.4 lists the principal management problems posed by developing international systems. It is interesting to note that these problems are the chief difficulties managers experience in developing ordinary domestic systems as well! But these are enormously complicated in the international environment.

A Typical Scenario: Disorganization on a Global Scale

Let us look at a common scenario. A traditional multinational consumer-goods company based in the United States and operating in Europe would like to expand into Asian markets and knows that it must develop a transnational strategy and a supportive information systems structure. Like most multinationals it has dispersed production and marketing to regional and national centers while maintaining a world headquarters and strategic management in the United States. Historically, it has allowed each of the subsidiary foreign divisions to develop its own systems. The only centrally coordinated system is financial controls and reporting. The central systems group in the United States focuses only on domestic functions and production. The result is a hodgepodge

TABLE 15.4 Management Challenges in Developing Global Systems
Agreeing on common user requirements
Introducing changes in business procedures
Coordinating applications development
Coordinating software releases
Encouraging local users to support global systems

of hardware, software, and telecommunications. The e-mail systems between Europe and the United States are incompatible. Each production facility uses a different manufacturing resources planning system (or different version with local variations), and different marketing, sales, and human resource systems. The technology platforms are wildly different: Europe is using mostly UNIX-based file servers and IBM PC clones on desktops. Communications between different sites are poor, given the high cost and low quality of European intercountry communications. The U.S. group is moving from an IBM mainframe environment centralized at headquarters to a highly distributed network architecture based on a national value-added network, with local sites developing their own local area networks. The central systems group at headquarters recently was decimated and dispersed to the U.S. local sites in the hope of serving local needs better and reducing costs.

What do you recommend to the senior management leaders of this company, who now want to pursue a transnational strategy and develop an information systems infrastructure to support a highly coordinated global systems environment? Consider the problems you face by reexamining Table 15.4. The foreign divisions will resist efforts to agree on common user requirements; they have never thought about much other than their own units' needs. The systems groups in American local sites, which have been enlarged recently and told to focus on local needs, will not easily accept guidance from anyone recommending a transnational strategy. It will be difficult to convince local managers anywhere in the world that they should change their business procedures to align with other units in the world, especially if this might interfere with their local performance. After all, local managers are rewarded in this company for meeting local objectives of their division or plant. Finally, it will be difficult to coordinate development of projects around the world in the absence of a powerful telecommunications network, and, therefore, difficult to encourage local users to take on ownership in the systems developed.

Strategy: Divide, Conquer, Appease

core systems Systems that support functions that are absolutely critical to the organization.

Figure 15.3 lays out the main dimensions of a solution. First, consider that not all systems should be coordinated on a transnational basis; only some core systems are truly worth sharing from a cost and feasibility point of view. **Core systems** are systems that support functions that are absolutely critical to the organization. Other systems should be partially coordinated because they share key elements, but they do not have to be totally common across national boundaries. For such systems, a good deal of local variation is possible and desirable. A final group of systems are peripheral, truly provincial, and are needed to suit local requirements only.

Define the Core Business Processes

How do you identify *core systems?* The first step is to define a short list of critical core business processes. Business processes were defined in Chapter 3, which you should review. Briefly, business processes are sets of logically related tasks such as shipping out correct orders to customers or delivering innovative products to the market. Each business process typically involves many functional areas, communicating and coordinating work, information, and knowledge.

The way to identify these core business processes is to conduct a workflow analysis. How are customer orders taken, what happens to them once they are taken, who fills the orders, how are they shipped to the customers? What about suppliers? Do they have access to manufacturing resource planning systems so that supply is automatic? You should be able to identify and set priorities in a short list of 10 business processes that are absolutely critical for the firm.

Next, can you identify centers of excellence for these processes? Is the customer order fulfillment superior in the United States, manufacturing process control superior in Germany, and human resources superior in Asia? You should be able to identify some areas of the company, for some lines of business, where a division or unit stands out in the performance of one or several business functions.

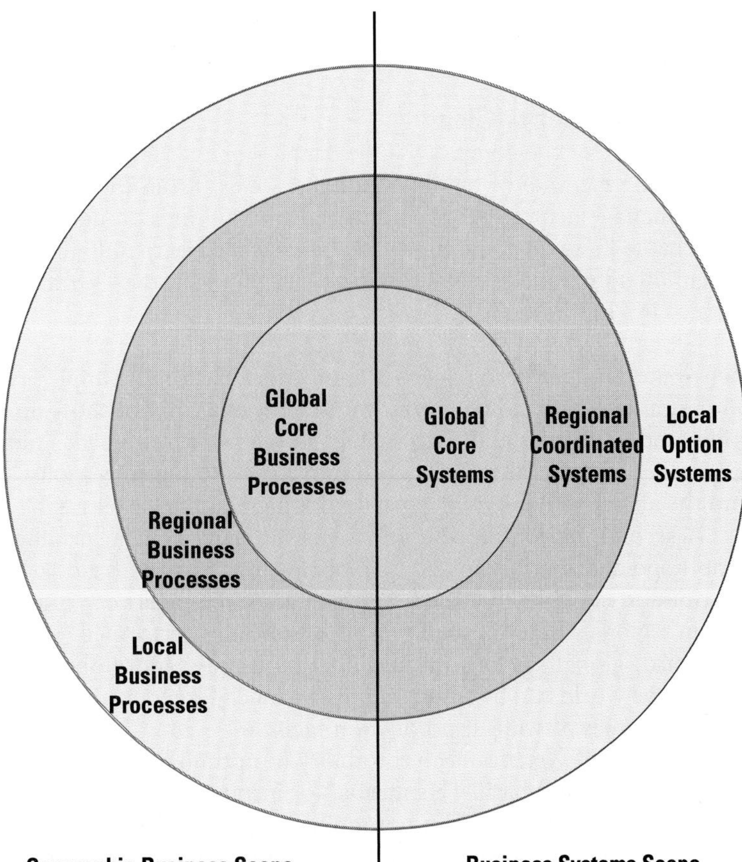

FIGURE 15.3

Agency and other coordination costs increase as the firm moves from local option systems toward regional and global systems. On the other hand, transaction costs of participating in global markets probably decrease as firms develop global systems. A sensible strategy is to reduce agency costs by developing only a few core global systems that are vital for global operations, leaving other systems in the hands of regional and local units. *Source: From* Managing Information Technology in Multinational Corporations *by Roche, Edward M., © 1993. Adapted by permission of Prentice-Hall, Inc., Upper Saddle River, NJ.*

When you understand the business processes of a firm, you can rank-order them. You then can decide which processes should be core applications, centrally coordinated, designed, and implemented around the globe, and which should be regional and local. At the same time, by identifying the critical business processes, the really important ones, you have gone a long way to defining a vision of the future that you should be working toward.

Identify the Core Systems to Coordinate Centrally

By identifying the critical core business processes, you begin to see opportunities for transnational systems. The second strategic step is to conquer the core systems and define these systems as truly transnational. The financial and political costs of defining and implementing transnational systems are extremely high. Therefore, keep the list to an absolute minimum, letting experience be the guide and erring on the side of minimalism. By dividing off a small group of systems as absolutely critical, you divide opposition to a transnational strategy. At the same time, you can appease those who oppose the central worldwide coordination implied by transnational systems by permitting peripheral systems development to progress unabated, with the exception of some technical platform requirements.

Choose an Approach: Incremental, Grand Design, Evolutionary

A third step is to choose an approach. Avoid piecemeal approaches. These surely will fail for lack of visibility, opposition from all who stand to lose from transnational development, and lack of power to convince senior management that the transnational systems are worth it. Likewise, avoid grand design approaches that try to do everything at once. These also tend to fail, due to an inability to focus resources. Nothing gets done properly, and opposition to organizational change is needlessly strengthened because the effort requires huge resources. An alternative approach is to evolve transnational applications from existing applications with a precise and clear vision of the transnational capabilities the organization should have in five years.

Make the Benefits Clear

What is in it for the company? One of the worst situations to avoid is to build global systems for the sake of building global systems. From the beginning, it is crucial that senior management at headquarters and foreign division managers clearly understand the benefits that will come to the company as well as to individual units. Although each system offers unique benefits to a particular budget, the overall contribution of global systems lies in four areas.

Global systems—truly integrated, distributed, and transnational systems—contribute to superior management and coordination. A simple price tag cannot be put on the value of this contribution, and the benefit will not show up in any capital budgeting model. It is the ability to switch suppliers on a moment's notice from one region to another in a crisis, the ability to move production in response to natural disasters, and the ability to use excess capacity in one region to meet raging demand in another.

A second major contribution is vast improvement in production, operation, and supply and distribution. Imagine a global value chain, with global suppliers and a global distribution network. For the first time, senior managers can locate value-adding activities in regions where they are most economically performed.

Third, global systems mean global customers and global marketing. Fixed costs around the world can be amortized over a much larger customer base. This will unleash new economies of scale at production facilities.

Last, global systems mean the ability to optimize the use of corporate funds over a much larger capital base. This means, for instance, that capital in a surplus region can be moved efficiently to expand production of capital-starved regions; that cash can be managed more effectively within the company and put to use more effectively.

These strategies will not by themselves create global systems. You will have to implement what you strategize and this is a whole new challenge.

Implementation Tactics: Cooptation

cooptation Bringing the opposition into the process of designing and implementing the solution without giving up control over the direction and nature of the change.

The overall tactic for dealing with resistant local units in a transnational company is cooptation. **Cooptation** is defined as bringing the opposition into the process of designing and implementing the solution without giving up control over the direction and nature of the change. As much as possible, raw power should be avoided. Minimally, however, local units must agree on a short list of transnational systems and raw power may be required to solidify the idea that transnational systems of some sort are truly required.

How should cooptation proceed? Several alternatives are possible. One alternative is to permit each country unit the opportunity to develop one transnational application first in its home territory, and then throughout the world. In this manner, each major country systems group is given a piece of the action in developing a transnational system, and local units feel a sense of ownership in the transnational effort. On the downside, this assumes the ability to develop high-quality systems is widely distributed, and that, say, the German team can successfully implement systems in France and Italy. This will not always be the case. Also, the transnational effort will have low visibility.

A second tactic is to develop new transnational centers of excellence, or a single center of excellence. There may be several centers around the globe that focus on specific business processes. These centers draw heavily from local national units, are based on multinational teams, and must report to worldwide management—their first line of responsibility is to the core applications. Centers of excellence perform the initial identification and specification of the business process, define the information requirements, perform the business and systems analysis, and accomplish all design and testing. Implementation, however, and pilot testing occur in World Pilot Regions where new applications are installed and tested first. Later, they are rolled out to other parts of the globe. This phased roll-out strategy is precisely how national applications are successfully developed.

The Management Solution

We now can reconsider how to handle the most vexing problems facing managers developing the transnational information system infrastructures that were described in Table 15.4.

- *Agreeing on common user requirements:* Establishing a short list of the core business processes and core support systems will begin a process of rational comparison across the many divisions of the company, develop a common language for discussing the business, and naturally lead to an understanding of common elements (as well as the unique qualities that must remain local).
- *Introducing changes in business procedures:* Your success as a change agent will depend on your legitimacy, your actual raw power, and your ability to involve users in the change design process. **Legitimacy** is defined as the extent to which your authority is accepted on grounds of competence, vision, or other qualities. The selection of a viable change strategy, which we have defined as evolutionary but with a vision, should assist you in convincing others that change is feasible and desirable. Involving people in change, assuring them that change is in the best interests of the company and their local units, is a key tactic.

legitimacy The extent to which one's authority is accepted on grounds of competence, vision, or other qualities.

- *Coordinating applications development:* Choice of change strategy is critical for this problem. At the global level there is far too much complexity to attempt a grand design strategy of change. It is far easier to coordinate change by making small incremental steps toward a larger vision. Imagine a five-year plan of action rather than a two-year plan of action, and reduce the set of transnational systems to a bare minimum to reduce coordination costs.
- *Coordinating software releases:* Firms can institute procedures to ensure that all operating units convert to new software updates at the same time so that everyone's software is compatible.
- *Encouraging local users to support global systems:* The key to this problem is to involve users in the creation of the design without giving up control over the development of the project to parochial interests. Recruiting a wide range of local individuals to transnational centers of excellence helps send the message that all significant groups are involved in the design and will have an influence.

Even with the proper organizational structure and appropriate management choices, it is still possible to stumble over technological issues. Choices of technology,

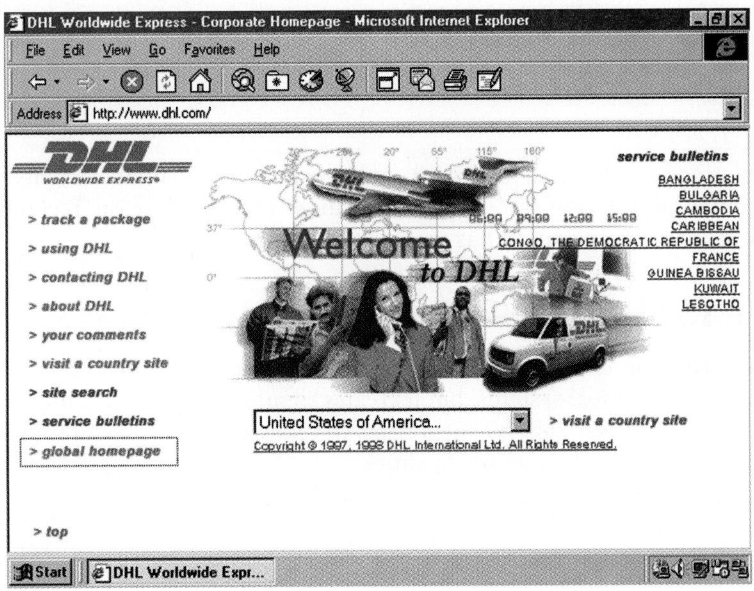

DHL Worldwide Express maintains a corporate Web site along with Web sites customized for dozens of countries outside the United States. DHL is creating a flexible information systems infrastructure that can meet both global and local requirements.

WINDOW ON TECHNOLOGY

DHL Thinks Global and Acts Local

What do businesspeople mean when they say "think global and act local?" And how does a business's information technology contribute to instituting such a strategy? This question confronted DHL Worldwide Express, the world's leading international air express organization with more than 40,000 employees and a presence in 80,000 cities in 220 countries worldwide.[1]

By acting locally, DHL means, for example, that its customers should be able to view their computer screens with their own language, that the computer databases will contain information and regulations that are important for each individual country where needed, that local information be up to date on the computer and on the World Wide Web, and that all local (i.e., national) information will be under the control of DHL offices serving each country. Acting globally means, for example, that the decentralized computer systems around the world be linked through DHLNET, a private global telecommunications network, that customers anywhere in the world can access to check on the status and location of their packages and get information that is timely and accurate.

To meet both global and local requirements, DHL developed global standards and systems with flexibility to enable regional or local units to meet their specific needs as well. Global coordination is accomplished by means of a DHL network technology group with representation from each of the key regions, which manages overall technology strategy, and additional task forces or steering groups, which address specific areas such as telecommunications. DHL also maintains a global information technology coordinating company, DHL Systems, Inc., in San Francisco, California, which manages DHL's global telecommunications and technologies. Certain software and systems are implemented globally (e.g., shipment tracing and tracking, e–mail). Regional and local DHL offices can and do develop applications to meet local needs according to the agreed systems architecture and standards.

In addition, the flexibility of the global databases enables local DHL offices to store only data needed locally. Some countries require additional data to support their local import regulations and their business practices. Thus, the common shipment database was specifically designed and built to enable local organizations to store local shipment data that will be seen only by the local unit that needs and stores it.

DHL standards also involve common application programming interfaces with local options which, for example, enable the Japanese group to display its DHL screens and information in Japanese characters rather than in some common "international" language such as English.

Satisfying both local and global information needs has not been easy. For example, localization of systems makes it difficult to handle a single brand image. Some global customers have become frustrated when systems have certain capabilities in some countries but not in others. But efforts are underway at DHL to coordinate systems better so that key customer interface systems have a common "look and feel."

DHL also maintains a central, global Web site (www.dhl.com), which gives customers information they need for shipping and also enables them to track packages. Specific information about each country is available on the global Web site. Some countries, including Australia, the United States, and Ireland have created their own, local Web sites for tracking and shipment information; each of these local Web sites is linked to the global home page.

To Think About: ***What management, organization, and technology issues do you think DHL faced in introducing the "think global and act local" approach?***

[1]DHL Worldwide Express is composed of DHL Airways, Inc, which serves all locations in the United States and its territories; and DHL International Ltd. and its agents and affiliated companies, which serve all locations outside the United States and its territories.

Sources: Gregory Dalton, "Ready to Go Global?" *InformationWeek,* February 9, 1998; and Anna Foley, "Global Shipper Is Ready for World's Special Delivery Needs," *Computerworld Global Innovators,* March 10, 1997.

platforms, networks, hardware, and software are the final elements in building transnational information system infrastructures. The Window on Technology describes how one global corporation has tackled these problems.

15.4 TECHNOLOGY ISSUES AND OPPORTUNITIES

Information technology is itself a powerful business driver for encouraging the development of global systems, but it creates significant challenges for managers. Global systems presuppose that business firms develop a solid technical foundation and are willing to continually upgrade facilities.

Main Technical Issues

Hardware, software, and telecommunications pose special technical challenges in an international setting. The major hardware challenge is finding some way to standardize the firm's computer hardware platform when there is so much variation from operating unit to operating unit and from country to country. Managers need to think carefully about where to locate the firm's computer centers and how to select hardware suppliers. The major global software challenge is finding applications that are user friendly and that truly enhance the productivity of international work teams. The major telecommunications challenge is making data flow seamlessly across networks shaped by disparate national standards. Overcoming these challenges requires systems integration and connectivity on a global basis.

Hardware and Systems Integration

The development of transnational information system infrastructures based on the concept of core systems raises questions about how the new core systems will fit in with the existing suite of applications developed around the globe by different divisions, different people, and for different kinds of computing hardware. The goal is to develop global, distributed, and integrated systems. Briefly, these are the same problems faced by any large, domestic, systems development effort. However, the problems are more complex because of the international environment. For instance, in the United States, IBM Corp. and IBM operating systems have played the predominant role in building core systems for large organizations, whereas in Europe, UNIX was much more commonly used for large systems. How can the two be integrated in a common transnational system?

The correct solution often will depend on the history of the company's systems and the extent of commitment to proprietary systems. For instance, finance and insurance firms typically have relied almost exclusively on IBM proprietary equipment and architectures, and it would be extremely difficult and cost ineffective to abandon that equipment and software. Newer firms and manufacturing firms generally find it much easier to adopt open UNIX systems for international systems. As pointed out in previous chapters, open UNIX-based systems are far more cost effective in the long run, provide more power at a cheaper price, and preserve options for future expansion.

After a hardware platform is chosen, the question of standards must be addressed. Just because all sites use the same hardware does not guarantee common, integrated systems. Some central authority in the firm must establish data, as well as other technical standards, with whom sites are to comply. For instance, technical accounting terms such as the beginning and end of the fiscal year must be standardized (review our earlier discussion of the cultural challenges to building global businesses), as well as the acceptable interfaces between systems, communications speeds and architectures, and network software.

Connectivity

The heart of the international systems problem is telecommunications—linking together the systems and people of a global firm into a single integrated network just like the phone system but capable of voice, data, and image transmissions. However, integrated global networks are extremely difficult to create (see Table 15.5). For example, many countries cannot fulfill basic business telecommunications needs such as obtaining

TABLE 15.5 Problems of International Networks
Costs and tariffs
Network management
Installation delays
Poor quality of international service
Regulatory constraints
Changing user requirements
Disparate standards
Network capacity

reliable circuits, coordinating among different carriers and the regional telecommunications authority, obtaining bills in a common currency standard, and obtaining standard agreements for the level of telecommunications service provided.

Despite moves toward economic unity, Europe remains a hodgepodge of disparate national technical standards and service levels. The problem is especially critical for banks or airlines that must move massive volumes of data around the world. Although most circuits leased by multinational corporations are fault-free more than 99.8 percent of the time, line quality and service vary widely from the north to the south of Europe. Network service is much more unreliable in southern Europe (Stahl, 1992).

Existing European standards for networking and EDI are very industry specific and country specific. Most European banks use the SWIFT (Society for Worldwide Interbank Financial Telecommunications) protocol for international funds transfer, while automobile companies and food producers often use industry-specific or country-specific versions of standard protocols for EDI. Complicating matters further, the United States standard for EDI is ANSI (American National Standards Institute) X.12. The Open Systems Interconnect (OSI) reference model for linking networks is more popular in Europe than it is in the United States. Various industry groups have standardized on other networking architectures, such as Transmission Control Protocol/Internet Protocol (TCP/IP), or IBM's proprietary Systems Network Architecture (SNA). Even standards such as ISDN (Integrated Services Digital Network) vary from country to country.

Firms have several options for providing international connectivity: Build their own international private network; rely on a network service based on the public switched networks throughout the world; or use the Internet and intranets.

One possibility is for the firm to put together its own private network based on leased lines from each country's PTT (post, telegraph, and telephone authorities). Each country, however, has different restrictions on data exchange, technical standards, and acceptable vendors of equipment. These problems magnify in certain parts of the world. Despite such limitations, in Europe and the United States, reliance on PTTs still makes sense while these public networks expand services to compete with private providers.

The second major alternative to building one's own network is to use one of several expanding network services. With deregulation of telecommunications around the globe, private providers have sprung up to service business customers' data needs, along with some voice and image communications.

Although common in the United States, IVANs (International Value-Added Network Services) are expanding in Europe and Asia. These private firms offer value-added telecommunications capacity usually rented from local PTTs or international satellite authorities, and then resell it to corporate users. IVANs add value by providing protocol conversion, operating mailboxes and mail systems, and offering integrated billing that permits a firm to track its data communications costs. Currently these systems are limited to data transmissions, but in the future they will expand to voice and image.

The third alternative, which is becoming increasingly attractive, is to create global intranets to use the Internet for international communication. However, the Internet is not yet a worldwide tool because many countries lack the communications infrastructure for extensive Internet use. Countries face high costs, government control, or government monitoring.

Western Europe faces both high transmission costs and lack of common technology because it is not politically unified and because European telecommunications systems are still in the process of shedding their government monopolies. The lack of an infrastructure and high costs of installing one is even more widespread in the rest of the world. In South Africa, for instance, a slow (14.4 kbps) modem costs more than a month's average wages. Where an infrastructure exists, as in China and Pakistan, it is often outdated, lacks digital circuits, and has very noisy lines. Figure 15.4 shows the uneven distribution of Internet host computers throughout the world and the disparities in Internet access among developing and developed nations.

Many countries monitor transmissions. The governments in China and Singapore monitor Internet traffic and block access to Web sites considered morally or politically offensive (Tan, Mueller, and Foster, 1997). Corporations may be discouraged from

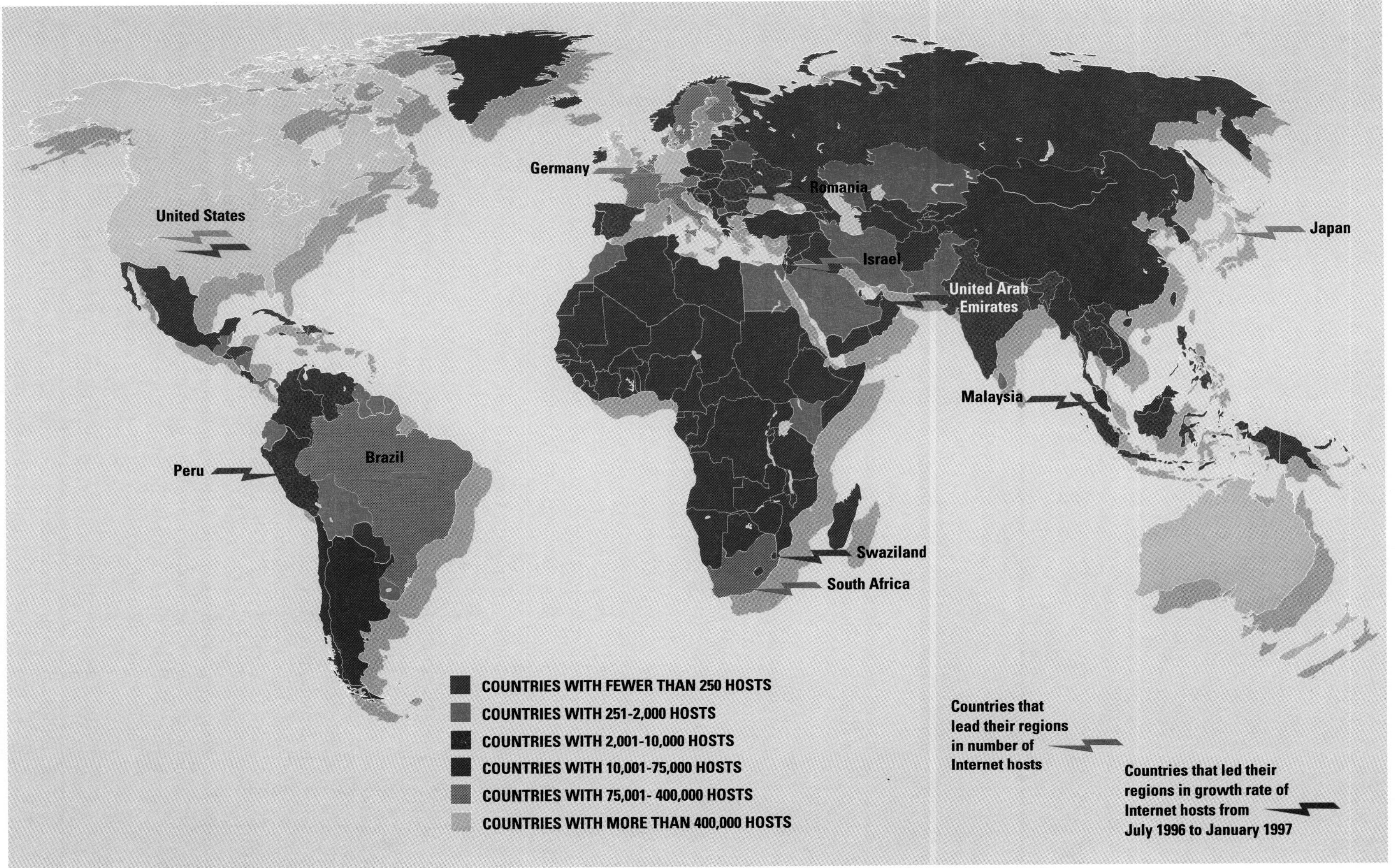

FIGURE 15.4 The world series. Most of the world is ready to do business on-line, but some countries are more ready than others. The map shows the number of Internet domains registered under country-specific domain names, such as ".uk" (United Kingdom) or ".fr" (France) as of January 1997. In all countries except the United States, the vast majority of Internet domains are registered under country-specific domain names. *Source: From Christopher Koch, "It's a Wired, Wired World" in* Webmaster, *March 1997. Reprinted through the courtesy of CIO. © 1997 CIO Communications, Inc.*

Software interfaces may have to be translated to accommodate users in East Asia or other parts of the world.

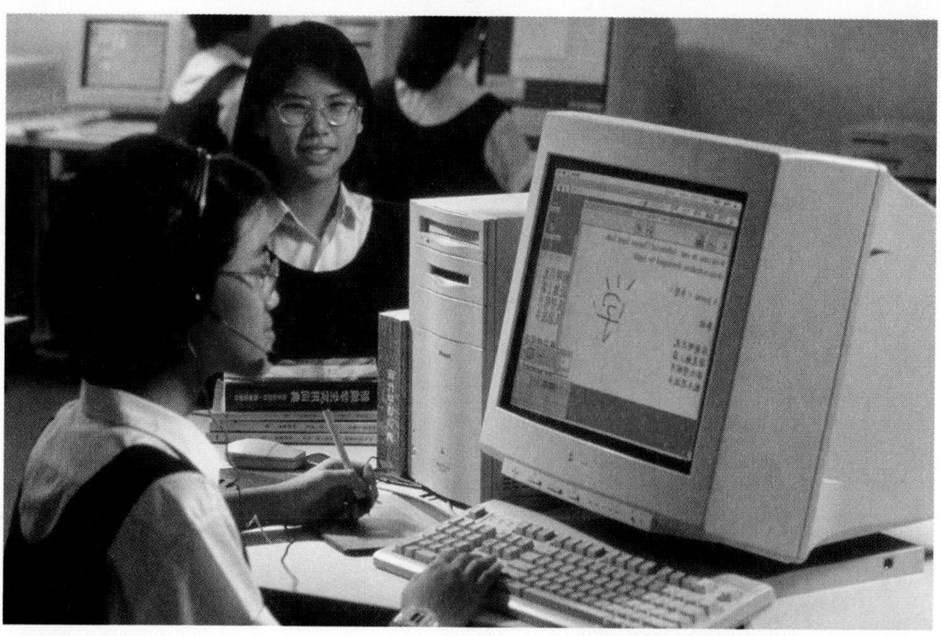

using this medium. Companies planning international operations through the Internet still will have many hurdles.

Software

Compatible hardware and communications provide a platform but not the total solution. Also critical to global core infrastructure is software. The development of core systems poses unique challenges for software: How will the old systems interface with the new? Entirely new interfaces must be built and tested if old systems are kept in local areas (which is common). These interfaces can be costly and messy to build. If new software must be created, another challenge is to build software that can be realistically used by multiple business units from different countries when these business units are accustomed to their unique procedures and definitions of data.

Aside from integrating the new with the old systems, there are problems of human interface design and functionality of systems. For instance, to be truly useful for enhancing productivity of a global work force, software interfaces must be easily understood and mastered quickly. Graphical user interfaces are ideal for this but presuppose a common language—often English. When international systems involve knowledge workers only, English may be the assumed international standard. But as international systems penetrate deeper into management and clerical groups, a common language may not be assumed and human interfaces must be built to accommodate different languages and even conventions.

What are the most important software applications? Although most international systems focus on basic transaction and MIS systems, there is an increasing emphasis on international collaborative work groups. EDI—electronic data interchange—is a common global transaction processing application used by manufacturing and distribution firms to connect units of the same company, as well as customers and suppliers on a global basis. Groupware systems such as electronic mail, videoconferencing, Lotus Notes, and other products supporting shared data files, notes, and electronic mail are much more important to knowledge- and data-based firms such as advertising firms, research-based firms in medicine and engineering, and graphics and publishing firms. The Internet will be increasingly employed for such purposes.

New Technical Opportunities and the Internet

Technical advances described in Chapter 8, such as ISDN and Digital Subscriber Line (DSL) services, should continue to fall in price and gain in power, facilitating the creation and operation of global networks. *Communicate and compute any time, any-*

The Asia Trade Network Web site assists companies that would like to do business with companies in Asia. It offers services such as a Yellow Pages telephone directory of over 7000 Asian businesses, an on-line business information library, on-line catalogue services for Asian companies, and a search capability for visitors to locate producers of items that interest them.

where networks based on satellite systems, digital cellular phones and personal communications services will make it even easier to coordinate work and information in many parts of the globe that cannot be reached by existing ground-based systems. Thus a salesperson in China could send an order-confirmation request to the home office in London effortlessly and expect an instant reply.

Companies are using Internet technology to construct **virtual private networks (VPNs)** to reduce wide-area networking costs and staffing requirements. Instead of using private, leased telephone lines or frame-relay connections, the company outsources the VPN to an Internet service provider. The VPN comprises WAN links, security products, and routers, providing a secure and encrypted connection between two points across the Internet to transmit corporate data. These VPNs from Internet service providers can provide many features of a private network to firms operating internationally. Companies

virtual private network (VPN) A secure and encrypted connection between two points across the Internet to transmit corporate data. Provides a low-cost alternative to a private network.

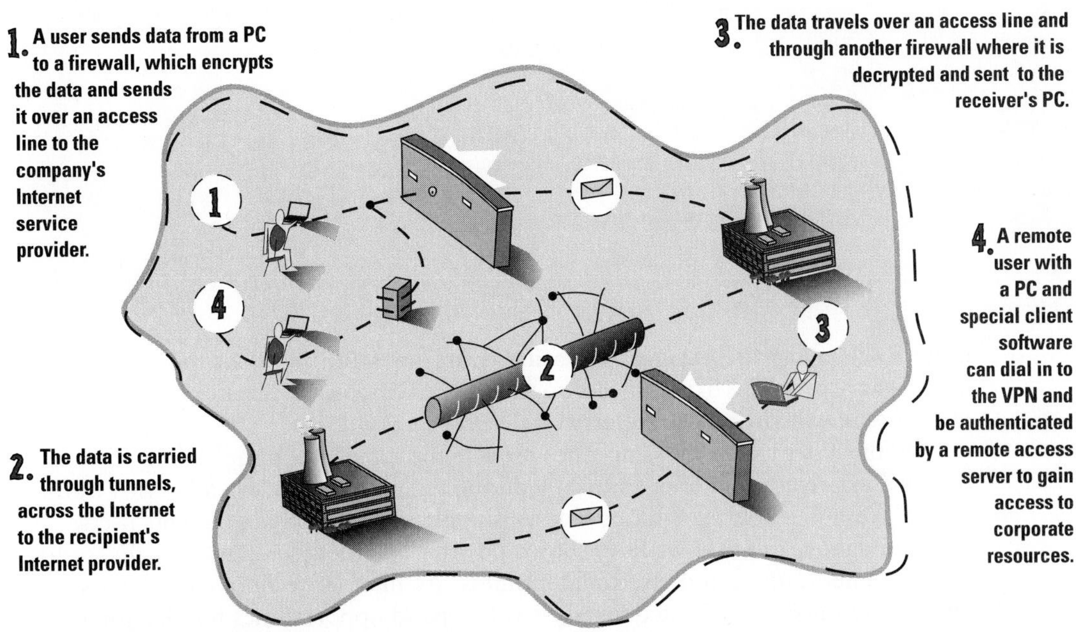

1. A user sends data from a PC to a firewall, which encrypts the data and sends it over an access line to the company's Internet service provider.
2. The data is carried through tunnels, across the Internet to the recipient's Internet provider.
3. The data travels over an access line and through another firewall where it is decrypted and sent to the receiver's PC.
4. A remote user with a PC and special client software can dial in to the VPN and be authenticated by a remote access server to gain access to corporate resources.
1
2
3
4

FIGURE 15.5 How a virtual private network (VPN) works. *Source: "How It Works,"* Computerworld, *February 2, 1998. Copyright ©1998 Computerworld, Inc. Framingham, MA 01701. Rights reserved. Reprinted with permission of* Computerworld *magazine.*

WINDOW ON TECHNOLOGY

Virtual Private Networks to the Rescue

What do you do when your company must have a wide-area network (WAN) but the costs are very high? One solution recently has emerged, reliance upon the Internet, using technology known as the virtual private network (VPN).

International Shipping Corporation was using a more traditional, frame-relay WAN to connect its Singapore office with its New Orleans headquarters. The connection was vital—employees needed to send financial and billing transactions back and forth. Their frame-relay WAN was expensive and very slow. Worst of all, it was exceedingly restrictive, allowing only a few users on the network simultaneously, and they all had to be working on the same application. With the new VPN, speed climbed from 56K bit/sec at both ends to 512K bit/sec in Singapore and 1.544M bit/sec in New Orleans. Multiple users now can access the network simultaneously and even can be working on different applications.

The cost of this improvement? Actually, it delivered a savings. This new, superior network cost International Shipping $120,000 per year less than their old WAN. The company also was able to cancel a planned $150,000 upgrade to add bandwidth to its old network.

What is a VPN and why are such savings possible? Instead of using private or leased lines like traditional networks such as frame-relay systems, VPNs use the worldwide Internet infrastructure to communicate with distant computers. Internet service providers (ISPs) assign subscribing companies a slice of their backbone bandwidth to use as a VPN. (By partitioning their networks, ISPs can provide VPNs to many corporate users.) Companies requiring a WAN pay their ISPs for the amount of bandwidth required. The company saves the cost of a private network and the staff needed to install and support it.

One key difficulty corporations face in relying upon the Internet is security. After all, companies like International Shipping send proprietary financial and company information through their WANs. If Internet security is not sufficient, that data can fall into the wrong hands. Moreover, the Net can be used by hackers to gain access to company computers. International Shipping purchased two high-end Cisco Systems Inc. PIX security systems to keep out hackers and encrypt Internet transmissions.

Omron Electronics, of Shaumberg, Illinois, produces factory automation and electronic components, shipping these products all over the world to manufacturers of all sizes. According to Barry Voltz, Omron's manager of information systems, the company needed to give its customers access to its AS/400 minicomputer at corporate headquarters to improve its ordering and shipping processes. He estimated that if they built their own WAN, annual operating costs would be about $360,000, and, "That doesn't include the salaries of staff I'd need to hire to run our own WAN," Voltz said. By going to a VPN through their ISP, they avoided the cost of building their own network, and their annual network costs are only $250,000.

Savvis Communications Corporation, a St. Louis ISP, sold Omron a lane on its national 45 megabits-per-second Asynchronous Transfer Mode highway. Savvis maintains such lanes for other subscribers as well. Omron provided the necessary data-access equipment. Workers encrypt their transmissions before sending them over the VPN, and Omron uses a hardware/software security firewall to lock out potential intruders. If Omron needs more transmission capacity, the company can call Savvis and have them increase bandwidth between remote sites and headquarters.

To Think About: ***What do you think were the technology, organization, and management implications of the decisions of the two companies to move to VPNs? If VPNs prove their value during the next few years, what might their impact be on the networking industry and on world trade?***

Sources: Bob Wallace, "Remote Users to Make Gains with New Network," *Computerworld,* February 2, 1998; "Virtual Private Network Saves Firm Big Money," *Computerworld,* August 4, 1997; and "Shipper Saves Money by Using the 'Net as Its WAN," *Computerworld,* July 14, 1997.

using VPNs avoid the expense of leasing entire lines and many of the technical and maintenance problems of private networks (see the Window on Technology). Figure 15.5 illustrates how a virtual private network (VPN) works.

On the other hand, VPNs may not provide the same level of quick and predictable response as private networks, especially during times of the day when Internet traffic is very congested. VPNs may not be able to support large numbers of remote users.

Throughout this text we have shown how the Internet facilitates global coordination, communication, and electronic business. As Internet technology becomes more widespread outside the United States, it will expand opportunities for electronic commerce and international trade. The global connectivity and low cost of Internet technology will further remove obstacles of geography and time zones for companies seeking to expand operations and sell their wares abroad. Small companies may especially benefit (Quelch and Klein, 1996).

Management Wrap-Up

Managers are responsible for devising an appropriate organizational and technology infrastructure for international business. Choosing a global business strategy, identifying core business processes, organizing the firm to conduct business on an international scale, and selecting an international information systems infrastructure are key management decisions.

MANAGEMENT

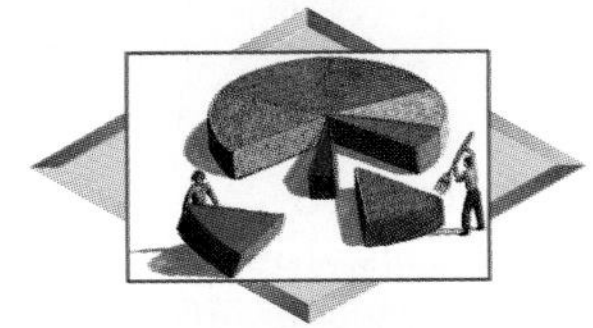

Cultural, political, and language differences magnify differences in organizational culture and standard operating procedures when companies operate internationally in various countries. These differences create barriers to the development of global information systems that transcend national boundaries.

ORGANIZATION

The main technology decision in building international systems is finding a set of workable standards in hardware, software, and networking for the firm's international information systems infrastructure. The Internet and intranets will increasingly be used to provide global connectivity and to serve as a foundation for global systems, but many companies will still need proprietary systems for certain functions, and therefore international standards.

TECHNOLOGY

For Discussion:

1. If you were a manager in a company that operates in many countries, what criteria would you use to determine whether an application should be developed as a global application or as a local application?
2. Describe ways the Internet can be used in international information systems.

SUMMARY

1. **Identify the major factors behind the growing internationalization of business.** There are general cultural factors and specific business factors to consider. The growth of cheap international communication and transportation has created a world culture with stable expectations or norms. Political stability and a growing global knowledge base that is widely shared contribute also to the world culture. These general factors create the conditions for global markets, global production, coordination, distribution, and global economies of scale.
2. **Compare global strategies for developing business.** There are four basic international strategies: domestic exporter, multinational, franchiser, and transnational. In a transnational strategy, all factors of production are coordinated on a global scale. However, the choice of strategy is a function of the type of business and product.
3. **Demonstrate how information systems support different global strategies.** There is a connection between firm strategy and information systems design. Transnational firms must develop networked system configurations and permit considerable decentralization of development and operations. Franchisers almost always duplicate systems across many countries and use centralized financial controls. Multinationals typically rely on decentralized independence among foreign units with some movement toward development of networks. Domestic exporters typically are centralized in domestic headquarters with some decentralized operations permitted.
4. **Plan the development of international systems.** Implementing a global system requires an implementation strategy. Typically, global systems have evolved without a conscious plan. The remedy is to define a small subset of core business processes and focus on building systems that could support these processes. Tactically, you will have to coopt widely dispersed foreign units to participate in the development and operation of these systems, being careful to maintain overall control.
5. **Evaluate the main technical alternatives in developing global systems.** The main hardware and telecommunications issues are systems integration and connectivity. The choices for integration are to go either with a proprietary architecture or with an open systems technology such as UNIX. Global networks are extremely

difficult to build and operate. Some measure of connectivity may be achieved by relying on local PTT authorities to provide connections, building a system oneself, relying on private providers to supply communications capacity, or using the Internet and intranets. Companies can use Internet services to create virtual private networks (VPNs) as low-cost alternatives to global private networks. The main software issue concerns building interfaces to existing systems and providing much needed group support software.

KEY TERMS

Business driver, 457
Cooptation, 468
Core systems, 466
Domestic exporter, 463
Franchiser, 463
Global culture, 459
International information systems infrastructure, 457
Legitimacy, 469
Multinational, 463
Particularism, 460
Transborder data flow, 460
Transnational, 463
Virtual private network (VPN), 475

REVIEW QUESTIONS

1. What are the five major factors to consider when building an international information systems infrastructure?
2. Describe the five general cultural factors leading toward growth in global business and the four specific business factors. Describe the interconnection among these factors.
3. What is meant by a *global culture?*
4. What are the major challenges to the development of global systems?
5. Why have firms not planned for the development of international systems?
6. Describe the four main strategies for global business and organizational structure.
7. Describe the four different system configurations that can be used to support different global strategies.
8. What are the major management issues in developing international systems?
9. What are three principles to follow when organizing the firm for global business?
10. What are three steps of a management strategy for developing and implementing global systems?
11. What is meant by *cooptation,* and how can it be used in building global systems?
12. Describe the main technical issues facing global systems.
13. Describe three new technologies that can help firms develop global systems.

GROUP PROJECT

With a group of students, identify an area of emerging information technology and explore how this technology might be useful for supporting global business strategies. For instance, you might choose an area such as digital telecommunications (e.g., electronic mail, wireless communications, value-added networks) or collaborative work group software or new standards in operating systems or EDI or the Internet. It will be necessary to choose a business scenario to discuss the technology. You might choose, for instance, an automobile parts franchiser or a clothing franchise such as the Limited Express as example businesses. What applications would you make global, what core business processes would you choose, and how would the technology be helpful?

TOOLS FOR INTERACTIVE LEARNING

■ **INTERNET**: The Internet Connection for this chapter will take you to a series of Web sites where you can complete an exercise to evaluate the capabilities of various global package tracking and delivery services. You can use the interactive software at a series of Web sites to complete an Electronic Commerce project for international marketing and pricing. You can also use the Interactive Study Guide to test your knowledge of the topics in this chapter and get instant feedback where you need more practice.

■ **CD-ROM**: If you purchase and use the Multimedia Edition CD-ROM with this chapter, you can complete an interactive exercise asking you to design a global network for a multinational corporation. You can also find a video clip illustrating the United Parcel Service International Shipping and Processing System (ISPS), an audio overview of the major themes of this chapter, and bullet text summarizing the key points of the chapter.

Pirelli's Drive Toward a Global Strategy

Although the global economy presents great opportunities for many companies, those heavily involved with it often are buffeted by its global ups and downs. The Pirelli Group, an international tire manufacturer headquartered in Milan, Italy, was forced to face the erratic nature of the global economy in the early 1990s. Automobile sales fell worldwide in those years, resulting in a concurrent drop in tire sales. Coincidentally, sales in Pirelli's second major product line, electronic cables, suffered the same fate when worldwide spending on telecommunications and energy also dropped sharply. To make matters worse, competition was intensifying as global markets developed and evolved.

Pirelli's management team had to find ways to return the company to its accustomed level of profitability and do so rapidly. The plan the team developed was not unusual in these circumstances: Focus on core products, cut costs, improve competitiveness by developing new technologies, and improve response to customer demands. The plan stressed the central role of information, including the need to access it and react to it very rapidly. Of necessity, the information technology (IT) group was vital to these changes.

In 1991, when these problems emerged, Pirelli had 102 plants in 14 countries and employed more than 51,000 people. The company also had a marketing and sales presence in many other countries. The information systems within all these countries were developed locally with no guidance from the corporate office because Pirelli had not established international standards for either hardware or software. The resulting lack of integration made data sharing across national borders difficult and left Pirelli as something less than a genuine global company despite its presence in so many countries. Arrigo Andreoni, Pirelli's corporate director of information, concluded that to respond to the new management plan, Pirelli's worldwide IT infrastructure needed to be redesigned and standardized. "The more standardization there is," he explained, "the easier it is to implement new ideas and respond to new opportunities." Key to his approach was his belief that IT "must be in tune with the overall business strategy."

One fundamental element of Andreoni's strategy was the establishment of a full-fledged global network. Each national unit is to be linked to the Milan headquarters by the year 2000 so that corporate management will have immediate and complete access to the information it needs to carry out its executive and planning functions. The infrastructure will be built upon open systems so that data can be moved from site to site with ease. The strategy also includes a companywide groupware platform that includes office automation, personal computing, e-mail, and workflow software. All of this is aimed at providing employees the tools they need while instituting standardization that enables communication from person to person regardless of the location of the employee.

The centerpiece of the new infrastructure is Andreoni's goal of installing the same comprehensive, integrated software at all Pirelli sites throughout the world. He selected SAP's R/3 as that software. R/3 is a client-server-based comprehensive system that includes integrated modules for production, factory automation, finance, sales, purchasing, and personnel (see the Chapter 11 Case Study). Andreoni hoped R/3 could act as a catalyst for companywide reengineering. However, finding and selecting the best software package was actually the easy part. Implementing R/3 in Pirelli's multinational environment of local control was the more challenging problem and is the stage at which many such projects flounder.

The most conspicuous problems to be faced were the different languages, currencies, legal systems, and tax laws in each of the locations. However, corporate culture presented an even more formidable hurdle because the local units were used to making their own decisions and building their own systems to meet their specific local needs. Andreoni decided that before he proceeded with the project, he must travel to Pirelli sites throughout the world, visiting and meeting with local Pirelli organizations. He needed not only to sell his approach, but also to gather information on the local systems and the stages of development at each site.

To implement his strategy, Andreoni developed an approach he calls "democratic governance." His goal was to achieve standardization in each of the core areas while leaving each local unit to maintain its local culture and projects. In this way, for example, the local unit would be able to address its own language, currency, and legal needs. He also did not want to impose an overly rapid companywide implementation of the new system in the core areas. He believes in moving ahead with small steps, explaining, "If a CEO of a particular unit does not view SAP as a real competitive weapon, we don't want to insist. We wait until the CEO is open to the idea, then we explain what the technology does and offer to implement the changeover." He adds, however, "We in information technology must be ready at the crucial time when the culture is changing." Pirelli companies are allowed to implement SAP in tune with their local requirements, but Andreoni encourages them to avoid unnecessary customizations. They must justify local differences in the system by demands in the local market.

Andreoni also believes in moving ahead at a carefully measured pace after a local unit is ready to make the changeover. His approach is to begin with a pilot project for one specific function within a specified Pirelli national unit. He is careful to select a function with a strong likelihood of success. In Spain, tire distribution was selected as the pilot project. In Scandinavia, because electronic commerce already is widely accepted, the pilot project was the use of the Internet for transacting business. After the pilot is successful, staff support will grow for the overall project, and the pilot becomes a prototype for the implementation of the rest of the system.

Pirelli units had to maintain their old systems as they made the changeover to R/3. In each country, they relied on outsourcing to handle both the new and old systems. Selection of outsourcing vendors was based on local conditions. In Italy, for example, IBM

Global Services helped Pirelli with its legacy mainframe applications. Pirelli staff were trained by working alongside the outsourcing consultants.

Pirelli is developing a full-fledged global network by linking a UNIX server in each country with the company's global headquarters in Milan. By the year 2000, this network will provide company management with complete and immediate access to information from its worldwide operations. Local units with appropriate management approval in turn will have total access to company information. This open systems environment, along with the integration in operations provided by R/3, will allow all information to move from and through fully integrated platforms. One platform is for queries, corporate reporting, data modeling, navigation, and financial systems. A groupware platform will feature office automation, personal computing, e-mail, multimedia, image processing, and workflow management. A research and development platform will include CAD/CAM, simulations, and test data systems.

What has been the effect of this global IT program? The Pirelli IT department itself has been reduced from 700 personnel down to 562, a drop of nearly 20 percent, and it is scheduled to fall to 490 (30 percent) by the year 2000. The decline in IT staff is a direct result of the growing standardization; software and hardware support are much less labor-intensive. For example, before standardization, Scandinavia, France, Switzerland, Austria, and the Benelux countries each had an independent, full-service, back-office operation to support its sales function. Today, they share one back-office operation located in Basel, Switzerland. However, the local front-end systems that were used to deal directly with customers were left intact. Today, Pirelli does rely more on information technology despite the drop in IT staff, as is clear from the fact that IT expenditures have grown from 1.5 percent of Pirelli revenues in 1993 to 1.64 percent in 1997. The IT effort has supported other changes within the company as Pirelli has reduced the number of plant facilities from 102 to 74. At the same time, Pirelli's staff has fallen by nearly 30 percent, from 51,572 to 36,534.

All of this has shown up on the bottom line. Company debt fell 56 percent between 1991 and 1995. Net income in 1996 was up 43 percent from the previous year. This is so despite the fact that the project was not yet fully implemented. As for Andreoni, he says that he spends a majority of his time interacting with top Pirelli management and with the CEOs in the various countries. His task, he says, is "explaining our proposals and the reasons for them. In short, I market IT's ideas to the rest of the company."

Source: Adapted from Dr. Edward Wakin, "Global Strategies Drive Pirelli," *Beyond Computing,* January–February 1998.

Case Study Questions

1. What kind of global business strategy is Pirelli pursuing?
2. Analyze Pirelli's problems using the competitive forces and value chain models. How well did Pirelli's information systems support its business strategy?
3. What problems did Pirelli's systems have? What management, organization, and technology factors were responsible for these problems?
4. Analyze Pirelli's strategy for dealing with these problems in relation to its global business strategy. Do you agree with this strategy?

CASE STUDY 1: Geelong & District Water Board to Barwon Water: An Integrated IT Infrastructure[1]

Joel B. Barolsky and Peter Weill, University of Melbourne (Australia)

Joe Adamski, the Geelong and District Water Board's (GDWB) executive manager of information systems, clicked his mouse on the phone messages menu option. Two messages had been left. The first was from an IT manager from a large Sydney-based insurance company confirming an appointment to "visit the GDWB and to assess what the insurance company could learn from the GDWB's IT experience." The second was from the general manager of another large water board asking whether Adamski and his team could assist, on a consultancy basis, in their IT strategy formulation and implementation.

The site visit from the insurance company was the thirty-fifth such request the Board had received since the completion of the first stage of their IT infrastructure investment strategy in January 1992. These requests were a pleasant diversion but the major focus of the GDWB's IT staff was to nurture and satisfy the increasing demands from the operational areas for building applications utilizing the newly installed IT infrastructure. The Water Board also faced the problem of balancing further in-house developments with external requests for consulting and demands from the GDWB's IT staff for new challenges and additional rewards.

ORGANIZATION BACKGROUND

The GDWB was constituted as a public utility of the Australian State of Victoria in July 1984 following an amalgamation of the Geelong Waterworks and Sewerage Trust and a number of other smaller regional water boards. The Board has the responsibility for the collection and distribution of water and the treatment and disposal of wastewater within a 1600 square mile region in the southwest part of the state. In 1991, the permanent population serviced by the Board exceeded 200,000 people, this number growing significantly in the holiday periods with an influx of tourists.

The GDWB financed all its capital expenditure and operational expenditure through revenue received from its customers and through additional loan borrowings. Any profits generated were reinvested in the organization or used to pay off long-term debt. For the financial year 1990–91 the Board invested over $35.3 million in capital works and spent over $25 million in operating expenditures. Operating profit for the year 1990–91 exceeded $62.4 million on total assets of $292.5 million.

In 1992, the GDWB was headed by a governing board with a state government-appointed chairperson and eight members, elected by the residents of the community, who each sat for a three-year term. Managerial and administrative responsibilities were delegated to the GDWB's Executive Group which consists of the CEO and executive managers from each of the five operating divisions, namely information systems, finance, corporate services, engineering development, and engineering operations. From 1981 to 1992, the number of GDWB employees across all divisions rose from 304 to 454.

The GDWB's head office, situated in the regional capital city of Geelong, housed most of the Board's customer service, administrative, engineering, IT, and other managerial staff. Complementing these activities, the GDWB operated five regional offices and a specialized 24-hour emergency contact service.

Commenting on the Board's competitive environment at the time, the GDWB's CEO, Geoff Vines, stated, "Although the organization operated in a monopolistic situation there still were considerable pressures on us to perform efficiently. Firstly, and most importantly, our objective was to be self-funding—our customers wouldn't tolerate indiscriminate rate increases as a result of our inefficiencies and we could not go cap in hand to the state government. Secondly, the amalgamation trend of water boards was continuing and the stronger the Board was the less likely it would be a target of a takeover. And thirdly, we did in a sense compare ourselves with private sector organizations and in some ways with other water boards. We had limited resources and we have to make the most of them."

KEY PROBLEM AREAS

Relating the situation up until the mid-1980s, Vines said that the Board faced a major problem in collectively identifying its largest assets—the underground pipes, drains, pumps, sewers, and other facilities. He explained that most of these facilities were installed at least two or three meters below the surface and therefore it was almost impossible to gain immediate physical access to them. The exact specifications of each particular asset could only be ascertained through a thorough analysis of the original installation documentation and other geophysical surveys and maps of the area.

The limitations on identifying these underground facilities impacted operational performance in a number of key areas:

- Most of the maintenance work conducted by the Board was based on reactive responses to leaks and other faults in the systems. It was difficult to introduce a coordinated preventative maintenance program because it was not possible to accurately predict when a particular pipe or piece of equipment was nearing the end of its expected life span.
- Only a limited number of hard copies of this facility information could be kept. This significantly reduced the productivity of the engineering and operations staff, especially in remote areas where they had to request this information from the central record-keeping systems. Backlogs and inaccuracies in filing also impacted

efforts to repair, upgrade, or install new piping, pumps, and other equipment. On numerous occasions changes would be made to one set of plans without the same changes being recorded on the other copies of the same plans. Engineers designing improvements to existing facilities were often confronted with the problem of not being sure whether they were using the most up-to-date information of the facilities currently installed in the area concerned.

- The Board could not place realistic replacement values and depreciation charges on these underground assets.

With over 100,000 rateable properties in its area of responsibility, the GDWB maintained a centralized paper filing system containing more than a billion pages of related property information. The documents, most of which were of different sizes, quality, and age, were divided into 95,000 different files and sorted chronologically within each file. Access to the documents was made difficult as larger documents were cumbersome to copy and older documents were beginning to disintegrate. Having only one physical storage area significantly increased the potential exposure to fire and other risks and limited the wider distribution and sharing of the information. In the early 1980s, it was commonplace for a customer request for a statement of encumbrances placed at one of the GDWB's regional offices to take in excess of four weeks. The delays usually centered on finding the appropriate documents at the Property Services' central files, making the necessary copies, and transferring the documents back to the regional offices.

THE INFORMATION SYSTEMS DIVISION

In 1985, PA Consulting was commissioned to conduct a comprehensive review of the Board's strategy, management, operations structures, and systems. One recommendation made by the consultants was that the Board should institute a more systematic approach to strategic planning. A major outcome of the planning process that followed was to create a new division for computing services and to recruit a new manager for this new area who reported directly to the CEO. The EDP Division was created with the objectives of "satisfying the Board's Information System needs through the provision of integrated and secure corporate computer systems and communication network." Vines said that the Board needed a stand-alone information services group that could be used as a resource center for all users and that could add value to the work conducted by each functional group within the Board.

In April 1987, Joe Adamski was employed to fill the new position of EDP manager (later changed to executive manager of information systems). At the time of his arrival, only a small part of the GDWB's work systems were computerized, the main components of which included:

- a "low-end" IBM System 38, primarily to run financial and other accounting software and some word processing applications. The system ran an in-house developed rate collection system which kept basic information on ratepayers including property details and consumption records;
- 19 "dumb" terminals—none of the Board's regional offices had terminal access to the central computer systems;
- a terminal link to the local university's DEC 20 computer to support the technical and laboratory services; and
- four stand-alone PCs, running some individual word processing packages as well as spreadsheet (Lotus 1-2-3), basic CAD, and database applications.

Computer maintenance, support, and development was allocated to the finance division and delegated to an EDP supervisor (and three staff) who reported to the finance manager. Adamski noted, "The computer set-up when I joined was pretty outdated and inefficient. For example, the secretarial staff at the Head Office were using the System 38's word processing facility and had to collect their dot matrix printouts from the computer room situated on the ground floor of the five-story building. In the technical area, some water supply network analysis data was available through the use of the DEC 20 system; however, hard copy output had to be collected from the University which was over five kilometers away. Most of the design engineers were using old drafting tables with rulers, erasers, and pencils as their only drafting tools."

Recognizing that some users required immediate solutions to problems they were facing, the Board purchased additional terminals, peripherals, and stand-alone microcomputers for the various areas thought to be in greatest need. Adamski said that these additional purchases further compounded some of the Board's computer-related problems. "We had a situation where we had at least four different CAD packages in use in different departments and we couldn't transfer data between them. There was a duplication of peripheral equipment with no sharing of printers, plotters, and other output devices. In addition, various managers began to complain that system expertise was too localized and that there was little compatibility between the various applications."

PLANNING THE NEW ROLE FOR IT

In July 1988, Adamski initiated a long-term computing strategy planning process with the establishment of a special planning project team with both IT and user representatives. The team embarked on a major program of interviews and discussion with all user areas within the Board. They investigated other similar public utilities across Australia to assess their IT strategies and infrastructures and made contact with various computer hardware and software vendors to determine the latest available technologies and indicative costs.

The Project Team developed a comprehensive corporate computing strategy that would provide, as Adamski put it, the "quantum leap forward in the Board's IT portfolio." Adamski said that central to the devised computing strategy was that there should be as much integration and flexibility as possible in all the Board's technical and administrative systems. "Linked to this strategy was the notion that we should strive for an 'open systems' approach with all our applications. This meant that each system had to have publicly specifiable interfaces or 'hooks' so that each system could talk to each other. From the users' perspective an open systems approach meant that all the different applications looked pretty much the same and it was simple and easy to cross over from one to the other. It also meant that if we weren't happy with one particular product within the portfolio or we wanted to add a new one we could do it without too much disruption to the whole system."

He continued, "A key decision was made that we should build on our existing IT investments. With this in mind we had to make sure that the new systems were able to use the data and communicate with the System 38. We wanted only one hardware platform using only one operating system and only one relational database management system (RDBMS). We also wanted only one homogenous network that was able to cater to a number of protocols and interfaces such as the network system for the microcomputers, workstations, and the Internet connection. There also had to be a high degree of compatibility and interaction with all the data files and applications that were proposed. In view of this, we chose a UNIX platform with a client/server architecture."

In addition to specifying the software components of the system, the Project Team outlined the hardware that was necessary to run the new systems and the additional staff that needed to be hired. To achieve the stated computing strategies and benefits, the Team also recommended that implementation take place over three key stages, with a formal progress review instituted at the end of each stage.

APPROVAL

In February 1989, the corporate computing strategy planning process was completed and Adamski presented the key recommendations to the governing Board. In his presentation, Adamski stated that the infrastructure cost of implementing the strategy was estimated to be about $5 million for the entire project (excluding data capture costs) and that the project would take up to the end of 1995 for full commissioning.

Vines stated, "From my perspective, the proposed IT strategy took into account the critical functions in the organization that needed to be supported, such as customer services, asset management, and asset creation. These were fundamental components of the Board's corporate objectives, and the computer strategy provided a means to realize these objectives and provide both short- and long-term benefits. There were some immediate short-term benefits, such as securing property services data that had no backup, and productivity gains in design and electronic mail. From a long-term perspective, I believe you can never really do an accurate rate-of-return calculation and base your decision solely on that. If you did you probably would never make such a large capital investment in IT. We did try to cost-justify all the new systems as best we could but we stressed that implementing IT strategy should be seen as providing long-term benefits for the entire organization that were not immediately measurable and would come to fruition many years later. Until all the information was captured and loaded on the IT facilities from the manual systems, the full benefits could not be realized."

Following an extensive and rigorous tendering process, it was decided that the Board should follow a multivendor solution as no one vendor could provide a total solution. Sun Microsystems was selected as the major hardware vendor and was asked to act as "prime contractors" in implementation. As prime contractors Sun was paid one project fee and then negotiated separate contracts with all other suppliers.

IMPLEMENTATION

In April 1990, the implementation of the IT strategy commenced with the delivery of the Sun file servers and workstations and installation of a homogenous network throughout the Board. Adamski said that the implementation stage went surprisingly smoothly. "We didn't fire anybody as a direct result of the new systems, but jobs were changed. There was some resistance to the new technology—most of it was born out of unfamiliarity and fear of not having the appropriate skills. Some people were very committed in doing things 'their way.' When some of these people started to perceive tangible productivity benefits, their perspectives started to change. We tried to counsel people as best we could and encourage them to experiment with the new systems. Most people eventually converted but there were still some objectors."

Adamski added that while they were implementing the new systems it was important for the IS Division not to lose sight of its key objectives and role within the organization. "We had to make sure that we didn't get carried away with the new whiz-bang technology and reduce our support and maintenance of the older, more conventional systems. For example, the Board went onto a new tariff system and we had to make significant changes to our rating system to accommodate this. Having an application generator in place significantly improved the systems upgrade time."

In May 1992, the Board's computer facilities included 4 Sun file servers, 80 Sun workstations, 100 microcomputers, 40 terminals, and the IBM System 38 Model 700. By this time, the IS Division had implemented the following components of the systems (see Figure 1 for a schematic of the systems):

1. A **Document Imaging Processing System** (DIPS) used for scanning, storing, and managing all documents on each property within the GDWB region which were being kept in the 95,000 separate paper files. This system was also used for the storage, backup, and retrieval of 25,000 engineering plans and drawings. DIPS gave designated Head Office departments and regional offices real-time access to all property documentation and allowed them to print out scanned images when required. The system had a sophisticated indexing system that facilitated easy retrieval of stored images by users and access by other programs. Figure 2 presents a copy of a scanned property plan from DIPS.
2. A digital mapping **Facilities Information System (FIS)** that provided for the storage, management, and ongoing maintenance of all graphic (map related) and nongraphic information relating to water and wastewater services, property information, property boundaries, and easements throughout the Board's region. The FIS provided a computerized "seamless" geographic map covering the entire GDWB region. The system encompassed the storing of all maps in digital form and attaching map coordinates to each digital point. Every point on a digital map was linked to a unique X and Y coordinate, based on the standard Australian Mapping Grid system, and had a specific address linked to it. Once each point on a map was precisely addressed and identified, specific attributes were attached to it. These attributes were then used as methods of recording information or used as indexes for access to or by other programs, for example, sewer pipe details, property details, water consumption, and vertical heights above sea level. The selected map area with all the related attributes and information was then displayed graphically in full color on a high resolution workstation monitor (see Figure 3).

   The FIS allowed cross referencing to financial, rating, and consumption data (through indexing) held on the System 38. It also enabled each underground facility to be numbered, catalogued, and identified as an asset with their associated data being integrated into other asset management systems. The FIS enabled data stored on a particular map to be "layered," with water pipes at one layer, sewer pipes at another, property boundaries at a third, future plans at another, and so on. This gave users the ability to recall maps in layers and to select the level and amount of detail they required. The

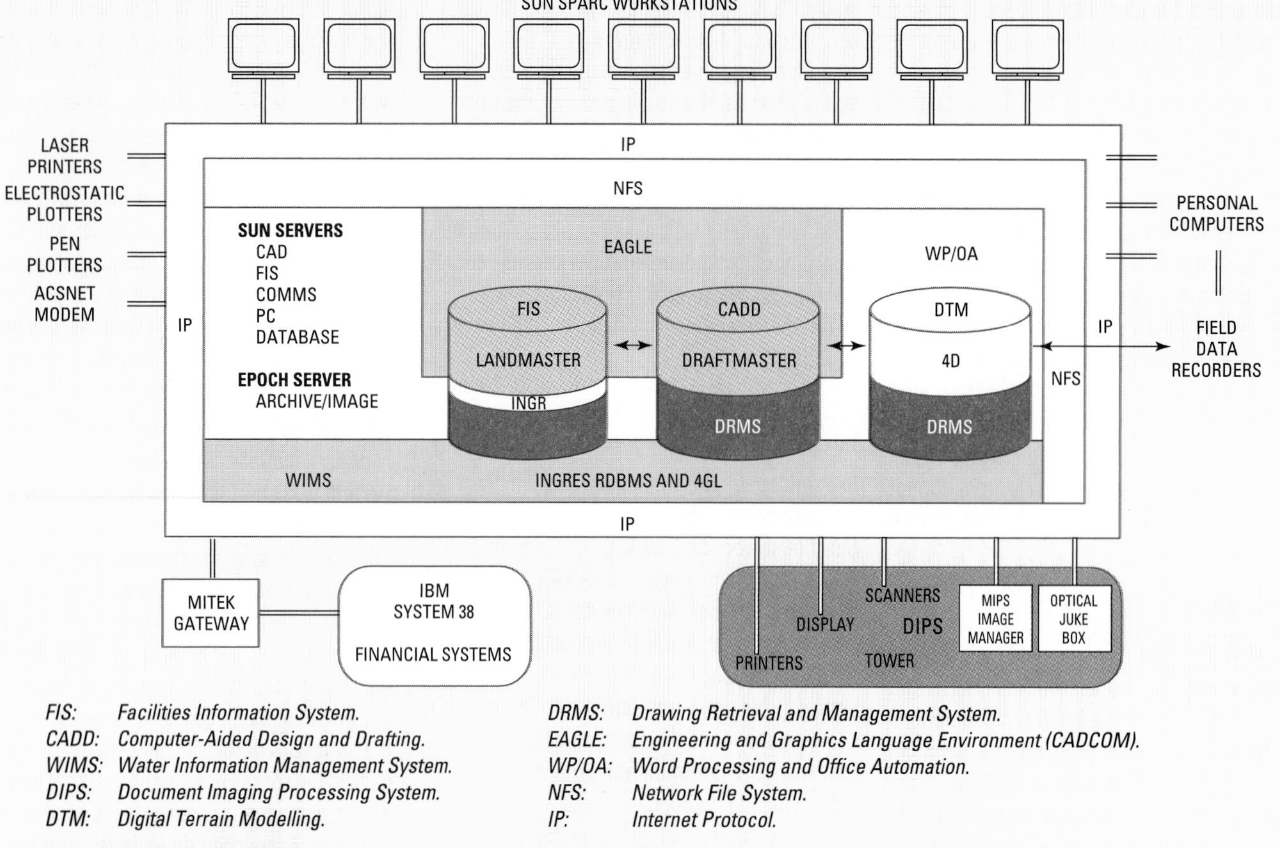

FIGURE 1 GDWB corporate computing system.

system was centered around a mouse-driven graphic interface where the user zoomed in and out and/or panned around particular areas—at the broadest level, showing the whole of southern Victoria, and at the most detailed, the individual plumbing and drainage plan of one particular property (through cross-referencing to the DIPS).

3. A **Computer-Aided Design and Drafting (CADD)** system that provided an integrated programmable 3-D environment for a range of civil, mechanical, electrical, surveying, and general engineering design and drafting applications. It offered the following features:
   - display manipulation, including multiple angle views, zooms, and pans;
   - geometric analysis, including automatic calculation of areas, perimeters, moments of inertia, and centroids; and
   - various customization features such as user-defined menus and prompts and a user-friendly macro language.
4. **Word Processing and Office Automation (WP/OA)** systems providing users the ability to prepare quality documentation integrating graphics, spreadsheets, mail merge, and databases, as well as other utilities such as electronic mail and phone message handling.
5. A **Relational Database Management System (RDBMS)** and a **Fourth-Generation Language** as a base foundation for the development of new applications. Some of the RDBMS applications included:
   - a Drawing and Retrieval Management System (DRMS) to control the development, release, and revision of all CADD projects and files; and
   - a Water Information Management System (WIMS) used for the storage and management of hydrographic engineering and laboratory data, both current and historical.

OUTCOMES

Vines said that one of the most important strategic outcomes of the changes introduced had been the way in which decision making at all levels with the organization had been enhanced. "This improvement is largely due to the fact that people have now got ready access to information they have never had before. This information is especially useful in enhancing our ability to forward plan. The flow and reporting of financial information has also speeded up and we now complete our final accounts up to two months earlier than we used to. In the areas that have come on-line there has been a definite improvement in productivity and in customer service. The CADD system, for example, is greatly enhancing our ability to design and plan new facilities. The turn-around time, the accuracy of the plans, and the creativity of the designers has been improved dramatically. In many departments there has been a change in work practices—some of the mundane activities are handled by the computer, allowing more productive work to be carried out, like spending more time with customers. Our asset management and control also started to improve. There was greater integrity in the information kept, and having just one central shared record meant that updating with new data or changes to existing data was far more efficient."

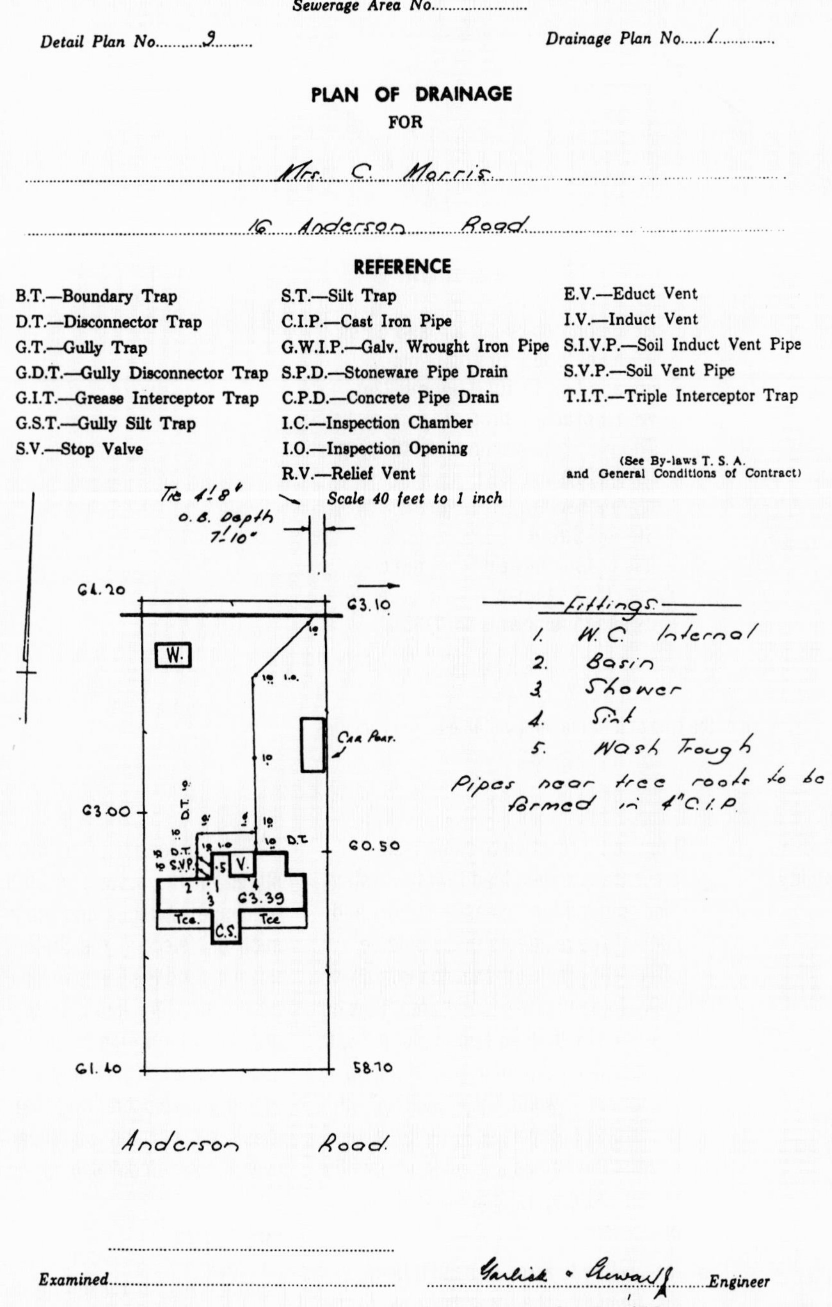
TORQUAY SEWERAGE AUTHORITY

Sewerage Area No.......................

Detail Plan No. 9 | Drainage Plan No. 1

PLAN OF DRAINAGE

FOR

Mrs. C. Morris

16 Anderson Road

REFERENCE

B.T.—Boundary Trap	S.T.—Silt Trap	E.V.—Educt Vent
D.T.—Disconnector Trap	C.I.P.—Cast Iron Pipe	I.V.—Induct Vent
G.T.—Gully Trap	G.W.I.P.—Galv. Wrought Iron Pipe	S.I.V.P.—Soil Induct Vent Pipe
G.D.T.—Gully Disconnector Trap	S.P.D.—Stoneware Pipe Drain	S.V.P.—Soil Vent Pipe
G.I.T.—Grease Interceptor Trap	C.P.D.—Concrete Pipe Drain	T.I.T.—Triple Interceptor Trap
G.S.T.—Gully Silt Trap	I.C.—Inspection Chamber	
S.V.—Stop Valve	I.O.—Inspection Opening	
	R.V.—Relief Vent	(See By-laws T. S. A. and General Conditions of Contract)

Scale 40 feet to 1 inch

Examined.......................

Garlick & Stewart Engineer

Date 10.2.72

FIGURE 2

Example of a building plan kept for each rateable property.

Adamski added that the initial reaction by Board staff to the whole corporate computing strategy "ranged from skepticism to outright hostility." He continued, "By the end of 1991, I would say that there had been a general reversal in attitude. Managers started to queue outside my office asking if we could develop specific business applications for them. They had begun to appreciate what the technology could do and most often they suddenly perceived a whole range of opportunities and different ways in which they could operate. One manager asked me, for example, if we could use document imaging technology to eliminate the need for any physical paper flows within his office. Technically this was possible but it was not really cost justifiable and the corporate culture would not really have supported it. Putting together the IS Division budget is now a difficult balancing act with a whole range of options and demands from users. I now ask the users to justify the benefits to be derived from new application proposals and I help out with the cost side. Cost-benefit justification usually drives the decisions as well as the 'fit' with the existing IT and other corporate objectives. What also must be considered is that these objectives are not written in stone. They are flexible and can and should adjust to changes in both the internal and external environment."

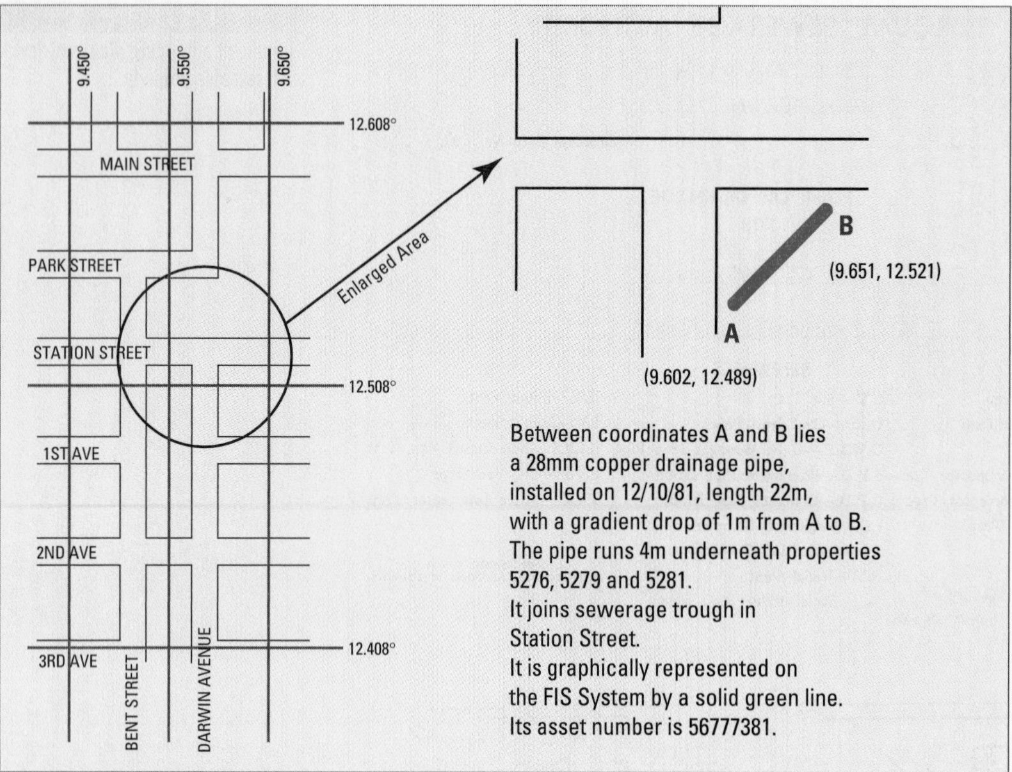
9.450°
9.550°
9.650°
12.608°
MAIN STREET
PARK STREET
Enlarged Area
STATION STREET
12.508°
1ST AVE
2ND AVE
3RD AVE
12.408°
BENT STREET
DARWIN AVENUE
B
(9.651, 12.521)
A
(9.602, 12.489)
Between coordinates A and B lies
a 28mm copper drainage pipe,
installed on 12/10/81, length 22m,
with a gradient drop of 1m from A to B.
The pipe runs 4m underneath properties
5276, 5279 and 5281.
It joins sewerage trough in
Station Street.
It is graphically represented on
the FIS System by a solid green line.
Its asset number is 56777381.

FIGURE 3 Illustration of the type of information available on the Facilities Information System.

A number of GDWB staff indicated that the new systems had enhanced their ability to fulfill their work responsibilities:

- A customer-service officer at one of the Board's regional offices stated that the DIPS had enabled her to respond to customer requests for encumbrance statements within a matter of minutes instead of weeks. She added that a number of customers had sent letters to their office complimenting them on the improvements in the service they received. She said that new DIPS had "flow on" benefits that weren't fully recognized. She cited the case in which local architects were able to charge their clients less because they had more ready access to information from the GDWB.
- A maintenance manager declared that the FIS had enabled his department to predict when pipes and drains should be replaced before they actually ruptured or broke down, by examining their installation dates and the types of materials used. He said this process over time started to shift the emphasis of his department's maintenance work from being reactive to being more preventative. He added that the system also enabled him to easily identify and contact the residents that would be affected by the work that the Board was going to do in a particular area. He said that the FIS enabled him to plot out with his mouse a particular area of a map on his screen. It would then "pick up" all the relevant properties in the area and identify the names and addresses of the current ratepayers residing in those properties.
- A secretary to a senior head office manager said that despite being a little daunted at first by the new word processing system, she felt the system had helped her considerably. She said that besides the obvious benefits in being able to prepare and edit documents on a WYSIWYG screen, she also had the ability of viewing as well as integrating scanned property plans, correspondence, and other documents from the DIPS.

Adamski said that one of the flow-on benefits from the FIS in particular was that the Board had the potential of selling the information stored on the system to authorities such as municipal councils and other public utilities such as Telecom, the State Electricity Commission, and the Gas and Fuel Corporation. He added that they had also considered marketing the information to private organizations such as building managers, architects, and property developers, and that the return from these sales could significantly reduce the overall costs in developing the FIS.

THE FUTURE

Commenting on the future prospects for the Board's IS Division, Adamski said, "There are some very complex applications that we are developing but we now have the skills, the tools, and the infrastructure to develop them cost effectively and to ensure that they deliver results. I think one of the main reasons why we are in this fortuitous position is that we chose a UNIX platform with client/server processing and a strong networking backbone. It gives us the flexibility and integration that we set out to achieve and we will need in the future to realize both our long- and short-term objectives. It's a lot easier now to cost-justify requests for new applications. The challenges ahead lie in three areas. Firstly, it's going to be difficult to consistently satisfy all our users' needs in that their expectations will be increasing all the time and they will become more demanding. We have to recognize these demands and at the same time keep investing in and maintaining our infrastructure. Secondly, we still have some way to go in developing a total corporate management information system. There are still some 'islands of data' floating around and the challenge is to get it all integrated. And thirdly, as the most senior IT manager at the Board I have to make sure that we retain our key IT staff and we compensate them adequately, both monetarily and in providing them stimulating and demanding work."

The Geelong and District Water Board changed its name to Barwon Water in February 1994. The name change reflected the change in the organization's governance structure with the appointment by the state government of a professional, "skills-based" governing board to replace the community-elected members. This initiative was part of a broader government strategy to commercialize state-owned utilities and to strive for greater efficiencies and productivity across the whole public service.

Four months after the name change, Geoff Vines retired and was replaced by Dennis Brockenshire as Barwon Water's chief executive. Brockenshire, formerly a senior manager with the State Electricity Commission, had considerable business and engineering experience relating to large-scale supply systems serving a large customer base. Commenting on Barwon Water's information technology (IT) infrastructure, Brockenshire stated, "Barwon Water has made and continues to make a significant investment in IT. The organization has spent something in the region of $7 to $10 million in building its IT infrastructure and has recurrent costs of 3 percent of total expenditure. I want to make sure we get an appropriate return for this investment. It is critical that IT delivers real business benefits. Since I've come into this role, I have insisted that my line managers justify any new IT investment on the grounds of the business value it will create."

From the period 1992 to 1995, Barwon Water's information systems (IS) department had focused most of its efforts in capturing all the relevant mapping, customer, and facilities data for its key systems. Significant resources were allocated to utilize the existing IT infrastructure to improve customer service and to streamline work flows. Improvements in security were also a major priority given the confidential and private nature of information stored on the various databases and the listing of Barwon Water's home page on the World Wide Web. In terms of hardware and software, the IBM System 38 was replaced by a Sun Sparcstation server running the Prophecy accounting package in a UNIX operating environment. The IS department had commenced work on an executive information system to assist with cost and performance measurement, particularly at the business unit level. This system would provide the core information to support a major benchmarking exercise in which Barwon Water compared its performance on key processes with other organizations, both within and external to the water industry.

Business processes were mapped and examined where steps could be eliminated or substituted by new IT applications. An interesting example of this was the introduction of a paperless, encumbrance certificating system. In this system a solicitor handling a property matter could interact with Barwon Water via the fax machine without the need to actually visit an office. All documents sent to and from Barwon Water and those transferred within the organization were accomplished entirely on the system with no need to print a hard copy. Processing times for these applications were reduced from an average of 10 days to a few hours.

A number of other efficiency gains were realized with the utilization of the IT infrastructure. The productivity of the engineering design staff increased by 20 to 50 percent for most drawings and by 90 percent for redrawings. The systems distributed computing design also reduced design cycles by enabling staff to share files and work on a common file to avoid duplicated effort. Overall staff numbers with Barwon Water had dropped to 400 by July 1995. Adamski said that although the total reduction in staff numbers could not be directly attributed to the new systems, there were several areas where staff had been made redundant or redeployed. He said that in many cases the systems "freed-up" front-line service personnel to spend more time listening and being responsive to customer concerns.

Barwon Water continued to receive acclaim for its innovative IT systems. In 1994 it was awarded the Geelong Business Excellence Award in the Innovation Systems/Development of Technology category. It also received a nomination for the award for innovation by the Washington-based Smithsonian Institute.[2]

A major organizational restructure in early 1995 saw Joe Adamski take over the responsibility for strategic planning as well as information systems. Adamski said that this restructure ensured that IT developments would be closely aligned with broader business objectives and strategies. He added that having the senior IT executive responsible for business planning symbolized how essential IT had become to the organization's operations and its management and control systems. As part of the restructure new business units were formed with the managers of these units made accountable for both revenue and cost items.

Commenting on future challenges, Adamski outlined his vision for Barwon Water as the computing center for the Greater Geelong region. "Geelong and district covers 4000 square kilometers. Within this region, there has recently been an amalgamation of councils into two super-councils—the City of Greater Geelong and the Surf Coast Council. These two organi[z]ations, serve the same customers as ourselves. We have articulated what we see as benefits of using common databases, mapping, and other information to serve these customers. Suggested benefits include a service shopfront where customers could pay rates, water tariffs, and apply for property approvals at the same place. These systems we now have in place at Barwon Water would be a good starting point in building this regional concept. Data is our most valuable asset and there is no point in duplicating it."[3]

 Funding for this research was provided by IBM Consulting (USA).

Case Study Questions

1. Describe the Geelong and District Water Board and the environment in which it operates. What problems did GDWB have before 1988? What were the management, organization, and technology factors that contributed to those problems?
2. Describe the role of information systems at GDWB and the GDWB's

information system portfolio before July 1988.

3. Describe and critique the process of upgrading GDWB's information systems portfolio.
4. How did the Water Board justify its investments in new information system technology? What were the benefits?

[1]This case was prepared by Joel B. Barolsky and Professor Peter Weill as part of the Infrastructure Study funded by *IBM Consulting Group (International)*. It should be read in conjunction with the *Geelong and District Water Board Information Technology Management* (CL298-1992) case. Both of these cases were written as the basis of discussion rather than to illustrate either effective or ineffective handling of a managerial situation. Copyright © 1995 Joel B. Barolsky and Peter Weill, Melbourne Business School Limited, The University of Melbourne.

[2]The original case study written by Barolsky and Weill on Geelong and District Water Board was awarded the Australian Computer Society Prize for best IT Case Study in 1993.

[3]"IT Manager Leads Corporate Plan to Water," *MIS* April 1994, 41–46.

CASE STUDY 2: Ginormous Life Insurance Company

Len Fertuck, University of Toronto (Canada)

Ginormous Life is an insurance company with a long tradition. The company has four divisions that each operate their own computers. The IS group provides analysis, design, and programming services to all of the divisions. The divisions are actuarial, marketing, operations, and investment. All divisions are located at the corporate headquarters building. Marketing also has field offices in 20 cities across the country.

- **The Actuarial Division** is responsible for the design and pricing of new kinds of policies. They use purchased industry data and weekly summaries of data obtained from the Operations Division. They have their own DEC VAX minicomputer, running the UNIX operating system, to store data files. They do most of their analysis on PCs and Sun workstations, either on spreadsheets or with a specialized interactive language called APL.
- **The Marketing Division** is responsible for selling policies to new customers and for follow-up of existing customers in case they need changes to their current insurance. All sales orders are sent to the Operations Division for data entry and billing. They use purchased external data for market research and weekly copies of data from operations for follow-ups. They have their own IBM AS/400 minicomputer with dumb terminals for clerks to enter sales data. There are also many PCs used to analyze market data using statistical packages like SAS.
- **The Operations Division** is responsible for processing all mission-critical financial transactions including payroll. They record all new policies, send regular bills to customers, evaluate and pay all claims, and cancel lapsed policies. They have all their data and programs on two IBM ES/9000 mainframes running under the OS/390 operating system. The programs are often large and complex because they must service not only the fifteen products currently being sold but also the 75 old kinds of policies that are no longer being sold but still have existing policy holders. Clerks use dumb terminals to enter and update data. Applications written in the last five years have used an SQL relational database to store data, but most programs are still written in COBOL. The average age of the transaction processing programs is about ten years.
- **The Investment Division** is responsible for investing premiums until they are needed to pay claims. Their data consists primarily of internal portfolio data and research data obtained by direct links to data services. They have a DEC minicomputer to store their data. The internal data are received by a weekly download of cash flows from the Operations Division. External data are obtained as needed. They use PCs to analyze data obtained either from the mini or from commercial data services.

A controlling interest in Ginormous Life has recently been purchased by Financial Behemoth Corp. The management of Financial Behemoth has decided that the firm's efficiency and profitability must be improved. Their first move has been to put Dan D. Mann, a hotshot information systems specialist from Financial Behemoth in charge of the Information Systems Division. He has been given the objective of modernizing and streamlining the computer facilities without any increase in budget.

In the first week on the job, Dan discovered that only seven junior members of the staff of 200 information systems specialists know anything about CASE tools, End-User Computing, or LANs. They have no experience in implementing PC systems. There is no evidence of any formal decision-support systems or executive information systems in the organization. New applications in the last five years have been implemented in COBOL on DB2, a relational database product purchased from IBM. Over two thirds of applications are still based on COBOL flat files. One of the benefits of using DB2 is that it is now possible to deliver reports quickly based on ad hoc queries. This is creating a snowballing demand for conversion of more systems to a relational database so that other managers can get similar service.

There have been some problems with the older systems. Maintenance is difficult and costly because almost every change to the data structure of applications in operations requires corresponding changes to applications in the other divisions. There has been a growing demand in other divisions for faster access to operations data. For instance the Investment Division claims that they could make more profitable investments if they had continuous access to the cash position in operations. Marketing complains that they get calls from clients about claims and cannot answer them because they do not have current access to the status of the claim. Management wants current access to a wide variety of data in summary form so they can get a better understanding of the business. The IS group says that it would be difficult to provide access to data in operations because of security considerations. It is difficult to ensure that users do not make unauthorized changes to the COBOL files.

The IS group complains that they cannot deliver all the applications that users want because they are short-staffed. They spend 90 percent of their time maintaining the existing systems. The programmers are mostly old and experienced and employee turnover is unusually low, so there is not likely to be much room for improvement by further training in programming. Employees often remark that the company is a very pleasant and benevolent place to work. At least they did until rumors of deregulation and foreign competition started to sweep the industry.

Dan foresees that there will be an increasing need for computer capacity as more and more applications are converted to on-line transaction processing and more users begin to make ad hoc queries. Dan is also wondering if intranets or the Internet should become part of any new software.

Dan began to look for ways to solve the many problems of the Information Systems Division. He solicited proposals from various vendors and consultants in the computer industry. After a preliminary review of the proposals, Dan was left with three broad options suggested by IBM, Oracle Corp. and Datamotion, a local consulting firm. The proposals are briefly described below.

IBM proposes an integrated solution using IBM hardware and software. The main elements of the proposal are:

- **Data and applications will remain on a mainframe.** The IBM ES/9000 series of hardware running their OS/390 operating system will provide mainframe services. Mainframe hardware capacity will have to be approximately doubled by adding two more ES/9000 series machines. The four machines will run under OS/390 with Parallel Sysplex clustering technology that allows for future growth. The Parallel Sysplex system can be scaled by connecting up to 32 servers to work in parallel and be treated as a single system for scheduling and system management. The OS/390 operating system can also run UNIX applications.
- **AS/400 minicomputers running under the OS/400 operating system** will replace DEC minicomputers.
- **RS/6000 workstations running AIX**—a flavor of the UNIX operating system—can be used for actuarial computations. All hardware will be interconnected with IBM's proprietary SNA network architecture. PCs will run under the OS/2 operating system and the IBM LAN Server to support both Microsoft Windows applications and locally designed applications that communicate with mainframe databases.
- **A DB2 relational database will store all data on-line.** Users will be able to access any data they need through their terminals or through PCs that communicate with the mainframe.
- **Legacy systems will be converted using reengineering tools,** like Design Recovery and Maintenance Workbench from Intersolv, Inc. These will have the advantage that they will continue to use the COBOL code that the existing programmers are familiar with. New work will be done using CASE tools with code generators that produce COBOL code.
- **Proven technology.** The IBM systems are widely used by many customers and vendors. Many mission-critical application programs are available on the market that address a wide variety of business needs.

Oracle Corp. proposed that all systems be converted to use their Oracle database product and its associated screen and report generators. They said that such a conversion would have the following advantages:

- **Over 90 hardware platforms are supported.** This means that the company is no longer bound to stay with a single hardware vendor. Oracle databases and application programs can be easily moved from one manufacturer's machine to another manufacturer's machine by a relatively simple export and import operation as long as applications are created with Oracle tools. Thus the most economical hardware platform can be used for the application. Oracle will also access data stored in an IBM DB2 database.
- **Integrated CASE tools and application generators.** Oracle has its own design and development tools called Designer/2000 and Developer/2000. Applications designed with Designer/2000 can be automatically created for a wide variety of terminals or for the World Wide Web. The same design can be implemented in Windows, on a Macintosh, or on X-Windows in UNIX. Applications are created using graphic tools that eliminate the need for a language like COBOL. The designer works entirely with visual prototyping specifications.
- **Vertically integrated applications.** Oracle sells a number of common applications, like accounting programs, that can be used as building blocks in developing a complete system. These applications could eliminate the need to redevelop some applications.
- **Distributed network support.** A wide variety of common network protocols like SNA, DecNet, Novell, and TCP/IP are supported. Different parts of the database can be distributed to different machines on the network and accessed or updated by any application. All data are stored on-line for instant access. The data can be stored on one machine and the applications can be run on a different machine, including a PC or workstation, to provide a client/server environment. The ability to distribute a database allows a large database on an expensive mainframe to be distributed to a number of cheaper minicomputers.

Datamotion proposed a data warehouse approach using software tools from Information Builders Inc. Existing applications would be linked using EDA, a middleware data warehouse server that acts as a bridge between the existing data files and the users performing enquiries. New applications would be developed using an application tool called Cactus. The advantages of this approach are:

- **Data Location Transparency** EDA Hub Server provides a single connection point from which applications can access multiple data sources anywhere in the enterprise. In addition, users can join data between any supported EDA databases—locally, cross-server, or cross-platform. Users can easily access remote data sources for enhanced decision-making capabilities.

- **The EDA server can reach most non-relational databases** and file systems through its SQL translation engine. EDA also supports 3GL, 4GL, static SQL, CICS, IMS/TM, and proprietary database stored procedure processing.
- **Extensive network and operating system support.** EDA supports 14 major network protocols and provides protocol translation between dissimilar networks. EDA also runs on 35 different processing platforms. EDA servers support optimized SQL against any RDBMS. And the EDA server can automatically generate the dialect of SQL optimal for the targeted data source. It is available on: Windows 3.x, Windows 95, Windows NT, OS/2, MVS, UNIX, CICS, VM, OpenVMS, Tandem, and AS/400.
- **Comprehensive Internet Support.** With EDA's Internet services, users can issue requests from a standard Web browser to any EDA-supported data source and receive answer sets formatted as HTML pages.
- **Cactus promotes modern development methods.** Cactus allows the developer to partition an application, keeping presentation logic, business logic, and data access logic separate. This partitioning of functionality can occur across a large number of enterprise platforms to allow greater flexibility in achieving scalability, performance, and maintenance. Cactus provides all the tools needed to deal with every aspect of developing, testing, packaging, and deploying client/server traditional applications or Web-based applications.

Dan is not sure which approach to take for the future of Ginormous Life. Whichever route he follows, the technology will have an enormous impact on the kinds of applications his staff will be able to produce in the future and the way in which they will produce them. While industry trends toward downsizing and distribution of systems may eventually prove to be more efficient, Dan's staff does not have much experience with the new technologies that would be required. He is uncertain about whether there will be a sufficient payoff to justify the organizational turmoil that will result from a major change in direction. Ideally he would like to move quickly to a modern client/server system with minimal disturbance to existing staff and development methods, but he fears that both of these are not simultaneously possible.

Source: Reprinted by permission of Len Fertuck, University of Toronto, Canada.

Case Study Questions

Dan must prepare a strategy for the renewal of the Information Systems Division over the next three years. As his assistant, prepare an outline, in point form, containing the following items:

1. A list of factors or issues that must be considered in selecting a technology platform for the firm.
2. Weights for each factor obtained by dividing up 100 points among the factors in proportion to their importance.
3. A score from 0 to 10 of how each of the three proposals performs on each factor.
4. A grand score for each proposal obtained by summing the product of the proposal score times the factor weight for each proposal.
5. The technology that you would recommend that Dan adopt and the reason for choosing the particular technology that you recommend.
6. The order in which each component of the technology should be introduced and the reason for selecting the order.

CASE STUDY 3: Analysis to Interface Design—The Example of Cuparla

Gerhard Schwabe, Stephan Wilczek, and Helmut Krcmar
University of Hohenheim (Germany)

Like in other towns, members of the Stuttgart City Council have a large workload: In addition to their primary professions (e.g., an engineer at Daimler Benz) they devote more than 40 hours a week to local politics. This extra work has to be done under fairly unfavorable conditions. Only council sessions and party meetings take place in the city hall; the deputies of the local council do not have an office in the city hall to prepare or coordinate their work. This means, for example, that they must read and file all official documents at home. In a city with more than 500,000 inhabitants, they receive a very large number of documents. Furthermore, council members believe they could be better informed by the administration and make better use of their time. Therefore Hohenheim University and partners launched the Cuparla project to improve the information access and collaboration of council members.[1]

A detailed analysis of their work revealed the following characteristics of council work:

- Council members need support available to them any time and in any place as they are very mobile.
- Council members collaborate and behave differently in different contexts: While they act informally and rather open in the context of their own party, they behave more controlled and formal in official council sessions.
- A closer investigation of council work reveals a low degree of process structure. Every council member has the right of initiative and can inform and

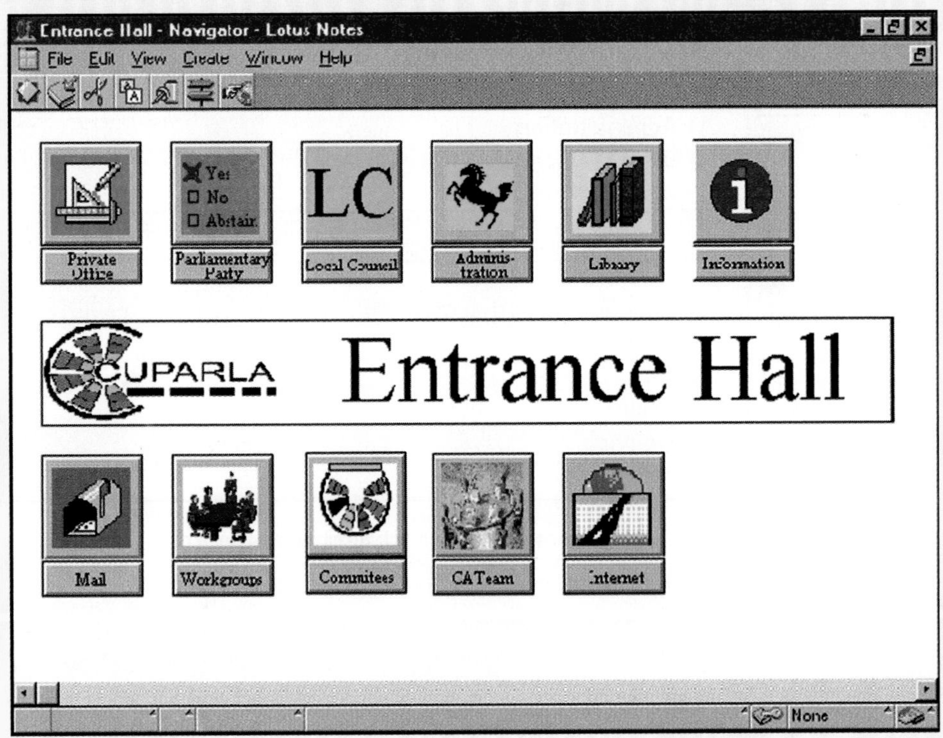

FIGURE 1

Entrance hall.

involve other members and members of the administration in any order.

- Council members rarely are power computer users. Computer support for them has to be straightforward and intuitive to use.

When designing computer support we initially had to decide on the basic orientation of our software. We soon abandoned a workflow model as there are merely a few steps and little order in the collaboration of local politicians. Imposing a new structure into this situation would have been too restrictive for the council members. We then turned to pure document orientation, imposing absolutely no structure on the council members' work. We created a single, large database with all the documents the city council ever needs. However, working with this database turned out to be too complex for the council members. In addition, they need to control the access to certain documents at all stages of the decision-making process. For example, a party may not want to reveal its proposals to other parties before it has officially been brought up in the city council. Controlling access to each document individually and changing the access control list were not feasible.

Therefore, the working context was chosen as a basis of our design. Each working context of a council member can be symbolized by a "room." A private office corresponds to the council member working at home; there is a party room, in which the member collaborates with party colleagues, and a committee room symbolizes the place for committee meetings. In addition, there is a room for working groups, a private post office, and a library for filed information. All rooms hence have an electronic equivalent in the Cuparla software. When opening the Cuparla software, a council member sees all the rooms from the entrance hall (see Figure 1).

The council member creates a document in one room (e.g., a private office) and then shares it with other council members in other rooms. If the member moves a document into the room of his party, the member shares it with his party colleagues; if he hands it on to the administration, he shares it with the mayors, administration officials, all council members, and so forth.

The interface of the electronic rooms resembles the setup of the original rooms. Figure 2 shows the example of the room for a parliamentary party. On the left side of the screen are document locations, and on the right side are the documents of the selected location. Documents that are currently worked on are displayed on the "desk." These documents have the connotation that they need to be worked on without an additional outside trigger. If a document is in the files, it belongs to a topic that is still on the political agenda; however, a trigger is necessary to move it out of the shelf. If a topic is no longer on the political agenda, all documents belonging to it are moved to the archive.

The other locations support the collaboration within the party. The conference desk contains all documents for the next (weekly) party meeting. Any council member of the party can put documents there. When preparing for the meeting, the council member simply has to check the conference desk for relevant information. The mailbox for the chairman contains all documents about which the chairman needs to decide. In contrast to the e-mail account, all members have access to the mailbox. Duplicate work is avoided as every council member is aware of the chairman's agenda. The mailbox of the assistant contains tasks for the party assistants—the mailbox for the secretary, assignments for the secretary (e.g., a draft for a letter). The inbox contains documents that have been moved from other rooms into this room.

Thus, in the electronic room all locations correspond to the current manual situation. Council members do not have to relearn their work. Instead, they collaborate in the shared environment to which they are accustomed,

FIGURE 2

Parliamentary party room.

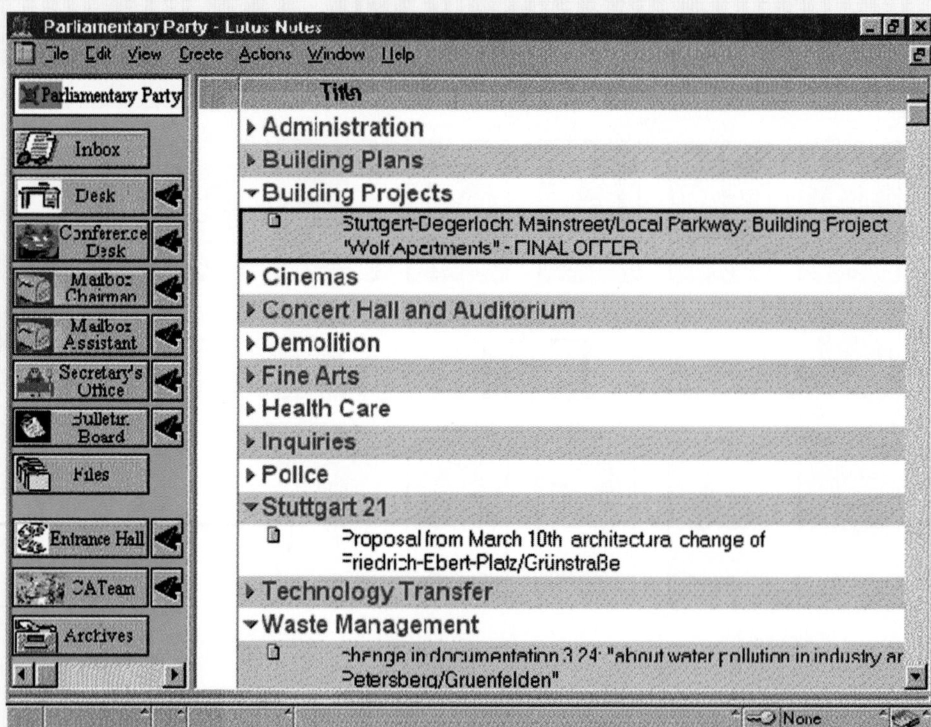

with shared expectations on the other peoples' behavior. Feedback from the pilot users indicates that this approach is appropriate.

Some specific design features make the software easy to use. The software purposely does not have a fancy 3-D interface that has the same look as a real room. Buttons (in the entrance hall) and lists (in the rooms) are much easier to use and do not distract the user from the essential parts. Each location (e.g., the desk) has a small arrow. If a user clicks on this arrow, a document is moved to the location. This operation is much easier for a beginner than proceeding by "drag and drop."

Furthermore, software design is not restricted to building an electronic equivalent of a manual situation. If a user wants to truly benefit from the opportunities of electronic collaboration support systems, one has to include new tools that are not possible in the manual setting. For example, additional cross-location and room search features are needed to make it easy for the council member to retrieve information. The challenge of interface design is to give the user a starting point that is similar to a familiar situation. A next step is to provide users with options to improve and adjust their working behaviors to the opportunities offered by the use of a computer.

Source: Reprinted by permission of Gerhard Schwabe, Stephen Wilczek, and Helmut Krcmar, University of Hohenheim (Germany).

Case Study Questions

1. Analyze the management, organization, and technology issues that had to be addressed by the Cuparla project.
2. Analyze the interface and design of the Cuparla system. How easy is it to use? What problems does it solve? What organizational processes does the system support? How effective is it? Would you make any changes? If so, what would they be?
3. Could the Cuparla software be used for other applications in business? Why or why not? What modifications would be required?

[1]The project partners are Hohenheim University (Coordinator), Datenzentrale Baden-Wüttemberg, and Group Vision Softwaresysteme GmbH. The project is funded as part of its R&D program by DeTeBerkom GmbH, a 100 percent subsidiary of German Telekom.

CASE STUDY 4: Citibank Asia-Pacific: Rearchitecting Information Technology Infrastructure for the Twenty-First Century

Boon Siong Neo and Christina Soh
Information Management Research Center (IMARC), Nanyang Business School
Nanyang Technological University (Singapore)

I. CITICORP

> Citicorp in 1991 recorded a net loss of $457 million,[1] suspended the dividend on its common stock, and saw the price of that stock fall to a long-time low before rebounding after year end. Nevertheless, and despite the magnitude of our problems, 1991 for Citicorp was in key respects a transitional, turnaround year.

John Reed, Citicorp's chairman, acknowledged Citicorp's problems in his letter to stockholders in the 1991 annual report. The bank had been struggling with a large Third-World loan portfolio, as well as significant problems with its commercial property loans, and with its financing of highly leveraged transactions in the United States. The bank needed more equity but Third-World debt costs prevented Citicorp from increasing its equity through retention of earnings.

The severe storms to which Citicorp had been subjected prompted significant changes. To combat the slowdown in revenue growth and the rise in consumer and credit write-offs, Citicorp aggressively reduced expenses to improve the operating margin, and issued stock to improve their capital ratio. Structural changes were aimed at providing more focused direction to the business. John Reed articulated three requirements for being a "great bank in the 1990s"—meeting customer needs, having financial strength, and "marshalling human and *technological* resources . . . *more imaginatively and cost-effectively* than one's competitors."

In the midst of this organizational turbulence, one of Citicorp's undisputed strengths was its global presence. It is unrivaled in its network of banks in more than 90 countries. Its overseas consumer banking operations in particular were showing healthy growth. Global consumer banking includes mortgage and insurance business and non-U.S. credit card business. Citicorp only entered the field of consumer banking in the mid-70s. John Reed's vision was to pursue growth in the consumer banking area, and to pursue it through global expansion and leveraging IT.

The primary vision in consumer banking is "Citibanking"—combining relationship banking with technology that enables Citibank to serve its customers anywhere anytime with the same high standard of service that they receive in their home countries. Some examples of the manner in which technology enables the Citibanking vision include having a one-stop account opening, paperless transactions, instant card and check issuance, and instant account availability; having a customer relationship database that supports cross-product relationships, creation of hybrid products and customized products, and relationship pricing that more closely matches the value to the customer. The Citicard is the key to Citibanking services such as checking, money market, and bankcard accounts. Consumer banking products are distributed through bank branches, Citicard centers, and Citiphone banking, which gives 24-hour, 7-day-a-week service. The global services available to customers were augmented in 1991 when Citibank joined the CIRRUS ATM network, allowing Citicard holders access to cash around the world.

The results of operating and structural changes, as well as the impact of the growing Asian consumer market, contributed to a turnaround at Citicorp, where the 1992 net earning was $772 million. This earned it an A-minus credit rating from *Standard and Poor,* which also upgraded the bank's outlook from negative to stable. Their performance continued to improve each year (see Figure 1). In early 1994, the bank was also given permission by the U.S. regulatory agency to resume issuing

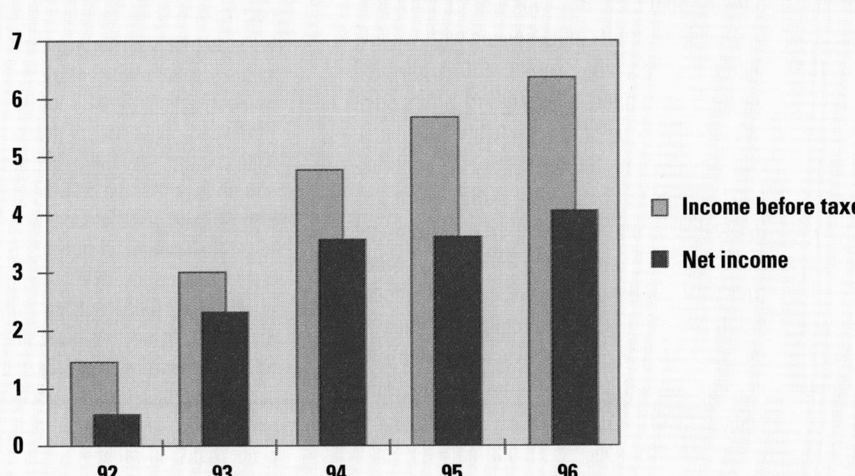

FIGURE 1
Income in billions. *Source: Citicorp Annual Report, 1996.*

dividends. These improvements were reflected in Citicorp's share price, which moved up to \$36.88 during 1993, from a low of \$23 in 1990. By 1997, the stock price was 10 times its low in 1990.[2]

II. CITIBANK IN ASIA-PACIFIC

Even in 1991, the profit that Citicorp made on its Asian business was a healthy \$400m, if one excludes the loan write-offs for Australia and New Zealand, and their slow progress in the difficult Japanese retail banking market. This compares well with the \$894m loss in the United States, and the \$132m profit in Europe, Africa, and the Middle East.[3] The Asian market also had a high growth potential. Asian consumer deposits grew six-fold to \$13.6 billion between 1983 and 1992, while loans grew seventeen-fold to \$10.8 billion over the same period.[4] This growth is a reflection of the region's high gross savings rate (about 35 percent) and high GNP growth.

Citicorp has been in Asia since 1902 when it set up finance houses in a number of Asian ports, such as Shanghai and Singapore. It has built up an understanding of these local markets. Today, consumer banking in the Asia-Pacific is organized into three regions—North Asia (Korea, Taiwan, Hong Kong, and the Philippines), South Asia (Thailand, Malaysia, Singapore, Indonesia, and Australia), and Central Europe/Middle Eastern Asia (India, Pakistan, Saudi Arabia, United Arab Emirates, Eastern Europe). The regional directors report to New York–based Executive Vice President De Sousa, who also heads the Private Bank. Besides the country managers, functions reporting to the regional directors include financial control, marketing and business development, technology and operations, treasury, credit, human resources, and service quality. Citicorp's major competitors in terms of established presence throughout Asia are Hong Kong Bank and Standard Chartered Bank, but neither has the global reach that Citicorp offers.

Citibank began pursuing consumer banking in Asia in earnest in 1986, and since then Asian accounts have increased from 1 million to 6 million in 1997 and are expected to reach 13 million by the year 2000. Critics suggest that Citicorp may run into credit problems because Asians have little experience with personal debt. Nonetheless, Citicorp continues to pioneer the concept of consumer credit in Asia—beside the usual mortgage and auto loans, Citicorp offers round-the-clock phone banking and automated teller cards that can be used in Singapore as well as New York.[5] Interestingly, some innovations such as phone banking were motivated by local regulations that severely restricted the number of branches that it may operate. To compete with the local banks, Citibank has had to be very focused in its customer base.

Citibank has made significant innovations in packaging financial services for the relatively rich customer and has managed to corner the market. Part of the underlying philosophy is that its market position requires continual research into local customer needs—what one senior Citibank officer called the "let a hundred flowers bloom" approach. That approach has resulted in each country having its own IT infrastructure and unique applications. Although it has worked adequately in the past, the local markets approach does not allow Citibank to integrate its products, services, and information to serve its highly sophisticated, mobile, and increasingly demanding global customers. Further, there were substantial economies of scale that may be gained from standardizing and consolidating bank products and processing across the diverse countries of the Asia-Pacific region. The key to achieving these goals lies in rearchitecting the technology infrastructure that enables the consumer banking business.

III. TECHNOLOGY INFRASTRUCTURE IN CITIBANK ASIA-PACIFIC

In the early 1990s, each of Citibank's Asia-Pacific countries belonged to one of three automation platforms—MVS, AS/400, or UNIX—and had one of two consumer banking applications—COSMOS or CORE. COSMOS was an earlier set of applications and was fairly typical of most U.S. banks' off-shore banking applications. It was written in COBOL to provide flexibility in complying with varying regulatory reporting formats, and it provided back-office support for standard areas such as current accounts, general ledger, and some loans processing. Subsequently, Citibank began to replace COSMOS with CORE, which was to provide a comprehensive system to run on AS/400s. CORE was used in a number of countries with smaller operations, such as Indonesia. It was not suitable for countries, such as India, where IBM did not have a presence, and in countries with high volumes, such as Hong Kong. Both COSMOS and CORE were subject to many country-specific modifications over time, as each country operation responded to varying regulatory and business requirements. The result was significant differences in each country's basic banking software.

A two-pronged strategy was adopted: First, rearchitect the IT infrastructure by standardizing and centralizing all back-office banking functions; and second, develop centers of excellence by encouraging individual countries to take the lead in developing products and processes where they have significant leadership and competitive advantages in the marketplace. The only rule in the latter strategy is that the lead country should develop products and processes that meet the requirements for all countries in the region and must provide ongoing support for the systems in which such products and processes are embedded.

IV. REGIONAL CARD CENTER AS PROTOTYPE OF THE NEW STRATEGY

A significant piece of Citibank's Asia-Pacific IT infrastructure that provided the prototype for further subsequent consolidation in consumer banking is the Regional Card Center (RCC). The RCC was set up in Singapore in 1989 to support start-up credit card businesses in Southeast Asia. Country managers whose credit card data processing were to be centralized demanded exacting performance standards from the center because of its direct impact on their operating performance. Ajit Kanagasundram, who used to run the data center for Citibank Singapore, was given the mandate to set up and run the center:

> The purpose of the RCC was to jump-start the credit card businesses in Citibank countries in Southeast Asia. Setting up the processing infrastructure before offering credit card services in each country would take too long and be too costly for start-up businesses. According to the sentiment at that time, we had planned the RCC for the initial three years, and then put processors in each country after that. The time constraint to make the RCC operational also dictated our approach, which was to get the operational software requirements from a couple of lead businesses, in this case, Citibank Hong Kong and Singapore. Trying to get requirements from all countries would be too time consuming and result in missed market opportunities. Further, 80 percent of credit card operational requirements

are stipulated by the card associations and were common across countries. We recruited a few staff experienced in credit card operations, used our own production experience, plus on-site consultants to modify the software, and got the RCC operational in eight months.

By 1990, we had reduced the processing cost per credit card by 45 percent and we were given the mandate to extend our operations to cover the Middle East and North Asia, excluding Hong Kong. In 1991, credit card software that had been developed by Citicorp in London and that was scheduled for implementation in Thailand was scrapped in favor of CARDPAC, the package used by the RCC. By 1994, in the midst of heightened cost consciousness because of corporate financial troubles, our cost per card was down to 32 percent of the 1989 cost. None of the country managers asked for decentralization of the credit card operations—who wants cost per card to triple overnight? We are now processing cards for 15 countries and the number of cards processed have increased from 230,000 in 1990 to 5 million in 1996. We have also decreased the time it took to launch a new business from 14 months to 3 months.

In 1993, Citibank beat out other regional rivals to become the issuer of affinity Visa and MastercCard for Passages, a joint frequent-flyer program of 15 Asian airlines. Citibank credits its ability to launch and support the cards regionally, enabled by the RCC, as being a key factor for being selected. By the end of 1996, the RCC was processing credit cards for 5 million customers in 15 countries from Japan in the north to New Zealand in the south, and from Turkey in the west to Guam in the east. The cost economies offered by the RCC made it obvious for countries to join it rather than go on their own. Citibank projects that, by 1999, its cost per card would drop by a further one-third from the current levels, the benefits of which would be reflected in each country's bottom line.

The RCC concept combines both centralization and decentralization ideas to meet specific local business needs and low costs of processing at the same time. The business strategy, marketing, credit evaluation, and customer service for credit cards continue to be decentralized in each country to cater to local market conditions and needs. The front-end data capture and printing of customer statements are also decentralized to each country. What is centralized is the back-end transaction processing and data repository. The control and active management of credit card businesses continue to be with country managers and the business gains are reflected in the financial performance of each country. The RCC provides the technology infrastructure for lowering operational costs, diffusing best practices, and attracting the needed technical talent. RCC's accumulated experience and infrastructure also enable Citibank to launch the card business in new countries within four months.

The strategic architecture of the RCC is shown in Figure 2. An IBM ES/9000 Model 821 designed for high-volume, on-line, and batch transaction processing formed the main platform for the system. Input/output operations performed at Citibank branches, ATMs, and other electronic systems include new account opening, collections, authorizations, printing of reports and monthly statements, and customer service. These input/output operations at individual countries are linked via leased lines of different capacities (2.4 kbps to 64 kbps). The databases and transaction history are stored centrally at the RCC.

The decreasing costs of telecommunications and the cost savings from standardizing hardware, software, and procedures enable RCC to reap ever-increasing economies of scale as each new country joins its fold, and as businesses of member countries grow. The centralization of credit card operations in the RCC provided other benefits as well:

FIGURE 2

Key systems in Citibank.

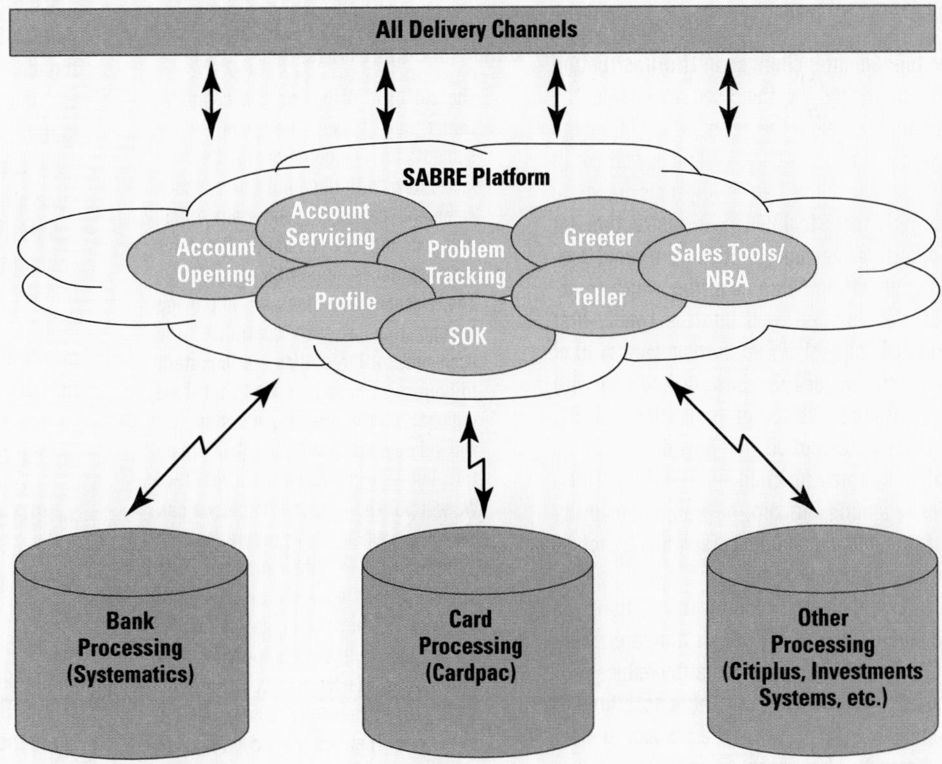

- It could devote the necessary resources to ensure superior service levels around the clock (100 percent availability and four-second terminal response time 99 percent of the time).
- It could recruit and retain talent from the best in the region because of the size of its operations; its 60 professional staff have developed in-depth knowledge and expertise in credit card operations and operations of the IBM S/390 platform.

The major concern of the RCC is that of telecommunication costs. Although the RCC has employed advanced data compression techniques, the current costs of leased land/sea circuits are significantly higher than equivalent lines in the United States. Although costs are expected to come down when fiber-optic submarine cables are put in place, the RCC's heavy reliance on telecommunications makes it vulnerable to corporate pressure to locate network processing in areas that minimize its total operating costs. The RCC experience provided the experiential base for subsequent rearchitecting of the technology of the consumer bank. The experience and expertise that RCC had built up would be repositioned to serve the processing requirements of the Asia-Pacific Consumer Bank.

V. REARCHITECTING THE *IT* INFRASTRUCTURE

The fundamental changes in IT infrastructure were motivated by the need to enable the Citibanking vision. The appointment of George DiNardo as the new chief technology officer in 1993 signaled the bank's strategic intent to develop a new technology infrastructure for capitalizing the opportunities from rapid economic growth in Asian countries which is expected to continue well into the twenty-first century. Recipient of *Information Week's* CIO of the Year Award for 1988, DiNardo had been with Mellon Bank in Pittsburgh from 1969 to 1991, and was its executive vice president of information systems function from 1985 to 1991. Prior to joining Citicorp, he was a consulting partner for Coopers and Lybrand and a professor of information systems at a leading U.S. university. DiNardo's plan for IT in Citibank is to enable Citibanking, through standardization of the IT platform, to significantly reduce processing costs per transactions through economies of scale, to reduce product to market times by 50 percent, and to increase systems reliability. He crisply summed up his job portfolio at Citibank:

> My job is to introduce the most advanced technology possible in Asia and I spent 35 years doing that for other banks, Bankers Trust and Mellon Bank. I am truly a bank businessman and a technologist. The vision requires that a customer going anywhere in the world be able to transact the same way wherever he goes. It is moving to (the concept of) Citibank recognizes you, and relationship manages you. If you have $100,000 with Citibank, you have certain services free, and it will be the same wherever you go. It's the ability to use the ATM wherever you are.

Moving toward this level of global banking requires that a Citibank branch anywhere in the world will have access to the customer's addresses, customary services, and relationships anywhere else in the world. It would have been costly to achieve this with the then decentralized computing structure, where each country in the Asia-Pacific has its own host computer and where each country has a different technology platform. It would also be difficult to ensure simultaneous rollout across countries of new products. Hence, the foundational changes to computing at Citibank Asia-Pacific began with the centralization of processing and a uniform back-office platform. The bank standardized on an IBM MVS platform. DiNardo explained the logic of centralization for Citibank Asia:

> The old days of having the computer center next to you are gone. Where should your computer center be—remote! Now, with fiber, put your console, command center in your main office, and your big box is remote. Our command center is here in Singapore . . . . The telecommunications are improving enough that we can centralize. The economies of large IBMs are important to banking. I have promised that if we regionalize on a new single system, we will get savings. It will cost $50m to do this, but we will break even in year two. We will put the largest IBM box we can get in a center in Singapore. I have promised a 10 to 20 percent computing reduction every year. How am I going to do that? You buy the biggest building, so you can pull any computer in any time, backup for 100 percent up-time, 99.9 percent on-time completion of batch jobs. Then you don't need backup all over Asia. You put in all the other countries account processing, and transmit all the rest.

Initially, the major saving will come from avoiding the need to build a computer center in Hong Kong. Savings arise also from having all processing in one site, with only one other hot backup site, as compared with having processing distributed in 14 countries, and with each country having its own backup. Citibank will be leveraging off the networks that are already in place as a result of the regional card center. Another significant source of savings comes from the centralization of software development.

Citibank is aiming for uniformity in its back-room processing software. Previously, each country controlled its own systems development efforts, so that while each country started out with the same basic software, over time the plethora of systems development efforts resulted in significantly different systems. The advent of PCs and client/server computing compounded the rate of change. Citibank replaced individual country systems that have evolved over time with a $20-million integrated back-office banking applications package from Systematics.

The strength of the Systematics package is that it has evolved significantly through its sale to more than 400 banks, and therefore offers many functions and features. It uses a traditional design based on the MVS/CICS/COBOL platform and has been proved capable of supporting high volumes. According to DiNardo, the idea is to not reinvent the wheel by writing yet another in-house back-office processing system, but to take this package and "turn the 2000 Citibank systems professionals loose on innovation . . . it's delivery and panache that counts . . . to create reusable modules to be called in through Systematics user exits. Systematics have promised to keep the exits constant through time." The plan also calls for eventual conversion of all other programs to the Systematics format, for example, using the same approach to data modeling, COBOL programming, and naming conventions.

A new Asia-Pacific data center running an IBM ES/9000 model 821 mainframe was set up in Singapore's Science Park on the western part of the island in October 1994. The hot-site backup running an IBM ES/9000 model 500 was located in Singapore's Chai Chee Industrial Park on the eastern part of the island. The intent is to relocate the backup site to another country to mitigate against country risks once the conversion is complete and the systems are running smoothly. Investments are also made to increase programmer productivity at development centers in Singapore, India, and the Philippines. Citibank is planning to spend $5 million on tools that will increase programmer productivity by 5 to 10 percent each year. Programmers in the centers will do remote TSO development using terminals with channel connects in all countries. Citibank is also considering putting in hyper channels if necessary.

By the first quarter of 1997, six countries have been converted to the Systematics platform—Australia, Singapore, Turkey, Guam, the Philippines, and Malaysia. The other countries are expected to be converted by 1998. By 1999 when the data center consolidation and regionalization are complete, Citibank expects to save about $17.6 million and reduce its staff by about 96 people. Its unit cost for banking transactions is expected to drop by 44 percent from 1996 levels.

VI. BUILDING COMMON FRONT-END SYSTEMS

Peter Mills, director for business improvement, is a 26-year Citibank veteran who has worked in most of the Citibank Asian divisions in his career and has oversight responsibilities for developing common processes for all Asia-Pacific businesses.

> Citibanking is our business vision. We have consolidated on a common platform for efficient back-room processing. My role is to create common business processes that may result in common front-end systems that are compatible with our back-end platforms. As part of the rearchitecting of Citibank's technology infrastructure, we initiated several process reengineering projects to develop new process templates for the Asia-Pacific. It is thus crucial that we manage our key reengineering projects very carefully.

A common thread that has emerged from both the reengineering and infrastructural change efforts is the idea of incorporating best practice—what Citibank calls "centers of excellence." In the area of software development, the emphasis on adopting best practice among the Citibank countries is a guard against the common trap of settling for the lowest common denominator in the process of standardization. The commitment to develop a reengineering template incorporating the best redesigned processes from each country, for use in developing common systems, is another embodiment of this idea. DiNardo explains what is being practiced in Citibank Asia-Pacific:

> The purchase of the Systematics package provides the bank with increased functionality and standardized processing without significant systems development effort. In-house development effort will be focused on strategic products such as those for currency trading, Citiplus, and the SABRE front-end teller and platform systems. The approach to future systems development will no longer be one of letting "a hundred flowers bloom." There will no longer be systems development or enhancement only for individual countries. Any country requiring any change needs to convince at least two other countries to support it. Any changes made would then be made for all Citibank countries in Asia. Several countries have now been identified as likely centers of excellence for front-end software development: Taiwan for auto loans processing, Australia for mortgage products, Hong Kong for personal finance products, India, the Philippines, and Singapore will become centers for application software development, design, and the generation of high-quality code at competitive cost.

The reengineering of business processes in Singapore provides a glimpse of how Citibank intends to introduce best practices in banking products and service delivery, which would be built into common front-end systems. Citibank has been in Singapore for more than 90 years. It started out as a wholesale bank. The consumer bank business was started later in the 1960s. Being a foreign bank, it is allowed to set up only three branches in Singapore. Nonetheless, Citibank has done very well in Singapore. Customer accounts have more than tripled since 1989, largely due to the successful introduction of Citibank's Visa card business. There has been an accompanying ten-fold increase in profit in the same period.

Citibank's retail customers in Singapore represent the more affluent segment of the population. The bank's fees and rates are not the lowest, but they feel that they are able to offer a higher level of service and more innovative banking products. This image of innovation and customer service is reinforced through a series of advertisements in print and on television. Innovative products include ready credit and Citiphone banking. The Citiphone service is Citibank Singapore's attempt to provide a high level of customer service despite the regulations that limit its number of branches to three. The vice president in charge of customer service, and the person responsible for implementing Citiphone, calls it their branch in the sky. This is a 24-hour, 7-day-a-week service that is manned by accredited Citibank officers, who are empowered to make decisions on the spot.

The increase in account volume, however, has been accomplished without any major increase in staff or changes in processes. Staff, processes, and infrastructure that were originally designed to support about 50,000 accounts, were strained when they had to support an account volume of about 250,000. This has contributed to a drop in customers' perception of service levels. Annual surveys indicated that customer satisfaction has dropped from a high of 90 percent in 1987 to a low of 65 percent in 1993. Some departments are experiencing high overtime and employee turnover. A cultural assessment study conducted by consultants confirmed that some employees did not feel valued and trusted. Front-line operations were also paper intensive and perceived to have significant opportunities for improvements. In addition, there was the need to achieve the vision of Citibanking, which required cross-product integration as a basis for relationship banking.

The project was carried out in three phases: (1) building the case for action, (2) design, and (3) implementation. In the first two phases, the consultants worked closely with four Citibankers who were assigned full time to the reengineering project. After six months, the team completed phase two and composed a list of 28 recommended process changes. Three core processes were identified for change—delivery of services to the customer, marketing, and transaction processing. The delivery process included account opening and servicing, credit, and customer problem resolution. The team found that it was encumbered with many hand-offs, a "maker-checker" mindset where transactions had to be checked by someone other than the originating employee, and unclear accountability for problem resolution. The transaction processing process was basically the back-end processing for the transactions originating in the branches. The major observation here was that the processing was fragmented by product or system. The marketing processes were currently also product focused, and there was limited understanding of customer segments and individual customers.

The vision which the team presented included a streamlined front-end delivery process with clear accountability and quick turnaround on customer problem resolution, a unified approach to transaction processing, and segment-focused, cross-product marketing. They felt that the most radical change required would be that of the organizational culture. One aspect of culture manifested in the "maker-checker" was a legacy of the days when the bank was a wholesale bank, and each transaction value was very high while volume was relatively low. In the retail bank business, the high volume and low individual value of transactions required a different mindset. Other aspects of Citibank culture that would need to change include the emphasis and the incentive system that rewarded product innovation and individuality. The process changes required a culture that focused more on relationships with customers and on team efforts.

The team also set detailed targets for each of the core processes. Among the many targets set for the delivery process, a rise in the percentage of customers who were highly satisfied from 64 to 80 percent, an increase in percentage of customers served within five minutes from 71 to 80 percent, and an improvement in transactions processing accuracy from 2 errors per 5000 transactions to 1 error per 5000 transactions. Detailed targets for productivity and cost improvements were also set. These targets that were in effect also listed measures that would be used to evaluate each process on a recurring basis.

Phase three involved the formation of three implementation teams—service delivery, operations, and product development and marketing—and many more employees. Each team was headed by the vice president in charge of the function. The role of the consultants in phase three was scaled back and they resisted some recommended changes. George DiNardo and Peter Mills addressed the problem of resistance by having discussions with key stakeholders of the processes to be reengineered, and by focusing on a number of projects. Before the end of the first year, the consultants had been phased out. The Citibank implementation teams were driving their own implementation.

A major part of implementation was to develop and implement the information systems needed to support the reengineered processes. Figure 3 is a representation of the key front-end systems within Citibank. One resulting new system is Strategic Asia-Pacific Branch Retail Environment (SABRE). SABRE consists of two complementary subsystems: SABRE I is at the teller level and provides automated support for signature verification, paperless teller transactions, and Citicard transactions. SABRE II includes the phone banking systems, together with facilities for telemarketing and cross-product marketing at the branches. The bank is developing the SABRE system in-house, because it considers this to be a strategic product.

The process change efforts, in tandem with the ongoing changes to the IT systems, have resulted in measurable improvements. Citibank tracks performance indicators before and after process changes (see Table 1) to assess the extent of the improvements.

VII. MANAGING IMPLEMENTATION AND CHANGE

It is evident that the structure of computing in Citibank is undergoing significant change. The changes are not trivial and will have "strategic impacts on the future business of the bank." The credibility and experience of George Di-

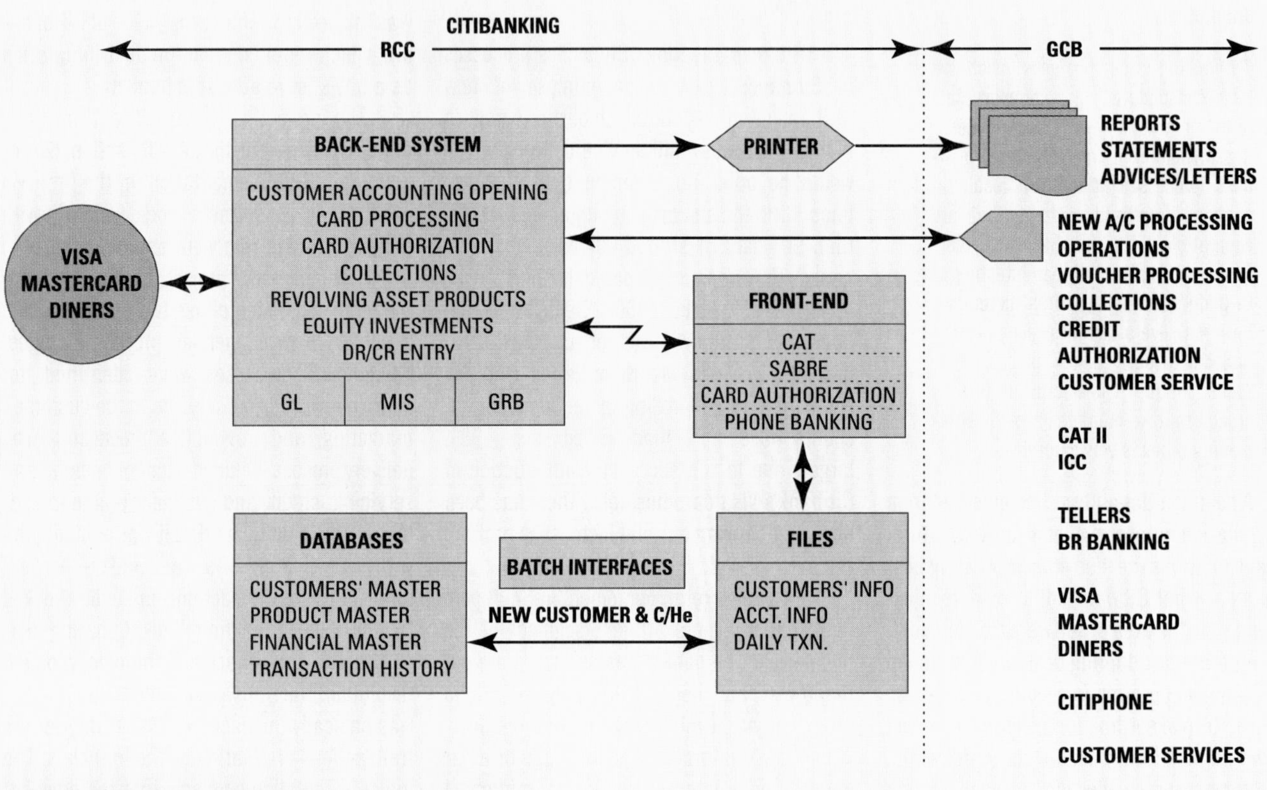

FIGURE 3 Strategic architecture.

TABLE 1

Results of Citicard Benchmarking Program

	Cycle Time		No. of Hand-offs		Paperless	
	Before	After	Before	After	Before	After
Statement rendition	41 hrs	24 hrs	2	1	—	—
Duplicate charges	6 days	24 hrs	3	1	no	yes
Card not received charges	6 days	24 hrs	3	1	no	yes
Address change	24 hrs	instant	2	none	no	yes
Payment status inquiry	1-3 days	instant	3	none	no	yes
Account cancellation	24 hrs	instant	2	none	no	yes
Application status inquiry	1-2 days	instant	3	none	no	yes
Expired card charges	2 days	instant	2	1	—	—

Nardo were crucial in convincing senior officers of the bank in corporate headquarters and in Asia of the need for drastic change to the IT infrastructure. He has the backing of Citibank's top management and since taking the job, has already brought a different perspective to technology management. He starts from the premise that the IT infrastructure will be standardized to obtain the maximum benefit for the bank. Countries wanting to be different will have to justify it, quite a change from the days when country managers decide the types of technology they want for each country. The IT management team is charging ahead at great speed. When asked for the planned sequence of change activities, DiNardo replied that his approach was "to get all changes bubbling along at the same time . . . get a few good people who know what they are doing."

The RCC experience provides a useful model for the current consumer bank consolidation. The in-depth technical expertise gained from running a regional data center would be directly relevant to the new infrastructure that Citibank is putting in place for consumer banking. Not surprisingly, Ajit now directs and runs the data center for the new Asia-Pacific Consumer Bank technology infrastructure. However, the new infrastructure is more than just scaling up to process more transactions. The business of Citibanking in Global Consumer Banking is more diverse and complex than cards and requires the internalization of many business parameters in developing software to support back-end banking operations. Correspondingly, the business impact is also far greater. Citibank, as an American bank operating in Asia, is subjected to restrictions in the number of branches allowed in each country. The reliance on an electronic interface with customers and for an electronic channel for delivery of banking services is significantly higher than many local banks. Citibank sees the new technological infrastructure as a key enabler for flexibility and integration in its product and service offerings throughout Asia at a competitive cost.

The conversion approach is to first bring the bank's internal processes into conformity with the Systematics process flow. Reengineering principles were applied to streamline and standardize these processes. The Systematics package also has a customer information systems module that will be used by the bank to support its relationship banking strategy. The conversion to a new technology infrastructure at Citibank Asia-Pacific spells some loss of control over computing for the Citibank country managers. Surprisingly, there has not been serious opposition to the changes, although country managers are understandably "nervous" about the sweeping changes. DiNardo offered a few reasons:

> It's an idea whose time has come. The Asia Pacific high profit margin must be maintained! They all know this. They know the value of what we're doing. Computer costs will be down for them, it will affect their bottom line. There is no longer any desire for the sophisticated manager to have his/her own mainframe computer. They know that I have done it 700 times already. No one objects to the logic of the idea. We will insist on a postimplementation audit. The country managers in Asia did see that to survive the next 10 years something like this is necessary. It's all about customer service.

However, it is the level of service and support from the center that country managers are concerned about. The standardization and centralization strategy obviously restricted some flexibility in individual country operations. The strategy was adopted consciously and the gain in integrated customer service and economies of scale is substantial. From experience in other areas of business activities, there is a tendency for most centralized operations to develop a life of their own that over time makes it less responsive to the needs of the end users. Will the Citibank Asia-Pacific data center go the same way eventually? Citibank is putting in place processes to ensure that country needs are not neglected. "Through the conversion and development, we know their needs very well. For example, we will even help them get support from the two other countries needed to justify enhancements," DiNardo explained. The issue of responsiveness to local needs is unlikely to go away despite such assurances. There is also a related concern about how priorities for enhancements will be handled if there are not enough resources and capacity to meet requests in a timely manner.

A number of factors may impede the progress of the plans. First is the risk that the Systematics conversion may surface unexpected technical problems, as Citibank experienced in converting operations in the Philippines. "We are learning as we go," commented one member of the technical staff. The conversion and implementation schedule may need to be stretched and the expected payback delayed. The Asia-Pacific conversion that was originally supposed to be completed by 1997 was pushed to 1998. Part of the reason is the shortage of technical personnel in the region. Further, those who have "cut their teeth" doing the technical implementation are being lured away by other international banks beginning to embark on similar strategies.

Second, the Asian technical staff, although skilled and highly motivated, are, in DiNardo's opinion, conservative. This makes it more difficult to push for the adoption of certain technologies that are perceived to be new in the region. "They tend to be too conservative in planning change—they are not aggressive in their time and payoff targets." DiNardo's experience and confidence have provided the needed leadership to his technical staff in setting the pace and standards for change. The question is whether the pace of change will continue at the same rate after DiNardo retires.

Third, the standardization and consolidation of technologies and systems have created a sophisticated but highly complex operation at Citibank's Asia-Pacific headquarters. For example, the Asia-Pacific data center has to deal with the integration of various operating systems such as MVS, Stratus, and UNIX. DiNardo admitted that "there are very few people able to run such massive data centers in the region." The high level of operational complexity presents challenges in maintaining consistently high availability, reliability, and quick response times.

Characteristically, DiNardo considers these minor problems that will not affect the overall success of the planned change. Although the implementation is still in progress, the plans have been well received by top management at Citicorp, and it is making plans for similar technology regionalization strategies for Europe, the United States, and Latin America. The Asia-Pacific Consumer Bank is setting the pace and direction for Citicorp in its technology strategy. The Citiplus multicurrency time deposits and Systematics product processes have now been adopted as standards for Citicorp worldwide. One important unanticipated gain accruing to Citibank as a result of the massive infrastructural change is that it has finessed its Year 2000 problems in the process. Once the 15 Asia-Pacific countries are converted by 1998, there will be no legacy systems and no Year 2000 problems to worry about, saving Citibank an estimated $60 million. The new architecture has also eliminated the need to find programmers with very rare operating system skills needed by the old systems. The successful implementation of the changes will reduce the cost of IT services and increase the ability of IT to support product innovation and integration. Today, Citibank services primarily the high-networth customers in Asia. IT may enable the bank to also offer its brand of services to the growing middle class.

Source: From Boon Siong Neo and Christina Soh, Information Management Research Center (IMARC), Nanyang Business School, Nanyang Technological University, Singapore. Reprinted by permission.

Case Study Questions

1. What business strategy is Citicorp pursuing in Asia?
2. Evaluate Citibank's Asia-Pacific information systems in light of this strategy. How well do they support it?
3. Evaluate Citibank's strategy for managing its Asia-Pacific information systems infrastructure.

[1]All financial figures are in U.S. $ unless otherwise stated.

[2]"Citicorp Credit Card Chief to Retire," *Business Times*, April 21, 1997.

[3]"Citicorp in Asia: Eastward Look," *The Economist*, October 24, 1992, p. 90.

[4]"Thinking Globally, Acting Locally," *China Business Review*, May–June, 1993, pp. 23–25.

[5]"For Citibank, There's No Place Like Asia," *Business Week*, March 30, 1992, pp. 66–69.

CASE STUDY 5: Heineken Netherlands B.V.: Reengineering IS/IT to Enable Customer-Oriented Supply Chain Management

Donald A. Marchand, Thomas E. Vollmann, and Kimberly A. Bechler,
International Institute for Management Development
(Switzerland)

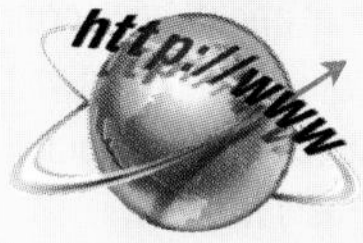

In June 1993, Jan Janssen, financial manager of Heineken Netherlands B.V. and the person responsible for Information Systems (IS) and Information Technology (IT), and his IS manager, Rob Pietersen, faced the challenge of developing an IS/IT configuration that would add value to the business and support the ongoing transformation of Heineken's supply chain management system. This system was extensive, not only supplying the Dutch home market, but also providing a significant part of the supply to more than 100 export countries served by the Heineken Group. Supply chain management was central to enterprise-wide transformation.

Management was committed to a process-driven organization, customer-service partnerships, 24-hour delivery lead time, major innovations in the transport system, and resulting changes in the way people worked. And Janssen knew that all of these—and more—required fundamental changes in the way this new work was to be supported by information systems and technology.

Janssen was convinced that the effective management of information as well as a more appropriate IT infrastructure were critical to achieving Heineken's goals of increased flexibility, greater coordination, and a sharper focus on customer needs.

In his mind, the change program initiated in 1990 in the IS/IT area had just been the beginning. Now, he and Pietersen needed to design an information systems and technology backbone that would be flexible enough to evolve with the changing business needs and adapt to continuous changes in technology.

HEINEKEN NETHERLANDS B.V.

Heineken Netherlands B.V. was the principal operating company responsible for operations in Heineken's home market. It also accounted for a significant part of Heineken N.V.'s worldwide exports. Of the 60.4 million hectoliters[1] of beer produced worldwide under the supervision of the Heineken Group in 1994, a significant portion was produced in the company's two Dutch breweries—Zoeterwoude and 's-Hertogenbosch (Den Bosch). Likewise, 11 percent of the Heineken Group's sales took place in the domestic market, and more than 5400 employees worked for Heineken Netherlands.

Supply Chain Management

The supply chain at Heineken Netherlands began with the receipt of the raw materials that went into the brewing process, and continued through packaging, distribution, and delivery. Brewing took six weeks; it began with the malt mixture of barley and ended with the filtering of the beer after fermentation. Depending on the distribution channel, the beer was then packaged in "one-way" or returnable bottles or cans of different sizes and labels, put in kegs, or delivered in bulk.

The variety of outlets meant that the company had to manage differences in response time (beer for the domestic market was produced to stock, while exported beer was produced to order) and three distinct distribution channels. While each channel consisted mainly of the same steps from the receipt of raw materials through brewing, they differed greatly in packaging and distribution. Beer could be distributed to either on-premise outlets (hotels, restaurants, and cafes, where it was delivered in kegs or poured directly into cellar beer tanks), off-premise outlets (supermarkets, grocery and liquor stores, where it was sold in a variety of bottle and package sizes for home consumption), or to export markets (export deliveries were made to order).

Ongoing Transformation

With key customers requesting faster response times, the development of a process-driven view of Heineken's supply chain activities became critical. The company started the transformation of its supply chain management system by creating customer-service partnerships with its largest domestic customers. The overall objective was to improve the logistics chain dramatically for these customers. In response, delivery lead times were reduced and the transport system was changed. However, the supply chain transformation was seen as a never-ending process.

New Customer-Service Partnerships

In these new service partnerships, Heineken was requested to reduce the time from the placement of the product order to the actual delivery. Before, this delivery lead time had been three days, but the supermarket chains wanted Heineken to supply their warehouses in the Netherlands in 24 hours. Each of the warehouses carried only 8 hours of stock at any time, so the supermarket chains depended on quick and flexible delivery to maintain low inventories and fast response times.

To further enhance its close cooperation with customers, Heineken had embarked on a pilot test of a new logistics improvement called "Comakership" with Albert Heijn, the largest supermarket chain in the Netherlands. Comakership was part of Albert Heijn's Efficient Customer Response project, "Today for Tomorrow." The Albert Heijn retail stores sent their sales information as scanning data to the computer in their central head office. There, the data for Heineken products were scanned out and separated. The beer sales information was then relayed via a standard EDI system (provided by a value-added network operator) from the central office of Albert Heijn directly to Heineken's Zoeterwoude brewery. Heineken was usually able to deliver within 18 hours. Although the pilot had been initiated in only one of Albert Heijn's distribution centers (and the set of stores it served), it had already resulted in lower lead times, decreased costs, and less complexity in the distribution system.

Moving to a 24-Hour Delivery Lead Time

As a result of these successes, top management concluded that delivery lead time could be cut to 24 hours for most domestic customers. However, it would require major shifts in the company's stock levels, distribution centers, work organization, transport system, organizational structure, and information systems.

The 24-hour lead time allowed for greater stock turnover and for lower stock levels in the customer distribution centers. There was, however, more interdepot traffic and higher stocks of packaging material ("returnables") on the brewery premises (which had been located elsewhere along the supply chain). But management believed that as less total inventory was held in the system, these packaging material stocks might be reduced over time.

New Transport System

Until 1991, Heineken Netherlands had contracted out the transportation of its products from the two breweries to about 50 transporters. All of them used a lorry-trailer system with "dedicated" drivers—a driver and his "truck" could make an average of 2.1 deliveries per day. To meet the 24-hour lead time, Heineken had to completely change the fleet used for transport and reduce the number of transporters from 50 to 10. Heineken then contracted 4 cabin trucks from each transporter (40 cabin trucks in total) and paid them for the use of the trailers. The ability of the driver to move from one trailer to another without waiting for unloading meant that he could make an average of 2.4 deliveries per day (a cost reduction of approximately G1.5 million).[2]

New Information Management (IM) Needs

Heineken's customer-service partnership with Albert Heijn and the other changes Heineken had implemented in its supply chain activities brought new information requirements to support the more stringent delivery dictates. With the pilot testing of the Comakership logistics improvement, Heineken needed to implement systems which could manage this new transfer of information, and make appropriate modifications in work activities and organizational structure. Furthermore, the new IS/IT infrastructure needed to be flexible enough to handle and reflect individual retailer and customer beer purchasing patterns.

In the context of these changes in supply chain activities, Janssen reflected on the beginnings of the transformation of IS/IT:

> The transformation of IS/IT and the shifts occurring in our supply chain activities were concurrent without causality. That is very strange, but it just happened that way. I can't say to you that it is a "chicken and egg" kind of story. Of course, there was a link but not an explicit one. Somewhere in our minds, when you do one you do the other, too.

Janssen knew that the relationship between information management, information systems, and information technology had to be clearly defined to have optimum support for the new approaches to value creation. Information management focused on supporting customers and creating new "bundles of goods and services." Information systems focused on developing applications software, managing data, and supporting the new business processes. Finally, information technology related primarily to data and text services, and the underlying operating systems, interfaces, hardware, and networks.

PHASE 1: RECOGNIZING THE NEED FOR CHANGE

In July 1989, at the beginning of all the changes at Heineken, Janssen (then at headquarters and responsible for IS/IT worldwide) received a request for a second mainframe at Heineken Netherlands, costing G6 million (with another G6 million required in three to four years); Janssen brought in the consulting firm Nolan, Norton, Inc. to evaluate the IS/IT infrastructure, first at the corporate level and then at the operating company level for Heineken Netherlands:

> A proposal to purchase a second mainframe focused everybody on our IS/IT infrastructure. You have to have some kind of crisis to get people thinking.

IS/IT Benchmarking

Nolan, Norton, Inc. benchmarked Heineken's IS/IT cost structure against the beverage industry IS/IT average and it was clear that Heineken was indeed not competitive—the company was spending twice the money for half the functionality. "The Nolan, Norton report confirmed what a very wide group of the users thought," Janssen commented. In response, management recommended decentralizing the data center and having each business area manage its own computing resources.

At the same time, Janssen asked Heineken Netherlands, the largest operating company, to develop a new IS/IT plan based on new computer technology, "which meant looking for mid-range platforms, decentralized computing, and standard software packages, rather than developing customized programs for every new application—previously the standard practice." Before determining an appropriate IS/IT plan, Janssen made sure that information management scans were conducted in every functional area. Managers were asked, "What do you need and how can that support our business?" The results were used to create information plans. Working with KPMG Management Consultants and Nolan, Norton, Inc., Janssen developed a list of priorities for IS/IT and selected a new IT platform (IBM AS/400)—both were accepted in July 1990:

> The AS/400 became the core of our new IT platform for two reasons: first, we had been a client with IBM for roughly 40 years, and it was not their fault that we used their mainframes in the wrong way; second, we already knew that huge masses of application software were being written for the AS/400, as a quick scan easily confirmed. Furthermore, we were starting to think about an appropriate IT architecture and we were considering the possibility of using personal computers as peripherals linked together through local area and wide area networks.

Implementation of the New IS/IT Plan

Before the end of 1990, Janssen was appointed financial manager. He became the person responsible for IS/IT at Heineken Netherlands and was to oversee the implementation of the new IS/IT plan. Janssen concluded that outsourcing would play a critical role in this process:

> The decision to outsource was part of the plan. When we came to the conclusion that a major change was necessary, that we should look for mid-range computers, that we should go for standard software, that we should not go for dumb terminals but for personal computers as peripherals, it became clear to us that this was a big operation and we could not evolve to it. We could not manage just to keep the old systems in the air with all the problems and have enough management attention for building up the new systems. So we told the organization, "Gentlemen, we are going to outsourcers, and we are going to freeze the applications to free up management time."

PHASE 2: OUTSOURCING TO DEVELOP THE NEW IS/IT INFRASTRUCTURE

Outsourcing enabled the IS group to keep the "old" mainframe applications running while it developed a new IT approach—focusing on the development of its client/server distributed processing infrastructure, the appropriate new IT architecture, and the IS people and skills to achieve these new objectives.

Outsourcing

In 1991, after scanning the outsourcers' market, Janssen chose Electronic Data Systems (EDS), the largest provider of computer services in the United States. EDS provided the *expertise* and *infrastructure* required to meet Heineken's information systems and technology needs, and *career possibilities* for Heineken's mainframe personnel, both vital to the successful transformation of its IS/IT infrastructure. Finally, the five-year contract (with declining involvement each year) provided "guaranteed continuity" while Heineken maintained control. The plan indicated that the last mainframe program would be replaced in 1996 and the contract with EDS would end.

Development of the New IT Architecture

The development of the new IT architecture took place almost concurrently:

> We moved in two directions—one, to outsource our operational concerns, and two, to focus on our new architecture development, eventually replacing everything which was on the mainframe with standard packages on AS/400s.

With the decision to downsize—to move off the mainframe platform—and to decentralize the information management and systems, Janssen chose a comprehensive client/server strategy using a combination of workstations, local and wide area networks, mid-range systems such as AS/400s, and local area servers to complete the technology architecture. (Refer to Figure 1 for Heineken's IT architecture.) "Personal Computers" became "Heineken workstations" to eliminate the confusion and "mess" of having 2000 "personal" workstations—in this way, every workstation had the same setup. Furthermore, the sales force began using "Notebooks" for customer sensing and information sharing.

Changing Over to Standard Packages and Developing Greater Flexibility to Serve the Business

In 1993, Rob Pietersen became IS manager at Heineken Netherlands. He believed that the decentralized IS/IT operations gave more "computer power to the people," and enabled the "user" to become the process owner. Old mainframe programs were replaced with new standard application packages that covered all the functions in the supply chain. Heineken started this "changeover" by focusing on the software applications dealing with clients: or-

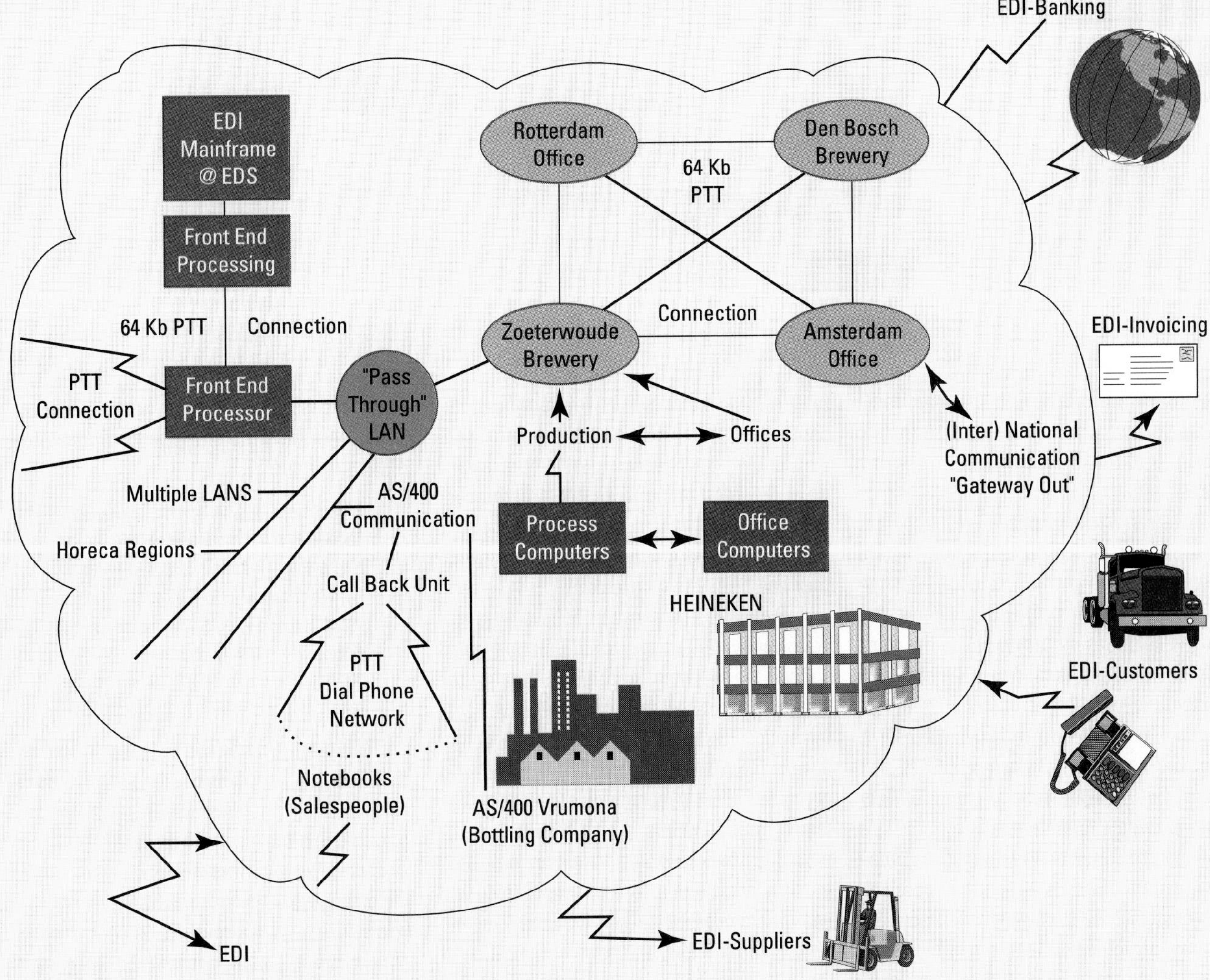

FIGURE 1 Heineken network era WAN/LAN.

der entry, delivery, transport, invoicing, and accounts receivable.

Selecting Standard Software Packages

To increase flexibility and customer responsiveness, Pietersen knew that Heineken had to shift from the "waterfall approach" to the development of standard software packages:

> At that time in the mainframe world, we were developing software applications using a methodology often referred to as the "waterfall." You started with a requirements definition from the users, developed a design and the code to implement that design (getting signoffs at each point along the way). You put the code in production, tested the code, released the code into operation and then you maintained it. When you adopted the code, you went back to the users and asked them if this was what they wanted, and often they said "What?" This waterfall process took 18 to 36 months or more, and by the time it was completed, the users' requirements often had changed.

Pietersen began using the PILS (Project Integral Logistics)—named after the successful approach developed to select appropriate logistics software—to test and select standard software packages (refer to Figure 2). The PILS approach involved:

- identifying appropriate software packages;
- setting the top two package vendors against one another in a "shoot-out"—as in the American "Wild West"—where the specific elements of each software package were compared and contrasted;
- creating a business pilot;
- implementing it;
- evaluating its performance.

For IS people, this meant moving from COBOL programming to developing a thorough knowledge of the business.

Pietersen chose PRISM for the logistics area and JD Edwards for the financial area. Pietersen found that the new systems and policies better fit the information needs of the company:

> We needed more flexibility, more power, and less cost. Our current systems have scored high in each of those areas. Computer power is now where it belongs: not with the IT people, but in the hands of the people who need it.

IS Group Reconfiguration

Outsourcing the mainframe and mainframe applications to EDS led to a change in the configuration of the IS group as well. Contracts with employees from software houses were stopped, and many of the individuals working

FIGURE 2

Project Integral Logistics (PILS) stages. *Heineken Netherlands (Courtesy of Marcam/PRISM).*

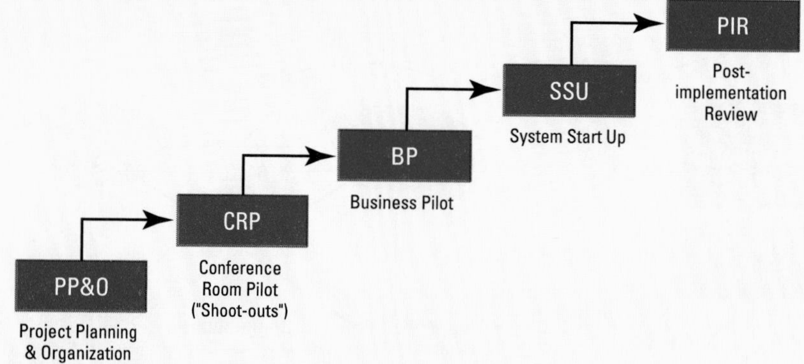

on the mainframe went with the mainframe systems to EDS while other staff shifted to other areas of the IS group, such as systems management.

Pietersen was convinced that the competencies and capabilities of the IS group had to be expanded to align the use of IT with the evolving supply chain, rather than simply promoting IT solutions as "answers" to the company's information management "problems." Pietersen understood that this change in approach for the IS group required not only a deeper knowledge of business processes and strategy, but also an understanding of how people used the information.

Pietersen therefore transformed the IS department from units for application development, customer support, and operations (a functional structure) to teams servicing production, commercial, distribution, and customer-service areas—the "process owners" (a team-oriented business approach). (Refer to Figures 3 and 4 for the IS organization before and after 1993.) The information management needs of the business areas were thus defined by people from both the business areas and IS. These *account teams* helped select standard application packages and, afterwards, adapt the business process to the software package *or* adapt the software package to the business process. These teams thus developed and implemented systems that gave the required support for the respective business processes and delivered information to enable a better control of the supply chain. Shrinking from 130 to 40 people, the IS group was now "doing what they had been doing differently."

Pietersen and Janssen believed that increasing overall access to information would support management's efforts to enhance the employees' empowerment. Client/server systems also fostered teamwork and horizontal decision making. They were fast, flexible, and permitted greater communication with customers and suppliers, which resulted in improved customer service. And they promoted the development of a "process view" (focusing on total processes rather than on discrete tasks). Furthermore, the new configuration of the IS group, with its more team-oriented business approach, also promoted a spirit of greater cooperation and communication. Pietersen commented, "If we still had the mainframe, all this would not be possible."

Evaluating IS Performance

In 1995, Pietersen and Janssen were still trying to determine how to measure the performance of the IS/IT department. They agreed that IS/IT needed to serve the business, and different service level agreements were to be negotiated with the different functional areas (as shown in Figure 5):

> What is our business? Is it information technology? No, our business is brewing and selling premium beer of high quality. We changed our IT policy to make it clear that IT *supports* the business, but doesn't *drive* the business. We started to focus on having a beautiful bottom line rather than beautiful IT applications.

Currently, IS performance was based on the timely and successful completion of projects. The most important *measure* was the improvement of the business process for which a system or service was meant. In the future, Pietersen and Janssen would be trying to develop criteria to measure the impact of an IS project on improving *overall business performance.*

PHASE 3: LEVERAGING INFORMATION ASSETS IN THE BUSINESS

Executive Information Systems (EIS)

By 1995, Heineken's operational supply chain system—from supplier to end customer—was in its final phase, and the company had begun to add the decision-support element. Decision-support or executive information sys-

FIGURE 3

IS organization before 1993. *Heineken Netherlands.*

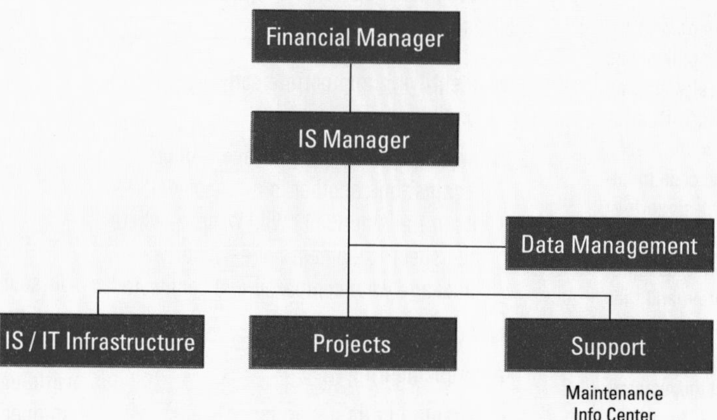

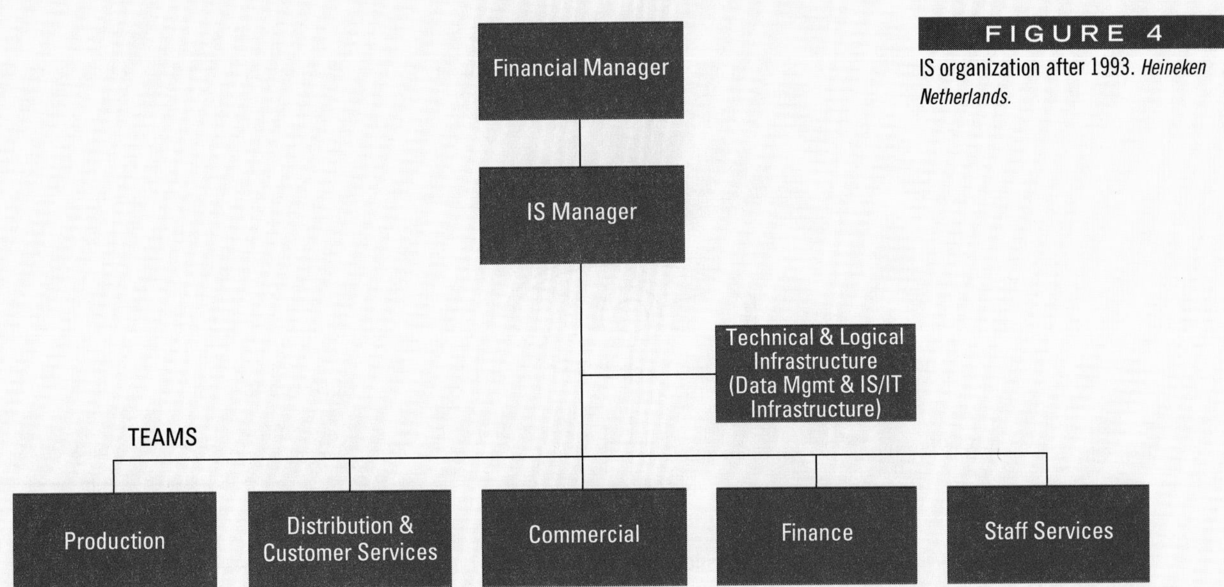

FIGURE 4

IS organization after 1993. *Heineken Netherlands.*

tems would make it possible for managers to express their information requirements directly. Pietersen hoped that their ease of use would encourage managers to analyze past performance in greater depth and enable them to simulate the possible consequences of proposed actions more accurately. When it came to selecting the appropriate software, Pietersen had chosen EIS Express:

> I call it the technical infrastructure; the basic logical infrastructure of all these systems is in place, and now we come to enabling real improvement, not just the EDI links we have with our retailers, but also such things as installing executive information systems (EIS) to give our management team the control instruments they need to navigate us through the more turbulent business environments we will face in the coming years. The executive information systems gather their data from the data warehouses of the different business systems in all areas and can show this easily through different (graphical) viewpoints.

One of Janssen and Pietersen's goals for the use of executive information systems was to have unity in the data. Janssen explained:

> Having unity in our data is crucial. Only a few years ago we discovered some departments were using different unit volumes than we were. And that just should not happen in any organization.

Better Planning Tools

A key part of the IS/IT strategy was to develop an integrated set of systems to plan and control

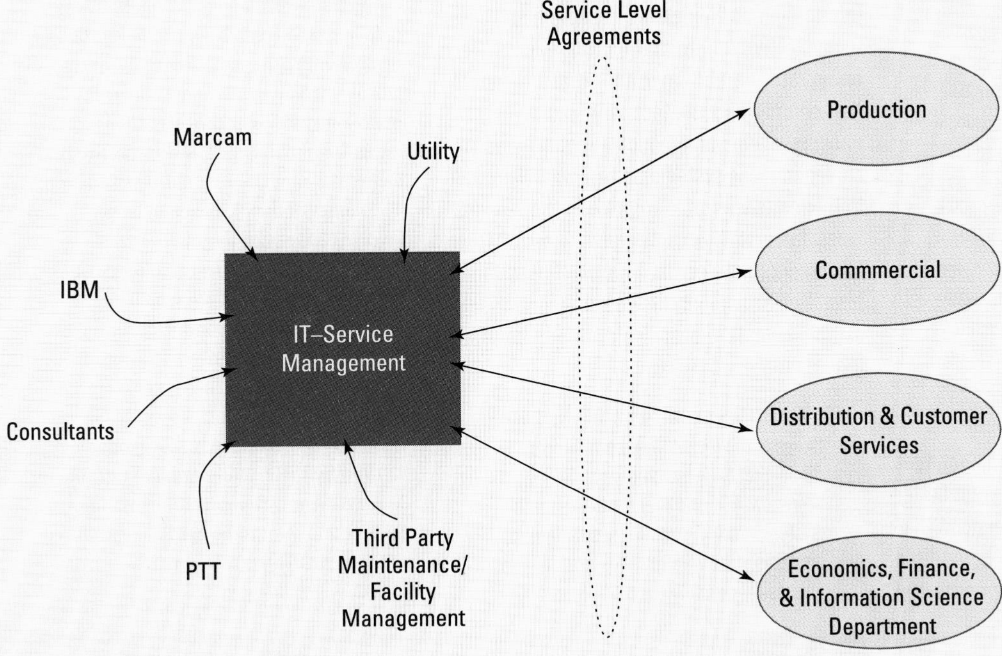

FIGURE 5

(Courtesy of Pink Elephant).

What is service management? "To assemble and offer." *Heineken Netherlands*

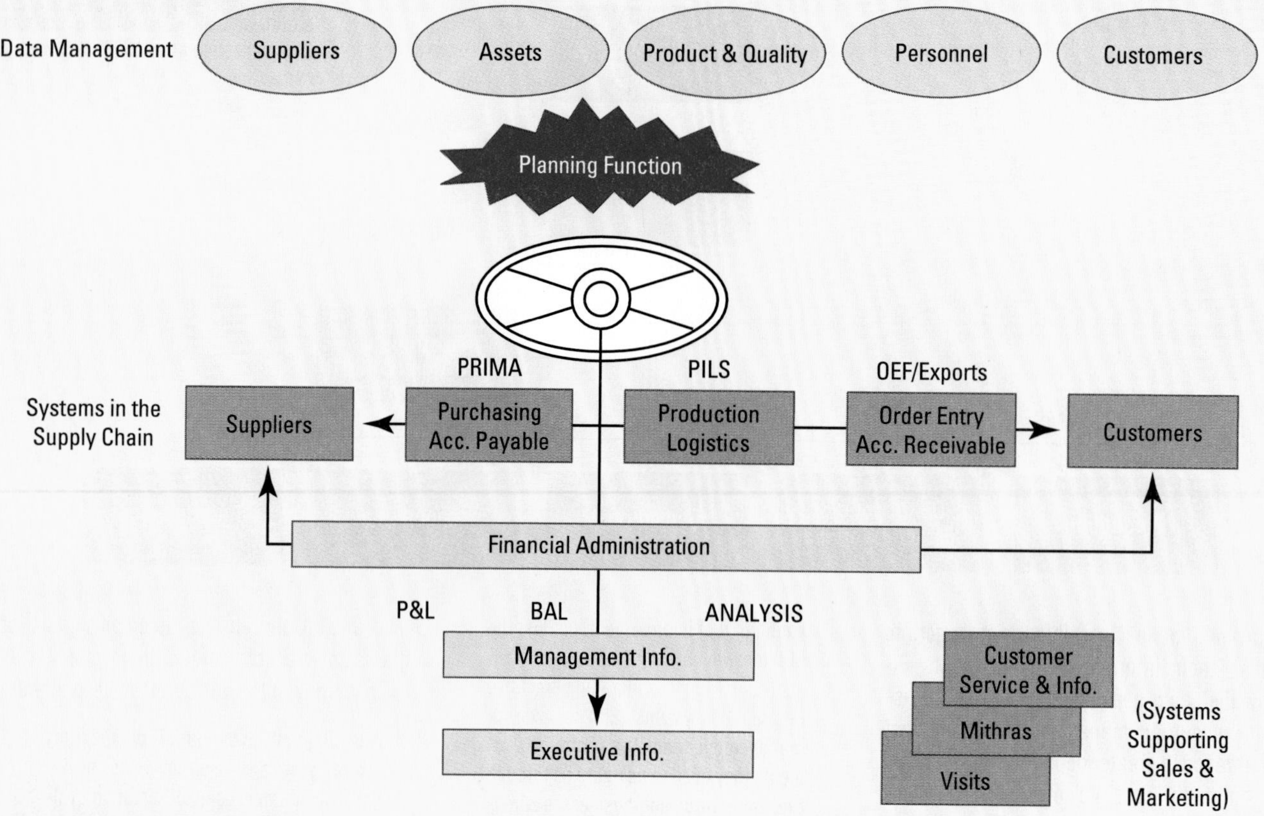

FIGURE 6 Information systems. *Heineken Netherlands.*

the overall supply chain, both in the short run (bottle-line scheduling and daily operations) and over a longer horizon (sales forecasts and long-term operations research). The aim was faster and more flexible control of supply chain activities. Jan Janssen elaborated:

> What we are working toward is a coherent and consistent set of planning and scheduling tools which are more or less compatible and interconnectible so that you can build up or build down the basic data. Our goal is to be able to model business processes and to have the data, like sales forecasts, to support our decisions about capacity, bottling lines, and stocks. We want to be in a position where, if you have to make a decision, you can run simulations based on actual data.

The concept of supply chain management ultimately served as the driver for better planning tools. Management understood that an overall planning function with multiple time horizons was essential to optimize the supply chain activities as well as to ensure better information management. (Refer to Figure 6 for Heineken's information systems.)

Janssen and Pietersen had put in place information systems to collect and integrate information on Heineken's "on-premise" customer activity. Information on each hotel, restaurant, and cafe/pub that Heineken Netherlands had contact with (as owner, financing agent, or product supplier) was included in these systems. In this way, Heineken Netherlands was able to provide the relevant sales force with an integrated view of their customers (large or small) as well as with information on competitors catering to the same establishments, beer sold, and contract terms. Janssen elaborated:

> We are thinking about what the "next stage of the rocket" will be. We have defined the baseline and are looking at workflow, EDI and planning information systems—how should these planning systems interrelate? We are in the process of defining the next phase of the vision for Heineken as a business in the Netherlands and for the IS/IT fit to that. The current debate is just how far to go.

This case is a condensed version of Heineken Netherlands B.V. A&B. It was prepared by Research Associate Kimberly A. Bechler under the supervision of Professors Donald A. Marchand and Thomas E. Vollmann, as a basis for class discussion rather than to illustrate either effective or ineffective handling of a business situation. The names of the Heineken managers involved have been disguised. It was developed within the research scope of Manufacturing 2000, a research and development project conducted with global manufacturing enterprises. The authors wish to acknowledge the generous assistance of Heineken management, especially IS manager Gert Bolderman.

Case Study Questions

1. Analyze Heineken Netherlands using the value chain and competitive forces models. Why did the company feel it needed to transform its supply chain?
2. Analyze all the elements of the new IT infrastructure that Heineken selected for its new business processes. Were Heineken's technology choices appropriate? Why or why not?
3. What management, organization, and technology issues had to be addressed when Heineken Netherlands reengineered its supply chain?

[1]Hectolitre = 22 Imperial gallons = 26.418 U.S. gallons; *Heineken 1994 Annual Report.*

[2]1000 Guilders (G) = approximately £368 = U.S.$575 (at December 31, 1994); *Heineken 1994 Annual Report.*

BUSINESS PROCESS REDESIGN PROJECT

Healthlite Yogurt Company

Healthlite Yogurt Company is a market leader in the expanding U.S. market for yogurt and related health products. Healthlite is experiencing some sharp growing pains. With the growing interest in low-fat, low-cholesterol health foods, spurred on by the aging of the baby boomers, Healthlite's sales have tripled over the past five years. At the same time, however, new local competitors, offering fast delivery from local production centers and lower prices, are challenging Healthlite for retail shelf space with a bevy of new products. Without shelf space, products cannot be retailed in the United States, and new products are needed to expand shelf space. Healthlite needs to justify its share of shelf space to grocers and is seeking additional shelf space for its new yogurt-based products such as frozen desserts and low-fat salad dressings.

Healthlite's biggest challenge, however, has not been competitors but the sweep of the second hand. Yogurt has a very short shelf life. With a shelf life measured in days, yogurt must be moved very quickly.

Healthlite maintains its U.S. corporate headquarters in Danbury, Connecticut. Corporate headquarters has a central mainframe computer that maintains most of the major business databases. All production takes place in processing plants that are located in New Jersey, Massachusetts, Tennessee, Illinois, Colorado, Washington, and California. Each processing plant has its own minicomputer, which is connected to the corporate mainframe. Customer credit verification is maintained at corporate headquarters, where customer master files are maintained and order verification or rejection is determined. Once processed centrally, order data are then fed to the appropriate local processing plant minicomputer.

Healthlite has 20 sales regions, each with approximately 30 sales representatives and a regional sales manager. Healthlite has a 12-person marketing group at corporate headquarters and a corporate director of sales and marketing. Each salesperson is able to store and retrieve data for assigned customer accounts using a terminal in the regional office linked to the corporate mainframe. Reports for individual salespeople (printouts of orders, rejection notices, customer account inquiries, etc.) and for sales offices are printed in the regional offices and mailed to them.

Sometimes, the only way to obtain up-to-date sales data is for managers to make telephone calls to subordinates and then piece the information together. Data about sales and advertising expenses and customer shelf space devoted to Healthlite products are maintained manually at the regional offices. Each regional office maintains its own manual records of customer shelf space and promotional campaigns. The central computer contains only consolidated, company-wide files for customer account data and order and billing data. The aging mainframe runs programs built back in the early 1980s.

The existing order processing system requires sales representatives to write up hard-copy tickets to place orders through the mail or by FAX. Each ticket lists the amount and kind of product ordered by the customer account. Approximately one hundred workers at Healthlite corporate headquarters open, sort, keypunch, and process 500,000 order tickets per week. Frequently orders are delayed when the FAX machines break down. This order information is transmitted every evening from the mainframe to a minicomputer at each of Healthlite's processing sites. This daily order specifies the total yogurt and yogurt product demand for each processing center. The processing center then produces the amount and type of yogurt and yogurt-related products ordered and then ships the orders out. Shipping managers at the processing centers assign the shipments to various transportation carriers, who deliver the product to receiving warehouses located in the regions.

Rapid growth, fueled by Healthlite's "health" image and its branching into new yogurt-based products, has put pressures on Healthlite's existing information systems. By mid-1998, growth in new products and sales had reached a point where Healthlite was printing new tickets for the sales force every week. The firm was choking on paper. For each order, a salesperson filled out at least two forms per account. Some sales representatives have more than 80 customers.

As it became bogged down in paper, Healthlite saw increased delays in the processing of its orders. Since yogurt is a fresh food product, it could not be held long in inventory. Yet Healthlite had trouble shipping the right goods to the right places in time. It was taking between four and fourteen days to process and ship out an order, depending on mail delivery rates. Healthlite also found accounting discrepancies of $1.5 million annually between the sales force and headquarters.

Communication between sales managers and sales representatives has been primarily through the mail or by telephone. For example, regional sales managers have to send representatives letters with announcements of promotional campaigns or pricing discounts. Sales representatives have to write up their monthly reports of sales calls and then mail this information to regional headquarters.

Healthlite is considering new information system solutions. First of all, the firm would like to solve the current order entry crisis and develop immediately a new order processing system. Management would also like to make better use of information systems to support sales and marketing activities and to take advantage of new Web-based information technologies. In particular, management wants a sales-oriented Web site to help market the products but is unsure how this will fit into the sales effort. Management wants to know how these new technologies can assist the local groceries and large chains who sell the product to the actual consumer.

Senior management is prepared to make a considerable investment in a plan for rescuing the company's systems and business operations. However, management is looking for a modest reduction in sales force head count as new, more effective systems come on line and to help pay for the systems investment. While senior management wants the company to deploy contemporary systems, they do not want to experiment with new technologies and are only comfortable using technology that has proven itself in real-world applications.

Sales and Marketing Information Systems: Background

Sales and marketing are vital to the operation of any business. Orders must be processed and related to production and inventory. Sales of products in existing markets must be monitored and new products developed for new markets. The firm must be able to respond to rapidly changing market demands, proliferation of new products and competing firms, shortened product life spans, changing consumer tastes, and new government regulations.

Firms need sales and marketing information in order to do product planning, make pricing decisions, devise advertising and other promotional campaigns, forecast market potential for new and existing products, and determine channels of distribution. They must also monitor the efficiency of the distribution of their products and services.

The sales function of a typical business captures and processes customer orders and produces invoices for customers and data for inventory and production. A typical invoice is illustrated here.

Healthlite Yogurt, Inc.

Customer:

Highview Supermarket

223 Highland Avenue

Ossining, New York 10562

Order Number:	679940
Customer Number:	#00395
Date:	04/15/98

Quantity	SKU#	*Description*	*Unit Price*	*Amount*
100	V3392	8 oz Vanilla	.44	44.00
50	S4456	8 oz Strawberry	.44	22.00
65	L4492	8 oz Lemon	.44	28.60
Shipping:				10.00
Total Invoice:				104.60

Data from order entry are also used by a firm's accounts receivable system and by the firm's inventory and production systems. The production planning system, for instance, builds its daily production plans based on the prior day's sales. The number and type of product sold will determine how many units to produce and when.

Sales managers need information to plan and monitor the performance of the sales force. Management also needs information on the performance of specific products, product lines, or brands. Price, revenue, cost, and growth information can be used for pricing decisions, for evaluating the performance of current products, and for predicting the performance of future products.

From basic sales and invoice data, a firm can produce a variety of reports with valuable information to guide sales and marketing work. For weekly, monthly, or annual time periods, information can be gathered on which outlets order the most, on what the average order amount is, on which products move slowest and fastest, on which salespersons sell the most and least, on which geographic areas purchase the most of a given product, and on how current sales of a product compare to last year's product.

The Assignment

Either alone, or with a group of three or four of your classmates, develop a proposal for redesigning Healthlite's business processes for sales, marketing, and order processing that would make the company more competitive. Your report should include the following:

- An overview of the organization—its structure, products, and major business processes for sales, marketing, and order processing.
- An analysis of Healthlite's problems: What are Healthlite's problems? How are these problems related to existing business processes and systems? What management, organization, and technology factors contributed to these problems?
- An overall management plan for improving Healthlite's business and system situation. This would include a list of objectives, a time-frame, major milestones, and an assessment of the costs and benefits of implementing this plan.

- Identification of the major changes in business processes required to achieve your plan.
- Identification of the major new technology components of your plan that are required to support the new business processes. If your solution requires a new system or set of systems, describe the functions of these systems, what pieces of information these systems should contain, and how this information should be captured, organized, and stored.
- A sample data entry screen or report for one of the new systems, if proposed.
- A description of the steps you would take as a manager to handle the conversion from the old system to the new.
- Quality assurance measures.

Your report should also describe the organizational impact of your solution. Consider human interface issues, the impact on jobs and interest groups, and any risks associated with implementing your solution. How will you implement your solution to take these issues into account?

It is important to establish the scope of the system. It should be limited to order processing and related sales and marketing activities. You do not have to redesign Healthlite's manufacturing, accounts receivable, distribution, or inventory control systems for this exercise.

References

CHAPTER 1

Ackoff, R. L. "Management Misinformation System." *Management Science* 14, no. 4 (December 1967), B140–B116.

Alavi, Maryam, and **Patricia Carlson.** "A Review of MIS Research and Disciplinary Development." *Journal of Management Information Systems* 8, no. 4 (Spring 1992).

Allen, Brandt R., and **Andrew C. Boynton.** "Information Architecture: In Search of Efficient Flexibility." *MIS Quarterly* 15, no. 4 (December 1991).

Anthony, R. N. *Planning and Control Systems: A Framework for Analysis.* Cambridge, MA: Harvard University Press (1965).

Applegate, Lynda, and **Janice Gogan.** "Electronic Commerce: Trends and Opportunities." Harvard Business School, 9-196-006 (October 6, 1995).

Applegate, Lynda M., Clyde W. Holsapple, Ravi Kalakota, Franz J. Radermacher, and **Andrew B. Whinston.** "Electronic Commerce: Building Blocks of New Business Opportunity." *Journal of Organizational Computing and Electronic Commerce* 6, no. 1 (1996).

Armstrong, Arthur, and **John Hagel, III.** "The Real Value of On-line Communities." *Harvard Business Review* (May–June 1996).

Bakos, J. Yannis. "A Strategic Analysis of Electronic Marketplaces." *MIS Quarterly* 15, no. 3 (September 1991).

Barrett, Stephanie S. "Strategic Alternatives and Interorganizational System Implementations: An Overview." *Journal of Management Information Systems* (Winter 1986–1987).

Benjamin, Robert, and **Rolf Wigand.** "Electronic Markets and Virtual Value Chains on the Information Superhighway." *Sloan Management Review* (Winter 1995).

Brown, Carol V., and **Sharon L. Magill.** "Alignment of the IS Functions with the Enterprise: Toward a Model of Antecedents." *MIS Quarterly* 18, no. 4 (December 1994).

Brynjolfsson, E. T., T. W. Malone, V. Gurbaxani, and **A. Kambil.** "Does Information Technology Lead to Smaller Firms?" *Management Science* 40, no. 12 (1994).

Cash, James I., F. Warren McFarlan, James L. McKenney, and **Lynda M. Applegate.** *Corporate Information Systems Management,* 4th ed. Homewood, IL: Irwin (1996).

Clark, Thomas D., Jr. "Corporate Systems Management: An Overview and Research Perspective." *Communications of the ACM* 35, no. 2 (February 1992).

Davis, Gordon B., and **Margrethe H. Olson.** *Management Information Systems: Conceptual Foundations, Structure, and Development,* 2nd ed. New York: McGraw-Hill (1985).

Deans, Candace P., and **Michael J. Kane.** *International Dimensions of Information Systems and Technology.* Boston, MA: PWS-Kent (1992).

Fedorowicz, Jane, and **Benn Konsynski.** "Organization Support Systems: Bridging Business and Decision Processes." *Journal of Management Information Systems 8,* no. 4 (Spring 1992).

Feeny, David E., and **Leslie P. Willcocks.** "Core IS Capabilities for Exploiting Information Technology." *Sloan Management Review* 39, no. 3 (Spring 1998).

Feitzinger, Edward, and **Hau L. Lee.** "Mass Customization at Hewlett-Packard: The Power of Postponement." *Harvard Business Review* (January–February 1997).

Garud, Raghu, and **Henry C. Lucas, Jr.** "Welcome to the Virtual Organization." *Stern Business* (Summer 1998).

Gilmore, James H., and **B. Joseph Pine, II.** "The Four Faces of Mass Customization." *Harvard Business Review* (January–February 1997).

Gorry, G. A., and **M. S. Scott Morton.** "A Framework for Management Information Systems." *Sloan Management Review* 13, no. 1 (1971).

Hardwick, Martin, and **Richard Bolton.** "The Industrial Virtual Enterprise." *Communications of the ACM* 40, no. 9 (September 1997).

Johnston, Russell, and **Michael J. Vitale.** "Creating Competitive Advantage with Interorganizational Information Systems." *MIS Quarterly* 12, no. 2 (June 1988).

Keen, Peter G. W. *Shaping the Future: Business Design Through Information Technology.* Cambridge, MA: Harvard Business School Press (1991).

King, John. "Centralized vs. Decentralized Computing: Organizational Considerations and Management Options." *Computing Surveys* (October 1984).

Kling, Rob, and **William H. Dutton.** "The Computer Package: Dynamic Complexity." In *Computers and Politics,* edited by James Danziger, William H. Dutton, Rob Kling, and Kenneth Kraemer. New York: Columbia University Press (1982).

Laudon, Kenneth C. "A General Model for Understanding the Relationship Between Information Technology and Organizations." Working paper, Center for Research on Information Systems, New York University (1989).

Leonard-Barton, Dorothy. *Wellsprings of Knowledge.* Boston, MA: Harvard Business School Press (1995).

Liker, Jeffrey K., David B. Roitman, and **Ethel Roskies.** "Changing Everything All at Once: Work Life and Technological Change." *Sloan Management Review* (Summer 1987).

Lucas, Henry C., Jr., and **Jack Baroudi.** "The Role of Information Technology in Organization Design." *Journal of Management Information Systems* 10, no. 4 (Spring 1994).

Malone, T. W., and **J. F. Rockart.** "Computers, Networks and the Corporation." *Scientific American* 265, no. 3 (September 1991).

Malone, Thomas W., JoAnne Yates, and **Robert I. Benjamin.** "Electronic Markets and Electronic Hierarchies." *Communications of the ACM* (June 1987).

———. "The Logic of Electronic Markets." *Harvard Business Review* (May–June 1989).

McFarlan, F. Warren, James L. McKenney, and **Philip Pyburn.** "The Information Archipelago—Plotting a Course." *Harvard Business Review* (January–February 1983).

———. "Governing the New World." *Harvard Business Review* (July–August 1983).

McKenney, James L., and **F. Warren McFarlan.** "The Information Archipelago—Maps and Bridges." *Harvard Business Review* (September–October 1982).

Niederman, Fred, James C. Brancheau, and **James C. Wetherbe.** "Information Systems Management Issues for the 1990s." *MIS Quarterly* 15, no. 4 (December 1991).
Orlikowski, Wanda J., and **Jack J. Baroudi.** "Studying Information Technology in Organizations: Research Approaches and Assumptions." *Information Systems Research* 2, no. 1 (March 1991).
Rayport, J. F., and **J. J. Sviokla.** "Managing in the Marketspace." *Harvard Business Review* (November–December 1994).
Roach, Stephen S. "Technology and the Services Sector: The Hidden Competitive Challenge." *Technological Forecasting and Social Change* 34 (1988).
———. "Services Under Siege—The Restructuring Imperative." *Harvard Business Review* (September–October 1991).
Roche, Edward M. "Planning for Competitive Use of Information Technology in Multinational Corporations." AIB UK Region, Brighton Polytechnic, Brighton, UK, Conference Paper (March 1992). Edward M. Roche, W. Paul Stillman School of Business, Seton Hall University.
Rockart, John F. "The Line Takes the Leadership—IS Management in a Wired Society." *Sloan Management Review* 29, no. 4 (Summer 1988).
Rockart, John F., and **James E. Short.** "IT in the 1990s: Managing Organizational Interdependence." *Sloan Management Review* 30, no. 2 (Winter 1989).
Scott Morton, Michael, ed. *The Corporation in the 1990s.* New York: Oxford University Press (1991).
Strassman, Paul. *The Information Payoff—The Transformation of Work in the Electronic Age.* New York: Free Press (1985).
Tornatsky, Louis G., J. D. Eveland, Myles G. Boylan, W. A. Hertzner, E. C. Johnson, D. Roitman, and **J. Schneider.** "The Process of Technological Innovation: Reviewing the Literature." Washington, DC: National Science Foundation (1983).
Upton, David M., and **Andrew McAfee.** "The Real Virtual Factory." *Harvard Business Review* (July–August 1996).
Warson, Albert. "Tool Time." *Forbes ASAP* (October 7, 1996.)
Weill, Peter, and **Marianne Broadbent.** *Leveraging the New Infrastructure.* Cambridge, MA: Harvard Business School Press (1998).
———. "Management by Maxim: How Business and IT Managers Can Create IT Infrastructures," *Sloan Management Review* (Spring 1997).
Winter, Susan J., and **S. Lynne Taylor.** "The Role of IT in the Transformation of Work: A Comparison of Post-Industrial, Industrial, and Proto-Industrial Organization." *Information Systems Research* 7, no. 1 (March 1996).

CHAPTER 2

Allen, Brandt R., and **Andrew C. Boynton.** "Information Architecture: In Search of Efficient Flexibility." *MIS Quarterly* 15, no. 4 (December 1991).
Anthony, R. N. *Planning and Control Systems: A Framework for Analysis.* Cambridge, MA: Harvard University Press (1965).
Bakos, J. Yannis, and **Michael E. Treacy.** "Information Technology and Corporate Strategy: A Research Perspective." *MIS Quarterly* (June 1986).
Barua, Anitesh, Charles H. Kriebel, and **Tridas Mukhopadhyay.** "An Economic Analysis of Strategic Information Technology Investments." *MIS Quarterly* 15, no. 5 (September 1991).
Beath, Cynthia Mathis, and **Blake Ives.** "Competitive Information Systems in Support of Pricing." *MIS Quarterly* (March 1986).
Berry, Leonard L., and **A. Parasuraman.** "Listening to the Customer—the Concept of a Service-Quality Information System." *Sloan Management Review* (Spring 1997).
Bower, Joseph L., and **Thomas M. Hout.** "Fast-Cycle Capability for Competitive Power." *Harvard Business Review* (November–December 1988).
Caldwell, Bruce. "A Cure for Hospital Woes." *InformationWeek* (September 9, 1991).
Cash, J. I., and **Benn R. Konsynski.** "IS Redraws Competitive Boundaries." *Harvard Business Review* (March–April 1985).
Cash, J. I., and **P. L. McLeod.** "Introducing IS Technology in Strategically Dependent Companies." *Journal of Management Information Systems* (Spring 1985).
Chan, Yolande E., Sid L. Huff, Donald W. Barclay, and **Duncan G. Copeland.** "Business Strategic Orientation, Information Systems Strategic Orientation, and Strategic Alignment." *Information Systems Research* 8, no. 2 (June 1997).
Clemons, Eric K. "Evaluation of Strategic Investments in Information Technology." *Communications of the ACM* (January 1991).
Clemons, Eric K., and **Michael Row.** "McKesson Drug Co.: Case Study of a Strategic Information System." *Journal of Management Information Systems* (Summer 1988).
———. "Sustaining IT Advantage: The Role of Structural Differences." *MIS Quarterly* 15, no. 3 (September 1991).
———. "Limits to Interfirm Coordination through IT." *Journal of Management Information Systems* 10, no. 1 (Summer 1993).
Clemons, Eric K., and **Bruce W. Weber.** "Segmentation, Differentiation, and Flexible Pricing: Experience with Information Technology and Segment-Tailored Strategies." *Journal of Management Information Systems* 11, no. 2 (Fall 1994).
Copeland, Duncan G., and **James L. McKenney.** "Airline Reservations Systems: Lessons from History." *MIS Quarterly* 12, no. 3 (September 1988).
Culnan, Mary J. "Transaction Processing Applications as Organizational Message Systems: Implications for the Intelligent Organization." Working paper no. 88-10, Twenty-second Hawaii International Conference on Systems Sciences (January 1989).
Dhar, Vasant, and **Roger Stein.** *Intelligent Decision Support Methods.* Upper Saddle River, NJ: Prentice Hall (1997).
Eardley, Alan, David Avison, and **Philip Powell.** "Developing Information Systems to Support Flexible Strategy." *Journal of Organizational Computing and Electronic Commerce* 7, no. 1 (1997).
Evans, Philip P., and **Thomas S. Wurster.** "Strategy and the New Economics of Information." *Harvard Business Review* (September–October 1997).
Fabris, Peter. "Going South." *Webmaster* (April 1997).
Feeny, David E., and **Blake Ives.** "In Search of Sustainability: Reaping Long-Term Advantage from Investments in Information Technology." *Journal of Management Information Systems* (Summer 1990).
Fisher, Marshall L. "What Is the Right Supply Chain for Your Product?" *Harvard Business Review* (March–April 1997).

Henderson, John C., and **John J. Sifonis.** "The Value of Strategic IS Planning: Understanding Consistency, Validity, and IS Markets." *MIS Quarterly* 12, no. 2 (June 1988).

Hopper, Max. "Rattling SABRE—New Ways to Compete on Information." *Harvard Business Review* (May–June 1990).

Houdeshel, George, and **Hugh J. Watson.** "The Management Information and Decision Support (MIDS) System at Lockheed Georgia." *MIS Quarterly* 11, no. 1 (March 1987).

Huber, George P. "Organizational Information Systems: Determinants of Their Performance and Behavior." *Management Science* 28, no. 2 (1984).

Ives, Blake, and **Gerald P. Learmonth.** "The Information System as a Competitive Weapon." *Communications of the ACM* (December 1984).

Ives, Blake, and **Michael R. Vitale.** "After the Sale: Leveraging Maintenance with Information Technology." *MIS Quarterly* (March 1986).

Johnston, H. Russell, and **Shelley R. Carrico.** "Developing Capabilities to Use Information Strategically." *MIS Quarterly* 12, no. 1 (March 1988).

Johnston, Russell, and **Paul R. Lawrence.** "Beyond Vertical Integration—The Rise of the Value-Adding Partnership." *Harvard Business Review* (July–August 1988).

Johnston, Russell, and **Michael R. Vitale.** "Creating Competitive Advantage with Interorganizational Information Systems." *MIS Quarterly* 12, no. 2 (June 1988).

Kambil, Ajit, and **James E. Short.** "Electronic Integration and Business Network Redesign: A Roles-Linkage Perspective." *Journal of Management Information Systems* 10, no. 4 (Spring 1994).

Keen, Peter G. W. *Competing in Time: Using Telecommunications for Competitive Advantage.* Cambridge, MA: Ballinger Publishing Company (1986).

———. *Shaping the Future: Business Design Through Information Technology.* Cambridge, MA: Harvard Business School Press (1991).

Keen, Peter G. W., and **M. S. Morton.** *Decision Support Systems: An Organizational Perspective.* Reading, MA: Addison-Wesley (1978).

Kettinger, William J., Varun Grover, Subashish Guhan, and **Albert H. Segors.** "Strategic Information Systems Revisited: A Study in Sustainability and Performance." *MIS Quarterly* 18, no. 1 (March 1994).

King, John. "Centralized vs. Decentralized Computing: Organizational Considerations and Management Options." *Computing Surveys* (October 1984).

"Komag Chooses MES for Production Control." *Datamation* (September 15, 1994).

Konsynski, Benn R., and **F. Warren McFarlan.** "Information Partnerships—Shared Data, Shared Scale." *Harvard Business Review* (September–October 1990).

Korzeniowski, Paul. "Boosting Bandwidth." *Beyond Computing* (September 1997).

LaPlante, Alice. "For IS, Quality is Job None." *Computerworld* (January 6, 1992).

Lasher, Donald R., Blake Ives, and **Sirkka L. Jarvenpaa.** "USAA–IBM Partnerships in Information Technology: Managing the Image Project." *MIS Quarterly* 15, no. 4 (December 1991).

Lederer, Albert L., Dinesh A. Mirchandani, and **Kenneth Sims.** "The Link Between Information Strategy and Electronic Commerce." *Journal of Organizational Computing and Electronic Commerce* 7, no. 1 (1997).

Levy, David. "Lean Production in an International Supply Chain." *Sloan Management Review* (Winter 1997).

McFarlan, F. Warren. "Information Technology Changes the Way You Compete." *Harvard Business Review* (May–June 1984).

Main, Thomas J., and **James E. Short.** "Managing the Merger: Building Partnership Through IT Planning at the New Baxter." *MIS Quarterly* 13, no. 4 (December 1989).

Mata, Franciso J., William L. Fuerst, and **Jay B. Barney.** "Information Technology and Sustained Competitive Advantage: A Resource-Based Analysis." *MIS Quarterly* 19, no. 4 (December 1995).

Olian, Judy D., and **Sara L. Rynes.** "Making Total Quality Work: Aligning Organizational Processes, Performance Measures, and Stakeholders." *Human Resource Management* 30, no. 3 (Fall 1991).

Porter, Michael. *Competitive Strategy.* New York: Free Press (1980).

———. *Competitive Advantage.* New York: Free Press (1985).

———. "How Information Can Help You Compete." *Harvard Business Review* (August–September 1985a).

Rackoff, Nick, Charles Wiseman, and **Walter A. Ullrich.** "Information Systems for Competitive Advantage: Implementation of a Planning Process." *MIS Quarterly* (December 1985).

Rekello, Joseph. "State Street Boston's Allure for Investors Starts to Fade" *The Wall Street Journal* (January 4, 1995).

Rockart, John F., and **Michael E. Treacy.** "The CEO Goes On-line." *Harvard Business Review* (January–February 1982).

Short, James E., and **N. Venkatraman.** "Beyond Business Process Redesign: Redefining Baxter's Business Network." *Sloan Management Review* (Fall 1992).

Sprague, Ralph H., Jr., and **Eric D. Carlson.** *Building Effective Decision Support Systems.* Englewood Cliffs, NJ: Prentice Hall (1982).

"USAA Insuring Progress." *InformationWeek* (May 25, 1992).

Vitale, Michael R. "The Growing Risks of Information System Success." *MIS Quarterly* (December 1986).

Wiseman, Charles. *Strategic Information Systems.* Homewood, IL: Richard D. Irwin (1988).

CHAPTER 3

Allison, Graham T. *Essence of Decision—Explaining the Cuban Missile Crisis.* Boston: Little Brown (1971).

Alter, Steven, and **Michael Ginzberg.** "Managing Uncertainty in MIS Implementation." *Sloan Management Review* 20, no. 1 (Fall 1978).

Anthony, R. N. *Planning and Control Systems: A Framework for Analysis.* Cambridge, MA: Harvard University Press (1965).

Argyris, Chris. *Interpersonal Competence and Organizational Effectiveness.* Homewood, IL: Dorsey Press (1962).

Attewell, Paul, and **James Rule.** "Computing and Organizations: What We Know and What We Don't Know." *Communications of the ACM* 27, no. 12 (December 1984).

Beer, Michael, Russell A. Eisenstat, and **Bert Spector.** "Why Change Programs Don't Produce Change." *Harvard Business Review* (November–December 1990).

Bell, Daniel. *The Coming of Post-Industrial Society.* New York: Basic Books (1973).

Bikson, T. K., and **J. D. Eveland.** "Integrating New Tools into Information Work." The Rand Corporation (1992). RAND/RP-106.

Blau, Peter, and **W. Richard Scott.** *Formal Organizations.* San Francisco: Chandler Press (1962).

Charan, Ram. "How Networks Reshape Organizations—For Results." *Harvard Business Review* (September–October 1991).

Cohen, Michael, James March, and **Johan Olsen.** "A Garbage Can Model of Organizational Choice." *Administrative Science Quarterly* 17 (1972).

Davenport, Thomas H., and **Keri Pearlson.** "Two Cheers for the Virtual Office." *Sloan Management Review* 39, no. 4 (Summer 1998).

DiMaggio, Paul J., and **Walter W. Powell.** "The Iron Cage Revisited: Institutional Isomorphism and Collective Rationality in Organizational Fields." *American Sociological Review* 48 (1983).

Drucker, Peter. "The Coming of the New Organization." *Harvard Business Review* (January–February 1988).

Earl, Michael J., and **Jeffrey L. Sampler.** "Market Management to Transform the IT Organization." *Sloan Management Review* 39, no. 4 (Summer 1998).

El Sawy, Omar A. "Implementation by Cultural Infusion: An Approach for Managing the Introduction of Information Technologies." *MIS Quarterly* (June 1985).

Etzioni, Amitai. *A Comparative Analysis of Complex Organizations.* New York: Free Press (1975).

Fayol, Henri. *Administration industrielle et generale.* Paris: Dunods (1950, first published in 1916).

Freeman, John, Glenn R. Carroll, and **Michael T. Hannan.** "The Liability of Newness: Age Dependence in Organizational Death Rates." *American Sociological Review* 48 (1983).

Fritz, Mary Beth Watson, Sridhar Narasimhan, and **Hyeun-Suk Rhee.** "Communication and Coordination in the Virtual Office." *Journal of Management Information Systems* 14, no. 4 (Spring 1998).

Fulk, Janet, and **Geraldine DeSanctis.** "Electronic Communication and Changing Organizational Forms." *Organization Science* 6, no. 4 (July–August 1995).

Garvin, David A. "The Processes of Organization and Management." *Sloan Management Review* 39, no. 4 (Summer 1998).

George, Joey. "Organizational Decision Support Systems." *Journal of Management Information Systems* 8, no. 3 (Winter 1991–1992).

Gorry, G. Anthony, and **Michael S. Scott Morton.** "A Framework for Management Information Systems." *Sloan Management Review* 13, no. 1 (Fall 1971).

Gurbaxani, V., and **S. Whang,** "The Impact of Information Systems on Organizations and Markets." *Communications of the ACM* 34, no. 1 (Jan. 1991).

Hinds, Pamela, and **Sara Kiesler.** "Communication across Boundaries: Work, Structure, and Use of Communication Technologies in a Large Organization." *Organization Science* 6, no. 4 (July–August 1995).

Hitt, Lorin M., and **Erik Brynjolfsson.** "Information Technology and Internal Firm Organization: An Exploratory Analysis." *Journal of Management Information Systems* 14, no. 2 (Fall 1997).

Huber, George P. "Cognitive Style as a Basis for MIS and DSS Designs: Much Ado About Nothing?" *Management Science* 29 (May 1983).

———. "The Nature and Design of Post-Industrial Organizations." *Management Science* 30, no. 8 (August 1984).

Huff, Sid L., and **Malcolm C. Munro.** "Information Technology Assessment and Adoption: A Field Study." *MIS Quarterly* (December 1985).

Isenberg, Daniel J. "How Senior Managers Think." *Harvard Business Review* (November–December 1984).

Ives, Blake, and **Margrethe H. Olson.** "Manager or Technician? The Nature of the Information Systems Manager's Job." *MIS Quarterly* (December 1981).

Jensen, M., and **W. Mekling.** "Theory of the Firm: Managerial Behavior, Agency Costs, and Ownership Structure." *Journal of Financial Economics* 3 (1976).

Johnston, David Cay. "A Kinder, Smarter Tax System for Kansas." *The New York Times* (June 22, 1998).

Keen, P. G. W. "Information Systems and Organizational Change." *Communications of the ACM* 24, no. 1 (January 1981).

Keen, Peter. G. W. *The Process Edge.* Boston, MA: Harvard Business School Press (1997).

King, J. L., V. Gurbaxani, K. L. Kraemer, F. W. McFarlan, K. S. Raman, and **C. S. Yap.** "Institutional Factors in Information Technology Innovation." *Information Systems Research* 5, no. 2 (June 1994).

Kling, Rob. "Social Analyses of Computing: Theoretical Perspectives in Recent Empirical Research." *Computing Survey* 12, no. 1 (March 1980).

Kling, Rob, and **William H. Dutton.** "The Computer Package: Dynamic Complexity." In *Computers and Politics,* edited by James Danziger, William Dutton, Rob Kling, and Kenneth Kraemer. New York: Columbia University Press (1982).

Kolb, D. A., and **A. L. Frohman.** "An Organization Development Approach to Consulting." *Sloan Management Review* 12, no. 1 (Fall 1970).

Kotter, John T. "What Effective General Managers Really Do." *Harvard Business Review* (November–December 1982).

Kraemer, Kenneth, John King, Debora Dunkle, and **Joe Lane.** *Managing Information Systems.* Los Angeles: Jossey-Bass (1989).

Laudon, Kenneth C. *Computers and Bureaucratic Reform.* New York: Wiley (1974).

———. *Dossier Society: Value Choices in the Design of National Information Systems.* New York: Columbia University Press (1986).

———. "Environmental and Institutional Models of Systems Development." *Communications of the ACM* 28, no. 7 (July 1985).

———. "A General Model of the Relationship Between Information Technology and Organizations." Center for Research on Information Systems, New York University. Working paper, National Science Foundation (1989).

Lawrence, Paul, and **Jay Lorsch.** *Organization and Environment.* Cambridge, MA: Harvard University Press (1969).

Leavitt, Harold J. "Applying Organizational Change in Industry: Structural, Technological, and Humanistic Approaches." In *Handbook of Organizations,* edited by James G. March. Chicago: Rand McNally (1965).

Leavitt, Harold J., and **Thomas L. Whisler.** "Management in the 1980s." *Harvard Business Review* (November–December 1958).

Lee, Ho-Geun. "Do Electronic Marketplaces Lower the Price of Goods?" *Communications of the ACM* 41, no. 1 (January 1998).

Leifer, Richard. "Matching Computer-Based Information Systems with Organizational Structures." *MIS Quarterly* 12, no. 1 (March 1988).

Lindblom, C. E., "The Science of Muddling Through." *Public Administration Review* 19 (1959).

Maier, Jerry L., R. Kelly Rainer, Jr., and **Charles A. Snyder.** "Environmental Scanning for Information Technology: An Empirical Investigation." *Journal of Management Information Systems* 14, no. 2 (Fall 1997).

Malcolm, Andrew H. "How the Oil Spilled and Spread: Delay and Confusion Off Alaska." *The New York Times* (April 16, 1989).

Malone, Thomas W. "Is Empowerment Just a Fad? Control, Decision-Making, and IT." *Sloan Management Review* (Winter 1997.)

March, James G., and **Herbert A. Simon.** *Organizations.* New York: Wiley (1958).

Markus, M. L. "Power, Politics, and MIS Implementation." *Communications of the ACM* 26, no. 6 (June 1983).

McKenney, James L., and **Peter G. W. Keen.** "How Managers' Minds Work." *Harvard Business Review* (May–June 1974).

Michels, Robert. *Political Parties.* New York: Free Press (1962; original publication, 1915).

Millman, Zeeva, and **Jon Hartwick.** "The Impact of Automated Office Systems on Middle Managers and Their Work." *MIS Quarterly* 11, no. 4 (December 1987).

Mintzberg, Henry. "Managerial Work: Analysis from Observation." *Management Science* 18 (October 1971).

———. *The Nature of Managerial Work.* New York: Harper & Row (1973).

———. *The Structuring of Organizations.* Englewood Cliffs, NJ: Prentice Hall (1979).

Olson, Margrethe H. "The IS Manager's Job." *MIS Quarterly* (December 1981).

Parsons, Talcott. *Structure and Process in Modern Societies.* New York: Free Press (1960).

Pindyck, Robert S., and **Daniel L. Rubinfield.** *Microeconomics.* Upper Saddle River, NJ: Prentice Hall (1997).

Porat, Marc. *The Information Economy: Definition and Measurement.* Washington, DC: U.S. Department of Commerce, Office of Telecommunications (May 1977).

Robey, Daniel, and **Sundeep Sahay.** "Transforming Work through Information Technology: A Comparative Case Study of Geographic Information Systems in County Government." *Information Systems Research* 7, no. 1 (March 1996).

Schein, Edgar H. *Organizational Culture and Leadership.* San Francisco: Jossey-Bass (1985).

Scott Morton, Michael S., ed. *The Corporation of the 1990s.* New York: Oxford University Press (1991).

Shore, Edwin B. "Reshaping the IS Organization." *MIS Quarterly* (December 1983).

Simon, H. A. *The New Science of Management Decision.* New York: Harper & Row (1960).

Simon, Herbert A. "Applying Information Technology to Organization Design." *Public Administration Review* (May–June 1973).

Starbuck, William H. "Organizations as Action Generators." *American Sociological Review* 48 (1983).

Straub, Detmar, and **James C. Wetherbe.** "Information Technologies for the 1990s: An Organizational Impact Perspective." *Communications of the ACM* 32, no. 11 (November 1989).

Turner, Jon A. "Computer Mediated Work: The Interplay Between Technology and Structured Jobs." *Communications of the ACM* 27, no. 12 (December 1984).

Turner, Jon A., and **Robert A. Karasek, Jr.** "Software Ergonomics: Effects of Computer Application Design Parameters on Operator Task Performance and Health." *Ergonomics* 27, no. 6 (1984).

Tushman, Michael L., William H. Newman, and **Elaine Romanelli.** "Convergence and Upheaval: Managing the Unsteady Pace of Organizational Evolution." *California Management Review* 29, no. 1 (1986).

Tushman, Michael L., and **Philip Anderson.** "Technological Discontinuities and Organizational Environments." *Administrative Science Quarterly* 31 (September 1986).

Tversky, A., and **D. Kahneman.** "The Framing of Decisions and the Psychology of Choice." *Science* 211 (January 1981).

Weber, Max. *The Theory of Social and Economic Organization.* Translated by Talcott Parsons. New York: Free Press (1947).

Williamson, Oliver E. *The Economic Institutions of Capitalism.* New York: Free Press, (1985).

Wrapp, H. Edward. "Good Managers Don't Make Policy Decisions." *Harvard Business Review* (July–August 1984).

CHAPTER 4

Anderson, Ronald E., Deborah G. Johnson, Donald Gotterbarn, and **Judith Perrolle.** "Using the New ACM Code of Ethics in Decision Making." *Communications of the ACM* 36, no. 2 (February 1993).

Andrews, Edmund L. "AT&T Will Cut 15,000 Jobs to Reduce Costs." *The New York Times* (February 11, 1994).

Association of Computing Machinery. "ACM's Code of Ethics and Professional Conduct." *Communications of the ACM* 36, no. 12 (December 1993).

Barlow, John Perry. "Electronic Frontier: Private Life in Cyberspace." *Communications of the ACM* 34, no. 8 (August 1991).

Bjerklie, David. "Does E-Mail Mean Everyone's Mail?" *InformationWeek* (January 3, 1994).

Brod, Craig. *Techno Stress—The Human Cost of the Computer Revolution.* Reading MA: Addison-Wesley (1982).

Brown Bag Software vs. Symantec Corp. 960 F2D 1465 (Ninth Circuit, 1992).

Carvajal, Dorren. "Book Publishers Worry about Threat of Internet." *The New York Times* (March 18, 1996).

Cavazos, Edward A. "The Legal Risks of Setting up Shop in Cyberspace." *Journal of Organizational Computing* 6, no. 1 (1996).

Chabrow, Eric R. "The Internet: Copyrights." *InformationWeek* (March 25, 1996).

Chen, David W. "Man Charged with Sabotage of Computers." *The New York Times* (February 18, 1998).

Cheng, Hsing K., Ronald R. Sims, and **Hildy Teegen.** "To Purchase or to Pirate Software: An Empirical Study." *Journal of Management Information Systems* 13, no. 4 (Spring 1997).

Collins, W. Robert, Keith W. Miller, Bethany J. Spielman, and **Phillip Wherry.** "How Good Is Good Enough? An Ethical Analysis of Software Construction and Use." *Communications of the ACM* 37, no. 1 (January 1994).

Computer Systems Policy Project. "Perspectives on the National Information Infrastructure." (January 12, 1993).

Couger, J. Daniel. "Preparing IS Students to Deal with Ethical Issues." *MIS Quarterly* 13, no. 2 (June 1989).

Cranor, Lorrie Faith, and **Brian A. LaMacchia.** "Spam!" *Communications of the ACM* 41, no. 8 (August 1998).

Dejoie, Roy, George Fowler, and **David Paradice,** eds. *Ethical Issues in Information Systems.* Boston: Boyd & Fraser (1991).

Denning, Dorothy E., et al., "To Tap or Not to Tap." *Communications of the ACM* 36, no. 3 (March 1993).

Diamond, Edwin, and **Stephen Bates.** "Law and Order Comes to Cyberspace." *Technology Review* (October 1995).

Furger, Roberta. "In Search of Relief for Tired, Aching Eyes." *PC World* (February 1993).

Gabriel, Trip. "Reprogramming a Convicted Hacker." *The New York Times* (January 14, 1995).

Gopal, Ram D., and **G. Lawrence Sanders.** "Preventive and Deterrent Controls for Software Piracy." *Journal of Management Information Systems* 13, no. 4 (Spring 1997).

Graham, Robert L. "The Legal Protection of Computer Software." *Communications of the ACM* (May 1984).

Green, R. H. *The Ethical Manager.* New York: Macmillan (1994).

Harrington, Susan J. "The Effect of Codes of Ethics and Personal Denial of Responsibility on Computer Abuse Judgments and Intentions." *MIS Quarterly* 20, no. 2 (September 1996).

Huff, Chuck, and **C. Dianne Martin.** "Computing Consequences: A Framework for Teaching Ethical Computing." *Communications of the ACM* 38, no. 12 (December 1995).

Joes, Kathryn. "EDS Set to Restore Cash-Machine Network." *The New York Times* (March 26, 1993).

Johnson, Deborah G. "Ethics Online." *Communications of the ACM* 40, no. 1 (January 1997).

Johnson, Deborah G., and **John M. Mulvey.** "Accountability and Computer Decision Systems." *Communications of the ACM* 38, no. 12 (December 1995).

King, Julia. "It's CYA Time." *Computerworld* (March 30, 1992).

Kling, Rob. "When Organizations Are Perpetrators: The Conditions of Computer Abuse and Computer Crime." In *Computerization & Controversy: Value Conflicts & Social Choices,* edited by Charles Dunlop and Rob Kling. New York: Academic Press (1991).

Laudon, Kenneth C. "Ethical Concepts and Information Technology." *Communications of the ACM* 38, no. 12 (December 1995).

Levinson, Marc. "Thanks. You're Fired." *Newsweek* (May 23, 1994).

Lohr, Steve. "A Nation Ponders Its Growing Digital Divide." *The New York Times* (October 21, 1996).

Markoff, John. "In the Data Storage Race, Disks Are Outpacing Chips." *The New York Times* (February 23, 1998).

Mason, Richard O. "Applying Ethics to Information Technology Issues." *Communications of the ACM* 38, no. 12 (December 1995).

Mason, Richard O. "Four Ethical Issues in the Information Age." *MIS Quarterly* 10, no. 1 (March 1986).

McPartlin, John P. "A Question of Complicity." *InformationWeek* (June 22, 1992).

———. "The Terrors of Technostress." *InformationWeek* (July 30, 1990).

Memon, Nasir, and **Ping Wah Wong.** "Protecting Digital Media Content." *Communications of the ACM* 41, no. 7 (July 1998).

Milberg, Sandra J., Sandra J. Burke, H. Jeff Smith, and **Ernest A. Kallman.** "Values, Personal Information Privacy, and Regulatory Approaches." *Communications of the ACM* 38, no. 12 (December 1995).

Mykytyn, Kathleen, Peter P. Mykytyn, Jr., and **Craig W. Slinkman.** "Expert Systems: A Question of Liability." *MIS Quarterly* 14, no. 1 (March 1990).

Neumann, Peter G. "Inside RISKS: Computers, Ethics and Values." *Communications of the ACM* 34, no. 7 (July 1991).

———. "Inside RISKS: Fraud by Computer." *Communications of the ACM* 35, no. 8 (August 1992).

Nissenbaum, Helen. "Computing and Accountability." *Communications of the ACM* 37, no. 1 (January 1994).

Okerson, Ann. "Who Owns Digital Works?" *Scientific American* (July 1996).

Oz, Effy. "Ethical Standards for Information Systems Professionals," *MIS Quarterly* 16, no. 4 (December 1992).

———. *Ethics for the Information Age.* Dubuque, Iowa: W. C. Brown (1994).

Pollack, Andrew. "San Francisco Law on VDTs Is Struck Down." *The New York Times* (February 14, 1992).

Ramirez, Anthony. "AT&T to Eliminate Many Operator Jobs." *The New York Times* (March 4, 1992).

Redman, Thomas C. "The Impact of Poor Data Quality on the Typical Enterprise." *Communications of the ACM* 41, no. 2 (February 1998).

Rifkin, Glenn. "The Ethics Gap." *Computerworld* (October 14, 1991).

Rifkin, Jeremy. "Watch Out for Trickle-Down Technology." *The New York Times* (March 16, 1993).

Rigdon, Joan E. "Frequent Glitches in New Software Bug Users." *The Wall Street Journal* (January 18, 1995).

Rotenberg, Marc. "Communications Privacy: Implications for Network Design." *Communications of the ACM* 36, no. 8 (August 1993).

———. "Inside RISKS: Protecting Privacy." *Communications of the ACM* 35, no. 4 (April 1992).

Samuelson, Pamela. "Computer Programs and Copyright's Fair Use Doctrine." *Communications of the ACM* 36, no. 9 (September 1993).

———. "Copyright's Fair Use Doctrine and Digital Data." *Communications of the ACM* 37, no. 1 (January 1994).

———. "Digital Media and the Law." *Communications of the ACM* 34, no. 10 (October 1991).

———. "First Amendment Rights for Information Providers?" *Communications of the ACM* 34, no. 6 (June 1991).

———. "Liability for Defective Electronic Information." *Communications of the ACM* 36, no. 1 (January 1993).

———. "Self Plagiarism or Fair Use?" *Communications of the ACM* 37, no. 8 (August 1994).

———. "The Ups and Downs of Look and Feel." *Communications of the ACM* 36, no. 4 (April 1993).

———. "Updating the Copyright Look and Feel Lawsuits." *Communications of the ACM* 35, no. 9 (September 1992).

Schnorr, Teresa M. "Miscarriage and VDT Exposure." *New England Journal of Medicine* (March 1991).

Sipior, Janice C., and **Burke T. Ward.** "The Ethical and Legal Quandary of E-mail Privacy." *Communications of the ACM* 38, no. 12 (December 1995).

Smith, H. Jeff. "Privacy Policies and Practices: Inside the Organizational Maze." *Communications of the ACM* 36, no. 12, (December 1993).

Smith, H. Jeff, Sandra J. Milberg, and **Sandra J. Burke.** "Information Privacy: Measuring Individuals' Concerns about Organizational Practices." *MIS Quarterly* 20, no. 2 (June 1996).

Stevens, William K. "Major U.S. Study Finds No Miscarriage Risk from Video Terminals." *The New York Times* (March 14, 1991).

Straub, Detmar W., Jr., and **William D. Nance.** "Discovering and Disciplining Computer Abuse in Organizations: A Field Study." *MIS Quarterly* 14, no. 1 (March 1990).

Straub, Detmar W., Jr., and **Rosann Webb Collins.** "Key Information Liability Issues Facing Managers: Software Piracy, Proprietary Databases, and Individual Rights to Privacy." *MIS Quarterly* 14, no. 2 (June 1990).

Tabor, Mary W., with **Anthony Ramirez.** "Computer Savy, with an Attitude." *The New York Times* (July 23, 1992).

The Telecommunications Policy Roundtable. "Renewing the Commitment to a Public Interest Telecommunications Policy." *Communications of the ACM* 37, no. 1 (January 1994).

Thong, James Y. L., and **Chee-Sing Yap.** "Testing an Ethical Decision-Making Theory." *Journal of Management Information Systems* 15, no. 1 (Summer 1998).

Turner, Jon. "Will Telecommuting Ever Get Off the Ground? *Stern Business* (Summer 1998).

Tuttle, Brad, Adrian Harrell, and **Paul Harrison.** "Moral Hazard, Ethical Considerations, and the Decision to Implement an Information System." *Journal of Management Information Systems* 13, no. 4 (Spring 1997).

United States Department of Health, Education, and Welfare. *Records, Computers, and the Rights of Citizens.* Cambridge: MIT Press (1973).

Wang, Huaiqing, Matthew K. O. Lee, and **Chen Wang.** "Consumer Privacy Concerns about Internet Marketing." *Communications of the ACM* 41, no. 3 (March 1998).

Wilder, Clinton. "Feds Allege Internet Scam." *InformationWeek* (June 10, 1996).

Wilson, Linda. "Devil in Your Data." *InformationWeek* (August 31, 1992).

Weisband, Suzanne P., and **Bruce A. Reinig.** "Managing User Perceptions of E-mail Privacy." *Communications of the ACM* 38, no. 12 (December 1995).

Wolinsky, Carol, and **James Sylvester.** "Privacy in the Telecommunications Age." *Communications of the ACM* 35, no. 2 (February 1992).

CHAPTER 5

Bell, Gordon. "Ultracomputers: A Teraflop Before Its Time." *Communications of the ACM* 35, no. 8 (August 1992).

Camp, W. J., S. J. Plimpton, B. A. Hendrickson, and **R. W. Leland.** "Massively Parallel Methods for Engineering and Science Problems." *Communications of the ACM* 37, no. 4 (April 1994).

Feder, Barnaby J. "For Amber Waves of Data." *The New York Times* (May 4, 1998).

Fitzmaurice, George W. "Situated Information Spaces and Spatially Aware Palmtop Computers." *Communications of the ACM* 36, no. 7 (July 1993).

Freeman, Eva. "No More Gold-Plated MIPS: Mainframes and Distributed Systems Converge." *Datamation* (March 1998).

Halfhill, Tom R. "Cheaper Computing." *Byte* (April 1997).

Hardaway, Don, and **Richard P. Will.** "Digital Multimedia Offers Key to Educational Reform." *Communications of the ACM* 40, no. 4 (April 1997).

Jacobs, April. "The Network Computer: Where It's Going." *Computerworld* (December 23, 1997/January 2, 1998).

Jenkins, Avery. "The Right Time for RAID." *Computerworld* (March 14, 1994).

Kay, Emily. "Hello Mr. Chips! Multimedia in the Classroom." *Technology Training* (June 1997).

Lambert, Craig. "The Electronic Tutor." *Harvard Magazine* (November–December 1990).

Lieberman, Henry. "Intelligent Graphics." *Communications of the ACM* 39, no. 8 (August 1996).

Lohr, Steve. "The Network Computer as the PC's Evil Twin," *The New York Times* (November 4, 1996).

Markoff, John. "Inside Intel, the Future Is Riding on a New Chip." *The New York Times* (April 5, 1998).

Peleg, Alex, Sam Wilkie, and **Uri Weiser.** "Intel MMX for Multimedia PCs." *Communications of the ACM* 40, no. 1 (January 1997).

Press, Larry. "Compuvision or Teleputer?" *Communications of the ACM* 33, no. 3 (September 1990).

———. "Personal Computing: Dynabook Revisited—Portable Computers Past, Present, and Future." *Communications of the ACM* 35 no. 3 (March 1992).

Selker, Ted. "New Paradigms for Using Computers." *Communications of the ACM* 39, no. 8 (August 1996).

Smarr, Larry, and **Charles E. Catlett,** "Metacomputing." *Communications of the ACM* 35, no. 6 (June 1992).

Strassman, Paul. "40 Years of IT History." *Datamation* (October 1997).

Thomborson, Clark D. "Does Your Workstation Computation Belong to a Vector Supercomputer?" *Communications of the ACM* 36, no. 11 (November 1993).

Vaughan-Nichols, Steven J. "To NC or Not to NC?" *NetWorker* 1, no. 1 (March/April 1997).

Weiser, Mark. "Some Computer Science Issues in Ubiquitous Computing." *Communications of the ACM* 36, no. 7 (July 1993).

Williamson, Miday. "High-Tech Training." *Byte* (December 1994).

Wood, Elizabeth. "Multimedia Comes Down to Earth." *Computerworld* (August 1, 1994).

CHAPTER 6

Apte, Uday, Chetan S. Sankar, Meru Thakur, and **Joel E. Turner.** "Reusability-Based Strategy for Development of Information Systems: Implementation Experience of a Bank." *MIS Quarterly* 14, no. 4 (December 1990).

Barrett, Jim, Kevin Knight, Inderject Man, and **Elaine Rich.** "Knowledge and Natural Language Processing." *Communications of the ACM* 33, no. 8 (August 1990).

Bochenski, Barbara. "GUI Builders Pay Price for User Productivity." *Software Magazine* (April 1992).

Clark, Don. "Sun Microsystems Still Has a Legion of Believers." *The Wall Street Journal* (March 23, 1998).

Fayad, Mohamed, and **Marshall P. Cline.** "Aspects of Software Adaptability." *Communications of the ACM* 39, no. 10 (October 1996).

Flynn, Jim, and **Bill Clarke.** "How Java Makes Network-Centric Computing Real." *Datamation* (March 1, 1996).

Greenbaum, Joshua. "The Evolution Revolution." *InformationWeek* (March 14, 1994).

Haavind, Robert. "Software's New Object Lesson," *Technology Review* (February–March 1992).

Jalics, Paul J. "Cobol on a PC: A New Perspective on a Language and Its Performance." *Communications of the ACM* 30, no. 2 (February 1987).

Johnson, Ralph E. "Frameworks = (Components + Patterns)." *Communications of the ACM* 40, no. 10 (October 1997).

Kappelman, Leon A., Darla Fent, Kellie B. Keeling, and **Victor Prybutok.** "Calculating the Cost of Year 2000 Compliance." *Communications of the ACM* 41, no. 2 (February 1998).

Korson, Timothy D., and **Vijay K. Vaishnavi.** "Managing Emerging Software Technologies: A Technology Transfer Framework." *Communications of the ACM* 35, no. 9 (September 1992).

Korson, Tim, and **John D. McGregor.** "Understanding Object-Oriented: A Unifying Paradigm." *Communications of the ACM* 33, no. 9 (September 1990).

Layer, D. Kevin, and **Chris Richardson.** "LISP Systems in the 1990s." *Communications of the ACM* 34, no. 9 (September 1991).

Littlewood, Bev, and **Lorenzo Strigini.** "The Risks of Software." *Scientific American* 267, no. 5 (November 1992).

Mandelkern, David. "Graphical User Interfaces: The Next Generation." *Communications of the ACM* 36, no. 4 (April 1993).

Monarchi, David E., and **Gretchen I. Puhr.** "A Research Typology for Object-Oriented Analysis and Design." *Communications of the ACM* 35, no. 9 (September 1992).

Morse, Alan, and **George Reynolds.** "Overcoming Current Growth Limits in UI Development." *Communications of the ACM* 36, no. 4 (April 1993).

Mukhopadhyay, Tridas, Stephen S. Vicinanza, and **Michael J. Prietula.** "Examining the Feasibility of a Case-Based Reasoning Model for Software Effort Estimation." *MIS Quarterly* 16, no. 2 (June 1992).

Nielsen, Jakob. "Noncommand User Interfaces." *Communications of the ACM* 36, no. 4 (April 1993).

Nilsen, Kelvin. "Adding Real-Time Capabilities to Java." *Communications of the ACM* 41, no. 6 (June 1998).

Purao, Sandeep, Hemant Jain, and **Derek Nazareth.** "Effective Distribution of Object-Oriented Applications." *Communications of the ACM* 41, no. 8 (August 1998).

Schonberg, Edmond, Mark Gerhardt, and **Charlene Hayden.** "A Technical Tour of Ada," *Communications of the ACM* 35, no. 11 (November 1992).

Semich, Bill, and **David Fisco.** "Java: Internet Toy or Enterprise Tool?" *Datamation* (March 1, 1996).

Sheetz, Steven D., Gretchen Irwin, David P. Tegarden, H. James Nelson, and **David E. Monarchi.** "Exploring the Difficulties of Learning Object-Oriented Techniques." *Journal of Management Information Systems* 14, no. 2 (Fall 1997).

Tyma, Paul. "Why Are We Using Java Again?" *Communications of the ACM* 41, no. 6 (June 1998).

Vassiliou, Yannis. "On the Interactive Use of Databases: Query Languages." *Journal of Management Information Systems* 1 (Winter 1984–1985).

White, George M. "Natural Language Understanding and Speech." *Communications of the ACM* 33, no. 8 (August 1990).

Wiederhold, Gio, Peter Wegner, and **Stefano Ceri.** "Toward Megaprogramming." *Communications of the ACM* 35, no. 11 (November 1992).

Wilkes, Maurice V. "The Long-Term Future of Operating Systems." *Communications of the ACM* 35, no. 11 (November 1992).

CHAPTER 7

Belkin, Nicholas J., and **W. Bruce Croft.** "Information Filtering and Information Retrieval: Two Sides of the Same Coin?" *Communications of the ACM* 35, no. 12 (November 1992).

Butterworth, Paul, Allen Otis, and **Jacob Stein,** "The GemStone Object Database Management System." *Communications of the ACM* 34, no. 10 (October 1991).

Carmel, Erran, William K. McHenry, and **Yeshayahu Cohen.** "Building Large, Dynamic Hypertexts: How Do We Link Intelligently?" *Journal of Management Information Systems* 6, no. 2 (Fall 1989).

Chang, Shih-Fu, John R. Amith, Mandis Beigi, and **Ana Benitez.** "Visual Information Retrieval from Large Distributed On-line Repositories." *Communications of the ACM* 40, no. 12 (December 1997).

Clifford, James, Albert Croker, and **Alex Tuzhilin.** "On Data Representation and Use in a Temporal Relational DBMS." *Information Systems Research* 7, no. 3 (September 1996).

Date, C. J. *An Introduction to Database Systems,* 6th ed. Reading, MA: Addison-Wesley (1995).

Everest, G. C. *Database Management: Objectives, System Functions, and Administration.* New York: McGraw-Hill (1985).

Fiori, Rich. "The Information Warehouse." *Relational Database Journal* (January–February 1995).

Francett, Barbara. "Data Warehousing Is the Sum of Its Marts." *Software Magazine* (February 1997).

Gardner, Stephen R. "Building the Data Warehouse." *Communications of the ACM* 41, no. 9 (September 1998).

Garvey, Martin J. "A New Face on Legacy Data," *InformationWeek* (July 28, 1997).

Goldberg, Michael, and **Jaikumar Vijayan.** "Data 'Wearhouse' Gains." *Computerworld* (April 8, 1996).

Goldstein, R. C., and **J. B. McCririck.** "What Do Data Administrators Really Do?" *Datamation* 26 (August 1980).

Goodhue, Dale L., Judith A. Quillard, and **John F. Rockart.** "Managing the Data Resource: A Contingency Perspective." *MIS Quarterly* (September 1988).

Goodhue, Dale L., Laurie J. Kirsch, Judith A. Quillard, and **Michael D. Wybo.** "Strategic Data Planning: Lessons from the Field." *MIS Quarterly* 16, no. 1 (March 1992).

Goodhue, Dale L., Michael D. Wybo, and **Laurie J. Kirsch.** "The Impact of Data Integration on the Costs and Benefits of Information Systems." *MIS Quarterly* 16, no. 3 (September 1992).

Grosky, William I. "Managing Multimedia Information in Database Systems." *Communications of the ACM* 40, no. 12 (December 1997).

Grover, Varun, and **James Teng.** "How Effective Is Data Resource Management?" *Journal of Information Systems Management* (Summer 1991).

Gupta, Amarnath, and **Ranesh Jain.** "Visual Information Retrieval." *Communications of the ACM* 40, no. 5 (May 1997).

Hoffman, Thomas. "Improved Analytics Drive Office Depot Sales." *Computerworld* (February 9, 1998).

Inman, W. H. "The Data Warehouse and Data Mining." *Communications of the ACM* 39, no. 11 (November 1996).

Kahn, Beverly K. "Some Realities of Data Administration." *Communications of the ACM* 26 (October 1983).

Kahn, Beverly, and **Linda Garceau.** "The Database Administration Function." *Journal of Management Information Systems* 1 (Spring 1985).

Kent, William. "A Simple Guide to Five Normal Forms in Relational Database Theory." *Communications of the ACM* 26, no. 2 (February 1983).

King, John L., and **Kenneth Kraemer.** "Information Resource Management Cannot Work." *Information and Management* (1988).

Kroenke, David. *Database Processing: Fundamentals, Design, and Implementation,* 6th ed. Upper Saddle River, NJ: Prentice Hall (1997).

Lange, Danny B. "An Object-Oriented Design Approach for Developing Hypermedia Information Systems." *Journal of Organizational Computing and Electronic Commerce* 6, no. 2 (1996).

Madnick, Stuart E., and **Richard Y. Wang.** "Evolution Towards Strategic Application of Databases through Composite Information Systems." *Journal of Management Information Systems* 5, no. 3 (Winter 1988–1989).

March, Salvatore T., and **Young-Gul Kim.** "Information Resource Management: A Metadata Perspective." *Journal of Management Information Systems* 5, no. 3 (Winter 1988–1989).

Qing, Li, and **Frederic H. Lochovsky,** "Advanced Database Support Facilities for CSCW Systems." *Journal of Organizational Computing and Electronic Commerce* 6, no. 2 (1996).

Ricciuti, Mike. "Winning the Competitive Game." *Datamation* (February 15, 1994).

Silberschatz, Avi, Michael Stonebraker, and **Jeff Ullman,** eds. "Database Systems: Achievements and Opportunities." *Communications of the ACM* 34, no. 10 (October 1991).

Smith, John B., and **Stephen F. Weiss.** "Hypertext." *Communications of the ACM* 31, no. 7 (July 1988).

Watson, Hugh J., and **Barbara J. Haley.** "Managerial Considerations." *Communications of the ACM* 41, no. 9 (September 1998).

Watterson, Karen. "When It Comes to Choosing a Database, the Object Is Value." *Datamation* (December-January 1998).

CHAPTER 8

Bikson, Tora K., Cathleen Stasz, and **Donald A. Monkin.** "Computer-Mediated Work: Individual and Organizational Impact on One Corporate Headquarters." Rand Corporation (1985).

Brandel, Mary. "Videoconferencing Slowly Goes Desktop." *Computerworld* (February 20, 1995).

Chatterjee, Samir. "Requirements for Success in Gigabit Networking." *Communications of the ACM* 40, no. 7 (July 1997).

Dertouzos, Michael. "Building the Information Marketplace." *Technology Review* (January 1991).

Donovan, John J. "Beyond Chief Information Officer to Network Manager." *Harvard Business Review* (September–October 1988).

Duchessi, Peter, and **InduShobha Chengalur-Smith.** "Client/Server Benefits, Problems, Best Practices." *Communications of the ACM* 41, no. 5 (May 1998).

Fisher, Sharon. "TCP/IP." *Computerworld* (October 7, 1991).

Frye, Colleen. "Talking Heads: Coming to a Desktop Near You." *Software Magazine* (May 1995).

Gefen, David, and **Detmar W. Straub.** "Gender Differences in the Perception and Use of E-Mail: An Extension to the Technology Acceptance Model." *MIS Quarterly* 21, no. 4 (December 1997).

Gilder, George. "Into the Telecosm." *Harvard Business Review* (March–April 1991).

Grover, Varun, and **Martin D. Goslar.** "Initiation, Adoption, and Implementation of Telecommunications Technologies in U.S. Organizations." *Journal of Management Information Systems* 10, no. 1 (Summer 1993).

Hall, Wayne A., and **Robert E. McCauley.** "Planning and Managing a Corporate Network Utility." *MIS Quarterly* (December 1987).

Hammer, Michael, and **Glenn Mangurian.** "The Changing Value of Communications Technology." *Sloan Management Review* (Winter 1987).

Hansen, James V., and **Ned C. Hill.** "Control and Audit of Electronic Data Interchange." *MIS Quarterly* 13, no. 4 (December 1989).

Hart, Paul J., and **Carol Stoak Saunders.** "Emerging Electronic Partnerships: Antecedents and Dimensions of EDI Use from the Supplier's Perspective." *Journal of Management Information Systems* 14, no. 4 (Spring 1998).

Huff, Sid, Malcolm C. Munro, and **Barbara H. Martin.** "Growth Stages of End User Computing." *Communications of the ACM* (May 1988).

Imielinski, Tomasz, and **B. R. Badrinath.** "Mobile Wireless Computing: Challenges in Data Management." *Communications of the ACM* 37, no. 10 (October 1994).

Keen, Peter G. W. *Competing in Time.* Cambridge, MA: Ballinger Publishing Company (1986).

Keen, Peter G. W., and **J. Michael Cummins.** *Networks in Action: Business Choices and Telecommunications Decisions.* Belmont, CA: Wadsworth Publishing Company (1994).

Kim, B. G., and **P. Wang.** "ATM Network: Goals and Challenges." *Communications of the ACM* 38, no. 2 (February 1995).

Laudon, Kenneth C. "From PCs to Managerial Workstations." In Matthias Jarke, *Managers, Micros, and Mainframes.* New York: John Wiley (1986).

Lee, Denis M. "Usage Pattern and Sources of Assistance for Personal Computer Users." *MIS Quarterly* (December 1986).

Lee, Sunro, and **Richard P. Leifer.** "A Framework for Linking the Structure of Information Systems with Organizational Requirements for Information Sharing." *Journal of Management Information Systems* 8, no. 4 (Spring 1992).

Massetti, Brenda, and **Robert W. Zmud.** "Measuring the Extent of EDI Usage in Complex Organizations. Strategies and Illustrative Examples." *MIS Quarterly* 20, no. 3 (September 1996).

Mueller, Milton. "Universal Service and the Telecommunications Act: Myth Made Law." *Communications of the ACM* 40, no. 3 (March 1997).

Nakamura, Kiyoh, Toshihiro Ide, and **Yukio Kiyokane.** "Roles of Multimedia Technology in Telework." *Journal of Organizational Computing and Electronic Commerce* 6, no. 4 (1996).

Ngwenyama, Ojelanki, and **Allen S. Lee.** "Communication Richness in Electronic Mail: Critical Social Theory and the Contextuality of Meaning." *MIS Quarterly* 21, no. 2 (June 1997).

"Plans and Policies for Client/Server Technology." *I/S Analyzer* 30, no. 4 (April 1992).

Premkumar, G., K. Ramamurthy, and **Sree Nilakanta.** "Implementation of Electronic Data Interchange: An Innovation Diffusion Perspective." *Journal of Management Information Systems* 11, no. 2 (Fall 1994).

Railing, Larry, and **Tom Housel.** "A Network Infrastructure to Contain Costs and Enable Fast Response." *MIS Quarterly* 14, no. 4 (December 1990).

Raymond, Louis, and **Francois Bergeron.** "EDI Success in Small- and Medium-sized Enterprises: A Field Study." *Journal of Organizational Computing and Electronic Commerce* 6, no. 2 (1996).

Richardson, Gary L., Brad M. Jackson, and **Gary W. Dickson.** "A Principles-Based Enterprise Architecture: Lessons from Texaco and Star Enterprise." *MIS Quarterly* 14, no. 4 (December 1990).

Roche, Edward M. *Telecommunications and Business Strategy.* Chicago: The Dryden Press (1991).

Sinha, Alok. "Client-Server Computing." *Communications of the ACM* 35, no. 7 (July 1992).

Teo, Hock-Hai, Bernard C. Y. Tan, and **Kwok-Kee Wei.** "Organizational Transformation Using Electronic Data Interchange: The Case of TradeNet in Singapore." *Journal of Management Information Systems* 13, no. 4 (Spring 1997).

Torkzadeh, Gholamreza, and **Weidong Xia.** "Managing Telecommunications Strategy by Steering Committee." *MIS Quarterly* 16, no. 2 (June 1992).

Vetter, Ronald J. "ATM Concepts, Architectures, and Protocols." *Communications of the ACM* 38, no. 2 (February 1995).

Westin, Alan F., Heather A. Schweder, Michael A. Baker, and **Sheila Lehman.** *The Changing Workplace.* New York: Knowledge Industries (1995).

CHAPTER 9

Applegate, Lynda, and **Janice Gogan.** "Paving the Information Superhighway: Introduction to the Internet," *Harvard Business School* 9-195-202 (August 1995).

Bakos, Yannis. "The Emerging Role of Electronic Marketplaces and the Internet." *Communications of the ACM* 41, no. 8 (August 1998).

Barua, Anitesh, Sury Ravindran, and **Andrew B. Whinston.** "Efficient Selection of Suppliers over the Internet." *Journal of Management Information Systems* 13, no. 4 (Spring 1997).

Berners-Lee, Tim, Robert Cailliau, Ari Luotonen, Henrik Frystyk Nielsen, and **Arthur Secret.** "The World-Wide Web." *Communications of the ACM* 37, no. 8 (August 1994).

Bowman, C. Mic, Peter B. Danzig, Udi Manger, and **Michael F. Schwartz.** "Scalable Internet Resource Discovery: Research Problems and Approaches." *Communications of the ACM* 37, no. 8 (August 1994.)

Buchanan, Lee. "Procurative Powers." *Webmaster* (May 1997).

Caldwell, Bruce. "Can It Be Saved?" *InformationWeek* (April 8, 1996).

Chabrow, Eric R. "On-line Employment," *InformationWeek* (January 23, 1995).

Choi, Soon-Yong, Dale O. Stahl, and **Andrew B. Whinston.** *The Economics of Electronic Commerce.* Indianapolis, IN: Macmillan Technical Publishing (1997).

Cole-Gomolski. "Groupware Gives Lift to Reebok Site." *Computerworld* (January 19, 1998).

Cortese, Amy. "Here Comes the Intranet." *Business Week* (February 26, 1996).

Crede, Andreas. "Electronic Commerce and the Banking Industry: The Requirement and Opportunities for New Payment Systems Using the Internet." *JCMC* 1, no. 3 (December 1995).

Cronin, Mary. *The Internet Strategy Handbook.* Boston, MA: Harvard Business School Press (1996).

Dahle, Cheryl. "Sellular Chemistry." *Webmaster* (January 1997).

Darling, Michael. "The Internet: Hot or Just Cool?" *Stern Business* (Spring 1996).

Dearth, Jeffrey, and **Arnold King** "Negotiating the Internet," *InformationWeek* (January 9, 1995).

Deutsch, Claudia. "Businesses Explore Cyberauctions." *The New York Times* (June 1, 1998).

Downes, Larry, and **Chunka Mui.** *Unleashing the Killer App: Digital Strategies for Market Dominance.* Boston, MA: Harvard Business School Press (1998).

Eckerson, Wayne. "Doing Business on the Web." Patricia Seybold Group's Notes on Information Technology (April 1996).

Elofson, Greg, and **William N. Robinson.** "Creating a Custom Mass Production Channel on the Internet." *Communications of the ACM* 41, no. 3 (March 1998).

Ghosh, Shikhar. "Making Business Sense of the Internet." *Harvard Business Review* (March–April 1998).

Goodman, S. E., L. I. Press, S. R. Ruth, and **A. M. Rutkowski.** "The Global Diffusion of the Internet: Patterns and Problems." *Communications of the ACM* 37, no. 8 (August 1994.)

Halper, Mark. "Meet the New Middlemen." *Computerworld Emmerce* (May 5, 1997).

Hardman, Vicky, Martina Angela Sasse, and **Isidor Kouvelas.** "Successful Multiparty Audio Communication over the Internet." *Communications of the ACM* 41, no. 5 (May 1998).

Hoffman, Donna L., William D. Kalsbeek, and **Thomas P. Novak.** "Internet and Web Use in the U.S." *Communications of the ACM* 39, no. 12 (December 1996).

Hoffman, Donna L., Thomas P. Novak, and **Patrali Chatterjee.** "Commercial Scenarios for the Web: Opportunities and Challenges." *JCMC* 1, no. 3 (December 1995).

Horwitt, Elisabeth. "Intranet Intricacies." *Computerworld Client/Server Journal* (February 1996).

"How to Use Intranets to Support Business Applications." *I/S Analyzer Case Studies* 35, no. 5 (May 1996).

Isakowitz, Tomas, Michael Bieker, and **Fabio Vitali.** "Web Information Systems." *Communications of the ACM* 41, no. 7 (July 1998).

Jahnke, Art. "It Takes a Village." *CIO WebBusiness* (February 1, 1998).

Kalakota, Ravi, and **Andrew B. Whinston.** *Electronic Commerce: A Manager's Guide.* Reading MA: Addison-Wesley (1997).

———. *Frontiers of Electronic Commerce.* Reading, MA: Addison-Wesley (1996).

Kanan, P. K., Ai-Mei Chang, and **Andrew B. Whinston.** "Marketing Information on the I-Way. *Communications of the ACM* 41, no. 3 (March 1998).

Kautz, Henry, Bart Selman, and **Mehul Shah.** "ReferralWeb: Combining Social Networks and Collaborative Filtering." *Communications of the ACM* 40, no. 3 (March 1997).

Korzeniowski, Paul. "IP Telephony: Ready for Prime Time?" *Datamation* (April 1998).

Lee, Ho Geun. "Do Electronic Marketplaces Lower the Price of Goods?" *Communications of the ACM* 41, no. 1 (January 1998).

Lee, Ho Geun, and **Theodore H. Clark.** "Market Process Reengineering through Electronic Market Systems: Opportunities and Challenges." *Journal of Management Information Systems* 13, no. 3 (Winter 1997).

Leiner, Barry M. "Internet Technology," *Communications of the ACM* 37, no. 8 (August 1994).

Levitt, Lee. "Intranets: Internet Technologies Deployed Behind the Firewall for Corporate Productivity." Process Software Corporation (1996).

Lohr, Steve. "Business to Business in the Internet." *The New York Times* (April 28, 1997).

Lohse, Gerald L., and **Peter Spiller.** "Electronic Shopping." *Communications of the ACM* 41, no. 7 (July 1998).

Maddox, Kate. "On-line Data Push." *InformationWeek* (February 24, 1997).

Markoff, John. "Commerce Comes to the Internet," *The New York Times* (April 13, 1994).

Meeker, Mary, and **Chris DePuy.** "The Internet Report." New York: Morgan Stanley & Co. (1996).

Mougayar, Walid. *Opening Digital Markets,* 2nd ed. New York: McGraw-Hill (1998).

Nouwens, John, and **Harry Bouwman.** "Living Apart Together in Electronic Commerce: The Use of Information and Communication Technology to Create Network Organizations." *JCMC* 1, no. 3 (December 1995).

O'Leary, Daniel E., Daniel Koukka, and **Robert Plant.** "Artificial Intelligence and Virtual Organizations." *Communications of the ACM* 40, no. 1 (January 1997).

Palmer, Jonathan W., and **David A. Griffith.** "An Emerging Model of Web Site Design for Marketing." *Communications of the ACM* 41, no. 3 (March 1998).

Price Waterhouse. "Technology Forecast: 1996." Menlo Park, CA: Price Waterhouse World Technology Centre (1995).

Quelch, John A., and **Lisa R. Klein.** "The Internet and International Marketing." *Sloan Management Review* (Spring 1996).

Richard, Eric. "Anatomy of the World-Wide Web." *Internet World* (April 1995).

Row, Heath. "Personnel Best." *Webmaster* (September 1996).

Sarkar, Mitra Barun, Brian Butler, and **Charles Steinfield.** "Intermediaries and Cybermediaries: A Continuing Role for Mediating Players in the Electronic Marketplace." *JCMC* 1, no. 3 (December 1995).

Semich, J. William. "The World Wide Web: Internet Boomtown?" *Datamation* (January 15, 1995).

Smarr, Larry, and **Charles E. Catlett.** "Metacomputing." *Communications of the ACM* 35, no. 6 (June 1992).

Sprout, Alison L. "The Internet Inside Your Company." *Fortune* (November 27, 1995).

Steinfield, Charles. "The Impact of Electronic Commerce on Buyer-Seller Relationships." *JCMC* 1, no. 3 (December 1995).

Sterne, Jim. "Customer Interface." *CIO WebBusiness* (February 1, 1998).

———. *World Wide Web Marketing.* New York: John Wiley (1995).

———. "The Premier 100: On Track to Internet Success." *Computerworld* (February 24, 1997).

Ubois, Jeffrey. "CFOs in Cyberspace." *CFO* (February, 1995).

Verity, John W., with **Robert D. Hof.** "The Internet: How It Will Change the Way You Do Business." *Business Week* (November 14, 1994).

Wigand, Rolf T., and **Robert Benjamin.** "Electronic Commerce: Effects on Electronic Markets." *JCMC* 1, no. 3 (December 1995).

Withers, Suzanne. "The Trader and the Internet." *Technical Analysis of Stocks & Commodities* (March 1995).

CHAPTER 10

Alter, Steven, and **Michael Ginzberg.** "Managing Uncertainty in MIS Implementation." *Sloan Management Review* 20 (Fall 1978).

Bacon, C. James. "The Uses of Decision Criteria in Selecting Information Systems/Technology Investments." *MIS Quarterly* 16, no. 3 (September 1992).

Barki, Henri, and **Jon Hartwick.** "User Participation, Conflict, and Conflict Resolution: The Mediating Roles of Influence." *Information Systems Research* 5, no. 4 (December 1994).

Baroudi, Jack, Margrethe H. Olsen, and **Blake Ives.** "An Empirical Study of the Impact of User Involvement on System Usage and Information Satisfaction." *Communications of the ACM* 29, no. 3 (March 1986).

Barua, Anitesh, Sophie C. H. Lee, and **Andrew B. Whinston.** "The Calculus of Reengineering." *Information Systems Research* 7, no. 4 (December 1996).

Beath, Cynthia Mathis, and **Wanda J. Orlikowski.** "The Contradictory Structure of Systems Development Methodologies: Deconstructing the IS-User Relationship in Information Engineering." *Information Systems Research* 5, no. 4 (December 1994).

Bostrom, R. P., and **J. S. Heinen.** "MIS Problems and Failures: A Socio-Technical Perspective. Part I: The Causes." *MIS Quarterly* 1 (September 1977); "Part II: The Application of Socio-Technical Theory." *MIS Quarterly* 1 (December 1977).

Bullen, Christine, and **John F. Rockart.** "A Primer on Critical Success Factors." Cambridge, MA: Center for Information Systems Research, Sloan School of Management (1981).

Buss, Martin D. J. "How to Rank Computer Projects." *Harvard Business Review* (January 1983).

Cerveny, Robert P., Edward J. Garrity, and **G. Lawrence Sanders.** "A Problem-Solving Perspective on Systems Development." *Journal of Management Information Systems* 6, no. 4 (Spring 1990).

Clement, Andrew, and **Peter Van den Besselaar.** "A Retrospective Look at PD Projects." *Communications of the ACM* 36, no. 4 (June 1993).

Cooper, Randolph B., and **Zmud, Robert W.** "Information Technology Implementation Research: A Technological

Diffusion Approach." *Management Science* 36, no. 2 (February 1990).

Davenport, Thomas H., and **James E. Short.** "The New Industrial Engineering: Information Technology and Business Process Redesign." *Sloan Management Review* 31, no. 4 (Summer 1990).

Davidson, W. H. "Beyond Engineering: The Three Phases of Business Transformation." *IBM Systems Journal* 32, no. 1 (1993).

Davis, Fred R. "Perceived Usefulness, Ease of Use, and User Acceptance of Information Technology." *MIS Quarterly* 13, no. 3 (September 1989).

Davis, Gordon B. "Determining Management Information Needs: A Comparison of Methods." *MIS Quarterly* 1 (June 1977).

———. "Information Analysis for Information System Development." In *Systems Analysis and Design: A Foundation for the 1980's,* edited by W. W. Cotterman, J. D. Cougar, N. L. Enger, and F. Harold. New York: Wiley (1981).

———. "Strategies for Information Requirements Determination." *IBM Systems Journal* 1 (1982).

Dennis, Alan R., Robert M. Daniels, Jr., Glenda Hayes, and **Jay F. Nunamaker, Jr.** "Methodology-Driven Use of Automated Support in Business Process Reengineering." *Journal of Management Information Systems* 10, no. 3 (Winter 1993–1994).

Desmarais, Michel C., Richard Leclair, Jean-Yves Fiset, and **Hichem Talbi.** "Cost-Justifying Electronic Performance Support Systems." *Communications of the ACM* 40, no. 7 (July 1997).

Doll, William J. "Avenues for Top Management Involvement in Successful MIS Development." *MIS Quarterly* (March 1985).

Dos Santos, Brian. "Justifying Investments in New Information Technologies." *Journal of Management Information Systems* 7, no. 4 (Spring 1991).

Ein-Dor, Philip, and **Eli Segev.** "Strategic Planning for Management Information Systems." *Management Science* 24, no. 15 (1978).

El Sawy, Omar, and **Burt Nanus.** "Toward the Design of Robust Information Systems." *Journal of Management Information Systems* 5, no. 4 (Spring 1989).

Emery, James C. "Cost/Benefit Analysis of Information Systems." Chicago: Society for Management Information Systems Workshop Report No. 1 (1971).

Franz, Charles, and **Daniel Robey.** "An Investigation of User-Led System Design: Rational and Political Perspectives." *Communications of the ACM* 27 (December 1984).

Gerlach, James H., and **Feng-Yang Kuo.** "Understanding Human-Computer Interaction for Information Systems Design." *MIS Quarterly* 15, no. 4 (December 1991).

Ginzberg, Michael J., "Improving MIS Project Selection." *Omega, Internal Journal of Management Science* 6, no. 1 (1979).

Goodhue, Dale L., Laurie J. Kirsch, Judith A. Quillard, and **Michael D. Wybo.** "Strategic Data Planning: Lessons from the Field." *MIS Quarterly* 16, no. 1 (March 1992).

Gould, John D., and **Clayton Lewis.** "Designing for Usability: Key Principles and What Designers Think." *Communications of the ACM* 28 (March 1985).

Grudnitski, Gary. "Eliciting Decision Makers' Information Requirements." *Journal of Management Information Systems* (Summer 1984).

Grover, Varun. "IS Investment Priorities in Contemporary Organizations." *Communications of the ACM* 41, no. 2 (February 1998).

Hammer, Michael. "Reengineering Work: Don't Automate, Obliterate." *Harvard Business Review* (July–August 1990).

Hammer, Michael, and **James Champy.** *Reengineering the Corporation.* New York: HarperCollins Publishers (1993).

Hammer, Michael, and **Steven A. Stanton.** *The Reengineering Revolution.* New York: HarperCollins (1995).

Helms, Glenn L., and **Ira R. Weiss.** "The Cost of Internally Developed Applications: Analysis of Problems and Cost Control Methods." *Journal of Management Information Systems* (Fall 1986).

Hirscheim, R. A. "User Experience with and Assessment of Participative Systems Design." *MIS Quarterly* (December 1985).

Hunton, James E., and **Beeler, Jesse D.,** "Effects of User Participation in Systems Development: A Longitudinal Field Study." *MIS Quarterly* 21, no. 4 (December 1997).

Huizing, Ard, Esther Koster, and **Wim Bouman.** "Balance in Business Process Reengineering: An Empirical Study of Fit and Performance." *Journal of Management Information Systems* 14, no. 1 (Summer 1997).

Ives, Blake, Margrethe H. Olson, and **Jack J. Baroudi.** "The Measurement of User Information Satisfaction." *Communications of the ACM* 26 (October 1983).

Janz, Brian D., James C. Wetherbe, Gordon B. Davis, and **Raymond A. Noe.** "Reengineering the Systems Development Process: The Link between Autonomous Teams and Business Process Outcomes." *Journal of Management Information Systems* 14, no. 1 (Summer 1997).

Joshi, Kailash. "A Model of Users' Perspective on Change: The Case of Information Systems Technology Implementation." *MIS Quarterly* 15, no. 2 (June 1991).

Karat, John. "Evolving the Scope of User-Centered Design." *Communications of the ACM* 40, no. 7 (July 1997).

Keen, Peter W. "Information Systems and Organizational Change." *Communications of the ACM* 24 (January 1981).

Kendall, Kenneth E., and **Julie E. Kendall.** *Systems Analysis and Design,* 4th ed. Upper Saddle River, NJ: Prentice Hall (1998).

King, Julia. "Reengineering Slammed." *Computerworld* (June 13, 1994).

King, William R. "Alternative Designs in Information System Development." *MIS Quarterly* (December 1982).

Kolb, D. A., and **A. L. Frohman.** "An Organization Development Approach to Consulting." *Sloan Management Review* 12 (Fall 1970).

Laudon, Kenneth C. "CIOs Beware: Very Large-Scale Systems." Working paper, Center for Research on Information Systems, New York University Stern School of Business (1989).

Lederer, Albert L., Rajesh Mirani, Boon Siong Neo, Carol Pollard, Jayesh Prasad, and **K. Ramamurthy.** "Information System Cost Estimating: A Management Perspective." *MIS Quarterly* 14, no. 2 (June 1990).

Lederer, Albert, and **Jayesh Prasad.** "Nine Management Guidelines for Better Cost Estimating." *Communications of the ACM* 35, no. 2 (February 1992).

Lientz, Bennett P., and **E. Burton Swanson.** *Software Maintenance Management.* Reading, MA: Addison-Wesley (1980).

Lucas, Henry C., Jr. *Implementation: The Key to Successful Information Systems.* New York: Columbia University Press (1981).

———. *Why Information Systems Fail.* New York: Columbia University Press (1975).

Mahmood, Mo Adam, and **Gary J. Mann.** "Measuring the Organizational Impact of Information Technology Investment." *Journal of Management Information Systems* 10, no. 1 (Summer 1993).

Markus, M. Lynne, and **Robert I. Benjamin.** "Change Agentry—the Next IS Frontier." *MIS Quarterly* 20, no. 4 (December 1996).

Markus, M. L. "Power, Politics, and MIS Implementation." *Communications of the ACM* 26 (June 1983).

Markus, M. Lynne, and **Mark Keil.** "If We Build It, They Will Come: Designing Information Systems That People Want to Use." *Sloan Management Review* (Summer 1994).

Matlin, Gerald. "What Is the Value of Investment in Information Systems?" *MIS Quarterly* 13, no. 3 (September 1989).

McFarlan, F. Warren. "Portfolio Approach to Information Systems." *Harvard Business Review* (September–October 1981).

McKeen, James D., and **Tor Guimaraes.** "Successful Strategies for User Participation in Systems Development." *Journal of Management Information Systems* 14, no. 2 (Fall 1997).

Moad, Jeff. "Does Reengineering Really Work?" *Datamation* (August 1993).

Mumford, Enid, and **Mary Weir.** *Computer Systems in Work Design: The ETHICS Method.* New York: Wiley (1979).

Nolan, Richard L. "Managing Information Systems by Committee." *Harvard Business Review* (July–August 1982).

Parker, M. M. "Enterprise Information Analysis: Cost-Benefit Analysis and the Data-Managed System." *IBM Systems Journal* 21 (1982).

Premkumar, G., and **William R. King.** "Organizational Characteristics and Information Systems Planning: An Empirical Study." *Information Systems Research* 5, no. 2 (June 1994).

Raghunathan, Bhanu, and **T. S. Raghunathan.** "Adaptation of a Planning System Success Model to Information Systems Planning." *Information Systems Research* 5, no. 3 (September 1994).

Rai, Arun, Ravi Patnayakuni, and **Nainika Patnayakuni.** "Technology Investment and Business Performance." *Communications of the ACM* 40, no. 7 (July 1997).

Robey, Daniel, and **M. Lynne Markus.** "Rituals in Information System Design." *MIS Quarterly* (March 1984).

Rockart, John F. "Chief Executives Define Their Own Data Needs." *Harvard Business Review* (March–April 1979).

Rockart, John F., and **Michael E. Treacy.** "The CEO Goes On-Line." *Harvard Business Review* (January–February 1982).

Shank, Michael E., Andrew C. Boynton, and **Robert W. Zmud.** "Critical Success Factor Analysis as a Methodology for MIS Planning." *MIS Quarterly* (June 1985).

Sia, Siew Kien, and **Boon Siong Neo.** "Reengineering Effectiveness and the Redesign of Organizational Control: A Case Study of the Inland Revenue Authority in Singapore." *Journal of Management Information Systems* 14, no. 1 (Summer 1997).

Swanson, E. Burton. *Information System Implementation.* Homewood, IL: Richard D. Irwin (1988).

Tait, Peter, and **Iris Vessey.** "The Effect of User Involvement on System Success: A Contingency Approach." *MIS Quarterly* 12, no. 1 (March 1988).

Tornatsky, Louis G., J. D. Eveland, M. G. Boylan, W. A. Hetzner, E. C. Johnson, D. Roitman, and **J. Schneider.** *The Process of Technological Innovation: Reviewing the Literature.* Washington, DC: National Science Foundation (1983).

Teng, James T. C., Seung Ryul Jeong, and **Varun Grover.** "Profiling Successful Reengineering Projects." *Communications of the ACM* 41, no. 6 (June 1998).

Thompson, Sian Hin Teo, and **William R. King.** "Integration between Business Planning and Information Systems Planning: An Evolutionary-Contingency Approach." *Journal of Management Information Systems* 14, no. 1 (Summer 1997).

Turner, Jon A. "Computer-Mediated Work: The Interplay Between Technology and Structured Jobs." *Communications of the ACM* 27 (December 1984).

Vessey, Iris, and **Sue Conger.** "Learning to Specify Information Requirements: The Relationship between Application and Methodology." *Journal of Management Information Systems* 10, no. 2 (Fall 1993).

Vitalari, Nicholas P. "Knowledge as a Basis for Expertise in Systems Analysis: Empirical Study." *MIS Quarterly* (September 1985).

Yin, Robert K. "Life Histories of Innovations: How New Practices Become Routinized." *Public Administration Review* (January–February 1981).

Vankatraman, N. "Beyond Outsourcing: Managing IT Resources as a Value Center." *Sloan Management Review* (Spring 1997).

Zachman, J. A. "Business Systems Planning and Business Information Control Study: A Comparison." *IBM Systems Journal* 21 (1982).

Zmud, Robert W., William P. Anthony, and **Ralph M. Stair, Jr.** "The Use of Mental Imagery to Facilitate Information Identification in Requirements Analysis." *Journal of Management Information Systems* 9, no. 4 (Spring 1993).

CHAPTER 11

Ahituv, Niv, and **Seev Neumann.** "A Flexible Approach to Information System Development." *MIS Quarterly* (June 1984).

Aiken, Peter, Alice Muntz, and **Russ Richards.** "DOD Legacy Systems: Reverse Engineering Data Requirements." *Communications of the ACM* 37, no. 5 (May 1994).

Alavi, Maryam. "An Assessment of the Prototyping Approach to Information System Development." *Communications of the ACM* 27 (June 1984).

Alavi, Maryam, R. Ryan Nelson, and **Ira R. Weiss.** "Strategies for End-User Computing: An Integrative Framework." *Journal of Management Information Systems* 4, no. 3 (Winter 1987–1988).

Anderson, Evan A. "Choice Models for the Evaluation and Selection of Software Packages." *Journal of Management Information Systems* 6, no. 4 (Spring 1990).

Arthur, Lowell Jay. "Quick and Dirty." *Computerworld* (December 14, 1992).

Baskerville, Richard L., and **Jan Stage.** "Controlling Prototype Development through Risk Analysis." *MIS Quarterly* 20, no. 4 (December 1996).

Bersoff, Edward H., and **Alan M. Davis.** "Impacts of Life-Cycle Models on Software Configuration Management." *Communications of the ACM* 34, no. 8 (August 1991).

Blum, Bruce I. "A Taxonomy of Software Development Methods." *Communications of the ACM* 37, no. 11 (November 1994).

Booch, Grady. *Object-Oriented Design with Applications.* Redwood City, CA: Benjamin Cummings (1991).

Caldwell, Bruce. "Blue Cross, in Intensive Care, Beeps EDS." *InformationWeek* (January 27, 1992).

Carr, Houston H. "Information Centers: The IBM Model vs. Practice." *MIS Quarterly* (September 1987).

Cerveny, Robert P., Edward J. Garrity, and **G. Lawrence Sanders.** "The Application of Prototyping to Systems Development: A Rationale and Model." *Journal of Management Information Systems* 3 (Fall 1986).

Christoff, Kurt A. "Building a Fourth-Generation Environment." *Datamation* (September 1985).

Clermont, Paul. "Outsourcing Without Guilt." *Computerworld* (September 9, 1991).

Coad, Peter, with **Edward Yourdon.** *Object-Oriented Analysis.* Englewood Cliffs, NJ: Prentice Hall (1989).

Cotterman, William W., and **Kuldeep Kumar.** "User Cube: A Taxonomy of End Users." *Communications of the ACM* 32, no. 11 (November 1989).

Davenport, Thomas H. "Putting the Enterprise into the Enterprise System." *Harvard Business Review* (July–August 1998).

Davis, Sid A., and **Robert P. Bostrum.** "Training End Users: An Experimental Investigation of the Role of the Computer Interface and Training Methods." *MIS Quarterly* 17, no. 1 (March 1993).

Dekleva, Sasa M. "The Influence of Information Systems Development Approach on Maintenance." *MIS Quarterly* 16, no. 3 (September 1992).

DeMarco, Tom. *Structured Analysis and System Specification.* New York: Yourdon Press (1978).

DiRomualdo, Anthony, and **Vijay Gurbaxani.** "Strategic Intent for IT Outsourcing." *Sloan Management Review* 39, no. 4 (Summer 1998).

Dijkstra, E. "Structured Programming." In *Classics in Software Engineering,* edited by Edward Nash Yourdon. New York: Yourdon Press (1979).

Earl, Michael J. "The Risks of Outsourcing IT." *Sloan Management Review* (Spring 1996).

Flatten, Per O., Donald J. McCubbrey, P. Declan O'Riordan, and **Keith Burgess.** *Foundations of Business Systems,* 2nd ed. Fort Worth, TX: Dryden Press (1992).

Fraser, Martin D., Kuldeep Kumar, and **Vijay K. Vaishnavi.** "Strategies for Incorporating Formal Specifications in Software Development." *Communications of the ACM* 37, no. 10 (October 1994).

Fuller, Mary K., and **E. Burton Swanson.** "Information Centers as Organizational Innovation." *Journal of Management Information Systems* 9, no. 1 (Summer 1992).

Gane, Chris, and **Trish Sarson.** *Structured Systems Analysis: Tools and Techniques.* Englewood Cliffs, NJ: Prentice Hall (1979).

Gould, John D., and **Clayton Lewis.** "Designing for Usability: Key Principles and What Designers Think." *Communications of the ACM* 28 (March 1985).

Grant, F. J. "The Downside of 4GLs." *Datamation* (July 1985).

Green, Jesse. "Productivity in the Fourth Generation." *Journal of Management Information Systems* 1 (Winter 1984–1985).

Harel, Elie C., and **Ephraim R. McLean.** "The Effects of Using a Nonprocedural Computer Language on Programmer Productivity." *MIS Quarterly* (June 1985).

Harrison, Allison W., and **R. Kelly Rainer, Jr.** "The Influence of Individual Differences on Skill in End-User Computing." *Journal of Management Information Systems* 9, no. 1 (Summer 1992).

Henderson-Sellers, Brian, and **Julian M. Edwards.** "The Object-Oriented Systems Life Cycle." *Communications of the ACM* 33, no. 9 (September 1990).

Holtzblatt, Laren, and **Hugh Beyer.** "Making Customer-Centered Design Work for Teams." *Communications of the ACM* 36, no. 10 (October 1993).

Huff, Sid L., Malcolm C. Munro, and **Barbara H. Martin.** "Growth Stages of End-User Computing." *Communications of the ACM* 31, no. 5 (May 1988).

Janson, Marius, and **L. Douglas Smith.** "Prototyping for Systems Development: A Critical Appraisal." *MIS Quarterly* 9 (December 1985).

Jenkins, A. Milton. "Prototyping: A Methodology for the Design and Development of Application Systems." *Spectrum* 2 (April 1985).

Johnson, Richard T. "The Infocenter Experience." *Datamation* (January 1984).

Jones, T. C. "The Limits of Programming Productivity." Guide and Share Application Development Symposium, Proceedings. New York: Share (1979).

Kiel, Mark, Richard Mixon, Timo Saarinen, and **Virpi Tuunairen.** "Understanding Runaway IT Projects." *Journal of Management Information Systems* 11, no. 3 (Winter 1994–1995).

Korson, Tim, and **John D. McGregor.** "Understanding Object Oriented: A Unifying Paradigm." *Communications of the ACM* 33, no. 9 (September 1990).

Kozar, Kenneth A., and **John M. Mahlum.** "A User-Generated Information System: An Innovative Development Approach." *MIS Quarterly* (June 1987).

Kraushaar, James M., and **Larry E. Shirland.** "A Prototyping Method for Applications Development by End Users and Information Systems Specialists." *MIS Quarterly* (September 1985).

Lacity, Mary C., Leslie P. Willcocks, and **David Feeny.** "The Value of Selective IT Outsourcing." *Sloan Management Review* (Spring 1996).

Livingston, Dennis. "Outsourcing: Look Beyond the Price Tag." *Datamation* (November 15, 1992).

Loh, Lawrence, and **N. Venkatraman.** "Determinants of Information Technology Outsourcing." *Journal of Management Information Systems* 9, no. 1 (Summer 1992).

Loh, Lawrence, and **N. Venkatraman.** "Diffusion of Information Technology Outsourcing: Influence Sources and the Kodak Effect." *Information Systems Research* 3, no. 4 (December 1992).

Lucas, Henry C., Eric J. Walton, and **Michael J. Ginzberg.** "Implementing Packaged Software." *MIS Quarterly* (December 1988).

Madsen, Kim Halskov, and **Peter H. Aiken.** "Experience Using Cooperative Interactive Storyboard Prototyping." *Communications of the ACM* 36, no. 4 (June 1993).

Martin, James. *Application Development without Programmers.* Englewood Cliffs, NJ: Prentice Hall (1982).

Martin, J., and **C. McClure.** "Buying Software Off the Rack." *Harvard Business Review* (November–December 1983).

Martin, James, and **Carma McClure.** *Structured Techniques: The Basis of CASE.* Englewood Cliffs, NJ: Prentice Hall (1988).

Mason, R. E. A., and **T. T. Carey.** "Prototyping Interactive Information Systems." *Communications of the ACM* 26 (May 1983).

Matos, Victor M., and **Paul J. Jalics.** "An Experimental Analysis of the Performance of Fourth-Generation Tools on PCs." *Communications of the ACM* 32, no. 11 (November 1989).

Mazzucchelli, Louis. "Structured Analysis Can Streamline Software Design." *Computerworld* (December 9, 1985).

McIntyre, Scott C., and **Lexis F. Higgins.** "Object-Oriented Analysis and Design: Methodology and Application." *Journal of Management Information Systems* 5, no. 1 (Summer 1988).

McMullen, John. "Developing a Role for End Users." *InformationWeek* (June 15, 1992).

Moran, Robert. "The Case Against CASE." *InformationWeek* (February 17, 1992).

Nerson, Jean-Marc. "Applying Object-Oriented Analysis and Design." *Communications of the ACM* 35, no. 9 (September 1992).

Norman, Ronald J., and **Jay F. Nunamaker, Jr.** "CASE Productivity: Perceptions of Software Engineering Professionals." *Communications of the ACM* 32, no. 9 (September 1989).

Pancake, Cherri M. "The Promise and the Cost of Object Technology: A Five-Year Forecast." *Communications of the ACM* 38, no. 10 (October 1995).

Rivard, Suzanne, and **Sid L. Huff.** "Factors of Success for End-User Computing." *Communications of the ACM* 31, no. 5 (May 1988).

Roche, Edward M. *Managing Information Technology in Multinational Corporations.* New York: Macmillan Publishing Company (1992).

Rockart, John F., and **Lauren S. Flannery.** "The Management of End-User Computing." *Communications of the ACM* 26, no. 10 (October 1983).

Schmidt, Douglas C., and **Mohamed E. Fayad.** "Lessons Learned Building Reusable OO Frameworks for Distributed Software." *Communications of the ACM* 40, no. 10 (October 1997).

Timmreck, Eric M. "Performance Measurement: Vendor Specifications and Benchmarks." In *The Information Systems Handbook,* edited by F. Warren McFarlan and Richard C. Nolan. Homewood, IL: Dow-Jones–Richard D. Irwin (1975).

Trauth, Eileen M., and **Elliot Cole.** "The Organizational Interface: A Method for Supporting End Users of Packaged Software." *MIS Quarterly* 16, no. 1 (March 1992).

White, Clinton E., and **David P. Christy.** "The Information Center Concept: A Normative Model and a Study of Six Installations." *MIS Quarterly* (December 1987).

Willis, T. Hillman, and **Debbie B. Tesch.** "An Assessment of Systems Development Methodologies." *Journal of Information Technology Management* 2, no. 2 (1991).

Vessey, Iris, and **Sue A. Conger.** "Requirements Specification: Learning Object, Process, and Data Methodologies." *Communications of the ACM* 37, no. 5 (May 1994).

Yourdon, Edward, and **L. L. Constantine.** *Structured Design.* New York: Yourdon Press (1978).

Zahniser, Richard A. "Design by Walking Around." *Communications of the ACM* 36, no. 10 (October 1993).

CHAPTER 12

Adhikari, Richard. "Virtually Superior." *InformationWeek* (November 3, 1997).

Allen, Bradley P. "CASE-Based Reasoning: Business Applications." *Communications of the ACM* 37, no. 3 (March 1994).

Amaravadi, Chandra S., Olivia R. Liu Sheng, Joey F. George, and **Jay F. Nunamaker, Jr.** "AEI: A Knowledge-Based Approach to Integrated Office Systems." *Journal of Management Information Systems* 9, no. 1 (Summer 1992).

Applegate, Linda. "Technology Support for Cooperative Work: A Framework for Studying Introduction and Assimilation in Organizations." *Journal of Organizational Computing* 1, no. 1 (January–March 1991).

Asakawa, Kazuo, and **Hideyuki Takagi.** "Neural Networks in Japan." *Communications of the ACM* 37, no. 3 (March 1994).

Balasubramanian, V., and **Alf Bashian.** "Document Management and Web Technologies: Alice Marries the Mad Hatter." *Communications of the ACM* 41, no. 7 (July 1998).

Bansal, Arun, Robert J. Kauffman, and **Rob R. Weitz.** "The Modeling Performance of Regression and Neural Networks." *Journal of Management Information Systems* 10, no. 1 (Summer 1993).

Barker, Virginia E., and **Dennis E. O'Connor.** "Expert Systems for Configuration at Digital: XCON and Beyond." *Communications of the ACM* (March 1989).

Bair, James H. "A Layered Model of Organizations: Communication Processes and Performance." *Journal of Organizational Computing* 1, no. 2 (April–June 1991).

Beer, Randall D., Roger D. Quinn, Hillel J. Chiel, and **Roy E. Ritzman.** "Biologically Inspired Approaches to Robots." *Communications of the ACM* 40, no. 3 (March 1997).

Bikson, Tora K., J. D. Eveland, and **Barbara A. Gutek.** "Flexible Interactive Technologies for Multi-Person Tasks: Current Problems and Future Prospects." Rand Corporation (December 1988).

Black, George. "Taking Notes, Big Sixer Aims for Head of the Class." *Software Magazine* (March 1995).

Blanning, Robert W., David R. King, James R. Marsden, and **Ann C. Seror.** "Intelligent Models of Human Organizations: The State of the Art." *Journal of Organizational Computing* 2, no. 2 (1992).

Bobrow, D. G., S. Mittal, and **M. J. Stefik.** "Expert Systems: Perils and Promise." *Communications of the ACM* 29 (September 1986).

Bohn, Roger E. "Measuring and Managing Technological Knowledge." *Sloan Management Review* (Fall 1994).

Braden, Barbara, Jerome Kanter, and **David Kopcso.** "Developing an Expert Systems Strategy." *MIS Quarterly* 13, no. 4 (December 1989).

Brutzman, Don. "The Virtual Reality Modeling Language and Java." *Communications of the ACM* 41, no. 6 (June 1998).

Brynjolfsson, Erik. "The Contribution of Information Technology to Consumer Welfare." *Information Systems Research* 7, no. 3 (September 1996).

———. "The Productivity Paradox of Information Technology." *Communications of the ACM* 36, no. 12 (December 1993).

Brynjolfsson, Erik, and **Lorin M. Hitt.** "Beyond the Productivity Paradox." *Communications of the ACM* 41, no. 8 (August 1998).

———. "New Evidence on the Returns to Information Systems." MIT Sloan School of Management (October 1993).

Burtka, Michael. "Generic Algorithms." *The Stern Information Systems Review* 1, no. 1 (Spring 1993).

Busch, Elizabeth, Matti Hamalainen, Clyde W. Holsapple, Yongmoo Suh, and **Andrew B. Whinston.** "Issues and Obstacles in the Development of Team Support Systems." *Journal of Organizational Computing* 1, no. 2 (April–June 1991).

Byrd, Terry Anthony. "Implementation and Use of Expert Systems in Organizations: Perceptions of Knowledge Engineers." *Journal of Management Information Systems* 8, no. 4 (Spring 1992).

Carlson, David A., and **Sudha Ram.** "A Knowledge Representation for Modeling Organizational Productivity." *Journal of Organizational Computing* 2, no. 2 (1992).

Churchland, Paul M., and **Patricia Smith Churchland.** "Could a Machine Think?" *Scientific American* (January 1990).

Clifford, James, Henry C. Lucas, Jr., and **Rajan Srikanth.** "Integrating Mathematical and Symbolic Models through AESOP: An Expert for Stock Options Pricing." *Information Systems Research* 3, no. 4 (December 1992).

Cole, Kevin, Olivier Fischer, and **Phyllis Saltzman.** "Just-in-Time Knowledge Delivery." *Communications of the ACM* 40, no. 7 (July 1997).

Cole-Gomolski, Barbara. "Customer Service with a :-)" *Computerworld* (March 30, 1998).

Creecy, Robert H., Brij M. Masand, Stephen J. Smith, and **Davis L. Waltz.** "Trading MIPS and Memory for Knowledge Engineering." *Communications of the ACM* 35, no. 8 (August 1992).

Davenport, Thomas H., David W. DeLong, and **Michael C. Beers.** "Successful Knowledge Management Projects." *Sloan Management Review* 39, no. 2 (Winter 1998).

Davenport, Thomas H., and **Lawrence Prusak.** *Working Knowledge: How Organizations Manage What They Know.* Boston, MA: Harvard Business School Press (1997).

Dhar, Vasant. "Plausibility and Scope of Expert Systems in Management." *Journal of Management Information Systems* (Summer 1987).

Dhar, Vasant, and **Roger Stein.** *Intelligent Decision Support Methods: The Science of Knowledge Work.* Upper Saddle River, NJ: Prentice Hall (1997).

El Najdawi, M. K., and **Anthony C. Stylianou.** "Expert Support Systems: Integrating AI Technologies." *Communications of the ACM* 36, no. 12 (December 1993).

Etzioni, Oren, and **Daniel Weld.** "A Softbot-Based Interface to the Internet." *Communications of the ACM* 37, no. 7 (July 1994).

Favela, Jesus. "Capture and Dissemination of Specialized Knowledge in Network Organizations." *Journal of Organizational Computing and Electronic Commerce* 7, nos. 2 and 3 (1997).

Feigenbaum, Edward A. "The Art of Artificial Intelligence: Themes and Case Studies in Knowledge Engineering." *Proceedings of the IJCAI* (1977).

Fryer, Bronwyn. "Visa Cracks Down on Fraud." *InformationWeek* (August 26, 1996).

Gelernter, David. "The Metamorphosis of Information Management." *Scientific American* (August 1989).

Gill, Philip J. "A False Rivalry Revealed." *InformationWeek* (May 20, 1996).

Giuliao, Vincent E. "The Mechanization of Office Work." *Scientific American* (September 1982).

Goldberg, David E. "Genetic and Evolutionary Algorithms Come of Age." *Communications of the ACM* 37, no. 3 (March 1994).

Grant, Robert M. "Prospering in Dynamically-Competitive Environments: Organizational Capability as Knowledge Integration." *Organization Science* 7, no. 4 (July–August 1996).

Grief, Irene. "Desktop Agents in Group-Enabled Projects." *Communications of the ACM* 37, no. 7 (July 1994).

Griggs, Kenneth. "Visual Aids that Model Organizations." *Journal of Organizational Computing* 2, no. 2 (1992).

Hayes-Roth, Frederick. "Knowledge-Based Expert Systems." *Spectrum IEEE* (October 1987).

Hayes-Roth, Frederick, and **Neil Jacobstein.** "The State of Knowledge-Based Systems." *Communications of the ACM* 37, no. 3 (March 1994).

Hibbard, Justin. "Knowing What We Know." *InformationWeek* (October 20, 1997).

Hinton, Gregory. "How Neural Networks Learn from Experience." *Scientific American* (September 1992).

Holland, John H. "Genetic Algorithms." *Scientific American* (July 1992).

"How Organizations Use Groupware to Improve a Wide Range of Business Processes." *I/S Analyzer* 35, no. 2 (February 1996).

Jacobs, Paul S., and **Lisa F. Rau.** "SCISOR: Extracting Information from On-line News." *Communications of the ACM* 33, no. 11 (November 1990).

Johansen, Robert. "Groupware: Future Directions and Wild Cards." *Journal of Organizational Computing* 1, no. 2 (April–June 1991).

Kanade, Takeo, Michael L. Reed, and **Lee E. Weiss.** "New Technologies and Applications in Robotics." *Communications of the ACM* 37, no. 3 (March 1994).

Kock, Ned, and **Robert J. McQueen.** "An Action Research Study of Effects of Asynchronous Groupware Support on Productivity and Outcome Quality in Process Redesign Groups." *Journal of Organizational Computing and Electronic Commerce* 8, no. 2 (1998).

Lee, Soonchul. "The Impact of Office Information Systems on Power and Influence." *Journal of Management Information Systems* 8, no. 2 (Fall 1991).

Leonard-Barton, Dorothy, and **John J. Sviokla.** "Putting Expert Systems to Work." *Harvard Business Review* (March–April 1988).

Lieberman, Henry. "Intelligent Graphics." *Communications of the ACM* 39, no. 8 (August 1996).

Liker, Jeffrey K., Mitchell Fleischer, Mitsuo Nagamachi, and **Michael S. Zonnevylle.** "Designers and Their Machines:

CAD Use and Support in the U.S. and Japan." *Communications of the ACM* 35, no. 2 (February 1992).

Lin, Frank C., and **Mei Lin.** "Neural Networks in the Financial Industry." *AI Expert* (February 1993).

Lou, Hao, and **Richard W. Scannell.** "Acceptance of Groupware: The Relationships Among Use, Satisfaction, and Outcomes." *Journal of Organizational Computing and Electronic Commerce* 6, no. 2 (1996).

Maes, Pattie. "Agents that Reduce Work and Information Overload." *Communications of the ACM* 38, no. 7 (July 1994).

Malhotra, Yogesh. "Toward a Knowledge Ecology for Organizational White-Waters." Keynote Presentations for the Knowledge Ecology Fair '98 (1998).

Mann, Marina M., Richard L. Rudman, Thomas A. Jenckes, and **Barbara C. McNurlin.** "EPRINET: Leveraging Knowledge in the Electronic Industry." *MIS Quarterly* 15, no. 3 (September 1991).

Marsden, James R., David E. Pingry, and **Ming-Chian Ken Wang.** "Intelligent Information and Organization Structures: An Integrated Design Approach." *Journal of Organizational Computing* 2, no. 2 (1992).

McCarthy, John. "Generality in Artificial Intelligence." *Communications of the ACM* (December 1987).

McCune, Jenny C. "All Together Now." *Beyond Computing* (May 1996).

Meyer, Marc H., and **Kathleen Foley Curley.** "An Applied Framework for Classifying the Complexity of Knowledge-Based Systems." *MIS Quarterly* 15, no. 4 (December 1991).

Motiwalla, Luvai, and **Jay F. Nunamaker, Jr.** "Mail-Man: A Knowledge-Based Mail Assistant for Managers." *Journal of Organizational Computing* 2, no. 2 (1992).

Munakata, Toshinori, and **Yashvant Jani.** "Fuzzy Systems: An Overview." *Communications of the ACM* 37, no. 3 (March 1994).

Mykytyn, Kathleen, Peter P. Mykytyn, Jr., and **Craig W. Stinkman.** "Expert Systems: A Question of Liability." *MIS Quarterly* 14, no. 1 (March 1990).

Naj, Amal Kumar. "Virtual Reality Isn't a Fantasy for Surgeons." *The Wall Street Journal* (March 3, 1993).

Nash, Jim. "State of the Market, Art, Union, and "Technology." *AI Expert* (January 1993).

Newquist, Harvey P. "AI at American Express." *AI Expert* (January 1993).

O'Leary, Daniel, Daniel Kuokka, and **Robert Plant.** "Artificial Intelligence and Virtual Organizations." *Communications of the ACM* 40, no. 1 (January 1997).

Orlikowski, Wanda J. "Learning from Notes: Organizational Issues in Groupware Implementation." Sloan Working Paper, no. 3428. Cambridge, MA: Sloan School of Management, Massachusetts Institute of Technology.

Panko, Raymond R. "Is Office Productivity Stagnant?" *MIS Quarterly* 15, no. 2 (June 1991).

Porat, Marc. "The Information Economy: Definition and Measurement." Washington, DC: U.S. Department of Commerce, Office of Telecommunications (May 1977).

Press, Lawrence. "Lotus Notes (Groupware) in Context." *Journal of Organizational Computing* 2, nos. 3 and 4 (1992b).

Roach, Stephen S. "Industrialization of the Information Economy." New York: Morgan Stanley and Co. (1984).

———. "Making Technology Work." New York: Morgan Stanley and Co. (1993).

———. "Services Under Siege—The Restructuring Imperative." *Harvard Business Review* (September–October 1991).

———. "Technology and the Service Sector." *Technological Forecasting and Social Change* 34, no. 4 (December 1988).

———. "The Hollow Ring of the Productivity Revival." *Harvard Business Review* (November–December 1996).

Ruhleder, Karen, and **John Leslie King.** "Computer Support for Work Across Space, Time, and Social Worlds." *Journal of Organizational Computing* 1, no. 4 (1991).

Rumelhart, David E., Bernard Widrow, and **Michael A. Lehr.** "The Basic Ideas in Neural Networks." *Communications of the ACM* 37, no. 3 (March 1994).

Schatz, Bruce R. "Building an Electronic Community System." *Journal of Management Information Systems* 8, no. 3 (Winter 1991–1992).

Schultze, Ulrike, and **Betty Vandenbosch.** "Information Overload in a Groupware Environment: Now You See It, Now You Don't." *Journal of Organizational Computing and Electronic Commerce* 8, no. 2 (1998).

Searle, John R. "Is the Brain's Mind a Computer Program?" *Scientific American* (January 1990).

Self, Kevin. "Designing with Fuzzy Logic." *Spectrum IEEE* (November 1990).

Selker, Ted. "Coach: A Teaching Agent that Learns." *Communications of the ACM* 37, no. 7 (July 1994).

Sheng, Olivia R. Liu, Luvai F. Motiwalla, Jay F. Nunamaker, Jr., and **Douglas R. Vogel.** "A Framework to Support Managerial Activities Using Office Information Systems." *Journal of Management Information Systems* 6, no. 3 (Winter 1989–1990).

Sibigtroth, James M. "Implementing Fuzzy Expert Rules in Hardware." *AI Expert* (April 1992).

Simon, H. A., and **A. Newell.** "Heuristic Problem Solving: The Next Advance in Operations Research." *Operations Research* 6 (January–February 1958).

Sproull, Lee, and **Sara Kiesler.** *Connections: New Ways of Working in the Networked Organization.* Cambridge, MA: MIT Press (1992).

Starbuck, William H. "Learning by Knowledge-Intensive Firms." *Journal of Management Studies* 29, no. 6 (November 1992).

Stein, Eric W. "A Method to Identify Candidates for Knowledge Acquisition." *Journal of Management Information Systems* 9, no. 2 (Fall 1992).

Stirland, Sarah. "Armed with Insight." *Wall Street and Technology* 16, no. 8 (August 1998).

Storey, Veda C., and **Robert C. Goldstein.** "Knowledge-Based Approaches to Database Design," *MIS Quarterly* 17, no. 1 (March 1993).

Stuart, Anne. "Under the Hood at Ford." *WebMaster* (June 1997).

Stylianou, Anthony C., Gregory R. Madey, and **Robert D. Smith.** "Selection Criteria for Expert System Shells: A Socio-Technical Framework. *Communications of the ACM* 35, no. 10 (October 1992).

Sviokla, John J. "An Examination of the Impact of Expert Systems on the Firm: The Case of XCON." *MIS Quarterly* 14, no. 5 (June 1990).

———. "Expert Systems and Their Impact on the Firm: The Effects of PlanPower Use on the Information Processing

Capacity of the Financial Collaborative." *Journal of Management Information Systems* 6, no. 3 (Winter 1989–1990).

Tam, Kar Yan. "Automated Construction of Knowledge-Bases from Examples." *Information Systems Research* 1, no. 2 (June 1990).

Tank, David W., and **John J. Hopfield.** "Collective Computation in Neuronlike Circuits." *Scientific American* (October 1987).

Trippi, Robert, and **Efraim Turban.** "The Impact of Parallel and Neural Computing on Managerial Decision Making." *Journal of Management Information Systems* 6, no. 3 (Winter 1989–1990).

Turban, Efraim, and **Paul R. Watkins.** "Integrating Expert Systems and Decision Support Systems." *MIS Quarterly* (June 1986).

Wallich, Paul. "Silicon Babies." *Scientific American* (December 1991).

Waltz, David L. "Artificial Intelligence." *Scientific American* (December 1982).

Weitzel, John R., and **Larry Kerschberg.** "Developing Knowledge Based Systems: Reorganizing the System Development Life Cycle." *Communications of the ACM* (April 1989).

Weizenbaum, Joseph. *Computer Power and Human Reason—From Judgment to Calculation.* San Francisco: Freeman (1976).

White, George M. "Natural Language Understanding and Speech Recognition." *Communications of the ACM* 33, no. 8 (August 1990).

Wijnhoven, Fons. "Designing Organizational Memories: Concept and Method." *Journal of Organizational Computing and Electronic Commerce* 8, no. 1 (1998).

Widrow, Bernard, David E. Rumelhart, and **Michael A. Lehr.** "Neural Networks: Applications in Industry, Business, and Science." *Communications of the ACM* 37, no. 3 (March 1994).

Zadeh, Lotfi A. "Fuzzy Logic, Neural Networks, and Soft Computing." *Communications of the ACM* 37, no. 3 (March 1994).

Zadeh, Lotfi A. "The Calculus of Fuzzy If/Then Rules." *AI Expert* (March 1992).

CHAPTER 13

Alavi, Maryam, and **Erich A. Joachimsthaler.** "Revisiting DSS Implementation Research: A Meta-Analysis of the Literature and Suggestions for Researchers." *MIS Quarterly* 16, no. 1 (March 1992).

Anthes, Gary H. "Notes System Sends Federal Property Data Nationwide." *Computerworld* (August 8, 1994).

Bonzcek, R. H., C. W. Holsapple, and **A. B. Whinston.** "Representing Modeling Knowledge with First Order Predicate Calculus." *Operations Research* 1 (1982).

Brachman, Ronald J., Tom Khabaza, Willi Kloesgen, Gregory Piatetsky-Shapiro, and **Evangelos Simoudis.** "Mining Business Databases." *Communications of the ACM* 39, no. 11 (November 1996).

Caouette, Margarette J., and **Bridget N. O'Connor.** "The Impact of Group Support Systems on Corporate Teams' Stages of Development." *Journal of Organizational Computing and Electronic Commerce* 8, no. 1 (1998).

Chidambaram, Laku. "Relational Development in Computer-Supported Groups." *MIS Quarterly* 20, no. 2 (June 1996).

Chidambaram, Laku, Robert P. Bostrom, and **Bayard E. Wynne.** "A Longitudinal Study of the Impact of Group Decision Support Systems on Group Development." *Journal of Management Information Systems* 7, no. 3 (Winter 1990–1991).

Dennis, Alan R. "Information Exchange and Use in Group Decision Making: You Can Lead a Group to Information, but You Can't Make It Think." *MIS Quarterly* 20, no. 4 (December 1996).

Dennis, Alan R., Sridar K. Pootheri, and **Vijaya L. Natarajan.** "Lessons from Early Adopters of Web Groupware." *Journal of Management Information Systems* 14, no. 4 (Spring 1998).

Dennis, Alan R., Jay F. Nunamaker, Jr., and **Douglas R. Vogel.** "A Comparison of Laboratory and Field Research in the Study of Electronic Meeting Systems." *Journal of Management Information Systems* 7, no. 3 (Winter 1990–1991).

Dennis, Alan R., Joey F. George, Len M. Jessup, Jay F. Nunamaker, and **Douglas R. Vogel.** "Information Technology to Support Electronic Meetings." *MIS Quarterly* 12, no. 4 (December 1988).

Dennis, Alan R., Craig K. Tyran, Douglas R. Vogel, and **Jay Nunamaker, Jr.** "Group Support Systems for Strategic Planning." *Journal of Management Information Systems* 14, no. 1 (Summer 1997).

DeSanctis, Geraldine, Marshall Scott Poole, Howard Lewis, and **George Desharnias.** "Computing in Quality Team Meetings." *Journal of Management Information Systems* 8, no. 3 (Winter 1991–1992).

DeSanctis, Geraldine, and **R. Brent Gallupe.** "A Foundation for the Study of Group Decision Support Systems." *Management Science* 33, no. 5 (May 1987).

Dhar, Vasant, and **Roger Stein.** *Intelligent Decision Support Methods: The Science of Knowledge Work.* Upper Saddle River, NJ: Prentice Hall (1997).

Dutta, Soumitra, Berend Wierenga, and **Arco Dalebout.** "Designing Management Support Systems Using an Integrative Perspective." *Communications of the ACM* 40, no. 6 (June 1997).

Easton, George K., Joey F. George, Jay F. Nunamaker, Jr., and **Mark O. Pendergast.** "Two Different Electronic Meeting Systems." *Journal of Management Information Systems* 7, no. 3 (Winter 1990–1991).

Edelstein, Herb. "Technology How To: Mining Data Warehouses." *InformationWeek* (January 8, 1996).

El Sawy, Omar. "Personal Information Systems for Strategic Scanning in Turbulent Environments." *MIS Quarterly* 9, no. 1 (March 1985).

El Sherif, Hisham, and **Omar A. El Sawy.** "Issue-Based Decision Support Systems for the Egyptian Cabinet." *MIS Quarterly* 12, no. 4 (December 1988).

Etzioni, Oren. "The World-Wide Web: Quagmire or Gold Mine?" *Communications of the ACM* 39, no. 11 (November 1996).

Fayyad, Usama, Gregory Piatetsky-Shapiro, and **Padhraic Smyth.** "The KDD Process for Extracting Useful Knowledge from Volumes of Data." *Communications of the ACM* 39, no. 11 (November 1996).

Fjermestad, Jerry. "An Integrated Framework for Group Support Systems." *Journal of Organizational Computing and Electronic Commerce* 8, no. 2 (1998).

Gallupe, R. Brent, Geraldine DeSanctis, and **Gary W. Dickson.** "Computer-Based Support for Group Problem-Finding: An Experimental Investigation." *MIS Quarterly* 12, no. 2 (June 1988).

Gerber, Cheryl. "Excavate Your Data." *Datamation* (May 1, 1996).

Ginzberg, Michael J., W. R. Reitman, and **E. A. Stohr,** eds. *Decision Support Systems.* New York: North Holland Publishing Co. (1982).

Gopal, Abhijit, Robert P. Bostrum, and **Wynne W. Chin.** "Applying Adaptive Structuration Theory to Investigate the Process of Group Support Systems Use." *Journal of Management Information Systems* 9, no. 3 (Winter 1992–1993).

Grobowski, Ron, Chris McGoff, Doug Vogel, Ben Martz, and **Jay Nunamaker.** "Implementing Electronic Meeting Systems at IBM: Lessons Learned and Success Factors." *MIS Quarterly* 14, no. 4 (December 1990).

Henderson, John C., and **David A. Schilling.** "Design and Implementation of Decision Support Systems in the Public Sector." *MIS Quarterly* (June 1985).

Hiltz, Starr Roxanne, Kenneth Johnson, and **Murray Turoff.** "Group Decision Support: Designated Human Leaders and Statistical Feedback." *Journal of Management Information Systems* 8, no. 2 (Fall 1991).

Ho, T. H., and **K. S. Raman.** "The Effect of GDSS on Small Group Meetings." *Journal of Management Information Systems* 8, no. 2 (Fall 1991).

Hogue, Jack T. "Decision Support Systems and the Traditional Computer Information System Function: An Examination of Relationships During DSS Application Development." *Journal of Management Information Systems* (Summer 1985).

Hogue, Jack T. "A Framework for the Examination of Management Involvement in Decision Support Systems." *Journal of Management Information Systems* 4, no. 1 (Summer 1987).

Houdeshel, George, and **Hugh J. Watson.** "The Management Information and Decision Support (MIDS) System at Lockheed, Georgia." *MIS Quarterly* 11, no. 2 (March 1987).

Imielinski, Tomasz, and **Heikki Mannila.** "A Database Perspective on Knowledge Discovery." *Communications of the ACM* 39, no. 11 (November 1996).

Jessup, Leonard M., Terry Connolly, and **Jolene Galegher.** "The Effects of Anonymity on GDSS Group Process with an Idea-Generating Task." *MIS Quarterly* 14, no. 3 (September 1990).

Jones, Jack William, Carol Saunders, and **Raymond McLeod, Jr.,** "Media Usage and Velocity in Executive Information Acquisition: An Exploratory Study." *European Journal of Information Systems* 2 (1993).

Kalakota, Ravi, Jan Stallaert, and **Andrew B. Whinston.** "Worldwide Real-Time Decision Support Systems for Electronic Commerce Applications." *Journal of Organizational Computing and Electronic Commerce* 6, no. 1 (1996).

Kasper, George M. "A Theory of Decision Support System Design for User Calibration." *Information Systems Research* 7, no. 2 (June 1996).

Keen, Peter G. W., and **M. S. Scott Morton.** *Decision Support Systems: An Organizational Perspective.* Reading, MA: Addison-Wesley (1982).

King, John. "Successful Implementation of Large Scale Decision Support Systems: Computerized Models in U.S. Economic Policy Making." *Systems Objectives Solutions* (November 1983).

Kraemer, Kenneth L., and **John Leslie King.** "Computer-Based Systems for Cooperative Work and Group Decision Making." *ACM Computing Surveys* 20, no. 2 (June 1988).

Laudon, Kenneth C. *Communications Technology and Democratic Participation.* New York: Praeger (1977).

Le Blanc, Louis A., and **Kenneth A. Kozar.** "An Empirical Investigation of the Relationship Between DSS Usage and System Performance." *MIS Quarterly* 14, no. 3 (September 1990).

Leidner, Dorothy E., and **Joyce Elam.** "Executive Information Systems: Their Impact on Executive Decision Making." *Journal of Management Information Systems* (Winter 1993–1994.)

Leidner, Dorothy E., and **Joyce Elam.** "The Impact of Executive Information Systems on Organizational Design, Intelligence, and Decision Making." *Organization Science* 6, no. 6 (November–December 1995).

Lewe, Henrik, and **Helmut Krcmar.** "A Computer-Supported Cooperative Work Research Laboratory." *Journal of Management Information Systems* 8, no. 3 (Winter 1991–1992).

Lou, Hao, and **Richard W. Scannell.** "Acceptance of Groupware: The Relationships among Use, Satisfaction, and Outcomes." *Journal of Organizational Computing and Electronic Commerce* 6, no. 2 (1996).

McLeod, Poppy Lauretta, and **Jeffry R. Liker.** "Electronic Meeting Systems: Evidence from a Low Structure Environment." *Information Systems Research* 3, no. 3 (September 1992).

Meador, Charles L., and **Peter G. W. Keen.** "Setting Priorities for DSS Development." *MIS Quarterly* (June 1984).

Miranda, Shaila M., and **Robert P. Bostrum.** "The Impact of Group Support Systems on Group Conflict and Conflict Management." *Journal of Management Information Systems* 10, no. 3 (Winter 1993–1994).

Mohan, Lakshmi, William K. Holstein, and **Robert B. Adams.** "EIS: It Can Work in the Public Sector." *MIS Quarterly* 14, no. 4 (December 1990).

Nidumolu, Sarma R., Seymour E. Goodman, Douglas R. Vogel, and **Ann K. Danowitz.** "Information Technology for Local Administration Support: The Governorates Project in Egypt." *MIS Quarterly* 20, no. 2 (June 1996).

Niederman, Fred, Catherine M. Beise, and **Peggy M. Beranek.** "Issues and Concerns about Computer-Supported Meetings: The Facilitator's Perspective." *MIS Quarterly* 20, no. 1 (March 1996).

Nunamaker, J. F., Alan R. Dennis, Joseph S. Valacich, Douglas R. Vogel, and **Joey F. George.** "Electronic Meeting Systems to Support Group Work." *Communications of the ACM* 34, no. 7 (July 1991).

Nunamaker, Jay, Robert O. Briggs, Daniel D. Mittleman, Douglas R. Vogel, and **Pierre A. Balthazard.** "Lessons from a Dozen Years of Group Support Systems Research: A Discussion of Lab and Field Findings." *Journal of Management Information Systems* 13, no. 3 (Winter 1997).

O'Keefe, Robert M., and **Tim McEachern.** "Web-based Customer Decision Support Systems." *Communications of the ACM* 41, no. 3 (March 1998).

Panko, Raymond R. "Managerial Communication Patterns." *Journal of Organizational Computing* 2, no. 1 (1992).

Post, Brad Quinn. "A Business Case Framework for Group Support Technology." *Journal of Management Information Systems* 9, no. 3 (Winter 1992–1993).

Rockart, John F., and **David W. DeLong.** "Executive Support Systems and the Nature of Work." Working Paper: Management in the 1990s. Sloan School of Management (April 1986).

Rockart, John F., and **David W. DeLong.** *Executive Support Systems: The Emergence of Top Management Computer Use.* Homewood, IL: Dow-Jones Irwin (1988).

Sambamurthy, V., and **Marshall Scott Poole.** "The Effects of Variations in Capabilities of GDSS Designs on Management of Cognitive Conflict in Groups." *Information Systems Research* 3, no. 3 (September 1992).

Sanders, G. Lawrence, and **James F. Courtney.** "A Field Study of Organizational Factors Influencing DSS Success." *MIS Quarterly* (March 1985).

Sharda, Ramesh, and **David M. Steiger.** "Inductive Model Analysis Systems: Enhancing Model Analysis in Decision Support Systems." *Information Systems Research* 7, no. 3 (September 1996).

Silver, Mark S. "Decision Support Systems: Directed and Nondirected Change." *Information Systems Research* 1, no. 1 (March 1990).

Sprague, R. H., and **E. D. Carlson.** *Building Effective Decision Support Systems.* Englewood Cliffs, NJ: Prentice Hall (1982).

Stefik, Mark, Gregg Foster, Daniel C. Bobrow, Kenneth Kahn, Stan Lanning, and **Luch Suchman.** "Beyond the Chalkboard: Computer Support for Collaboration and Problem Solving in Meetings." *Communications of the ACM* (January 1987).

"The New Role for 'Executive Information Systems.' " *I/S Analyzer* (January 1992).

Turban, Efraim and **Jay E. Aronson.** *Decision Support Systems and Intelligent Systems: Management Support Systems*, 5th ed. Upper Saddle River, NJ: Prentice Hall (1998).

Turoff, Murray. "Computer-Mediated Communication Requirements for Group Support." *Journal of Organizational Computing* 1, no. 1 (January–March 1991).

Tyran, Craig K., Alan R. Dennis, Douglas R. Vogel, and **J. F. Nunamaker, Jr.** "The Application of Electronic Meeting Technology to Support Senior Management." *MIS Quarterly* 16, no. 3 (September 1992).

Vandenbosch, Betty, and **Michael J. Ginzberg.** "Lotus Notes and Collaboration: Plus ca change . . ." *Journal of Management Information Systems* 13, no. 3 (Winter 1997).

Varney, Sarah E. "Database Marketing Predicts Customer Loyalty." *Datamation* (September 1996).

Vogel, Douglas R., Jay F. Nunamaker, William Benjamin Martz, Jr., Ronald Grobowski, and **Christopher McGoff.** "Electronic Meeting System Experience at IBM." *Journal of Management Information Systems* 6, no. 3 (Winter 1989–1990).

Volonino, Linda, and **Hugh J. Watson.** "The Strategic Business Objectives Method for EIS Development." *Journal of Management Information Systems* 7, no. 3 (Winter 1990–1991).

Walls, Joseph G., George R. Widmeyer, and **Omar A. El Sawy.** "Building an Information System Design Theory for Vigilant EIS." *Information Systems Research* 3, no. 1 (March 1992).

Watson, Hugh J., Astrid Lipp, Pamela Z. Jackson, Abdelhafid Dahmani, and **William B. Fredenberger.** "Organizational Support for Decision Support Systems." *Journal of Management Information Systems* 5, no. 4 (Spring 1989).

Watson, Hugh J., R. Kelly Rainer, Jr., and **Chang E. Koh.** "Executive Information Systems: A Framework for Development and a Survey of Current Practices." *MIS Quarterly* 15, no. 1 (March 1991).

Watson, Richard T., Geraldine DeSanctis, and **Marshall Scott Poole.** "Using a GDSS to Facilitate Group Consensus: Some Intended and Unintended Consequences." *MIS Quarterly* 12, no. 3 (September 1988).

Watson, Richard T., Teck-Hua Ho, and **K. S. Ramar.** "Culture: A Fourth Dimension of Group Support Systems." *Communications of the ACM* 37, no. 10 (October 1994).

Wreden, Nick. "Business Intelligence: Turning on Success," *Beyond Computing* (September 1997).

Zigurs, Ilze, and **Kenneth A. Kozar.** "An Exploratory Study of Roles in Computer-Supported Groups." *MIS Quarterly* 18, no. 3 (September 1994).

CHAPTER 14

Abdel-Hamid, Tarek K. "The Economics of Software Quality Assurance: A Simulation-Based Case Study." *MIS Quarterly* (September 1988).

Alberts, David S. "The Economics of Software Quality Assurance." Washington, DC: National Computer Conference, 1976 Proceedings.

Anderson, Ross J. "Why Cryptosystems Fail." *Communications of the ACM* 37, no. 11 (November 1994).

Anthes, Gary H. "Viruses Continue to Wreak Havoc at Many U.S. Companies." *Computerworld* (June 28, 1993).

Banker, Rajiv D., Srikant M. Datar, Chris F. Kemerer, and **Dani Zweig.** "Software Complexity and Maintenance Costs." *Communications of the ACM* 36, no. 11 (November 1993).

Banker, Rajiv D., Robert J. Kaufmann, and **Rachna Kumar.** "An Empirical Test of Object-Based Output Measurement Metrics in a Computer-Aided Software Engineering (CASE) Environment." *Journal of Management Information Systems* 8, no. 3 (Winter 1991–1992).

Banker, Rajiv D., and **Chris F. Kemerer.** "Performance Evaluation Metrics in Information Systems Development: A Principal-Agent Model." *Information Systems Research* 3, no. 4 (December 1992).

Boehm, Barry W. "Understanding and Controlling Software Costs." *IEEE Transactions on Software Engineering* 14, no. 10 (October 1988).

Boockholdt, J. L. "Implementing Security and Integrity in Micro-Mainframe Networks." *MIS Quarterly* 13, no. 2 (June 1989).

Borning, Alan. "Computer System Reliability and Nuclear War." *Communications of the ACM* 30, no. 2 (February 1987).

Buss, Martin D. J., and **Lynn M. Salerno.** "Common Sense and Computer Security." *Harvard Business Review* (March–April 1984).

Chaum, David. "Security Without Identification: Transaction Systems to Make Big Brother Obsolete." *Communications of the ACM* 28 (October 1985).

Corbato, Fernando J. "On Building Systems that Will Fail." *Communications of the ACM* 34, no. 9 (September 1991).

Davis, Beth. "In Certificates We Trust." *InformationWeek*, (March 23, 1998).

Dekleva, Sasa M. "The Influence of Information Systems Development Approach on Maintenance." *MIS Quarterly* 16, no. 3 (September 1992).

DeMarco, Tom. *Structured Analysis and System Specification.* New York: Yourdon Press (1978).

Dijkstra, E. "Structured Programming." In *Classics in Software Engineering,* edited by Edward Nash Yourdon. New York: Yourdon Press (1979).

Dutta, Soumitra, Luk N. Van Wassenhove, and **Selvan Kulandaiswamy.** "Benchmarking European Software Management Practices." *Communications of the ACM* 41, no. 6 (June 1998).

Fraser, Martin D., and **Vijay K. Vaishnavi.** "A Formal Specifications Maturity Model." *Communications of the ACM* 40, no. 12 (December 1997).

Forrest, Stephanie, Steven A. Hofmeyr, and **Anil Somayaji.** "Computer Immunology." *Communications of the ACM* 40, no. 10 (October 1997).

Gane, Chris, and **Trish Sarson.** *Structured Systems Analysis: Tools and Techniques.* Englewood Cliffs, NJ: Prentice Hall (1979).

Halper, Stanley D., Glenn C. Davis, Jarlath P. O'Neill-Dunne, and **Pamela R. Pfau.** *Handbook of EDP Auditing.* Boston: Warren, Gorham, and Lamont (1985).

Hoffman, Lance. *Rogue Programs.* New York: Van Nostrand Reinhold (1990).

Jarzabek, Stan, and **Riri Huang.** "The Case for User-Centered CASE Tools." *Communications of the ACM* 41, no. 8 (August 1998).

Johnson, Philip M. "Reengineering Inspection." *Communications of the ACM* 41, no. 2 (February 1998.)

Kahane, Yehuda, Seev Neumann, and **Charles S. Tapiero.** "Computer Backup Pools, Disaster Recovery, and Default Risk." *Communications of the ACM* 31, no. 1 (January 1988).

Kaplan, David, Ramayya Krishnan, Rema Padman, and **James Peters.** "Assessing Data Quality in Accounting Information Systems." *Communications of the ACM* 41, no. 2 (February 1998.)

Kemerer, Chris F. "Progress, Obstacles, and Opportunities in Software Engineering Economics." *Communications of the ACM* 41, no. 8 (August 1998).

Keyes, Jessica. "New Metrics Needed for New Generation." *Software Magazine* (May 1992).

King, Julia. "It's C.Y.A. Time." *Computerworld* (March 30, 1992).

Klein, Barbara D., Dale L. Goodhue, and **Gordon B. Davis.** "Can Humans Detect Errors in Data?" *MIS Quarterly* 21, no. 2 (June 1997).

Knowles, Ann. "EDI Experiments with the Net." *Software Magazine* (January 1997).

Laudon, Kenneth C. "Data Quality and Due Process in Large Interorganizational Record Systems." *Communications of the ACM* 29 (January 1986a).

———. *Dossier Society: Value Choices in the Design of National Information Systems.* New York: Columbia University Press (1986b).

Lientz, Bennett P., and **E. Burton Swanson.** *Software Maintenance Management.* Reading, MA: Addison-Wesley (1980).

Littlewood, Bev, and **Lorenzo Strigini.** "The Risks of Software." *Scientific American* 267, no. 5 (November 1992).

———. "Validation of Ultra-high Dependability for Software-based Systems." *Communications of the ACM* 36, no. 11 (November 1993).

Loch, Karen D., Houston H. Carr, and **Merrill E. Warkentin.** "Threats to Information Systems: Today's Reality, Yesterday's Understanding." *MIS Quarterly* 16, no. 2 (June 1992).

Mazzucchelli, Louis. "Structured Analysis Can Streamline Software Design." *Computerworld* (December 9, 1985).

McPartlin, John P. "The True Cost of Downtime." *InformationWeek* (August 3, 1992).

Needham, Roger M. "Denial of Service: An Example." *Communications of the ACM* 37, no. 11 (November 1994).

Nerson, Jean-Marc. "Applying Object-Oriented Analysis and Design." *Communications of the ACM* 35, no. 9 (September 1992).

Neumann, Peter G. "Risks Considered Global(ly)." *Communications of the ACM* 35, no. 1 (January 1993).

Oppliger, Rolf. "Internet Security, Firewalls, and Beyond." *Communications of the ACM* 40, no.7 (May 1997).

Orr, Kenneth. "Data Quality and Systems Theory." *Communications of the ACM* 41, no. 2 (February 1998.)

Parsons, Jeffrey, and **Yair Wand.** "Using Objects for Systems Analysis." *Communications of the ACM* 40, no. 12 (December 1997).

Post, Gerald V., and **J. David Diltz.** "A Stochastic Dominance Approach to Risk Analysis of Computer Systems." *MIS Quarterly* (December 1986).

Putnam, L. H., and **A. Fitzsimmons.** "Estimating Software Costs." *Datamation* (September 1979, October 1979, and November 1979).

Rainer, Rex Kelley, Jr., Charles A. Snyder, and **Houston H. Carr.** "Risk Analysis for Information Technology." *Journal of Management Information Systems* 8, no. 1 (Summer 1991).

Redman, Thomas. "The Impact of Poor Data Quality on the Typical Enterprise." *Communications of the ACM* 41, no. 2 (February 1998.)

Rettig, Marc. "Software Teams." *Communications of the ACM* 33, no. 10 (October 1990).

Slaughter, Sandra A., Donald E. Harter, and **Mayuram S. Krishnan.** "Evaluating the Cost of Software Quality." *Communications of the ACM* 41, no. 8 (August 1998).

Straub, Detmar W. "Controlling Computer Abuse: An Empirical Study of Effective Security Countermeasures." Curtis L. Carlson School of Management, University of Minnesota (July 20, 1987).

Strong, Diane M., Yang W. Lee, and **Richard Y. Wang.** "Data Quality in Context." *Communications of the ACM* 40, no. 5 (May 1997).

Swanson, Kent, Dave McComb, Jill Smith, and **Don McCubbrey.** "The Application Software Factory: Applying Total Quality Techniques to Systems Development." *MIS Quarterly* 15, no. 4 (December 1991).

Tate, Paul. "Risk! The Third Factor." *Datamation* (April 15, 1988).

Tayi, Giri Kumar, and **Donald P. Ballou.** "Examining Data Quality." *Communications of the ACM* 41, no. 2 (February 1998.)

Thyfault, Mary E., and **Stephanie Stahl.** "Weak Links." *InformationWeek* (August 10, 1992).

United States General Accounting Office. "Computer Security: Virus Highlights Needed for Improved Internet Management." GAO/IMTEC-89-57 (June 1989).

———. "Patriot Missile Defense: Software Problem Led to System Failure at Dharan, Saudi Arabia." GAO/IMTEC-92-26 (February 1992).

Wand, Yair, and **Richard Y. Wang.** "Anchoring Data Quality Dimensions in Ontological Foundations." *Communications of the ACM* 39, no. 11 (November 1996).

Wang, Richard. "A Product Perspective on Total Data Quality Management." *Communications of the ACM* 41, no. 2 (February 1998).

Wang, Richard Y., Yang W. Lee, Leo L. Pipino, and **Diane M. Strong.** "Manage Your Information as a Product." *Sloan Management Review* 39, no. 4 (Summer 1998).

Weber, Ron. *EDP Auditing: Conceptual Foundations and Practice,* 2nd ed. New York: McGraw-Hill (1988).

Wilson, Linda. "Devil in Your Data." *InformationWeek* (August 31, 1992).

Yourdon, Edward, and **L. L. Constantine.** *Structural Design.* New York: Yourdon Press (1978).

CHAPTER 15

Cash, James I., F. Warren McFarlan, James L. McKenney, and **Lynda M. Applegate.** *Corporate Information Systems Management,* 4th ed. Homewood, IL: Irwin (1996).

Chismar, William G., and **Laku Chidambaram.** "Telecommunications and the Structuring of U.S. Multinational Corporations." *International Information Systems* 1, no. 4 (October 1992).

Cox, Butler. *Globalization: The IT Challenge.* Sunnyvale, CA: Amdahl Executive Institute (1991).

Deans, Candace P., and **Michael J. Kane.** *International Dimensions of Information Systems and Technology.* Boston, MA: PWS-Kent (1992).

Deans, Candace P., Kirk R. Karwan, Martin D. Goslar, David A. Ricks, and **Brian Toyne.** "Key International Issues in U.S.-Based Multinational Corporations." *Journal of Management Information Systems* 7, no. 4 (Spring 1991).

Dutta, Amitava. "Telecommunications Infrastructure in Developing Nations." *International Information Systems* 1, no. 3 (July 1992).

Holland, Christopher, Geoff Lockett, and **Ian Blackman.** "Electronic Data Interchange Implementation: A Comparison of U.S. and European Cases." *International Information Systems* 1, no. 4 (October 1992).

Ives, Blake, and **Sirkka Jarvenpaa.** "Applications of Global Information Technology: Key Issues for Management." *MIS Quarterly* 15, no. 1 (March 1991).

———. "Global Business Drivers: Aligning Information Technology to Global Business Strategy. *IBM Systems Journal* 32, no. 1 (1993).

———. "Global Information Technology: Some Lessons from Practice." *International Information Systems* 1, no. 3 (July 1992).

Karin, Jahangir, and **Benn R. Konsynski.** "Globalization and Information Management Strategies." *Journal of Management Information Systems* 7 (Spring 1991).

Keen, Peter. *Shaping the Future.* Cambridge, MA: Harvard Business School Press (1991).

King, William R., and **Vikram Sethi.** "An Analysis of International Information Regimes." *International Information Systems* 1, no. 1 (January 1992).

Levy, David. "Lean Production in an International Supply Chain." *Sloan Management Review* (Winter 1997).

Mannheim, Marvin L. "Global Information Technology: Issues and Strategic Opportunities." *International Information Systems* 1, no. 1 (January 1992).

Nelson, R. Ryan, Ira R. Weiss, and **Kazumi Yamazaki.** "Information Resource Management within Multinational Corporations: A Cross-Cultural Comparison of the U.S. and Japan." *International Information Systems* 1, no. 4 (October 1992).

Neumann, Seev. "Issues and Opportunities in International Information Systems." *International Information Systems* 1, no. 4 (October 1992).

Palvia, Shailendra, Prashant Palvia, and **Ronald Zigli,** eds. *The Global Issues of Information Technology Management.* Harrisburg, PA: Idea Group Publishing (1992).

Quelch, John A., and **Lisa R. Klein.** "The Internet and International Marketing." *Sloan Management Review* (Spring 1996).

Roche, Edward M. *Managing Information Technology in Multinational Corporations.* New York: Macmillan (1992).

Sadowsky, George. "Network Connectivity for Developing Countries." *Communications of the ACM* 36, no. 8 (August 1993).

Stahl, Stephanie. "Global Networks: The Headache Continues." *InformationWeek* (October 12, 1992).

Steinbart, Paul John, and **Ravinder Nath.** "Problems and Issues in the Management of International Data Networks." *MIS Quarterly* 16, no. 1 (March 1992).

Straub, Detmar W. "The Effect of Culture on IT Diffusion: E-Mail and FAX in Japan and the U.S." *Information Systems Research* 5, no. 1 (March 1994).

Tan, Zixiang (Alex), Milton Mueller, and **Will Foster.** "China's New Internet Regulations: Two Steps Forward, One Step Backward." *Communications of the ACM* 40, no. 12 (December 1997).

Tractinsky, Noam, and **Sirkka L. Jarvenpaa.** "Information Systems Design Decisions in a Global Versus Domestic Context." *MIS Quarterly* 19, no. 4 (December 1995).

Watson, Richard T., Gigi G. Kelly, Robert D. Galliers, and **James C. Brancheau.** "Key Issues in Information Systems Management: An International Perspective." *Journal of Management Information Systems* 13, no. 4 (Spring 1997).

Name Index

Organizations Index

International Organizations Index

International Organizations Index

Subject Index

Photo Credits

Photo and Screen Shot Credits
Page Photographer/Source

CHAPTER 1

3 Volkswagen de Mexico, S. A. de C. V.
10 United Parcel Service.
17 Donna Cox/Robert Patterson. National Center for Supercomputing Applications—University of Illinois.
21 Reprinted by permission of The New York Times.
26 Sabre.

CHAPTER 2

37 Hubble, Inc.
46 A. Smith. Intergraph Corporation.
53 Stein Roe and Farham.
56 Nina Barnett. Nina Barnett Photography.
61 Courtesy of 1-800-FLOWERS.

CHAPTER 3

69 Schneider Logistics.
77 Pat McDonogh.
86 Courtesy of International Business Machines Corporation. Unauthorized use not permitted.

CHAPTER 4

103 Adrian Bradshaw. SABA Press Photos, Inc.
107 Don Mason. The Stock Market.
118 © The San Francisco Chronicle. Reprinted with permission.
124 Frank Herholdt. Tony Stone Images.
125 Hacker Mobile Research Center.
128 Stephen Ferry/ Gamma-Liaison, Inc.

CHAPTER 5

135 Roger Tully. Tony Stone Images.
146 Intel Corporation.
149 Courtesy of International Business Machines Corporation. Unauthorized use not permitted.
153 NEC Technologies, Inc.
155 Elographics.
158 Courtesy of CBC Newsworld.

CHAPTER 6

167 Reprinted by permission of Australian Chamber of Manufactures.
175 Screen shot reprinted by permission of Microsoft Corp.
183 (*top*) Schwartz Communications Inc.
183 (*bottom*) Screen shot reprinted by permission of Microsoft Corp.
185 Screen shot reprinted by permission of Microsoft Corp.
186 Lotus Developmental Corp.
188 Courtesy of International Business Machines Corporation. Unauthorized use not permitted.

CHAPTER 7

199 SAAB Cars USA, Inc.
220 Hyperion Solutions

CHAPTER 8

231 Robert E. Daemmrich. Tony Stone Images.
238 Motorola Paging Products, Inc., Motorola, Inc.
252 (*top*) Copyright 1994–1998, America Online, Inc. All Rights Reserved.
252 (*bottom*) John Feingersh. Tony Stone Images.
253 Courtesy of Liz Claiborne.

CHAPTER 9

265 Mazda Corp.
272 (*top*) Text and artwork copyright © 1998 by Yahoo! Inc. All rights reserved. YAHOO! and the YAHOO! logo are trademarks of YAHOO!, Inc.
272 (*bottom*) BackWeb
277 Copyright 1994–1998. Net Contents, Inc., dba Virtual Vineyards.
278 Lycos, Inc.
280 Reebok International
282 Marshall Industries.
292 Copyright 1998. Avon Products, Inc.

CHAPTER 10

301 John Riley. Tony Stone Images.
309 Cigna Insurance Co.
315 Matthew Borkoski. Stock Boston.
325 Toshiba.
326 Dennis Craig, Bellevue Industries Co.

CHAPTER 11

339 Don Spiro. Tony Stone Images.
348 Copyright by SAP AG. All Rights Reserved.
351 George Haling. Photo Researchers, Inc.
361 Information Builders.

CHAPTER 12

369 Howard Grey. Tony Stone Images.
374 Shelly R. Harrison. Shelly R. Harrison Photography.
377 Copyright Planet 9 Studios, San Francisco.
387 Countrywide.
397 Excite and Jango are trademarks of Excite, Inc., and may be registered in various jurisdictions. Excite screen display copyright 1995–1998 Excite, Inc.

CHAPTER 13

403 Courtesy of Reynolds Metal Company.
411 Pedestal Capital, Inc.
415 Group Systems®, courtesy of Ventana Corp.
420 (*top*) Fuld & Co., Inc. Reprinted with permission.
420 (*bottom*) Platinum Technology.

CHAPTER 14

427 Courtesy of Pacific Exchange
432 Symantec Corp.
442 Lan Optics, Inc.
444 Copyright ©1998 DigiCash Inc. All rights reserved. www.digicash.com
449 Steven Peters. Tony Stone Images.

CHAPTER 15

455 Kellogg's® and package designs are registered trademarks of Kellogg Company. All rights reserved. Used with permission.
457 Charles Thatcher. Tony Stone Images.
469 Reprinted with permission of DHL International Ltd.
474 Stanley Yip. Apple Computer, Inc.
475 Asia Trade Network

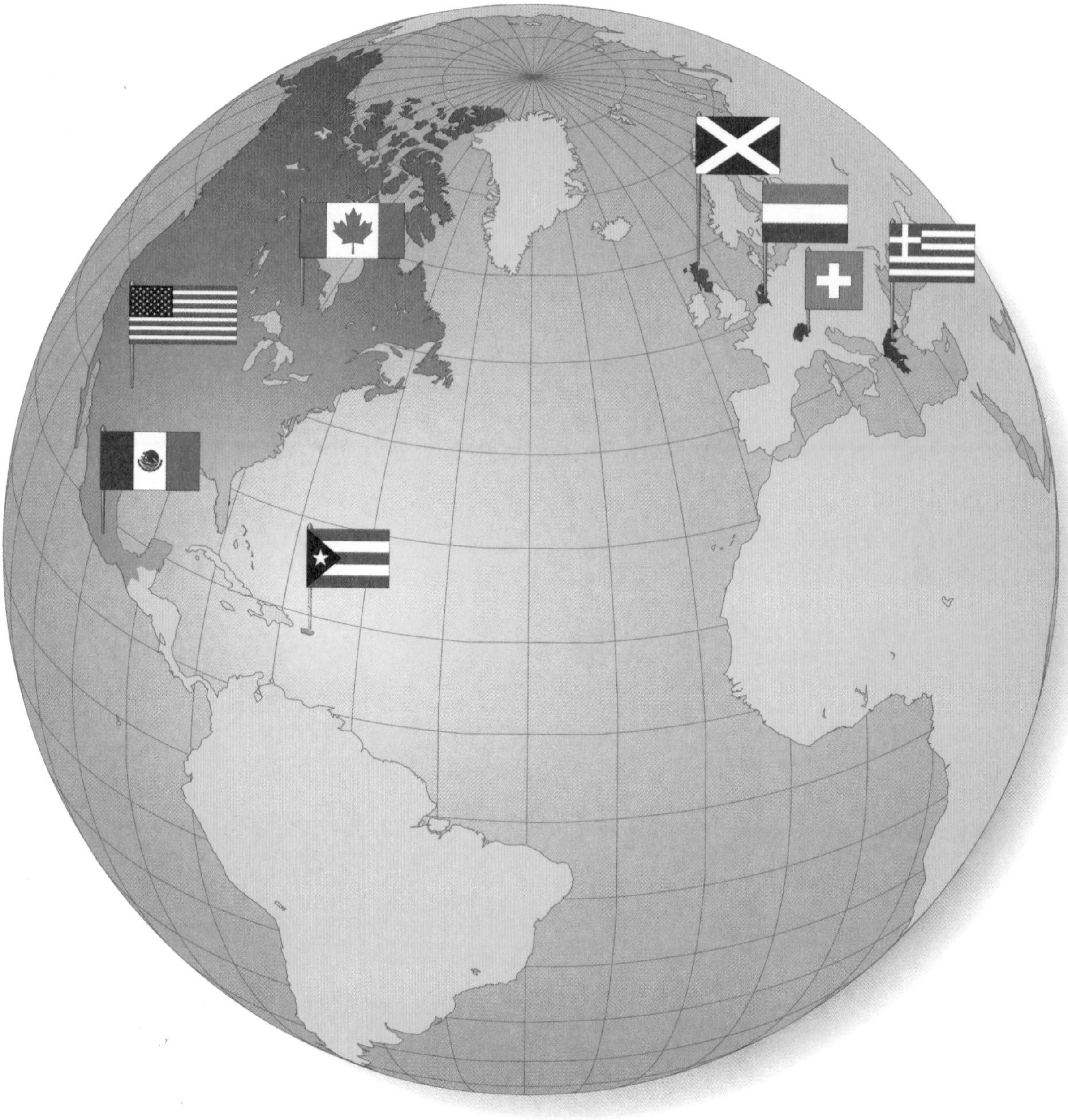

Contributors

AUSTRALIA

Joel B. Barolsky, University of Melbourne
Peter Weill, University of Melbourne

CANADA

Len Fertuck, University of Toronto

GERMANY

Helmut Krcmar, University of Hohenheim
Gerhard Schwabe, University of Hohenheim
Stephen Wilczek, University of Hohenheim

SINGAPORE

Boon Siong Neo, Nanyang Technological University
Christina Soh, Nanyang Technological University

SWITZERLAND

Kimberly A. Bechler, International Institute for Management Development
Donald A. Marchand, International Institute for Management Development
Thomas E. Vollmann, International Institute for Management Development

Consultants

AUSTRALIA

Robert MacGregor, University of Wollongong
Alan Underwood, Queensland University of Technology
Peter Weill, University of Melbourne

CANADA

Wynne W. Chin, University of Calgary
Len Fertuck, University of Toronto
Robert C. Goldstein, University of British Columbia
Rebecca Grant, University of Victoria
Kevin Leonard, Wilfrid Laurier University
Anne B. Pidduck, University of Waterloo

GREECE

Anastasios V. Katos, University of Macedonia

HONG KONG

Enoch Tse, Hong Kong Baptist University

INDIA

Sanjiv D. Vaidya, Indian Institute of Management, Calcutta

ISRAEL

Phillip Ein-Dor, Tel-Aviv University
Peretz Shoval, Ben Gurion University

MEXICO

Noe Urzua Bustamante, Universidad Tecnológica de México

NETHERLANDS

E.O. de Brock, University of Groningen
Theo Thiadens, University of Twente
Charles Van Der Mast, Delft University of Technology

PUERTO RICO, Commonwealth of the United States

Brunilda Marrero, University of Puerto Rico

SWEDEN

Mats Daniels, Uppsala University

SWITZERLAND

Andrew C. Boynton, International Institute for Management Development